Collins

Period House

Albert Jackson & David Day

IN ASSOCIATION WITH ENGLISH HERITAGE

COLLINS PERIOD HOUSE
was created exclusively for HarperCollins Publishers by
Albert Jackson, David Day and Simon Jennings
trading as Inklink

Authors
Albert Jackson
David Day

Design
Simon Jennings
Alan Marshall
Elizabeth Standley

Editor
Peter Leek

Illustrators
Robin Harris
David Day

Location photographer
Shona Wood

Studio photographers
Neil Waving
Ben Jennings

Indexer and proofreader
Mary Morton

Originally published as
Collins Complete Home Restoration Manual in 1992, then as
Collins Care & Repair of Period Houses in 1998 and
Collins Period House in 2002

This edition first published in 2005
by HarperCollins Publishers, London
in association with English Heritage

This paperback edition published in 2008

For English Heritage
David Pickles

**The CIP catalogue record for this book is available from
the British Library**

ISBN-13 978 0 00 727103 0

Printed by
Printing Express Ltd, Hong Kong

Copyright © 2005
HarperCollins Publishers

CONTENTS

INTRODUCTION

FROM THE STATELY HOME TO THE HUMBLE COTTAGE, there is a growing interest in the care and protection of historic buildings. Every old house has its own individual character and, despite the potential problems, more and more people are attracted to owning and living in period properties.

Before the boom in house prices in the 1960s, many people rented their homes – partly because houses were frequently built for renting, but also because owning a house was considered to be a liability. Since there was no incentive to invest money in aesthetic improvements when house prices were static, landlords in particular tended to sanction only repairs that were necessary in order to prevent a building deteriorating to the point where it would begin to depreciate. One consequence of this was that old houses tended to remain more or less as built, albeit often in a somewhat dilapidated condition. Subsequently, rising prosperity engendered new confidence in the long-term benefits of home ownership. This led to a profound change of attitude, and we now take it for granted that sympathetic improvements to a house are likely to be financially advantageous. However, people are now more mobile and houses change hands more frequently – and a succession of different owners, each eager to make their own mark and each making alterations, can quickly erode the character of a house. The patina of age is a subtle feature, and one that is only too easily destroyed.

Many of us dream of buying and refurbishing an old house. Making that dream a reality can often be a struggle, but the rewards are many. Not only can you take pride in what you have achieved, but there is also the satisfaction of helping to save part of the country's heritage. Even so, finding sufficient finance to undertake the work can be daunting, and sustained patience is needed to see the project through without being tempted by short cuts – which could result in inappropriate work and so accelerate deterioration. An old house complete with its period fixtures and fittings can be regarded as a composite work of art and document of history. Despite the best of intentions, it is easy to impair the integrity of your house by misguided alterations – but often, by analysing and understanding its special qualities, such mistakes can be avoided.

Sometimes damage can occur through removing too much historic fabric, so that the building loses some of its appeal. It is better to have a worn and carefully patched old door than a modern replica, however faithfully copied. Old buildings vary greatly in the extent to which they are able to accommodate change without loss of character. Some are sensitive to even seemingly minor alterations, particularly externally or if they retain original interior fixtures, fittings and details. Others may have been modified to such an extent that putting them back to a previous state is not a feasible or sensible option. A conservative approach is fundamental to good conservation – so retaining as much of the original fabric and keeping changes to a minimum are of key importance when carrying out work on a period house.

Serious damage can result from the use of inappropriate or incompatible materials. Where possible, materials matching the original should therefore always be used. Also, old houses are often damaged by lack of care. Regular maintenance is both cost-effective and an important part of looking after an old building. Often, prompt action can prevent decay and avoid the need for major repairs.

Period buildings constitute a precious non-renewable legacy that needs to be sustained. Owning one implies responsibility – in the history of a 300-year-old cottage an individual's residency is but a short event. We are looking after these buildings for our children and their children, so that they will have something worthwhile to inherit. William Morris, who founded the Society for the Protection of Ancient Buildings, urged his contemporaries to 'hand them down instructive and venerable to those that come after us'. That is no less true today. The stock of old buildings is finite, and every loss or instance of serious damage is significant.

This book provides practical guidance about maintaining and repairing the older house and how to reinstate missing features authentically. It explains what you need to consider before embarking on any work, and when necessary how to obtain expert advice. It also indicates which tasks you may be able to tackle yourself, and gives information about techniques and materials so you can discuss aspects of repairs or restoration in detail when briefing professionals to do work for you.

PHOTOGRAPHS & ILLUSTRATIONS

The authors are grateful to the following companies and individuals for additional photographs and illustrations:

Photographs

Peter Aprahamian/Traditional Homes Magazine
Pages 201BR; 204C

Chris Challis/Traditional Homes Magazines
Page 202

Paul Chave
Pages 16R; 157B

Crown Berger Ltd
Page 172T

Edifice
Pages 10T, CL; 11; 25; 27CR, BL; 41BL; 47TL; 58CL; 59BR; 61CL; 64C; 75BR; 76BR; 89TL; 91; 102; 103BR; 104CL; 175TL, CL, BL, C, TR; 180TL

English Heritage Photographic Library
Pages 18; 19; 22; 23TL, BL; 24; 27TC; 28CL, CR; 64TR, CR, BR; 65; 105TR; 224; 228; 229TL, BR

Tony Herbert
Pages 153BR; 156CR; 157TL

John Heseltine/Traditional Homes Magazine
Pages 152CL; 184T; 205BL

Hugh Howard
Page 211L

Inklink
Pages 27TR, BR; 28TR, CL, C, BL; 29TL, TC, TR, C, BL, BR; 57BR; 176CR

Albert Jackson
Pages 13C, BL, BR; 14; 15; 17CR; 23TR, B; 31BL, C, TR; 32; 33R; 34; 35; 36L; 39TR, BR; 40; 42BL; 46CR; 48C, BL; 50; 61BC, BR; 62; 66CL

Simon Jennings
Pages 16T; 17TL; 25TL; 33TR; 63TR; 66CR, B; 68; 89TC; 92CR; 114; 120BR; 122B; 195L

Richard Littlewood/Traditional Homes Magazine
Page 184B

Alan Marshall
Page 158

Ian Parry/Traditional Homes Magazine
Pages 36R; 152C, CR; 154; 183; 189; 204BL, BR; 212BR; 214T

Rentokil Ltd
Pages 28BC, BR; 29CR; 227

Traditional Homes Magazine
Page 153TL

Adele Bishop/Carolyn Warrender Stencil Designs
Page 190

Neil Waving
Pages 9R; 125BR; 146; 162; 195

Historical illustrations

B. T. Batsford Ltd
Pages 9T; 12B

Bexley Library & Museums Department
Pages 17CL; 20CR

Chiswick Library
Pages 9BL; 20T, B

Mary Evans Picture Library
Pages 12T; 38TL; 61T; 151T; 152T

Ironbridge Gorge Museum Trust
Pages 31T; 32CL; 41T; 45TL; 62TL; 75T; 111CL, TR; 113TR; 131TR; 141; 159T; 191T; 200L

Warwick Leadlay
Page 12C

Marflex International Ltd
Pages 211T; 212T; 213T

KEY TO CREDITS
T=TOP, B=BOTTOM, L=LEFT, R=RIGHT, TL=TOP LEFT, TR=TOP RIGHT, C=CENTRE, TC=TOP CENTRE, CL=CENTRE LEFT, CR=CENTRE RIGHT, BL=BOTTOM LEFT, BR=BOTTOM RIGHT, BC=BOTTOM CENTRE.

MATERIALS

The authors are indebted to the following companies and individuals who generously supplied samples or products for photography:

Stonework

The Carving Workshop

Doors & windows

The Antique Hardware Store
Ball & Ball
Clayton-Munroe Ltd
Comyn Ching Ltd
Peter Cornish
Dorset Restoration
GKN Crompton Ltd
Joseph Tipper Ltd

Ornamental glass

Lamont Antiques Ltd
Sam Towers

Plasterwork

E. J. Harmer & Co.

Decorative woodwork

Cumberland Woodcraft Co. Inc.

Wall panelling

Desfab
Winther Browne & Co. Ltd

Tiling

Chris Blanchett
H. & R. Johnson Tiles Ltd
Dennis Ruabon Ltd

Decorative metal

R. Bleasdale (Spirals)
Britannia Architectural Metalwork & Restoration
County Forge Ltd

Fireplaces

Westcombe Antiques

CONSULTANTS AND CONTRIBUTORS

The authors are grateful to the following experts who generously contributed their time and expertise:

Chimneys & fireplaces

Christian Pederson,
Marflex International Ltd
Eddie Gidding,
Stoneage

Ornamental glass

Peter McDonnell,
Gray & McDonnell Ltd
Sam Towers

Plasterwork & stucco

Ernest Millar,
E. G. Millar (Plastering) Ltd
Karl Walters,
British Gypsum Ltd

CHAPTER ONE

ARCHITECTURAL STYLES

W E ARE BECOMING MORE SENSITIVE *to the importance of protecting our heritage. Yet in the not so distant past many old houses were subjected to indiscriminate assault, with relatively little protest.*

During that period many house owners would simply discard what were thought of as unfashionable fittings and decoration in the belief that by 'modernization' they were increasing the market value of their homes. But attitudes have changed. Today, period houses retaining all their original features are highly marketable, and those of us who own old houses that have not been ruined by ill-considered alterations now make every effort to repair and maintain them.

Often these houses require extensive repairs and improvements, such as new wiring and plumbing or the installation of full central heating. But such considerations seldom dissuade the eager house hunter from acquiring a period home that attracts them.

What they find irresistible are those elegant façades with their perfectly proportioned windows, the carved wood and stonework, the delightful moulded plasterwork, the colourful stained glass and floor tiles – all those decorative elements that our forebears were able to fashion with such consummate skill and confidence, and which give every old house its distinctive appeal. The process of preserving, re-creating or repairing such features can provide a great deal of satisfaction.

By describing the development of house construction over the centuries, this chapter aims to help you understand the way your house is built and give you a fuller appreciation of what you have and how it may have changed over time.

A lithograph of 1882 depicting the Victorian suburb of Bedford Park

Thoughtful conservation has preserved Bedford Park for over 100 years

EARLY BRITISH HOUSES
Timber frames to masonry

Jettied wealden house

HOUSES CAME INTO BEING *as soon as people began to settle into communities and cultivate the land. The development of domestic architecture reflects their increasing desire for comfort and privacy. In Britain, Roman housing eventually reached a high state of sophistication, based on classical ideas. Then, following the departure of the Romans, the standard of domestic building declined until after the Norman conquest, when the invaders, with their passion for masonry, introduced stone houses.*

EARLY TIMBER HOUSES

From earliest times, houses have been constructed from a series of prefabricated timber frames (cross frames, wall frames, floor and roof frames) that were joined, one to another, dividing the building into bays. One type of cross frame is known as a cruck, which comprises a pair of long curved timbers joined by tie beams or 'collars'. In some places it is still possible to find examples of cruck houses, which display the distinctive frame prominently on the outside.

Cruck-house timber construction

MEDIEVAL AND VERNACULAR HOUSES

Few, if any, examples of humble housing have survived from the twelfth and thirteenth centuries, as the peasants' simple wattle-and-daub houses and outbuildings have now largely perished. But by the beginning of the fourteenth century the timber-frame house had become established, and this form of construction continued to be widely used for the next 300 years.

The medieval house was generally divided into three sections. At its nucleus was the hall, usually with an entrance at one end and a dais at the other. At the upper end of the hall was the 'master's' accommodation; and at the lower end, beyond the through passage, or 'screens passage', were the servants' quarters and household services. Hall houses, which were normally rectangular in plan, were constructed with a series of wooden trusses that divided the building into bays.

One of the most distinctive types of timber-frame house to develop during the fourteenth century was the wealden house. This type of dwelling, which was particularly common in the south-eastern counties of England, continued to be built until the late sixteenth century. The chief characteristic of the wealden house is the 'jettied' (overhanging) upper storey of the end bays of the house. In towns the jetties often continued round the sides of the house and sometimes round the back as well – a feature less common in rural houses. The entrance, opening into the through passage formed by screens, was at the lower end of the hall.

In early hall houses the hearth had been in the centre of the hall, with the smoke escaping through open timber

The timber-frame house has developed over hundreds of years

Attractive raised pargeting

louvres in the roof. The four-teenth century witnessed the advent of wall fireplaces, but external chimneys built of brick or stone were not a common feature until the sixteenth century.

The changes in living habits in early Tudor times can be seen in the alterations that were made to hall houses – because the great hall had ceased to be a vital centre of daily life, it began to change. During the sixteenth and seventeenth centuries, in many houses upper floors were built into the hall and over a period of time other changes were introduced, too. Bay windows were often added to the dais end of the hall, making a small space that could be screened off for dining. Oriels and bays became popular stylistic features, and windows and doorways imitated the prevailing style of church architecture. During the six-teenth century, houses were still predominantly made of timber, but brick began to be used, particularly as infilling for the timber framework.

By the seventeenth cent-ury, the desire for improved comfort and weatherproofing began to change the way houses were constructed. Windows were glazed and interior walls plastered. Externally, plaster was often used to cover the frame and frequently it was ornamented with incised or raised pat-terns, known as pargeting. The plaster was usually lime-washed, with the addition of a pigment to provide colour. But plastering was not the only method of covering the timber frame. In Kent and Sussex, hung tiles became a common feature, mainly on the upper storey. In some counties wooden weather-boarding was popular, often disguising the presence of an earlier house.

The plan of the vernacular house remained much the same – seldom more than one room deep and two storeys high. Additional rooms were accommodated by extending the slope of the main roof or in wings built at right angles to the main part of the house.

THE IMPACT OF THE RENAISSANCE

During the seventeenth century, building gradually passed out of the hands of carpenters into the hands of masons and bricklayers. Improved transport began to make bricks more accessible, especially when canal systems were introduced. Much of the once plentiful supply of timber was being reserved for the navy, and during the latter part of the century legislation on fire prevention began to have an impact.

The spread of Renaissance style to the smaller house was slow, and traditional building methods continued to be used in the north and west of the country long after they had declined in the south. However, the growth of classical ideas gradually began to impact on vernacular building. This usually manifested itself in the introduction of a sym-metrical show front when houses were altered inter-nally. The hierarchy of the house now began to shift away from the end-to-end plan of the medieval house, with its hall as the main living space, to the deeper front-and-back arrangement – which is still how most houses are organized.

Timber frame infilled with brick

Relatively small town house, exhibiting the impact of Renaissance style

THE GEORGIAN PERIOD
Classicism & elegant proportion

THE STYLE OF ENGLISH HOUSES *when George I came to the throne in 1714 was largely derived from classically inspired architects, particularly* the sixteenth-century Venetian, Andrea Palladio.

The English Palladian movement began with Inigo Jones, who built the nation's first Palladian mansion, the Queen's House in Greenwich, in the early seventeenth century. But the most formative influence on early-Georgian architecture was probably Palladio's QUATTRO LIBRI DELL' ARCHITETTURA, *which was translated into English in 1715. This was a detailed study of the ruins of ancient Rome, interpreting building style and proportion in terms of the five classical orders of architecture – Tuscan, Doric, Ionic, Corinthian and Composite.*

Inigo Jones, architect, 1573–1652

PALLADIANISM AND PROPORTION

The classical orders embodied a set of guidelines and rules that enabled an architect or builder to determine the proportions of a building with confidence. Once the key dimensions were established, the rest could be calculated with ease. An early-Georgian building or terrace was conceived like an ancient Graeco-Roman façade. The ground floor, which was often rusticated to give an impression of solidity, represented a plinth

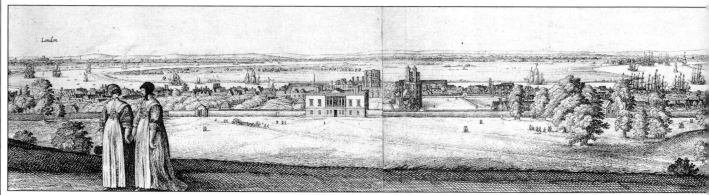

A detail from an engraving by Wenceslaus Hollar, showing the newly built Queen's House, Greenwich

The classical orders of architecture

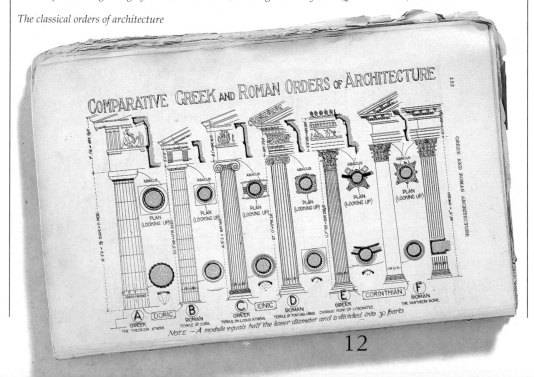

upon which was constructed a row of columns or pilasters extending through perhaps two storeys to a classical entablature incorporating a cornice, frieze and architrave. Some façades were even capped with a pedimented gable reminiscent of an ancient temple.

This literal interpretation, which was acceptable for large public buildings and grand mansions, was too much for the average house built on a smaller scale. Yet the same principles of proportion were applied – the line of the plinth, capitals and entablature being defined by simple stone courses and by the placing of the windows, in what was otherwise a simple unadorned brick or stone

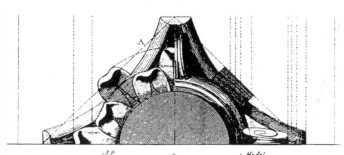

Grand stone-built façade based on Graeco-Roman architectural concepts

façade. Recognizable references to the classical orders were largely restricted to window and door surrounds – especially doorcases comprising pilasters or engaged columns in one of the accepted styles, surmounted by a pediment enclosing a semi-circular fanlight. Classically inspired motifs are to be found inside houses of the period, too, particularly in the form of plaster ceiling cornices incorporating dentils, modillions, rosettes or paterae.

NEO-CLASSICISM

The followers of Palladianism were convinced to the point of dogmatism that the tenets of the movement were based on irrefutable principles. But Palladianism itself was derived from yet another revival movement, a Romanized version of ancient-Greek architecture. By the middle of the eighteenth century, a passion for foreign travel and research into ancient cultures had led to a rediscovery of the Greek originals. This inevitably brought about a reassessment of accepted principles, which in turn led to the movement known as Neo-classicism and eventually to the stricter Greek revival. Proponents of the Greek revival rejected the Tuscan and Composite orders as Roman interlopers, and defined a purer Greek form of the Doric, Ionic and Corinthian orders.

Neo-classicism supplemented the existing Palladian repertoire with a delightful range of new ornamental motifs, including scrolling, foliage, strings of husks, classical urns, mythical beasts, abstract enrichments, such as the Greek key pattern, and the ubiquitous anthemion motifs, most commonly based on honeysuckle flowers and leaves.

THE REGENCY PERIOD

Historically the Regency period is defined as those few years between 1811 and 1820 when the future George IV ruled as Prince Regent in place of his deranged father. However, the architectural style of the first 30 years of the nineteenth century is generally known as Regency.

The lingering influence of Neo-classicism, particularly the Greek-revival movement, is discernible in typical late-Georgian bow-fronted houses, which sometimes boast rusticated-stucco ground floors. However, the taste for painted stucco led to bright, colourful urban vistas, which began to reflect more flamboyant influences brought from the Far East – particularly the passion in fashionable circles for so-called chinoiserie. Perhaps the most famous example of Regency whimsy is the Royal Pavilion in Brighton, with its domes, minarets and elaborate pseudo-oriental interior decoration. The more ordinary houses of the period show little trace of these extravagant flights of fancy, apart from occasional references – such as canopies over porches or balconies with a hint of oriental style.

C18th terrace embodying simple yet precise Georgian proportions

Bow-fronted Regency houses

Regency adaptation of exotic style

THE VICTORIAN PERIOD
Confident opulence

ASPIRATIONS AND TASTE *do not change automatically with the death of a monarch. Early-Victorian buildings were no different from late-Georgian ones. Some conservative institutions, for example, continued to opt for time-honoured classical styles and ornamentation throughout the nineteenth century, presumably to proclaim their permanence and dependability; and the popular stuccoed Italianate villas of the early nineteenth century, which were inspired by Renaissance architecture, still reflected classical themes. However, many Victorians were eventually to reject the classically inspired homogeneity and traditionalism of the eighteenth century and boldly adopted new forms that were more in step with the endemic confidence of the era.*

 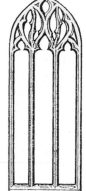

A large family house with Gothic-revival features

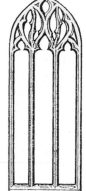

This splendid house epitomizes the sombre romanticism of the Gothic revival

THE GOTHIC REVIVAL

The Victorians were intensely nationalistic in their attitudes and aspirations, and many architects and designers of the era consistently strived to develop a distinctive British style. However, just what that style should be was vigorously debated and contested. If there was ever a victor in the early days of what is sometimes called 'the battle of the styles', it was the Gothic-revival movement, which exerted a dominant influence on Victorian architecture until the latter part of the nineteenth century.

Although the epitome of high-Victorian taste and ideals, the Gothic-revival movement had its roots in the mid eighteenth century. The architects of that time had experimented with romantic Gothic symbolism, but always as a fairly light-hearted parody of medieval style. The Victorians were to take Gothic architecture much more seriously. The Palace of Westminster had been destroyed by fire in 1834. When two years later it was decided to rebuild it in Gothic-revival style, the movement gained respectability and it was adopted enthusiastically for important public buildings – especially churches, for which the Victorians considered the style more appropriate than pagan classicism.

Based as it was on medieval church architecture, pure

Gothic revivalism did not translate easily for the mass of smaller houses built in the Victorian era. Very often these were built by speculators who adopted vaguely Gothic forms to give their houses a fashionable appearance. Lancet windows, stained glass, battened doors in oak, and bay windows with elegant medieval-style pillars are all typical features of speculative Victorian housing.

Less austere references were inspired by the publication in 1851 of *The Stones of Venice*, John Ruskin's studies of Italian Gothic architecture. Among other developments, the book led to widespread use of polychromatic and patterned brickwork, which were ideally suited to the average-size house.

Although the Gothic-revival movement attracted its share of dedicated purists, Victorian architecture in general was self-indulgent compared with the disciplined practices of the eighteenth century. Indeed, houses were frequently an amalgam of styles and motifs borrowed from different ages and cultures, simply because an architect, builder or client found them attractive. To some extent this eclectic approach to design is what gives mid-Victorian architecture its peculiar charm – although that is not the way it was viewed by some contemporary critics.

An archetypal Victorian terrace of polychromatic-brick houses

THE DOMESTIC REVIVAL

Some artists, designers and architects disapproved of the more obvious mid-Victorian excesses in the decorative arts. From the late 1860s onwards, a number of groups began to form in an attempt to shift the emphasis away from eclecticism and mass production towards a revival of vernacular architectural forms and traditional craftsmanship. It can be argued that the fruits of such movements were as derivative as those they sought to replace. Although it had a strong appeal to Victorian middle-class romantics, the idealized image of rural life in the sixteenth and seventeenth centuries was far from historical truth. But what cannot be faulted was the earnest endeavour to promote materials and workmanship of the highest quality.

Groups such as the Arts and Crafts movement, led by William Morris, and the Aesthetic movement were influential in furthering their cause in every aspect of the visual arts, from architecture and interior decoration to wallcoverings and carpets. Among the popular motifs of the period were exotic birds (such as peacocks and cranes), traditional Japanese themes (such as cherry and apple blossom), medieval symbolism, and botanical subjects (especially lilies and sunflowers).

Several architectural styles were spawned at about this time, all of them reminiscent of Tudor or Stuart England. One of the most potent yet unpretentious fashions, the Queen Anne revival, seemed ideally suited to the smaller town house. Simple red brick became popular again, sometimes accented with stone mouldings. There were

A charming Queen-Anne-revival house built in the late 1870s

distinctive Flemish gables, decorative stucco or pargeting, and a return to sash windows with thick white-painted glazing bars and small panes of glass.

Some considered the 'Old English' style to be the rural equivalent of the rather more mannered Queen Anne style, which was perhaps better suited to urban settings. Inspired by Elizabethan or Jacobean architecture, 'Old English' houses frequently combined motifs and forms from both periods, with little consideration for historical verisimilitude. Some houses were tasteful fusions of half-timbering and roughcast, tile-hung gables and leaded-light casements. Others included even more overt references to the past, such as diaper-pattern brickwork and tall chimneys, carved bargeboards and linenfold panelling, stone mullions, and drip mouldings over the windows.

Such houses, invariably set in delightful surroundings, marked a return to a human scale of domestic architecture. People felt comfortable with the so-called Domestic-revival movement. As a result, it became an enduring influence, lasting well into the twentieth century.

Craftsman-built Victorian house in the Old English style

TWENTIETH CENTURY
Art Nouveau & Art Deco

EARLY TWENTIETH-CENTURY HOUSES, *especially those built for the middle classes during Edward VII's short reign, were often similar in style to their Victorian precursors, though generally smaller in scale and with less decoration. However, the Edwardians themselves would probably have considered their houses to be relatively sophisticated compared with the highly ornate, even ostentatious, fashions of the previous era, and much of the architecture of the early twentieth century is epitomized by styles and forms that broke new ground – styles that owed little to the past and which appealed to the more avant-garde Edwardian architects and designers.*

Art Deco architecture seemed extraordinarily avant-garde in the 1930s

Art Nouveau ceramic porch tiles

Art Deco interiors relied on bold shapes and simple fittings for their impact

ART NOUVEAU

Art Nouveau, which is one of the most distinctive design styles, originated in France in the 1880s. Although it was adopted in Europe with some enthusiasm, it made hardly any impact in Britain until the turn of the century – and even then only for furnishings and decorative detail rather than as a full-blown architectural style.

Art Nouveau is characterized by sinuous lines, especially the so-called whiplash curves that frequently appear in compositions. Subjects such as luxuriant foliage and young women with long flowing hair were consciously chosen in order to exploit their linear qualities. Asymmetry was the other conspicuous trademark of the Art Nouveau movement – one that demanded considerable skill on the part of an artist or a designer in order to achieve a composition that was both pleasing and balanced.

It was clearly a style that the average builder would have had some difficulty in mastering. As a result, perhaps, Art Nouveau rarely features as an architectural style in British housing. However, being an idiom that appealed to artists and professional designers, it appears not infrequently in the form of stained glass, cast-iron fire surrounds, light fittings and, above all, wallcovering patterns.

ART DECO

The other remarkable innovative movement of the early twentieth century was also of European origin. Art Deco took its name from the *Exposition Internationale des Arts Décoratifs et Industriels Modernes* held in Paris in 1925. Uncompromisingly modern in its approach, Art Deco was ideally suited to the contemporary passion for homes that were clean, simple and full of light. The style is notable for bold geometric shapes and highly stylized natural forms. Typically, touches of intense colour, in the form of ornamental glass, tiles or paint, are used to accentuate larger white or pale-coloured textured surfaces or to contrast with natural materials such as marble and wood. Built-in furniture became a coveted feature, often constructed from bent or moulded plywood to create striking curvilinear forms.

During the 1920s and 1930s, Art Deco percolated through all strata of society and various types of edifice, from the modernist homes of the fashionable elite to public buildings such as underground-railway stations and cinemas. Sometimes one can even discern a passing reference to Art Deco ideas in local-authority housing projects of the time.

Semi-detached dream homes were built in their thousands between the two world wars

Some Edwardian garden-city developments were highly sophisticated

Village charm was the model for this estate on the outskirts of London

SEMI-DETACHED SUBURBIA

The late-Victorian ideal of the village-style cottage estate was no doubt the inspiration for the county-council garden-suburb developments built just before and after the First World War. These schemes were designed to alleviate the pressure on chronically outdated housing by demolishing the Victorian slums of the major cities and transposing their inhabitants to the outskirts.

The better developments were highly successful, with the houses built to a modest budget yet with an emphasis on individuality. In place of the straight terraces of identical houses, there were meandering avenues and small squares or courts lined with vaguely 'Old English' style cottages, each seemingly built to a slightly different specification.

Between the two world wars, the housing boom continued at an unprecedented rate. Improved transport systems and new-found prosperity led to a doubling of Britain's housing stock, largely by extending city-suburb developments in all directions. These comprised the now familiar semi-detached mock-Tudor houses, with their bay windows at the front and French windows at the rear. Built to a formula that was enormously popular, such houses embodied everything that would appeal to the aspiring home owner. They were easy to

clean and heat (they included the latest labour-saving appliances), and had indoor toilets and tiled bathrooms as standard. These were thoroughly desirable and up-to-date residences, with no small measure of prestige.

The suburban 'semi' has been much maligned for its image of dreariness and stuffy conservatism. Such houses have probably suffered most from the ravages of modernization, not the least because they have been considered unworthy of conservation. An unspoilt example of a 1930s semi-detached house has now become almost as difficult to find as a Victorian or Georgian house in similar condition.

However, the undoubted qualities of these soundly built houses are now at long last being appreciated. Thanks to their somewhat unsophisticated charm and the fact that they can be restored comparatively cheaply, they are one of the more recent additions to the catalogue of desirable period homes.

THE POSTWAR PERIOD
Prefabs to high-rise blocks

IN THE AUTUMN OF 1939 *the outbreak of war interrupted building in Britain, and for the next six years only airfields and other military installations were built. With the cessation of hostilities the government's first priority was to house people who had lost their homes to bombing, and simple prefabricated dwellings were erected on waste ground in many towns and cities. Surprisingly, some of these 'prefabs' survive to this day and many are now legally protected.*

Temporary accommodation built in the 1940s is still in use today

Simple forms are a feature of 1950s housing

High-rise flats are now desirable residences

Architects delighted in designing one-off houses

THE FESTIVAL OF BRITAIN
Rebuilding on a large scale presented architects with many new and exciting opportunities. One of the most important single factors to influence contemporary design was the Festival of Britain, an international showcase for British culture, described as a 'tonic to the nation', held in 1951. However, this celebration of the new era was set against a backdrop of postwar austerity, with a system of building licences in force due to the shortages of building materials. Despite these constraints, the 1950s saw a burst of creative thinking in Britain. Advances in construction and the use of a wide variety of materials – timber, plastics, steel and concrete – were the major influences on the form of postwar buildings. Simplicity combined with a variety of surface finish and texture became a feature of house design during the 1950s.

HIGH-RISE DEVELOPMENTS
Most of the building work in the period immediately after the war was publicly funded. The need for schools and public housing had drawn many talented architects to work for local authorities. Several new towns had been designated soon after the war ended, and Britain continued to play a pioneering role in the design and planning of suburban housing. At the same time, much publicly funded housing in towns and cities was being built in the form of 'high-rise' blocks of flats. Although many of the high-rise blocks became – and remain – objects of hatred and derision, some of them are now viewed as desirable residences and are legally protected.

ONE-OFF DESIGNS
As the 1960s approached, shortages of money and materials eased. Throughout this decade many new ideas were explored in the building of small 'one-off' private houses alongside public-sector architecture. No single overall style or movement emerged, but the chance to build a completely original house provided an attractive alternative to the then unfashionable houses of the Victorian and Edwardian eras, which at that time were often remodelled internally to create a more 'contemporary' ambience. The fundamental elements of house design were being questioned, both in the way the house functioned and in how it looked.

By the 1970s, house design had moved on from large-scale redevelopment schemes. There was growing interest in the rehabilitation of old buildings, alongside new ecological concerns and a search for a more humane environment born out of a new pragmatism that respected place and local materials.

CHAPTER TWO

TAKING STOCK

WE ALL HAVE OUR REASONS *for wanting to find out more about older houses. Maybe you are actively looking for a period house* or already have a property in mind and are wondering whether you're making the right decision in taking on what could be a long-term refurbishment project. Or perhaps you live in an old house or have inherited the family home, and are concerned about how to go about putting the building in good order. In any of these situations, you may be asking yourself whether it is going to be worth the time and effort involved. With so many important considerations to weigh up, the worst possible course of action is to make hasty decisions that you might have cause to regret in the future.

When you are caught up in the excitement and anticipation of buying a house, there are strong pressures to make a snap decision before somebody else gets there first or the price of the property escalates out of your reach. But before buying any house, especially an old one, it is essential to have it surveyed professionally in order to ascertain its true value and ensure that there are no unforeseen problems.

Even when you are over these initial hurdles and you have actually moved into the house, it is worth living in it for a while before deciding how to adapt, renovate or modernize your new home. Getting to know your house more intimately will give you an opportunity to discover and appreciate its best attributes, and also to identify aspects of the house you cannot live with. It may be difficult to curb your enthusiasm, but a period of careful reflection will help you take stock of the situation and then move forward confidently.

Old houses should be surveyed to ensure there are no unexpected problems

Living in a house for a while helps you appreciate its best attributes

GETTING TO KNOW YOUR HOUSE

Having recently purchased *or inherited an old house, you probably can't wait to turn it into your dream home. But do you really know enough about the house to make the most of what you now own, and to avoid costly mistakes? Naturally there are going to be practical considerations with regard to the structural condition of the building — but putting those aside for the moment, try to find out all you can about the history of your house. What was it like when it was built, and what changes has it gone through? Answers to these questions will provide valuable clues as to how you can best preserve the essential qualities of the house, while modifying it for a contemporary lifestyle.*

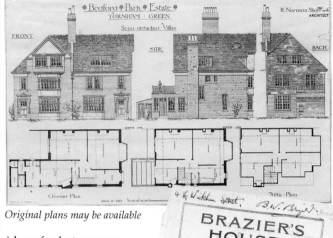

Original plans may be available

Old advertisements are informative

HISTORICAL RESEARCH

Discovering the history of your house and, in particular, how it has evolved over time will help you identify the important features that should be preserved or reinstated. Similarly, understanding how the house was constructed or has been modified may shed light on some of the problems that exist today.

You could engage the services of a professional architectural historian, who will be familiar with all the relevant sources of information and who may be able to spot clues that are not obvious to an untrained eye.

However, there's a great deal of research you can do yourself. For example, there are numerous books on domestic architecture, including some that are aimed specifically at helping house owners research the history of their homes.

Once you have a general idea of what you are looking for, you can begin to broaden your search. Original plans, site maps and deeds may still exist, and there may be other valuable documentary evidence, such as old letters, legal transactions, electoral registers and census returns, that could tell you something about the people who built your house or lived there before you. Ask around to see if there are people living in your neighbourhood who can give you a first-hand account of how things have changed over the years.

The local reference library might have an archive of photographs and paintings, which may include pictures of your house. Estate agents' advertisements that appear in old newspapers are another source of detailed information.

Visit your local-authority planning department to see if they have records and plans of work carried out on your house, including applications for planning permission and listed-building consent.

The National Monuments Record contains brief descriptions of listed buildings and, in some cases, photographs of older properties.

Though not entirely reliable, a contemporary painting will give some idea of what your street may have looked like

ORIGINAL FEATURES

One of the pleasures of first-hand investigation is discovering delightful features, such as walled-up fireplaces or nicely pro-portioned panelled doors, hidden beneath sheets of painted hardboard. But too

Original Victorian tiled panel

often the owner of an old house is left wondering what the original windows or plaster mouldings might have looked like.

You may come across pictures or perhaps written descriptions, but more direct evidence can often be found by studying neigh-bouring houses of similar design to your own. On the outside, see if attractive brickwork, stonework and, especially, stuccowork could have been covered over or removed at some time in the past. Carved or fretted woodwork might have been discarded as a cost-saving exercise or in a misguided attempt at modernization. Internal features such as decorated plaster surfaces, window shutters, doors and door-cases, and finger plates might all have suffered a similar fate. If features such as these have survived, it is worth making an effort to repair and preserve them.

Neighbouring buildings may hold valuable clues

ALTERATIONS AND EXTENSIONS

As you consult various plans and records, try to establish the changes that have occurred over the life of the building. Have walls been removed or added? Perhaps internal partitioning has been rearranged.

There may well be clues in the house itself, such as interruptions to the run of ceiling cornices, picture rails and dadoes. Similarly, you may be able to detect a change in floor levels or floorcoverings. Blocked door-ways could provide a clue to how rooms or passages were laid out in the past. Perhaps you will discover a simple

way to reinstate the original interior, or you may perhaps decide that the present arrangement is a distinct improvement.

An extension is usually easy to identify. There may be a case for dismantling a poorly designed or badly constructed extension that spoils the appearance of the house, but not every exten-sion is detrimental. A well-designed extension not only reflects the way previous owners used and adapted the house, but can be seen as integral to the building and part of its architectural history.

Even simple unadorned features contribute to the appeal of an old house

Reinstate items that have survived

WORTHWHILE IMPROVEMENTS

T HE GENERAL LEVEL OF PROSPERITY *in this country engenders confidence in the long-term benefits of home ownership. For the most part, we take it for granted that improving a house can be financially advantageous. Nevertheless, opinion is divided as to precisely what kind of improvements are worthwhile.*

GETTING IT RIGHT

It is generally preferable to buy a house that has not been completely modernized, even if it is in poor condition. You will have the satisfaction of owning an authentic, unspoilt period house, and will find that repairing dilapidated features is usually cheaper than having to locate and install suitable replacements. It also avoids having to pay for previous 'improvements' that can unduly inflate the purchase price of a house.

However, basically sound, untouched period houses have become scarce, and most people in search of an old house have to settle for one that is not only in need of some repair but has also been stripped of at least some of its original features. In today's market it often makes financial sense to reinstate them, provided you resist the temptation to spend more on refurbishments than is warranted by the house's market value. To attempt to enhance its status by introducing uncharacteristically ornate fittings or decorative elements is as inappropriate as ripping out original features in the name of modernization.

Each type of house within a given locality has a maximum value and no one, especially an experienced estate agent, is going to be fooled into accepting an inflated price for a house that is pretending to be something it isn't. A shrewd investor will put back only what was there in the first place, while ensuring that all repairs and restoration work are done to the highest standard. That way, the house will command the best price in return for the minimum investment.

Don't embark on extensive refurbishments until you have a clear idea of what you want to achieve and what it is going to cost. From the start, work out how much you can realistically afford and, if you are on a limited budget, spend money first on essential repairs that will keep the building watertight and structurally sound. Also, make sure the water, gas and electrical services are operating efficiently and are in a safe condition. Don't forget to put aside money for ongoing maintenance.

New work and modernization

If you need to extend the building or feel you want to install new fixtures or fittings, there's no need to copy slavishly the original style of the house. In these circumstances, it is often best to consult an architect (or an experienced builder) who is sensitive enough to reflect the character and qualities of your house without creating a second-rate pastiche. This is also an opportunity to establish which elements of the building are structural and cannot be removed without substituting some other means of support. This type of information is vital to formulating realistic plans for redesigning the interior of your house.

Unless you are intent on creating a living museum, it makes perfect sense to take advantage of modern technology. In theory, we might enjoy the romance of candlelight, but few of us would seriously contemplate forgoing modern lighting or hesitate to install labour-saving laundry and kitchen appliances. And although accommodating radiators discreetly in an old house may take ingenuity, central heating has become a welcome and universally accepted advance.

Nowadays we consider hygienic functional bathrooms plumbed with hot and cold water a necessity, and would scarcely entertain the notion of doing without an indoor toilet.

When making repairs, retain as much original material as possible

It is worth making every effort to reinstate original features

Stone cladding destroys the integrity of a terrace

Drastic refurbishments have all but obliterated the character of these Victorian houses

GETTING IT WRONG

Provided the work is carried out tastefully and to a good standard, genuine improvements not only add to our comfort and wellbeing but also have a positive effect on the value of the property. On the other hand, it pays to think twice before spending large sums of money on what are at best fashionable whims that ultimately could detract from the sale price of your house.

Don't buy a house unless you are prepared to accept what it has to offer. Most old cottages, for example, are built with small rooms and low ceilings, often with modest windows that were never meant to flood the interior with daylight. The doors may be made from rough boards and fitted with worn iron latches and hinges. But that's what makes these houses special.

Replacing original windows and doors not only destroys the character of the building, but also makes little financial sense when they can be repaired and reinstated at no extra cost. No future buyer is likely to object to authentic windows and doors in good condition – the same cannot necessarily be said of PVCu or aluminium replacements.

Cladding the exterior of a house with colourful fake stone, or pebble-dashing what was supposed to be exposed brickwork are irreversible measures that have limited appeal. Apart from the visual disruption they cause to a terrace or group of buildings, the costs involved are unlikely to be recoverable when it comes to selling the house after such treatments have fallen from favour. Similarly, garish paint schemes may dissuade a potential buyer, particularly when the bricks or stonework are painted in bright colours and the pointing is picked out with white or black paint. Restoring painted masonry to its original condition is likely to be expensive.

Every old house has a unique quality, or at least it shares that quality with its immediate neighbours. It is important to recognize and respect those aspects of older houses that distinguish them from run-of-the-mill modern homes and to refrain from transforming them into something that was never intended.

Painting brickwork is a mistake

Colourful but inappropriate paintwork may not appeal to prospective buyers

SURVEYING YOUR HOUSE

H OW YOU GO ABOUT SURVEYING *your house depends on the condition of the building and also on whether you already own the house or intend to buy it. If you have lived in the house for some time and know it sufficiently well to be sure there are no serious defects, you could draw up a schedule of repairs, making a note of which jobs you can tackle yourself and which are best left to professionals.*

If, on the other hand, you are thinking about purchasing a property, then it is advisable to have it surveyed professionally before making up your mind.

Peeling wallpaper is often the first indication of damp in an old building

PROFESSIONAL SURVEYS

If you are applying for a mortgage, the initial survey will probably be carried out by a mortgage-valuation surveyor. A basic valuation survey simply gives the lender a guide as to whether the property is worth the amount of money you have requested. The valuation survey is unlikely to be very detailed and may not even mention certain serious defects. Even if the surveyor finds signs of damp or infestation, the valuation report is unlikely to provide any detailed diagnosis or recommendations, but will probably suggest that the building be inspected by a damp-proofing company or a firm that specializes in spraying to eradicate woodboring insects. Surveyors and valuers undertaking a mortgage valuation of an old house usually refer to what is known as the 'Red Book' (the RICS/ISBA Appraisal and Valuation Manual), which provides guidance on what valuers should look for when inspecting listed or historic buildings.

Another type of survey is the 'Home Buyers' Survey and Valuation Report', which follows a standard format set out by the Royal Institute of Chartered Surveyors (RICS). This is suitable for properties that are in reasonable condition and no more than 150 years old.

In the long run, it is worth investing in an independent full-condition survey, often referred to as a 'building survey'. This

should be undertaken by an expert who is fully conversant with the problems associated with older buildings and who can accurately diagnose defects and make recommendations for correcting them. This type of survey provides a detailed guide to long-term refurbishment and may even furnish ammunition to enable you to negotiate a fair purchase price. A thorough survey is a sound basis for establishing what repairs are necessary, and it should help you devise a realistic timetable for carrying out the work.

Commission a comprehensive survey

UNDERSTANDING A SURVEY

A building survey, which can cover everything from the state of the foundations to the condition of the interior decoration, can at first sight make depressing reading – until you can put it all into perspective. Your first step is to decide which faults are serious and require urgent attention, and which ones can be tackled as part of a long-term strategy.

If you are applying for a mortgage, a building society or bank may insist that you carry out essential repairs highlighted in the surveyor's report before they advance the entire sum you have applied for. And they will almost certainly demand that the repairs are carried out by a contractor who is prepared to furnish guarantees. However, depending on who has carried out the survey, it may be worth getting a second opinion to make sure the defects highlighted in the report are a genuine cause for concern.

Dilapidation and its causes

Weathering is a fundamental cause for dilapidation in all houses, regardless of their age. The combined effects of wind, rain, frost and sunshine create stresses that cause paint to flake, wood to split, masonry to spall, and roofcoverings to fall off. The list of possible defects caused by weathering is long. However, most can be eradicated without too much trouble and can even be prevented by regular maintenance. Indeed, lack of maintenance can be the root cause of a number of problems. A blocked gutter that allows rainwater to spill over and soak the wall below can lead to blown internal plaster or, worse still, an outbreak of dry rot. An airbrick blocked with moss or leaves could be the reason why your floor joists are suffering from fungal attack or mould is growing in your bathroom.

Ill-considered measures carried out in the past can be the cause of your problems today. If earth is piled up against the walls or paving has been laid above recommended levels, water may saturate the masonry, eventually rotting structural timbers below the floor. Poorly executed repairs, including the use of hard cement renders and mortar, can allow moisture to penetrate the structure with similar results.

Though potentially ruinous, none of these problems is insoluble. However, one should be aware that houses subjected to problems such as severe rising damp for prolonged periods can take a long time to recover, even after the initial cause has been identified and remedied.

Why is your house damp?
Damp is high up on the list of concerns for owners of period houses, and it features in a great many surveys. However, the causes of damp are often misunderstood and, as a result, the measures taken to eradicate it are frequently ineffective or unnecessary. There are three main categories of damp – rising damp, penetrating damp and condensation – and each can be mistaken for the others.

Condensation is caused by warm saturated air coming into contact with a cold surface. If that happens to be a windowpane, the nature of the problem is easy to diagnose. But if it happens to be an external wall, a great deal of money can be spent on damp-proofing measures when all that's required is better ventilation, heating and possibly insulation.

Any defect that allows water to make its way through to the inside of the building can be the reason why damp patches or stains are appearing on the inside of your walls and ceilings. Defective seals around doors and windows, missing roof slates or broken flashings, damaged masonry and defective gutters or downpipes are among the most common reasons why there's widespread penetrating damp in your home.

If, however, signs of damp are restricted to an area that extends no more than about 1m (3ft) above skirting level, there's a strong possibility that moisture is being drawn up from the ground below. From the mid 1870s, houses were built with impervious damp-proof courses to prevent moisture rising above critical levels. At later stages, damp-proof membranes were included in concrete floors, for similar reasons. If either a DPC or a DPM has been breached, the simple answer is to have it repaired or replaced – but before opting for such drastic action, you would want to make sure that the surrounding ground level is at least 150mm (6in) below the DPC. Similarly, check that external render that extends below the level of a DPC is not acting as a bridge for rising damp.

Distinguishing one form of damp from another is not always as straightforward as you might imagine. If you are in any doubt, you should consult a professional who has in-depth knowledge of damp in old houses.

Is a DPC necessary?
Before the Public Health Act of 1875, houses were built without damp-proof courses. Moisture rising from the ground into the walls and floors simply evaporated, often without causing the kinds of problems we see today. This was because the materials used in constructing these older buildings were more permeable than their modern equivalents and the structure could 'breathe' more effectively.

Problems tend to occur when attempts are made to upgrade these old houses with modern building standards – walls are covered with impervious paints and renders, lime mortars are replaced with cement-rich mortars, and floors get sealed with DPMs. This all tends to trap moisture within the fabric of the building, and the damp is driven further up the walls. Rising damp usually contains salts that have been carried up from lower levels and, being highly absorbent, the salts exacerbate the problem.

The installation of a DPC may be an appropriate measure to correct rising damp in your home – but before you make a decision, obtain independent expert advice from someone other than a damp-proofing contractor, who may have vested interests (see PROFESSIONAL HELP and ROT & INFESTATION). Dampness is one of the most damaging problems associated with period buildings, and accurate diagnosis is vital to finding the right solution.

Structural movement
Alarm bells start ringing whenever the term subsidence is mentioned in a building survey. Structural movement in old houses can be attributed to a number of causes. It could be the result of rot or infestation, or possibly distortion caused by the movement of materials that react differently to changes in temperature and humidity. Bad practice and ineptitude also contribute to structural instability – partly dismantled chimney breasts, overloaded floors, and poorly supported door and window openings are the sorts of problems often highlighted in survey reports. Period houses were frequently built on shallow foundations, which are not always capable of accommodating natural expansion and contraction of the ground beneath them.

These are all potentially serious defects that could threaten the stability of the building, but in reality a great many old houses move to some degree without it ever becoming a problem. In some cases, settlement has occurred in the past but at some point the building has stabilized again. Only when

Subsidence may need expert attention

Movement may have stabilized

Get expert advice from a surveyor

movement is ongoing and threatens the safety of the structure should the owner be concerned. To reassure yourself, seek the advice of a structural engineer who is familiar with the construction and behaviour of old houses (see PROFESSIONAL HELP).

MAINTENANCE & REPAIR

COMMISSIONING A PROFESSIONAL SURVEY *is merely the first step in getting your house in good order. You now have to act on that advice and draw up a schedule of repairs. Following your survey point by point, make an inspection yourself to ascertain which tasks you can tackle personally and make notes of those jobs you will put out to professionals. Even if you have been living in your house for years, a similar exercise will help you plan a programme of regular maintenance.*

REGULAR MAINTENANCE

On founding the Society for the Protection of Ancient Buildings in 1877, William Morris spoke of the need to 'stave off decay by daily care, to prop a perilous wall or mend a leaky roof'. Morris was stressing the importance of tending to minor defects before they get out of hand and become expensive repairs.

Routine maintenance is designed to tackle the defects that occur during the life of any building – it is a form of insurance against more serious problems and, as such, should be adopted by every home owner. It may seem like a tedious chore, but a building that is looked after properly retains its maximum value and enriches the neighbourhood. At the same time, you avoid the stress and expense of dealing with unexpected emergency repairs and may prevent accidents to your family and members of the public.

It is convenient to divide a programme of maintenance into three parts:
● Inspection – assessing the condition of the building and checking that the services are working satisfactorily.
● Remedial action – drawing up a list of minor repairs and specific tasks, such as clearing leaves and debris from blocked gutters, that you are able to undertake yourself.
● Instituting long-term repairs – undertaking work needed in order to rectify more serious defects that will return the building to good condition. You may decide to employ professionals for this type of work, which falls outside your programme of day-to-day maintenance.

Inspecting the property

Ideally you should inspect your house twice a year: in the autumn, to safeguard the house throughout the winter, and again in spring to see what maintenance can be done outside when the weather is more favourable. Take a look at the building after heavy rain, when defective gutters, downpipes and leaky roofs are going to be easier to spot.

Work safely. If you have to climb a ladder to check the roof or look into the loft, make sure that the ladder is propped at a safe angle and is secured on firm ground. Where access is particularly difficult, consider employing a professional.

You will need some basic equipment to help you inspect your house and note defects: binoculars that will enable you to inspect the roof and chimneys from the ground, a penknife for probing timber to see if it is hard or spongy, a pocket notebook, a torch, and a compact camera to record defects, especially those you want to show to a professional.

It is worth starting a log in which you can make a record of your inspection and then document all the repairs you make to your house. Any professional surveys can be filed together with your personal log. You could store the information and scanned photographs on a personal computer, but a scrapbook serves the same purpose and will no doubt prove to be a fascinating document in years to come, perhaps even being handed over to the next occupier.

No two houses are ever exactly the same, but knowing where to look and what to look for may help you spot potential problems. The illustrated check list on the following pages will serve as a guide to analysing the condition of your house and preparing a plan of action.

DOING IT YOURSELF

Fees for professional labour often constitute the largest proportion of the costs involved in repairing an old house. It is therefore not surprising that the DIY trade has mushroomed dramatically in order to serve the ever growing numbers of amateur builders, decorators and plumbers. But no matter how enterprising you are, there will always be some aspects of the work where it is expedient to hire contractors, simply because they can do the job better, faster and more safely than someone who is not a skilled tradesperson.

To help you decide on the most appropriate approach to maintaining and repairing your house, keyed illustrations are included, both in the pages that follow and throughout the book, suggesting which jobs are so straightforward that even a beginner can achieve satisfactory results, which ones require a reasonable level of competence, and which are best left to a professional contractor.

DRAWING UP A CHECK LIST

Old houses are built *primarily from three kinds of material – wood, stone and brick – with a variety of roof coverings. In addition, some are rendered and many are plastered internally. Each of these materials deteriorates in a particular way, and this determines how well a house is able to stand up to natural weathering. Being able to recognize the various forms of decay and dilapidation is the key to instigating an effective programme of regular maintenance.*

Be systematic when inspecting your house, so you don't miss anything. It is often best to start at the top, making a note of any roof or chimney defects, then gradually work down through the structure, inside and out. Once you have inspected the building itself, lift the manhole covers to see whether there are any blockages within the drainage system, and clean out debris and leaves from the gullies at the foot of your rainwater downpipes. At the same time, cut back any plant growth that is causing physical damage or encouraging damp conditions. Finally, check the condition of boundary walls and fences.

ROOF AND CHIMNEYS

Check your roof regularly, especially after storms or strong winds. If you notice slate or tile fragments on the ground, inspect your roof from all angles (including from inside the roof space) for indications of damage. Be sure to inspect the gutters and downpipes, to make sure they are not leaking and saturating the wall below.

Unstable chimney
An unstable chimney should be repaired before it topples, causing extensive damage and possibly injuries to pedestrians.
▲ Exposed masonry is susceptible to weathering. Repair or rebuild (pages 72–3).

Climbers out of control
Ivy and other climbing plants left to grow unchecked can block gutters and damage roof coverings and chimneys.
● Cut back climbers at least once a year, making sure you have a safe platform to work from.

Moss growing on the roof
On a thatched roof, moss indicates moisture retention. Get expert advice.
▲ Have the roof inspected by a master thatcher (page 65).
● Scrape moss from other roofcoverings before it blocks the gutters.

ASSESSING REPAIRS

● Easy even for beginners.
■ Fairly difficult. Good practical skills required.
▲ Difficult. Hire a professional.
◆ Various levels of skill required.

Broken downpipe
Staining and algae are often signs of a leaking downpipe.
■ Have corroded downpipes repaired or replaced. Clean and repaint stained walls. Check inside the house for signs of damp (page 25).

Damaged gutters
Broken or blocked gutters cause penetrating damp when rainwater soaks the wall.
■ Repair the gutter and check for signs of damp (page 25).
● Check the condition of parapet and valley gutters.

Loose slates or tiles
Corroded fixings allow slates and tiles to slip out of place.
◆ Reinstate or replace slates or tiles (pages 67–9).

Poorly maintained flashing
Inappropriate repairs are likely to deteriorate rapidly.
▲ Have an expert replicate the original flashing (page 70).
● Check all lead flashings and mortar fillets for signs of dilapidation.

WALLS

Masonry in good condition stands up well to weathering, and will usually dry out quickly after heavy rain. However, as soon as defects are allowed to go unattended, water begins to seep into the structure and serious deterioration can develop. Check for signs of damage outside, and for damp patches and stains on internal plasterwork.

ASSESSING REPAIRS
● Easy even for beginners.
■ Fairly difficult. Good practical skills required.
▲ Difficult. Hire a professional.
◆ Various levels of skill required.

Eroded pointing
Mortar can deteriorate and fall out of the joints.
■ Repoint the wall (pages 36–7).

Cracked pointing
Brittle cement mortar tends to crack and allow moisture to penetrate the wall.
◆ Cut out the cracked mortar and repoint (pages 36–7).

Spalled brickwork
Low-strength bricks are susceptible to frost damage.
■ Insert replacements in severe cases (page 38). Repoint with lime mortar (page 37).

Cracked masonry
This may not be serious.
■ Replace individual cracked bricks (page 38).
▲ Have extensive cracking checked (pages 24–5, 230).

Damaged wattle and daub
Carry out prompt repairs where daub is missing and wattle framework exposed.
▲ Seek expert advice on suitable repair materials.

Delaminating stone
Poorly laid stone can flake.
▲ Consolidate serious flaking with epoxy resin (page 50).
▲ Have badly damaged stone replaced by a contractor.

Mould growth
Organic growth proliferates in damp conditions.
● Scrape off the mould and try to determine why the wall is damp. If necessary, treat the wall with a biocide (page 34).

STRUCTURAL TIMBERS AND WOODWORK

Old houses incorporate a great many timber components, ranging from structural beams and joists to decorative woodwork. Like wooden windows and doors, these components suffer from the effects of weathering and rot. Because carved and fretted woodwork can be expensive to replace, decorative features are often in poor condition or have been discarded.

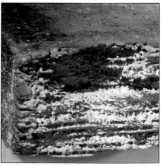

Dry rot
Timber that is allowed to get wet in poorly ventilated areas of a building is subject to fungal attack.
▲ Get expert advice on remedial treatment (pages 24–5, 227).

Woodworm
Woodboring insects consume house timbers.
● Treat minor outbreaks with preservative (page 226).
▲ Have seriously infested timber treated by experts (page 226).

Broken render
Cracked and loose render can fall from the wall.
■ Patch damaged render before damp develops (page 52).

DOORS AND WINDOWS

Because they are vulnerable to decay and corrosion, doors and windows require special attention. Not only should you attend to any defects in the wood or metalwork, but make sure the seals around the frames and doorcases are well maintained, in order to prevent penetrating damp and wood rot.

ASSESSING REPAIRS

● Easy even for beginners.
■ Fairly difficult. Good practical skills required.
▲ Difficult. Hire a professional.
◆ Various levels of skill required.

Overpainted woodwork
Layers of old paint can obscure fine details.
● Before you strip and repaint the wood, make sure you are not erasing historical evidence (pages 81–2).

Damaged doors
Weathering affects wooden doors that have not been painted regularly.
■ Repair loose joints (page 83).
■ Bottom rails are particularly prone to rot (page 85, 114).

Poorly maintained joinery
Often, doors and windows are in need of attention. Expect to redecorate every three to five years.
■ Repair and repaint (pages 81–91, 109–15, 118).

Corroded metal frames
Rust sheds paint from metal casements.
◆ Treat and repaint (page 118).

Wet rot
Neglect causes water to rot wooden frames and sills.
■ Repair or replace rotted wood (pages 114–15).

SERVICES

Serious water damage can occur if pipes burst after freezing, so check that cold-water pipes are insulated. Employ a qualified contractor to service your boiler and other appliances annually.

Mains electrical installations are dangerous if they have not been updated and are not kept in good working order.

Old wiring and equipment
Unsafe wiring and electrical equipment must be replaced at the earliest opportunity.
▲ Get a competent electrician to test your circuits and fuse board.

FENCES AND BOUNDARY WALLS

Fences and garden walls are an integral part of your property. Wooden components can be replaced and treated for rot, and masonry repointed. Many of the problems associated with metalwork you can tackle yourself, and there are plenty of skilled contractors able to carry out more major repairs or reinstate missing components.

Rusty or broken metalwork
Corrosion is the most common cause of metal deterioration.
◆ Paint, repair or replace shabby metalwork (pages 191–200).

LEGAL PROTECTION FOR OLD HOUSES

LEGISLATION EXISTS TO PROTECT BUILDINGS *of special interest and to control building development and the methods and materials used for construction. The relevant items of legislation tend to be complex, and they are often amended and reviewed. The information given here should not be taken as an* authoritative interpretation of the law, and you should always check with the relevant authorities for information and clarification. Most householders sensibly employ a professional to make the necessary applications, including the preparation of the drawings that are often required for the various forms of consent.

LISTED BUILDINGS
Since the nineteenth century, amenity societies such as the Society for the Protection of Ancient Buildings have existed to encourage the preservation of old houses and other structures. However, it was not until 1947 that significant numbers of houses were given legal protection. Part of the purpose of the legislation was to ensure that buildings of special architectural or historical interest could not be demolished or altered without consent.

In England and Wales, there are three main grades: Grade I (the highest grade), Grade II* (known as two-star listing), and Grade II. In Scotland and Northern Ireland, there are slightly different grades.

Listed status does not just cover features mentioned in the listing description. It covers the entire building, inside and out, and may also include other structures that are attached or close by.

If your house is listed, it does not mean that all alterations are precluded, but you must apply to your local planning authority for listed-building consent before making any alterations. To proceed without consent is a criminal offence. If you are in any doubt as to whether the work you propose may require consent, contact the Conservation Officer at your local authority.

If the owner of a listed building neglects to keep it in good condition, the local authority can serve a repairs notice to enforce proper upkeep; and if the owner then continues to ignore legitimate requests, the local authority may issue a compulsory-purchase order.

Grants are sometimes available to help owners of listed buildings meet the costs of necessary repairs (see PROFESSIONAL HELP).

CONSERVATION AREAS
Regardless of whether or not it contains listed buildings, a locality that merits preservation can be designated a conservation area by a local authority. A conservation area has additional planning protection to safeguard the area's special character. This ranges from protection of trees to consent for demolition, new developments and alterations to buildings. The authority is required to pay special attention to preserving the character and appearance of the area. With a few minor exceptions, it is illegal to demolish any building within such an area or to alter the external appearance of the building without consent from the local planning authority. In some cases, the local authority may use an 'Article 4 Direction' to remove permitted development rights; this enables it to control alterations that affect the character of the area, such as the removal or alteration of doors or windows.

National Parks also have special consent procedures.

PLANNING PERMISSION
Planning permission is needed before you carry out any alteration that affects the use or siting of a building or other structure. In addition, any development that does not blend sympathetically with its surroundings may require consent. However, your proposed development may fall within permitted development rights, for which planning consent is not required. Extensions and conversions generally require planning permission – but even building a garden wall can be subject to approval if, for example, it blocks a right of way. Therefore, it pays to contact the planning department at the outset, before making detailed plans.

Having submitted your application, you can expect a decision within eight weeks. Once granted, planning permission remains valid for five years. If permission is refused, the authority has to give you a full explanation – so that, if you wish to do so, you can amend your plans and resubmit them for further consideration. Alternatively, you can submit an appeal against the decision, using a form obtainable from the planning authority. Should you proceed without consent, the planning authority can insist you restore the building to its previous state.

BUILDING REGULATIONS
Even if planning permission or listed-building consent is not needed, you will have to obtain Building Regulations approval (Building Standards in Scotland) for structural alterations and for any other alterations that fall within the scope of the regulations. The applicability of Building Regulations depends on the extent and type of changes proposed and on considerations such as whether the property is a single dwelling and whether the work may affect neighbouring properties. The regulations are designed to implement adequate construction and health-and-safety standards, and also govern issues such as access to buildings. If you are unsure about the need for approval, speak to your local Building Control Officer. If your building is listed or in a conservation area, you may be able to obtain special concessions from Building Control in order not to compromise historic features.

You are obliged either to supply 'full plans' showing all constructional details or to complete a form called a 'building notice', which you can obtain from your local Building Control Office. Scale drawings have to accompany a building notice, but they need not be as detailed as the ones required for a full-plans application.

Apply for approval well in advance, so you have time to discuss your proposals with the Building Control Officer. He or she will also advise on relevant local legislation and tell you whether you need to approach other authorities concerning sanitation, fire escapes and so on. So that the Building Control Officer can arrange an inspection, you must give at least 48 hours' notice before starting work and 24 hours' notice before covering foundations or laying drains. You must also let the officer know when the work has been finished.

PARTY-WALL AWARDS
If you plan to carry out work on or near to a wall shared with neighbours, a party-wall agreement may be required. A booklet explaining the provisions of the Party Wall Act 1996 is available on the website of the Office of the Deputy Prime Minister under 'Building Regulations'.

CHAPTER THREE

BRICKWORK

DURING THE LATE EIGHTEENTH CENTURY towns expanded rapidly as builders constructed acres of densely packed terraces to house the thousands drawn from the countryside by the promise of employment in factories, mills and workshops. Brick was frequently the material chosen to satisfy this demand for housing that could be built quickly and cheaply. The result was often rows of overcrowded houses lacking basic amenities. These became the notorious Victorian slums, many of which were cleared for the rebuilding schemes of the 1950s and 1960s.

However, brick was by no means an exclusively working-class material. On the other side of town, the

merchants and industrialists who had prospered from the new technology erected luxurious villas. In parts of the country where good local building stone was lacking, brick was just as likely to have been used for these houses built by the new middle class.

The better-quality houses boasted fine ornamental brickwork, with moulded terracotta tiles, decorative coursing and finely gauged arches. Yet with its subtle colours and texture enhanced by age and weathering, even plain bonded brickwork is often a delight to the eye. These are qualities well worth preserving, especially as shaped and decorative bricks and terracotta panels can be replicated easily by specialist suppliers.

The warm glow of London stocks

Victorian moulded-brick tiles

Care and attention was often lavished on the smallest of brick houses

Beautifully detailed brick almshouse

Fine early C18th rubbed brickwork

COLOURS & TEXTURES

BEFORE INDUSTRIAL CHANGES *made mass production feasible and transport easier, bricks were produced for a particular locality, using the clays occurring in that part of the country. Local clays lent a distinctive colour to the brickwork of the region.*

When improved transportation systems were introduced in the nineteenth century, it became possible to buy bricks made at the other end of the country. Often bricks were named after the town or district in which they were made. The list must once have been extremely long and included evocative names such as Accrington Bloods, Staffordshire Blues and Leicester Reds. The ready availability of a variety of coloured bricks helped to bring to an end clearly defined regional characteristics. It also contributed to the spread of the spectacular polychrome brickwork much loved by the Victorians.

BRICK MANUFACTURING
Although the local clay gave a brick its distinctive colour, the subtleties of shape and hue were to a large extent determined by the method of manufacture.

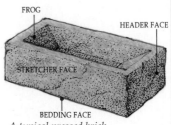

A typical pressed brick

Hand-moulded bricks
Although there were early attempts at mechanization, before the mid nineteenth century all bricks were made by hand in individual wooden moulds. The clay was 'pugged' (mixed with water and kneaded to a smooth consistency), often in a horse-driven pug mill.

Sand, or sometimes water, was sprinkled into open-top moulds to prevent the clay sticking to them. Then the moulds were filled, and the clay levelled with a steel or wooden straightedge. After the 'green' bricks had been turned out of the moulds, they were often stacked on layers of straw to dry naturally before being fired.

Pressed bricks
Bricks with sharper arrises (edges) and a smoother surface texture were produced mechanically by pressing semi-dry clay into moulds. Since they were dense and hard-wearing, pressed bricks were frequently employed as facing bricks for façades.

Wire-cut bricks
The other common mechanized method of production was to extrude a long bar of clay and use wires to slice it into bricks. Wire-cut bricks do not have the distinctive recesses known as 'frogs' often found on pressed bricks. The frog fills up with mortar, thus keying the brick into the wall, and also reduces the weight of the brick.

Some pressed bricks have a recess in the top face only; others have a frog in the bedding face as well. Wire-cut bricks are sometimes made with holes passing through them that perform a similar function.

The mottled colours of old handmade bricks

Patterned polychromatic brickwork

Colourful brickwork incorporating projecting headers

CLEANING & WEATHERPROOFING

An impressive Gothic-revival façade built from coloured bricks and stone

BEFORE EMBARKING *on an ambitious and irreversible cleaning programme, it is worth pausing to consider why you should want to clean the brickwork of your house at all. There's every reason to remove stains, spilled paint and graffiti, but it would be disastrous to lose the mellow character of nicely weathered brickwork in the pursuit of total renovation. Harsh methods of cleaning that involve sandblasting or powerful chemicals have the most detrimental effects and they tend to leave brickwork looking unpleasantly raw.*

An overcleaned detached house looks bad enough. It is even worse to spoil the appearance of a lovely old terrace by cleaning or stripping individual dwellings.

Yellow London stocks show the dramatic results of cleaning brickwork

Firing bricks

Once the clay had dried out, the bricks had to be baked to make them hard enough for building purposes. The earliest method of firing bricks was to pile them in rows in a stack or 'clamp'. Channels left between the rows were filled with timber (or, later, with coal or coke), and the entire stack was surrounded with previously fired bricks daubed with clay. The whole clamp was then set alight and was left to burn, sometimes for weeks. The method produced unevenly fired bricks that varied in colour according to their position within the clamp. Hand-made bricks were fired in clamps until the process was industrialized, at which point firing in brick-built kilns became the preferred method of production, as it produced bricks of a more consistent hardness and colour. The early kilns were tiny compared with modern continuous kilns, normally consisting of a simple brick chamber with an opening at one end that was sealed before firing.

BRICK CLASSIFICATION

Modern firing techniques are designed to produce bricks with specific characteristics – but with earlier methods the bricks from a single firing varied in quality and had to be sorted according to their properties.

The most regular bricks (the ones that were most evenly fired) were classified as 'facings' or face bricks. These attractive weather-resistant bricks were generally used for building exposed exterior walls. The less uniform, poorly fired bricks were designated as common or place bricks and were normally used for constructing walls that were to be covered with plaster or stucco. Overburnt bricks, from the hottest parts of the clamp or kiln, were reserved for flue linings or for headers in diaper-pattern brickwork.

WASHING BRICKWORK

An old brick house in any environment will eventually develop a patina due to airborne dirt and pollution. This 'natural' weathering simply reflects the history of the building. However, if you are really bothered by the appearance of your brick-work, it is often possible to wash off surface grime with water.

Starting at the top of the wall, wet an area of bricks with a garden hose and scrub the brickwork with a stiff-bristle brush. Never use a wire brush, which can damage the surface of the bricks. Clean the wall in horizontal bands, gradually working your way down to the bottom.

Heavy deposits that have combined with the brick surface chemically can usually only be removed by professional masonry-cleaning contractors, using hydrofluoric acid.

STRIPPING A PAINTED WALL

Brickwork in good condition does not need painting, rendering or any other form of weatherproofing – but sadly there are plenty of houses with once beautiful brickwork hidden beneath layers of paint.

Probably unnecessary in the first place, the paint is now expensive to remove. There are professionals who will undertake this work for you, but before proceeding consult your local Conservation Officer to ensure that it won't have adverse effects on the brickwork.

Stripping painted brickwork

There are several reasons why it may be advisable to hire a reliable professional company to strip old paint from brickwork. First of all, it is usually necessary to erect scaffolding, perhaps around an entire building that may be several storeys high. Also, experience of applying and removing chemical stripper is essential in order to remove every trace of paint from a deeply textured surface. In addition, paint stripping on this sort of scale can be a time-consuming and messy business, involving the use of toxic materials that have to be handled with care and disposed of safely. Most oil-based paints, for example, can be softened using a methylene-chloride paint stripper applied as a thick paste, or by applying other proprietary pastes that contain sodium hydroxide. Thick coatings of paint may require several applications of a stripper. This type of treatment can leave harmful salts in the mortar joints if paint stripper is not washed away adequately.

To determine whether the outcome is likely to be satisfactory, ask the company or contractor you are thinking of hiring to strip a small inconspicuous patch of brickwork, using the chemicals they recommend for the job. In certain cases the results may indicate that it is better to repaint, in which case you should use a paint suitable for masonry (see PAINT FOR PERIOD HOUSES).

Alternatives to painting

Once the old paint has been removed (or if you want to preserve unpainted brickwork), your best option is to prevent moisture permeating the wall by repointing or by repairing or replacing cracked and spalled bricks. But there are situations where a whole wall has become porous due to natural erosion, or because the brickwork has been subjected to abrasive cleaning. Blasting with sand or grit should be avoided, as it tears and pits the surface of the brickwork, accelerating decay.

Water ingress is usually through poor pointing, and rarely through the bricks themselves. Consequently, it is nearly always more appropriate and effective to repoint the wall than to coat it with a water repellent. Some repellents can trap moisture within the walls, and can also exacerbate salt damage to soft bricks. After a while, repellents cease to be effective and can attract dirt. In the rare cases where water repellents can be justified, the wall should be coated after repointing with porous lime mortar, which allows salts and moisture to escape through the joints. Brick walls should never be coated with a water repellent immediately after chemical paint stripping or cleaning with water, as this risks trapping moisture in the masonry.

Heavy organic growth on brickwork should be treated with a biocide

REMOVING STAINS

Tar, grease and oil can often be softened by applying white spirit, paraffin or a proprietary grease solvent. Since there is a slight risk that the softened stain will be spread further if you attempt to wash it from the surface, apply a poultice to absorb the oil or grease. To make a poultice, saturate an absorbent material (such as whiting, fuller's earth, sawdust, or even talcum powder) with solvent. Follow the maker's recommendations when handling and disposing of solvents. Also, always wear protective gloves and goggles.

Dampen the stain with the solvent, then cover it immediately with a layer of poultice about 12mm (½in) thick. Tape a sheet of plastic over the poultice, and leave it to dry out and absorb the stain. When the poultice is dry, use a wooden or plastic spatula to lift it off the wall. Finally, scrub the bricks with water and a bristle brush.

EFFLORESCENCE

A white crystalline deposit that commonly appears on new and old brickwork, efflorescence is caused by soluble salts within the masonry migrating to the surface. This occurs as saturated masonry dries out. Efflorescence can also occur within the bricks – the salt crystals damage the surface of the brickwork, particularly if the bricks are underfired. Locate and cure the cause of the dampness within the wall (such as a failed damp-proof course), then brush the crystals from the bricks with a stiff-bristle brush. You may also have to brush the wall periodically as the masonry dries out.

ORGANIC GROWTH

Since moulds and lichens tend to grow in moist conditions, their presence may indicate a source of damp that needs to be eradicated before any surface treatment is considered.

To remove heavy organic growth from a wall, scrape it from the bricks with a non-metallic spatula; then apply a clear proprietary biocide specifically formulated for masonry. Paint on a generous application of the biocide, starting at the top of the wall. After a couple of days, when the wall has dried, brush off the dead growth and treat the wall a second time.

BRICK BONDS

MORTAR, *though strong under compression, has practically no tensile strength. If a wall was built by stacking bricks one directly above the other, creating continuous vertical joints, movement within the wall would tend to pull the joints apart and seriously weaken the structure. Bonding (staggering the vertical joints) ties the bricks together and spreads any load over a wide area. Brick bonding is primarily functional and the patterns created by staggering the joints can be most attractive.*

TRADITIONAL BRICK BONDS

Modern cavity walls consist of two individual leaves of masonry that are separated by a gap spanned by metal or plastic ties. Most frequently, the outer leaf consists of brickwork built with a stretcher bond. In contrast, up to at least the end of the nineteenth century, since most brick walls were solid, they were constructed with a variety of traditional bonding patterns that utilized different combinations of stretchers and headers. Stretchers are the bricks that run parallel with the face of the wall; headers run from front to back, tying the stretcher courses together.

In the eighteenth century, façades were frequently only one brick thick. These façades were tied to the structural brickwork of the building with true headers in every fifth or sixth course; the rest of the 'headers' were simply half-bricks.

There is no real evidence to suggest that one bond is significantly stronger than another. It must therefore be assumed that the popularity of any particular style was primarily due to its visual appeal. English bond, Flemish bond and English garden-wall bond were all developed in the fifteenth and sixteenth centuries, and have been used for solid-brick walls ever since. The Flemish bond was especially popular in Georgian times.

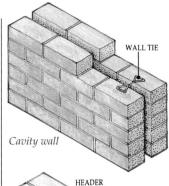
Cavity wall

WALL TIE

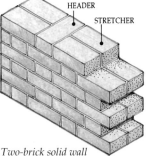
HEADER
STRETCHER
Two-brick solid wall

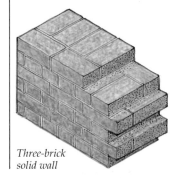
Three-brick solid wall

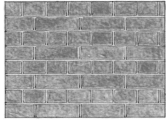
English bond

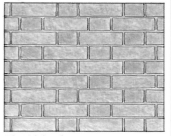
Flemish bond

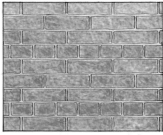
English garden-wall bond

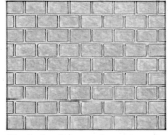
Header bond

DECORATIVE BONDS

Purely decorative bonds were used to relieve large areas of unbroken brickwork, typically in the form of basket-weave or herringbone panels.

Traditional diaper work (which used dark headers to produce diamond patterns against paler brickwork) is just one example of how bricks of contrasting colour or tone were incorporated into a decorative bond. Similar patterns were also created by allowing headers to project slightly from a wall so that they would cast attractive shadows.

C19th diaper-pattern brickwork

Combination of basket-weave and herring-bone panels

REPOINTING BRICKWORK

S KILLED BRICKLAYERS *have always taken pride in their ability to build regular bonds with precise joints. Much relies on the consistency of the mortar. It must neither be so firm that it prevents the bricklayer tapping each course into alignment nor so soft that it slumps under the weight of the bricks. In addition, each mortar joint must be shaped to complement the style of the building and the type of bricks used in its construction. The collective name for these shaped joints is pointing.*

Early-C19th tuck pointing used to simulate rubbed brickwork

Eroded pointing weakens the wall

Cement-rich mortar is liable to crack

WHEN TO REPOINT

Repointing is a laborious job that is expensive if you hire a bricklayer to do the work and time-consuming if you do it yourself. Consequently, it is advisable only to repoint when necessary and to limit repairs to as small an area as possible, matching the old pointing in shape, colour and texture. Within a fairly short time, the new and old pointing will be practically indistinguishable, provided the work is done properly. But if say three-quarters of the pointing has decayed, then it makes sense to rake out what's left and repoint the entire wall – or, if need be, the whole building.

If recent repointing is too unsightly to ignore, there may be a case for raking out the mortar and starting again. Otherwise, look for signs of deterioration likely to lead to penetrating damp or to the disintegration of the bricks themselves.

Natural erosion

Under the combined assault of wind and driving rain, soft mortar tends to erode, especially on the windward side of exposed buildings. Erosion can lead to deep crevices in the pointing that not only allow rainwater to soak deeply into the wall but may eventually lead to loose brickwork.

Damp and frost

Excessive damp caused by leaking gutters and down-pipes can exacerbate the effects of erosion, and the action of frost tends to make matters even worse.

Cracked mortar

As often as not, cracked mortar is the result of using an inflexible cement-rich mortar that is unable to absorb the slightest movement within the masonry. In a relatively short time, cracked mortar falls out, leaving vulnerable open joints.

JOINT STYLES

Unless it is leading to deterioration of the brickwork, it is best to copy the existing style of joint when repointing a small area of wall. However, if complete repointing seems inevitable, choose the style most appropriate for the age of the house and the condition of the brickwork.

The joints described below are probably those most often used for the brickwork of old houses. If you have walls pointed with one of the less common styles (such as beaded or V-shaped pointing) that may be original, then it is worth finding a bricklayer able to replicate them.

Flush joint

Before the second half of the nineteenth century most brickwork was pointed with flush joints. In practice, many so-called flush joints are slightly recessed or concave to allow for the rounded arrises of old handmade or worn bricks.

Weatherstruck joint

This joint has only been in use since the 1850s or 1860s. It sheds water efficiently and enhances the appearance of bricks with sharp arrises. It is not suitable for repointing very old brickwork.

Tuck pointing

Tuck pointing was used, in the eighteenth century especially, to simulate the exactness of rubbed brickwork (see OPENINGS IN BRICKWORK).

The joints were filled flush, using mortar coloured to match the brickwork. Fine grooves, scored along the centres of the joints, were filled with a slightly projecting strip of lime putty. This was normally white and was sometimes mixed with silver sand. Less commonly, soot was used to stain it black. When repairs are necessary, it pays to hire a bricklayer with experience of replacing tuck pointing.

Penny-round pointing

As proper tuck pointing was expensive, bricklayers were sometimes persuaded to substitute penny-round pointing. Although a narrow groove was scored along each joint (presumably with a coin), to save money the lime putty was omitted.

1 Flush joint *2 Weatherstruck* *3 Tuck pointing* *4 Penny-round*

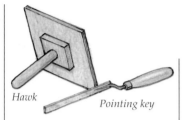

Hawk　*Pointing key*

PREPARING THE WALL

Rake out the old mortar to a depth at least twice the width of the joint, using a piece of wood shaped to fit the joints. If necessary, chop out hard mortar with a mason's quirk (plugging chisel) – a special tool that you can rent from a tool-hire company. Take care not to damage the edges of the bricks. Never use a power tool, such as a chain saw or an angle grinder.

Brush out all loose material, then hose the wall lightly so that the new mortar will not dry too quickly.

Chop out hard pointing

FILLING AND SHAPING THE JOINTS

Many builders use a small pointing trowel to push mortar into the open joints, but a better method is to use a tool called a pointing key or jointer that fits between the bricks. Carry a small quantity of mortar to the wall on a hawk (a hand-held board with a wooden handle underneath). Holding the hawk against the wall, fill each joint flush with mortar, compacting it with the pointing key **(1)**. Try not to smear mortar onto the faces of the bricks. Leave the mortar to stiffen until it will retain a clear impression of your thumb, then shape the joints as appropriate. As soon as the pointing has set, use a dry scrubbing brush to clean any specks of mortar from the faces of the bricks.

Flush joints

Flush joints need no further shaping; but if the finish left by the tool looks smoother than the old mortar, you can stipple the joints with a stiff-bristle brush to expose the sand aggregate **(2)**.

Weatherstruck joints

Use the pointing key to shape the mortar, leaving each joint with a sloping profile. The vertical joints, which should be shaped first, can slope to either right or left – look at the original pointing and make the new joints consistent.

Bricklayers remove excess mortar from the base of the joints with a tool called a Frenchman that has a blade with a right-angled tip. You can make one from a narrow strip of thin metal.

Use a wood straightedge to guide the Frenchman's blade. Nail plywood scraps to the straightedge to serve as spacers, so there's a gap through which the excess mortar can drop as you draw the tool along the joints.

1 Use a pointing key to fill joints

2 Stipple flush joints with a brush

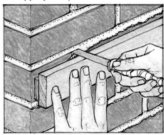

Scrape off mortar with a Frenchman

MORTAR

Old brickwork was usually built using lime mortar. Even when set, this mortar is flexible enough to withstand slight movement in a wall without cracking. Also, lime-based mortar allows moisture within the wall to evaporate harmlessly. When cement-based mortar is used to repoint soft brickwork, it prevents evaporation except through the bricks themselves. This can result in the surfaces of the bricks spalling (flaking).

Lime for mortar

Lime is classified as either hydraulic or non-hydraulic, and is sold in various forms.

Non-hydraulic or 'fat lime' hardens slowly when exposed to the air. Nowadays it is available as lime putty in sealed tubs and can also be obtained premixed with sand.

Hydrated or 'bagged lime' is non-hydraulic lime, the water having been removed. It is sold as a powder in bags at builders' merchants. It needs to be soaked in water for 24 to 48 hours to 'fatten up' to a putty with the consistency of yoghurt before it is ready to be used for mortar.

Naturally hydraulic lime, also supplied as a powder, sets by chemical reaction with water. It sets faster than non-hydraulic lime and is not so entirely dependent on contact with the air. Naturally hydraulic lime is available in various strengths.

Matching colour and texture

To match original pointing, choose the ingredients of the new mortar carefully. Sand varies a great deal in colour, and grade. A mortar made with a relatively coarse grade of sharp sand usually matches the appearance of old weathered pointing.

Even with the correct materials, it is difficult to get a precise match unless you prepare some test samples of mortar and let them dry. However, the only way to determine the make-up of the old mortar exactly is to have it analysed by a specialist.

Mixing mortar

Of all the mixes available, the one you might consider using is a weak naturally hydraulic lime supplied as a powder for mixing with water and sand. Mix the mortar in the proportions of 1 part lime to 2.5 parts sand, and add water until the mixture has the consistency of cottage cheese. As lime is caustic, always wear gloves and goggles when mixing and handling it.

Don't apply lime mortars in either freezing, very wet, very dry or windy conditions. Once applied, lime mortar should be protected from wet weather with plastic sheeting for 2 or 3 days. In a hot dry atmosphere use dampened hessian sacking instead.

REPAIRING BRICKWORK

EXTENSIVELY CRACKED BRICKWORK *and bulging walls should be inspected by a surveyor, architect or structural engineer (see* PROFESSIONAL HELP) *to ascertain the cause of the damage and to determine whether the structure has stabilized. Even serious faults such as defective foundations, broken lintels or detached bonding can be corrected, but the remedial work should always be carried out by an experienced contractor.*

You may find the professional's report indicates that there has been minimal movement, and it is always possible that the movement may have been arrested by a previous owner. In such cases, you will probably be able to repoint or replace the damaged bricks yourself.

REPLACING SPALLED BRICKS

In freezing conditions the expansion of water trapped just below the surface of bricks often causes spalling (flaking) since the moisture cannot evaporate evenly.

If spalling is widespread, hard cement pointing may have cracked, allowing moisture to penetrate. Or there could be drainage problems at the base of the wall, or a defective damp-proof course allowing rising damp. These defects should be eradicated before further treatment is considered.

More often, spalling affects only a small area of the wall, and individual bricks can be cut out and replaced. There's a limit to the number of bricks you can take out without destabilizing the structure of the wall. If more than two or three bricks have to be removed at a time, hire a builder.

POINTING WORN BRICKS

As soft mortar is eroded the corners and arrises (edges) of the bricks are exposed to the elements, and eventually they will become worn and rounded. If worn bricks are pointed so that the mortar is flush with their stretcher faces, the joints look much wider than intended. Also, the mortar presents weak feathered edges that quickly deteriorate (**1**).

When you are repointing worn bricks, recess the joints to retain their original width. Recessed joints look best if they are flat or slightly concave (**2**). Special tools are made for shaping concave joints, but you can improvise with a short length of bent copper tubing. Finally, stipple the mortar with a brush to match weathered pointing.

1 *Flush joint with weak edges* **2** *Recessed joint is preferable*

Cutting out a spalled brick
Rake out the mortar joints around the spalled brick. If need be, loosen the mortar by boring into it with a masonry drill (**1**) and chop out what remains with a quirk (plugging chisel). After you have removed the brick, brush dust from the cavity and dampen the inside.

1 *Loosen mortar with a drill*

Inserting a replacement
Spread mortar on the bottom of the cavity and up one side. Wet the replacement brick, spread mortar on top of the brick and on one end, then insert it into the cavity (**2**). Compact the mortar and, once it begins to get firm, shape the joints to match the rest of the pointing.

2 *Insert a mortared brick*

FINDING REPLACEMENT BRICKS

Finding replacement bricks that will blend with period brickwork is not easy. With their clean, sharp edges, mass-produced bricks are usually too perfect; they are also unlikely to be the same size as the ones you are replacing. On the other hand, you can have hand-moulded bricks made to any specification you require, although you will need to track down a specialist brick manufacturer operating in your part of the country.

Most people restoring old brickwork try to acquire some second-hand bricks (seconds) from a building of a similar age and style that has undergone alterations or partial demolition. Whenever possible, avoid buying seconds that have been repointed with cement-rich mortar. It usually has to be hacked off with a cold chisel, which often results in bricks being broken.

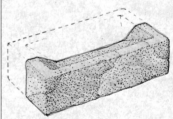

Cut bricks lengthwise for economy

If you are repairing a small area of brickwork, you can make your supply of second-hand replacement bricks go twice as far by cutting them in half with an angle grinder fitted with a stone-cutting disc. This provides you with two brick 'slips' that you can back up with mortar and fit into the wall with their good face outwards.

Similarly, if you are able to remove a spalled brick without breaking it, you can turn the brick round, so the flaking face is hidden and the intact face exposed, and then mortar it back in place.

OPENINGS IN BRICKWORK

Tʜᴇ ʙʀɪᴄᴋᴡᴏʀᴋ *above windows and doors has to be supported in some way, otherwise the wall would collapse. Very often this is achieved by the insertion of a stone or wooden lintel, but frequently a brick arch is used instead. The two methods are also sometimes combined, a lintel being concealed behind a brick arch.*

Brick arches are invariably carefully designed and constructed, and they contribute significantly to the character of terraces and individual façades. The effect is further enhanced if openings are given additional embellishment in the form of coloured-brick jambs.

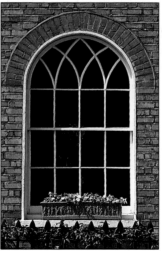
Late C18th semi-circular brick arch

Exquisite elliptical-arched doorway

BRICK ARCHES
A true arch is composed of a number of bricks that support each other as weight is applied from above, transmitting the load to the brickwork on each side of the door or window opening. Purpose-made shaped bricks are now used to construct arches, but better-quality structures were once made from soft bricks that were individually cut and rubbed (ground to shape on an abrasive stone). A skilled bricklayer could shape these 'rubbers' so accurately that the joints between them were no more than 2–3mm (⅛in) wide. Superior-quality 'gauged' (rubbed-brick) arches were pointed either with 'fat' lime putty or with a mixture of lime putty and silver sand (which is very fine). For cheaper work, ordinary bricks were sometimes cut to a tapered shape or uncut bricks were built into an arch, using tapered mortar joints.

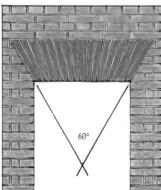
1 Arch based on equilateral triangle

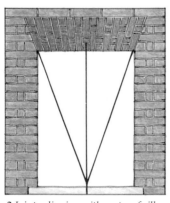
2 Joints aligning with centre of sill

Flat gauged arch
An elegantly constructed flat gauged arch is a pleasing feature of classic Georgian straight-head windows.

The lower edge of this type of arch has to be raised with a slight curve in order to counteract an optical illusion – if it was perfectly straight, the arch would appear to sag in the middle.

Each brick in each half of a flat gauged arch is a different shape. The joints radiate from the apex of an imaginary inverted equilateral triangle plotted below the arch (**1**). Alternatively, they may align with a point in the centre of the window sill (**2**).

Segmental arch
A segmental arch is built with identical tapering bricks, known as voussoirs, once again centred on the apex of an equilateral triangle. Although there are notable exceptions, few segmental arches seem to have been built with the same care lavished on most flat gauged arches and they are often constructed with whole or crudely cut bricks.

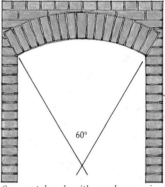
Segmental arch with equal voussoirs

Semi-circular and elliptical arches
Semi-circular arches were used for spanning not only windows but also doorways with fanlights. The elliptical arch is more subtle in shape and consequently requires a variety of accurately made rubbed voussoirs for its construction. It is mostly used to span fairly wide openings.

Pointed arch
Pointed arches, sometimes picked out in soft red bricks, became popular during the Gothic-revival period.

Soldier arch
The soldier arch (or 'brick lintel') is nothing more than a row of upright standard bricks. This structure, which is inherently weak, is usually supported from below by a sturdy steel angle or flat metal bar.

Classic Gothic-revival pointed arch

POINTING RUBBED BRICKWORK

The extremely fine joints in rubbed brickwork cannot be repointed in the usual way. The process described below demands patience and care, but it will ensure that the bricks are not smeared with lime putty.

Ready-made lime putty is sold in tubs, and if need be it can be mixed with fine silver sand (about 1 part lime putty to 3 parts sand) to make a mortar matching the texture of the original pointing.

Sometimes in gauged work the joints are so narrow that the blade of a pointing key is too wide to enter the joint, so you may have to improvise with something like a steel ruler that fits snugly between the bricks.

Rake out loose pointing with a hacksaw blade – taking care not to damage the edges of the very soft bricks – then dampen the open joints.

To keep the bricks clean, apply strips of heavy-duty adhesive tape over the joints and then cut a slit along the centre of each joint, using a sharp knife. Introduce the lime putty/mortar, through the slits in the tape, into the joints and compress it with the pointing tool. Then carefully peel away the tape.

Flat gauged arches composed of soft red rubbed bricks

REPAIRING BRICK ARCHES

Whenever there is a structural failure of a building's foundations, cracks tend to develop at the corners of window and door openings. If this happens, the integrity of the window or door arch is compromised and there is a danger that the voussoirs will fall out. This is a situation that must be remedied without delay.

Get an experienced builder to correct the original cause of the collapse. It will then be possible to insert a beam through the wall above the arch to support the brickwork while the arch itself is dismantled. Rubbers should be handled with care, as they are easily chipped or broken.

The builder will erect a timber-and-plywood former to support the arch while it is being rebuilt. This should not be removed until the mortar or lime putty has set hard.

SHAPED BRICKS & TERRACOTTA

BRICKLAYERS *were adept at constructing decorative detailing from ordinary bricks. Dentil courses beneath the eaves or dogtooth brickwork created by laying bricks at an angle to the face of the wall are typical of the ornamentation found on even the humblest of Victorian workers' cottages. However, much more elaborate embellishments were possible using special-purpose shaped or moulded bricks and terracotta tiles or panels.*

Special-purpose brick voussoirs

Doorway with terracotta panels

SPECIAL BRICKS

Rubbed brickwork, which was extremely laborious to produce, gradually gave way to factory-made shaped bricks. By the second half of the nineteenth century, brick manufacturers were offering a vast selection of profiles and 'specials' for creating all manner of plinths, cornices, arches, chamfered borders and moulded jambs.

There is still a wide range of special-purpose bricks in production, from which you may be able to select suitable replacements for damaged originals. But if you are unable to find appropriate substitutes, then it is generally preferable to live with ornamentation that is in less than perfect condition, rather than allow a builder to cut away or render over original decorative brickwork.

MOULDED BRICKWORK

The Victorians frequently used moulded-brick tiles or slips to make cornices, string courses and other classical-style mouldings. Much of the detailing was extremely elaborate, making it possible to create extravagant ornamentation that was previously only possible with expensive hand carving.

Purely decorative panels composed of soft pinkish-red abstract or figurative brick tiles are a familiar feature of better-quality Victorian and Edwardian housing. If such decorative tiles have been hacked away in the course of insensitive refurbishment, it is very often possible to find modern reproductions of moulded brickwork that will enable you to re-create perfectly acceptable period-style panelling.

CHAPTER FOUR

STONEWORK

BECAUSE WE ARE ACCUSTOMED to seeing impressive public buildings and gentrified houses constructed from dressed stone, many of us tend to equate stonework with quality and wealth. And yet to someone living in an area where stone is plentiful, it is a commonplace material used for practically every house, cottage, workshop and barn in the vicinity. But this in no way diminishes the importance of stone as a building material. Being built from indigenous stone, using local methods of construction, vernacular architecture becomes virtually part of the landscape – a quality which we cannot help but admire.

Houses that are built from limestone, sandstone or granite reflect the local geology, and are most commonly found in areas where such stone predominates. A relatively small number of houses incorporate cobble and knapped flint, which can be found near the coast and on chalk downlands. Generally, vernacular buildings are built of rubble masonry, sometimes plastered or rendered in lime; more refined buildings are of dressed ashlar and often of imported stone. Native and imported marbles are costly, so tend to have been reserved for decorative floor tiles, fireplaces and other features.

Dressed and carved stone has always been expensive, and builders would often substitute cast imitation stone. Some early examples look so authentic that only an expert can tell them from the real thing.

A charming rubble-built cottage

Sophisticated carved stone doorway

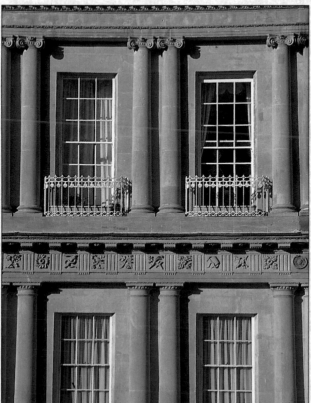

Mellowed limestone ashlar masonry in the neo-classical manner

Squared rubble makes for precision

C19th surround with transom lights

RUBBLE & DRESSED STONE

Nowadays machinery and power tools *take much of the hard labour out of the quarrying of stone. Until the mid nineteenth century, however, quarrying had hardly changed since ancient times. Although the harder building stones would have been extracted by controlled blasting, huge slabs of softer stratified rocks were still being split from the bed using metal wedges driven into the rock. These slabs were then split or sawn into building blocks, which perhaps received a surface dressing, depending on the requirements of the builder or mason.*

Beautifully proportioned cottages built with squared rubblework

FLINT WALLING

For centuries, nodules of flint have been dug out from soft chalk deposits or collected from seashores or river beds for this delightful form of rubble walling. When quarried, a nodule is covered with a pale-grey crust of lime. It's only when the stone is split that the glassy black or brown-coloured flint core is revealed.

Relatively smooth flint cobbles are selected for building purposes and are laid in courses with their rounded ends projecting from the face of the wall. Alternatively, the cobbles are snapped in half to expose the core. For better-quality work, snapped cobbles are then knapped (dressed) on all four sides to make building blocks, approximately 100mm (4in) square, which are laid in bonded courses with relatively fine joints.

Although a flint facing is extremely hard-wearing, an all-flint wall is not particularly strong and it's impossible to build one with accurate square corners. Consequently, most flint buildings have brick or stone quoins at each corner, usually tied together at regular intervals with narrow lacing courses and piers of brick, stone or tiles. As a result, flint-built houses are a delightful blend of colours and textures, with the various structural elements creating attractive geometric patterns.

Typical flint and brick combination

Square-knapped flintwork

RUBBLEWORK

Although the name might suggest otherwise, rubble walls are not shoddy structures. Even with random rubblework (1), the irregular stones must be carefully selected and arranged to build stable masonry walls with staggered joints. In addition, transverse stones that extend for at least two-thirds of the thickness of a wall are incorporated to bond the masonry securely. For slightly better-quality work, the stones are laid in courses (2), creating a level bed every 450mm (1ft 6in) or so. Random-rubble walling is frequently finished at the corners with quoins constructed from blocks of dressed stone.

Random rubblework is most often found in rural areas, but the better-quality housing, particularly in villages and country towns, tends to be constructed from squared rubble (3). This type of rubblework is composed of split blocks, which are sometimes roughly dressed with a hammer or steel chisel. With squared rubble, it was possible to construct masonry with regular courses (4) that are constant in height, although the stones themselves vary in length.

1 Random rubblework

2 Coursed random rubble

3 Squared rubblework

4 Regular-coursed squared rubble

Surface dressings
1 Tooled finish
2 Punched
3 Picked
4 Furrowed
5 Vermiculated
6 Rock-faced

ASHLAR

Ashlar is the name given to masonry constructed from accurately cut and jointed blocks of stone. Usually, each block is sawn on all sides and the face (the outer exposed surface) is sometimes rubbed to a flat finish.

Ashlar walls are almost always laid to regular courses, and are frequently built with an accurate bond. Due to the high cost of ashlar, dressed blocks were often used as a facing backed by rubble or bricks. This type of construction is known as compound walling.

Joints in ashlar

The majority of ashlar blocks are flush-faced and butted together, with lime mortar used as a bedding material **(1)**. The mortar joints can be as narrow as 3mm (⅛in) wide, but normally range from between 5 to 15mm (¼ to ⅝in) wide. However, stonework is often 'rusticated' to emphasize the joints, the edges of each block either being chamfered to form V-jointing **(2)** or rebated to create channelling **(3)**.

1 Square-cut flush-faced ashlar

2 V-jointed rustication

3 Deep rebates cut in the edges of each ashlar block form chanelled joints

Surface dressings

Masons cut a variety of textures into the face of building stones by hand in order to draw the eye to features such as doors and windows, or to give a building the impression of strength and solidity at street level.

One of the simplest textures comprises little more than a hand-tooled flat surface covered with fine, closely packed lines made with the edge of a chisel **(1)**. A punched texture **(2)** or the even finer picked dressing **(3)** are made with a pointed tool, and a gouge is used to incise a furrowed dressing with 6 to 9mm (¼ to ⅜in) parallel flutes **(4)**. Deeply carved vermiculation **(5)**, which is supposed to look like worm tracks, is often employed to lend visual emphasis to openings and quoins. Rock-faced masonry **(6)** is deliberately left rough, usually in contrast to smooth margins carved around the edges of each block of stone.

CLEANING STONEWORK

AUTHORITIES AND ASSOCIATIONS *concerned with the preservation of period buildings normally advise against the cleaning of stonework unless it is absolutely necessary. This advice is primarily intended to prevent irreversible damage caused by insufficiently skilled operatives or use of unnecessarily harsh cleaning methods. There are also those who feel that cleaning stonework reduces its aesthetic appeal by eliminating all the subtleties of colour and tone built up over the years, which give the building its patina.*

However, some limestone houses – particularly in urban areas – would undoubtedly benefit from cleaning in order to remove black deposits caused by pollution. Cleaning may be essential in order to prevent or halt physical deterioration of the stone by removing harmful salts that cause or exacerbate decay.

Cleaning parts of a building may not be entirely satisfactory

SELECTING THE BEST METHOD

It is important to select the appropriate treatment for a particular type of stone. Consequently, if you are concerned about the condition of your house, it pays to get expert advice before you make a decision. The Conservation Officer attached to your local planning department will certainly lend a sympathetic ear, but will usually only get involved if a house is listed or is in a conservation area. The Society for the Protection of Ancient Buildings may be able to give you names of architects or surveyors practising in your part of the country who offer advice on the cleaning of stone.

Having established that cleaning would be beneficial, it is vital to find a responsible company that will clean a sample area before undertaking the task. The Stone Federation will put you in touch with members that can recommend the most appropriate treatment and give you an estimate of the costs, which vary depending on the size and complexity of the job, the sensitivity of the stone and the type and degree of soiling.

The principal methods for cleaning masonry are outlined here. Together with the recommendations of your professional advisers, they will serve as a guide to selecting the most suitable process for your house.

WASHING STONEWORK

Dirty limestone generally responds well to washing with water. In fact, it is possible to clean a fairly small house yourself, using a stiff-bristle brush and a garden hose (see WASHING BRICKWORK). However, scrubbing stone by hand is hard work and professionals usually resort to some form of spraying. The gentlest method involves rigging up a series of spray heads that direct a fine mist of droplets onto the surface of the stone to soften the dirt before it is scrubbed from the masonry with bristle brushes or ones made from phosphor-bronze. Steel-wire brushes should not be used for cleaning stone, as they may create a metallic brown staining.

A jet of water forced under low pressure from a hand-held lance is often extremely effective – but experience is needed in order to avoid damaging mortar joints and soft stonework.

Steam cleaning may be recommended for removing oily stains, but in practice it is not much more effective than hosing down the stonework with water.

Whichever method of cleaning you decide on, it is always essential to use as little water as possible and to prevent water penetrating between the joinery and the surrounding masonry.

Water should not be used on stonework when there is any likelihood of frost.

CHEMICAL CLEANING

Chemical cleaners must only be applied to stonework under the supervision of an expert. This is especially important since careless use of chemicals can cause local environmental pollution. Moreover, it is necessary to ascertain the effects of a particular chemical on the stone in order to avoid irreversible damage, such as staining, discoloration and disintegration.

Acidic cleaning agents, for example, are recommended for cleaning granite and most sandstones, but are not suitable for calcareous or chalky sandstone and would probably dissolve limestone or marble. You therefore need to make sure that a professional conducts a test before applying a cleaner to a wide area of stone. Even a few drops of diluted hydro-chloric acid cause soluble stone to bubble and foam.

Alkali or caustic cleaners are used on heavily soiled terracotta, limestone and marble. Chemical cleaning may be recommended for these materials when there's a danger that washing the stonework with water might result in oversaturation.

The normal procedure for chemical cleaning involves spraying the grimy masonry with water before the chosen cleaner is either brushed or sprayed onto the surface. Once the dirt has dissolved, the stone is washed down with low-pressure jets.

Traditional mason's handtools

REPOINTING STONEWORK

ALTHOUGH MANY GOOD BUILDERS *know how to repoint brickwork, they often lack experience of similar work on stone-built houses. This is evident from the many examples of walls where mortar has been spread over the edges of the stones or where the joints project beyond the face of the masonry, creating what is known as ribbon or strap pointing. Both of these methods spoil the appearance of a wall by emphasizing the joints at the expense of the stones.*

Whether a wall is built of ashlar or rubble, the mortar should generally be as close to the colour of the stone as possible and may be very slightly lighter in tone. It should usually be slightly gritty in texture.

It's a mistake to be too eager to repoint an old wall. Even slightly recessed pointing is acceptable, provided the original mortar has not become too soft and friable. If there are obvious signs that the pointing is being eroded, leaving deep open joints, carefully rake out and replace the loose mortar.

Ribbon pointing is unsightly

Well-executed recessed pointing

USING ABRASIVES

Indiscriminate sandblasting and the use of power tools fitted with wire brushes or grinders have been responsible for serious damage to old stone and brickwork. As a result, very few authorities will now contemplate granting permission for the use of abrasives on listed buildings. In the hands of a careless operative, harsh abrasives can totally destroy carved or moulded detail and may leave the surface of soft stone pitted and scoured.

However, for a number of years conservators have been cleaning valuable stone sculpture with extremely fine abrasive particles that can be used for removing surface dirt only. Some companies are developing this 'microparticle' system on a commercial scale for cleaning dirty buildings without most of the hazards of abrasive cleaning or the risk of staining and discoloration associated with other techniques. Nevertheless, it must be stressed that all abrasive materials have to be adequately controlled and contained in order to safeguard the health not only of the operative and the occupants of the house but also other people working or living nearby.

LIME-PUTTY MORTAR

Old masonry was invariably constructed with a weak lime-putty mortar, which was plastic enough to absorb any slight movements within the structure. A modern cement-rich mortar – which is often misguidedly used for repointing stonework – has little flexibility and cracks easily, leading to the ingress of water and eventually to the disintegration of the masonry. There is no advantage in using such a strong mortar, even for hard stone such as flint.

When repointing a rubble wall that is in an exposed situation, use a mortar comprising 1 part white Portland cement, 2 parts hydrated lime and 9 parts aggregate (sand or crushed stone) mixed with water. For similar stonework that's in a sheltered position, use a weaker 1:3:12 mix. Alternatively, use a mix of naturally hydraulic lime with 2.5 parts of selected sand. For how to mix mortars to match the original pointing, see REPOINTING BRICKWORK.

Ashlar walls are normally repointed using a fat lime-putty mortar made by mixing lime with an equal amount of crushed stone.

REPOINTING RUBBLE WALLING

Use a strong pointed stick to rake out the joints to a depth double their width. Wet the wall, in order to reduce its suction, then press fresh mortar between the stones, leaving the joint very slightly recessed (see POINTING WORN BRICKS).

When the mortar begins to stiffen, stipple the joints with a stiff-bristle brush to expose the texture of the aggregate.

REPOINTING ASHLAR

Repointing a finely jointed ashlar wall would tax the patience of most amateurs. The joints can be filled flush with lime putty which, to keep the stones clean, is applied through slit tape that is removed once the putty is in place (see POINTING RUBBED BRICKWORK).

REPOINTING FLINT WALLING

Cobbles can be repointed in the same way as rubble walling. However, the joints between square-knapped flints are sometimes so fine that they have to be pointed like ashlar – a job that is best left to a skilled professional.

GALLETING

Wide mortar joints were sometimes filled with small stones or flint flakes. Known as galleting, this is not just an attractive detail – it also helps the mortar to resist weathering. When repointing galleted work, collect the small stones and rebed them while the new mortar joints are still soft.

CARVED STONEWORK

V ERNACULAR STONE HOUSES AND COTTAGES *have a charm and character that relies more on skilful construction and the colours and textures of the natural materials than on unnecessary embellishment. But this was not so with the average urban dwelling – for even when a town house was constructed mainly from brick, stonemasons and carvers were frequently employed to create decorative features in the form of classically inspired mouldings or elaborately carved door and window surrounds.*

Traditional hand skills still continued to be used even on quite humble dwellings well into the twentieth century, but from early-Georgian times genuine carved stone had already begun to be rivalled by the introduction of cast artificial-stone enrichments.

DOOR AND WINDOW OPENINGS

The stone components used in the construction of door and window openings were not simply decorative linings. Each element has a specific structural function and was shaped and installed accordingly.

Nevertheless, typical of builder craftsmen, stonemasons decorated practically every stone-built opening to some extent, even if only with chamfers to relieve the sharp edges. Much of the carving was done at the mason's own yard then later transported to the building site. Very little carving was actually done *in situ*.

Window and door openings have to be made precisely in order to accommodate the necessary joinery. Consequently, rubble-built houses normally incorporate dressed-stone openings. Brick houses are also frequently built with stone lintels above the windows and doors, and some even have complete surrounds of carved stonework.

Typically Victorian entrance with deeply carved foliage and bird motifs

Carved stone lintels and mullion

An unusual form of vermiculation

Lintels

A lintel is a beam that spans an opening, supporting the weight of the masonry above a window or door.

Stone lintels are normally cut as a single block. However, if there was a risk that a long lintel might crack under load, it would be made from three separate blocks joined with sloping joggle joints (which are designed to tighten as weight is applied to them). This type of lintel is also known as a flat arch.

The lintels even on fairly modest terraced houses, particularly in the Victorian era, are frequently decorated, if only with shallow carvings.

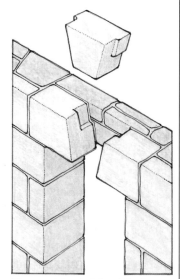
Three-part joggle-jointed lintel

Arches

An arch is the alternative method of spanning window or door openings. It is constructed from accurately cut tapering stones, called voussoirs, that support each other and transfer the load to the section of wall on each side of the opening.

The voussoir at the centre of the arch, which locks the other stones in place, is known as the keystone and is usually singled out for special decorative treatment. Very often keystones are embellished with a carved mask representing a minor classical deity or an animal. Alternatively, the stone may simply be vermiculated to distinguish it visually from the other voussoirs.

A relieving arch is built into the masonry above an opening when it is necessary to deflect the load away from a lintel that is too slim to bear the weight without support. Relieving arches are not always visible on the outside of the house.

Sometimes the presence of a relieving arch is incorrectly assumed to be evidence that the shape of an opening has been altered. But don't be tempted to remove the lintel, since the arch may not be strong enough on its own.

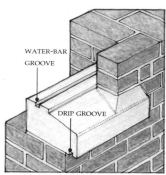

Weathered stone subsill

Sills

A stone sill (or, strictly speaking, subsill) is used to cap the section of wall at the base of a window. The wooden window frame sits directly on the stone sill and the joint is weatherproofed with a metal water bar fitted into a groove in each component. The ends of a stone sill are normally built into the brick or stone wall on both sides of the window. The top surface is weathered (sloped) to drain water away from the wooden window frame. In addition, a drip groove cut along the underside causes rainwater to drop to the ground before it can run back to soak the wall behind. Drip grooves should be raked out periodically to ensure that they do not become bridged by paint, moss or lichen.

Jambs

The stone jambs flanking door and window openings are usually constructed from quoins (alternate headers and stretchers of dressed stone). These are particularly obvious when they are built into rubble walls or when picked out with distinctive surface dressings.

The jambs in ashlar walls, in particular, are sometimes lined with narrow dressed stones that form reveals. Known as upstarts, these stones often project slightly from the face of the wall and are carved to create decorative architraves.

Jambs may be splayed to provide more natural light.

Mullions and piers

Stone mullions are used to divide a window opening in order to accommodate two or more individual windows and provide additional support to the lintel above. Larger vertical supports, such as those at the corners of a bay window, are called piers. Piers and mullions are frequently decorated with ornamental carvings.

Carved stone door surround

Stone courses contrast with brick

Painted stone arch with keystone and capitals

STONE COURSES

Many stone-built or brick façades are broken by horizontal moulded bands of stone that project beyond the face of the wall. As well as dividing a building into aesthetically pleasing proportions, these stone courses have a more prosaic function. Like a window sill, stone courses are weathered so they shed rainwater, which would otherwise saturate or stain the wall.

Cornices

A cornice is normally situated just below the parapet at the top of a house. Often the junctions between the individual blocks of stone were saddled (raised) to encourage water to flow away from the actual joints; alternatively, the top of the entire cornice was protected with a lead flashing.

Architraves

An architrave is a similar but smaller moulding situated just below the cornice. The section of wall between the two is known as a frieze.

String courses

A string course is a narrow horizontal band of moulded stones. A square-faced one is called a band course.

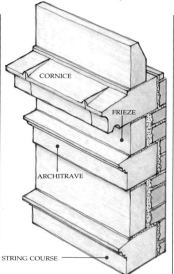

Horizontal stone courses

COPINGS

A coping is a row of capping stones designed to shed rainwater from the top of a brick or stone wall. Coping stones, which may be either saddled or weathered, are wider than the wall itself and have drip grooves on the underside.

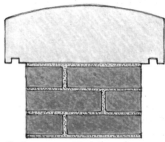

Coping stone with drip grooves

ARTIFICIAL STONE

WE TEND TO REGARD IMITATIVE MASONRY *as a relatively modern phenomenon restricted to garden paving and cast-concrete walling. However, by the beginning of the nineteenth century artIficial cast stonework was already fairly commonplace as a cheaper alternative to hand carving, and the earliest experiments in processing artificial stone were carried out perhaps a century earlier.*

In the eighteenth century the public was intrigued by artificial-stone products, not just because of their convincing natural appearance but also because of the mystery surrounding their manufacture. Richard Holt, who took out a patent for artificial stone in 1722, went so far as to claim that he had succeeded in rediscovering a lost formula possessed by our ancestors long ago, who used it for manufacturing building materials for such well-known monuments as the pyramids of ancient Egypt and the megaliths of Stonehenge.

COADE STONE

The artificial-stone market was potentially so lucrative that processes and exact compositions were jealously guarded secrets. However, recent scientific analysis has revealed that Coade stone, perhaps the most famous of all artificial stones, was composed of nothing more exotic than china clay mixed with finely ground aggregates and linseed oil.

Founded in the 1760s, the Coade Company established a reputation for manufacturing artificial stonework of the highest quality, and time has proved the durability of their products. Coade's output included copies of well-known classical stonework, but most of their products were designed specially for their catalogue. The company produced a vast range of cast architectural features, including their now familiar door surrounds complete with masked keystone and vermiculated quoins. Even though Coade-stone artifacts were made in quantity, the more intricate castings were finished by hand – which is perhaps why it is sometimes difficult to tell Coade-stone castings from genuine stone.

The Coade family together with their various associates traded successfully for about seventy years, eventually exporting their products as far afield as America and the West Indies.

A Coade-stone door surround incorporating quoins and masked keystone

Vermiculated window opening

Terracotta is rich and colourful

TERRACOTTA

Terracotta arguably has more in common with brick so far as its composition and manufacture are concerned. Nevertheless, for architectural purposes it is generally classified as an artificial stone. It had already been in use for centuries when the Victorians, with their characteristic enthusiasm for ornamentation, took to terracotta and its glazed version 'faience', exploiting the potential of industrial production to full advantage.

We are perhaps used to thinking of terracotta as a decorative facing for large public buildings and department stores, but it was also used in better-quality houses to embellish entrances and for sculptured panels, cornices and other mouldings. Manufacturers experimented with different colours, but castings for both commercial and domestic buildings were mostly brick red or beige.

Normally made as hollow blocks, terracotta and faience in particular are extremely durable unless water is able to seep behind them, rusting steel or iron fixings, which eventually expand and crack the castings. It is possible to order replacement castings, although the cost is likely to be prohibitive. However, depending on the nature of the damage, you may be able to repair cracked terracotta with epoxy adhesive.

REPAIRING DEFECTIVE STONE

DESPITE ITS REPUTATION FOR DURABILITY, *stone is surprisingly susceptible to wear and decay. In addition to the more obvious defects resulting from accidental breakages, stonework can be eaten away by atmospheric impurities caused by the coal fires and furnaces of the past or today's acid rain. Occasionally the erosion is very gradual and may be acceptable, even attractive, but when stone begins to flake, the disintegration can be rapid and urgent treatment may be essential.*

In most cases, especially when you are dealing with carved stonework or ashlar, professional skills are required to produce a sound and inconspicuous repair. However, most of the better-known stone-restoration companies are used to working on public buildings, such as city halls or churches, and are usually not geared to small-scale work. There are both individual masons and carvers and small groups that are happy to undertake domestic commissions, but they are not always easy to find. The best way to track down suitable repairers is to consult a directory such as the Building Conservation Directory, which lists skilled contractors.

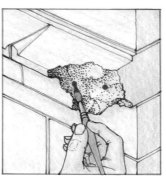

1 Mark pin positions with paint

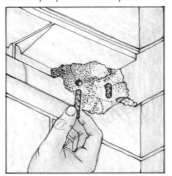

2 Insert keyed and glued pins

MECHANICAL REPAIRS

If a small fragment of stone breaks away – from a carving or moulded course, for example – you can glue it back in place with epoxy adhesive. This type of adhesive only begins to set once its constituents have been mixed. Low-viscosity epoxy glues are available from specialists, but most DIY shops stock a standard two-part adhesive that can be thinned sufficiently by warming the tubes on a radiator. Large pieces of stone need to be reinforced with non-ferrous metal pins.

Reinforcing a repair

Make the reinforcing pins by cutting stainless-steel or brass rod into short lengths. File notches along each pin to form keys for the adhesive. Mark the position of the pins on one half of the repair with small spots of paint **(1)**. Reposition the broken piece of stone to transfer the spots.

Dismantle the repair again and use a masonry drill to bore holes in each half of the repair that are slightly larger in diameter than the pins. Make a dry assembly, with the pins in place, to ensure that the joint fits snugly.

Scrub the mating surfaces with acetone (nail-varnish remover), then glue the pins into one half **(2)**. Spread a thin layer of adhesive on the other half, and also onto the projecting pins. Assemble the joint, rocking the stone slightly to squeeze out excess adhesive, then wipe it off immediately with cotton-wool buds wetted with acetone. If possible, bind the repair with string or self-adhesive parcel tape until the adhesive has set hard.

THE EFFECTS OF INCORRECT BEDDING

Sedimentary rocks, such as sandstone and limestone, are the products of materials that have been deposited in geological beds (strata) by water or wind. As a result, when cut or split blocks are laid, their erosion may be exacerbated if the mason fails to allow for the effect of this bedding.

When a block of stone is laid with its strata horizontal **(1)**, the weight of subsequent masonry prevents the block from delaminating. Laying stones in this way is known as 'natural bedding'. It is the method that should be used in most situations.

When a stone block is face-bedded **(2)**, with the strata on edge and parallel to the face of the wall, the action of spalling tends to shear flakes from the

surface of the stone – rather like shedding individual playing cards from a deck. Gradually the disintegration eats deeper and deeper into the wall until it seriously compromises the stability of the masonry.

Courses, such as cornices, that project from a wall should be constructed from edge-bedded stones **(3)** in order to prevent delamination. For the same reason, stone lintels above window and door openings should also be edge-bedded.

Even skilled stonemasons sometimes have difficulty in identifying the direction of the bedding on a newly cut block. The direction is therefore normally marked on the stone itself, either at the quarry or once the block has been sawn roughly to size.

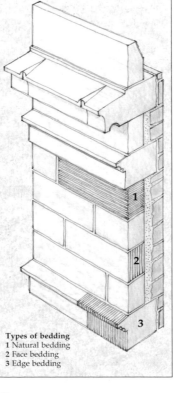

Types of bedding
1 Natural bedding
2 Face bedding
3 Edge bedding

Face-bedded stone that begins to delaminate can be consolidated by an expert

REPAIRING WITH MORTAR

Patching stonework with mortar is simpler and cheaper than having to cut out and replace damaged stones. In fact, as long ago as the early nineteenth century builders used Roman cement (see INGREDIENTS OF RENDER AND STUCCO) for such repairs. Provided that the damaged stones have a simple profile, it is possible to undertake 'plastic' repairs yourself – however, since it is difficult to obtain an exact match, you may prefer to hire a professional mason unless the stonework is painted.

Depending on the nature and colour of the original stonework, a mason will probably select silver sand or even crushed stone as the aggregate for a suitable repair mortar. Some masons include cement in the mortar, but you might consider using a weak naturally hydraulic lime or a fat lime-putty mix instead of the cement. If necessary, consult your district Conservation Officer or an experienced architect or surveyor practising in your area.

Gluing delaminating stone
It is possible to consolidate flaking face-bedded stones by injecting a thin epoxy adhesive into holes drilled through the laminations. Reinforcing pins are then introduced into the same holes. However, this is a skilled repair best left to a professional conservator.

Injecting adhesive for reinforcing pins

Indenting
Replacing damaged stone blocks with new ones is known as indenting. Since it is difficult even for an experienced mason to guarantee an exact match of colour and texture, it may be preferable to live with slightly blemished stonework rather than risk having a repair done that could prove more noticeable than the blemish itself.

One stone at a time can be cut out and replaced without propping, but if a number of adjacent blocks are affected, the surrounding masonry should be supported while the work is in progress.

An entire facing stone can be removed with a hammer and chisel, but it is often only necessary to cut back the stone by a minimum of 100mm (4in) in order to make sufficient room for a shallow block to be mortared in place.

Unless the stonework has been face-bedded, it may be possible to dismantle an eroded section of the wall and then turn the blocks round so as to expose the undamaged faces.

Use shallow blocks to repair headers

Preparing the masonry
The decayed stone should be cut back by at least 25mm (1in) to sound material. Cut a regular shape with undercut edges, except for the bottom edge which should be left square **(1)**. Treat each individual stone separately, using strips of wood to form appropriate joints in the mortar until it has set (the strips are then removed and the joints repointed in the usual way).

Reinforce the repair by gluing non-ferrous pins or wire into holes drilled in the stone **(2)**. Brush off loose material and wet the stone to reduce suction.

Applying the mortar
Apply a coat of mortar 12 to 18mm (½ to ¾in) thick and scratch the surface to provide a key. Two to four hours later, apply a second coat and smooth its surface with a wooden float. Once the top coat has begun to get firm, stipple it with a damp sponge or a bristle brush in order to expose the aggregate.

When repairing cornices and other moulded courses, you can use a running mould to shape them (see STUCCO MOULDINGS).

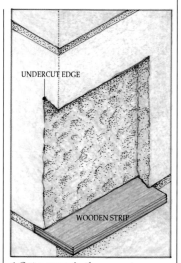
1 Cut a recess in the worn stone

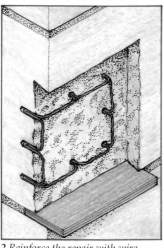
2 Reinforce the repair with wire

CHAPTER FIVE

RENDER & STUCCO

RENDER USUALLY DENOTES *a plain external-wall coating. It has been in use from the very earliest times. Renders used for the walls of old houses range from single low-strength lime coatings applied over wattle or lath to high-strength cement-based renders applied to brickwork.*

The term stucco encompasses many different applications – from covering exterior walls in imitation stone to fine plaster applied to interior walls or ceilings and the creation of all manner of decorative mouldings. The term is now often employed to describe the high-quality renders used to provide a cheap yet convincing substitute for stonework – brick or rubble masonry being coated to look like best-quality ashlar, complete with mouldings, quoins and cornices.

Stucco became highly fashionable in the late eighteenth century and was to remain popular throughout the Victorian era, being widely used for decorative window and door surrounds. Although the illusion was frequently reinforced by painting to resemble nicely weathered masonry, there was keen competition to produce stuccos that would dry naturally to match the colours of building stones. The materials used for stucco varied considerably, but in England in the early nineteenth century stucco finishes were generally lime-based renders applied as either two-part or three-part coatings to façades.*

Towards the end of the nineteenth century a very different type of render, known as roughcast, became fashionable for mock-Tudor houses. The top coat of this coarsely textured rustic-looking render is mixed with gravel. Pebble dash, a slightly later type of render, is similar in composition but a dry aggregate is thrown onto the wet render so that the aggregate remains exposed on the surface.

Painted stucco contrasts with brick

Plain-rendered seaside terrace

Fully stuccoed early-C19th house with rusticated ground floor

Unpainted stucco with white details

Semi-rusticated Regency façade

REPAIRING RENDER

BEFORE EMBARKING ON REPAIRS, *it's important to establish whether the old render is lime-based or cement-based.*

Cement renders are generally hard and impervious, whereas lime renders are normally weaker and can accommodate slight movement. It is essential to make repairs with a compatible material.

Before starting work, try to establish why the render has failed. An unsuitable material may have been used to repair the wall, or damp may be causing the render to detach itself from the background masonry.

FILLING CRACKS
Rake out large cracks – 2mm (⅛in) wide or more – with a cold chisel, undercutting the edges to form a key. If you discover that the brickwork behind is cracked too, seek professional advice. Clean out loose debris with a stiff-bristle brush, then wet the crack and fill it flush with new lime-based or cement mortar to match the rest of the render.

PATCHING HOLES
If you neglect to repair damaged render (particularly cement-based render), rainwater penetrates and soaks the wall behind, leading to damp and decay internally. The wetting and drying cycle may cause efflorescence. Also, trapped moisture expands during frosty weather, causing the render to break away.

Preparing the wall
Tap the wall in the vicinity of obvious damage with a wooden mallet, listening for the hollow sound that indicates loose render.

Use a bolster chisel and a heavy hammer to hack off loose render. Cut the edges straight, to avoid a patchy appearance, and try to align them with features of the building that will disguise joins between old and new stucco. Undercut all but the bottom edge, which should be left square. Rake out the mortar joints between bricks to a depth of about 16mm (⅝in), then brush all loose material from the wall.

Applying the render
Thoroughly wet the area that is to be patched and use a plasterer's trowel to apply the first layer of render. Sweep the render onto the wall with upward strokes of the trowel, using fairly firm pressure **(1)**, then smooth it out to a depth of between 10 and 12mm (⅜ and ½in). As the render begins to set firm, scratch the surface to form a key for the next coat and leave it till the following day to set.

Depending on the thickness of the original render, repeat the procedure – adding a second layer of render approximately 10mm (⅜in) thick – before applying a 6mm (¼in) finishing coat.

Before you trowel on the finishing coat, wet the keyed surface of the previous layer. Use a wooden straightedge to scrape the render flush **(2)**, working with a zigzag action from the bottom upwards, then fill any low spots with fresh render.

Finally, smooth the finishing coat with a wooden float, using circular and figure-of-eight strokes.

INGREDIENTS OF RENDER AND STUCCO

Before the latter part of the eighteenth century, most exterior render was a mixture of lime and sand, sometimes reinforced with chopped animal hair. It set slowly, drying out over a period of days while the lime absorbed carbon dioxide from the atmosphere. During the eighteenth and nineteenth centuries, other ingredients were used in an attempt to create a high-quality but inexpensive material. These stuccos or 'mastics' were made using fine aggregates (limestone, various sands, crushed pottery, glass) bound with linseed oil and other additives.

Experiments aimed at making faster-setting renders, led to the development of more durable and water-resistant materials. One of these was called Roman cement. Used as a render material from the 1790s, it was a form of natural cement that dried to a distinctive pink/brown colour. These developments culminated with the patenting in 1824 of Portland cement. Cement sets by a chemical reaction that begins as soon as it is mixed with water. As a result, render containing cement sets hard in a matter of hours and continues to gain strength over a period of weeks.

Depending on the strength of the render to be repaired, there are a number of mixes you might consider. For lime/cement-based renders, mix the undercoats using 1 part cement, 2 parts lime, and 9 parts sand. For the top coat, a weaker mix of 1:3:12 is suitable. When repairing a lime-based render, you can use either a naturally hydraulic lime mixed with sand or a lime-putty/sand mix. For the hydraulic-lime mix, use 2 parts lime mixed with 5 parts well-graded sharp sand as an undercoat, with 1 part lime and 3 parts soft sand for the top coat. When using lime putty, make the undercoat of 1:2.5 lime putty and sand; and for the top coat, use a mix of 1:3.5.

Mixing the ingredients
If you are preparing render from dry ingredients, mix them thoroughly first, then form a well in the centre of the pile and pour in some water. Shovel the ingredients from around the edges of the well into the water until it has been absorbed, then gradually turn the mixture over until the consistency is even – the render should retain marks left by the shovel without slumping or crumbling. When handling lime, wear a face mask, goggles and gloves.

1 Trowel on first layer of render

2 Scrape level with a straightedge

RUSTICATION

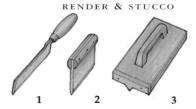

1 **2** **3**

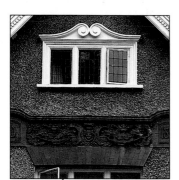

Late-Victorian roughcast

PATCHING PEBBLE DASH AND ROUGHCAST

The method for patching a hole in a pebble-dash wall is the same as for plain stucco – but while the top coat is still soft, pick up some 6mm (¼in) washed pebbles on the toe of your plasterer's trowel and flick them onto the render **(1)**. Spread a dust-sheet at the foot of the wall to catch fallen pebbles. When you have filled the patch evenly, tap the pebbles light-ly with a float to bed them into the render **(2)**.

When patching roughcast, mix equal parts of sand and 6mm (¼in) crushed-stone aggregate into the top-coat render, using slightly more water than normal. Soak the keyed undercoat and flick the roughcast mixture onto it, covering the patched area evenly so as to match the surrounding wall.

1 Flinging pebbles with a trowel

2 Bed them in with a float

O N CLOSER EXAMINATION, *what appear to be ashlar (dressed stone) blocks making up the ground floor of an early-nineteenth-century house often prove to be nothing more than an illusion created by a plasterer drawing a tool through wet stucco in an attempt to disguise cheap brickwork.*

The horizontal and vertical joints of closely fitting ashlar blocks are frequently represented in the stucco-work of the period. Alternatively, pronounced grooves are incised – often as banded rustication, which does not include vertical joints. When executed by a skilled plasterer, it is difficult to distinguish rusticated stucco from genuine stonework unless part of the render has broken away to reveal a telltale brick background.

VERMICULATION

Some plasterers went to even greater lengths to deceive the eye by reproducing vermiculation – a deep irregular texture, similar in appearance to worm tracks, which was a tradition-al stonemason's surface dressing. Vermiculation was most commonly used to decorate door or window surrounds and to create fake quoins on the corners of buildings.

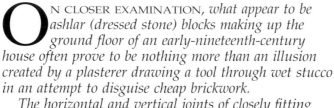

Half-stuccoed late-Georgian houses with banded rustication

RE-CREATING VERMICULATION

If you are sufficiently skilled, it is possible to cut vermicul-ation by hand in wet stucco, using modelling tools or old chisels. However, it is easier to take an impression from an identical 'stone' and to cast vermiculated blocks in sand-and-cement render (see CASTING VERMICULATION).

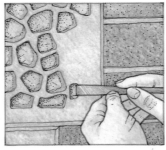

Cutting vermiculation by hand

1 Chop back to nearest joint lines

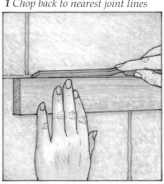

2 Rule lines with a jointing tool

RESTORING RUSTICATION

Square-cut ashlar rustication was created by marking stucco with a steel jointing tool, but there's no need to buy special tools. You can make a jointing tool of your own from wood; and to re-create deep V-grooves you can screw an improvised wooden template to the end of a float.

Use a bolster chisel and hammer to cut loose rustic-ated stucco back to the nearest joint lines in sound render **(1)**. Fill flush with fresh stucco and finish the surface with a wooden float.

Using a straight batten as a guide, slowly draw a joint-ing tool through the stucco **(2)**. For the time being leave any specks of render that are dragged out onto the surface, then carefully rub them off with a float when the stucco begins to harden.

STUCCO MOULDINGS

STUCCO REALLY COMES INTO ITS OWN *when it is used to simulate the mouldings and other enrichments associated with carved stonework. In Georgian times entire façades were often covered with ornamental stucco, whereas the Victorians tended to favour the contrast of brickwork with stucco details.*

Classically inspired stucco cornice and string course

Decorative moulding and pediment

Stucco architrave with keystone

RESTORING MOULDINGS

Classically inspired cornice mouldings running just below the parapet of a house or near the top of a porch are design-ed to shed water clear of the face of the wall. Their top surfaces are therefore 'weathered' (sloped) to ensure that rainwater drains away from the masonry. Similar, though smaller, mouldings known as string courses are used to provide horizontal emphasis and improve the visual propor-tions of a façade. Architraves in stucco often surround window openings, and many a doorway is flanked with stucco pilasters.

Mouldings were either fabricated directly on the wall or cast on a bench then fixed to the building once they had set. As with internal plasterwork, stucco mouldings frequently include beds for accommodating separately moulded decorative features.

RUNNING MOULDINGS ON THE WALL

It is normally easier to work on a horizontal bench than on the vertical surface of a wall. However, there are times when it makes more sense to repair mouldings *in situ* – for example, when a moulding is built around an integral support of brick or tile corbelling (1), or only a short section of a long moulding is damaged, or a moulding is simply too large to be lifted into place.

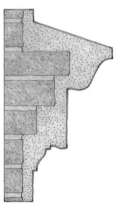

1 Brick-corbelling reinforcement

The running mould

A stucco moulding is shaped by using a zinc template screwed to a running mould. This is made in a similar way to the moulds used for making interior plaster cornices (see RUNNING A PLAIN CORNICE). Wooden battens, known as rules, are nailed to the masonry to guide the running mould (2).

2 Running mould with fixed rules

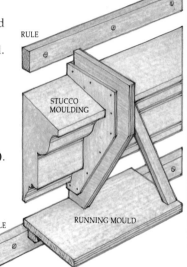

RULE

STUCCO MOULDING

RULE

RUNNING MOULD

EMPLOYING PROFESSIONALS

You should seriously consider whether it is worth attempting to restore stucco mouldings yourself or whether it is advisable to employ a professional plasterer. Considerable skill is needed to restore some mouldings, especially those that have to be run *in situ*. Also, there are inherent risks in working at the height at which some of these features are located, and mouldings installed high up on a building constitute a safety risk unless they are securely attached. Scaffolding is normally required to provide a safe working platform for the duration of the work – and as you are likely to take longer to complete the job than a professional, the saving on scaffold hire makes at least some contribution towards the cost of paying a plasterer.

However, there is a degree of satisfaction in restoring one's own house – and provided that you can reach damaged stucco from a low platform constructed from hired slot-together scaffold frames, there is no practical reason why you shouldn't tackle the work.

Fabricating a moulding

If you are fabricating mouldings that form part of a larger area of stucco, you should use a mix for the mouldings that is compatible with the rest of the render. For separate mouldings, a mix of 1 part Portland cement, 1 part hydrated lime and 2.5 parts plasterer's sand might be suitable.

After the masonry background has been wetted, the approximate shape of the moulding is built in stucco. A professional plasterer would use a gauging trowel – a tool shaped like a bricklayer's trowel but with a round-tip blade. However, a pointing trowel can be used instead. The running mould is then slid along the rules, scraping the stucco to create the profile of the finished moulding (1). Any slight blemishes are smoothed out with a wooden float. All

mitres and returns must be shaped by hand as the work progresses.

Deep mouldings are built up gradually in layers approximately 12mm (½in) thick by making 'muffle' runs. A muffle is a smaller template that is run in advance of a finished-profile one. Several muffles, each increasing in size, may be needed in order to build a large moulding.

Each layer is scratched to provide a key for the next (which is normally applied about 24 hours later), the keyed surface having first been dampened with water.

Some plasterers prefer to apply a subsequent coat while the previous one is slightly wet – when it's still 'green'. This is possible if you make one run early in the morning and a second run sometime after lunch.

Creating a stonelike texture

To create a stucco moulding with a convincing stonelike texture, mix roughly equal proportions of dry sand and cement together – then while the finished moulding is still wet, flick the dry mixture onto the surface of the stucco with a plasterer's trowel. When you see the mixture change colour as it absorbs moisture from the moulding, make one final pass with the running mould.

Including reinforcement

Repairs to deep mouldings are sometimes reinforced with metal rod and wire bent into a suitable armature (2). Choose non-ferrous metal and use an epoxy adhesive to glue the rods into holes drilled in the masonry. Before gluing them, file the ends of the reinforcement rods in order to provide a key for the adhesive.

1 Slide the running mould sideways

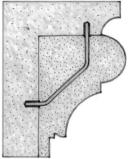

2 Bent-metal reinforcement

MAKING MOULDINGS ON A BENCH

The alternative method for making mouldings was to cast them on site then apply them to the walls. The same procedure can be used when replacing damaged sections, or to re-create entire cornices or other mouldings. When installing replacement mouldings, it pays to attach them to the wall with fixings such as non-ferrous expanding-anchor screws.

Making a reverse mould.

A replacement moulding is cast in a reverse mould (1) run in plaster of Paris (see RUNNING A PLAIN CORNICE).

Traditionally once the plaster of Paris has set, the reverse mould is sealed with three coats of shellac.

However, to produce a casting with a better surface finish, seal the mould with a coat of PVA bonding agent then paint a film of cooking oil over it. If the bonding agent sticks to the stucco, it will peel off easily, due to the presence of the oil, without harming the surface of the casting.

Casting the moulding

Make a semi-dry mixture of 1 part cement and 3 parts sand. Add just enough water for a ball of stucco squeezed in your hand to retain the impression of your fingers.

Evenly cover the inside of the mould with stucco to a depth of about 25mm (1in), then use a piece of wood to tamp it into all the crevices. Lay longitudinal reinforcement in the mould (such as galvanized-metal rods or non-ferrous expanded-metal strips), then fill the mould with more stucco.

Push lengths of wooden dowel through the stucco to

form clearance holes for wall fixings (2). Next day, lift the casting out of the mould and leave it on the bench for 48 hours or so to harden. Spray it with water from time to time to prevent cracking.

Installing the moulding

You will probably need at least one assistant when installing a stucco moulding. It also helps if you nail a wooden batten to the wall to support the moulding (3).

Countersink the clearance holes, then drill through them into the wall behind. Insert and tighten the fixings before removing the batten.

Depending on the style of stuccowork, either render up to the moulding or fill gaps between the moulding and the wall with a mortar paste. Also, cover the screwheads with mortar.

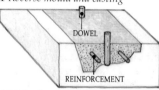

1 Reverse mould and casting

2 Make clearance holes for fixings

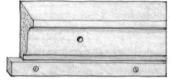

3 Support the moulding on a batten

CASTING ORNAMENTS IN STUCCO

BROKEN OR MISSING CONSOLES, *scrolls and other ornaments cast in stucco can be reproduced by taking an 'impression' from an original that is still intact. A flexible mould made from cold-cure silicone rubber is normally used – but it is possible to reproduce simple textures, such as vermiculation, using plaster of Paris alone.*

Decorative painted-stucco gable

Ornamental lintel in painted stucco

USING A FLEXIBLE MOULD

Brush loose dust off the original ornament and spray it with the release agent supplied. Mix the silicone rubber following the manufacturer's directions, including a thixotropic additive that enables the material to cling to vertical surfaces without slumping. Build a 3mm (⅛in) layer of silicone rubber, embed a light scrim and then add a further layer of rubber about 3 to 6mm (⅛in to ¼in) thick. Leave it to set for 12 hours or so.

An unsupported silicone-rubber mould is often too flexible and tends to distort when filled with stucco. Consequently, you usually need to apply a fairly thick layer of reinforced plaster of Paris to the outside of the flexible mould while it is still in place. Remove the plaster backing once it has set hard, then peel the flexible mould off the wall.

Making the casting

Reunite the flexible mould with its plaster backing and lay them on a workbench. Brush a fairly liquid mixture of 1 part cement to 3 parts sand onto the inside face of the mould, then fill it to the brim with more stucco.

Heavy castings may need reinforcing with non-ferrous expanded metal, and they should be attached to the wall with screws or expanding bolts. Disguise the wall fixings with mortar.

Classical pilasters with ornate capitals

CASTING VERMICULATION

To re-create vermiculation, first brush the original clean then paint it with a cooking-oil release agent. Coat the stone with a 30mm (1¼in) layer of plaster of Paris, including some jute scrim to reinforce it. When the plaster has set, ease the mould off the wall and lay it flat on a bench. Coat the inside of the mould with cooking oil.

Half-fill the mould with stucco. Place a strip of non-ferrous expanded metal on top and cover it with stucco, filling the mould to the brim. Leave the stucco to set hard, then remove the casting and screw it to the wall. Finally, fill the edges and cover the screwheads with mortar.

Impeccably restored vermiculated arches and dentil cornice

PAINTING STUCCO

New stucco must be dry before it's painted. Non-hydraulic-lime stuccos will require between 7 and 21 days, depending on the type of mix, the ambient temperature and level of humidity. Stucco based on hydraulic lime dries faster – perhaps in a few days. New stucco should be protected with plastic sheets to stop it drying too quickly in hot, dry weather. Use damp hessian to prevent it drying too slowly if humidity is high.

Most lime-based stucco was painted with limewash or lead paint. Limewash is still used, as it allows the building fabric to 'breathe'. Masonry paint is suitable for most cement-based renders.

CHAPTER SIX

TIMBER CLADDING

TIMBER-FRAME HOUSES *are among the earliest buildings still standing. The familiar picturesque 'half-timbered' house is often constructed with a stout oak framework infilled with wattle and daub or sometimes with bricks.*

From the sixteenth century, it became fashionable to cover timber frames with lime render, which also provided additional weatherproofing. At around the same time, some houses, particularly in south-east England, were clad with planks of wood known as weatherboarding. The boards were usually cut from oak or elm, but by the late eighteenth century sawn softwood boards were increasingly being imported from the Baltic and North America. Gradually weatherboarding became less widely used in Britain, except for the decorative cladding of gable ends and bay windows.

Early cladding in oak or elm may have been left unfinished, but the poorer-quality softwood needed protection in the form of wood tar or limewash mixed with pigments. In the early nineteenth century, coal tar was sometimes used, although mainly for agricultural buildings. Up to the 1950s, weatherboarding was often finished with white lead paint.

When repairing weatherboarding, disturb as few boards as possible. Old boards are likely to be of a better-quality timber and should be reused where possible. Replacing slightly irregular older boards with modern machine-cut ones may detract from the character of a building.

Early weatherboarded house that has been maintained in perfect condition

Partially clad timber-frame cottage

WEATHERBOARDING

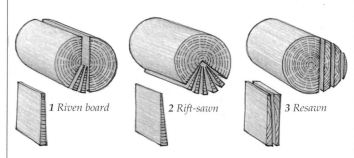

1 Riven board   2 Rift-sawn   3 Resawn

WEATHERBOARDING *is essentially a means of cladding a building effectively against the weather – and perhaps it is this honest 'no frills' appearance, with its neat horizontal shadow lines, that we find so appealing. There are plenty of examples of houses totally clad in weatherboarding, from eaves to ground level, but in certain areas it was a common practice to use timber cladding for the first floor only, which was supported by a lower storey of brick or stone; also, cladding is sometimes nailed to battens to protect substandard brickwork. This combination of painted weatherboarding and natural-coloured masonry is particularly handsome.*

From the earliest times, softwoods such as white pine, hemlock and spruce were used for weatherboarding. But it was not until the start of the twentieth century that red cedar – perhaps today's most fashionable timber for exterior cladding – became widely available.

BOARD PROFILES

The earliest boards were wedge-shape planks, riven from logs like slicing a cake. The result was a more-or-less symmetrical feather-edged board **(1)** with the grain running directly across its thickness. By the late nineteenth century similar boards were being produced by machine. Turned logs, suspended above a circular saw, were rotated fractionally between cuts, producing rift-sawn boards **(2)**.

Due to the orientation of the grain, riven and rift-sawn boards are relatively stable and are rarely susceptible to the splitting and warping that often results from shrinkage. Riven boards were seldom more than about 100mm (4in) in width, whereas much wider boards could be cut by machine. Typically, rift-sawn boards were 125 to 150mm (5 to 6in) wide, but widths of 225mm (9in) or more were available.

Another method for producing feather-edged boards was to saw logs into thick planks, which in turn were resawn to make two bevelled boards **(3)**. With this type of board, the grain direction varies and the worst effects of shrinkage are common.

Riven and sawn boards were usually planed on one face. At the same time, some boards were machined with a moulding along their bottom edges **(4)**.

Shiplap boarding **(5)** has been popular since the late nineteenth century and is still in use today. Tongue-and-groove boards **(6)**, used since the 1920s, were often machined with a profile that made a wide board look like two narrower ones, thus halving the time it took to clad a house.

Rare unpainted weatherboarding

  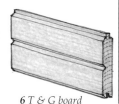

4 Machined   5 Shiplap   6 T & G board

NAILS FOR WEATHERBOARDING

In the eighteenth century, weatherboarding would have been fixed in place with handmade iron nails with large raised heads. Although most iron nails will have rusted away by now, it is preferable when replacing boards to use nails made in the traditional manner by a blacksmith specializing in the production of wrought-iron door fittings. However, it is generally more practical to use modern galvanized nails for repairs, or other non-ferrous nails that will not corrode. With their superior grip, ring-shank nails are good for fixing weatherboarding, too.

Typical combination of painted weatherboarding and red bricks

FIXING WEATHERBOARDING

There is some debate about the best way to fix weatherboarding. Traditionalists follow the time-honoured method, whereas others favour an approach that is designed to cope with modern mass-produced boards.

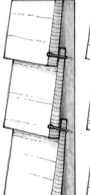   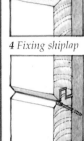

4 Fixing shiplap

1 Double-fixed　　*2 Single-fixed*　　*3 Blind-nailed*　　*5 Hidden fixing*

CORNERS AND EDGE DETAILS

In theory it is possible to mitre the ends of boards where they meet at a corner, but such detailing requires skilful carpentry. And even when boards are fitted perfectly, the joints are likely to open up in time – which is not only unsightly but exposes the vulnerable end grain to wet rot.

Corner posts

The most common method of finishing weatherboarding at corners, both internal and external, is to butt the ends of the boards against a vertical wooden corner post nailed to the underlying framework. An internal-corner post is simply a square batten **(1)**. Two strips of wood are nailed together at right angles to cap an external corner **(2)**.

Nailing procedures

Feather-edged boards overlap by about 25 to 38mm (1 to 1½in). Traditionally, nails were driven right through the overlap, pinning both boards to the framework **(1)**. Because riven and rift-sawn boards tend to shrink and swell across their thickness only, fixing them rigidly in this manner leads to few problems.

The modern practice is to hammer each nail through one board only, just missing the board below **(2)**. This permits the boards to move unrestrictedly and prevents splitting if the timber shrinks across its width. However, even some professional installers are of the opinion that driving nails in this way is likely to cause a board to cup (bend across its width), which is in itself sufficient to promote a split.

With 'blind' nailing, each board is nailed along the top edge only, so that the overlap hides the fixings **(3)**. This method has the advantage of being neat in appearance, but there's nothing to stop the lower edges of the boards bowing or twisting.

It is normal to fix shiplap cladding with a single row of nails for each board **(4)**.

When nailing tongue-and-groove boards, hidden fixings are more usual **(5)**.

Drip mouldings

Some early boarded houses have cladding running right down to the ground – an unsatisfactory solution that inevitably leads to rotting timber. The weatherboarding on later houses, which were normally built on masonry foundations, begins just above the ground with some kind of drip moulding to shed rainwater. This may be nothing more than a wooden starter strip nailed under the first board to hold the bottom edge away from the wall **(3)**, but better-quality houses often have purpose-made drip mouldings **(4)**.

Fascia boards

At the eaves, the cladding is lapped by a flat fascia board. Occasionally, the top board is tucked into a rebate planed along the bottom edge of the fascia board.

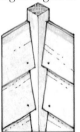

1 Internal

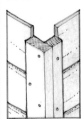

2 External

Boards bent around a corner

3 Starter strip

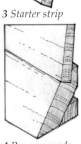

4 Purpose-made

Drip moulding fixed above windows

Conjunction of boards and hung tiles

REPAIRING WEATHERBOARDING

EXPERIENCE HAS PROVED *that provided a timber-clad house is maintained regularly it can last for centuries. What is perhaps even more encouraging is the fact that few if any of the repairs that may be necessary are beyond the skills of any reasonably competent carpenter. The repairs described below refer mainly to feather-edged weatherboarding, but you can adapt the techniques for other varieties of horizontal timber cladding.*

ROUTINE MAINTENANCE

You will find it pays to inspect weatherboarding at least once a year, and also immediately after periods of storms or high winds. If you are able to spot potential problems early enough, they need never develop into costly or time-consuming repairs.

Old iron nails are bound to corrode, until eventually they are too weak to hold the boards securely. Look out for loose boards and, before the wind does further damage, tap back and renail any that have dropped. Check to see if it's time to recaulk around window and door frames and along the butt joints between boards and corner posts.

REPLACING A ROTTED SECTION

The end grain of any piece of timber is particularly prone to wet rot. As a result, it is quite common to find that an otherwise sound length of weatherboarding has rotted at one or both ends. Rather than discard perfectly serviceable boards, replace only the rotten sections with new wood.

Prise up the bottom edge of the board above the one that has rotted, then make a sawcut over the nearest stud, so you can remove the rotten section (1). Keep the saw upright and make the last few strokes with the point of the blade, in order to avoid damaging the board below.

Use a chisel to split out the decayed wood (2), which you can remove piece by piece. Don't drive the chisel too deep, or you will tear the building paper that may lie beneath timber cladding.

A strip of wood still held by the nails under the edge of the board above is now all that remains of the rotted section. Slide a hacksaw blade up behind the board to cut through the nails, then prise out this last piece of wood. If necessary, patch any building paper that is

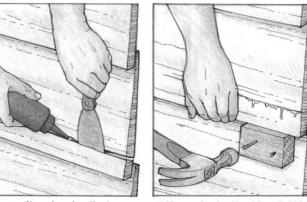

1 *Open split and apply adhesive*   2 *Clamp glued split with nailed block*

REPAIRING SPLIT BOARDS

A crack running along the centre of a board can be caulked or filled to prevent water getting in behind the cladding, but if a split occurs near the end of a board it is best to repair it with glue. Prise the split apart carefully (1) and apply an exterior wood glue to the exposed edge. To clamp the split together, temporarily nail a block of wood against the underside of the damaged board (2). You may have to slip a hacksaw blade up behind the board to cut the nails, so that the section below is free to move. Wipe excess glue from the surface of the cladding. Then, once the glue has set, remove the block and if necessary renail the repaired board.

torn. Next, cut a new piece of board to length. Treat both sides of the board with preservative, coating the end grain thoroughly, before you tap the new piece into place, using a block of wood to protect the edge (3). Since you will have to nail very close to the ends of the new piece of board, drill pilot holes first to avoid splitting the wood. If the rest of the siding is fixed with hidden nails, drive the new fixings just below the surface and cover their heads with either exterior wood filler or putty before painting the timber.

PAINTING BOARDS

If you fail to paint a timber-clad house regularly, sooner or later you will be faced with serious deterioration – wet rot and split timbers that may have to be replaced.

When repainting the boards, you need to match the existing finish. If it is tar, then this can still be obtained from specialist suppliers, but you will need to check that it is compatible with the old finish.

When exterior paintwork deteriorates, it tends to dry out and flake – so, before redecorating, all you need do is scrape it off and rub down the woodwork with abrasive paper.

Areas of sound paintwork may simply need washing down with a solution of sugar soap to remove the dirt and grease that would prevent new paint adhering. Cladding should be finished with a compatible paint or with limewash.

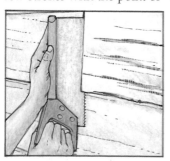

1 *Cut off the rotted section*

2 *Split out decayed wood with chisel*

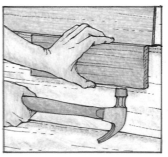

3 *Tap the new board in place*

CHAPTER SEVEN

ROOF COVERINGS

IN THE DAYS OF RUDIMENTARY TRANSPORT *heavy building materials such as masonry were not usually taken great distances, so roofs and walls had a distinctive local character.*

This changed with the spread of cheaper machine-made materials made possible by the Industrial Revolution and the growth of the railways and canal systems. Nor was this diversification of materials restricted to just one or two nations, or to the products of machines alone – for, as well as architectural styles, European settlers spread their craft skills and manufacturing methods around the world.

Most roofs are pitched in order to shed water efficiently and have a large surface area, which makes them a prominent feature. The type of roof covering is therefore important to the character of the building. Like brickwork, most roof coverings are made up from small units that together form an aesthetically pleasing pattern. And the majority of traditional coverings have a naturally attractive quality of colour and texture which, like other building materials, mellow with age to enhance the appearance of a period house.

Roofs require sympathetic maintenance to preserve their original character. With the resurgence of interest in older buildings, many trade manufacturers are able to supply traditional roof coverings, such as handmade clay tiles. As a result, it is usually possible to repair or recover an old roof in the appropriate style.

The thatched roof enhances this charming half-timbered house

An impressive 1920s hipped and gabled plain-tiled roof

Plain-tiled roof with dormer window

Slate roofing harmonizes with stone and rendered walls

Gable roof with tile-hung walls

TYPES OF ROOF

Flat   *Mono-pitch*

Gable   *Hipped*

Dutch gable   *Mansard*

T HE FUNCTION OF THE ROOF *is to shelter the fabric and contents of a building from the weather. The shape of the roof and the type of material used to cover it are largely determined by historical precedents evolved over the centuries to meet local conditions and architectural fashion and style.*

ROOF SHAPES

The shape of a roof is important not only to its function but also to the architectural style of the house. A flat roof affords good shelter from wind and sun, but is not very efficient for shedding rain. Pitched roofs are more common, as they are better able to withstand rain or snow. The pitch can vary considerably, depending on the type of covering used and the complexity of the roof shape.

The simplest form of pitched roof is the mono-pitched type, but the most common is the duo-pitched or gable roof. Hipped roofs, which are a variant of the latter, have one or both ends pitched as well as the front and rear slopes. Various combinations of these two types are frequently used.

The Mansard roof, which originated in France, is a variation of the pitched roof incorporating two angles on each side in order to create a greater volume of habitable space within the roof area.

Conical, hexagonal or octagonal roofs are all used for capping decorative turrets. Some pitched roofs have dormers, projecting structures that usually include a window to allow light into the attic space.

Victorian mechanized tile production

Decorative slate-covered tower

Functional needs

The design of a roof has to take into account the exposure of the site, the architectural style of the building, and the loading on the structure. The roof load is not restricted to the static load of the covering alone. Wind forces apply pressure on the windward side and suction on the lee side, so adequate covering and fixings are important. Weight of snow may need to be taken into account, and also thermal movement caused by extremes of temperature in different seasons. The fire resistance of some coverings may be a consideration.

When it comes to repairing or renewing an existing roof, most of these factors will already have been established by the original design and the performance of the roofing materials over the years. However, if you are planning modifications or a change of roof covering, then it is best to obtain advice from an experienced roofing specialist. Also, get advice from your local planning authority as to whether any consent is required. A new roof or major alterations have to comply with building regulations and may require consent if your house is listed or in a conservation area. Regular maintenance of an old roof is not subject to controls.

Components of a pitched roof

The terminology used to describe the individual parts of a roof can become quite complex when different elements are combined in its construction. The principal terms used in the roofing trade are illustrated here.

ASSESSING REPAIRS

● Easy even for beginners.
■ Fairly difficult. Good practical skills required.
▲ Difficult. Hire a professional.

Tiled roofs
Tiles can fracture, spall, or suffer from weak fixings.
■ Check the condition of the fixings (page 66).
■ Replace damaged or dislodged tiles (page 67).

Thatched roofs
Thatching deteriorates over time.
▲ Check for slipped or thinning thatch (page 65).
▲ Look for eroded abutments with chimneys or gables (page 65).
▲ Complete renewal may be your only option (page 65).

Slate roofs
Cracked or missing slates can allow water to enter.
■ Remove and replace broken slates (page 69).
▲ If fixings fail, have slates in good condition stripped and relaid (page 68).

Ornamental features
Damaged or missing details mar the integrity of a roof.
■ Refix or replace damaged or loose ridge tiles (page 69).
▲ Have damaged or missing details replaced (page 69).

Metal roofing
Corrosion and thermal movement can weaken sheet-metal roofs.
● Keep the roof clear of debris and moss (page 70).
● Check condition of flashings regularly (page 70).
▲ Get a specialist to carry out repairs promptly (page 70).

Roof terminology
1 Roof covering
2 Ridge
3 Gable end
4 Verge
5 Bargeboard
6 Eaves
7 Fascia
8 Soffit
9 Hip
10 Hipped end
11 Valley
12 Stepped flashing
13 Back gutter
14 Apron
15 Dormer window
16 Flat roof
17 Parapet

ROOF COVERINGS

Traditional roof coverings still in use today include clay tiles, slates, thatch and, to a lesser extent, metal sheeting. Their durability, cost-effectiveness, and fitness for purpose have been responsible for their continued use. Appearance, too, has played a part in their survival, particularly in the case of thatching. This centuries-old craft, using straw or reeds as a roof covering, is much appreciated for its charm and character. Although its use has been restricted in the past (it was banned in London in 1212 as a fire hazard), thatch is now enjoying a revival. Thatching follows regional styles and needs to be undertaken by a skilled thatcher experienced in the appropriate local traditions.

Steep-pitched plain-tiled roof c.1911

Beautifully crafted thatched roof

Weathered terracotta pantiles complement the old stone walls

Thick natural-stone roof slates

Roof pitch

The type of covering must be suitable for the pitch of the roof, which is determined by the exposure of the site and the local weather conditions.

The pitch of tiled and slate roofs depends on the size and overlap of the individual tiles or slates. Small plain tiles or slates are typically pitched at 40 to 45 degrees, though they can be used on steeper slopes and even on vertical surfaces. Roofs covered with large slates or profiled single-lap tiles need a pitch of no more than 30 degrees. Thatch needs a steeper angle (at least 50 degrees), so that it will shed rainwater quickly.

Flat roofs or ones with a shallow pitch require a continuous covering, such as metal or asphalt.

Double-lap coverings

Shingles, slates and plain tiles are known as double-lap coverings. They are laid in 'broken-bond' courses – staggered so that, with a slate roof, for example, the vertical joints between slates are centred over the slates in the row below. As a result, the 'head' of each slate is partly overlapped by the two courses above. In this way, the nail fixings are covered and the gaps between the exposed parts of the slates are always backed up by a whole slate, thus rendering the covering waterproof.

Double-lap roof coverings are fairly expensive, since a lot of material is involved and installing them is labour-intensive, particularly if the roof shape is complex.

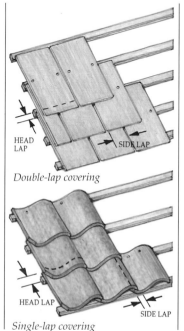

Double-lap covering

Single-lap covering

Single-lap coverings

Single-lap roof coverings are made of specially shaped tiles. The profile of each tile is designed to overlap or interlock at the sides to stop rainwater penetrating the vertical joints. Some tiles are made to interlock at the head and tail in order to provide a barrier between the courses.

Each course only has to lap the one below, and in most cases the vertical joints are not staggered. Single-lap coverings are relatively quick to lay, compared with double-lap roofing.

Single-lap coverings were traditionally made of clay pantiles, but there are also modern types made of concrete and finished in various colours.

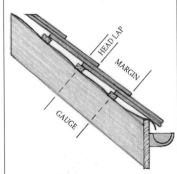

Spacing of battens determines lap

Lap and gauge

If double-lap and single-lap coverings are to perform properly, the head lap must fall within certain limits. The minimum lap dimensions that suppliers recommend depend on the size of the unit, the pitch of the roof and the degree of exposure.

The lap is adjusted by the spacing or 'gauge' of the battens to which the roof covering is fixed. With modern materials, the maximum specified gauge is usually given in the manufacturer's literature. The exposed part of the tile or slate is called the margin and is the same dimension as the gauge.

SAFETY

- Roof work is hazardous, so every care must be taken to ensure that safe working platforms are erected and barriers provided to prevent tools and materials falling or being knocked off the work area.
- For routine repair work, use a stable scaffold tower and a roof ladder – a special lightweight ladder that hooks over the ridge.
- For major work, have full scaffolding erected by an independent installer. Roofing contractors are required by law to provide safe working platforms and will either put up scaffolding themselves or arrange for it to be erected by a scaffolding firm.

THATCHED ROOFS

THE COTTAGE OR FARMHOUSE *with a thatched roof is one of the most enduring images of our countryside. Indeed, Britain probably has the greatest concentration of thatched buildings anywhere in the world: an estimated 50,000, half of which are listed buildings. Until the end of the Middle Ages, nearly all smaller houses were thatched. But the use of thatch gradually declined with the growth of industrialization and the increasing availability of other building materials, such as slate, brought about by cheap transport. Thatch is usually made from straw or water reed, though in parts of Britain other materials, such as heather and bracken, are used. Being an organic material, it is truly sustainable.*

One of the most enduring images of the English countryside

CHOOSING THATCH

When repairing thatch, the first problem is deciding which type to use. Over the centuries a house may have been thatched with a variety of different materials, which can make the decision difficult.

Your local planning authority may well have a policy concerning which type of thatch is appropriate, and if your building is listed or in a conservation area you may need consent to change from one type of thatch to another. It is therefore important to speak to their Conservation Officer at the outset, not least because the lower layers of thatch – which can date back hundreds of years – may provide valuable historical information, such as medieval smoke blackening on the underside of the thatch. Consent may also be required for any change in the external appearance of the roof or a change to another material.

Types of thatch

The three main types of thatch all consist of plant stems laid sloping downwards, towards the outer edge of the thatch. Water is therefore shed from the surface of the roof as quickly and directly as possible, minimizing the rotting process to which all thatch is eventually prone. The overall pitch of the roof, the pitch of the stems and the design of the roof should work together to achieve this end.

Water reed is a wetland plant. By the nineteenth century it was being used in Norfolk, the Fens, parts of south Dorset, and some other areas. Nowadays a lot of water reed is imported.

Combed wheat reed is a variety of thatching straw, sometimes grown specially for thatching. The straw is combed mechanically to remove the grain and other waste material without crushing the stems.

Long straw was at one time the commonest form of thatching in most parts of England. As with combed wheat reed the basic material is wheat straw, but long straw retains the heads and butts.

With some materials, patching is a viable option

REPAIRING THATCH

Recognizing when rethatching is essential and judging whether to repair or replace are not easy decisions and require an expert inspection from a master thatcher. To find one in your area, contact the Thatching Information Service.

Your thatcher will be able to assess how much of the top surface of the thatch has eroded. This tends be most evident at abutments with chimneys or gables. He or she will also be able to tell whether some of the thatch has slipped, determine the thickness of covering left over the fixings, and gauge the condition of the fixings and the tightness of the thatch.

Repair methods differ from one type of thatch to another. With long straw and combed wheat reed, successive coats are often added when the top layer wears down. With water reed, the thatch is usually taken back to the rafters.

Unlike water reed, straw thatches are often repaired by patching, rather than replacing the entire thatch. Patching particular areas in need of repair can substantially extend the life of the main coat.

In all cases, the ridge and the areas around chimneys, where the thatch tends to sink after a time, are the most vulnerable parts of the roof and are likely to require replacement sooner than the main coat (they usually need replacing every 15 to 20 years). Only when partial repairs become uneconomic should complete rethatching be considered. Endeavour to retain as much of the existing thatch as possible, while ensuring that the building remains watertight. It may be possible to extend the life of a thatched roof by reridging and redressing plus some localized repair work.

Thatching is a job for an expert

When the thatch does eventually need complete renewal, it is worth laying a fire-resistant barrier between the rafters – but be sure to provide a ventilated gap, in order to allow ventilation to the thatch. Also, consult your house insurers, as they may have specific guidelines to reduce the risk of fire.

Unlike other forms of roofing material, thatched roofs have wide eaves that shed water clear of the building, so gutters and downpipes are not required. However, it is important to provide adequate drainage, so that rainwater does not saturate the base of the walls.

ROOF VENTILATION

MANY PERIOD HOUSES *are made of porous materials that tend to absorb more moisture than modern building materials do. It is therefore important that the whole building is allowed to 'breathe', so the moisture can evaporate. A crucial part of this process occurs within the roof space, where moisture can easily accumulate – which is why ventilation is an important characteristic of traditionally detailed tile and slate roofs. In modern times, the performance of many roofs has been compromised by the use of inappropriate roofing felts and by badly placed insulation. Until recently most roofing felt was impervious – but over the past few years vapour-permeable membranes have been introduced, which help disperse moisture.*

ROOFING FELT

Roofing felt was first used in the 1930s, in the form of a thin building paper laid beneath the slates or tiles. It acted as a secondary barrier, to keep out wind-driven rain and snow. Not long after, bitumen and plastic felts were introduced. These types of roofing felt provide a high level of resistance to the passage of water vapour and constitute a cold contact surface upon which warm moist air can condense. In severe cases, this can cause decay to the roof rafters.

More modern roofing felts permit the passage of some water vapour. However, in order to install vapour-permeable felt, the roof needs to be stripped of its slates or tiles – so it is most conveniently fitted when the roof needs to be re-covered.

You can install proprietary roof ventilators that allow the passage of air between the overlapping sheets of underlay without intruding above the roofline. Ideally, the airflow should be from the top to the bottom of the roof, which may necessitate counterbattening. Ventilators that protrude above the roofline are not recommended for period houses.

INSULATING THE ROOF

The insulation of roof spaces started to become widespread in the 1970s. The placing of insulation within a roof space requires some careful thought. When it is laid just above the ceiling, it may make the roof space colder and increase the risk of condensation, particularly if there is no ventilation. Care also has to be taken to ensure that the insulation doesn't inhibit the passage of air at the eaves. If insulation installed between the rafters is next to an impervious roofing felt, condensation can make the insulation damp. Many modern insulation quilts retain moisture and do not dry out readily – which may cause decay to the tile battens and roof timbers.

As an alternative to the many types of manufactured roof insulation, you can use natural sheep's wool. If it is used in conjunction with a vapour-permeable felt, the risk of decay induced by condensation is thought to be significantly less.

To reduce the amount of water vapour in your home, consider providing mechanical ventilation, particularly in the kitchen and bathrooms.

TILED ROOFS

C LAY TILES, *which have been in use for centuries, had their origins in the great civilizations of the East and the Mediterranean. The latter had the greater influence in the countries of Europe, and subsequently in their colonies.*

Until labour-saving mechanization was introduced in the nineteenth century, plain and profiled tiles were made by hand. Today there is a resurgence of interest in the qualities of the original materials – and, though they never completely died out, handmade tiles are once more available for those who can afford them.

Glazed coloured profile tiles on a C20th hipped roof

PLAIN TILES

Plain tiles make up a double-lap covering that produces a pleasing overall texture similar to that of a slated roof. The colour, character and durability of clay tiles soon came to be appreciated, and they began to be used as a fireproof alternative in areas where thatched roofs had predominated.

The small size and overall regular pattern of the tiles, albeit with some variation due to their handmade nature, produced an attractive covering that mellowed with age. Plain tiles look equally at home on rural houses and barns and on sophisticated town houses.

Decorative tiled gable roof

Verge detail of swept valley

Handmade   *Machine-made*

Types of plain tile

Made from processed clay, plain tiles are mostly made to a standard size of 265mm (10½in) by 165mm (6½in) by 12mm (½in). These dimensions were established by Edward IV in the fifteenth century. Nowadays, larger plain tiles and specials are also available.

The tiles are simple rectangles moulded with a slight curve or 'camber' from head to tail. Early handmade tiles also had a cross-camber that gave the roof an attractive texture and a measure of ventilation, while shedding rainwater efficiently. Modern machine-made tiles are produced without a cross-camber, but it is still possible to obtain handmade cross-cambered clay tiles.

Fixing methods

Early handmade plain tiles were punctured with two holes close to the top edge or head, through which oak pegs were fitted. The pegs hooked over riven tiling battens, and the tiles were generally known as peg tiles **(1)**. Later versions had nibs of clay formed in the top edge **(2)**, although nail holes were provided for extra security in exposed situations. Sometimes the head laps were sealed on the inside with lime mortar known as 'torching'.

Tile-hung walls, for which ordinary or shaped plain tiles were often used **(3)**, also required nail fixings. In this case, every tile was twice-nailed, whereas in roof work it was usual only to nail the perimeter tiles at the eaves, verge and ridge and at every fourth course.

Shaped tiles

During the earlier part of the nineteenth century, shaped versions of the simple plain tile began to appear. These were used to create attractive repeat-pattern tile-hung walling as well as decorative roof coverings.

On walls, as with some ornamental roofs, shaped tiles were often laid with alternating courses of plain tiles or tiles of a different colour to produce interesting decorative treatments.

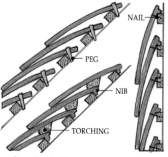

NAIL
PEG
NIB
TORCHING

1 Peg-fixed tiles
2 Nibbed tiles with torching
3 Nail-fixed wall-hung tiles

Decorative tile-hung walling

Coloured tiles

Although red-toned tiles are the most common in many parts of the country, other colours, such as blues and beige, were produced from clays of different regions. These were sometimes combined to create diaper patterns or other polychrome designs. If you are fortunate to own such a feature, take reference photographs of it in case it should have to be stripped for renovation purposes in the future.

Hips and valleys

Tiled roofs have the benefit of specially shaped tiles for hips and valleys which are laid to bond neatly with each course. However, one of the most attractive features of a plain-tiled roof is the swept valley, where the tiles are cut to a tapered shape so the courses can be run round in a curve (1). A less expensive alternative is the laced valley, where the tiles are not cut but laid to butt up to wide tile-and-a-half tiles set diagonally (2). Although even a laced valley is quite costly to reproduce, it is worth the expense in order to preserve the style of an old tiled roof. Hire the services of a specialist roofing company familiar with historic craft practices to help maintain the roof's original features.

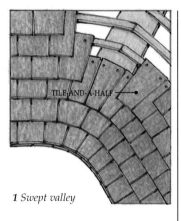

1 Swept valley

2 Laced valley

REPLACING TILES

Although clay tiles are very durable, they can fracture if struck or undue pressure is applied to them; and if they become porous, they may suffer frost damage. Also, it's inevitable that with time the nail fixings will fail.

Traditional peg-tiled roofs are unusual. Should the pegs break or perish, they can be replaced and the tiles refitted.

If nibbed tiles are broken, replacements can be hooked onto the tile battens. Use copper, aluminium-alloy or silicon-bronze roofing nails to fix those that can be nailed. Slide the tiles of the last course into position, while using wooden wedges to lift the course above. If the tiles do not have nibs, use a wire or sheet-metal hook (see FITTING A SLATE).

A modern fixing method for old roof coverings, involves spraying a foam onto the underside of the slates or tiles, where it sets into a hard layer. Much is claimed for these foams. They are said to improve insulation and weatherproofing, stop tiles or slates slipping and prevent condensation, but they can cause problems in old buildings. Since the tiling battens and the upper parts of the rafters are covered with foam, normal airflow into the roof space is restricted and rotting can occur. Also, you can't salvage the slates or tiles when you want to reroof the property.

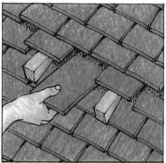

Use wooden wedges to lift the tiles

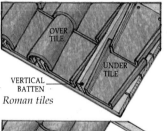

Roman tiles

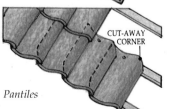

Pantiles

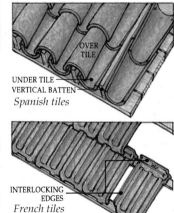

Spanish tiles

French tiles

PROFILED TILES

Profiled tiles are single-lap coverings that are shaped to overlap or interlock with one another. The principal traditional types are Roman tiles, Spanish or mission tiles, pantiles, and French or Marseilles tiles. These coverings, which in most cases are laid in unbonded courses, produce a boldly textured roof.

Roman tiles

Roman-tiled roofs are made up of flat 'under tiles' and half-round barrel-shaped 'over tiles'. Most are tapered from head or tail so that they nest together along their side edges and between courses. The under tiles are nailed flat on tiling battens or close boarding, while the over tiles are nailed to vertical battens run between them.

Spanish tiles

Spanish or 'mission' tiles (so called because they were introduced into the southern states of America by Spanish missionaries) are similar in principle to the Roman type. The main difference is that the under tile of the Spanish type is concave. The under tiles are nailed sideways into the vertical battens on each side, and the over tiles are single-nailed to the top of the battens.

Pantiles

The pantile is a simpler variation of the Spanish tile, the trough of the under tile being combined with the curve of the over tile to produce an S-shaped profile. The opposite diagonal corners are cut away to allow

Multi-coloured Spanish tiles

the tiles to fit together in the same plane where the head and tail meet between courses. The tiles are located on tiling battens by a single wide nib at the head and are fixed with a single nail.

French tiles

The French tile is one of many machine-made interlocking tiles that became widely used in the early part of the twentieth century. It provides an efficient and visually pleasing roof covering that is fairly easy to install.

Most French tiles were a natural terracotta red, but some were coloured and glazed. They were hung on tile battens and rarely nailed, as their interlocking shape helped keep them in place.

SLATE ROOFS

LATE ROOFING *provides a highly durable and relatively maintenance-free roof covering. This type of roofing uses naturally occurring fissile stone that can be converted into thin slabs or sheets.*

True slate – as opposed to the sedimentary limestone or sandstone slabs used in some regions – is a hard metamorphic rock formed from clay sediments. Due to immense pressure millions of years ago, it has a laminated structure that enables it to be readily split into sheets. This type of stone has been quarried or mined for centuries.

Smooth blue-grey slate from Wales is perhaps the best known, because with the advent of industrialization it was produced in great quantities and transported to all parts of the country and exported abroad. Its fine grain meant it could be split into thin, even thicknesses and mass-produced in uniform sizes, which made it particularly suitable for roofing the houses of the rapidly developing towns and cities.

As well as Welsh slate, there are many other types of regional slates, such as Collyweston, Horsham, Pennine and Delabole. Although the slate industry has diminished in recent times, natural slates are still available for renovation work if you are unable to reuse your own slates.

Traditional slate roof laid in diminishing courses

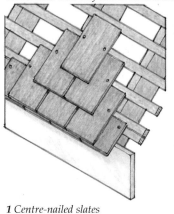

BATTEN

COUNTERBATTEN

BOARDING

ROOFING FELT

1 *Centre-nailed slates*

2 *Counterbattens on boarded roof*

SHAPED SLATES

After splitting, the edges of each slate are cropped to bring the slate to the finished length and width. This process is known as dressing. The dressed edge gives the characteristic bevelled finish to the face of natural-slate roofing. Slates were cut and dressed by hand but are now mostly machine-processed.

Most are cut to standard rectangular sizes, although sometimes the tail of the slate is shaped to form a decorative pattern when laid.

Slates that cannot readily be worked and thick stone slates are sold as 'random sizes' for thickness grading and sorting by the roofer. This type of roofing is laid with the largest slates at the eaves and the smallest at the ridge. As it takes skill to install, it is expensive.

COLOUR AND TEXTURE

The colour and texture of slate varies according to its origin. The surface of some slates is smooth; others have a distinct riven texture to the face. The colours can vary from cool greens, blues and greys to warmer purples and russet reds in a range of tones. Some are variegated, with stripes or mottled patterns, while others are plain. In most cases just one type of slate was used, giving a pleasing natural colour and texture to the roof. However, in the mid nineteenth century different-coloured slates were sometimes combined to create a decorative effect.

If you need to replace old slates, take a sample slate or fragment to a supplier of roofing materials to help you match the colour and size.

FIXING METHODS

Slate roofing is a double-lap covering laid in bonded courses. Usually each slate is fixed with two nails, though sometimes old stone slates were simply located on battens with wooden pegs.

The holes for the nails are punched through by hand or machine from the underside. This produces countersunk holes on the face of the slate in which the nailheads sit. Slates are sometimes head-nailed, but are more commonly centre-nailed to prevent them being lifted by the wind **(1)**.

Slates may be fixed to battens or to close boarding. If the roof is boarded, the current practice is to lay roofing felt then fix vertical counterbattens up the slope of the roof to raise the horizontal battens clear of

the surface **(2)**. This allows any penetrating moisture to drain down freely.

Many old slate roofs were fixed with iron nails, though more durable copper nails were used on better-quality houses. Good slates will last for generations, but a slate roof covering can fail due to corroded fixings.

Whenever carrying out repairs, or if you have your roof re-covered, make sure stainless-steel or copper roofing nails are used. The nails should be 20mm (¾in) to 25mm (1in) longer than the thickness of the slate. Galvanized nails can be used for the battens. If the fixings perish but the slates are still in good condition, have the roof stripped and re-laid with the original slates rather than new ones.

1 Cut fixing nails   *2 Nail strip to batten*   *3 Bend tail of strip*

Perfectly matched group of slated buildings

REPAIRING A SLATE ROOF

Before tackling the work, you will need to find a supply of matching slates with which to make the repairs. If they are to function properly and look right, the thickness of the slates must be the same as that of the original. If they are too thick, the overlapping courses will not lie flat.

The overall size is less of a problem, because new slates are available in a wide variety of sizes. If individual slates are too large, you can cut them down to the required dimensions. The width should allow a gap of about 3mm (⅛in) between each vertical joint.

Removing a broken slate

Nail-fixed slate roofing is laid in such a way that each course covers the fixings of the course below. In order to remove an individual slate it is necessary to release the hidden fixing. This is done with a special tool called a slater's ripper.

Slide the end of the tool under the damaged slate and hook it onto one of the nails. Give the hilt of the handle a sharp tap with a hammer to cut or pull out the nail (1). Remove the second nail in the same way. If you aren't able to hire a slater's ripper, try cutting the nails with a hacksaw blade. You should now be able to pull the broken part of the slate free.

Fitting a slate

Cut a strip of lead about 25mm (1in) wide. The strip should be 50mm (2in) or so longer than the head lap of the roofing. Nail the strip to the slate-fixing battens or boarding between the slates of the course below, just clearing the head of the next course down (2). Slide the new slate into place and then bend the tail of the strip over the edge to form a hook (3).

Cutting to size

Provided it is not too thick, you can cut a slate to a smaller size. Hold it face down on a straight board, with the edge of the slate overhanging by the amount that is to be trimmed off. Use the edge of a brick-layer's trowel to chop off the waste, working towards you and using the edge of the board as a guide (4).

4 Cut slate with a trowel

ORNAMENTAL FEATURES

The roofs of many Victorian and Edwardian houses were embellished with decorative metal cresting and terra-cotta ridge tiles and finials. Unfortunately, as a result of poor maintenance, many of these are now missing – but you can buy suitable replicas from roofing-tile manufacturers.

For any major repairs to an ornamental cresting, call in a roofing company. If you are used to working at heights, you may be able to fix loose ridge tiles yourself. First, lift off the loose tiles and chisel off the weak old mortar. Mix a bedding mortar of 1 part lime, 1 part

Lay mortar carefully in bands

cement and 6 parts sand. Lay a band of mortar on each side of the ridge and at each end. Carefully set the tiles into the mortar and bed them down. Remove excess mortar with a trowel, taking care not to smear the roof tiles or slates.

Decorative terracotta ridge tiles and finials

METAL ROOFS

L EAD AND COPPER SHEETING *have been used as roof coverings for generations. Both metals are soft, malleable and highly durable, and were principally used for important public buildings.*

In the domestic context, lead was most commonly used for covering roofs, doorhoods and porch or balcony canopies where other traditional coverings were unsuitable because of the pitch or shape of the roof. Lead sheeting is manufactured by a rolling or casting process. Cast lead is considered to be the best, but is more expensive than rolled-sheet lead.

TYPES OF METAL ROOFING

Metal expands and contracts with changes in temperature. To overcome movement problems, sheet roofing is made up from panels of metal. Where the panels meet on vertical edges, they are joined by weathertight rolled or flat seams; on horizontal edges, they are joined by lapped or drip joints. In both cases, the joints are formed by hand.

Sheet iron began to be used for roofing in the eighteenth century. Corrugated iron, patented in England in the early nineteenth century, was in common use for commercial buildings by the middle of the century. It was also used for colonial domestic buildings and outhouses.

Lightweight tin-plate roofing was in use in the eighteenth century, and became popular in the United States towards the end of the nineteenth century with the introduction of interlocking embossed machine-made tin-plate tiles.

FLASHINGS

Flashings are used to weatherproof the junctions between the roof covering and wall abutments, chimneys, or other elements that interrupt the roof surface. These junctions, which may be either mortar fillets or strips of metal, are often the most vulnerable part of the roof. They therefore require regular inspection, and prompt attention if repairs are needed. Metal flashings are superior and mostly made *in situ* to suit the type of roof covering. If they are beyond repair, get a specialist to replicate the original pattern.

Double-lap covering

The abutment flashings for double-lap coverings, such as tiles, slates or shingles, are made up with 'soakers' and stepped cover flashing (1). Soakers are thin sheets of metal that are turned up at right angles and fitted under each tile. The top edge generally hooks over the head of the tile to keep the soaker securely in place.

The step flashing is made from a 150mm (6in) strip of lead, no more than 1.5m (5ft) long. This is cut into a stepped shape to follow the pitch of the roof and is tucked into the mortar joints. Lead wedges are used to fix the flashing, and the joints are then pointed with mortar.

Single-lap covering

Flashings for single-lap coverings, such as profiled tiles, are made without soakers. A wide step-and-cover flashing is used instead, the extra width being formed into the contour of the roofing (2).

MAINTAINING METAL ROOFING

In time all metal roofing deteriorates, mainly due to fatigue or chemical action. The latter may occur as a result of atmospheric pollution or contact with corrosive substances in other materials or in organic matter. Corrosion can also take place when dissimilar metals are used together (for example, when copper sheeting is fixed with iron nails). It is therefore advisable to use compatible materials – such as copper nails for fixing copper or lead sheeting, and galvanized fixings for galvanized iron.

Repairs to lead and copper sheeting require the services of a metal-roofing specialist. Pinholes in lead caused by corrosion can be patch-repaired; so can splits caused by thermal movement. It is not usually necessary to have the entire covering stripped and replaced. Splits can be welded successfully using oxyacetylene (known as lead burning); or a patch of matching material can be let in using the same technique.

Lead burning allows the repair to expand and contract at the same rate. Stringent fire precautions must be followed when this process is being used.

Mastics and repair tapes are rarely successful, even as a temporary repair, and can make a permanent repair to metal roofing more difficult.

Always keep flat roofs free from debris and build-up of mosses – both can reduce water flow, and the latter causes corrosion. If organic growth is a persistent problem on a lead roof, apply a chemical treatment available from builders' merchants. Copper will not sustain organic growth. Wear soft shoes when walking over a flat roof, and take care not to damage the surface when brushing or scraping the surface of the covering.

Iron-based roof coverings will rust if the protective galvanizing or tin plating breaks down, so keep them well painted to prolong their working life.

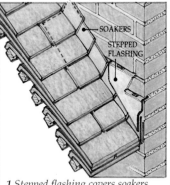

1 Stepped flashing covers soakers

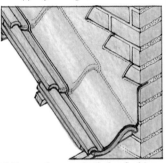

2 Step-and-cover single-lap flashing

CHIMNEY FLASHING

A flashing round a chimney is more complex than other roof flashings, as it has to be waterproof on four sides. This is done with an apron flashing at the front (1), step flashing at the sides (2), and a back gutter at the rear (3).

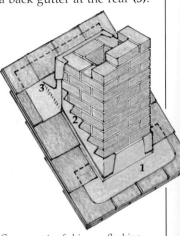

Components of chimney flashing

CHAPTER EIGHT

CHIMNEYS

BEFORE CHIMNEYS EXISTED *the smoke from fires simply escaped through a central covered hole in the roof. Funnel-shaped hoods of lime-plastered timber were used in houses when fireplaces began to be sited against walls. Eventually the hood evolved into the brick or stone chimney, either built onto the outside of the wall or projecting inside the room to form a chimney breast. In some houses the centrally placed fire continued with the introduction of massive brick or stone fireplaces, either single or back-to-back, that divided the house.*

The chimney became an important feature of domestic architecture from early medieval times, when the roofs of houses were graced

with magnificent moulded-brick examples. But by the early eighteenth century the imposing chimney stack had lost its importance, thanks to the influence of classical architectural styles. The chimney, along with the low-pitched roof, was now set back and hidden or masked by the parapet of the symmetrical façade. Whereas formerly chimneys had been built separately, although often set in groups, they were now combined into a relatively plain rectangular mass of brick or stone. However, the reintroduction of steeply pitched roofs and decorative chimneys, along with the vogue for fancy terracotta chimney pots, gave added interest to the rooflines of Victorian houses.

Simple well-proportioned stone chimney

Imposing pair of brick-built chimneys with decorative coursing

CHIMNEY STYLES

CHIMNEYS *are generally constructed of brick, although stone was used for grand houses and in areas where it was a common local material. In most cases, the only visible part of a chimney is the chimney stack protruding from the roof. However, some chimneys show as imposing monoliths, rising majestically on the outside of the house.*

Stone chimneys are usually built of smooth ashlar (dressed-stone) blocks, although rusticated and rubble stone with ashlar quoins are also used. More often than not, the upper part is moulded in the manner of a plain column; or sometimes the top is castellated.

Brick chimneys, like stone ones, may be square, octagonal, rectangular or round in plan, although the brick types tend to be more ornamental. The Victorian revival movements produced some impressive decorative structures based on Tudor models. The flanks of towering brick-built chimneys were often relieved by recessed brick panels and brick strapwork, while oversailing courses added decorative relief at the top. If this was not enough, coloured-brickwork patterns were sometimes included, too.

Castellated dressed-stone stacks

Decorative brickwork chimney

CHIMNEY CONSTRUCTION

Single-storey dwellings require only a simple chimney. In early country houses this took the form of a massive fireplace with a proportionally large straight flue. The chimneys of houses with more than one floor were more complex. The plan of Georgian and Victorian town houses had the fireplaces of individual rooms built against the side walls so the flues could be grouped into single chimney structures.

The interior masonry of each chimney was corbelled or 'gathered over' above the fireplace to form a funnel shape leading into the flue. In order for the flue of the lower fireplace to circumvent the fireplace in the room above, it had to be bent to one side. Although theoretically a long straight flue is the most efficient, it was found that the bend stopped rain falling on the

fire. It was also, erroneously, believed that bends reduced down draughts. Even flues that had no need to avoid obstacles above were therefore built with bends, too.

Where the flues converged in the chimney stack, they were separated by brick or stone divisions known as withes or midfeathers. The insides of the flues were 'pargeted' or rendered with a 12mm (½in) lining of mortar. This helped to seal each flue and make a smoother passage for the smoke.

At the point where the chimney stack emerged through the roof, a fillet of mortar or a dressed-lead flashing provided a waterproof seal around the base. The top of the stack may be finished with shaped brickwork or stone, or each flue may terminate with a chimney pot bedded in an angled fillet of mortar known as a flaunching.

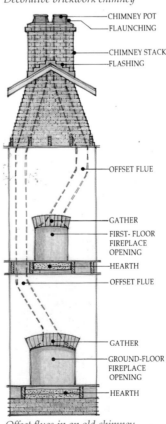

CHIMNEY POT
FLAUNCHING
CHIMNEY STACK
FLASHING
OFFSET FLUE
GATHER
FIRST-FLOOR FIREPLACE OPENING
HEARTH
OFFSET FLUE
GATHER
GROUND-FLOOR FIREPLACE OPENING
HEARTH

Offset flues in an old chimney

CHIMNEY REPAIRS

Because of their exposed position, chimneys are particularly susceptible to the effects of wind, rain and frost – including exfoliated stonework or brickwork, eroded pointing, cracked flaunching, damaged pots and perished flashing.

They are also susceptible to sulphate attack from inside. Water vapour, given off as a by-product of burning fuel, condenses on the cooler upper regions of the flue and combines with other products of the combustion process to form sulphuric acid and other corrosive chemicals. These acids cause masonry, mortar joints and pargeting to decay.

In some cases the condensation is concentrated on the windward side of the flue, resulting in uneven erosion of the lining and mortar joints – which makes the chimney lean in the direction of the prevailing wind. Repointing may arrest the problem, or it may be possible to stabilize the structure by reinforcing it with a concrete liner. Failing this, the chimney can be rebuilt, using the original masonry plus a new liner – which is often the best solution.

Acid attack also causes erosion of the withes, leading to cracks in the structure or bulging, or poor draught due to leakage between the flues.

Erosion of masonry

Badly exfoliated bricks or stone blocks may have to be cut out and replaced. Try to match the original material, and point new brickwork in the appropriate style. If you have difficulty finding suitable replacement material, use a colour-matched mortar to fill the surface (see REPAIRING DEFECTIVE STONE).

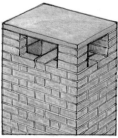

Wire binding   *Stone-slab capping*   *Ridge-tile capping*

Flush roofing-slate capping   *Terracotta chimney-pot inserts*

CHIMNEY POTS

C HIMNEY POTS *generally started to transform the appearance of chimneys in the eighteenth century, although earlier examples existed. However, a wide range of decorative patterns did not become available until the nineteenth century. Made of terracotta, an unglazed fired clay that has excellent durability and resistance to heat, they were used to improve the efficiency of the chimney.*

You can still buy chimney pots made using traditional methods and patterns. The shapes are produced either by hand on a potter's wheel or by pressing kneaded clay into plaster moulds. The moulding is removed while the clay is still workable, then finished by hand and left to dry out before being fired in a kiln.

CHIMNEY POT REPAIRS

Although terracotta is fairly durable, it can decay (especially if underfired in manufacture) and, being relatively brittle, it cracks quite easily. However, it is worth trying to preserve old chimney pots, even on a chimney that is disused.

Chimney pots are surprisingly large when seen close up, and need careful handling. Although it may be feasible to carry out repairs *in situ*, it is often safer to remove the pot from the stack and either work on it on a securely constructed scaffold platform or lower the pot by rope to the ground.

Cracks in brickwork

Differential settlement or erosion of the mortar joints may result in cracks opening up in the stack. Where these follow the joints, they can be raked out and repointed. If the bricks themselves are cracked, have them replaced.

Small brick-built chimneys that have suffered cracking can be reinforced by binding them with stainless-steel wire. This entails raking out the horizontal joints around the upper part of the chimney in order to receive the wire, which is then discreetly hidden with new pointing.

If the old lime mortar is badly perished and the brickwork is in a poor state, you may have to have the chimney rebuilt. Should that be necessary, it is important that the original details are recorded before the stack is dismantled, so they can be reproduced. Have reusable bricks re-laid, preferably with the weathered face showing, using a 1:2:9 mortar mix of sulphate-resistant cement, lime and sand. Use a 1:1:6 mix for the flaunching around replaced chimney pots and the top edges of oversailing courses.

Damp chimneys

Since chimneys are open to the elements, rain is able to enter them. When the chimney is in use, the heat from the fire normally keeps the system relatively dry. So, to some extent, does the through draught when the fire is not alight.

A stone slab set on brick piers is a traditional form of capping for a large working stack that provides ventilation when the chimney is not in use. Disused chimneys should be capped in a way that prevents the ingress of water while allowing ventilation. Half-round ridge tiles bedded in mortar can be used. Where the chimney would look better with a flush top, roofing slates can be mortared in place and an airbrick built into opposite sides of the stack to provide the necessary ventilation. A variety of terracotta tops and hood inserts are available that provide ventilated covering for chimney pots.

In all cases, air must be allowed to enter at fireplace level to provide a through draught. If the fireplace opening has been sealed off, fit a vent in the form of an airbrick or grille.

Repairing cracks

Fix cracks with a two-part epoxy resin adhesive. Reinforce the repair by binding the pot with fine stainless-steel wire. Twist the ends of the wire together with pliers to tighten it, and fold the twisted end back against the face. Position the wire to lie in a groove or under a bead to disguise its presence.

Weathered pots

You may be able to prolong the life of a decaying pot by refitting it so the eroded side faces in a sheltered direction. If it has to be replaced, try to match the style and colour. Architectural-salvage firms generally have a variety of pots in stock, and you may be lucky enough to find one that is naturally weathered.

Otherwise, try a company that sells new pots; or if you are really dedicated, have a replica made to order.

Fitting pots

Chimney pots must be well seated and securely fitted. The method will depend on the size of the pot and the shape of the base. Tall pots should be set into the top courses of the brickwork, to make them less vulnerable to high winds. The top of the stack is then finished with a mortar flaunching sloped to shed water. Although short pots are very often set in the flaunching, they are better built into the brickwork, too.

Terminals and inserts

A selection of terminals and inserts is available today, mostly in terracotta or metal. They are designed to assist performance or prevent rainwater entering the flue. Bird guards are available, too.

When fitting a pot or an insert, check with the supplier that the design won't restrict flow of smoke from the flue.

FLUE LINERS

I F A FLUE IS INEFFICIENT, *that can lead to erosion of the mortar joints, causing potentially dangerous fumes and tars to escape. It also boosts the build-up of soot and so increases the risk of fire.*

All new chimneys now have to be built with a flue lining to protect the masonry from harmful flue gases. The lining is usually made of refractory concrete or impervious clay. It has long been realized that a flue lining improves the flow of combustion gases, and it was not uncommon for old flues to be pargeted (lined) with lime-mortar as the chimney was erected. However, many were not lined at all.

A modern flue liner can replace perished pargeting in an old flue, reduce the size of the flue in order to make it more efficient, or add stability to a frail chimney structure. A specialist installer will advise you about the most suitable and cost-effective type of liner.

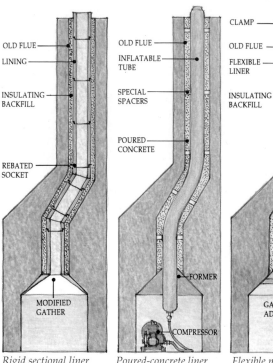

Rigid sectional liner   *Poured-concrete liner*   *Flexible metal liner*

RIGID SECTIONAL LINERS

This type of liner, which may be made of ceramic, light-weight pumice or refractory concrete, is well established because of its durability and is commonly used for new installations. It is suitable for all types of fuel.

Manufactured in short round or square lengths of various sizes, these liners are installed in sections, which are then mortared together. Ideal for straight flues, they can be adapted to offset ones either by cutting the ends to an angle or using standard elbow sections. Usually the meeting edges of the parts simply interlock, the rebated socket always being placed uppermost, but some types have a locating collar too.

The chimney pot has to be removed in order to reline a flue using this method. Also, holes have to be made at key points in the chimney wall, particularly at bends, in order to gain access to the flue. For a straight chimney this may only be at the bottom of the flue, where a support is needed for the liner and insulating backfill.

The sections are lowered down the flue from the top of the chimney. The top joint of each piece is coated with mortar to receive the next section as it is lowered down the flue. Once the openings have been rebuilt, the void around the new liners is usually backfilled with light-weight concrete – although this is not always needed, as sectional liners have good insulation properties. The chimney pot and capping are finished in the normal way.

POURED CONCRETE

This fairly recent innovation for lining old chimneys uses a lightweight concrete that is pumped into the flue around an inflatable tube. The concrete is specially formulated to provide a fire-resistant insulative lining that seals the old brickwork while reinforcing the structure.

First of all, the contractors will clean and inspect the chimney. Where bends are located, an opening is made so the former can be centred using special spacers. The toughened-rubber former is passed down the flue and inflated to suit the size of the appliance or fireplace. Then, after all the openings have been sealed, the concrete mix is pumped into the chimney from the top to fill the void around the tube.

When the mix has set, the former is removed, leaving a smooth, efficient cylindrical flue that can be used for all types of fuel. Once installed, it is virtually permanent. It is a good lining for single flues but may not be suitable for a multi-flued system, as the dividing masonry may be too weak to bear the weight of the poured concrete.

FLEXIBLE METAL LINERS

Of the three basic kinds of chimney lining, flexible stainless-steel liners are the simplest to install. The best of these is the spirally wound double-skinned type. Made of austenitic stainless steel, which is particularly resistant to corrosion as well as heat, it has a smooth inner surface and can be used for appliances that burn coal, wood, oil or gas, as well as for open fires. Made as a continuous length, it can be fitted easily to both straight and offset chimneys.

A rope, which is passed down the flue, is attached to the liner by a nose cone. The liner is then fed down the chimney and carefully pulled through from below. The bottom end is sealed and secured into a flue-pipe adaptor, for connecting to an appliance, or a gather-type adaptor (a funnel-shaped hood) for an open fire. At the top of the chimney, the liner is cut to length and fitted with a clamp and a closing plate, after backfilling the old flue with a lightweight insulation such as perlite or vermiculite. The closing plate is finished with a cement mortar flaunching, into which a chimney pot may be set. Gas boilers require an approved flue terminal, which can be set inside the chimney pot.

Single-skin flexible steel liners are usually designed for use with gas-fired boilers or room heaters only. They should never be used with solid-fuel or wood-burning fires or stoves.

CHAPTER NINE

DOORS

THE FRONT DOOR OF A HOUSE *is much more than a means of entry or a barrier against intrusion. The porch or doorway becomes the focus of attention as visitors approach the house, and the door itself creates a first impression of the building and its occupants. And while the visitor waits to be admitted, there's time to admire the decorative mouldings and ornamental glass or fine metalwork of the door and its surround.*

The front door is usually designed to impress and is singled out for special treatment. This may take the form of nothing more than a bold splash of colour in an otherwise plain façade. More often, even in comparatively modest houses, a great deal of money is lavished on embellishing the door and its surround.

Imposing columns and canopies, classically inspired pediments, and elaborate hoods and porches have all been used at one time or another to enhance the visual impact of the main entrance. To 'modernize' or remove such important features detracts from the character of a house and will probably reduce its monetary value as well.

Although interior doors are generally less ostentatious, they make an equally valuable contribution to the character of a building. Yet it is disturbingly common to find that they have been ruined or superficially disfigured by ill-advised attempts to modernize the décor. Fortunately, however, doors are sturdy pieces of joinery that are rarely prone to serious deterioration and they are relatively easy to repair.

Sturdy solid-oak door

Victorian brick-built doorway

It is difficult to imagine a more impressive approach to any house

Georgian taste and elegance

Exquisite Edwardian door and window

BATTENED DOORS

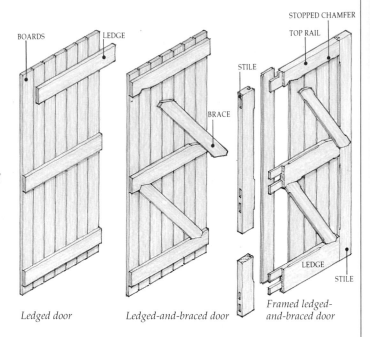

Ledged door · Ledged-and-braced door · Framed ledged-and-braced door

THE BATTENED DOOR *dates from the Middle Ages, but the design is so practical that it has been employed in one form or another, especially in country houses and cottages, right up to the present day. Battened doors were fitted in internal as well as external doorways; at first oak and other hardwoods were used, but many of the later doors were made from softwoods.*

As more sophisticated designs became fashionable, a battened front door was sometimes relegated to the rear entrance of the house or cut down to fit an attic or cellar doorway. Consequently, some battened doors have been in continuous use for centuries.

LEDGED DOORS

The simplest and earliest type of battened door was made from vertical boards approximately 18 to 30mm (¾ to 1¼in) thick, nailed to three horizontal rails known as ledges.

Stronger doors, primarily for the main entrance of a house, were sometimes made with an internal skin of horizontal boards instead of the three ledges.

LEDGED-AND-BRACED DOORS

In the nineteenth century the construction of battened doors was improved by the addition of wooden braces, to prevent sagging. To be effective, a brace must run diagonally downwards towards the hinged edge of the door. Preferably, each end of the brace should be notched into the ledges and secured with a nail.

FRAMED LEDGED-AND-BRACED DOORS

An even more sophisticated form of construction was used for better-quality work, the facing boards being surrounded on three sides by substantial framing, so as to present a flush surface on the outside. The top rail is joined to the vertical stiles with haunched mortise-and-tenon joints, and the stiles and rail are rebated or grooved on the inner edges to hold the boards. Two ledges run behind the boards and are joined to the stiles with pairs of barefaced mortise-and-tenon joints. The braces, as on the simpler versions of the door, run diagonally downwards towards the hinged edge of the door. As a decorative feature, stopped chamfers were sometimes planed on the inside of the frame and along the ledges and braces.

BOARD JOINTS

On early battened doors square-edged vertical boards were simply butted together, the joints being covered on the outside with strips of wood to keep out draughts **(1)**. Alternatively, the boards could be rebated to create weatherproof joints **(2)**.

The Industrial Revolution was responsible for the introduction of machine-cut tongue-and-groove joints. Tongue-and-groove boards had both edges chamfered to form a V-joint **(3)**, or a bead **(4)** was cut along one edge of the board. These details were designed to mask the effects of shrinkage, which could result in unsightly gaps opening up between the boards.

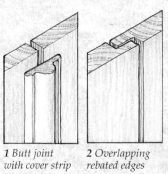

1 Butt joint with cover strip · *2 Overlapping rebated edges*

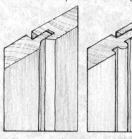

3 Tongue-and-groove joint · *4 Beaded edge disguises joint*

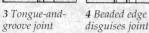

This battened door is a comfortable partner for a weathered-stone wall

PANELLED DOORS

PANELLED DOORS, *constructed in a similar way to the wooden wall panelling of the time, were made, in relatively small numbers, as early as the sixteenth century. However, it took a further two hundred years for the style to gain widespread acceptance.*

By the middle of the eighteenth century the panelled door had become commonplace – and, although from time to time whims of fashion have resulted in changes in its appearance, its basic construction has remained unaltered to the present day.

C18th fielded-panel door

Typically simple Georgian door

An impressive combination of bevelled-glass lights and bolection mouldings

PANEL ARRANGEMENTS

The basic design comprises a frame of rails, stiles and muntins infilled with thin panels of solid wood. The classic Georgian front door had six rectangular panels (1), although various arrangements of five or seven panels were also used by Georgian architects.

Most Victorian doors, especially interior ones, were of the four-panel type (2) still widely used today. Panels were sometimes arched (3) or circular (4), in which case they were usually surrounded by heavy wooden mouldings.

After the First World War panelled doors became simpler in appearance, and there was a tendency to dispense with mouldings in favour of solid-wood or plywood panels (5).

1 Six-panel

2 Four-panel

3 Arched

4 Circular

5 Plywood

Victorian studded entrance door

Panelled door of the 1920s or 1930s

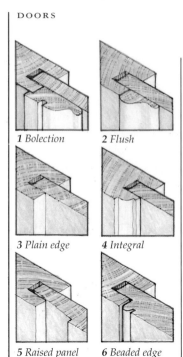

1 Bolection *2 Flush*

3 Plain edge *4 Integral*

5 Raised panel *6 Beaded edge*

MOULDINGS AND PANELS

The joints between panels and the surrounding frame were masked with planted (separate) mouldings. These are nailed to the frame, never to the panels, and are always mitred at the corners.

Bolection mouldings were planted mouldings rebated to cover the edge of the frame (1) and disguise the effects of shrinkage. Flush mouldings (2) that do not project beyond the face of the frame were also popular, especially for internal doors. The inside face of a door for a minor bedroom or for a cupboard was frequently left plain, without any mouldings (3). Other doors were made with integral mouldings cut on the inside of the frame members (4).

Door panels are usually flat on both sides, but sometimes, particularly in the Georgian period, raised-and-fielded panels (5) were used. On entrance doors, the bottom panels were often made to be flush with the frame and were edged with a small bead moulding (6). These relatively thick panels were stronger than the raised-and-fielded type and tended to shed rainwater more efficiently.

Springing hinges
Badly fitted hinges prevent the door closing properly.
● Fit correct-size screws (page 84).
● Pack out hinge leaf (page 84).

Creaking hinges
Hinges often creak loudly when dry or under strain.
● Apply oil (page 83).
■ Realign hinges (page 83).

Loose hinges
A door will drop if hinge screws work loose or knuckle joints wear.
● Renew screw fixings (page 82).
● Swap hinges (page 83).

Bowed mouldings
Mouldings can bow because of uneven shrinkage, creating unsightly gaps.
● Renail mouldings (page 85).
■ Replace mouldings (page 85).

Wet rot
If rainwater can run under the door, the wood around the end grain rots.
● Treat with timber preservative (page 114).
■ Fit weatherboard (page 85).

Components of a panelled door
1 Stile
2 Top rail
3 Bottom rail
4 Lock rail
5 Frieze rail
6 Muntins
7 Mortise-and-tenon joint
8 Wedges
9 Panel
10 Groove
11 Moulding

Loose joints
Shrinkage or failed glue can cause gaps to open up along shoulders or joints.
■ Reglue joints (page 83).

Warped door
A warped door is difficult to close.
● Move doorstops (page 84).
■ Flatten the door (page 84).

ASSESSING REPAIRS
● Easy even for beginners.
■ Fairly difficult. Good practical skills required.
▲ Difficult. Hire a professional.

Split panel
If a solid-wood panel is not free to move, it may split.
■ Repair panel (page 85).

Rattling door
A door may rattle if it is not held firmly against its stops.
● Fit draught excluders.
■ Move staple or striker plate (pages 95 and 96).

Sticking door
A door will jam in its frame if the wood swells or the edge of the stile is caked with paint.
● Shave door with plane (page 83).
● Strip paint from edge (page 81).

HOW PANELLED DOORS WERE CONSTRUCTED

Hardwoods such as oak and mahogany have been used at various times for making panelled doors. But they are more often constructed from softwood, which is almost invariably painted.

A typical panelled door has a vertical stile (1) on each side. The one that is hinged is known as the hanging stile, the other as the closing or lock stile.

Between the stiles are the top rail (2), bottom rail (3) and middle or lock rail (4). The fourth rail of a six-panel door is known as the frieze rail (5). Running down the centre of the door are vertical muntins (6).

The frame is constructed using mortise-and-tenon joints (7) throughout, and those that pass right through the stiles are secured with wedges from outside (8). The panels (9) are held loosely in grooves (10) cut along the inside edges of all the frame members. In order to avoid splitting when the wood shrinks, the panels are not glued or fixed in any way.

On most types of panelled door, mouldings (11) are used to cover the joints around the panels. They also disguise any shrinkage.

GLAZED DOORS

THE FANLIGHT *above the front door that became a delightful feature of Georgian architecture was designed to admit light to the hall. For the same reason, narrow windows were sometimes incorporated in the surround. But only rarely, if ever, was the front door itself glazed, although the two upper panels were sometimes subsequently replaced with glass.*

DECORATIVE GLASS PANELS

From Victorian times, glass panels became widely used for all sorts of doors and were especially popular for entrance doors, where acid-etched or stained glass could be employed to impressive decorative effect.

Glazing was generally restricted to the upper half of the door. Often it took the form of a single large panel; but sometimes several small panes were used, divided by wooden glazing bars. A common alternative was to insert glass instead of wood in one of the conventional door-panel arrangements.

Traditional battened doors were never glazed, but many of the country-style 'revival' houses that were popular after the First World War have a small rectangular or diamond-shape window placed centrally in the upper half of battened doors.

SAFE GLASS FOR DOORS

Before modern safety standards were introduced, doors were glazed using whatever thickness of glass suited the glazier or the client. However, for greater safety, if you have to replace glass in a door, you should comply with British Standards recommendations. (This does not mean you are obliged to replace old glass that is still intact – for example, when you remove a panel from a door in order to carry out extensive repairs to the woodwork.)

Provided that there is more than one pane of glass in the door or a single pane does not take up the greater part of the door's area, you can install ordinary (annealed) glass, which must be at least 6mm (¼in) thick. However, this stipulation regarding thickness does not apply to leaded lights, because even a large leaded window is constructed from relatively small pieces of glass held in a lead or copper lattice – and the lattice tends to buckle under impact, which reduces the risk of injury from shattered glass.

Recommendations regarding fully glazed doors are particularly stringent, and you may have to fit toughened glass. For more detailed advice, contact the Glass and Glazing Federation.

Glazed cottage door with side lights

Edwardian glazed entrance door

Glazed lobby doors admit light to a Victorian hallway

Glazed doors frequently incorporate painted lights

79

FLUSH DOORS

A GREAT MANY OLD HOUSES *have been spoilt by replacing original panelled doors with modern plywood or hardboard flush doors. But, thankfully, thoughtless vandalism of that kind is no longer encouraged and, apart from more modern uses, flush doors are now considered appropriate only for some of the flats and houses built in the 1920s and 1930s.*

When they made their first appearance, flush doors were considered extremely smart and fitted perfectly with fashionably stark Art Deco styling. The cheaper, plywood-faced doors were painted, but flush doors were also frequently finished with hardwood veneer.

HOW PANELLED DOORS WERE CONSTRUCTED

Earlier flush doors were often made by gluing strips of solid wood together (1) then applying a plywood sheet (2) to each face. Hardwood lipping (3) along the edges protected the surface veneer from damage.

Framed flush doors
Framed flush doors were developed in order to reduce the overall weight. The outer frame comprises softwood top (1) and bottom (2) rails joined to vertical stiles (3). Narrow regularly spaced intermediate rails (4) form the core, with heavier blocks of wood (5) inserted at strategic points in order to accommodate a mortise lock and, in the case of external doors, a letter plate. A plywood skin (6) on each side adds rigidity to the door. Slots (7) cut across the intermediate rails ventilate the core, to prevent changes of atmospheric pressure bowing the plywood skins, and disperse moisture-laden air. As on the earlier flush doors, hardwood lipping (8) protects the plywood veneer from wear and tear.

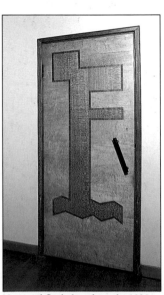

Veneered flush door from the 1930s

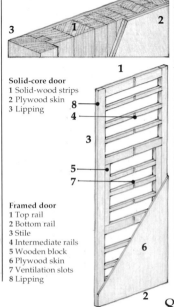

Solid-core door
1 Solid-wood strips
2 Plywood skin
3 Lipping

Framed door
1 Top rail
2 Bottom rail
3 Stile
4 Intermediate rails
5 Wooden block
6 Plywood skin
7 Ventilation slots
8 Lipping

HOW DOORS WERE FITTED

TRADITIONALLY THE DOOR OPENING *was lined with a wooden frame, within which the door was hung. Although the structure of the wall itself varied considerably, the construction of door linings was generally consistent.*

INTERNAL DOORS
The lining of an internal door opening is known as the casing. It comprises two vertical jambs (1) joined by barefaced housings to the soffit (2), which runs across the top of the opening. The door hangs from one of the jambs. Sometimes the casing was rebated to create a doorstop, but more often the doorstop took the form of separate strips of wood nailed to the jambs and soffit (3). An architrave (4) was nailed all round to cover the joints between the casing and the wall.

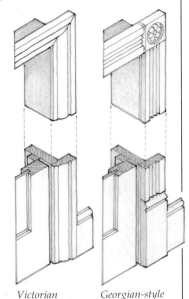

Door-casing components
1 Jamb
2 Soffit
3 Doorstop
4 Architrave

Architrave details
Victorian architraves usually take the form of tapered mouldings that extend down to the floor on each side of the door and are mitred at the top corners. The skirting boards butt against this type of moulding.

Frequently late-Georgian doorways were graced by fluted rectangular-section architraves. These had separate decorated square blocks nailed into the top corners. Skirting blocks were fitted each side of the door to finish the foot.

Wide door casings
Wide framed casings were used to line door openings in thick internal walls.

Victorian architrave

Georgian-style architrave

STRIPPING DOORS

EXTERNAL DOORS

Door-surround designs vary enormously, but in principle an external door was hung from a substantial wooden frame comprising a head **(1)** across the top, a post **(2)** on each side and, sometimes, a wooden threshold **(3)** at the bottom. A transom **(4)** was included if there was a fanlight above the door. The posts and head or transom were usually rebated to form a doorstop **(5)**. If the wooden threshold was omitted, a metal dowel was sometimes used to attach the bottom end of each post to the stone doorstep.

Usually, the frame was fixed to the surrounding structure by nailing through the posts into strips of wood or plugs built into the wall. Alternatively, bent metal lugs **(6)** screwed to the outside of the frame were bedded in mortar joints as the wall was being built. Like window frames, doorframes were often fitted in a recess built in the surrounding masonry.

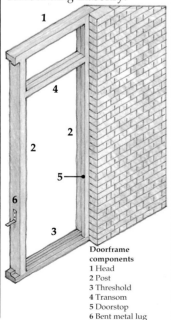

Doorframe components
1 Head
2 Post
3 Threshold
4 Transom
5 Doorstop
6 Bent metal lug

ATTRACTIVE DETAILS *such as mouldings and carving are often obscured by layers of old paint. Clumsy application can also spoil the appearance of woodwork, leaving unsightly runs and sagging paint. You may have to consider stripping the old paint and starting again – but stop and think before you go ahead. Sometimes, as well as destroying the door's character, stripping the paint will erase a record of all the finishes that have been applied since the house was built. And it is a mistake to imagine that stripped pine looks authentic, because most was painted from the outset. In some rare cases, you may require consent to remove historic paint from a listed building – so, before proceeding, speak to a Conservation Officer.*

Although this section focuses on doors, most of the information is relevant to stripping other items of woodwork, too. For industrial stripping, they need to be portable and small enough to be immersed in a tank.

USING HEAT TO STRIP PAINT

Burning the paint off with a blowlamp or propane torch used to be the normal way to strip wood, but apart from a few professional decorators hardly anyone uses this method today. Unless you are fairly experienced, it is easy to scorch areas of woodwork and there is always the risk of causing a fire. Also, blowlamps vaporize the lead contained in old paints, so you could find yourself breathing toxic fumes. A modern electric hot-air stripper is not only safer, it is also easier to handle and there is less risk of scorching. Although these strippers will lift paint while operating at a relatively low temperature, you should still wear a respirator when burning off old paint.

Hold the nozzle of a hot-air stripper about 50mm (2in) from the surface, and move it from side to side until the paint begins to blister. As soon as it does so, remove the softened paint with a flat scraper,

or with a shavehook if you are stripping a moulding **(1)**. When working on a door, it is usually best to strip mouldings first then the flat areas. If you use a hot-air stripper close to a window, fit a heat deflector to avoid cracking the glass **(2)**.

If you plan to repaint a door, there's no need to extract the specks of paint trapped in the pores of the wood. Just rub down the stripped wood lightly with a medium-grade abrasive paper, then redecorate. If you intend to use a clear finish, however, remove the residue of paint with small balls of fine wire wool dipped in chemical stripper. Rub the wood in the direction of the grain only, then wash the surface with white spirit or water to neutralize the stripper.

STRIPPING WITH CHEMICALS

Chemical strippers soften old paint until it is liquid enough to be scraped and washed from the surface. Thick gel-like strippers are

1 *Strip mouldings with a shavehook*

2 *Protect glass with a heat deflector*

ideal for doors, because they are stiff enough to cling to vertical surfaces. The average chemical stripper will dissolve old oil-based and modern resin-based paints, but there are also specific varnish strippers that are formulated to remove tough polyurethane varnishes.

Chemical strippers are potentially hazardous, so they must be handled with caution and the maker's recommendations observed very carefully. Wear vinyl gloves and protect your eyes with safety spectacles or goggles. Many strippers emit unpleasant fumes – it is therefore essential to ventilate the area in which you are working and wear a face mask. Never smoke in the vicinity, and keep pets and children away from all chemical strippers. If you splash stripper on your skin, wash it immediately with plenty of cold water. If it gets in your eyes, rinse them thoroughly under running water and seek medical advice without delay.

Safer all-purpose strippers have been developed that are fume-free and will not burn your skin, although they may take a little longer to soften the paint. Read the manufacturer's instructions before you buy one, to make sure it is not one of the more common caustic strippers.

Using chemical strippers
The procedure described below will serve as a guide to using chemical strippers safely and efficiently, but always follow the detailed recommendations supplied by the manufacturer.

Lay a polyethylene dust sheet under the door, then brush on a liberal coat of stripper. Stipple the gel into mouldings to make sure all surfaces are covered. Leave it for 10 to 15 minutes, then scrape a small section to see if the paint is soft enough to remove easily. If the paint is still resistant, apply more stripper – but this time stipple it onto the whole area, so the chemicals come into contact with all the still-unsoftened paint.

Five minutes later, scrape off the paint and wrap up the scraped-off paint in newspaper. Dispose of it carefully at a toxic-waste disposal point at your local council rubbish dump.

Unless the wood is oak, use wire-wool balls dipped in fresh stripper to remove stubborn patches of paint and clean up mouldings. For oak, use coarse sacking since wire wool can stain the wood and detract from its appearance.

Finally, wash the surface with water or white spirit, depending on the maker's recommendations. Allow the wood to dry thoroughly before rubbing down and repainting.

INDUSTRIAL STRIPPING
Most people derive great satisfaction from stripping paint from a beautiful door and revealing the natural wood beneath. But faced with the prospect of having to strip perhaps half a dozen doors, many people turn to industrial stripping.

The cheapest method involves dipping the door in a tank of hot caustic stripper, which then has to be washed off by hosing the wood with water. The combination of heat and water can be detrimental and, although most doors emerge from the process relatively unscathed, occasionally solid-wood panels split, joints open up, and mouldings distort.

Another drawback is that hot dipping always raises the grain, leaving a furry surface that has to be rubbed down with abrasive paper before you can proceed to refinish the wood.

To avoid most of these problems, you need to go to a company that dips wood in cold chemicals only. Cold dipping does not discolour the wood and it is ready for refinishing after 24 hours, whereas after hot dipping it may not be ready for weeks. With cold chemicals the grain may be raised slightly, but you are unlikely to be faced with the worst side effects of hot dipping. The only disadvantage is that, because the chemicals are expensive, you have to pay more for cold dipping.

Most firms will collect a door and deliver it back to you after stripping. If you're having a front door stripped, same-day service is essential. Never submit a veneered door to industrial stripping unless the company can guarantee that the veneers will not delaminate.

CURING MINOR DOOR PROBLEMS

*S*OME DOORS *have to be shouldered open, others catch on the floor or doorframe whenever you use them. These irritating problems can occur for a number of reasons, so you need to check the door carefully to determine the appropriate course of action.*

CURING LOOSE HINGES
If the screws holding the top hinge work loose, the door sags and its top corner binds against the frame. Open the door partially and lift it by the closing stile. If you can see the hinge moving, examine it more closely.

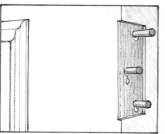
1 Leave dowels until glue sets

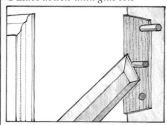
2 Then pare them flush with a chisel

Tightening loose screws
If the screw heads are protruding, try tightening them with a screwdriver; and if that's successful, check whether the screws in the other hinges need to be tightened, too.

You may find the screws are loose because repetitive movement has caused the screw threads to tear the wood and lose their grip. If the door has a substantial frame or the screws have worked loose from the door itself, it may be possible to substitute longer screws of the same gauge.

However, the jambs of most interior doorframes are too thin for this solution to work. In which case,

remove the screws and fold the hinge out of the way. Use a sharp knife to shape softwood strips into tapered dowels that will fit the screw holes. Glue the dowels and tap them into the holes. Leave them untrimmed **(1)** until the glue sets, then cut them off and pare them flush with a chisel **(2)**. Finally, fold the hinge back, then drill pilot holes for the screws and replace them.

Swapping worn hinges
The hinges may be screwed firmly in place, yet when you lift the closing stile you may still be able to detect movement. This is probably due to wear on the hinge pins and knuckles. Since the weight of the door puts uneven strain on the top and bottom hinges, it is sometimes possible to correct the fault by simply swapping the top and bottom hinges, thus reversing the wear on the pins.

REMOVING THICK PAINT
If the closing stile binds regularly against the frame, along its entire length, it is probably due to a build-up of paint over the years. If you are planning to strip the door entirely for some other reason, the problem will be solved in the process. Otherwise, use a hook scraper to remove paint from the edge of the door.

REPAIRING LOOSE JOINTS

Wood shrinks considerably during very dry hot spells, then swells again when wet weather returns. This movement can break down the glue in the joints of a door. If the mortise-and-tenon joints of a panelled door work loose and the securing wedges fall out, the joints can gradually open up until the door is fractionally too wide for its opening.

Check carefully for gaps along the shoulders of the joints (they may have been filled in the past). If necessary, strip the paint around the joints and rake out any debris lodged between the shoulders. Chop out any wedges that remain in through mortise-and-tenon joints. Inject PVA woodworking glue between the shoulders and into the ends of the joints (1). Tap the joints home, using a mallet and protective softwood block (2), or hire a large sash cramp to pull them together. Glue and insert overlength hardwood wedges, tapping them in with a hammer (3). When the glue has set, trim the wedges flush with a chisel.

If a door is made with stopped mortise-and-tenon joints, it may be impossible to inject sufficient glue between the shoulders to secure the joints. Having closed the glued joints with a cramp, insert a locking dowel (4) and trim it flush when the glue has set.

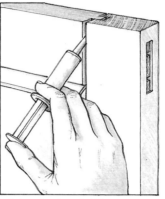
1 Inject glue into the joint

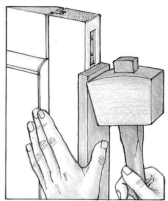
2 Tap the joint home with a mallet

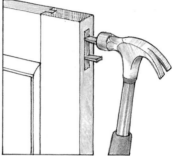
3 Glue and insert hardwood wedges

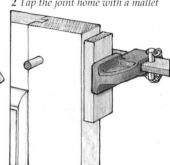
4 Secure stopped tenon with a dowel

CREAKING AND RATTLING DOORS

Most people find creaking doors annoying, and doors that rattle with the slightest draught can be positively infuriating to live with. As well as removing a source of constant irritation, it pays to rectify these relatively minor faults before wear on the door furniture increases.

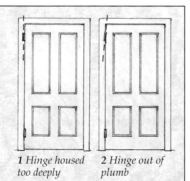
1 Hinge housed too deeply   *2 Hinge out of plumb*

Stopping a door creaking

In most cases a creaking door can be cured with a drop of oil on the hinges. Place the oil on the top of the hinge pins, then swing the door gently back and forth so the lubricant works down into the hinge.

Occasionally, oiling fails to silence the creaking. In which case, examine both hinges carefully to see if their pins are out of line with each other. Use strips of thin card to pack out a hinge housed too deeply in the wood (1). To align a hinge pin that is out of plumb (2), pare the bottom of the hinge housing with a chisel.

Stopping a door rattling

The easiest way to cure a rattling door is to stick soft-plastic or foam draught-excluding strips to the doorstops. If fitting draught-excluding material would make the door difficult to close, you can prise off the stops and reposition them closer to the door. Alternatively, move the striker plate of the lock slightly so the latch fits snugly (see LOCKS).

DEALING WITH EXPANSION

If a door only sticks during humid weather or after a lot of rain, the cause of the problem is probably the swelling of the wood. The answer is to trim the edge of the closing stile while the weather is still wet. Don't wait for dry weather to return, or the door will shrink and you won't be able to judge how much wood to remove.

Take the door off its hinges and support it on edge, with the closing stile uppermost. Remove the latch or lock, and trim the edge of the door with a plane. You may find that it is necessary to adjust the fit of the lock when you replace it.

STOPPING A DOOR CATCHING

People often fit rising butt hinges (which lift the door as it swings open) to stop a door catching on an uneven floor or thick carpet. However, there are other causes that can make the bottom of a door catch – and other solutions worth considering before you go to the expense of fitting new hinges.

Detecting a loose bottom hinge

When a door normally opens and closes smoothly, you may well not suspect that it has a loose bottom hinge. However, once the door swings past a certain point, a loose bottom hinge tends to dislocate, allowing the bottom of the door to drag on the floor.

Check whether the screws are loose or the bottom hinge is worn – and if necessary, either tighten the screws or swap or replace the hinge (see opposite page).

Adjusting the bottom hinge

If the bottom edge of a door is jamming on a bump in the floor, you can sometimes overcome the problem by adjusting the position of the lowest hinge.

First, open the door and remove the screws from the hinge leaf fixed to the frame.

Move the leaf sideways, away from the doorstop, so that the hinge pin projects slightly further from the frame than the pin of the hinge above does. Replace the screws to hold the hinge in its new position. To prevent the door creaking, you may have to adjust the top hinge slightly, so that both hinge pins are at the same angle.

Trimming the bottom

You may have no option but to trim the bottom of a door that is catching, especially if it is already fitted with rising butt hinges.

Professional carpet layers use a special power saw with a horizontally mounted circular blade that can trim a specified amount off a door *in situ*. However, in order to do the job yourself, you will have to take the door off its hinges and either plane the bottom edge or trim it with an ordinary circular saw.

You can use a sharp bench plane, with the door held in the vice jaws of a folding workbench – but there is a lot less effort with a portable power planer. Whichever type of plane you use, work from both ends towards the middle, to avoid splitting the end grain.

Trimming the top

You may find that a door fitted with rising butt hinges scrapes the frame above as it opens. To provide the necessary clearance, plane a shallow bevel on the corner of the door.

Plane a shallow bevel on the door

Support a door with a folding bench

ENSURING A DOOR CLOSES PROPERLY

You should be able to close a door without having to apply force. There are several problems that can make a door keep springing open, but they are mostly fairly easy to resolve.

Relieving springing hinges

A door that resists closing just before it latches is most probably 'hingebound'. As a result, it tends to spring open again as you release pressure against it. If that is happening, check whether the hinges are being levered out of their housings by the act of pressing on the door.

It may be that projecting screw heads are stopping the leaves of the hinges closing properly **(1)**. Try driving the screws home; or if someone has inserted screws that are too large, swap them for ones with smaller heads that nestle flush with each leaf.

Inaccurately fitted hinges are another possible cause. If one or more of the leaves have been housed too deeply in the wood **(2)**, unscrew them and place strips of thin card behind each hinge to pack it out flush.

If both the hinges appear to have been fitted correctly, try scraping or stripping any thick paint from the edge of the hanging stile and, if need be, from the doorframe too.

Easing tight doorstops

You may find that a door won't latch properly because the stops, and perhaps the door as well, are caked with layers of paint. If scraping the closing face of the stops fails to cure the problem, strip the frame and, if need be, the door itself.

Firm draught-excluding strips sometimes prevent a door closing properly. In which case, either substitute soft-plastic or foam strips or move the doorstops slightly to accommodate the existing draught excluders.

Flattening a warped door

Temperature variation on each side of a door can dry the timber unevenly. As a result, the door may twist or warp so that it will no longer rest against its stops without being forced shut. Leaving a door to dry in the sun after industrial stripping can also cause warping.

Strip the paint from the warped door and soak both sides with water. To reverse the effects of warping, place the door on the floor with a block of wood under one corner then load the door with heavy weights. After 24 hours remove the block, but leave the weights in place for a similar period.

A much simpler, though less satisfactory, solution is to move the doorstops to accommodate the warping.

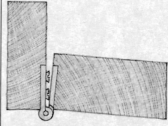

1 *Screw heads prevent hinge closing*

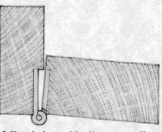

2 *Deeply housed leaf has same effect*

REPAIRING DOORS

R EPAIRING THE FABRIC OF A DOOR *often requires considerable exertion and skill, but the high cost of an authentic replacement or acceptable replica more than compensates for the effort involved.*

CORRECTING BOWED MOULDINGS
When the mouldings on a panelled door bow, unsightly gaps are left between the mouldings and the stiles, rails and muntins (1).

To get rid of the gaps, nail the mouldings back against the framework, working from the middle of each length of moulding. Drive the nailheads below the surface with a nail set (2) and fill the holes before redecorating.

With luck, the mitre joints at the corners of each panel will close up as you renail the mouldings. If the mouldings have shrunk, leaving open mitres, you can buy replacement mouldings from a DIY store or builders' merchant. Alternatively, if you want something special, choose a moulding from the catalogue of a specialist joinery supplier or ask a joiner to make a replica of the original.

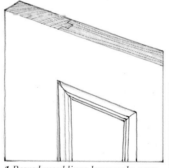

1 Bowed mouldings leave ugly gaps

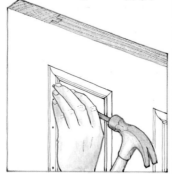

2 Sink nailheads with a nail set

Settlement can distort a doorframe

REPLACING A WEATHERBOARD

Moulded weatherboards are frequently fixed to external doors to shed rainwater away from the threshold. A drip groove machined along the underside of the weatherboard prevents water running back to the base of the door and rotting the wood.

In the past, many a householder found it expedient to discard a damaged or rotted weatherboard rather than repair or replace it. But nowadays you can purchase stock weatherboard mouldings from many builders' merchants and timber suppliers.

Measure the width of the opening between the doorstops and cut the weatherboard moulding to this length. Plane the end near the latch side of the door to a slight angle, so that it clears the stop when the door swings open (1).

To make a weatherproof seal between the moulding and the door, paint the back of the weatherboard with a thick coat of primer. While the paint is still wet, screw the weatherboard to the door (2). Fill or plug the screw holes, then prime and paint the moulding.

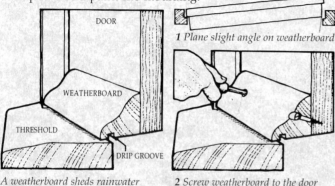

DOOR
WEATHERBOARD
THRESHOLD
DRIP GROOVE

A weatherboard sheds rainwater

1 Plane slight angle on weatherboard

2 Screw weatherboard to the door

REPAIRING SPLIT PANELS
If a solid-wood door panel has been fixed inadvertently with nails or glue, there's a chance that it will split if the wood shrinks. Incompetent industrial paint stripping can also cause splitting. You may be able to reglue a split panel *in situ* (see REPAIRING PANELLING). If not, you will have to dismantle the door to remove and repair the panel. Having chopped out any securing wedges, steam the door joints with a kettle to soften the glue. Then tap them apart with a hammer, using a block of softwood to protect the components from damage.

Fixed door panels tend to split

FILLING AN UNEVEN GAP
One characteristic indication of building settlement is the distortion of doorframes, resulting in a tapering gap between the top of the door and the head or soffit. If the settlement is recent, consult a professional who will be able to advise you on whether there's subsidence that requires remedial action (see PROFESSIONAL HELP).

However, an old house may have settled years ago then restabilized, albeit in a less-than-perfect condition. In which case, the simplest solution is to cut a softwood wedge to fill the gap and screw it to the top of the door. Plane the wedge flush with the door before painting.

DEALING WITH WET ROT
Doors are less susceptible than windows to wet rot attack. However, if a door is neglected and its finish is allowed to deteriorate, water can penetrate and soften the fibres, especially around areas of end grain.

For methods of treating wet rot, see DEALING WITH ROTTED WINDOWS.

REPLACING DOORS

WHATEVER *the cost of repair or maintenance, it pays to do everything you can to retain the doors that were installed when the house was built. They were made to fit openings that almost certainly do not conform to modern notions of stand-ardization and they are, of course, authentic in style.*

However, not everyone holds the same opinion. For example, it was once fashionable to install a brand-new front door in the mistaken belief that it would increase the value of a property; and panelled doors, which were considered old-fashioned, were frequently replaced with mass-produced flush doors. As a result, many home owners are now faced with the task of reinstating old doors in order to restore the character of the building.

With luck, you may be be able to buy an old door from a local architectural-salvage company exactly like one that once hung in your home, but the further afield *you have to search the less chance there is of obtaining a perfect match. Alternatively, you may be able to find a similar door and plane or cut it to fit the opening, though there is a limit to the amount of wood you can remove without weakening the structure of the door or spoiling its proportions.*

Another option is to buy a modern reproduction door, but it is extremely difficult to find a mass-produced door that is entirely suitable for an old house. However, there are joinery companies that specialize in making doors to order, using traditional methods and authentic styles, including external doors, interior room doors and a variety of doors with glazed panels. Although custom-made doors are relatively expensive, they are usually made to the highest standards.

1 Drive a wedge under the door

2 Clear slots with a screwdriver

REMOVING AN OLD DOOR

First, secure the door in an open position by driving a wedge under it **(1)**. If the doorframe is painted, uncover the screw heads that hold the hinges to the frame by scraping off the paint. It is important to dig out paint clogging screw slots before you attempt to turn the screws. Place a corner of a screwdriver tip at one end of each slot and tap the screwdriver sideways with a hammer to cut out the paint **(2)**. With the tip in position, tap the end of the handle with the hammer to break the paint seal around the screw head, then extract the screw. Remove all but one screw from each hinge, then get an assistant to support the door while you extract the last screws.

If a screw slot becomes so badly damaged that it is impossible to engage it with the blade of a screwdriver, drill out the head in stages, using progressively larger bits. Lift off the hinge and remove the remains of the screw by turning its shank with a plier wrench.

HANGING A NEW DOOR

New doors are sometimes supplied with extended stiles, known as horns, to ensure that the corners are not damaged during trans-portation. You need to saw off the horns before fitting the door in its opening.

A custom-made door may need nothing more than a light trimming with a plane, but other doors may have to

Saw the horns off a new door

be cut down with a saw in order to obtain a perfect fit. Ideally, there should be a 3mm (⅛in) clearance at the top and sides of a door, and a gap of at least 6mm (¼in) at the bottom. A gap of up to 12mm (½in) may be needed to accommodate a thick carpet. When planing the top or bottom of a door, always plane inwards towards the middle, to avoid splitting the end grain.

Mark the position of the hinges on the door, using the existing housings in the doorframe as a guide. Cut hinge housings in the door (see HINGES).

Hang the door with a single screw holding each hinge to the doorframe, and check the swing and fit of the door. Make any adjust-ments that may be needed, then insert the other screws. Finally, fit the lock and other hardware (see DOOR FURNITURE).

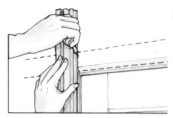
1 Draw alongside each component

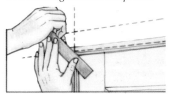
2 Mark the positions of the mitres

1 Mark the height of the architrave

2 Mark the length of the top member

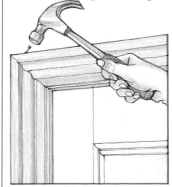
3 Nail the moulding to the casing

4 Drive a nail into the mitre joint

Composite architrave as seen below

Wide decorative door architraves embellish a Victorian hallway

REPLACING ARCHITRAVES

R EPLACING *door or window architraves that are damaged or unsightly is a very straightforward procedure. Standard architrave mouldings in softwood can be purchased from DIY stores and timber merchants. If you need to obtain a more elaborate or wider-than-average moulding, choose one from the stock of a specialist joinery supplier. A good joinery supplier will also make a replica of a moulding for you.*

REMOVING AN ARCHITRAVE

To remove a damaged architrave, drive a bolster chisel behind each piece until you can lever it off with a claw hammer. Pull out any nails left in the frame or casing.

Picture rails and skirting boards often butt against an architrave. If the new architrave is wider than the one you are replacing, trim the ends of the picture rail or skirting with a tenon saw. If you are unable to saw a skirting board *in situ*, you will need to lever it off the wall (see SKIRTING REPAIRS).

INSTALLING AN ARCHITRAVE

Hold an upright in position about 6mm (¼in) from the face of the jamb. Mark its length with a pencil, allowing for the width of the top member and 6mm (¼in) clearance (1). Cut a 45-degree mitre on the marked line; then, using a spirit level to keep the upright vertical, nail it to the casing every 300mm (1ft) or so with 50mm (2in) lost-head nails. Don't drive the nails all the way home at this stage, in case you have to move the architrave. Install the second upright using the same procedure.

Rest the top member upside down on the ends of the uprights and mark its length (2). Cut a mitre at each end and nail the moulding between the uprights (3). Drive a nail through the edge of the top member into the mitre joints at each end (4). Drive all nailheads below the surface, then fill the holes and joints before painting; if you plan to varnish the wood, use a coloured wood filler instead.

Fitting an architrave to an out-of-square frame

If your doorway is not quite square, 45-degree mitre joints will not fit snugly. Instead, hold each component in position against the wall and draw a pencil line against each edge where the joints will occur (1). Mark the mitres where the lines cross (2), then transfer these points onto the architrave members. Cut the mitres and fit the components as described left.

DOORCASES & DOORHOODS

MEDIEVAL BUILDERS *began the practice of setting dripstone mouldings into the masonry above doors and windows in order to divert rainwater to each side of the opening, where it could drip harmlessly to the ground.*

By the beginning of the eighteenth century the dripstone above the front door had been superseded by a cantilevered hood beneath which visitors could shelter while waiting to be admitted. But eventually practicality took second place to aesthetic considerations, and special emphasis was given to the front door by surrounding it completely with a decorative wooden doorcase. By Georgian times the demands of the shipbuilding industry had made oak a scarce commodity for the building trade. As a result, all but the earliest hoods and doorcases were made from imported softwoods.

Wooden doorcases are often extremely elaborate, mimicking styles originally intended for stonework. The restoration of masonry and stucco surrounds is described elsewhere in this book; only wooden hoods and doorcases are included here.

DOORHOODS
A doorhood consists of a wooden frame, often with a deep moulded edge, supported on two stout beams projecting from the wall. The exposed part of each beam was typically carved into a decorative scroll, creating what appears to be a bracket on each side of the door.

The shallow sloping 'roof' of the hood had a sheet-lead covering which, in order to prevent rainwater running behind the hood, was formed into a flashing against the wall. The lead was folded over the edges of the hood to protect the timber. The door opening below the hood was usually surrounded by a relatively simple wooden architrave.

Later, the supporting wooden beams were concealed within the structure of the doorhood itself. As a result, the brackets became purely decorative and were frequently made from separate, deeply carved elements.

CONSOLES
Eventually, Georgian doorcase brackets evolved into vertical wooden consoles that appeared to support narrow cornices or pointed classical-style pediments above the door. Consoles were often elaborately carved and even pierced.

PILASTERS AND COLUMNS
Narrow pilasters, running from bracket to ground level on each side of the opening, were frequently used to give consoled doorcases an impression of strength and solidity. Pilasters were to become increasingly complex, often resembling fluted piers that appeared to support classically inspired pediments or entablatures. A pilaster of this sort might include a carved capital and a moulded base.

Some doorcases had semi-circular staved-timber columns constructed the same way as a barrel. On larger houses, the canopy above the front door might project sufficiently to form a shallow porch supported by freestanding columns. A second pair of semi-circular columns would usually flank the door opening itself.

When painted, doorcases constructed from separate wooden elements nailed together could be difficult to distinguish from genuine stone surrounds.

Carved brackets support a doorhood

Vertical wooden consoles

Beautifully proportioned doorcase with fluted Ionic columns

REPAIRING DOORCASES

O N A SURPRISING NUMBER *of eighteenth-century houses, what looks like a stone door surround is in fact a wooden doorcase.*

Any wooden structure that has stood in the open for a couple of centuries is bound to have suffered to some extent from the effects of weathering. Usually, the greatest harm is inflicted by the ingress of water, which can in turn lead to wet rot. Damaged flashings allow rainwater to run behind hoods and canopies; open joints between a doorcase and the wall or between wooden components also provide routes for water to penetrate; and rising damp in masonry walls can saturate the timbers from behind.

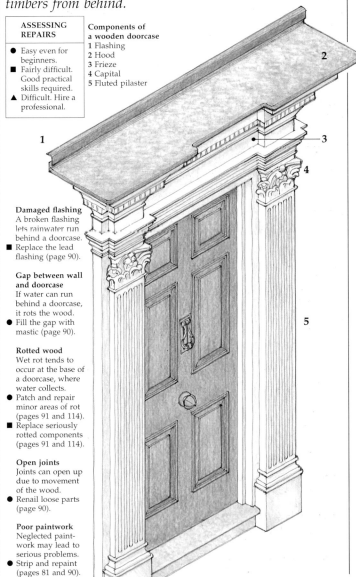

Carved stone door surround

C18th engaged wooden columns

Freestanding staved columns support this substantial canopy

ASSESSING REPAIRS

● Easy even for beginners.
■ Fairly difficult. Good practical skills required.
▲ Difficult. Hire a professional.

Components of a wooden doorcase
1 Flashing
2 Hood
3 Frieze
4 Capital
5 Fluted pilaster

Damaged flashing
A broken flashing lets rainwater run behind a doorcase.
■ Replace the lead flashing (page 90).

Gap between wall and doorcase
If water can run behind a doorcase, it rots the wood.
● Fill the gap with mastic (page 90).

Rotted wood
Wet rot tends to occur at the base of a doorcase, where water collects.
● Patch and repair minor areas of rot (pages 91 and 114).
■ Replace seriously rotted components (pages 91 and 114).

Open joints
Joints can open up due to movement of the wood.
● Renail loose parts (page 90).

Poor paintwork
Neglected paintwork may lead to serious problems.
● Strip and repaint (pages 81 and 90).

REGULAR MAINTENANCE

If an old doorcase has survived unscathed, it has probably been maintained regularly throughout its life. If paintwork is beginning to flake, craze or crack, attend to it before it deteriorates further and lets in water to rot the timbers. Except for very minor blemishes that can be rubbed down then filled and repainted, you may have to strip the doorcase down to the bare wood – which will allow you to make good any defects and redecorate with a superior finish. However, there may be historic paint layers that are worth retaining, along with a beautiful old patina that is impossible to reproduce.

A partially stripped doorcase in the process of being restored

STRIPPING A DOORCASE

Most period doorcases are too elaborate to be stripped using a hot-air gun alone, so the only practicable solution is to use a chemical stripper. However, what looks like low-relief carving on panels, brackets and pilasters may in fact be moulded plaster, which could be damaged by the scrapers and wire wool used for removing softened paint from wood.

To be on the safe side, it's best to scrape a small area of paintwork with a very sharp blade. If you detect plaster below the paint, use the type of chemical stripper that is recommended for painted plaster ceilings.

Treating and painting the wood

Once you have exposed the wood, treat the whole doorcase with clear preservative in order to protect it from rot in the future. Then nail back any open joints or loose components. Before repainting the doorcase, sink the nailheads, using a nail set, and fill the holes.

WEATHERPROOFING A DOORCASE

Take whatever measures are required to prevent water saturating a wooden doorcase. Cure rising damp as a matter of priority, and if possible allow the doorcase to dry out thoroughly before further treatment.

Filling open joints

If nailing doesn't close up a joint satisfactorily, fill it with a flexible exterior wood filler before painting. Use flexible mastic to seal gaps between the doorcase and wall. You can buy it in cartridge form and inject it into the gap with a gun **(1)**, or as a strip sealant that you press into place with your fingers **(2)**.

Renewing the flashing

A doorhood or canopy has a sheet-lead covering, which is turned up against the wall. A strip of lead flashing is inserted in a mortar joint just above the canopy and bent down to cover the upstand, forming a weatherproof joint. It's common to see a damaged flashing replaced by a mortar fillet. However, over a period of time a fillet may shrink, leaving a gap between it and the wall. In the long run it therefore pays to renew the flashing.

Chop out the mortar joint to a depth of 25mm (1in) and remove any scraps of the old flashing that remain. Buy a strip of flashing lead 1.8mm (¹⁄₁₆in) thick from a builders' merchant. Use tinsnips to cut it to width so that it reaches from the canopy to the mortar joint, plus 25mm (1in).

Clamp the lead between two wooden battens, leaving a 25mm (1in) strip projecting **(1)**. Bend this over to form a right-angle lip and gently hammer it flat, using another batten to protect the lead **(2)**. Insert the lip in the mortar joint above the canopy and wedge it in place with small rolled strips of lead **(3)**. Use a soft hammer to tap the flashing against the upstand, shaping it to fit against the wall snugly. Finally, repoint the mortar joint.

Pointed pediments require stepped lead flashings that are best replaced by a skilled professional roofer.

1 Clamp lead strip between battens

1 Inject mastic into the gap

2 Or introduce a strip sealant

2 Hammer strip over to form a lip

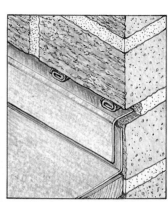

3 Wedge flashing with rolled strips

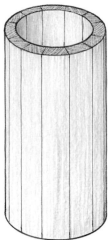 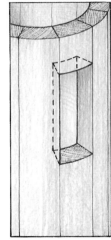 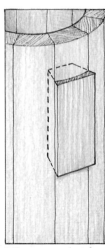

A wooden column is staved like a barrel

1 Cut a hole bevelled on all four sides

2 Tap an oversize plug into the hole

REPAIRING COLUMNS

Owing to their shape and construction, columns are particularly difficult to repair. Most of them are hollow, comprising a number of narrow strips of wood or staves with bevelled edges glued together then shaped on the outside. A staved column is fairly stable, but unless the joints are reinforced with splines they tend to open up as a result of glue failure or shrinkage.

Having supported a porch roof, it is possible to remove an entire column and close a reglued joint with heavy-duty strap cramps. However, this type of repair work is best left to a professional restorer who has the experience to judge whether clamping a joint is likely to create additional strains and splits in the column.

Filling a split column

A vertical split or gaping joint in a semi-circular doorcase column would be difficult to repair using the method described above, but provided the wood is relatively stable it is possible to fill a narrow gap with a sliver of softwood.

If necessary, open up the split with a power jigsaw. Shape the sliver with a sharp plane so that it will fill the gap. Plane a shallow bevel on both sides of the sliver to form a wedge, then glue it in place with waterproof exterior adhesive. Tap it home firmly with a hammer (but not too hard, or you may expand the column). Leave enough of the wedge projecting to plane once the glue has set, so that it will fit flush following the curve of the column.

Inserting a plug

An isolated patch of wet rot in a column can be cut out and replaced with a tapered plug of matching timber.

After drilling an insertion hole, insert the blade of a power jigsaw and cut out the rotted wood, leaving a rectangular hole bevelled on all four sides (1).

Make a plug of wood with the grain running vertically, shaping it so that it fits the hole but protrudes slightly from the column (2).

Apply waterproof exterior adhesive to the edges of the plug, then tap it into the hole with a hammer. Either use a strap cramp to hold the plug in place or nail it with long panel pins, driving them below the surface with a nail set. Once the glue has set, plane the plug to match the shape of the column.

TREATING WET ROT

Wet rot most frequently occurs near the end grain of timber, where water is able to penetrate more easily. It also often breaks out near the base of columns and pilasters, where water tends to collect. Check for wet rot by pressing the wood with the tip of a screwdriver. Rotted wood is soft and spongy when wet, and becomes dry and crumbly during warm weather.

To preserve, harden and fill areas of wet rot, see DEALING WITH ROTTED WINDOWS. Badly affected wood has to be cut out and replaced. Because a doorcase is an assembly of several pieces of wood, it is feasible to replace individual components with preservative-treated timber. It is also possible to splice wood onto a component to replace a short section of rotted timber.

Wooden columns constructed from narrow staves

REINSTATING DOORCASES AND COLUMNS

Don't be tempted to buy scaled-down mock-Georgian door surrounds designed to enhance modern town houses. A good specialist joiner is capable of making accurate replica doorcases and freestanding columns, using traditional materials and methods of construction. However, it is essential to employ a professional who is conversant with period proportion and detailing.

DOOR FURNITURE

OOR FURNITURE *is the collective name used for hardware made for doors, both external and internal. Each piece of hardware is primarily functional – yet for the past 250 years or so, being specifically designed to enrich the main entrance and principal rooms of our homes, most door furniture has been extremely handsome. Attractive and sometimes costly materials were used for period door furniture, and as a rule it was expertly crafted and finished.*

Finding and renovating door furniture is perhaps one of the most pleasurable activities associated with restoring old houses. Antique hardware and good-quality reproductions are both widely available, and the level of skill required to fit, clean and finish just about any piece of door furniture is well within the capabilities of any householder with the slightest practical experience.

A pair of cast-iron knockers complements this ornate Victorian door

Suitably dignified brass fittings

Iron fittings are perfect for a cottage

CHOOSING DOOR FURNITURE

With such a wealth of products to choose from, it is not always easy to decide which is the right hardware for a particular door.

The heaviest (and usually most expensive) hardware was normally reserved for the main entrance of the house. However, one should always respect the age, style and character of a building and select the door furniture accordingly.

A country house with battened doors looks best with simple wrought-iron fittings, whereas a Victorian villa can take more elaborate cast-iron or brass door furniture without appearing overornamented. Similarly, it makes sense to reserve heavily ornate hardware for the principal rooms and install more modest fittings in what would perhaps have been the servants' quarters in earlier times.

You can learn a great deal about period styles from contemporary magazine advertisements and trade catalogues. However, it pays to exercise a little caution before replacing what at first sight appear to be historically inappropriate additions or modifications.

Whereas few would argue against replacing a 1950s plastic handle added to an Edwardian drawing-room door, it makes little sense to discard a good-quality Victorian mortise lock on an early-Georgian door simply because it is not 'authentic'.

Our predecessors were just as keen to improve their homes and take advantage of the latest advances in technology as we are – and, provided an item has been fitted properly, looks well and is still in working order, there's a great deal to be said for retaining it.

Authentic weathered door furniture

DOOR LATCHES AND HANDLES

When door handles, knobs and latches were replaced in the past, they frequently found their way into the second-hand market. As a result, it is possible to buy matching sets of original door knobs from architectural-salvage companies, market stalls, house-clearance sales and other antiques-trade outlets. And if you can't obtain an item of door furniture from any of these sources, there is a vast range of excellent reproduction hardware to choose from.

LATCHES

One of the earliest methods of keeping a door closed was with a short horizontal beam, pivoted at one end, that dropped onto a hook fixed to the doorframe. The beam, which in its crudest form was made from timber, would have been lifted by means of a length of string or leather thong that passed through a hole in the door to the outside.

More sophisticated latches based on the same principle were made in wrought iron by blacksmiths. The more successful versions were eventually mass-produced and are still to be found in manufacturers' catalogues. Handmade wrought latches that are perfect replicas of ones made by early black-smiths can be obtained from specialist suppliers.

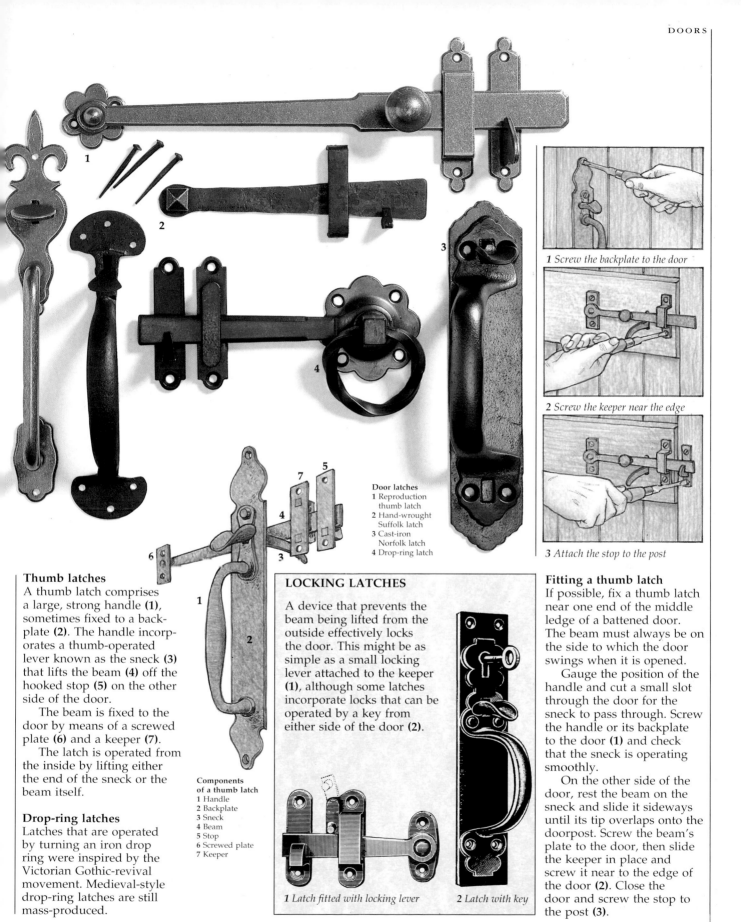

Door latches
1 Reproduction
   thumb latch
2 Hand-wrought
   Suffolk latch
3 Cast-iron
   Norfolk latch
4 Drop-ring latch

Components
of a thumb latch
1 Handle
2 Backplate
3 Sneck
4 Beam
5 Stop
6 Screwed plate
7 Keeper

1 Screw the backplate to the door

2 Screw the keeper near the edge

3 Attach the stop to the post

Thumb latches

A thumb latch comprises a large, strong handle (1), sometimes fixed to a backplate (2). The handle incorporates a thumb-operated lever known as the sneck (3) that lifts the beam (4) off the hooked stop (5) on the other side of the door.

The beam is fixed to the door by means of a screwed plate (6) and a keeper (7).

The latch is operated from the inside by lifting either the end of the sneck or the beam itself.

Drop-ring latches

Latches that are operated by turning an iron drop ring were inspired by the Victorian Gothic-revival movement. Medieval-style drop-ring latches are still mass-produced.

LOCKING LATCHES

A device that prevents the beam being lifted from the outside effectively locks the door. This might be as simple as a small locking lever attached to the keeper (1), although some latches incorporate locks that can be operated by a key from either side of the door (2).

1 Latch fitted with locking lever

2 Latch with key

Fitting a thumb latch

If possible, fix a thumb latch near one end of the middle ledge of a battened door. The beam must always be on the side to which the door swings when it is opened.

Gauge the position of the handle and cut a small slot through the door for the sneck to pass through. Screw the handle or its backplate to the door (1) and check that the sneck is operating smoothly.

On the other side of the door, rest the beam on the sneck and slide it sideways until its tip overlaps onto the doorpost. Screw the beam's plate to the door, then slide the keeper in place and screw it near to the edge of the door (2). Close the door and screw the stop to the post (3).

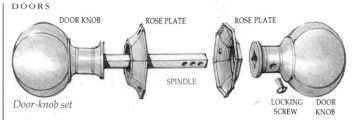

DOOR KNOB   ROSE PLATE   ROSE PLATE

SPINDLE

Door-knob set

LOCKING   DOOR
SCREW   KNOB

DOOR KNOBS

With the invention of rim locks and mortise locks, the latch was incorporated into the lock's mechanism in the form of a sliding latch bolt. A latch bolt is retracted by turning one of a pair of handles attached to each end of a square metal bar or spindle that passes through the lock.

From the Georgian period onwards, these handles usually took the form of door knobs that were roughly circular or oval in shape. A wide variety of materials was used in their manufacture, including brass, ceramic, glass, wood and even plastic, which was first used for door furniture in the early twentieth century. The principal rooms of a house, particularly throughout the Victorian period, were frequently furnished with impressive pairs of door knobs that were enhanced with cast or printed decoration.

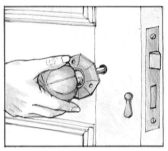

1 Pass spindle through lock

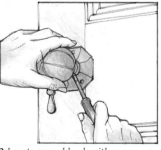

2 Locate second knob with screw

3 Some spindles are slotted

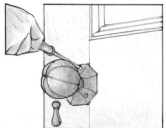

4 Fix rose plates with woodscrews

Fitting a door knob

Door knobs are normally sold in pairs, complete with either one or two rose plates (depending on whether they are intended for a door fitted with a rim lock or a mortise lock). A square spindle links the pair, and one of the knobs is usually fixed to the spindle. Slide this knob's rose plate up to it, then pass the spindle through the lock (1).

Slide the second knob and rose plate onto the other end of the spindle. In most cases the knob is secured by inserting a small machine screw through the neck of the knob into one of a series of threaded holes in the spindle (2).

Instead of screw holes, some spindles have a row of machined slots into which a pivoting 'key' on the knob locates (3).

Screw the rose plates to the door (4). Some knobs are made with integral rotating rose plates and fit onto each end of a plain spindle. Screwing both plates to the door is sufficient to hold the knobs onto the spindle. Since the fixing screws are very small, use a bradawl to make pilot holes in the wood so that it is easier to insert them without damaging the screw slots.

1

2

3

4

5

6

Door handles
1 Ceramic knob
2 Early-C20th copper lever handle
3 Copper-plated oval door knob
4 Cast-metal knob
5 Pressed-brass knob
6 Victorian door pull

DOOR PULLS

Door pulls for external doors are substantial iron or brass handles used to pull the door closed. Georgian and Victorian front doors were furnished with a single round or faceted knob or with a bar fixed to a backplate.

Fitting a door pull

Door pulls are invariably positioned centrally at about waist height and are fixed to the door with bolts. Round door pulls are often made with cast lugs on the back that are designed to bite into the wood and prevent the handle spinning and unscrewing itself. You will need to drill shallow holes in a hardwood door in order to accommodate the lugs.

LEVER HANDLES

Lever handles were not common in Georgian or Victorian homes except on double doors in the grander houses. However, chromed or bronzed lever handles became fashionable in the 1920s and 1930s, when they were fitted to flush and panelled doors of the period. Like door knobs, lever handles are attached to square spindles that operate sliding latch bolts.

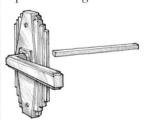

Art Deco lever handle with spindle

FINGER PLATES

To keep the paintwork fresh and free from fingerprints, house-proud Victorians screwed metal, ceramic or glass plates to the closing stiles of internal doors.

Bedrooms normally had simple finger plates. Much more elaborate plates were available for drawing rooms and parlours.

Finger plates were sometimes sold in pairs, the larger one being positioned above the door handle and the smaller one (presumably for children) below the handle. Finger plates were also made that combined the function of door-knob backplate and keyhole escutcheon.

Late-Victorian finger plates

Art Nouveau door set, including finger plate, knob and escutcheon

LOCKS AND BOLTS

Before the seventeenth century, the only way to secure an ordinary house against intruders was to attach wooden or iron bolts to the inside of the door. However, since it is impossible to bolt a door from the outside, unattended houses remained insecure until the invention of a lock that could be operated from either side of the door with a removable key.

RIM LOCKS

Early locks were built into boxes screwed to the face of the door. The majority of these rim locks were purely utilitarian, being encased in iron, but by the eighteenth century the better-quality houses were being furnished with beautifully made brass-cased locks with sliding latch bolts retracted by turning a drop-ring handle or a small knob on the lock.

Rim locks, most of them manufactured from folded or pressed steel, were to be found in practically every home throughout the whole of the nineteenth century and the earlier part of the twentieth century. Wealthier householders fitted discreet mortise locks on some of their more important doors, but rim locks were used for the bedrooms and servants' quarters of Victorian villas.

A typical rim lock has what is known as a deadbolt, which is thrown by turning a key and locates in a cast-metal staple screwed to the door jamb. When the deadbolt is withdrawn, the door is prevented from swinging open by a sliding latch bolt. The latch bolt is not only operated by turning a handle but, because the end is bevelled, it is retracted automatically by being pressed against the staple as the door is closed.

Normally, a small brass or ceramic knob was fixed to the lock itself. Another knob, usually rather grander in design, was screwed to the other side of the door and connected to the lock by means of a metal spindle.

Fitting a rim lock

Place the lock on the middle rail, with its endplate hooked over the edge of the door (1). If you are fitting a heavy Victorian lock, cut a recess in the edge of the door to accommodate the endplate. Early-twentieth-century locks were made from thinner sheet metal so the endplate would fit easily between the edge of the door and the jamb without being let into the wood.

Mark the position of the keyhole and handle on the door, then cut holes through the stile for them, using a drill and padsaw. Replace the lock and insert the key and spindle from the other side of the door, so that you can position the fitting accurately.

Drill through the holes in the lock to bore pilot holes for round-head fixing screws (2). Screw the lock to the door and fix the endplate to the edge of the door with small countersunk screws.

Screw the staple to the jamb opposite the lock (3). If necessary, chop a recess in the architrave moulding to accommodate the staple. Screw or pin an escutcheon to the other side of the door to finish the keyhole.

Pass the spindle of the door knob through the lock and fit a handle to the other side (see opposite page).

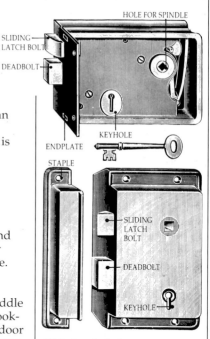

Victorian rim locks

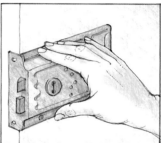

1 Hook endplate over edge of door

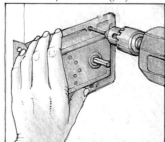

2 Drill holes for fixing screws

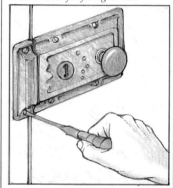

3 Screw the staple to the jamb

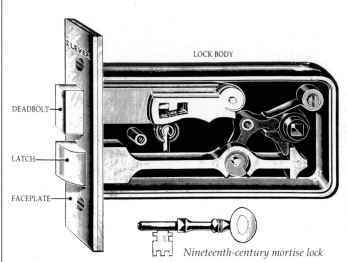

LOCK BODY

DEADBOLT

LATCH

FACEPLATE

2 LEVER

Nineteenth-century mortise lock

MORTISE LOCKS

It is impossible to fit anything but a surface-mounted lock to a ledged-and-braced door (except the framed variety). But the greater thickness of panelled doors made it feasible to install a lock in a mortise cut within the edge of the closing stile. The mechanism is contained in the body of the lock. Only the faceplate is visible when the lock is in place. The deadbolt and latch engage a striker plate let into the jamb or doorpost.

Fitting a mortise lock

Draw a line centrally on the edge of the stile and mark the top and bottom of the lock body on the door (1) to denote the extent of the mortise. Use a drill that matches the thickness of the lock body to bore out most of the waste (2), then square up the edges of the mortise with a chisel (3). Insert the lock and mark the perimeter of the faceplate (4). Chop a series of shallow cuts across the recess and pare out the waste till the plate fits flush with the edge of the door.

Holding the lock against the face of the stile, mark the centre of the keyhole and the hole for the spindle (5). Drill and cut both holes, then install the lock and fix escutcheons to both sides of the door.

Extend the deadbolt and use it to mark the edge of the jamb or doorpost (6), then transfer these marks to the face so you can gauge the position of the striker plate. Cut a mortise and recess for the striker plate, then screw it in place.

1 Mark centre line on door

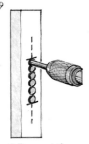

2 Bore out the waste wood

3 Trim mortise with a chisel

4 Mark the edge of the faceplate

5 Mark keyhole and spindle

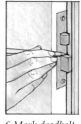

6 Mark deadbolt on doorpost

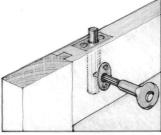

1 Unobtrusive key-operated rack bolt

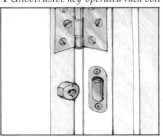

2 Fixed hinge bolts strengthen a stile

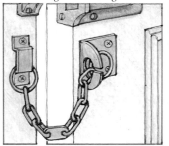

3 A security chain is essential

4 A viewer helps to identify callers

MODERN SECURITY RECOMMENDATIONS

When installing antique or period-style door furniture, don't ignore modern home-security recommendations. Surface-mounted locks, for example, are only as strong as the screw fixings in the wood – whereas mortise locks, being buried in the wood, are considerably stronger. An entrance door with an antique rim lock should be fitted with either a mortise lock or modern security bolts, as well.

Key-operated rack bolts (1) sunk into the edge of a door are extremely efficient. They are also unobtrusive, since a small escutcheon is all that is visible when the door is closed.

Inserting fixed hinge bolts (2) in the edge of the hanging stile prevents the hinged edge of a door being levered open from outside.

A security chain (3) that prevents an intruder pushing open an entrance door when you unlatch it and a small telescopic viewer (4) that allows you to identify callers before opening the door are also discreet and worthwhile precautions.

ESCUTCHEONS

An escutcheon is used to cover the keyhole slot cut through a door. In its simplest form an escutcheon is a flat metal plate, but most escutcheons are made with a pivoting cover to prevent draughts. Stamped or cast-metal escutcheons are highly decorative and are much sought after by people restoring period houses.

A selection of period escutcheons

Original brass bell pull

KNOCKERS AND BELL PULLS

It has been customary at least since Georgian times for tradesmen and other callers to announce their presence by rapping on the front door with a metal knocker or by ringing a bell.

Door knockers

Old brass door knockers are usually very handsome. But, although good-quality replicas are made, modern reproductions sometimes look tawdry compared to mellow antique brass – and black-painted cast-iron knockers are better suited to many old houses.

Door knockers look best mounted centrally on a muntin at about head height. They are normally fixed to the door by bolts that pass through the wood, from the inside, into threaded bosses cast on the reverse of the knocker.

Bell pulls

In larger Georgian homes a bell inside the house was attached to a cable that ran to the front door via a conduit buried in the wall plaster. The bell was rung by pulling on a knob mounted on the doorcase or the surround. It was a system that was easily converted to electricity during the nineteenth century.

Devotees of the Arts and Crafts movement delighted in fitting twisted wrought-iron bell pulls, which were mounted vertically beside the front door.

Door knockers and letter plates
1 Cast-iron letter plate
2 Medieval-style door knocker
3 Reproduction iron knocker
4 Victorian-pattern brass knocker
5 Combined letter plate and knocker

LETTER PLATES

After the introduction of prepaid postage stamps in 1840, it was no longer necessary for a messenger to collect a fee from the recipient. Consequently, the letter plate became a desirable addition to the door furniture of a house, so mail could be delivered without disturbing the household. You hardly ever see a Georgian front door that has not had a letter plate added to it, although there was no genuine Georgian equivalent.

A stylish alternative to a letter plate

TYPES OF LETTER PLATE

The earliest letter plates were probably of simple design cut from thick sheet brass, but the Victorians were never slow to embellish any item of door furniture. A householder was able to choose from a variety of fretted, stamped, pressed and cast-metal versions. Knockers or door pulls were often combined with letter plates to make attractive and convenient single fittings.

Original letter plates are invariably too small for much of the mail that is delivered nowadays. The postal authorities recommend a slot measuring 254 x 38mm (10 x 1½in).

Fitting a letter plate

A letter plate can be mounted vertically in the centre of a door muntin or horizontally on the lock rail, whichever is most convenient and aesthetically pleasing. Letter plates should never be fixed to a door panel.

Mark out the position of the plate on the door and measure the size of the slot to be cut through the rail or muntin. You need to make the slot slightly larger than the flap of the letter plate.

Drill a small insertion hole in each corner of the marked rectangle, then insert the blade of a power jigsaw and cut out the slot. Clean up the inside of the slot with a file. Mark the centre of the letter-plate fixing bolts on each side of the slot and bore through the wood. Attach the plate by passing the bolts through the holes from the inside of the house.

You can reduce draughts and also enhance the appearance of the letter plate by screwing a simple cover flap over the slot on the inside of the door.

NUMERALS

As communities grew larger, especially with the building of rows of terraced houses, it became desirable to be able to identify individual houses at a glance. Householders therefore began applying numerals to the front door, doorcase or door surround.

Sometimes a signwriter was employed to paint the number on the woodwork or masonry; or a small enamelled or engraved plate was fixed to the front door or to the wall of the house. Black wax was rubbed into engraved designs to make the numerals stand out. More often, individual cast or pressed metal numerals were screwed centrally to the door muntin, while transom lights provided an ideal location for numerals etched or painted in reverse on the glass.

Early-C20th carved keystone

HINGES

Unlike most other items of door furniture, hinges are not usually chosen for aesthetic reasons, since they are primarily functional pieces of hardware. The hinge that works best in a given situation is therefore likely to look right, since our predecessors were also mainly influenced by functional considerations when selecting hinges.

FACE-MOUNTED HINGES

All early hinges were face-mounted, being visible on the door and frame when the door was closed. They were invariably rather crudely made in wrought iron and were usually nailed in place.

Strap hinges

Long tapering strap hinges were used for hanging ledged-and-braced doors. With a T-hinge, the strap is fixed to one of the ledges and joined by a knuckle joint to a relatively wide leaf attached to the doorframe.

The knuckle joints of this kind of handmade hinge were rather slack compared to those of modern machine-made hinges, but as soon as two or three hinges were fitted to a door all slackness was eliminated.

Other types of strap hinge were made by curling the end of the strap to form an eye that dropped over the vertical pin of a pintle – an L-shaped fitting with a spike **(1)** that was driven like a nail into a doorpost. Some pintles were made to screw into the wood **(2)**. Pintle hinges are difficult to fit accurately.

Strap hinges have been made continuously for centuries and they are still mass-produced, primarily for use on sheds and other outbuildings. However, accurate reproductions of old hinges are made for house-restorers who want an authentic-looking hinge.

Ideally, the length of a strap hinge should be about two-thirds the width of the door – although shorter hinges can be fitted near the bottom, where less strain is imposed by the weight of the door.

1 Spiked pintle   *2 Woodscrew pintle*

H and HL hinges

These face-mounted hinges were sometimes used in place of strap hinges to hang ledged-and-braced doors. They are also found on early panelled doors. An H-hinge has a pair of identical leaves joined by a knuckle joint. Fancier versions were made for wealthy clients. An HL or 'Holy Lord' hinge has an extended leaf that lends greater support to a door.

Both H and HL hinges were fixed with handmade nails or screws. Replicas can be obtained from specialist ironmongers. Choose 150 to 200mm (6 to 8in) hinges for an average door.

Fitting face-mounted hinges

Authentic-looking nails are sold by the suppliers of handmade wrought hinges for those who want to nail face-mounted hinges to a door in the traditional manner. The old joiners would 'deaden' a nail by holding a metal block, such as a hammer head, against the reverse of the door so that the point of a long nail would be bent back into the wood, thus improving the grip and preventing the wood splitting.

Two hinges are usually sufficient to support even a heavy door, but a third is often fitted to help prevent warping.

Fix a strap hinge centrally on one of the ledges, with just the knuckle overhanging the edge of the door **(1)**. H and HL hinges are fixed near the top and bottom of a door. The extended leaf of an HL-hinge aligns with the centre of the top or bottom rail **(2)**.

Fix face-mounted hinges to the door first. Then, with the door wedged securely in its opening, nail or screw the flaps to the doorpost.

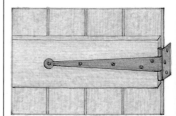

1 Screw a strap hinge to the ledge

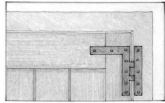

2 Align an HL-hinge with the rail

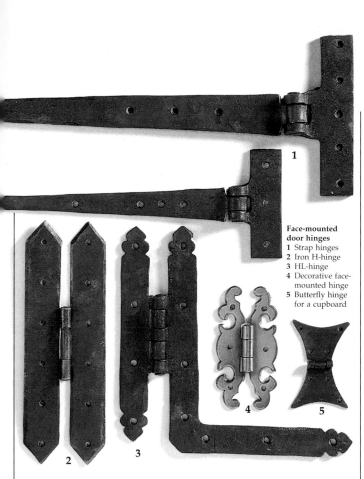

Face-mounted door hinges
1 Strap hinges
2 Iron H-hinge
3 HL-hinge
4 Decorative face-mounted hinge
5 Butterfly hinge for a cupboard

BUTT HINGES

The cast-metal butt hinge (1) was patented in 1775. This revolutionary hinge was designed to fit between the door stile and the jamb, so only the knuckle was visible when the door was closed. Not surprisingly its discreetness appealed to Georgian architects and builders, and by 1800 it was commonplace.

Early butt hinges were made of cast iron and were painted along with the door, but brass was used for more handsome hinges for show-wood doors. By the middle of the nineteenth century, cheaper hinges were being made by stamping them from sheet metal. Decorative brass butt hinges (2) became popular later in the century.

Improvements in manufacturing led to the lift-off hinge that allowed the door to be removed without un-screwing the hinges (3).

The rising butt hinge (4) was a further development. The spiralling shoulders of this type of hinge cause the door to rise as it is opened, so it clears carpets and rugs. All butt hinges are screwed to the door and frame.

Fitting butt hinges

You will find two 100mm (4in) butt hinges are strong enough to hang the average panelled door. Add a third if the door is particularly heavy. Lightweight flush doors can be hung with two 75mm (3in) hinges.

First, wedge the door in its opening and mark the position of the hinges on the door stile and the jamb. The top hinge should be about 175mm (7in) from the top of the door and the bottom hinge about 250mm (10in) from the bottom edge. The recesses cut into the stile and jamb for each hinge must be an equal depth.

Support the door on edge and lay each hinge on the stile. With the knuckle over-hanging, mark the position of the hinge by drawing round it (1). Mark the depth of each hinge recess on the side of the stile, using a marking gauge (2).

Make a series of shallow cuts with a chisel (3), then pare out the waste (4) to leave a shallow recess for each hinge leaf. Neaten the edges and corners of the recess with a bevel-edge chisel, then insert the hinge to check the fit.

Screw the hinges to the door and then wedge it in an open position with the hinges aligned with the marks on the jamb. Draw round the hinges (5). Mark the depth of the recesses and chop out the waste wood, as before.

Hang the door with one screw only in each leaf to check that the door swings and closes properly, then make any adjustments that are needed (see ENSURING A DOOR CLOSES PROPERLY). Once the door swings and latches to your satisfaction, insert the remaining screws.

1 Butt hinge   2 Decorative hinge   3 Lift-off hinge   4 Rising butt hinge

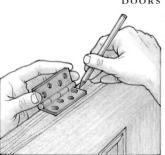

1 Mark the position of the hinge

2 Mark the depth of the hinge recess

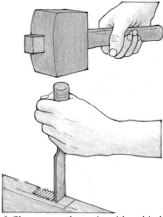

3 Chop across the grain with a chisel

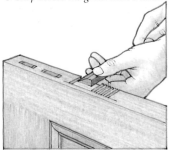

4 Pare out the waste wood

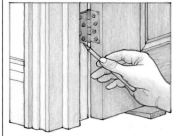

5 Mark the hinge on the jamb

CLEANING & FINISHING DOOR FURNITURE

W HETHER DOOR FURNITURE *should be cleaned and polished is a matter of controversy. There is no question that metalware that is seriously corroded or disfigured by layers of paint needs to be restored, but some people argue that cleaning old brass is ill-advised since the metal loses the mellow patina built up over the years. However, there are no hard and fast rules and, provided you follow the maxim that in restoration one should never do anything that cannot be undone in the future, there is no reason why you should not follow your own inclination.*

STRIPPING PAINTED HARDWARE

Even if you intend to strip a door, it is best to remove the hardware, so that the door and its furniture can be treated more effectively.

Arrange the hardware in one or more metal-foil dishes and pour chemical paint stripper into them. Stipple the stripper onto each piece of door furniture with an old paintbrush to ensure that the chemicals penetrate all the crevices. Leave the stripper to do its work for 10 to 15 minutes, then check that the paint has begun to soften.

Wearing protective gloves, remove the softened paint from each item with fine wire wool. If there is still paint adhering to the fitting, return it to the dish and apply fresh stripper. Wash the stripped metal in hot water and dry it thoroughly with thick kitchen paper. If the fitting is hollow, stand it on a wad of newspaper to allow any water trapped inside to drain away.

STRIPPING METALWARE SAFELY

Follow the manufacturer's safety recommendations whenever you use chemical paint strippers.

Stipple stripper onto the fittings

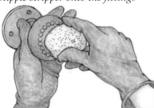
Soften corrosion with a salted lemon

CLEANING TARNISHED BRASS

Brass (which is an alloy of copper and zinc) develops a brown patina when left unprotected. It is a patina that does not lead to further corrosion, and many people find it attractive. Polishing brass door furniture that has been exposed to the elements for some time can be hard work, especially if it has begun to develop traces of green verdigris as a result of a higher-than-average copper content.

One traditional method for cleaning tarnished brass is to sprinkle some salt onto the cut surface of half a lemon and rub the metal vigorously with the fruit until the corrosion softens.

Another method is to make a cleaning solution of one level tablespoon of salt plus a tablespoon of vinegar in half a pint of hot water. Dip a pad of fine wire wool in the solution and use it to swab the corroded brass.

Before polishing, rinse the brass in clean water and dry it thoroughly.

POLISHING DOOR FURNITURE

Metal polishes are mildly abrasive cleaning agents that remove small amounts of metal along with the dirt and corrosion. They should therefore be used sparingly on plated door furniture, since frequent polishing will eventually wear through to the base metal. It is safer to clean items such as copper-plated finger plates by washing off greasy marks with lighter fluid, then buff them with a clean soft cloth.

Burnish brass door furniture with a 'long-term' brass polish that leaves an invisible chemical barrier on the metal and inhibits corrosion, so the metal needs polishing less frequently.

Clean grimy chromium-plated door furniture with lighter fluid, or wash it in warm soapy water containing a few drops of household ammonia. Then burnish the metal with a mild cream chrome polish.

Protecting the paintwork

Clearly, it would be too much of a chore to remove door furniture every time you want to polish it. To protect the surrounding paintwork from abrasive cleaners, cut a template from thin card to slip over each item of door furniture or stick low-adhesive masking tape over the paintwork.

If you don't want to remove door furniture with raised edges, such as a letter plate or the number of the house, you can leave the fittings *in situ* when you repaint the door. Allow the paint to coat the edges of the fittings, but wipe it from their surface, using a cloth dampened with white spirit.

Once the paint is dry, you can polish the exposed metal without spoiling the newly painted woodwork.

CLEANING RUSTY IRON

Remove rusty wrought-iron or cast-iron fittings from the door and soak them in paraffin for several hours to soften the corrosion, then clean them with fine wire wool. Dry the metal and treat it immediately with a chemical rust inhibitor before priming and painting.

FINISHING DOOR FURNITURE

You can protect polished brass with clear acrylic lacquer. Paint it on fairly quickly with a soft artist's brush. If you can't avoid leaving brush marks in the lacquer, stand the door furniture on a warm radiator before the lacquer sets really hard. The heat will soften the lacquer sufficiently for the brush marks to flow out naturally. If lacquer becomes discoloured or gets chipped, remove it with acetone then repolish the metal and apply fresh lacquer.

Iron door furniture is usually protected by applying a calcium-plumbate or zinc-phosphate primer followed by one or two coats of semi-matt black paint. However, some restorers prefer to keep wrought-iron hinges free from rust by wiping them occasionally with an oily rag.

CHAPTER TEN

WINDOWS

B Y THE EIGHTEENTH CENTURY *there were two designs for domestic windows in common use. The side-hung casement – which swings open like a door – was probably of medieval origin and at the beginning of the century it was the chosen style for humble cottage and grand house alike. However, the last quarter of the seventeenth century saw the introduction of the sliding-sash window, which revolutionized building design and remained the most popular type of window, in Britain for the next two hundred years.*

Probably of British origin, although some maintain that the Dutch were the inventors, the sliding-sash window consists of two overlapping glazed frames, or 'sashes', that slide vertically. The earliest versions had a single sliding sash, which was held open with wedges or by inserting pegs in holes drilled in the wooden frame that lined the window

opening. However, the double-hung sash window, which has two movable sashes, was to become the standard model within a few years of its invention. Save for a few minor variations, it has remained unchanged ever since.

A double-hung sash window is a sophisticated piece of design, the sliding sashes being suspended from pulleys on weighted cords or chains so that they will remain in any position required. Leaving the window open at top and bottom provides an ideal means of promoting efficient circulation of air within the room.

One notable variation on the sash window was the horizontally sliding version. Although its use was largely restricted to modest dwellings, it can be found in most parts of the country. This type of window generally had only one movable sash. Since it was horizontal, there was no need for counterweights or supports of any kind.

Metal-frame Modern-movement windows

Bowed sashes exhibit Georgian skill

C20th metal casements resemble earlier window styles

Simple unspoilt rural casements

Nicely proportioned fixed lights

GEORGIAN SASH WINDOWS

EARLY SASH WINDOWS *were divided by thick wooden glazing bars, or astragals, into anything from 16 to 24 almost-square panes. But as the eighteenth century progressed, the classic twelve-pane or 'six-over-six' sash window became a universally accepted norm.*

The classic six-over-six or twelve-pane sliding-sash window

PROPORTIONS

The shapes of window openings were based on simple geometric proportions that appealed to refined Georgian architects, builders and clients alike. The width and status of a particular window determined the height of the opening. A window on the main floor, or *piano nobile*, which was normally located at first-floor level in the grander houses, was usually a double square, being twice as high as it was wide. The height of a window on the 'chamber' or bedroom floor was often 1¼ times its width, while windows at attic level, where the majority of the servants' rooms were situated, tended to be square. These proportions are largely responsible for the elegant appearance of Georgian houses.

Attic level
Servants' quarters and nursery

Second floor
Family bedrooms

First floor
Formal reception rooms

Ground floor
Dining room and parlour

Cellar
Kitchen and scullery

Window proportions

The elevation of a typical late-Georgian house demonstrates the principles of geometry used to arrive at the proportions of the windows. These principles were not adhered to rigidly but served as useful rules of thumb. Wide windows were divided by extra vertical glazing bars to keep the size of the panes constant.

Tall windows need additional panes

1 Ovolo

2 Astragal and hollow

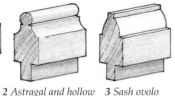
3 Sash ovolo

4 Lamb's tongue

1 Basic straight-head sash window

2 C18th segmental-head window

3 Late-Georgian semi-circular head

4 Elliptical-head sash window

GLAZING BARS

The glazing bars, or astragals, that divide each sash are rebated on the exterior to support a pane of glass on each side. The putty that holds the glass in place is shaped to form simple bevels. Glazing bars are moulded on the inside and are perhaps the most decorative elements of the design. Although there were innumerable local variations, certain styles of glazing-bar moulding can be identified as typical for different stages in Georgian sash-window development.

Early Georgian windows were made with thick square-ovolo mouldings **(1)**. The number of glazing bars decreased when larger panes of glass became fashionable. At the same time, they became thinner and thinner, with more refined mouldings. The astragal and hollow **(2)** was popular from about the 1730s, followed in quick succession by the sash-ovolo **(3)** and lamb's-tongue **(4)** mouldings – all of them remaining in use well into the nineteenth century.

Although the majority of windows were made with a straightforward grid of glazing bars, late-Georgian windows were enhanced by rearranging the astragals to create narrow marginal lights, and semi-circular-head and elliptical-head windows afforded the opportunity for decorative radial and curved patterns of glazing bars.

VARIATIONS ON THE SASH WINDOW

Although one thinks of a typical Georgian house as having a more or less symmetrical façade with regularly placed individual windows, architects rang the changes by grouping sash windows, usually in combinations of three.

The Venetian or Palladian window is the most obvious example. A semi-circular-head sash window is flanked by narrow, slightly lower, sashes that are sometimes fixed. In order to keep the mullions between the windows as narrow as possible, the counterweight cords for the moving sashes in the middle often ran over the top of the flanking windows so that the weights could hang on each side of the group.

Bow and bay windows were often a combination of three separate windows, and in many cases all three of them were working sash windows.

WINDOW SHAPES

The basic rectangular straight-head window **(1)** is common-place in Georgian houses, but in the early eighteenth century windows with segmental heads were fashionable, too **(2)**. Late-Georgian houses were often built with semi-circular-head **(3)** or elliptical-head windows **(4)**.

BLIND WINDOWS

Fake sashes or plain recesses in the masonry are often found in Georgian houses where, from the outside, one would expect to see a genuine window. Some of these were, in fact, once real windows but were blocked up to avoid the infamous eighteenth-century window taxes, which were levied according to the number of windows in a house. More often, blind windows were inserted so as not to disturb the rhythm of a façade when a real window would have broken into a flue or some other internal feature. Although a blind window is often no more than a simple recess in the wall, sometimes part of the masonry is set back slightly to cast a shadow resembling a lower sash. More elaborate examples are constructed with glazed but non-working sashes in the recess and may even include a painted facsimile of a window blind to complete the illusion.

Early-eighteenth-century Venetian window

VICTORIAN & EDWARDIAN SASH WINDOWS

WINDOW STYLES *did not, of course, suddenly change as the Georgian period drew to a close. However, the prevailing feature that distinguished Victorian windows from Georgian ones was the larger panes of cheap mass-produced glass, supported by fewer and fewer glazing bars. Four-over-four, two-over-two, and eventually one-over-one are all typical Victorian windowpane arrangements. Earlier windows were frequently 'modernized' by removing the original glazing bars in order to install larger sheets of glass, which is why you find horned windows in some Georgian buildings.*

Four-over-four   *Two-over-two*   *One-over-one*

Edwardian sashes with original glass

Gothic-revival lancet window

Composite sashes admit more light

THE INTRODUCTION OF HORNED SASHES

The elimination of glazing bars put an additional strain on the relatively slim meeting rail of the upper sash, especially on the joint at each end of the rail. From about 1840 this joint was modified to include a wedged through tenon, and so the vertical stile had to be extended in order to reinforce the joint. This extension, known as the 'horn', was either bevelled or moulded.

Horns strengthen the meeting rail

VICTORIAN WINDOW SHAPES

The Victorians continued to employ semi-circular and segmental-head windows, and the Gothic-revival movement was responsible for the widespread use of the pointed-head or lancet window. However, since rectangular window openings were easier to build, these shapes were frequently incorporated within a rectangular sash, creating 'triangular' lights in the top corners of the window.

COMPOSITE SASH WINDOWS

The desire for larger areas of glass, which would admit more light, is reflected in Victorian and Edwardian housing by the combination of sash windows in pairs and groups of three. In the majority of cases, all the sashes slide and the counter-weights are housed in the dividing mullions. Palladian windows feature regularly in more grandiose and ornate houses throughout the Victorian period.

BAY WINDOWS

Curved (bow), square and canted bay windows, often running the full height of the house, up to the eaves, occur so frequently that they are practically synonymous with Victorian and Edwardian housing. Bay windows enrich the seemingly endless rows of terraced houses built during both periods. They also have the practical advantage of greatly increasing the field of view from inside.

Oriel windows, cantilevered from the upper storeys, are charming variations of the traditional bay. Square and canted oriels with windows on three sides are used to light major bedrooms. Small triangular oriels illuminate small bedrooms and staircases. Oriel windows recur from time to time in later revival styles, particularly in the neo-Tudor housing of the 1920s and 1930s.

Canted bay window

Stone-built oriel window

Restricting glazing bars to the upper sash was a typically Victorian practice

The ubiquitous brick terrace with full-height square bays

GLAZING-BAR ARRANGEMENTS

With their characteristic enthusiasm for anything decorative, the Victorians employed a much greater variety of glazing-bar arrangements than their Georgian predecessors had done, and they delighted in marginal lights incorporating coloured glass. Often, however, decorative arrangements of astragals were restricted to the upper sash, with a single undivided pane of glass in the sash below. The Queen Anne revival during the last quarter of the nineteenth century saw the reintroduction of the early-Georgian-style multi-pane sash with thick glazing bars.

Elegant glazing-bar arrangement

Imaginative use of glazing bars

HOW SASH WINDOWS WERE MADE

DOUBLE-HUNG SASH WINDOWS *vary in the details of their construction, but the basic principles described here are common to all windows of this type. A sash window is a complicated piece of joinery, yet is designed in such a way that it can be dismantled easily when it is necessary to carry out maintenance and repairs. Most windows are made from softwood, although oak and mahogany have been used for better-quality windows.*

CONSTRUCTION OF THE SLIDING SASHES

Each sash comprises two vertical stiles **(1)**, a top rail **(2)** or bottom rail **(3)**, and a meeting rail **(4)**. The meeting rails oppose each other when the sashes are closed, and their adjoining faces are bevelled **(5)** so they close together relatively tightly in order to keep draughts and rattles to a minimum. They are sometimes bevel-rebated to prevent a knife blade or similar implement being slipped between the window rails to open the window fastener from outside.

Sash rails are rebated on the outside (the lower-sash meeting rail is grooved) to accept the glass, and they are moulded on the inside. The glass is retained with sprigs (small nails) or glazing points (flat triangular metal fixings) and linseed-oil putty.

The top rail of the upper sash and the bottom rail of the lower sash are joined to the stiles with through mortise-and-tenon joints **(6)**. Joints are glued and usually reinforced with wedges from the outside or with locking dowels through the sides of the joints.

Meeting rails are wider than stiles in order to close the gap between sliding sashes. They are joined to the stiles with a form of dovetailed bridle joint **(7)**. Often a stronger mortise-and-tenon joint is used for the upper sash, and the stile is extended to form a 'horn' that strengthens the bottom of the mortise.

Glazing bars

Narrow wooden glazing bars **(8)** are used to hold relatively small panes of glass within the sashes. These are rebated for the glass and moulded on the inside. Vertical glazing bars are usually continuous, and are jointed into the rails **(9)** with mortise-and-tenon joints. The shorter horizontal bars are made with similar joints. Alternatively, all the glazing bars may be continuous, in which case they are joined with halving joints **(10)** where they cross. A single vertical glazing bar may be joined to the meeting rail of the upper sash with a wedged through tenon.

CONSTRUCTION OF THE WINDOW FRAME

The frame within which the sashes slide comprises two vertical jambs (one on each side), a head across the top and a sill across the bottom. Because a jamb needs to be hollow to house the sash weights, it is made in three parts – the inner lining **(11)**, the outer lining **(12)** and the the pulley lining **(13)** – which together form a three-sided box. With better-quality work, a rough-sawn back lining **(14)**, nailed to the inner and outer linings,

strengthens the jamb and prevents the sash weights getting caught on any projections from the wall behind. The weights are separated from each other by a narrow strip of wood, called a parting slip **(15)**, which is housed in a slot in the head and suspended from a nail or peg. The parting slip stops about 100mm (4in) short of the sill.

The head is constructed in a similar way to a jamb, with inner and outer linings plus a soffit lining **(16)**. Since there is no top lining, glued triangular blocks **(17)** are used to strengthen the head.

The sill **(18)** is cut from a single piece of solid wood, and is shaped so that water flows away from the sashes to the outside.

A recess is formed for the upper sash by the projecting lips of the outer linings together with the two parting beads **(19)** that are nailed into grooves cut in the pulley stiles and a similar bead running across the soffit lining. Stop beads **(20)** nailed all round the frame hold the lower sash in place.

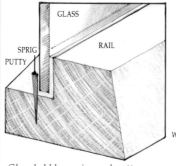

Glass held by sprigs and putty

Joint between bottom rail and stile

Halving joint for glazing bars

Joint between glazing bar and rail

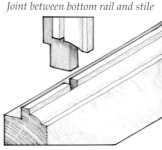

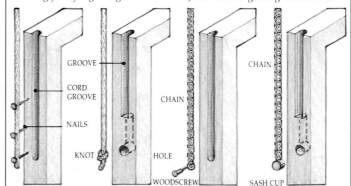

Attaching cord to sashes

Attaching chain to sashes

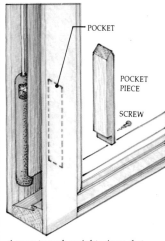

Access to sash weight via pocket

WEIGHTS AND PULLEYS

A pair of counterweights **(21)** is attached to each sash with waxed cords **(22)** or chains that pass over pulley wheels **(23)** screwed to the jambs. Cheap pulleys have plain axles, but better-quality ones are made with roller or ball bearings. Each cord is nailed into a groove cut in the sash stile or, alternatively, the knotted end of the cord may be located in a hole drilled into the stile. Chains are attached with woodscrews or by means of a metal lining (sash cup) for the hole in the stile.

Access to sash weights is by means of openings known as 'pockets' **(24)** cut through the pulley stiles. Each pocket is closed by a strip of wood, or 'pocket piece', which may be fixed by a single screw at the bottom – although often pocket pieces are simply held in place by the beads and lower sliding sash.

TAPE BALANCES

Tape balances have been used since the latter part of the nineteenth century as an alternative to the weight-and-cord method of hanging sliding sashes. A spring-loaded steel tape, wound into a metal drum, is hooked onto the sash stile. The drum is screwed into the pulley recess in the jamb.

● Easy even for beginners.
■ Fairly difficult. Good practical skills required.
▲ Difficult. Hire a professional.

Broken glass
■ Try to find matching glass to replace broken windowpanes (page 112).

Damaged weatherseal
Mortar used to seal around the frame shrinks and falls out.
● Seal the joints as soon as possible (page 115).

Seized pulley wheel
Paint can jam a pulley, making a sash difficult to open and close.
● Lubricate or strip pulley (page 110).

Broken cords
■ It is worth replacing all the sash cords when one breaks (page 109).

Loose joints
Sash joints shrink and work loose.
■ Repair them before water penetrates and rots the wood (page 110).

Loose putty
Loose putty is a security risk and encourages wood rot.
● Replace it with fresh putty (page 113).

Dry rot
Dry rot can develop inside the jamb.
▲ Have it inspected and treated by an expert (page 114).

Tape balance

Rotted sill
Being the lowest horizontal member, the sill often rots.
■ Dig out and patch the rotten wood (page 114).
▲ Have the old sill replaced with a new hardwood sill.

Components of a sash window
1 Vertical stile
2 Top rail
3 Bottom rail
4 Meeting rail
5 Bevelled face
6 Through mortise-and-tenon joint
7 Dovetailed bridle joint
8 Glazing bar
9 Mortise-and-tenon joint
10 Halving joint
11 Inner lining
12 Outer lining
13 Pulley lining
14 Back lining
15 Parting slip
16 Soffit lining
17 Triangular block
18 Sill
19 Parting bead
20 Stop bead
21 Counterweight
22 Sash cord
23 Pulley wheel
24 Pocket

Bevelled meeting rails

Bevel-rebated meeting rails

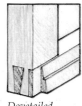

Dovetailed bridle joint for meeting rail

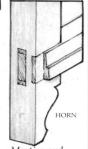

Mortise-and-tenon with horn

Rotted rails and glazing bars
Condensation and rainwater run down the glass and seep behind loose putty. Wet rot develops.
● Patch and preserve (page 114).
■ Replace the rotted wooden components (page 115).

Sticking sashes
Swollen sashes or a build-up of paint can cause a wooden window to jam.
● Ease sash (page 110).

An unusual sash in a wooden wall

SASH WINDOWS IN MASONRY WALLS

From the last quarter of the eighteenth century, wooden window frames were made to be a close fit in the window opening, and the jambs and head were recessed behind the brickwork on each side and behind a stone lintel or brick arch above. Sometimes wedges were inserted around the frame to centre it in the opening. The wooden sill sits on top of a stone subsill built into the wall. A metal strip forms a weatherproof joint between both sills. The head might be nailed to a wooden lintel that supports the masonry behind the stone lintel or brick arch. Once the internal wall is plastered and architraves (cover mouldings) are fitted, the window frame is firmly fixed in place.

SASH WINDOWS IN TIMBER-FRAME WALLS

When a sash window was fitted in a timber-frame wall, it was centred in the opening with wooden shims, then the soffit lining was nailed to a header or lintel and the sill similarly nailed to a subsill. The inner and outer linings form a casing that hides the joint between the window frame and the wall.

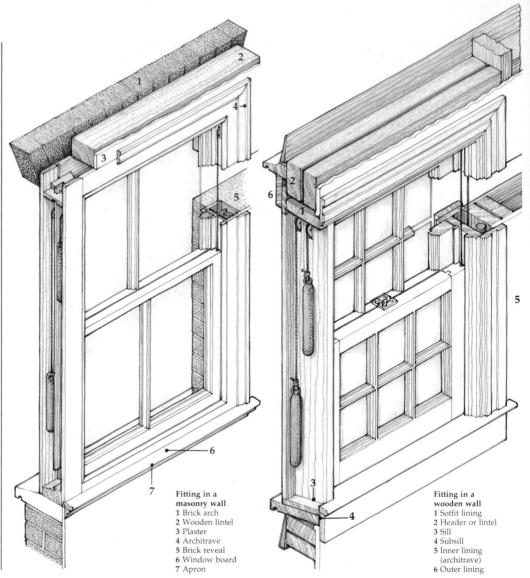

Fitting in a masonry wall
1 Brick arch
2 Wooden lintel
3 Plaster
4 Architrave
5 Brick reveal
6 Window board
7 Apron

Fitting in a wooden wall
1 Soffit lining
2 Header or lintel
3 Sill
4 Subsill
5 Inner lining (architrave)
6 Outer lining

EIGHTEENTH-CENTURY BUILDING ACTS

Before 1709 sash-window frames were set practically flush with the façade of a house (1). The Building Act of that year stipulated that the frame should be set back by 100mm (4in) to reduce the risk of fire spreading (2). The act was strengthened in 1774, and from then on frames had to be recessed behind the brickwork (3). These regulations were only enforced in London, where the risk was greatest – and even there you can find later houses with the earlier types of window frames.

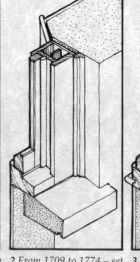
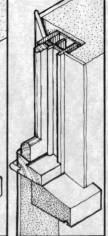

1 Before 1709 – flush with brickwork

2 From 1709 to 1774 – set back 100mm (4in)

3 After 1774 – set back and recessed

REPAIRING SASH WINDOWS

CONTRARY TO THE PROPAGANDA *put out by some manufacturers and installers of replacement windows, it is nearly always possible to repair wooden-sash windows. It is also very satisfying to preserve what are important features of a period house, especially when it proves to be much cheaper than replacing them. Some aspects of the work are quite time-consuming, but most of it is well within the capabilities of a reasonably competent woodworker.*

CORDS AND CHAINS

Waxed-cotton sash cords are made in a range of diameters numbered 6 to 12, but sizes 7 and 8 are the ones most commonly used for domestic windows. Don't be tempted to economize by fitting lightweight cords to a heavy window. You could find you have to replace them again in a matter of weeks.

Very heavy windows may be hung from chains. The cheaper chains are made with folded metal links. Better-quality ones are made with riveted links, like a bicycle chain.

Try not to smear paint onto cords or chains when redecorating. Paint clogs chain links and weakens cotton cord.

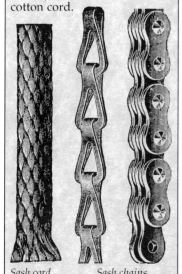

Sash cord   Sash chains

Broken sash cords

When one or both sash cords break, a sash window becomes difficult to open. A sash with weight on one side only may be out of balance; and if both cords are broken, the sash may be too heavy to lift. If you have to dismantle a sash window, it is worth taking the opportunity to replace both the cords before reinstalling it.

Drive a wide paint scraper between the stop bead and the jamb on one side of the window (1). Then, starting halfway up the window, use the same tool to begin prising the bead away from the frame. Once a few nails lose their grip, bend the bead by hand until you can free the mitre joint at each end. This will allow you to swing the lower sash out of the frame. Disconnect intact cords or chains and lower the sash weights to the bottom of the jambs.

To remove the upper sash, prise out the parting beads (2) and disconnect cords or chains as before.

Retrieve the weights by opening the pocket in the pulley stile on each side of the window (3). Pull the parting slips aside to reach the outer weights.

Using an old cord as a guide, mark off its length on the new replacement cord, but don't cut it to length at this stage. Tie a bent nail or a similar small weight to a length of string and pass it over the pulley into the hollow jamb (4). Lower the weight until it appears at the open pocket, then tape the other end of the string to the new cord. Pull on the string while feeding the cord over the pulley until you can retrieve it from the pocket.

Tie the cord to the ring on the end of the sash weight (5), or make a figure-of-eight knot to locate in the recess cast in some weights (6).

Pull the weight up to the pulley on the inside of the jamb, then lower it by about 100mm (4in). With the sash resting on the sill, nail the premarked cord into the groove in the sash stile, using three large blued tacks. Fix the lower 150mm (6in) only (7), then cut off excess cord with a sharp knife. Alternatively, fit a knotted cord in the sash stile – or screw a sash chain to the stile, instead.

Attach other weights and cords, then replace the sashes, checking that they run smoothly before nailing the parting beads and stop beads to the jamb.

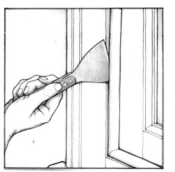

1 Break paint seal with a scraper   *2 Prise out the parting beads*

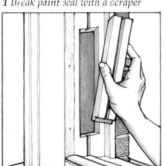

3 Take out the pocket piece

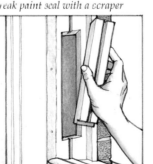

4 Pass weight over pulley wheel

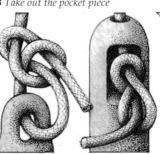

5 Tie cord to the sash weight   *6 Or tie a figure-of-eight knot*

7 Nail the sash cord in the groove

EASING A STICKING SASH

One of the most common and frustrating properties of sliding-sash windows is their refusal to budge or to open and close smoothly. Not only is a sticking sash window annoying to live with, but the strain imposed by forcing it to move puts additional load on joints that may be weak already. There are several reasons why a sash can stick, so it pays to try the simpler solutions first.

OVERPAINTING

Unless a freshly painted sash is moved regularly while the paint is drying, there is every possibility that the wet paint will act as an adhesive. When this happens, if the next painter does not bother to free the sash and simply paints it *in situ*, that makes matters even worse.

Take a sharp craft knife and carefully score around the sash, then work the blade of a wide paint scraper (or, better still, a flexible filling knife) between the sash and the surrounding beads. You may find that you also have to ease the sash from the outside.

Grasp the meeting rail and try shaking the sash from side to side in order to break the paint seal.

Misplaced beads

A sash may be difficult to move because a misplaced stop bead is virtually clamping it against the parting beads. Prise suspect beads from the frame and reposition them.

Seized pulley

If a pulley is not running freely, the friction will impede the movement of the sash cord. A drop of penetrating oil may be all that's needed to free the pulley – but you are more likely to find that it has been overpainted at some time, causing it to seize up. If so, disconnect the sash cord and remove the pulley, which is normally fixed to the stile with two woodscrews. Use paint stripper to dislodge the paint, then lightly oil the pulley before reassembly.

Swollen or distorted sash

During humid or damp weather, a wooden window can expand considerably, especially if it has been neglected and the paintwork is in poor condition. If you have a sliding sash that sticks intermittently, wait for dry weather then prepare and paint it to seal the wood.

A twisted or bowed sash probably sticks most of the time, and it will usually exhibit signs of wear or scuffing in areas that are rubbing against the frame. Take the distorted sash out of its frame (see BROKEN SASH CORDS) and shave the worn areas with a sharp block plane. Before you reinstall it, lubricate the sash by rubbing a candle along its running surfaces.

Trim a twisted sash with a plane

Loose sash joints

South-facing windows are particularly susceptible to the effects of weathering. With the alternate swelling and shrinking of the wood, glued joints begin to work loose, exhibiting wide gaps along their shoulders. An expanding sash may jam in its frame, but more serious problems can arise when rainwater and condensation penetrate the joint and rot the wood.

As a temporary measure, rake out loose material from the gap along each shoulder and close up the joint as best you can. Screw an L-shaped metal plate onto the outside of the sash to clamp the joint and prevent it deteriorating further. To make a more permanent repair, you should dismantle the sash and reglue the joints. Remove the sash and lay it flat on a convenient surface, so you can remove the glass without breaking it. Lay the glass aside, then clamp the frame to a bench.

Inspect the joints to see if there are any wedges or locking dowels that would prevent them coming apart. If necessary, chop wedges out with a small chisel. However, you may find they are loose or missing. Locking dowels can be drilled out.

Try tapping the joints apart with a hammer, using a softwood block to protect the sash (1). Work alternately, first at one end of the stile then the other, to avoid breaking a joint. If any of the joints are stuck fast, play steam from a kettle along the shoulder line to soften the glue – then tap again.

Using a sharp chisel, scrape old glue from the joints. Before proceeding to reassemble the sash, consider stripping the paint

Mend a sash temporarily with a plate

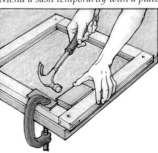

1 Tap joints apart with a hammer

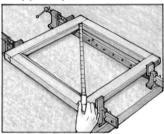

2 Check the sash is square

and applying a liquid preservative to all surfaces, including the joints.

Use a waterproof synthetic-resin adhesive to glue the sash, and hire long sash cramps to pull the joints together. Measure from one corner to another (2) to check that the sash is square. Both diagonals should be identical. Replace wedges or dowels as required. When the glue has set, replace the glass and reinstall the sash.

CURING RATTLING SASHES

Our forebears used to stop sash windows rattling by driving small rubber wedges between the sashes and the beads. Another solution is to fit a fastener that has a cam action, which will pull the two meeting rails together.

110

REPLACING GLASS

I T IS DIFFICULT TO APPRECIATE *the quality old glass gives to a building until you see a façade with all its original glazing, each pane catching the light at a different angle and distorting reflections. It pays to preserve any antique glass you find intact and to replace it with a similar form of glazing when broken. The various types of glass described below were used for glazing domestic windows from the eighteenth century onwards.*

Making cylinder glass in the traditional manner

CROWN GLASS

Until about 1830 windows were glazed with handmade crown glass. This was produced by blowing a bubble of molten glass, which was then attached to a metal rod, called a pontil, directly opposite the glass-blower's pipe. Once the blowpipe was cut from the bubble, the glass was heated again and spun on the pontil until it formed a disc about 1.5m (4 to 5ft) in diameter. The disc was then cut into square, rectangular or diamond-shape panes for glazing windows. The centre of the disc, which had a scar left by the pontil, was either thrown back into the furnace or sold as cheap glazing for poorer houses or agricultural buildings. The popular belief that bull's-eye panes were fitted for decorative reasons is a modern idea. Crown glass is thin and brittle, and the spinning process left curved ridges or striations in the glass that distort the view through a window. It is these subtle flaws and imperfections, coupled with its highly fire-polished surface and variations in colour, that endow crown glass with its special character.

Spinning crown glass

CYLINDER GLASS

Cylinder, or 'broad glass', was the only real alternative to crown glass for windows until the middle of the nineteenth century. Although not of the same quality as crown glass, larger panes could be made from cylinder glass. A large sausage-shape bubble of glass some 1.5m (4 to 5ft) long and 250 to 300mm (10 to 12in) in diameter was blown over a pit, which provided room for the extending cylinder. The two ends of the cylinder were removed, then it was split lengthwise before being reheated and opened out to make a flat sheet about 900mm (3ft) wide. The top surface of the sheet was relatively flat, but the underside inevitably puckered as the cylinder was unrolled, creating a slightly wavy surface that breaks up reflections in a most attractive manner when cylinder glass is installed in a window.

Genuine crown or cylinder glass enlivens a façade

PLATE GLASS

As a result of mechanization, manufacturers were able to make larger and larger cylinders of glass. But there was clearly a need for a process that could produce large flat sheets.

Plate glass was invented as early as the seventeenth century, but its production was so labour-intensive that it was almost exclusively used for making mirrors for the wealthy.

Molten glass was poured onto a metal casting table. Then, after cooling, it was painstakingly ground and polished to make a sheet that was optically almost perfect.

During the second half of the nineteenth century improvements were made whereby the glass was rolled flat, but the texture left on both sides of the sheet by the rolling process still had to be laboriously ground out before polishing.

DRAWN-SHEET GLASS

Although rolled-plate glass was popular for shopfronts, it was too expensive to be at all widely used for houses. However, the development of drawn-sheet glass early in the twentieth century made it possible to manufacture large flat sheets much more economically.

A ribbon of molten glass was drawn vertically from the melting pot and allowed to cool. Since the thickness of the glass was determined by the speed at which it was drawn from the pot, it was impossible to guarantee a uniform thickness.

As a result, although early drawn-sheet glass lacked many of the imperfections of handmade glass, it still tended to distort reflections and so produce a distorted view through a window.

Early-Victorian plate-glass rolling mill

FLOAT GLASS

Float glass is a relatively modern development, having been pioneered in the 1950s. This optically superb glass has a highly polished surface, made by floating it on molten metal. Float glass tends to look a little too perfect when installed in an old house, especially if it can be compared with old glass in other windows.

CURVED GLASS

If you have to replace curved glass – in a bow window, for example – you will need to employ a specialist glazier. The making of curved glass demands considerable skill, as it cannot be cut to size once it has been shaped and must therefore be measured accurately beforehand. A flat sheet of glass is heated in a furnace and allowed to sag onto a curved metal mould. Making a new mould is costly, but an experienced glazier may be able to adapt existing stock. Measure the window sash carefully and make an accurate cardboard template of the required curve. Alternatively, take the sash itself to the glazier.

FINDING REPLACEMENT GLASS

You can buy genuine old glass from an architectural-salvage company, but it is expensive and you will find that it's quite difficult to cut antique glass without breaking it. If you use crown glass, it looks best with the convex side outwards.

Cylinder glass is made for restoration purposes, in the traditional manner, in sheets 3mm (⅛in) thick measuring up to 600 x 900mm (2 x 3ft). Although it is far more expensive than modern float glass, cylinder glass will integrate perfectly with original glazing and is often used for restoring coloured leaded lights.

A cheaper alternative for clear glazing is to use imported horticultural glass made for greenhouses. This is 3mm (⅛in) thick and is sold in sheets measuring 750 x 1425mm (2ft 6in x 4ft 9in). Being a second-quality glass, it exhibits some of the imperfections of Victorian drawn-sheet glass.

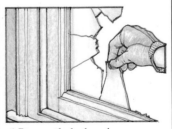

1 Remove the broken glass

2 Chop out the remaining putty

REPLACING A BROKEN PANE

Wearing goggles and thick work gloves to protect your eyes and hands, remove the broken glass piece by piece, rocking it gently backwards and forwards to loosen the putty (1). Chop out what remains of the putty from the rebates with a glazier's hacking knife (2) or an old chisel. Using pincers, remove the sprigs or glazing points that hold the glass in place, then clean out the rebates with a stiff bristle brush. (Glass is held in rolled-steel windows with small spring clips.)

Apply primer to the rebates, to prevent oil being soaked out of the new putty; or use linseed oil diluted 50 per cent with turpentine.

Measure the height and width of the opening. If you don't want to cut the glass yourself (see opposite), you will need to order replacement glass 3mm (⅛in) smaller from top to bottom and from side to side.

Knead a fist-size ball of linseed-oil putty until it has an even consistency. Remove some of the oil from sticky

3 Secure the glass with sprigs

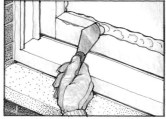

4 Smooth the putty with a knife

fresh putty by rolling it in newspaper. Conversely, soften stiff putty with a drop of linseed oil.

Shape the putty into a thin 'rope' and press it firmly into the rebates all round the opening. Set the new pane of glass into this bedding putty, pressing around the edges only to squeeze excess putty from the rebates. Secure the glass every 200mm (8in) or so with sprigs or glazing points, tapping them into the wood with the edge of a firmer chisel (3). Cut excess putty from the inside of the window with a putty knife.

Press more putty into the rebate to cover the fixings, smoothing it to form an even bevel with the point of a putty knife (4). Dip the knife in water from time to time to prevent it sticking to the putty. Clean putty smears from the glass with methylated spirits.

Leave the putty for a week or so to harden, then paint it (at least with an undercoat) within a month. To seal the edge of the putty, let the paint overlap very slightly onto the glass.

RENEWING OLD PUTTY

Old putty is often so loose you can pick it out with your fingers. Not only does loose putty admit water to rot the woodwork, it is also a security risk since it enables a pane of glass to be removed silently. Old putty is extremely hard; and if sections are still firmly attached to the sash, trying to chop it out in the conventional manner may crack the glass. Soften hard putty with a coat of chemical paint stripper. A paste stripper is best because it can be covered with strips of plastic sheeting to keep it moist and active, for up to 48 hours, until the putty is soft enough to scrape from the rebates. Prime the rebate, then apply new putty (see left).

Glaziers at work

CUTTING GLASS

If you have never cut glass before, practise on some spare glass before you start a job in earnest.

Lay a sheet of glass on a flat worktable covered with a blanket, then thoroughly clean the area to be cut with methylated spirits to remove traces of grease, which can cause a glass cutter to skid. An ordinary glass cutter has a steel wheel that scores the glass, but better-quality diamond-tipped cutters are also available. Use a wooden straightedge (preferably a T-square) to guide the cutter.

Lubricate the tip of a wheeled glass cutter by dipping it in light oil. Then, holding the tool between your index and middle fingers (1), draw it towards you with one continuous movement that scores the glass from edge to edge. A harsh grating sound means you are pressing too hard, sending shock waves through the glass that could cause the cut to wander; a light irregular sound may mean you are not scoring a continuous line.

Slide the glass towards you until it overhangs the edge of the worktable, then tap the glass directly under the scored line (2) to start the cut. Place a gloved hand on each side of the line (3) and snap the glass with a twist of the wrists.

Cutting shapes

To cut a shaped piece of glass, make a thick card-board template that fits the window opening but is 1.5mm (1⁄16in) smaller all round (not forgetting to allow for the thickness of the glass cutter).

Hold the template on the glass with double-sided adhesive tape and score a cut line along each edge (4). Run each cut out to the edge of the glass (5) and cut the waste alongside a curved edge into segments.

Snap the glass, holding it as previously described, or use ordinary pliers padded with masking tape to grip awkward pieces (6).

1 Hold a cutter between your fingers

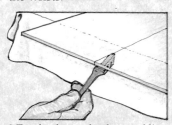

2 Tap the glass under the scored line

3 Grip glass on each side of the line

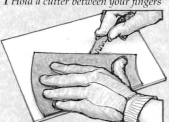

4 Score alongside a template

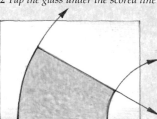

5 Run each cut out to an edge

6 Snap a strip with padded pliers

DEALING WITH ROTTED WINDOWS

DRY ROT BREAKS OUT *only in dark, unventilated enclosed spaces where moisture is present. It may start inside the hollow parts of a sash-window frame and then gradually invade neighbouring components. Alternatively, a window can be affected by dry rot creeping from some other source.*

In practice dry rot occurs comparatively rarely in window frames, but wooden windows do frequently suffer from the effects of wet rot. Wet rot most often occurs at points where moisture is able to penetrate the end grain of timber, such as the ends of the sill, the bottom of both jambs and the joints.

Neglected paintwork is one of the most common causes of wet rot, as are the breakdown of the mortar seal around the frame, bad pointing, loose putty and rising damp – in fact, anything that is responsible for the wood becoming saturated regularly.

Before attempting to treat the symptoms of rot, always locate and eradicate the source of the dampness that has caused the fungus to develop.

Neglected paintwork and missing putty lead to wet rot

Checking for wet rot
Peeling paint, where the wood has expanded beneath, is often the first sign of wet rot. Wood suffering from wet rot is spongy when wet, but becomes dry and crumbly as it dries out in warm weather. It is always relatively soft, and areas of rot can be pinpointed by probing with the point of a screwdriver.

Checking for dry rot
If you become aware of a strong musty smell when you are changing a sash cord or making some other repair to a wooden window, open the pocket and inspect the inside of the jamb with a torch and a small mirror. If you notice a dusting of red spores or any of the other signs of dry rot, have the window inspected and treated by a professional as soon as possible.

TREATING AREAS OF WET ROT
Gouge out decayed wood until you reach relatively sound material, then apply preservative and consolidate the affected area by painting a liquid wood hardener onto it. One coat of hardener is enough to reinforce weakened fibres and seal the wood against future penetration.

After six hours, fill holes, cracks and crevices with a flexible exterior wood filler.

Patching a deep hole
Having gouged out soft decayed wood to investigate the extent of the damage, chisel out a cavity that is slightly larger than the damaged area and, if possible, undercut the edges to lock the new patch in place (1).

Cut a patch from timber similar to that of the component, with the grain running in the same direction. Shape the patch to match any undercuts and leave it very slightly oversize, both in thickness and in width, for planing down after fitting (2). Paint the prepared area and the new timber with a chemical preservative before gluing the patch in place with a waterproof synthetic-resin adhesive.

When the glue has set, plane the patch flush then coat it with preservative again before filling any gaps with a flexible wood filler.

1 Chisel out a cavity with undercuts   2 Plane the patch repair to fit

REPLACING ROTTED TIMBER
If the extent of the wet rot has structurally weakened a component of a wooden window, cut out the damaged wood and repair it by inserting a new section or replace the entire component.

114

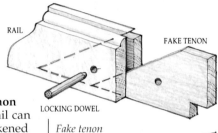

RAIL

FAKE TENON

LOCKING DOWEL

Repairing
a broken sash-rail tenon
The tenon of a sash rail can become severely weakened by wet rot. Once you have dismantled the sash, you could replace the entire component, but that would involve having a matching moulding cut into the rail. However, provided serious damage goes no further than the tenon itself, the joint can be repaired relatively simply by installing a fake tenon. The same repair is also appropriate for the tongue of a meeting-rail bridle joint.

Set a mortise gauge to the width of the tenon and mark an angled housing for the fake tenon on the outer edge of the rail (1). Cut off the remnants of the tenon flush with the shoulder of the joint, then mark the housing on the end grain (2).

Saw down each side of the housing with a tenon saw (3), then pare out the waste with a mortise chisel. Use similar timber to make a fake tenon that fits the housing but is slightly wider than the sash rail (4).

Treat both components with preservative, then glue the tenon into the housing. When the glue has set, plane and shape the tenon.

Last of all, insert a glued locking dowel to reinforce the joint (5).

Making
replacement components
An entire rail, stile or glazing bar can be copied from the original. Whether you do the work yourself or employ a professional joiner, it is important to reproduce the mouldings exactly. Some joiners use antique moulding planes for this type of work, but it is probably easier to have an electric-router cutter ground to match the profile.

Fake tenon

1 Mark out the housing

2 Mark out housing on end grain

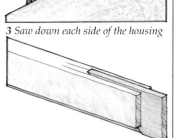

3 Saw down each side of the housing

4 Make the tenon slightly oversize

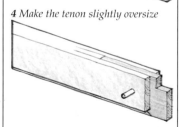

5 Shape tenon and fit a dowel

PREVENTATIVE TREATMENT
Considering the expense and time involved in curing the effects of rot in wooden windows, it pays to take preventative measures whenever possible.

Chemical preservatives
Having stripped a window for repainting, you might take the opportunity to treat the bare timber with a chemical preservative. Two or three applications are ideal. You will need to leave it for between two and five days before painting, depending on drying conditions.

For replacements, either use pressure-treated timber or paint the wood with a preservative yourself.

Repairing
a damaged weatherseal
If a window has a decayed weatherseal, rake out loose mortar to expose the joint between the window frame and the masonry surround. The traditional way to fill large gaps was to stuff them with wet newspaper before reinstating the mortar seal, but it's probably simpler and more efficient to inject an expanding polyurethane foam, provided there is no possibility of it impeding the movement of sash weights.

Finally, seal the joint with a gun-applied mastic (1) or press-in-place strip sealant (2). To preserve the original appearance, you can cover a mastic seal with mortar.

SAFETY WITH PRESERVATIVES
- Follow the preservative maker's instructions very carefully.
- Wear protective gloves to handle preservatives, and goggles when applying them. Use a face mask if you are working indoors.
- Make sure that there is adequate ventilation while preservatives are drying.

1 Apply mastic with a gun

2 Or use a press-in-place strip

REPLACING AN ENTIRE WINDOW
It is rarely necessary to replace an entire window, but if decay is so extensive that repairs are not practicable then replacement may be your only option. However, resist any temptation to install inappropriate modern-style windows in a period house. It isn't necessary, given that any competent joiner is capable of reproducing sliding-sash or casement windows, and there are several companies that specialize in making exact replicas of individual windows in treated softwoods or hardwoods (some types of window can even be supplied fully draughtproofed). If you have sufficient experience, you might want to install the windows yourself; or you can get the supplier to fit them for you.

CASEMENT WINDOWS

DESPITE THE POPULARITY *of the double-hung sash window, hinged casements have never really been out of fashion. They have remained in use in one form or another since medieval times, especially for smaller houses and workers' cottages. They are likely to comprise simple wooden frames divided by one or two glazing bars, constructed as individual windows or in pairs that close together with rebated stiles down the centre. Alternatively, there might be a single casement that opens within a group of fixed sashes. French windows are perhaps the most extreme example of twin casements, being in effect pairs of glazed doors opening onto a terrace, patio or balcony.*

Edwardian bay with leaded-light casement windows

THE REVIVAL OF THE CASEMENT WINDOW

The earliest casements had wrought-iron or wooden frames surrounding a tracery of cames (grooved lead strips) that held small diamond-shape or square glass panes. Similar forms of casement reappeared in Victorian times with the revival of Gothic and Queen Anne styles.

The same nostalgic sentiments were expressed in the fenestration of the late-Victorian and Edwardian 'Old English' styles and neo-Tudor interwar housing. Elegant mass-produced rolled-steel casement windows represented an opposing taste during the interwar decades, their uncluttered and severely practical lines being ideally suited to the avant-garde Art Deco architecture of the 1930s.

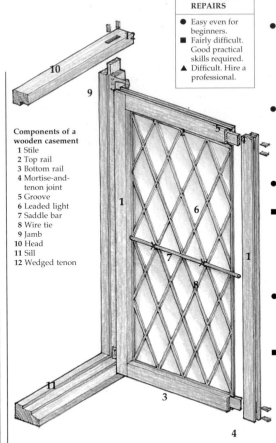

ASSESSING REPAIRS
● Easy even for beginners.
■ Fairly difficult. Good practical skills required.
▲ Difficult. Hire a professional.

Components of a wooden casement
1 Stile
2 Top rail
3 Bottom rail
4 Mortise-and-tenon joint
5 Groove
6 Leaded light
7 Saddle bar
8 Wire tie
9 Jamb
10 Head
11 Sill
12 Wedged tenon

Swollen casement
A wooden casement may swell and jam.
● Plane the frame (page 118).

Loose hinge
A loose or worn hinge allows the casement to drop and jam.
● Repair the hinge (page 118).

Rotted wood
Wet rot develops in poorly maintained wood components.
● Patch and repair minor areas of rot (page 114).
■ Replace rotted components (page 115).

Damaged weatherseal
Mortar falls out around frame.
● Reseal to prevent water seeping in (page 115).

Broken glass
■ Replace broken glass (page 112) or leaded lights (page 132).

Loose putty
Old putty no longer holds the glass or leaded lights securely in place.
● Replace the putty (page 113).

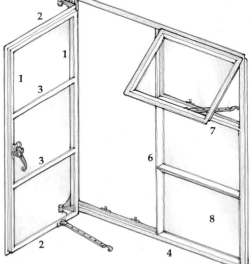

Glass held with putty

Components of a metal casement
1 Stile
2 Top and bottom rails
3 Glazing bar
4 Frame
5 Corner joint
6 Mullion
7 Transom
8 Fixed light

Corrosion
Some corrosion is present in all metal casements.
● Unless extremely advanced, it is fairly easy to treat (page 118).

Broken glass
■ Replacing broken panes in metal casements is quite straightforward (page 119).
■ Repairing a leaded light requires different skills (page 132).

Bent sections
Hinged casements are difficult to close if metal sections are bowed or distorted.
▲ Expert treatment may be required (page 119).

Damaged weatherseal
A deteriorating seal between the wall and window frame can cause serious corrosion.
● Seal with mastic (page 119).

HOW CASEMENTS WERE MADE

ALTHOUGH RELATIVELY SIMPLE *in construct-ion, a wooden-casement window is similar to a sliding-sash window in that the various components are jointed together and, when necessary, can be dismantled for repair or replacement.*

A rolled-steel casement window, on the other hand, is made in complete sub-assemblies at the factory. The hinged casement itself can be removed, but it is impossible to replace individual components except by cutting and rewelding sections.

WOODEN-CASEMENT CONSTRUCTION

A hinged wooden casement comprises two vertical stiles **(1)** and horizontal top **(2)** and bottom rails **(3)** jointed at the corners with wedged through mortise-and-tenon joints **(4)**. The outer faces of the stiles and rails are rebated to accept the glass and are usually moulded decoratively on the inside A groove **(5)** around the outer edge stops water seeping in.

Although they may be divided by wooden glazing bars, casement windows are often glazed with leaded lights **(6)**. These consist of a lattice of lead 'cames' (grooved strips) holding square or diamond-shape panes of glass. To support this relatively weak lattice against wind pressure, 6mm (¼in) steel or iron saddle bars **(7)** are placed at strategic intervals. Each end of a saddle bar is located in a hole in the stile, and lengths of copper wire soldered to the lead cames **(8)** are twisted around the bar to tie the glazed panel securely in place.

Most casements are side-hung, like a door, being attached by hinges to a vertical stile. You sometimes find small wooden casements placed above larger ones, such as door-height French windows. They are usually hinged at the bottom and open inwards. When open, they are supported by metal stays or chains.

METAL-CASEMENT CONSTRUCTION

Early metal-casement windows were handmade from wrought iron, but late-nineteenth-century technology made it possible to mass-produce window casements and frames from rolled-steel sections. The stiles **(1)** and top and bottom rails **(2)** are made from identical Z-section pieces of metal. T-section glazing bars **(3)** divide the casement and support the glass panes, which are held in place with spring clips and a special putty formulated for use with metal.

Construction of the frame

The surrounding frame **(4)** is constructed from the same metal section used for the casement. The corner joints **(5)** are welded. Frames may be divided by T-section mullions **(6)** and transoms **(7)**, and often include fixed lights **(8)** as well as the hinged casement.

Wooden casement windows

Construction of the frame

A simple casement is hinged from a surrounding wooden frame comprising two vertical jambs **(9)**, a top rail or head **(10)**, and a sill **(11)** across the bottom. If the frame was to hold two or more casements, it was divided vertically by a mullion and, if need be, horizontally by a transom. A tenon on each end of the jamb passes right through the head and sill, and is secured with glue and wedges **(12)**. These joints are sometimes pinned with dowels in the manner of sliding-sash mortise-and-tenon joints. The frame is rebated externally to receive the casement.

Metal casement windows

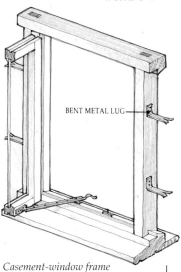

BENT METAL LUG

Casement-window frame

HOW WOODEN WINDOWS WERE FITTED

Wooden window frames were nailed directly to a timber-frame wall or to preservative-treated pallets (wooden strips), which were built into the mortar joints at 600mm (2ft) intervals as a masonry wall was being constructed. Another method was to nail into wooden plugs driven into holes cut in a finished masonry wall. Alternatively, bent metal lugs screwed to the frame at strategic points were bedded in mortar joints during the building of the opening. As well as being bedded in mortar, frames may also have been sealed with mastic.

HOW METAL WINDOWS WERE FITTED

Rolled-steel windows were either screwed to a wooden surround or to plugged masonry or, alternatively, bent metal lugs bolted to the metal frame were built into the mortar joints.

The window frames were bedded in mastic.

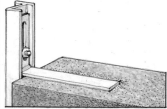

Fixing lug bolted to a metal frame

RESTORING CASEMENT WINDOWS

WOODEN-CASEMENT WINDOWS *generally suffer from problems very similar to those associated with sliding-sash windows, although leaded lights need special care and you may have to hire an expert to deal with extensive deterioration to the leadwork and the glass itself.*

REPAIRING WOODEN CASEMENTS

As with sash windows, rotted wood may have to be consolidated and either filled, patched or replaced, joints may need to be dismantled and reglued, loose putty replaced, and new panes of glass inserted. Joints around a frame can be resealed with mastic.

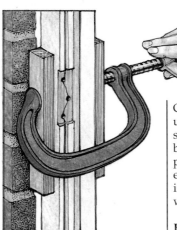

Glue a split frame and apply a cramp

CORRECTING A LOOSE HINGE

You may find that a hinged casement is binding against its frame because a loose hinge is allowing it to drop.

First of all, inspect the upper hinge to see if there are missing or loose screws; then lift the casement *in situ* to check whether the hinge knuckles are worn and have become slack. Swapping the top and bottom hinges may be enough to even out the wear and correct the fault.

Alternatively, the screws may have lost their grip as a result of the wooden frame splitting. The best solution in this case is to remove the casement, then work some waterproof glue into the split with a knife blade.

Close the split with a cramp until the glue has set. If the split will no longer close because the wood has expanded, fill it flush using an exterior wood filler that is tough enough to accept a woodscrew.

EASING A SWOLLEN CASEMENT

If a casement sticks or is difficult to open, inspect its edges for signs of abrasion where it is rubbing against the frame. Skim those areas with a finely set block plane until the window opens and closes smoothly. Take care not to remove too much wood, especially if the swelling could be due to humid conditions.

REPLACING A WOODEN CASEMENT

If a window has deteriorated beyond repair, have a joiner make an exact replica. Avoid the temptation to buy a cheaper ready-made casement window from a builders' merchant. The chances of it being a suitable style for an old house are very remote indeed.

Rolled-steel casements are often sadly neglected and needlessly replaced, largely due to a widely held view that metal windows are not worthy of conservation. But a rolled-steel window may be no less important to the integrity of a building than a Georgian sash window in a different context.

REPAIRING METAL CASEMENTS

Many people are under the impression that metal-casement windows are more difficult to restore than wooden ones, but with basic metalwork skills and equipment it is possible to do a great deal of repair work and restoration before it is necessary to replace a window.

DEALING WITH CORROSION

Corrosion, or rust, begins whenever moisture is able to penetrate the protective paint that coats a rolled-steel window. Neglected decoration is perhaps the most obvious cause of corrosion, but defective putty can lead to even worse symptoms, allowing corrosion to eat away at the metal section beneath. A faulty weatherseal around the perimeter of a metal frame is equally damaging, allowing rust to develop unnoticed until it eventually breaks through the paintwork.

Flaking or blistered paintwork is often the first sign of corrosion. Probing the affected area with a pointed tool will detect the degree and extent of the rust, which in turn determines the required treatment.

Light rust

If the metal is firm and flaking paint is due simply to a light accumulation of rust on the surface, rub it down with silicon-carbide paper dipped in white spirit to remove the rust, feathering the edges of sound paintwork surrounding it. Wipe away the dust with a cloth dampened in methylated spirits, then paint the

bare metal immediately with a rust-inhibiting primer. Repaint the window with two coats of paint that is compatible with the primer. It often pays to use a paint and primer made by the same manufacturer.

Medium rust

If the metal flakes when probed, wire-brush all corroded surfaces until you reach sound metal. For extensive corrosion, use a wire-brush attachment in a power drill. Wear goggles and a face mask, and protect adjacent masonry and glass. First neutralize the rust by applying an anti-corrosion acid-based gel, then fill pitted metal with an epoxy-based car-body filler. Prime and paint the window.

Heavy corrosion

If corrosion is ignored for a long time, it can weaken metal-window components to such an extent that your only recourse is to cut out damaged sections and weld new ones in their place. The casement or even the frame itself may have to be transferred to a workshop to be repaired by an expert. Replacing a rolled section of metal can be difficult unless you have an identical scrap window from which to plunder parts.

118

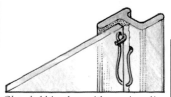

Glass held in place with a spring clip

REPLACING BROKEN GLASS

To reglaze a rolled-steel casement, follow the instructions for removing broken glass and installing new panes in a wooden window. However, the glass is held in place by spring clips, which you should remove and put aside for replacement. Use a special metal-window putty, available from a glazier or a builders' merchant.

STRAIGHTENING BENT COMPONENTS

Bent components can make it impossible to close a metal casement properly, perhaps leaving gaps that cannot be draughtproofed successfully. A badly distorted window will have to be repaired professionally, but you may be able to straighten a slightly bent component *in situ* yourself. After removing the glass, apply pressure to the bent component, using a stout wooden batten to spread the load evenly and prevent the metal kinking.

REPLACING A DECAYED WEATHERSEAL

Rake out any loose material from around the metal window frame, then seal the gap between the frame and the surrounding masonry with a gun-applied mastic.

REPLACING STEEL WINDOWS

Some manufacturers have continued to produce rolled-steel windows unchanged since their introduction in the 1920s and 1930s, which can be used as replacements for earlier versions. They are also available with superior galvanized or stoved finishes and can be ordered with draughtproofing and double glazing.

SHUTTERS

WINDOW SHUTTERS *have now largely fallen out of fashion, and sadly many have been rendered inoperable or ripped out. Yet it is hard to imagine why this should be so, considering that shutters are extremely practical, screening out harsh sunlight and noise, preventing draughts, and providing welcome additional security.*

Folding shutters
1 Folding leaves
2 Shutter box
3 Splayed reveal
4 Panelled wall
5 Staple
6 Rebated edge

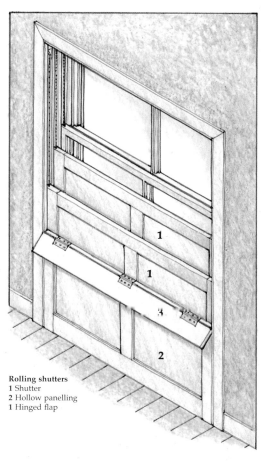

Rolling shutters
1 Shutter
2 Hollow panelling
1 Hinged flap

INTERNAL SHUTTERS

Folding or rolling shutters were a feature of many Georgian and Victorian interiors. Yet they were so ingeniously designed to be unobtrusive that sometimes householders are completely unaware of their presence.

Folding shutters

Panelled shutters, which generally comprise a pair of leaves on each side of the window **(1)**, fold back into deep shutter boxes **(2)** in the reveals. The reveals may be square to the window, but often they are splayed **(3)** to admit more daylight. The wall below the shutter boxes **(4)** and the window is usually panelled to match the shutters themselves. Once folded out flat against the window, the shutters are secured by metal bars that engage strong staples **(5)** fixed to the back of the leaves. Leaf stiles are rebated **(6)** to make lightproof joints.

Rolling shutters

Rolling shutters are comparatively rare and are even more unobtrusive. They work on the same principle as a sliding-sash window, being counterbalanced by cords and weights.

The shutters **(1)** are housed behind panelling **(2)** constructed between the window and the floor, and are accessible by means of a hinged flap **(3)** that forms the internal window board.

REINSTATING INTERNAL SHUTTERS

If you have wood-panelled reveals or unusually deep window boards, it might be worth stripping a small section to see if there are shutters hidden beneath layers and layers of paint. There's every chance that the shutters themselves are in perfect condition, perhaps requiring a drop of oil on the hinges or a new set of cords.

If you decide to strip all the paint from panelled shutters, either do it yourself or make sure a professional stripper uses a cold-chemical dip – since a hot-caustic stripping solution can split the relatively thin panelling used for shutters.

EXTERNAL SHUTTERS

With outward-opening casements it is difficult, if not impossible, to reach exterior shutters from the upper floors of a house. This problem has been overcome in some houses by the use of an ingenious worm gear that controls the position of each shutter by cranking a handle on the inside.

Small houses and cottages are most likely to be fitted with shutters of frame-and-panel construction or simple ledged-and-braced boarded shutters with strap hinges that are either screwed to the wooden window frame or hung from hooked pins driven into the wall.

Routine maintenance is all that's required with these types of shutter, and even complete replacement is no problem to a reasonably competent joiner. Unless they are traditional in the area where you live, avoid having shutters made with cutouts – which can make an attractive cottage look unconvincingly twee.

Panelled shutters fold out of deep shutter boxes

Adjustable louvred shutters control the light

LOUVRED SHUTTERS

Louvred shutters or blinds are to be found both internally and externally on Georgian and early-Victorian villas. Especially valuable are the ones with pivoting slats that are operated simultaneously by a vertical wooden rod, attached to the edge of each slat with staples.

Banks of small louvred shutters are sometimes mounted one above the other to provide a greater degree of flexibility when in use. The bottom half of a window, for example, can be screened for privacy while the top half is left partly open for light and ventilation.

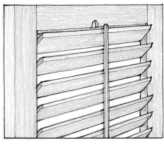

A stapled rod operates pivoting slats

Attractive external louvred shutters

Sturdy framed shutters with raised-and-fielded panels

FANLIGHTS

THE TERM FANLIGHT *was coined in the eighteenth century to describe a semi-circular fixed light or window with a radiating pattern of glazing bars. It was installed above a doorway to admit light to the hallway or passage beyond. In time, 'fanlight' became a general term for similar fixed lights of any pattern, including rectangular ones.*

FANLIGHT PATTERNS

A simple fan of wooden glazing bars was probably the earliest fanlight pattern. It was developed sometime during the first quarter of the eighteenth century. The techniques required to make this type of fanlight would have been familiar to a joiner used to constructing semi-circular-head or segmental-head sash windows.

Fanlights of similar design were made by fretting the pattern of glazing bars from a single piece of solid wood. However, fretted fanlights that break with tradition are often extremely decorative. Wooden fanlights were often embellished with 'compo' (a mixture of whiting and glue) and hand carving.

The introduction of metal fanlights in the 1770s made it possible to produce the delicately beautiful traceries that are a feature of classic Georgian design. There were countless variations on the original fan, and patterns such as the umbrella and the batswing and its derivative the teardrop were extremely popular, too.

Traditional patterns were frequently adapted to suit rectangular fanlights; and abstract patterns such as intersecting circles or Gothic arches were devised to make the most of the increasingly fashionable rectangular fanlight shape.

A relatively early fretted and carved fanlight

Variation on the fan motif in a wooden doorcase

Delicate umbrella-pattern fanlight

Gothic-style fanlight with simple wooden glazing bars

Simple rectangular fanlight

Classic metal fanlight above a Georgian door

Typical metal teardrop fanlight

Batswing with hinged ventilator

METHODS OF CONSTRUCTION

A wooden fanlight has a substantial outer frame **(1)** enclosing glazing bars **(2)** that accommodate the glass in the usual way. But, unlike most wooden windows, the moulded side of a fanlight faces the street.

A metal fanlight has brass or tinned wrought-iron ribs **(3)** fixed inside a wooden sash. Decorative lead-alloy strips **(4)** soldered to the leading edges of the ribs form the glazing rebates. Very often they incorporate rosettes or scrolls, or other ornamental motifs, that do not support the glass in any way. The metal framework is attached to the sash by means of thin strips of tin **(5)** nailed to the wood. The sash itself either locates in rebates cut in the doorframe or may be fixed directly to the masonry and plastered in.

REPLACING FANLIGHTS

There are relatively few professionals with the skill and knowledge required to repair, let alone reconstruct, authentic metal fanlights. As a result, the space above many a Georgian door is now filled with a blank sheet of glass or a cheap imitation of a period fanlight.

Look for a craftsperson who will remake corroded ribs, attach new tin fixing strips, and resolder cast-lead ornamentation. A first-class workshop will even cast new sections from existing fragments to reproduce missing ornamentation. A craftsperson with this type of experience will probably be able to make a copy of a neighbour's fanlight if your own has been discarded at some time in the past.

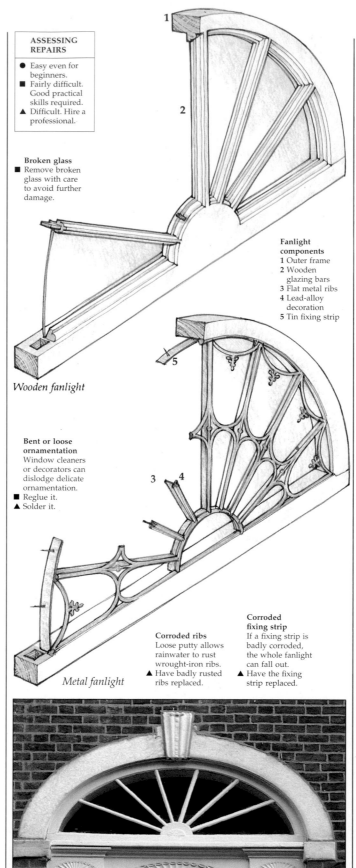

> **ASSESSING REPAIRS**
> ● Easy even for beginners.
> ■ Fairly difficult. Good practical skills required.
> ▲ Difficult. Hire a professional.

Broken glass
■ Remove broken glass with care to avoid further damage.

Wooden fanlight

Bent or loose ornamentation
Window cleaners or decorators can dislodge delicate ornamentation.
■ Reglue it.
▲ Solder it.

Metal fanlight

Fanlight components
1 Outer frame
2 Wooden glazing bars
3 Flat metal ribs
4 Lead-alloy decoration
5 Tin fixing strip

Corroded ribs
Loose putty allows rainwater to rust wrought-iron ribs.
▲ Have badly rusted ribs replaced.

Corroded fixing strip
If a fixing strip is badly corroded, the whole fanlight can fall out.
▲ Have the fixing strip replaced.

Elliptical-head fanlight designed to fit above a wide doorcase

Some fanlights incorporate lanterns

REPAIRING FANLIGHTS

Restoring a wooden fanlight is no more difficult than working on any other similar window, except that if you need to remove the whole sash you will probably have to hack away some interior plasterwork. Look for signs of filler covering the sash-fixing nails, and drive them right through the outer frame with a punch.

Metal fanlights, especially ones that have reached an advanced stage of corrosion, can be extremely fragile; and clumsy attempts to repair them can make matters even worse. Inspect a fanlight closely before you start work to ascertain whether you need expert help or advice.

Avoiding damage to the glass

Old fanlights sometimes still contain the original crown glass, which should be preserved if at all possible. When you are removing glass, especially from a metal fanlight, soften the putty with paint stripper to avoid distorting the frame and cracking other panes.

Replacing loose cast-metal ornamentation

You frequently find cast-lead strips and ornamentation that are bent or peeling away from the metal glazing ribs behind them. Straighten the components, and refit them with an epoxy glue or get an expert to resolder them.

WINDOW FURNITURE

THE APPROPRIATE HARDWARE *or 'furniture' is important to the security and smooth operation of both casement and sliding-sash windows. It is preferable to restore antique hardware; but if you need to replace a broken or missing fitting, you can buy reproductions that are almost indistinguishable from original pieces. Whenever possible, it is best to remove fittings for cleaning, lubricating or stripping. So you can put back the fittings in their original positions, don't fill fixing holes when decorating. Brass screws should be used for attaching brass fittings.*

SASH FASTENERS

Antique fasteners made to secure double-hung sash windows provide minimal security and prevent sashes rattling in the wind. Some fasteners were designed in such a way that they could not be opened by a blade slipped between the meeting rails, but by themselves they do not conform to modern standards of home security. It is therefore recommended that you fit a lock or security bolt with a removable key to any accessible window, in addition to a traditional sash fastener.

Cam fastener

Cam fasteners have been fitted to sash windows since Georgian times. A lever on one half of the fitting engages a cam-shape lug on the other, pulling the meeting rails together. Cam fasteners, originally made in bronze or brass, are often very decorative, with brass or ceramic knobs fitted to the lever.

Screw the fitting to the tops of the meeting rails, as close to the centre of the window as possible. Fit the lever first (on the upper sash) and use it to position the lug, making allowance for the cam action.

Fitch fastener

A Fitch or crescent fastener is even better for windows with loose sashes. The rim of a helical metal cam engages a hook on the other half of the fitting. Turning the cam forces the sashes apart vertically while pulling the meeting rails together.

Screw the hook to the upper sash first, then use it to position the cam on the other meeting rail.

Always remember to turn the cam back completely before opening the window, or the fastener may gouge wood out of glazing bars in the upper sash.

Screw fastener

Like other sash fasteners, a screw fastener pulls the meeting rails together – this time by means of a knurled nut on the end of a pivoting lever. Unless the lever is raised properly when the window is opened, it will get caught under the meeting rail of the lower sash when you close the window.

Victorian sash screw

Sash screw

A sash screw passes right through one meeting rail into the other so that neither sash can be opened. Period brass sash screws are most attractive – however, unlike modern ones that can only be extracted with a key, security is compromised if a pane of glass is broken.

SASH LIFTS

Sash lifts are screwed to the bottom rails of heavy lower sashes to make them easier to open. They are fitted approximately 150mm (6in) from each end of the rail.

Hook lift

Simple brass lifts are still manufactured today, but antique hook lifts with cast decoration are even more attractive. On some lifts the hook forms a complete ring, but they offer little practical advantage over the simple hooked variety.

Flush lift

Flush lifts provide a more positive grip, but because a recess has to be cut in the wood in order to set them into the rail they are more difficult to fit.

SASH HANDLES

Upper sashes without horizontal glazing bars that form finger grips are difficult to open. One solution is to screw a pair of D-shaped handles to the underside of the meeting rail, close to the stiles. Sash handles can only be reached by raising the lower sash.

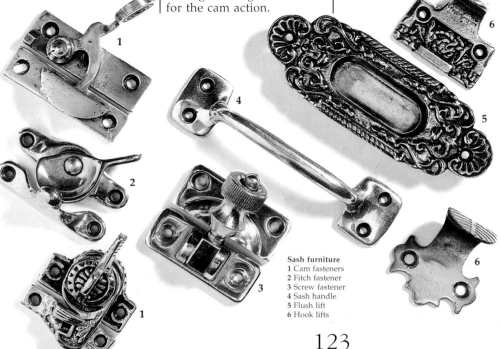

Sash furniture
1 Cam fasteners
2 Fitch fastener
3 Screw fastener
4 Sash handle
5 Flush lift
6 Hook lifts

123

CASEMENT FASTENERS

A hinged casement is held closed by a one-piece pivoting handle known as a cockspur fastener. The window is held open in a number of positions by means of a metal bar or stay.

Cockspur fastener

A cockspur fastener comprises a metal handle with a projecting spur that engages a slotted striker plate screwed to the frame or, alternatively, a hook screwed to the face of an adjacent fixed casement.

The traditional iron rat-tail fastener with its coiled handle looks well on a casement of any period up to the end of the nineteenth century. Twentieth-century casements are generally fitted with cast-metal cockspur fasteners, made from either sherardized iron, bronze, or aluminium alloy. Similar fasteners for rolled-steel casement windows are frequently of the 'two-point' or 'three-point' types with slotted spurs. The slots locate on the edge of the window muntin or stile, holding the casement ajar to provide ventilation.

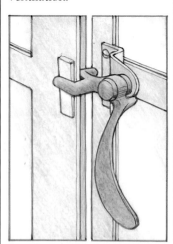

A two-point cockspur locates on the muntin to hold the window ajar

Casement stay

A casement or peg stay is a flat, rigid metal bar pivoting on a metal plate screwed to the bottom rail of a hinged casement. A short peg screwed to the sill engages one of a series of holes that run the length of the bar, holding the window open. When the window is closed, a second peg holds the bar parallel to the bottom rail. You can buy stays made to match the various styles of cockspur fasteners.

Sliding stays that are fixed permanently to rolled-steel casements are secured in an open or closed position by a thumbscrew or lever.

Sliding casement-window stay

CASEMENT HINGES

Standard butt hinges are fitted to many wooden-casement windows. However, special extension hinges are sometimes used to facilitate cleaning both sides of the glass, especially on windows situated on the upper floors of a house.

Extension hinge

When a window is open, extension hinges provide a clearance of about 100 to 125mm (4 to 5in) between the hinge stile and the frame, making it possible to clean the outside of the window from inside the room. Rolled-steel windows are invariably fitted with extension hinges.

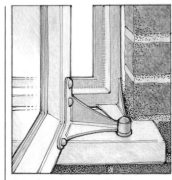

Metal-window extension hinge

ESPAGNOLETTE BOLTS

Victorian and Edwardian door-height French windows are frequently fitted with espagnolette bolts. Turning a centrally fitted door handle simultaneously closes two substantial bolts running parallel with the closing stile of the window. One bolt shoots into the window head, the other into the sill.

Casement furniture
1 Rat-tail cockspur fastener
2 Rat-tail stay
3 Iron peg stay
4 Simple cockspur fastener
5 Brass two-point fastener

Espagnolette bolt secures door-height French windows

CHAPTER ELEVEN

ORNAMENTAL GLASS

WHETHER IT IS THE FEELING OF OPTIMISM conjured by the early-morning sunshine streaming through a colourful landing window or the welcoming sight of a back-lit stained-glass door on a winter's evening, ornamental glass can influence our emotional attachment to a house in a most direct and effective manner.

In fact, decorative glass is such a valuable asset, financially as well as aesthetically, that any householder would be well advised to preserve even the most modest items and to replace any that have been removed.

For a period of a hundred years or so, from the early nineteenth century onwards, grand and humble houses alike were enriched with all manner of decorative glass. But the beginnings of handcrafted glass are very much earlier. Stained glass, for example, has a pedigree stretching back to before medieval times. Nevertheless, crucial aspects of the technology had to be rediscovered by the Victorians before the craft could be exploited with a fresh momentum that would carry it beyond the ecclesiastical tradition into the wider domestic context.

The technical innovations of the Industrial Revolution introduced more and more possibilities for using glass cheaply as well as decoratively in practically every Victorian home. In particular, with the increased density of urban housing, various forms of acid-etched, sandblasted and machine-rolled glass were used instead of clear glazing to preserve Victorian and Edwardian sensitivities.

A spectacular Art Deco door panel

The welcoming sight of stained glass is most appealing

Typical Victorian landing light

Late-C19th hand-painted glass panel

PATTERNED GLASS

S O-CALLED PATTERNED GLASS *was made by passing it in a molten state between water-cooled rollers, one of which was embossed in order to press a texture on one side of the sheet. A notable feature of patterned glass is that it's impossible to see anything through it save for vague distorted images. Sometimes known as obscured glass, from Victorian times onwards it has been used in bathrooms, toilets and elsewhere to afford privacy.*

But it was not only its practical applications that appealed to the Victorians. They were also quick to recognize the aesthetic qualities of patterned glass. It was used extensively in door panels and fanlights; and in windows it was often employed in the form of marginal lights or as small decorative panes across the top of a sliding sash, thus providing a contrast to large panes of clear glass.

Even in the early twentieth century its popularity was such that literally hundreds of patterns were offered for sale. However, very few are stocked today, even by specialist glaziers, and the number of patterns available varies according to the whims of the market. The ones listed below are modern copies of original patterns that can be used as substitutes for old glass no longer produced.

Muffled and waterglass
Muffled glass, which closely resembles rippled water, was widely used in Victorian and Edwardian leaded lights. Fortunately, there is still a reasonable range of colours to choose from.

Waterglass is a modern glass similar to some old versions of muffled glass that are no longer manufactured. Several colours are available.

Cathedral
Cathedral, also known as 'German cathedral', is a subtly textured glass used for decorative leaded lights. 'Rolled cathedral' is a version that includes flecks and air bubbles.

You can buy a wide range of single-colour and 'streaky' (two-colour) cathedrals from specialist glass suppliers.

Muranese
A deep-textured machine-rolled glass, Muranese has a pattern resembling a crystal-line structure. The modern version is slightly smaller than its Victorian equivalent. As well as clear glass, you can buy a limited range of colours.

Reeded
Victorian and Edwardian glaziers employed the unremarkable texture of reeded glass to spectacular effect in leaded lights by arranging quarries (small panes of glass) in such a way that the flutes made a variety of linear patterns. However, it may be difficult to match using modern glass, which is generally made with comparatively wide flutes. It is only produced as clear glass.

Edwardian patterned-glass window

Rich combination of patterned glass

Muffled glass

Waterglass

Cathedral glass

Muranese glass

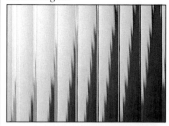
Reeded glass

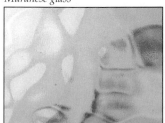
Flemish glass

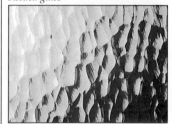
Hammered glass

Ice-crystal glass

LEADED LIGHTS

Detail from a 1930s door panel

THE TERM STAINED GLASS *is commonly used for any coloured window – but unless the window includes painted glass, strictly speaking it is a leaded light. This does not imply that leaded lights are inferior. The 'palette' of glass available to Victorian and Edwardian artisans was such that many a house is enriched with coloured windows and door panels that do not contain a single pane of painted glass.*

Leaded lights were all constructed in a similar way, the only real difference being the way the lead was incorporated. The leadwork for clear-glass windows is invariably constructed from straight cames only. But coloured glass arrests the eye and focuses attention on the dark lines created by the leadwork – so artists and craftsmen tended to form the lead into sinuous shapes, almost as if they were drawing with it.

Clear-glass leaded lights

Flemish
Another clear 'commercial' glass available from high-street glaziers. Our forebears could choose between 'big' and 'little' Flemish, but you will probably be offered only one size today.

Hammered
This Victorian textured glass is still available from good high-street glaziers. Its closely dimpled texture makes it look as if it has been struck repeatedly with a ball-peen hammer. Hammered glass is usually clear, but you may come across coloured versions.

Ice-crystal
Clear glass with a texture resembling crushed ice has been manufactured for decades under various names. The modern version has a relatively small-scale texture compared with some Victorian examples.

CUTTING AND FITTING PATTERNED GLASS
When cutting patterned glass, score the flat side (not the textured side).

For ease of cleaning, fit the glass with the textured surface facing the inside of the house.

A beautiful example of free-flowing linework and coloured glass

GLASS FOR LEADED LIGHTS

If you look closely at a decorative leaded light, you may be surprised to see just how many different types of glass have been used in a single window. Victorian stained-glass artists in particular had a vast range of both handmade and mass-produced glass to choose from. Although today the selection is much more limited, many of the original types of glass are still manufactured, so you stand a good chance of finding a similar pattern, colour or texture, if not an exact replica of the original glass.

Antique glass

Leaded lights were once commonly fashioned from handmade glass, either spun into a disc (crown glass) or formed into a large tube that was split lengthwise then opened to make a flat sheet (cylinder glass). Today, clear and coloured handmade 'antique' glass is still being produced, using precisely the same methods employed by our forebears. These traditional processes imbue the coloured varieties in particular with interesting characteristics not found in mass-produced glass.

Even clear glass can be bought as 'plain' (free from blemishes and of uniform thickness), 'reamy' (rippled due to variations in density) or 'seedy' (containing trapped air bubbles).

Coloured types (1) include 'pot colours' (strong even colour throughout), 'tints' (pale tones) and 'streaky' (two or more colours mixed in one sheet). Some colours, such as deep red or blue, are too dense to use as pot colours. Instead, they are applied as a thin layer over a sheet of clear or coloured glass. These are known as 'flashed' colours (2). Glass is flashed with pure gold to create dramatic pink or ruby hues. 'Opal' glass is made by flashing opaque white on clear glass. 'Opalescent' is opal glass mixed with at least one other colour to create a marbled appearance.

Rolled glass

As if the range of handmade glass was not sufficient, leaded-light artists availed themselves of the variety of patterns and textures created commercially in the form of machine-rolled glass.

Roundels

A roundel (3), or 'bullion', is a small disc of spun crown glass that includes the scar left at its centre by the glass blower's pontil. Roundels were, and still are, made specially for leaded lights.

Jewels

Jewels (4) are faceted square and circular pieces of glass that were set among flat quarries to catch and break up the light You can buy modern 'jewels' – but some professionals consider them to be inferior to nineteenth-century examples, which are sold at a premium whenever an old window is broken up for scrap.

A bold yet simple abstract design

Formalized fruit-bowl motif

Art Nouveau transom light incorporating a floral wreath and swags

CAMES

Each piece of glass in a leaded window is surrounded by H-section strips of lead known as cames (5). These are made either with a convex surface (round lead) or with a flat one (flat lead). Flat lead is the earlier type.

Because lead is a very soft metal, the cames are practically unmanageable until they have been stretched. This both straightens and work-hardens the came. It is done by holding one end in a vice and pulling the other end sharply with pliers.

Towards the end of the nineteenth century a new technique for joining glass quarries was developed in America by Louis Tiffany. A strip of copper foil was wrapped round the edges of each quarry. With the foiled quarries butted together, a bead of solder was run along both sides of the window to make a neat continuous joint. It is an ideal method for joining small pieces of glass However, the cost of restoring or remaking a copper-foiled window is likely to be higher than for a conventional leaded light.

Jewels and roundels

Round lead

Flat lead

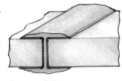
Copper foil

**Components of
a leaded light**
1 Coloured glass
2 Flashed glass
3 Roundel
4 Jewel
5 Cames
6 Soldered joint
7 Cement seal
8 Saddle bar

Loose wire ties
The solder breaks
from joints.
■ Replace the wire
   ties (page 131).

Cracked quarry
Slamming a door
or window can
crack the quarries.
■ Strap with lead
   (page 132).

Broken joint
Weak lead cracks
near joint.
■ Resolder joint
   (page 132).
▲ Have lead replaced
   (page 133).

Corroded lead
Lead becomes
brittle due to
pollution.
▲ Have lead replaced
   (page 133).

**Seriously
damaged panel**
Severe damage
can be caused by
a break-in.
▲ Have the panel
   professionally
   repaired (page 133).

Missing panel
Panel discarded or
sold by a previous
owner.
▲ Have replacement
   made (page 133).

SOLDER

The joints between lengths
of came are secured with
solder **(6)** made from 60 per
cent lead and 40 per cent tin.
Professionals tend to use gas
soldering irons to melt the
solder, but you may find
a thermostatically controlled
electric iron more convenient. Tallow, cast in stick
form, is the flux favoured
by professional stained-glass
artists and restorers.

CEMENT

To create a weatherproof
seal, a mixture of whiting
(powdered chalk), linseed oil
and turpentine known in the
trade as 'cement' is packed
into the gaps between the
glass and lead **(7)**. Vegetable
black or grate polish is included to colour the mixture.

You can buy ready-made
cement, in the form of a
special quick-setting putty,
but for a single repair it is
cheaper to use ordinary
glazier's putty mixed with
grate polish.

SADDLE BARS

Vulnerable leaded lights are
supported on the inside by
steel or iron rods, 6 to 9mm
(¼ to ⅜in) in diameter,
known as saddle bars **(8)**.
Copper-wire ties soldered to
strategic joints in the lead are
twisted round each bar to
secure the window.

If straight saddle bars
would spoil the appearance
of a leaded light, they can be
shaped to follow the line of
the leading. Alternatively,
steel inserts, known as lead
strengtheners, can be run
inside the cames.

**Dirty
glass and lead**
Airborne pollution
leaves deposits
on leadwork and
dirties the glass.
● Clean and polish
   (page 133).

Loose quarries
Brittle old cement
falls out. Quarries
rattle if you tap the
window with your
fingertips.
● Seal with fresh
   cement (page 131).

Broken quarry
A quarry may get
broken as a result
of an accident or
vandalism.
■ Replace the quarry
   (page 132).

Buckled panel
A buckled window
or door panel
can be caused by
slamming or wind
pressure.
■ Straighten panel
   (page 131).
■ Install saddle bar
   (page 131).

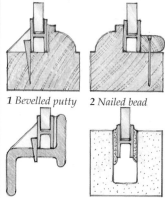

1 Bevelled putty *2 Nailed bead*

3 Lead peg *4 Grooved stone*

HOW LEADED LIGHTS WERE FITTED

Leaded lights were installed in the same way as ordinary window glass. The panel was bedded in linseed-oil putty and secured in the rebates with sprigs or tacks, then more putty was added and shaped to form a bevel all round **(1)**. When leaded lights were installed in sliding sashes, relatively large counterweights were required to counterbalance the weight of the lead.

Interior leaded lights were often secured with wooden beads screwed or nailed to the rebates **(2)**.

Lead pegs driven into holes in the frame held leaded lights in metal casements, and putty was used to fill the rebates **(3)**. If the leaded light has been repaired in the past, the pegs may have been cut off flush with the frame and the plugged lead used as fixing points for nails or tacks.

A leaded light fixed in a stone surround was located in grooves (or sometimes in rebates) cut in the masonry all round the opening **(4)**. Deep grooves allowed the panel to be slid into place then centralized. If the grooves were shallow, the lead flanges around the panel were bent back for fitting then straightened out into the grooves. Pointing with mortar made the joints surrounding the window waterproof.

REPAIRING LEADED LIGHTS

ALTHOUGH MINOR REPAIRS *to leaded lights can often be undertaken by a reasonably competent amateur, full-scale restoration requires the skills of a professional. Don't expect your high-street glazier to be able to restore stained glass. It is a craft that takes years of training and experience to perfect.*

Consequently, stained-glass artists are a relatively rare breed. When looking for a professional to work for you, it is therefore worth contacting associations such as the British Society of Master Glass Painters and the Guild of Master Craftsmen who can recommend experts practising in your part of the country.

You will find that most professionals have a port-folio of their work to show you. You should also ask to see an actual job in progress, in order to ascertain the quality of the detailing.

PLYWOOD SUPPORT   LEADED PANEL

1 Support a leaded panel on a piece of padded plywood

REMOVING A LEADED LIGHT

Try to disturb an old leaded light as little as possible. Careless repair work or clumsy handling may cause further damage, requiring expensive restoration.

Though some jobs can be done with the leaded light *in situ*, many repairs can only be tackled efficiently with the window laid flat on a bench.

If possible, take the whole casement or door off its hinges and lay it on a work-bench with the leaded panel supported from below by a piece of plywood cut to fit the opening **(1)**. If necessary, use wads of newspaper to raise the support slightly.

If the leaded light is in a fixed frame or surround, or has to be dismantled to facilitate a repair, you have no alternative but to remove it from the opening. Cut wire ties with pliers, then remove wooden beads or use an old chisel to chop out the putty holding the leaded

panel in place. If the putty is very hard, it is probably safer to soften it first with paint stripper (see RENEWING OLD PUTTY).

Remove any nail fixings, then run a blade all round the leaded panel to loosen it.

If necessary, use a sharp-ened paint scraper to gently lever out the panel, working from the other side of the window **(2)**. Insert the blade of the scraper as close as possible to joints in the lead, and work alternately on opposite sides of the frame.

Carry a leaded light on edge, keeping it as vertical as possible. If you cannot lay the panel flat on the bench immediately, rest it in an upright position against a wall and place a weight on the ground to prevent the bottom sliding outwards.

If a leaded light has to be removed for more than a day, as a security measure temporarily install ordinary glass in its place.

Specialized tools, glass and other materials are available from stained-glass suppliers, who advertise in trade or craft magazines and may be listed in Yellow Pages.

WHERE TO BUY TOOLS AND MATERIALS

Specialized tools, glass and other materials are available from stained-glass suppliers, who advertise in trade or craft magazines and may be listed in Yellow Pages.

2 Gently lever out the panel

WORKING SAFELY WITH LEADED LIGHTS

- You have to work with lead for relatively long periods before the metal presents a serious threat to your health. Nevertheless, it pays to wear barrier cream and to wash your hands thoroughly after handling it. Do not eat or prepare food in the workshop, and always work in a well-ventilated environment.
- Wear protective gloves when handling glass, and protect your eyes with safety goggles when you are cutting it.
- Be careful not to exert too much pressure on a leaded light – if the lead suddenly buckles, you may thrust your hand or arm right through the window.

RECEMENTING LOOSE QUARRIES

If glass quarries are loose because of damaged cames, you will need to have the window releaded. However, you are more likely to find that the quarries are rattling because expansion and contraction of the lead has caused brittle old cement to fall out.

There's no need to spend money on special cement for just one or two quarries. Instead, you can knead a ball of ordinary linseed-oil putty to a fairly stiff consistency (if need be, removing some of the oil by pressing it between newspaper) and mix in black grate polish until the putty is dark grey.

Use your thumbs to push the putty under the edges of the cames surrounding the loose quarries (1). You can do this with the window *in situ*, but don't forget to fill both sides.

Remove excess putty by running a pointed tool along the edges of the cames (2), then consolidate the putty by brushing in all directions with a bristle brush.

1 Push putty under the cames

2 Scrape off excess putty

FLATTENING A BUCKLED PANEL

The force generated by the repeated slamming of a door or window gradually bows the lead outwards, and even strong winds have been known to distort a large leaded light. If there are no other obvious signs of damage, it may be possible to straighten out a bowed or distorted panel – but consider first whether this is really desirable.

Slight buckling of the lead creates interesting reflections that add to the character of a window. Furthermore, it is not always possible to flatten a leaded light satis-factorily. If the lead has been buckled for some time, it may have become inflexible and brittle and will resist any attempt to straighten it out. This is often exacerbated by the sharp edges of the glass cutting into the inside of the cames as you attempt to move them.

Taking great care, try to push the cames back into position with the window in place. Wear thick protective gloves, and press very gently and evenly. If the glass does not flex, do not try to force it – remove the leaded light and leave it in the sun for a day with a weight such as a book carefully placed on the leadwork. Once the panel has been flattened, you may need to renew the cement.

Before reinstalling the panel, consider whether adding a saddle bar might prevent a recurrence of the bulging in future.

If the window already has a saddle bar, renew the wire ties (see right) before you put the panel back *in situ*.

INSTALLING A SADDLE BAR

Most movable windows and doors, and any fixed light that is over 600mm (2ft) in height, are likely to benefit from the addition of a saddle bar. It is therefore worth installing one when leaded lights are removed for repair. You may need to fit several bars if the panel is very large.

Select a position for the bar (or bars) that will not detract from the design of the window. Saddle bars usually look best running alongside a continuous horizontal came or a row of soldered joints. Mark the chosen position on the inside of the window frame.

The length of the saddle bar should be the width of the frame plus 12mm (½in) at each end (1).

Drill holes for the bar (2) on both sides of the window. One hole should be 12mm (½in) deep; the other should be 25mm (1in). The deeper hole will allow you to slide the bar into place then adjust its position until it is located at both ends.

Cut 75mm (3in) lengths of copper wire to serve as ties, and solder their centres to conveniently placed joints that will align with the bar (3). Space the ties as regularly as possible.

Install the leaded light and saddle bar, then wrap each tie around the bar and twist the ends of the wire together with pliers (4).

Cut off excess wire and fold the twisted tail under the bar. Apply putty all round the window on the outside (see REPLACING A BROKEN PANE).

If beads are used on the inside to secure the panel, notch them so they fit over the saddle bar.

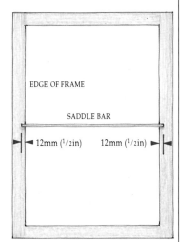

EDGE OF FRAME

SADDLE BAR

◀– 12mm (½in)　　12mm (½in) –▶

1 Allow extra on length of bar

2 Drill holes in the frame

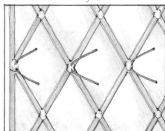

3 Solder wires to the joints

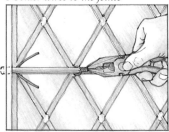

4 Twist wire ties with pliers

1 Score broken quarry

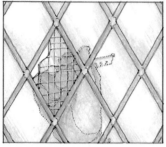

2 Tap the quarry to break the glass

3 Cut the joints with a knife

4 Bend back the lead flanges

5 Rub down the cames

REPLACING
A BROKEN QUARRY

If only one or two quarries are broken, provided the lead is in good condition you can replace them *in situ*.

Make a tracing of the broken quarry by drawing along the inner edge of the surrounding cames. This tracing will serve as a template for cutting the replacement glass.

Support the back of the window and, using a glass cutter, score what remains of the quarry with a series of crisscross lines **(1)**. Wearing protective gloves and safety goggles, tap the back of the glass in the middle of the quarry to break out most of the fragments **(2)**. Use a penknife to loosen small pieces of glass trapped in the cames, then scrape out the residue of old cement with a small screwdriver.

Cut the corner joints, on the inside only, with a stout craft knife **(3)**. Because you are cutting through solder, which is harder than lead, it is important to keep the knife blade at an angle that doesn't put sideways pressure on the leaded panel, making it buckle.

Use a small pair of pliers (ordinary engineer's pliers are too large), with the jaws padded with tape, to bend back the flanges all round **(4)**. Don't bend the flanges too far or they will crease, making it impossible to close them up neatly.

Select a piece of glass that matches the broken quarry and cut it to size (see CUTTING GLASS). The new piece should be 2mm (⅟₁₆in) larger all round than the tracing you made from the original quarry.

Insert the new glass and close up the cames, using a home-made tool known as a lathykin or larrikin. This is a round-pointed stick made from a piece of wood about 6mm (¼in) thick and 40mm (1½in) wide. Rub down the cames all round **(5)**, and make sure the corners are closed up neatly.

As this operation is performed on the inside of the window, it is not absolutely essential to resolder the joints. If you want to complete the job with solder, take the door or window off its hinges and lay it flat on the floor or workbench.

Seal the cames with cement (see RECEMENTING LOOSE QUARRIES). For at least the next week, close the door or window very gently.

STRAPPING
A CRACKED QUARRY

Strapping entails soldering a flat piece of lead over cracked glass, in effect creating a false came. Although individual quarries can be replaced, it is sometimes desirable to strap cracked glass, especially if it is rare and expensive. Strapping a narrow strip of glass in a border, for example, is relatively simple and the repair is hardly noticeable.

Shorten the blade of an ordinary paint scraper and sharpen it to make a lead-cutting knife. Use this knife to make a strap by slicing off one flat side of a came **(1)**.

Clean a section of came next to each end of the crack in the glass by scraping the lead with a blade. Lay the strap over the crack and solder one end to the edge of the came **(2)**. Pull the strap taut and cut off the other end flush with the opposite came **(3)**. Solder it, then repeat the process on the other side of the window and darken the lead with grate polish.

1 Slice a flat strap from a lead came

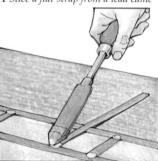

2 Solder one end of the strap

3 Cut strap flush with other came

REPAIRING
A BROKEN LEAD JOINT

When a soldered joint in a leaded light cracks, it is not normally the joint itself that breaks but the piece of lead next to the solder.

You can repair the joint with solder; but if it breaks again, it's a sure sign that the lead is weak and you should consider having the window releaded.

REPLACING CORRODED CAMES

Decades of airborne pollution can seriously weaken lead-work. It becomes brittle, and pieces gradually break away until whole sections of glass are in danger of falling out. If you have a window in this state, get a professional to remove it and take it away for releading. He or she will make a rubbing of the window as an exact guide to the layout of the cames. A full-size drawing called a 'cutline' is made from the rubbing, each line representing the position of the central web or 'heart' of each piece of leading.

The leaded light is carefully dismantled and each piece of glass laid out in the correct pattern. The old cement is then scraped from around the edges of the glass with a lead-cutting knife. Any damaged quarries are replaced at this stage.

The full-size drawing is laid on the bench and two wooden battens are nailed through it, one aligning with the bottom of the drawing, the other with the left-hand side. Starting with the corner formed by the battens, new lead is cut and the old glass refitted, using the drawing as a guide. Horseshoe nails are used to clamp the loose cames in place as, piece by piece, the panel is rebuilt.

When it is complete, the joints are cleaned with a wire brush, and tallow flux is wiped across each joint before soldering. Then the panel is turned over and the joints are soldered on the other side.

Using a small scrubbing brush, cement is brushed in all directions on both sides of the panel until the lead is sealed. Dry whiting is then sprinkled onto the panel to absorb excess oil.

About two hours later a pointed tool is used to remove cement from around the edges of the cames, then the panel is scrubbed again with a clean soft-bristle brush. After another two hours the lead is darkened with grate polish.

Jewel about to fall from brittle lead

RE-CREATING A BADLY DAMAGED PANEL

A badly damaged leaded light, perhaps one that has been smashed by a burglar, can be re-created exactly by a professional stained-glass artist. He or she will take critical measurements, note the types of glass used and make a rubbing of what's left of the leaded light.

If you happen to have another identical window, the artist can use that as a pattern for restoring badly damaged sections. Otherwise, he or she will have to deduce what the window looked like from the remaining fragments.

If the original window has been completely destroyed, then your only recourse is to find a restorer able to design a replacement (see below).

REPLACING A MISSING PANEL

You often come across clear-glass door panels and fanlights where a previous owner was not prepared to pay for the repair of leaded lights. If you want to have a new window made to the original style, you need to find a stained-glass artist with creative skills equal to his or her craftsmanship. Together, you can research the subject and may be able to track down an example in your neighbourhood to serve as a model.

If you can't find a suitable authentic pattern or original to copy, you will need to discuss with the artist the style of design you want and the types of glass to be used. The artist will then prepare a coloured drawing for your approval and will submit an estimate for making and fitting the window.

Make sure the artist gives you a date for starting the work and an estimate of how long the job will take. Also, any savings in cost or alterations to the design must be clearly agreed at this stage.

Each job is different, but normally you can expect to pay one-third of the fee in advance.

ENLARGING OR REDUCING A PANEL

Salvaged leaded lights and stained-glass panels bought from a dealer are unlikely to fit your window opening without modification. However, a professional may be able to enlarge a panel by adding sympathetic borders.

Reducing the size tends to be more difficult – so if a panel is too large, it may be necessary to keep the best parts only and have the surround redesigned to fit.

PROTECTING FINISHED WINDOWS

Rare painted windows in churches and other public buildings are sometimes protected with a sheet of clear polycarbonate. If you are thinking of protecting your glass in a similar way, consult a professional about the technical problems of sandwiching a sheet of plastic in the existing rebates. You may also want to check whether your window is valuable enough to warrant the extra expense.

CLEANING LEADED LIGHTS

Even if leaded lights are cleaned regularly, dirt tends to collect around the edges of each quarry. In addition, pollution affects the lead, which develops a white powdery deposit. Not only does this make the cames unsightly; rainwater and condensation tend to wash it onto the glass, too.

Unless the glass is etched or sandblasted, clean the cames with a soap-filled pad or with a small brass-wire brush (such as a suede brush) dipped in moistened scouring powder. Wipe the lead with a rag, then wash the glass carefully with warm soapy water.

Darken the cleaned lead with a touch of grate polish on a shoe brush. Brush across the cames, not along them. Grate polish will not adhere to clean glass, even if it is painted. It also polishes the glass. If the glass is dirty, you may need to wipe the polish off, using a rag dampened with white spirit.

STAINED & PAINTED GLASS

Glass painting *is one of the foremost skills in a tradition of craftsmanship in glass that is centuries old – but in terms of its use in relatively ordinary houses the Victorian era must surely rank as its heyday. At that time, an artisan's labour was so cheap that even the aspiring middle classes could afford exquisitely painted windows and door panels for their villas. Floral motifs and animals and birds were particularly fashionable themes, but a client could choose any subject from landscape to portraiture. Although the demand for true stained glass has declined steadily since the First World War, skilled glass painters practising today can restore or reproduce even the best of their predecessors' work.*

Birds and flowers have always been popular subjects

An exceptionally detailed autumnal scene

Bright luminous colours with the minimum of modelling

A landscape is the centrepiece of this circular door panel

REPRODUCING PAINTED GLASS

Developing the necessary skills for restoring stained glass is out of the question for the average amateur, especially if you only have to repair one or two pieces. Furthermore, the cost of the specialized brushes and vitreous paints needed (let alone a kiln in which to fire the glass) would almost certainly be higher than an expert's fee for restoring the glass. Nevertheless, it pays to familiarize yourself with glass-painting techniques so you are able to discuss the various options with a professional.

A skilled glass painter can reproduce damaged portions of a window, using broken fragments or undamaged areas of glass as a guide. If you need to re-create an entire stained-glass window, the painter will either copy a suitable existing example or design a new window for you that is in character with your house.

Tracing

The glass painter's first task, known as tracing, is to paint outlines and other linework onto each piece of glass, using dark pigments (either brown, green, red or black) thinned with various media and mixed with a binder that makes the paint adhere to the glass.

After tracing, most artists fire the glass to fuse the paint to the surface of the

The linework is traced with a fine brush

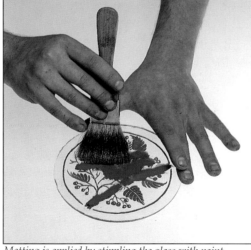

Matting is applied by stippling the glass with paint

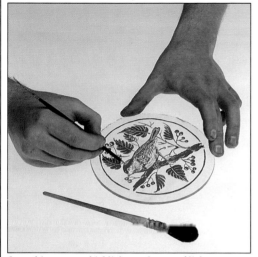

Scratching creates highlights and areas of light tone

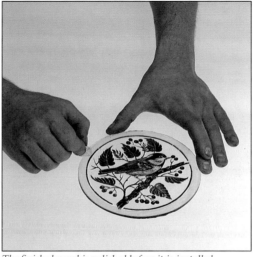

The finished panel is polished before it is installed

glass permanently. But some mix the pigments for subsequent layers of paint with a different medium that will not disturb the tracing, and delay firing till a later stage.

Matting
Areas of tone and modelling are applied to the painting using a process known as matting. An even layer of paint is brushed or stippled over the tracing. When it has dried, part of the paint is removed with a variety of brushes, pointed sticks and pens, creating areas of lighter tone and highlights. After firing, a second matt, possibly in another colour, can be applied over the first.

Colouring glass
Enamels are used to colour areas of glass and for painting details. These paints are opaque when applied, but become transparent when fired at a relatively low temperature. Considerable experience is required to determine the end result with any degree of certainty. Enamels are not as permanent as other vitreous paints.

Staining glass
A range of yellows, from pale lemon to a deep amber, can be achieved by staining glass with silver nitrate. Mixed with water, silver stain is milky in appearance when applied to the back of the glass. Firing causes the

stain to change colour and permeate the glass. Inexplicably, this single process has been responsible for the term 'stained glass' being used for the entire craft of making windows in coloured glass, despite the multiplicity of techniques involved.

Etching
Hydrofluoric acid is used to modify the colour of flashed glass. Depending on how long the glass is immersed in the acid, it is possible to grade tones or remove the coloured surface entirely. Hard edges are created by masking areas of colour, and acid can be painted on freehand in order to create a modelled effect.

AGEING THE APPEARANCE
Even though a stained-glass artist will attempt to match the glass, colours and style of a window exactly, a restored window may still look too 'new' when compared with an original. If the window is to be viewed from a distance, no one may ever notice the difference. But if it is to be fitted where it can be inspected closely (in a door, for example) then a stained-glass artist may decide to age its appearance artificially.

Metalling
Metalling is the term used by glass painters to describe the effect of overfiring silver stain – which acquires a darker, more opaque appearance as a result.

A painter normally strives to avoid metalling, but it may sometimes be the only way to match the colour of old stained glass.

Heavy matting
A heavy application of paint during the matting process can reproduce the mellow colours typical of ancient painted glass.

Etching the glass
Careful use of hydrofluoric acid dulls the glass slightly to mimic etching caused by long-term pollution.

Distressing the lead
If you want to simulate the distressed look of old leadwork, tap new cames here and there with the blade of a knife or screwdriver before colouring them with grate polish (see CLEANING LEADED LIGHTS).

ACID ETCHING & SANDBLASTING

ACID ETCHING (ALSO KNOWN AS EMBOSSING) imparts a matt-white 'frosted' texture to glass. By applying an acid-resistant mask to selected areas, it is possible to create patterns with alternating clear and textured glass. Very beautiful subtly toned etched images are made by repeating the process two or three times using different masks. Acid etching was developed towards the end of the eighteenth or early in the nineteenth century. But, apart from the types of mask or 'resist' used to protect the glass, the process remains virtually unchanged, and modern production methods can reproduce old embossed glass exactly.

Sandblasting, which was patented in 1870, is a comparatively new industrial process. Bombarding the surface of the glass with fine aluminium-oxide grit (sharp sand was used originally) leaves a texture similar in appearance to acid etching. Although it is possible to vary the texture by the depth of cut, sandblasting cannot reproduce the subtlety of two-tone or three-tone embossing. However, it is much cheaper, and only an expert eye can distinguish between sandblasting and single-tone etching.

Authentic Art Nouveau design

Overall patterns are still available

BUYING FROSTED GLASS FROM STOCK

Semi-obscured frosted glass was installed in Victorian and Edwardian bathroom windows, landing skylights, and doors of almost every conceivable kind.

Glazing with an overall repeat pattern, similar to wallpaper, was cheap and could be cut to fit any size or shape of window. Several original patterns are still made as stock sheet glass.

A frosted background provides maximum privacy, while a fine pattern etched on a clear background is the ideal form of glazing for conservatories and other areas where an unobscured view is required

You can buy antique-style frosted-glass transom lights and door panels from a good glazier. Only a limited range is available, but if you are fortunate you may be able to find an item that is an exact fit. Should that prove to be impossible, there are lights without borders designed to fit most locations.

Triple-etched Victorian door panel

INSTALLING FROSTED GLASS

Sandblasted and acid-etched textures attract dirt, which is why the textured face of a decorative window always faces inwards.

Mask the outer edges of the textured face to prevent linseed oil from fresh putty spreading and staining the frosted area. Brush washing-up liquid onto the outermost 50mm (2in) of the glass all round the panel (or rub a cake of soap onto it).

When the liquid becomes tacky, fit the panel in the normal way, taking care not to touch the textured face with oily fingertips. Leave the putty to dry for a couple of weeks before washing off the protective soap.

CLEANING FROSTED GLASS

A new replacement pane installed next to old frosted glass often looks too white by comparison. Clean the old glass with a soft-bristle brush dipped in undiluted household bleach. Rub the bleach into the texture with small circular brush strokes. After half an hour, repeat the process and then wash the window. You can remove specks of paint from frosted glass with chemical paint stripper, but don't touch the surface with an abrasive or a metal blade.

FINDING PROFESSIONALS

It isn't practicable for an amateur to reproduce an antique embossed or sandblasted window – not least because both processes are subject to strict health and safety regulations.

Sandblasting can only be performed inside a specially built enclosed cabinet, and hydrofluoric acid (the medium used by professional etchers) is so corrosive that it's never sold to the general public. A weaker acid paste is available in kit form for etching small items of glassware, but it is not really suitable for reproducing the majority of antique embossed windows.

Unless your local glazier is able to recommend a reliable firm, your best chance of finding professional acid etchers or sandblasters is to approach an association such as the Glass and Glazing Federation, the British Society of Master Glass Painters, or the Guild of Master Craftsmen. Alternatively, look through the advertisements in a good trade magazine.

REPLACING AN ACID-ETCHED WINDOW

If one of a pair of embossed door panels is broken, a professional acid etcher can make an exact reproduction of the surviving window. It may be possible to make a rubbing of the glass, but if the etching is too shallow a professional will have to trace the design, instead. At the same time, he or she will make a note of the different textures involved and measure the opening where the glass is to be installed.

Back at the workshop, the rubbing or tracing is converted into an accurate drawing before transferring the design to a sheet of glass. This is achieved by masking all areas that are to remain clear with a resist. Most professionals employ a form of screen printing to apply an acid-resistant coating, but simple shapes can be cut from self-adhesive film stuck to the glass. Areas to be etched are peeled off before the glass is immersed in acid. To create a second tone, acid-resistant paint is brushed over selected areas before the glass is returned to the acid. The etched glass is then washed thoroughly to remove the resist.

REPLACING A SANDBLASTED WINDOW

Sandblasted glass can be copied using methods similar to those employed for acid etching. However, sandblasted designs are hardly ever deep enough to be picked up as a rubbing, so it is usually necessary to make a tracing.

Provided the design is relatively simple, such as a numbered transom light, you can cut your own mechanical mask from the type of self-adhesive film used to cover kitchen shelves. As the textured surface always faces the inside of the house, remember to reverse your design so that it appears the right way round from outside. Having stuck the film to the glass, draw your design on it; then cut the film and peel it from areas you want to be textured. Rub down all the edges of the mask before taking the glass to be sandblasted.

If the window you want to reproduce has a very fine or complicated pattern, ask a professional to print a resist onto the glass and sandblast it for you.

BRILLIANT-CUT GLASS

BRILLIANT CUTTING, *a craft that was introduced to Britain from America in the middle of the nineteenth century, consists of grinding a pattern or motif into glass with a stone then polishing the cut until it sparkles. It is a highly skilled process that demands near-perfect hand and eye coordination, with little room for error. The effect is luxuriant, especially when deeply cut polished decoration is set off by matt-white acid etching.*

Brilliant cutting is often found in commercial premises such as banks, department stores and public houses. But, apart from the ubiquitous 'glory stars' that were set into the corners of thousands of doors and windows, it was seldom used in private homes except for those built on a relatively grand scale. In keeping with that type of house, brilliant cutting is frequently found in glazed doors leading from an entrance lobby into a hallway.

BEVELLED GLASS

Examples of bevelling (a poor relation of brilliant cutting) can be found in practically every home in the country. Until comparatively recently mirrors were almost always made with bevelled edges, the glass being ground to a shallow angle then polished since it was felt that they gave a mirror a 'finished' appearance. For the same reason, windows and leaded lights were invariably bevelled as part of the brilliant-cutting process.

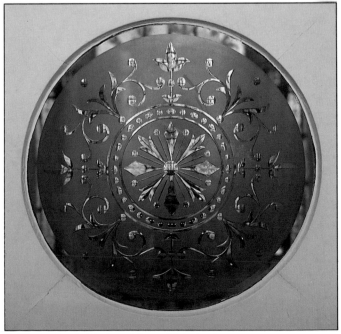

Brilliant-cut and etched panel from a Victorian door

Brilliant-cutting by hand in 1840

REPLACING GLORY STARS

Decorative marginal lights were often enhanced with corner panes of flashed ruby, blue or green glass featuring brilliant-cut star-shaped motifs. You can buy perfect reproductions inexpensively from most decorative-glass suppliers to replace missing or damaged originals.

Modern reproduction glory stars

REPLACING BRILLIANT-CUT WINDOWS

Brilliant-cut glass is not as vulnerable as some other forms of ornamental glass. It is too tough to wear out and usually too thick to break easily; and if it's mounted indoors, it will not be affected by atmospheric pollution. However, if a brilliant-cut window does get broken, unless you can find a suitable reproduction, you have no choice but to find a professional able to make a replacement.

Brilliant cutting was always done by hand and, although modern computer-controlled machines can cut very intricate patterns, they can't reproduce hand-cut glass exactly. The furniture trade relies on cutters and bevellers to reproduce old mirrors and glazed doors for display cabinets, and a good antique-furniture dealer will almost certainly be able to recommend a small firm who can copy hand-cut glass. A high-street glazier may also have contacts, but the price is likely to be lower if you deal with a brilliant cutter direct.

Copying the design

Take the broken glass to the cutter, who will tape the fragments together and make a rubbing of the decoration. This rubbing is laid under a sheet of plate glass, and the outline traced onto the glass with a felt-tip pen.

Cutting the glass

The sheet of glass is pressed against the edge of a vertically mounted sandstone wheel that revolves slowly. Straight lines and flowing curves are cut on the corner of a square-edged wheel (1), while round-edged wheels are employed for grinding hollows (2) and 'mitre' wheels for incising V-shaped grooves (3). The brilliant cutter may use any of these wheels in combination in order to follow the pen lines traced from the original window onto the new sheet of glass.

Polishing the cut

Grindstones leave a striated grey finish that has to be polished out of the glass in two stages. Traditionally the first stage of polishing was done on willow or elm wheels, but nowadays many cutters use a synthetic-rubber wheel, with pumice powder mixed with water as a polishing agent. The result is very attractive, though it is still matt and parts of the design may be left untouched after this first stage of polishing. But for the true brilliant-cut finish, a cork wheel is used with cerium-oxide powder to buff the cut until it's gleaming and the glass is clear.

BEVELLING

Today straight edges, and even simple curves, are usually ground by machines with built-in diamond-grit wheels and felt polishers. However, bevellers in the antique-restoration trade can still employ traditional methods when called for.

Hand bevelling is similar in principle to brilliant cutting, but larger, horizontally mounted stone wheels are used and the glass is ground on the sides of the wheels, not on the edges. The glass is shaped initially on a silicon-carbide wheel lubricated with water, followed by a sandstone wheel that smooths the bevel. A thick wooden wheel coated with pumice is used for the first stage of polishing, then the job is completed on a hard-felt wheel dressed with rouge.

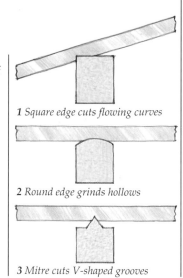

1 Square edge cuts flowing curves

2 Round edge grinds hollows

3 Mitre cuts V-shaped grooves

RESILVERING MIRRORS

Antique mirrors are often 'fogged' by damp that has penetrated the silvered backing. Resilvering an antique mirror may reduce its value; but if you want to restore a mirror so that it's usable, you can have the damaged silvering stripped and replaced. Glass bevellers frequently include resilvering as part of their service.

First, they strip off the old silver, using acid, and wash the glass thoroughly with distilled water. They then brush tinning solution onto the back of the mirror before spraying on silver nitrate. This is much faster than the traditional method of pouring it from a jug onto a sheet of glass supported on timber wedges. The wedges were then adjusted to control the flow of nitrate until it covered the back of the mirror.

The silver was once coated with varnish to protect it from damp, but nowadays it is sprayed with a copper solution then dried by being passed under a blower. Last of all paint is rolled onto the back of the mirror and any residue of silver washed from the face with acid.

CHAPTER TWELVE

PLASTERWORK

LINING THE INTERIOR WALLS *and especially the ceilings of a house with decorative plasterwork was a common practice even in ancient times, but in Britain it was not till the sixteenth or seventeenth century that plastering developed as the highly skilled craft we recognize today.*

The Georgian plasterwork of the eighteenth century was elegant, tasteful and, very often, classically inspired. All the features familiar today were employed, including the ceiling centrepiece, the moulded cornice masking the junction between wall and ceiling, the decorative frieze below the cornice, and strip mouldings delineating wall and ceiling panels.

In the Victorian period, especially after the introduction of mass-produced reinforced fibrous-plaster mouldings, plasterwork became ever more ornate. This new manufacturing process made it possible to prefabricate elaborate cornices, ceiling roses, overdoors and other mouldings that could be installed by general tradesmen, rather than calling for expensive specialist plasterers as in earlier times.

The First World War marked the end of decorative plasterwork in the average home. Fashionable taste dictated starker lines, the principal rooms of a house often being distinguished by nothing more than a simple cornice and, at most, a matching centrepiece.

Delicate mid-Victorian plaster centrepiece restored to perfect condition

Expertly painted and gilded ceiling with grapevine enrichments

Overdoors enhance a landing

Elaborate frieze upgrades a cornice

Cornice with modillions and rosettes

Highly ornate plaster corbels

THE STRUCTURE OF PLASTERWORK

Three-coat plaster *was trowelled directly onto solid masonry walls or applied to laths (wooden slats) nailed across wall studs or ceiling joists. The first coat was squeezed through the spaces between the laths so it spread out behind them to form keys that, when set, held the plaster in place.*

Prefabricated plasterboard became available towards the end of the First World War but was rarely used in houses until the late 1940s.

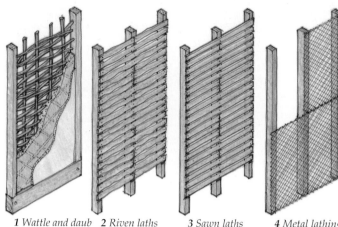

1 *Wattle and daub*　**2** *Riven laths*　**3** *Sawn laths*　**4** *Metal lathing*

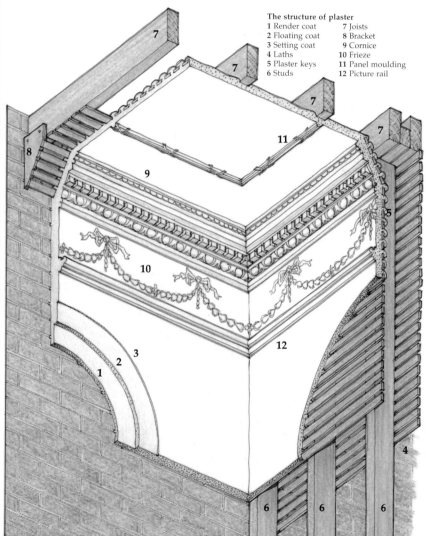

The structure of plaster

1 Render coat	7 Joists
2 Floating coat	8 Bracket
3 Setting coat	9 Cornice
4 Laths	10 Frieze
5 Plaster keys	11 Panel moulding
6 Studs	12 Picture rail

ASSESSING REPAIRS

● Easy even for beginners.
■ Fairly difficult. Good practical skills required.
▲ Difficult. Hire a professional.

Overpainted mouldings
Moulded plasterwork may become clogged with paint.
● Wash off distemper (page 142).
■ Remove paint with chemical stripper (page 142).

Damaged or missing mouldings
Mouldings may be damaged or missing due to neglect or modernization.
■ Run a new cornice (pages 146–8).
■ Cast and install new enrichments (page 148–9).
■ Fit new fibrous-plaster mouldings (pages 147, 149–50).

Sagging ceiling
Ceilings sag when nail fixings decay or plaster keys are damaged.
■ Screw back the detached laths (page 143).
■ Secure ceiling from above (page 143).

Delaminated setting coat
The setting coat may flake due to damp or poor adhesion.
■ Seal and replaster (page 145).

Stains
Dampness and pollution stain plasterwork.
● Seal stains before you decorate (page 141).

Holes in plaster
Damp or vibration can make patches of plaster fall from walls and ceilings.
■ Fill holes with fresh plaster (page 144).

Cracked plaster
Shrinkage causes cracks, most of them harmless.
■ Fill cracks before you decorate (page 143).

LATH-AND-PLASTER WALLS AND CEILINGS

Lath-and-plaster walls and ceilings are a development of wattle and daub **(1)**, the age-old practice of infilling timber-frame walls by smearing a mixture of lime, sand, straw and dung onto a lattice of interwoven hazel twigs and upright oak or willow slats.

The earliest laths **(2)** were riven (split by hand) from baulks of timber, which produced strips 3 to 6mm (⅛ to ¼in) thick and 25 to 35mm (1 to 1½in) wide. These were nailed to the structural timbers, leaving 'keyway' slots approximately 10mm (⅜in) wide between the slats. In order to stop cracks developing as the plaster dried out, the laths were staggered and the butt joints between them positioned over the wall studs or the ceiling joists.

In the 1820s machine-sawn laths **(3)** were introduced and increasingly became the norm. These had similar dimensions to hand-riven laths but were more regular.

Wire-mesh lathing was patented as early as 1797. However, expanded metal **(4)** was not widely employed as a plastering support until the end of the nineteenth century – and even after that a great many plasterers continued using the traditional wooden laths for at least another 30 or 40 years.

INGREDIENTS OF PLASTER

Up to the 1930s the normal practice was to apply plaster to walls and ceilings in three flat coats or layers.

First a 'render' coat about 8mm (⅜in) thick was trowelled on in order to grip the wall or ceiling securely, then the surface of the render coat was scored to create a key for the second layer.

The second or 'floating' coat, which was about 6mm (¼in) thick, provided an even surface for the final layer. Like the render coat, the floating coat was keyed in order to achieve more effective adhesion.

The last layer, known as the 'setting' coat, was about 3mm (⅛in) thick and was trowelled perfectly smooth to provide a suitable surface for decoration.

Traditional three-coat plaster was composed of lime and sand mixed with water. Animal hair was mixed into the first two coats in order to bind the material together. Quicklime (crushed limestone heated to a high temperature) was mixed with water on site and then left to slake (hydrate) for a minimum of three weeks. Thoroughly slaked lime, which had the consistency of soft butter, was known in the trade as lime putty. To make 'coarse stuff' for the render and floating coats, 1 part lime putty was mixed with 3 parts sharp plasterer's sand.

Pure lime putty was sometimes used for the setting coat. Alternatively, 3 parts putty was mixed with 2 parts fine sand.

Lime plaster took about three weeks to dry between each coat. This considerably delayed the completion of any building. Consequently, towards the end of the nineteenth century the practice

Early-C20th representation of a tradesman mixing plaster

of 'gauging' lime plaster by adding gypsum or cement was introduced in order to speed up the setting time.

Patching plaster

When repairing plasterwork, there are two important issues to consider. First, how to eradicate the cause of the deterioration of the plaster; and then what material to use for making the repairs.

If the plaster in need of repair is lime-based, then it is often best to replace it with the same type of material, particularly if the plaster is to be applied to the inner face of an external wall, from which it needs to exude moisture.

Lime putty can be bought ready-mixed with various grades of sand for use as a top-coat render, or mixed with sand and hair as a base-coat render. Lime render is easy to apply to the irregular surfaces found in many old houses. Wear goggles and gloves when working with lime plasters.

If you decide on a gauged lime plaster for the first two coats, mix 1 part gypsum (Class B hemihydrate plaster) with 1 part lime putty and 6 parts sand. For the setting coat, mix equal parts of gypsum and lime putty. You don't have to add animal hair to the mixture when patching small areas of old plaster.

BASIC REPAIRS & RESTORATION

H OUSE RESTORERS *are often, understandably, reluctant to tackle traditional plastering. However, cleaning and stripping or minor repairs to plasterwork do not require specialized skills and are well within the capability of most people.*

DEALING WITH SURFACE STAINS

Plaster can become stained for a variety of reasons. Dampness is a major cause of staining. As the moisture spreads, it tends to draw impurities to the surface of the plaster, where they create permanent stains that are evident even when the plaster dries out. Damp conditions may also lead to black mould or efflorescence (white crystals), which spoil the appearance of plastered walls and ceilings. Nicotine and airborne dust both cause widespread staining, while wood preservative seeping from an attic leaves the most stubborn stains. Always seal stained plaster before redecorating, otherwise the stains are likely to bleed through the paint.

Damp and nicotine stains

Locate and cure the source of damp, then let the plaster dry out before applying an aluminium spirit-based sealer to the affected area. Use the same sealer to prime a yellow nicotine-stained ceiling before redecorating it.

Preservative stains

When treating an attic for rot or insect attack, avoid flooding the ceiling with preservative. If it does soak through the ceiling, wait till it is dry then paint the stain with an aluminium wood primer before redecorating.

Efflorescence

This is the result of mineral salts from building materials being drawn to the surface by dampness, which must be eradicated before treating the condition. These same crystals can form on fresh plaster as it dries out.

Brush the crystals from the plaster with sacking or a stiff bristle brush. If you try to wash them off, the salts will be reabsorbed by the plaster and re-emerge when it dries. Keep removing efflorescence until crystals stop forming; then if you are planning to redecorate with an oil-based paint, seal the plaster with an alkali-resistant primer.

Mould

Black specks of mould can appear on damp plaster anywhere, but they often occur on ceilings below an inadequately insulated loft as a result of water vapour condensing on cold plasterwork. When this happens, since the mould tends to grow less vigorously on the comparatively warm and dry plaster directly below the joists, it may create pale stripes between the areas blackened by the mould.

The remedy is to brush a sterilizing solution of one part household bleach mixed with 16 parts water onto the ceiling (use a 1:10 solution if the mould growth is very heavy). It is advisable to wear goggles to protect your eyes. Four hours later scrape off the mould, then wash the ceiling again with sterilizing solution. Allow the plaster to dry naturally.

To stop mould recurring, think about how you can improve your heating, ventilation and insulation (see SURVEYING YOUR HOUSE).

STRIPPING PAINT FROM PLASTERWORK

Before modern emulsion paints were available, distemper was the preferred finish for plastered walls and, especially, ceilings. The friable nature of distemper, combined with the fact that it is soluble in water, makes it a very poor base for redecorating with modern paints or wallcoverings. You can bind distemper to plasterwork by painting over it with a proprietary stabilizing solution. But if layers of distemper have been applied to decorative plasterwork, the fine detail of the original may be almost obliterated. So should you strip all the paint back to the plaster finish? Before embarking on this tedious and time-consuming task, consider whether it will result in the loss of historic paint that could give clues to the original decorative scheme. It any case, it's worth working on a trial area in order to establish what method is suitable for the type of plaster.

Late-Victorian cornice all but obliterated by layers of old paint

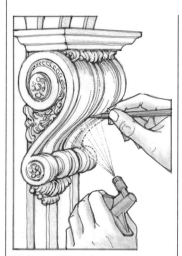

Pick out softened distemper

Removing distemper with water

You can sponge distemper from flat plasterwork with water containing a little proprietary wallpaper stripper. Cleaning decorative plaster takes greater care and effort.

Working on a small area at a time, moisten the distempered plaster with water from a plant spray and, as the paint softens, scrape it from the mouldings with an old toothbrush. You will have to pick thick distemper out of the deeper crevices with a sharpened stick. Finally, wash the plaster with clean water and apply a stabilizing solution to bind any traces of distemper.

Steam-cleaning plaster

Stripping a ceiling rose or an ornate cornice by hand with water is a laborious, back-breaking task. To save yourself several days of work on each room, you may be able to hire a specialist contractor to strip the distemper with steam. It is not easy to find professionals able to undertake this type of work safely and proficiently. Make sure they can protect the fabric of your house and collect the copious amounts of water generated by the process. A steam generator in unskilled or inexperienced hands can destroy irreplaceable plasterwork, so insist on references from recent customers.

Steam leaves plaster clean and crisp

1 Stipple stripper onto plasterwork

2 Peel away fibrous-tissue covering

Using a chemical stripper

Special ready-mixed paste strippers will remove any combination of distemper, emulsion and oil-based paints. Sheets of laminated plastic and fibrous tissue, supplied with the stripper, are used to cover the paste while it softens and absorbs the paint. If you can't face the prospect of stripping a ceiling yourself, there are specialists who will do the work for you.

When buying this type of stripper, check the details on the container to make sure it is suitable for use on plaster. Follow the manufacturer's safety recommendations carefully when handling these chemicals. Wear long plastic gloves taped to your sleeves and protect your eyes, face and hair from falling paint, dust and stripper.

Stipple the paste into the nooks and crannies of moulded plasterwork with an old paintbrush (1); then trowel it onto flat and convex surfaces, building up a layer of stripper 3 to 6mm (⅛ to ¼in) thick. Straightaway, lay the sheets (plastic side outward) over the pasted plaster and press each sheet into the stripper, rubbing the plastic gently in order to expel air bubbles.

Leave the sheets in place for 24 to 48 hours, during which time the stripper will emulsify the paint and draw it away from the plaster. Lift the edge of one of the sheets from time to time and, when all the layers of paint appear to have been absorbed into the fibrous tissue, peel away the sheets (2) and dispose of them carefully.

Wash the stripped plaster with water, using a scrubbing brush or sponge, then leave it to dry out for a few days.

1 Drag filler across crack

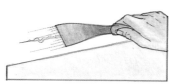

2 Then smooth it lengthwise

FILLING CRACKS

Hairline cracks in plaster are usually the result of shrinkage and require nothing more than filling followed by redecoration. However, wide cracks should be investigated to make sure that they are not a sign of serious structural movement.

With a masonry wall, probe the crack with a screwdriver or pencil to see if the damage extends farther than the depth of the plaster. If in doubt, chop out a small section of plaster on each side of the crack to determine whether the wall behind is affected. If you discover cracked masonry, get a surveyor to inspect it.

It is more difficult to tell with cracked plaster on a wooden loadbearing wall. If there are extensive cracks more than 3mm (⅛in) wide, have it inspected by a surveyor, unless the damage has an obvious cause such as a burst pipe.

Filling hairline cracks

Widen fine cracks by raking out loose material with the corner of a scraper. Moisten them with a paintbrush, then press plasterboard-joint filler or cellulose wall filler into the cracks. Drag the blade of a filling knife across the cracks (1), then smooth the filler by drawing the blade along them (2). When the filler has set, use medium-grade abrasive paper to sand it flush with the plaster.

Filling wider cracks

Use a bolster chisel to undercut the edges of a wide crack, then brush out loose debris. Thoroughly wet the crack, using a paintbrush, and fill with a proprietary wall filler, building it up gradually in layers until it is very slightly proud. Let the filler set hard, then sand it flush. Fill deep cracks almost completely with plaster of Paris, which sets quickly, then finish the repair with a sandable filler.

REFIXING A SAGGING CEILING

When the lath fixings fail, a lath-and-plaster ceiling will sag under its own weight (1), although the laths themselves provide some measure of reinforcement. If the plaster keys become detached or are broken due to damp conditions or physical damage (2), the unsupported plaster hangs free and the ceiling is likely to be in imminent danger of collapse. Go into the loft or lift a few floorboards in the room above, as appropriate, in order to inspect the ceiling and ascertain the most suitable course of action.

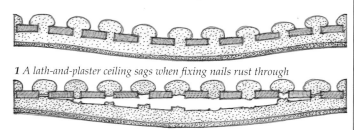

1 A lath-and-plaster ceiling sags when fixing nails rust through

2 Broken plaster keys leave a ceiling completely unsupported

Screwing back detached lath and plaster

Screw sagging lath and plaster to the joists with stainless-steel screws and washers. Vacuum debris from beneath the joists, then shore up the ceiling with several stout softwood props wedged between the ceiling and the floor below. Protect the plaster with plywood panels about 1m (3ft) square, placing a square of carpet underlay between the panels and the ceiling. Drill pilot holes through the lath and plaster into the joists, then twist a coin into the plaster to make depressions for the washers and screw heads. Insert the screws, remove the props and cover the screw heads with filler.

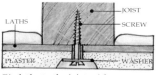

Fix laths to the joist with screws

Securing unsupported plaster

When the plaster has broken away from the laths, you can use lengths of stainless steel wire and washers to support a sagging ceiling. This method merely holds the plaster in place, instead of pulling it up against the joists. It accommodates a certain amount of flexing, and so may prevent loss of plaster from a fragile or valuable ceiling.

Drill holes through the plaster on each side of the joists and make depressions for washers as described left. Cut lengths of wire and bend one end over to 90 degrees. Pass the other end through a washer and then up through one of the holes into the void above. Pull the washer up against the plaster, then bind the other end of the wire over a narrow strip of perforated metal laid across the joists and screwed to the wood.

Another method, which makes the ceiling rigid but at the cost of adding weight, is to secure the plaster from above with a bonding agent. This is perhaps more suitable for an ordinary flat-plastered ceiling. Support the ceiling on stout props (see far left), and then paint the upper surface of the lath and plaster with diluted PVA bonding agent. Spread a 12mm (½in) deep layer of retarded plaster of

Paris (see RUNNING A PLAIN CORNICE) between each pair of joists above the damaged ceiling. Bed strips of jute-scrim reinforcement into the wet plaster (the strips need to be wide enough to span the space between the joists and turn up the sides). Trap the jute with battens screwed to the joists, then add a second layer of plaster before the first has set. Don't remove the props until the plaster is hard.

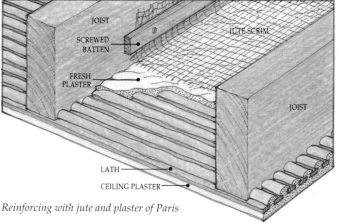

Reinforcing with jute and plaster of Paris

PATCHING HOLES IN GYPSUM PLASTER

To plaster a large expanse *of wall or ceiling successfully requires a skill that can only be developed with a great deal of experience. However, patching damaged plaster is not difficult, and satisfactory results are practically guaranteed with a modicum of practice.*

Before embarking on a repair, tap the wall or ceiling in the vicinity of the hole to check that the area of loose plaster does not extend too far. If it sounds 'hollow' over quite a wide area, get advice from a professional plasterer before you dislodge any more plaster.

The only specialized tools you need are a plasterer's steel trowel and a hawk – a small square sheet of wood or metal with a handle mounted beneath it, which is used for carrying the plaster to the wall or ceiling.

PATCHING HOLES OVER MASONRY

If plaster has broken away down to a masonry background, chop the loose plaster from the perimeter of the hole with a bolster chisel until you reach sound material.

Exterior walls

Before you start to patch plaster on the inside of a brick or stone exterior wall, find out what has caused the plaster to deteriorate in the first place. If the wall has been damp, make sure the problem has been resolved and that moisture within the wall has had plenty of time to dry out. Salts may migrate to the surface of the wall during the process of drying out, and if you replaster too soon the salts can spoil the new plaster surface.

Pick up some fresh plaster on your hawk, then tip the hawk towards you slightly so you can scoop plaster onto your trowel (1). Holding the trowel at a slight angle to the wall, spread the plaster on the masonry with a sweeping upward action (2). Cover the masonry to an even depth of about 8mm (⅜in) and, as the plaster begins to get firm, score it with shallow scratches (3) to form a key for the next coat.

Let the render coat set for about two hours, then apply the floating coat in the same way – but this time there is no need to add a waterproofer to the plaster. Build the coat almost flush with the surrounding plaster, then scrape it level with a length of wooden architrave or some similar straightedge (4). You will find a zigzag action works best. Fill in any hollows with fresh plaster, then scrape again. Once the floating coat begins to get firm, use the trowel to scrape the outermost 150mm (6in) or so of the new plaster, so that it is about 3mm (⅛in) lower than the edge of the old plaster around it (5).

Hammer some panel pins through a piece of softwood so that the points of the pins are just protruding. Using this improvised tool, key the floating coat with circular strokes (6).

About two hours later trowel on a setting coat of renovating finish plaster. It is easier to achieve an even

MIXING PLASTER

As a rough guide, you need to mix approximately equal proportions of clean water and dry powdered plaster.

Almost half-fill a plastic bucket with clean water and sprinkle plaster into it until the bucket is nearly full. Leave the plaster for a few minutes to absorb the water, then stir vigorously until it has a uniform creamy consistency. If you overstir the plaster, that will accelerate its setting time.

Plasterer's trowel   Hawk

thickness if you make two applications of plaster. Spread the first quite firmly (almost like buttering toast) to fill any hollows, then immediately apply more plaster, leaving it as smooth as possible and flush with the old plasterwork. When this coat is firm but has not yet set hard, dampen the trowel and use it to 'polish' the plaster. Holding the face of the tool at a very shallow angle, sweep the trowel in all directions across the patch (7).

Interior walls

You can patch dry interior walls in the same way. But use a Class B hemihydrate hardwall undercoat plaster for the render and floating coats, and a similar general-purpose finish plaster or a universal one-coat plaster for the setting coat. Seal the wall with a bonding agent – there is no need to add a waterproofer to the plaster.

1 Scoop plaster onto a trowel

2 Sweep plaster onto the wall

3 Key the render coat by scoring it

4 Level the floating coat

5 Scrape back the edge with a trowel

6 Lightly key the floating coat

7 Polish with circular strokes

CORNICE PATTERNS

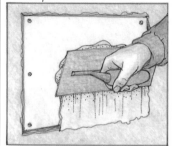

1 Screw plasterboard to studs

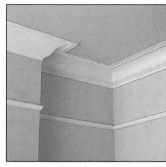

2 Finish with one-coat plaster

PATCHING HOLES IN LATH AND PLASTER

Chop away the plaster at the edge of the hole to reveal the nearest studs or joists at each side. Cut a plasterboard panel to fit the hole and fix it over the laths using plaster-board screws driven into the studs or joists (1). Paint the edge of the surrounding plaster with diluted bonding agent, then trowel on universal one-coat plaster to form a smooth flush surface (2).

REPAIRING DELAMINATED PLASTER

Areas of the setting can break away from a wall or ceiling even when the underlying plaster is perfectly sound. This may result from poor adhesion or from badly mixed plaster.

Provided that the plaster behind is sound and dry, scrape off any loose setting-coat plaster, then make sure the suction is consistent and stabilize the floating coat by painting on two coats of diluted PVA bonding agent.

While the second coat of bonding agent is still tacky, apply a fresh setting coat (see opposite page), using either a Class B hemihydrate gypsum finishing plaster or a universal one-coat plaster.

FROM THE EIGHTEENTH CENTURY *until the First World War no principal room would have been considered complete without a decorative cornice running around the edge of the ceiling. As a result, cornices are among the most common plaster features that house restorers have to contend with.*

Cornices can be categorized into two main groups – plain run and enriched mouldings. Plain run cornices rely on a combination of concave flutes, convex beads and square corners for their visual appeal. They were fashioned by plasterers who either ran metal templates through plaster in situ or created cornices on a bench and then fixed them in place at a later stage.

Basically, enriched cornices were run mouldings that incorporated flat areas to which separately cast decoration was applied in the form of continuous strips or individual brackets, rosettes and other motifs. With the invention of fibrous plasterwork, it became possible to design an elaborate ornamental cornice that was cast as one long piece.

Plain-run Edwardian cornice

Mid-C19th enriched cornice

Reproduction plaster cornices
1 Victorian-style enriched cornice
2 Deep cornice with modillions and rosettes
3 Georgian-pattern cornice
4 Dentil cornice
5 Plain-run cornice

1

2

3

4

5

Anthemion

Swags or festoons

Leaf and dart

Acanthus leaves

Greek-key design

Egg and dart

Bead and reel

Fluting

DECORATIVE MOTIFS

It is impossible to assign a specific date to motifs employed in decorative plasterwork, since many of them have been used in one form or another for centuries

However, Georgian enriched cornices were invariably based on classical orders. The Ionic dentil cornice, with its row of small square 'teeth', is a typical example; so are the decorative brackets known as modillions (often interspersed with paterae or rosettes) found on Corinthian cornices. Pictorial motifs such as the anthemion (stylized honeysuckle flower), elegant vases, human figures and festoons (better known as swags) were also favourite Georgian motifs. All these motifs are also found on Victorian cornices, along with deeply modelled fruit, flowers and foliage – but Victorian cornices are generally larger and more elaborate than the Georgian versions.

Other motifs commonly incorporated into cornices are egg and dart, leaf and dart, bead and reel, Greek key, fluting and acanthus leaves.

FRIEZES

Deep decorative panels or friezes were added on the wall below a cornice to make it more impressive. Similarly, narrow mouldings were often run or stuck on the ceiling to increase the visual width of a cornice.

Deeply modelled plaster frieze with Art Nouveau influence

RUNNING A PLAIN CORNICE

IF YOUR ORIGINAL CORNICE HAS BEEN REMOVED *and discarded, it is perhaps easiest to buy a suitable fibrous-plaster replacement. However if you have a badly damaged plain run cornice, or one with fairly simple enrichments, you can copy an intact fragment and make a reproduction of the original cornice.*

Only a skilled plasterer can run a cornice in situ, but an amateur who is prepared to accept a certain amount of trial and error before achieving satisfactory results should be capable of running a cornice on a bench for fixing in place once the plaster has set.

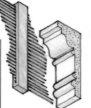
1 Profile gauge

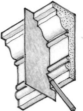
2 Card template

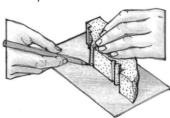
3 Draw round a plaster template

DUPLICATING THE PROFILE

To match a cornice accurately it is necessary to copy its profile and reproduce the shape in the form of a metal template. Professional plasterers refer to the process of copying the profile as 'taking a squeeze'. You may be able to use a DIY profile gauge, pressing its retractable steel pins against the moulding (**1**) – but you are unlikely to find a profile gauge that is large enough to accommodate the majority of cornices.

If you can saw a shallow slot in the cornice, insert a piece of card and trace around the moulding with a pencil (**2**).

Alternatively, coat a small section of cornice with a film of cooking oil, to act as a release agent, then coat it with a layer of plaster of Paris 50mm (2in) thick. When the plaster has set, ease it off the cornice and saw through it to produce a section that can be used for tracing the outline onto the template (**3**).

MAKING A RUNNING MOULD

Cut the template from a zinc sheet with tinsnips and shape it with files. Burnish the cut edge with a nail to remove any burrs, which would create striations in the plaster. Cut a thick plywood backing board roughly to the shape of the template and cut back the edge to about 45 degrees (**1**). Pin or screw the template to the board, then screw a baseboard onto the backing board and secure it with a triangular brace (**2**).

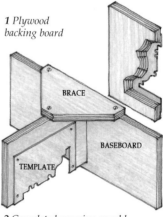
1 Plywood backing board

BRACE

BASEBOARD

TEMPLATE

2 Completed running mould

LINING THE BENCH

Make the running surface for your mould from a smooth melamine-faced board fixed to a workbench. The running surface must be kept flat, so a thick kitchen worktop is ideal. The baseboard needs to project sufficiently to run against the edge of your running surface (1). In order to reduce the weight of a wide cornice, build a melamine-faced backing board on your running surface and add a triangular wooden fillet (2), which should be coated with a film of cooking oil. Add to the mould a second triangular brace running along the top of the backing board.

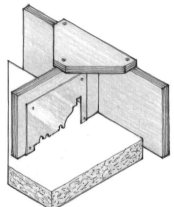

1 Baseboard runs against front edge

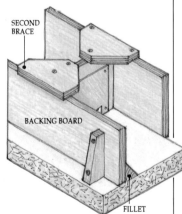

2 Running surface for wide cornice

RUNNING THE CORNICE

Sections of cornice approximately 3m (10ft) long are a convenient size to mould and install. You will find that plaster of Paris is the best material to use for running a cornice. Neat plaster is suitable for a smallish cornice, but since it sets in only a few minutes you may prefer to retard it slightly if you are moulding a cornice that is large or complex. One pinch of cream of tartar in half a bucket of plaster should give you plenty of time (though some plasterers prefer to add wallpaper size). After a little experimenting, you will discover how much retardant suits your particular speed of operation. Mix the plaster of Paris to the consistency of pourable cream.

It is best to have an assistant mix and pour the plaster, so that you can concentrate your attention on running the cornice and washing the template between passes.

To reinforce the cornice, place one or two laths on the running surface along the line of the moulding. Temporarily nail the laths at each end. Lay a strip of jute scrim dipped in plaster on top and rub it down so that it sticks to the laths.

Pour the first coat of plaster onto the running surface and make the first pass with the mould, keeping it firmly pressed against the front edge of the running surface (1). Straightaway, wash the remaining plaster from your mould in a bucket of water while your assistant pours another layer of plaster over the first. Then make another pass with the mould.

As the plaster begins to set, the shape of the casting starts to form rapidly. Continue adding more plaster to the hollows between passes until the cornice appears to be complete.

Once the plaster is firm, splash water along the cornice and make a pass without adding fresh plaster. This will skim the cornice as the plaster swells during the setting process. Repeat the process as often as necessary until the plaster is stable.

Remove minor blemishes from the set cornice with a scraper or chisel dipped in water. Fill any tiny holes or irregularities. After about 20 minutes, scrape off excess plaster left on the running surface on each side of the moulding (2) and remove the finished cornice.

1 Make a pass with running mould

2 Scrape off excess plaster

INSTALLING THE CORNICE

When installing lengths of plain run cornice to match an existing moulding that is still *in situ*, strip and clean what remains of the original and cut the ends square so you can butt the new cornice against them. (The procedure described here is also used when installing ready-made fibrous-plaster mouldings.) Before commencing work, you will need to erect a sturdy platform for you and an assistant to stand on.

Paint some PVA bonding agent, diluted following the manufacturer's instructions, along the junction between walls and ceiling to ensure that the suction is consistent. While it is drying, cut off a short section of cornice to use as a template for marking out guidelines.

Starting with the longest run of wall that is visible as you enter the room, hold the template in the corner so it fits snugly against the wall and the ceiling. Trace along the top and bottom of the cornice with a pencil (1), then repeat the procedure at the other end of the wall and join the marks by snapping a chalked string against the plaster. Continue in the same way around the room until you have marked every run, including the sides of any chimney breast or alcoves.

Using a tenon saw or a fine-tooth panel saw, cut the first length of cornice to fit between the two walls. With the help of your assistant, lift the moulding into position and transfer the ceiling guideline onto the front edge of the cornice at each end (2).

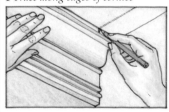

1 Trace along edges of cornice

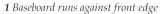

2 Transfer guideline to cornice

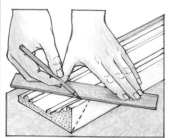

3 Mark compound mitre at each end

5 Then mark the corner itself

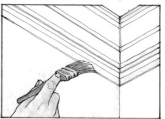

7 Clean off excess filler with a brush

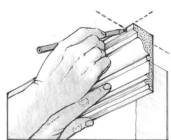

4 Mark ceiling line at a corner

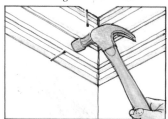

6 Support cornice on nails

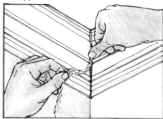

8 Fill wide gaps with jute scrim

CASTING ENRICHMENTS

MUCH OF THE ORNAMENTATION *that is found on cornices consists of individual castings glued in place with plaster. Even what appears to be continuous moulded decoration is often made from short sections of cast plaster butted end to end. The same can be said of elaborate early ceiling roses, which were in fact constructed from dozens of individual castings glued together on the ceiling. Damaged or missing enrichments of this sort can be replaced by taking castings from specimens that are still intact.*

Lay the cornice on its back and, using a straightedge, draw a line from the mark to the bottom corner (3). After doing this at both ends, cut along these lines to form a mitre joint. Irregularities can be filled after the cornice is installed. Repeat the whole procedure for the lengths of cornice on adjacent walls.

For external corners, cut the cornice a bit longer than required and mark on it the ceiling line (4) and corner of the wall (5). Join these marks across the face of the cornice and cut along this line.

On a very long wall, you will need to butt two lengths of cornice end to end.

Use diluted PVA bonding agent to seal the back of each section and plasterboard-joint filler to glue it in place. Spread the filler on the back of the first length of cornice, then lift it into position and press it against the wall and ceiling, squeezing out excess filler. The suction created will help to hold the cornice in place. Nevertheless, to keep it secure while the filler

is setting, it is best to drive galvanized nails or masonry pins through it at strategic points, carefully punching the nailheads below the surface of the plaster.

Alternatively, in order to avoid damaging a delicate moulding, drive nails into the wall and ceiling so they support the top and bottom edges of the cornice, then remove them once the filler has set (6). Very heavy cornices should be fixed with brass woodscrews driven into joists or wall studs.

Before the filler sets, use a damp brush to clean off any filler that has squeezed out around the edges (7); brushing the edges also helps fill any gaps between the cornice and the wall.

After fitting each length of cornice, fill any gaps and disguise all nailheads with joint filler. Fill wide gaps at corner joints with rolls of jute scrim dipped in joint filler (8). Use your finger to fill the joints flush, then smooth the filler with a damp cloth or paintbrush.

REMOVING AN ENRICHMENT

It is essential to strip paint from an enrichment in order to obtain a clean casting, so the newly made replicas will resemble the original enrichments still *in situ*.

Once all the paint has been removed, you should be able to insert the tip of a screwdriver or old chisel behind the selected enrichment and prise it carefully away from the plaster so you can make a mould on a bench.

Cornice with applied enrichments

MAKING A MOULD

Any number of individual enrichments can be cast from a custom-made flexible mould. Cold-cure silicone rubber is perhaps the easiest to use. Furthermore, if it is impossible to take down an enrichment without damaging it, you can buy a thixotropic additive that enables you to brush the silicone rubber onto the ceiling or wall. Admittedly, hot-melt mould-making compounds are cheaper, but they require very careful handling and you need a special melting pot in order to use them.

Construct a softwood box with a melamine-faced base to surround the enrichment, leaving a generous margin all round so that the mould will have strong walls. Stick the original to the base of the box with plaster and fill any

gaps to prevent moulding compound flowing beneath the casting. Spray the original with the sealer/release agent supplied as part of the moulding kit. Mix the cold-cure silicone rubber with its catalyst, following the manufacturer's instructions, then pour it slowly and steadily into the bottom of the box until the enrichment is covered completely. Leave the rubber to set overnight, then dismantle the box and peel off the flexible mould.

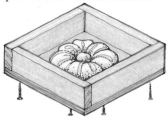

Make a softwood box with a base

FIBROUS PLASTER

1 *Level the plaster with a spatula*

2 *Score the plaster when it has set*

IT IS NOT DIFFICULT TO IMAGINE *the enthusiasm with which fibrous plaster was greeted when it was patented in 1856. For the first time it became possible to mass-produce u large, complex and detailed moulding as a comparatively lightweight single piece that could be fitted on site without special skills.*

Fibrous plaster was also relatively cheap to produce, and the range of standard castings was extensive. As a result, it was not long before decorative plasterwork was common even in fairly humble homes.

MAKING A CASTING
Lay the mould on a level bench and fill it to the brim with plaster of Paris. Tap the sides in order encourage air bubbles to rise to the surface. Draw a spatula across the mould to level up the plaster **(1)**. As soon as the plaster begins to get firm, score the surface to form a key **(2)**. After 10 minutes or so peel off the mould, which can be used immediately to cast further identical copies.

**INSTALLING
AN ENRICHMENT**
Use a pencil to mark the positions of the individual enrichments on the plaster, then key the spots where they are to be installed by scoring them with a pointed tool. Paint the scored plaster and the backs of the enrichments with slightly thinned PVA bonding agent.

Spread plasterboard-joint filler onto the back of each enrichment and press it into position, sliding it back and forth slightly to squeeze out excess filler. The suction thus created will grip the enrichment – nevertheless, it's best to hold it in place while you remove excess filler with a scraper and clean up with a damp paintbrush.

Fibrous-plaster reproductions
1 Oval centrepiece
2 Corbels
3 Wall plaque
4 Overdoor
5 Fluted pilaster with Ionic capital

FIBROUS-PLASTER MOULDINGS

Fibrous-plaster mouldings, made from ordinary plaster but reinforced with scrim and strips of wood, are still manufactured in the traditional way and are sometimes cast from original moulds. If plasterwork in your home has been removed or damaged, you can therefore take comfort from the fact that there is an enormous variety of authentic-looking fibrous-plaster mouldings available – ranging from the simplest coves to richly embellished combinations that include deep friezes and decorative ceiling plates.

Ceiling roses, for example, from which to hang pendant light fittings or chandeliers, range from elaborate centrepieces as much as 1350mm (4ft 6in) in diameter to plain discs a mere 200mm (8in) across. Most are circular, but it's possible to buy roses that are octagonal or elliptical. Unlike earlier ceiling roses, which were often made by plastering individual enrichments together on the ceiling, fibrous-plaster roses are manufactured in one piece and so are very much easier to install.

Strips of delicate plasterwork that can be combined with cast plaques and fancy corner mouldings are available for constructing wall or ceiling panels – which were considered vital for dividing up plain plaster surfaces into acceptable proportions.

In addition, there are more unusual items such as complete archway sections and ornate supporting brackets or corbels – and there is a huge selection of columns, pilasters and capitals, wall niches, overdoor mouldings, fire surrounds, and even classical urns and statues.

FITTING A CEILING ROSE

A central ceiling 'rose' made from plaster was a feature of practically every Victorian drawing room and parlour, from large country houses to modest terraced working-class cottages. The earliest ones were intended for use with gas lighting and provided a means of extracting unpleasant fumes: small holes that formed part of the moulded pattern led, via pipes, to an airbrick in an outside wall. However, the prime function of the ceiling rose was to act as a focal point or to enrich what would otherwise have been a plain ceiling. The procedure for fitting a ceiling rose involves the same methods as fitting any simple fibrous-plaster moulding.

Originally roses were often built up on the ceiling from separate enrichments

Accommodating an electrical fitting

Reproduction plaster centrepieces are often designed to house a light fitting. Sometimes there is just a circular recess at the centre of the rose that accommodates a standard plastic backplate and a screw-on cover. However, the more elaborate ceiling roses are made with decorative plaster bosses mounted on the plastic cover, concealing the whole fitting except for the flex, which hangs from a hole in the centre of the boss.

Always make sure that an electrical fitting is screwed securely to a ceiling joist – not just into the plaster rose. Unless you have the knowledge and experience to fit it yourself, get an electrician to install and wire the light fitting. The electricity supply must be switched off at the mains while you are fitting the ceiling rose itself.

Preparing the ceiling

If necessary, strip paper and paint from the area where the rose is to be fitted. Hold the rose against the ceiling in the required position and draw a circle round it with a pencil (1). Score the plaster within the circle and seal it with diluted PVA bonding agent. Treat the back of the rose in the same way.

Probe the plaster with a pointed tool to locate at least one joist within the circle. Mark the position of the joist with a pencil (2).

Fixing the rose

Orientate the rose so you can bore two holes through it to align with the centre of the joist, preferably within an area of pattern that disguises their presence. These holes are for brass woodscrews, which will need to be long enough to reach through the rose and ceiling plaster into the joist itself.

Spread plasterboard-joint filler or ceramic-tile adhesive on the back of the rose. Press the rose against the ceiling, moving it slightly from side to side to squeeze out excess adhesive and to align the screw-fixing holes with the joist. Insert the screws (3) and clean off the excess adhesive with a damp sponge or paintbrush, then cover the screwheads with filler.

1 Draw round the ceiling rose

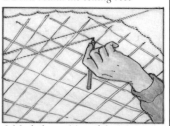

2 Mark the position of the joist

3 Screw through rose into joist

CHAPTER THIRTEEN

PAVING & WALL TILES

VIRTUALLY ALL THE EARLIEST FLOORS – *which were no more than rammed earth, frequently compounded with ashes and ox blood – have* long been covered over with riven-flagstone paving, square quarry tiles or brick-shaped paviours. Many of these surfaces have survived unaltered for hundreds of years, except that generations of footsteps have endowed them with a subtle patina of colour and texture. The majority of them are utilitarian floors found in kitchens, workshops and cellars – but with increased affluence, ostentatious or aesthetically minded house owners chose to have entrance halls, vestibules and

passageways laid with patterned floors constructed from coloured stone or marble slabs.

Ceramic tiles were used initially for flooring, and at a later date as wallcoverings. Glazed wall tiles (both plain and decorative) were particularly popular with the hygiene-conscious Victorians, and they have remained the most practical surface finish for bathrooms ever since.

In the recent past, tiled surfaces were not infrequently carpeted over or obliterated with paint. Being hard-wearing and durable, many of them will have survived relatively undamaged, only waiting for someone to rediscover and restore them.

Colourful paving is an asset that should be preserved at all costs

Exceptionally well-preserved Edwardian wall tiling and mosaic floor

PAVED FLOORING

ORIGINALLY PAVED FLOORING *was a luxury only the wealthy could afford. But from the late seventeenth or early eighteenth century, with increased affluence and the availability of cheaper materials, it was adopted by all strata of society.*

Stone paving, one of the costliest forms of flooring to lay today, was most often used in humble dwellings or in the service areas of more prosperous households.

Man-made tiles were equally practical, and with improved industrial processes quite ordinary home owners found they were able to afford elaborate floors composed of decorative ceramic tiles.

Attractive unfinished random-flagstone floor

Slate floors are often found in period kitchens

Quarry-tile floor in a Norfolk farmhouse

STONE PAVING

Sedimentary rocks that split easily along the planes of natural bedding or cleavage were ideal for making flag-stones, which could be anything from 25 to 100mm (1 to 4in) thick. Before the days of damp-proof courses, flagstones were laid over an earth floor on a bed of ash or coarse sand. As a result, porous limestone or sand-stone floors were invariably subject to rising damp in all but the driest conditions.

Slate, on the other hand, being impervious to water, was ideally suited to paving, and houses with slate floors were always comparatively dry. Originally it was only used for domestic paving in areas where there were slate quarries within easy reach. But in the nineteenth century, thanks to vastly improved transportation, slate became readily available to Victorian builders in all parts of the country. As a result, many of them used it for paving base-ments and cellars in larger houses, where it is still to be found in perfect condition.

Marble, whether imported or one of the native varieties, was used for effect in the more public areas of a house.

Marble slabs were laid with tight-fitting joints and set out with precision. Often they ran diagonally across a room or hallway, with contrasting colours employed to make a chequerboard pattern.

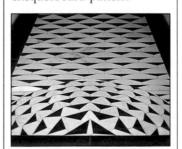

Early-C20th mixed-marble hallway

QUARRY TILES

Where stone was not a local commodity, our forebears tended to use quarry tiles when a hard-wearing floor was required. Traditionally made from yellow or brick-red kiln-fired clay, quarry tiles were normally unglazed and laid to a grid pattern.

Old quarry tiles were not as standardized as modern mass-produced ones. They were mostly larger, being up to 300mm (1ft) square and some 38mm (1½in) thick; but smaller square, octagonal and hexagonal tiles, which tended to be thinner, were also produced.

Manufacturer's floor-tile pattern

Medieval-style encaustic tile of 1845

Fully glazed Victorian encaustic tile

Interlocking patent mosaic tile

ENCAUSTIC TILES

The medieval practice of making inlaid clay floor tiles was lost with the dissolution of the monasteries in the sixteenth century. Hundreds of years later it was revived by Victorian tile makers inspired by the Gothic-revival movement, who developed mechanical methods for reproducing the designs that Cistercian monks had once made by hand.

A tile body, usually of soft red clay, was pressed into a mould that left an indented pattern. Once fired, the indentations were filled flush with slip (liquid clay) of different colours, then the tile was fired a second time.

Initially these unglazed tiles were manufactured for Victorian churches built in the fashionable neo-Gothic style and for paving other large-scale public buildings. But they were so striking and attractive in appearance that encaustic tiling was enthusiastically adopted for late-Victorian and Edwardian domestic use. As a result, there are still a great many houses that have encaustic paving in the entrance hall and corridors, frequently extending to conservatories and exterior pathways and patios. True encaustic tiles were sometimes mixed with simpler plain-coloured tiles of different sizes and shapes known as 'geometrics'. Laid with consummate skill and patience, these paved areas are one of the most delightful legacies from the Victorian era.

This encaustic-tile floor has retained its fresh colours since it was laid in 1869

An intricate late-Victorian pattern of geometrics and small encaustic tiles

MOSAICS

Mosaics composed of tiny coloured ceramic tesserae are also to be found on the floors of Victorian buildings, but are much less common in domestic interiors. They were painstakingly pieced together in factories where female workers pasted the tesserae one at a time onto a full-size drawing to build up the required design. When complete, the mosaic was cut into convenient pieces and transported to the house, or other building, for laying.

Typical of Victorian ingenuity were the 'patent mosaic tiles'. These were relatively large coloured floor tiles manufactured with deeply incised grooves. Once a complete area of tiling had been laid, the grooves were filled with cement to create the impression of genuine mosaic paving.

Patent mosaics pass for real tesserae

PRESERVING FLAGSTONE FLOORS

FLAGSTONES *are fairly large slabs of stone used to provide a hard-wearing floor. Most old stone floors have a mellow, rustic quality well worth preserving. They are an important period feature, and minor problems such as an irregular surface or a somewhat cold feel are a small price to pay for preserving such an attractive form of flooring.*

DEALING WITH WORN FLAGSTONES

Worn flags are an intrinsic feature of an old stone floor and, unless they are dangerous, should be accepted as part of the character of a house. If a stone has sunk unevenly, it may be sensible to lift and re-lay it. Similarly, a badly worn slab can be lifted, turned over and reset in mortar. When lifting out a slab, take care not to damage it or the surrounding stones with the levering tools.

CLEANING STONE FLOORS

Stone floors generally need nothing more than regular sweeping to keep them in good order. However, some stones are more porous than others and, particularly in work areas, may become heavily soiled.

Wash a lightly soiled stone floor with a bucket of water containing two tablespoons of washing soda. For a dirty waxed floor, use a cupful of soda and detergent to a bucket of water. Coat the whole floor first, then work back over it with a scrubbing brush before rinsing.

A tablespoon of caustic soda to 4.5 litres (8 pints) of water removes deep grease stains and heavy soiling. Rinse the floor thoroughly after scrubbing the surface. Protect your eyes and skin.

Treat organic growths such as mildew with dilute household bleach or a biocide.

For removing stains from marble, see FIREPLACES.

FINISHING STONE FLOORS

In most cases it is unnecessary to apply a surface finish or sealant to flagstones. In fact, some authorities advise against it on the grounds that it can create a dangerously slippery surface on impervious stones, and trap moisture in more porous ones, leading to structural breakdown.

However, polishes and sealants are available for finishing stone. These need to be applied to a dry, dust-free surface. Generally two even coats of sealant are recommended, applied with a radiator paint roller. Always follow the manufacturer's instructions carefully. To maintain the slight sheen produced by a sealant, you can apply wax polish from time to time. All finishes will darken and enrich the natural colour.

To bring out the colour of slate, apply a 1:4 mixture of linseed oil and white spirit, then wipe dry.

SAFETY

Handling stone flooring is hard and heavy work.
- Always wear gloves when handling stone slabs.
- Bend your knees and keep your back straight when lifting flagstones.
- Wear goggles and a mask when cutting stone, using a hammer and chisel or an angle grinder fitted with a stone-cutting disc.

New flagstones can coexist with old weathered paving

DEALING WITH DAMP

If a stone floor is damp, try to establish the underlying cause and determine whether other parts of the building have been affected. It may be that external ground levels are too high, or rainwater pipes may be leaking and soaking the ground.

Old stone floors were often laid directly upon bare earth, but with adequate ventilation any moisture that rose through the floor evaporated naturally. However, impervious floor-coverings can prevent evaporation, so try removing them and see whether the stone dries out – this may take some time. Similarly, modern impervious floor finishes and sealers can prevent natural evaporation.

Dampness in kitchens and laundries may be the result of condensation – in which case, better ventilation and heating may go some way towards solving the problem.

Lifting and re-laying an old stone floor with a new sub-floor that incorporates a damp-proof membrane (DPM) is not something to tackle yourself unless you have the relevant building experience. It is hard time-consuming work, and there is always a risk of driving the damp into the walls. Also, replacing old stone slabs may destroy historical evidence in the process.

CERAMIC FLOOR TILES

W HEN REPAIRING A TILED FLOOR, *take the damaged tile, or tile fragments, to the supplier so that you can buy a close match in size, colour and pattern.*

QUARRY TILES

Since quarry tiles are usually laid in a regular grid pattern, any replacement has to be an exact fit. However, old quarry tiles were made in a range of sizes and could be anything from 12 to 38mm (½ to 1½in) thick. Modern quarry tiles, on the other hand, are generally 12mm (½in) thick.

Should you need to make patch repairs to an old quarry-tile floor, you may find you have to pack out replacement tiles that are too thin with bedding mortar, or even cut back the sub-floor to accommodate ones that are too thick.

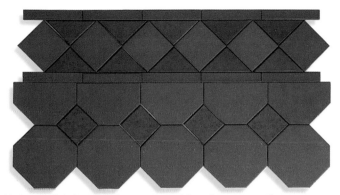

Victorian-style floors can be re-created with modern quarry tiles

Cutting quarry tiles

The thickness and hardness of quarry tiles makes them difficult to cut. You can score the surface and edges of a single tile with a tile cutter and give the back a sharp tap with a cross-peen hammer, but if you have to cut a number of tiles it is easier to hire a heavy-duty commercial tile-cutting jig.

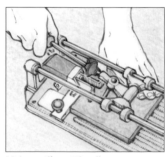

Using a tile-cutting jig

CLEANING TILES

Quarry tiles in good condition require practically no maintenance. To keep them clean, simply sweep the floor then wash the tiles with warm water and household detergent. After washing, rinse the surface of the floor with clean water and a sponge mop.

For ingrained heavy soiling, apply a proprietary tile cleaner, using plastic scouring pads or a hired scrubbing machine. Always follow the manufacturer's instructions and wear protective clothing when using these products.

Encaustic and geometric tiles have similar properties to unglazed quarry tiles, and so can be maintained in a similar way.

Reproduction encaustic tiles and small geometrics

ENCAUSTIC AND GEOMETRIC TILES

Encaustic tiles are still made by hand. Each tile is based on a moulded body, to which different coloured clays are painstakingly added to build up a polychromatic decorative pattern. After firing for 24 hours, the tiles are measured for accuracy then cut on a diamond wheel to precise dimensions.

Encaustic and geometric tiles are made to special order for restoration work. The reinstatement of a traditional floor takes great skill and is a job for a flooring specialist.

Special-purpose border tiles

Making repairs

Although very hard-wearing, both encaustic and geometric tiles frequently work loose. Fancy floors are particularly likely to have loose or missing tiles, since the small shaped tiles that make up the pattern do not bond so well. The close fit of the tiles helps keep them in place, but this should not be relied on since in time dirt and grit will build up under them. The edges exposed then get damaged, and small pieces may become dislodged and get lost.

Fixing the pieces

Carefully prise out loose pieces from the floor, using either the blade of a knife or a narrow scraper. If the paving is indoors, glue them back in place with a PVA bonding agent.

For an exterior repair or if a large patch has become detached, make a reference drawing of the pattern before you lift the loose pieces. Chisel away the old mortar to a depth of about 6mm (¼in). Vacuum the surface and dampen it with water. Apply a bed of cement-based flooring adhesive, then replace the tiles, tamping them down level with the surrounding surface. Once the adhesive has set, apply grouting to the patch if necessary.

Tamp tiles level with the surface

CERAMIC WALL TILES

Hand-painted Victorian porch tiles

DECORATED CERAMIC TILES, *especially those made in Victorian times and earlier, are highly prized by collectors, and considerable sums change hands even for individual examples. If this is a measure of their value, one can appreciate how important it is to preserve areas of tiling that are still intact. Happily, unless damaged by acts of deliberate vandalism or as a result of woeful ignorance, ceramic wall tiles are practically indestructible, and they also require very little maintenance.*

Dutch delftware overlaid with an English tile of 1750

Seventeenth-century Dutch polychrome delftware

DELFTWARE

Holland and Flanders had a thriving ceramic industry in the seventeenth century that exported tin-glazed earthenware, including handmade blue-and-white tiles, to all parts of Europe. At around that time, Dutch and Flemish potters set up workshops in England in order to manufacture these tiles, which became known as delftware after the most celebrated production centre of the day. Before long, English potters began to compete with the immigrant tile makers, copying typical Dutch designs depicting figures, animals, landscapes and birds. By the middle of the eighteenth century, English tile makers had cultivated a substantial market for their own wares and were confidently designing tiles that were much less dependent on the traditional Dutch themes.

Delftware tiles were made by cutting squares from clay that had been rolled flat like pastry. These blanks were fired in a kiln, then coated with a liquid glaze that dried leaving a powdery surface on the face of each tile. The design was freely painted onto the absorbent surface, then the tile was fired for a second time, which fused the colour into what became a hard, opaque white glaze. Blue or sometimes purple were the colours most often painted onto delftware, but yellow, green or orange were also used occasionally.

In England the success of delftware was short-lived, as the increasing popularity of other types of ceramic began to force a decline in the manufacture of tin-glazed pottery and tiles. By the turn of the century, not one delftware manufacturer was still in business in this country.

VICTORIAN WALL TILES

In the first quarter of the nineteenth century, tile production in Britain was virtually nonexistent. Initially Victorian manufacturers built their businesses on the production of encaustic floor tiles, and it was not until the 1860s and 1870s that they started to make decorated glazed wall tiles in earnest. However, towards the end of of the century the demand for tiles of every description was simply enormous, and the larger manufacturers exported their wares all over the world, including parts of Asia and America.

Glazed tiles were especially practical in kitchens and bathrooms, where washable surfaces were essential. Decorative tiles would often be used to form borders or to break up areas of cheaper white or plain-coloured tiles. It was not regarded as necessary, particularly in a bathroom, to tile entire walls. Very often ceramic tiling was restricted to the lower part of a wall, forming a dado, or was simply used to create splashbacks behind the bathtub and washbasin.

Tiled dadoes were a fairly common feature in blocks of flats, as well as public buildings, and exterior porches were often flanked with tiled panels that were sometimes decorated with painted landscapes or floral themes.

Sets of tiles that formed a design were also made for inserting in cast-iron fire grates (see TILED FIREPLACES) and were incorporated in washstands, coat racks, and other items of furniture.

New methods of production were required to meet the demand. Experiments in printing onto tiles had been fairly successful as early as 1756, when John Sadler

Transfer-printed tiles of c.1780

developed the process of transfer printing. An image incised into a wood block or engraved on a copper plate was transferred to the face of a tile by means of a soft-paper tissue. The printing on early tiles was vulnerable to wear, but the images on Victorian tiles were protected by a coat of transparent glaze. The basic design was normally printed in one colour, usually black or dark brown, and areas of colour were often added by hand.

An alternative method for mass-producing tiles was block printing, whereby simple areas of colour were transferred from a metal plate on which the image had been created in relief. Each colour used in a block-printed pattern required a separate plate.

Dust-pressing, invented in 1840, was yet another significant breakthrough in tile production. Slightly moist powdered clay was compressed between two metal dies, creating beautifully smooth, even tiles. It was a method ideally suited to the manufacture of embossed tiles, a shaped die being employed to create the same low-relief image on the face of each tile. Once fired, an embossed tile was either coated with a single glossy translucent glaze or parts of the image were picked out with different colours.

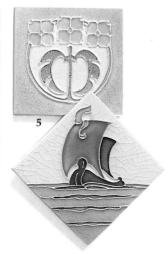

1 Block-printed tile made in 1880
2 Transfer-printed hand-coloured tile
3 Multicoloured block-printed tile
4 Art Nouveau embossed tile
5 Glazed wall tiles manufactured between 1930 and 1935

Fully tiled bathroom originating from the late 1930s

TWENTIETH-CENTURY WALL TILES

From the turn of the century, tile production continued unabated until the First World War. During that time the Art Nouveau movement had a notable effect on the tile-making industry, and many of the tiles, especially embossed ones, exhibit Art Nouveau influences.

In the 1920s and 1930s taste changed dramatically. Tiling became more austere, often comprising nothing more than a field of plain white tiles with a border of slim red, blue or black tiles. Fireplaces were still tiled, but gone were the ornamental side panels – instead, the whole surround was usually faced with mottled tiles in subdued colours. The last spark of the decorative tradition was kept alive by devotees of the Art Deco movement who designed colourful tiles, some of them embossed, that incorporated bold geometric shapes.

PRESERVING CERAMIC WALL TILES

WALL TILES, *like ceramic floor tiles, are very hard-wearing and need little maintenance. Although generally the same standard size as most floor tiles, they can be recognized by their thinner body and glazed finish. Tile glazes vary in thickness, and cleaning methods should take the thickness of the glaze into account. If the surface is crazed or you are unsure how thick the glazing is, seek expert advice before cleaning with strong chemicals.*

Victorian embossed tiles languishing beneath a coat of red paint

CLEANING WALL TILES

The glasslike surface of glazed wall tiles not only enhances their decorative effect but also makes them easy to clean. However, the ceramic body of wall tiles is not as impervious as that of most floor tiles. Care must therefore be taken, particularly if the glaze is crazed, that dirt is not absorbed into the tile during the cleaning process. It is best not to bleach tiles *in situ*, in case the stains are absorbed. But if you have unfixed tiles that need cleaning, you can soak them in water (preferably distilled) then apply dilute household bleach since presoaking the tiles will prevent dirt or stains being drawn into the ceramic body.

Tiled walls need to be cleaned regularly in order to maintain their surface finish. All that's usually needed is to wipe the surface with a damp cloth or sponge. If dirt has been allowed to build up, wash it off with a household washing-up liquid, or use a teaspoonful of washing soda in a bucket of warm water. Rinse the surface and wipe dry as you go.

For heavy soiling, use a proprietary tile cleaner and rinse the surface thoroughly. Tile cleaners are caustic and must be used with care, as they can cause some Victorian ruby lustre glazes or gold finishes to fade. When working with them,

wear rubber gloves and protect your eyes. Always try out cleaning agents on an inconspicuous area of tiling before you proceed with cleaning. Use a fibre scouring pad to remove stubborn deposits of dirt. In some cases a pad of very fine wire wool can be used on thick-glazed tiles, but generally it is advisable not to use abrasive materials and cleaners at all on glazed ceramic tiles. If you use wire wool, all traces of metal particles must be removed so rust staining doesn't occur.

Cleaning grout

Grout is a cementitious material that is used to fill and seal the joints between tiles. The appearance of a field of light-coloured tiles can be spoilt by old dirty grout. To refresh sound grout, apply a tile cleaner or household cream cleaner with a stiff nylon toothbrush, working along the joint lines. Rinse down thoroughly as you go. Mould growth can be treated with a solution of household bleach and hot water.

If grout is in a poor state, remove it and regrout the joints. Use a dental pick or suitable pointed tool. Control the tool carefully, so as not to damage the surface. Leave any part of the grouting that is in good condition intact. Brush and vacuum out all loose material, and then apply new matching grout.

Gently scrape off paint with scalpel

Removing paint

You may find that ceramic wall tiles have been splashed with paint, or even painted over entirely in an attempt to alter the character or colour scheme of the interior.

As a general rule, it's safer to use mechanical methods to remove paint rather than resort to chemical strippers. For example, it is possible to gently remove splashes of paint with a sharp scalpel.

However, if a sizeable area of tiling has been painted over, you have little choice but to use a water-washable stripper. Apply it following the maker's instructions and remove the softened paint with a wooden or plastic scraper. Wash off the residue with water, working a bristle brush into crevices, and then wipe the surface dry.

DRILLING TILED WALLS

When appliances or fixtures need to be fixed to a wall, try to avoid drilling into the face of old tiles – especially ones that are decorative or rare. If you do have to drill the wall, position the hole or holes on a joint line or corner whenever possible.

To prevent a masonry drill bit skidding on the face of a tile, before drilling mark the centre of the hole on the tile with a felt-tip pen and then stick a patch of clear adhesive tape over the mark. Run the drill at a slow speed and apply light pressure. Drill the hole to match the length of a suitably sized wall plug plus the thickness of the tile. Insert the plug into the hole fully, so when the screw is tightened the expansion of the plug will not fracture the glazed surface of the tile.

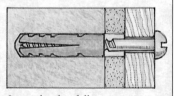

Insert the plug fully

REPLACING DAMAGED TILES

Having first removed the surrounding grout, carefully chisel out a cracked or broken tile with a narrow cold chisel and a club hammer, working from the centre. Chisel a recess into the background, then vacuum away all loose material.

Apply a wall-tile adhesive to the back of the replacement and press it into place. Allow the adhesive to set, then finish with matching grout.

CHAPTER FOURTEEN

WALL PANELLING

WOODEN WALL PANELLING, *sometimes known as wainscoting, was usually made from painted softwood when used for finishing the walls of the entrance hall and principal rooms in many of the better-class eighteenth-century houses. It was classical in style, influenced by the pattern books of the Renaissance architects, and used sophisticated frame-and-panel joinery.*

The use of wood panelling as an attractive and practical wall lining was not new, having been employed both for this purpose and as partitioning in much earlier times. This early panelling consisted of hand-wrought vertical planks that were either nailed in place or slotted into grooved studs or muntins and held by a sill and a head member. By the end of the fifteenth century a refinement in joinery techniques led to the development of Tudor frame-and-panel wainscoting. Although the style had declined by the close of the seventeenth century, it enjoyed something of a revival in the mid-Victorian period, when it was widely imitated.

Tongue-and-groove matchboarding was also used in the eighteenth century. It was simpler to make and install, and was more refined than earlier boarding of this type. It usually featured a bead moulding, and was most commonly found in provincial houses.

Elegant painted C18th wall panelling

Late-C19th Tudor-style oak panelling in an Arts and Crafts interior

TYPES OF PANELLING

T HE EARLY FRAME-AND-PANEL WAINSCOTING *was made from oak, using small plain panels set in a simple pegged mortise-and-tenon framework. The frame consisted of a top rail and bottom rail and a number of intermediate rails, all jointed into vertical stiles. Muntins (short vertical members) were jointed into the rails, usually spaced at equal intervals across the width of the frame. The inner edges of all the frame members were grooved to hold the panels without use of glue, so they were able to expand and contract freely without splitting.*

Traditionally the edges of the frame that surrounded and held the panels were shaped with a simple stuck moulding, which was cut by hand into the edge of the

wood, using a scratch stock. Where the moulding of the muntins met the edge of the rails, mitred corners had to be carved in the rails after the fashion of a mason's mitre joint.

The top edges of the intermediate rails were often finished with a stopped-chamfer detail. This detail was almost certainly influenced by masons' work too, as it recalls the sloping top face of a stone sill. Some panels were decorated with low-relief carving, the linenfold pattern being a typical design.

Tudor-style panelling has been widely copied. However, although later versions sometimes have handmade joints and mouldings, more often the mouldings are machined and the shoulders of the joints are scribed.

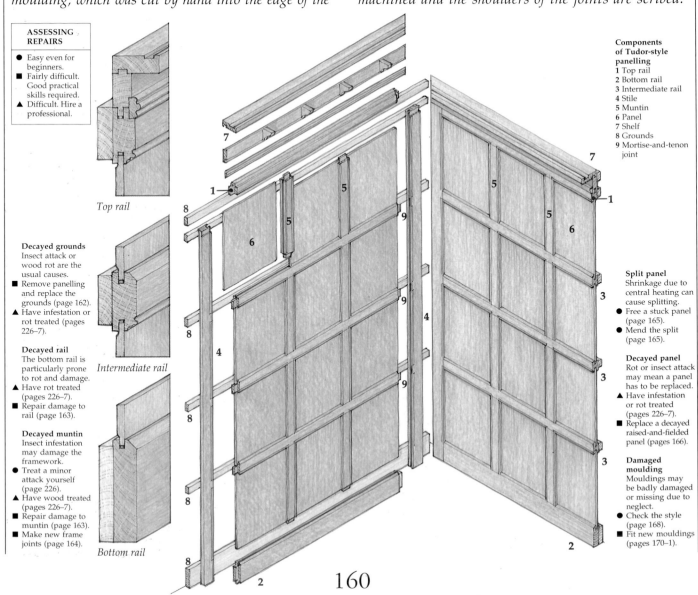

ASSESSING REPAIRS

- ● Easy even for beginners.
- ■ Fairly difficult. Good practical skills required.
- ▲ Difficult. Hire a professional.

Top rail

Decayed grounds
Insect attack or wood rot are the usual causes.
- ■ Remove panelling and replace the grounds (page 162).
- ▲ Have infestation or rot treated (pages 226–7).

Decayed rail
The bottom rail is particularly prone to rot and damage.
- ▲ Have rot treated (pages 226–7).
- ■ Repair damage to rail (page 163).

Intermediate rail

Decayed muntin
Insect infestation may damage the framework.
- ● Treat a minor attack yourself (page 226).
- ▲ Have wood treated (pages 226–7).
- ■ Repair damage to muntin (page 163).
- ■ Make new frame joints (page 164).

Bottom rail

Components of Tudor-style panelling
1 Top rail
2 Bottom rail
3 Intermediate rail
4 Stile
5 Muntin
6 Panel
7 Shelf
8 Grounds
9 Mortise-and-tenon joint

Split panel
Shrinkage due to central heating can cause splitting.
- ● Free a stuck panel (page 165).
- ● Mend the split (page 165).

Decayed panel
Rot or insect attack may mean a panel has to be replaced.
- ▲ Have infestation or rot treated (pages 226–7).
- ■ Replace a decayed raised-and-fielded panel (pages 166).

Damaged moulding
Mouldings may be badly damaged or missing due to neglect.
- ● Check the style (page 168).
- ■ Fit new mouldings (pages 170–1).

CLASSICAL INFLUENCES

By the late seventeenth century wider panels (known as wide-board panelling in America) had become fashionable, and their vertical dimensions reflected the proportions of the classical orders of architecture.

Solid oak was still in use, but increasingly pine was used for large and painted panelling. The panels were either plain or raised-and-fielded. The framing was worked with stuck moulding, or the joins between the panels and the frame might be finished with a planted or a bolection moulding.

Pilasters in the classical style were often used to add relief to a run of panelling or to serve as an architrave that hid the join between the stiles of meeting sets of panels.

This style of solid-wood panelling remained fashionable until the nineteenth century. However, only the owners of relatively grandiose houses could afford it, and painted plaster and wallpapers became more commonly used.

Classical orders influenced styles

THE PANELLING REVIVAL

Wall panelling was revived by members of the Arts and Crafts movement, whose influence continued into the early twentieth century.

Started by William Morris in England, the ideas of the movement were taken up with enthusiasm by Gustav Stickley and the Greene brothers, among others, in America.

The movement embraced artists, designers and architects whose aim was to return to the simple 'honest' styles of earlier times as a reaction against the excesses of mass-produced ornamentation. Well-executed, functional designs employing tradition-al methods and materials were the principles on which they based their work.

Natural oak was widely used both for panelling and furniture. The designs were deliberately plain, with only restrained decoration to complement the natural features of the wood. Arts and Crafts wall panelling tended to stop round about door or head height, often terminating with a shelf, the upper part of the wall being finished with painted plaster. This design was not adopted for purely aesthetic reasons: it also gave light to interiors that would other-wise have been gloomy in view of the dark wood and small windows favoured by architects working in the new style.

Although the aim of the Arts and Crafts movement was to keep the old craft skills alive, it did not halt the progress of mechanization. By the early twentieth cent-ury traditional panelling had become rare and machine-made plywood panels had taken over from solid wood.

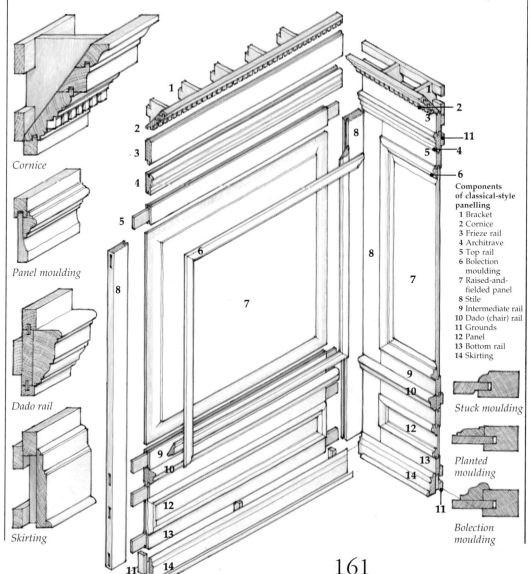

Cornice

Panel moulding

Dado rail

Skirting

Components of classical-style panelling
1 Bracket
2 Cornice
3 Frieze rail
4 Architrave
5 Top rail
6 Bolection moulding
7 Raised-and-fielded panel
8 Stile
9 Intermediate rail
10 Dado (chair) rail
11 Grounds
12 Panel
13 Bottom rail
14 Skirting

Stuck moulding

Planted moulding

Bolection moulding

DADOES

By Victorian times wainscoting generally only extended up to the chair-rail moulding, forming a dado. The moulding and dado protected the walls from being damaged by chair backs and general traffic. It also provided a visual division of the wall following classical principles. Dadoes were constructed using frame-and-panel methods or, in some cases, tongue-and-groove boarding.

By the mid nineteenth century the dado rail began to go out of fashion for main rooms, but it continued to be used as a finishing detail for embossed-paper dadoes in stairways and entrance halls. The last vestiges of the classical panelled wall were the picture rail and the skirting. Picture rails were a common feature of 1930s interiors, and skirting boards are still in use today.

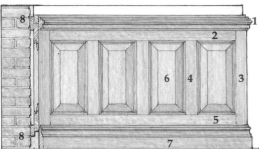

Components of a frame-and-panel dado
1 Dado rail
2 Top rail
3 Stile
4 Muntin
5 Bottom rail
6 Panel
7 Skirting
8 Grounds

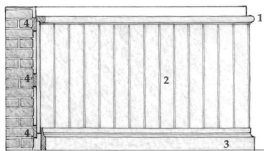

Components of a tongue-and-groove dado
1 Dado rail
2 Tongue-and-groove boarding
3 Skirting
4 Grounds

Oak raised-and-fielded panelled dado on a late-nineteenth-century staircase

HOW PANELLING IS FIXED

Wooden battens or 'grounds' are used for fixing panelling to brick or stone walls. The battens are levelled and nailed or screwed to plugs set in the wall. The fixings used to hold the panelling to the grounds are either discreetly placed or hidden by wooden pellets cut to match the grain of the wood, or they may be disguised with a coloured filler.

REMOVING PANELLING

It's worth making strenuous efforts to preserve original panelling – but only remove it from the wall for repair when absolutely necessary.

If you have to remove panelling to make a repair and your house is recorded as a listed building, you will first need to obtain consent from the relevant authority. If you think your house may be a listed building but are not certain, contact the Conservation Officer in your local planning office.

Seek out fixing points and remove them carefully. If you have to prise the frame from the wall, place the lever close to the fixing. Even if you exercise great care, you may find that the grounds to which the panelling is fixed pull away from the wall and need to be refixed.

The procedure for removing panelling should be the reverse of the way it was installed. Remove skirtings, dado rails and cornice mouldings first. These are usually nailed in place, but take care when dismantling them since some components may be fixed together with tongue-and-groove joints. Always try to make minor repairs *in situ*, since removing panels can create further damage.

PANELLED CEILINGS

The earliest ceilings were little more than the underside of the roof covering or the floorboards of the rooms above. Plaster was sometimes used to finish the underside of the boards, leaving the beams exposed – a common feature of many cottages over the centuries.

In the Tudor period the structural beams were decoratively carved, and wooden panels and mouldings were often used to fill the spaces between them. Eventually this developed into similar plaster forms. Tongue-and-groove boarding was also used as an infilling between the beams, and sometimes plain boards were fixed over the joists to provide a flat ceiling that could be painted. Frame-and-panel ceilings, made and fitted in a similar way to wall panelling, were employed for some interiors but were not as common.

By the late sixteenth century plaster had become the standard material for ceilings, although timber panelling saw a revival during the Victorian era and timber-boxed beams and strapwork (a grid of flat strips of wood) were used by architects of the Arts and Crafts movement.

Late interpretation of beamed ceiling

MAKING REPAIRS TO THE FRAME

Splits, chipped edges and general bruising and discoloration are normally regarded as part of the character of old panelling. However, where wood rot or insect attack has seriously weakened the framework, you may have no option but to remove the panelling and replace the infected timber.

Try to retain as much of the original panelling as possible. Before you begin work on repairs, take reference photographs of the panelling and make measured drawings of the components. Use a profile gauge to record the shape of the mouldings, and transfer it to your drawing in the form of full-size sections. Cut out the affected timber and make a new section to replace it. Make the new components from the same species of wood, with grain that closely matches the original.

The new wood will not, of course, be the correct colour – but you can tone it down with wood stain or bleach it, as appropriate. This is less important when dealing with painted panelling. Some argue that new work should not be disguised in any way. However, if the colour blends with the original, that helps maintain the harmony of the panelling as a whole, instead of drawing attention to the repair. Distressing the wood in order to age it is perhaps less justifiable.

Repairing a bottom rail

Support the panelling on a bench or trestles, depending on its size. Use lengths of wood spanning the trestles for extra support. The repair described here is for damage around the bottom rail, which is the most vulnerable area, but the method can be used for other parts of the panelling, too.

Carefully saw or router across the rail to remove the infected area back to sound wood (1). If there is a muntin tenoned into the part to be removed, carefully drive out or drill out any pegs holding the joint together. You can then knock the joint apart, using a hammer and a scrap of wood to take the blows. Should the joint be glued, soften the glue with steam from a kettle. A jet of steam from a flexible neoprene tube attached to the spout gives greater control. Wear protective gloves and take care not to scald yourself when working with steam.

Lap-joint the new wood into the old. First, cut the shoulder of the lap in the ends of the old wood at 45 degrees to the face of the rail (2). Cut the shoulder lines not less than 50mm (2in) from the ends, and stop at the groove. Then pare off the waste to this level.

Cut the new wood to size. Plane a groove in the top edge to match the old one. Chamfer or cut a matching moulding in the front edge. Shape the moulding with a scratch stock, multi-plane or power router, as appropriate. Cut away the back of the rail at each end to match the lap in the old material. Bevel the ends of the new lap to fit the angled shoulder already cut (3). If necessary, mark out and cut a mortise for a muntin tenon (4).

Try the new work for fit. If all is well, glue the lap joints and the mortise and tenon. Take care to keep the glue away from the panel, which must be free to move. If need be, remake or reuse the peg for the joint, drill a new hole for it and glue it in place.

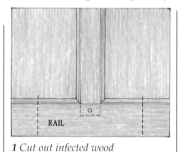

1 Cut out infected wood

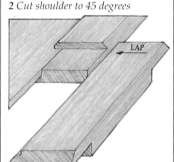

2 Cut shoulder to 45 degrees

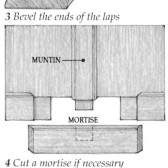

3 Bevel the ends of the laps

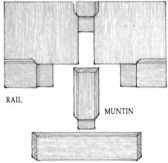

4 Cut a mortise if necessary

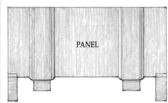

5 Repair muntin as for rail

Muntin repair

If the muntin members are damaged, proceed as for repairing the bottom rail (see left) then cut away the muntin and repair it with new wood lap-jointed into place (5).

Cut rail on outside of muntins

Panel repair

In order to take out a panel for repair, cut the bottom rail outside the muntins on each side, then remove the rail and slide out the panel. For how to make a replacement for a damaged raised-and-fielded panel that is beyond repair, see MAKING A RAISED-AND-FIELDED PANEL.

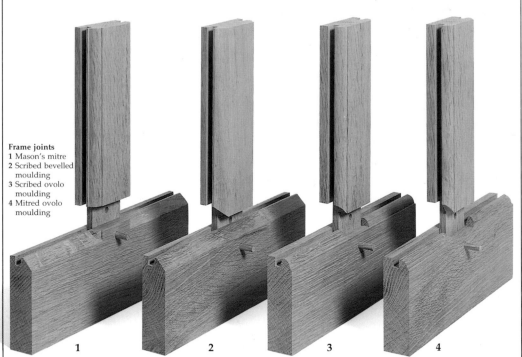

Frame joints
1 Mason's mitre
2 Scribed bevelled moulding
3 Scribed ovolo moulding
4 Mitred ovolo moulding

1   2   3   4

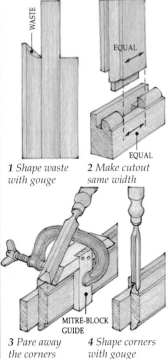

1 Shape waste with gouge   *2 Make cutout same width*

MITRE-BLOCK GUIDE

3 Pare away the corners   *4 Shape corners with gouge*

FRAME JOINTS
Traditionally the framework for panelling was constructed with hand-cut mortise-and-tenon joints – the top, bottom and intermediate rails being tenoned into the stiles, while the muntins are tenoned into the rails.

Although the basic principles of making the joint apply to all periods, the techniques for dealing with the mouldings vary. Early examples had the moulding stopped or run out, or were given the appearance of a mitred corner by the use of a mason's mitre.

Various methods for treating the moulding are shown, using a muntin-to-rail joint as an example.

MASON'S MITRE JOINT
This was a technique used by masons for carving a mitre in stone blocks where two mouldings met at an internal angle. Early joiners adopted the method, using a scratch stock and moulding planes and chisels.

To make this type of joint, run the moulding the length of the tenon member. On the mortise member you can't run the moulding through, so work the moulding with the scratch stock and stop close to the mortise. Using small chisels and carving gouges, carve the remaining 'corner' in the form of a mitre to meet the shape of the other member when the joint is assembled.

SCRIBED JOINTS
Joiners ran the moulding plane through on the edges of both workpieces, then scribed the shoulder of the tenon member to the reverse contour of the mortise member. This method gave the appearance of a mitred joint when two matching moulded edges, such as a bevel or an ovolo, met. It had the advantage over true mitred joints in that cross-grain shrinkage was less apparent.

The technique is still used today for moulded joinery, since the edges of the parts and the end-grain shoulders of the tenons can quickly and accurately be shaped by machine.

Bevelled moulding
To make this joint by hand, you have to cut a tenon member with one long and one short shoulder. The difference between the two shoulders is determined by the size of the moulding. A simple bevelled edge is shown above.

Plane the groove, cut the mortise, and form the bevel on the front edge of the mortise member. Groove the edges of the tenon member, then mark and cut the long-and-short shouldered tenon as required. Make the saw-cuts the same length **(1)**. Saw out the waste to match the bevel on the mating rail **(2)**.

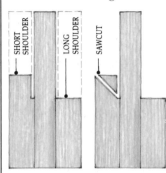

SHORT SHOULDER   LONG SHOULDER   SAWCUT

1 Tenon for bevelled-edge joint   *2 Saw out waste on short shoulder*

Ovolo moulding
This joint can be made in a similar fashion to a bevelled moulding, but you have to shape the bevelled shoulder of the tenon further, using an in-cannel gouge **(1)**.

However, an alternative method for making a moulding such as an ovolo is to cut away part of the moulding from the mortise member.

Make the width of the cutout the same width as the face of the tenon member **(2)**. Now, instead of shaping the full width of the short tenon shoulder, it only remains to pare away the corners of the moulding carefully.

To produce the required contour, first mitre the end of the moulding with the aid of a simple home-made mitre-block guide. Clamp the guide block to the work level with the long shoulder. Pare away the corner with a chisel to form a mitre **(3)**. Remove the guide block and, making vertical cuts with an in-cannel gouge, carefully pare away the wood in order to shape the corners, finishing on the line created by the mitre cut **(4)**.

REPAIRING PANELLING

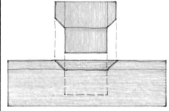

Mitre muntin and rail moulding

MITRED JOINTS

You can use mitred joints for mouldings with any kind of profile – including under-cut mouldings, for which a scribed joint cannot be used.

First, cut a long-and-short shouldered tenon. Then cut away the moulding on the mortise member to the width of the face of the tenon piece. Using the mitre block as a guide, pare away the corners of the moulding on the tenon member. Clamp the guide to the mortise member, and mitre the moulding in the same way.

MITRING APPLIED MOULDINGS

When mitred corners are to be used, make sure applied mouldings have a stable moisture content. If the wood should shrink after the mitres are made, they will open up on the inside of the corner (1); if it takes up moisture and expands, they open up on the outside (2).

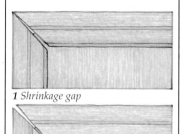

1 Shrinkage gap

2 Expansion gap

WOOD EXPANDS AND CONTRACTS *because of changing moisture conditions, the greatest movement taking place across the grain. The grain of the panels nearly always runs vertically; so, to allow for movement, more clearance is usually allowed in the side grooves of the frame than at the top and bottom. In order to keep the framework relatively light, it was necessary for the panels to be thin. This was not at all easy to achieve, since early panels were cut by hand and the edges had to be thinned down considerably to fit into the grooves in the framework. The thinning of the edges may be worked on the back, as with flat or sunken panels, or featured on the front to form a fielded panel.*

SPLIT PANELS

To allow for movement, solid-wood panels should never be fixed in their grooves. Nevertheless, distortion in the frame members or applied finishes can cause them to stick. Should a stuck panel shrink due to excessive drying out, it is likely to split. The decision then has to be made as to whether a split should be repaired or left as part of the panel's ageing character. Also, any repair must take account of the need for the wood to move. But, first of all, you need to try to free the panel in the groove.

Freeing a panel

Should a panel be held fast by a distorted frame, there is not much you can do to free it short of removing the entire assembly – a remedy that is hardly justified by the problem. However, usually the problem only arises if the wood shrinks drastically due to dry conditions, as caused by central heating.

If the panel is stuck with paint or varnish, carefully tap around the edge to try to free it. Don't strike the panel itself, but place a batten along the edge to protect the wood. Otherwise, try sliding a thin knife blade between the panel and the frame.

Dealing with splits

Splits in naturally finished show-wood panels can look quite acceptable. The split is likely to follow a weakness in the wood that relates to the grain (1). If the split runs

in from one edge and tapers off, it would be difficult to close up, anyway, and filling with a coloured stopper would not be acceptable.

In the case of a wide painted panel where a butt joint between two narrow boards has opened up, it may be visually desirable to close the 'split'. If the panel is free to move, clean the joint by scraping it with a narrow blade and work woodworking glue into the joint. Push the parts together with the palms of your hands (2), wearing rubber gloves to increase friction. Tape the joint while it sets.

Alternatively, use two narrow chisels to lever one part up to the other (3), protecting the frame with card. Wipe away any excess glue and, when it has set, fill the indentations in the wood before repainting.

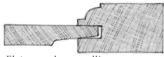

Flat or sunken panelling

Raised-and-fielded panelling

1 Split is likely to follow the grain

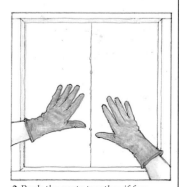

2 Push the parts together if free

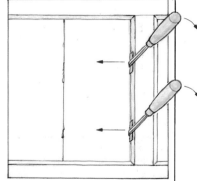

3 Carefully lever panel with chisels

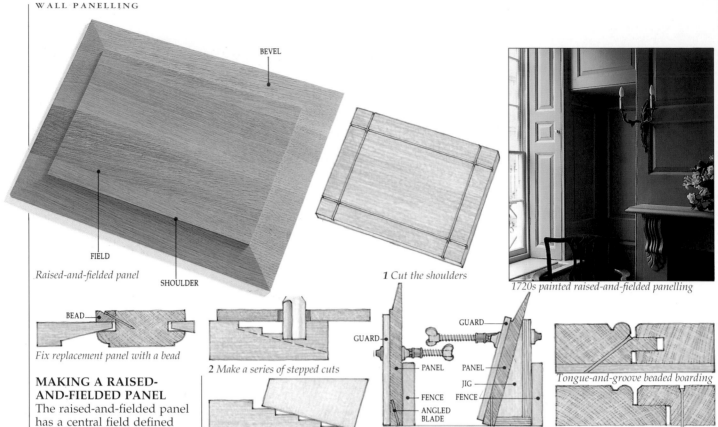

BEVEL

FIELD

SHOULDER

Raised-and-fielded panel

1 Cut the shoulders

1720s painted raised-and-fielded panelling

BEAD

Fix replacement panel with a bead

2 Make a series of stepped cuts

3 Use rebate plane to finish surface

GUARD

GUARD

PANEL

PANEL

JIG

FENCE

FENCE

ANGLED
BLADE

4 Always guard the saw blade

5 Use a jig on a non-tilting saw

Tongue-and-groove beaded boarding

Rebated beaded boarding

MAKING A RAISED-AND-FIELDED PANEL

The raised-and-fielded panel has a central field defined by a shallow raised shoulder combined with a bevelled border. If you have a panel of this type that is beyond repair (due to insect attack, for example), make a replacement to match the original.

The panelling will need to be removed and the frame dismantled to make replacement possible. Alternatively, particularly in the case of a middle panel, free the damaged panel by routing out the back of the groove in the frame. You can then drop the new panel into the resulting rebate and pin a bead behind the panel to secure it.

Preparing the wood

If possible, use the old panel as a pattern; if not, take the dimensions from adjacent panels. Select new wood that closely matches the original (take the old panel or a piece of it with you to your timber supplier) and have it machined to thickness. If you are unable to find wood that is wide enough, you can butt-joint pieces together. Leave the panel to acclimatize for several weeks in the room

where it is to be fitted. Hire a moisture meter to check the moisture content of the new wood against that of the old panelling.

Cut the panel to width and length. Then use a marking gauge to mark the width of the fielded border on the face of the panel and to mark the depth of the bevel all round the edge.

Cutting the bevel

Originally raised-and-fielded panels were shaped with purpose-made panel-raising planes. These wooden planes had the sole shaped to the contour of the border, with the blade set at a skew so that they cut cleanly across the grain at the ends of the panel. Although some craftsmen still use these planes, it is possible to shape the edge with a rebate plane, power router or table saw, or to use a combination of these.

First, cut the shoulders using a table saw or a power router (1). You can continue

to remove much of the waste in this way by resetting the depth of cut and making a series of steps (2). Use a rebate plane to finish the stepped surface (3). In order to save all the resetting, use the rebate plane by itself to shape the bevel

If you decide to cut the bevel on a table saw, use a stiff tungsten-carbide-tipped blade; if your table saw has a tilting facility, set it to the required angle and depth of cut. Clamp a piece of board to the face of the panel to act as a guard when cutting the bevel (4). If your saw table is non-tilting, make a jig to hold the work at the desired angle (5). Plane the sawn surface to finish it.

Finishing the panel

Sand all the faces with fine abrasive paper, then apply the finish to both sides. This will help to keep the panel stable. When it is thoroughly dry, install the panel in the framework.

BEADED WAINSCOTING

Beaded wainscoting is a form of panelling that uses either tongue-and-groove or rebated boarding. The boards are nailed into place along one edge, the beaded side being held by the fixed edge of the adjacent board. In this way each board is free to move. The moulded bead forms a definite visual break that helps mask the variable gaps at the joints.

Replacing a damaged board

Beaded wainscoting is still a popular wall finish and is available from most timber suppliers. However, you can't be sure that a modern pattern will match an old one exactly. If you need to replace a few boards, you can have them made to order or make them yourself.

Have new boards machined to the required size by your supplier. Use a power router or combination plane to tongue and groove the edges. Cut the bead moulding with a scratch stock.

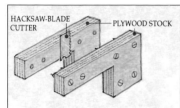

HACKSAW-BLADE CUTTER   PLYWOOD STOCK

HOW TO MAKE A SCRATCH STOCK

This is a simple home-made tool used for shaping small mouldings or parts of larger mouldings.

Make the stock of the tool from two L-shaped pieces cut from 150 x 75 x 18mm (6 x 3 x ¾in) plywood. Fix them together with 32mm (1¼in) countersunk screws. Fashion the cutter from a piece of old hacksaw blade. This is made of very hard steel and can be snapped to length. File the reverse shape of the bead profile in the end of the cutter blade. Clamp the cutter between the stock pieces at the desired setting.

To shape the moulding, hold the shoulder of the scratch stock firmly against the edge and push the tool away from you, working the tool with even strokes.

Work the tool with even strokes

MAINTAINING A WOODEN CEILING

Little maintenance is needed for sound wooden ceilings other than general cleaning, preservative treatment and, if appropriate, repainting. Exposed oak beams should not be stained black, as there is no historical precedent for this. Painted woodwork that would originally have been a natural colour should be chemically stripped (see STRIPPING DOORS) and either left unfinished or waxed.

FINISHING THE REPAIR

Unless you plan to strip the entire wall of its finish, you will need to use a compatible finish for your repair so as to preserve the original patina.

Oil-based resin varnishes were introduced early in the sixteenth century and are to be found on panelling of the period, although they may have been applied at a later date.

By the early nineteenth century spirit-based shellac polishes were available, but by this time paint (which was in effect a pigmented varnish) had become the fashionable finish for wood panelling. If you are lucky enough to discover panelling finished with early casein (milk-based) paint, it should be preserved.

Testing the finish

To determine which finish to use, test a small unobtrusive area of panelling. Clean dirt and wax polish from the surface, using a cotton cloth dampened with a solution of 4 parts spirit to 1 part linseed oil. Next, wipe the surface with a cloth dampened with methylated spirit, which is the solvent of shellac. If the finish softens and can be wiped off, then it is spirit-based shellac. Oil-based varnishes and paints will not react to meths in this way – and white spirit, which is their solvent, won't redissolve them.

If you are aiming for total authenticity, have a slice of the finish analysed by an expert to establish its type and date. A national or local conservation organization will tell you who to contact for this specialist service.

Preparing the new wood

To prepare the new wood for a natural finish, you will

Wax polish gives natural-wood panelling a subtle sheen

need to stain it to tone down its colour.

Water-based stains are simple to apply, and wipe off easily if the colour proves to be too strong; however, they may raise the grain. Spirit-based stains do not raise the grain; but they dry rapidly, so they are difficult to apply evenly. Oil-based stains are thinned with white spirit. They are easy to apply and will not affect the grain, but they may bleed into an oil-based varnish.

You can buy stains in a variety of common wood shades. To test the colour of a stain, apply it to offcuts of the wood used for the repair. Dilute the stain if necessary; or for darker shades apply extra coats. Different colours can be obtained by mixing stains of the same type. When dry, apply a wax or varnish finish to evaluate the darkening effect it has on the colour. Modify the stain accordingly.

When you have achieved a match with the original material, proceed to colour and finish the repair. Make sure the stain is dry before applying the finish.

Wax finish

For a wax finish, prepare the newly stained wood with a coat of clear sanding sealer. This prevents the first coat of polish sinking in excessively. A range of ready-prepared traditional wax polishes is available. Apply two or three coats of polish, using a pad of fine wire wool or a cloth. Allow each coat to dry, then buff with a soft cloth.

Varnish finish

Newly applied varnish can never match the worn patina of an old finish, nor will it have the subtle character of a wax finish. However, if you are trying to match an old varnish finish, use a compatible oil-based varnish (never a modern polyurethane one).

Apply an oil varnish with a brush, laying the finish on evenly in thin coats. Let each coat dry, and rub down with fine silicon-carbide paper between coats.

After varnishing, apply a wax polish on a pad of fine wire wool.

Paint finish

Colour matching is never easy, and matching old paint can be particularly difficult. If you think your interior finish is original, discuss the work with a specialist or an adviser from a historical society before embarking on any repairs.

ARCHITECTURAL MOULDINGS

MOULDED SKIRTINGS, *dado rails, picture rails and cornices play an important part in creating the attractive character of an old house, and deserve to be preserved or reinstated if they have been removed. Although their use may have been primarily functional, they were also employed to give balance and enrichment to the wall surface to which they were applied.*

Traditional wooden moulding planes

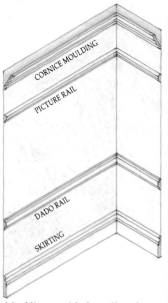
Mouldings enrich the wall surface

Stuck moulding

Applied moulding

Wooden interior mouldings
1 Victorian-style skirting
2 Torus skirting
3 Cornice mouldings
4 Straight-run dado rail
5 Carved-type dado rails
6 Small straight-run dado rail
7 Small carved-type dado rail
8 Astragal panel moulding
9 Picture rail

Wooden interior mouldings

Mouldings are produced by making a series of shaped parallel cuts that combine to give a contoured form to the edge or face of a workpiece. There are two types: either the moulding is worked directly into the component, in which case it is known as a stuck moulding, or it can take the form of an applied moulding (a moulded length of wood that has to be fixed to the background).

Most wooden mouldings are intended to be painted and are therefore made from an inexpensive softwood. Nevertheless, good-quality selected timber is used, in order to avoid knots that are difficult to cut. Before the woodworking trade became mechanized, all mouldings were laboriously fashioned by hand using moulding planes. Each one needed an individual size or shape of plane, and some required the use of several special planes.

Early interior mouldings were relatively simple and were worked in vernacular styles by local craftsmen. But from the early seventeenth century mouldings began to be influenced by classical styles, and by the eighteenth century wooden mouldings inspired by Roman and Greek architecture were the standard forms.

The Roman versions were rather heavier in style than the Greek ones – the former being based on segments of a circle, while the latter were based on elliptical curves.

Skirtings

Skirtings or baseboards are used to line, or 'skirt', the base of interior walls. They help conceal the junction between the wall and floor and protect the surface of the wall from impact damage.

The size and complexity of the moulding and the materials from which it is made are dependent on the quality of the house. Most old skirtings are made from single softwood boards up to 200mm (8in) in height and shaped with a simple classical moulding. Some Victorian skirtings, however, can be up to 350mm (14in) in height and made from two or three elaborately moulded softwood or hardwood sections. The shoulders of the tongue-and-groove edges fall on a line of the moulding to disguise the joint.

Main rooms and hallways were fitted with impressive decorative skirtings, while bedrooms were mostly fitted with a simpler style. Attic and basement rooms were normally fitted with plain square-edged boards.

Standard mouldings are generally available, but you may need to have elaborate skirtings purpose-made by a specialist joinery company. Give them a sample of the moulding or a dimensioned sketch to serve as a guide.

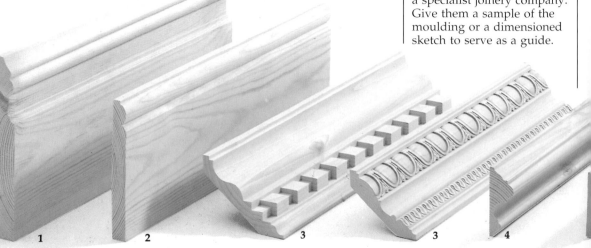

1   2   3   3   4

Dado rails

Dado rails, sometimes called chair rails, are a legacy from classical panelling and the wainscot or dado panelling of Victorian times. The cap moulding of dado panelling served as a rubbing strip that protected the wall finish from wear and tear by chair backs. The dado rail, which was usually set about 1 to 1.2m (3 to 4ft) from the floor, continued this tradition after the use of wood panelling had declined. Dado rails did not feature in rooms beyond the nineteenth century, but they were still widely used as a trim for the fashionable embossed wallcoverings that lined the dadoes of so many halls and stairways in late-Victorian and Edwardian times. Dadoes had ceased to be a common architectural feature by the mid 1920s.

Straight-run and carved mouldings in hardwoods and softwoods are available from specialist sources.

Picture rails

Like the dado moulding, the picture rail is an echo of the earlier panelled walls. The position of the rail varied according to the height of the room, but it was usually positioned 300 to 500mm (1ft to 1ft 8in) below the ceiling cornice to form a frieze. For this reason, it is sometimes known as a frieze moulding. The true picture rail had a quirk (narrow groove) in the top edge, into which picture hangers fitted.

The picture rail figured widely in Victorian interiors and is a common feature in many houses well beyond the 1930s. The later versions tend to be smaller and less fussy than the Victorian ones. Traditional mouldings are available from specialist suppliers in softwoods and a limited range of hardwoods.

Cornice mouldings

Wooden cornice mouldings were used to finish the top of panelling that terminated below ceiling level. For full-height panelling, they were fitted up to the ceiling. The moulding formed an integral part of the panelling.

They were also sometimes fitted in place of the more widely used plaster cornice at the junction between un-adorned plastered walls and the ceiling. Wooden cornices are generally smaller than the plaster versions.

Suppliers who specialize in reproduction mouldings stock a range of ornamental hardwood cornices.

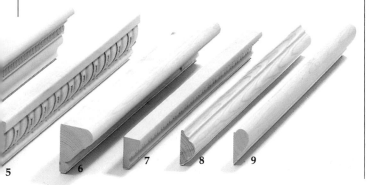

RESTORING MOULDINGS

I F THE ORIGINAL STYLE *of the interior of your house is not known, you will need to find references to serve as a guide for repair work. The chances are that your house will be one of a number in your street built in the same style. Not all of the houses will have been altered in the same way, and with luck you may find original mouldings to copy.*

Decorative mouldings used to perfection in a late-Victorian sitting room

DETECTING MISSING MOULDINGS

Unless your walls have been replastered, you will be able to detect the use and original position of missing mouldings when the wallpaper has been stripped. Parallel streaks of varnish or paint on the plaster of the wall will indicate the exact location of a dado or picture rail. You can also use the patches of plaster covering the original fixing points as a guide. If the walls have been painted over, you may find that you can detect the patches by shining a light obliquely across the surface to show up irregularities.

DADO AND PICTURE-RAIL FIXINGS

Picture rails and dado rails were fixed with cut nails, either driven directly into the masonry or into wooden plugs set in the vertical joints of the plastered brickwork. Timber-frame walls had the rails nailed directly to the studs. The plugs are unlikely to have survived – so when fitting new rails to masonry, either use cut nails or modern masonry nails or drill and plug the walls for screw fixings. Use oval nails for timber-frame walls.

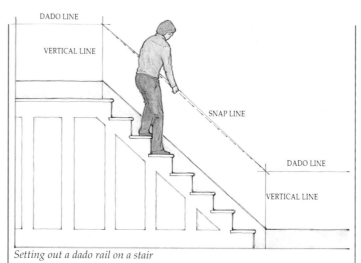

Setting out a dado rail on a stair

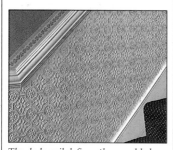

The dado rail defines the panel below

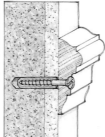

Plug and screw fixing

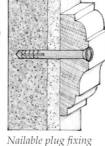

Nailable plug fixing

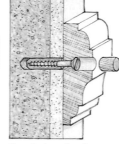

Counterbored and plugged screw fixing

Fitting a new rail

Using a long straight batten and a spirit level, mark a horizontal fixing line at the required height. If you have no original marks to go by, position a dado rail about 1 to 1.2m (3 to 4ft) from the floor. For a rail following the slope of a staircase, use a length of chalked string to snap a straight line onto the wall. Hold each end of the string at a point where vertical lines level with the end of the skirting of the hall and landing meet the line of the horizontal dado at the top and bottom of the staircase.

The position of the picture rail depends on the period of the house. Houses at the turn of the century had high ceilings, and the rail was generally positioned about 300 to 500mm (1ft to 1ft 8in) below the cornice moulding.

Later interiors usually had lower ceilings, so the picture rail was fitted at door height.

Cut the rails to length as you work round the room, and mitre or scribe the ends where they meet. With the aid of an assistant, hold the rail on the marked line and nail it in place. Sink the nailheads below the surface with a nail punch.

For a screw fixing, first drill countersunk or counterbored clearance holes in the rail, at 600mm (2ft) intervals, for No8 50mm (2in) screws. Temporarily fix the rail in place by partly driving in a few nails. Mark the position of the holes on the wall and remove the rail. Drill the plug holes, then insert the wall plugs and screw the rail in place.

For a larger rail, you can use nailable plugs. Drill the wood and plug hole together, and drive the fixing through the face of the rail.

Fill the fixing holes with a fine plaster filler and, when it is set, sand it smooth ready for painting. Alternatively, use a coloured wood filler for a natural wood finish.

For a superior finish, you can use counterbored screw fixings and make matching wooden plugs to fill the holes. Cut the plugs from offcuts of the wood, using a plug-cutting bit and a power drill set up in a drill stand. Alternatively, turn the plugs on a lathe, with the grain running across the width of the plug. Glue the plugs into the holes, ensuring that the grain aligns with that of the rail. When the glue has set, carefully pare off the waste.

Joining lengths of moulding

Try to buy the mouldings in lengths that will cut up economically – but always allow extra for waste, particularly if you are having the mouldings specially made.

For a long wall, you will no doubt have to join lengths together. Cut the meeting ends to form a mitred butt joint, as this is neater and more effective than a plain butt joint. Mark the top back edges of both pieces of moulding where they will join. Cut the angles accurately, with the moulding held vertically in a mitre box.

For wide mouldings such as skirtings a mitre box is impractical, so use a circular saw or power jigsaw with the blade set to 45 degrees. Mark the required length on the bottom edge of each piece. Mark off the angle with a mitre square, and square the line across the face. Pin a wooden strip to the surface to guide the sole plate of the saw. Set it the required distance from the cut line **(1)**. Make sure you cut on the waste side of the line on each piece **(2)**.

1 *Pin guide strip to surface*

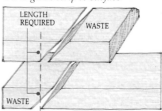

2 *Cut on waste side of each piece*

SKIRTING REPAIRS

Whereas seemingly redundant dado and picture rails may have been stripped out by fashion-conscious home owners, the skirting boards are likely to remain as they still perform a necessary function. However, you may find that an attractive period skirting has been ripped out and replaced by a plain modern version.

Most original skirtings suffer some form of damage, such as dents, or from over-painting. A certain amount of denting is acceptable; but if the skirting boards are badly dented, repair them with a fine plaster filler prior to repainting. When the filler has set, wrap abrasive paper around shaped blocks and sand the filler to the contour of the moulding.

Blurring of the moulding's detail due to overpainting or poorly applied paint (often incorporating dust from the floor) can be remedied by stripping the paint back to bare wood then repainting. Use a hot-air gun (but not on old lead paint) or a chemical stripper to soften the paint, then scrape it off carefully. Remove the paint from fine decorative moulding with a pad of wire wool dipped in chemical stripper. Most strippers are hazardous, so protect your eyes and skin and ventilate the room when working with them.

Skirting fixings

The method used for fixing skirting boards will usually depend on the quality of the building. Cut nails may be used to fix the boards directly to a plastered masonry wall or driven into wooden plugs set into the wall to receive them. In better-class houses softwood grounds are fixed to the wall and the plaster is worked up to them. The grounds consist of horizontal battens, one of them set close to the top of the skirting, and vertical blocks known as 'soldiers' set 600 to 900mm (2 to 3ft) apart. In Victorian houses that have elaborate built-up skirtings, stepped soldiers may be used.

If the grounds pull away from the wall when you are removing a skirting board, they can be refixed with masonry nails or screws and wall plugs. Make sure the grounds are level and true. Replace any that are rotten or badly infested with wood-worm. Treat the wood with an insecticide before fitting.

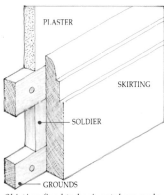

PLASTER
SKIRTING
SOLDIER
GROUNDS

Skirting fixed to horizontal grounds

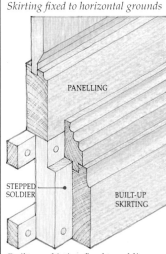

PANELLING
STEPPED SOLDIER
BUILT-UP SKIRTING

Built-up skirting fixed to soldiers

1 Tap chisel behind skirting

2 Protect the plaster with plywood

Removing skirting

You may be forced to remove more of the skirting than you want to if the damaged section is trapped behind an adjacent scribed board.

Starting at an end or at an external corner, tap a bolster chisel between the top of the skirting and the plaster **(1)**. Level the skirting away from the wall, taking care not to split short lengths. Wedge it with a thin strip of wood, and work along the edge to the next fixing point. Use a crowbar if better leverage is required. Place a piece of 6mm (¼in) plywood behind the crowbar to protect the plaster **(2)**. Expect some bruising and scuffing of the plaster at the edge where it meets the skirting, but try to minimize the damage. Continue in this way until the skirting pulls free.

If you are going to reuse the skirting board, pull the old nails out through the back with pincers. If you try to knock them out from behind, you risk splitting the face of the board.

Fitting skirting boards

When replacing a damaged piece of skirting, you can use the old piece as a template. This is particularly helpful if the end is scribed. It is best to check that the old skirting was a good fit, as gaps may have opened up if the building structure has moved due to settlement. In any event, you will need to measure the relevant length of wall.

Mark and cut the board to length. Scribe or mitre the end, if required. Mark the position of soldiers, if fitted, on the face. Level the board, and nail it in place with oval nails. If you are replacing all the skirting boards, follow the sequence shown below. Scribe internal corners and mitre external ones.

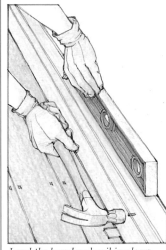

Level the board and nail in place

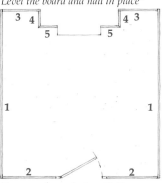

Sequence for replacing skirting

EMBOSSED WALLCOVERINGS

DECORATED PAPER *began to be used as a cheaper alternative to canvas and leather hangings or wood panelling during the sixteenth century. It was handmade and by the eighteenth century it had become a fashionable wall finish, although only found in the grandest houses.*

However, this was to change when in 1841 Potters of Darwin, in Lancashire, manufactured the first continuous machine-made wallpaper, thus making printed wallcoverings widely available at an affordable price.

Then in 1877 Frederick Walton invented Lincrusta, a high-relief wallcovering that quickly became popular because of its durability and washability (both selling points attractive to Victorian householders) as well as its decorative appeal. Some 10 years later Anaglypta, a lighter-weight embossed paper, appeared. Both were intended for painting and were widely used for dadoes and friezes and as general wallcoverings.

Should you strip a wall, particularly in a hallway or beside a staircase, and discover a dado-height band of different plaster or numerous patches, you can be sure that an embossed wallcovering has been removed. In which case, using a Lincrusta or period Anaglypta wallcovering will restore the original decorative style.

LINCRUSTA

Frederick Walton had been involved with the manufacture of linoleum for some years, and Lincrusta was a dense and moderately stiff material based on a similar formula to linoleum. A mixture of oxidized linseed oil, resin, paraffin wax, fibre and whiting was applied to a canvas backing (this was later changed to waterproof paper) then passed through rollers under high pressure. One roller was decoratively engraved, leaving a continuous impression in the soft compound. The material was then left to dry in a heated environment for two weeks.

When, in 1883, Lincrusta was manufactured under licence in America, it quickly established itself as a very popular wallcovering and a variety of new patterns were introduced specifically for the US market. Lincrusta went out of fashion in the second quarter of the twentieth century and ceased to be produced – until recently, when British manufacturers reintroduced a limited range of panels, rolls and borders featuring original patterns.

The late-Victorian patterns were inspired by classical decorative themes (one was called 'Italian Renaissance'). Several of the later patterns had Art Nouveau motifs.

A Lincrustra frieze provides an attractive border to the upper part of a wall

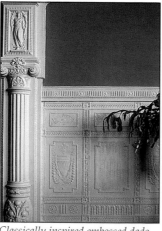

Classically inspired embossed dado

Painted Anaglypta stairway dado

ANAGLYPTA

At the time when Lincrusta was finding a ready market in America the launching of its rival, Anaglypta, was being proposed in Britain. It was Thomas Palmer, one of Walton's employees, who suggested making a cheaper, lighter and more flexible embossed wallcovering from cotton and paper pulp. When Walton rejected the idea, Palmer patented the process, left the company (in 1886) and together with the Storey brothers developed the material, which became available for sale by 1888.

Like Lincrusta, Anaglypta was intended for painting and was washable; however, it was not so durable. Being relatively easy to hang, it was particularly suitable for friezes and ceilings. It very soon became widely used in place of Lincrusta and has continued to be available, in modern as well as traditional designs, to this day.

You can detect whether an old embossed wallcovering is Lincrusta or Anaglypta by pressing the raised surface. If it is compressible, then it is Anaglypta, which is hollow.

As with Lincrusta, the embossed patterns reflected current fashions, and Palmer employed leading artists and architects to devise fine Art Nouveau and floral designs.

1 Wet the back of each piece

2 Trim off waste with craft knife

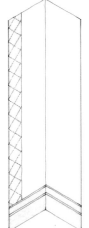

*3 Measure
the width*

*4 Bevel the
cut edge*

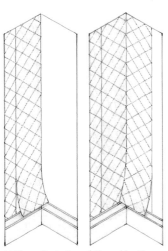

*5 Hang first piece, followed by the
offcut set on a plumbed line*

HANGING LINCRUSTA

Although it is relatively stiff and heavy and requires careful handling, Lincrusta is not a particularly difficult material to hang. As with other decorating techniques, thorough preparation of the surface and careful setting out is necessary.

Since it is a fairly expensive wallcovering, calculate your requirements accurately. Most patterns are a straight match, but some have offset or random designs – in which case, you will need to make sufficient allowance for waste.

Papered walls

Remove traces of old wallpaper and paste, and inspect the bare plaster surface for holes or loose patches. Make good where necessary with plaster filler. When it is dry, apply a wallpaper size.

Painted walls

Scrape off powdery, flaking or blistered emulsion paint, and bind the surface with a clear stabilizing primer.

Wash off most of a water-based distemper-type finish from the wall before you apply a stabilizing primer.

Key the surface of sound oil-based paintwork with abrasive paper, then wash it down with sugar soap.

Lining the walls

If the wall plaster has been unevenly patched, lining paper will help to even out suction and create a smooth surface for the wallcovering.

Cross-line the walls with a good-quality lining paper. Use a heavy-duty wallpaper paste containing a fungicide.

Applying the covering

Measure and cut individual lengths from a roll, taking note of any pattern-matching required and allowing about 50mm (2in) for waste on each length. Trim the selvage from the rolled material with a straightedge and sharp craft knife. Hold the knife at a slight angle to undercut the edge of the material.

Using a plumb line, mark a vertical line on the wall. Hold the edge of the first piece of wallcovering on the line and check the fit of the top end against the ceiling, cornice moulding or picture rail. If need be, mark and cut the edge to fit any irregularities. Trim the other pieces to match, if required.

Sponge the back of each piece with warm water and leave it to soak for up to 30 minutes (**1**). This allows the material to soften and fully expand, so that it doesn't blister when you are hanging it. Wipe off any surplus water before applying the special Lincrusta glue. Stir

the glue thoroughly and apply it evenly with a wide paintbrush or paint roller, depending on the length of the piece. Ensure the edges are well covered with glue.

Apply the first piece to the wall level with the vertical line and butting the top edge. Press it into place with a cloth pad or rubber roller. Mark the line of the skirting on each edge of the piece, then peel it back just far enough to place a piece of hardboard under it on which to cut the end. Trim off the waste with the craft knife and straightedge (**2**), then press the edge down and clean off surplus glue with a damp sponge. Continue in this way, butting subsequent pieces together.

Dealing with corners

At the end of a run you will meet an internal or external corner. You can work the material round a curved corner without cutting it, but not round an angled one. The cut edges will need to be mitred, and an allowance made on the width for the thickness of the material.

If the wallcovering is to continue onto the adjacent surface of an angled corner, first measure the distance between the edge of the last piece and the corner. Take

measurements from the top, middle and bottom (**3**). Mark the widths at corresponding heights on a length of the wallcovering (for an external corner, adding the thickness of the material). Cut it to size with a craft knife, holding a straightedge on the marks.

Control the knife carefully, as it will have a tendency to follow the pattern. Make the cut with a series of knife strokes. Bevel the edge with a sanding block (**4**). Hold the length flush with the edge of your worktable to provide good support. Hold the material face down when shaping an external-corner piece (the thinner parts are brittle and likely to crumble, so handle with care).

Hang the prepared piece of wallcovering in the usual way. The remaining offcut is now used to turn the corner. The pattern will then follow through, but there will be a slight mismatch because of the cut edges. The corner may not be quite vertical, so mark a plumbed line on the adjacent wall on which to set the straight edge of the offcut (**5**). Trim and level the cut edge as required.

After hanging this piece, continue to hang the covering as before. Fill the joints with plaster filler, and make good any broken edges.

DADO PANELS

Lincrusta dado panels come ready trimmed to width and length (you can also buy a moulded border). Applying them to a plain wall is therefore quite straightforward. However, if the wall has a dado rail, you may need to trim the height of the panels or even reposition the rail.

The panel designs form a complete pattern, so avoid reducing the height if you can. If you have to trim the panels, remove the surplus from the bottom edge only. Before hanging the panels, prepare the wall as required and cross-line it.

In order to hang Lincrusta dado panels on a plain wall, mark a horizontal guideline at panel height **(1)** then set out and apply the covering as already described. If there is to be a border, after hanging the panels cut the border to length and glue it in place to finish the top edge **(2)**.

1 Mark horizontal guideline

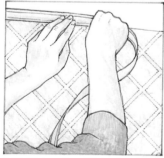

2 Finish top edge with border strip

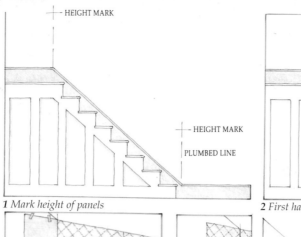

1 Mark height of panels

3 Crease the paper into the angle

4 Hang the half-panel

5 Hang the corner piece

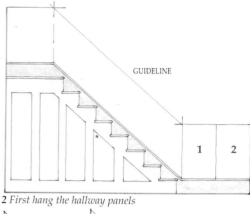

2 First hang the hallway panels

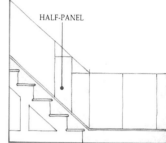

6 Cut and hang other half-panel

DEALING WITH STAIRWAYS

To set out dado panels for a stairway wall, first mark a plumbed line at the foot and top of the stairs where the stringboard meets the skirting. Mark the height of the panels on the vertical lines measured up from the skirting **(1)**. On a long stair, set out intermediate marks in the same way, then join them up with a straightedge – or snap a line, using a chalked taut length of cord or twine.

Hanging the panels

Hang the panels in the hall first, working away from the vertical line at the foot of the stairs **(2)**. The panels that follow the slope of the stairs must be cut to the required angle before hanging. Cut the first panel vertically into equal halves. Make the cut dead straight, guiding the knife with a straightedge.

Cut a sheet of paper to the exact size of one of the half-panels in order to make a pattern (lining paper is handy for this). Temporarily tape the paper to the wall, with the long edge against the vertical line and level with the top of the dado at the foot of the staircase. Crease the paper into the angle of the stringboard **(3)**. Remove the paper, and fold the end along the crease line. Trim off the triangular end along the line.

Lay the paper pattern over the half-panel, with the top and side edges flush. Mark the panel where the slope of the pattern meets its edge. Place a straightedge from the corner to the edge mark, and cut off the corner. Take care to make a clean cut and not to damage the triangular offcut, as it will be needed.

Prepare the panel and offcut for gluing, as already described. Hang the half-panel, with the angled cut edge butted up to the stringboard **(4)**. Then add the triangular piece to the top of the half-panel level with the guideline and the long edge of the panel **(5)**. Cut and hang the other half-panel in the same way **(6)**. Follow this method up to the vertical line at the top of the staircase (you may have to make the last piece a narrower infill panel), then continue with full panels on the landing. You can finish the top edge with a border strip, mitring the ends of the strip at the top and bottom of the stair.

REPAINTING LINCRUSTA

Avoid stripping paint from Lincrusta unless absolutely necessary. Should you have to strip paint from the wallcovering, don't use a strong chemical stripper (which could dissolve the material). Before proceeding, test an inconspicuous corner of the wallcovering to make sure that the paint stripper is not too strong. Never remove old paint with a hot-air gun – Lincrusta is flammable and will soften with heat.

HANGING ANAGLYPTA

Anaglypta is hung on walls and ceilings in the same way as a conventional wallpaper.

After cutting the lengths to size, apply heavy-duty wallpaper paste and leave it to soak for about 10 minutes. Fold the paper on itself, then carry it to the wall or ceiling and apply it to the surface with a paperhanger's brush. Avoid using excessive pressure, so you don't flatten the embossing. Cut off the waste with scissors.

Let the paper dry out for a few days before finishing. Use an eggshell oil paint for walls, and an emulsion paint for a ceiling.

CHAPTER FIFTEEN

DECORATIVE WOODWORK

WOOD IS BOTH A VERSATILE MATERIAL and one that is relatively easy to work. These properties, coupled with the desire of craftsmen over the centuries to decorate their work, have resulted in all manner of shaped, carved and fretted woodwork. In the past, decoration was regarded as a sign of wealth, and elaborate carved work was frequently commissioned for both interior and exterior joinery in the stylish houses of the rich.

In Victorian times, speculative builders, encouraged by increasing prosperity and the new manufacturing methods brought about by industrialization, often indulged in widespread use of flamboyant decorative woodwork to embellish even fairly modest homes.

Most household joinery is made from the cheaper softwoods, which suffer from weathering if not adequately maintained. In addition, later house owners viewed Victorian styles as grotesquely old-fashioned. As a result, many fine examples of decorative woodwork have been reduced to a shadow of their original glory or ripped out and replaced by modern substitutes. However, with a fairly modest outlay it is possible to re-create period woodwork in appropriate style – restoring an important part of a house's character.

Carved solid-oak bargeboard

Pierced canopy with dogtooth edges

Porch made from painted laths

A delightful combination of balusters and fretted porch brackets

Unusual layered bargeboard

Carved console supporting a jetty

Superb detail in good condition

BARGEBOARDS

BARGEBOARDS *(also known as vergeboards) are used to finish and protect the verge of a gabled roof, porch or dormer. They provide a striking exterior feature and were first used to full effect in the medieval period, when important houses had decorative carved oak bargeboards.*

Simple modern versions are little more than wide plain boards, but elaborately fretted and carved bargeboards were fashionable during the Gothic revival of the nineteenth century. Indeed, the bargeboard's original function was sometimes almost forgotten in the enthusiasm for decorative extravagance.

A simple but striking design cut into the edge of a bargeboard

Carved-oak Tudor-style bargeboard

Sturdy white-painted bargeboard

TYPES OF BARGEBOARD

Bargeboards can be fitted close to the wall, or may project forward – in which case they are known as oversailing gables. Usually, these are supported by shaped brackets and the underside is finished with a soffit board. Turned or shaped wooden finials or fretted panels may be fitted at the apex to complete the decorative effect. Extensive use of cutouts produced highly ornate tracery designs. These were often structurally weak, so were sometimes applied to a backing board – a style known as appliqué.

GABLE CONSTRUCTION

A simple gable roof consists of ordinary rafters notched over wooden wall plates, which are supported by the load-bearing side walls. The top ends of the rafters are nailed to a ridge board, while the bottom ends are tied together by the ceiling joist, forming a rigid triangular structure. A horizontal timber support, called a purlin, may be used to brace the rafters if they are likely to bend under the weight of the roof covering.

At a gable end of a brick-built house the ridge board and wall plates, and possibly the purlins as well, extend through the brickwork to provide fixing points for the bargeboard.

For an oversailing gable, rafters are usually fixed outside the wall on extended wall plates and ridge board.

Intermediate supports may be fitted between the inner and outer rafters, and a soffit board added to finish the underside **(1)**. The shaped bargeboard is nailed to the outside rafters to cover the ends of the battens used for fixing the tiles or slates, and is set slightly proud of the top face of the battens in order to tilt the roof covering at the edge. This is to direct water away from the face of the board. A fascia moulding is usually applied at the top of the board under the overhanging edge of the roof covering.

In some timber-frame houses the bargeboard may be nailed directly to the side wall in order to cover roof sheathing boards **(2)**; or to extended boarding, in order to form an oversailing or boxed gable **(3)**.

Components of a gable roof
1 Common rafter
2 Wall plate
3 Ridge board
4 Ceiling joist
5 Purlin
6 Bargeboard
7 Intermediate support
8 Fascia moulding
9 Finial
10 Soffit

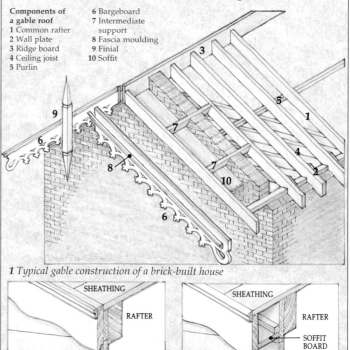

1 Typical gable construction of a brick-built house

SHEATHING
RAFTER

2 Bargeboard nailed to sheathing

SHEATHING
RAFTER
SOFFIT BOARD

3 Bargeboard forming boxed gable

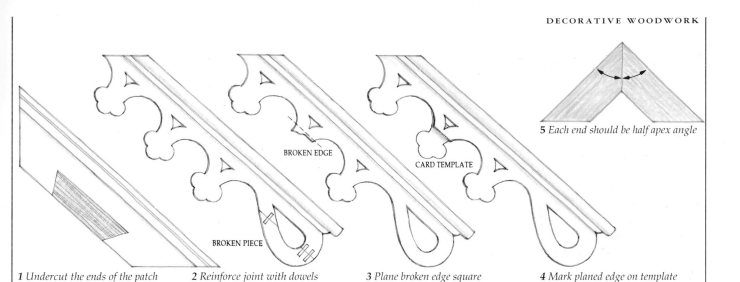

5 *Each end should be half apex angle*

1 *Undercut the ends of the patch* 2 *Reinforce joint with dowels* 3 *Plane broken edge square* 4 *Mark planed edge on template*

BROKEN EDGE

BROKEN PIECE

CARD TEMPLATE

REPAIRING A BARGEBOARD

Victorian and Edwardian bargeboards were made from soft-wood and finished with paint. Repainting the bargeboards is not infrequently omitted from general redecoration because of their height from the ground. Nevertheless, it is important to maintain the paintwork regularly, as the boards are in an exposed position and can weather badly.

If you have a decorative bargeboard that has decayed, it's worth making the effort to repair it in preference to fitting a cheaper, plain replacement. Try to make repairs *in situ* – but if the wood is beyond repair, remove it and make a new bargeboard to the old pattern.

Removing a bargeboard

Unless you have a single-storey house, working on a bargeboard is a tricky operation because of the height. Most bargeboards are large and awkward to handle, so it generally takes two people to remove them.

Always work from a safe platform, such as a scaffold tower, and make sure it is stable and well secured. If you are not confident when working at heights, call in a professional.

Nails are normally used to fix the joinery together, although screws may be used where short-grained wood is present. Locate the fixing points. Then if the bargeboard is fitted with a fascia moulding, remove it using a bolster chisel. Tap the chisel between the moulding and the board, and lever it off close to the fixings. Further fixings may now be revealed, in which case you will need to prise the bargeboard free from the roof timbers.

Fitting a plain patch

If you find a minor patch of rot, rake out the infected wood and treat it with a preservative, a proprietary hardener and a wood filler. Where the rot has occurred along a plain edge, cut it away back to sound wood. Undercut the ends to give improved holding. Make a patch of matching wood to fit your cutout (1). Fix the patch in place with an exterior woodworking glue. When it is set, treat the new wood with a preservative in readiness for painting.

Repairing a shaped edge

The projecting details of a decorative sawn edge sometimes break away because of weak short grain. If that has happened, you may be able to make the repair *in situ*, assuming you still have the piece that has broken away.

Hold the piece in place and mark one or two lines at right angles across the break line. Square the lines across the broken edges of the two parts. Set a marking gauge to half the thickness of the wood and mark a centre line on each part. Drill 10mm (⅜in) dowel holes where the lines cross. Finally, glue the broken piece in place, inserting wooden dowels to reinforce the joint (2).

Replacing missing parts

Bargeboards are often decorated with a repeat pattern. If part of the pattern has rotted or broken off and is lost, you can replace the missing part.

Take a rubbing of part of the decoration that is still intact, using a wax crayon and plain paper. Tape the paper onto the bargeboard for easier handling. Cut out a card template, following the outline of the rubbing.

Plane the broken edge of the bargeboard square (3). Holding the card template behind the bargeboard at the point where the section is missing, draw the position of the planed edge on it (4).

Mark the shape of the new section on a suitably sized board and cut it out with a power jigsaw or a coping saw. If the pattern includes pierced details, drill a hole in the waste so you can insert the saw blade. Smooth the sawn edges. Dowel and glue the new piece in position, and treat it with a timber preservative before priming and finishing with paint.

MAKING A REPLACEMENT

Neglected bargeboards in an exposed position can decay beyond reasonable repair, making replacement necessary. Remove the old one as carefully as possible, to keep it in one piece. If it looks too weak to survive removal intact, first record its size and shape with full-size drawings and photographs. Buy new boards of knot-free straight-grained wood. Give your supplier the finished dimensions and have the timber machined to size.

Lay the original bargeboards or your drawing of them on the new boards and mark out the shape. Check the angle of the mitred ends with a sliding bevel. Each end should be half the angle of the apex (5).

Cut the board to shape with a power jigsaw or a coping saw, including cutouts. If the boards are bevelled and carved, use chisels and gouges to shape them (see CARVED WOODWORK).

Bring all the surfaces to a smooth finish, then treat them with a wood preservative, following the maker's instructions. When the preservative is dry, finish all the surfaces with a good paint system and nail the finished boards in place. Sink the nailheads, fill the recesses, and paint to match. Refit the original fascia moulding or, if need be, replace it.

FINIALS

The apex of a gabled roof is often fitted with a turned or square-sided wooden post called a finial that protrudes above the roof line. Sometimes the bottom end of the post extends downwards and is detailed in a similar way (the part that projects downwards is known as a pendant). The post may also be embellished with decorative wrought ironwork.

Reinstating a finial

Finials and pendants can be cut from flat board or from square-sectioned wood. They may either be nailed to the bargeboard or fixed to structural roof members with the bargeboards butted up to them.

If your roof has a not very interesting stub of wood at its apex, it is probably the remains of a finial that has been sawn off due to decay. If the remaining wood is sound, you can purchase a ready-made turned finial from a specialist supplier or have one made to order. Either dowel and glue the new component or use a screw dowel to fix it to the end of the old wood (1).

You can make square-sectioned finials with sawn decorative profiles yourself, using either a band saw or a powered fret saw. Mark the profile, based on a suitable pattern, on two adjacent sides of the wood. Cut along the guide lines on one face. Tape the waste in place, then turn the wood over to present the other marked face and cut the second pair of sides (2). Fix the new finial in place, using the same type of fixing used for the original. Last of all, treat the finial with a timber preservative and apply a good paint system.

Finial with pendant fitted at apex

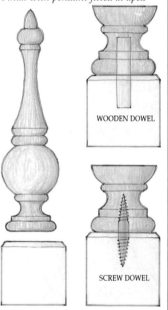

WOODEN DOWEL

SCREW DOWEL

1 Dowel and glue or use screw dowel

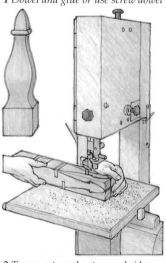

2 Tape waste and cut second sides

BRACKETS

B RACKETS *are normally fitted to provide support between horizontal and vertical members, but fretted brackets are often used for decorative rather than functional purposes – to add richness and texture to gables, porches or door openings.*

Shaped with a saw, fretted brackets are relatively easy to make. Interior examples are generally made of thinner wood than exterior ones. You can have fancy brackets made to order or buy them ready-made from specialist suppliers. Choose a style that suits your house – don't be tempted by a design that is readily available but out of character.

MAKING A BRACKET

Make a pattern by tracing the shape of an existing bracket onto stiff paper. If you don't have a suitable bracket available, draw one to your own design, basing it on a pictorial reference from a library source or catalogue. You may perhaps be able to determine the size of the missing original by looking at fixing marks left on the adjacent woodwork. If you need to produce a number of brackets, make a template. Transfer the shape of the pattern onto hardboard, and cut it to shape with a jigsaw or coping saw. Smooth the edge with abrasive paper.

Prepare straight-grained knot-free wood to the size and thickness required. If need be, glue several boards together to make up the thickness, using interior or exterior woodworking glue as appropriate. Mark out the shape of the bracket on the wood, positioning the pattern so that it follows the direction of the grain (1). This avoids short weak grain that can break easily (2).

Cut the bracket to shape, using a power jigsaw or a band saw. Finish the cut edges with a spokeshave, plane or files, as appropriate. Use screws to fix brackets – in preference to nails, which

1 Position pattern to follow grain

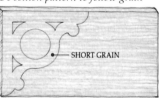

SHORT GRAIN

2 Short weak grain can break easily

may split the ends. Drill counterbored clearance holes for suitably sized screws.

Fitting a bracket

Hold the bracket in position, and mark the position of the screw holes with an awl. Drill appropriately sized pilot holes in the adjoining woodwork. If the holes are set at an angle, use the bracket as a guide for the drill. Apply mastic sealant to the joining faces of the bracket, then fix it in place with zinc-coated screws. Fill the counterbored holes with glued wooden plugs. When set, trim the plugs to the contour of the bracket and apply a primer. Finish the new work with paint, making sure the end grain is well covered.

Fretted brackets help support the porch roof

Decorative wooden brackets
1 Fretted porch bracket with spindles
2 Fretted porch brackets
3 Moulded exterior consoles
4 Carved console

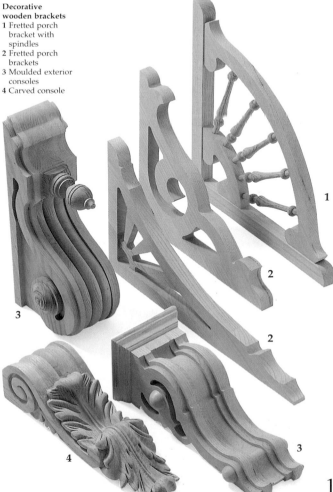

CONSOLES

Consoles are fretted or carved solid-wood brackets. They were commonly used as an exterior feature under soffits in imitation of the stone corbels used in Italianate architecture.

Wooden consoles were also often used as interior features, and may be found under mantel shelves and in door openings or supporting beams.

A range of designs for replacing missing consoles is available, in both softwoods and hardwoods, from specialist suppliers.

Maintaining consoles

Both interior and exterior consoles are likely to suffer from overpainting, which obliterates the crisp edges and details of the carved decoration. Where this has occurred, use a chemical stripper to soften and clean off the build-up of paint. When clean and dry, repaint the wood.

Making a console

Wet rot can cause deterioration of exterior consoles exposed to the weather. If the damage cannot be successfully treated with a preservative and repaired with wood filler, make a new one.

Make a pattern for the profile, based on another console. Fretted consoles sometimes comprise a central section of thicker wood sandwiched between decorative scrolls or pierced side pieces, made of thinner wood. If the central section is to stand proud of the side pieces, or the side pieces are to protrude beyond the central section, make a second pattern from the first, increasing or reducing the size as required.

Wooden consoles decorating a soffit

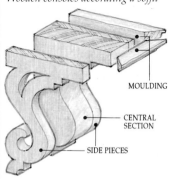

MOULDING

CENTRAL SECTION

SIDE PIECES

Fretted-console construction

Mark out the profiles on wood prepared to the correct thickness and cut them to shape. Smooth the edges. Pin and glue the side pieces to the centre piece, with the back and top edges flush. Cut a suitable decorative moulding to size with the meeting ends mitred. Pin and glue the moulding around the front and side edges of the top part of the console.

Exterior wooden consoles are usually painted; interior ones may either be painted or stained and varnished. Apply a timber preservative and the finish to an exterior console before fitting it; an interior console can be finished after fitting.

Fix the bracket securely with counterbored nonferrous screws. Then plug the holes with wooden pellets and trim them to shape. If the console is already painted, finish the pellets to match.

BALUSTRADES

WOODEN PORCHES, *verandas and balconies are a delightful feature most commonly found in coastal and colonial-style houses. They were also frequently used, largely for decorative effect, by the architects of Victorian and Edwardian suburban 'villas'. Designed to provide shade or shelter from inclement weather, and as a vantage point in seaside houses, with their turned or slatted balusters they add charm and character to a building.*

Turned posts and balusters create a most attractive veranda

Ornate fretted softwood balusters

Balustrade with turned balusters

BALUSTERS

Slats and balusters – which simultaneously give a sense of security and allow air to flow – are often used decoratively, having shaped edges that in turn make shapes of the gaps between them. Sometimes cutouts within the width of the balusters add to the decorative effect.

Normally the top ends of the balusters are nailed to the underside of the handrail, which may be grooved to receive them, and are either fixed or jointed to a horizontal rail at the bottom.

If a flat baluster is broken or missing, it is usually a straightforward matter to make a replacement. Simply make a pattern from a sound identical baluster and cut a new one to match. Treat the new wood with a timber preservative, ensuring that the porous end grain is well covered. Paint the surfaces with primer and, when it is dry, nail the new baluster in place. Fill the nail holes and apply a paint finish. For repairs to turned balusters, see WOODEN STAIR REPAIRS.

CARVED WOODWORK

CARVING IS A METHOD *of shaping and decorating wood with special chisels and gouges. The techniques are centuries old and have been applied to wooden artifacts and furniture as well as being used to embellish internal and external features of houses. Stylistically, woodcarving can range from abstract or naturalistic low-relief work to more sculpted high-relief or fully three-dimensional features.*

The techniques for carving low-relief decorative motifs are relatively easy to master, but carving in the round and high-relief work call for a keen eye and a well-developed sense of form. All early carved work was hand cut, and repeat patterns often display subtle differences in shape. It is this human touch that makes early work more interesting and valuable than the machine-cut versions of recent times.

With practice you can undertake woodcarving yourself – but if the features are particularly ornate or important, it's best to have the work carried out by a professional. You may also be able to use ready-made carved woodwork available from specialist suppliers.

Decorative beam with relief-carved mythical beasts and painted motifs

A porch made of oak and decorated with low-relief carving

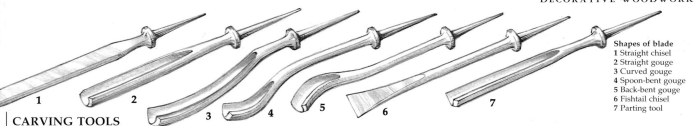

Shapes of blade
1 Straight chisel
2 Straight gouge
3 Curved gouge
4 Spoon-bent gouge
5 Back-bent gouge
6 Fishtail chisel
7 Parting tool

CARVING TOOLS

Woodcarving is so versatile that generations of craftsmen have developed hundreds of different tools to meet their needs. The blades are made in a variety of length shapes, cross-section profiles and cutting-edge widths. There are five basic length shapes: straight, curved, spoon-bent (also known as front-bent), back-bent, and fishtail (or spade) tools. Eighteen cross-section profiles are available, most of them in a range of sizes from 2mm (1/16in) to 50mm (2in).

The principal categories of carving tools are chisels, gouges and parting tools.

Chisels are ground with a square or skewed cutting edge and are used for general shaping, cutting straight lines, detailing and finishing.

Gouges are the main tools for shaping. They constitute the largest group of carving tools, having a comprehensive range of shallow to deep sweeps (curved profiles). All the sweeps are true radius curves except for the veiner type, which has straighter sides. The larger gouges are used for taking the wood off quickly, the medium-size and smaller ones for general and fine shaping.

Parting tools are V-shaped in section and are made in three profiles. They are used for outlining, lettering and detail work.

A basic set of carving tools might comprise a range of gouges, one or two straight chisels, a skew chisel, a parting tool and possibly a veining tool for fine work. You will need a round-headed carver's mallet, which is heavier and more versatile than a carpenter's mallet. A selection of flat, round and half-round rasps and files is desirable for shaping and finishing sculptural work. Rotary rasps held in a flexible drive or in the chuck of a power drill are handy for shaping. Punches are used for adding texture to the surface of the wood and for refining detail, but are not essential for most work.

Carved and painted Phoenix motif

Using the tools

Carving tools can be driven by hand pressure or with a mallet. When using hand pressure for lighter work, grip the handle with one hand and steady the blade and the thrust of the tool with the other (1). Use the mallet for difficult woods or larger cuts. Hold the carving tool low down the handle, with the mallet in your driving hand (2).

Carving tools have fine cutting edges and are prone to damage if driven into cross-grain hardwood. When a vertical cut on a line is required (known as setting in), use a small deep gouge or parting tool to carve a groove adjacent to the line. The remaining waste will then cut away cleanly with little effort (3).

The tools will readily cut across the grain. In fact, cross-grain cutting is generally preferred for roughing in the shape – since there is less chance of the grain tearing ahead of the tool or of the blade wandering off, which can easily happen when cutting with the grain.

Follow the grain for fine finishing cuts. When cutting at a tangent to the grain (if you are carving a groove around a circular motif, for example), work in the direction that will give a smooth cut on the motif side (4).

Use curved gouges to work the bottom of hollows where a straight tool would tend to dig into the wood (5). Spoon-bent tools are used for similar but more detailed work (6).

1 Steady the blade and thrust of the tool

2 Hold the tool low down the handle if using a mallet

3 Cut waste

4 Cut in the right direction

5 Use a bent gouge for hollows   *6 Use a spoon-bent gouge for details*

HOLDING THE WORK

Unless the wood is being cut *in situ* (when making a patch repair, for example), the work has to be held securely. Specialized vices, pivoting clamps and a screw-in holding device known as a carver's screw are helpful. However, they are by no means essential, as you can use most woodworking and metalworking vices and cramps quite effectively.

CARVING IN THE ROUND

CARVINGS IN THE ROUND *are pieces that are fully three-dimensional and intended to be seen from all sides. They are not as common as relief carvings in most houses but may be used for finials, pendants, stair newel posts, brackets, or overmantel ornamentation. Some may be turned shapes that are then carved and decorated with floral motifs. The subject matter for sculptural carvings can be inspired by either naturalistic or fanciful forms.*

If original carved work has been stripped out in an attempt to modernize the interior, you may want to re-create the missing details. Take note of the style of ornamentation appropriate for the period, and seek out references on which to base your design from libraries and from houses of a similar type. You can then either commission a professional carver or, if the work is not too demanding, attempt it yourself.

Carved doorhood console

1 Cut profile with a saw

2 Rough in the shape *3 Shape the contours* *4 Refine the shape*

CHOOSING THE WOOD

Virtually any wood can be carved, but some species are more difficult to carve than others. The best woods are those with a fine even grain. Lime, a favourite of the master carver Grinling Gibbons, is a light-coloured hardwood that carves and finishes extremely well. Softwoods such as ponderosa pine, yellow pine and sitka spruce carve well, too.

If the work has to match an existing feature, then the choice is made for you. However, many tropical hardwoods are now classified as endangered species – so if a tropical hardwood such as mahogany was used for the original feature, make sure the new wood comes from a sustainable source.

If you cannot find a single piece of wood large enough for a particular carving, one solution is to glue sections of timber together. Gluing sections together also helps reduce the risk of shrinkage problems, such as splitting, which are often encountered with large or thick balks of partially seasoned timber.

Though it's possible to carve 'green' (unseasoned) wood, there's a much greater risk of splitting. Reducing the bulk of the timber and hollowing out the centre helps to promote even drying out – but it is best to use seasoned wood whenever possible.

SETTING OUT

A good eye for form and well-developed drawing and craft skills are required for carving in the round. It is essential to have a clear idea of the shape to be cut, and preparatory sketches and elevation drawings will help you to achieve satisfactory results. Some carvers also find that it is helpful to make a maquette, so they can see the shape and take scaled measurements from it.

Make full-scale drawings of the form, showing the front and side elevations and possibly the back and plan views too. You can either use printed grid paper or draw a grid with 25mm (1in) squares over your design. Use carbon paper to transfer the design to the faces of a prepared block of wood.

BASIC SHAPING

Although you can use a gouge, it is usually quicker to do the rough shaping with a band saw or a powered fret saw. Saw round the profiles marked on the faces of the block. With some shapes, only one profile may be cut in this way **(1)**.

When two faces are cut, the waste from the first is likely to carry the profile for the other. Temporarily tape the waste offcuts back in position, then cut the second profile with the saw.

After sawing, remove the waste and draw in the outlines of the shapes that fall within the shaped block as a guide for carving.

CARVING THE SHAPE

Begin to rough in the shape using a straight medium-sweep gouge and a mallet **(2)**. As the work progresses, use suitably shaped smaller and flatter gouges to shape the contoured planes and hollows **(3)**. Keep viewing the work from all sides. Refine the modelling and add textures and small details, using small gouges, chisels, parting tools, punches and files **(4)**. You may want to retain the tool marks to create an interesting texture. Otherwise, take the surface to a smooth finish with progressively finer abrasive paper, folding the paper to finish fine inside details.

CHAPTER SIXTEEN

WOOD FLOORING

ARLY WOODEN FLOORS *used random-sized hand-cut boards of oak, elm, pine or fir. The boards were usually wide and of varying thickness. It is not uncommon to find thinner ones resting on packing over a joist, or the underside of thicker ones trimmed with an adze to make the floor level. By the eighteenth century the size of floorboards had become more regular. Boards about 100mm (4in) wide were used in better-quality houses to avoid shrinkage and distortion problems, while houses of lesser quality had boards 200 to 250mm (8 to 10in) wide. However, it was not until the earlier part of the nineteenth century that the introduction of mechanized production methods made consistent floorboard sizes generally available.*

Georgian houses often had tongue-and-groove pine floorboards, but their light colour was not looked on with favour so they were usually painted to resemble more expensive hardwoods. Other

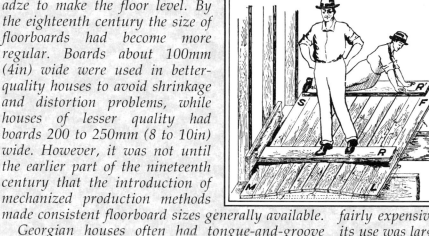

materials were imitated, too, including marble, stone and slate set out in geometric patterns. Sometimes the boards were simply finished with a plain matt colour. Floor coverings of carpet, painted cloth or matting were also used. These were often fitted wall to wall, unless laid over a quality hardwood floor, in which case the boards would usually be exposed to form a border. As a cheaper alternative to carpeting, sometimes floors were painted overall and then decorated with attractive free-hand or stencilled designs.

Parquet, a flooring made from strips or blocks of wood laid in a geometrical pattern, appealed to the Victorians because of its decorative nature. Since it was fairly expensive to lay, as it still is today, initially its use was largely confined to better-quality houses. Nevertheless, parquet became increasingly fashionable and it retained its popularity throughout the Edwardian period and the 1920s and 1930s.

The pale-coloured walls harmonize well with the unfinished pine boards

The dark stained and polished floorboards suit this cottage interior

TYPES OF FLOORING

A WOOD FLOOR, *like other features and materials in a period house, derives its character from the patina of age. Provided the material has been well maintained, the inevitable scrapes, wear, light stains and all-over mellow tone combine to give an acceptable – indeed, often desirable – appearance that is worth preserving. Well-worn boards in high-traffic areas such as halls and doorways tell a story, and so long as they are not structurally weak they don't need to be replaced.*

Nevertheless, age and neglect can take their toll, and there are times when the introduction of 'new' wood is unavoidable in order to preserve the floor.

MATCHING OLD WOOD

Always try to obtain the appropriate species of wood when making a patch repair or replacing part of an old floor. This may not always be easy, but flooring specialists stock many of the species used traditionally and often keep reclaimed wood for repairs of this kind. It is also worth trying timber suppliers, who stock a wide range of woods from which boards can be cut.

New and even resawn old wood will not have the mellow colour of the original, so you may find that the replacement has to be toned down with a wood stain, or needs bleaching if a lighter colour is required.

TYPES OF WOOD

The majority of floors are constructed from softwoods, such as yellow-heart pine, Columbian pine, pitch pine, spruce and fir. However, a number of hardwoods are used too, particularly for the types of parquet that are laid on a sub-floor. Hardwood species used for flooring range from blond and dark-brown woods – including maple, ash, beech, elm, oak, walnut and teak – to redder woods such as cherry, mahogany, utile and jarrah.

Handsome wide elm boards

Wood usually changes colour as it ages, which can make identification difficult. If you are not sure of the species used for your floor, take a sample to a timber supplier, who should be able to identify it for you. If the underside of a board does not show the original colour, plane off a shaving to reveal the true colour beneath.

Herringbone-pattern parquet floor

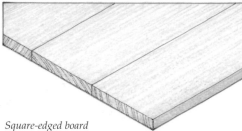

Square-edged board

ASSESSING REPAIRS

- Easy even for beginners.
- ■ Fairly difficult. Good practical skills required.
- ▲ Difficult. Hire a professional.

WOOD FLOORING

Poor finish
An unsuitable or worn finish spoils the appearance of a wooden floor.
- Clean the surface (pages 189–90).
- Apply a suitable finish (pages 188–9).

Squeaking boards
Weak fixings can cause loose or warped boards.
- Fix with nails or screws (page 187).

Damaged flooring
Patched or rough wood may make repairs necessary.
- Sand the surface (page 188).
- Fill gaps (page 186).
- Repair splits (page 187).
- Treat minor insect infestation yourself (page 226).
- ▲ Have rot or serious infestation treated (pages 226–7).
- ■ Lift and replace boards (page 186).
- ■ Repair parquet floors (page 187).

Tongue-and-groove board

Tongue-and-groove strip flooring

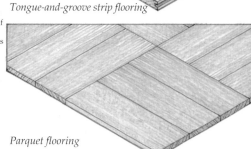

Parquet flooring

TYPES OF BOARD

You can buy wood flooring in the form of boards, strips and parquet. Boards come in long lengths and are planed to a finished thickness of about 18mm (¾in) or more. Their width can vary from 100 to 300mm (4 to 12in), and the edges may either be planed square (plain-edged) or tongued and grooved.

Strip flooring is normally made from hardwoods in narrow tongue-and-groove widths of about 75mm (3in). Strips for laying directly onto joists have a nominal thickness of 25mm (1in). Thinner versions are made for laying on a sub-floor.

Parquet is made in various forms. The thicker versions are sometimes referred to as woodblock flooring. These have plain-edged or tongue-and-groove blocks approx-imately 75mm (3in) wide and 225 to 300mm (9 to 12in) long, with a nominal thick-ness of 18mm (¾in). The thinner versions of parquet are made from strips about 25 to 50mm (1 to 2in) wide and 225 to 300mm (9 to 12in) long. You can also buy par-quet panels, with short strips of wood bonded to a backing sheet. These are produced in various configurations and are laid like tiles.

FIXING METHODS

SELECTING BOARDS

Because it is a porous material, wood expands and contracts as it reacts to changes in its moisture content. The amount of 'movement' also depends on the species of the wood and how the wood is cut from the log. The latter is a particularly important consideration for flooring.

Most logs, for reasons of economy, are flat-sawn **(1)**. This produces wide boards with an attractive sweeping figure. However, they are prone to warping, splitting and uneven wear. When boards are cut in this way, the annual growth rings run more or less across the width of the board or from edge to edge. Because wood shrinks more in the direction of the growth rings than across them, this leads to a greater reduction on the width of a board than on the thickness. Also, shrinkage is uneven, since the 'longer' growth rings shrink more than those on the heart side (the side nearest to the centre of the tree), which causes the board to distort or cup **(2)**. The movement of the wood can cause nails to loosen; if the board is securely held, the movement may make it split.

Using boards that have been converted by the

Traditional log cutting Saw

quarter-sawn or rift sawn method overcomes these problems. The log is cut more or less radially **(3)**. This produces boards known as edge-grain timber with short even-length growth rings that appear as lines on the face sides. Since shrinkage is minimal across the growth rings, the effect on the width of the board is negligible.

Quarter-sawn boards are more expensive than flat-sawn ones, since the method of milling is more wasteful, but their greater stability and resistance to wear far outweighs the extra cost.

To check the cut of your old boards, look at the end grain **(4)**. Always choose quarter-sawn boards for repairs, unless you are matching the figure of old flat-sawn floorboards.

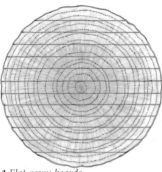
1 Flat-sawn boards

2 Shrinkage causes boards to cup

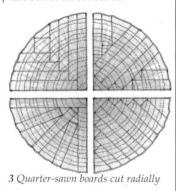
3 Quarter-sawn boards cut radially

4 Look at end grain to check cut

WOODEN FLOORING IS USUALLY FIXED *with nails or glue, or both. The method will depend on the type, quality and profile of the flooring. The profile can be plain-edged, rebated (shiplapped) or tongued and grooved. Where nails are used as a feature, try to match their type and spacing when making repairs.*

PLAIN-EDGED AND REBATED BOARDS

The most common method for fixing plain-edged and rebated boards is to nail them through the face, using cut floorboard nails. These are rectangular in section and are driven in with the wider face parallel to the grain. The square-cut tip is designed to sever the fibres as it punches through the wood – instead of parting the fibres, causing the wood to split, as can happen with pointed round wire nails.

Plain-edged board fixing

Rebated board fixing

TONGUE-AND-GROOVE FLOORBOARDS

Tongue-and-groove boards are secret-nailed through the tongue. The grooved edge is held by the tongue of the previous board. Lost-head finishing nails are driven in at an angle of about 45 degrees. A nail punch must be used to sink the nails, as it is easy to mar the edges with a hammer. Nowadays professional floorlayers use a powered nail gun, which drives the nails in quickly and neatly at a set angle.

Tongue-and-groove board fixing

PARQUET FLOORING

Traditionally, the thicker type of parquet flooring was laid using hot bitumen. After the pieces of wood had been cut to shape, each piece was dipped in a shallow tray filled with the hot adhesive and laid in place. Once the bitumen had set, the surface of the wood was planed and scraped level ready for finishing. Nowadays a cold-set flooring adhesive is used for parquet flooring. The adhesive is spread over the sub-floor with a serrated-edge trowel, then the wood blocks are set in it.

Thinner parquet flooring is usually pinned or glued. If individual parquet strips need to be replaced, apply a flooring adhesive and fix with 20mm (¾in) panel pins through the face. Sink the nailheads and fill them with a coloured filler. In order to avoid splitting close-grained hardwoods, drill holes for the nails before fixing. The backing fabric of parquet panels provides a generous surface area for gluing, so they do not require pinning.

FLOATING FLOORS

Modern woodstrip 'floating floors' are constructed from thin tongued and grooved hardwood boards. These are not secured to the sub-floor in any way, but are usually glued together edge to edge.

Although it isn't a traditional type of wood flooring, the style and quality of a floating floor can make it acceptable in a period house.

REPAIRING WOODEN FLOORS

WOODEN FLOORS *are subjected to considerable daily wear and tear, which may ultimately necessitate repairs. However, the patina of wood improves with age and a floor only looks old if it bears visible signs of its past. So, before undertaking repairs, consider whether there is a case for preserving the floor in its present state, especially if it contributes significantly to the character of the house.*

Gaps between boards, surface damage, splits and insect infestation are the most frequently encountered problems that mar old floors. Not all of these will need attention if you are planning to cover the floor, but they can look unattractive if exposed.

DEALING WITH GAPS

As well as being unsightly, gaps between plain-edged floorboards admit draughts. Gaps are the result of shrink-age, usually caused by the introduction of a modern heating system. Provided that the wood has stabilized, they can be filled.

From the point of view of appearance, the most satis-factory solution is to lift all the boards and re-lay them so they fit snugly together, filling the space remaining at the end of the operation with an additional board or two. However, lifting and re-laying the boards demands considerable effort and can cause further damage to the floor – so it's best to have the work done by a tradesman unless you have some exper-ience yourself, and only to have an old wood floor re-laid if absolutely necessary.

To fill wide gaps without lifting the boards, use strips of matching wood cut with a slight taper **(1)** on a table saw or with a circular saw. Not all the gaps will be the same size, and they may not all be parallel throughout the length of the floor. So you will need to make the strips slightly wider than the gaps and plane them down to fit.

Before cutting the strips, scrape the edges of the floor-boards to clean them. You can make an ideal scraper tool with an angled end from a strip of steel. The angled end should be ground to a 1-in-20 taper **(2)**; the taper that you cut on the wooden strips needs to be the same.

Apply some woodworking glue to the angled face of the wooden strip and tap the strip into place. Wipe off the surplus glue and, when set, plane the top edge flush with the surface of the floor. If need be, apply wood stain.

For narrow gaps, use a flexible wood filler. Clean the gaps with an old saw blade and vacuum out loose material. Press the filler into place with a filling knife. To keep filler off the surface of the boards, lay strips of masking tape on each side of the gaps. When set, sand the filler to a smooth finish.

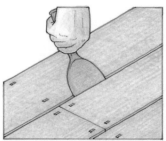
1 Lever up the end of the board

2 Cut the tongues to release board

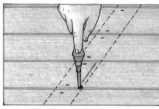
3 Saw at a shallow angle

4 Set depth of cut to board thickness

5 Cut board level with the joist

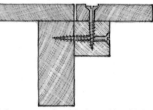
6 Screw wooden block to side of joist

LIFTING FLOORBOARDS

To lift plain-edged boards, insert a wide-bladed bolster chisel into the gap between the boards, close to the end. Start to lever up one edge of the board, trying to avoid crushing the edge of the one next to it **(1)**. Change sides, and repeat the operation in order to ease the end free. Move to the next fixing point along the board, and do the same again. Place a batten under the loose end to help the board pull free as you continue working along it.

To lift a damaged tongued and grooved board it is necessary to cut through the tongue on one or both sides of the board to be removed **(2)**. You can use a tenon saw or circular saw. If you use a tenon saw, the gap between the boards can serve as a guideline or you can tack a straight batten along the cut line to guide the saw. Make the cut at a shallow angle **(3)**. If using a circular saw, fit it with a carbide-tipped blade and fix a guide batten to the floor against which to run the baseplate. Position the batten so that the sawcut will

be just clear of the adjacent board. Set the depth of cut to the thickness of the board **(4)**. Prise out the cut board with a wide chisel. If you need to lift the neighbouring floorboards, they can now be levered up from below.

Before inserting a replace-ment, you will need to plane off the tongue to allow the board to drop into place. Fix the new board in position with finishing nails driven through the face.

When a section of board needs to be replaced, it is often simplest to remove the whole board and saw off the damaged part. However, if the board is continuous and is trapped at each end, you may have no alternative but to cut it to length *in situ*. To locate the joist nearest to the proposed cutting point, insert a knife blade between the boards. Drill a hole next to the side of the joist, insert a padsaw or power jigsaw and cut the board level with the joist **(5)**. Screw a wooden block to the side of the joist to provide support for the new floorboard **(6)**.

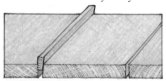
1 Fill gaps with tapered strips

1-in-20
TAPER
2 Make a scraper tool from steel strip

DEALING WITH SPLITS

Splits occur where the fibres of the wood have parted, either at the end of a board or within the face, depending on the grain structure. They are usually caused by shrinkage, but sometimes occur where nails have been driven in. Unless they are disfiguring or likely to cause splinters, they don't necessarily require attention.

If the boards do need to be repaired, glue the parts that have split (if need be, applying pressure by inserting wooden wedges between the boards); or use wood filler if the wood is stable and not liable to splinter.

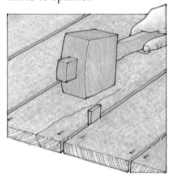

Use a wedge to apply pressure

Square brick pattern

Diagonal brick pattern

Herringbone pattern

Square basket pattern

Diagonal basket pattern

CURING SQUEAKING BOARDS

Over a period of time, the flexing of the floor or expansion and contraction of the timber may loosen the floorboard nails. It is the resulting movement of the wood against the nails or against the neighbouring boards that produces the typical irritating squeak.

The simplest cure is to drive the floorboard nails in deeper with a nail punch, which allows the tapered edges of the nails to grip the wood more securely. However, this may not be a lasting solution. If the problem persists, use either larger or ring-shank nails. The latter are designed to give a better grip, but are not traditional and require clearance holes drilled through the boards. Fill any redundant holes with a matching wood filler.

If the boards can't be renailed satisfactorily (for example, because of twisting or bowing), use countersunk stainless-steel woodscrews. Bury the heads of the screws deep enough to cover them with filler or with matching wooden plugs. Dampening the wood thoroughly before fixing will help it to 'give' as the boards are screwed down.

PARQUET FLOORS

Parquet flooring is usually made from quality materials and, unless neglected, does not require major repairs. However, sections of a thick parquet floor laid on a concrete base can lift due to expansion of the wood. This may be caused by deterioration of the damp-proof membrane (DPM) beneath the floor, or by water that has been allowed to soak into the wood from leaking plumbing.

Eliminating the water leak and letting the wood dry out while pressed down flat with a weighted board may effect a satisfactory solution, but the area that has lifted may have to be refixed and will no doubt need to be refinished.

If the source of moisture is from below, consult a surveyor or specialist contractor. It is possible that the entire floor will have to be taken up and a new bituminous or epoxy damp-proof membrane applied before the blocks can be re-laid. If you re-lay the floor yourself, number the blocks in sequence with chalk or a wax crayon before taking them up.

Patch repairs

If individual blocks get damaged, they can be replaced with blocks of matching wood cut to fit. First drill out most of the old wood, using a large drill bit, then trim out the remainder of the waste with a chisel. If the blocks are tongued and grooved, you will need to remove the tongues so the new blocks can be dropped into place. Spread flooring adhesive into the recesses, and tap the blocks down with a mallet and a block of scrap wood.

A neglected thin parquet floor generally has a number of loose, warped or missing strips. If it is laid on a wood sub-floor, refix loose strips with woodworking glue and fine nails, which must be punched below the surface.

It may be possible to fix a slightly warped strip in the same way. If it is too badly distorted to respond to this treatment, prise the strip out and dampen it with water, then press it flat between two pieces of particle board held in a vice. Let the strip dry out completely before you fix it back in place.

Missing strips should be replaced with timber of the same species, bought from a flooring specialist or timber merchant. Unless you have machine tools for planing it, have the wood cut to size with the dimensions slightly larger all round than those of the finished piece. Leave the wood to acclimatize in the room for several weeks.

Make a paper pattern of the recess and transfer the dimensions to the wood. Trim it to size with a tenon saw and plane. Use a mitre box for sawing the 45-degree angle needed on end pieces for parquet floors that have a diagonal pattern. Glue and nail the new strips in place. Then plane them flush with the surrounding wood, taking care not to mar the surface. Finish the new strips to match the rest of the floor.

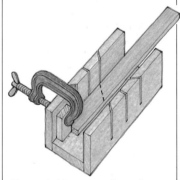

Use a mitre box to cut the angle

FINISHING FLOORS

IT IS ALWAYS POSSIBLE THAT *originally an exposed wooden floor in an old house, particularly if made of softwood, may not have been treated with a finish of any sort. Over the years the bare boards would have acquired a patina produced by the effect of light on the colour absorption of dirt plus burnishing from use and the 'natural' finish imparted by regular scrubbing.*

Nevertheless, you are unlikely to find a wood floor that has remained untreated to the present day – since, with changes in fashion and ownership, virtually all uncarpeted floors have now been treated with a stain, oil, wax, varnish or paint.

Which is the 'right' finish to adopt now is debatable, so let the floor itself be your guide. If you have an old floor that's in good condition, use a traditional finish. But if the wood has been replaced or low maintenance is important, you may prefer to use a modern finish.

Reproduction of a decorative boarded floor made for a Georgian house

SANDING FLOORS

Think carefully before sanding an old floor – the room may lose some of its character as a result. Although wood changes colour with age, it doesn't do so all the way through. So, unless the wood is very deeply stained, removing the surface by sanding will reveal the original colour beneath, which will look more like a new floor than an old one. Also, if the floor has had woodworm, their tunnels may be exposed by sanding.

The only efficient way to sand a wooden floor is to hire a commercial drum sander and, for the edges, a rotary floor-sanding machine.

Preparing for work
Make sure all the boards are fixed down securely, and use a nail punch to drive the nail heads below the surface of the boards. Clear the room and seal the gaps around the door. Always work with the windows open and wear a face mask.

Operating a drum sander
Fit an appropriate abrasive paper to the drum of the sanding machine, following the supplier's instructions. To operate the machine, tilt it backwards and switch on. Gently lower the drum until it comes into contact with the floor. Don't push the machine, but keep it under control, so it moves forward at an even pace. Don't stop with the drum in contact with the floor, or it will cut a hollow that is difficult to remove. Each 'band' of sanding should overlap the previous one.

If the boards are very uneven, start by working across the room diagonally, using a coarse abrasive paper (1). Then sand the floor diagonally with coarse paper again, working across your first sanding (2). Change the paper and sand along the boards, using first a medium grade and then a fine grade to smooth the wood (3). Vacuum the dust from the floor between each sanding.

Cleaning up
Using the rotary sander, sand the borders missed by the drum sander. Finally, use a long-handled scraper to finish the corners. A sanded surface marks easily, so it is advisable to wear soft shoes throughout the entire sanding operation.

Once sanding is complete, vacuum the entire floor area thoroughly and wipe the surface with white spirit in readiness for finishing. If you are unable to proceed with finishing straightaway, cover the floor with clean paper. Rolls of wall-lining paper provide a handy way of protecting a large area.

An alternative to sanding
To avoid sanding altogether, remove surface dirt and old finishes with a plastic scouring pad dipped in a proprietary agent used for cleaning antique furniture. This leaves the floor almost intact, retaining the scars and patina that the wood has acquired over a long period.

1 Work diagonally across the room

2 Then sand the other way

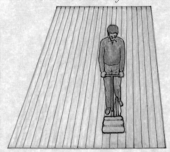

3 Follow the boards to finish

TYPES OF FINISH

Floor finishes can be divided into two main groups: those that penetrate the wood and those that form a protective film on the surface.

Oil finishes such as linseed oil, tung oil, Danish oil and teak oil are all penetrating finishes. Both traditional and modern lacquers and varnishes are surface finishes, as are paints – which are, in fact, pigmented varnishes. A wax finish can be either. It can be employed as a penetrating finish on bare wood, but it is more often used on surfaces that have already been sealed with one of the other types of finish.

Oil finishes

Oil is a traditional finish for wood, especially for woods that are naturally oily, such as teak and afrormosia. Suitable both for hardwoods and softwoods, an oil finish gives wood a natural-looking and pleasingly mellow quality. It is ideal for most board and parquet floors.

Commercially prepared oil finishes such as Danish oil and teak oil are fairly quick-drying and simple to apply. Like all oil finishes, they are easy to maintain.

Varnishes and lacquers

Traditional varnishes were based on natural oils and resins, whereas modern ones are based on synthetic resins. Most varnishes use white spirit as a solvent – but they are not solvent-reversible and need a chemical stripper to remove them.

Polyurethane is a modern hard-wearing, heat-resistant and waterproof synthetic-resin finish available in gloss and matt versions. It is best suited to new dirt-free floors, as careful preparation of the surface is required in order

Mellow early-C19th sealed and waxed pine board floor

to ensure good adhesion. Its hard-wearing properties are useful in high-traffic areas, such as hallways or kitchens.

Catalysed lacquers give an extremely hard-wearing surface that is resistant to heat, solvents and scratches. They are a modern invention, and cure by chemical action. Precatalysed lacquers include a hardener and set on exposure to air; two-part lacquers cure when a separate hardener is added.

All 'clear' varnishes darken the wood to some degree, and some are pretinted. Oil-based ones mellow with age.

Paint

When painting a bare wood floor with a traditional paint system, a primer has to be applied first, followed by an undercoat and top coat; on previously painted floors, the primer can be omitted. Some paints are now formulated in one-coat versions.

Old decoratively painted floors are now quite rare and should be preserved. If you have one that needs restoration, ask a specialist from a historical society for advice.

Wood stains

Stains are used to change the colour of wood but do not act as a finish. You can buy ready-made water-based, spirit-based and oil-based stains in a variety of shades.

Wax

A traditional finish for floors that protects and enhances the qualities of the wood, wax can be used either on bare wood or as a finish for sealed floors. It is available both as a paste and in liquid form. Liquid waxes are less laborious to apply, so most people prefer them for polishing floors.

CLEANING FLOORS

Whichever finish you decide on, you will need to clean the surface thoroughly as a preparatory measure. In fact, you may find that cleaning is all that is required and that the original finish is still in good condition.

Unfinished wood floors

Vacuum an unfinished floor to remove loose dust and grit, then wash it with warm water and detergent. To treat

light soiling, use a sponge and the minimum amount of water. To remove ingrained dirt, scrub the floor with a bristle brush, using scouring powder for bad patches. Rinse the surface as you go, then mop up the water quickly with a sponge and leave the floor to dry.

Waxed floors

Remove dust regularly with a soft brush, vacuum cleaner or dry mop. When necessary, use a liquid cleaning wax to improve the appearance of a floor that is lightly scratched or soiled but otherwise in good condition. Apply the wax with a clean soft cloth, working a small area at a time. The cleaning wax contains solvents that soften the finish sufficiently for the dirt to be absorbed by the cloth and leaves a film of polish on the floor. Let the finish dry, then buff to a soft sheen. An application of floor wax can follow if required.

To remove a wax finish, use white spirit and wire wool, working in the direction of the grain. Wipe up any residue of wet wax with a clean cloth and white spirit.

Oiled floors

Remove dust with a vacuum cleaner or soft brush. Wipe the surface with a lightly oiled cloth to give the finish new life. If necessary, wash the floor with soap suds, using a well-wrung mop and working a small area at a time. Rinse with clean water, in the same way, then dry the floor with a clean cloth. Allow the surface to dry thoroughly before applying a fresh coat of oil.

Varnished floors

Varnished floors should not be washed unless absolutely necessary, as there is always a chance that the water will penetrate under the finish and cause staining. Instead, use a solvent cleaner made of 4 parts white spirit to 1 part linseed oil. Apply the cleaner with a cloth, or fine wire wool for stubborn dirt, then wipe the surface dry with a clean cloth. If a varnished floor has been heavily coated with a wax polish, clean it like a waxed floor (see previous page).

Painted floors
Wash painted floors with a solution of warm soapy water or with a commercial paint cleaner. Working only a small area at a time, apply the solution or paint cleaner sparingly with a cloth or sponge mop, then wipe dry.

If a floor is to be repainted, rub the surface down, using fine silicon-carbide paper, and wipe clean with a tack rag before painting.

Clean decoratively painted floors with great care. After cleaning, apply a coating of wax floor polish to preserve the surface.

SAFETY
- Fumes from varnishes, paints and cleaners can be harmful when inhaled and should not be allowed to build up in a room. When using these materials, work with the windows open and wear a mask.
- Spirit-based finishes and finishes that have an oil or resin base are highly flammable. Extinguish all naked flames before working with them; and clean or destroy all used rags or cloths, especially ones that have been used to apply linseed oil, since they are liable to catch fire due to spontaneous combustion.

Pine floor decorated with attractive stencilled design in muted colours

APPLYING A FINISH
Before finishing a wood floor, all new work or repairs must be completed, the surface needs to be smoothed or cleaned, and colour applied if not in the finish itself. When applying finishes, always follow the manufacturer's instructions.

Oil
When using a proprietary oil finish, apply a generous coat with a cloth or paintbrush. Allow it to soak in for a few minutes, then wipe off the excess. Let the wood dry for up to eight hours, depending on drying conditions, before applying a second and third coat in the same way. When dry, buff to a soft sheen.

Wax
On a bare wood floor, apply two coats of sealer, using either thinned varnish or a proprietary sanding sealer. Sand down the surface with very fine silicon-carbide paper. The sealer stops the wax sinking in too deeply, which would draw dirt into the wood.

Brush on a liberal coat of liquid wax and leave it to soak in. About an hour later, work over the surface with an electric floor polisher. Apply further thin coats with a cloth pad charged with wax and buff each in turn. Leave the surface to harden, then burnish with the polisher next day.

Paste waxes need to be applied sparingly, using a cloth pad and building up the wax in layers until you have obtained a satisfactory finish. Never apply thick coats of paste in an attempt to achieve quick results – it will remain soft, hold the dirt and look dull. Between coats, burnish the wood with an electric floor polisher.

Varnish
New wood should first be sealed with a thinned coat of varnish, containing about 30 per cent solvent. Brush it in well, working with the grain. On a previously finished surface, use the varnish full strength for the first coat.

When it has set, apply two or three coats of unthinned varnish, allowing each to set before applying the next one. Work first across the grain, to spread the varnish evenly, then finish by brushing with the grain. Between each coat, rub down the surface with fine silicon-carbide paper.

If you can't complete the job in a single session, finish on a joint between boards. Don't work back over varnish that's partly set, as it will pick up brush marks.

Catalysed lacquers
Mix a two-part catalysed lacquer carefully, using the proportions recommended by the manufacturer. Apply an even coat of lacquer with a well-loaded brush, working with the grain. Do not brush the lacquer too much; allow it to flow freely from the brush so that it forms a smooth surface. Work quickly – to maintain a wet edge, so you can blend in each brushload without leaving brush marks. The coating should set in two hours.

Apply a second and third coat at two-hourly intervals. Rub down the surface with fine silicon-carbide paper before applying the last coat.

Paint and wood stains
Apply paint in even coats, using a brush 75mm (3in) wide and laying off with the grain. Allow the paint to set, and rub down between coats as required. Semi-matt paints are best for floors, as their texture makes them easier to work. Always work towards a door if you are painting the whole floor, so you will have a means of exit without treading on the newly painted surface. Let the paint dry thoroughly before walking on it.

To create a decorative pattern, prepare the floor then set out the design, painting it freehand or using stencils purchased from a specialist supplier. For the decorative elements, use a fast-drying acrylic paint to speed up the work, particularly if the pattern is multi-coloured. Use a stippling technique for the smaller details; for the larger elements, brush away from the edges of the stencil.

You can apply wood stains with a stencil, too, using a cloth pad and the minimum amount of colour so the stain doesn't bleed into the wood and blur the pattern.

Protect newly painted floors with a polyurethane varnish. Stained floors can be varnished or waxed.

CHAPTER SEVENTEEN

DECORATIVE METALWORK

IRON – which had previously been employed primarily for functional purposes – began to be used for decorative architectural work around the beginning of the eighteenth century. Up to that time iron had been smelted in relatively limited quantities, its production relying on charcoal-fuelled furnaces that required a ready supply of timber. This restricted the development of the material until in 1709 the iron founder Abraham Darby pioneered the use of coke for smelting iron ore.

Beautifully crafted wrought-iron gates and railings were produced by master craftsmen patronized by the wealthy. The work of migrant blacksmiths such as Jean Tijou was to have a profound influence on English wrought iron during the first quarter of the eighteenth century, and by the end of the century the production of iron for both wrought and cast work was well established. Without it, industrial development would have been impossible.

Although wrought iron was still employed for railings, porches and balconies until the mid nineteenth century, by this time cast iron had become the preferred material for decorative purposes. It was regarded not as a substitute for wrought iron, although designs were copied, but as a more substantial-looking material offering better value. Iron founders were now able to produce ornate castings cheaply in any number of identical pieces. This meant that architects could choose decorative ironwork from pattern books, instead of relying on the relatively expensive work of blacksmiths. It also gave them the freedom to create their own designs.

A C19th decorative balcony with cast-iron balustrade

Beautifully preserved 1830s wrought-iron hollow-urn newel post

TYPES OF METAL

METALS USED FOR TRADITIONAL BUILDINGS *can be divided into two main groups: ferrous metals (metals that contain iron, including wrought iron, cast iron and steel in its various forms) and non-ferrous metals (including copper, lead and brass). Non-ferrous metals generally resist corrosion better than ferrous metals do.*

Wrought iron
Being handmade by crafts-men, authentic wrought iron is no longer widely available. Its fibrous structure gives it good tensile strength and bending properties. A mal-leable iron, it is easily work-ed by forging and can be worked hot or cold. It can also be readily welded with modern welding methods.

Because wrought iron is a relatively corrosion-resistant metal, its traditional uses ranged from nails, locks, hinges and strapwork to fine examples of gates, railings, brackets and balustrades.

Cast iron
A heavy and relatively corrosion-resistant metal, cast iron is strong in compression but does not have good tensile strength. Cast-iron components are not easily worked, but can be machined and welded to make a repair.

Cast iron has been used for a wide variety of house-hold fitments, including weights and pulleys for sash windows, door fittings, fire-places and stoves, staircases, decorative brackets, railings, gates, balustrades, porches, roof crestings, and rainwater pipes and gutters.

Steel
Steel is a refined form of iron. It is a hard, tough and malleable metal. Although steel is very much a modern material, traditional 'carbon steel' was produced in the eighteenth century.

The most common type of steel today is mild steel. A general-purpose steel that can be worked hot or cold, it bends readily when heated and is available in various sections as well as in sheet form. In addition to its many other uses, it is now used as a substitute for traditional wrought iron.

Mild steel machines well and can be welded, but it is more difficult to forge-weld than traditional wrought iron. It does not have good corrosion resistance.

Copper
Copper was one of the first metals used by Man. In fact, there is evidence that it was being annealed and worked as early as 4,000 B.C. A soft metal that can be welded, brazed or soldered, it is both strong and malleable. Copper has excellent thermal and electrical conductivity and resistance to corrosion.

Brass
Brass is a yellow-coloured alloy of copper and zinc. Available in strip, bar, rod and sheet form, it is a common material for cast architectural fittings.

Lead
Lead is a heavy, malleable metal that is a bright silver colour when cut, but quickly oxidizes to a matt grey. It has excellent resistance to corrosion and is used for sheet roofing, flashings, pipes and gutters, as well as for decorative cast work.

IDENTIFYING THE METAL

IT IS NOT NECESSARY TO UNDERSTAND *the technical properties of metals, but it is useful to be able to identify the type of material used so that you can maintain it in an appropriate manner. Most examples of decorative metalwork, such as railings, balconies and brackets, are made of iron. However, since they are invariably thickly painted, it is not always easy to tell whether the metal is wrought iron or cast iron. Also, some of the decorative details may be made of other metals (for example, brass rosettes or finials cast in lead).*

Built-up construction and tapered scrolls are typical of wrought iron

Finely crafted wrought iron with delightful scrolls and repoussé work

Complex shapes and moulded surfaces are readily reproduced in cast iron

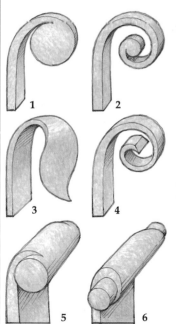

Wrought-iron scroll-work shapes
1 Halfpenny snub end
2 Solid snub end
3 Blow-over leaf
4 Ribbon end
5 Bolt end
6 Fishtail snub end

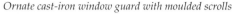

Ornate cast-iron window guard with moulded scrolls

1930s Art Deco decorative wrought-iron panel

Wrought and cast iron

To distinguish wrought iron from cast iron, first look at the style of the metalwork and the proportions of the elements that make up the design. Wrought iron is mostly based on standard square and rectangular sections of iron bar that are worked into decorative scrolls, twists and motifs. The ends of the bars are usually tapered or flattened and worked into snub ends or scrolls, each being individually shaped and subtly different from its neighbour. The overall appearance is crisp and elegant.

In contrast to wrought iron, each part of cast iron-work is precisely reproduced. Components tend to be thicker, incorporating a variety of sections and shapes, including turned forms. Look for 'flash lines' – the seams that run down the sides of a casting at the join between the moulds. The presence of flash lines provides conclusive evidence that a piece of ironwork is cast, not wrought, though on better-quality work these lines are filed away.

Typically the components of wrought ironwork are joined with rivets and collars, and incorporate joints familiar to wood-workers, such as mortise-and-tenon and cross halving joints. Forge or fire welding is also used to blend one part into another. Cast iron is joined by lead-caulked sockets or nuts and bolts fixed through cast lugs.

The surface texture also differs. Wrought iron tends to be smooth, albeit with some roller or hammer marks, whereas cast iron has a more granular feel.

Cracked or broken iron-work indicates the use of cast iron. If you examine the break, you will see the brittle crystalline nature of the material. Wrought iron, on the other hand, is malleable, so impact damage takes the form of bent rather than broken components.

Mild steel

Introduced in the latter part of the nineteenth century, mild steel is now commonly used for 'wrought' iron-work. Sections tend to be slimmer than traditional wrought iron. Also, if gas or electric-arc welding has been used for the joints, then that indicates that the metal is mild steel.

Copper

Polished copper has a rich pinkish-red colour, which oxidizes to a matt brown. With long exposure to the atmosphere, copper forms a green protective patina. Its main use in old buildings is as a sheet roof covering and for guttering, but it was also used for decorative details in Victorian interiors.

Weather vanes use various metals

Decoratively worked lead cladding

Brass

When stripped, the yellow colour of brass clearly distinguishes it from iron and lead, which are grey. When decorative brass details are found, it can be assumed that they were intended as additional ornamentation to contrast with painted ironwork. These should be cleaned carefully and protected from the elements with a clear lacquer.

Lead

Cast lead details can cause problems when stripping paint from old metalwork, since the softness of lead means that they are easily damaged. You may be able to detect the presence of lead under the paint by testing the metal with a sharp spike, to find out whether it is hard or soft, or by scraping the surface of the metal to reveal the bright silver colour beneath.

In order to preserve lead components, when stripping them don't try to burn off the paint or use abrasive stripping methods. Soften the paint with a chemical stripper, then wash it off with a bristle brush. Protect your eyes and hands when using paint strippers.

DECORATIVE IRONWORK

WELL-PRODUCED CHEAP CAST IRONWORK *was a boon to speculative builders, and from the early eighteenth century many town houses boasted a display of prefabricated decorative ironwork.*

Handmade wrought ironwork was revived by Arts and Crafts designers, who abhorred Victorian taste and machine-made products and valued traditional craftsmanship. The vogue only lasted until the 1920s, but their influence continues to this day.

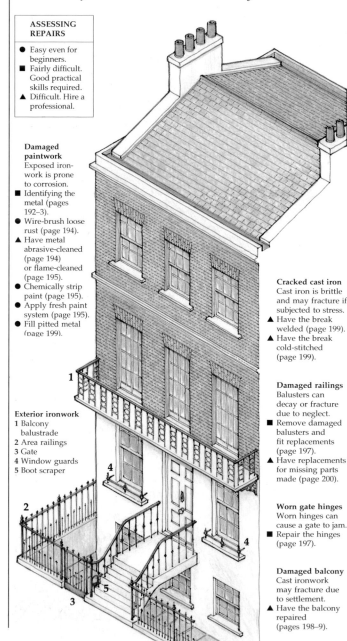

ASSESSING REPAIRS

- ● Easy even for beginners.
- ■ Fairly difficult. Good practical skills required.
- ▲ Difficult. Hire a professional.

Damaged paintwork
Exposed iron-work is prone to corrosion.
- ■ Identifying the metal (pages 192–3).
- ● Wire-brush loose rust (page 194).
- ▲ Have metal abrasive-cleaned (page 194) or flame-cleaned (page 195).
- ● Chemically strip paint (page 195).
- ● Apply fresh paint system (page 195).
- ● Fill pitted metal (page 199).

Exterior ironwork
1 Balcony balustrade
2 Area railings
3 Gate
4 Window guards
5 Boot scraper

Cracked cast iron
Cast iron is brittle and may fracture if subjected to stress.
- ▲ Have the break welded (page 199).
- ▲ Have the break cold-stitched (page 199).

Damaged railings
Balusters can decay or fracture due to neglect.
- ■ Remove damaged balusters and fit replacements (page 197).
- ▲ Have replacements for missing parts made (page 200).

Worn gate hinges
Worn hinges can cause a gate to jam.
- ■ Repair the hinges (page 197).

Damaged balcony
Cast ironwork may fracture due to settlement.
- ▲ Have the balcony repaired (pages 198–9).

PAINTING METAL

UNLIKE METALS *that form a protective oxide film, iron requires regular painting to protect it from corrosion. Good adhesion of the paint system is essential, and it is vital that the surface is thoroughly cleaned and prepared.*

A conventional paint system comprises a primer, an undercoat and a top coat, although you can now buy some paints for metal that form a protective barrier in a single coat.

Preparing painted surfaces
The only preparation necessary for previously painted surfaces is to clean them before repainting. Wash the surfaces with a sugar-soap solution to remove all traces of dirt and grease. If there is a high-gloss finish, wash the paintwork then key it by rubbing down with fine wet-and-dry paper. Rinse and dry well before repainting.

Damaged paintwork
If the paintwork is damaged and localized corrosion has set in, causing blisters or flaking, remove the loose material with a scraper. Scrape away paint around the damaged area to expose all traces of rust. Clean the rusted areas to a bright finish, either by hand with a wire brush or using a brush attachment fitted into the chuck of a power drill (1). Feather the edges of the old paint with abrasive paper.

If the metal is pitted, it is very difficult to eradicate all traces of rust. To overcome the problem, apply a rust inhibitor (available from car accessory shops), which will convert the rust into an inert form of iron phosphate (2).

1 Wire-brush the rust

2 Apply a rust inhibitor

Abrasive cleaning
Dry abrasive cleaning (grit or shot blasting) offers an efficient and effective way to clean rusted metal. If you have a large area to clean, it could be worth employing a contractor.

The process creates a lot of dust, and if the work is being carried out *in situ* the contractor should provide some form of protective barrier around the work area. Old lead-based paints are poisonous and it is harmful to inhale the dust, so keep away from the area until the job is completed.

Thoroughly cleaned iron rerusts quickly, so the work should be prepared in stages and it is essential to apply a primer as soon as possible after cleaning.

Flame cleaning

Use an oxypropane torch to help remove loose rust and scale from wrought iron and steel (but not cast iron, since it suffers from intense local-ized heating). Wire-brush the metal immediately after heating and remove fine dust prior to priming.

Thin metal sections may distort with this method, and fumes from burning lead-painted surfaces can be a health hazard.

Chemical stripping

Over a long period normal routine maintenance causes a considerable build-up of paint that can mask the fine detail of decorative pieces. Where this has occurred or the paint has been damaged or neglected, causing corros-ion to set in, it may be better to strip the paintwork and repaint completely.

You can apply a paste or gel stripper to interior and exterior ironwork *in situ* or, if the item is portable, send it to an industrial stripping company.

Apply strippers according to the maker's instructions. It's usually best to brush stripper onto fancy shaped work, so you can work the paste or gel into the crevices. Take care not to brush it on too thinly. Leave the stripper to soften the paint fully before scraping it off. You will find a stiff-bristle brush is best for cleaning paint from decorative details.

Most stripping agents are toxic. They therefore need to be handled with care during application, and materials contaminated by them must be disposed of according to local regulations. Wear eye protection, a face mask, vinyl gloves and, possibly, rubber boots when working with these materials.

APPLYING PAINT

Brush-applied oil-based paints provide a good serviceable treatment for most interior and exterior decorative metal-work. Treat derusted iron and steel with a rust-neutralizing inhibitor (some inhibitors require rinsing after treatment, others are self-priming). Then apply one or two even coats of zinc-phosphate primer. Always treat welded repairs with an additional coat. When the primer has set, brush on two layers of undercoat followed by one or two top coats.

Choosing a colour

Black has now become the standard colour for painted ironwork. However, in the Georgian period railings, balustrades and decorative metalwork were often painted dull green, a colour inspired by the patinated bronzes of antiquity. Other colours, including blue, brown and dark red, have also been used in the past.

If you plan to change the colour of decorative metal-work that is in a conserv-ation area or part of a listed building, you may need to obtain consent from the appropriate authority.

Gloss paints give better weather protection than matt paints for exterior work.

Finishing non-ferrous metals

Brass and copper take on a mellow natural patina that can look attractive without treatment. However, where the atmosphere or degree of exposure is likely to cause corrosion, the metal should be protected with a clear varnish.

Clean the surface with a metal polish, then wash with a mild liquid detergent in warm water and rinse well. Dry the metal with a soft cloth, then apply a clear varnish or acrylic lacquer with a soft brush.

Lead develops an attract-ive coating of grey oxide that protects the metal, so does not need painting. However, new leadwork can discolour unevenly and stain adjacent materials, so a patination oil is used in order to provide a protective film while the natural patina is forming.

Although galvanization is a relatively modern process, you may find zinc-plated (galvanized) iron and steel have been introduced into an old building. When new, the surface provides a poor key for most paints, though it will improve if allowed to weather for at least six months. However, if you apply a calcium-plumbate primer, the surface can be painted in the normal way. Check that the finishing paints you plan to use are compatible with the primer.

Blue paint used as an alternative to the usual black

Late-C19th gilded wrought-iron railing

RAILINGS

RAILINGS ARE THE MOST COMMON FORM *of traditional decorative wrought and cast iron-work in city and urban areas. If you walk down a street lined with Georgian or Victorian houses that have basements, you are likely to find wrought-iron or cast-iron railings designed to prevent pedestrians falling into the basement 'area'. Iron railings were also used to flank gateways of town houses or country estates, to fence in small domestic gardens and enclose communal gardens in city squares. Sadly, many of the latter have disappeared from the streets of Britain, having been requisitioned by the government during 1941–2 to provide metal for munitions. However, the stubs of these railings often still remain in the coping stones of the low supporting walls from which they were removed.*

Wrought-iron and cast-iron railings can be made to original patterns by blacksmiths or iron foundries that specialize in supplying traditional cast ironwork. A varied selection of ready-made cast-iron railings is available, too. Nowadays some manufacturers use cast aluminium, which can be cheaper for small runs of elaborate designs.

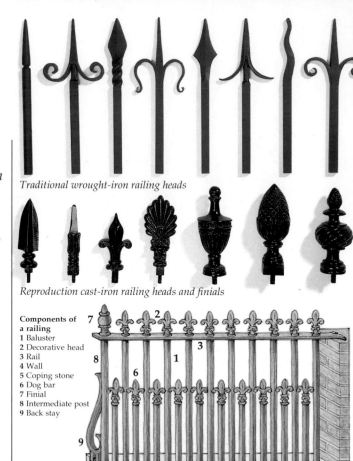

Traditional wrought-iron railing heads

Reproduction cast-iron railing heads and finials

Components of a railing
1 Baluster
2 Decorative head
3 Rail
4 Wall
5 Coping stone
6 Dog bar
7 Finial
8 Intermediate post
9 Back stay

Handsome C19th cast-iron panelled area railing

The popular anthemion motif, used here for cast-iron railing heads

Construction

A typical iron railing has a run of uprights, or balusters, topped with decorative heads. The uprights are joined together just below the heads by a horizontal rail, through which they pass. The tops of wrought-iron balusters would be forged into decorative shapes, or cast-iron decorative heads applied. The heads of cast-iron balusters were either cast as part of the baluster itself or made separately and screwed on.

The bottom end of the railing was usually supported by a low wall capped with a coping stone, but sometimes a stone plinth was used instead of a wall. The traditional method for joining the metal balusters to the stone was to set them in lead poured into drilled holes. The soft lead allows the metal a certain amount of thermal movement without damage to the stone and provides protection against corrosion. In some cases, lead was also run into the joints between the rail and balusters. The ends of the rail were fixed to metal posts or to brick or stone piers.

An elaborate railing may have short uprights (known as dog bars) between the main balusters, as well as additional rails and decorative details.

Railings that had balusters fixed into a supporting wall or plinth were assembled on site. However, railings were also often made as panels, with rails near the top and the bottom for fixing to a post. Where there was a long span between end posts or piers, a lighter intermediate post or a decorative panel fitted with a back stay was used to give extra support.

GATES

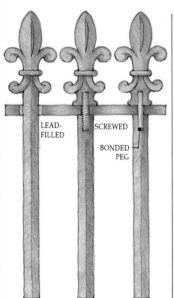

LEAD-FILLED SCREWED BONDED PEG

Fixing methods for railing heads

Replacing a baluster

Corrosion can set in where the base of a baluster is set into the stonework or around the joint with the top rail. If the baluster is badly corroded, you may be able to find a matching replacement from an architectural-salvage company or reproduction manufacturer. Otherwise, you can have a new baluster made to order.

Chisel out the lead from the stonework socket. Use an old (but sharp) narrow wood chisel for this operation.

If there is a detachable head, detach it and remove the baluster. Some detachable heads unscrew; but if the head is fixed to a peg, you will have to cut the peg in order to free the baluster.

If the head is an integral part of the baluster, remove the lead from the top joint (either melt it, using a blow torch, or trim it out with a chisel) then pull the baluster through the rail.

Fit the new baluster into place, and either set it in lead or use a two-part epoxy adhesive. If there is a detachable head, screw it in; or if it fits onto a peg, drill out the remains of the old peg and bond the head to a new one with the epoxy adhesive.

IN ADDITION TO PROVIDING SECURITY, *gates present the first impression of a property. Consequently, magnificent examples have been made in wrought and cast iron for grand country houses. These were often very large and topped with a decorative arch spanning the gateway, known as an overthrow. But for most domestic architecture, the gates were no more than waist or head height.*

Traditional iron gates are usually hung on cast-iron posts or brick piers. They are normally fitted with a wrap-round hinge at the top and a ground pivot at the base. Because iron gates are heavy, the pivots tend to suffer from wear.

Bold cast-iron railing panels make up this impressive pair of gates

Maintenance and repair

Keep the paintwork in good condition and grease the pivot points regularly in order to reduce wear and stop annoying squeaks.

Should the hinges be seriously worn, they may need to be replaced. The 'strap' of the top hinge, which wraps around a turned section of the gate-frame member, is usually bolted in place. Remove the bolts to inspect the condition of the parts. You may have to drill them out or cut them free with a hacksaw, in which case replace with a similar fitting.

Some assemblies include a bronze bush. If the strap or bush is badly worn and you are unable to do the

work yourself, you can have a new one made by a blacksmith or foundry – or maybe by a local garage. Give the repairer the old part and, if possible, a dimensioned drawing of the assembly.

The bottom of the gate pivots in a metal collar or in a cup set in the ground, which should be kept free from dirt. If a cast-iron cup is broken, have a replacement cast by a specialist.

If an iron gate is missing, you can have a replacement made in the traditional manner by a blacksmith or foundry, either to an old design or to a new design in keeping with the character of the building.

Grand pair of iron entrance gates

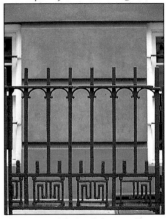

Area gate with Greek-key motif

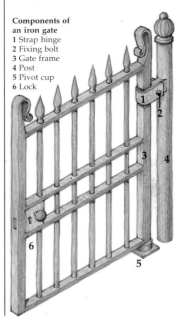

Components of an iron gate
1 Strap hinge
2 Fixing bolt
3 Gate frame
4 Post
5 Pivot cup
6 Lock

BALCONIES

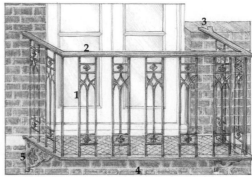
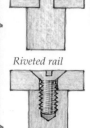

Riveted rail

Screwed rail

RENAISSANCE ARCHITECTURE *was the inspiration for the balconies that became such a popular feature of Georgian and Victorian town houses. At first-floor level, they provided a projecting terrace that enabled the occupants to step outside to enjoy the open air or view the scene below. Some balconies ran the entire width of the building, forming a continuous design with those of neighbouring houses, while others were only one window wide.*

Although stone was often used for the grander houses, most balconies were constructed of wrought iron or cast ironwork. These elegant and attractive structures were cantilevered from the façade, some having a projecting stone base surmounted by an iron balustrade while others were made entirely of iron. The latter type were usually constructed of panels of decorative cast iron. The heavier balconies were often supported by ornamental brackets, and sometimes by elegant cast-iron columns. Columns or traceried panel supports were also sometimes used when a balcony was surmounted by a roof or canopy.

Balcony construction

The stone bases of some balconies were built into the wall as the house was erected and formed an extension to the string course. The mass of the upper brickwork was used to counter the weight of the projecting stone, while brackets of stone or iron gave additional support. The supports for the iron balustrade panels were set into the slab and secured with lead. The ends of the handrail were fixed into a stone wall in the same way but would be built into a brick wall. In the latter case, the ends were split to form a 'fishtail' fork in order to provide a stronger grip in the mortar.

Balconies constructed entirely of iron were usually supported by the string course or window sill and fixed by the handrail at the top and by embedded lugs at the base. Cantilevered arms built into the wall or decorative brackets held by lead-packed lugs or bolts provided extra support for heavier versions.

Elegant iron balconettes complement the tall first-floor windows

BALCONETTES AND WINDOW GUARDS

The small bow or flat-fronted balconies, or balconettes, that grace a single window are often little more than window guards, their real function being to provide a barrier for the tall first-floor sash windows that almost touched the floor.

Window guards are lighter in construction than balconies and normally are not supported by brackets. Some have a platform consisting of a metal grille or open bars. They may be little more than a flat panel across a window opening or a decorative rail fitted to a deep stone window sill.

A lead-covered canopy provides shelter for this attractive balcony

Cast-iron anthemion balconette

Lattice-pattern window guard

Elegant cast-iron balconies, providing an ideal support for wisteria

REPAIRING & REPLACING IRON

METAL IS A TOUGH AND DURABLE *material, but if neglected it decays. Regular maintenance is therefore needed to keep it in good order and avoid expensive repairs. Although it is not particularly easy to work, you can carry out certain repairs yourself – and fortunately there are specialists who are able to deal with most problems and remake parts that are missing or beyond repair.*

Cold repairs to cast iron

Large hollow-sectioned porch or veranda columns, cast-iron newel posts and heavy-gauge brackets (for example, in a conservatory) can crack when subjected to subsidence stresses or impact damage. In order to avoid having to heat a large mass of metal, cracks in cast iron that is not less than 6mm (¼in) thick can be repaired by a specialist contractor using a technique known as cold stitching **(1)**.

If a non-structural part, such as a decorative detail, has broken off a cast-iron component, you can repair it with a two-part epoxy adhesive. For small pieces, simply mix the adhesive according to the maker's instructions, apply it to the broken surfaces and fix in place. For larger pieces, drill holes in each part and fit pegs cut from stainless-steel rod to reinforce the joint.

Pitting in rusted cast iron can be filled with an epoxy car-body filler. Clean the metal thoroughly and apply a rust inhibitor. Mix the filler and apply it with a plastic spatula so it is just proud of the surface **(2)**. When it has set, shape the filler with a file and rub it down with abrasive paper to follow the contour of the metal, as required. Prime and paint the repair to match the finish of the work.

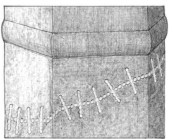

1 Cold stitching on thick cast iron

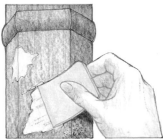

2 Apply filler proud of the surface

Maintaining a balcony

A decorative iron balcony adds considerable character to a house. However, if it isn't maintained properly its prominent position can make it a distinct liability. Chipped or worn paint may result in rusting, which can stain the walls of the house and, if untreated, lead to structural failure. Broken or missing rails create an aura of neglect, and weak fixings may cause structural problems that are costly to repair.

Keep paintwork in sound condition and repaint regularly. Replace missing or seriously decayed elements, using matching parts bought from specialist suppliers or made to order.

From time to time, check the joints where a stone base meets the wall. The slab should slope away from the wall slightly in order to shed rainwater. If water is lying against the wall, it is likely to create penetrating damp. Have a surveyor inspect the structure, as settlement may be causing the problem and require the attention of a builder.

Stresses caused by settlement can crack brittle cast iron. If balusters or decorative iron panels are cracked, have them welded *in situ*. Continuous balconies with large panels of ironwork need to expand and contract to some degree. It is therefore important that welding repairs should not restrict thermal movement, otherwise the ironwork may suffer from further fractures. Large platform grids in need of repair may require strapping with bolted stainless steel plates rather than welding.

If a balcony is beyond repair or has been removed by a previous owner, consult a specialist supplier able to reproduce and install a new balcony for you. If the house is listed or in a conservation area, you will need approval for the replacement balcony.

Welding broken cast iron

Cast iron is brittle and may fracture when struck sharply or weakened by rust. If the break is simple, provided the metal is still in reasonable condition, you can normally have it arc-welded *in situ* either by a blacksmith or a welding service that undertakes cast-iron repairs.

In order to avoid setting up stresses in the metal, cast iron has to be heated as part of the welding process. The edges of the crack are ground into a 'V', which is filled with weld metal. The weld should be continuous, without holes (which can encourage corrosion), ground flat, and thoroughly primed ready for painting.

IRONWORK MADE TO ORDER

If ironwork is missing or beyond repair, you can have a replacement made by a specialist. A number of blacksmiths and specialist foundries still exist, but sadly not as many as when ironwork was in its heyday.

Ordering wrought ironwork

Wrought ironwork is made by artist blacksmiths, using traditional craft skills. Now a rare breed, they fashion plain lengths of iron into beautiful forms by heating the metal and beating it on the anvil and on a variety of shaped stakes. This type of work has always been fairly expensive compared with mass-produced cast ironwork, but for one-off items it may be competitive. You can ask the blacksmith to reproduce an old pattern or to create a new design in a traditional style.

Ordering cast ironwork

Because cast iron is made in a mould, any number of identical pieces can be cast from the same pattern.

If you use an existing component as a pattern, you need to bear in mind that cast iron shrinks by about 1 per cent on cooling. For small items, the difference is insignificant. However, if a baluster or other item is 1m (3ft) long, the reproduction would be 10mm (⅜in) or so shorter than the original.

When a single baluster needs replacing, you may prefer to make up the difference with packing rather than spend money on having a special pattern made. If, on the other hand, you have a number of balusters that need to be replaced, you may consider it is worth getting the blacksmith or foundry to make a new pattern for you.

The patterns are normally machined and carved from wood, but clay and resins are used too. To make the casting, a special type of sand is packed all round the pattern in a two-part mould. Various channels are formed in the sand and the pattern is removed, leaving a hollow into which the molten iron is poured.

When the iron has set, the sand is cleaned away, leaving the casting and attached sprues (the iron solidified in the channels). These are cut away and the casting is fettled (filed) to remove the mould marks. Threads may then be 'tapped' (cut) into the component, depending on the method of fixing.

Reproductions of decorative cast iron
1 Porch brackets
2 Railing or column panels
3 Anthemion balustrade panel
4 Gothic-style balustrade panel
5 Late-Victorian window guard

CHAPTER EIGHTEEN

STAIRCASES

EARLY HOUSES RARELY HAD STAIRS, *simple ladders being used to gain access to upper levels such as lofts. However, important medieval buildings often had internal or external stairs, most of them constructed from masonry, although some had wooden treads built into the walls.*

Wooden framed staircases had generally replaced stone stairs by the late sixteenth century. At first these were robustly constructed from heavy sections of timber and featured rudimentary decoration, although handsomely carved staircases are found in Elizabethan and Jacobean mansions. The position of interior staircases varied, but as often as not they were tucked away in a corner or else advantage would be taken of a convenient alcove or chimney breast.

By the eighteenth century staircase building was highly developed, employing sophisticated building and joinery techniques. Main staircases were now generally made of wood, although stone stairs with iron balustrades were used in the grandest Georgian and Victorian houses. Since the foot of the main staircase was normally situated in the entrance hall, designers and makers took the opportunity to demonstrate their skills by constructing eye-catching straight or curving staircases. Some were relatively simple in style, while others featured ornate balustrades and finely carved decorative details.

Stairs leading to a basement were frequently made of wood or of stone and metal, and some were entirely constructed from metal. These were usually plainer than the main stairs, but cast-iron types were invariably produced in decorative designs. Cellar stairs were of the simplest kind, mostly being open-tread straight flights made of thick sections of wood.

The staircase is an important feature of this C18th entrance hall

A fine early-C18th mahogany balustrade with moulded handrail

TYPES OF STAIR

T HE SIMPLEST TYPE OF STAIRWAY *comprises a single straight flight of stairs. However, short flights linked by landings are quite common. This type of stairway may be known as a quarter-turn or half-turn stair, depending on whether the turn is made through 90 or 180 degrees. Some staircases have tapered steps, known as winders, instead of landings.*

Dog-leg and open-well stairs are types of half-turn stair. The former, which began to be used in small houses around the late seventeenth century, gets its name from its elevational shape. It is used where the width of the stairway is restricted, and has the upper balustrade in the same plane as the lower one. The open-well stair has a space between the balustrades, providing a more satisfactory arrangement for the layout of the handrail.

NEWEL STAIRS

The majority of staircases are constructed of wood, using a system of structural posts called newels or newel posts.

These are positioned at the ends of each flight in order to transfer the weight of the stair to the floor and support the balustrades, which are jointed into the newel posts at each turn. An open-well stair therefore has two posts at landing level, whereas the simpler dog-leg type needs only one landing post.

Late-C19th newel staircase

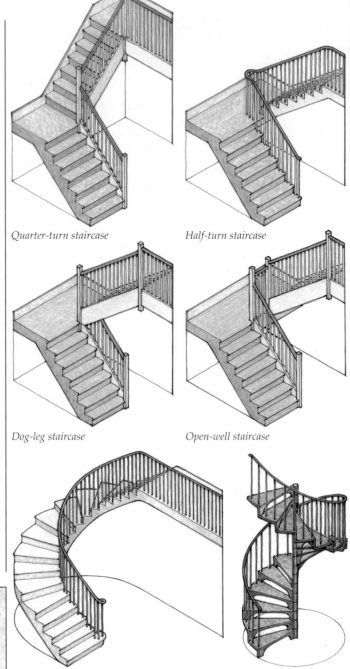

Quarter-turn staircase

Half-turn staircase

Dog-leg staircase

Open-well staircase

Winding geometrical staircase

Spiral staircase

BUILDING REGULATIONS

All stairs present a hazard to the user. To make them as safe as possible, the Building Regulations include a number of rules governing their size and layout.

The rules relate to the shape, depth, height, level and number of the steps, the pitch of the staircase, the clearance above it, and the width of the landings. The provision of hand-rails and balustrades as well as their related heights and the space between balusters are also covered.

The regulations apply to all new work, including installing stairs in a building when there is a change of use – such as a barn conversion – and may affect the reinstatement of a traditional-style staircase in an old house (but not repairs to an existing stair). This can make the re-creation of a staircase in an old building problematic, if not impossible, although you may be able to obtain a relaxation of the rules in special circumstances. In addition, any work to staircases (including repairs) will need approval if your house is a listed building. Contact your local Building Control Officer for advice.

GEOMETRICAL STAIRS

Geometrical staircases are designed and constructed in such a way that supporting posts are unnecessary. The balustrade and inner string of this type of open-well stair form a continuous curving structure In grandiose late-Georgian and Regency houses they were sometimes made of stone. Wide sweeping geometrical staircases with radiating tapered steps are known as winding stairs. Elliptical stairs are of similar construction.

Spiral stairs are simply a form of geometrical stair with radiating tapered steps. Most are metal and have a central supporting column. Spiral stairs that are made on the open-well principle are called helical stairs.

WOODEN STAIRS

T HE INTERIOR STAIRCASES *of the mid eighteenth century were mostly constructed of softwood, such as pine, though oak (which had generally been used earlier) continued to be used in the larger houses. Mahogany, at that time regarded as an exotic timber, began to be used for handrails and newel posts in better-quality houses, in combination with painted softwood balusters and framing.*

By the Victorian period mahogany had become much more commonplace. Most staircases were now fitted with mahogany handrails, and in some cases the entire balustrade was made of the wood. Oak was popular too thanks to the Arts and Crafts movement, which used it to revive styles of earlier times.

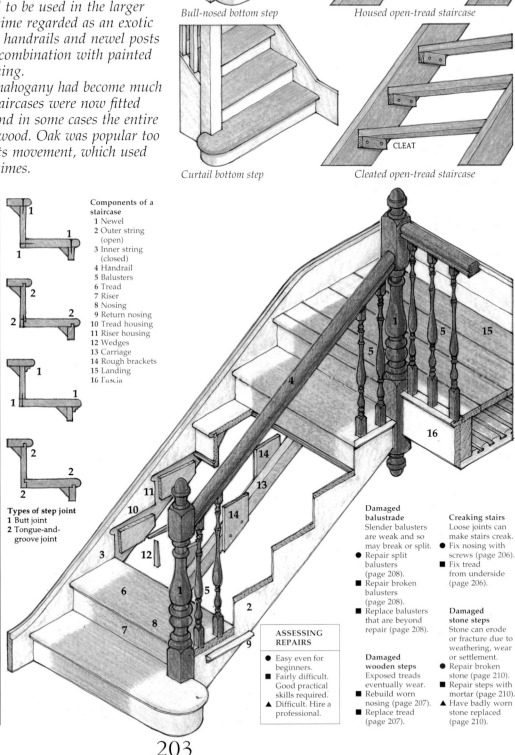

Bull-nosed bottom step

Housed open-tread staircase

HOUSING

Curtail bottom step

Cleated open-tread staircase

CLEAT

Steps

The steps of most wooden staircases are made in two parts, each step consisting of a horizontal tread board and a vertical riser. The risers are fitted between consecutive treads and are usually fixed to the treads with nail-fixed butt joints or with tongue-and-groove joints. Variations on these types of joint are also sometimes used for step assemblies.

The riser, which is about 18mm (¾in) in thickness, provides a closed back to the step. This allows the tread to be relatively lightweight, so the board is normally only 28mm (1⅛in) or so thick. The front edge of the tread, which is called the nosing, projects beyond the riser and is often rounded over.

The bottom step is usually made as a separate part that is added to the main flight. As it isn't fitted between the strings, it often has a shaped outer end. Bull-nosed and curtail steps are examples that are commonly found.

The steps of a traditional open-tread staircase are of very simple construction, merely having a thick tread that is either housed into both stringboards or fixed to them with cleats.

Components of a staircase
1 Newel
2 Outer string (open)
3 Inner string (closed)
4 Handrail
5 Balusters
6 Tread
7 Riser
8 Nosing
9 Return nosing
10 Tread housing
11 Riser housing
12 Wedges
13 Carriage
14 Rough brackets
15 Landing
16 Fascia

Types of step joint
1 Butt joint
2 Tongue-and-groove joint

Damaged balustrade
Slender balusters are weak and so may break or split.
● Repair split balusters (page 208).
■ Repair broken balusters (page 208).
■ Replace balusters that are beyond repair (page 208).

Damaged wooden steps
Exposed treads eventually wear.
■ Rebuild worn nosing (page 207).
■ Replace tread (page 207).

Creaking stairs
Loose joints can make stairs creak.
● Fix nosing with screws (page 206).
■ Fix tread from underside (page 206).

Damaged stone steps
Stone can erode or fracture due to weathering, wear or settlement.
● Repair broken stone (page 210).
■ Repair steps with mortar (page 210).
▲ Have badly worn stone replaced (page 210).

ASSESSING REPAIRS
● Easy even for beginners.
■ Fairly difficult. Good practical skills required.
▲ Difficult. Hire a professional.

Strings

The ends of the treads and risers are jointed into thick inclined boards known as strings (also as stringboards or stringers). These are the structural members that run up each side of the stairs. Two types are commonly used. The closed string has straight parallel edges with the inner face housed to take the ends of the treads and risers. The open or 'cut' string, introduced in the late seventeenth century, has a straight lower edge but is notched to the step shape along its upper edge to bear the treads and risers.

The stringboard fitted to the wall is of the closed type and is usually referred to as the inner or wall string. The other one, which carries the balusters, is usually called the outer string and may be either closed or open.

On some staircases an intermediate string, called a carriage, is fitted under the centre to give support. This is necessary for a stair more than 1m (3ft) wide. The carriage may be a thick notched board, but more often it is a bearer with rough brackets nailed to it. These brackets, which are short lengths of board, support the treads and are fixed to alternate sides of the carriage in order to distribute the load evenly.

On stairs that have a lath-and-plaster soffit, carriage bearers placed on one or both sides and at the centre provide support for the laths, which are nailed across them. Sometimes the laths run vertically, following the slope of the stair, and are nailed only to the underside edge of the steps.

Closed strings have the treads and risers housed into them. The housings are cut some 12mm (½in) deep, with a tapering bottom edge. Glued hardwood wedges are driven into the housings from the back to secure the treads and risers tightly. Triangular softwood 'glue blocks', measuring about

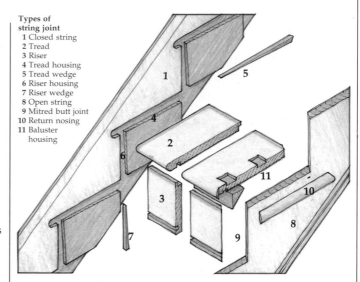

Types of string joint
1 Closed string
2 Tread
3 Riser
4 Tread housing
5 Tread wedge
6 Riser housing
7 Riser wedge
8 Open string
9 Mitred butt joint
10 Return nosing
11 Baluster housing

100 x 38mm (4 x 1½in), are rub-jointed into the angles between the tread boards and risers for extra support.

On open-string stairs, the joints between the outer string and the treads and risers are different from those of the closed wall string – the treads being simply glued and nailed to the horizontal edge of the stepped outer string. A 'return' nosing is nailed onto the end of the tread board to cover the end grain and the baluster joints. A fretted bracket is sometimes fitted under the nosing for decorative purposes. To conceal the end grain of the riser, a mitred butt joint is made between the outer end of the riser and the vertical edge of the string.

Late-C19th decorative string

C18th carved string brackets

C18th baluster-type newel made from mahogany

Mid-C19th staircase with solid newel post

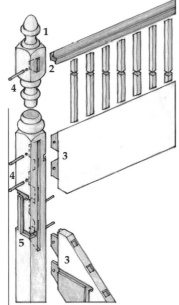

Construction details
of a newel post
1 Intermediate
  newel
2 Mortise-and-
  tenoned handrail
3 Mortise-and-
  tenoned strings
4 Dowels
5 Tread and riser
  housings

Newel posts

Newels were included in the construction of the earliest framed staircases. Placed at the foot and the head or turn of the stair, they support the staircase and balustrade. They are usually cut from solid wood, though panelled versions are also found.

The newel at the foot is a prominent feature of most newel staircases by virtue of its material and its form or surface decoration, as well as its size. However, instead of ending with a large post, eighteenth-century staircases frequently culminated in a cluster of balusters, which often included a fine newel.

Bulbous solid-hardwood newels, often turned and richly carved, were fashionable in the grand houses of the early nineteenth century. These inspired the vogue for turned newels, found even in modest houses until the beginning of the twentieth century. Eventually, simpler square-sectioned newels, in the manner of the earlier seventeenth-century style, were to supersede the turned forms. Some, however, were capped with a turned knob.

The newel at the bottom of the stair and usually the first intermediate post, too, are fixed to the floor. Often they are nailed to floorboards, but fixing to a joist gives greater rigidity. Hollow newels are sometimes fixed with a long threaded rod inside. The top newels of a dog-leg or open-well stair are fixed to the top floor and cut short, forming a decorative drop detail.

The newels are housed to receive the steps, and if the post is panelled the outer string as well. The string is tenoned into a solid newel and pegged for security. The handrail is housed or tenoned into the post.

Typical patterns for round and square-turned balusters

Balustrades

The type of balustrade used for staircases from the seventeenth century until modern times consisted of a series of vertical balusters fixed to the top edge of the outer string or stair treads and to the underside of a handrail. On a newel stair the run of the balustrade is punctuated at every turn by the newel posts, while on a geometrical staircase the balustrade is uninterrupted.

The curving style of the geometrical stair became popular around the second quarter of the eighteenth century and continued into the Victorian era. The handrails are moulded or oval in section and relatively lightweight. At the foot of the stair, the rails often terminate with a volute supported by a group of balusters set on a curtail step.

Early-nineteenth-century balustrades have a handrail that terminates in a turned bun-shape cap attached to a slim newel post. Where the stairway changes direction or meets a landing, shaped handrail sections – called turns, ramps or swan necks, as appropriate – are used to cope with the change of level and direction. The various parts of the handrail are usually fixed together with dowel pegs or special bolts.

The balusters for newel and geometrical staircases may be decoratively turned (with a column-and-vase or twist pattern, for example) or they may simply be plain square sticks.

On well-constructed stairs the balusters are housed into the underside of the handrail and into the top edge of the closed string. Otherwise, they are simply butt-jointed and nailed in place.

Open-string stairs may have either two or three balusters fitted to a tread. These are normally secured with housing or dovetail joints, which are concealed by a return nosing fitted to the side of each step.

Painted mid-C18th Chinese Chippendale balustrade

C18th twist-pattern balustrade

WOODEN STAIR REPAIRS

MOST STAIRCASES ARE WELL CONSTRUCTED *and only require light repairs that can be carried out as part of your routine painting and decorating programme. However, structural repairs may become necessary as a result of infestation or rough treatment. Loose or weak parts should be repaired or replaced as soon as they are discovered.*

FIXING CREAKING STAIRS

Creaking stairs can be irritating and give the impression that a house is not properly maintained. The source is likely to be loose or flexing components rubbing together at their joints because of shrinkage or wear and tear. The most satisfactory repairs are achieved by working from the back of the step – however, if the stair has a plastered soffit it is much simpler to work from the front.

To identify the source of the creaking, remove the stair covering and walk up the stairs. Tread on and off each step, applying your weight to different parts to find out where the loose joints are situated.

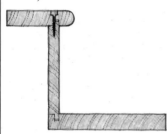

1 Screw the tread to the riser

Working from the front

One likely cause of creaking is a weak joint between the tread nosing and the riser. This is usually a tongue-and-groove joint, or a butt joint with a scotia moulding set into the angle between the riser and the tread. In either case, the easiest solution is to drill and counterbore the tread to take two or three 38mm (1½in) screws set directly above the centre line of the riser **(1)**. Inject woodworking adhesive into the holes and flex the board to help it penetrate the joint as far as possible. Insert the screws, which will pull the joint tightly together, and fit matching wooden plugs to cover the heads.

If the stair has featured hardwood treads, try not to

use screws. Prise the joint apart a little and work glue into it with a brush. If this fails to get rid of the creaking, you will need to work from the underside.

Working from the back

If the underside of the staircase has a lath-and-plaster soffit, it will be necessary to cut into it to gain access to the problem area. To reduce the damage, locate the weak steps and note the position in relation to the underside. Chop away the plaster with a bolster chisel, then saw through or pull out the laths **(2)**. You will have to make good the plaster after completing the repair.

In many period houses the underside of the staircase leading up from the ground floor is enclosed with a partition between the outer string and the floor called a spandrel. This may be a lath-and-plaster stud wall or a wood-panelled frame. A door provides access to the cellar stairs or a cupboard space below the staircase. The underside of the stair is usually unfinished.

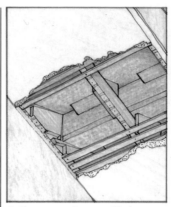

2 Clear away plaster and laths

3 Inject glue into the opened joint

4 Rub-joint blocks into place

5 Glue and screw back joint

Fixing the tread

Glue blocks are normally fitted into the angle between the tread and the riser. If old glue has failed, knock the blocks off and clean the glue from the surfaces.

Use a chisel to prise apart the joint between the front of the tread board and the riser. Inject woodworking glue **(3)** and rub-joint the blocks in place **(4)**. To strengthen the joint, make and fit additional glue blocks.

Similarly, prise apart the joint between the back of the tread and the riser. Inject glue into the joint and insert screws to pull it tight **(5)**.

Do not use the stairs until the glue has set.

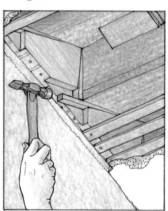

6 Fit new riser and tread wedges

Fixing the housing joint

If the ends of the tread or riser are loose in their housings, prise out the wedges that help to hold the boards securely in position.

Use a narrow chisel to chip or pare out any hardened glue or splintered fragments of the old wedges that may remain in the housings.

Make new wedges from hardwood; apply woodworking glue and drive them into place. Fit the vertical wedge for the riser first and cut it to length, then fit the horizontal wedge for the tread **(6)**.

1 Guide the saw with a pinned batten

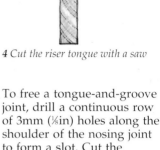

2 Saw in from front edge of tread

3 Prise off the nosing moulding

4 Cut the riser tongue with a saw

REPAIRING DAMAGED STEPS

The treads of a wooden stair eventually wear at the nosing, especially if they are unprotected and made of softwood. Badly worn treads are dangerous and should be repaired or replaced without delay.

Treads are difficult to replace, since they may be held with tongue-and-groove joints across their width and the treads of closed-string stairs can only be removed from the back. Unless you have the necessary experience, it is therefore best to employ a builder or a carpenter – particularly if the staircase has carriage bearers, which makes replacement an even trickier operation.

Rebuilding the nosing

Mark cutting lines around the worn area. Hold a drill at 60 degrees to the surface, and at one end of the section that needs replacing drill four 3mm (⅛in) holes close together to form a slot. Set a power jigsaw to 60 degrees and make a sawcut along the line. To help make a straight cut, pin a guide batten to the tread (1).

At each end of the marked section, saw in from the front edge of the nosing to meet the first cut at right angles (2). You will need to reset the cutting angle of the saw for the second end. Tap the worn piece from below to free the waste. The end sawcuts will have cut into the riser, so these will need to be filled.

Cut a new section of wood to fit the cutout. If the riser board has a tongue, work a groove into the underside of the new section to receive it. Shape the front edge of the nosing, then check the fit and glue the new section in place. When the glue has set, plane the surfaces flush.

Replacing a tread

Tread and riser assemblies may either be tongued and grooved or butt-jointed and nailed. In either case, the parts will probably need to be cut to free the tread.

Remove the glue blocks from under the tread and if there is a scotia moulding under the nosing prise it free with a wide wood chisel (3). Also, remove any screws or nails. Try to pull out nail fixings – however, if the tread has a butt joint, you can cut through nails by sliding a hacksaw blade into the joint.

To free a tongue-and-groove joint, drill a continuous row of 3mm (⅛in) holes along the shoulder of the nosing joint to form a slot. Cut the tongue either by hand, using first a padsaw and then a panel saw, or by inserting a powered sabre saw or jigsaw into the slot (4). If it is an open-string stair, cut the rear tongue from the underside in a similar way.

How you remove the tread will depend on whether the staircase is a closed-string or open-string type (see below).

Closed-string stair

Remove the wedges from under each end of the tread. Using a hammer and a block of wood, give the tread a sharp tap from above to free the back joint and housing joints (5). The tread should now be clear of the riser tongue at the rear, so you can drive it out of its housings from the front (6).

Make a new tread, but do not cut a groove on the underside. Build up the cut edge of the front riser with glued veneer or a thin strip of wood cut from a board with a machine saw. Apply glue, then insert the tread from the back and secure it with new hardwood wedges glued into place. Fit glue blocks inside the nosing. If needed, refit a scotia moulding under the front edge.

5 Strike the tread to free it

6 Drive out the tread from the front

Open-string stair

Prise off the return nosing carefully (7). Free and remove the balusters from the tread and handrail. Chisel out the wedge from under the tread housed in the wall string. Tap the open-string end of the tread from the rear to free it, then extract the board from the front (8).

Make a new tread of well-seasoned wood to match the shape of the old one and cut the joints for the balusters. Build up the cut edges of the risers with glued strips of wood. Glue and screw the tread to the risers and wedge the housing joint in the wall string. Fit the balusters, then fix the return nosing with a dab of glue and a nail at the mitred front end and a nail at the other.

7 Prise off the return nosing

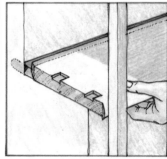

8 Pull the tread out from the front

REPAIRING BALUSTRADES

Much of the character of a staircase is provided by the balustrade. The repetition of the balusters, whether ornately turned or merely plain sticks, gives a pleasing decorative effect. If one or two balusters are damaged or missing, or have been replaced by non-matching ones, the symmetry is disturbed and the appearance spoilt.

Broken balusters are potentially dangerous, so should be repaired or replaced without delay. Try to preserve original turned ones. If they are beyond repair, either make replacements on a lathe yourself or have new ones made to order.

Baluster fixings

On well-constructed stairs the balusters are housed into the underside of the handrail and the top edge of a closed string **(1)**. However, you often come across staircases where the balusters are simply butt-jointed and nailed in place **(2)**.

Open-string stairs may have two or three balusters to a tread. Usually, housing or dovetail joints are used to secure them and the joints are covered with a return nosing **(3)**.

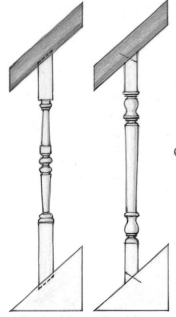
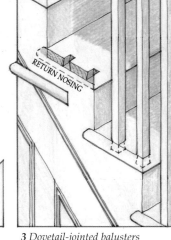

1 Housing joint *2 Butt joint* *3 Dovetail-jointed balusters*

Repairing a split baluster

Turned or slender wooden balusters tend to be fairly weak, and may break if they are struck from the side. A split baluster that has a long tapering break is simple to repair and there is normally no need to remove it from the balustrade.

Apply an even coating of woodworking glue to the surfaces of the break, then pull them together tightly with self-adhesive tape **(4)**. Wipe off surplus glue with a damp cloth before binding up the repair. When the glue has set, peel off the tape. Clean up with a scraper and abrasive paper, then finish to match the other balusters.

Repairing a broken baluster

If a break – at a narrow section of a turned baluster **(5)**, for example – is short due to a weakness in the structure of the grain, gluing alone may not make a sufficiently strong repair. It is therefore better to remove the baluster and reinforce the repair with a wooden dowel.

To enable you to drill a stopped hole that will accurately align in both parts, first drill a 9mm (⅜in) diameter hole about 50mm (2in) deep down the centre of one of the parts **(6)**. Make sure that the part you choose has beads and coves or similar details close to the end.

Saw off the broken end with a fine dovetail saw. Make the cut on a shoulder line of the turned decoration **(7)**, having made a pencil mark across the shoulder so you can align the parts when reassembling the baluster. Then glue the broken ends together carefully.

When the glue is set, drill down the other part of the baluster **(8)**, using the glued-on piece as a guide – and again making the hole about 50mm (2in) deep. If need be, glue a piece of veneer to the end to make up the sawcut waste. Trim out the centre to reopen the hole.

Cut a length of 9mm (⅜in) dowel, then chamfer the ends and cut a groove along its length. Apply glue to the parts and assemble the dowelled joint, using the pencil mark to help you realign the parts correctly **(9)** Wipe away surplus glue with a damp cloth.

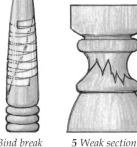

4 Bind break with tape *5 Weak section of baluster*

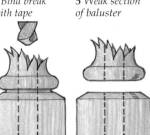
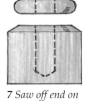

6 Drill a hole down one part *7 Saw off end on a shoulder line*

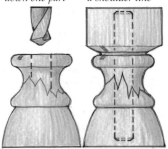

8 Drill the other part of baluster *9 Glue and dowel the parts*

Replacing a baluster

If a baluster is beyond repair or missing, you will need to replace it. Select matching wood unless the baluster is to be painted. Plain square-sectioned sticks can easily be planed to size if they are not a standard timber section.

Making decorative turned balusters involves the use of a lathe. If you have access to one and have the necessary woodturning experience, either make a card template of the baluster's profile or take out a sound baluster to act as a guide. You can construct the template profile with drawing instruments, or use a profile gauge to take an impression of the shape.

If you lack the facilities to make a replacement yourself, take a sample baluster to a specialist woodturner and have a reproduction of it made. Some woodturning companies have copy lathes that reproduce the shape of an original automatically.

Whether you make a replacement yourself or have one made to order, the new baluster should be made overlength for cutting to size before fitting and finishing.

STONE STAIRS

1860s stone staircase with sweeping spandrel steps and cast-iron balustrade

STONE IS PRIMARILY *an exterior building material and is not commonly employed indoors. However, it can be used to provide attractive interior features. Grand stone geometrical staircases are occasionally found in large late-eighteenth-century and nineteenth-century houses, as well as secondary stone stairs leading to the basement. Decorative wrought-iron or cast-iron balustrades were generally used to complement the solidity of stone staircases.*

Many houses of this period have a basement or semi-basement. To enable a large window and a doorway to be built at the front, an open 'area' was created between the footpath and the front of the basement wall. Usually stone steps and a stone platform bridged the gap between the path and the front door, while a decorative iron or stone balustrade guarded the open area. The basement itself was reached by descending a stone or metal stairway that led down into the area.

STONE STAIR CONSTRUCTION

The design of stone steps can range from thick rectangular blocks (1) or thinner slabs forming treads and risers (2) to the more sophisticated carved wedge-shaped sections of spandrel steps (3).

Spandrel steps are used in the construction of interior open-well geometrical stairs. The inner ends of these steps are left square and built into the wall for support. Each step sits on the back edge of the one below and is located by a mortared splayed rebate cut in the lower front edge.

The shaping of the nosing usually follows the conventional rounded form used on wooden stairs, including the return nosing detail at the side and sometimes a scotia moulding at the front.

Landings are made from slabs of stone built into the wall. To make installation easier they are constructed from pieces of a manageable size, which are locked together with 'joggle joints' (a kind of stopped tongue-and-groove joint).

1 Rectangular-block stone steps

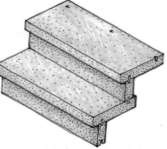

2 Stone slabs form treads and risers

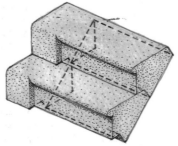

3 Wedge-shaped spandrel steps

Balustrades

Decorative iron balustrades are commonly used with stone stairs. The balusters are set in dovetail-shaped holes cut in the treads and secured by pouring molten lead into each hole. The solidified lead is then caulked and a stone-coloured mortar used to fill and finish the recess (4).

Sometimes, where the stairs are narrow or simply for visual effect, the balusters are made to oversail the ends of the steps (5). These are fixed into the side face of the step with caulked lead in a similar way.

The handrail of an iron balustrade may be made of iron, in which case it is attached to the top ends of the balusters with countersunk machine screws (6). Alternatively, an interior stone staircase may have an elegantly moulded handrail made of a hardwood such as mahogany. A wooden handrail is secured with woodscrews through an iron strip that is fixed to the balusters with machine screws (7).

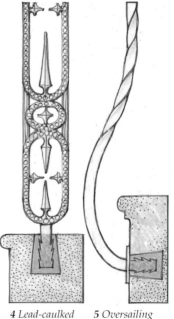

4 Lead-caulked metal baluster

5 Oversailing metal baluster

6 Metal handrail fixing

7 Wooden handrail fixing

REPAIRING STONE STAIRS

Even indoors stone eventually wears; and if settlement takes place in the supporting material, it may crack. Interior open-well stairs showing signs of distortion should be checked by a surveyor. If it is not possible to cut out and reset or replace individual steps, a specialist builder may be able to build a framework of steel beams to reinforce the structure and box it in discreetly with a plaster soffit.

Worn exterior steps, especially when covered with ice, are dangerous and should be repaired or replaced. An outdoor metal balustrade needs regular maintenance if it is to remain a safe and attractive feature (see DECORATIVE METALWORK).

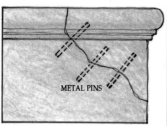

Reinforce the joint with metal pins

Repairing a damaged step

Working stone is a special-ized skill and for any major repairs you need to employ an experienced craftsman, but it is possible to under-take simple repairs yourself.

To refix a small piece of broken stone, mix a two-part epoxy adhesive and apply a very thin coat to both faces. Press the broken piece into place and, if need be, secure it with adhesive tape until the glue has set. Many glues will only set at a specified temperature, so do the work on a warm, dry day.

If there is still a gap along the break line, mix some crushed-stone dust with a little adhesive to make a filler. Apply it to the crack with a knife, taking care not to spread it on the surface.

A larger broken piece can be replaced in a similar way, but needs reinforcing with non-ferrous metal pegs. Use a power drill fitted with a masonry bit to bore two or three 3mm (⅛in) stopped holes about 12mm (½in) deep in each part. Rock the

drill to open up the inside of the holes slightly. Drill the holes in the broken piece first. Position it and give it a tap to deposit some residual stone dust from the holes onto the other half. Remove the piece carefully and mark around the spot of dust, then drill matching holes on the marked positions.

Cut short lengths of 3mm (⅛in) stainless-steel or brass rod for the pegs. Apply resin adhesive to the holes and to the broken faces of the stone. Insert the pegs and position the piece, then tape or clamp until the adhesive has set.

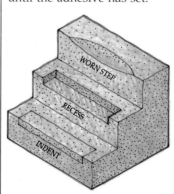

Indenting makes an effective repair

Fitting new stone

Indenting is an effective method for repairing steps that are badly worn. The damaged area is cut away to form a recess, then a stone 'indent' is fitted and resin-bonded into it. This is a job for an experienced builder or a flooring specialist.

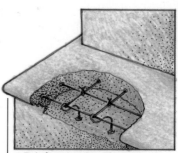

1 Reinforce repair with metal rod

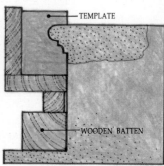

2 Make a running mould

Mortar repair

Patching the stone with mortar (commonly known as a 'plastic' repair) is a possible method for repairing worn or damaged steps. However, very careful preparation of the old surface is necessary. In addition, it is important that the mortar is capable of standing up to the physical demands put upon it, and it has to be compatible with the original stone.

Mixing a suitable mortar is the most difficult part of the operation, requiring a good deal of trial and error. Most mortars are mixes of lime, cement and sand or stone dust (see REPAIRING DEFECTIVE STONE). A local stonemason should be able to supply small quantities of dust from common types of stone.

Mix small portions of the materials to test the strength, colour and texture. Make up a number of mixes, varying the ingredients slightly and keeping a careful note of each. Leave them to mature and weather for some weeks (the longer, the better). Test their hardness by scraping the surface; also, judge their appearance against the natural stone. The strength of the mortar should always be weaker than the material being filled. To match a rough surface, use a coarser aggregate. To give a more weathered appearance, dry brush the surface lightly before the mortar sets.

Using masonry chisels and a club hammer, cut back the worn area to sound stone to form a level recess. Undercut the edges to provide a key

and a well-defined cutout, as mortar laid to finish with a feathered edge is likely to break away.

For recesses that are larger than 38mm (1½in), metal reinforcement is necessary, particularly at the edges of steps. Use non-ferrous metal, such as brass rod and wire bent to shape, and set in epoxy-resin-filled holes (1). The reinforcement should be not less than 18mm (¾in) from the finished surface.

To help form steps with a shaped nosing, make a tem-plate from thin steel plate. Take the shape from a sound section of the step, using a profile gauge. Transfer the outline onto the metal and cut it to shape. Mount the plate in a running mould (2) (see PLASTERWORK). Square-edged steps can be shaped with a trowel.

Apply the mortar in layers or 'coats' to prevent shrink-age and cracking. Dampen the stone, and then apply the first coat. Build up the full thickness with coats no more than 9mm (⅜in) thick. Key the surface of each and allow it to set hard. Dampen the previous coat before applying the next one.

Apply the last coat of a moulded step so it finishes proud of the surface. Set up a straight wooden batten on which to run the mould. Shape the mortar to the finished profile. In order to stop the mortar drying out too rapidly, cover the repair with plastic sheeting or dampen it occasionally with a light spray of water.

CHAPTER NINETEEN

FIREPLACES

WITH THE INTRODUCTION of gas and electric appliances and central heating systems in the late nineteenth century, the open fire gradually ceased to be the focus of family activity. For centuries the solid-fuel fire had provided warmth, energy for cooking, and in some cases light. Early open-hearth fireplaces were literally at the centre of the household, but as buildings and chimney systems developed the fireplace took up its now familiar place against the wall.

In medieval times logs were burned on the hearth within large fireplace openings, and this style continued to be popular in country houses for generations. But as timber became scarcer and coal fires more common

the size of the opening was gradually reduced. Nevertheless, the architectural importance of the fireplace did not diminish. With the coming of the Industrial Revolution designers and manufacturers devised all kinds of patent grates and stoves, and these helped to ensure that the fireplace remained the focus of attention in the room until its decline in recent times.

Some fireplaces are grandiose and ornate, others elegantly stylish or plainly functional. All have character and add a certain charm to the home. As a result, many period fireplaces, stripped out to make way for central heating or modernized décor, are now being reinstated to bring back the original character of the interior.

A restored late-C18th open fireplace with moulded surround

Late-Victorian fireplace with classically styled mantelpiece

MANTELPIECES

THE MANTELPIECE *forms a decorative 'fireplace surround' – a term frequently used today – that frames the fireplace opening. Traditionally the surround was made from stone (often marble or slate) or from wood or cast iron.*

Early rural fireplaces were simply large functional openings, without any surround. The inglenook type, with its massive timber lintel supported by exposed or plastered brickwork, provided a wide enclosure for heating and cooking and sometimes for seating, too. In more formal interiors, the fireplace was shaped in the current architectural style and had simple mouldings carved into the stone that formed the opening.

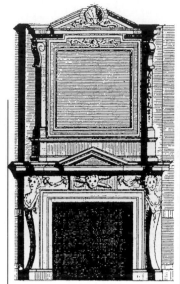

Inigo Jones-style chimneypiece

MANTELPIECE STYLES

In England, ornamental mantelpieces began with the Renaissance-style chimneypieces found in important houses of the late sixteenth century. The classical detailing served as an inspiration for architects such as Inigo Jones and Robert Adam in the following centuries and had a lasting influence on the style of the mantelpiece.

Inigo Jones established the fireplace as an architectural feature with his grandiose chimneypieces. The jambs were treated as columns, pilasters or volutes supporting a lintel or frieze in the style of an entablature. This was surmounted by an overmantel that continued the decorative detail to form a pedimented frame, which was sometimes filled with a painting or later a mirror.

In less grand houses, the treatment was simpler but followed classical forms. Late-seventeenth-century and early-eighteenth-century fireplaces had simple wood or stone surrounds with bold bolection mouldings. This type of mantelpiece did not always provide a shelf.

The eighteenth century

By the mid eighteenth century the use of decorative columns, pilasters and consoles to support a mantelshelf had become common. Elaborate rococo decoration featuring naturalistic forms came into vogue for a short time. Mirror glass, which had formerly been a luxury that only the very rich could afford, was now available in large sheets from France and was used to make richly decorative overmantels that reflected light into the room.

Mirrored overmantels and other mantelpieces inspired by Robert Adam were less ornate, being embellished with sophisticated low-relief classical decoration.

Victorian mantelpieces

The Victorian mantelpiece reflected a number of styles, including bolder interpretations of the classical forms. Marble surrounds were shaped to accommodate the cast-iron arched grate introduced around 1850. Mirrored overmantels also adopted an arched top. White and coloured marble continued to be used widely and, to cater for the fashionable black colour, slate was introduced too. This was sometimes artfully painted to simulate black marble, and gilding was often added to highlight incised mouldings. Frequently, softwood mantels were painted to simulate marble or hardwoods.

Elaborate cast-iron mantelpieces also appeared. Some were made entirely of iron, while others had wooden shelves. Ornate overmantels that had mirrored panels and fancy display shelves became fashionable in the late-Victorian period.

The twentieth century

The influence of the Arts and Crafts movement was reflected in the designs of the early twentieth century. Natural materials such as oak, stone and brick were now once again used for mantelpieces. The wooden mantels of the period were often ornamented with Art Nouveau fretted brackets and panels. Art Nouveau decoration was also applied to brass and copper hoods and to tiles used in cast-iron grates. But by the 1930s taste had changed, and marble, brick or plainly tiled mantelpieces had become the rage.

Impressive Edwardian painted-wood chimneypiece

Elegantly carved C18th stone mantelpiece

212

COMPONENTS OF A MANTELPIECE

The basic components of a mantelpiece are the jambs **(1)**, which support the frieze or lintel **(2)**, which in turn carries the mantelshelf **(3)**. The jambs may be in the form of columns, pilasters, carved caryatid figures or simple architectural mouldings. The frieze or lintel may be a matching architrave moulding or a plain or decorated panel. The degree of ornamentation is dependent on the grandeur and style of the mantel. The shelf may be plain-edged or moulded.

Most marble mantelpieces are supplied as separate elements for assembly on site. The jambs and frieze are usually constructed from marble panels or slips (narrow strips), which are held together with plaster of Paris and reinforced with plaster-bonded spacer blocks fitted inside. Wooden fireplace surrounds are made up of boards glued together and assembled for fitting as a single piece. Cast-iron surrounds are made in one piece, except for the separate bolt-on shelf.

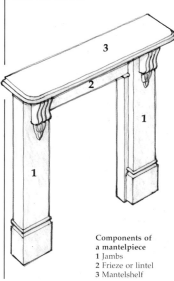

Components of a mantelpiece
1 Jambs
2 Frieze or lintel
3 Mantelshelf

HOW A MANTELPIECE IS FIXED

Marble mantelpieces are attached to the wall with steel-wire ties or hooks fixed into the back edge of the parts. These are set in plaster or tied with wire to screws or nail hooks set in the wall.

Wooden mantels are held in place with screws or nails fitted through metal plates attached to the jambs.

Cast-iron mantelpieces have cast lugs at the top and foot of the jambs for screw fixing. If there is a shelf, it is bolted to the top of the casting before the mantelpiece is positioned against the wall.

With all types, plaster is applied around the mantelpiece to conceal the fixings and help hold it firm.

Grand stone mantelpiece with carved frieze and caryatid jambs

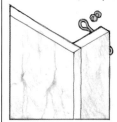  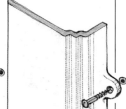

Marble fixing   *Wood fixing*   *Cast-iron fixing*

CLEANING MARBLE

Marble's variety of subtle colours and markings and ease of working have made it a favourite material for mantelpieces for centuries. However, it is a porous stone that can easily become dowdy or stained – which is why you sometimes come across marble mantelpieces that have been painted over. With care, marble can be stripped and cleaned to bring it back to its original finish.

General soiling

Use a soft brush and cloth to remove loose dust from the surface and crevices. Wash off surface dirt with warm soapy distilled water, working up from the bottom to avoid leaving streaks. Use a bristle brush to clean mouldings, and a toothbrush for fine detail. Rinse with clean water, then dry with a cloth.

For more persistent dirt, a commercial marble cleaner is often effective. Alternatively, use a solution of household ammonia, or try hydrogen peroxide (100 volume) in a solution of 1 part peroxide to 3 parts water (a few drops of ammonia can be added to it). Wear rubber gloves, a mask and eye protection when working with any of these substances. Wet the surface before applying the solution to prevent dirt being drawn into the marble. Don't use household bleach, as it can etch the marble. Also, don't mix bleach with ammonia, as toxic fumes are produced.

Removing stains

To remove deep stains, you need to apply a poultice. Commercial poultice materials are available, or you can make your own. A poultice consists of an absorbent substance (such as fuller's earth, powdered chalk or talc, or pulped white blotting paper or paper tissues) to which a stain solvent is added. Use baking powder mixed with distilled water as the solvent for soot stains; white spirit or acetone for oily stains; and ammonia or hydrogen peroxide for organic stains.

Mix the absorbent and solvent to make a paste and apply a layer, not less than 6mm (¼in) thick, over the stain. Tape plastic film over the poultice to stop it drying too rapidly. Leave for a day or two before removing the plastic covering. The solvent will be absorbed into the marble to activate the stain; then as the poultice dries, the stain substance is drawn out with the solvent. When the poultice is completely dry, scrape it off. You may have to repeat the process and change the solvent several times if more than one type of stain substance is present.

Finishing marble

Apply a thin film of marble polish or a fine white-wax polish and buff to a natural sheen. Maintain the surface by periodically washing with a mild soap solution then applying a little polish.

FIRE GRATES

NTIL THE EARLY EIGHTEENTH CENTURY *wood was the fuel most commonly used for open fires. Although it will readily burn on the hearth, large logs were usually supported on a pair of andirons or firedogs.*

When timber became scarce in and around towns and cities, it was more economical to burn coal. Coal burns at a higher temperature than wood and needs a good flow of air. Wrought-iron fire baskets were therefore produced to contain the fuel and concentrate the heat. They also kept the coals clear of the floor, improving air flow and combustion while allowing ash to fall away. Although it is often possible to date a fireplace by the type of grate, this can be misleading since many old fireplaces have been modified over the years.

FIREBACKS

The early wood-burning open fires were simply laid in stone or brick-built fireplaces. In order to protect the masonry at the back of the fire, cast-iron firebacks were introduced. Produced in various sizes, with ornamental tops and decorated with allegorical subjects, they were very widely used. As a result, a great many eighteenth-century firebacks have survived to the present day. Excellent replicas are also readily available, taken from original patterns.

FROM A SMOKY LIFE
AND A SCOULDINGE WIFE
ALL MEN THAT DOE ME SE
TAKE PETIE AND DELIVER ME

Inscription on C17th fireback

DOG GRATES

Dog grates (also known as basket or stove grates) were introduced in the early part of the eighteenth century and were used to burn coal. A freestanding fire basket, which incorporated a fireback and had iron or steel bars in front, was supported on legs similar in style to firedogs – hence the name.

By the middle of the eighteenth century these grates had been transformed into refined examples of metalwork, with polished steel bars at the front and decorative steel or brass legs, which were joined by a handsome pierced-metal apron. Late-eighteenth-century designs intended for quality houses followed neo-classical styles and sometimes included Adam motifs. Today this type of grate can be found in period-style houses that have a large brick-built open fireplace, although the modern interpretation is likely to be a gas-fuelled coal-effect or log-effect fire.

FITTED GRATES

The decline in the use of wood as a domestic fuel, coupled with a better understanding of fireplace technology and the development of mass-produced cast iron, led to a proliferation of novel designs for more efficient fitted grates in the late eighteenth century.

Hob grates

During this period the hob grate, which was fitted into the lower half of the fireplace opening, became popular. This type of grate featured wide decorative cast-iron front panels, fitted on each side of a high fire basket, and hob plates that provided a useful surface for keeping pots and kettles hot.

Register grates

The register grate was a further development. This had a front frame or plate that fitted the opening. The early examples had cast-iron back and side panels, which lined the upper part of the fireplace. Above, a closure plate sealed off the chimney opening except for an aperture controlled by an adjustable

Hob-style register grate in a Georgian house

Attractive reproduction cast-iron grate

Stylish 1930s marble-faced fireplace

plate known as a register. However, the name 'register grate' eventually came to mean any grate with a front plate that fitted the fireplace opening, regardless of whether a register was fitted. Today, this type is often referred to as an insert grate.

Late-eighteenth-century register grates in polished steel sometimes had wide baskets with small side hobs, under which ran a pierced decorative apron.

Although the register plate offered some control of heat loss up the chimney and slowed the rate of burning by restricting the air flow, it didn't solve all the problems – especially since the basket was still set high.

Arched grates
Until the mid nineteenth century, fire grates were generally either square or rectangular and most were still made entirely of cast iron. The second half of the century saw the introduction of the arched grate. This had a smaller fire basket set at a lower level and lined with firebricks, while the register became a semi-circular flap or damper that was opened once the fire was alight. The style remained popular until the end of the century.

Splay-sided fireplaces
Around 1870 a new style emerged that had a narrow rectangular opening with splayed sides decorated with tiled panels. The fire basket was now set very low, and the front bars lifted out as a single unit. An ash pan, fitted underneath, helped control the flow of air.

One-piece units
By the 1930s cast-iron grates had been ousted by plainer one-piece units, combining fireplace and mantelpiece as a single entity. Some of these were made of cast concrete and faced with marble or plain tiles, while others were constructed from brick.

MAINTAINING A GRATE
When open fires were in constant use, it was considered necessary that the grate was polished daily with black lead. Grate polish is still available, although modern heat-proof paints can now be used to reduce regular maintenance.

Blacking the grate
If you need to brighten up your grate, use a traditional-style graphite grate polish. This imparts an attractive silver-black finish that is ideal for highlighting decorative details. Apply it evenly with a brush, then polish with a soft cloth.

If a cast-iron grate shows signs of rusting, remove the rust with a wire brush – then either use grate polish or, for a stronger finish, apply stove paint. The latter is specially designed to withstand high temperatures and produces a matt black finish.

Polishing metal
Dull or lightly rusted polished steel can be revived with fine wire wool dipped in thin oil. Wear rubber gloves to protect your hands. Rub the surface to a bright finish, always working in the same direction, then use a cloth to wipe it dry. Alternatively, apply a proprietary abrasive liquid cleaner with a cloth.

Polish dull brass or copper with a suitable metal polish, following the maker's directions. If need be, use a heat-resistant transparent lacquer in order to protect the newly polished surface.

SOLID-FUEL STOVES
Wood-burning stoves are efficient space heaters that have been a popular means for heating homes in country areas of Europe and America since the eighteenth century. Made of cast iron or steel plate, and in some cases incorporating heat-retentive soapstone, they have been manufactured in a great variety of sizes and styles. Restored originals and reproductions of old designs are available from specialist suppliers.

The basic stove
Solid-fuel stoves are mostly designed to be freestanding, although you do sometimes see one fitted into a fireplace opening. Essentially, a stove is an enclosed chamber that is provided with a regulator for controlling the air flow. The fuel burns slowly and completely, the heat being absorbed by the casing then radiated out into the room. A stovepipe fitted into the top or rear carries away the smoke and also helps to radiate the heat. A hinged door, which may be glazed, or a removable top plate gives access for loading the fuel. Some stoves have a decorative top, while others provide a flat surface that can serve as a hotplate.

The general trend towards the use of cleaner fuels and central heating systems in the early twentieth century meant that old fireplaces and stoves became redundant in many homes. However, there is now a resurgence of interest in traditional heating methods and many disused fireplaces are being opened up or fitted with stoves.

Old stoves
It's easy to be tempted by an attractive antique stove – but make sure when buying one that it has been restored properly or is in genuinely good order. If you purchase an antique stove and intend to use it, establish that it is safe to use and that it meets

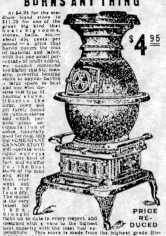

your heating requirements. Consult a stove specialist should you have any doubts.

A modern reproduction that can burn a variety of fuels may be a better option if you are planning to use a stove as your main source of heating, since most antique stoves are not airtight and are therefore much less efficient producers of heat.

Installation
In theory it is possible to fit a freestanding solid-fuel stove yourself. Nevertheless, it is advisable to employ or fully consult a specialist installer, as the relevant installation standards and regulations are constantly changing.

Most stove suppliers offer advice, plus an installation service designed to suit their customers' needs.

TILED FIREPLACES

Types of tile
1 Five-tile set
2 Geometric design
3 Delft-style design
4 Naturalistic floral
5 Stylized floral
6 Art Nouveau

T HE IMPORTANCE OF FIREPLACES *to interior design is evident from the degree of decoration applied to them throughout history. Mantelpieces of stone, wood and, later, cast iron – which relied as much on the colour and texture of the material as on carved embellishment for their effect – provided an ornamental frame around plain functional fireplace openings or sombre cast-iron grates. However, this was to change during the first half of the nineteenth century, as the use of coloured glazed tiles for grates and mantelpieces became increasingly popular.*

Fireplace tiles

The production of tin-glazed tiles had been developed in Holland during the sixteenth century. The Dutch designs and techniques inspired and influenced the English tile industry, which became established in the eighteenth century. The fire-resistant properties of clay tiles, as well as their tough easy-to-clean surface and decorative qualities, made them ideally suited for fireplace use.

As well as plain tiles and tiles in the Dutch 'Delft blue' style, decoratively moulded tiles were produced and a variety of fine tiles depicting domestic scenes, ancient and modern stories, animals and plants. Tile-manufacturing techniques newly introduced as a result of industrialization, combined with the mass production of cast-iron grates, meant that tiled grates could be produced fairly cheaply. They were soon to feature in the parlours of even modest homes. By the 1930s, fancy tiled cast-iron grates had finally given way to plainer types of fireplace.

Tiled grates

The typical tiled Victorian grate had splayed side panels with five 150mm (6in) square picture tiles fitted one above the other, although sometimes these were separated by plain or patterned half-tiles or quarter-tiles. It was also possible to buy sets of decorative tiles that, when assembled, made up a complete panel. The tiles were fixed with plaster into a pair of metal backing frames.

REPAIRING TILES

In order to extract a cracked tile for repair, it is necessary to remove the entire fireplace. Consequently, unless the break is particularly unsightly (if, for example, the tile is smashed and the parts have become dislodged), you may be better advised to live with the cracked tile.

If, on the other hand, you have bought a damaged grate from an architectural-salvage company or have to take out a fireplace temporarily for any reason, then it is clearly worth repairing any broken tiles.

Removing tiles

Remove any rust from the threaded fixing studs on the back of the grate with a wire brush. Apply penetrating oil to the threads to help free the nuts fitted on the studs. Remove the metal backing frame and prise out the tiles very carefully.

Cleaning tiles

Scrape off the old plaster from the backs of the tiles. These tiles are not grouted, so very little plaster will need to be cleaned from the edges. Wash them with a solution of detergent and distilled water. If tarry soot deposits have marked the surfaces, apply a coating of water-washable paint stripper. This will, of course, also remove paint if the tiles have been painted over.

Soak the tiles in distilled water before applying the stripper. This prevents the dirt being absorbed into the ceramic body. Remove the residue of the stripper from smooth-surfaced tiles with a plastic or wooden scraper, or with a bristle brush from textured ones. Wash the tiles in clean water and leave them to dry.

The grate is enhanced by the tile-panelled overmantel

Floral tiles decorate the sides and hood of the grate

Gluing the break

Dry-assemble the fragments to check the fit. If the tile is broken into several pieces, it may only be possible to re-assemble it in a certain order.

PVA is a good choice of adhesive for bonding a clean break in thick earthenware, and will dry clear. Wet the broken edges, then apply the glue to them evenly. Wipe squeezed-out glue from the surface of the tile with a damp cloth. Hold the pieces together with strips of sticky tape till the glue has set (1).

A two-part epoxy-resin adhesive mixed with a little titanium dioxide (available from pharmacists) will give a strong joint and is suitable for coloured tiles with a white ceramic body. Heat the tubes on a radiator to make the glue flow better, then mix the two components together and add the white titanium-dioxide powder. Apply the glue and assemble the pieces on a flat worktop covered with polyethylene sheeting. Wipe any glue from the surface of the tile with a cloth dampened with methylated spirits. Tape the join until the glue has set. If a white line remains, you can touch in the colour with enamel paint available from model shops (2).

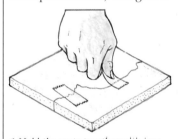

1 Hold the parts together with tape

2 Touch in colours with paint

Patching chipped edges

If the coloured glaze has been chipped at the edge as a result of the break, add some talcum powder to the epoxy adhesive to make a filler. Using a knife, apply the filler so it is just proud of the surface. When it has set, scrape it flush with a sharp knife blade. Paint the patch with enamel to match the colour of the tile.

Fitting the tiles

Set out the repaired tiles on the two backing frames and bolt them to the rear of the grate's side frames. Pack out the back of the tiles with small pieces of wood so that they butt snugly against the front (1). Apply plaster of Paris over the back of the tiles to fix them in place (2).

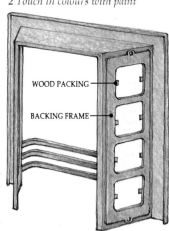

WOOD PACKING

BACKING FRAME

1 Pack out the back of the tiles

2 Fix the tiles with plaster

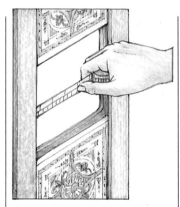

1 Measure the depth of the groove

REPLACING TILES

When you need to replace a tile but removing the entire fireplace is impractical, it is sometimes possible to work from the front. The replacement has to be cut down in width slightly – so if the tile is a rare one this may not be an appropriate repair.

Protecting your eyes, chip out the broken tile with a cold chisel; then clean out the grooves in each side of the iron frame. Measure the depth of the grooves (you will need to measure the deepest one if they are different) to determine how much to cut from the new tile (1). Reduce the width of the tile by half the depth of the groove, taking the material off both side edges, so that the design remains symmetrical (2). Wearing a mask and eye protection, remove the waste with a power grinder or with coarse abrasive paper.

Remove just enough to allow the tile to be fitted into the hole when one edge is pushed fully into the side groove. Apply a strip of self-adhesive tape to the face of the tile to form a tab, so you can hold the tile (3). Apply plaster of Paris to both side grooves and the back of the tile. Insert the tile fully into the side groove, then slide it back halfway into the other. Hold the tile until the plaster has set. Before it hardens, clean away the surplus from the face of the tile.

2 Ensure the design is symmetrical

3 Apply an adhesive-tape holding tab

HEARTH TILES

Cracked hearth tiles are common, as they tend to get broken by falling objects, such as fire irons. Loose ones also frequently occur, due to failure of the original cement adhesive. Old hearth tiles are not normally grouted. As a result, it is often possible to lift out loose tiles cleanly for replacement or repair.

Use a chisel and hammer to chip out some of the old cement to make sufficient room for fresh ceramic-tile adhesive, taking care not to damage the edges of the tiles still *in situ*.

Apply a thin bed of adhesive and press the new or repaired tiles into place. Use a straight batten to check that they are flush with the surrounding ones. If the old bedding cement is hard and difficult to remove, bond them in place by brushing on PVA adhesive.

ANATOMY OF A FIREPLACE

MANTELPIECE AND GRATE STYLES *have varied according to fashion, but the basic structural elements of a fireplace have not changed radically over the centuries. The early combination of a large stone or brick opening with a chimney built over it evolved from the obvious fact that smoke rises, rather than from a scientific understanding of how a well-devised flue system functions.*

Open wood and, later, coal-burning fires were very inefficient and it was not until Benjamin Thompson, known as Count Rumford, produced his thesis on the principles of fireplace design in 1799 that smaller grates and improvements in the internal shape of the opening were introduced.

ELEMENTS OF A FIREPLACE

A brick or stone enclosure **(1)** forms the basis of the fireplace. Variously known as the fireplace opening or recess or builder's opening, it may be set flush with the wall itself or built out into the room, forming a chimney breast **(2)**. A chimney breast rises through the height of the house, emerging through the roof to form a chimney stack. The gather **(3)** and flue **(4)** carry the smoke up the chimney. If the chimney is shared by several fireplaces on different floors, it may contain more than one flue.

The masonry over the fireplace opening is supported by a lintel or a brick arch **(5)**. Old inglenook fireplaces used massive oak beams, whereas a sturdy iron strap usually supports an early brick arch. Later fireplaces may have a straight arch supported by angle iron (an L-shaped iron bar), and early-twentieth-century ones often have a cast-concrete lintel. On no account should these structural beams and lintels be cut into or taken out without expert advice.

Constructed from non-combustible materials such as stone or tile-faced concrete, the hearth projects out into the room to protect the floor from falling embers **(6)**. In most old houses the hearth was set flush with the floor, although sometimes a superimposed hearth was used to raise the level. The area within the fireplace opening, which is known as the back hearth **(7)**, is usually level with the hearth itself.

A dog grate **(8)**, for burning wood or coal, may be placed on the back hearth. However, by the mid nineteenth century the cast-iron register grate, which filled in the opening, had become the fashion (see FIRE GRATES).

To complete the assembly, a mantelpiece – or fireplace surround, as it is often called today – is fitted to frame the grate or fireplace opening **(9)**. The mantelpiece itself may be constructed from stone, slate, marble, wood or cast iron. The walls around it may be finished with wood panelling, or more commonly with plaster, and in some instances the mantelpiece extends upwards to form an impressive chimneypiece. Mirrored overmantels were introduced in the late eighteenth century, and these became a common feature of Victorian sitting rooms.

Fireplaces
Poor design or lack of maintenance can cause smoke.
- Modify fireplace opening (page 219).

Mantelpieces
The mantelpiece may be missing or in poor condition.
- Clean a soiled or stained marble mantel (page 213).
- Strip a painted mantelpiece, if appropriate (page 220).
- Glue a cracked cast-iron surround (page 221).
- ▲ Or have it welded (pages 220, 221).
- Replace a missing mantelpiece (page 222).

Components of a fireplace
1 Fireplace opening
2 Chimney breast
3 Gather
4 Flue
5 Brick arch
6 Hearth
7 Back hearth
8 Dog grate
9 Mantelpiece

Flues
Blocked or decayed flues are unable to function properly.
- ▲ Have the chimney swept (page 219).
- ● Check that the flue is clear (page 72).
- ▲ Have the flue lined (page 74).
- ▲ Have the chimney repaired or rebuilt (pages 72, 73).

Grates
The grate may be damaged or missing.
- ● Maintain a grate regularly in order to preserve it (page 215).
- ■ Repair a damaged grate (page 220).
- ■ Replace missing or badly damaged decorative tiles (page 217).
- ■ Replace cracked or loose hearth tiles (pages 217, 221).
- ■ Choose and fit a replacement grate (pages 221, 222).

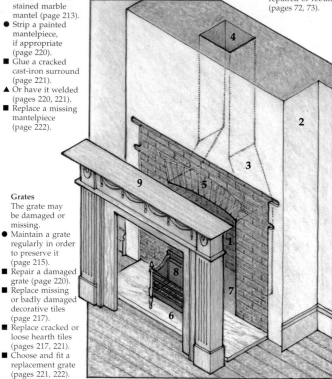

SOLID-FUEL OPEN FIRES

An open fire burning wood or coal is a cheerful sight, but if it is your only source of heat, as it was for centuries, the romantic image can soon fade – especially if the fire does not burn properly. Getting a fire started and keeping it alight then becomes a challenge, if not a chore.

How the system works

For wood and coal fires to burn well a good supply of air is needed under the grate **(1)**, as well as a means of escape for the hot gases and smoke **(2)**. The fireplace opening **(3)** safely contains the fuel, which is laid on an iron grate **(4)**. The barred grate holds the fuel clear of the hearth and allows air to circulate through it. As the fuel is consumed, waste ash drops through the grate so the fire isn't stifled. If the chimney is inadequate or the flow of air restricted, the fire will not function effectively.

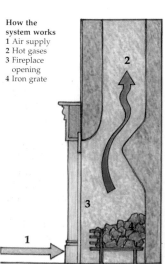

How the system works
1 Air supply
2 Hot gases
3 Fireplace opening
4 Iron grate

SMOKING FIREPLACES

The efficiency of an open fire depends not only on the supply of air but also on the size of the flue compared with the size of the fireplace opening. Count Rumford (see right) recommended that the cross-sectional area of the flue should be about a tenth of the size of the opening. However, fireplaces tended to be smaller after the mid nineteenth century. Modern flue-liner manufacturers favour a ratio of one to seven, and there are sizing charts published that give details of current standards.

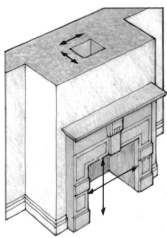

Check flue and fireplace opening dimensions (flue area/opening area ratio should be about 1:7 or 1:10).

Improving ventilation

If your fire smokes or won't burn properly, see if opening a window improves matters. If it does, you need better ventilation in the room.

One solution is to install a window vent, although this may cause an uncomfortable cross draught. A much more efficient form of ventilation is either a single ducted vent set into the floor in front of the fireplace or twin ducted vents set into the floor or external walls on each side of the chimney breast.

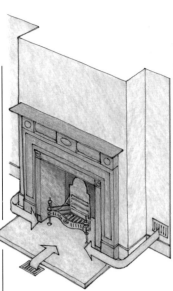

Alternative positions for air vents

Improving air flow

When wood and coal are burned, flammable gases, tarry substances, acids and dust are given off. However, because domestic fires are relatively inefficient not all of these substances are consumed. Instead, they rise up the chimney and some of them condense on the inside of the flue. Unburned carbon combines with these tars and acids, creating soot – which builds up over a period of time and effectively reduces the size of the flue.

Have chimneys that are regularly used swept at least twice a year – ideally before, during and at the end of the heating season. A soot-laden flue is a fire hazard, since the unburned elements of the soot can ignite, causing a chimney fire which may reach high temperatures and damage the chimney.

Modifying the flue

If a flue is too large, it can be reduced by fitting a flue liner. A variety of methods and materials are used (see FLUE LINERS), including liners made of flexible stainless steel, ceramic, lightweight concrete sections, or concrete cast *in situ*.

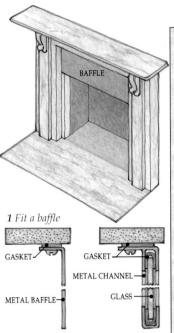

1 Fit a baffle

GASKET — METAL BAFFLE

GASKET — METAL CHANNEL — GLASS

2 Mount with discreet screw fixings

Modifying the fireplace opening

One way to reduce the size of the fireplace opening is to raise the hearth, though this may look out of character with the fireplace. In fact, it is probably both easier and more acceptable to install a baffle. This is fitted across the width of the opening (1) and can be made of steel, copper or heatproof glass.

In order to establish the size of the baffle panel, with the fire alight, temporarily tape a metal or thoroughly dampened plywood sheet across the top of the fireplace opening – and then adjust it up and down to determine the most effective position.

Make or commission a panel of the required size in a style and material that will harmonize with the mantelpiece. Mount the panel with discreet screw fixings and fit a fibreglass tape around the joint to act as a gasket (2).

Fitting a hood or canopy

If a baffle is unsuitable or installing one is problematic, it may be worth asking a fireplace specialist whether fitting a metal smoke hood or canopy in the opening is the best solution.

RUMFORD'S REFORMS

Count Rumford in his essays on fireplaces proposed that the flue should be a specified proportion of the fireplace opening and that the area immediately above the fire should be narrowed down to form a throat. The throat causes the rising air to speed up as it passes through the constriction, thus improving the draught up the chimney.

To improve the efficiency of the fire further, he argued that the fireplace itself ought to be smaller and it should be lined with firebrick. The sides, he suggested, should be splayed to reflect the heat into the room, and the fireback made one-third the width of the opening. Also, the upper part of the fireback was to slope forward to reflect the heat. A smoke shelf formed at the throat by the sloping back helped prevent rainwater falling into the fire and was also thought to improve the air circulation within the flue.

Some large fireplaces in houses built before the late eighteenth century were modified in accordance with Rumford's principles. Some of these have splayed sides with marble or tiled panels around the fireplace opening, the original opening having been reduced.

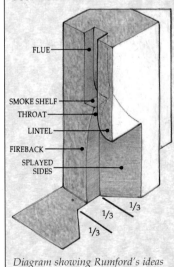

FLUE
SMOKE SHELF
THROAT
LINTEL
FIREBACK
SPLAYED SIDES
1/3 1/3 1/3

Diagram showing Rumford's ideas

RESTORING FIREPLACES

A**LTHOUGH FIREPLACES** *contribute significantly to the character of a house, years of neglect can reduce a fine example to a poor state. Fortunately, however, the damage is often superficial.*

STRIPPING A MANTELPIECE

The efficiency of commercial chemical stripping processes and DIY stripping products has created a fashion for stripping painted fireplaces and mantelpieces. However, stripping them is not always appropriate, as some mantelpieces were intended to be painted. Stripping paint from a marble mantelpiece would seem to be an obvious improvement – but beware, a marbled paint finish on wood or slate can look like the real thing. It was also a common practice to treat softwood mantelpieces with wood grain effects imitating the appearance of the more expensive hardwoods.

Before proceeding to strip the paint, always try to detect which materials have been used in the construction of a mantelpiece. A wooden surround will feel warmer to the touch than one made of stone or cast iron. See if it feels as warm as the skirting.

The decorative mouldings applied to an Adam-style mantel were often made of plaster or gesso, and they can quite easily be damaged by stripping tools. If you discover a marbling paint finish that has been painted over, it is best either to seek the services of a specialist or to leave well alone.

Chemical stripping, as shown on this partly stripped fireplace, will remove thick old paint to reveal the fine detail of the cast iron

Adam-style details made of gesso

REPAIRING A GRATE

Cast iron is brittle and prone to cracking if struck sharply. As a result, the lift-off bars of grates are frequently missing, having been damaged and then discarded. Fortunately, however, missing or broken parts can be repaired or remade.

Grate bars

Cast iron can be welded. So if you have a grate that has broken bars, a blacksmith or a garage repair shop or fireplace specialist may well be able to repair them for you.

If the bars are missing, measure the size of the grate and prepare a dimensioned drawing to enable a fireplace specialist to supply or reproduce a replacement.

Architectural-salvage companies may also be of help. They sometimes keep useful parts from old grates that are no longer serviceable.

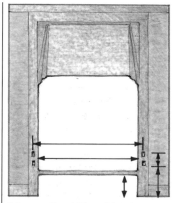

Measure the width and height between the locating holes, and the height above the floor or grate

Stripping methods

Cast-iron mantelpieces that have been removed can be efficiently stripped by an industrial stripping company, but it is better to strip all other materials by hand.

Modern chemical strippers can be used to remove paint from marble, wood and cast-iron mantelpieces. Use a gel or paste stripper, applying it according to the manufacturer's instructions. Try out the stripper on a small unobtrusive area first – and even if the test proves satisfactory, proceed carefully. Scrape off the softened paint (using a wooden or plastic spatula for marble) and clean out mouldings and carved detail with a bristle brush.

Apply fresh stripper in order to remove any residual film of paint, particularly from open-grained timber such as oak, then wash the wood down and wipe dry.

Chipped edges

On a decoratively moulded grate a chipped edge may not show sufficiently to be a problem, but on a plain grate the defect may be obvious.

Providing the chip is not likely to be exposed to high temperatures, fill it with an epoxy metal filler. Overfill the defect slightly and, when the filler has set, rub down flush with the surface. Apply stove paint and grate polish to disguise the repair.

STRIPPING A GRATE

You sometimes come across grates no longer in use that have been painted to blend in with the décor. If you wish to restore the original finish, remove the paint with a chemical stripper. Hot-air stripper guns aren't suitable for this purpose, as the mass of metal dissipates the heat.

Cover the area around the fireplace with polyethylene sheeting and apply a gel or paste stripper, following the manufacturer's instructions. Remove the softened paint from flat surfaces with a scraper, and from moulded ones with a bristle brush. Wipe down and then apply grate polish or stove paint.

A grate that has been removed can be taken away for dipping in a chemical stripping tank – or for a bright finish you can have it sandblasted and polished. Remove any decorative tiles from a grate before you send it for sandblasting – and if vulnerable, for stripping, too.

Fill the crack with fire cement

BROKEN FIREBRICKS

Firebricks can be repaired *in situ*, but seriously decayed bricks need to be replaced.

Rake out a crack with the tip of a pointed trowel after wire-brushing to remove soot. Dampen the brick with clean water and fill the crack with fire cement or mould-able firebrick compound specially designed for this purpose. Press the cement in well with the trowel, and then smooth it flush with the surface. Do not use the fire for several days.

It is sometimes possible to repair a decayed brick in a similar way – but if it needs to be replaced, you will have to remove the grate in order to make the replacement. You may be able to purchase a matching firebrick from a fireplace specialist or from an architectural-salvage company. If not, cast one yourself using fire cement.

REPAIRING CAST IRON

If you lever out a cast-iron fireplace surround without removing the fixings from the lugs cast in the vertical edge of the jambs, that may cause the metal to fracture.

Have cracks in cast iron welded – or if the damaged part will not be subjected to high temperatures, repair it with a two-part epoxy glue.

Before gluing them, clean the surfaces with methylated spirits. Arrange the broken parts so gravity will hold them together or so they can be cramped properly.

Apply the adhesive to the broken edges and assemble the parts, making sure they are well seated. Cramp the parts or bind them with adhesive tape. Wipe off excess glue with methylated spirits.

FITTING A FIREPLACE

WITH THE DECLINE OF OPEN FIRES *in favour of more efficient or convenient methods – such as gas and electric appliances or central-heating systems – many old fireplaces were removed and the opening was filled in. Sometimes the fireplace was left in place and panelled over, making restoration a relatively straightforward job. Fortunately, there is a ready supply of original and reproduction grates and mantelpieces, so replacing a fireplace that has been taken out is not too difficult either, provided that the flue is in good order.*

REINSTATING AN OLD FIREPLACE

Before reinstating a fireplace, it is advisable to check that the fireplace opening, hearth and chimney are all in good condition, and that proposed alterations will comply with the Building Regulations.

These stipulate minimum requirements for the size and thickness of the hearth; the proximity to the chimney breast of combustible materials, such as joinery, joists and floorboards; the thickness of the brickwork; height of chimney stacks, air supply, and type of flue lining. A certain amount of flexibility may be allowed in special circumstances, so it is worth seeking professional advice.

Clearing the opening

It is safer to leave chimney repairs to a professional, but you can prepare the opening and fit a fireplace yourself.

Demolition work always creates a lot of dust, so cover the floor and any furniture that cannot be removed from the room. Chop away the plaster with a club hammer and bolster chisel to expose the brickwork. Note the out-line of the original opening where it contrasts with the brick or blockwork infill. Cut out the infill material, taking care not to chip the original brickwork, especially the lintel. Remove all traces of

old rubble, leaving a clear opening. If the opening has been sealed with plaster-board over a timber frame, you will need to strip it out with a crow bar.

Selecting a fireplace

When choosing a grate or mantelpiece, keep in mind the type and size of room as well as the date of the house. Original examples can be bought from architectural-salvage companies, either fully restored or in need of some work. The price will reflect their condition and rarity. Alternatively, you could buy one of the many excellent reproductions that are available.

A register grate will need to be the right size – that is slightly larger than the mantelpiece opening. If this proves difficult, you could fill the space with marble, slate or tiled slips (narrow panels) plaster-bonded to the wall around the grate.

With luck, the overall size of the mantel can be deter-mined by the outline left in the old plaster where the original was removed.

Preparing the wall

Chop away plaster around the fireplace opening back to the brickwork, to leave a clearance of about 50mm (2in) all round the new mantelpiece when it is fitted.

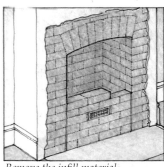

Remove the infill material

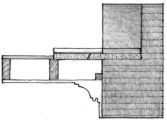

1 Fit a superimposed hearth

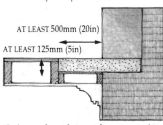

AT LEAST 500mm (20in)

AT LEAST 125mm (5in)

2 A new hearth must be correct size

Preparing the hearth

An inadequate hearth con-stitutes a fire risk. Cracked stone hearths should either be replaced or covered with a superimposed hearth **(1)**. To make one, have a slab of marble cut to size and set it level on a bed composed of 1 part cement, 1 part lime and 6 parts sand mortar. Build up the back hearth flush with the surface of the slab, using 1 part cement and 4 parts sand mortar.

If you are using tiles for the hearth and plan to have an open recess with a dog grate, lay the front and back hearth together on a 1:4 mix.

If alterations to the fire-place constitute new work, the constructional hearth **(2)** must be made to project at least 500mm (20in) in front of the fireplace opening and 150mm (6in) on each side. It must be at least 125mm (5in) thick, as stipulated in the Building Regulations.

FITTING A REGISTER GRATE

Before installing a register grate, make sure that the size of the flue is appropriate for the grate opening, and that there is a proper gather and throated lintel to divert the smoke into the flue.

Position the grate on the hearth, placing it centrally in the fireplace opening (or the chimney breast if they differ) and setting it against the wall. Check that it is plumb and square. If the opening is larger than the front plate, fill in the space at the sides with mortared brick. Should the top fall short, add a concrete lintel supported by the side brickwork (1).

Temporarily position the mantelpiece to see whether it fits snugly against the grate. If need be, pull the grate forward to butt up to the back edge of the mantel opening. Remove the mantelpiece, and then seal and secure the front plate to the wall with fire cement (2).

FITTING A MANTELPIECE

The method for fitting the mantelpiece will depend on its construction. Wooden and cast-iron types are relatively straightforward. Offer the mantel up to the grate and centralize it. Check that it is plumb and level. Mark the position of the screw holes through the fixing plates or lugs fitted to the side jambs (1). Remove the mantelpiece, then drill and plug the wall. Replace and fix the mantel with brass screws.

Backfill the area behind the grate with a lightweight concrete mixture of 6 parts perlite or vermiculite aggregate to 1 part cement. Fill the space through the damper aperture, and trowel the top surface so it slopes towards the opening (2).

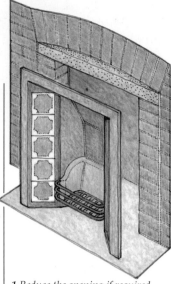

1 Reduce the opening if required

2 Seal the front plate with cement

1 Mark the fixing holes

2 Fill the space through damper hole

Marble mantelpieces

Installing a marble mantelpiece requires a different technique, since the jambs, frieze and mantelshelf are usually separate pieces. If corbels located on wooden dowels or metal pins are to be fitted, bond them in place with fine casting plaster. Fit the jambs first. These have to be set the right distance apart. Also, check that they are plumb – at the same level at the top and in the same plane across the front (1).

Before fixing the mantelpiece in place, drill and plug the wall and fit fixing screws to fall inside the jambs close to the wire ties or hooks in the back edge. If no fixings are provided in the marble, use strips of expanded metal bonded with plaster.

First apply fine casting plaster on the hearth inside the base of each jamb. This sets quickly, so work fast. Bind the jambs with copper wire to the screws in the wall. Set them up accurately and apply a generous dab of plaster over the fixings. Apply generous fillets of the plaster adhesive inside the jambs, positioning them where you can reach to hold them securely.

Spread a fairly thin bed of plaster on the top meeting surfaces and place the frieze member across the jambs (2). Set the mantelshelf in place on a thin bed of plaster and bond it to the wall (3). Prop the shelf, if necessary, and check that it is level before the plaster sets.

Clean away excess plaster from the joints before it sets hard, using a wooden tool or a damp cloth if the plaster is still wet. Finally, make good the plasterwork around the mantelpiece with gypsum plaster before proceeding to redecorate the wall.

1 Check jambs are set true

2 Place frieze member across jambs

3 Set mantelshelf in place

REFERENCE

ENERGY CONSERVATION

GOVERNMENT AND PRESSURE GROUPS *are tireless in their attempts to persuade society to reduce carbon-dioxide emissions by limiting the use of fossil fuels through improvements to the energy efficiency of buildings.*

If you own a period house, you should consider how you can make improvements to assist in the effort to conserve energy – but at the same time you should ensure that any measures you take are not detrimental to the character of the house, and you also need to avoid the possibility of long-term deterioration to the fabric of the building. Architects, surveyors and local-authority Conservation Officers are able to offer specialist advice to assist you in your deliberations.

Shutters in good working order prevent draughts and reduce heat loss

BUILDING REGULATIONS

Energy efficiency comes within the scope of the Building Regulations (see LEGAL PROTECTION FOR OLD HOUSES), which are divided into various parts, each designated by a letter. Energy conservation is referred to as Part L, Conservation of Fuel and Power. The regulations apply to existing buildings when they are altered, extended or subjected to a new use. However, Part L makes it clear that the special characteristics of a historic building must be recognized. The aim of this revised part of the Building Regulations is to improve energy efficiency where it is practical to do so.

For existing buildings, Part L (2002) generally requires energy-conservation upgrading only for elements that are to be 'substantially replaced' as part of the work. The requirements do not apply to general repairs or to elements that do not need replacing.

Where proposed alterations or replacements could trigger Part L of the Building Regulations, care must be exercised in deciding whether or not such work will affect the building's character. If your house is listed, listed-building consent may be required. In some instances, a historic building may be in an almost totally original state and like-for-like replacement will be the only appropriate solution. In many cases, however, some thermal upgrading may be practicable – for example, between the joists within roof spaces and under suspended floors – provided it doesn't pose technical problems such as inhibiting ventilation. It may even be reasonable for this insulation to exceed the recommendations in Part L, in order to help make up for shortcomings elsewhere.

In terms of ventilation and moisture control, old houses can have quite different requirements from newer buildings. Houses built with solid walls without a damp-proof course and from permeable materials function differently from buildings constructed using modern standards and practices. As a result, these older buildings may require comparatively more ventilation to ensure their wellbeing. Nevertheless, a new extension to an old house will normally be expected to have a higher degree of thermal performance than the original building to which it is attached.

SAVING ENERGY

There are two ways to save energy. You can change the way you live – for example, by maintaining lower room temperatures and taking fewer baths or showers – although that is unlikely to be a popular choice. Or you can find ways to prevent heat escaping and also install more energy-efficient heating and lighting, then use these services more effectively. When weighing up the options for a period house, however, there are other important issues to bear in mind, too:

- Don't make unnecessary alterations to the building.
- Avoid making changes that could increase the risk of damage to other parts of the structure.
- Don't destroy important architectural features or spoil their appearance.

There are various measures open to you, ranging from inexpensive draughtproofing to efficient roof insulation, but each must be evaluated in the context of preserving the building's architectural style while saving energy.

Windows

Windows contribute greatly to the appearance of a house, and you should avoid taking any measures that would alter their proportions or details. Even the depth of the window opening and the position of the frame within it can be important historical features that need to be respected.

Double glazing is often cited as a desirable cost-saving improvement, but most systems on the market are unsuited to a period house. Double-glazed plastic (PVCu) windows can greatly detract from the appearance of an old house. And sealed double-glazed units are often made with thick glazing bars that are poorly proportioned compared with those of the original window. Worse still are poor facsimiles of glazing bars glued to the face of the glass.

Draughtproofing is cheap and effective

There is little point in replacing a venerable old window with a modern double-glazed unit if it's possible to repair and draughtproof the original. Draughtproofing and weatherstripping can be effective in reducing heating bills and noise levels and keeping dust out of the house.

Secondary glazing, fitted on the inside of the window, has similar advantages and, if the glazing is carefully designed, it can be relatively unobtrusive.

Shutters are charming and practical features that should never be discarded. Close-boarded or panelled shutters help to minimize heat loss at night and, when rooms are not in use, they can reduce or exclude harsh sunlight during the day. Internal shutters can also be draughtproofed. Hanging good-quality lined curtains is another effective way to reduce heat loss.

Doors
Original doors, especially those of historical value, should always be preserved and kept in good condition. Solid doors, in particular, have fairly good insulating properties, but a lot of heat may be wasted through gaps around the perimeter. Draughtproofing greatly improves matters.

Provided its design is in keeping with the interior, a draughtproof lobby might be a possibility, whereas the addition of a new external porch tends to look out of place on the majority of old houses.

Walls
Opportunities to improve the thermal performance of walls with external insulation is limited – it inevitably spoils the appearance of most period houses. Even insulating internally is likely to be a problem, as dimensional changes around window and door openings make the proposition

unacceptable. The detailing around original features such as dadoes and cornices may be another difficulty.

Floors
The floors are often a distinctive feature of an old house, and so it is only when they have to be lifted – to install new services, for example – that there is a realistic opportunity to improve insulation.

Suspended floors constructed from floorboards can be insulated with comparative ease, either by installing sheet insulating material between the joists or by suspending blanket insulation on netting fixed to the underside of the joists. However, it's important to ensure that underfloor ventilation is not compromised as a result.

Solid floors can't be insulated successfully without first excavating beneath them, which is best avoided unless it becomes necessary in order to remedy some serious defect.

Roofs
Proposals to improve the thermal performance of the roof space have to be considered in relation to the use and performance of the rest of the building. Modern living tends to introduce more moisture into a house, especially the roof space, so effective measures may be required to ensure that the additional water vapour is able to escape harmlessly before it damages the fabric of the building (see ROOF VENTILATION).

There are a great many economical solutions to insulating roofs, and it is one of the most effective ways to reduce domestic fuel bills.

BUILDING SERVICES
People's expectations of comfort and convenience are higher now than in the past, and we all require central heating, electric lighting and power to run our modern appliances. When you live in an older property, it all requires careful planning to ensure the proposed work will be beneficial without compromising the essential character of your house.

The past few years have seen significant advances in efficient heating boilers and controls – so much so that the expense of replacing old worn-out equipment can often be recouped quickly in fuel savings. Long-life lamps (bulbs and strips) may be relatively expensive to buy, but they too save money in the long term.

Most hot-water storage cylinders are now supplied preinsulated, having a layer of foam sprayed on the outside. However, a lot of houses are still plumbed with older uninsulated copper cylinders that waste considerable amounts of heat. Wrapping a proprietary insulating jacket around the cylinder will start to have an effect on your heating bills within just a few months. Similarly, wrapping exposed hot-water pipes in foamed-plastic tubing is another energy-saving measure. Look especially for pipes running through unheated areas of the house, such as the cellar and roof space.

Preserving period fittings
In the rush to improve our plumbing and electrics, it is sometimes forgotten that period fixings and fittings are themselves of historic interest. You may have attractive cast-iron radiators, authentic period bathroom appliances, or antique light fittings and switches. Such appliances and fittings are all worthy of preservation.

There are various options to consider:

● Continue to use the fittings in their original state. However, this will probably not be possible in the case of electrical fittings – which are unlikely to comply with modern safety standards.
● It may be possible to have such fittings refurbished and brought up to standard.
● You could have unsafe or inefficient period fittings disconnected but left in place for their aesthetic appeal, and supplement the lighting or heating with other means.
● As a last resort, you could have fittings or appliances removed and put them into storage.

Avoiding unnecessary damage
When plumbing or rewiring older properties, take precautions to avoid damaging the fabric of the building.

Electrical wiring should be concealed whenever possible, but the cutting of the necessary holes and chases in plaster and woodwork must be done with care to keep damage to a minimum. Never cut through mouldings – and if possible, route the wires through existing voids in the walls and under suspended floors.

Plumbing can be even more destructive, but there are microbore and flexible pipes that are much easier to install in confined spaces.

It is also important to ensure there is no direct or indirect damage to period features resulting from the close proximity of services that emit heat or light.

ROT & INFESTATION

HOUSE TIMBERS *subjected to damp conditions with little or no ventilation are susceptible to decay. Prevention being better than cure, the best policy is to keep the house as watertight as possible and to undertake regular inspection and maintenance.*

Most period houses are likely to have had some form of insect infestation in their lifetime, so don't be overly alarmed if you see evidence of woodboring insects in your own home – there's a possibility that remedial treatment has been carried out already. Similarly, an outbreak of rot may have been rendered inactive by eradicating the damp conditions.

CHECKING FOR WOODWORM ATTACK

Insect attack manifests itself as flight holes produced by the emerging adult insects and possibly as a telltale layer of 'frass' – light-coloured droppings from woodboring beetle larvae. The wood can be unsound even when the flight holes are not extensive, since its interior may have been seriously weakened by a honeycomb of tunnels. Test the strength of the wood by probing it with the blade of a penknife. If in doubt about the seriousness of the problem, call in a specialist. It is usually possible to treat the wood with a preservative that will eradicate the woodworm and provide long-term protection against further outbreaks.

Treating a minor attack

If the outbreak is minor, you can use a fluid woodworm-treatment insecticide available from DIY stores. Brush a liberal coating onto the bare wood (painted or varnished surfaces have to be stripped first). Also, inject the fluid into flight holes, using an aerosol applicator or a can with a pointed spout.

Follow the manufacturer's instructions carefully, as these chemicals are hazardous. Most wood-preservative fluids are flammable, so avoid naked lights and don't smoke while working with them. Wear protective gloves, goggles and a respirator. Make sure the room is well ventilated.

Professional treatment

If the outbreak is extensive, your best bet is to call in an independent expert who has no vested interest in possible remedial work; or you can contact a specialist treatment company, but make sure the company is a member of the British Wood Preserving and Damp Proofing Association. In either case, someone will inspect the property and give you an initial report. When the job is finished, you should expect to receive a guarantee for the work. Specialist operatives will clean then pressure-spray the infested wood. Where it is desirable to preserve a surface (if it has an original finish, for example), it is sometimes possible to have the preservative injected.

Completing the work

After treatment, consolidate any friable wood by applying a wood hardener to strengthen the fibres. There's no need to disguise the holes in old bare wood, but you can fill painted woodwork with cellulose filler when you redecorate.

WOODBORING INSECTS

Although most woodboring insects are beetles, they are generally known as woodworm, since it is usually the larvae that do the damage. The most common woodboring insects are the common furniture beetle, the deathwatch beetle, the house longhorn beetle and the powder-post beetle.

Seasoned but untreated house timbers – both softwoods and the sapwood of various hardwoods – are prone to infestation. Old plywood is also susceptible to attack, because the beetle larvae are partial to the glue that was used during the manufacturing process.

COMMON FURNITURE BEETLE

This small brown beetle, only about 3mm (⅛in) long, attacks joinery and the sapwood of structural timbers. It spends up to three years as a larva burrowing destructively through the wood, then emerges as an adult, leaving a flight hole about 1.5mm (1/16in) in diameter. If it is not treated, the infected wood can suffer from serious attack by generations of beetle larvae.

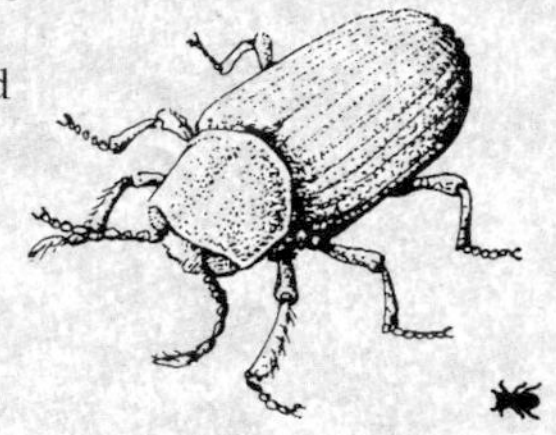

ACTUAL SIZE

DEATHWATCH BEETLE

The deathwatch beetle mainly attacks old decaying hardwoods such as oak. Its life cycle varies from five to twelve years, and the beetle emerges between April and June. It is brown in colour and about 6mm (¼in) in length. It produces a round flight hole approximately 3mm (⅛in) across.

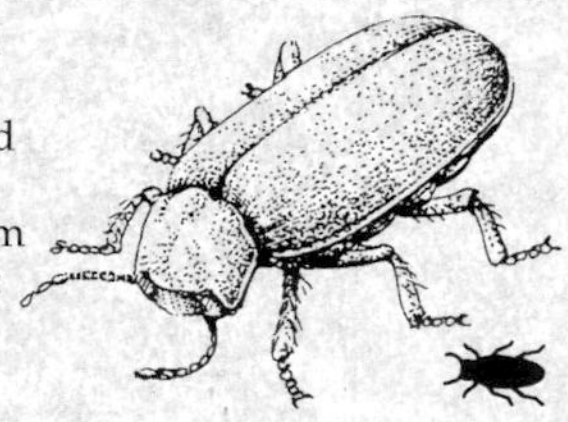

ACTUAL SIZE

HOUSE LONGHORN BEETLE

The house longhorn beetle is the largest of the woodboring insects. About 12mm (½in) long, it tends to attack the sapwood of modern softwoods. The beetle emerges in mid to late summer. It produces an oval hole measuring about 9 x 5mm (⅜ x 3/16in). Its life cycle is from three to eleven years.

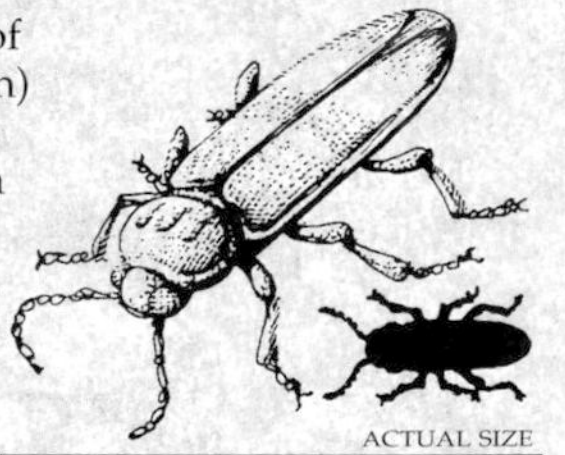

ACTUAL SIZE

POWDER-POST BEETLE

The powder-post beetle is approximately 6mm (¼in) long and leaves a small flight hole about 1.5mm (1/16in) in diameter. It only attacks the sapwood of hardwoods. The beetle emerges during the summer and has a life cycle of about ten months.

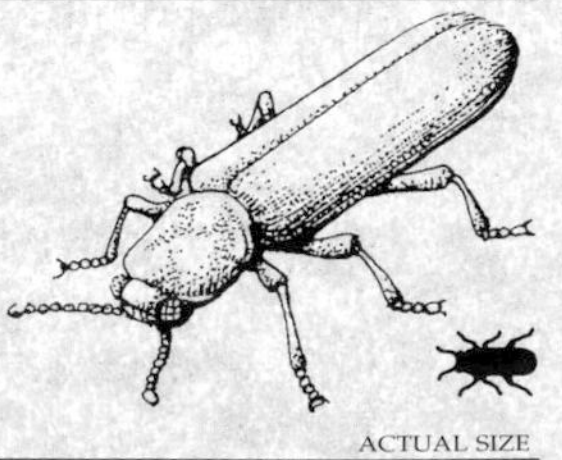

ACTUAL SIZE

WOODBORING WEEVIL

The woodboring weevil is no more than 3mm (⅛in) long and produces a small elongated hole. It thrives on decaying wood in damp conditions. Unlike other woodboring insects, the adults as well as the larvae infest the wood. The weevil is active throughout the year and has a life cycle of seven to nine months.

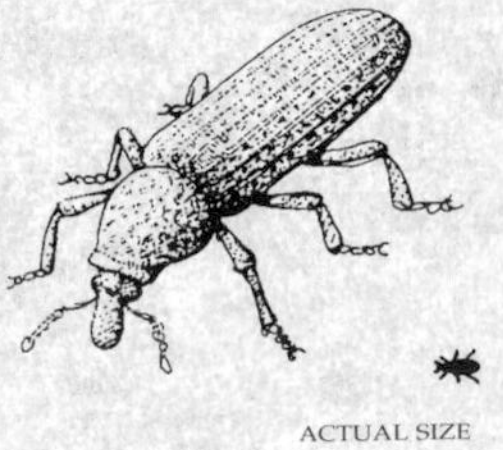

ACTUAL SIZE

WOOD ROT

Wood that's kept dry will not rot. All wood-rotting fungi, including dry rot, require a continuous supply of moisture in order to develop. Provided the source of water is removed, the fungus will die once the wood dries out. Wet rot and dry rot are the two main types of fungus that attack building timbers. The terms wet and dry can be misleading. For example, some people are under the false impression that building timbers are susceptible to dry rot as they dry out – and it is quite wrong to believe that the fungus can produce enough water to sustain itself after the original source of moisture has been removed. Dry rot is potentially the more serious, but only under specific conditions in a poorly maintained building. Get expert advice on the cause of the rot (usually rising or penetrating damp, but sometimes leaking plumbing) and have it rectified.

Wet-rot fungus under floorcovering

Mature fruiting body of dry rot

Wet rot

Many fungi will attack damp building timbers, but none is specially adapted to do so. All are basically woodland fungi and, to them, wet joists and skirting boards are no different to a pile of logs in the forest. Any type of decay other than dry rot is classed as wet rot, which frequently infects exposed and unprotected wood, such as window and door frames. It can also break out in damp cellars and where plumbing is leaking. Wet rot makes wood become soft and spongy, often exhibiting horizontal and cross-grain cracks. The fungus itself may take the form of grey-brown or black threadlike strands and, as the fungus grows, flat fruiting bodies may develop.

Depriving the fungus of moisture inhibits its further growth and stops continued deterioration of the wood.

Dry rot

Outbreaks of dry rot occur on damp wood in dark unventilated conditions. Unlike wet rot, it cannot survive in well-ventilated areas.

Once established, dry rot spreads over timber and other materials as a network of fine tubular strands. These can spread very widely – even passing through cracks in building materials, such as plaster, stone, brick and concrete.

You may be able to detect an outbreak of dry rot by the pungent smell of the fungus. Painted wood may exhibit signs of buckling, and the surface may collapse due to decomposition of the wood.

The infected wood turns dark brown and, as it shrinks and splits, deep cracks form both with and across the grain, breaking the timber up into fine cubelike pieces. Dry rot

appears as light-grey to black strands fanning out across infected surfaces.

The mature fungus develops a brown pancake-shaped fruiting body with a rough surface and a smooth white outer margin When the spores are released, they tend to cover surrounding surfaces with a layer of fine rust-red dust.

The fungus can grow rapidly – as much as 150mm (6in) in a month.

DEALING WITH WET ROT

First eradicate the cause of the damp – wet-rot fungus will only continue growing if the area stays wet.

If necessary, cut away structurally weakened wood and replace it with new preservative-treated timber, possibly sandwiching a strip of damp-proof membrane between the wood and any adjacent masonry.

Alternatively, treat the new sections of wood yourself after you have installed them. Brush on three generous coats of fungicidal wood preservative. Cover all wood in any surrounding area where moisture has been present. Wear protective gloves, goggles and a respirator when handling preservatives.

Pressure injection of timber

For the treatment of larger sections of timber *in situ*, such as structural timbers, it is possible to have the wood impregnated, using a high-pressure injection system. This is undertaken by specialists, using one-way-valve plastic injectors that are inserted into holes drilled in the vulnerable areas. A special gun is connected that injects the fluid until it fully permeates the cells of the wood.

DEALING WITH DRY ROT

If you notice signs of dry rot, call in an independent expert who can identify the source of the damp, evaluate the extent of the damage, and tell you what needs to be done. This sometimes involves having to remove much of the surrounding material, and you should seek advice from your local Conservation Officer before allowing anyone to do that kind of work in a protected building.

Once the source of the moisture has been eliminated, the usual treatment recommended by many contractors involves stripping and replacing infected wood and plastered surfaces up to 1m (3ft) beyond the last sign of fungal attack, and applying a fungicidal solution to sterilize all woodwork, masonry and associated materials in the infected area. You may have little choice but to accept such drastic measures if a treatment guarantee is required. However, once the damp is eradicated and possibly extra ventilation provided, dry-rot growth will cease and chemical treatment may not be required – but be sure to get expert advice.

PAINT FOR PERIOD HOUSES

Period houses sometimes retain evidence of successive decorative schemes

PAINT HAS TWO PURPOSES – *to protect and decorate. All paints are made up of three components: pigments, which provide colour; binder, which holds the pigments together and bonds them to the surface; and solvents, which act as a thinner for the mixture of pigment and binder.*

The protective properties of paint became more important in the seventeenth century as the use of imported softwoods, rather than more durable hardwoods, became more common. By the late nineteenth century making paint had become an industrial process, and the emerging chemical industry developed a wide range of synthetic pigments and media that were used in the manufacture of ready-made paints.

Period houses usually retain evidence of successive decorative schemes applied over the course of time, which reflect the changing fashions in interior decoration and the tastes of the occupants. If your house is of particular historic or architectural interest or has not undergone modernization in the recent past, you may wish to conserve old finishes and decorative schemes that have survived. If you find rare or historically interesting paint finishes or wallpapers, consider preserving them under modern lining paper, rather than stripping them or obliterating them with paint. Your local Conservation Officer will be able to give advice on how these finishes might be protected or conserved.

PAINT BEFORE INDUSTRIALIZATION

Until the early twentieth century, house paints were traditionally either limewash, distempers or lead-based oil paints. All these paints are characterized by their water-permeable elastic qualities, which make them highly suitable for many older buildings.

Limewash

Limewash was applied as a decorative finish to a wide variety of different materials: stone, brickwork and timber framing. A cheap material, it provided protection, inside and outside, and was also an effective means of cleansing and disinfecting. The basic ingredients, still used today, were water and lime putty made from burnt limestone (calcium hydroxide). Often, coloured pigments were added.

Limewash is highly permeable – water vapour can escape easily, allowing the substrate to 'breathe'. Limewash can also be applied as a shelter coat to vulnerable materials, such as decayed stonework or old timber framing, where it acts as a 'sacrificial layer' and affords protection to the surface underneath.

Unlike modern masonry paints, limewash has a soft, subtle texture and varies in tone, which makes it a particularly attractive finish for many older buildings. It also weathers differently from modern paints, which tend to crack and blister in extremes, and can trap water in damp masonry. In contrast, limewash simply erodes gradually until a new coating is required.

Limewash has a subtlety of texture and tone that suits old buildings

But it can be as colourful as modern masonry paints

Making limewash

Limewash is a mixture of water and non-hydraulic lime putty. The lime putty can be purchased in tubs ready prepared. Generally, 1 part lime putty mixed with 2 parts water is sufficient, but you may need to adjust the mix to suit the porosity of the surface. You may also wish to add a coloured pigment, such as red or yellow ochre. A pigment should never be more than 10 per cent of the mix.

Wear goggles and gloves

Before brushing on limewash, the surface needs to be wetted well, so that the surface will not absorb water from the limewash too quickly. It is important to wear goggles and gloves when mixing and applying limewash, as lime is a caustic substance.

Depending on the weather, it can take several hours, or even days, for limewash to dry.

Distemper

A mixture of chalk and glue, 'soft' distemper – usually called simply 'distemper' – can be tinted with pigments and is very permeable. Because it can be brushed onto freshly applied plaster, distemper was commonly used as 'a builder's finish' – the temporary decoration applied to a house while the plaster carbonated and before the application of oil paints. It is an inexpensive finish, but having been mixed has to be applied within a few days. Distemper is not washable and takes marks easily, but it is perfectly suitable as a finish for ceilings and cornices.

Mixing distemper with materials such as casein – a binder of milk solids – produces what is sometimes referred to as 'milk paint'. Mixing it with linseed oil makes 'oil-bound distemper'. Being relatively hard, oil-bound distemper was the first washable permeable paint. It is still available from specialist paint manufacturers. These modified distempers, the forerunners of modern emulsions, are not as permeable as soft distemper.

Oil paints

Until the 1950s the basic ingredients of most oil paints were lead white and linseed oil. Oil paints were applied to a wide range of materials – wood, metal, stone and plaster – both internally and externally. Lead-based oil paint is an extremely durable and attractive finish, which weathers better than many modern gloss paints. Lead is no longer added to paint, and since 1992 its use is prohibited except for approved applications on Grade I and II* listed buildings (Grade A in Scotland).

MODERN PAINTS

Today, paints contain non-toxic pigments such as zinc and titanium instead of lead; and fast-drying alkyd resins have replaced traditional linseed oil. Vinyl emulsions provide a washable and more durable alternative to distemper.

Silicate (mineral) paints

Modern silicate paints are porous and soak into the substrate, where they bond with minerals within the underlying structure. As a result, they will last for at least 15 years.

HISTORICALLY ACCURATE SCHEMES

If you want to reinstate a historically accurate paint scheme or would just like to know the kind of colours likely to have been used during the history of your house, you could try to identify the dates when major alterations were carried out, as they may furnish clues to the styles fashionable at the time. To get a feel for a particular era, it is worth consulting books of contemporary paintings that illustrate decorative schemes popular during the relevant periods.

However, a more accurate record may exist in the accumulated layers of paint within the house itself, although teasing out the information can only be done by a skilled professional. After reviewing the historical and structural evidence, a specialist architectural-paint researcher will remove small sections of paint and substrate. These fragments are then examined under high magnification to determine the sequence of paints applied. This reveals the full story of how your house was decorated. The practice of taking 'paint scrapes' is now considered to be an old-fashioned method of paint analysis, and one that can be highly inaccurate.

Armed with your detailed analysis, you may be able to conserve or re-create one of the original colour schemes. Whether you decide to do this or prefer to decorate rooms in colours that reflect your own taste, there is now a wide range of historically matched colours and wallpapers available, some of them from specialist suppliers.

Whatever you decide to do, it is recommended that whenever possible you leave existing paint layers and any traces of old wallcoverings in place, as they constitute valuable evidence of what was done in the past. Areas of flaking paint and damaged woodwork have to be refurbished, but there is usually no need to strip well-bonded paint. Furthermore, old lead-based oil paint can be a health hazard should it ever become necessary to remove it. When rubbing down old paintwork, it is therefore best to assume it is lead-based. Use wet-and-dry paper dipped in water and wear a face mask. Burning off old lead paint creates toxic fumes.

The detail of decorative cornices and mouldings may be obscured by layers of soft distemper, which can be removed safely with water and a scrubbing brush.

Sympathetic modern colour scheme

History trapped in layers of paint

Changing colours and finishes

Unless your house is a Grade I or Grade II* listed building, changing the interior colour scheme is unlikely to require consent. But if you live in a listed building or in a conservation area, or if your house forms part of a significant group, it is advisable to consult a Conservation Officer before you make major changes to exterior colours or introduce new finishes.

PROFESSIONAL HELP

THERE ARE A NUMBER OF KEY PROFESSIONALS who can help you plan and carry out work on an old house. It is tempting to dispense with professional services in order to save money, but that often proves to be a false economy. You need people who are experienced in dealing with older properties, and who understand what you want to do and why you want to do it. Regrettably, many building professionals are trained and experienced in modern construction methods but are unable to handle the complexities and special requirements of repairing or modifying a period house.

FINDING THE RIGHT PROFESSIONAL

Depending on the size, complexity and nature of your building project, you may need to consult or employ one or more of the following.

Architect
The term architect is a protected title in the UK. Only a person registered with the Architects Registration Board can be called an architect. There are more than 20,000 architects registered in the UK, but only a small percentage specialize in the repair of old buildings. The Royal Institute of British Architects (RIBA) keeps a register of such specialists and can supply you with a list of recommendations. You may also wish to consult the list of Architects Accredited in Building Conservation (RIBA/AABC), which is held by RIBA, or the lists of architects held by the Society for the Protection of Ancient Buildings (SPAB).

As well as RIBA, there are regional organizations you can turn to, such as the Royal Society of Architects in Wales (RSAW), the Royal Incorporation of Architects in Scotland (RIAS), who run their own accreditation scheme, and the Royal Society of Ulster Architects (RSUA). All architects are trained in building design, but those who specialize in working on older buildings bring specific expertise to the project. They have a broad knowledge of past construction methods, and should be skilled at blending new work with old. An architect can prepare all the documentation you need to apply for listed-building consent, planning permission or Building Regulations approval. If you wish, you can entrust on-site supervision and administration of the contract to your architect.

Building surveyor
Surveyors of this type can play a role similar to an architect's, but generally they are not trained as designers. Within the Royal Institute of Chartered Surveyors there is a building conservation group that maintains its own list of members accredited in building conservation.

Structural engineer
This type of specialist will carry out a structural survey of a property you are thinking of buying, or help you decide on the most suitable structural repairs for an old building. It is best to employ an engineer who has had experience of surveying older houses. The Institution of Civil Engineers (ICE) and the Institution of Structural Engineers (IStrucE) hold lists of engineers accredited in building conservation – the Conservation Accreditation Register of Engineers (CARE).

Quantity surveyor
For a large project, you might consider hiring a quantity surveyor who will deal with the financial control of the work and contractual issues.

Services engineer
Also known as mechanical or electrical engineers, these professionals can provide advice on heating, drainage, plumbing and electrics.

Project manager
This is someone you can employ either to coordinate a team of professionals or to act as your agent on a large building project.

Builder
Most architects or surveyors can help you find a suitable builder, but if you are running the job yourself it is essential to employ a builder who has the expertise and knowledge to work on an old house. Ask for personal recommendations, check up on references, and look at other jobs the builder has done in the past. Have a contract drawn up, which includes dates for starting and finishing the work. If possible, get a firm price, not just an estimate; but if certain aspects are difficult to cost in advance, establish with the builder how any additional work is to be costed. If at any stage you suspect a builder of serving his own interests by proposing unnecessary work, you should seek independent professional advice from an architect or building surveyor.

Specialist supplier
There is a wide range of suppliers who stock materials appropriate for repairing period houses – lime putty, plasters and renders, bricks and roofcoverings to match old stock, traditional paints, and so on. These suppliers can also give advice on how the materials should be used.

One useful source of such information is the website **www.buildingconservation. com**.

Conservation specialist
Materials and fittings used in building period houses are often vulnerable and could be irretrievably damaged by inexpert treatment. To find specialists for tasks such as the cleaning of masonry or paint, mortar analysis, or the installation of services in protected houses, try **www.buildingconservation. com**.

Conservation Officer
The Conservation Officer employed by your local planning authority is an invaluable source of technical advice on repairs and improvements, and can also give advice on proposed extensions and alterations to old buildings.

GRANTS
Although financial help is not widely available, grant schemes are operated by some local authorities. If your period house is listed Grade I or Grade II*, the work may be eligible for a grant from English Heritage as part of their Historic Buildings, Monuments and Designed Landscapes grants scheme. The grant application is more likely to be successful if it meets national and regional priorities, which are outlined in the application pack. The application must demonstrate that there is financial need for a grant and that the work will be undertaken within two years.

You may also wish to visit the website of the Funds for Historic Buildings (**www. ffhb.org.uk**). This provides a guide to funding for anyone seeking to repair, restore or convert a historic building and includes all the material previously contained in the Architectural Heritage Fund's Directory of Funding Sources.

GLOSSARY OF TERMS

A

Acanthus
Classical decorative motif based on the large deeply cut leaves of a plant native to the Mediterranean region.

Aggregate
Particles of sand or stone, mixed with materials such as cement or lime to make concrete or mortar.

Annealing
The process of removing stresses in a material, usually by heating.

Anthemion
Stylized floral motif derived from Greek and Roman architecture, widely used in neo-classical ornamentation. The most common form was based on honeysuckle flowers and leaves.

Architrave
A moulding that surrounds a door or window. *or* The lowest horizontal moulding of a classical entablature.

Arris
The sharp edge at the meeting of two flat surfaces.

Ashlar
Dressed and finely jointed stonework

Astragal
Another term for glazing bar. *or* A moulding comprising a half-round raised central spine with a cove or square fillet on each side.

B

Band course
A square-faced horizontal moulding in stucco or stone.

Bead
A narrow strip of wood with a half-round profile.

Bevel
A surface that meets another at an angle of less than 90 degrees. See also CHAMFER.

Binding
A term used to describe a door or

hinged casement that is rubbing against the surrounding frame.

Bolection moulding
Wooden moulding used to cover the joint between members that have surfaces at different levels.

Bonding
A method of interlocking bricks or stone blocks in order to create a stable structure.

Bow
To bend as a result of uneven shrinkage – usually in reference to wood.

Brace
A diagonal member used to prevent a battened door from sagging.

Brushing out
Spreading paint finishes to avoid runs or uneven coverage.

Burr
A rough raised edge left on metal after cutting or filing.

Butt
To fit snugly against.

C

Cantilever
A projecting beam that is secured at one end only.

Capital
The topmost part of a column or pilaster.

Caryatid
A supporting column or pilaster in the form of a female figure.

Caulking
Weatherproofing a joint by sealing with a non-setting mastic.

Cement
A combination of powdered calcined limestone and clay mixed with water and an aggregate to make mortar or concrete.

Chair rail
Another term for dado rail.

Chamfer
A 45-degree bevel.

Clamp
A primitive kiln for firing, comprising a stack of unbaked bricks and fuel encased in a mound of old bricks and clay.

Compo
A mixture of materials such as whiting and glue used to fashion raised decoration on a frame etc.

Conservation
Work done to ensure that a building retains its historical or architectural character.

Console
A decorative bracket used to support a doorhood, soffit, etc.

Conversion
Altering the whole or part of a building to serve a different purpose.

Coping stones
Stone slabs laid on top of a masonry wall to shed rainwater.

Corbel
A bracket, usually of stone, brick or plaster.

Corbelling
A projection in masonry, formed by building successive courses outwards in a stepped fashion, one above the other.

Cornice
A decorative moulding forming a junction between the walls of a room and the ceiling. *or* The uppermost horizontal moulding of a classical entablature.

Cove
A concave moulding.

Cross grain
Wood grain that deviates from the main axis of a length of timber.

Cup
To bend, usually as a result of shrinkage. Cupping occurs across the width of a piece of wood.

D

Dado
A decorative or protective panel

applied to the lower part of an interior wall.

Damp-proof course (DPC)
A layer of impervious material that prevents moisture rising from the ground into the walls of a building.

Damp-proof membrane (DPM)
A sheet of impervious material that prevents moisture rising through a floor.

Dentil
One of a row of small toothlike blocks that form part of a classical cornice.

Distressing
The act of giving something an aged appearance by various measures, such as staining and denting.

Dormer
A structure projecting from a roof, usually housing a window.

Dressing
The act of cutting, shaping and finishing masonry or metal etc.

Drip groove
A groove cut in the underside of a projection such as a moulding or sill to cause rainwater to drip to the ground.

Dripstone
A moulding placed above a door or window opening to deflect rainwater. Also known as a label or hood mould.

Duo-pitched roof
A roof that slopes in two directions.

E

Edge grain
Grain (growth rings) running at not less than 45 degrees to the faces of a piece of wood. Also known as quarter-sawn timber.

Efflorescence
A white powdery deposit on masonry or plaster caused by mineral salts migrating to the surface as a result of evaporation.

GLOSSARY OF TERMS

Elevation
Side view of a building or other structure.

End grain
The surface of wood exposed after cutting across the fibres.

Engaged
Attached to a wall (e.g. an engaged column).

Enrichments
Decorative features, usually added separately to a cornice, frieze, etc.

Entablature
The band of mouldings near the top of a façade, divided into cornice, frieze and architrave.

Exfoliation
See SPALLING.

Expanded metal
A type of lathing for plasterwork made by slitting and stretching metal sheet.

F

Fabric
The material(s) from which a building or part of a building is constructed.

Façade
The exterior face of a building.

Facings
Weather-resistant bricks used for constructing exterior brickwork.

Faience
Glazed terracotta.

Feathering
Brushing out the edge of paint or other finishes.

Festoon
See SWAG.

Fettling
Cleaning up a casting by removing excess material.

Fillet
Strip of mortar used to seal the junction between two surfaces, such as a roof and a wall. *or* A small square-section moulding, usually in wood.

Finial
A decorative spike or post set at the apex of a gable or on the point of a spire, tower, etc.

Flashing
A weatherproof strip (usually of metal) used to cover the junction between a roof and a wall or chimney, or between one part of a roof and another.

Frieze
The strip of wall between a ceiling cornice and a picture rail. *or* The central panel of a classical entablature.

Frog
The recess in the top face of a brick. Some bricks have a frog in the bedding face, too.

G

Gable
The triangular section of wall at the end of a duo-pitched roof. Also known as a gable end.

Gable roof
Another, commonly used, term for a duo-pitched roof.

Galvanized
Protected with an electroplated or dipped zinc coating.

Gather
The funnel-shaped smoke outlet leading to the flue above a fireplace.

Gauging
The mixing of a little cement or gypsum with lime mortar or plaster to hasten setting time.

Gesso
A mixture of plaster and size used as a base coat for gilding or painting.

Glazing points
Small triangular fixings used to hold window glass in a rebate.

Grounds
Rough strips of wood attached to masonry as fixing points for panelling, skirting, etc.

H

Hardwood
Wood cut from broadleaved (mostly deciduous) trees belonging to the botanical group *Angiospermae.*

Head
The topmost horizontal component of a casement-window or exterior-door frame.

Header
A brick or stone block laid so the end is visible.

Hingebound
A term used to describe a door or casement that cannot be closed properly due to a misaligned or poorly fitted hinge.

Hip
The external sloping corner formed by two angled faces of a pitched roof.

Horn
An extension of a sliding-sash stile that strengthens the joint between it and the meeting rail. *or* The extension of a door stile, designed to protect a new door from accidental damage during transportation.

Housing
A groove cut across the grain of a wooden component.

I

Indenting
Patching damaged masonry by cutting out a worn area and inserting new stone.

Intervention
Any action that modifies the fabric of a building.

J

Jamb
The vertical side member of a doorframe or casement-window frame.

K

Keying
Abrading or incising a surface to provide a better grip for gluing or plastering etc.

Knapping
The process of shaping a flint by chipping flakes from its edges.

L

Laying off
Finishing an application of paint or varnish etc. with upward brush strokes.

Lintel
A beam supporting the masonry above a door or window opening.

Lipping
Protective solid-wood strip glued to the edge of a man-made board.

M

Maintenance
Regular upkeep of a building, to prevent it requiring major repairs.

Mitre
A joint between two pieces of wood formed by cutting bevels of equal angle (usually 45 degrees) at the ends of both pieces.

Modillion
One of a row of brackets, usually decorated with acanthus leaves, forming part of a cornice.

Mortar
A mixture of cement or lime with an aggregate and water for bonding bricks or blocks of stone.

Mullion
A vertical member separating two windows.

Muntin
A vertical member between panels (e.g. of a door).

N

Newel
A substantial post at either end of a balustrade.

O

Orders
The five classical architectural

GLOSSARY OF TERMS

styles that provided the basis for the proportions and detailing of neo-classical buildings.

Overmantel
A framed mirror surmounting a fireplace.

Overthrow
A decorative metal archway, often incorporating a lantern, spanning a gateway.

Ovolo
A quarter-round convex moulding.

Oxidize
To form a layer of metal oxide, as in rusting.

P

Pallets
Wooden plugs built into masonry joints on each side of a door or window opening to serve as fixing points for the frame.

Parapet
A low wall at the edge of a roof or balcony.

Pargeting
Decorative low-relief stuccowork. *or* Lime mortar flue lining.

Paterae
Floral motifs, often alternating with modillions when used to decorate cornices.

Pediment
A triangular structure forming a gable on a Greek or Roman temple. Neo-classical doors and windows were often surmounted by a pediment.

Pilaster
A shallow square-section engaged column.

Pilot hole
A small-diameter hole drilled before inserting a screw to act as a guide for the thread.

Pin holes
Small holes caused by cutting into voids made by gas bubbles formed in cast metal during the casting process.

Pitch
The slope of a roof.

Plan
Top view of a building, room, piece of furniture, etc.

Planted moulding
A wooden moulding applied separately. Also known as an applied moulding.

Pointing
The act of shaping the mortar joints between bricks or stone blocks. *or* The mortar joints themselves.

Pontil
Iron rod used for spinning glass.

Poultice
An absorbent paste applied to masonry to draw out stains.

Preservation
Retaining a building in its present condition by retarding deterioration.

Pugging
The act of mixing and kneading clay with water to produce an even consistency. *or* Material inserted between wooden flooring and ceiling to reduce transmission of sound.

Purlin
A horizontal beam providing intermediate support for rafters or sheet roofing.

Q

Quarry
A square or diamond-shape pane of glass for a leaded light.

Quirk
A continuous groove in an architectural moulding.

Quoin
Masonry forming the outer corner of a wall.

R

Rafter
One of a set of parallel sloping beams that form the main structural element of a roof.

Raised grain
Roughening of the surface of a piece of wood, caused by the fibres swelling due to the presence of water.

Rebate
A stepped recess along the edge of a workpiece or component. Also known as a rabbet.

Reconstruction
The process of returning a building to a previous condition or style on the basis of documentary or physical evidence.

Relieving arch
A masonry arch built above a door or window to deflect the load away from a lintel.

Render
A mixture of cement, lime and sand (or lime and sand) used for coating the exterior of a wall. *or* To coat a wall with render.

Renovation
Making as new. Renovation usually involves more work than is required to repair the fabric of the building.

Repair
Work that is beyond the scope of regular maintenance, done in order to remedy defects such as significant decay or damage. Repairing involves returning a building to good order without significant alteration.

Repoussé work
Thin decorative metalwork raised in relief by hammering the metal from behind.

Restoration
Reinstating parts of a building to return it to its original appearance.

Reveal
The vertical side of a door or window opening, between the frame and the face of the wall.

Reversible
Capable of being returned to the present state or condition without any significant damage or alteration.

Ridge
The horizontal joint line at the apex of a pitched roof.

Ridge board
The horizontal beam to which the rafters are joined at the apex of a roof.

Roof cresting
A decorative ceramic or metal strip running along the ridge of a roof.

Rose plate
A backing plate for a door knob.

Roundel
A small circular piece of crown glass containing the pontil mark, used as a decorative element in leaded lights.

Rub joint
A joint made by sliding one glued component from side to side on another until suction causes the joint to stick.

Running mould
A template used for shaping stucco or plaster mouldings.

Rustication
Bevelled or chanelled joints between blocks of masonry.

S

Saddle bar
A metal bar used to reinforce a leaded light.

Sandblasting
The process of cleaning a surface (usually metal or masonry) with a jet of abrasive grit or sand. See also SHOT BLASTING.

Sapwood
New wood surrounding the denser heartwood of a tree.

Sash
A glazed frame forming part of a window, sometimes fixed but more often made to slide or to pivot on hinges.

Scribe
To mark and shape the edge of a workpiece so that it will fit exactly against another surface. *or* To mark by scratching with a pointed tool.

GLOSSARY OF TERMS

Scrim
Open-weave fabric used for reinforcing plasterwork.

Seasoning
Reducing the moisture content of wood.

Secret nailing
A method of securing wooden components with concealed nail fixings.

Selvage
The irregular untrimmed edge on each side of a length or roll of wallcovering.

Setting in
Making vertical cuts with a chisel or gouge to establish the outline of a motif carved in relief.

Sherardized
Covered with a protective coating produced by heating iron or steel in a container together with zinc dust.

Shim
A thin packing piece.

Short grain
This occurs where the general direction of the wood fibres runs across a narrow section of timber.

Shot blasting
A similar process to sandblasting but using iron or steel particles instead of sand or grit.

Show wood
Wood intended to be seen, often coated with a clear finish.

Sill
The lowest horizontal member of a window frame.

Skirting
A board used to cover the junction between an interior wall and the floor.

Soffit
The underside of a structure such as an arch, stair or beam.

Softwood
Wood cut from coniferous trees belonging to the botanical group *Gymnospermae*.

Soldiers
Vertical wooden grounds to which a skirting is fixed.

Spalling
Flaking of the outer face of masonry, often caused by expanding moisture in freezing conditions.

Spandrel
Panelling used to fill the triangular shape below a stair string.

Sprigs
Small cut nails used for fixing a window pane in a rebate.

Sprue
Excess metal left on a casting due to the metal solidifying in the channel through which it was introduced into the mould.

Stile
The vertical member on each side of a door or window sash.

Stippling
Applying paint or other finishes as spots, using the tip of a brush.

Straight grain
Grain (wood fibres) aligning with the main axis of timber.

Straightedge
A length of timber or metal that has at least one true edge – used for drawing straight lines or for scraping a surface level.

Stretcher
A brick or stone block laid so that one of its long faces is visible.

String
A board running from one floor level to another into which the treads and risers of a staircase are jointed. Also known as a stringer or stringboard.

String course
A horizontal strip of moulded stone or stucco (similar to a cornice but smaller in scale) that extends across a façade.

Stucco
A type of render used to imitate stone, often with details such as mouldings and cornices.

Stuck moulding
A moulding that is cut into a piece of wood. Also known as a struck or integral moulding.

Stud wall
An interior timber-frame wall sheathed with lath and plaster or plasterboard.

Studs
The vertical wooden posts within a timber-frame wall.

Swag
An ornamental motif depicting a hanging garland. Also known as a festoon.

T

Template
A cut-out pattern used to help shape a workpiece accurately.

Thixotropic
A term used to describe paints that have a gel-like consistency until stirred or applied, at which point they liquefy.

Throat
The narrow aperture at the base of a flue, designed to cause rising air and smoke to speed up.

Timber-frame wall
A wall composed of structural wooden components, sheathed on both sides or infilled with masonry or wattle and daub.

Transom
A horizontal rail separating a fanlight from a door. *or* A horizontal window-frame member.

U

Undercutting
Cutting away material from the edges of a recess to form a dovetail-shape cavity.

V

Valley
Trough formed at the junction of two sloping roof surfaces.

Vapour barrier
A layer of impervious material that prevents the passage of moisture-laden air.

Vermiculation
A form of carved surface dressing for stonework, composed of closely packed shallow recesses separated by wavy ridges said to resemble worm tracks.

Volute
A decorative spiral scroll found on column capitals, consoles, etc.

Voussoir
A wedge-shape member of a brick or stone arch.

W

Wainscoting
Wall panelling made of painted oak or softwood.

Wall plate
A horizontal wooden member placed along the top of a wall to support the ends of joists and rafters, thus spreading their load.

Wet-and-dry paper
An abrasive paper consisting of silicon-carbide particles glued to a waterproof backing, used to smooth new paintwork or varnish between coats.

Window guard
A low metal panel, grille or railing placed across a window at sill level on the outside.

Withe
A masonry partition dividing one flue from another in a chimney. Also known as a midfeather.

Work hardening
Increasing the strength or hardness of a metal workpiece by manipulation, such as stretching, bending, hammering, etc.

INDEX

INDEX

INDEX

INDEX

ACKNOWLEDGMENTS

The authors and producers are grateful to the following companies, organizations and individuals for their assistance in the production of this book.

Acquisitions Fireplaces Ltd
The Fan Museum
Aristocast Originals Ltd
Artisan
BCM Contracts Ltd
Brighton Borough Council
Chris Blanchett
The Brooking Collection Trust
R. Bleasdale (Spirals)
Phillip Bradbury Glass
Brickmatch Ltd
Britannia Architectural Metalwork
 & Restoration
British Gypsum Ltd
British Society of
 Master Glass Painters
R. W. Brunskill
Building Adhesives Ltd
The Building Conservation Trust
Richard Burbidge Ltd
Barbara & Tony Burrough
C. D. (UK) Ltd
Constance & Jack Cairns
Capricorn Architectural
 Ironwork Ltd
The Carving Workshop
Cattles Precision Woodwork
Cement & Plaster Mouldings Ltd
Cico Chimney Linings Ltd
Pat & Jim Clark

Classic Designs
Classical Concrete Ltd
Clayton-Munroe Ltd
Clean Walls Ltd
Comyn Ching Ltd
Cookson Industrial Materials Ltd
Peter Cornish
County Forge Ltd
Crittal Windows Ltd
Anthony Cross
Crown Berger Ltd
The Department of the Environment
Barbara Doig
Exchem Mining & Construction Ltd
Feltham Glass Works
Geoff & Mareszka Fleming
Forgeries Ltd
The Georgian Group
Gray & McDonnell Ltd
The Hardwood Flooring Co. Ltd
E. J. Harmer & Co. Ltd
Harrison Thompson & Co. Ltd
Haslemere Design Ltd
Hayes & Howe
Tony Herbert
James Hetley & Co. Ltd
Allen Charles Hill
Hodkin & Jones Ltd
Ibstock Building Products Ltd
ICI Chemicals & Polymers Ltd

Jackfield Tile Museum
Jackson & Cox Architectural
 Restoration Ltd
H. & R. Johnson Tiles Ltd
K.C.C. Planning Department
Lamont Antiques Ltd
Langlow Products Ltd
The Lead Development Association
Warwick Leadlay
J. Legge & Co. Ltd
Luminaries Stained Glass Studio
Marflex International Ltd
Marston & Langinger Ltd
The Metalock Organisation
The Michelmersh
 Brick & Tile Co. Ltd
E. G. Millar (Plastering) Ltd
Mr & Mrs Scovell
Mumford & Wood Ltd
National Corrosion Service
Nero Designs
The Original Box Sash Window Co.
The Paint Research Association
Mr & Mrs Pery-Knox-Gore
Pilkington Glass Ltd
Plantation Shutters
The Post Office Archives
Protim Services Ltd
The Rainbow Glass Co.
Red Bank Manufacturing Co. Ltd

Rentokil Ltd
Ridout Associates Ltd
Dennis Ruabon Ltd
John Sambrook
B. C. Sanitan Ltd
The Society for the Protection
 of Ancient Buildings
Solaglass Technical Advisory Service
Stag Polymer & Sealants Ltd
Stained Glass Supplies
Staircase Solutions
Sterling Roncraft
The Stone Federation
Stovax Ltd
London Regional Planning, DOE
Thames Moulding Co.
The Tiles & Architectural
 Ceramics Society
Joseph Tipper Ltd
Jenny Todd
Top Knobs Ltd
Townsends (London) Ltd
The Universal Railings Co. Ltd
Hans van Lemmen
Vermont Castings
Webb & Kempf Ltd
Wellington Tile Co.
Westcombe Antiques
John Williams & Co. Ltd
Winther Browne & Co. Ltd

Owners of period houses may find the following sources of information useful.

National amenity societies
Amenity societies are a valuable source of information when repairing period houses. They produce many technical leaflets as well as organizing courses and lectures. Contact the following:

Society for the Protection of Ancient Buildings
www.spab.org.uk
Victorian Society
www.victorian-society.org.uk
Georgian Group
www.georgiangroup.org.uk
Twentieth Century Society
www.c20society.demon.co.uk
Ancient Monuments Society
www.ancientmonumentssociety.org.uk

Local authority guidance
Many local authorities provide guidance on historic buildings and the types of materials used in their area. Contact your local authority to see what services they can provide.

Conservation information available online
The internet is a rich source of information on conservation specialists and suppliers as well as useful technical information. The following websites are particularly useful:

www.buildingconservation.com
www.oldhouse.info
www.periodproperty.co.uk

Government advisors on heritage matters
Government agencies produce a wide range of publications on the historic environment. Some of this information is supplied free of charge.

English Heritage
www.english-heritage.org.uk
Historic Scotland
www.historic-scotland.gov.uk
Cadw (Welsh Historic Environment Agency)
www.cadw.wales.gov.uk
Environment and Heritage Service (Northern Ireland)
www.ehsni.gov.uk

Fourth Edition

INTRODUCING PHYSICAL GEOGRAPHY

Fourth Edition

Introducing Physical Geography

Alan Strahler

Boston University

Arthur Strahler

John Wiley & Sons, Inc.

Acquisitions Editor	Jerry Correa
Associate Editor	Denise Powell
Production Editor	Sandra Dumas
Marketing Manager	Jeffrey Rucker
Senior Designer	Karin Kincheloe
Photo Editor	Kathy Bendo/Jennifer MacMillan
Illustration Editor	Sigmund Malinowski
Production Management Services	Hermitage Publishing Services
Text Design	Jerry Wilke
Cover Design	David Levy
Cover Photo	Chris Noble/Photographer's Choice/Getty Images
Cover Inset Illustration	Precision Graphics

This book was typeset in 10/12 Times New Roman by Hermitage Publishing Services and printed and bound by Von Hoffmann Corporation. The cover was printed by Lehigh Press Corporation.

The paper in this book was manufactured by a mill whose forest management programs include sustained yield harvesting of its timberlands. Sustained yield harvesting principles ensure that the number of trees cut each year does not exceed the amount of new growth.

This book is printed on acid-free paper. ⊗

Strahler, Alan, N., Strahler, Arthur/Introducing Physical Geography, Fourth Edition
ISBN 0-471-67950-X

Printed in the United States of America.

10 9 8 7 6 5 4 3 2 1

PREFACE

It is with great pleasure that we present the Fourth Edition of *Introducing Physical Geography.* Our new edition builds on the considerable strengths of our prior editions, but also adds much that is new:

- *Expanded coverage of global change*, including three new multiple-page features on climate change that document regional impacts of climate change predicted for North America (in Chapter 7); global climate change and agriculture (Chapter 10); and global change and coastal environments (Chapter 18). In addition, our feature on the IPCC report of 2001 has been expanded (Chapter 3), along with our coverage of the Aral Sea environmental disaster (Chapter 15).
- *More remote sensing for global change*, including features on monitoring of global productivity from space (Chapter 8) and mapping global land cover by satellite (Chapter 9).
- *New environmental coverage,* including a new *Eye on the Environment* feature on the December 2004 Indian Ocean tsunami (Chapter 13), updates on the Florida hurricanes of 2004 (Chapter 6), and a discussion of transcurrent fault earthquakes in Turkey in 2002 and 2003 (Chapter 13).
- *New "A Closer Look" feature* that positions nine longer essays between chapters. These interchapter features include selected *Geographer's Tools, Eye on the Environment,* and *Eye on Global Change* boxes. End-of-chapter positioning allows these multipage features to be read independently of the text and without interrupting the flow of in-chapter material.
- *Expanded "Showcase" photo spreads,* now appearing in eight more chapters. These two-page layouts group large photos together to communicate concepts visually in a direct and striking fashion.
- *Ten new Eye on the Landscape features* to help build student interest. In this feature, shown on our cover, an inset image marks locations of interest on landscape photos and queries students about what geographers might observe or infer from them, helping students to learn how to view the landscape in an informed manner. Answers are at the end of each chapter.
- *Eight new chapter opener photos* add visual interest while illustrating main chapter themes.
- *A new location for GeoDiscoveries,* our multimedia learning supplement, which is now on the Wiley web site for our book. Material on the web site includes the animations, interactivities, film and video clips, quizzes, and other features previously available on our GeoDiscoveries CD-ROM, as well as new and updated ones. Special materials for instructors are available on a second tier of the web site. More detail is shown on the following pages.
- *Enhanced integration of GeoDiscoveries,* including short references located within the main text that guide students to specific activities and features on the web site.

We have also improved the text narrative in a number of areas, large and small:

- *A revised introduction to geography as a discipline* in our Prologue that follows themes developed in both the National Academy panel report *Rediscovering Geography: New Relevance for Science and Society* and the new AAG volume *Geography in American at the Dawn .*

of the 21st Century, edited by Gary Gaile and Cort Willmott.

- **Specific reference to the geographic themes of scale, process, and pattern** in a new section in the Prologue, as well as in each chapter in opening or closing discussions.
- **An enhanced discussion of past temperature reconstruction and paleotemperatures** in Chapters 3 and 19, with two new figures.
- **Revisions in the treatment of precipitation,** including recognition of convergence as a separate process of precipitation and an improved description of how raindrops form in Chapter 4.
- **New discussion of the Pacific decadal oscillation**, accompanied by a new figure, in Chapter 5.
- **A new section on highland climates** in Chapter 7.
- **Addition of the nitrogen cycle** to Chapter 8.
- **A new section on disturbance,** including fire, in Chapter 8.
- **Expanded coverage of periglacial processes** in Chapter 14, including two new figures and a new table.
- **Enhanced treatment of lakes** in Chapter 15, including a new *Eye on the Environment* feature focusing on the Great Lakes.
- **A new section on wave characteristics** in Chapter 18, including three new figures and a new table.
- **Major revision of the Canadian soils appendix,** adding four new photos and revised tables and figures to a rewritten text.
- **An updated graphic of topographic map symbols** in the topographic map appendix.
- **Fine-tuning of the text throughout** with many small changes to improve and clarify wording. Includes selected new and replacement photos to better illustrate concepts and phenomena.

THE LEARNING ENVIRONMENT

Visualization

Introducing Physical Geography uses a strategy of *visualization* to enhance the student learning environment. Today's students are accustomed to learning visually and interactively, and our text is designed specifically to help students visualize concepts as they learn them. The strategy involves three components: illustrations, word pictures, and *GeoDiscoveries*—our collection of animations, video clips, and interactivities located on the Wiley web site for our book.

Our illustrations include an art program of large, detailed, and professional photos that attract student interest while clearly demonstrating the process or phenomenon at hand. In addition to the many in-chapter photos, we provide full- or double-page "showcase" photo spreads in each chapter that group three or four striking photos together based on a chapter theme. By placing the photos together, the student

has the chance to compare and contrast them, viewing the theme from different perspectives.

Another visualization feature is *Eye on the Landscape*, which identifies features in landscape photos that demonstrate concepts and linkages across the fields of physical geography. For example, cloud patterns may be identified as a point of interest in a photo of a landform, or glacial features may be indicated in a photo illustrating a forest biome. An inset graphic identifies locations in the photo and queries, "What else would the geographer see?" Answers are provided at the end of the chapter. The objective is to help students learn how to view the landscape in an informed manner.

Remote sensing provides yet another visualization tool to enhance learning. Our *Focus on Remote Sensing* features provide examples of Earth phenomena viewed from space, as well as insight into how remote sensing is used as a tool in geography to study global and regional processes ranging from climate change to floods and fires. The synoptic view from Earth orbit provides the opportunity to examine landforms and landscapes in plan view, helping students better understand the workings of the spatial processes that differentiate the Earth's surface.

Word pictures are essential to learning, and throughout the text we have striven to build word pictures that will stay in students' minds to serve as milestones along a journey of discovery. Clear word pictures lay out and connect scientific ideas and images and place them in the context of other processes and concepts. This involves not only accurate descriptions of processes within the main body of the text, but also virtual images in which the students experience the processes directly.

To build on this learning domain, we have developed the *Putting You in the Picture* feature. This series of chapter-opening essays directly involves the student, personalizing the chapter with an experience or topic relevant to the chapter's main themes. The first such feature, in our prologue chapter *Introducing Physical Geography*, puts the student in the place of an astronaut stationed on the Moon who embarks on a journey home to Earth. By following this journey, the student sees the planet at ever-increasing scales, first as a whole, then as a realm of the four great spheres, then as regions differentiated by climate, vegetation, and soils, and finally as a collection of individual landscape features as the return spacecraft proceeds to a touchdown. The journey is both a metaphor and model for the learning to come.

Other *Putting You in the Picture* features are shorter, but still continue to involve the student in the chapter content. For example, in Chapter 6 the student reads an account of a hurricane watcher experiencing the fury of Hurricane Andrew as it devastated the South Florida coast. In Chapter 16, the student experiences the erosive power of rivers by riding a raft down the Colorado River through the Grand Canyon. Most of these essays are written in the second person to draw the student in more directly.

The third leg of our visualization strategy is *GeoDiscoveries*, our interactive web site. Here the student adds motion to visual learning by viewing animations and video clips. For example, a visualization illustrates the Earth as it rotates on its axis and revolves around the Sun, developing the concept of the seasons from the viewpoint of an observer in space. Another animation illustrates the path of the Sun in the sky as seen by an observer at the surface at different latitudes and seasons, showing the same phenomena but from a different viewpoint. Digital video clips, created specifically for our book by the well-known team of Mary Lee and Sid Nolan of Academic Media Network, show real-world phenomena from breaking waves to flowing glaciers as seen from the ground and air.

Serving not only our visualization strategy, *GeoDiscoveries* also furthers our goals of presenting clear learning structures and enhanced comprehension. Organized on topics oriented to specific chapters, it reviews and strengthens the understanding of the key concepts of each chapter in a dynamic, interactive fashion. Exploration modules, such as a simulation of climate in response to variations in the Earth's albedo or solar output, put the concepts of the chapter and visualizations to work in a way that enhances logical thinking and comprehension. *GeoDiscoveries* was designed and coordinated by Professor S. Mary P. Benbow of the University of Manitoba, and more specifics are provided on following pages.

Geography, Environment, and Global Change

Global change is also a recurring theme in our text. Geographers, perhaps more than scientists from other fields, are particularly aware of human impact on the Earth and its environment. Global change is, of course, a two-way street. Humans change the Earth in many ways—by clearing and cultivating its lands, harvesting its wildland resources, damming its rivers, and polluting its air. But the Earth changes the situations of its human inhabitants in return when volcanic eruptions bury human settlements, tornadoes and hurricanes level towns and villages, and floods erode agricultural lands. An understanding of global change requires not just a familiarity with the latest climatic change projections, but also an understanding of the many processes that shape the human physical environment, both natural and human-induced.

To facilitate this understanding, we provide two types of boxed features: *Eye on Global Change* and *Eye on the Environment*. These illustrated essays focus the concepts of the chapter on specific topics in environmental and global change, ranging from the ozone layer to ice sheets and global warming. The book concludes with an *Epilogue* that raises the environmental implications of the physical geography that the student has learned. In an extended script for a news broadcast from the mid-twenty-first century, students picture how life might change in the future as human impacts continue to reshape our planet. The news broadcast leads into a discussion of the most serious environmental issues facing the human species and the prognosis for the Earth's immediate future.

Learning Tools

To help students master text material, we provide a number of learning tools. To help build the necessary vocabulary, we have identified the dozen or so key terms that are most important in each chapter with the use of boldface. Less important terms are identified in italics. All terms are defined in our glossary, which contains over 1000 individual entries and includes many terms that are part of a basic science vocabulary.

As another aid to learning, we have embedded brief key statements in the text that summarize important concepts in one or two sentences. They are set as type blocks between text columns.

Our suite of end-of-chapter materials is also designed to reinforce key concepts and ideas of the chapter. A summary, *In Review*, is written like a bulleted abstract and covers all the major concepts of the chapter. The list of *Key Terms* gathers together the critical vocabulary of the chapter. *Review Questions* are designed as oral or written exercises that require description or explanation of important ideas and concepts. They are provided both for text and *Eye on the Environment and Eye on Global Change* boxes. *Visualizing Exercises* are review questions that utilize sketching or graphing as a way of focusing attention on key illustrations. Also provided are *Essay Questions* that require more synthesis or the reorganization of knowledge in a new context.

GEODISCOVERIES

The GeoDiscoveries media program offers a rich electronic medium for exploring the core concepts of physical geography. This robust assembly of media resources allows students and professors to move beyond the textbook with interactive exercises, animations, videos, self-assessments and an interactive globe.

Building off the success of our present/interact/assess framework, our GeoDiscoveries program has been integrated into our on-line book companion web sites. Web sites tailored to the needs of both students and instructors include the following resources:

Resources specific to the study of physical geography have been created and developed by S. Mary P. Benbow of the University of Manitoba.

For Students:

Animated Globe: This 3D interactive globe allows you to overlay different layers of geographic information, including plate tectonics, topography, political boundaries, and population to help visualize the spatial relationships between these features and elements.

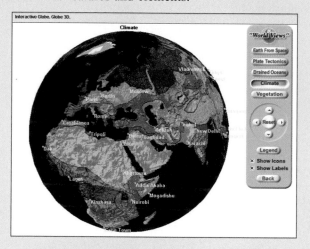

Interactive Globe. Globe 3D.

Animations: Key diagrams and drawings from our rich signature art program have been animated to provide a virtual experience of difficult concepts. These animations have proven crucial to the understanding of this content for visual learners.

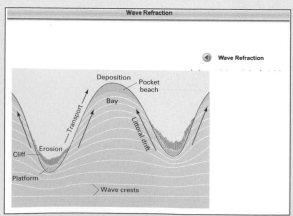

Videos: Brief video clips provide real-world examples of geographic features, and put these examples into context with the concepts covered in the text.

Simulations: Computer-based models of geographic processes allow you to manipulate data and variables to explore and interact with virtual environments.

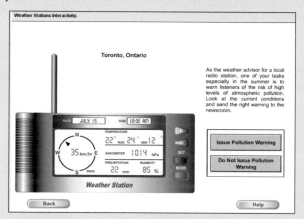

Weather Stations Interactivity.

Interactive Exercises: Learning activities and games build off our presentation material. They give students an opportunity to test their understanding of key concepts and explore additional visual resources.

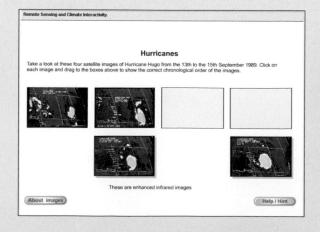

Remote Sensing and Climate Interactivity.

For Instructors:
Our animations, videos, simulations, and interactive exercises provide ideal in-class presentation tools to help engage students in the classroom. All these resources can be easily integrated into instructors' customized PowerPoint presentations.

In addition to our multi-media content, we offer an on-line image gallery, containing both line art and comprehensive photographic materials. These resources can be easily uploaded into PowerPoint presentations, course management systems, and on-line tutorials and web sites.

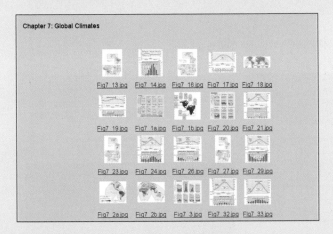

We also offer prepared PowerPoint presentations centered on key concepts and hot topics in the field of physical geography. These lecture materials can be customized to suit the instructor's individual needs, or can be used as is to add context and relevancy to any lecture.

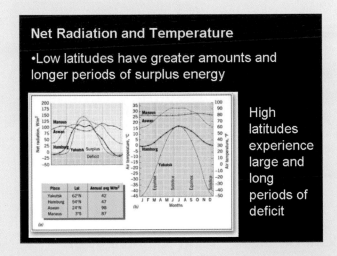

GeoDiscoveries also offers a wealth of assessment and assignment tools that can be used for tutorials as well as quizzes purposes. These question banks are closely tied to our multi-media materials to help gauge understanding of the resources. Easy integration of this content into course management systems and homework assignments gives instructors the opportunity to integrate multimedia with their syllabuses and with more traditional reading and writing assignments.

BOOK COMPANION SITE

In addition to our GeoDiscoveries multimedia content, our student companion site offers a wealth of study and practice materials, including:

Student On-line Resources:
- *Self-Quizzes*—chapter based multiple choice and fill-in-the-blank questions
- *Annotated Weblinks*—useful weblinks selected to enhance chapter topics and content
- *Chapter Summaries*—brief overviews of chapter content
- *Flashcards*—drill and practice application to help study key terms
- *Learning Objectives*—list of key concepts covered in each chapter
- *Learning Styles Survey*—a survey developed to help determine your own particular way of learning, and study skill suggestions to help each kind of learner
- *Virtual Field Trips*—web sites devoted to the exploration and virtual experience of landscapes and environments around the world.

Instructor Resources:
- *PowerPoint Lecture Slides*—chapter-oriented slides including lecture notes and text art
- *Computerized Test Bank*—including multiple choice and fill-in-the-blank test items
- *Teaching Tips*—for enhancing the classroom experience
- *On-line Essay and In-class Activities*—Materials for in-class projects, with corresponding essay-based homework assignments
- *Instructor's Manual*—including lecture notes, chapter objectives, and guides to additional resources

eGRADE PLUS

To aid both our students and instructors, our publisher has made available eGrade Plus, a state-of-the-art web-based information interface. eGrade Plus helps students to study more effectively by presenting interactive simulations, study guides, and queries that provide rapid feedback. An on-line multimedia copy of the text is linked to assignments while a personal gradebook keeps track of each student's own work. For instructors, eGrade Plus provides all the tools needed to administer the course, including preparing and displaying presentations and assignments, and tracking, testing, and grading. The next four pages, provided by Wiley, provide more information on eGrade Plus.

eGrade Plus

www.wiley.com/college/strahler
Based on the Activities You Do Every Day

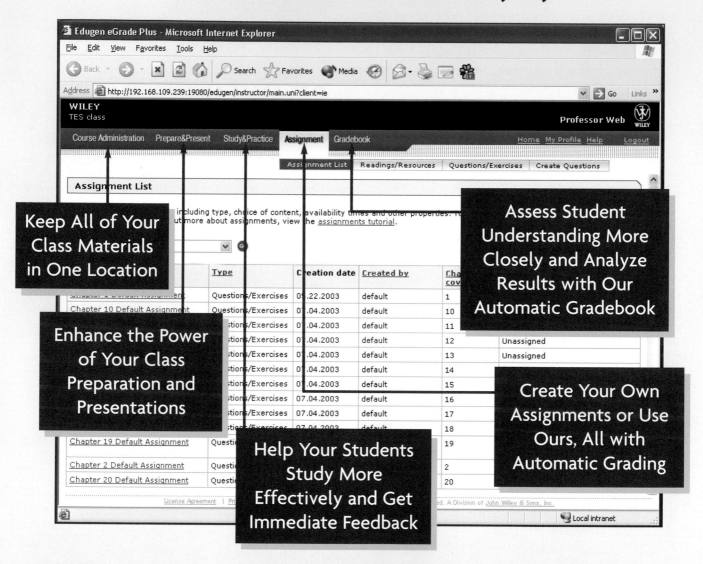

Keep All of Your Class Materials in One Location

Enhance the Power of Your Class Preparation and Presentations

Help Your Students Study More Effectively and Get Immediate Feedback

Assess Student Understanding More Closely and Analyze Results with Our Automatic Gradebook

Create Your Own Assignments or Use Ours, All with Automatic Grading

All the content and tools you need, all in one location, in an easy-to-use browser format.
Choose the resources you need, or rely on the arrangement supplied by us.

Now, many of Wiley's textbooks are available with eGrade Plus, a powerful online tool that provides a completely integrated suite of teaching and learning resources in one easy-to-use website. eGrade Plus integrates Wiley's world-renowned content with media, including a multimedia version of the text, PowerPoint slides, and more. Upon adoption of eGrade Plus, you can begin to customize your course with the resources shown here.

See for yourself!
Go to www.wiley.com/college/egradeplus for an online demonstration of this powerful new software.

Keep All of Your Class Materials in One Location

Course Administration tools allow you to manage your class and integrate your eGrade Plus resources with most Course Management Systems, allowing you to keep all of your class materials in one location.

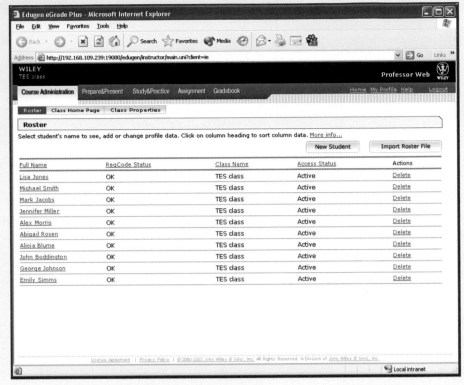

Enhance the Power of Your Class Preparation and Presentations

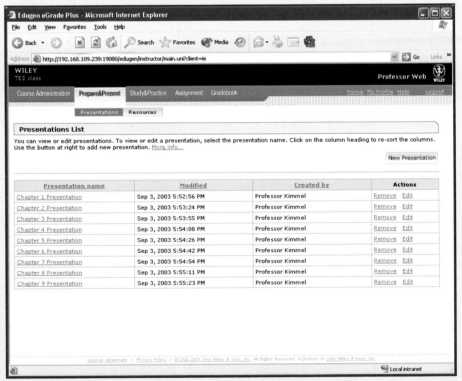

A **Prepare and Present tool** contains all of the Wiley-provided resources, such as **PowerPoint slides** and **student activities,** making your preparation time more efficient. You may easily adapt, customize, and add to Wiley content to meet the needs of your course.

Create Your Own Assignments or Use Ours, All with Automatic Grading

An **Assignment** area allows you to create **student home-work** and **quizzes** by using **Wiley-provided question banks,** or by writing your own. You may also assign readings, activities and other work you want your students to complete. One of the most powerful features of eGrade Plus is that student assignments will be automatically graded and recorded in your gradebook. This will not only save you time but will provide your students with immediate feedback on their work.

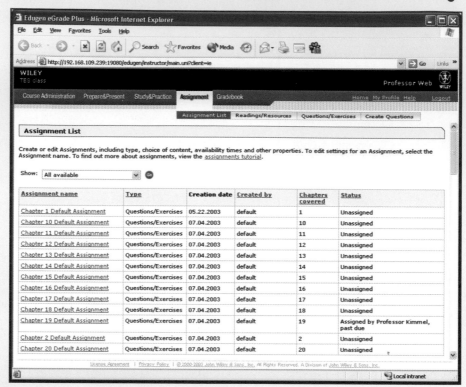

Assess Student Understanding More Closely

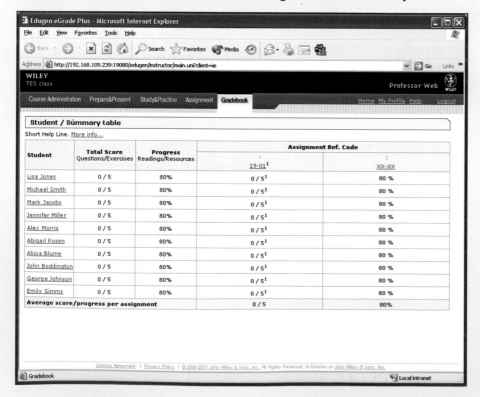

An **Instructor's Gradebook** will keep track of your students' progress and allow you to analyze individual and overall class results to determine their progress and level of understanding

Students,
eGrade Plus Allows You to:

Study More Effectively

Get Immediate Feedback When You Practice on Your Own

eGrade Plus problems link directly to relevant sections of the **electronic book content,** so that you can review the text while you study and complete homework online. Additional resources include **interactive simulations, study guide** and other problem-solving resources.

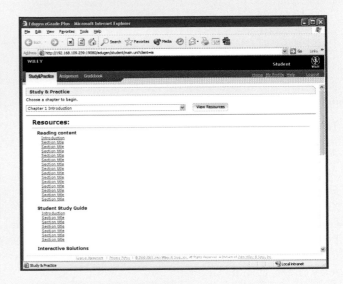

Complete Assignments / Get Help with Problem Solving

An **Assignment** area keeps all your assigned work in one location, making it easy for you to stay "on task." In addition, many homework problems contain a **link** to the relevant section of the **multimedia book,** providing you with a text explanation to help you conquer problem-solving obstacles as they arise. You will have access to a variety of **interactive problem-solving tools,** as well as other resources for building your confidence and understanding.

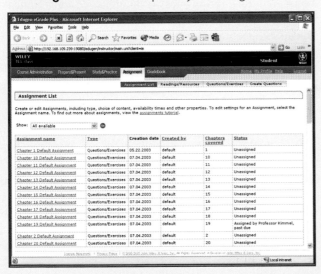

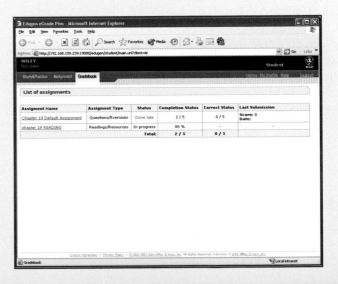

Keep Track of How You're Doing

A **Personal Gradebook** allows you to view your results from past assignments at any time.

ACKNOWLEDGMENTS

The preparation of *Introducing Physical Geography, Fourth Edition*, was greatly aided by the following reviewers who read and evaluated the various parts of the manuscript:

William M. Buhay, University of Winnipeg
Christopher Justice, University of Maryland, College Park
Robert M. Hordon, Rutgers University
Francis A. Galgano, United States Military Academy, West Point
Thomas A. Terich, Western Washington University

We would also like to thank the reviewers who read and commented on prior editions:

Tanya Allison, Montgomery College
Joseph M. Ashley, Montana State University
Roger Balm, Rutgers State University
David Bixler, Chaffey Community College
Peter Blanken, University of Colorado, Boulder
Kenneth L. Bowden, Northern Illinois University
David Butler, University of North Carolina, Chapel Hill
Les Dean, Riverside Communicty College
Christopher H. Exline, University of Nevada
Jerry Green, Miami University
Clarence Head, University of Central Florida
Peter W. Knightes, Central Texas College
Christopher S. Larsen, State University of New York, Buffalo
Robert E. Lee, Seattle Central Community College
Denyse Lemaire, Rowen University
Eugene J. Palka, U.S. Military Academy, West Point
James F. Petersen, Southwest Texas State University
Clinton Rowe, University of Nebraska-Lincoln
Carol Shears, Ball State University
Carol I. Zinser, State University of New York, Plattsburgh

It is with particular pleasure that we thank the staff at Wiley for their long hours of careful work in the preparation and production of our Fourth Edition. They include our editor, Jerry Correa, our associate editor Denise Powell, photo researchers Jennifer MacMillan and Kathy Bendo, designer Karin Kincheloe, illustration editor Sigmund Malinowski, the artists of Precision Graphics illustration studio, marketing manager Jeffrey Rucker, new media product manager Tom Kulesa, Larry Meyer and the staff of Hermitage Publishing Services for production services and page layout, and our production editor Sandra Dumas, who made it all come together.

Alan Strahler
Boston, Massachusetts
January 1, 2005

ABOUT THE AUTHORS

It is with great sadness that we mark the passing of Arthur Strahler in December, 2002. Through five decades of bringing science to geography students, he held the highest of standards in his writing, making accuracy and clarity his primary goals. Throughout, he strived to make the many subfields of physical geography both accessible and exciting to successive generations of learners. His heritage persists not only in our books written for Wiley, but in the table of contents of every major textbook used in physical geography today.

Arthur Strahler will also be remembered for his contributions to geomorphology, which are still frequently cited. He pioneered the quantitative approach to geomorphology, emphasizing the direct study of landform-making processes rather than the descriptive interpretation of landforms. He was among the first researchers to apply statistical techniques to analysis of landforms, and his work on streams and erosion laid the foundation for much of modern fluvial geomorphology. He later applied general systems theory to geomorphology, bringing a new paradigm to the field. His research achievements were honored by his election to the rank of Fellow in both the Association of American Geographers and the Geological Society of America.

He was truly a giant of geographers.

Alan Strahler received his B.A. degree in 1964 and his Ph.D degree in 1969 from The Johns Hopkins University, Department of Geography and Environmental Engineering. He has held academic positions at the University of Virginia, the University of California at Santa Barbara, and Hunter College of the City University of New York, and is now Professor of Geography at Boston University. With Arthur Strahler, he is a coauthor of seven textbook titles with ten revised editions on physical geography and environmental science. He has published over 250 articles in the refereed scientific literature, largely on the theory of remote sensing of vegetation, and has also contributed to the fields of plant geography, forest ecology, and quantitative methods. His research has been supported by over $6 million in grant and contract funds, primarily from NASA. In 1993, he was awarded the Association of American Geographers/Remote Sensing Specialty Group Medal for Outstanding Contributions to Remote Sensing. In 2000, he received the honorary degree Doctorem Scientiarum Honoris Causa (D.S.H.C) from the Université Catholique de Louvain, Belgium, for his academic accomplishments in teaching and research. In 2004, he was honored by election to the rank of Fellow in the American Association for the Advancement of Science.

Arthur Strahler (1918–2002) received his B.A. degree in 1938 from the College of Wooster, Ohio, and his Ph.D. degree in geology from Columbia University in 1944. He was appointed to the Columbia University faculty in 1941, serving as Professor of Geomorphology from 1958 to 1967 and as Chairman of the Department of Geology from 1959 to 1962. He was elected as a Fellow of both the Geological Society of America and the Association of American Geographers for his pioneering contributions to quantitative and dynamic geomorphology, contained in over 30 major papers in leading scientific journals. He was the author or coauthor with Alan Strahler of 16 textbook titles with 16 revised editions in physical geography, environmental science, the Earth sciences, and geology.

BRIEF CONTENTS

An astronaut on the Moon would see the Earth suspended in space in a similar perspective to this Meteosat photo, which records clouds, water vapor patterns, and land masses as seen from a geostationary orbit.

INTRODUCING PHYSICAL GEOGRAPHY

PUTTING YOU IN THE PICTURE

Physical geography is the study of the surface of our home planet, Earth. It is not just a catalog of mountains and rivers, but rather a branch of science that investigates how and why the surface changes from day to day, from year to year, and over millions of years.

Perhaps the easiest way to introduce physical geography is to examine the features of our planet—first as a whole and then by zooming in on continents, regions, and, finally, local areas. But to make it more interesting, imagine that the year is 2050 and that you are an astronaut ending a tour of duty on a lunar base station. Relax and follow along as you move from the lunar base to a space station orbiting the Earth and finally to the descent and landing of a space shuttle carrying you safely home.

It's eight hundred hours, on December 17, Houston time, and your duty watch is just beginning. Taking your place at the lab's environmental control desk, you check the oxygen and carbon dioxide balances and review the pressure and water vapor concentration log from the previous watch. All is well. You rise from your desk and turn. A small push on your right foot produces a giant but graceful step. You are standing in front of the viewport, looking out across the moonscape. Not much scenery here at Lunar Base Alpha, at least not when you're in the middle of the long lunar night. But in the black sky above, there is a truly majestic sight—a huge blue, green, and brown disk veiled by swirls and films of white. It is Earth, your home.

From your lunar viewpoint, the Earth's environmental realms are easily identified by their colors. The blue of the world oceans—the hydrosphere—dominates the area of the disk. Rich browns characterize the lithosphere—the solid rocky portion of the planet—where it rises above the seas. Vast white cloud expanses form and fade in the gaseous portion of the planet—the atmosphere. The lush greens of plants are the visible portion of the biosphere, the realm of life on

Earth, which dominates the life layer—the interface between air, land, and ocean.

The right-hand edge of the disk is in shadow, and you see the dramatic contrast between the day and night portions of the globe. The land and water masses of the illuminated side bask in the sunlight, and here the temperature of the life layer is increasing. On the shadowed side of the planet, however, the heat of the oceans, atmosphere, and continents is continuously being lost—radiated into outer space. Without sunlight, the Earth's surface cools.

Over the next few hours, you notice the planet's slow rotation. The continent of South America glides across the center of the disk to its edge, then disappears. Australia emerges from behind the curtain of night and makes its way out onto the illuminated portion of the disk. As you watch, each land and water mass slowly takes its turn in the Sun, absorbing and reflecting its quota of solar energy.

Africa and South America receive the lion's share of the sunlight striking the Earth. These continents lie near the equator, where they meet the strong, near-vertical rays of the Sun. North America and Europe, on the other hand, are short-changed because they intercept the Sun's rays at a low angle. At the lower rim of the Earth's disk, the stark, white continent of Antarctica rotates slowly but remains sunlit, experiencing 24-hour daylight.

As the Earth days go by, you often gaze at your planet, marking the changes. Away from the equator, huge swirls of clouds form, dissolve, and reform in its atmosphere, making their way eastward across the disk. First one portion of a continent, and then another, is obscured. These swirls mark the passage of weather fronts and storms that are moved eastward by persistent westerly winds above the surface.

Near the Earth's equator in Africa you notice a band of patchy, persistent cloudiness bracketed by reddish-brown areas of earth that are normally clear. The clouds result when warm, moist air is heated by excess solar energy and rises. As the air rises, it cools, and the

moisture it contains condenses, forming clouds and producing rain. The lush, green landscape that is occasionally visible underneath the cloud belt seems to thrive on the warm temperature and abundant rainfall it receives. The reddish-brown areas are vast deserts. These receive the air that rises over the equator and becomes depleted of moisture. As the air descends toward the desert, it warms. Showing the colors of rock and soil, the hot, dry deserts are barren of plants.

During the remainder of your six-month tour of duty at the lunar base, you watch the slow changes of the planet with the season. By June, the Earth has changed its position in the Sun. Antarctica has moved below the southern rim. The sunlit northern rim of the disk now includes northern Canada, Siberia, and the Arctic Ocean. In previous months, you watched the green wave of vegetation sweep northward, up and across North America, Europe, and eastern Asia, following the warming temperatures of spring. The band of tropical cloudiness has also moved northward, bringing a green wave in Africa along with it as well. Clearly, each region of the Earth has its unique climate, responding to the rhythms of the season in different

ways. You remember fondly the days of June on Earth—the smell of warm soil mixed with the scent of flowers, the hot sidewalks and streets at noon, the long evenings and warm nights alive with quiet rustlings. As the end of your tour draws near, you count the days eagerly, thinking of your return to your true home, planet Earth.

It's sixteen hundred hours, June 18, Houston time, aboard the Space Station *Enterprise,* in low earth orbit. Your duty watch is just over. Being an environmental specialist in orbit around the Earth is not the hardest job on the space station, but it isn't the easiest either. Today's shift required changing the filter on the nutrient pump for the algae, and in the weightlessness of orbit, it was a ticklish, delicate job.

It's been quite a trip so far. You recall the events of the last few weeks—the arrival of the new crew on the lunar shuttle at Moon Base Alpha's spaceport, the preparations for the departure of your crew, the relaunch of the lunar shuttle, the slow days in transit to Earth orbit, and, at long last, the docking of the lunar craft at the space station. But the most memorable part of the return trip was approaching the Earth ever

Deforestation from space *A satellite image of deforestation in the Rondonia region, Brazil. In this false-color image, vegetation appears red and forest clearings appear blue. The light green lines, laid out in a rectangular pattern, are areas cleared for cultivation or pasture.*

The San Francisco Bay area *A Landsat satellite view from Earth orbit.*

green islands are visible, but you know that from this distance they are actually ranges of hills or diked cities. Where the Yangtze meets the sea, a plume of sediment-laden river water curls lazily across the ocean waters. In this view, the work of rivers is especially evident—moving sediment from highlands to lower lands and the ocean, under the power of rains generated ultimately by unequal solar heating of the globe.

The following day, your view is of the San Francisco Bay area. The San Andreas fault is clearly visible on the peninsula as a line marked by narrow valleys and linear lakes at the eastern edge of the Santa Cruz mountains. Crossing seaward of the Golden Gate, it heads northwest, producing the long arm of Tomales Bay. As you have

closer. With each day and hour, it grew larger and larger. Continents became regions of forests and deserts, mountain ranges, and inland seas. At last the planet became a sphere, its edges falling away and out of view as the lunar shuttle neared the space station. Now, in low Earth orbit, finer detail is visible—systems of rivers, agricultural patterns, large cities.

Still drawn to the majesty and serenity of the Earth turning below you, you float gently to the viewport for yet another few minutes of observation. Beneath you stretches Amazonia, its lush green rainforests visible through gaps in the clouds. The verdant pattern is interrupted by patches and streaks of recently cleared land, some with hazy smoke plumes at their edges. The rainforest is but one of the many types of vegetation covers you have noted from space, ranging from spruce forests to tropical grasslands. The vegetation patterns have fit the cloud patterns well and have also marked the seasonal changes of solar illumination you noted from your lunar base.

Some hours later, your view is of China. Finally, the clouds have cleared, and a disaster is in view—the Yangtze River is in flood. The river is now a wide, shining ribbon, filling its broad valley from edge to edge. A few tiny

Touchdown view *The Space Shuttle runway at Edwards Air Force Base, California, as photographed from the Space Shuttle Challenger.*

I.2 Eye on the Landscape *Vancouver, British Columbia This cosmopolitan city enjoys a spectacular setting on the Strait of Georgia, flanked by the Pacific and Vancouver Island Ranges.* **What else would the geographer see?...Answers at the end of the chapter.**

weather, we can think of climate as a description of average weather and its variation at places around the world. Chapters 1–7 will familiarize you with the essentials of climatology, including the processes that control the weather we experience daily. Climatology is also concerned with climate change, both past and future. One of the most rapidly expanding and challenging areas of climatology is global climate modeling, which we touch on in several chapters. This field attempts to predict how human activities, such as converting land from forest to agriculture or releasing CO_2 from fossil fuel burning, will change global climate.

Geomorphology is the science of Earth surface processes and landforms. The Earth's surface is constantly being altered under the combined influence of human and natural factors. The work of gravity in the collapse and movement of Earth materials, as well as the work of flowing water, blowing wind, breaking waves, and moving ice, acts to remove and transport soil and rock and to sculpt a surface that is constantly being renewed though volcanic and tectonic activity. The closing chapters of our book (Chapters

14–19) describe these geomorphic processes, while the basic geologic processes that provide the raw material are covered in Chapters 11–13. Modern geomorphology also focuses on modeling landform-shaping processes to predict both short-term, rapid changes, such as landslides, floods, or coastal storm erosion, and long-term, slower changes, such as soil erosion in agricultural areas or as a result of strip mining.

Coastal and marine geography combines the study of geomorphic processes that shape shores and coastlines with their application to coastal development and marine resource utilization. Chapter 18 describes these processes and provides some perspectives on problems of human occupation of the coastal zone.

Geography of soils includes the study of the distribution of soil types and properties and the processes of soil formation. It is related to both geomorphic processes of rock breakup and weathering, and to biological processes of growth, activity, and decay of organisms living in the soil (Chapter 10). Since both geomorphic and biologic processes are influenced by the sur-

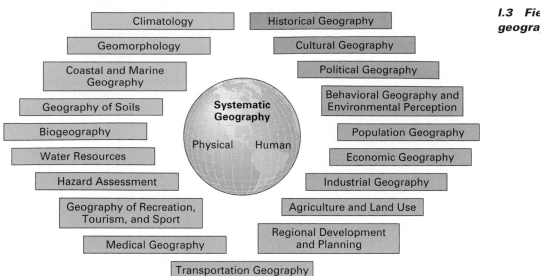

I.3 Fields of systematic geography

face temperature and availability of moisture, broad-scale soil patterns are often related to climate.

Biogeography, covered in Chapters 8 and 9, is the study of the distributions of organisms at varying spatial and temporal scales, as well as the processes that produce these distribution patterns. Local distributions of plants and animals typically depend on the suitability of the habitat that supports them. In this application, biogeography is closely aligned with *ecology,* which is the study of the relationship between organisms and environment. Over broader scales and time periods, the migration, evolution, and extinction of plants and animals are key processes that determine their spatial distribution patterns. Thus, biogeographers often seek to reconstruct past patterns of plant and animal communities from fossil evidence of various kinds. *Biodiversity*—the assessment of biological diversity from the perspective of maintaining the diversity of life and life-forms on Earth—is a biogeographic topic of increasing importance as human impact on the environment continues. The present global-scale distribution of lifeforms as the great biomes of the Earth provides a basic context for biodiversity.

In addition to these five main fields of physical geography, two others are strongly involved with applications of physical geography—water resources and hazards assessment. **Water resources** is a broad field that couples both basic study of the location, distribution, and movement of water, for example, in river systems or as ground water, with the utilization and quality of water for human use. This field involves many aspects of human geography, including regional development and planning, political geography, and agriculture and land use. We touch on water resources briefly in this book by discussing water wells, dams, and water quality in Chapters 15 and 16.

Hazards assessment is another field that blends physical and human geography. What are the risks of living next to a river, and how do inhabitants perceive those risks? What is the role of government in protecting citizens from floods or assisting them in recovery from flood damages? Answering questions such as these requires not only knowledge of how physical systems work, but also how humans perceive and interact with their physical environment as both individuals and as societies. In this text, we develop an understanding of the physical processes of floods, earthquakes, landslides, and other disaster-causing natural events as a background for appreciating hazards to humans and their activities.

The many remaining fields of human geography are also shown in Figure I.3. Although they are not covered in this book, most have linkages with physical geography. For example, climatic and biogeographic factors may determine the spread of disease-carrying mosquitoes (medical geography). Or mountain barriers may isolate populations and increase the cost of transporting goods from one place to another (cultural geography, transportation geography). Or unique landforms and landscapes may be the objects of tourism (geography of recreation, tourism, and sport). Nearly all human activities take place in a physical environment that varies in space and time, so the physical processes that we examine in this text provide a background useful for further learning in any of geography's fields.

> **Five major fields of physical geography include climatology (study of climate), geomorphology (study of landforms), coastal and marine geography, geography of soils, and biogeography (study of the distribution patterns of plants and animals). Water resources and hazards assessment are important applied fields of physical geography.**

Tools in Geography

As we saw earlier, the representation of spatial phenomena is a primary interest of geographers. Many of the modes of representation allow geographers to examine, explore, and interact with spatial data. In this way, we can regard them as tools that are especially useful to geographers (Figure I.5). The map is a common example. A **map** is a paper

a...Climatology Climate is largely dependent on atmosphere-surface interaction.

b...Geomorphology Geomorphology is the study of landform-making processes.

c...Eye on the Landscape Coastal and marine geography Coastal and marine geography examines coastal processes, marine resources, and their human interface. **What else would the geographer see?...Answers at the end of the chapter.**

d...**Eye on the Landscape
Biogeography** *Biogeography
examines the distribution patterns of
plants and animals and relates them
to environment, migration, evolution,
and extinction.* **What else would the
geographer see?...Answers at the end of
the chapter.**

e...***Geography of soils*** *Soils are
influenced by their parent material,
climate, biota, and time.*

1.5 Tools of Physical Geography

a...Cartography *A portion of the U.S. Geological Survey 1:24,000 topographic map of Green Bay, Wisconsin. Using symbols, the map shows creeks and rivers, a bay, swampy regions, urban developed land, streets, roads, and highways.*

b...Geographic information systems (GIS) *Computer programs that store and manipulate geographic data are essential to modern applications of geography. This screen from the ARCInfo GIS program package shows earthquake centers in eastern Asia superimposed on a political map underlain by a shaded relief map of undersea topography.*

c...Remote sensing *Remote sensing includes observing the Earth from the perspective of an aircraft or spacecraft. Wildfires on the Greek island of Peloponnesos, seen in a Landsat image from July 2000, are an example.*

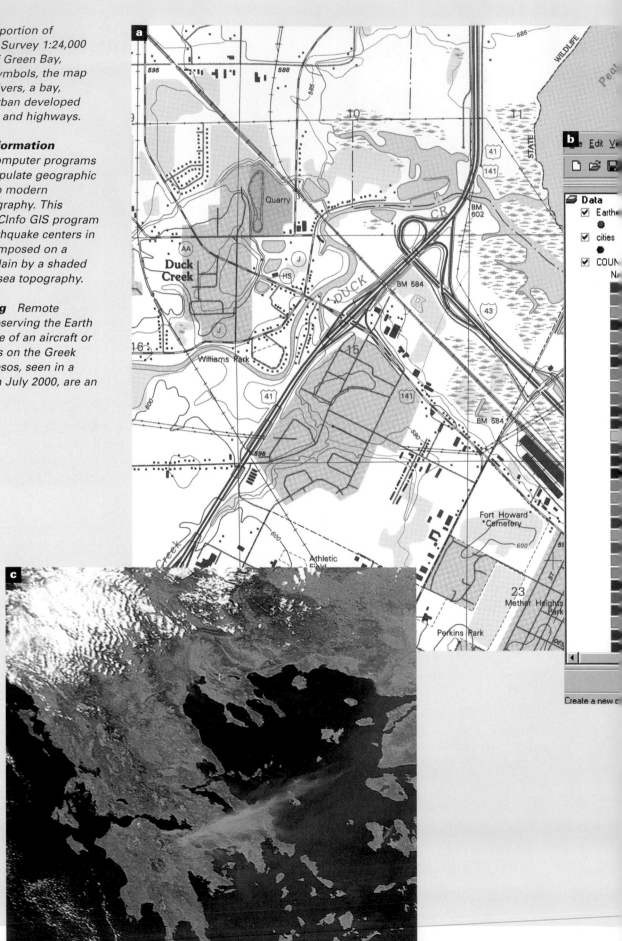

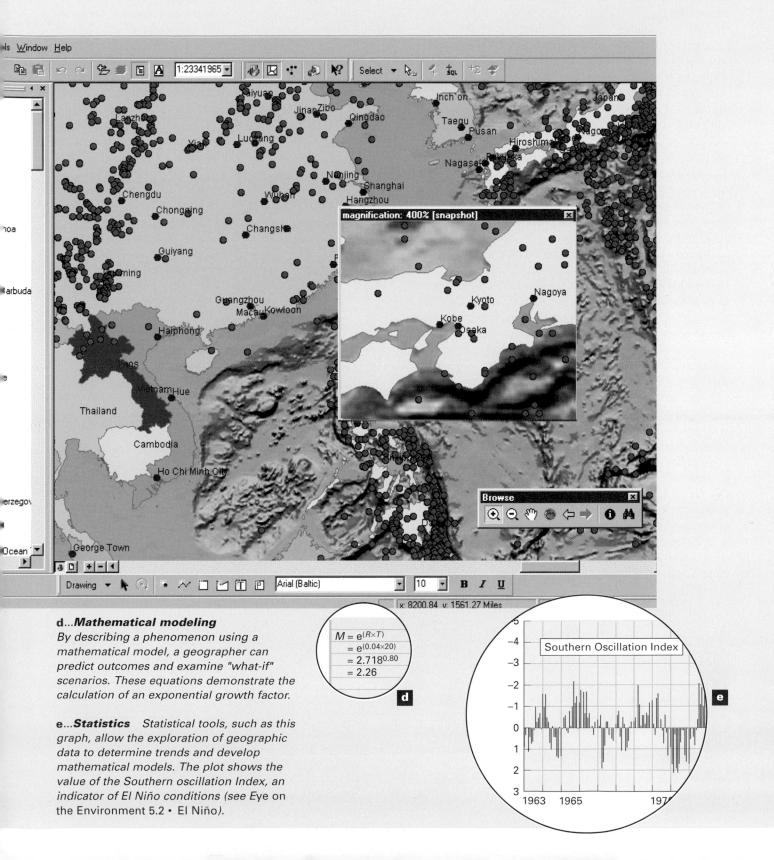

d...Mathematical modeling
By describing a phenomenon using a mathematical model, a geographer can predict outcomes and examine "what-if" scenarios. These equations demonstrate the calculation of an exponential growth factor.

$$M = e^{(R \times T)}$$
$$= e^{(0.04 \times 20)}$$
$$= 2.718^{0.80}$$
$$= 2.26$$

d

e...Statistics Statistical tools, such as this graph, allow the exploration of geographic data to determine trends and develop mathematical models. The plot shows the value of the Southern oscillation Index, an indicator of El Niño conditions (*see Eye on the Environment 5.2 • El Niño*).

Southern Oscillation Index

e

representation of space showing point, line, or area data—that is, locations, connections, and regions. It typically displays some characteristics or features of the Earth's surface that are positioned on the map in much the same way that they occur on the surface. The map's scale links the true distance between places with the distance on the map. The art and science of map-making is called **cartography.** Chapter 1 provides some basic information about maps as well as a special supplement, *Geographer's Tools 1.2 • Focus on Maps,* that adds depth on this important subject.

Maps, like books, are very useful methods for storing information, but they have limitations. In the past two decades, striking advances in data collection, storage, analysis, and display have led to the development of **geographic information systems (GISs).** These spatial databases rely on computers for analysis, manipulation, and display of spatial data. We will turn to an examination of GISs in Chapter 1 with our special supplement, *Geographer's Tools 1.3 • Geographic Information Systems.*

Another important geographic technique for acquiring spatial information is **remote sensing,** in which aircraft or spacecraft provide images of the Earth's surface. Depending on the scale of the remotely sensed image, the information obtained can range from fine local detail—such as the arrangement of cars in a parking lot—to a global-scale picture—for example, the "greenness" of vegetation for an entire continent. As you read this textbook, you will see many examples of remote sensing, especially images from orbiting satellites, as well as boxed features highlighting applications of remote sensing in physical geography. We will return to remote sensing in our special supplement, *Geographer's Tools 2.1 • Remote Sensing for Physical Geography,* which is included in Chapter 2.

Tools in geography also include **mathematical modeling and statistics.** Using math and computers to model geographic processes is a powerful approach to understanding both natural and human phenomena. Statistics provides methods that can be used to manipulate geographic data so that we can ask and answer questions about differences, trends, and patterns. Because these tools rely heavily on specialized knowledge, we only touch on them lightly in this book.

Maps, geographic information systems (GISs), and remote sensing are important geographic tools to acquire, display, and manipulate spatial data. Mathematical modeling and statistics are also helpful tools for the geographer.

As another aid to comprehension and understanding of our text material, we have placed **summary statements** on many pages. These short statements restate the most important concepts of physical geography as they are being explained and described in the text. They should help you keep focused on the key points as you read along.

We have also included a series of *Eye on the Environment* and *Eye on Global Change* features that highlight particular topics of environmental interest. These range from human impact on the ozone layer to the effect of global warming on ice sheets Greenland and the Antarctic.

Our *GeoDiscoveries* CD-ROM, along with its associated worldwide web site and web links, is yet another important resource that will help you to understand physical geography. It includes animations, movies, photos, diagrams, and interactive text in modules keyed to each chapter. Throughout this book you will find icons and pathways pointing to topics in *GeoDiscoveries* that are particularly appropriate to the text material. We've worked very hard on *GeoDiscoveries* and hope that it can make a real difference in your mastery of physical geography.

SPHERES, SYSTEMS, AND CYCLES

As a part of your introduction to physical geography, it will be useful to take a look at the big picture and examine some ideas that arch over all of physical geography—that is, spheres, systems, and cycles. The first of these ideas is that of the four great physical realms, or *spheres* of Earth—atmosphere, lithosphere, hydrosphere, and biosphere. These realms are distinctive parts of our planet with unique components and properties. Another big idea is that of *systems*—viewing the processes that shape our landscape as a set of interrelated components that comprise a system. The systems viewpoint stresses linkages and interactions and helps to understand complex problems, such as global climate change or loss of biodiversity. The last big idea is that of *cycles*—regular changes in systems that recur in a fixed period of time.

Understanding Physical Geography

From the start of your study of physical geography, you will find that it differs from other sciences in that it focuses on the world around you, from the changes in the weather to the landforms you travel over every day. When you finish your study, you should be able to see the landscape in a new way. To help you preview what you will learn about our environment, we provide a new feature—Eye on the Landscape—which takes many of our photos and identifies prominent features that a physical geographer would recognize and understand.

The Spheres—Four Great Earth Realms

The natural systems that we will encounter in the study of physical geography operate within the four great realms, or **spheres,** of the Earth. These are the atmosphere, the lithosphere, the hydrosphere, and the biosphere (Figure I.6).

The **atmosphere** is a gaseous layer that surrounds the Earth. It receives heat and moisture from the surface and redistributes them, returning some heat and all the moisture to the surface. The atmosphere also supplies vital elements—carbon, hydrogen, oxygen, and nitrogen—that are needed to sustain life-forms.

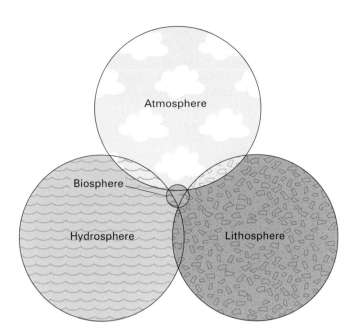

I.6 The Earth realms *The Earth realms, shown as intersecting circles.*

The outermost solid layer of the Earth, or **lithosphere,** provides the platform for most Earthly life-forms. The solid rock of the lithosphere bears a shallow layer of soil in which nutrient elements become available to organisms. The surface of the lithosphere is sculpted into landforms. These features—such as mountains, hills, and plains—provide varied habitats for plants, animals, and humans.

The liquid realm of the Earth is the **hydrosphere,** which is principally the mass of water in the world's oceans. It also includes solid ice in mountain and continental glaciers, which, like liquid ocean and fresh water, is subject to flow under the influence of gravity. Within the atmosphere, water occurs as gaseous vapor, liquid droplets, and solid ice crystals. In the lithosphere, water is found in the uppermost layers in soils and in ground water reservoirs.

The **biosphere** encompasses all living organisms of the Earth. Life-forms on Earth utilize the gases of the atmosphere, the water of the hydrosphere, and the nutrients of the lithosphere, and so the biosphere is dependent on all three of the other great realms. Figure I.6 diagrams this relationship.

Most of the biosphere is contained in the shallow surface zone called the **life layer.** It includes the surface of the lands and the upper 100 meters or so (about 300 ft) of the ocean (Figure I.7). On land, the life layer is the zone of interactions among the biosphere, lithosphere, and atmosphere. The hydrosphere is represented on land by rain, snow, still water in ponds and lakes, and running water in rivers. In the ocean, the life layer is the zone of interactions among the hydros-

> Scale, pattern, and process are three interrelated geographic themes. Scale refers to the level of structure or organization at which a phenomenon is studied; pattern refers to the variation in a phenomenon seen at a particular scale; and process describes how the factors that affect a phenomenon act to produce a pattern at a particular scale.

phere, biosphere, and atmosphere. Here, photosynthesis by marine organisms provides the base of the oceanic food chain. The lithosphere is represented by nutrients dissolved in the upper layer of sea water. Throughout our exploration of physical geography, we will often refer to the life layer and the four realms that interact within it.

Scale, Pattern, and Process

As we saw earlier, geographers have unique perspectives that characterize a geographic approach to understanding the physical and human organization of the Earth's surface. Three interrelated themes that often arise in geographic study are scale, pattern, and process. **Scale** refers to the level of structure or organization at which a phenomenon is studied. **Pattern** refers to the variation in a phenomenon that is seen at a particular scale. **Process** describes how the factors that affect a phenomenon act to produce a pattern at a particular scale.

To make these ideas more real, let's discuss them in the context of the essay that opens this chapter—the space voyage of an astronaut from the Moon back to the Earth. Putting yourself in the place of the astronaut, your view of our planet takes in scales ranging from global to local as you make the trip. As the scale changes, so do the patterns and processes that you observe. At the *global scale,* you see the Earth's major physical features— oceans of blue water, continents of brown Earth, green vegetation, and white snow and ice, and an atmosphere of white clouds and clear air (chapter opening photo). The pattern of land and ocean is created by the processes of plate tectonics, which shape land masses and ocean basins across the eons of geologic time. The pattern of white clouds, which includes a band of persistent clouds near the Earth's equa-tor and spirals of clouds moving across the globe, is created by atmospheric circulation processes that depend on solar heating coupled with the Earth's slow rotation on its axis.

I.7 The life layer *As this sketch shows, the life layer is the layer of the Earth's surface that supports nearly all of the Earth's life. This includes the land and ocean surfaces and the atmosphere in contact with them.*

These processes act more quickly and on a finer spatial scale than those of plate tectonics.

At the *continental scale*, we see the broad differentiation of land masses into regions of dry desert and moister vegetated regions, a pattern caused by atmospheric processes that provide some areas with more precipitation than others. In some regions, air temperatures keep liquid water frozen, producing sea ice and glaciers. Air temperature and precipitation are the basic elements of climate, and so we may regard climate as major factor affecting the landscape on a continental level.

At a *regional scale*, mountain ranges, deserts, lakes, and rivers create a varied pattern caused by interaction between geologic processes that raise mountains and lower valleys with atmospheric processes that provide water to run off the continents while supporting the growth of vegetation. Also evident at the regional scale are patterns of human activity, such as the deforestation of the Amazon (shown in our image in the essay) or the development corridor of the eastern United States from Washington to Boston. Agricultural regions are clearly visible, distinguished by repeating geometric patterns of fields.

At the *local scale*, we zoom in on a landscape showing a distinctive pattern in fine detail. For example, our image of the San Francisco Bay region reveals both the natural processes that carve hillslopes and canyons from mountain masses and the human processes that superimpose city and suburb on the natural landscape. At the finest scale, we see *individual-scale* landscape features, such as Rogers Lake, California, visible from a Space Shuttle landing at Edwards Air Force Base in the Mojave desert north of Los Angeles. The patterns of gray and green that surround the basin of the dry salt lake are related to ground relief interacting with salty ground water reaching the surface in low places.

Our example above, zooming in from a view of the whole Earth to that of a few landforms in the California desert, illustrates the themes of scale, pattern, and process as they apply to the landscapes of our planet. Keep in mind, however, that these themes are quite general ones. Throughout this book, we will see many examples of scale, pattern, and process applied to such diverse phenomena as climate, vegetation, soils, and landforms. We will zoom in and out, examining processes at local scales and applying them to regions to create and explain broad patterns observed at continental and global scales. In this way, you will gain a better understanding of how the Earth's surface changes and evolves in response to natural and human activities.

Systems in Physical Geography

The processes that interact within the four realms to shape the life layer and differentiate global environments are varied and complex. A helpful way to understand the relationships among these processes is to study them as **systems.** "System" is a common English word that we use in everyday speech. It typically means a set or collection of things that are somehow related or organized. An example is the solar system—a collection of planets that revolve around the Sun. In the text, we will use the word *system* in this way quite often. Sometimes it refers to a scheme for naming things. For example, we will introduce a climate system in Chapter 7 and a soil classification system in Chapter 10. However, we will also use *system* to mean a group of interrelated processes that operate simultaneously in the physical landscape.

When we study physical geography using a *systems approach* we look for linkages and interactions among processes. For example, global warming should enhance the process of evaporation of water from oceans and moist land surfaces, generating more clouds. But an increase in clouds also affects the process of solar reflection, in which white, fleecy clouds reflect solar radiation back out to space. This leaves less radiation to be absorbed by the atmosphere and surface and so should tend to cool our planet, reducing global warming. This is actually an example of negative feedback, in which one process counteracts another process to reduce its impact. (We'll present more information about this topic in Chapter 6.) Throughout the text there will be more examples of this systems viewpoint in physical geography.[2]

Time Cycles

Many natural systems show **time cycles**—rhythms in which processes change in a regular and repeatable fashion. For example, the annual revolution of the Earth around the Sun generates a time cycle of incoming solar energy flow. We speak of this cycle as the rhythm of the seasons. The rotation of the Earth on its axis sets up the night-and-day cycle of darkness and light. The Moon, in its monthly orbit around the Earth, sets up its own time cycle. We see the lunar cycle in the range of tides, with higher high tides and lower low tides ("spring tides") occurring both at full moon and at new moon.

The astronomical time cycles of Earth rotation and solar revolution will appear at several places in our early chapters. Other time cycles with durations of tens to hundreds of thousands of years describe the alternate growth and shrinkage of the great ice sheets. Still others, with durations of millions of years, describe cycles of the solid Earth in which supercontinents form, break apart, and reform anew.

PHYSICAL GEOGRAPHY, ENVIRONMENT, AND GLOBAL CHANGE

Physical geography is concerned with the natural world around us—in short, with the human environment. Because natural processes are constantly active, the Earth's environments are constantly changing (Figure I.8). Some-

---

[2] For a more careful and rigorous treatment of systems as flow systems of energy and matter, see our *Focus on Systems* features in *Physical Geography: Science and Systems of the Human Environment,* 3rd ed., Wiley, 2005.

a...Global climate change
Is the Earth's climate changing?
Nearly all global change scientists
have concluded that human
activities have resulted in climate
warming and that weather
patterns, shown here in this
satellite image of clouds and
weather systems over the Pacific
ocean, are changing.

b...Carbon cycle Clearcutting
of timber, shown here near the
Grand Tetons, Wyoming, removes
carbon from the landscape,

c...Biodiversity Reduction in the area
and degradation of the quality of natural
habitats is reducing biodiversity. The
banks of this stream in the rainforest of
Costa Rica are lined with several
species of palms.

d...Pollution Human activity can create
pollution of air and water, causing change
in natural habitats as well as impacts on
human health. The discharge from this
pulp mill near Port Alice, British Columbia,
is largely water vapor, but pulp mill pollutants often include harmful sulfur oxides.

e...Extreme events Hurricanes, severe storms, droughts,
and floods may be becoming more frequent as global climate
warms. A tornado flattened this neighborhood in Kansas City,
Kansas, May 2003.

times the changes are slow and subtle, as when crustal plates move over geologic time to create continents and ocean basins. At other times, the changes are rapid, as when hurricane winds flatten vast areas of forests or even tracts of houses and homes.

Environmental change is now produced not only by the natural processes that have acted on our planet for millions of years but also by human activity. The human race has populated our planet so thoroughly that few places remain free of some form of human impact. Global change, then, involves not only natural processes, but also human processes that interact with them. Physical geography is the key to understanding this interaction.

Environment and global change are sufficiently important that we have set off these topics from ordinary text in this book by placing them in special sections identified with **Eye on the Environment.** As you read, watch for these sections as your key to the application of physical geography to environmental and global change topics.

What are some of the important topics in global change that lie within physical geography? Let's examine a few.

Environmental change is produced by both natural and human processes. Human activities are currently changing both the Earth's climate and the global flows of carbon from Earth to ocean to atmosphere.

Global Climate Change

Are human activities changing global climate? It seems that almost every year we hear that it has been the hottest year, or one of the hottest years, on record. But climate is notoriously variable. Could such a string of hot years be part of the normal variation? This is the key question facing scientists studying global climate change. Over the past decade, most scientists have come to the opinion that human activity has, indeed, begun to change our climate. How has this happened?

The answer lies in the greenhouse effect. As human activities continue to release gases that block heat radiation from leaving the Earth, the greenhouse effect intensifies. The most prominent of these gases is CO_2, which is released by fossil fuel burning. Others include methane (CH_4), nitrous oxide (NO), and the chlorofluorocarbons that until recently served as coolants in refrigeration and air conditioning systems and as aerosol spray propellants. Taken together, these gases are acting to raise the Earth's surface temperature, with consequences including dislocation of agricultural areas, rise in sea level, and increased frequency of extreme weather events, such as severe storms or record droughts.

Climate change is a recurring theme throughout this book, ranging from the urban heat island effect that tends to raise city temperatures (Chapter 3) to the El Niño phenomenon that alters global atmospheric and ocean circulation (Chapter 5), to the effect of clouds on global warming (Chapter 6), and to rising sea level due to the expansion of sea water with increasing temperature (Chapter 18).

The Carbon Cycle

One way to reduce human impact on the greenhouse effect is to slow the release of CO_2 from fossil fuel burning. In fact, the Kyoto Protocol of 1997, an international agreement first proposed at the 1992 Earth Summit in Rio de Janeiro, commits many of the world's industrialized nations to limit current CO_2 emissions to levels at or below those of 1990. But since modern civilization depends on the energy of fossil fuels to carry out almost every task, reducing fossil fuel consumption to stabilize the increasing concentration of CO_2 in the atmosphere is not easy. However, some natural processes reduce atmospheric CO_2. Plants withdraw CO_2 from the atmosphere by taking it up in photosynthesis to construct plant tissues, such as cell walls and wood. In addition, CO_2 is soluble in sea water. These two important pathways, by which carbon flows from the atmosphere to lands and oceans, are part of the carbon cycle. So, biogeographers and ecologists are now focusing in detail on the global carbon cycle in order to better understand the pathways and magnitudes of carbon flow. They hope that this understanding will suggest alternative actions that can reduce the rate of CO_2 buildup without penalizing economic growth.

As nations work to determine how much CO_2 they release and to develop plans to reduce that amount, scientists are focusing on the role of CO_2 uptake by natural vegetation. An important question now under study concerns the balance between forest growth and organic matter decay in the northern hemisphere forest zone. At present, there are large areas of young forests that are actively growing and taking up significant amounts of CO_2. In an opposite effect, this uptake is offset by the decay of organic matter in soils, which releases CO_2. Because the decay process depends on temperature, global warming is thought to be increasing the rate of decay and thus CO_2 release. Scientists have not yet determined the balance between these two pathways but are intensively studying these flows. The processes of carbon fixation and release are covered in Chapter 8. This chapter also describes how changes in temperature and CO_2 concentration affect plant growth and decay, and documents the process of succession by which plant communities change through time.

Biodiversity

Among scientists, environmentalists, and the public, there is a growing awareness that the diversity in the plant and animal forms harbored by our planet—the Earth's biodiversity—is an immensely valuable resource that will be cherished by future generations. One important reason for preserving as many natural species as possible is that, over time, species have evolved natural biochemical defense mechanisms against diseases and predators. These defense mechanisms involve bioactive compounds that can sometimes be very useful, ranging from natural pesticides that increase crop yields to medicines that fight human cancer.

Another important reason for maintaining biodiversity is that complex ecosystems with many species tend to be more stable and to respond better to environmental change. If human activities inadvertently reduce biodiversity significantly, there is a greater risk of unexpected and unintended human effects on natural environments.

Biogeographers focus on both the processes that create and maintain biodiversity and the existing biodiversity of the Earth's many natural habitats. These topics are treated in Chapters 8 and 9.

Human activity is reducing the biodiversity of many of the Earth's natural habitats. Environmental pollution degrades habitat quality for humans as well as other species. Extreme weather events, which are thought to be more frequent with human-induced climate change, as well as other rare natural events, are increasingly destructive to our expanding human population.

Pollution

As we all know, unchecked human activity can degrade environmental quality. In addition to CO_2 release, fuel burning can release gases that are hazardous to health, especially when they react to form such toxic compounds as ozone and nitric acid in photochemical smog. Water pollution from fertilizer runoff, toxic wastes of industrial production, and acid mine drainage can severely degrade water quality. Such degradation impacts not only the ecosystems of streams and rivers, but also the human populations that depend on rivers and streams as sources of water supply. Ground water reservoirs can also be polluted or turn salty in coastal zones when drawn down excessively.

Environmental pollution, its causes, its effects, and the technologies used to reduce pollution, form a subject that is broad in its own right. As a text in physical geography that emphasizes the natural processes of the Earth's land surface, we touch on air and water pollution in several chapters—Chapter 4 for air pollution and Chapter 15 for surface water pollution, irrigation effects, and ground water contamination.

Extreme Events

Catastrophic events—floods, fires, hurricanes, earthquakes, and the like—can have great and long-lasting impacts on both human and natural systems. Are human activities increasing the frequency of these **extreme events**? As our planet warms in response to changes in the greenhouse effect, global climate modelers predict that weather extremes will become more severe and more frequent. Droughts and consequent wildfires and crop failures will happen more often, as will spells of rain and flood runoff. In the last decade, we have seen numerous examples of extreme weather events, from Hurricane Andrew in 1992—the most costly storm in U.S. history—to the southeast drought of 2000, which devastated crops in large parts of the southeastern United States. Is human activity responsible for the increased occurrence of these extreme events? Significant evidence now points in that direction. (See *Eye on the Environment 3.2 • The IPCC Report of 2001.*)

Other extreme events, such as earthquakes, volcanic eruptions, and seismic sea waves (wrongly called tidal waves), are produced by forces deep within the Earth that are not affected by human activity. But as the human population continues to expand and comes to rely increasingly on a technological infrastructure ranging from skyscrapers to the Internet, we are becoming more sensitive to damage and disruption of these systems by extreme events.

This text describes many types of extreme events and their causes. In Chapters 4 and 6, we discuss thunderstorms, tornadoes, cyclonic storms, and hurricanes. Droughts in the African Sahel are presented in Chapter 7. Earthquakes, volcanic eruptions, and seismic sea waves are covered in Chapter 13. Floods are described in Chapter 15, including the great Mississippi flood of 1993.

A LOOK AHEAD   The past few pages have presented an introduction to geography, to physical geography, to some of the tools and approaches that physical geographers use in studying the landscape, and to some of the big ideas that overarch physical geography. We have also introduced some of the key environmental and global change topics that will appear in our text.

With this introduction now complete, we can turn to our topical coverage of physical geography. We begin in Chapter 1 with some fundamental principles about Earth–Sun relationships that drive global climate, which in turn is a key factor in many fields of physical geography, ranging from biogeography to geomorphology.

Humans are now the dominant species on the planet. Nearly every part of the Earth has felt human impact in some way. As the human population continues to grow and rely more heavily on natural resources, our impact on natural systems will continue to increase. Each of us is charged with the responsibility to treat the Earth well and respect its finite nature. Understanding the processes that shape our habitat as they are described by physical geography will help you carry out this mission.

In Review | Introducing Physical Geography

- **Geography** is the study of the evolving character and organization of the Earth's surface. Geography has a unique set of perspectives. Geographers look at the world from the **viewpoint** of geographic space, focus on the **synthesis** of ideas from different disciplines, and develop and use special techniques for the **representation** and manipulation of spatial information.

- **Human geography** deals with social, economic, and behavioral processes that differentiate places, and **physical geography** examines the natural processes occurring at the Earth's surface that provide the physical setting for human activities. **Climatology** is the science that describes and explains the variability in space and time of the heat and moisture states of the Earth's surface, especially its land surfaces. **Geomorphology** is the science of Earth surface processes and landforms. **Coastal and marine geography** combines the study of geomorphic processes that shape shores and coastlines with their application to coastal development and marine resource utilization. **Geography of soils** includes the study of the distribution of soil types and properties and the processes of soil formation. **Biogeography** is the study of the distributions of organisms at varying spatial and temporal scales, as well as the processes that produce these distribution patterns. **Water resources** and **hazards assessment** are applied fields that blend both physical and human geography.

- Important tools for studying the fields of physical geography include **maps, geographic information systems, remote sensing, mathematical modeling,** and **statistics.**

- Scale, pattern, and process are three interrelated geographic themes. **Scale** refers to the level of structure or organization at which a phenomenon is studied, **pattern** refers to the variation in a phenomenon seen at a particular scale, and

process describes how the factors that affect a phenomenon act to produce a pattern at a particular scale. The processes of physical geography operate at multiple scales, including *global, continental, regional, local,* and *individual.*

- **Spheres, systems,** and **cycles** are three overarching themes that appear in physical geography. The four great Earth realms are **atmosphere, hydrosphere, lithosphere,** and **biosphere.** The **life layer** is the shallow surface layer where lands and oceans meet the atmosphere and where most forms of life are found.

- Physical processes often act together in an organized way that we can view as a **system.** A *systems approach* to physical geography looks for linkages and interactions between processes.

- Natural systems may undergo periodic, repeating changes that constitute **time cycles.** Important time cycles in physical geography range in length from hours to millions of years.

- Physical geography is concerned with the natural world around us—the human environment. Natural and human processes are constantly changing that environment. Global climate is changing in response to human impacts on the greenhouse effect. Global pathways of carbon flow can influence the greenhouse effect and are the subject of intense research interest. Maintaining global biodiversity is important both for maintaining the stability of ecosystems and guarding a potential resource of bioactive compounds for human benefit. Unchecked human activity can degrade environmental quality and create pollution. Extreme events take ever-higher tolls on life and property as populations expand. Extreme weather—storms and droughts, for example—may be more frequent with global warming caused by human activity.

Key Terms

geography, p. 6
viewpoint, p. 6
synthesis, p. 7
representation, p. 7
human geography, p. 7
physical geography, p. 7
climatology, p. 7
geomorphology, p. 9

coastal and marine
   geography, p. 9
geography of soils, p. 9
biogeography, p. 9
water resources, p. 9
hazards assessment, p. 9
map, p. 9
cartography, p. 14

geographic information
   system (GIS), p. 14
remote sensing, p. 14
mathematical modeling
   and statistics, p. 14
scale, p. 15
pattern, p. 15
process, p. 15

spheres, p. 14
atmosphere, p. 14
lithosphere, p. 15
hydrosphere, p. 15
biosphere, p. 15
life layer, p. 15
systems, , p. 16
time cycles, p. 16

Review Questions

1. What is geography? Identify three perspectives used by geographers in studying the physical and human characteristics of the Earth's surface.
2. How does human geography differ from physical geography?
3. Identify and define five important subfields of science within physical geography.

4. Identify and describe three tools that geographers use to acquire, display, and manipulate spatial data.
5. Identify and define three interrelated themes that often arise in geographic study.
6. Name and describe each of the four great physical realms of Earth. What is the life layer?

7. Provide two examples of processes or systems that operate at each of the following scales: global, continental, regional, local, and individual.

8. How is the word *system* used in physical geography? What is a systems approach?

9. What is a time cycle as applied to a system? Give an example of a time cycle evident in natural systems.

10. Identify and describe two interacting components of global change.

11. How is global climate change influenced by human activity?

12. Why are current research efforts focused on the carbon cycle?

13. Why is loss of biodiversity a concern of biogeographers and ecologists?

14. How does human activity degrade environmental quality? Provide a few examples.

15. How do extreme events affect human activity? Is human activity influencing the size or reoccurrence rate of extreme events?

Essay Question

1. Go to the extended table of contents for this book. With a pencil, check off every topic listed that you know something about. Now think about where you learned about these topics. Which of the following sources has provided you with the most information about physical geography? television, books and magazines, schoolwork, courses in college or university, learning by experience, other? How do you think the information sources by which you have learned about physical geography have affected what you have learned?

Eye on the Landscape

I.2 Vancouver, British Columbia With its deep embayments and steep topography, this is a coastline of submergence **(A)**. Much of the terrain was carved into steep slopes and wide valleys by glacial ice descending from nearby peaks during the Ice Age, when sea level was as much as 100 m (about 300 ft) lower. With the melting of ice sheets, sea level rose, drowning the landscape. Also note the snowcapped peaks in the far distance **(B)**. Rugged landscapes like this often indicate recent plate tectonic activity in which immense crustal plates collide to push up mountain chains like the Cascade Range. Chapters 18 and 19 describe coastlines and glacial erosion features. Plate tectonics is covered in Chapter 12.

I.4c Coastal and marine geography (A) This rock platform, shown at low tide, is a feature formed by wave action and is found on many rocky shorelines. At times of high water and surf, waves attack the cliffs, releasing rock fragments that are carried back and forth by the waves, thus cutting the flat bench. Chapter 18 provides more information on wave action. At **(B)**, horizontal lines revealed in the rock faces of these cliffed promontories mark individual layers (beds) of sedimentary rock. These beds were probably formed when silt and clay settled from turbid waters in a shallow arm of the ocean or in an inland sea. After millions of years of burial and consolidation into rock, the beds were uplifted and are now being eroded by waves. Sedimentary rock formation is covered in Chapter 11, and uplift (tectonic processes) is covered in Chapters 12 and 13.

I.4d Biogeography These patches of fog at **(A)** illustrate that fog is simply cloud touching the ground. They are probably patches of morning fog, formed when the moist air of the rainforest is chilled below the dew point by radiation cooling on a clear night. As the air warms, they will evaporate. Chapter 4 covers clouds, fog, and radiation cooling.

Stonehenge, England

1 | THE EARTH AS A ROTATING PLANET

PUTTING YOU IN THE PICTURE

This chapter is about the two great rhythms of solar illumination that affect every location on Earth—the daily rhythm of daylight and darkness, and the annual rhythm of lengthening and shortening of the daylight period with the seasons. They are vital to life on Earth, and nearly every form of life is adapted in some way to these solar rhythms. As we will see, these two rhythms arise from the Earth's rotation on its axis and its revolution around the Sun. To an observer at a fixed point on the Earth, however, the motions appear to be those of the Sun, not the Earth. As the Sun moves through the heavens, it rises and sets each day, marking the daily cycle of rotation. But its position of rising and setting on the horizon changes slowly day by day on an annual cycle, as does its elevation above the horizon at noon and the length of time that it remains in the sky. This annual rhythm marks the revolution of the Earth around the Sun during a year.

The motions of the Sun in the sky have been the subject of observation and study by human civilizations for thousands of years. An example is Stonehenge, a collection of huge rock slabs put in place thousands of years ago by a long-lost culture in a remote part of southwest England. Imagine yourself now at Stonehenge in the early morning of the first day of summer, waiting for first light…

At last the sky is brightening. Perhaps it won't be much longer now, you think, until the first rays of the Sun become

visible on the horizon next to the Slaughter Stone. Exhaling slowly, you watch the condensation from your breath float away on the still air. A shiver overwhelms you and you grasp your jacket more tightly, pulling it closer to your body.

Although the morning is cold, the sky is mostly clear. June weather in the southwest corner of England is notoriously changeable, but it looks like the viewing conditions will be good. According to the information you noted yesterday on your visit to the Greenwich Observatory, the summer solstice will occur at 3:28 P.M. this afternoon. So, today will be the longest day of the year—almost sixteen and a half hours at this latitude of more than 50 degrees north. It will also be the day of the year on which the Sun rises at its most northerly position from due east. You check your watch. Sunrise will be at 4:59. Still about 10 minutes to go.

You pause for a moment to survey your surroundings. Not far away is a trilithon—two immense vertical slabs of brown sandstone crowned by a massive horizontal sandstone called a lintel. This trilithon is one of five, arranged in a horseshoe. Three are still standing, and two are represented only by a single, still-erect stone. Surrounding the trilithons by four or five yards are the remaining vertical slabs of the sarsen circle, arranged in a ring of about 100 feet in diameter. Stonehenge was quite an accomplishment, considering that it was built three to four thousand years ago using only the most primitive methods.

The low voices of the crowd are suddenly quiet in anticipation as a ruby gleam brightens the sky. The first solar rays are soon visible. Slowly, the red solar disk emerges. Beyond the Sun, the sky is washed with red and pink, fading to deep blue. Small, puffy clouds above glow a spectacular rosy pink. What a sight!

From your location near the center of the ruin, the red solar ball is visible just to the left of the immense Slaughter Stone that marks the entrance to the ancient structure. You visualize the missing twin slab to the Slaughter Stone, nothing that the Sun would have been centered perfectly between the two huge vertical monoliths. The long shadow of the Slaughter Stone to your right would have been joined by a second shadow on your left, marking a broad sunlit path extending from the entrance to the center of the structure. Quite amazing, you think, that the ancient peoples that built Stonehenge were so fascinated with the paths of the Sun and the Moon in the sky that they marked them by hauling huge stones hundreds of miles to this hallowed place. Suddenly, a wave of reverence for Earth and nature hits you, and you realize that the scene has touched something primitive deep inside you that springs from the common heritage of humanity. ∎

THE EARTH AS A ROTATING PLANET

Since the dawn of civilization, humans have observed the movements of the Sun in the sky. However, only since the time of Copernicus—the sixteenth century—have we known that the daily and seasonal motions of the Sun are a consequence of the motion of the Earth rather than the Sun. From day to day, the Earth's rotation on its axis produces the alternation of the light and darkness that we experience in 24 hours. From month to month, the revolution of the Earth around the Sun produces slow changes in the length of daylight that create the rhythm of the seasons. These two great cycles continue, day after day, year after year, regulating the processes of Earthly life. We begin our systematic study of physical geography by devoting a chapter to the motions of the Earth and Sun and the implications of these motions for Earth location, timekeeping, and the seasons.

The Earth rotates on its axis and revolves around the Sun. The rotation produces the day–night cycle, while the revolution produces the seasonal cycle.

GEODISCOVERIES **Observing Earth-Sun Relationships.** Watch a video to learn how ancient peoples used the position of the rising and setting Sun on the horizon to devise annual calendars to predict wet and dry seasons, planting, and harvesting.

THE SHAPE OF THE EARTH

The Earth's shape is very close to that of a sphere, as we all learn early in school (Figure 1.1). Pictures taken from space by astronauts and by orbiting satellites also show us that the Earth is a round body. We learn this fact so early in life that it seems quite unremarkable.

Many of our ancestors, however, were not aware of our planet's spherical shape. To sailors of the Mediterranean Sea in ancient times, the shape and breadth of the Earth's oceans and lands were unknown. On their ships and out of sight of land, the sea surface looked perfectly flat and bounded by a circular horizon. Given this view, many sailors concluded that the Earth had the form of a flat disk and that their ships would fall off if they traveled to its edge. Of course, had the telescope been invented, they could have seen a distant ship with its decks seemingly below the water line—a demonstration of the curvature of the Earth's surface.

The curvature of the Earth is also evident as you view a sunset with clouds in the sky (Figure 1.1*d*). Although the Sun is below the horizon from your viewpoint and no longer illuminates the land around you, it is above the horizon at

1.1 Our Spherical Earth

a...Photo of Earth curvature   This astronaut photo shows the Earth's curved horizon from low-Earth orbit.

b...Eye on the Landscape   Space view of Earth   From a geostationary weather satellite, the Earth is a disk obscured by swirls of moving clouds.   What else would the geographer see?...Answers at the end of the chapter.

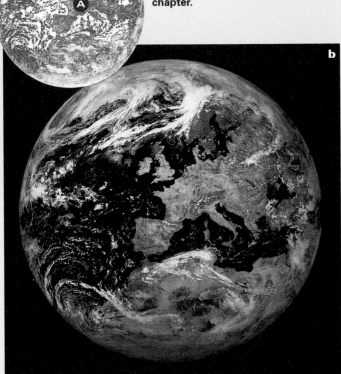

d...Sunset photo
In this dramatic sunset photo, the far distant clouds are still directly illuminated by the Sun's last red rays. For the clouds directly overhead, however, the Sun has left the sky.

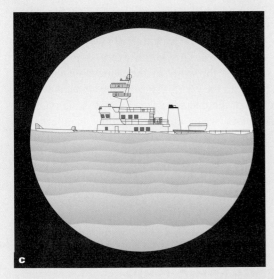

c...Distant Ship   Seen through a telescope, the decks of a distant ship seem to be under water.

the altitude of the clouds and still bathes them in its red and pinkish rays. As the Sun progressively washes the clouds overhead in red light, the red band of illumination slowly moves farther and farther toward your horizon. Soon only the far distant clouds can still "see" the Sun. This movement of solar illumination across the clouds is easily explained by a rotating spherical Earth.

Actually, the Earth is not perfectly spherical. Because the outward (centrifugal) force of the Earth's rotation causes the Earth to bulge slightly at the equator and flatten at the poles, the Earth assumes the shape of an *oblate ellipsoid.* ("Oblate" means flattened.) Thus, the Earth's equatorial diameter, about 12,756 km (7926 mi), is very slightly larger than the polar diameter, about 12,714 km (7900 mi). The difference (42 km, 26 mi) is very small—about three-tenths of 1 percent.

Scientists still study the Earth's shape and attempt to measure it as precisely as possible. Satellite navigation systems need this important information for aircraft, ocean vessels, and ground vehicles seeking to determine their exact location (see *Focus on Remote Sensing 1.1* • *The Global Positioning System,* later in this chapter).

EARTH ROTATION

Another fact about our planet that we learn early in life is that it spins slowly, making a full turn with respect to the Sun every day. We use the term **rotation** to describe this motion. One complete rotation with respect to the Sun defines the *solar day.* By convention, the solar day is divided into exactly 24 hours.

The Earth rotates on its *axis,* an imaginary straight line through its center. The two points where the axis of rotation intersects the Earth's surface are defined as the poles. To distinguish between the two poles, one is called the *north pole.* and the other, the *south pole.*

To determine the direction of Earth rotation, you can use one of the following guidelines (Figure 1.2):

- Imagine yourself looking down on the north pole of the Earth. From this position, the Earth is turning in a counterclockwise direction (Figure 1.2*a*).
- Imagine yourself off in space, viewing the planet much as you would view a globe in a library, with the north pole on top. The Earth is rotating from left to right or in an eastward direction (Figure 1.2*b*).

The Earth's rotation is important for three reasons. First, the axis of rotation serves as a reference in setting up the geographic grid of latitude and longitude, which we will discuss later in the chapter. Second, it provides the day as a convenient measure of the passage of time, with the day in turn divided into hours, minutes, and seconds. Third, it has important effects on the physical and life processes on Earth.

> The direction of the Earth's rotation is counterclockwise when viewed from above the north pole, or from west to east if viewed with the north pole up.

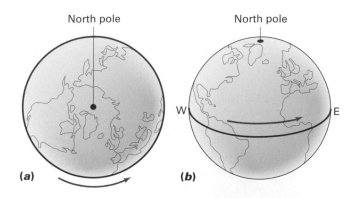

1.2   Direction of Earth rotation *The direction of rotation of the Earth can be thought of as (a) counterclockwise at the north pole, or (b) from left to right (eastward) at the equator.*

Environmental Effects of Earth Rotation

The first—and perhaps most obvious—effect of the Earth's rotation is that it imposes a daily, or *diurnal,* rhythm in daylight, air temperature, air humidity, and air motion.

All surface life responds to this diurnal rhythm. Green plants receive and store solar energy during the day and consume some of it at night. Among animals, some are active during the day, others at night. The daily cycle of incoming solar energy and the corresponding cycle of fluctuating air temperature are topics for analysis in Chapters 2 and 3.

A second environmental effect is that the flow paths of both air and water are turned consistently in a sideward direction because of the Earth's rotation. Flows in the northern hemisphere are turned toward the right and in the southern hemisphere toward the left. This phenomenon is called the *Coriolis effect.* It is of great importance in studying the Earth's systems of winds and ocean currents and is discussed in Chapter 5.

A third physical effect of the Earth's rotation is the movement of the tides. The Moon exerts a gravitational attraction on the Earth, while at the same time the Earth turns with respect to the Moon. These forces induce a rhythmic rise and fall of the ocean surface known as the *tide.* The tide in turn causes water currents to flow in alternating directions in the shallow salty waters of the coastal zone. This ebb and flow of tidal currents is a life-giving pulse for many plants and animals that live in coastal saltwater environments. The tidal cycle is a clock regulating many daily human activities in the coastal zone as well. When we examine the tide and its currents further in Chapter 18, we will see that the Sun also has an influence on the tides.

THE GEOGRAPHIC GRID

The geographic grid provides a system for locating places on the Earth's surface. Because the Earth's surface is curved, and not flat, we cannot divide it into a rectangular grid, like

Focus on Remote Sensing | 1.1

The Global Positioning System

The latitude and longitude coordinates of a point on the Earth's surface describe its position exactly. But how are those coordinates determined? For the last few hundred years, we have known how to use the position of the stars in the sky coupled with an accurate clock to determine the latitude and longitude of any point. Linked with advances in mapping and surveying, these techniques became highly accurate, but they were impractical for precisely determining desired locations in a short period of time.

Thanks to new technology originally developed by the U.S. Naval Observatory for military applications, there is now in place a *global positioning system (GPS)* that can provide location information to an accuracy of about 20 meters within a minute or two. The system uses 24 satellites that orbit the Earth every 12 hours, continuously broadcasting their position and a highly accurate time signal.

To determine location, a receiver listens simultaneously to signals from four or more satellites. The receiver compares the time readings transmitted by each satellite with the receiver's own clock to determine how long it took for each signal to reach the receiver. Since the radio signal travels at a known rate of speed, the receiver can convert the travel time into the distance between the receiver and the satellite. Coupling the distance to each satellite with the position of the satellite in its orbit at the time of the transmission, the receiver calculates its position on the ground to within about 20 m (66 ft) horizontally and 30 m (98 ft) vertically.

The accuracy of the location is affected by several types of errors. First are small perturbations in the orbits of the satellites, caused by such unpredictable events as solar particle showers. These cause errors in the information about satellite position. Another source of error is small variations in the atomic clock that each satellite carries. A larger source of error, however, is the effect of the atmosphere on the radio waves of the satellite signal as they pass from the satellite to the receiver. The layer of charged particles at the outer edge of the atmosphere (ionosphere) and water vapor in the lowest atmospheric layer (troposphere) act to slow the radio waves. Since the conditions in these layers can change within a matter of minutes, the speed of the radio waves varies in an unpredictable way. Another transmission problem is that the radio waves may bounce off local obstructions and then reach the receiver, causing two slightly different signals to arrive at the receiver at the same time. This "multipath error" creates noise that confuses the receiver.

There is a way, however, to determine location within about 1 m (3.3 ft) horizontally and 2 m (6.6 ft) vertically. The method uses two GPS units, one at a base station and one that is mobile and used to determine the desired locations. The base station unit is placed at a position that is known with very high accuracy. By comparing its exact position with that calculated from each satellite signal, it determines the small deviations from orbit of each satellite, any small variations in each satellite's clock, and the exact speed of that satellite's radio signal through the atmosphere at that moment. It then broadcasts that information to the GPS field unit, where it is used to calculate the position more accurately. Because this method compares two sets of signals, it is known as *differential GPS*.

Differential GPS is now in wide use for coastal navigation, where a few meters in position can make the difference between a shipping channel and a shoal. It is also required for the new generation of aircraft landing systems that will allow much safer instrument landings with equipment that is much lower in cost than existing systems.

As GPS technology has developed, costs have fallen exponentially. It is now possible to buy a small, hand-held GPS receiver for less than $100. Worldwide sales of GPS products and services reached $8 billion in 2000 and are expected to double by 2003. Besides plotting your progress on a computer-generated map as you drive your car or sail your boat, GPS technology can even keep track of your children at a theme park. With the coupling of wireless telephones and GPS, you may never have the chance to claim you're at a client meeting when the readout shows your employer that you're on the golf links!

GEODISCOVERIES **Global Positioning Systems.** Watch an animation on the Navstar Global Positioning System to learn more about how the system works.

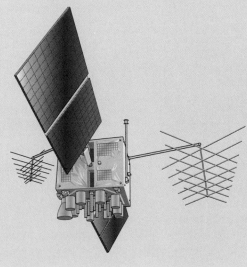

A GPS satellite as it might look in orbit high above the Earth.

a sheet of graph paper. Instead, we divide it using imaginary circles set on the surface that are perpendicular to the axis of rotation in one direction and parallel to the axis of rotation in the other direction.

Parallels and Meridians

Imagine a point on the Earth's surface. As the Earth rotates, the point traces out a path in space, following an *arc*—that is, a curved line that forms a portion of a circle. With the completion of one rotation, the arc forms a full circle. This circle is known as a parallel of latitude, or a **parallel** (Figure 1.3a). Imagine cutting the globe much as you might slice an onion to produce onion rings— that is, perpendicular to the onion's main axis. Each cut creates a circle or parallel crosswise through the globe. The Earth's longest parallel of latitude lies midway between the two poles and is designated the **equator.** The equator is a fundamental reference line for measuring the position of points on the globe.

Imagine now slicing the Earth with a plane that passes through the axis of rotation instead of across it. This is the way you might cut up a lemon to produce wedges. Each cut outlines a circle on the globe passing through both poles. Half of this circular outline, connecting one pole to the other, is known as a meridian of longitude, or, more simply, a **meridian** (Figure 1.3b).

Meridians and parallels define geographic directions. Meridians are north-south lines, so if you walk north or south you are following a meridian. Parallels are east-west lines, and so if you walk east or west you are following a parallel. Any number of parallels and meridians are possible. Every point on the globe is associated with a unique combination of one parallel and one meridian. The position of the point is defined by their intersection. The total system of parallels and meridians forms a network of intersecting circles called the **geographic grid.**

Looking more closely at meridians and parallels, we see that they are made up of two types of circles—great and

> The geographic grid consists of an orderly system of circles—meridians and parallels—that are used to locate position on the globe. Parellels are east-west lines, while meridians are north-south lines.

small (Figure 1.4). A **great circle** is created when a plane passing through the center of the Earth intersects the Earth's surface. A great circle always has the Earth's center as its own center, and it bisects the globe into two equal halves. A **small circle** is created when a plane passing through the Earth, but not through the Earth's center, intersects the Earth's surface. By looking at Figure 1.3, you can easily see that meridians are actually halves of great circles, while all parallels, except the equator, are small circles. Great circles can be aligned in any direction on the globe. This means that if we choose two points on the globe, we can always find a great circle that passes through both points. As we will see shortly in our discussion of map projections, the portion of the great circle between the two points is the shortest distance between them.

Latitude and Longitude

To label parallels and meridians, we use a special system— latitude and longitude. Parallels are identified by latitude and meridians by longitude. **Latitude** is an indicator of how far north or south of the equator a parallel is situated. The latitude of a parallel is measured by the angle between a point on the parallel, the center of the Earth, and a point on the equator intersected by a meridian passing through the point of interest on the parallel (Figure 1.5a). Note that

1.4 *Great and small circles* A great circle is created when a plane passes through the Earth, intersecting the Earth's center. Small circles are created when a plane passes through the Earth but does not intersect the center point.

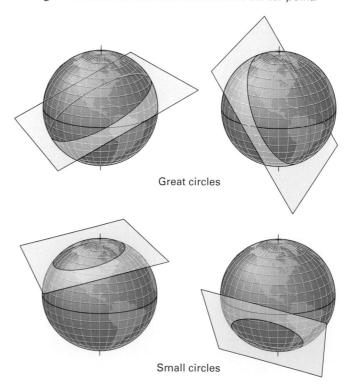

Great circles

Small circles

1.3 *Parallels and meridians* (a) Parallels of latitude divide the globe crosswise into rings. (b) Meridians of longitude divide the globe from pole to pole.

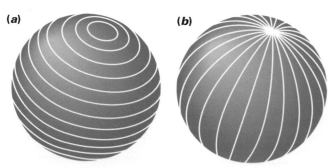

(a) *(b)*

(a)

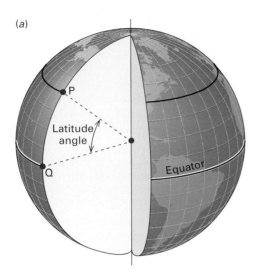

(b)

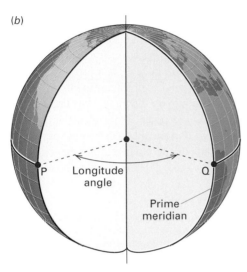

1.5   Latitude and longitude angles *(a) The latitude of a parallel is the angle between a point on the parallel (P) and a point on the equator at the same meridian (Q) as measured from the Earth's center. (b) The longitude of a meridian is the angle between a point on that meridian at the equator (P) and a point on the prime meridian at the equator (Q) as measured at the Earth's center.*

1.6   The prime meridian *This photograph, taken at dusk at the old Royal Observatory at Greenwich, England, shows the prime meridian, which has been marked as a stripe on the forecourt paving.*

the equator divides the globe into two equal portions, or *hemispheres*. All parallels north of the equator—that is, in the *northern hemisphere*—are designated as having north latitude, and all points south of the equator—in the *southern hemisphere*—are designated as having south latitude (N or S).

Longitude is a measure of the position of a meridian eastward or westward from a reference meridian, called the *prime meridian*. As Figure 1.5*b* shows, longitude is the angle, measured in degrees, between a plane passing through the meridian and a plane passing through the prime meridian. The prime meridian passes through the

> **Latitude and longitude uniquely determine the position of a point on the globe. Latitude records the parallel, and longitude the meridian, associated with the point.**

location of the old Royal Observatory at Greenwich, near London, England (Figure 1.6). For this reason it is also referred to as the Greenwich meridian. It has the value long. 0°. The longitude of a meridian on the globe is measured eastward or westward from the prime meridian, depending on which direction gives the smaller angle. Longitude thus ranges from 0° to 180°, east or west (E or W).

Figure 1.7 shows how the location of a point on the Earth's surface is determined by its latitude and longitude. The point *P* lies on the parallel of latitude at 50 degrees north, which we can abbreviate as lat. 50° N. It also lies on the meridian of longitude at 60 degrees west, which we can abbreviate as long. 60° W. When both the latitude and longitude of a point are known, it can be accurately and precisely located on the geographic grid.

When latitude or longitude angles are measured other than in full-degree increments, *minutes* and *seconds* can be used. A minute is 1/60 of a degree, and a second is 1/60 of a minute, or 1/3600 of a degree. Thus, the latitude 41°, 27 minutes (′), and 41 seconds (″) north (lat. 41° 27′ 41″ N) means 41° north plus 27/60 of a degree plus 41/3600 of a degree. This cumbersome system has now largely been replaced by decimal notation. In this example, the latitude 41° 27′ 41″ N translates to 41.4614° N.

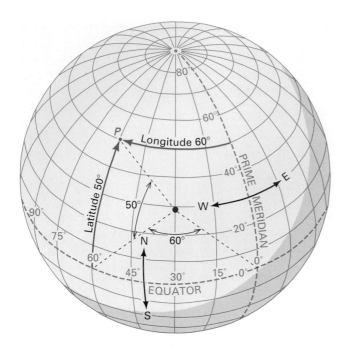

1.7 Latitude and longitude of a point *The point P lies on the parallel of latitude at 50° north (50° from the equator) and on the meridian at 60° west (60° from the prime meridian). Its location is therefore lat. 50° N, long. 60° W.*

Degrees of latitude and longitude can also be used as distance measures. A degree of latitude, which measures distance in a north-south direction, is equal to about 111 km (69 mi). The distance associated with a degree of longitude, however, will be progressively reduced with latitude because meridians converge toward the poles. For example, at 60° latitude, a degree of longitude has a length exactly half of that at the equator, or 55.5 km (34.5 mi).

The latitude and longitude of any point can now be determined quickly and accurately with the help of the *global positioning system (GPS)*—a system of satellites that constantly sends radio signals to Earth with information that allows a GPS receiver to calculate its position on the Earth's surface. *Focus on Remote Sensing 1.1 • The Global Positioning System* provides more information about GPS and how it works.

MAP PROJECTIONS

With a working understanding of the geographic grid, we can consider how to display the locations of continents, rivers, cities, islands, and other geographic features on maps. This will take us briefly into the realm of *cartography,* the art and science of making maps. The discussion in the main text will focus on a few simple types of maps that are used widely and found in our chapters. At the end of this chapter we provide a special supplement, *Geographer's Tools 1.2 • Focus on Maps,* with more information about how maps are made and how they display information.

As we observed earlier, the Earth's shape is nearly spherical, and so the Earth's surface is curved. However, maps are flat. It is impossible to copy a curved surface onto a flat surface without cutting, stretching, or otherwise distorting the curved surface in some way. So, making a map means devising an orderly way of changing the globe's geographic grid of curved parallels and meridians into a grid that lies flat. We refer to a system for changing the geographic grid to a flat grid as a **map projection.**

GEODISCOVERIES **Map Projections.** Watch an animation showing how map projections are constructed.

Associated with every map is a *scale fraction*—a ratio that relates distance on the map to distance on the Earth's surface. For example, a scale fraction of 1:50,000 means that one unit of map distance equals 50,000 units of distance on the Earth.

Because a curved surface cannot be projected onto a flat surface without some distortion, the scale fraction of a map holds only for one point or a single line on the map. Away from that point or line, the scale fraction will be different. However, this variation in scale is a problem only for maps that show large regions, such as continents or hemispheres.

We will concentrate on the three most useful map projections. The first is the polar projection, which pictures the globe from top or bottom and is essential for scientific uses like weather maps of the polar regions. Second is the Mercator projection, a navigator's map invented in 1569 by Gerhardus Mercator. It is a classic that has never gone out of style. Third is the Goode projection, named for its designer, Dr. J. Paul Goode. It has special qualities not found in the other two projections.

Polar Projection

The *polar projection* (Figure 1.8) can be centered on either the north or the south pole. Meridians are straight lines radiating outward from the pole, and parallels are nested circles centered on the pole. Spacing of the parallels increases outward from the center. The map is usually cut off to show only one hemisphere so that the equator forms the outer edge of the map. Because the intersections of the parallels with the meridians always form true right angles, this projection shows the true shapes of all small areas. That is, the shape of a small island would always be shown correctly, no matter where it appeared on the map. However, because the scale fraction increases in an outward direction, the island would look larger toward the edge of the map than near the center.

Mercator Projection

The *Mercator projection* (Figure 1.9) is a rectangular grid of meridians as straight vertical lines and parallels as straight horizontal lines. Meridians are evenly spaced, but the spacing between parallels increases at higher latitude so that the spacing at 60° is double that at the equator. Closer to the poles, the spacing increases even more, and the map must be cut off at some arbitrary parallel, such as

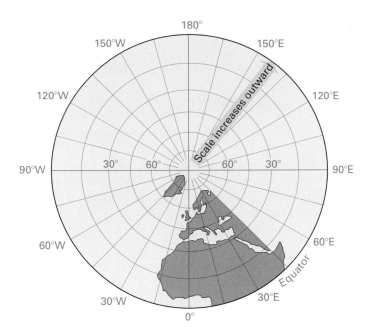

1.8 A polar projection *The map is centered on the north pole. All meridians are straight lines radiating from the center point, and all parallels are concentric circles. The scale fraction increases in an outward direction, making shapes toward the edges of the map appear larger.*

80° N. This change of scale enlarges features when they near the pole, as can easily be seen in Figure 1.9. There Greenland appears larger than Australia and is nearly the size of Africa! In fact, Greenland is very much smaller, as you can see on a globe.

The Mercator projection has several special properties. One is that a straight line drawn anywhere on the map is a line of constant compass direction. A navigator can therefore simply draw a line between any two points on the map and measure the *bearing,* or direction angle of the line, with respect to a nearby meridian on the map. Since the meridian is a true north-south line, the angle will give the compass bearing to be followed. Once aimed in that compass direction, a ship or an airplane can be held to the same compass bearing to reach the final point or destination.

This line will not necessarily follow the shortest actual distance between two points. As we noted earlier, the shortest path between two points on the globe is always a portion of a great circle. On a Mercator projection, a great circle line curves (except on the equator) and can falsely seem to represent a much longer distance than a compass line.

Because the Mercator projection shows the true compass direction of any straight line on the map, it is used to show many types of straight-line features. Among these features are flow lines of winds and ocean currents, directions of

1.9 The Mercator projection *The compass line connecting two locations, such as Portland and Cairo, shows the compass bearing of a course directly connecting them. However, the shortest distance between them lies on a great circle, which is a longer, curving line on this map projection. The diagram at the right shows how rapidly the map scale increases at higher latitudes. At lat. 60°, the scale is double the equatorial scale. At lat. 80°, the scale is six times greater than at the equator.*

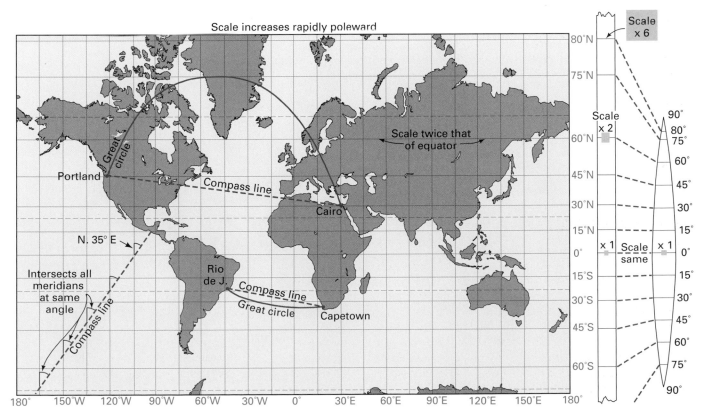

crustal features (such as chains of volcanoes), and lines of equal values, such as lines of equal air temperature or equal air pressure. This explains why the Mercator projection is chosen for maps of temperatures, winds, and pressures.

The Mercator projection shows a line of constant compass bearing as a straight line and so is used to display directional features such as wind direction.

Goode Projection

The *Goode projection* (Figure 1.10) uses two sets of mathematical curves (sine curves and ellipses) to form its meridians. Between the 40th parallels, sine curves are used, and beyond the 40th parallel, toward the poles, ellipses are used. Since the ellipses converge to meet at the pole, the entire globe can be shown. The straight, horizontal parallels make it easy to scan across the map at any given level to compare regions most likely to be similar in climate.

The Goode projection has one very important property—it indicates the true sizes of areas of the Earth's surface. That is, if we drew a small circle on a sheet of clear plastic and moved it over all parts of the Goode world map, all the areas enclosed by the circle would have the same value in square kilometers or square miles. Because of this property, we use the Goode map to show geographical features that occupy surface areas. Examples of useful Goode projections include maps of the world's climates, soils, and vegetation.

The Goode map suffers from a serious defect, however. It distorts the shapes of areas, particularly in high latitudes and at the far right and left edges.

The Goode projection displays the relative areas of land masses correctly but distorts their shape—especially near the poles.

To minimize this defect, Dr. Goode split his map apart into separate, smaller sectors, each centered on a different vertical meridian. These were then assembled at the equator. This type of split map is called an *interrupted projection*. Although the interrupted projection greatly reduces shape distortion, it separates parts of the Earth's surface that actually lie close together, particularly in the high latitudes.

Maps are in wide use today for many applications as a simple and efficient way of compiling and storing spatial information. However, in the past two decades, maps are being supplemented by more powerful computer-based methods for acquiring, storing, processing, analyzing, and outputting spatial data. These are contained within *geographic information systems (GISs)*. Our special supplement, *Geographer's Tools 1.2 • Geographic Information Systems,* presents some basic concepts of geographic information systems and how they work.

GLOBAL TIME

Maps and map projections are a practical application of the Earth's geographic grid. Another practical application, which involves both the grid and the Earth's rotation, is global time.

Our planet requires 24 hours for a full rotation with respect to the Sun. Put another way, humans long ago decided to divide the solar day into 24

1.10 *The Goode projection* *The meridians in this projection follow sine curves between lat. 40° N and lat. 40° S, and ellipses between lat. 40° and the poles. Although the shapes of continents are distorted, their relative surface areas are preserved. (Copyright © by the University of Chicago. Used by permission of the Committee on Geographical Studies, University of Chicago.)*

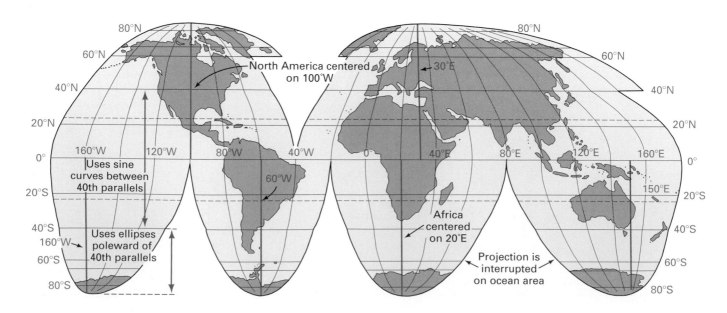

units, called hours, and devised clocks to keep track of hours in groups of 12. Yet, different regions set their clocks differently. For example, when it is 10:03 A.M. in New York, it is 9:03 A.M. in Chicago, 8:03 A.M. in Denver, and 7:03 A.M. in Los Angeles. Note that these times differ by exactly one hour. How did this system come about? How does it work?

Our global time system is oriented to the Sun. Think for a moment about how the Sun appears to move across the sky. In the morning, the Sun is low on the eastern horizon, and as the day progresses, it rises higher until at *solar noon* it reaches its highest point in the sky. If you check your watch at that moment, it will read a time somewhere near 12 o'clock (12:00 noon). After solar noon, the Sun's elevation in the sky decreases. By late afternoon, the Sun appears low in the sky, and at sunset it rests on the western horizon.

Imagine for a moment that you are in Chicago, the time is noon, and the Sun is at or near its highest point in the sky. Imagine further that you call a friend in New York and ask about the time there and the position of the Sun. You will receive a report that the time is 1:00 P.M. and that the Sun is already past solar noon, its highest point. Calling a friend in Vancouver, you hear that it is 10:00 A.M., there and that the Sun is still working its way up to its highest point. However, a friend in Mobile, Alabama, will tell you that the time in Mobile is the same as in Chicago and that the Sun is at about solar noon. How can we explain these different observations?

The difference in time between Chicago, New York, and Vancouver makes sense because solar noon can occur simultaneously only at locations with the same longitude. In other words, only one meridian can be directly under the Sun and experience solar noon at a given moment. Locations on meridians to the east of Chicago, like New York, already will have passed solar noon, and locations to the west of Chicago, like Vancouver, will not yet have reached solar noon. Since Mobile and Chicago have nearly the same longitude, they experience solar noon at approximately the same time.

Figure 1.11 indicates how time varies with longitude. In this figure, the inner disk shows a polar projection of the world, centered on the north pole. Meridians are straight lines (radii) ranging out from the pole. The outer ring indicates the time in hours. The figure shows the moment in time when the prime meridian is directly under the Sun—that is, the 0° meridian is directly on the 12:00 noon mark. This means that, at this instant, the Sun is at the highest point of its path in the sky in Greenwich, England. The alignment of meridians with hour numbers tells us the time in other locations around the globe. For example, the time in New York, which lies roughly on the 75° W meridian, is about 7:00 A.M. In Los Angeles, which lies roughly on the 120° W meridian, the time is about 4:00 A.M.

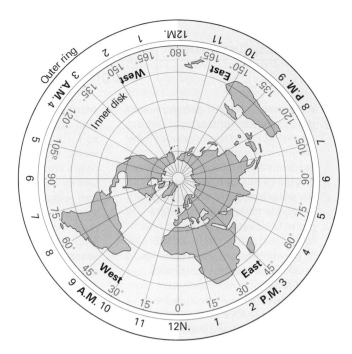

1.11 *The relation of longitude to time* The outer ring shows the time at locations identified by longitude meridians on the central map. The diagram is set to show noon conditions in Greenwich, England—that is, on the prime meridian. Clock time is earlier to the west of Greenwich and later to the east.

Notice that 15° of longitude equates to an hour of time. Since the Earth turns 360° in a 24-hour day, the rotation rate is 360° ÷ 24 = 15° per hour.

Standard Time

We've just seen that locations with different longitudes experience solar noon at different times. But consider what would happen if each town or city set its clocks to read 12:00 at its own local solar noon. All cities and towns on different meridians would have different local time systems. In these days of instantaneous global communication, chaos would soon result.

The use of standard time simplifies the global timekeeping problem. In the **standard time system,** the globe is divided into 24 **time zones.** All inhabitants within a zone keep time according to a *standard meridian* that passes through their zone. Since the standard meridians are usually 15 degrees apart, the difference in time between adjacent zones is normally one hour. In some geographic regions, however, the difference is only one-half hour.

Seven time zones cover the United States and its Caribbean possessions. Six zones cover Canada. Their names and standard meridians of longitude are as follows:

> In the standard time system, we keep global time according to nearby standard meridians that normally differ by one hour from each other.

U.S. Zones	Meridian	Canadian Zones
	52½°	Newfoundland
Atlantic	60°	Atlantic
Eastern	75°	Eastern
Central	90°	Central
Mountain	105°	Mountain
Pacific	120°	Pacific-Yukon
Alaska-Bering	135°	
Hawaii	150°	

If carried out strictly, the standard time system would consist of belts exactly 15°, extending to meridians 7½° east and west of each standard meridian. However, this system could be inconvenient since the boundary meridians could divide a state, county, or city into two different time zones. As a result, time zone boundaries are often routed to follow agreed-upon natural or political boundaries.

Figure 1.12 presents a map of time zones for the contiguous United States and southern Canada. From this map, you can see that most time zone boundaries are conveniently located along an already existing and widely recognized line. For example, the eastern time–central time boundary line follows Lake Michigan down its center, and the mountain time–Pacific time boundary follows a ridge-crest line also used by the Idaho–Montana state boundary.

World Time Zones

Figure 1.13 shows the 24 principal standard time zones of the world. In the figure, 15° meridians are dashed lines, while the 7½° meridians, which form many of the boundaries between zones, are bold lines. The figure also shows the time of day in each zone when it is noon at the Greenwich meridian. The country spanning the greatest number of time zones from east to west is Russia, with 11 zones, but these are grouped into eight standard time zones. China spans five time zones but runs on a single national time using the standard meridian of Beijing.

A few countries keep time by a meridian that is midway between standard meridians, so that their clocks depart from those of their neighbors by 30 or 90 minutes. India and Iran are examples. The Canadian province of Newfoundland and the interior Australian states of South Australia and Northern Territory are examples of regions within countries that keep time by 7½° meridians.

World time zones are numbered to indicate the number of hours difference between time in a zone and time in Greenwich. A number of –7, for example, indicates that local time is seven hours behind Greenwich time, while a +3 indicates that local time is three hours ahead of Greenwich time.[1]

---

[1]Instructors should note that the sign convention for time zones has changed in this edition.

1.12 Time zones of the contiguous United States and southern Canada The name, standard meridian, and number code are shown for each time zone. Note that time zone boundaries often follow preexisting natural or political boundaries.

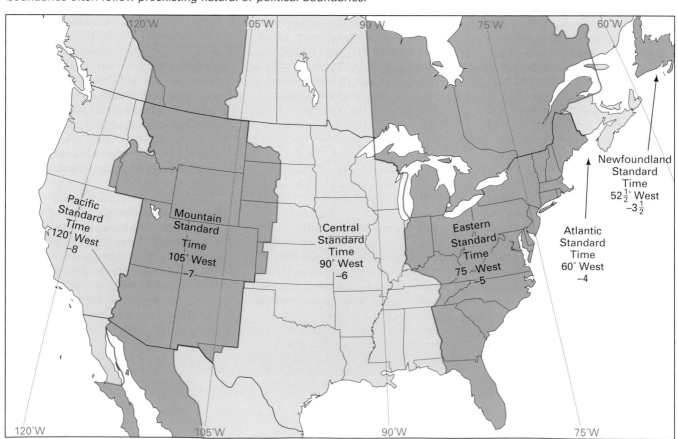

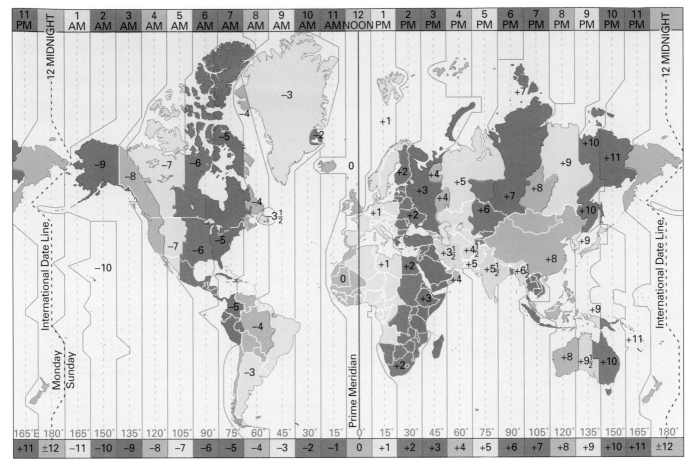

1.13 Time zones of the world *Dashed lines represent 15° meridians, and bold lines represent 7¹/₂° meridians. Alternate zones appear in color. (U.S. Navy Oceanographic Office.)*

International Date Line

When we take a world map or globe with 15° meridians and count them in an eastward direction, starting with the Greenwich meridian as 0, we find that the 180th meridian is number 12 and that the time at this meridian is therefore 12 hours later than Greenwich time. Counting in a similar manner westward from the Greenwich meridian, we find that the 180th meridian is again number 12 but that the time is 12 hours earlier than Greenwich time. How can the same meridian be both 12 hours ahead of Greenwich time and 12 hours behind? This paradox is explained by the fact that different days are observed on either side of this meridian.

Imagine that you are on the 180th meridian on June 26th and it is exactly midnight. Let's stop the world for a moment and examine the situation. On the 180th meridian at the exact instant of midnight, the same 24-hour calendar day covers the entire globe. Stepping east will place you in the very early morning of June 26, while stepping west will place you very late in the evening of June 26. You are in the same calendar day on both sides of the meridian but 24 hours apart in time.

Doing the same experiment an hour later, at 1:00 A.M., stepping east you will find that you are in the early morn-

ing of June 26. But if you step west you will find that midnight of June 26 has passed, and it is now the early morning of June 27. So on the west side of the 180th meridian, it is also 1:00 A.M. but one day later than on the east side. For this reason, the 180th meridian serves as the *International Date Line*. This means that if you travel westward across the date line, you must advance your calendar by one day. If traveling eastward, you set your calendar back by a day.

Air travelers between North America and Asia cross the date line. For example, flying westward from Los Angeles to Sydney, Australia, you may depart on a Tuesday evening and arrive on a Thursday morning after a flight that lasts only 14 hours. On an eastward flight from Tokyo to San Francisco, you may actually arrive the day before you take off, taking the date change into account!

Actually, the International Date Line does not follow the 180th meridian exactly. Like many time zone boundaries, it deviates from the meridian for practical reasons. As shown in Figure 1.13, it has a zigzag offset between Asia and North America, as well as an eastward offset in the South Pacific to keep clear of New Zealand and several island groups.

Daylight Saving Time

Especially in urban areas, many human activities being well after sunrise and continue long after sunset. Therefore, we adjust our clocks during the part of the year that has a longer daylight period to correspond more closely with the modern pace of society. This adjusted time system, called *daylight saving time,* is obtained by setting all clocks ahead by one hour. The effect of the time change is to transfer the early morning daylight period, theoretically wasted while schools, offices, and factories are closed, to the early evening, when most people are awake and busy. Daylight saving time also yields a considerable savings in power used for electric lights. In the United States, daylight saving time comes into effect on the first Sunday in April and is discontinued on the last Sunday of October. Arizona, certain counties in Indiana, Puerto Rico, Hawaii, U.S. Virgin Islands, and American Samoa do not observe daylight saving time.

Precise Timekeeping

Many scientific and technological applications require precise timekeeping. Today, a worldwide system of master atomic clocks measures time to better than one part in 1,000,000,000,000. However, our Earth is a much less precise timekeeper, demonstrating small changes in the angular velocity of its rotation on its axis and variations in the time it takes to complete one circuit around the Sun. As a result, constant adjustments to the timekeeping system are necessary. The legal time standard recognized by all nations is Coordinated Universal Time, which is administered by the Bureau International de l'Heure, located near Paris.

THE EARTH'S REVOLUTION AROUND THE SUN

So far, we have discussed the importance of the Earth's rotation on its axis. Another important motion of the Earth is its **revolution,** or its movement in orbit around the Sun.

GEODISCOVERIES The Earth's Revolution Around the Sun. Watch a narrated animation to see how the Earth revolves around the Sun to cause the seasons.

The Earth completes a revolution around the Sun in 365.242 days—about one-fourth day more than the calendar year of 365 days. Every four years, the extra one-fourth days add up to about one whole day. By inserting a 29th day in February in leap years, we largely correct the calendar for this effect. Further minor corrections are necessary to perfect the system.

The Earth's orbit around the Sun is shaped like an ellipse, or oval. This means that the distance between the Earth and Sun varies somewhat through the year. The Earth is nearest to the Sun at *perihelion,* which

1.14 *Revolution of the Earth and Moon* *Viewed from a point over the Earth's north pole, the Earth both rotates and revolves in a counterclockwise direction. From this viewpoint, the Moon also rotates counterclockwise.*

occurs on or about January 3. It is farthest away from the Sun at *aphelion,* on or about July 4. However, the distance between Sun and Earth varies only by about 3 percent during one revolution because the elliptical orbit is shaped very much like a circle. For most purposes we can regard the orbit as circular.

In which direction does the Earth revolve? Imagine yourself in space, looking down on the north pole of the Earth. From this viewpoint, the Earth travels counterclockwise around the Sun (Figure 1.14). This is the same direction as the Earth's rotation.

The Moon rotates on its axis and revolves about the Sun in the same direction as the Earth. However, the Moon's rate of rotation is such that one side of the Moon is always directed toward the Earth. Thus, astronomers had never seen the far side of the Moon until a Soviet spacecraft passing the Moon transmitted photos back to Earth in 1959. The phases of the Moon are determined by the position of the Moon in its orbit around the Earth, which in turn determines how much of the sunlit Moon is seen from the Earth. In Figure 1.14, the Moon is behind the Earth and we see the Moon as full. In Figure 1.15, the Moon is nearly full. From the way that the Sun illuminates the Moon as a sphere, it is easy to see that the Sun is to the right.

Tilt of the Earth's Axis

The seasons we experience on Earth are related to the orientation of the Earth's axis of rotation as it revolves around the Sun. We usually describe this situation by stating that the Earth's axis is tilted with respect to the *plane of the ecliptic*—the plane containing the Earth's orbit around the Sun. Figure 1.16 shows the plane of the ecliptic as it intersects the Earth, and Figure 1.17 shows the full Earth orbit traced on the plane of the ecliptic.

Now consider the angle of the axis of the Earth's rotation as shown in Figure 1.16. Note that the axis is tilted at an angle of $23\frac{1}{2}°$ away from a right angle to the plane of the ecliptic. That is, the angle between the axis and the plane of the ecliptic is

> The axis of the Earth's rotation is titled by $23\frac{1}{2}°$ away from the plane of the ecliptic. This tilt causes the seasons.

1.15 Eye on the Landscape   Midnight in June, Lake Clark National Park, Alaska *Although it is midnight, the Sun is only just below the horizon, bathing the scene in soft twilight. The way the spherical Moon is lit by the Sun also shows that the Sun is located below the horizon and to the right.* **What else would the geographer see? ... Answers at the end of the chapter.**

$66^{1}/_{2}°$, not 90°. In addition, the direction toward which the axis points is fixed in space—it aims toward Polaris, the north star. The direction of the axis does not change as the Earth revolves around the Sun. Let's investigate this phenomenon in more detail.

Solstice and Equinox

Figure 1.17 diagrams the Earth as it revolves in its orbit through the four seasons. Because the direction of the Earth's axis of rotation is fixed, the

> At the June solstice, the north pole is tilted toward the Sun. At the December solstice, it is tilted away from the Sun.

north pole is tilted away from the Sun during one part of the year and is tilted toward the Sun during the other part. Consider first the event on December 22, which is pictured on the far right. On this day, the Earth is positioned so that the north polar end of its axis leans at the maximum angle away from the Sun, $23^{1}/_{2}°$. This event is called the **winter solstice** in the northern hemisphere. (While it is winter in the northern hemisphere, it is summer in the southern hemisphere, so you can use the term *December solstice* to avoid any

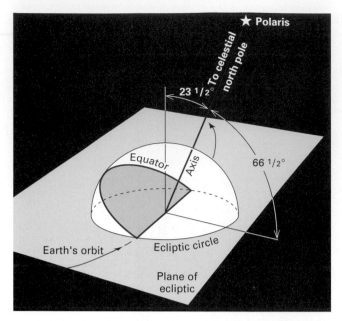

1.16 The tilt of the Earth's axis of rotation with respect to its orbital plane *As the Earth moves in its orbit on the plane of the ecliptic around the Sun, its rotational axis remains pointed toward Polaris, the north star, and makes an angle of 66¹/₂° with the ecliptic plane.*

confusion.) At this time, the southern hemisphere is tilted toward the Sun and enjoys strong solar heating.

Six months later, on June 21, the Earth is on the opposite side of its orbit in an equivalent position. At this event, known as the ***summer solstice** (June solstice)* in the northern hemisphere, the north polar end of the axis is tilted at 23¹/₂° toward the Sun. Thus, the north pole and northern hemisphere are tilted toward the Sun, while the south pole and southern hemisphere are tilted away.

Midway between the solstice dates, the equinoxes occur. At an **equinox,** the Earth's axial tilt is neither toward nor away from the Sun. The axis makes a right angle with a line drawn to the Sun, and neither the north nor south pole is tilted toward the Sun. The *vernal equinox* occurs on March 21, and the *autumnal equinox* occurs on September 23. Conditions are identical on the two equinoxes as far as Earth–Sun relationships are concerned. We should also note that the date of any solstice or equinox in a particular year may vary by a day or so, since the revolution period is not exactly 365 days. Let's look at equinoxes and solstices in more detail.

1.17 The four seasons *The four seasons occur because the Earth's tilted axis keeps a constant orientation in space as the Earth revolves about the Sun. This tips the northern hemisphere toward the Sun for the summer solstice and away from the Sun for the winter solstice. Both hemispheres are illuminated equally at the spring equinox and the fall equinox.*

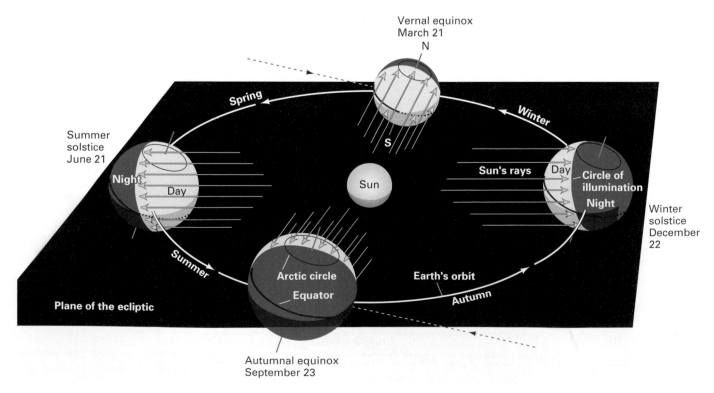

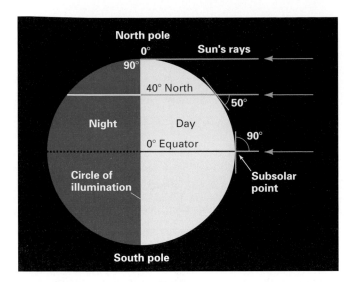

1.18 Equinox conditions *At this time, the Earth's axis of rotation is exactly at right angles to the direction of solar illumination. The subsolar point lies on the equator. At both poles, the Sun is seen at the horizon. Note that the viewpoint for this diagram is away from the plane of the ecliptic, as shown in Figure 1.17, so that both poles may be seen.*

Equinox Conditions

The conditions at an equinox, shown in Figure 1.18, form the simplest case. The figure illustrates two important concepts of global illumination that we use for describing equinoxes and solstices. The first concept is the *circle of illumination*. Note that the Earth is always divided into two hemispheres with respect to the Sun's rays. One hemisphere (day) is lit by the Sun, and the other (night) lies in the darkness of the Earth's shadow. The circle of illumination is the circle that separates the day hemisphere from the night hemisphere. The second concept is the *subsolar point,*

the single point on the Earth's surface where the Sun is directly overhead at a particular moment.

At equinox, the circle of illumination passes through the north and south poles, as we see in Figure 1.18. The Sun's rays graze the surface at either pole, and the surface there receives little or no solar energy. The subsolar point falls on the equator. Here, the angle between the Sun's rays and the Earth's surface is 90°, and the solar illumination is received in full force. At an intermediate latitude, such as 40° N, the rays of the Sun at noon strike the surface at a lesser angle. This *noon angle*—the elevation of the Sun above the horizon at noon—can be easily determined. Some simple geometry shows that the noon angle is equal to 90° minus the latitude, or 50° in this example, for equinox conditions.

Imagine yourself at a point on the Earth, say, at a latitude of 40° N. Visualize the Earth rotating from left to right, so that you turn with the globe, completing a full circuit in 24 hours. At the equinox, you spend 12 hours in darkness and 12 hours in sunlight. This is because the circle of illumination passes through the poles, dividing every parallel exactly in two. Thus, one important feature of the equinox is that day and night are of equal length everywhere on the globe.

The Sun's declination describes the latitude of the subsolar point as it ranges from 23½° S (December solstice) to 23½° N (June solstice) throughout the year.

Solstice Conditions

Now examine the solstice conditions shown in Figure 1.19. Summer solstice is on the left. Consider yourself back at a point on the lat. 40° N parallel. The circle of illumination does not divide your parallel in equal halves because of the tilt of the northern hemisphere toward the Sun. Instead, the larger part is in daylight. For you, the day is now considerably longer (about 15 hours from sunrise to sunset) than the night (about 9 hours).

The farther north you go, the more the effect increases. In fact, the entire area of the globe north of lat. 66½° is on the daylight side of the circle of illumination. This parallel is known as the

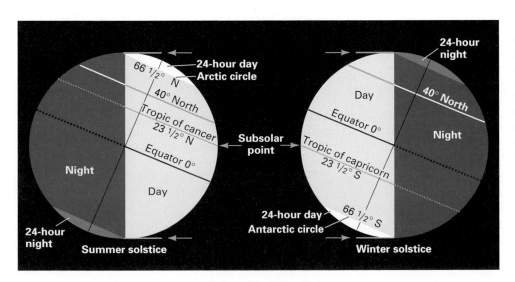

1.19 Solstice conditions *At the solstice, the north end of the Earth's axis of rotation is fully tilted either toward or away from the Sun. Because of the tilt, polar regions experience either 24-hour day or 24-hour night. The subsolar point lies on one of the tropics, at lat. 23½° N or S.*

arctic circle. Even though the Earth rotates through a full cycle during a 24-hour period, the area north of the arctic circle remains under continuous direct solar illumination. We also see that the subsolar point is at a latitude of $23\frac{1}{2}°$ N. This parallel is known as the **tropic of cancer.** Because the Sun is directly over the tropic of cancer at this solstice, solar energy is most intense here.

At the winter solstice, conditions are exactly reversed from those of the summer solstice. If you imagine yourself back at lat. 40° N, you find that the night is now about 15 hours from sunset to sunrise while daylight lasts about 9 hours. All the area south of lat. $66\frac{1}{2}°$ S lies under the Sun's rays, inundated with 24 hours of direct illumination. This parallel is known as the **antarctic circle.** The subsolar point has shifted to a point on the parallel at lat. $23\frac{1}{2}°$ S, known as the **tropic of capricorn.**

Note that we have carefully used the term *daylight* to describe the period of the day during which the sun is above the horizon. When the sun is not too far below the horizon, scattering of solar rays by atmospheric particles still lights the sky and we observe *twilight*. At high latitudes during the polar night, a twilight period of some hours length provides enough illumination for many human activities.

The solstices and equinoxes represent conditions at only four times of the year. Between these times, the latitude of the subsolar point travels northward and southward in an annual cycle between the tropics of cancer and capricorn. We refer to the latitude of the subsolar point as the Sun's *declination*. Figure 1.20 plots the Sun's declination through the year. As the year progresses, the declination varies between $23\frac{1}{2}°$ S lat. at the December solstice and $23\frac{1}{2}°$ N lat. at the June solstice.

As the seasonal cycle progresses in polar regions, areas of 24-hour daylight or 24-hour night shrink and then grow. At other latitudes, the length of daylight changes slightly from one day to the next, except at the equator. In this way, the Earth experiences the rhythm of the seasons as it continues its revolution around the Sun.

GEODISCOVERIES   Web Quiz. Take a quick quiz on the key concepts of this chapter.

A LOOK AHEAD

This chapter has focused at a planetary scale on the daily rotation of the Earth on its axis and annual revolution of the Earth around the Sun. The daily rotation provides the basis for the geographic grid — latitude and longitude — as well as for timekeeping in units of hours, minutes, and seconds. The annual revolution, coupled with the tilt of the Earth's axis at $23\frac{1}{2}°$ from the plane of the ecliptic, provides the basis for the seasons.

The daily and annual rhythms of the Earth's motion create a global pattern of energy flow from the Sun to the Earth that changes from minute to minute, day to day, and season

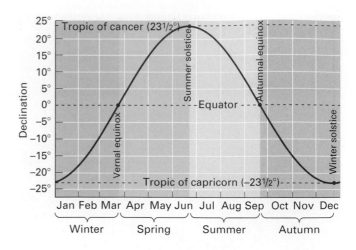

1.20 The Sun's declination through the year *The latitude of the subsolar point marks the Sun's declination, which changes slowly through the year from $-23\frac{1}{2}°$ to $+23\frac{1}{2}°$ to $-23\frac{1}{2}°$. Solstices and seasons are labeled for the northern hemisphere.*

to season. This flow powers most of the natural processes that we experience every day, from changes in the weather to the work of streams in carving the landscape. Our next chapter examines in detail solar energy and its interaction with the Earth's atmosphere and surface. The solar radiation intercepted by the Earth constitutes the biggest and most important energy flow system for us, the land dwellers of the Earth.

What have we learned about the Sun–Earth energy flow system thus far? Here are two simple, important facts we can glean from this chapter that are important for the next:

- *Half of the Earth is always receiving solar energy.* So, there is a constant flow of light and heat from Sun to Earth.
- *However, the solar energy flow is not received uniformly over the surface.* This is because of the Earth's spherical shape, its constant rotation on its axis, the tilt of its axis, and its constant revolution around the Sun.

As we will see in Chapter 2, the amount of incoming solar energy at a location depends on the length of the daylight portion of the day and on the height of the Sun's path in the sky during the daylight period. Both of these factors depend on the latitude and season of the location. So, your understanding of the Earth's rotation and revolution will come in quite handy in the chapter to come.

GEODISCOVERIES   Web Links. Visit web sites to find out more about longitude, maps, and globes. Find the time at any location in the world. Find the position of the Sun in the sky for any location, time, and date. Learn more about GPS.

In Review | The Earth as a Rotating Planet

- The **rotation** of the Earth on its axis and the revolution of the Earth in its orbit about the Sun are fundamental topics in physical geography. The Earth is nearly spherical—it is slightly flattened at the poles into the shape of an *oblate ellipsoid*. It rotates on its *axis* once in 24 hours. The intersection of the axis of rotation with the Earth's surface marks the *north* and *south poles*. The direction of rotation is counterclockwise when viewed from above the north pole.

- The Earth's rotation provides the first great rhythm of our planet—the daily alternation of sunlight and darkness. The tides, and a sideward turning of ocean and air currents, are further effects of the Earth's rotation.

- The Earth's axis of rotation provides a reference for the system of location on the Earth's surface—the **geographic grid,** which consists of **meridians** and **parallels.** This system is indexed by our system of **latitude** and **longitude,** which uses the **equator** and the *prime meridian* as references to locate any point on Earth.

- We require a **map projection** to display the Earth's curved surface on a flat map. The *polar projection* is centered on either pole and pictures the globe as we might view it from the top or bottom. The *Mercator projection* converts the curved geographic grid into a flat, rectangular grid and best displays directional features. The *Goode projection* distorts the shapes of continents and coastlines but preserves the areas of land masses in their correct proportion.

- We monitor the Earth's rotation by daily timekeeping. Each hour the Earth rotates by 15°. In the **standard time system** we keep time according to a nearby *standard meridian*. Since standard meridians are normally 15° apart, clocks around the globe usually differ by whole hours. At the *International Date Line,* the calendar day changes—advancing for westward travel, dropping back a day for eastward travel. *Daylight saving time* advances the clock by one hour.

- The seasons are the second great Earthly rhythm. They arise from the **revolution** of the Earth in its orbit around the Sun, combined with the fact that the Earth's rotational axis is tilted with respect to its orbital plane. The **solstices** and **equinoxes** mark the cycle of this revolution. At the **summer** *(June)* **solstice,** the northern hemisphere is tilted toward the Sun. At the **winter** *(December)* **solstice,** the southern hemisphere is tilted toward the Sun. At the equinoxes, day and night are of equal length.

Key Terms

rotation, p. 26	great circle, p. 28	standard time system, p. 33	equinox, p. 40
parallel, p. 28	small circle, p. 28	time zones, p. 33	arctic circle, p. 42
equator, p. 28	latitude, p. 28	revolution, p. 38	tropic of cancer, p. 42
meridian, p. 28	longitude, p. 29	winter solstice, p. 39	antarctic circle, p. 42
geographic grid, p. 28	map projection, p. 30	summer solstice, p. 40	tropic of capricorn, p. 42

Review Questions

1. What is the approximate shape of the Earth? How do you know? What is the Earth's true shape?
2. What is meant by Earth rotation? Describe three environmental effects of the Earth's rotation.
3. Describe the geographic grid, including parallels and meridians.
4. How do latitude and longitude determine position on the globe? In what units are they measured?
5. Name three types of map projections and describe each briefly. Give reasons why you might choose different map projections to display different types of geographical information.
6. Explain the global timekeeping system. Define and use the terms *standard time, standard meridian,* and *time zone* in your answer.
7. What is meant by the "tilt of the Earth's axis"? How is the tilt responsible for the seasons?

Geographer's Tools 1.2 • Geographic Information Systems

1. What is a geographic information system?
2. Identify and describe three types of spatial objects.
3. What are the key elements of a GIS?

A Closer Look:
Geographer's Tools 1.3 • Focus on Maps

1. Explain three types of map "projections" as they might occur by projecting a wire globe onto a flat sheet of paper.
2. What is the scale fraction of a map or globe? Can the scale of a flat map be uniform everywhere on the map? Do large-scale maps show large areas or small areas?
3. What types of symbols are found on maps, and what types of information do they carry?
4. How are numerical data represented on maps? Identify three types of isopleths. What is a choropleth map?

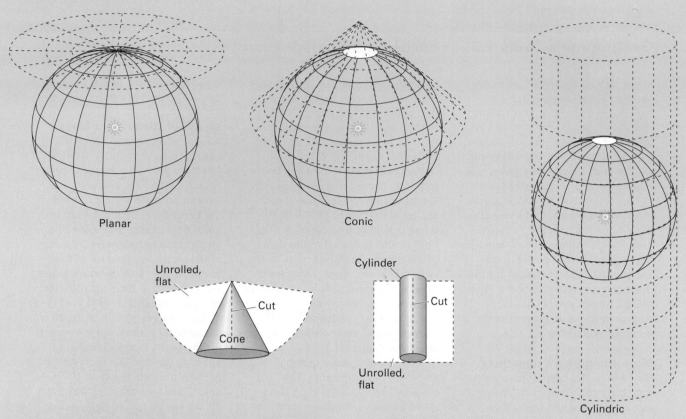

Planar   Conic

Unrolled, flat   Cut   Cylinder   Cut   Cylindric

Cone   Unrolled, flat

S1.1 Simple ways to generate map projections *Rays from a central light source cast shadows of the spherical geographic grid on target screens. The conical and cylindrical screens can be unrolled to become flat maps. (A. N. Strahler.)*

we can't say about any world map: "Everywhere on this map the scale is 1:65,000,000." It is, however, possible to select a meridian or parallel—the equator, for example—for which a scale fraction can be given, relating the map to the globe it represents. In Figure 1.9, the scale of the Mercator projection along its equator is about 1:325,000,000.

Small-Scale and Large-Scale Maps

When geographers refer to small-scale and large-scale maps, they refer to the value of the scale fraction. For example, a global map at a scale of 1:65,000,000 has a scale fraction value of 0.00000001534, which is obtained by dividing 1 by 65,000,000. A hiker's topographic map might have a scale of 1:25,000, for a scale value of 0.000040. Since the global scale value is smaller, it is a small-scale map, while the hiker's map is a large-scale map. Note that this contrasts with many persons' use of

the terms *large-scale* and *small-scale.* When we refer in conversation to a large-scale phenomenon or effect, we typically refer to something that takes place over a large area and that is usually best presented on a small-scale map.

Maps of large scale show only small sections of the Earth's surface. Because they "zoom in," they are capable of carrying the enormous amount of geographic information that is available and that must be shown in a convenient and effective manner. Most large-scale maps carry a *graphic scale,* which is a line marked off into units representing kilometers or miles. Figure S1.2 shows a portion of a large-scale map on which sample graphic scales in miles, feet, and kilometers are superimposed. Graphic scales make it easy to measure ground distances.

For practical reasons, maps are printed on sheets of paper usually less than a meter (3 ft) wide, as in the case of the ordinary highway map or navigation chart. Bound

books of maps—atlases, that is— consist of pages usually no larger than 30 by 40 cm (about 12 by 16 in.), whereas maps found in text-books and scientific journals are even smaller.

Conformal and Equal-Area Maps

Thinking more about the map projections shown in Figure S1.1, it seems obvious that the shape and area of a small feature, like an island or peninsula, will change as the feature is projected from the surface of the globe to a map. With some projections, the area will change, but the shape will be preserved. Such a projection is referred to as *conformal.* The Mercator projection (Figure 1.9) is an example. Here, every small twist and turn of the shoreline of each continent is shown in its proper shape. However, the growth of the continents with increasing latitude shows that the Mercator projection does not depict land areas uniformly. A projection that does

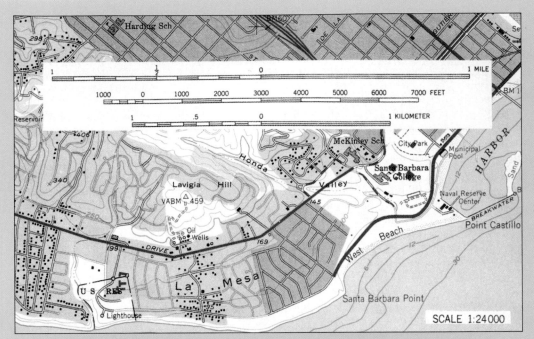

S1.2 Graphic scales on a topographic map *A portion of a modern, large-scale topographic map for which three graphic scales have been provided. (U.S. Geological Survey.)*

show area uniformly is referred to as *equal-area*. An example is the Goode projection (Figure 1.10). Here continents show their relative areas correctly, but their shapes are distorted. No projection can be both conformal and equal-area — only a globe has that property.

In general, equal-area maps are used to show surface extent. Examples are the double-page Goode projections of precipitation, climate, vegetation, and soils we use in this text (Figures 7.2, 7.6, 9.3, and 10.13). Conformal maps are often used to show true shape or direction. Our Mercator projections of global winds and pressures (Figure 5.18) are examples.

Informational Content of Maps

The information conveyed by a map projection grid system is limited to one category only: absolute location of points on the Earth's surface. To be more useful, maps also carry other types of information. Figure S1.2 is a portion of a large-scale *multipurpose map*. Map sheets published by national governments, such as this one, are usually multipurpose maps. Using a great variety of symbols, patterns, and colors, these maps carry a high information content. A larger example of a multipurpose map is reproduced on the last pages of this book. It is a portion of a U.S. Geological Survey topographic quadrangle map for San Rafael, California.

In contrast to the multipurpose map is the *thematic map*, which shows only one type of information, or *theme*. We use many thematic maps in this text. Some examples include Figure 4.23, mapping the frequency of severe hailstorms in the United States; Figure 5.17, atmospheric surface pressures; Figure 7.2, mean annual precipitation of the world; and Figure 7.6 world climates.

Map Symbols

Symbols on maps associate information with points, lines, and areas. To express points as symbols, they can be renamed "dots." Broadly defined, a dot can be any small device to show point location. It might be a closed circle, open circle, letter, numeral, or a lit- tle picture of the object it represents (see "church with tower" in Figure S1.3). A line can vary in width and can be single or double. The line can also consist of a string of dots or dashes. A specific area of surface can be referred to as a "patch." The

S1.3 Multipurpose map *A multipurpose map of an imaginary area with 10 villages illustrating the use of dots, lines, and patches. (After J. P. Cole and C.A.M. King, Quantitative Geography, copyright © John Wiley & Sons, London. Used by permission.)*

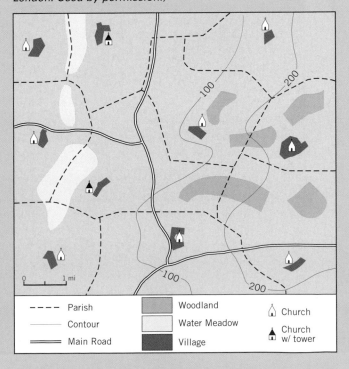

EYE ON THE LANDSCAPE

*A beach on Bora Bora,
French Polynesia, near
sunset.* What else would the
geographer see? … Answers
at the end of the chapter.

2 | THE EARTH'S GLOBAL ENERGY BALANCE

. . . .
PUTTING YOU IN THE PICTURE

The Sun is deliciously warm on your back. The sound of the surf is subdued as you lie stretched full-length on your towel. The beach here at Cancun is everything you thought it would be—soft, fine sand and clear blue water, with hazy tropical skies overhead. What a place to spend spring break!

It's not long before the Sun on your back seems a little too warm, and so you roll over, pulling the brim of your hat down over your eyes to screen out the bright sunlight. Soon you are hot all over, and the sound of the gently breaking waves seems very inviting. Shaking off a few clinging grains of sand, you head for the surf. A wave breaks over your feet, splashing cool drops of foam on your legs. A few quick steps, a shallow dive, and your skin is tingling with the shock of the Gulf waters. What a marvelous feeling!

Thoroughly refreshed, you emerge from the waves and walk back up to your place on the beach. As you towel the water from your skin, the tropical breeze takes on a cool edge. You lie down again, keeping low, and exposing your body to the direct rays of the sun overhead. Soon your skin dries, and you are warm once more.

Later, in the evening, you return to the beach. The stars are out now, and the white crescent is framed by palm trees behind you and the dark ocean in front. The gentle breakers splash phosphorescent foam up the beach, which quickly sinks into the fine sand. After a few minutes, you notice that your shoulders and arms are a bit cold. The sand, however, is still warm to your feet. You lie down, burrowing slightly into the soft surface to create a smooth support for your back and legs. Comfortable now, you relax and watch the sky overhead. Slowly, the stars grow brighter and the night behind them deepens to a velvet black. A shooting star flashes across the sky. This will be a spring break you'll always remember.

This description of a beach holiday probably seems far from the subject of this chapter—the Earth's global energy balance. But, in fact, many of the principles involved in the global radiation balance are the same as those that warm or cool your skin on a Polynesian beach. Like your skin, the Earth's surface absorbs sunlight and is warmed. At night, lacking sunlight, it loses heat and is cooled. The surface, as well as your skin, also loses heat when cooled by evaporation. And the surface can be cooled or warmed by direct contact with a cool or warm atmosphere—just as your skin can be cooled or warmed by direct contact with beach sand or ocean water.

No matter whether the surface is your skin or a layer of grass-covered soil, it is constantly emitting radiation. For example, our bodies emit radiation in the form of heat. Very hot objects, such as the Sun or the filament of a light bulb, give off radiation that is nearly all in the form of light. The surface and atmosphere of our planet constantly emit heat energy. Of course, the Earth also receives a flow of energy—radiation from the Sun, largely in the form of light. Over the long run, the Earth emits exactly as much energy as it absorbs, forming a global energy balance.

In this chapter, we examine the energy balance of the Earth, including the energy balances of land and ocean surfaces and the atmosphere. These balances control the seasonal and daily changes in the Earth's surface temperature. They also produce differences in energy flow rates from place to place that drive currents of air and ocean water. These, in turn, produce the changing weather and rich diversity of climates we experience on the Earth's surface. ■

THE EARTH'S GLOBAL ENERGY BALANCE

Lounging on an exotic tropical beach, you might be particularly aware of the Sun. Basking in its glow, you might be impressed by its ability to light your world and warm your body across millions of miles of black space. Actually, the Sun's power is even more impressive, considering that most natural phenomena that take place at the Earth's surface are directly or indirectly solar-powered. From the downhill flow of a river to the movement of a sand dune to the growth of a forest, solar radiation drives nearly all of the natural processes that shape the world around us. As we will see here and in many other chapters of this book, it is the power source for wind, waves, weather, rivers, and ocean currents. This chapter examines the flow of energy from Sun to Earth at a global scale, describing the process by which solar radiation is intercepted by our planet, flows through the Earth's atmosphere, and interacts with the Earth's land and ocean surfaces. This process produces a pattern in which different latitude belts receive different amounts of energy flow from the Sun. We will also see a pattern of energy transport from lower to higher latitudes driven by ocean currents and atmospheric circulation.

A primary topic of this chapter is the *energy balance* of the Earth. The energy balance refers to the balance between the flows of energy reaching the Earth, which includes land and ocean surfaces and the atmosphere, and flows of energy leaving it. The Earth's energy balance controls the seasonal and daily changes in the Earth's surface temperature. Differences in energy flow rates from place to place also drive currents of air and ocean water. All these, in turn, produce the changing weather and rich diversity of climates we experience on the Earth's surface.

Human activities now dominate many regions of the Earth, and we have irreversibly modified our planet by changing much of its surface cover and adding carbon dioxide to its atmosphere. Have we shifted the balance of energy flows? Is our Earth absorbing more solar energy and becoming warmer? Is it absorbing less and becoming cooler? Before we can understand human impact on the Earth–atmosphere system, we must examine the global energy balance in detail.

ELECTROMAGNETIC RADIATION

Our study of the global energy system begins with the subject of radiation—that is, **electromagnetic radiation.** This form of energy is emitted by all objects. Light and radiant heat are two familiar examples of electromagnetic radiation. Light is radiation that is visible to our eyes. Heat radiation, though not visible, is easily felt when you hold your hand near a warm object, such as an oven or electric stove burner. In this chapter, we are concerned primarily with electromagnetic energy in the forms of light and heat.

Think of electromagnetic radiation as a collection, or spectrum, of waves of a wide range of wavelengths traveling quickly away from the surface of an object. *Wavelength* describes the distance separating one wave crest from the next wave crest (Figure 2.1). The unit we will use to measure wavelength is the *micrometer* (formerly called the micron). A micrometer is one millionth of a meter, or 10^6 m. This is such a small unit that the tip of your little finger is about 15,000 micrometers wide. In this text, we use the abbreviation μm for the micrometer. The first letter is the

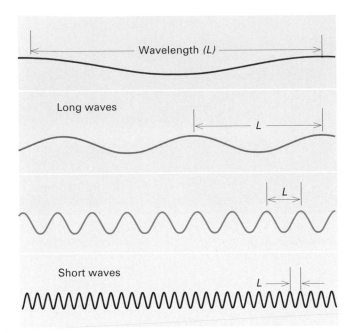

2.1 Wavelength of electromagnetic radiation
Electromagnetic radiation can be described as a collection of energy waves with different wavelengths. Wavelength L is the crest-to-crest distance between successive wave crests.

Figure 2.2 shows how electromagnetic waves differ in wavelength throughout their entire range, or *spectrum*. At the short wavelength end of the spectrum are *gamma rays* and *X rays*. Their wavelengths are normally expressed in *nanometers*. A nanometer is one one-thousandth of a micrometer, or 10^{-9} m, and is abbreviated nm. Gamma and X rays have high energies and can be hazardous to health. Gamma and X-radiation grade into *ultraviolet* radiation, which begins at about 10 nm and extends to 400 nm or 0.4 μm. Like gamma and X rays, ultraviolet radiation can be damaging to living tissues.

The **visible light** portion of the spectrum starts at about 0.4 μm with violet. Colors then grade through blue, green, yellow, orange, and red, reaching the end of the visible spectrum at about 0.7 μm. Next is *near-infrared* radiation, with wavelengths from 0.7 to 1.2 μm. This radiation is very similar to visible light in that most of it comes from the Sun. However, human eyes are not sensitive to radiation beyond about 0.7 μm, so we do not see near-infrared light. Healthy plant leaves and green tissues reflect near-infrared light strongly, a fact that is often used in remote sensing with near-infrared light.

Shortwave infrared radiation lies in the range of 1.2 to 3.0 μm. Like near-infrared light, it comes mostly from the Sun. In remote sensing, this radiation can distinguish clouds from snow. It is also useful for differentiating rock types, which may have different "colors" in this portion of the spectrum. From 3 μm to about 6 μm is *middle-infrared* radiation. It comes from the Sun as well but is also emitted by fires burning at the Earth's surface, such as forest fires or gas well flames.

Greek letter μ, or mu. It is used in metric units to denote micro-, meaning one-millionth (10^{-6}). Radiant energy can exist at any wavelength. Heat and light are identical forms of electromagnetic radiation except for their wavelengths.

Visible light includes colors ranging from violet to red and spans the wavelength range of about 0.4 to 0.7 μm.

2.2 The electromagnetic spectrum *Electromagnetic radiation can exist at any wavelength. By convention, names are assigned to specific wavelength regions as shown in the figure.*

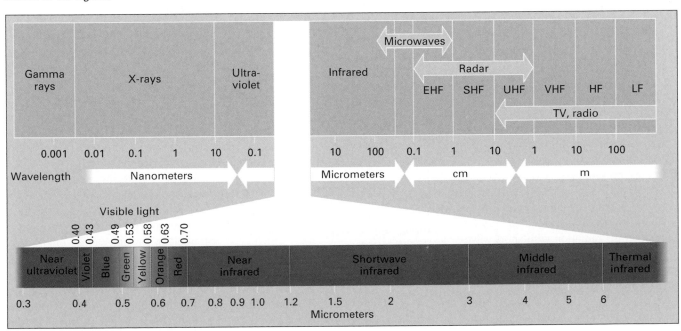

2.3 A thermal infrared image *This suburban scene was imaged at night in the thermal infrared spectral region. Black and blue tones show lower temperatures, while yellow and red tones show higher temperatures. Ground and sky are coldest, while the windows of the heated homes are warmest.*

At wavelengths between 6 and about 300 nm, we have *thermal infrared* radiation. This radiation includes the heat radiation given off by bodies at temperatures normally found at the Earth's surface. As we'll see shortly, most heat radiation lies in the range of 8 to 12 μm. Beyond infrared wavelengths lie the domains of microwaves, radar, and communications transmissions, such as radio and television.

Thermal infrared radiation is no different in principle from visible light radiation. Although photographic film is not sensitive to thermal radiation, it is possible to acquire an image of thermal radiation using a special sensor. Figure 2.3 shows a thermal infrared image of a suburban scene obtained at night. Here the image brightness is displayed using color, with red tones indicating the warmest temperatures and black tones the coldest. Windows appear red because they are warm and radiate more intensely. House walls are intermediate in temperature and appear blue. Roads and driveways are cool, as are the trees, shown in purple tones. Ground and sky are coldest (black).

GEODISCOVERIES The Electromagnetic Spectrum. Expand your vision! Go to this animation and click on parts of the electromagnetic spectrum to reveal images that can't be sensed directly with your eyes.

Radiation and Temperature

There are two important physical principles that concern the emission of electromagnetic radiation. The first is that an inverse relationship exists between wavelengths of the radiation that an object emits and the temperature of the object. For example, the Sun, a very hot object, emits radiation with short wavelengths. In contrast, the Earth, a much cooler object, emits radiation with longer wavelengths.

The second principle is that hot objects radiate more energy than cooler objects—much more. In fact, the flow of

> Hotter objects radiate energy at shorter wavelengths than cooler objects. Hotter objects also radiate substantially more energy than cooler objects.

radiant energy from the surface of an object is directly related to the absolute temperature of the surface raised to the fourth power. (Absolute temperature is temperature measured on the Kelvin scale, with zero being the absence of all heat.) Thus, if the absolute temperature of an object is doubled, the flow of radiant energy from its surface will be 16 times larger. Because of this relationship, a small increase in temperature can mean a large increase in the rate at which radiation is given off by an object or surface. For example, water at room temperature emits about one-third more energy than when it is at the freezing point.

Solar Radiation

Our Sun is a ball of constantly churning gases that are heated by continuous nuclear reactions. It is about average in size compared to other stars, and it has a surface temperature of about 6000°C (about 11,000°F). Like all objects, it emits energy in the form of electromagnetic radiation. The energy travels outward in straight lines, or rays, from the Sun at a speed of about 300,000 km (about 186,000 mi) per second. At that rate, it takes the energy about $8\frac{1}{3}$ minutes to travel the 150 million km (93 million mi) from the Sun to the Earth.

As solar radiation travels through space, none of it is lost. However, the rays spread apart as they move away from the Sun. This means that a planet farther from the Sun, like Mars, receives less radiation than one located nearer to the Sun, like Venus. The Earth intercepts only about one-half of one-billionth of the Sun's total energy output.

The Sun's interior is the source generating solar energy. Here, hydrogen is converted to helium at very high temperatures and pressures. In this process of nuclear fusion, a vast quantity of energy is generated and finds its way to the Sun's surface. Because the rate of production of energy is nearly constant, the output of solar radiation is also nearly constant. So, given the average distance of the Earth from the Sun, the amount of solar energy received on a small, fixed area of surface held at right angles to the Sun's rays is almost constant. This rate of incoming energy, known as the *solar constant,* is measured beyond the outer limits of the Earth's atmosphere, before energy has been lost in passing through the atmosphere. The solar constant has a value of about 1370 watts per square meter (W/m^2).

The *watt* (W), which describes a rate of energy flow, is a familiar measure of power. You've probably seen it applied to light bulbs or to home appliances, such as stereo amplifiers or microwave ovens. When we use the watt to measure the intensity of a flow of radiant energy, we must specify the unit of surface area that receives or emits the energy. This cross section is assigned the area of 1 square meter (1 m^2). Thus, the measure of intensity of received (or emitted) radiation is given as watts per square meter (W/m^2). Because there are no common equivalents for this energy flow rate in the English system, we will use only metric units.

The intensity of solar radiation is greatest in the visible portion of the spectrum. In this range, most of the solar radiation penetrates the Earth's atmosphere to reach the surface.

Characteristics of Solar Energy

Let's look in more detail at the Sun's output as it is received by the Earth, which is shown in Figure 2.4. Energy intensity is shown on the graph on the vertical scale. Note that it is a logarithmic scale—that is, each whole unit marks an intensity 10 times greater than the one below. Wavelength is shown on the horizontal axis, also on a logarithmic scale.

The left side of Figure 2.4 shows how the Sun's incoming electromagnetic radiation varies with wavelength. The uppermost line shows how a "perfect" Sun would supply solar energy at the top of the atmosphere. By "perfect," we mean a Sun radiating as a *blackbody,* which follows physical theory exactly. The solid line shows the actual output of the Sun as measured at the top of the atmosphere. It is quite close to the "perfect" Sun, except for ultraviolet wavelengths, where the real Sun emits less energy. Note that the Sun's output peaks in the visible part of the spectrum. Thus, our human vision

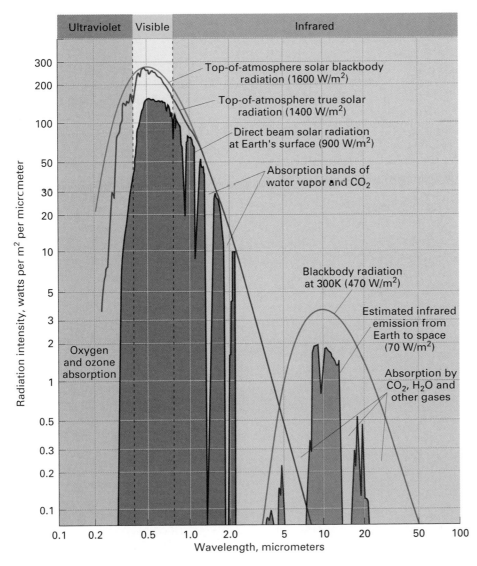

2.4 Spectra of solar and Earth radiation *This figure plots both shortwave radiation, which comes from the Sun (left side), and longwave radiation, which is emitted by the Earth's surface and atmosphere (right side). (After W. D. Sellers, Physical Climatology, University of Chicago Press. Used by permission.)*

system is adjusted to the wavelengths where solar light energy is most abundant.

The line showing solar radiation reaching the Earth's surface is quite different from the others, however. As solar radiation passes through the atmosphere, it is affected by **absorption** and scattering. Absorption occurs when molecules and particles in the atmosphere intercept and absorb radiation at particular wavelengths. This absorption is shown by the steep "valleys" in the graph—for example, at about 1.3 μm and 1.9 μm. At these wavelengths, molecules of water vapor and carbon dioxide absorb solar radiation very strongly and keep nearly all of it from reaching the Earth's surface. Note also that oxygen and ozone absorb almost all of the ultraviolet radiation at wavelengths shorter than about 0.3 μm. Atmospheric absorption is important because it warms the atmosphere directly and constitutes one of the flows of energy in the global energy balance that we will discuss toward the end of this chapter.

Solar radiation passing through the atmosphere can also be scattered. By **scattering,** we refer to a turning aside of radiation by a molecule or particle so that the direction of a scattered ray is changed. Scattered rays may go upward toward space or downward toward the surface. The line on Figure 2.4 is for direct beam energy only, so it does not include any scattered radiation that makes its way to the surface.

From the wavelengths shown on the horizontal axis, we see that solar energy received at the surface ranges from about 0.3 μm to 3 μm. This is known as **shortwave radiation.** These wavelengths are "short" as compared to the longer wavelengths of energy that are emitted by the Earth and atmosphere, which we discuss next.

Shortwave radiation refers to wavelengths emitted by the Sun, which are in the range of about 0.3 to 3 μm. Longwave radiation refers to wavelengths emitted by cooler objects, such as Earth surfaces, and ranges from about 3 to 30 μm.

---

much of the Earth's surface radiation is absorbed by the atmosphere, especially between about 6 and 8 μm and between 14 and 17 μm, where absorption is nearly complete. Above 21 μm, absorption is also essentially complete. Absorption of Earth radiation by the atmosphere is an important part of the greenhouse effect, which we will discuss shortly. Water and carbon dioxide are the primary absorbers.

The atmospheric absorption regions of the spectrum leave three regions in which outgoing energy flow is significant—4 to 6 μm, 8 to 14 μm, and 17 to 21 μm. We can call these *windows* through which longwave radiation leaves the Earth and flows to space.

An examination of Figure 2.4 shows that significant amounts of radiant energy, both shortwave by scattering and longwave by radiation, leave the Earth's surface and pass upward through the atmosphere. This energy, whose wavelength ranges from visible to thermal infrared, is therefore available for aircraft and satellite instruments to measure and compose into images of the Earth's surface through the process of remote sensing. Our interchapter feature, *A Closer Look: Geographer's Tools 2.1 ● Remote Sensing for Physical Geography,* provides some basic concepts of remote sensing that will prove useful in understanding both our *Focus on Remote Sensing* features and the uses of remotely sensed images in the main text.

The Global Radiation Balance

As we have seen, the Earth constantly absorbs solar shortwave radiation and emits longwave radiation. Figure 2.5 presents a diagram of this energy flow process, which we refer to as the Earth's **global radiation balance.**

The Sun provides a nearly constant flow of shortwave radiation toward Earth that is received at the top of the atmosphere. Part of this radiation is scattered away from the Earth and heads back into space without absorption. Clouds and dust particles in the atmosphere contribute to this scattering. Land and ocean surfaces also reflect some shortwave radiation back to space. The shortwave energy from the Sun that is not scattered or reflected is absorbed by either atmosphere, land, or ocean. Once absorbed, solar energy raises the temperature of the atmosphere as well as the surfaces of the oceans and lands.

The atmosphere, land, and ocean also emit energy in the form of longwave radiation. This radiation ultimately leaves the planet, headed for outer space. The longwave radiation outflow tends to lower the temperature of the atmosphere, ocean, and land, and thus cool the planet. In the long run, these flows balance—incoming energy absorbed and outgoing radiation emitted are equal. Since the temperature of a surface is determined by the amount of energy it absorbs and emits, the Earth's overall temperature tends to remain constant.

Longwave Radiation from the Earth

Recall that both the range of wavelengths and the intensity of radiation emitted by an object depend on the object's temperature. Since the Earth's surface and atmosphere are much colder than the Sun's surface, we can deduce that our planet radiates less energy than the Sun and that the energy emitted has longer wavelengths.

The right side of Figure 2.4, which shows outgoing radiation, confirms these deductions. The upper line shows the radiation of a blackbody at a temperature of about 300 K (23°C, 73°F), which is not a bad approximation for the Earth as a whole. At this temperature, radiation ranges from about 3 to 30 μm and peaks at about 10 μm in the thermal infrared region. We refer to the thermal infrared radiation emitted by the Earth as **longwave radiation.**

Beneath the blackbody curve is an irregular line, shaded underneath, that shows upwelling energy emitted by the Earth and atmosphere as measured at the top of the atmosphere. Comparing this line with the blackbody curve shows that

2.5 The global radiation balance *Shortwave radiation from the Sun is transmitted through space, where it is intercepted by the Earth. The absorbed radiation is then ultimately emitted as longwave radiation to outer space. (From A. N. Strahler, "The Life Layer," Journal of Geography, vol. 69, p. 72. Used by permission.)*

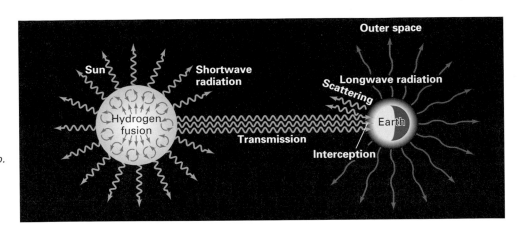

INSOLATION OVER THE GLOBE

The flow of solar radiation to the Earth as a whole remains constant, but the amount received varies from place to place and time to time. We turn now to this variation and its causes. In this discussion, we will refer to **insolation** (**in**coming **sol**ar radi**ation**)—the flow of solar energy intercepted by an exposed surface assuming a uniformly spherical Earth with no atmosphere. Insolation is a flow rate and has units of watts per square meter (W/m²). *Daily insolation* refers to the average of this flow rate over a 24-hour day. Annual insolation, discussed in a later section, is the average flow rate over the entire year. Insolation is important because it measures the amount of solar power available to heat the land surface and atmosphere.

Insolation depends on the angle of the Sun above the horizon. Figure 2.6 shows that insolation is greatest when the Sun is directly overhead and the Sun's rays are vertical (position *A*

> **Insolation refers to the flow rate of incoming solar radiation. It is high when the Sun is high in the sky.**

in the figure). When the Sun is lower in the sky, the same amount of solar energy spreads over a greater area of ground surface, so insolation is lower (position *B* in the figure).

Daily insolation at a location depends on two factors: (1) the angle at which the Sun's rays strike the Earth, and (2) the length of time of exposure to the rays. Recall from Chapter 1 that both of these factors are controlled by the latitude of the location and the time of year. For example, in midlatitude locations in summer, days are long and the Sun rises to a position high in the sky, thus heating the surface more intensely. Let's investigate these variations in more detail.

Refer back to Chapter 1 and Figure 1.18, showing equinox conditions. Only at the subsolar point does the Earth's spherical surface present itself at a right angle to the Sun's rays. To a viewer on the Earth at the subsolar point, the Sun is directly overhead. But as we move away from the subsolar point toward either pole, the Earth's curved surface becomes turned at an angle with respect to the Sun's rays. To the Earthbound viewer at a new latitude, the Sun appears to be nearer the horizon. When the circle of illumination is reached, the Sun's rays are parallel with the surface. That is, the Sun is viewed just at the horizon. Thus, the angle of the Sun in the sky at a particular location depends on the latitude of the location, the time of day, and the time of year.

GEODISCOVERIES **The Sun's Noon Angle and the Length of Day.** Imagine yourself watching the Earth from a point far out in space, where it is easy to see how both the Sun's angle at noon and the length of day vary with the seasons and latitude for any point on Earth. An animation.

2.6 Insolation and Sun angle *The angle of the Sun's rays determines the intensity of insolation on the ground. The energy of vertical rays A is concentrated in square a by c, but the same energy in the slanting rays B is spread over a larger rectangle, b by c.*

Insolation and the Path of the Sun in the Sky

How does the angle of the Sun vary during the day? The angle depends on the Sun's path in the sky. When the Sun is high above the horizon—near noon, for example—the Sun's angle is greater, and so insolation will be greater. Figure 2.7 shows the Sun's daily path in the sky at various latitudes and how this path changes from season to season.

whole. However, incoming and outgoing flows do not have to balance at any given surface location. At night, for example, there is no incoming radiation, yet the Earth's surface and atmosphere still emit outgoing radiation. In any one place and time, then, more radiant energy can be lost than gained, or vice versa.

Net radiation is the difference between all incoming radiation and all outgoing radiation. In places where radiant energy flows in faster than it flows out, net radiation is a positive quantity, providing an energy surplus. In other places, where radiant energy is flowing out faster than it is flowing in, net radiation is a negative quantity, yielding an energy deficit. Our analysis of the Earth's radiation balance has already shown that for the entire Earth and atmosphere as a unit, net radiation is zero on an annual basis.

In Figure 2.8, we saw that solar energy input varies strongly with latitude. What is the effect of this variation on net radiation? To answer this question, we will look at the net radiation profile spanning the entire latitude range from 90° N to 90° S. In this analysis we will use yearly averages for each latitude, so that the effect of seasons is concealed.

The lower part of Figure 2.16 presents a global profile of net radiation from pole to pole. Between about 40° N lat. and 40° S lat. there is a net radiant energy gain labeled "energy surplus." In other words, incoming solar radiation exceeds outgoing longwave radiation throughout the year. Poleward of 40° N and 40° S, the net radiation is negative and is labeled "energy deficit"—meaning that outgoing longwave radiation exceeds incoming shortwave radiation.

If you carefully examine the lower part of Figure 2.16, you will find that the area on the graph labeled "surplus" is equal in size to the combined areas labeled "deficit." The matching of these areas confirms the fact that net radiation for the Earth as a whole is zero and that global incoming shortwave radiation exactly balances global outgoing longwave radiation.

The pattern of energy surplus at low latitudes and energy deficit at high latitudes creates a flow of energy from low latitudes to high (upper part of Figure 2.16). This energy flow is in the form of sensible and latent heat in poleward movements of warm ocean water and warm, moist air that are part of the global circulation patterns of the ocean and the atmosphere. Heat is exchanged when oceanic and atmospheric currents move warm water and warm, moist air poleward and cooler water and cooler, drier air equatorward.

GEODISCOVERIES **Energy Balance** *Model Interactivity.* Work with a simple global energy balance model to see how solar output, albedo, and poleward atmospheric heat transport affect the Earth's surface temperature.

We'll return to these flows in later chapters, but keep in mind that this **poleward heat transfer,** driven by the imbalance in net radiation between low and high latitudes, is thus the power source for ocean currents and broad-scale atmospheric circulation patterns. Without this circulation, low latitudes would heat up and high latitudes would cool down until a radiative balance was achieved, leaving our planet with much more extreme temperature contrasts. Our Earth would be a far different place than it is now. Figure 2.17 illustrates

2.16 Annual surface net radiation from pole to pole *Where net radiation is positive, incoming solar radiation exceeds outgoing longwave radiation. There is an energy surplus, and energy moves poleward as latent heat and sensible heat. Where net radiation is negative, there is an energy deficit. Latent and sensible heat are lost in the form of outgoing longwave radiation.*

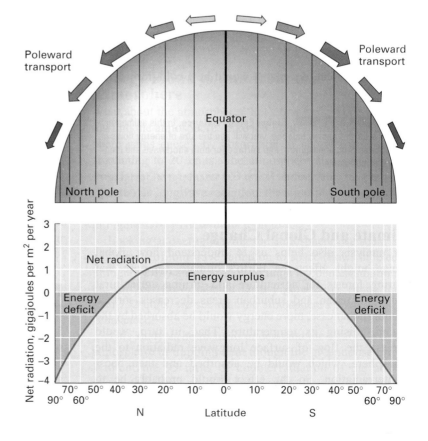

a...Solar-powered call box
This emergency telephone is powered by the solar cell atop its pole.

**b...Eye on the Landscape
Wave erosion**   Ocean waves, powered by the Sun through the Earth's wind system, have eroded the eastern bluffs of Cape Cod by hundreds of meters since the end of the Ice Age. **What else would the geographer see?...Answers at the end of the chapter.**

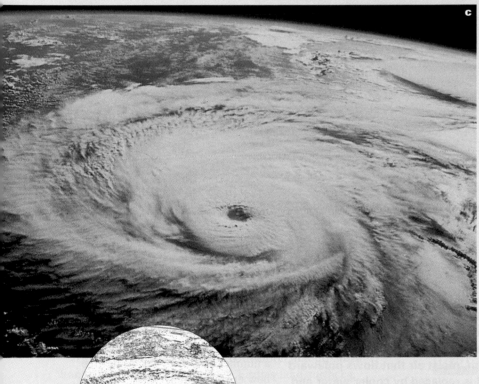

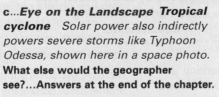

c...Eye on the Landscape Tropical cyclone   Solar power also indirectly powers severe storms like Typhoon Odessa, shown here in a space photo. **What else would the geographer see?...Answers at the end of the chapter.**

d...Water power   The hydrologic cycle, powered by solar evaporation of water over oceans, generates runoff from rainfall that erodes and deposits sediment.

71

the near-infrared—is the basis for much of vegetation remote sensing, as we will see in many examples of remotely sensed images throughout this book.

The soil spectrum shows a slow increase of reflectance across the visible and near-infrared spectral regions and a slow decrease through the shortwave infrared. Looking at the visible part of the spectrum, we see that soil is brighter overall than vegetation and is somewhat more reflective in the orange and red portions. Thus, it appears brown. (Note that this is just a "typical" spectrum—soil color can actually range from black to bright yellow or red.)

We refer to the pattern of relative brightness within spectral bands as the *spectral signature* of an object or substance. Spectral signatures can be used to recognize objects or surfaces in remotely sensed images in much the same way that we recognize objects by their colors. In computer processing of remotely sensed images, spectral signatures can be used to make classification maps, showing, for example, water, vegetation, and soil.

Aerial Photography

Aerial photography is the oldest form of remote sensing. Air photos have been in wide use since before World War II. Commonly, the field of one photograph overlaps the next along the plane's flight path, so that the photographs can be viewed stereoscopically for a three-dimensional effect. Because of its high resolution (degree of sharpness) and low cost, aerial photography is a widespread application of remote sensing.

Aerial photography often makes use of color infrared film. This special film is sensitive to near-infrared wavelengths in addition to visible wavelengths. Red color in the film is produced as a response to near-infrared light, green color is produced by red light, and blue color by green light. Because healthy, growing vegetation reflects much more strongly in the near-infrared than in the red or

green regions of the spectrum, vegetation has a characteristic red appearance. Figure S2.2 shows a color infrared photo image of an agricultural region in California. The distinctive red color identifies crop fields. The image also shows areas of abnormally high ground water and high soil salinity, both of which are agricultural problems in this region. Other examples of color infrared photos and images will be found in later chapters of this book.

Photography has been extended to greater distances through the use of cameras on orbiting space vehicles. An example is the large-format camera, which was designed to produce very large, very detailed transparencies of the Earth's surface suitable for precise topographic mapping. An excellent example, acquired in a mission aboard the Space Shuttle, is shown in Figure S2.3. Astronauts have also made a number of striking photos of the Earth from space using hand-held cameras.

Thermal Infrared Sensing

Recall from Figure 2.2 that radiation leaving the Earth's surface is concentrated in the thermal infrared spectral region, ranging from about 8 to 12 μm. The amount of radiation emitted by the surface of an object or substance is proportional to the fourth power of its absolute temperature. This means that warm objects emit more thermal radiation than cold ones, so warmer objects appear brighter in thermal infrared images. We have already noted this principle in our discussion of Figure 2.3 in the main chapter text.

Besides absolute temperature, the intensity of infrared emission depends on the *emissivity* of an object or substance. Whereas the blackbody is an ideal perfect radiator of energy, all substances are imperfect radiators and emit less energy. Emissivity is the ratio of the actual energy emitted by an object or substance to that of a blackbody at the same temperature. For most natural Earth sur-

faces, emissivity is comparatively high—between 0.85 and 0.99. Differences in emissivity affect thermal images. For example, two different surfaces might be at the same temperature, but the one with the higher emissivity will look brighter because it emits more energy.

Some substances, such as crystalline minerals, show different emissivities at different thermal infrared wavelengths. In a way, this is like having a particular color, or spectral signature, in the thermal infrared spectral region. In Chapter 11 we will see examples of how some rock types can be distinguished and mapped using thermal infrared images from several wavelengths.

Radar

There are two classes of remote sensor systems: passive and active. *Passive systems* acquire images without providing a source of wave energy. The most familiar passive system is the camera, which uses film that is sensitive to solar energy reflected from the scene. *Active systems* use a beam of wave energy as a source, sending the beam toward an object or surface. Part of the energy is reflected back to the source, where it is recorded by a detector. A simple analogy would be the use of a spotlight on a dark night to illuminate a target, which then reflects light back to the eye.

Radar is an example of an active sensing system. Radar systems in remote sensing use the *microwave* portion of the electromagnetic spectrum, so named because the waves have a short wavelength compared to other types of radio waves (Figure 2.2). (However, these wavelengths are much, much longer than those of solar shortwave radiation.) Radar systems emit short pulses of microwave radiation and then "listen" for a returning microwave echo. By analyzing the time and strength of the return pulse, an image is created showing the surface as it is illuminated by the radar beam.

S2.2 *High-altitude color infrared photograph* This color infrared photo of an area near Bakersfield, California, in the southern San Joaquin Valley, was taken by a NASA aircraft flying at approximately 18 km (60,000 ft). Photos such as this can be used to study problems associated with agriculture. Problems affecting crop yields arise in abnormally high ground water areas (A), which appear dark, and areas of high soil salinity (B), which appear light. The various red tones are associated with different types of crops. (Courtesy NASA, compiled and annotated by John E. Estes and Leslie W. Senger.)

S2.3 Color infrared photograph from low Earth orbit *A special large-format camera carried on a flight of the NASA Space Shuttle acquired this color infrared photograph. The area shown, about 125 km (77 mi) in width, includes the Sulaiman Range in western Pakistan (upper left). The Indus and Sutlej rivers, fed by snowmelt from the distant Hindu Kush and Himalaya Ranges, cross the scene flowing from northeast to southwest. A mottled pattern of green fields (red) interspersed with barren patches of saline soil (white) covers much of the lower fourth of the area. (Courtesy Geonex/Chicago Aerial Survey, Inc.)*

An advantage of radar systems is that they use wavelengths that are not significantly absorbed by liquid water. This means that radar systems can penetrate clouds to provide images of the Earth's surface in any weather. At some short wavelengths, however, microwaves are scattered by water droplets and can produce a return signal sensed by the radar apparatus. This effect is the basis for weather radars, which can detect rain and hail and are used in local weather forecasting.

Figure S2.4 shows a radar image of the folded Appalachian Mountains in south-central Pennsylvania. It is produced by an airborne radar instrument that sends pulses of radio waves downward and sideward as the airplane flies forward. Surfaces oriented most nearly at right angles to the slanting radar beam will return the strongest echo and therefore appear lightest in tone. In contrast, those surfaces facing away from the beam will appear darkest. The effect is to produce an image resembling a three-dimensional model of the landscape illuminated at a strong angle. The image shows long mountain ridges running from upper right to lower left and casting strong radar shadows to emphasize their three-dimensional form. The ridges curve and turn sharply, revealing the geologic structure of the region. Between the ridges are valleys of agricultural land, which are distinguished by their rougher texture in the image. In the upper left is a forested plateau that has a smoother appearance.

Digital Imaging

Modern remote sensing relies heavily on computer processing to extract and enhance information from remotely sensed data. This requires that the data be in the form of a *digital image* (Figure S2.5). In this format, the picture consists of a very large number of grid cells arranged in rows and columns to cover the scene. Each grid cell records a brightness value and is referred to as a *pixel*, a term that arises as a contraction of "picture element." Normally, low values code for dark (low reflectance), and high values code for light (high reflectance). To create an image that is viewable, as, for example, on a computer screen, the brightness values are fed to a special computer chip that generates a corresponding television signal fed to the monitor. Or the image is processed and sent to a computer printer to produce a hard copy print or transparency.

The great advantage of digital images over images on photographic film is that they can be processed by computer, for example, to increase contrast or sharpen edges (Figure S2.6). *Image processing* refers to the manipulation of digital images to extract, enhance, and display the information that they contain. In remote sensing, image processing is a very broad field that includes many methods and techniques for processing remotely sensed data.

S2.4 Side-looking radar image from south-central Pennsylvania *The image shows a portion of the folded Appalachians with zigzag ridges and intervening valleys. The area shown is about 40 km (25 mi) wide. Compare this with Figure 17.15, which is a Landsat image of this region. (SAR image courtesy of Intera Technologies Corporation, Calgary, Alberta, Canada.)*

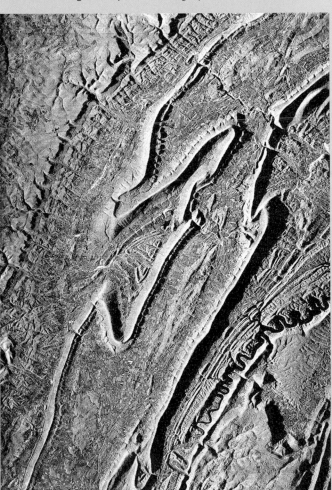

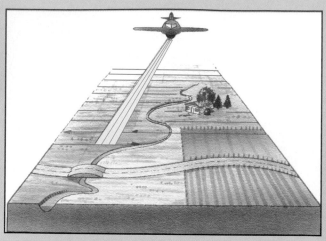

S2.7 Multispectral scanning from aircraft *As the aircraft flies forward, the scanner sweeps from side to side. The result is a digital image covering the overflight area. (A. H. Strahler.)*

S2.9 An area array of detectors *The center part of this computer chip is covered by an array of tiny light detectors arranged in rows and columns.*

Orbiting Earth Satellites

With the development of orbiting Earth satellites carrying remote sensing systems, remote sensing has expanded into a major branch of geographic research. Because orbiting satellites can image and monitor large geographic areas or even the entire Earth, global and regional studies have become possible that could not have been carried out in any other way.

How does a satellite sensor image the entire Earth? One way is to use a polar orbit. As the satellite circles the Earth, passing over each pole, the Earth rotates underneath it, allowing all of the Earth to be imaged after repeated passes. However, a polar orbit remains fixed in space with respect to the stars, not to the Sun. So as the Earth revolves around the Sun in its yearly cycle, the satellite passes overhead about four minutes later each solar day. This means that illumination conditions slowly

S2.8 Landsat image of Boston *An image of Boston, acquired by Landsat Thematic Mapper on September 27, 1991. In this false-color composite, the red color is from the shortwave infrared band (1.55 to 1.75 μm), the green from the near-infrared (0.79 to 0.91 μm), and the blue from the red band (0.60 to 0.72 μm). (A. H. Strahler.)*

(a)

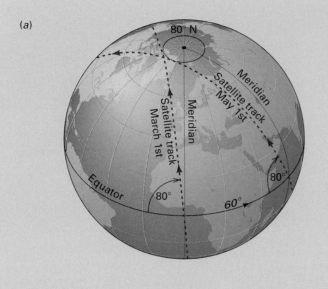

80° N

Meridian Satellite track May 1st

Satellite track March 1st

Meridian

Meridian

Equator

80°

80°

80°

60°

(b)

Equator

Satellite

S2.10 Satellite orbits *(a) Earth track of a Sun-synchronous orbit. With the Earth track inclined at 80° to the equator, the orbit slowly swings eastward at about 30° longitude per month, maintaining its relative position with respect to the Sun. Between March 1 and May 1 (shown) the orbit moves about 60°. (© A. N. Strahler.) (b) Motion of a geostationary satellite. Because the satellite revolves around the Earth above the equator at the same rate as the Earth's rotation, it appears fixed in the sky above a single point on the equator.*

change from day to day and quite a lot from month to month or season to season.

A solution to this problem is to use a *Sun-synchronous orbit* (Figure S2.10a). This type of near-polar orbit is oriented at a small angle to the polar axis and so crosses the equator at an angle less than 90 degrees. Recall from Chapter 1 that the Earth is not a perfect sphere but is slightly thicker at the equator than at the poles. Thus, the Earth's gravity is slightly greater at the equator. When the orbit crosses the equator at an angle, the difference in gravity acts to push the orbit very slightly eastward. This keeps the satellite orbit in time with the Sun instead of the stars, so that satellite overpasses continue to occur at the same time of day. Typical Sun-synchronous orbits take 90 to 100 minutes to cir-

cle the Earth and are located at heights of about 700 to 800 km (430 to 500 mi) above the Earth's surface.

Another orbit used in remote sensing is the *geostationary orbit* (Figure S2.10b). Instead of orbiting around the poles, a satellite in geostationary orbit constantly revolves above the equator. The orbit height, about 35,800 km (22,200 mi), is set so that the satellite makes one revolution in exactly 24 hours in the same direction that the Earth turns. Thus, the satellite always remains above the same point on the equator. From its high vantage point, the geostationary orbiter provides a view of nearly half of the Earth at any moment.

Geostationary orbits are ideal for observing weather, and the weather satellite images readily available on television and the

Internet are obtained from geostationary remote sensors. Geostationary orbits are also ideal for communications satellites. Since a geostationary orbiter remains at a fixed position in the sky for an Earthbound observer, a high-gain antenna can be pointed at the satellite and fixed in place permanently, providing high-quality, continuous communications.

Remote sensing is an exciting, expanding field within physical geography and the geosciences in general. This special supplement has provided some basic information about remote sensing that will come in handy as you read our special boxed features, *Focus on Remote Sensing*, and as you view the various examples of remotely sensed images throughout the text.

3 | AIR TEMPERATURE

. . . .
PUTTING YOU IN THE PICTURE

The stars are bright and clear tonight. From your vantage point here in the grassy meadow, it's easy to trace the outline of the Big Dipper, with the North Star high above its rim. In fact, you can even see the white blur of the Milky Way, arching across the sky and disappearing behind the peaks of the tall firs that surround the meadow. Brrr! It's getting chilly now. With regret, you decide to abandon your stargazing and return to the campsite, just a few minutes away in the midst of the conifer forest.

Entering the forest, you feel the chill leaving your body as the sheltering conifers shield you from the cold night sky. As you approach the camp, the fire is burning brightly. You step close to it, enjoying its warm glow. A friend offers you a mug of hot cocoa. "I'll bet we'll have frost in the meadow tonight," you think as you sip from the steaming cup. Sure enough, the next morning the grass in the meadow sparkles with white crystals that slowly turn to glistening beads as they absorb the Sun's first rays.

A few hours later in the day, you are well along on your journey to the mountain summit. Here, the trail is steep and you are sweating. Although it was cool in the forest below,

the low shrubs and scattered grasses nested in the cracks and crevices of the rocky, high terrain don't relieve the force of the Sun high overhead in the sky. A sudden breeze brings a pleasant cooling to your head and shoulders, as the moisture accumulating under your hat and shirt evaporates. You scramble over a low ledge, and the stark granite rocks are warm to your touch. Straightening up, you see the summit ahead, shimmering in the rising currents of hot air.

It is not long before you reach the summit, and the view is absolutely spectacular. In the thin, clear air, the surrounding peaks stand majestically against the deep blue sky, some with patches of white snow glistening in the intense sunlight. Below the peaks, the gray-brown tones of the barren summit slopes grade into the deep green mantle of conifer forests that line the valleys and lower slopes. It's been a long, hard climb, especially the last part up the crusted surface of the snowfield. The view, however, is worth every moment of exertion. You wouldn't have missed it for anything!

The subject of this chapter is air temperature, primarily the air temperature we experience every day within a few feet from the ground surface. What influences air temperature? Three factors are important. The first and most important one is the cyclic nature of solar radiation, produced by the two constant motions of the Earth—its daily rotation on its axis and its annual revolution in its solar orbit. These cycles produce cycles of air temperature that follow daily and annual rhythms.

The second is the nature of the ground surface. In our example above, the forest is a thick layer covering the surface that acts to insulate the ground from temperature changes. Thus, the grassy meadow loses heat more rapidly at night than does the forest, and frost forms first on the meadow grass.

The third is location on the continent. Locations near the ocean experience a narrower range of temperatures than locations in continental interiors. The reason is that water heats and cools more slowly than soil, so air temperatures near water bodies tend to change more slowly as well. Understanding air temperatures will be easy if you keep these three factors in mind. ■

AIR TEMPERATURE

This chapter focuses on **air temperature**—that is, the temperature of the air as observed at 1.2 m (4 ft) above the ground surface. Air temperature conditions many aspects of human life, from the clothing we wear to the fuel costs we pay. Air temperature and air temperature cycles also act to select the plants and animals that make up the biological landscape of a region. Even geological weathering and soil-forming processes are dependent on temperature over the long term. And air temperature, along with precipitation, is a key determiner of climate, which we will explore in more depth in Chapter 7.

Is air temperature changing? You may have heard that the Earth is becoming increasingly warmer and that, as a result, sea level is rising, climate boundaries are shifting, and severe weather is becoming more frequent. Global warming and its effects are a complicated story that we have already touched upon at several points and will return to again in future chapters. Toward the end of this chapter, we will examine the effect of increasing CO_2 and other gases on global warming and place the present record warmth in the perspective of the Earth's natural time cycles. But first you will need to understand how and why air temperature changes from day to day, month to month, and year to year.

What factors influence air temperatures? Five factors are important.

1. Insolation. The two motions of the Earth—its daily rotation on its axis and its annual revolution in its solar orbit—create the daily and annual cycles of insolation that we described in Chapter 2. In turn, these cycles produce the cycles of air temperature that distinguish day and night, winter and summer.

2. Latitude. As we noted in Chapter 2, daily and annual cycles of insolation vary systematically with latitude, causing air temperatures and air temperature cycles to vary as well. As shown in Figure 2.10, yearly insolation decreases toward the poles, so less energy is available to heat the air. Thus, temperatures generally fall as we move poleward. Temperatures also become more variable over the year as latitude increases. Recall from Figure 2.8 that as much, or more, solar energy may be received in a summer day at high latitudes than is received at the equator, while little or no solar energy is received at high latitudes during the winter. Because of this annual variation, high latitudes experience a much greater range in air temperatures through the year.

3. Surface type. Urban surfaces of asphalt, roofing shingles, and rubber are dry compared to the moist soil surfaces of rural areas and forests. They heat more rapidly because solar energy cannot be taken up in evaporation of water. They also absorb a greater portion of the Sun's energy than vegetation-covered surfaces. Because of these factors, urban air temperatures are generally higher than rural temperatures. The same is true for areas of barren or rocky soil surfaces, such as those of deserts.

Five key factors influence a station's air temperature, its daily variation, and its annual variation: insolation, latitude, surface type, coastal vs. interior location, and elevation.

4. Coastal vs. interior location. Locations near the ocean experience a narrower range of air temperatures than locations in continental interiors. The reason is that water heats and cools more slowly than land, so air temperatures over water bodies tend to be less extreme than temperatures over the land surface. And since winds can easily cause air to flow from water to land, a coastal location will more often feel the influence of the adjacent water.

5. Elevation. At high elevation, there is less atmosphere above the surface. This means that the greenhouse effect provides a less effective insulating blanket. Average temperatures are cooler because more surface heat is lost to space. This allows snow to accumulate and remain longer on high peaks, for example. The reduced greenhouse effect also results in greater daily temperature variation.

These five factors act at different scales. Insolation and latitude vary at the global scale, while location and elevation affect temperature at the continental or regional scale. Surface type affects both broad regions, like rainforests and deserts, and local areas, such as cities and their surroundings. In following sections we will explore how heating and cooling processes work to create patterns of temperature at these different scales.

SURFACE TEMPERATURE

Temperature is a familiar concept. It is a measure of the level of sensible heat of matter, whether it is gaseous (air), liquid (water), or solid (rock or dry soil). We know from experience that when a substance receives a flow of radiant energy, such as sunlight, its temperature rises. Similarly, if a substance loses energy, its temperature falls. This energy flow moves in and out of the substance at its **surface**—for example, the very thin surface layer of soil that actually absorbs solar shortwave radiation and radiates longwave radiation out to space.

The temperature of a surface is determined by the balance among the various energy flows that move across it. As we saw in Chapter 2, **net radiation**—the balance between incoming shortwave radiation and outgoing longwave radiation—produces a radiant energy flow that can heat or cool a surface. Recall that during the day, incoming solar radiation normally exceeds outgoing longwave radiation, so the net radiation balance is positive and the surface warms. Energy flows through the surface into the cooler soil below. At night, net radiation is negative, and the soil loses energy as the surface temperature falls and the surface radiates longwave energy to space.

Energy may also move to or from a surface in other ways. **Conduction** describes the flow of sensible heat from a warmer substance to a colder one through direct contact. When heat flows into the soil from its warm surface during the day, it flows by conduction. At night, heat is conducted back to the colder soil surface. **Latent heat transfer** is also important. When

water evaporates at a surface, it removes the heat stored in the change of state from liquid to vapor, thus cooling the surface. When water condenses at a surface, latent heat is released, warming the surface. Another form of energy transfer is **convection,** in which heat is distributed in a fluid by mixing. If the surface is in contact with a fluid, such as a soil surface with air above, upward and downward flowing currents can act to warm or cool the surface. (We'll return to convection in more detail in Chapters 4 and 5.)

AIR TEMPERATURE

Thus far, we've discussed the temperature of surfaces. However, in this chapter we are concerned with air temperature, which is measured a short distance above the ground surface. As we will see shortly, air temperature can be different from surface temperature. Walking across a parking lot in sandals on a clear summer day, you will certainly notice that the pavement is quite a lot hotter than the air you feel on the upper part of your body. But because conduction and convection transfer sensible heat to and from the surface to the air, air temperatures will tend to follow surface temperatures. So we can safely conclude that the temperature changes and trends experienced at the ground surface will be reflected in the air temperatures that are observed and recorded a short distance above the surface.

Measurement of Air Temperature

Air temperature is a piece of weather information that we encounter daily. In the United States, temperature is still widely measured and reported using the Fahrenheit scale. The freezing point of water on the Fahrenheit scale is 32°F, and the boiling point is 212°F. This represents a range of 180°F. In this book, we use the Celsius temperature scale, which is the international standard. On the Celsius scale, the freezing point of water is 0°C and the boiling point is 100°C. Thus, 100 Celsius degrees are the equivalent of 180 Fahrenheit degrees (1°C = 1.8°F; 1°F = 0.56°C). Conversion formulas between these two scales are given in Figure 3.1.

You are probably familiar with the *thermometer* as an instrument for measuring temperature. In this device, a liquid inside a glass tube expands and contracts with temperature, and the position of the liquid surface indicates the temperature. Since air temperature can vary with height, it is measured at a standard level—1.2 m (4 ft) above the ground. A *thermometer shelter* (Figure 3.2a) is a louvered box that holds thermometers or other weather instruments at proper height while sheltering them from the direct rays of the Sun. Air circulates freely through the louvers, ensuring that temperatures inside the shelter are the same as the outside air.

Surface air temperature is measured under standard conditions at 1.2 m (4 ft) above the ground. Maximum and minimum temperatures are typically recorded. The mean daily temperature is taken as the average of the minimum and maximum temperatures.

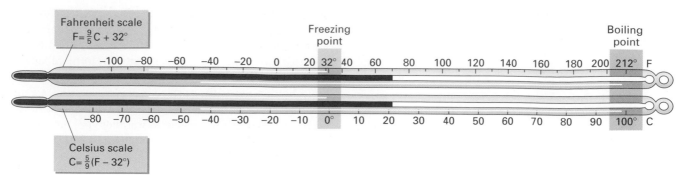

3.1 Celsius and Fahrenheit temperature scales compared *At sea level, the freezing point of water is at Celsius temperature (C) 0°, while it is 32° on the Fahrenheit (F) scale. Boiling occurs at 100°C, or 212°F.*

Liquid-filled thermometers are being replaced by newer instruments for the routine measuring of temperatures. Perhaps you have used a digital fever thermometer, which reads out your body temperature directly as a number on a display. It uses a device called a *thermistor,* which changes its electrical resistance with temperature. By measuring this resistance, the temperature may be obtained electronically. Many weather stations are now equipped with temperature measurement systems that use thermistors (Figure 3.2*b*).

Although some weather stations report temperatures hourly, most stations only report the highest and lowest temperatures recorded during a 24-hour period. These are the most important values in observing long-term trends in temperature.

Temperature measurements are reported to governmental agencies charged with weather forecasting, such as the U.S. Weather Service or the Meteorological Service of Canada. These agencies typically make available daily, monthly, and yearly temperature statistics for each station using the daily maximum, minimum, and mean temperature. Note that the mean daily temperature is defined as the average of the maximum and minimum daily values. These statistics, along with others such as daily precipitation, are used to describe the climate of the station and its surrounding area.

GEODISCOVERIES **Weather Stations Interactivity.** Check out a modern automatic weather station. See how it measures air and ground temperatures.

3.2 Weather recording instruments *la) An instrument shelter housing a pair of thermometers. The shelter is constructed with louvered sides for ventilation and painted white to reflect solar radiation. (b) A thermister-based maximum-minimum recording system (left) and a recording rain gauge (right).*

(a)   *(b)*

THE DAILY CYCLE OF AIR TEMPERATURE

Because the Earth rotates on its axis, incoming solar energy at a location can vary widely throughout the 24-hour period, while outgoing longwave energy remains more constant. During the day, net radiation is positive, and the surface gains heat. At night, net radiation is negative, and the surface loses heat by radiating it to the sky and space. Since the air next to the surface is warmed or cooled as well, air temperatures follow the same cycle. This results in the daily cycle of rising and falling air temperatures.

3.3 Daily cycles of insolation, net radiation, and air temperature *These three graphs show idealized daily cycles for a midlatitude station at a continental interior location. Insolation (a) is a strong determiner of net radiation (b). Air temperatures (c) respond by generally increasing, while net radiation is positive and decreasing when it is negative.*

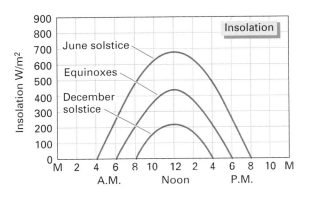

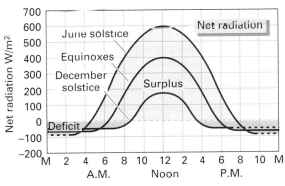

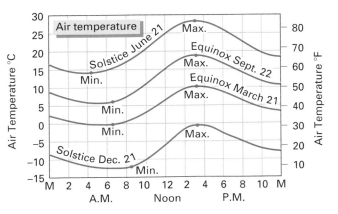

Daily Insolation and Net Radiation

Let's look in more detail at how insolation, net radiation, and air temperature are linked in this daily cycle. The three graphs in Figure 3.3 show average curves of daily insolation, net radiation, and air temperature that we might expect for a typical observing station at lat. 40° to 45° N in the interior of North America. The time scale is set so that 12:00 noon occurs when the Sun is at its highest elevation in the sky.

Graph *(a)* shows daily insolation. At the equinox (middle curve), insolation begins at about sunrise (6 A.M.), rises to a peak value at noon, and declines to zero at sunset (6 P.M.). At the June solstice, insolation begins about two hours earlier (4 A.M.) and ends about two hours later (8 P.M.). The June peak is much greater than at equinox, and the total insolation for the day is also much greater. At the December solstice, insolation begins about two hours later than the equinox curve (8 A.M.) and ends about two hours earlier (4 P.M.). Both the peak intensity and daily total insolation are greatly reduced in the winter solstice season.

Graph *(b)* shows net radiation for the surface. Recall that when net radiation is positive, the surface gains heat, and when negative, it loses heat. The curves for the solstices and equinox generally resemble those of insolation. Net radiation begins the 24-hour day at midnight as a negative value—a deficit. The deficit continues into the early morning hours. Net radiation shows a positive value—a surplus—shortly after sunrise and rises sharply to a peak at noon. In the afternoon, net radiation decreases as insolation decreases. A value of zero is reached shortly before sunset. With no incoming insolation, net radiation then becomes negative, showing a deficit, where it remains until morning.

Although the three net radiation curves show the same general daily pattern—negative to positive to negative—they differ greatly in magnitude. For the June solstice, the positive values are quite large, and the surplus period is much larger than the deficit period. This means that for the day as a whole, net radiation is positive. At the December solstice, the surplus period is short and the surplus is small. The total deficit, which extends nearly 18 hours, outweighs the surplus. This means that the net radiation for the entire day is negative. As we will see, this pattern of positive daily net radiation in the summer and negative daily net radiation in the winter drives the annual cycle of temperatures.

Daily Temperature

Graph *(c)* shows the typical, or average, air temperature cycle for a 24-hour day. The minimum daily temperature usually occurs about a half hour after sunrise. Since net radiation has been negative during the night, heat has flowed from the ground surface, and the ground has cooled the surface becomes positive, the surface warms quickly and transfers heat to the air above. Air temperature rises sharply in the morning hours and continues to rise long after the noon peak of net radiation.

We should expect the air temperature to rise as long as net radiation is positive. However, another process begins in

The second factor is that of coastal-interior contrasts. As we've noted, coastal stations that receive marine air from prevailing winds have more uniform temperatures—cooler in summer and warmer in winter. Interior stations, on the other hand, show a much larger annual variation in temperature. Ocean currents, discussed further in Chapter 5, can also have an effect. By keeping coastal waters somewhat warmer or cooler than expected, temperatures at maritime stations will be influenced in a similar manner.

Elevation is the third important factor. At higher elevations, temperatures will be cooler. Therefore, we expect world temperature maps to show the presence of mountain ranges, which will be cooler than surrounding regions.

World Air Temperature Patterns for January and July

With these factors in mind, let's look at some world temperature maps in more detail. Figure 3.20 consists of maps of world temperatures for two months—January and July. The Mercator projections show temperature trends from the equator to the midlatitude zones, and the polar projections give the best picture for high latitudes. From the maps, we can make six important points about the temperature patterns and the factors that produce them. Be sure to follow along by examining the maps carefully.

1. Temperatures decrease from the equator to the poles. Annual insolation decreases from the equator to the poles, thus causing temperatures to decrease. This temperature gradient is most clearly seen in the polar maps for the southern hemisphere in January and July. On these maps, the isotherms are nearly circular, decreasing to a center of low temperature on Antarctica near the south pole. The center is much colder in July, when most of the polar region is in perpetual night. We can also see this same general trend in the north polar maps, but the continents complicate the pattern. The general temperature gradient from the equator poleward is also evident on the Mercator maps.

2. Large land masses located in the subarctic and arctic zones develop centers of extremely low temperatures in winter. The two large land masses we have in mind are North America and Eurasia. The January north polar map shows these low-temperature centers very well. The cold center in Siberia, reaching $-50°C$ ($-58°F$), is strong and well defined. The cold center over northern Canada is also quite cold ($-35°C$, $-32°F$) but is not as well defined. Both features are visible on the January Mercator map. Greenland shows a low-temperature center as well, but it has a high dome of glacial ice, as discussed below in point 6. An important factor in keeping winter temperatures low in these regions is the high albedo of snow cover, which reflects much of the winter insolation back to space.

3. Temperatures in equatorial regions change little from January to July. Note the broad space between $25°C$ ($77°F$) isotherms on both January and July Mercator maps. In this region, the temperature is greater than $25°C$ ($77°F$) but less than $30°C$ ($86°F$). Although the two isotherms

move a bit from winter to summer, the equator always falls between them. This demonstrates the uniformity of equatorial temperatures. (An exception is the northern end of the Andes Mountains in South America, where high elevations, and thus cooler temperatures, exist at the equator.) Equatorial temperatures are uniform primarily because insolation at the equator does not change greatly with the seasons.

4. Isotherms make a large north-south shift from January to July over continents in the midlatitude and subarctic zones. Figure 3.21 demonstrates this principle. In the winter, isotherms dip equatorward, while in the summer, they arch poleward. This effect is shown in North America and Eurasia in the January and July Mercator maps. In January the isotherms drop down over these continents, and in June they curve upward. For example, the $15°C$ ($59°F$) isotherm lies over central Florida in January. But by July this same isotherm has moved far north, cutting the southern shore of Hudson Bay and then looping far up into northwestern Canada. In contrast are the isotherms over oceans, which shift much less. This striking difference is due to the contrast between oceanic and continental surface properties, which cause continents to heat and cool more rapidly than oceans.

5. Highlands are always colder than surrounding lowlands. You can see this by looking at the pattern of isotherms around the Rocky Mountain chain, in western North America, on the Mercator maps. In winter, the $-5°C$ ($23°F$) and $-10°C$ ($14°F$) isotherms dip down around the mountains, indicating that the center of the range is colder. In summer, the $20°C$ ($68°F$) and $25°C$ ($77°F$) isotherms also dip down, showing the same effect even though temperatures are much warmer. The Andes Mountains in South America show the effect even more strongly. The principle at work here is that temperatures decrease with an increase in elevation.

6. Areas of perpetual ice and snow are always intensely cold. Greenland and Antarctica contain our planet's two great ice sheets. Notice how they stand out on the polar maps as cold centers in both January and July. They are cold for two reasons. First, their surfaces are high in elevation, rising to over 3000 m (about 10,000 ft) in their centers. Second, the white snow surfaces have a high albedo, reflecting much of the incoming insolation. Since little solar energy is absorbed, little is available to warm the snow surface and the air above it. The Arctic Ocean, bearing a cover of floating ice, also maintains its cold temperatures throughout the year. However, the cold is much less intense in January than on the Greenland Ice Sheet, since ocean water underneath the ice acts as a heat reservoir to keep the ice above from getting extremely cold.

The Annual Range of Air Temperatures

Figure 3.22 is a world Mercator map showing the annual range of air temperatures. The lines, resembling isotherms, show the difference between the January and July monthly means. We can explain the features of this map by using

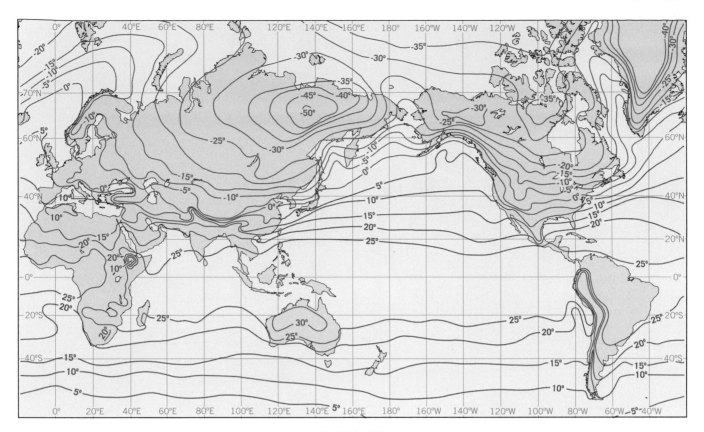

JANUARY

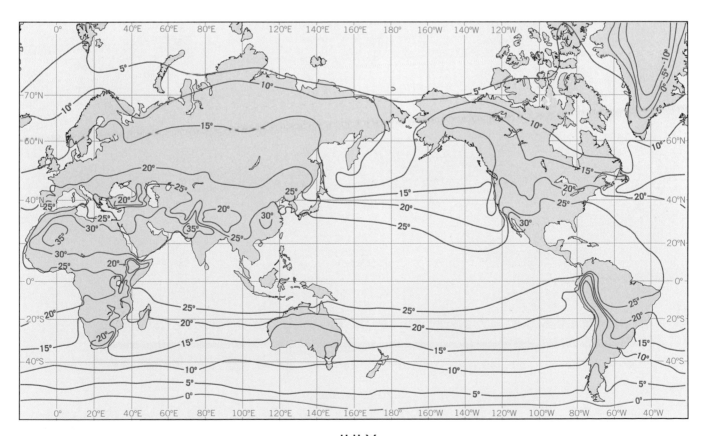

JULY

3.20 Mean monthly air temperatures (°C) for January and July, Mercator and polar
projections (Compiled by John E. Oliver.)

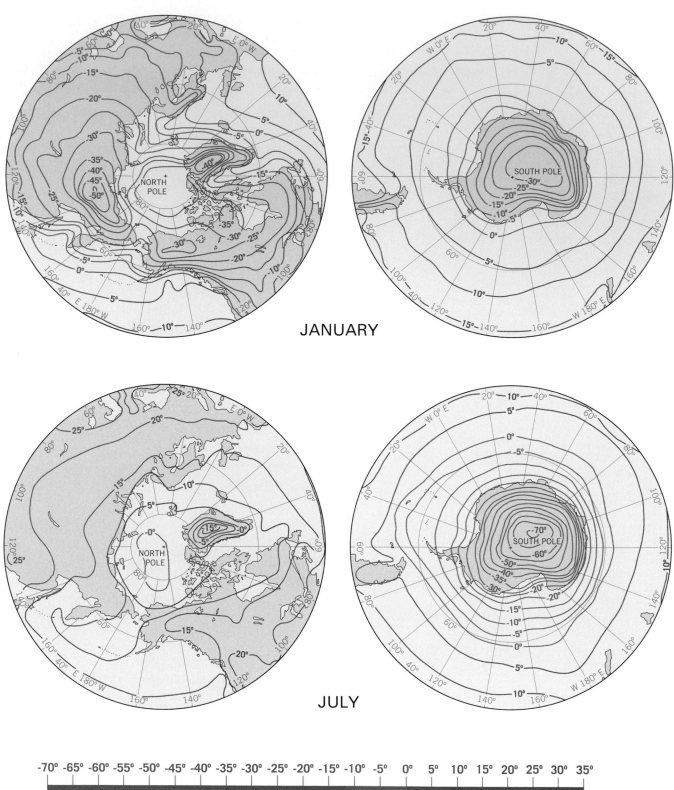

JANUARY

JULY

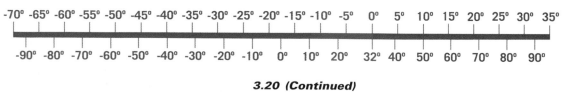

3.20 (Continued)

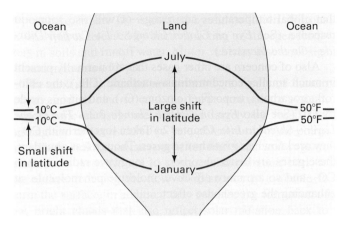

3.21 Seasonal migration of isotherms *Continental air temperature isotherms shift over a much wider latitude range from summer to winter than do oceanic air temperature isotherms. This difference occurs because oceans heat and cool much more slowly than continents.*

the same effects of latitude, interior-maritime location, and elevation.

1. The annual range increases with latitude, especially over northern hemisphere continents. This trend is most clearly shown for North America and Asia. This is due to the contrast between summer and winter insolation, which increases with latitude.

2. The greatest ranges occur in the subarctic and arctic zones of Asia and North America. The map shows two very strong centers of large annual range—one in northeast Siberia and the other in northwest Canada–eastern Alaska. In these regions, summer insolation is nearly the same as at the equator, while winter insolation is very low.

3. The annual range is moderately large on land areas in the tropical zone, near the tropics of cancer and capricorn. These are regions of large deserts—North Africa (Sahara), southern Africa (Kalahari), and Australia (interior desert) are examples. Dry air and the absence of clouds and moisture allow these continental locations to cool strongly in winter and warm strongly in summer, even though insolation contrasts with the season are not as great as at higher latitudes.

4. The annual range over oceans is less than that over land at the same latitude. This can be seen by following a parallel of latitude—40° N, for example. Starting from the right, we see that the range is between 5 and 10°C (9 and 18°F) over the Atlantic but increases to about 30°C (54°F) in the interior of North America. In the Pacific, the range falls to 5°C (9°F) just off the California coast and

> The global pattern of annual temperature range shows that tropical oceans have the smallest range, while northern hemisphere continental interiors show the largest range.

3.22 Annual range of air temperature in Celsius degrees *Data show differences between January and July means. The inset box shows the conversion of Celsius degrees to Fahrenheit for each isotherm value (Compiled by John E. Oliver.)*

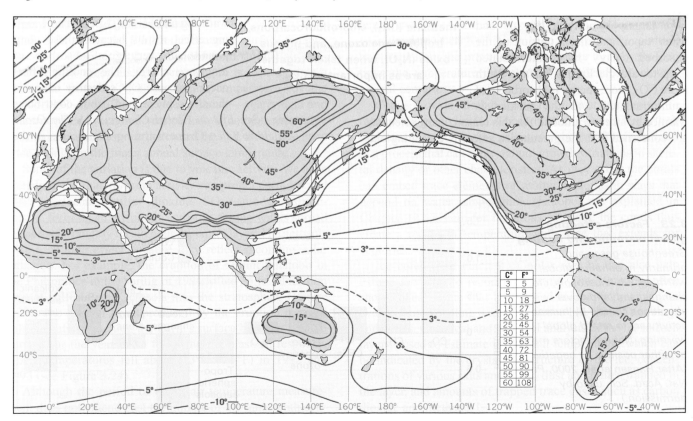

3.25 Eruption of Mount Pinatubo, Philippine Islands, April 1991 *Volcanic eruptions like this can inject particles and gases into the stratosphere, influencing climate for several years afterwards.*

the European Union, the United States, and Japan agreed to reduce average emissions during 2008 and 2012 to levels that were 6, 7, and 8 percent lower, respectively, than 1990 levels. Achieving such reductions could have economic consequences ranging from minor to severe, depending on the analysis.

Meeting again in Buenos Aires in 1998, the participating nations set timetables for the implementation of plans for greenhouse gas reduction in 1999–2000. Important breakthroughs occurred when the conference adopted a plan to allow countries to trade emission rights, as well as a "clean development" mechanism that would permit industrial

3.26 Temperature variation over the last thousand years *Compared to the reference temperature of the 1961–1990 average, northern hemisphere temperatures trended slightly downward until the beginning of the twentieth century. The line shown is a 40-year moving average obtained from thermometers, historical data, tree rings, corals, and ice cores. Annual data are shown after 1965. (IPCC, 2001. Used by permission.)*

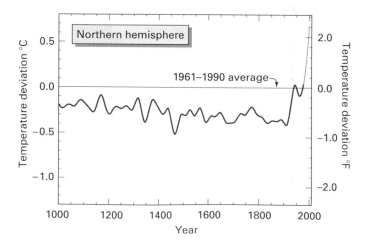

nations to invest in emissions-reducing enterprises in developing countries. For the first time, some developing countries pledged specific greenhouse gas reductions of their own.

The international effort to reduce releases of greenhouse gases suffered a setback in the spring of 2001, when President George W. Bush rejected American participation in the Kyoto Protocol. However, American resistance was not sufficient to keep 178 nations from pledging to join in the effort to reduce greenhouse gas emissions.

Although these efforts will slow the buildup of greenhouse gases, the ultimate solution will certainly involve greater reliance on solar, wind, and geothermal energy sources, which produce power without releasing CO_2. Energy conservation and development of new methods of utilizing fossil fuels that produce reduced CO_2 emissions will also be important.

GEODISCOVERIES **Web Quiz.** Take a quick quiz on the key concepts of this chapter.

A LOOK AHEAD In this chapter we have developed an understanding of both air temperatures and temperature cycles, along with the factors that influence them—insolation, latitude, surface type, continental-maritime location, and elevation. Air temperatures are a very important part of climate, and looking ahead, we will study the climates of the Earth in Chapter 7.

The other key ingredient of climate is precipitation–the subject covered in the next chapter. Here temperature plays a very important role, since moist air must cool before condensation forms water droplets and, eventually, precipitation.

GEODISCOVERIES **Web Links.** Visit a NASA site to see today's continental and global temperature maps. Check out global change sites to explore global warming and past climates. See how ice cores and tree rings are used to reconstruct climate. Explore the urban heat island effect.

In Review | Air Temperature

- **Air temperature**—measured at 1.2 m (4 ft) above the surface—is influenced by insolation, latitude, surface type, location, and elevation. The energy balance of the ground surface is determined by **net radiation, conduction** to the soil, and **latent heat transfer** and **convection** to and from the atmosphere.

- Air temperature is measured using a *thermometer* or *thermistor.* Stations make daily minimum, maximum, and mean temperature measurements.

- The two major cycles of air temperature—daily and annual—are controlled by the cycles of insolation produced by the rotation and revolution of the Earth. These cycles induce cycles of net radiation at the surface. When net radiation in the daily cycle is positive, air temperatures increase; when negative, air temperatures decrease. This principle applies to both daily and annual temperature cycles.

- Temperatures of air and soil at or very close to the ground surface are more variable than air temperature as measured at standard height.

- Surface characteristics also affect temperatures. Rural surfaces are generally moist and slow to heat and cool, while urban surfaces are dry and absorb and give up heat readily. This difference creates an urban heat island effect.

- Air temperatures normally fall with altitude in the **troposphere.** The average value of decrease with altitude is the **environmental temperature lapse rate,** 6.4°C/1000 m (3.5°F/1000 ft). At the *tropopause,* this decrease stops. In the **stratosphere** above, temperatures increase slightly with altitude.

- Air temperatures observed at mountain locations are lower with higher elevation, and day-night temperature differences increase with elevation.

- When air temperature increases with altitude, a **temperature inversion** is present. This can develop on clear nights when the surface loses longwave radiation to space.

- Annual air temperature cycles are influenced by the annual pattern of net radiation, which depends largely on latitude.

- Maritime or continental location is another important factor. Ocean temperatures vary less than land temperatures because water heats more slowly, absorbs energy throughout a surface layer, and can mix and evaporate freely. Maritime locations that receive oceanic air therefore show smaller ranges of both daily and annual temperature.

- Global temperature patterns for January and July show the effects of latitude, maritime-continental location, and elevation. Equatorial temperatures vary little from season to season. Poleward, temperatures decrease with latitude, and continental surfaces at high latitudes can become very cold in winter. At higher elevations, temperatures are always colder.

- **Isotherms** over continents swing widely north and south with the seasons, while isotherms over oceans move through a much smaller range of latitude. The annual range in temperature increases with latitude and is greatest in northern hemisphere continental interiors.

- Our planet's global temperature changes from year to year. Within the last few decades, global temperatures have been increasing. CO_2 released by fossil fuel burning is important in causing warming, but so are the other **greenhouse gases,** CH_4, CFCs, O_3, and N_2O. Aerosols scatter sunlight back to space and induce more low clouds, so they tend to lower global temperatures. Solar output and volcanic activity also influence global temperatures.

- Most scientists agree that the human-induced buildup of greenhouse gases has begun to affect global climate. However, natural cycles, such as variations in the Sun's output, still provide strong influences. If we continue to release large quantities of greenhouse gases at increasing rates, we can expect a significant rise in global temperatures that will be accompanied by shifts of climate zones and increasing sea level.

Key Terms

air temperature, p. 88
surface, p. 89
net radiation, p. 89
conduction, p. 89
latent heat transfer, p. 89

convection, p. 89
transpiration, p. 92
evapotranspiration, p. 94
heat island, p. 94

lapse rate, p. 95
environmental tempera-ture lapse rate, p. 95
troposphere, p. 96
stratosphere, p. 96

temperature inversion, p. 99
isotherms, p. 103
greenhouse gases, p. 108

Review Questions

1. Identify five important factors in determining air temperature and air temperature cycles.
2. What factors influence the temperature of a surface?
3. How are mean daily air temperature and mean monthly air temperature determined?
4. How does the daily temperature cycle measured within a few centimeters or inches of the surface differ from the cycle at normal air temperature measurement height?
5. Compare the characteristics of urban and rural surfaces and describe how the differences affect urban and rural air temperatures. Include a discussion of the urban heat island.
6. What are the two layers of the lower atmosphere? How are they distinguished? Name the two upper layers.
7. How and why are the temperature cycles of high mountain stations different from those of lower elevations?
8. Explain how latitude affects the annual cycle of air temperature through net radiation by comparing Manaus, Aswan, Hamburg, and Yakutsk.
9. Why do large water bodies heat and cool more slowly than land masses? What effect does this have on daily and annual temperature cycles for coastal and interior stations?
10. What three factors are most important in explaining the world pattern of isotherms? Explain how and why each factor is important, and what effect it has.
11. Turn to the January and July world temperature maps shown in Figure 3.20. Make six important observations about the patterns and explain why each occurs.

12. Turn to the world map of annual temperature range in Figure 3.22. What five important observations can you make about the annual temperature range patterns? Explain each.
13. Identify the important greenhouse gases and rank them in terms of their warming effect. What human-influenced factors act to cool global temperature? How?
14. Describe how global air temperatures have changed in the recent past. Identify some factors or processes that influence global air temperatures on this time scale.

Eye on Global Change 3.1 • Carbon Dioxide—On the Increase

1. Why has the atmospheric concentration of CO_2 increased in recent years?
2. How does plant life affect the level of atmospheric CO_2?
3. What is the role of the ocean in influencing atmospheric levels of CO_2?

A Closer Look:
Eye on Global Change 3.2 • The IPCC Report of 2001

1. What changes in global climate have been noted for the last half of the twentieth century in global temperature, snow and ice cover, precipitation, and greenhouse gas concentrations?
2. How is climate predicted to change by the end of the twenty-first century with respect to temperature, precipitation, snow and ice cover, and sea level?

Visualizing Exercises

1. Sketch graphs showing how insolation, net radiation, and temperature might vary from midnight to midnight during a 24-hour cycle at a midlatitude station such as Chicago.

2. Sketch a graph of air temperature with height showing a low-level temperature inversion. Where and when is such an inversion likely to occur?

Essay Questions

1. Portland, Oregon, on the north Pacific coast, and Minneapolis, Minnesota, in the interior of the North American continent, are at about the same latitude. Sketch the annual temperature cycle you would expect for each location. How do they differ and why? Select one season, summer or winter, and sketch a daily temperature cycle for each location. Again, describe how they differ and why.

2. Many scientists have concluded that human activities are acting to raise global temperatures. What human processes are involved? How do they relate to natural processes? Are global temperatures increasing now? What other effects could be influencing global temperatures? What are the consequences of global warming?

Eye on the Landscape

Chapter Opener Opabin Prospect, Yoho National Park This striking mountain landscape shows obvious evidence of recent glaciation. Glacial ice once filled this broad valley, scraping it bare of loose rock and leaving behind low piles of rock debris. The shallow lakes—called tarns **(A)**—occupy depressions scraped out by moving ice. At **(B)** is a cirque—a steep but rounded valley head where an alpine glacier once formed. Alpine glacial landforms are covered in Chapter 19. Note also the extensive conifer forest **(C)**, which is characteristic of high elevations in cool climates. Conifer forests are discussed in Chapter 9.

3.5a Urban surfaces Beyond the urban surfaces in the foreground is a distant view of a semiarid landscape in the western United States **(A)**. The sparse and low vegetation cover reflects the semiarid climate (see Chapters 7 and 9 for semiarid climate and vegetation). Note also the smooth profile of the land surface from the mountain peak to the base of the slope **(B)**. This shape indicates long-continued erosion by running water (fluvial erosion), which we describe in Chapter 16.

3.5b Rural surfaces The human influence on this agricultural landscape **(A)** is strong. A dam has created a small fire pond, providing water for both livestock and fire-fighting. The fields are mowed for hay, providing a groomed look by cutting all plants. Grazing by livestock would be more selective and give a more tufted appearance to the pasture. The young trees dotting the landscape are probably all planted and have been pruned to pleasing shapes. The split-rail fencing is attractively rustic but too expensive for most farm applications. In short, this is the spread of a gentleman farmer.

3.10 Clear air at high elevation—Mount Whitney The jagged topography of these high peaks **(A)** indicates glacial, rather than fluvial, erosion. Imagine a dome of glacial ice covering this entire scene, leaving only the tip of Mount Whitney uncovered. Ice flowing in and around the rock masses below the summit gouges the rock, tearing huge chunks loose along cracks and joints in the rock. Then the climate warms and the ice melts, revealing rugged slopes and sheer rock faces stripped by the ice action. We'll cover glacial landscapes in Chapter 19.

A CLOSER LOOK

Eye on Global Change   3.2 | The IPCC Report of 2001

In 2001, the United Nations Inter-governmental Panel on Climate Change (IPCC), a body of over 600 scientists nominated by countries from all over the globe, issued three major reports on human-induced changes in global climate. The reports concerned the scientific basis for anticipated climate change, the projected impacts of the change, and strategies for mitigating the impacts.

To estimate the degree of climate change with time and over the globe, scientists of the IPCC used several complex global climate models—mathematical models that predict the state of the atmosphere and land and water surfaces at short time steps for long periods. The models were driven by predicted releases of greenhouse gases under different scenarios of global economic growth and social evolution through the end of the twenty-first century. The two graphs on the facing page show global temperature change and sea-level rise as modeled under these scenarios. Although there is variation between outcomes, it is clear that both global temperature and sea level will rise significantly by 2100 based on their analysis.

Here are some of the panel's more specific findings, taken from *Climate Change 2001: The Scientific Basis, A Report of the Working Group I of the Intergovernmental Panel on Climate Change,* Summary for Policymakers, IPCC, Geneva, Switzerland, 2001.

Recent Climate Change
- Global average surface temperature increased about 0.6°C (1.1°F) during the twentieth century. The 1990s was the warmest decade and 1998 the warmest year since 1861. Nighttime daily minimum air temperatures rose about twice as fast as daytime maximum temperatures. Since 1950, the frequency of extreme low temperatures has decreased. The frequency of extreme high temperatures has increased a smaller amount.
- The lowest 8 km (5 mi) of the atmosphere has warmed at a rate of about 0.05°C (0.09°F) per decade since at least 1979.
- Snow and ice cover has decreased by about 10 percent since the late 1960s. The duration of snow cover has been reduced by about two weeks in the mid- and high latitudes of the northern hemisphere. The extent of sea ice in spring and summer in the northern hemisphere has decreased by 10 to 15 percent since the 1950s. Summer and fall sea ice is thinner.
- Global average sea level rose between 10 and 20 cm (4 and 8 in.) during the twentieth century. Global ocean heat content has increased since at least the late 1950s.
- Precipitation increased by 0.5 to 1 percent per decade in the twentieth century over the mid- and high latitudes of the northern hemisphere. Rainfall decreased in subtropical regions. There was an increase of 2 to 4 percent in the frequency of heavy precipitation events in the latter half of the twentieth century. The frequency and intensity of droughts in some parts of Africa and Asia have also increased in recent decades.
- Cloud cover increased by about 2 percent in the mid- and high latitudes of the northern hemisphere during the twentieth century.
- Since 1970, El Niño episodes have been more frequent, intense, and persistent, compared to those in the previous 100 years.
- Some important aspects of climate have not changed. Some parts of the southern hemisphere oceans and parts of Antarctica have not warmed in recent decades. No significant changes have occurred in Antarctic sea ice coverage since 1978. Tropical and extratropical cyclone frequencies have not been shown to be changing.
- Concentrations of greenhouse gases in the atmosphere have increased as a result of human activities. CO_2 has increased by 31 percent since 1750. For the past two decades, CO_2 concentration has increased by about 1.5 parts per million (ppm) per year. Methane (CH_4) concentration has increased by 151 percent since 1750; nitrous oxide (N_2O) by about 17 percent; and ozone (O_3) by about 36 percent.
- There is newer and stronger evidence that human activities are responsible for most of the warming observed since 1950.

Climate Change in the Twenty-first Century
The IPCC reports also offer these predictions for the rest of the twenty-first century. Although they may not all come true, they are considered likely given the state of present knowledge and current levels of confidence in global climate model predictions, as well as reasonable scenarios for economic growth, development, and emission control.

- Atmospheric composition will continue to change. CO_2 from fossil fuel burning will continue to increase. As this occurs, land and ocean will take up a decreasing fraction of CO_2 released, accentuating the increase. By 2100, CO_2

(a)

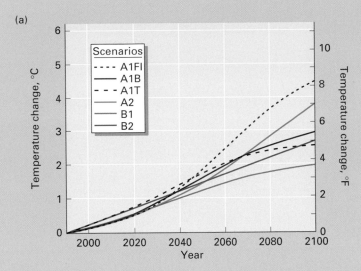

(b)

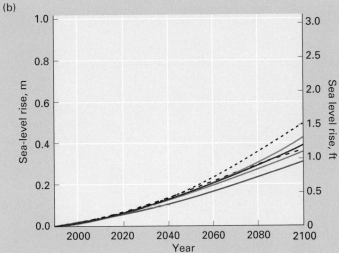

***Increases in temperature and sea-level
rise modeled by the IPCC*** *These graphs
show how temperature (a) and sea level
(b) are predicted to rise between now and
2100, based on global climate models.
Curves show means for several models
under six emissions scenarios. The A1
scenarios describe a world of rapid
growth with economic and social
convergence among regions leading to a
more uniform world. Scenario A1F1
projects heavy reliance on fossil fuels;
A1T on nonfossil energy sources; and A1B
a balance across all sources. The A2
scenario is a more heterogeneous world
with less convergence and greater
regional isolation. The B scenarios are
similar to A1 but move toward a service
and information economy that
emphasizes social and environmental
sustainability. B1 assumes more global
convergence, while B2 assumes more
independence among regions. (From
IPCC, Climate Change Report 2001:
Synthesis Report, copyright IPCC 2001,
used by permission of Cambridge
University Press.*

concentration will have increased
by 90 to 250 percent above the
1750 value, depending on the
scenario of economic growth,
development, and CO_2 release.

- Other greenhouse gas
concentrations are likely to
change, increasing under most
scenarios. Aerosols could
contribute significantly to
warming if their release is
unabated.

- Global average temperature will
rise between 1.4 and 5.8°C (2.5
and 10.4°F) from 1990 to 2100.
The projected rate of warming is
much larger than that of the late
twentieth century and is likely to
be greater than any warming
episode in the last 10,000 years.

- Land areas will warm more
rapidly than the global average,
especially northern latitudes in
the winter.

- Precipitation will increase in
northern mid- to high latitudes
and in Antarctica in winter.
Larger year-to-year variations in
precipitation are likely. At low
latitudes, there will be decreases
in precipitation in some areas
and increases in others.

- Over nearly all land areas, there
will be higher maximum
temperatures and more hot days;
higher minimum temperatures,
fewer cold days and frost days;
reduced daily temperature range;
more intense precipitation
events; increased risk of summer

drought; and an increase in peak
wind and precipitation intensities
of tropical cyclones.

- Snow and ice cover will decrease
further, and ice caps and glaciers
will continue their widespread
retreat of the late twentieth
century. The Antarctic Ice Sheet
will gain mass from increased
precipitation, while the
Greenland Ice Sheet will thin.

- Sea level will rise from 9 to 88
cm (3.5 to 34.6 in.) depending on
the scenario, due to thermal
expansion and a gain in volume
from melting ice.

- Human-generated climate change
will persist for many centuries
into the future. Even if
concentrations of greenhouse
gases are stabilized, oceans will
continue to warm; sea level will
continue to rise; and ice sheets
and glaciers will continue to melt.
Models suggest that a local
warming of 3°C (5.4°F) over the
Greenland ice cap, if sustained
over 10 centuries, would
completely melt the ice cap,
raising sea level by about 7 m
(9.8 ft).

Lightning heralds the approach of a summer thundershower.

4 | ATMOSPHERIC MOISTURE AND PRECIPITATION

• • • • • • • • • • • • • • • • • •
PUTTING YOU IN THE PICTURE

Rain is a common event in most parts of the world. We don't think much about a rainy day, other than perhaps to grumble a bit at having to grab a raincoat or umbrella before leaving the house. On the other hand, precipitation is a vital part of life, for without rain and snow we'd have no fresh water to meet our daily needs.

Precipitation, along with temperature, is an essential ingredient of climate. The timing and duration of rainy periods condition many human activities, especially agriculture. They also influence the nature of plant and animal communities in a region, as well as the soil processes that provide the substrate needed for natural and cultivated plant growth.

Another important role for precipitation is the shaping of the landscape through the processes of erosion and deposition. As rain and melting snow run off the landscape under the influence of gravity, water carries and deposits soil and sediment, both carving the landscape by removal and building it up by accumulation.

What causes precipitation? As we'll see in this chapter, rain and snow form when warm, moist air is chilled and condensation or deposition takes place. The chilling is usually the result of uplift, for example, as air passes up and over a mountain barrier or is carried upward by convection.

When visualizing a rainfall, what usually comes to mind is a soggy day of gray skies, showers, or drizzle. While most rainstorms are pretty routine, a thunderstorm can be an exciting, even dangerous, event. You might experience it like this…

Suddenly you notice that the thick, humid air is perfectly still. The songbirds and insects are strangely silent. Not a single leaf trembles in the huge, ancient oak shading your lawn chair. You look up from the book you've been reading and notice that the puffy white clouds that had filled the sky seem to have merged into a darkening blanket. Across the grassy field in front of you, the rambling old farmhouse where you are spending the holiday weekend with friends looks pale and somehow vacant of life in the flat, gray light.

A low, distant rumble shatters the stillness. A thunderstorm is approaching! Tucking your book under your arm, you fold up your lawn chair and head for the house. As you walk through the field, you begin to hear a rushing sound. Looking over your shoulder, you see the tops of the forest trees at the edge of the field shaking and swaying in a sudden wind. Then, the top of the old oak twists violently, its upper branches jerking chaotically as it is battered by strong gusts. A flood of cool air sweeps over you, lifting the lawn chair in your left hand. The sickly smell of ozone, now assaulting your nose, harkens of danger. Unconsciously, you quicken your steps toward the farmhouse.

The first large, heavy drops begin to fall as you reach the wide front porch. A rushing sound deepens as the first wave of heavy rainfall approaches through the distant trees and crosses the field. The sky explodes with light, and a loud crack of thunder startles you. The rain now drives intensely toward the ground, banging on the tin roof of the porch and swirling onto the porch in the strong gusts. The oak in the middle of the field is barely visible through the falling torrent.

A crackle pierces the din, and a blinding flash prints an image of the ancient oak onto your eyes. At the same moment, a deafening bang shatters the air. Lightning has struck the old oak! A huge branch crashes to the ground, the sound of its fall muffled by the wind and rain. That was too close for comfort! You retreat from the porch for the safety of the house to watch the storm from a window, hopeful that the lightning rods that project from the chimneys at either end of the house will save you from the fate of the ancient oak.

Later, you survey the damage. The top of the tree lies on the ground, its thick limbs splintered by the force of the lightning strike. The stout trunk is split almost to the base. Huge splinters are strewn on the surrounding ground. The smell of fresh-split green oak is pungent in the humid air. "Good thing I didn't decide to wait out the storm under the tree!" you think to yourself. ∎

ATMOSPHERIC MOISTURE AND PRECIPITATION

Water plays a key role in the energy flows that shape our planet's climate and weather. In Chapter 2 we noted how ocean currents act to carry the annual surplus of solar energy from equatorial regions toward the poles. Another water-assisted part of this global energy flow is the flow of latent heat in the form of water vapor conducted poleward by atmospheric circulation. When water evaporates over warm tropical oceans, it takes up latent heat. When it condenses, often in distant colder regions, that latent heat is released in a different location. Precipitation, then, is an important part of this global energy flow process. Precipitation over land also provides water (and ice) that can move under the influence of gravity, thus carving the landforms and landscapes that provide the Earth's varied human habitats. We will return to this role of water in Chapters 15–17.

In this chapter, we focus on water in the air, both as vapor and as liquid and solid water. **Precipitation** is the fall of liquid or solid water from the atmosphere to reach the Earth's land or ocean surface. It is formed when moist air is cooled, causing water vapor to form liquid droplets or solid ice particles. If cooling is sufficiently long and intense, liquid and solid water particles will grow to a size too large to be carried in the air by air motion. They can then fall to Earth.

What causes the cooling of moist air? The answer is upward motion. Whenever air moves upward in the atmosphere, it is cooled. This is not simply because surrounding air temperatures tend to get lower as you go up, as we saw in Chapter 3. It is because of a simple physical principle stating that when air expands, it cools. And because atmospheric pressure decreases with altitude, air moving upward expands—and so at the same time it gets cooler.

What makes air move upward? There are four major causes. One occurs when winds move air up and over a mountain barrier. The second takes place when unequal heating at the ground surface creates a bubble of air that is warmer than the surrounding air. Since it is less dense, it is buoyed upward—like a cork under water bobbing to the surface. This chapter focuses on these two causes of uplift. The third occurs when a mass of cooler, denser air slides under a mass of warmer, lighter air, lifting the warmer air aloft. This type of upward movement occurs in weather systems, which we will cover in Chapter 6. A fourth type of upward motion, also covered in Chapter 6, occurs when air converges at a common location and is thus forced aloft. But before we begin our study of atmospheric moisture and precipitation, we will briefly review the three states of water and the conversion of one state to another.

THREE STATES OF WATER

As shown in Figure 4.1, water can exist in three states—solid (ice), liquid (water), and gas (water vapor). A change of state from solid to liquid, liquid to gas, or solid to gas requires the input of heat energy. As we noted in Chapter 2, this energy is called *latent heat,* which is drawn in from the surroundings and stored within the water molecules. When

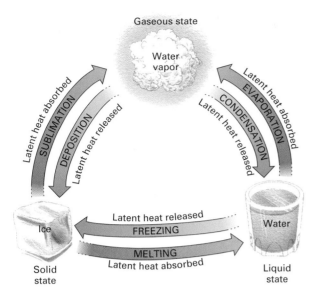

Gaseous state

Water vapor

Latent heat absorbed
SUBLIMATION

DEPOSITION
Latent heat released

Latent heat absorbed
EVAPORATION

CONDENSATION
Latent heat released

Latent heat released
FREEZING

MELTING
Latent heat absorbed

Ice

Water

Solid state

Liquid state

4.1 *Three states of water* *Arrows show the ways that any one state of water can change into either of the other two states. Heat energy is absorbed or released, depending on the direction of change.*

THE HYDROSPHERE AND THE HYDROLOGIC CYCLE

Let's now turn to the **hydrosphere,** the realm of water in all its forms, and the flows of water among ocean, land, and atmosphere. About 97.2 percent of the hydrosphere consists of ocean saltwater, as shown in Figure 4.2. The remaining 2.8 percent is fresh water. The next largest reservoir is fresh water stored as ice in the world's ice sheets and mountain glaciers. This water accounts for 2.15 percent of total global water.

Fresh liquid water is found both on top of and beneath the Earth's land surfaces. Water occupying openings in soil and rock is called *subsurface water.* Most of it is held in deep storage as *ground water,* at a level where plant roots cannot access it. Ground water makes up 0.63 percent of the hydrosphere, leaving 0.02 percent of the water remaining.

The right-hand portion of Figure 4.2 shows how this small remaining proportion of the Earth's water is distributed. This proportion is important to us because it includes the water available for plants, animals, and human use. *Soil water,* which is held in the soil within reach of plant roots, comprises 0.005 percent of the global total. Water held in streams, lakes, marshes, and swamps is called *surface water.* Most of this surface water is about evenly divided between freshwater lakes and saline (salty) lakes. An extremely small proportion is held in the streams and rivers that flow toward the sea or inland lakes.

the change goes the other way, from liquid to solid, gas to liquid, or gas to solid, this latent heat is released to the surroundings.

For each type of transition, there is a specific name, shown in the figure. *Melting, freezing, evaporation,* and *condensation* are all familiar terms. **Sublimation** is the direct transition from solid to vapor. Perhaps you have noticed that old ice cubes in your refrigerator's freezer seem to shrink away from the sides of the ice cube tray and get smaller with time. They shrink through sublimation, which is induced by the constant circulation of cold, dry air through the freezer. The ice cubes never melt, yet they lose bulk directly as vapor. **Deposition** is the reverse process, when water vapor crystallizes directly as ice.* Frost formed on a cold winter night is an example.

> Water exists in solid, liquid, and gaseous states as ice, water, and water vapor. Latent heat energy is released or absorbed as water changes from one state to another.

Note that the quantity of water held as vapor and cloud water droplets in the atmosphere is also very small—0.001 percent of the hydrosphere. Though small, this reservoir of water is of enormous importance. It provides the supply of precipitation that replenishes all freshwater stocks on land. And, as we will see in the next chapter, the flow of water vapor from warm tropical oceans to cooler regions provides a global flow of heat, in latent form, from low to high latitudes.

The movements of water among the great global reservoirs constitute the **hydrologic cycle.** In this cycle, water moves from land and ocean to the atmosphere as water vapor and returns as precipitation. Because precipitation over land exceeds evaporation, water also runs off the land to the oceans. We will return to the hydrologic cycle in more detail in Chapter 15.

---

* *Deposition* is a term used by chemists to describe the deposit of a solid directly from a vapor. Meteorologists generally use the term *sublimation* for both the change from vapor to solid and from solid to vapor, with the difference determined by the context. Since it is clearer to use a separate word for each process, we use the term *deposition* in this text.

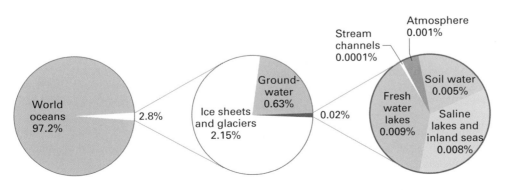

World oceans 97.2%

2.8%

Ice sheets and glaciers 2.15%

Ground-water 0.63%

Stream channels 0.0001%

0.02%

Atmosphere 0.001%

Soil water 0.005%

Fresh water lakes 0.009%

Saline lakes and inland seas 0.008%

4.2 *Volumes of global water in each reservoir of the hydrosphere* *Nearly all the Earth's water is contained in the world ocean. Fresh surface and soil water make up only a small fraction of the total volume of global water.*

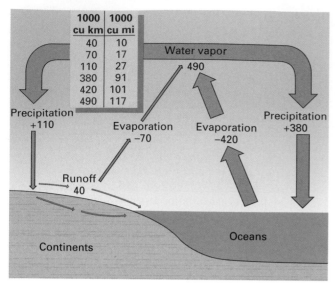

1000 cu km	1000 cu mi
40	10
70	17
110	27
380	91
420	101
490	117

4.3 The global water balance *Figures give average annual water flows in and out of world land areas and world oceans. Values are in thousands of cubic kilometers (cubic miles). Global precipitation equals global evaporation. (Based on data of John R. Mather.)*

For now, we will summarize the main features of the hydrologic cycle in the global water balance, shown in Figure 4.3. The cycle begins with evaporation from water or land surfaces, in which water changes state from liquid to vapor and enters the atmosphere. In the case of land, this evaporation is enhanced by transpiration. Total evaporation is still about six times greater over oceans than land, however. This is because the oceans cover most of the planet and because land surfaces are not always wet enough to yield much evaporated water. Once in the atmosphere, water vapor can condense or deposit to form precipitation, which falls to Earth as rain, snow, or hail. Precipitation over the oceans is nearly four times greater than precipitation over land.

Upon reaching the land surface, precipitation has three fates. First, it can evaporate and return to the atmosphere as water vapor. Second, it can sink into the soil and then into the surface rock layers below. As we will see in later chapters, this subsurface water emerges from below to feed rivers, lakes, and even ocean margins. Third, precipitation can run off the land, concentrating in streams and rivers that eventually carry it to the ocean or to a lake in a closed inland basin. This flow of water is known as *runoff.*

The Global Water Balance

Since our planet contains only a fixed amount of water, a global balance must be maintained among flows of water to and from the lands, oceans, and atmosphere. Let's examine this idea in more detail. For our analysis, we will assume that the volume of ocean waters and the overall volume of fresh

---

> The hydrologic cycle describes the global flow of water to and from oceans, land, and atmosphere. Water is exchanged between the atmosphere and oceans and atmosphere and land by evaporation and precipitation. Water moves from land to ocean by runoff.

---

water in surface and subsurface water remains constant from year to year. This is probably quite reasonable, unless climate is changing rapidly.

The global water balance is diagrammed in Figure 4.3. Let's consider the ocean first, shown on the right side of the diagram. There are three flows to and from the ocean: evaporation (out), precipitation (in), and runoff (in). For precipitation and runoff, water enters the ocean, while water leaves the ocean by evaporation. Since "in" and "out" must balance, we have

Precipitation + Runoff = Evaporation   (ocean)

Using the values in the figure, which are given as thousands of cubic kilometers, we find that $380 + 40 = 420$.

Now let's turn to the continents, shown on the left side of the figure. Again, there are three flows—precipitation (in), evaporation (out), and runoff (out). This time, precipitation is entering (falling onto) the land, while evaporation and runoff are leaving. Thus,

Precipitation = Evaporation + Runoff   (land)

Using the values in the figure, we observe that $110 = 70 + 40$.

If we rearrange this last equation to put evaporation first, we have

Evaporation = Precipitation – Runoff   (land)

compared to

Evaporation = Precipitation + Runoff   (ocean)

Taking the land and oceans together and considering only the flow of water from the planet's surface to the atmosphere and the reverse, we can conclude that the runoff terms within the last two equations cancel out. This leaves total evaporation to equal total precipitation, as it must:

Total Evaporation	Total Precipitation
70 (land) + 420 (ocean) =	110 (land) + 380 (ocean)
cubic kilometers	cubic kilometers

The point of this simple analysis is not to write equations, but to show that we have constructed a budget that accounts for the flows of water between the reservoirs of the hydrologic cycle. Like a household budget, it must balance. If it does not, then there must be some flow that is not being considered. This is why scientists use budgets as tools to help understand natural processes, like the hydrologic cycle.

For most of this chapter, we will be concerned with one aspect of the hydrologic cycle—the flow of water from the atmosphere to the surface in the form of precipitation. We will begin by examining how the water vapor content of air is measured and how clouds and precipitation form.

HUMIDITY

The amount of water vapor present in the air varies widely from place to place and time to time. It ranges from almost nothing in the cold, dry air of arctic regions in winter to as much as 4 or 5 percent of a given volume of air in the warm wet regions near the equator. The general term **humidity** refers to the amount of water vapor present in the air.

Understanding humidity and how the moisture content of air is measured involves an important principle—namely, that the maximum quantity of moisture that can be held at any time in the air is dependent on air temperature. Warm air can hold more water vapor than cold air—a lot more. Air at room temperature (20°C, 68°F) can hold about three times as much water vapor as air at freezing (0°C, 32°F).

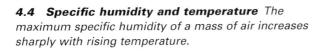

Humidity refers to the amount of water vapor present in air. Warm air can hold much more water vapor than cold air.

Specific Humidity

The actual quantity of water vapor held by a parcel of air is its **specific humidity.** This measure is important because it describes how much water vapor is available for precipitation. Specific humidity is stated as the mass of water vapor contained in a given mass of air and is expressed as grams of water vapor per kilogram of air (g/kg). Figure 4.4 shows the relationship between air temperature and the maximum amount of water vapor that air can hold. We see, for example,

The dew-point temperature of a mass of air is the temperature at which saturation will occur. The more water vapor in the air, the higher is the dew-point temperature.

that at 20°C (68°F), the maximum amount of water vapor that the air can hold—that is, the maximum specific humidity possible—is about 15 g/kg. At 30°C (86°F), it is nearly doubled—about 26 g/kg. For cold air, the values are quite small. At −10°C (14°F), the maximum is only about 2 g/kg.

Climatologists often use specific humidity to describe the moisture characteristics of a large mass of air. For example, extremely cold, dry air over arctic regions in winter may have a specific humidity as low as 0.2 g/kg. In comparison, the extremely warm, moist air of equatorial regions often holds as much as 18 g/kg. The total natural range on a worldwide basis is very wide. In fact, the largest values of specific humidity observed are from 100 to 200 times as great as the smallest.

Specific humidity is a geographer's yardstick for a basic natural resource—water. It is a measure of the quantity of water in the atmosphere that can be extracted as precipitation. Cold, moist air can supply only a small quantity of rain or snow, but warm, moist air is capable of supplying large amounts.

Figure 4.5 is a set of global profiles showing how specific humidity varies with latitude and how it relates to mean surface air temperature. Both humidity and temperature are measured at the same locations in standard thermometer shelters the world over, and also on ships at sea. Note that the horizontal axis of the graphs has an uneven scale of units—they get closer together toward both left and right edges, which represent the poles. In this case, the units are adjusted so that they reflect the amount of the Earth's surface present at that latitude. That is, since there is much more surface area between 0° and 10° latitude than between 60° and 70°, the region between 0° and 10° is allocated more width on the graph.

Let's look first at specific humidity (upper graph). The curve clearly shows the largest values for the equatorial zones, with values falling off rapidly toward both poles. This curve follows the pattern of insolation quite nicely (see Figure 2.8). More insolation is available at lower latitudes, on average, to evaporate water in oceans or on moist land surfaces. Therefore, specific humidity values are higher at low latitudes than at high latitudes.

The global profile of mean (average) surface air temperature (lower graph) shows a similar shape to the specific humidity profile. We would expect this to be the case, since air temperature and maximum specific humidity vary together, as shown in Figure 4.4.

Another way of describing the water vapor content of air is by its **dew-point temperature.** If air is slowly chilled, it eventually will reach *saturation*. At this temperature, the air holds the maximum amount of water vapor possible. If further cooling continues, condensation will begin and dew will form. The temperature at which satura-

4.4 Specific humidity and temperature *The maximum specific humidity of a mass of air increases sharply with rising temperature.*

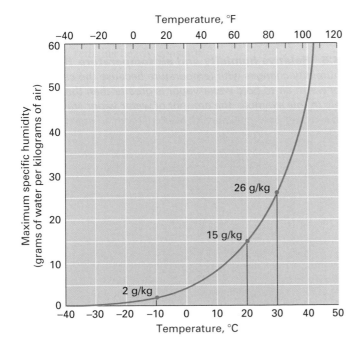

How is air chilled sufficiently to produce precipitation? One mechanism for chilling air is nighttime cooling. As we saw in Chapter 3, the ground surface can become quite cold on a clear night through loss of longwave radiation. Thus, still air near the surface can be cooled below the condensation point, producing dew or frost. However, this mechanism is not sufficient to form precipitation. Precipitation is formed only when a substantial mass of air experiences a steady drop in temperature below the dew point. This happens when an air parcel is uplifted to a higher level in the atmosphere, as we will see in the following section.

Dry Adiabatic Rate

An important principle of phsyics, which we can refer to as the *adiabatic principle,* is that when a gas is allowed to expand, its temperature drops. Conversely, when a gas is compressed, its temperature increases. If you have ever pumped up a bicycle tire using a hand pump, you have observed this latter effect yourself. As you pump vigorously, the metal pump gets hot. This occurs because air inside the pump is being compressed and therefore heated. In the same way, when a small jet of air escapes from a high-pressure hose, it feels cool. Perhaps you have flown on an airplane and noticed a small nozzle overhead that directs a stream of cool air toward you. When the air moves from higher pressure in the air hose that feeds the nozzle to lower pressure in

the cabin, it expands and cools. Physicists use the term **adiabatic process** to refer to a heating or cooling process that occurs solely as a result of pressure change. That is, the change in temperature is not caused by heat flowing into or away from a volume of air, but only by a change in pressure on a volume of air.

Given that air cools or heats when the pressure on it changes, how does that relate to uplift and precipitation? The missing link is simply that atmospheric pressure decreases with an increase in altitude. So, if a parcel of air is uplifted, atmospheric pressure on the parcel will be lower, and it will expand and cool. Conversely, if a parcel of air descends, atmospheric pressure will be higher, and it will be compressed and warmed (Figure 4.9). The **dry adiabatic lapse rate** describes this behavior for a rising air parcel that has not reached saturation. This rate has a value of about 10°C per 1000 m (5.5°F per 1000 ft) of vertical rise. That is, if a parcel of air is raised 1 km, its temperature will drop by 10°C. Or, in English units, if raised 1000 ft, its temperature will drop by 5.5°F. This is the "dry" rate because condensation does not occur.

Note that in the previous chapter we encountered the environmental temperature lapse rate. The temperature lapse rate is simply an expression of how the temperature of still air varies with altitude. This rate will vary from time to time and from place to place, depending on the state of the atmosphere. It is quite different from the dry adiabatic lapse rate. The dry adiabatic rate applies to a mass of air in vertical motion. It is always constant and is determined by physical laws. No motion of air is implied for the temperature lapse rate.

> The adiabatic principle states that compression warms a gas, while expansion cools it. In an adiabatic process, the temperature of a gas changes solely as a result of a change in pressure—not from an inflow or outflow of heat energy.

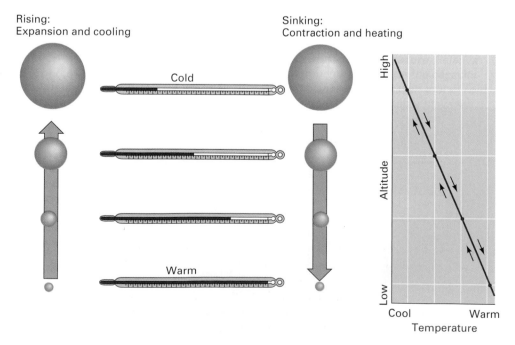

4.9 Adiabatic cooling and heating *A schematic diagram of adiabatic cooling and heating that accompanies the rising and sinking of a mass of air. When air is forced to rise, it expands and its temperature decreases. When air is forced to descend, its temperature increases. (A. N. Strahler.)*

Rising: Expansion and cooling

Sinking: Contraction and heating

Cold

Warm

High

Altitude

Low

Cool   Warm

Temperature

and are colder than surface features, they appear white. The oceans appear blue because they are dark in the visible bands but are still somewhat warm.

For weather forecasting, an important tool of the latest generation of GOES imagers is the water vapor image. The image at the right shows a global water vapor image for August 11, 2000, constructed from GOES-East and West

Earth from GOES-8 *The GOES-8 geostationary satellite acquired this image on September 2, 1994. (Courtesy NASA. Image produced by M. Jentoft-Nilsen, F. Hasler, D. Chesters, and T. Nielsen.)*

and attain a diameter of 50 to 100 μm (0.002 to 0... In collisions with one another, the droplets grow... 500 μm in diameter (about 0.02 in.). This is th... water droplets in drizzle. Further collisions and c... increase drop size and yield *rain*. Average raind... diameters of about 1000 to 2000 μm (about 0.04 t... but they can reach a maximum diameter of about... (about 0.25 in.). Above this value they... become unstable and break into smaller... drops while falling. This type of precip-... itation formation occurs in warm clouds... typical of the equatorial and tropical... zones.

Figure 4.14 diagrams the process of... formation of raindrops in a warm cloud.... Here, the updraft of rising air lifts tiny... suspended cloud droplets upward. By collisions... droplets, some grow in volume. These larger dropl... with other small droplets and continue to grow. N... droplet is kept aloft by the pressure of the updraft

4.12 Cloud photos *(a) Rolls of altocumulus clouds, also known as a "mackerel s... High cirrus clouds lie above puffy cumulus clouds in this scene from Holland. (c) Fi... cirrus clouds are drawn out in streaks by high-level winds to form "mare's tails." (d... layer: lenticular clouds, a type of altostratus formed when moist air is uplifted as it... a range of hills. Lower layer: cumulus clouds, also triggered by the uplift.*

delays and shutdowns because of fog bring economic losses to airlines and can inconvenience many thousands of travelers in a single day. For centuries, fog at sea has been a navigational hazard, increasing the danger of ship collisions and groundings. In addition, polluted fogs, like those of London in the early part of the twentieth century, can injure urban dwellers' lungs and take a heavy toll in lives.

One type of fog, known as *radiation fog,* is formed at night when the temperature of the air layer at the ground level falls below the dew point. This kind of fog is associated with a low-level temperature inversion (Figure 3.12). Another fog type, *advection fog,* results when a warm, moist air layer moves over a cold surface. As the warm air layer loses heat to the surface, its temperature drops below the dew point, and condensation sets in. Advection fog commonly occurs over oceans where warm and cold currents occur side by side. When warm, moist air above the warm current moves over the cold current, condensation occurs. Fogs of the Grand Banks off Newfoundland are formed in this way because here the cold Labrador current comes in contact with the warmer waters of the Gulf Stream.

> In warm clouds experiencing strong uplift, water droplets grow by condensation, then collide and coalesce to form raindrops. In colder clouds, ice particles grow from collisions with supercooled water droplets that freeze on contact.

Sea fog is freq... forms within a coo... colder water of th... fogs are found on... tude zones where... shoreline.

PRECIPITA...

Clouds are the sou... vides the fresh wa... life. Let's look in... inside clouds. Pre... clouds, fine water...

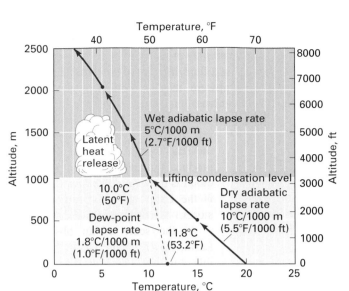

Temperature, °F
40 50 60 70

Altitude, m — 2500, 2000, 1500, 1000, 500, 0
Altitude, ft — 8000, 7000, 6000, 5000, 4000, 3000, 2000, 1000, 0

Wet adiabatic lapse rate 5°C/1000 m (2.7°F/1000 ft)
Latent heat release
10.0°C (50°F)
Lifting condensation level
Dew-point lapse rate 1.8°C/1000 m (1.0°F/1000 ft)
Dry adiabatic lapse rate 10°C/1000 m (5.5°F/1000 ft)
11.8°C (53.2°F)

Temperature, °C
0 5 10 15 20 25

4.10 Adiabatic cooling *Adiabatic decrease of temperature in a rising parcel of air leads to condensation of water vapor into water droplets and the formation of a cloud. (Copyright © A. N. Strahler.)*

Wet Adiabatic Rate

Let's continue examining the fate of a parcel of air that is moved upward in the atmosphere (Figure 4.10). We will assume that the parcel starts with a temperature of 20°C (68°F). As the parcel moves upward, its temperature drops at the dry adiabatic rate, 10°C/1000 m (5.5°F/1000 ft). At 500 m (1600 ft), the temperature has dropped by 5°C (9°F) to 15°C (59°F). At 1000 m (3300 ft), the temperature has fallen to 10°C (50°F). As the rising process continues, the air is cooled to its dew-point temperature, and condensation starts to occur. This is shown on the figure as the *lifting condensation level.*

Note, however, that the dew-point temperature changes slightly with elevation. Instead of remaining constant, it falls at the *dew-point lapse rate* of 1.8°C/1000 m (1.0°F/1000 ft). Suppose the dew-point temperature of the air mass is 11.8°C (53.2°F). Then at 1000 m (3300 ft), the dew-point temperature will be 10°C (50°F). That will also be the temperature of the parcel for the example above, so condensation will begin at that level. The lifting condensation level is thus determined by the initial temperature of the air and its dew point.

If cooling continues, water droplets will form, producing a cloud. If the parcel of saturated air continues to rise, however, a new principle comes into effect—latent heat release. That is, when condensation occurs, latent heat is released and warms the uplifted air. In other words, two effects are occurring at once. First, the uplifted air is being cooled by the reduction

> Rising air cools less rapidly when condensation is occurring, owing to the release of latent heat. This explains why the wet adiabatic cooling rate has a lesser value than the dry adiabatic cooling rate.

> A cloud consists of water droplets, ice particles, or a mixture of both. These form on tiny condensation nuclei, which are normally minute specks of sea salt or dust.

in atmospheric pressure. Second, it is being warmed by the release of latent heat from condensation.

Which effect is stronger? As it turns out, the cooling effect is stronger, so the air will continue to cool as it is uplifted. But because of the release of latent heat, the cooling will occur at a lesser rate. This cooling rate for saturated air is called the **wet adiabatic lapse rate** and ranges between 4 and 9°C per 1000 m (2.2 and 4.9°F per 1000 ft). Unlike the dry adiabatic lapse rate, which remains constant, the wet adiabatic lapse rate is variable because it depends on the temperature and pressure of the air and its moisture content. For most situations, however, we can use a value of 5°C/1000 m (2.7°F/1000 ft). The higher rates apply only to cold, relatively dry air that contains little moisture and therefore little latent heat. In Figure 4.10, the wet adiabatic rate is shown as a slightly curving line to indicate that its value increases with altitude.

CLOUDS

Clouds are frequent features of the atmosphere. Views of the Earth from space show that about half of the Earth is covered by clouds at any given time. We noted earlier that low clouds reflect solar energy, thus cooling the Earth–atmosphere system, while high clouds absorb outgoing longwave radiation, thus warming the Earth–atmosphere system. In Chapter 6 we will return to this topic in more detail. In this chapter, however, we are concerned with clouds as the source of precipitation.

A **cloud** is made up of water droplets, ice particles, or a mixture of both, suspended in air. These particles have a diameter in the range of 20 to 50 μm (0.0008 to 0.002 in.). Recall from Chapter 2 that μm denotes the *micrometer,* or one-millionth of a meter. Each cloud particle is formed on a tiny center of solid matter, called a *condensation nucleus.* This nucleus has a diameter in the range 0.1 to 1 μm (0.000004 to 0.00004 in.).

An important source of condensation nuclei is the surface of the sea. When winds create waves, droplets of spray from the crests of the waves are carried rapidly upward in turbulent air. Evaporation of sea water droplets leaves a tiny residue of crystalline salt suspended in the air. This aerosol strongly attracts water molecules. Another source of nuclei is the heavy load of dust carried by polluted air over cities, which substantially aids condensation and the formation of clouds and fog. But even very clean and clear air contains enough condensation nuclei for the formation of clouds.

In our everyday life at the Earth's surface, liquid water turns to ice when the surrounding temperature falls to the freezing point, 0°C (32°F), or below. However, when water is dispersed as tiny droplets in clouds, it remains in the liquid state at temperatures far below freezing. Such water is described as *supercooled*. Clouds consist entirely of water droplets at temperatures down to about −12°C (10°F). As cloud temperatures grow colder, a mix of water droplets and ice crystals occurs. The coldest clouds, with temperatures below −40°C (−40°F), occur at altitudes of 6 to 12 km (20,000 to 40,000 ft) and are formed entirely of ice particles.

Cloud Forms

Clouds come in many shapes and sizes, from the small, white puffy clouds often seen in summer to the dark layers that produce a good, old-fashioned rainy day. Meteorologists classify clouds into four families, arranged by height: high, middle, and low clouds, and clouds with vertical development. These are shown in Figures 4.11 and 4.12. Some individual types with their names are also shown.

Clouds are grouped into two major classes on the basis of form—stratiform, or layered clouds, and cumuliform, or globular clouds. *Stratiform* clouds are blanket-like and cover large areas. A common type is *stratus*, which covers the entire sky. Stratus clouds are formed when air layers are forced to rise gradually over large regions. This can happen when one air layer overrides another. As the overriding layer rises and is cooled, condensation occurs over a large area, and a blanket-like cloud forms. If the overriding layer is quite moist and rising continues, dense, thick stratiform clouds result that can produce abundant rain or snow.

Cumuliform c[louds] associated with s[...] parcels rise beca[use] air. Like bubbles [...] they are buoyed [...] process. When c[...] most common cl[...]

> **There are two major classes of clouds—stratiform (layered) and cumuliform (globular). Cumulonimbus clouds are dense, tall clouds that produce thundershowers.**

continental or gl[...] mark air motions [...] circulation. One [...] cloud patterns re[...] ary satellites. *Fo[...] Clouds from G[...]* images.

Fog

Fog is simply a cl[...] our industrialized [...] Dense fog on high[...] accidents, sometim[...] ing injury or deat[...]

4.11 Cloud families and types *Clouds are grouped into families on the basis o[f] height. Individual cloud types are named according to their form.*

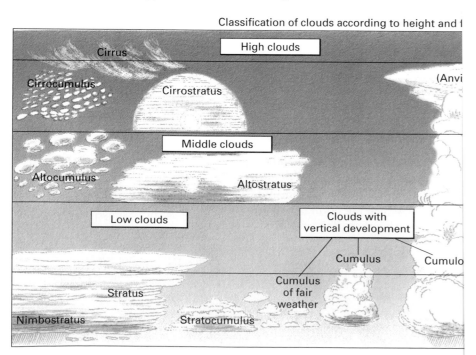

Classification of clouds according to height and [...]

Focus on Remote Sensing | 4.[...]

Some of the most familiar images of Earth acquired by satellite instruments are those of the Geostationary Operational Environmental Satellite (GOES) system. Images from the GOES series of satellites, and its pathfinding predecessors, Synchronous Meterological Satellite (SMS) −1 and −2, have been in constant use by meterologists and weather forecasters since 1974. The primary mission of the GOES series is to view cloud patterns and track weather systems by providing frequent images of the Earth from a consistent viewpoint in space. This capability is of great economic value in forecasting storms and severe weather.

A key feature of the GOES series is its geostationary orbit. Recall from *Geographer's Tools 2.1 ● Remote Sensing for Physical Geography* that a satellite in geostationary orbit rotates above the equator in the same direction as the Earth and at the same angular velocity—that is, it remains constantly above the same point on the equator. From this vantage

point, [...] consta[...] Earth [...] tiona[...] cloud[...]

Alt[...] three [...] place[...] have [...] ous s[...] points[...] 75°W [...] North[...] (GOES[...] tems [...] appro[...] acros[...] provi[...] weath[...] the ea[...] they [...] East [...] Atlan[...] tropic[...] they f[...] towar[...] south[...]

Th[...] platf[...] instru[...]

4.13 Eye on the Landscape Sea fog *A layer of sea fog along the Big Sur coast of California, south of San Francisco. A patch of fog has burned off in the center embayment, revealing the water surface and a pocket beach.* **What else would the geographer see? ... Answers at the end of the chapter.**

4.14 Formation of rain in warm clouds *As cloud droplets are formed and carried aloft in a rising cloud, they collide and coalesce, building drops that are large enough to fall downward (left). As a drop grows in size, its weight increases until it overcomes the upward force of the rising air and the drop begins to fall (right).*

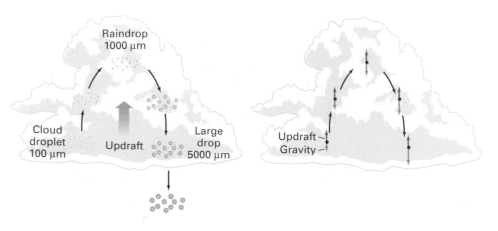

Raindrop 1000 μm

Cloud droplet 100 μm   Updraft   Large drop 5000 μm

Updraft Gravity

further, taking on shapes such as plates, columns, or needles. Under certain conditions, the ice crystals take the form of *dendrites*—delicate structures with six-sided symmetry (Figure 4.15).

When the underlying air layer is below freezing, snow reaches the ground as a solid form of precipitation. Otherwise, it melts and arrives as rain. A reverse process, the fall of raindrops through a cold air layer, results in the freezing

4.15 Snowflakes *These individual snow crystals, greatly magnified, were selected for their beauty.*

of rain and produces pellets or grains of ice. These are commonly referred to in North America as *sleet*. (Among the British, sleet refers to a mixture of snow and rain.)

Perhaps you have experienced an *ice storm*. This occurs when the ground is frozen and the lowest air layer is also below freezing. Rain falling through the layer is chilled and freezes onto ground surfaces as a clear glaze. Ice storms cause great damage, especially to telephone and power lines and to tree limbs pulled down by the weight of the ice. In addition, roads and sidewalks are made extremely hazardous by the slippery glaze. Actually, the ice storm is more accurately named an "icing" storm, since it is not ice that is falling but supercooled rain.

Hail, another form of precipitation, consists of lumps of ice ranging from pea- to grapefruit-sized—that is, with a diameter of 5 mm (0.2 in.) or larger. Most hail particles are roughly spherical in shape. The formation of hail will be explained in our discussion of the thunderstorm.

Precipitation is measured in units of depth of fall per unit of time—for example, centimeters or inches per hour or per day. A centimeter (inch) of rainfall would cover the ground to a depth of 1 cm (1 in.) if the water did not run off or sink into the soil. Rainfall is measured with a *rain gauge*. The simplest rain gauge is a straight-sided, flat-bottomed pan, which is set outside before a rainfall event. (An empty coffee can does nicely.) After the rain, the depth of water in the pan is measured.

A very small amount of rainfall, such as 2 mm (0.1 in.), makes too thin a layer to be accurately measured in a flat pan. To avoid this difficulty, a typical rain gauge is constructed from a narrow cylinder with a funnel at the top (Figure 4.16). The funnel gathers rain from a wider area than the mouth of the cylinder, so the cylinder fills more quickly. The water level gives the amount of precipitation, which is read on a graduated scale.

Snowfall is measured by melting a sample column of snow and reducing it to an equivalent in rainfall. In this way, rainfall and snowfall records may be combined in a single record of precipitation. Ordinarily, a 10-cm (or 10-in.) layer of snow is assumed to be equivalent to 1 cm (or 1 in.) of rainfall, but this ratio may range from 30 to 1 in very loose snow to 2 to 1 in old, partly melted snow.

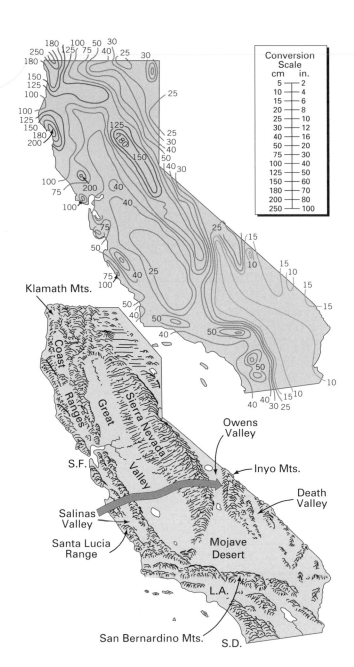

4.18 Orographic precipitation effects in California
The effect of mountain ranges on precipitation is strong in the state of California because of the prevailing flow of moist oceanic air from west to east. Centers of high precipitation coincide with the western slopes of mountain ranges, including the coast ranges and Sierra Nevada. To the east, in their rain shadows, lie desert regions.

Conversion Scale	
cm	in.
5	2
10	4
15	6
20	8
25	10
30	12
40	16
50	20
75	30
100	40
125	50
150	60
180	70
200	80
250	100

balloon. Because the heated air is less dense than the surrounding air, the balloon rises. The same principle will cause a bubble of air to form over the field, rise, and break free from the surface. Figure 4.19 diagrams this process.

As the bubble of air rises, it is cooled adiabatically and its temperature will decrease as it rises. However, we know that the temperature of the surrounding air will normally decrease with altitude as well. Nonetheless, as long as the bubble is still warmer than the surrounding air, it will be less dense and will therefore continue to rise.

If the bubble remains warmer than the surrounding air and uplift continues, adiabatic cooling chills the bubble below the dew point. Condensation occurs, and the rising air column becomes a puffy cumulus cloud. The flat base of the cloud marks the lifting condensation level at which condensation begins. The bulging "cauliflower" top of the cloud is the top of the rising warm-air column, pushing into higher levels of the atmosphere. Normally, the small cumulus cloud will encounter winds aloft that mix it into the local air. After drifting some distance downwind, the cloud evaporates.

UNSTABLE AIR Sometimes, however, convection continues strongly, and the cloud develops into a dense cumulonimbus mass, or thunderstorm, from which heavy rain will fall. Two environmental conditions encourage the development of thunderstorm: (1) air that is very warm and moist, and (2) an environmental temperature lapse rate in which temperature decreases more rapidly with altitude than it does for either the dry or wet adiabatic lapse rates. Figure 4.20, which diagrams the convection process in unstable air, shows this type of lapse rate as having a flatter slope than the dry or wet adiabatic

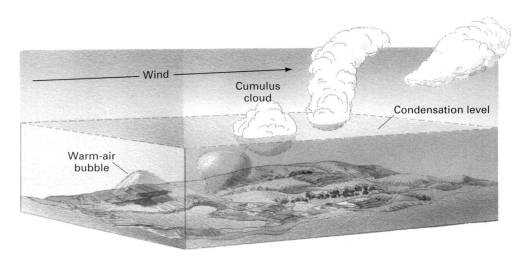

4.19 Formation of a cumulus cloud
A bubble of heated air rises above the lifting condensation level to form a cumulus cloud.

rates. Air with these characteristics is referred to as **unstable air.**

For the first condition, recall that there are two adiabatic rates—dry and wet (Figure 4.10). The wet rate is about half the dry rate. While condensation is occurring, the lesser wet rate applies. Thus, air in which condensation is occurring cools less rapidly with uplift. Furthermore, the wet rate is smallest for warm, moist air. This means that the temperature decrease experienced by warm, moist, rising, condensing air is quite small. And since the temperature decrease is small, the rising air is more likely to stay warmer than the surrounding air. Thus, uplift continues.

With regard to the second condition—an environmental temperature lapse rate value that exceeds the adiabatic rates—keep in mind that this rate describes the temperature of the surrounding, still air. Therefore, the temperature of the still air falls quite rapidly with altitude. This means that the condensing air in a rising parcel will stay warmer than the surrounding air. Again, uplift continues.

A simple example may make convection in unstable air clearer. Figure 4.20 shows how temperature changes with altitude for a parcel moving upward by convection in unstable air. The surrounding air is at a temperature of 26°C (78.8°F) at ground level and has a lapse rate of 12°C/1000 m (6.6°F/1000 ft). A parcel of air is heated by 1°C (1.8°F) to 27°C (80.6°F), and it begins to rise. At first, it cools at the

> **Unstable air—warm, moist, and heated by the surface—can produce abundant convectional precipitation. It is typical of hot summer air masses in the central and southeastern United States.**

dry adiabatic rate. At 500 m (1640 ft), the parcel is at 22°C (71.6°F), while the surrounding air is at 20°C (68°F). Since it is still warmer than the surrounding air, uplift continues. At 1000 m, the lifting condensation level is reached. The temperature of the parcel is 17°C (62.6°F).

As the parcel rises above the condensation level, the wet adiabatic rate applies, here using the value 5°C/1000 m (2.7°F/1000 ft). Now the parcel cools more slowly as it rises. At 1500 m (4920 ft), the parcel is 14.5°C (58.1°F), while the surrounding air is 8°C (46.4°F). Since the parcel is still warmer than the surrounding air, it continues to rise. Note that the difference in temperature between the rising parcel and the surrounding air now actually increases with altitude. This means that the parcel will be buoyed upward ever more strongly, forcing even more condensation and precipitation.

The key to the convectional precipitation process is latent heat. When water vapor condenses into cloud droplets or ice particles, it releases latent heat to the rising air parcel. By keeping the parcel warmer than the surrounding air, this latent heat fuels the convection process, driving the parcel ever higher. When the parcel reaches a high altitude, most of its water will have condensed. As adiabatic cooling continues, less latent heat will be released. As a result, the uplift will weaken. Eventually, uplift will stop, since the energy source, latent heat, is gone. The cell dies and dissipates into the surrounding air.

4.20 Convection in unstable air *When the air is unstable, a parcel of air that is heated sufficiently to rise will continue to rise to great heights.*

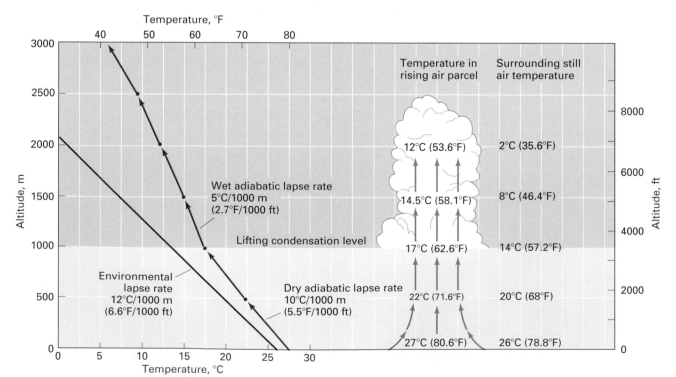

4.21 Thunderstorms

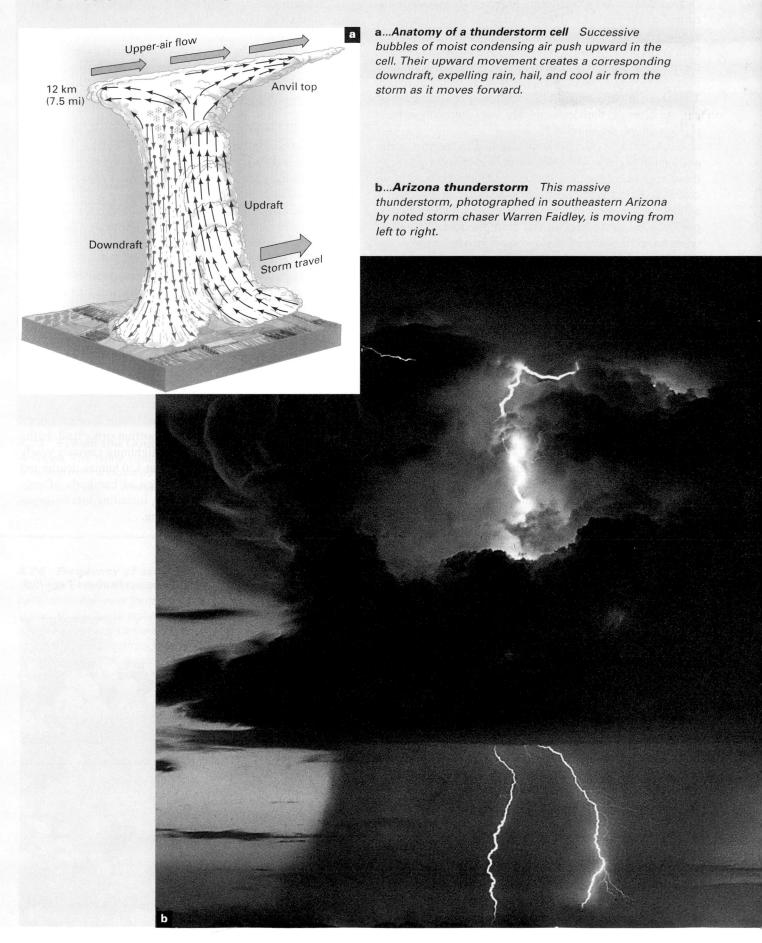

Upper-air flow

12 km
(7.5 mi)

Anvil top

Updraft

Downdraft

Storm travel

a...**Anatomy of a thunderstorm cell**   *Successive bubbles of moist condensing air push upward in the cell. Their upward movement creates a corresponding downdraft, expelling rain, hail, and cool air from the storm as it moves forward.*

b...**Arizona thunderstorm**   *This massive thunderstorm, photographed in southeastern Arizona by noted storm chaser Warren Faidley, is moving from left to right.*

5 | WINDS AND GLOBAL CIRCULATION

● ● ● ● ● ● ● ● ● ● ● ● ● ● ● ●
PUTTING YOU IN THE PICTURE

Coming about! You push the tiller hard to the opposite side of the boat, and the small craft turns easily into the wind. The sail goes slack and begins to swing across the boat. You duck under the boom, the long pole that holds the bottom of the sail taut, and you step neatly to the other side. The sail now catches the wind from the other side and begins to fill. You pull in the line attached to the sail and correct the rudder for your new course. The sail tightens, and the boat leans away from the wind, gathering speed. You quickly move to the boat's edge and, sitting on the rim, lean out over the water. Your weight is held in check by the strong pull of the sail on the line in your right hand. The boat swings upright, and you are skimming across the water again, thanks to the cool, southeast breeze.

What a marvelous setting for a sail! With the soaring skyscrapers of Boston on the south and the leafy Cambridge campus of MIT on the north, the mouth of the Charles River is the magnificent jewel in the center of the famed necklace of parks, green spaces, and beaches that frames the map of the city. Unfortunately, you're not the only one out for a sail. There are perhaps a dozen other boats sharing the water with you, and since it's still early in the afternoon, the fleet is sure to increase. Watching out for them requires attention.

Sailing on the Charles River in downtown Boston is always something of a challenge. Not only are there other sailors, but

151

along the Peruvian coast is greatly reduced. El Niño events normally occur on a three- to eight-year cycle and affect global patterns of precipitation in many regions. The causes of El Niño are not well understood.

- The Pacific decadal oscillation in sea surface temperature steers the polar jet stream over the Pacific, which alters winter storm tracks to create 20- to 30-year cycles of wet and dry years along the Pacific coast and arid interior western states.

- Slow, deep ocean currents are driven by the sinking of cold, salty water in the northern Atlantic. This *thermohaline circulation* pattern involves nearly all the Earth's ocean basins, and also acts to moderate the buildup of atmospheric CO_2 by moving CO_2-rich surface waters to ocean depths.

Key Terms

millibar, p. 153
barometer, p. 153
wind, p. 154
pressure gradient, p. 155

isobar, p. 155
Coriolis effect, p. 158
cyclones, p. 161
anticyclones, p. 161
Hadley cells, p. 162

intertropical convergence zone (ITCZ), p. 162
subtropical high-pressure belts, p. 162

monsoon, p. 166
Rossby waves, p. 170
jet streams, p. 171
gyres, p. 174

Review Questions

1. Explain atmospheric pressure. Why does it occur? How is atmospheric pressure measured and in what units? What is the normal value of atmospheric pressure at sea level? How does atmospheric pressure change with altitude?

2. Describe a simple convective wind system, explaining how air motion arises from a pressure gradient force induced by heating.

3. Describe land and sea breezes. How do they illustrate the concepts of pressure gradient and convection loop?

4. How do valley and mountain breezes arise? How are they related to land and sea breezes?

5. What are drainage winds? What local names are applied to them?

6. What is the Coriolis effect, and why is it important? What produces it? How does it influence the motion of wind and ocean currents in the northern hemisphere? in the southern hemisphere?

7. Define cyclone and anticyclone. How does air move within each? What is the direction of circulation of each in the northern and southern hemispheres? What type of weather is associated with each and why?

8. What is the Asian monsoon? Describe the features of this circulation in summer and winter. How is the ITCZ involved? How is the monsoon circulation related to the high- and low-pressure centers that develop seasonally in Asia?

9. Compare the winter and summer patterns of high and low pressure that develop in the northern hemisphere with those that develop in the southern hemisphere.

10. How does global-scale heating of the atmosphere create a pressure gradient force that increases with altitude?

11. What is the geostrophic wind, and what is its direction with respect to the pressure gradient force?

12. Describe the basic pattern of global atmospheric circulation at upper levels.

13. What are Rossby waves? Why are they important?

14. Identify five jet streams. Where do they occur? In which direction do they flow?

15. What is the general pattern of ocean surface current circulation? How is it related to global wind patterns?

16. What is the Pacific decadal oscillation? On what time scale does it operate? What are its effects?

17. How does thermohaline circulation induce deep ocean currents?

Eye on the Environment 5.1 • Wind Power, Wave Power, and Current Power

1. Discuss wind power as a source of energy. Include indirect use in tapping waves and ocean currents for energy.

Eye on Global Change 5.2 • El Niño

1. Compare the normal pattern of wind, pressure, and ocean currents in the equatorial Pacific with the pattern during an El Niño event.

2. What are some of the weather changes reported for El Niño events?

3. What is La Niña, and how does it compare with the normal pattern?

Visualizing Exercises

1. Sketch an ideal Earth (without seasons or ocean—continent features) and its global wind system. Label the following on your sketch: doldrums, equatorial trough, Hadley cell, ITCZ, northeast trades, polar easterlies, polar front, polar outbreak, southeast trades, subtropical high-pressure belts, and westerlies.

2. Draw four spiral patterns showing outward and inward flow in clockwise and counterclockwise directions. Label each as appropriate to cyclonic or anticyclonic circulation in the northern or southern hemisphere.

Essay Questions

1. An airline pilot is planning a nonstop flight from Los Angeles to Sydney, Australia. What general wind conditions can the pilot expect to find in the upper atmosphere as the airplane travels? What jet streams will be encountered? Will they slow or speed the aircraft on its way?
2. You are planning to take a round-the-world cruise, leaving New York in October. Your vessel's route will take you through the Mediterranean Sea to Cairo, Egypt, in early December. Then you will pass through the Suez Canal and Red Sea to the Indian Ocean, calling at Bombay, India, in January. From Bombay, you will sail to Djakarta, Indonesia, and then go directly to Perth, Australia, arriving in March. Rounding the southern coast of Australia, your next port of call is Auckland, New Zealand, which you will reach in April. From Auckland, you head directly to San Francisco, your final destination, arriving in June. Describe the general wind and weather conditions you will experience on each leg of your journey.

Eye on the Landscape

Chapter Opener Sailboats on the Charles River, Boston An urban landscape In a large city, such as Boston, very little of the landscape is in a natural state. Although the skyscrapers **(A)** are anchored firmly to Boston's bedrock, much of the city is built on fill brought in near the turn of the twentieth century. The Charles River, once a tidal estuary, is dammed and now amounts to a shallow freshwater lake **(B)**. The vegetation on the Esplanade that borders the river is nearly all planted with culvated trees chosen for their appearance and utility. In short, just about everything in this scene is a product of human activity.

5.11 Brushfire The dense, shrubby vegetation on this slope is chaparral, a mix of tough woody shrubs with leathery leaves **(A)** that is often found on steep slopes in Mediterranean climates (covered in Chapter 7). To reduce moisture loss during the hot, dry summer, many plants of the chaparral have waxy, oily leaves that can prove very flammable under the right conditions. Chaparral is a vegetation type that depends on burning at regular intervals to maintain itself, so the fire in this picture is merely part of a natural process.

5.29 Jet stream clouds A desert landscape seen from space. Large expanses of the Middle East are essentially devoid of vegetation, and so a space photo such as this shows variation in soil and surface color. Many of the white areas **(A)** are wind-blown sand sheets (see Dunes, Chapter 18), while the medium tones are weathered rock materials that have not been carried as far by wind or water from their origin (see Chapters 16 and 18 for sediment transportation by water and wind). Ranges of hills and low mountains **(B)** appear darker due to a sparse vegetation cover. The Nile River Valley cuts a wide swath through the region, with its broad band of irrigated agriculture (see Chapter 15 on rivers). The overall blue tint is produced by atmospheric scattering (Chapter 2), which is more intense in the blue region of the spectrum.

5.34 Sea-surface temperatures This image shows a temperature pattern over the land **(A)** as well as the water. The general gradient from yellow and red tones (hot) to dark tones (cold) shows land surface temperatures decreasing strongly from Florida to the Maritime Provinces, as we might expect for a week in April. Industrial and residential regions, such as the Washington to New York corridor, Hudson River Valley, and Connecticut River Valley show warmer temperatures due to human activity (see Chapter 3 on urban-rural surface temperature contrasts). Note the dark color of the Appalachians, which are colder because of their elevation (see Chapter 3 for how surface temperature varies with elevation).

EYE ON THE LANDSCAPE

Hurricane Ivan heading for the Florida panhandle on September 15, 2004, as observed by GOES-12. Ivan, joined by Charley, Frances, and Jeanne, was one of four hurricanes to make landfall in the state of Florida in 2004. **What else would the geographer see? … Answers at the end of the chapter.**

6 | WEATHER SYSTEMS

. . . .
PUTTING YOU IN THE PICTURE

Our day-to-day weather may occasionally be stormy, bringing the inconvenience of rain or snow to our daily activities. But rare storms, with high winds, high coastal ocean waters, and torrential rains or blizzards of snow can cause great destruction and loss of life. What is it like to experience a severe storm?

On August 23, 1992, Hurricane Andrew approached the coast of south Florida, near Miami. Following the path of the storm was veteran storm chaser and photographer, Warren Faidley, who decided to ride out the storm with two friends, Steve and Mike. For their shelter, they selected a sturdy parking garage, built of concrete and steel, in a coastal community south of Miami. Here is part of Faidley's account of the terrifying night of the storm.

At sunset, my friends and I gathered at the garage. Throughout the evening we monitored radio and television broadcasts. With ominous accuracy, Robert Sheets, director of the National Hurricane Center, gave hourly updates on Andrew, now a Category 4 … Like sentries awaiting an advancing army, we took turns scanning the Miami skyline from our borrowed fortress, searching for early signs of Andrew. Bright flashes from downed power lines on the horizon marked Andrew's imminent arrival.

Steve and I held an anemometer through the opening on the fourth floor. "Fifty-five miles per hour!" I yelled over the howling. "A gust to 65!" The meter almost flew out of my hand. The electrical explosions across the city grew more intense, yet the fury of the wind swallowed up all sound save the car alarms whining inside the garage. Eventually even the alarms were overwhelmed by the whistling wind.

Around 4 A.M. all hell broke loose. I have experienced severe storms with winds in excess of 75 m.p.h., but these gusts were blowing at well over 140 m.p.h. The anemometer and later damage surveys indicated even stronger gusts. By now only an occasional thud—some building collapsing or losing a roof—would punctuate the noise. Windows from the surrounding buildings imploded, scattering glass everywhere. I looked down at my arm and saw blood, not knowing when I'd been cut. Putting on my reading glasses to protect my eyes, I made a mental note: next time, bring goggles.

My senses were on red alert, a self-preservation mode I adopt only in the most extreme danger. Everything I see, hear, feel—even taste—goes by so quickly that my mind simply slows it all down to preserve rational thought. The alternative is sheer panic.

The infamous "hurricane wail" people talk about is in many ways unreal—"the scream of the devil," Steve and I agreed. The piercing sound alone is wicked enough, but mixed with breaking glass and crashing debris, it rattled me inside. I will never forget that sound…

In the garage, not all was well. The elevator shafts had begun to flood; water poured out between the doors and cascaded down the emergency stairwells. The lights in the garage flickered on and off and the fire alarm blared, yet it was hardly audible in the din. … I trusted the structural integrity of our fortress, but under Andrew's full force, the garage began to oscillate. After two hours of this swaying, I began to worry one of the floors might collapse…

For more than five hours Andrew pounded the garage and the rest of South Florida with everything it had. As the building shook and the storm raged all around, I felt as though I was inside a tornado and riding an earthquake at the same time.*

Hurricane Andrew was the most costly natural disaster to strike the United States, with some damage estimates as high as $40 billion in today's dollars. *Eye on the Environment 6.2 • Hurricane Andrew—Killer Cyclone* provides more information on this devastating storm. Hurricanes, or tropical cyclones, as they are termed by meteorologists, are but one of a number of types of weather systems that are the subject of this chapter. ∎

*From *Weatherwise,* vol. 45, no. 6, Copyright © Warren Faidley. Used by permission.

WEATHER SYSTEMS

As we saw in Chapter 5, the Earth's atmosphere is in constant motion, driven by the planet's rotation and its uneven heating by the Sun. The horizontal motion of the wind moves air from one place to another, allowing air to acquire characteristics of temperature and humidity in one region and then carry those characteristics into another region. The vertical motion affects clouds and precipitation. When air is lifted, it is cooled, enabling clouds and precipitation to form. When air descends, it is warmed, retarding the formation of clouds and precipitation. In this way, the Earth's wind system influences the weather we experience from day to day—the temperature and humidity of the air, cloudiness, and the amount of precipitation.

Some patterns of wind circulation occur commonly and so present recurring patterns of weather. For example, traveling low-pressure centers (cyclones) of converging, inspiraling air often bring warm, moist air in contact with cooler, drier air, with clouds and precipitation as the result. We recognize these recurring circulation patterns and their associated weather as **weather systems.**

Weather systems range in size from a few kilometers, in the case of the tornado, to a thousand kilometers or more, in the case of a large traveling anticyclone. They may last for hours or weeks, depending on their size and strength. Some forms of weather systems—tornadoes and hurricanes, for example—involve high winds and heavy rainfall and can be very destructive to life and property.

Recall that in Chapter 4, we recognized four types of precipitation, each arising from somewhat different causes: orographic, convectional, cyclonic, and convergent. In each case, moist air rises, condensation occurs, clouds form, and ultimately precipitation results. In this chapter we will examine cyclonic and convergent precipitation in more detail as they occur in weather systems. We will also see that more than one type of precipitation may be associated with a particular type of weather system.

AIR MASSES

Weather systems are often associated with the motion of air masses. An **air mass** is a large body of air with fairly uniform temperature and moisture characteristics. It can be several thousand kilometers or miles across, and it can extend upward to the top of the troposphere. A given air mass is characterized by a distinctive combination of surface temperature, environmental temperature lapse rate, and surface-specific humidity. Air masses range widely in temperature—from searing hot to icy cold—as well as in moisture content.

Air masses acquire their characteristics in *source regions.* In a source

---

Air masses are large bodies of air with fairly uniform temperature and moisture characteristics that are acquired from a source region. They are classified by latitudinal position (e.g., arctic, tropical), which largely determines temperature, and by underlying surface type (maritime, continental), which largely determines moisture content.

region, air moves slowly or stagnates, which allows the air to acquire temperature and moisture characteristics from the region's surface. For example, an air mass with warm temperatures and a high water vapor content develops over a warm equatorial ocean. Over a large tropical desert, slowly subsiding air forms a hot air mass with low humidity. A very cold air mass with a low water vapor content is generated over cold, snow-covered land surfaces in the arctic zone in winter.

Air masses move from one region to another under the influence of pressure gradients and upper-level wind patterns and are sometimes pushed or blocked by high-level jet stream winds. When an air mass moves to a new area, its properties will begin to change because it is influenced by the new surface environment. For example, the air mass may lose heat or take up water vapor.

Air masses are classified on the basis of the latitudinal position and the nature of the underlying surface of their source regions. Latitudinal position primarily determines surface temperature and the environmental temperature lapse rate of the air mass, while the nature of the underlying surface—continent or ocean—usually determines the moisture content. For latitudinal position, five types of air masses are distinguished, as shown in the following table.

Air Mass	Symbol	Source Region
Arctic	A	Arctic ocean and fringing lands
Antarctic	AA	Antarctica
Polar	P	Continents and oceans, lat. 50–60° N and S
Tropical	T	Continents and oceans, lat. 20–35° N and S
Equatorial	E	Oceans close to equator

For the type of underlying surface, two subdivisions are used:

Air Mass	Symbol	Source Region
Maritime	m	Oceans
Continental	c	Continents

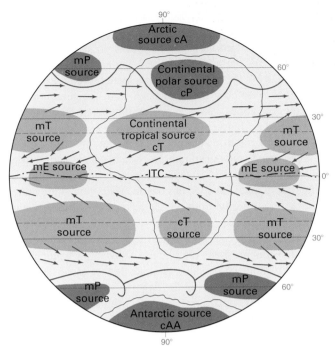

6.1 Global air masses and source regions *An idealized continent, producing continental (c) air masses, is shown at the center. It is surrounded by oceans, producing maritime air masses (m). Tropical (T) and equatorial (E) source regions provide warm or hot air masses, while polar (P), arctic (A), and antarctic (AA) source regions provide colder air masses of low specific humidity.*

Combining these two types of labels produces a list of six important types of air masses, shown in Table 6.1. The table also gives some typical values of surface temperature and specific humidity, although these can vary widely, depending on season. Air mass temperature can range from –46°C (–51°F) for continental arctic (cA) air masses to 27°C (81°F) for maritime equatorial air masses (mE). Specific humidity shows a very high range—from 0.1 g/kg for the cA air mass to as much as 19 g/kg for the mE air mass. In other words, maritime equatorial air can hold about 200 times as much moisture as continental arctic air.

Figure 6.1 shows schematically the global distribution of source regions of these air masses. An idealized continent is

Table 6.1 | Properties of Typical Air Masses

Air Mass	Symbol	Source Region	Properties	Temperature °C	(°F)	Specific Humidity (gm/kg)
Maritime equatorial	mE	Warm oceans in the equatorial zone	Warm, very moist	27°	(81°)	19
Maritime tropical	mT	Warm oceans in the tropical zone	Warm, moist	24°	(75°)	17
Continental tropical	cT	Subtropical deserts	Warm, dry	24°	(75°)	17
Maritime polar	mP	Midlatitude oceans	Cool, moist (winter)	4°	(39°)	4.4
Continental polar	cP	Northern continental interiors	Cold, dry (winter)	–11°	(12°)	1.4
Continental arctic (and continental antarctic)	cA (cAA)	Regions near north and south poles	Very cold, very dry (winter)	–46°	(–51°)	0.1

shown in the center of the figure surrounded by ocean. Note from the figure that the polar air masses (mP, cP) originate in the subarctic latitude zone, not in the polar latitude zone. Recall that in Chapter 2 we defined "polar" as a region containing one of the poles. However, meteorologists use the word "polar" to describe air masses from the subarctic and subantarctic zones, and we will follow their usage when referring to air masses.

The maritime tropical air mass (mT) and maritime equatorial air mass (mE) originate over warm oceans in the tropical and equatorial zones. They are quite similar in temperature and water vapor content. With their high values of specific humidity, both are capable of very heavy yields of precipitation. The continental tropical air mass (cT) has its source region over subtropical deserts of the continents. Although this air mass may have a substantial water vapor content, it tends to be stable and has low relative humidity when highly heated during the daytime.

The maritime polar air mass (mP) originates over midlatitude oceans. Since the quantity of water vapor it holds is not as large as maritime tropical air masses, the mP air mass yields only moderate precipitation. Much of this precipitation is orographic and occurs over mountain ranges on the western coasts of continents. The continental polar air mass (cP) originates over North America and Eurasia in the subarctic zone. It has low specific humidity and is very cold in winter. Last is the continental arctic (and continental antarctic) air mass type (cA, cAA), which is extremely cold and holds almost no water vapor.

North American Air Masses

The air masses that form in and near North America have a strong influence on North American weather. The source regions of these air masses are shown in Figure 6.2. The continental polar (cP) air mass of North America originates over north-central Canada. This air mass forms tongues of cold, dry air that periodically extend south and east from the source region to produce anticyclones accompanied by cool or cold temperatures and clear skies. The arctic air mass (cA) that develops over the Arctic Ocean and its bordering lands of the arctic zone in winter is extremely cold and stable. When this air mass moves southward, it produces a severe cold wave.

The maritime polar air mass (mP) originates over the North Pacific and Bering Strait, in the region of the persistent Aleutian low-pressure center. This air mass is characteristically cool and moist, with a tendency in winter to become unstable, giving heavy precipitation over coastal ranges. Another maritime polar air mass of the North American region originates over the North Atlantic Ocean. It, too, is cool and moist, and is felt especially in Canada's maritime provinces in winter.

Of the tropical air masses, the most common visitor to the central and eastern United States is the maritime tropical air mass (mT) from the Gulf of Mexico. It moves northward, bringing warm, moist, unstable air over the eastern part of the country. In the summer, particularly, this air mass brings

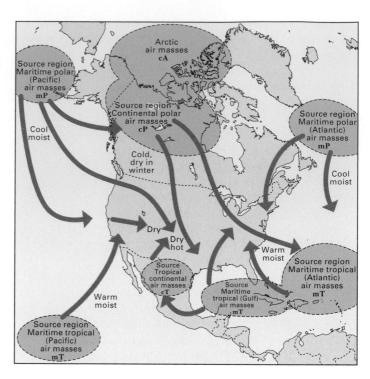

6.2   North American air mass source regions and trajectories *Air masses acquire temperature and moisture characteristics in their source regions, then move across the continent. (Data from U.S. of Dept. Commerce.)*

hot, sultry weather to the central and eastern United States. It also produces many thunderstorms. Closely related is a maritime tropical air mass from the Atlantic Ocean east of Florida, over the Bahamas.

Over the Pacific Ocean, a source region of another maritime tropical air mass (mT) lies in the cell of high pressure located to the southwest of lower California. Occasionally, in summer, this moist unstable air mass penetrates the southwestern desert region, bringing severe thunderstorms to southern California and southern Arizona. In winter, a tongue of mT air frequently reaches the California coast, bringing heavy rainfall that is intensified when forced to rise over coastal mountain ranges.

A hot, dry continental tropical air mass (cT) originates over northern Mexico, western Texas, New Mexico, and Arizona during the summer. This air mass does not travel widely but governs weather conditions over the source region.

Cold, Warm, and Occluded Fronts

A given air mass usually has a sharply defined boundary between itself and a neighboring air mass. This boundary is termed a **front.** We saw an example of a front in the contact between polar and tropical air masses, shown in Figures 5.16, 5.25, and 5.27. This feature is the *polar front,* and it is located below the axis of the jet stream in the upper-air waves.

Figure 6.3 shows the structure of a front along which a cold air mass invades a zone occupied by a warm air mass. A front of this type is called a **cold front.** Because the colder air

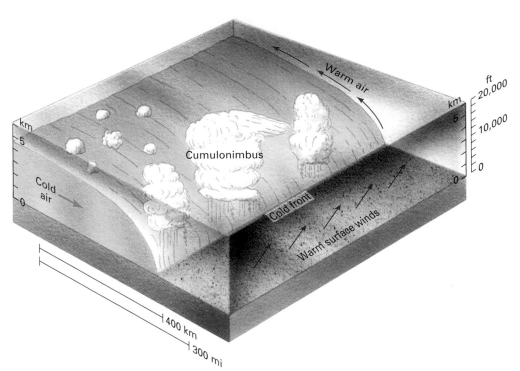

6.3 Cold front *At a cold front, a cold air mass lifts a warm air mass aloft. The upward motion sets off a line of thunderstorms. The frontal boundary is actually much less steep than is shown in this schematic drawing. (Drawn by A. N. Strahler.)*

mass is denser, it remains in contact with the ground. As it moves forward, it forces the warmer air mass to rise above it. If the warm air is unstable, severe thunderstorms may develop. Thunderstorms near a cold front often form a long line of massive clouds stretching for tens of kilometers (Figure 6.4).

> Fronts are boundaries between air masses. When cold air invades warmer air, the boundary is a cold front. When warm air invades colder air, the boundary is a warm front.

Figure 6.5 diagrams a **warm front** in which warm air moves into a region of colder air. Here, again, the cold air mass remains in contact with the ground because it is denser. The warm air mass is forced to rise on a long ramp over the cold air below. The rising motion causes stratus clouds to form, and precipitation

6.4 Cold front cumulus *A line of cumulus clouds marks the advance of a cold front, moving from left to right. The cold air pushes warmer, moister air aloft, triggering cloud formation.*

6.5 Warm front *In a warm front, warm air advances toward cold air and rides up and over the cold air. A notch of cloud is cut away to show rain falling from the dense stratus cloud layer. (Drawn by A. N. Strahler.)*

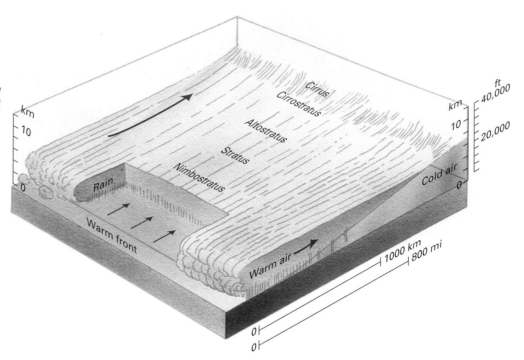

often follows. If the warm air is stable, the precipitation will be steady (Figure 6.5). If the warm air is unstable, convection cells can develop, producing cumulonimbus clouds with heavy showers or thunderstorms (not shown in the figure).

Cold fronts normally move along the ground at a faster rate than warm fronts. Thus, when both types are in the same neighborhood, a cold front can overtake a warm front. The result is an **occluded front,** diagrammed in Figure 6.6. ("Occluded" means closed or shut off.) The colder air of the fast-moving cold front remains next to the ground, forcing both the warm air and the less cold air ahead to rise over it. The warm air mass is lifted completely free of the ground.

Another type of front is the *stationary front,* in which two air masses are in contact but with little or no relative motion. Often a stationary front arises when a cold or warm front stalls and ceases forward motion. Clouds and precipitation associated with the earlier motion will often remain in the vicinity of the front.

> In an occluded front, a cold front overtakes a warm front, lifting a pool of warm, moist air upward. The result is a region of clouds and precipitation.

TRAVELING CYCLONES AND ANTICYCLONES

Air masses are set in motion by wind systems—typically, cyclones and anticyclones that involve masses of air moving in a spiraling motion. As we saw in Chapter 5, air spirals inward and converges in a *cyclone,* while air spirals outward and diverges in an *anticyclone.* Most types of cyclones and anticyclones

> In middle and higher latitudes, traveling cyclones and anticyclones bring changing weather systems. In cyclones, convergence and uplift typically cause condensation and precipitation, while in anticyclones subsidence causes air to be warmed, producing clear conditions.

are large features that move slowly across the Earth's surface, bringing changes in the weather as they move. These are referred to as *traveling cyclones* and *traveling anticyclones.*

In a cyclone, convergence and upward motion cause air to rise and be cooled adiabatically. If the air is moist, condensation or deposition can occur. This is **cyclonic precipitation.** Many cyclones are weak and pass overhead with little more than a period of cloud cover and light precipitation. However, when pressure gradients are steep and the inspiraling motion is strong, intense winds and heavy rain or snow can accompany the cyclone. In this case, the disturbance is called a **cyclonic storm.**

Traveling cyclones fall into three types. First is the wave cyclone of midlatitude, arctic, and antarctic zones. This type of cyclone ranges in intensity from a weak disturbance to a powerful storm. Second is the tropical cyclone of tropical and subtropical zones. This type of cyclone ranges in intensity from a mild disturbance to the highly destructive hurricane or typhoon. A third type is the tornado, a small, intense cyclone of enormously powerful winds. The tornado is much, much smaller in size than other cyclones, and it is related to strong convectional activity.

In an anticyclone, downward motion causes air to descend and be warmed adiabatically. Thus, condensation does not occur. Skies are fair, except for occasional puffy cumulus clouds that sometimes develop in a moist surface air layer. Because of these characteristics, anticyclones are often termed *fair-weather systems.*

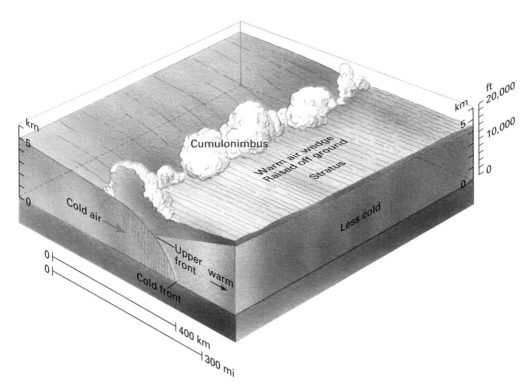

6.6 Occluded front In an occluded front, a warm front is overtaken by a cold front. The warm air is pushed aloft, and it no longer contacts the ground. Abrupt lifting by the denser cold air produces precipitation. (Drawn by A. N. Strahler.)

Toward the center of an anticyclone, the pressure gradient is weak, and winds are light and variable. Traveling anticyclones are found in the midlatitudes. They are typically associated with ridges or domes of clear, dry air that move eastward and equatorward. Figure 6.7 is a geostationary satellite image of eastern North America. A large anticyclone is centered over the area, bringing fair weather and cloudless skies.

6.7 Eye on the Landscape Picture of an anticyclone This geostationary satellite image of eastern North America shows a large anticyclone centered over the area, bringing fair weather and cloudless skies. The boundary between clear sky and clouds running across the Gulf of Mexico and the Florida peninsula delineates the leading edge of the cool, dry air mass. The cloud edge at the top of the photo marks the cold fronts of two cold air masses advancing eastward and southward. **What else would the geographer see? ... Answers at the end of the chapter.**

6.8 Conditions for formation of a wave cyclone
Two anticyclones, one with warm subtropical air and the other with cold polar air, are in contact on the polar front. The shaded area is shown in block (a) of the following figure as the early stage of development of a wave cyclone.

Wave Cyclones

In middle and high latitudes, the dominant form of weather system is the **wave cyclone,** a large inspiral of air that repeatedly forms, intensifies, and dissolves along the polar front. Figure 6.8 shows a situation favorable to the formation of a wave cyclone. Two large anticyclones are in contact on the polar front. One contains a cold, dry polar air mass, and the other a warm, moist maritime air mass. Airflow converges from opposite directions on the two sides of the front, setting up an unstable situation. The wave cyclone will begin to form between the two high-pressure cells in a zone of lower pressure referred to as a *low-pressure trough.*

How does a wave cyclone form, grow, and eventually dissolve? Figure 6.9 shows the life history of a wave cyclone. In block (*a*) (early stage), the polar-front region shows a wave beginning to form. Cold air is turned in a southerly direction and warm air in a northerly direction, so that each advances on the other. As these frontal motions develop, precipitation will form.

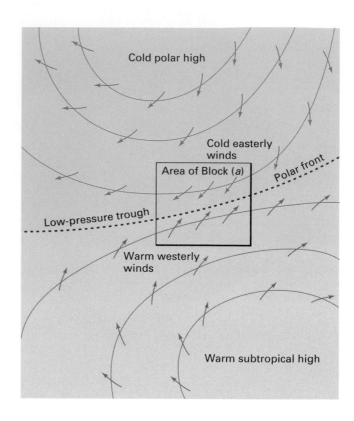

6.9 Development of a wave cyclone
In (a), a wave motion begins at a point along the polar front. The wave along the cold and warm fronts deepens and intensifies in (b). In (c), the cold front overtakes the warm front, producing an occluded front in the center of the cyclone. Later, the polar front is reestablished with a mass of warm air isolated aloft (d).

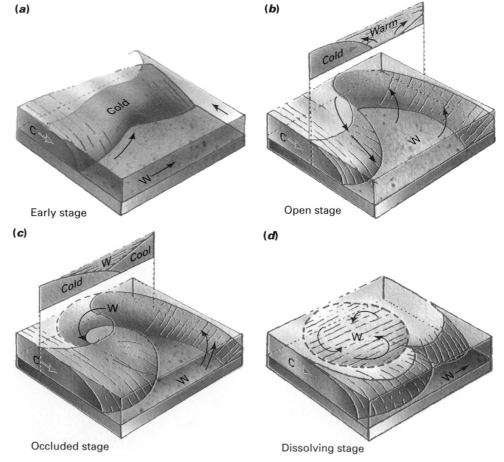

(a) Early stage

(b) Open stage

(c) Occluded stage

(d) Dissolving stage

In block (*b*) (open stage), the wave disturbance along the polar front has deepened and intensified. Cold air actively pushes southward along a cold front, and warm air actively moves northeastward along a warm front. The zones of precipitation along the two fronts are now strongly developed but are wider along the warm front than along the cold front.

In block (*c*) (occluded stage), the cold front has overtaken the warm front, producing an occluded front. The warm air mass at the center of the inspiral is forced off the ground, intensifying precipitation. Eventually, the polar front is reestablished (block (*d*), dissolving stage), but a pool of warm, moist air remains aloft. As the moisture content of the pool is reduced, precipitation dies out, and the clouds gradually dissolve.

Keep in mind that a wave cyclone is quite a large feature—1000 km (about 600 mi) or more across. Also, the cyclone normally moves eastward as it develops, propelled by prevailing westerlies aloft. Therefore, blocks (*a*)–(*d*) are like three-dimensional snapshots taken at intervals along an eastbound track.

In relatively moist air masses, weak, elongated cyclones can develop that are known as *low pressure troughs*. These are often produced when upper air flows along a curving path that causes air molecules to pick up speed and spread out, or *diverge*. The divergence creates an upper level region of lower pressure, and in response surface air below converges to move upward. The result is a weak cyclonic flow pattern of surface convergence associated with clouds and showers—an example of convergent precipitation.

······

GEO*DISCOVERIES* **Wave Cyclones.** Watch an animation of Figure 6.9 showing the life cycle of a wave cyclone with cold, warm, and occluded fronts.

······

Weather Changes within a Wave Cyclone

How does weather change as a wave cyclone passes through a region? Figure 6.10 shows two simplified weather maps of the eastern United States depicting conditions on successive days. The structure of the storm is defined by the isobars,

6.10 Simplified surface weather maps and cross sections through a wave cyclone *In the open stage (left), cold and warm fronts pivot around the center of the cyclone. In the occluded stage (right), the cold front has overtaken the warm front, and a large pool of warm, moist air has been forced aloft.*

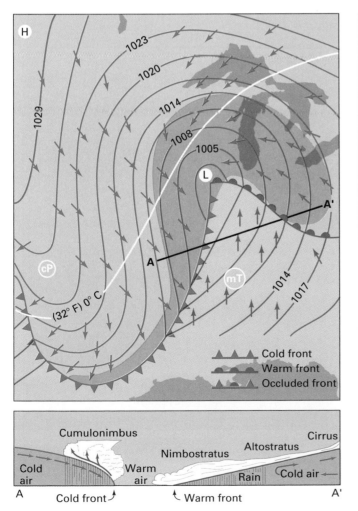

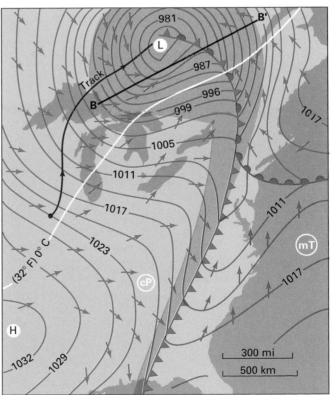

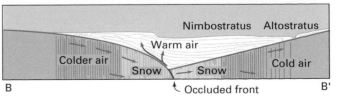

labeled in millibars. The three kinds of fronts are shown by special line symbols. Areas of precipitation are shown in gray.

The map on the left shows the cyclone in an open stage, similar to Figure 6.9, block (*b*). The isobars show that the cyclone is a low-pressure center with inspiraling winds. The cold front is pushing south and east, supported by a flow of cold, dry continental polar air from the northwest filling in behind it. Note that the wind direction changes abruptly as the cold front passes. There is also a sharp drop in temperature behind the cold front as cP air fills in. The warm front is moving north and somewhat east, with warm, moist maritime tropical air following. The precipitation pattern includes a broad zone near the warm front and the central area of the cyclone. A thin band of precipitation extends down the length of the cold front. Cloudiness generally prevails over much of the cyclone.

A cross section along the line A–A′ shows how the fronts and clouds are related. Along the warm front is a broad layer of stratus clouds. These take the form of a wedge with a thin leading edge of cirrus. (See Figures 4.11 and 4.12 for cloud types.) Westward, this wedge thickens to altostratus, then to stratus, and finally to nimbostratus with steady rain. Within the sector of warm air, the sky may partially clear with scat-

tered cumulus. Along the cold front are cumulonimbus clouds associated with thunderstorms. These yield heavy rains but only along a narrow belt.

The weather map on the right shows conditions 24 hours later. The cyclone has moved rapidly northeastward, its track shown by the red line. The center has moved about 1600 km (1000 mi) in 24 hours—a speed of just over 65 km (40 mi) per hour. The cold front has overtaken the warm front, forming an occluded front in the central part of the disturbance. A high-pressure area, or tongue of cold polar air, has moved in to the area west and south of the cyclone, and the cold front has pushed far south and east. Within the cold air tongue, the skies are clear. A cross section below the map shows conditions along the line B–B′, cutting through the occluded part of the storm. Notice that the warm air mass is lifted well off the ground and yields heavy precipitation.

Cyclone Tracks and Cyclone Families

Wave cyclones tend to form in certain areas and travel common paths until they dissolve. Figure 6.11 is a world map showing common paths of wave cyclones and tropical cyclones. (We will discuss tropical cyclones in detail later in

6.11 *Paths of tropical cyclones and wave cyclones* *This world map shows typical paths of tropical cyclones (red) and midlatitude wave cyclones (blue). (Based on data of S. Pettersen, B. Haurwitz and N. M. Austin, J. Namias, M. J. Rubin, and J-H. Chang.)*

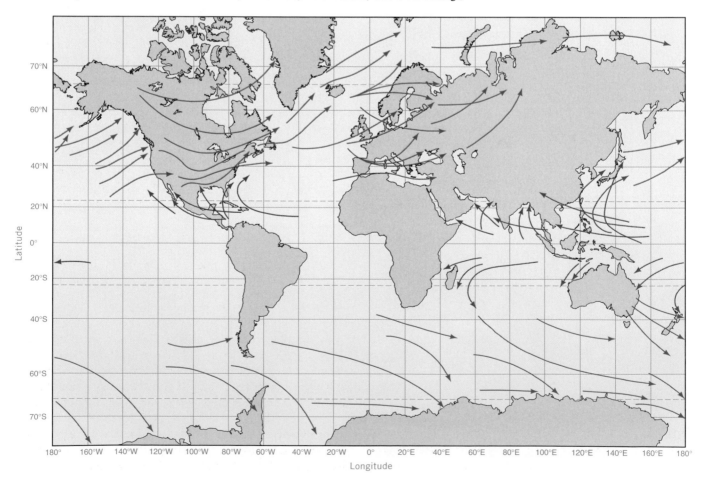

6.12   *Daily world weather map* *A daily weather map of the world for a given day during July or August might look like this map, which is a composite of typical weather conditions. (After M. A. Garbell.)*

this chapter.) The western coast of North America commonly receives wave cyclones arising in the North Pacific Ocean. Wave cyclones also originate over land, shown by the tracks starting in Alaska, the Pacific Northwest, the south-central United States, and along the Gulf coast. Most of these tracks converge toward the northeast and pass into the North Atlantic, where they tend to concentrate in the region of the Icelandic Low.

In the northern hemisphere, wave cyclones are heavily concentrated in the neighborhood of the Aleutian and Icelandic Lows. These cyclones commonly form in a succession, traveling as a chain across the North Atlantic and North Pacific oceans. Figure 6.12, a world weather map, shows several such cyclone families. Each wave cyclone moves northeastward, deepening in low pressure and occluding to form an upper-air low. For this reason, intense cyclones arriving at the western coasts of North America and Europe are usually occluded.

In the southern hemisphere, storm tracks are more nearly along a single lane, following the parallels of latitude. Three such cyclones are shown in Figure 6.12. This track is more uniform because of the uniform pattern of ocean surface circling the globe at these latitudes. Only the southern tip of South America projects southward to break the monotonous expanse of ocean.

The Tornado

A **tornado** is a small but intense cyclonic vortex in which air spirals at tremendous speed. It is associated with thunder-

storms spawned by fronts in midlatitudes of North America. Tornadoes can also occur inside tropical cyclones (hurricanes).

The tornado appears as a dark funnel cloud hanging from the base of a dense cumulonimbus cloud (Figure 6.13). At its lower end, the funnel may be 100 to 450 m (about 300 to 1500 ft) in diameter. The base of the funnel appears dark because of the density of condensing moisture, dust, and debris swept up by the wind. Wind speeds in a tornado exceed speeds known in any other storm. Estimates of wind speed run as high as 100 m/s (about 225 mi/hr). As the tornado moves across the countryside, the funnel writhes and twists. Where it touches the ground, it can cause the complete destruction of almost anything in its path.

> The tornado is a small but intense cyclonic vortex with very high wind speeds. Tornados occur within cumulonimbus clouds traveling in advance of a cold front, and are most common in spring and summer.

GEODISCOVERIES How Tornados Cause Damage. Visualize how tornado winds spiral inward and stream across houses, raising and wrecking roofs. Watch a minimovie of tornadoes in action.

Tornadoes occur as parts of cumulonimbus clouds traveling in advance of a cold front. They seem to originate where turbulence is greatest. They are most common in the spring and summer but can occur in any month. Where a cold front of maritime polar air lifts warm, moist maritime tropical air, conditions are most favorable for tornadoes. As shown in Figure 6.14, they occur in greatest numbers in the central and southeastern states and are rare over mountainous and forested regions. They are almost unknown west of the Rocky Mountains and are relatively less fre-

6.13 **Tornado** *This tornado touched down near Clearwater, Kansas, on May 16, 1991. Surrounding the funnel is a cloud of dust and debris carried into the air by the violent winds.*

quent on the eastern seaboard. Tornadoes are a typically American phenomenon, being most frequent and violent in the United States. They also occur in Australia in substantial numbers and are occasionally reported from other midlatitude locations.

6.14 **Frequency of occurrence of observed tornadoes in the conterminous United States and southern Canada** *The data shown in this map span a 30-year record, 1960–1989. (Courtesy of Edward W. Ferguson, National Severe Storms Forecast Center, National Weather Service.)*

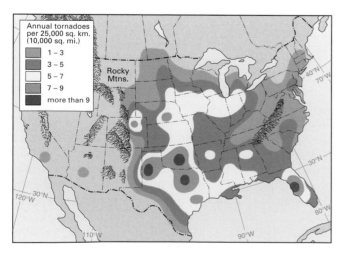

Annual tornadoes
per 25,000 sq. km.
(10,000 sq. mi.)

1 – 3
3 – 5
5 – 7
7 – 9
more than 9

Devastation from a tornado is often complete within the narrow limits of its path (Figure 6.15). Only the strongest buildings constructed of concrete and steel can withstand the extremely violent winds. The National Weather Service maintains a tornado forecasting and warning system. Whenever weather conditions favor tornado development, the danger area is alerted, and systems for observing and reporting a tornado are set in readiness.

GEODISCOVERIES Occurrence of Tornadoes. See a cold front develop a line of tornado-generating thunderstorms near Fort Worth, Texas, in this animation of GOES satellite imagery.

TROPICAL AND EQUATORIAL WEATHER SYSTEMS

So far, the weather systems we have discussed are those of the midlatitudes and poleward. Weather systems of the tropical and equatorial zones show some basic differences from those of the midlatitudes. Upper-air winds are often weak, so air mass movement is slow and gradual. Air masses are warm and moist, and tend to have similar characteristics. Thus, clearly defined fronts and large, intense wave cyclones are missing. On the other hand, intense convectional activity occurs because of the high moisture content of low-latitude maritime air masses. In these very moist air masses, even slight convergence and uplifting can be sufficient to trigger precipitation.

6.15 Tornado destruction *A very powerful tornado swept this broad path through Midwest City, Oklahoma, on May 3, 1999.*

Clouds and precipitation in tropical and equatorial regions have recently become the object of a remote sensing mission. Of special interest is the intensity and duration of rainfall over oceans, which is not well monitored. *Focus on Remote Sensing 6.1 ● TRMM—The Tropical Rainfall Monitoring Mission* provides more information.

> **Tropical weather systems include easterly waves and weak equatorial lows. Precipitation results when moist air converges in these systems, triggering convectional showers.**

rainy monsoon is in progress in Southeast Asia. It is marked by a weak equatorial low in northern India.

Polar Outbreaks

Another distinctive feature of low-latitude weather is the occasional penetration of powerful tongues of cold polar air from the midlatitudes into very low latitudes. These tongues are

Easterly Waves and Weak Equatorial Lows

One of the simplest forms of tropical weather systems is an *easterly wave,* a slowly moving trough of low pressure within the belt of tropical easterlies (trades). These waves occur in latitudes 5° to 30° N and S over oceans, but not over the equator itself. Figure 6.16 is a simplified upper-air map of an easterly wave showing wind patterns, the axis of the wave, isobars, and the zone of showers. At the surface, a zone of weak low pressure underlies the axis of the wave. The wave travels westward at a rate of 300 to 500 km (about 200 to 300 mi) per day. Surface airflow converges on the eastern, or rear, side of the wave axis. This convergence causes the moist air to be lifted, producing scattered showers and thunderstorms. The rainy period may last a day or two as the wave passes.

Another related weather system is the *weak equatorial low,* a disturbance that forms near the center of the equatorial trough. Moist equatorial air converges toward the center of the low, causing rainfall from many individual convectional storms. Several such weak lows are shown on the world weather map (Figure 6.12), lying along the ITCZ. Because the map is for a day in July or August, the ITCZ is shifted well north of the equator. During this season, the

6.16 Easterly wave *An easterly wave passing over the West Indies. (Data from H. Riehl,* Tropical Meteorology, *New York: McGraw-Hill.)*

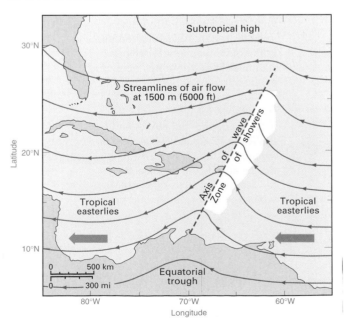

known as *polar outbreaks.* The leading edge of a polar outbreak is a cold front with squalls, which is followed by unusually cool, clear weather with strong, steady winds. The polar outbreak is best developed in the Americas. Outbreaks that move southward from the United States into the Caribbean Sea and Central America are called "northers" or "nortes," while those that move north from Patagonia into tropical South American are called "pamperos." One such outbreak is shown over South America on the world weather map (Figure 6.12). A severe polar outbreak may bring subfreezing temperatures to the highlands of South America and severely damage such essential crops as coffee.

Tropical Cyclones

The most powerful and destructive type of cyclonic storm is the **tropical cyclone,** which is known as the *hurricane* in the western hemisphere, the *typhoon* in the western Pacific off the coast of Asia, and the *cyclone* in the Indian Ocean. This type of storm develops over oceans in 8° to 15° N and S latitudes but not closer to the equator. The exact mechanism of formation is not known, but typically the tropical cyclone originates as an easterly wave or weak low, which then intensifies and grows into a deep, circular low. High sea-surface temperatures, over 27°C (81°F), are required for tropical cyclones to form. Once formed, the storm moves westward through the trade-wind belt, often intensifying as it travels. It can then curve northwest, north, and northeast, steered by westerly winds aloft. Tropical cyclones can penetrate well into the midlatitudes, as many residents of the southern and eastern coasts of the United States can attest.

An intense tropical cyclone is an almost circular storm center of extremely low pressure. Because of the very strong pressure gradient, winds spiral inward at high speed. Convergence and uplift are intense, producing very heavy rainfall (Figure 6.17). The storm gains its energy through the release of latent heat as the intense precipitation forms. The storm's diameter may be 150 to 500 km (about 100 to 300 mi). Wind speeds can range from 30 to 50 m/s (67 to 112 mi/hr) and sometimes much higher. Barometric

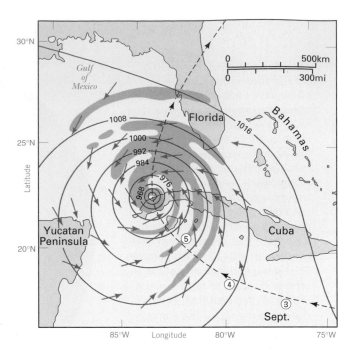

6.17   Hurricane weather map *A simplified weather map of a hurricane passing over the western tip of Cuba. Daily locations, beginning on September 3, are shown as circled numerals. The recurving path will take the storm over Florida. Shaded areas show dense rain clouds as seen in a satellite image.*

pressure in the storm center commonly falls to 950 mb (28.1 in. Hg) or lower.

A characteristic feature of the tropical cyclone is its central eye, in which clear skies and calm winds prevail (Figure 6.18). The eye is a cloud-free vortex produced by the intense spiraling of the storm. In the eye, air descends from high altitudes and is adiabatically warmed. As the eye passes over a site, calm prevails, and the sky clears. Passage of the eye may take about half an hour, after which the storm strikes with renewed ferocity, but with winds in the opposite direction. Wind speeds are highest along the cloud wall of the eye.

Tropical cyclones (hurricanes or typhoons) are the most powerful and destructive of cyclonic storms, with wind speeds ranging from 30 to 50 m/s (about 65 to 135 mi/hr) and above. In the central eye of the storm, barometric pressure may fall to 950 mb (28.1 in. Hg) or lower.

6.18   Anatomy of a hurricane *In this schematic diagram, cumulonimbus (Cb) clouds in concentric rings rise through dense stratiform clouds. Cirrus clouds (Ci) fringe out ahead of the storm. Width of diagram represents about 1000 km (about 600 mi). (Redrawn from NOAA, National Weather Service.)*

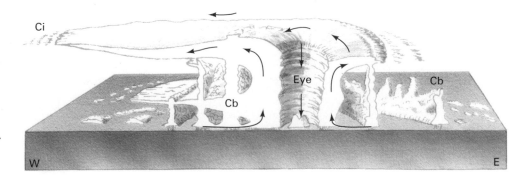

Table 6.2	Simpson–Saffir Scale of Tropical Cyclone Intensity		
Category	Central Pressure mb (in. Hg)	Storm Surge m (ft)	Mean Wind m/s (mph)
1 Weak	>980 (>29.0)	1.2–1.7 (4–5)	33–42 (74–95)
2 Moderate	965–979 (28.5–29.0)	1.8–2.6 (6–8)	43–49 (96–110)
3 Strong	945–964 (27.9–28.5)	2.7–3.8 (9–12)	50–58 (111–130)
4 Very Strong	920–944 (27.2–27.9)	3.9–5.6 (13–18)	59–69 (131–155)
5 Devastating	<920 (<27.2)	>5.6 (>18)	>69 (>155)

GEODISCOVERIES Hurricanes. A video shows how a hurricane, fueled by warm ocean water, develops extreme winds in its eye wall.

The intensity of tropical cyclones is rated on the Simpson–Saffir scale, shown in Table 6.2. This scale ranks storms based on the central pressure of the storm, mean wind speed, and height of accompanying storm surge. Category 1 storms are weak, while category 5 storms are devastating.

Refer to Figure 6.11, presented earlier, which shows typical paths of both wave cyclones and tropical cyclones. As you can see, tropical cyclones always form over oceans. In the western hemisphere, hurricanes originate in the Atlantic off the west coast of Africa, in the Caribbean Sea, or off the west coast of Mexico. Curiously, tropical cyclones do not form in the South Atlantic or southeast Pacific regions. As a result, South America is never threatened by these severe storms. In the Indian Ocean, cyclones originate both north

and south of the equator, moving north and east to strike India, Pakistan, and Bangladesh, as well as south and west to strike the eastern coasts of Africa and Madagascar. Typhoons of the western Pacific also form both north and south of the equator, moving into northern Australia, Southeast Asia, China, and Japan.

Tracks of tropical cyclones of the North Atlantic are shown in detail in Figure 6.19. Most of the storms originate at 10° to 20° N latitude, travel westward and northwestward through the trades, and then turn northeast at about 30° to 35° N latitude into the zone of the westerlies. Here their intensity lessens, especially if they move over land. In the tradewind belt, the cyclones travel 10 to 20 km (6 to 12 mi) per hour. In the zone of the westerlies, their speed is more variable.

Tropical cyclones are now tracked using satellite images. They are often easy to identify from their distinctive pattern of inspiraling bands of clouds and a clear central eye. Figure 6.20 provides a gallery of satellite images of tropical cyclones.

Tropical cyclones occur only during certain seasons. For hurricanes of the North Atlantic, the season runs from May through November, with maximum frequency in late summer or early autumn. In the southern hemisphere, the season is roughly the opposite. These periods follow the annual migrations of the ITCZ to the north and south with the seasons, and correspond to periods when ocean temperatures are warmest.

For convenience, tropical cyclones are given names as they are tracked by weather forecasters. Male and female names are alternated in an alphabetical sequence renewed each season. Two sets of names are used—one for hurricanes of the Atlantic and one for typhoons of the Pacific. Names are reused, but the names of storms that cause significant damage or destruction are retired from further use.

GEODISCOVERIES Remote Sensing and Climate Interactivity. Examine satellite images of Hurricanes Hugo and Andrew and watch the storms develop. Learn how cloud types are organized in the hurricane structure.

Impacts of Tropical Cyclones

Tropical cyclones can be tremendously destructive storms. Islands and coasts feel the full force of the high winds and flooding as tropical cyclones move onshore. The most serious effect of tropical cyclones is usually coastal destruction by storm waves and very high tides. Since the atmospheric pressure at the center of the cyclone is so low, sea level rises toward the center of the storm. High winds create a damaging surf and push water toward the coast, raising sea level even higher. Waves attack the shore at points far inland of the normal tidal range. Low pressure, winds, and the underwater shape of a bay floor can combine to produce a sudden rise of water level, known as a **storm surge.** During surges, vessels large and small are lifted by the high waters and can be stranded far inland.

If high tide accompanies the storm, the limits reached by inundation are even higher. This flooding can create enormous death tolls. At Galveston, Texas, in 1900, a sudden storm surge generated by a severe hurricane flooded

6.19 Tracks of typical hurricanes occurring during August The storms arise in warm tropical waters and move northwest. On entering the region of prevailing westerlies, the storms change direction and move toward the northeast.

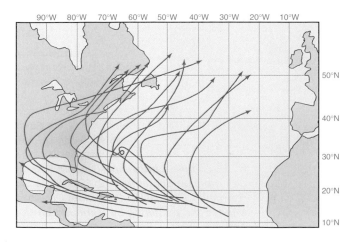

- Because global warming, produced by increasing CO_2 levels in the atmosphere, will increase the evaporation of surface water, atmospheric moisture levels will increase. This will tend to enhance the greenhouse effect. But more clouds are likely to form, and this should cool the planet. Increased moisture could also reduce temperatures by increasing the amount and duration of snow cover. Further research on the effect of global warming on climate is needed.

Key Terms

weather systems, p. 186
air mass, p. 186
front, p. 188
cold front, p. 188

warm front, p. 189
occluded front, p. 190
cyclonic precipitation, p. 190

cyclonic storm, p. 190
wave cyclone, p. 192
tornado, p. 195

tropical cyclone, p. 200
storm surge, p. 201

Review Questions

1. Define air mass. What two features are used to classify air masses?
2. Compare the characteristics and source regions for mP and cT air mass types.
3. Describe a tornado. Where and under what conditions do tornadoes typically occur?
4. Identify three weather systems that bring rain in equatorial and tropical regions. Describe each system briefly.
5. Describe the structure of a tropical cyclone. What conditions are necessary for the development of a tropical cyclone? Give a typical path for the movement of a tropical cyclone in the northern hemisphere.
6. Why are tropical cyclones so dangerous?
7. How does the global circulation of the atmosphere and oceans provide poleward heat transport?

8. How does water, as vapor, clouds, and precipitation, influence global climate? How might water in these forms act to enhance or retard climatic warming?

Eye on Environment 6.2 • Hurricane Andrew—Killer Cyclone

1. Where did Hurricane Andrew first form, and how did it develop and move?
2. What damage was sustained by south Florida and coastal Louisiana from Hurricane Andrew?
3. What were the maximum wind speeds of Andrew? How were they achieved?
4. How did Hurricane Andrew affect the Everglades?

Visualizing Exercises

1. Identify three types of fronts and draw a cross section through each. Show the air masses involved, the contacts between them, and the direction of air mass motion.
2. Sketch two weather maps, showing a wave cyclone in open and occluded stages. Include isobars on your sketch. Identify the center of the cyclone as a low. Lightly shade areas where precipitation is likely to occur.

Essay Questions

1. Compare and contrast midlatitude and tropical weather systems. Be sure to include the following terms or concepts in your discussion: air mass, convectional precipitation, cyclonic precipitation, easterly wave, polar front, stable air, traveling anticyclone, tropical cyclone, unstable air, wave cyclone, and weak equatorial low.
2. Prepare a description of the annual weather patterns that are experienced through the year at your location. Refer to the general temperature and precipitation pattern as well as the types of weather systems that occur in each season.

Eye on the Landscape

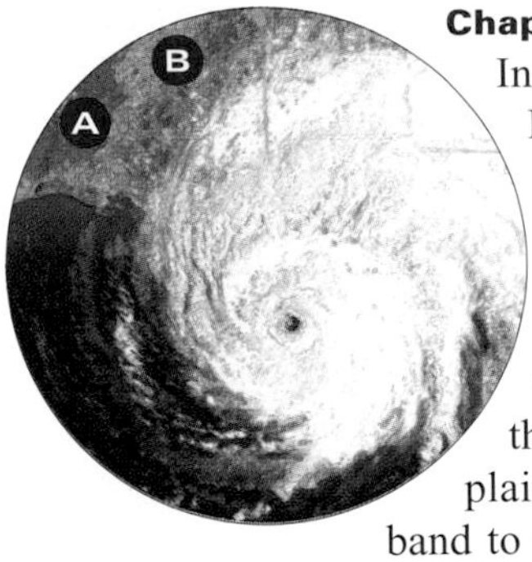

Chapter Opener Hurricane Ivan
In addition to the structure of Hurricane Ivan, this image also shows vegetation patterns. The curving band of dark olive tones in western Louisiana and eastern Texas **(A)** reveal the pine forests on the uplands of older coastal plain sediments. Compare this band to the light green tones of agricultural land along the Mississippi valley **(B)**. Natural vegetation is covered in Chapter 9, while soils and agriculture are the subject of Chapter 10.

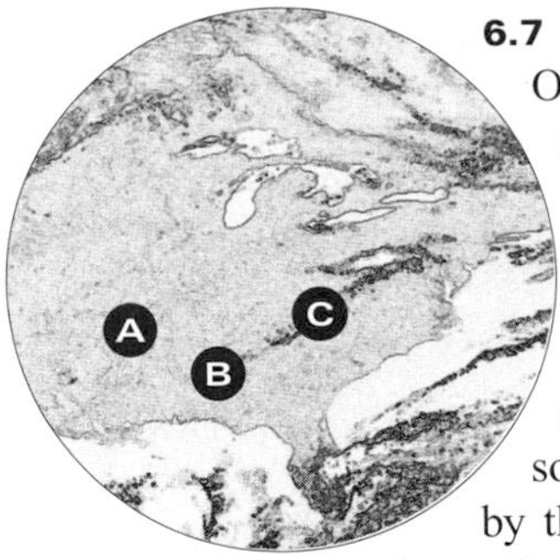

6.7 Picture of an anticyclone
On this clear satellite image, it is easy to see some of the major features of the eastern North American landscape. At **(A)**, note the difference in soil color along the Mississippi River. These are alluvial soils, deposited over millennia by the Mississippi during the Ice Ages. At **(B)**, note the curving arc that marks the boundary between soft coastal plain sediments to the south and the weathered rocks and soils of the piedmont, to the north. (Figure 17.8 diagrams this location.) Actually, this boundary can be traced all the way to New York City. Further inland lie the Appalachians **(C)**, showing puffy orographic cumulus clouds. (We covered orographic precipitation in Chapter 4.)

These residents of Mumbai (formerly known as Bombay) dress in light, bright clothing to keep cool and use umbrellas to ward off the strong tropical sun.

7 | GLOBAL CLIMATES

. . . .
PUTTING YOU IN THE PICTURE

London, Rome, Cairo, Delhi, Singapore, Tokyo, Honolulu, and Anchorage! An around-the-world tour! It was hard to believe that you were the winner of the sweepstakes drawing sponsored by the credit card company, but now that you've picked up your first-class air ticket, it's finally hitting home. Although you'll only spend a few days in each of these famous cities, it will be a real thrill to experience them first-hand.

But what kind of weather should you expect? Will it be hot or cold, sunny or rainy? Should you pack your overcoat and sweaters? Or will your lightweight clothes be more appropriate? Will you need an umbrella in any of these cities? You'll be leaving in January, so you know what to expect for your trip to the airport, but what happens after that? Fortunately, you still have your college physical geography textbook to refer to. That evening, you brush up on the climates you will encounter.

"Let's see, London. Oh yes, that's a marine west-coast climate type. Lots of occluded wave cyclones in January. Hmm.

I'd better have my raincoat and umbrella. Wool would be good. Perhaps that lightweight gray sweater will fit in my carry-on bag. Then on to Rome. That's the Mediterranean climate. Well, winter is the wet season for the Mediterranean climate, but the rainfall is so much lighter than in London that I'm likely to get away with just an umbrella. Still, I'll need some kind of light coat, since it won't be very warm. The raincoat will probably do fine.

"Cairo—now, that's the dry subtropical climate. Not much chance of rain in that climate, and the hottest temperatures aren't till later in the year, when the sun moves to the tropic of cancer and is nearly overhead. Better have something light and cool. And I'll need my swimsuit for lounging by the hotel pool. Then there's Delhi. It's dry tropical there as well. Hmm. With the winter monsoon bringing dry, continental air down the slope of the Himalayas, it should be pretty clear, with warm days and cool nights.

"Then on from Delhi to Singapore. Oh oh, Singapore is right on the equator, so that would be the wet equatorial climate. I'd better make sure my umbrella isn't buried too deeply in my suitcase. Those convectional showers don't last long, but they can be pretty intense. It'll certainly be hot and steamy. Now, Tokyo is in the moist continental climate, at about 35° N latitude. That's the same climate as New York. In January? Looks like I'll need those wool clothes again. And I'd better keep that umbrella handy.

"Now, Honolulu! That's the wet equatorial climate, the same as Singapore. But Hawaii's at about 20° N, so the ocean will be cooler and the daily temperature should be just perfect! Last of all is Anchorage. That's the boreal forest climate—and in January! I'll certainly need something warm. But I hate to lug my heavy winter coat around the world just for the last few days. Here's an idea! I've been putting off buying that new ski suit for a couple of years, but how about buying it in Anchorage? And skis, too. What a way to end the trip! Swimming in the warm Pacific and skiing in Alaska!"

Who said learning physical geography wouldn't come in handy some day? After finishing this chapter, you'll be set to pack your clothes for any destination, any time!

As we examine the Earth's climates, you will find that your earlier studies of air temperatures, precipitation, global winds and circulation patterns, air masses, and weather systems will all combine to help you understand the nature of global climates as they are located over the globe. Thus, this chapter will help you to bring together much of the knowledge of physical geography that you have already acquired in a focus on the breadth and diversity of the world's climatic regions. ■

GLOBAL CLIMATES

What do we mean by climate? In its most general sense, **climate** is the average weather of a region. To describe the average weather of a region, we could use many of the measures describing the state of the atmosphere that we have already encountered. These might include daily net radiation, barometric pressure, wind speed and direction, cloud cover and type, presence of fog, precipitation type and intensity, incidence of cyclones and anticyclones, frequency of frontal passages, and other such items of weather information. However, observations as detailed as these are not made regularly at most weather stations around the world. To study climate on a worldwide basis, we must turn to the two simple measurements that are made daily at every weather station—temperature and precipitation. We will be concerned with both their average values for each month of the year and their variation across the months of the year.

Note that temperature and precipitation strongly influence the natural vegetation of a region—for example, forests occur generally in moist regions, and grasslands in dry regions. The natural vegetation cover is often a distinctive feature of a climatic region and typically influences the human use of the area. Temperature and precipitation are also important factors in the cultivation of crop plants—a necessary process for human survival. And the development of soils, as well as the types of processes that shape landforms, are partly dependent on temperature and precipitation. For these reasons, we will find that climates defined on the basis of temperature and precipitation also help set apart many features of the environment, not just climate alone. This is why the study of global climates is such an important part of physical geography.

KEYS TO CLIMATE

A few simple principles discussed in earlier chapters are very helpful in understanding the global scope of climate. First, recall from Chapter 3 that three major factors influence the annual cycle of air temperature experienced at a station: latitude, coastal versus continental location, and elevation.

- *Latitude.* The annual cycle of temperature at a station depends on its latitude. Near the equator, temperatures are warmer and the annual range is low. Toward the poles, temperatures are colder and the annual range is greater. These effects are produced by the annual cycle of insolation, which varies with latitude.
- *Coastal-continental location.* Coastal stations show a smaller annual variation in temperature, while the variation is larger for stations in continental interiors. This effect occurs because ocean surface temperatures vary less with the seasons than do temperatures of land surfaces.

- *Elevation.* High elevation stations show cooler temperatures than sea-level stations. Temperatures are cooler because the atmosphere cools with elevation at the average environmental temperature lapse rate of 6.4°C/1000 m (3.5°F/1000 ft).

Air temperature also has an important effect on precipitation. Recall this principle from Chapter 4:

- *Warm air can hold more moisture than cold air.* This means that colder regions generally have lower precipitation than warmer regions. Also, precipitation will tend to be greater during the warmer months of the temperature cycle.

Another key idea associated with climate is the *time cycle,* which we discussed in our Introduction. The primary driving force for weather, as we have seen, is the flow of solar energy received by the Earth and atmosphere. Since that energy flow varies on daily cycles with the planet's rotation and on annual cycles with its revolution in orbit, it imposes these cycles on temperature and precipitation. Other time cycles appear in climate as well.

Keeping these key ideas in mind as you read this chapter will help make the climates easy to understand and explain.

Temperature Regimes

Let's look in more detail at the influence of latitude and location on the annual temperature cycle of a station. Figure 7.1 shows some typical patterns of mean monthly temperatures observed at stations around the globe. We can refer to these patterns as *temperature regimes*—distinctive types of annual temperature cycles related to latitude and location. In the figure, each regime has been labeled according to its latitude zone: equatorial, tropical, midlatitude, and subarctic. Some labels also describe the location of the station in terms of its position on a landmass—"continental" for a continental interior location, and "west coast" or "marine" for a location close to the ocean.

The equatorial regime (Douala, Cameroon, 4° N) is uniformly very warm. Temperatures are close to 27°C (81°F) year-round. There are no temperature seasons because insolation is nearly uniform through the year. In contrast, the tropical continental regime (In Salah, Algeria, 27° N) shows a very strong temperature cycle. Temperatures change from very hot when the Sun is high, near one solstice, to mild at the opposite solstice. However, the situation is quite different at Walvis Bay, Southwest Africa (23° S), which is at nearly the same latitude and so has about the same insolation cycle as In Salah. At Walvis Bay, we find the tropical west-coast regime, which has only a weak annual cycle and no extreme heat. The difference, of course, is due to the moderating effects of the maritime location of Walvis Bay. This moderating effect persists poleward, as shown in the two temperature graphs for the midlatitude west-coast regime—Monterey, California (36° N) and Sitka, Alaska (57° N).

In continental interiors, however, the annual temperature cycle remains strong. The midlatitude continental regime of Omaha, Nebraska (41° N), and the subarctic continental regime of Fort Vermilion, Alberta (58° N), show annual variations in mean monthly temperature of about 30°C (54°F) and 40°C (72°F), respectively. The ice sheet regime of Greenland (Eismitte, 71° N) is in a class by itself, with severe cold all year.

Other regimes can be identified, and, because they grade into one another, the list could be expanded indefinitely. However, what is important is that (1) annual variation in insolation, which is determined by latitude, provides the basic control on temperature patterns, and (2) the effect of location—maritime or continental—moderates that variation.

> The contrast in temperatures with season at a location depends on latitude, location, and elevation. At higher latitudes, in continental interiors, and at higher elevations, the contrast is greater.

Global Precipitation

Global precipitation patterns are largely determined by air masses and their movements, which in turn are produced by global air circulation patterns. To see this, let's look at the world map of precipitation, Figure 7.2, in more detail. This map of mean annual precipitation shows **isohyets**—lines drawn through all points having the same annual precipitation. Analyzing the map, we can recognize seven global precipitation regions as follows. (Note that for regions where all or most of the precipitation is rain, we use the word "rainfall." For regions where snow is a significant part of the annual total, we use the word "precipitation.") Table 7.1 summarizes the observations below.

1. **Wet equatorial belt.** This zone of heavy rainfall, over 200 cm (80 in.) annually, straddles the equator and includes the Amazon River Basin in South America, the Congo River Basin of equatorial Africa, much of the African coast from Nigeria west to Guinea, and the East Indies. Here the prevailing warm temperatures and high-moisture content of the mE air masses favor abundant convectional rainfall. Thunderstorms are frequent year-round.

2. **Trade-wind coasts.** Narrow coastal belts of high rainfall, 150 to 200 cm (about 60 to 80 in.), and locally even more, extend from near the equator to latitudes of about 25° to 30° N and S on the eastern sides of every continent or large island. Examples include the eastern coast of Brazil, Central America, Madagascar, and northeastern Australia. The rainfall of these coasts is supplied by moist mT air masses from warm oceans, brought over the land by the trade winds. As they encounter coastal hills and mountains, these air masses produce heavy orographic rainfall.

3. **Tropical deserts.** In striking contrast to the wet equatorial belt astride the equator are the two zones of

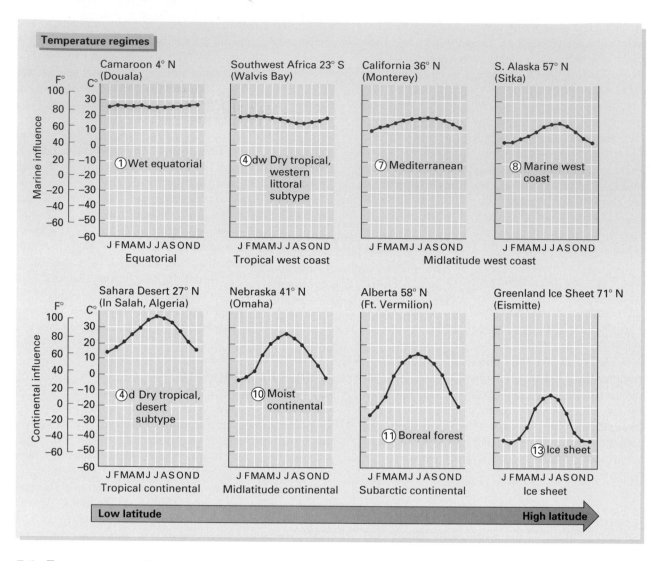

Temperature regimes

Camaroon 4° N (Douala)	Southwest Africa 23° S (Walvis Bay)	California 36° N (Monterey)	S. Alaska 57° N (Sitka)
① Wet equatorial	④dw Dry tropical, western littoral subtype	⑦ Mediterranean	⑧ Marine west coast
Equatorial	Tropical west coast	Midlatitude west coast	

Sahara Desert 27° N (In Salah, Algeria)	Nebraska 41° N (Omaha)	Alberta 58° N (Ft. Vermilion)	Greenland Ice Sheet 71° N (Eismitte)
④d Dry tropical, desert subtype	⑩ Moist continental	⑪ Boreal forest	⑬ Ice sheet
Tropical continental	Midlatitude continental	Subarctic continental	Ice sheet

Low latitude → High latitude

7.1 Temperature regimes *(above and right) Some important temperature regimes, represented by annual cycles of air temperature. (Based on the Goode Base Map.)*

vast tropical deserts lying approximately on the tropics of cancer and capricorn. These are hot, barren deserts, with less than 25 cm (10 in.) of rainfall annually and in many places with less than 5 cm (2 in.). They are located under and are caused by the large, stationary subtropical cells of high pressure, in which the subsiding cT air mass is adiabatically warmed and dried. These deserts extend off the west coasts of the lands and out over the oceans. Rain here is largely convectional and extremely unreliable.

4. **Midlatitude deserts and steppes.** Farther northward, in the interiors of Asia and North America between lat. 30° and lat. 50°, are great deserts, as well as vast expanses of semiarid grasslands known as *steppes.* Annual precipitation ranges from less than 10 cm (4 in.) in the driest areas to 50 cm (20 in.) in the moister

---

At low latitudes, annual rainfall is heavy in the wet equatorial belt and trade-wind coasts. In contrast, tropical deserts are very dry.

---

steppes. Dryness here results from remoteness from ocean sources of moisture.

Located in regions of prevailing westerly winds, these arid lands typically lie in the rain shadows of coastal mountains and highlands. For example, the Cordilleran Ranges of Oregon, Washington, British Columbia, and Alaska shield the interior of North America from moist mP air masses originating in the Pacific. Upon descending into the intermountain basins and interior plains, the mP air masses are warmed and dried. Similarly, mountains of Europe and the Scandinavian Peninsula obstruct the flow of moist mP air masses from the North Atlantic into western Asia. The great southern Asiatic ranges also prevent the entry of moist mT and mE air masses from the Indian Ocean.

The southern hemisphere has too little land in the midlatitudes to produce a true continental desert, but

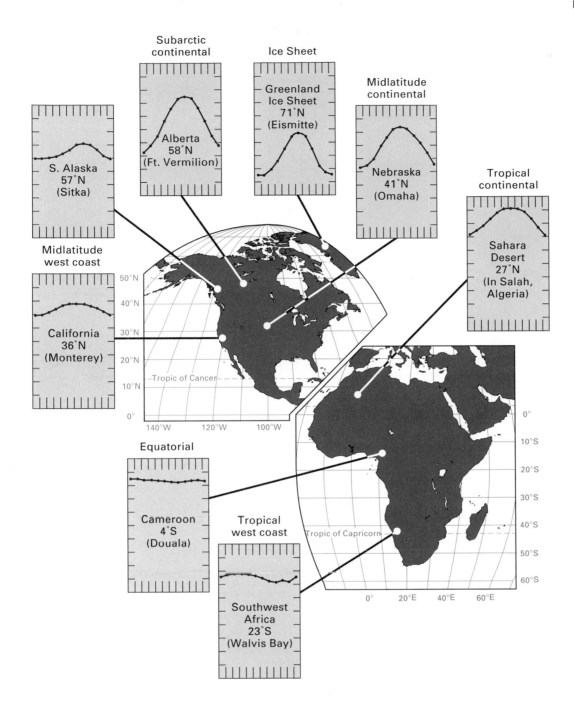

the dry steppes of Patagonia, lying on the lee side of the Andean chain, are roughly the counterpart of the North American deserts and steppes of Oregon and northern Nevada.

5. **Moist subtropical regions.** On the southeastern sides of the continents of North America and Asia, in lat. 25° to 45° N, are the moist subtropical regions, with 100 to 150 cm (about 40 to 60 in.) of rainfall annually. Smaller areas of the same kind are found in the southern hemisphere in Uruguay, Argentina, and southeastern Australia. These regions are positioned on the moist western sides of the oceanic subtropical

> At higher latitudes, east and west coasts have higher precipitation, while continental interiors and arctic and polar regions are drier.

high-pressure centers. As a result, the lands receive moist mT air masses from the tropical ocean that are carried poleward over the adjoining land. Commonly, too, these areas receive heavy rains from tropical cyclones.

6. **Midlatitude west coasts.** Another distinctive wet location is on midlatitude west coasts of all continents and large islands lying between about 35° and 65° in the region of prevailing westerly winds. In these zones, abundant orographic precipitation occurs as a result of forced uplift of mP air masses. Where the coasts are mountainous, as in Alaska and British Columbia, southern Chile, Scotland,

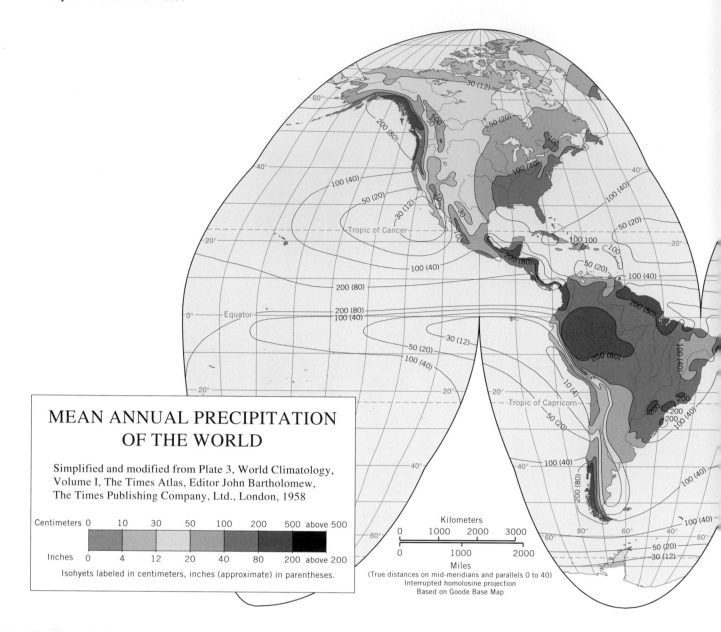

MEAN ANNUAL PRECIPITATION OF THE WORLD

Simplified and modified from Plate 3, World Climatology, Volume I, The Times Atlas, Editor John Bartholomew, The Times Publishing Company, Ltd., London, 1958

Centimeters 0   10   30   50   100   200   500 above 500

Inches   0   4   12   20   40   80   200 above 200

Isohyets labeled in centimeters, inches (approximate) in parentheses.

Kilometers
0   1000   2000   3000

Miles
0   1000   2000

(True distances on mid-meridians and parallels 0 to 40)
Interrupted homolosine projection
Based on Goode Base Map

7.2   World precipitation *Mean annual precipitation of the world. Isohyets are labeled in cm (in.)*

Table 7.1 | **World Precipitation Regions**

Name	Latitude Range	Continental Location	Prevailing Air Mass	Annual Precipitation Centimeters	Inches
1. Wet equatorial belt	10° N to 10° S	Interiors, coasts	mE	Over 200	Over 80
2. Trade-wind coasts (windward tropical coasts)	5–30° N and S	Narrow coastal zones	mT	Over 150	Over 60
3. Tropical deserts	10–35° N and S	Interiors, west coasts	cT	Under 25	Under 10
4. Midlatitude deserts and steppes	30–50° N and S	Interiors	cT, cP	10–50	4–20
5. Moist subtropical regions	25–45° N and S	Interiors, coasts	mT (summer)	100–150	40–60
6. Midlatitude west coasts	35–65° N and S	West coasts	mP	Over 100	Over 40
7. Arctic and polar deserts	60–90° N and S	Interiors, coasts	cP, cA	Under 30	Under 12

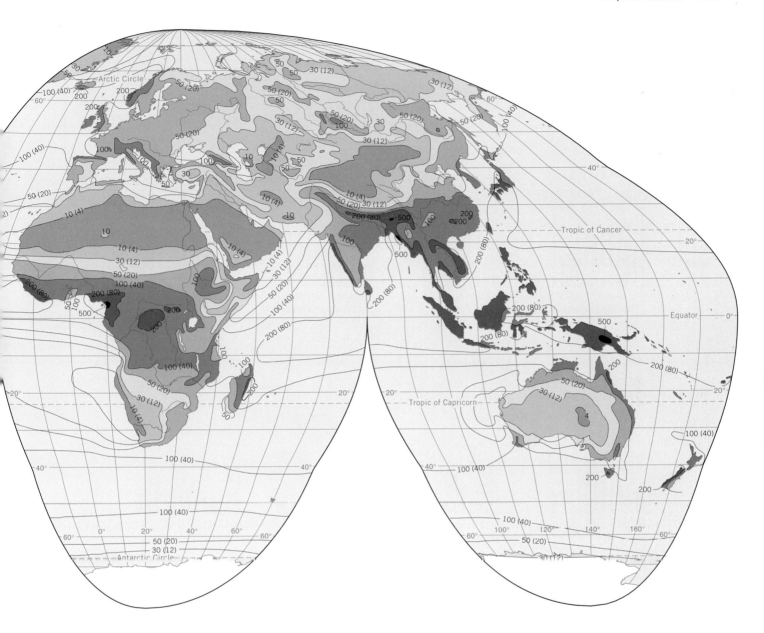

Norway, and South Island of New Zealand, the annual precipitation is over 200 cm (79 in.). During the Ice Age, this precipitation fed alpine glaciers that descended to the coast, carving the picturesque deep bays (fiords) that are so typically a part of the scenery there.

7. **Arctic and polar deserts.** A seventh precipitation region is formed by the arctic and polar deserts. Northward of the 60th parallel, annual precipitation is largely under 30 cm (12 in.), except for the west-coast belts. Cold cP and cA air masses cannot hold much moisture, and consequently, they do not yield large amounts of precipitation. At the same time, the relative humidity is high and evaporation rates are low.

Seasonality of Precipitation

Total annual precipitation is a useful quantity in establishing the character of a climate type, but it does not account for the seasonality of precipitation. The variation in monthly precipitation through the annual cycle is a very important factor in climate description. If there is a pattern of alternating dry and wet seasons instead of a uniform distribution of precipitation throughout the year, we can expect that the natural vegetation, soils, crops, and human use of the land will all be different. It also makes a great deal of difference whether the wet season coincides with a season of higher temperatures or with a season of lower temperatures. If the warm season is also wet, growth of both native plants and crops will be enhanced. If the warm season is dry, the stress on growing plants will be great and irrigation will be required for crops.

Monthly precipitation patterns can be described largely by three types: (1) uniformly distributed precipitation; (2) a precipitation maximum during the summer (or season of high Sun), in which insolation is at its peak; and (3) a precipitation maximum during the winter or cooler season (sea-

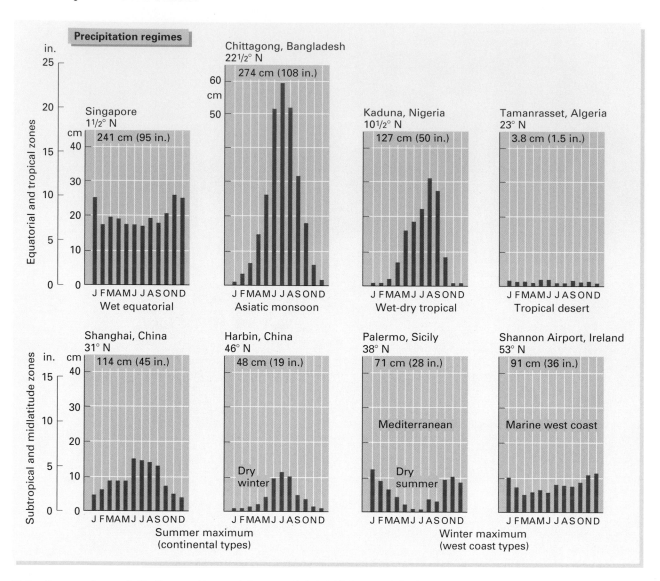

7.3 Seasonal precipitation patterns *(above and right) Eight precipitation types selected to show various seasonal patterns. (Based on the Goode Base Map.)*

son of low Sun), when insolation is least. Note that the uniform type of pattern can include a wide range of possibilities from little or no precipitation in any month to abundant precipitation in all months.

Figure 7.3 shows a set of monthly precipitation diagrams selected to illustrate the major types that occur over the globe. Two stations show the uniformly distributed pattern described above—Singapore, a wet equatorial station near the equator ($1^{1}/_{2}°$ N), and Tamanrasset, Algeria, a tropical desert station very near the tropic of cancer at 23° N. At Singapore, rainfall is abundant in all months, but some months have somewhat more than others. Tamanrasset has so little rain in any month that it scarcely shows on the graph.

Chittagong, Bangaladesh ($22^{1}/_{2}°$ N), and Kaduna, Nigeria ($10^{1}/_{2}°$ N), both show patterns of the second type—that is, a wet season at the time of high Sun (summer solstice) and a dry season at the time of low Sun (winter solstice).

Monthly patterns of precipitation are typically of three types— uniformly distributed, summer or high-Sun maximum, and winter or low-Sun maximum.

Chittagong is an Asian monsoon station, with a very large amount of precipitation falling during the high-Sun season. Kaduna, an African station with about half the total annual precipitation, shows a similar pattern and is also of the wet-dry tropical type. Both of these stations experience their wet season when the intertropical convergence zone (ITCZ) is nearby and their dry season when the ITCZ has retreated to the other hemisphere.

The summer precipitation maximum also occurs at higher latitudes on the eastern sides of continents. Shanghai, China (31° N), shows this pattern nicely in the subtropical zone. The same summer maximum persists into the midlatitudes. For example, Harbin, in eastern China (46° N), has a long, dry winter with a marked period of summer rain.

In contrast to these patterns are cycles with a winter precipitation maximum. Palermo, Sicily (38° N), is an example of the Mediterranean type, named for its prevalence in the

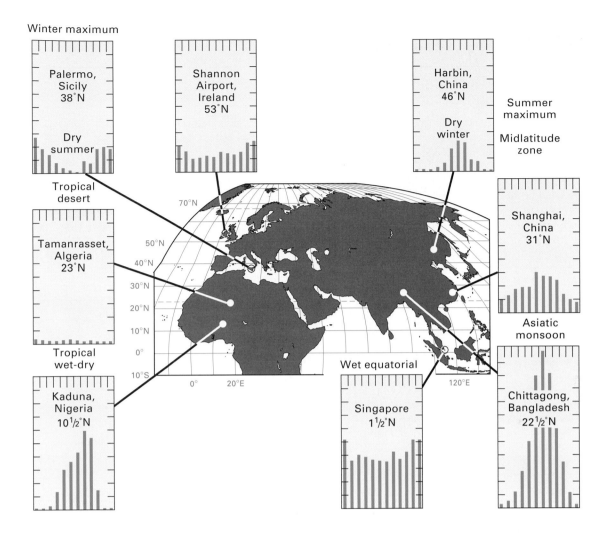

Winter maximum

Palermo, Sicily 38°N — Dry summer

Tropical desert

Shannon Airport, Ireland 53°N

Tamanrasset, Algeria 23°N

Tropical wet-dry

Kaduna, Nigeria 10½°N

Harbin, China 46°N — Dry winter

Summer maximum — Midlatitude zone

Shanghai, China 31°N

Asiatic monsoon

Chittagong, Bangladesh 22½°N

Wet equatorial

Singapore 1½°N

lands surrounding the Mediterranean Sea. This type experiences a very dry summer but has a moist winter. Southern and central California are also regions of this climate type. In Mediterranean climates, summer drought is produced by subtropical high-pressure cells, which intensify and move poleward during the high-Sun season. They extend into the regions of Mediterranean climate, providing the hot dry weather of their associated cT air masses and blocking the passage of other, moister, air masses. In the low-Sun season, the subtropical high-pressure cells move equatorward and weaken, allowing frontal and cyclonic precipitation to penetrate Mediterranean climate regions.

The dry-summer, moist-winter cycle is carried into higher midlatitudes along narrow strips of west coasts. Shannon Airport, Ireland (53° N), shows this marine west-coast type, although the difference between summer and winter rainfall is not as marked. Summers have less rainfall here for two reasons. First, the blocking effects of subtropical high-pressure cells tend to extend poleward into these regions, keeping moister air masses and cyclonic storms away. Second, the cyclonic storms that produce much of the winter precipitation are reduced in intensity during the high-Sun season. This occurs because the temperature and moisture contrasts between polar and arctic air masses and

tropical air masses are weaker in summer, owing to increased high-latitude insolation.

CLIMATE CLASSIFICATION

Mean monthly values of air temperature and precipitation can describe the climate of a weather station and its nearby region quite accurately. To study climates from a global viewpoint, climatologists classify these values into distinctive climate types. This requires developing a set of rules to use in examining monthly temperature and precipitation values. By applying the rules, the climatologist can use each station's data to determine the climate to which it belongs. This textbook recognizes 13 distinctive climate types that are designed to be understood and explained by air mass movements and frontal zones. The types follow quite naturally from the principles governing temperature and precipitation that we have discussed above.

An alternative climate classification is that devised by the Austrian climatologist Vladimir Köppen in 1918 and modified by Geiger and Pohl in 1953. It uses a system of letters to label climates. It is presented in *Special Supplement 7.1 • The Köppen Climate System.*

Special Supplement | 7.1

The Köppen Climate System

Air temperature and precipitation data have formed the basis for several climate classifications. One of the most important of these is the Köppen climate system, devised in 1918 by Dr. Vladimir Köppen of the University of Graz in Austria. For several decades, this system, with various later revisions, was the most widely used climate classification among geographers. Köppen was both a climatologist and plant geographer, so his main interest lay in finding climate boundaries that coincided approximately with boundaries between major vegetation types.

Under the Köppen system, each climate is defined according to assigned values of temperature and precipitation, computed in terms of annual or monthly values. Any given station can be assigned to its particular climate group and subgroup solely on the basis of the records of temperature and precipitation at that place.

Note that mean annual temperature refers to the average of 12 monthly temperatures for the year. Mean annual precipitation refers to the average of the entire year's precipitation as observed over many years.

The Köppen system features a shorthand code of letters designating major climate groups, subgroups within the major groups, and further subdivisions to distinguish particular seasonal characteristics of temperature and precipitation. Five major climate groups are designated by capital letters as follows:

A *Tropical rainy climates*
Average temperature of every month is above 18°C (64.4°F). These climates have no winter sea-son. Annual rainfall is large and exceeds annual evaporation.

B *Dry climates*
Evaporation exceeds precipitation on the average throughout the year. There is no water surplus; hence, no permanent streams originate in B climate zones.

C *Mild, humid (mesothermal) climates*
The coldest month has an average temperature of under 18°C (64.4°F) but above −3°C (26.6°F); at least one month has an average temperature above 10°C (50°F). The C climates thus have both a summer and a winter.

D *Snowy-forest (microthermal) climates*
The coldest month has an average temperature of under −3°C (26.6°F). The average temperature of the warmest month is above 10°C (50°F). (Forest is not generally found where the warmest month is colder than 10°C (50°F).)

E *Polar climates*
The average temperature of the warmest month is below 10°C (50°F). These climates have no true summer.

Note that four of these five groups (A, C, D, and E) are defined by temperature averages, whereas one (B) is defined by precipitation-to-evaporation ratios. Groups A, C, and D have sufficient heat and precipitation for the growth of forest and woodland vegetation. Figure S7.1 shows the boundaries of the five major climate groups, and Figure S7.2 is a world map of Köppen climates.

Subgroups within the five major groups are designated by a second letter according to the following code.

S Semiarid (steppe)
W Arid (desert)

(The capital letters S and W are applied only to the dry B climates.)

f Moist, adequate precipitation in all months, no dry season. This modifier is applied to A, C, and D groups.
w Dry season in the winter of the respective hemisphere (low-Sun season).
s Dry season in the summer of the respective hemisphere (high-Sun season).
m Rainforest climate, despite short, dry season in monsoon type of precipitation cycle. Applies only to A climates.

From combinations of the two letter groups, 12 distinct climates emerge:

A *Tropical rainforest climate*
The rainfall of the driest month is 6 cm (2.4 in.) or more.

Am *Monsoon variety of Af*
The rainfall of the driest month is less than 6 cm (2.4 in.). The dry season is strongly developed.

Aw *Tropical savanna climate*
At least one month has rainfall less than 6 cm (2.4 in.). The dry season is strongly developed.

Figure S7.3 shows the boundaries between Af, Am, and Aw climates as determined by both annual rainfall and rainfall of the driest month.

BS *Steppe climate*
A semiarid climate characterized by grasslands, it occupies an intermediate position between the desert climate (BW) and the more humid climates of the A, C, and D groups. Boundaries are deter-

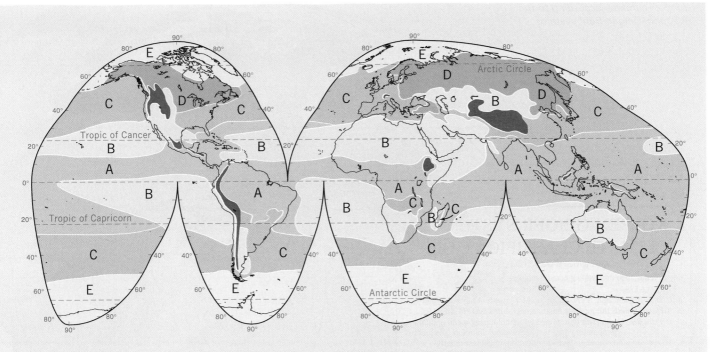

S7.1 Generalized Köppen climate map *Highly generalized world map of major climate regions according to the Köppen classification. Highland areas are in black. (Based on Goode Base Map.)*

mined by formulas given in Figure S7.4.

BW Desert climate
Desert has an arid climate with annual precipitation of usually less than 40 cm (15.7 in.). The boundary with the adjacent steppe climate (BS) is determined by formulas given in Figure S7.4.

C Mild humid climate with no dry season
Precipitation of the driest month averages more than 3 cm (1.2 in.).

Cw Mild humid climate with a dry winter
The wettest month of summer has at least 10 times the precipitation of the driest month of winter. (Alternative definition: 70 percent or more of the mean annual precipitation falls in the warmer six months.)

Cs Mild humid climate with a dry summer
Precipitation of the driest month of summer is less than 3 cm (1.2 in.). Precipitation is at least three times

as much as the driest month of summer. (Alternative definition: 70 percent or more of the mean annual precipitation falls in the six months of winter.)

Df Snowy-forest climate with a moist winter
No dry season.

Dw Snowy-forest climate with a dry winter

ET Tundra climate
The mean temperature of the warmest month is above 0°C (32°F) but below 10°C (50°F).

EF Perpetual frost climate
In this ice sheet climate, the mean monthly temperatures of all months are below 0°C (32°F).

To denote further variations in climate, Köppen added a third letter to the code group. The meanings are as follows:

a With hot summer; warmest month is over 22°C (71.6°F); C and D climates.

b With warm summer; warmest month is below 22°C (71.6°F); C and D climates.

c With cool, short summer; less than four months are over 10°C (50°F); C and D climates.

d With very cold winter; coldest month is below −38°C (−36.4°F); D climates only.

h Dry-hot; mean annual temperature is over 18°C (64.4°F); B climates only.

k Dry-cold; mean annual temperature is under 18°C (64.4°F); B climates only.

As an example of a complete Köppen climate code, BWk refers to a cool desert climate, and Dfc refers to a cold, snowy-forest climate with cool, short summer.

GEODISCOVERIES Generalized **Köppen Climate Map.** View an image of the map at the top of the page and click on the land regions to see representative climographs. An animation.

Table 7.2 | **Moist, Dry, and Wet-Dry Climate Types**

Climate Group	Climate Type		
	Moist	Dry	Wet-Dry
I: Low-latitude Climates	Wet equatorial ① Monsoon and trade-wind coastal ②	Dry tropical ④ (*s*, steppe; *a*, arid)	Wet-dry tropical ③
II: Midlatitude Climates	Moist subtropical ⑥ Marine west-coast ⑧ Moist continental ⑩	Dry subtropical ⑤ (*s*, *a*) Dry midlatitude ⑨ (*s*, *a*)	Mediterranean ⑦
III: High-latitude Climates	Boreal forest ⑪ Tundra ⑫	Ice sheet ⑬	

patterns. Table 7.2 summarizes moist, dry, wet-dry climates as they occur within the three main climate groups.

With our introduction to global climates now complete, we can describe each of the climates and their associated environments in turn. Keep in mind that the annual cycles of temperature and precipitation for each climate region can be easily related to the latitude and location (coastal or interior) of the region, as well as to the characteristic movements of air masses and fronts through the region as they are controlled by global-scale patterns of atmospheric circulation. Our description of the environments associated with the climate types will stress the natural vegetation covers, agricultural practices, and other climate-related human activities that occur in the regions of each climate type.

· ·
GEODISCOVERIES **Interaction of Climate, Vegetation and Soil.** View climate, vegetation, and soils maps superimposed to see common patterns. One animation for each of five global regions.
· ·

LOW-LATITUDE CLIMATES

The *low-latitude climates* lie for the most part between the tropics of cancer and capricorn. In terms of world latitude zones, the low-latitude climates occupy all of the equatorial zone (10° N to 10° S), most of the tropical zone (10–15° N and S), and part of the subtropical zone. In terms of prevailing pressure and wind systems, the region of low-latitude climates includes the equatorial trough of the intertropical convergence zone (ITCZ), the belt of tropical easterlies (northeast and southeast trades), and large portions of the oceanic subtropical high-pressure belt (Figure 7.4).

Figure 7.7 shows climographs for the four low-latitude climates. These climates range from extremely moist—the wet equatorial climate ①—to extremely dry—the dry tropical climate ④. They also vary strongly in the seasonality of their rainfall. In the wet equatorial climate ①, rainfall is abundant year-round. But in the wet-dry tropical climate ③,

----

The wet equatorial climate ① is dominated by warm, moist tropical and equatorial maritime air masses yielding abundant rainfall year-round. The monsoon and trade-wind coastal climate ② has a strong wet season occurring when the ITCZ is nearby.

----

rainfall is abundant for only part of the year. During the remainder of the year, little or no rain falls. The seasonal temperature cycle also varies among these climates. In the wet equatorial climate ①, temperatures are nearly uniform throughout the year. In the dry tropical climate ④, there is a strong annual temperature cycle. Table 7.3 summarizes some of the characteristics of these climates.

The Wet Equatorial Climate ① (Köppen: *Af*)

The **wet equatorial climate** ① is a climate of the intertropical convergence zone (ITCZ), which is nearby for most of the year. The climate is dominated by warm, moist maritime equatorial (mE) and maritime tropical (mT) air masses that yield heavy convectional rainfall. Precipitation is plentiful in all months, and the annual total often exceeds 250 cm (about 100 in.). However, there is usually a seasonal pattern to the rainfall, so that rainfall is greater during some part of the year. This period of heavier rainfall occurs when the ITCZ migrates into the region. Remarkably uniform temperatures prevail throughout the year. Both mean monthly and mean annual temperatures are typically close to 27°C (81°F).

Figure 7.8 shows the world distribution of the wet equatorial climate ①. This climate is found in the latitude range 10° N to 10° S. Its major regions of occurrence include the Amazon lowland of South America, the Congo Basin of equatorial Africa, and the East Indies, from Sumatra to New Guinea.

Figure 7.9 is a climograph for Iquitos, Peru (located in Figure 7.8), a typical wet equatorial station situated close to the equator in the broad, low basin of the upper Amazon River. Notice the very small annual range in temperature and the very large annual rainfall total. Monthly air temperatures are extremely uniform in the wet equatorial climate ①. Typically, mean monthly air temperature will range between 26° and 29°C (79° and 84°F) for stations at low elevation in the equatorial zone.

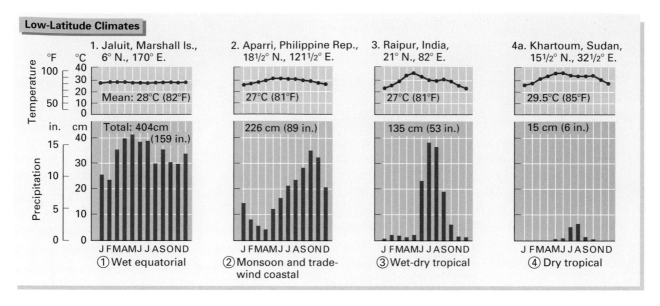

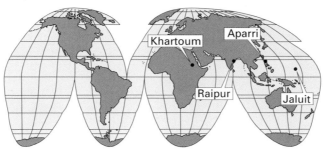

7.7 Low-latitude climographs *These four climographs show the key features of the four low-latitude climates.*

The Monsoon and Trade-Wind Coastal Climate ② (Köppen: *Af, Am*)

Like the wet equatorial climate ①, the **monsoon and trade-wind coastal climate** ② has abundant rainfall. But unlike the wet equatorial climate ①, the rainfall of the monsoon and trade-wind coastal climate ② always shows a strong seasonal pattern. This seasonal pattern is due to the migration of the intertropical convergence zone (ITCZ). In the high-Sun season ("summer," depending on the hemisphere), the ITCZ is nearby and monthly rainfall is greater. In the low-Sun season, when the ITCZ has migrated to the other hemisphere, subtropical high pressure dominates and monthly rainfall is less. Figure 7.8 shows the global distribution of the monsoon and trade-wind coastal climate ②. The climate occurs over latitudes from 5° to 25° N and S.

As the name of the monsoon and trade-wind coastal climate ② suggests, this climate type is produced by two somewhat different situations. On trade-wind coasts, rainfall is produced by moisture-laden maritime tropical (mT) and maritime equatorial (mE) air masses. These are moved onshore onto narrow coastal zones by trade winds or by

In the wet periods of the monsoon and trade-wind coastal climate ②, equatorial east coasts receive warm moist air masses from easterly trades while tropical south and west coasts receive moist air from southwesterly monsoon winds.

monsoon circulation patterns. As the warm, moist air passes over coastal hills and mountains, the orographic effect touches off convectional shower activity. Shower activity is also intensified by easterly waves, which are more frequent when the ITCZ is nearby. The east coasts of land masses experience this trade-wind effect because the trade winds blow from east to west. Trade-wind coasts are found along the east sides of Central and South America, the Caribbean Islands, Madagascar (Malagasy), Southeast Asia, the Philippines, and northeast Australia (see Figure 7.8).

The coastal precipitation effect also applies to the summer monsoon of Asia, when the monsoon circulation brings mT air onshore. However, the onshore monsoon winds blow from southwest to northeast, so it is the western coasts of land masses that are exposed to this moist airflow. Western India and Myanmar (formerly Burma) are examples. Moist air also penetrates well inland in Bangladesh, providing the very heavy monsoon rains for which the region is well known.

In central and western Africa, and southern Brazil, the monsoon pattern shifts the intertropical convergence zone

7.8 World map of wet equatorial ① and monsoon and trade-wind coastal climates ② (Based on Goode Base Map.)

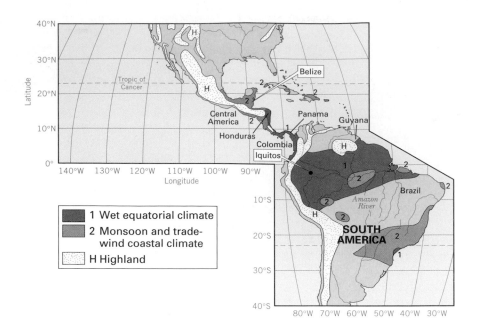

1 Wet equatorial climate
2 Monsoon and trade-wind coastal climate
H Highland

Table 7.3 | Low-Latitude Climates

Climate	Temperature	Precipitation	Explanation
Wet equatorial ①	Uniform temperatures, mean near 27 °C (81°F).	Abundant rainfall, all months, from mT and mE air masses. Annual total may exceed 250 cm (100 in.).	The ITCZ dominates this climate, with abundant convectional precipitation generated by convergence in weak equatorial lows. Rainfall is heaviest when the ITCZ is nearby.
Monsoon and trade-wind coastal ②	Temperatures show an annual cycle, with warmest temperatures in the high-Sun season.	Abundant rainfall but with a strong seasonal pattern.	Trade-wind coastal: Rainfall from mE and mT air masses is heavy when the ITCZ is nearby, lighter when the ITCZ moves to the opposite hemisphere. Asian monsoon coasts: dry air flowing southwest in low-Sun season alternates with moist oceanic air flowing northeast, producing a seasonal rainfall pattern on west coasts.
Wet-dry tropical ③	Marked temperature cycle, with hottest temperatures before the rainy season.	Wet high-Sun season alternates with dry low-Sun season.	Subtropical high pressure moves into this climate in the low-Sun season, bringing very dry conditions. In the high-Sun season, the ITCZ approaches and rainfall occurs. Asian monsoon climate: alternation of dry continental air in low-Sun season with moist oceanic air in high-Sun season brings a strong pattern of dry and wet seasons.
Dry tropical ④	Strong temperature cycle, with intense hot temperatures during high-Sun season.	Low precipitation. Sometimes rainfall occurs when the ITCZ is near.	This climate is dominated by subtropical high pressure, which provides clear, stable air for much or all of year. Insolation is intense during high-Sun period.

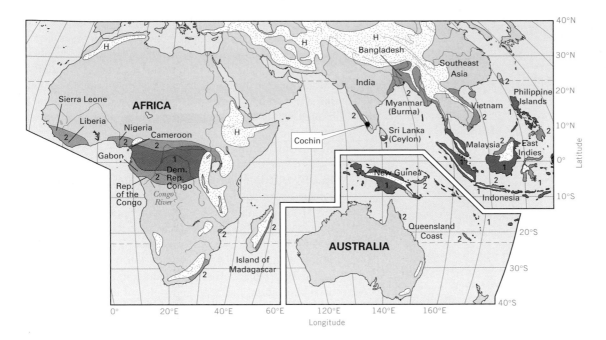

over 20° of latitude, or more (see Figure 5.19). Here, heavy rainfall occurs in the high-Sun season, when the ITCZ is nearby. Drier conditions prevail in the low-Sun season, when the ITCZ is far away.

Temperatures in the monsoon and trade-wind coastal climate ②, though warm throughout the year, also show an annual cycle. Warmest temperatures occur in the high-Sun

season, just before arrival of the ITCZ brings clouds and rain. Minimum temperatures occur at the time of low Sun.

Figure 7.10 is a climograph for the city of Belize, in the Central American country of Belize (Figure 7.8). This east-coast city, located at lat. 17° N, is exposed to the tropical easterly trade winds. Rainfall is abundant from June through November, when the ITCZ is nearby. Easterly waves are

7.9 Wet equatorial climate ① *Iquitos, Peru, lat. 3° S, is located in the upper Amazon lowland, close to the equator. Temperatures differ very little from month to month, and there is abundant rainfall throughout the year.*

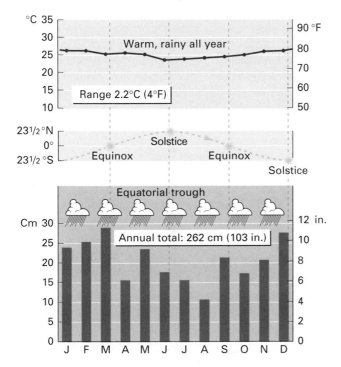

7.10 Trade-wind coastal climate ② *This climograph for Belize, a Central American east-coast city at lat. 17° N, shows a marked season of low rainfall following the period of low Sun. For the remainder of the year, precipitation is high, produced by warm, moist northeast trade winds.*

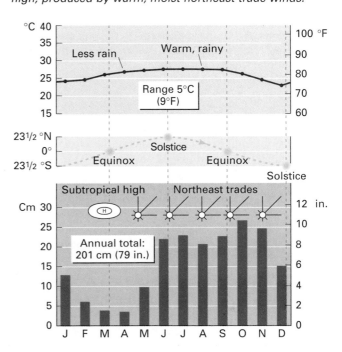

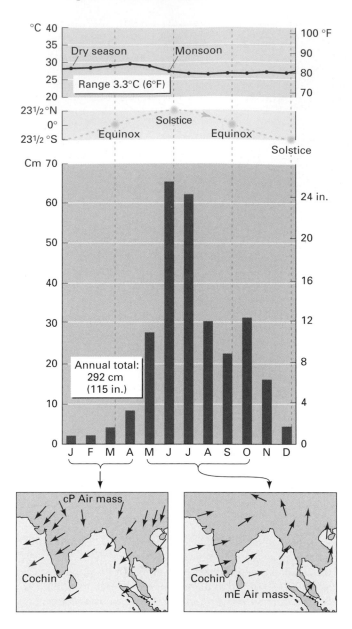

7.11 Monsoon coastal climate ② *Cochin, India, on a windward coast at lat. 10° N, shows an extreme peak of rainfall during the rainy monsoon, contrasting with a short dry season at time of low Sun.*

India, provides an example (Figure 7.11). Located at lat. 10° N on the west coast of lower peninsular India (see Figure 7.8), Cochin receives the warm, moist southwest winds of the summer monsoon. In this season, monthly rainfall is extreme in both June and July. A strongly pronounced season of low rainfall occurs at time of low Sun—December through March. Air temperatures show only a very weak annual cycle, cooling a bit during the rains, so the annual range is small at this low latitude.

THE LOW-LATITUDE RAINFOREST ENVIRONMENT   Our first two climates—wet equatorial ① and monsoon and trade-wind coastal ②—are quite uniform in temperature and have a high annual rainfall. These factors create a special environment—the *low-latitude rainforest environment* (Figure 7.12). In the rainforest, streams flow abundantly throughout most of the year, and river channels are lined along the banks with dense forest vegetation. Indigenous peoples of the rainforest once traveled the rivers in dugout canoes, although today most enjoy easier travel powered by outboard motor. Over a century ago, larger shallow-draft river craft turned the major waterways into the main arteries of trade, connecting towns and cities on the river banks. Aircraft have added a new dimension in mobility, criss-crossing the almost trackless green sea of forest to find landings in clearings or on broad reaches of the larger rivers.

Low-latitude rainforests, unlike higher latitude forests, possess a great diversity of plant and animal species. The low-latitude rainforest can contain as many as 3000 different tree species in an area of only a few square kilometers, whereas midlatitude forests possess fewer than one-tenth that number. The number of types of animals found in the rainforest is also very large. A 16 km² (6 mi²) area in Panama near the Canal, for example, contains about 20,000 species of insects, while all of France has only a few hundred.

Many products of the rainforest have economic value. Rainforest lumber, such as mahogany, ebony, or balsawood, is an important export. Quinine, cocaine, and other drugs come from the bark and leaves of tropical plants. Cocoa is derived from the seed kernel of the cacao plant. Natural rubber is made from the sap of the rubber tree. The tree comes from South America, where it was first exploited. Rubber trees also are widely distributed through the rainforest of Africa. Today, the principal production is from plantations in Indonesia, Malaysia, Thailand, Vietnam, and Sri Lanka (Ceylon).

common in this season, and on occasion a tropical cyclone will bring torrential rainfall. Following the December solstice, rainfall is greatly reduced, with minimum values in March and April. At this time, the ITCZ lies farthest away, and the climate is dominated by subtropical high pressure. Air temperatures show an annual range of 5° C (9° F) with maximum in the high-Sun months. The Asiatic monsoon shows a similar pattern, but there is an extreme peak of rainfall during the high-Sun period and a well-developed dry season with two or three months of only small rainfall amounts. The climograph for Cochin,

> The natural environment of the wet equatorial ① and monsoon and trade-wind coastal climates ② is a rainforest of broadleaf evergreen trees. The rainforest is complex and diverse and yields many useful products.

In many areas of the rainforest and its fringes, agriculture is practiced by the slash-and-burn method, in which small patches of forest are cut down and then burned on the site. The wood ashes contain nutrients, and when spread over the soil, they serve as a simple fertilizer. Crops are then grown in the soil for a few years, until the nutrients are gone. The now unproductive plot is abandoned and eventually returns to rainforest. *Eye on the Environment 9.1 • Exploitation of the Low-Latitude Rainforest Environ-*

7.12 Eye on the Landscape Rainforest of the western Amazon lowland, near Manaus, Brazil *The river is a tributary of the Amazon.* **What else would the geographer see? ... Answers at the end of the chapter.**

ment provides more detail on this process and discusses the effects of large-area clearing of the rainforest for mechanized agriculture and grazing.

The Wet-Dry Tropical Climate ③ (Köppen: *Aw, Cwa*)

In the monsoon and trade-wind coastal climate ②, we noted that the movements of the intertropical convergence zone into and away from the climate region produce a seasonal cycle of rainfall and temperature. As we move farther poleward, this cycle becomes stronger, and the monsoon and trade-wind coastal climate ② grades into the **wet-dry tropical climate** ③.

The wet-dry tropical climate ③ is distinguished by a very dry season at low Sun that alternates with a very wet season at high Sun. During the low-Sun season, when the equatorial trough is far away, dry continental tropical (cT) air masses prevail. In the high-Sun season, when the ITCZ is nearby, moist maritime tropical (mT) and maritime equatorial (mE) air masses dominate. Cooler temperatures accompany the dry season but give way to a very hot period before the rains begin.

Figure 7.13 shows the global distribution of the wet-dry tropical climate ③. It is found at latitudes of 5° to 20° N and S in Africa and the Americas, and at 10° to 30° N in Asia. In

> The wet-dry tropical climate ③ has a very dry season alternating with a very wet season. A typical vegetation cover in this climate is savanna woodland, a sparse cover of trees over grassland.

Africa and South America, the climate occupies broad bands poleward of the wet equatorial and monsoon and trade-wind coastal climates. Because these regions are farther away from the ITCZ, less rainfall is triggered by the ITCZ during the rainy season, and subtropical high pressure can dominate more strongly during the low-Sun season. In central India and Indochina, the regions of wet-dry tropical climate ③ are somewhat protected by mountain barriers from the warm, moist mE and mT air flows provided by trade and monsoon winds. These barriers create a rain shadow effect, so that even less rainfall occurs during the rainy season and the dry season is drier still.

Figure 7.14 is a climograph for Timbo, Guinea, at lat. 10° N in West Africa (Figure 7.13). Here the rainy season begins just after the March equinox and reaches a peak in August, about two months following the June solstice. At this time, the ITCZ has migrated to its most northerly position, and moist mE air masses flow into the region from the ocean lying to the south. Monthly rainfall then decreases as the low-Sun season arrives and the ITCZ moves to the south. Three months—December through February—are practically rainless. During this season, subtropical high pressure dominates the climate, and stable, subsiding continental tropical (cT) air pervades the region. The temperature cycle is closely linked to both the solar cycle and the precipitation pattern. In February and March, insolation

7.13 World map of the wet-dry tropical climate ③ *(Based on Goode Base Map.)*

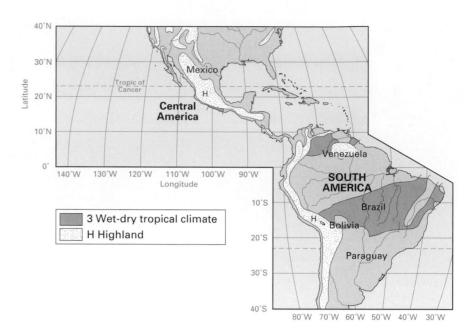

increases, and air temperature rises sharply. A brief hot season occurs. As soon as the rains set in, the effect of cloud cover and evaporation of rain causes the temperature to decline. By July, temperatures have resumed an even level.

The wet-dry tropical climate ③ is the home of the savanna environment. The native vegetation of this climate must survive alternating seasons of very dry and very wet

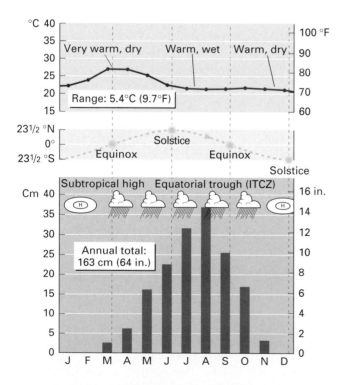

7.14 Wet-dry tropical climate ③ *Timbo, Guinea, at lat. 10° N, is located in West Africa. A long wet season at time of high Sun alternates with an almost rainless dry season at time of low Sun.*

weather. Most plants enter a dormant phase during the dry period, then burst forth into leaf and bloom with the coming of the rains. For this reason, the native plant cover can be described as *rain-green vegetation.*

Rain-green vegetation consists of two basic types. First is *savanna woodland* (Figure 7.15). By *woodland* we mean an open forest in which trees are widely spaced apart. In the savanna woodland, coarse grasses occupy the open space between the trees, which are often coarse-barked and thorny. Large expanses of grassland may also be present. In the dry season, the grasses turn to straw, and many of the tree species shed their leaves to cope with the drought. The second vegetation type is found in the more arid parts of the climate region. Here, small thorny trees and large shrubs form dense patches. This type of vegetation cover is referred to as *thorntree-tall-grass savanna.* (Further details are given in Chapter 9.) Because of the prevalence of the savanna vegetation in the wet-dry tropical climate ③, it can be identified as the savanna environment.

In the savanna environment, river channels that are not fed by nearby moist mountain regions are nearly or completely dry in the low-Sun dry season. In the rainy season, these river channels become filled to their banks with swiftly flowing, turbid water. The rains are not reliable, and agriculture without irrigation is hazardous at best. When the rains fail, a devastating famine can ensue. The Sahel region of Africa, discussed further in *Eye on Global Change 7.2 • Drought and Land Degradation in the African Sahel,* is a region well-known for such droughts and famines.

The Dry Tropical Climate ④ (Köppen: *BWh, BSh*)

The **dry tropical climate** ④ is found in the center and east sides of subtropical high-pressure cells. Here, air strongly subsides, warming adiabatically and inhibiting condensa-

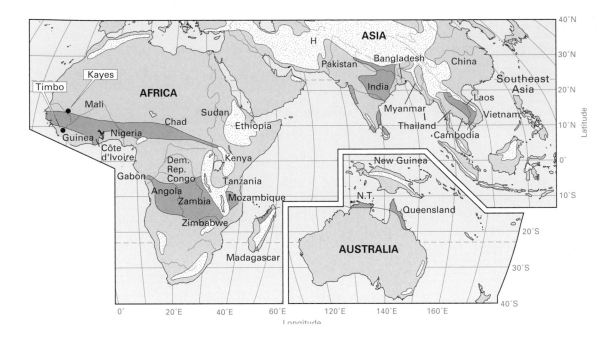

tion. Rainfall is very rare and occurs only when unusual weather conditions move moist air into the region. Since skies are clear most of the time, the Sun heats the surface intensely, keeping air temperatures high. During the high-Sun period, heat is extreme. During the low-Sun period, temperatures are cooler. Given the dry air and lack of cloud cover, the daily temperature range is very large.

The driest areas of the dry tropical climate ④ are near the tropics of cancer and capricorn. As we travel from the tropics toward the equator, we find that somewhat more rain

falls. Continuing in this direction, we encounter a short rainy season at the time of year when the ITCZ is near, and the climate grades into the wet-dry tropical ③ type.

Figure 7.16 shows the global distribution of the dry tropical climate ④. Nearly all of the dry tropical climate ④ areas lie in the latitude range 15° to 25° N and S. The largest region is the Sahara–Saudi Arabia–Iran–Thar desert belt of North Africa and southern Asia. This vast desert expanse includes some of the driest regions on Earth. Another large region of dry tropical climate ④ is the desert of central Aus-

7.15 Savanna woodland of the Serengeti Plains, Tanzania, East Africa *Acacia trees with flattened crowns are scattered on this grassy landscape.*

Eye on Global Change | **7.2**

Drought and Land Degradation in the African Sahel

The wet-dry tropical climate ③ is subject to years of devastating drought as well as to years of abnormally high rainfall that can result in severe floods. Climate records show that two or three successive years of abnormally low rainfall (a drought) typically alternate with several successive years of average or higher than average rainfall. This variability is a permanent feature of the wet-dry tropical climate ③, and the plants and animals inhabiting this region have adjusted to the natural variability in rainfall, with one exception: the human species.

The wet-dry tropical climate ③ of West Africa, including the adjacent semiarid southern belt of the dry tropical climate ④ to the north, provides a lesson on the human impact on a delicate ecological system. Countries of this perilous belt, called the *Sahel,* or *Sahelian zone,* are shown in the figure at the right. From 1968 through 1974, all these countries were struck by a severe drought. Both nomadic cattle herders and grain farmers share this zone. During the drought, grain crops failed and foraging cattle could find no food to eat. In the worst stages of the Sahel drought, nomads were forced to sell their remaining cattle. Because the cattle were their sole means of subsistence, the nomads soon starved. Some 5 million cattle perished, and it has been estimated that 100,000 people died of starvation and disease in 1973 alone.

The Sahelian drought of 1968–1974 was associated with a special phenomenon, which at that time was called *desertification*—the permanent transformation of the land surface by human activities to resemble a desert, largely through the destruction of grasses, shrubs, and trees by grazing animals and

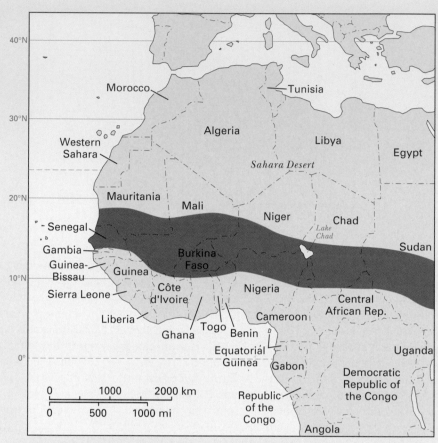

The African Sahel *The Sahel, or Sahelian zone, shown in color, lies south of the great Sahara Desert of North Africa.*

fuel wood harvesting. That term has now been abandoned in favor of *land degradation.* This degradation accelerates the effects of soil erosion, such as gullying of slopes and accumulations of sediment in stream channels. The removal of soil by wind is also intensified.

Periodic droughts throughout past decades are well documented in the Sahel, as they are in other world regions of wet-dry tropical climate ③. Presented at right is a graph showing the percentage of departures from the long-term mean of each year's rainfall in the western Sahel from 1901 through

1995. Note the wide year-to-year variation. Since about 1950, the durations of periods of continuous departures both above and below the mean seem to have increased substantially. The period of sustained high-rainfall years in the 1950s contrasts sharply with a series of severe drought episodes starting in 1971. To obtain an earlier record, scientists have examined fluctuations in the level of Lake Chad. In times of drought, the lake's shoreline retreats, while in times of abundant rainfall, it expands. The changes document periods of rainfall deficiency and

Sahelian drought *At the height of the Sahelian drought, vast numbers of cattle had perished and even the goats were hard pressed to survive. Trampling of the dry ground prepared the region for devastating soil erosion in the rains that eventually ended the drought.*

excess—1820–1840, below normal; 1870–1895, above normal; 1895–1920, below normal.

The sustained drought periods of the past show that droughts and wet periods are a normal phenomenon in the Sahel. In prior eras, the landscape was able to recover from the droughts during periods of abundant rainfall. Today, the pressure of increased populations of humans and cattle keeps the land degraded. As long as these populations remain high, the land degradation will be permanent.

The effect of an accelerated global warming in the coming decades on regions of wet-dry tropical climate ③ is difficult to predict. Some regions may experience greater swings between drought and surplus precipitation. At the same time, these regions may migrate poleward as a result of intensification of the Hadley cell circulation. Thus, the Sahel region may move northward into the desert zone of the Sahara. However, such changes are highly speculative. At this time, there is no scientific consensus on how climatic change will affect the Sahel or other regions of wet-dry tropical climate ③.

Rainfall in the Sahel *Rainfall fluctuations for stations in the western Sahel, 1901–1995, expressed as a percent departure from the long-term mean. (Courtesy of Sharon E. Nicholson, Department of Meteorology, Florida State University, Tallahassee.)*

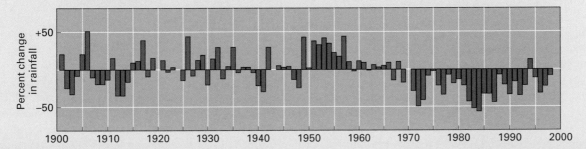

7.16 World map of the dry tropical ④, dry subtropical ⑤, and dry midlatitude ⑨ climates
The latter two climates are poleward and eastward extensions of the dry tropical climate ④ with cooler temperatures. (Based on Goode Base Map.)

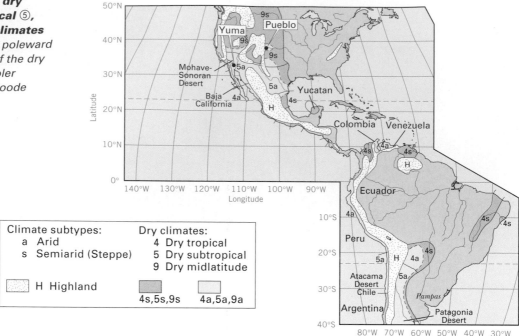

Climate subtypes:
  a Arid
  s Semiarid (Steppe)

  ☐ H Highland

Dry climates:
  4 Dry tropical
  5 Dry subtropical
  9 Dry midlatitude

  ▨ 4s,5s,9s   ☐ 4a,5a,9a

tralia. The west coast of South America, including portions of Ecuador, Peru, and Chile, also exhibits the dry tropical climate ④. However, temperatures there are moderated by a cool marine air layer that blankets the coast.

Figure 7.17 is a climograph for a dry tropical station in the heart of the North African desert. Wadi Halfa, Sudan (Figure 7.16), lies at lat. 22° N, almost on the tropic of cancer. The temperature record shows a strong annual cycle with a very hot period at the time of high Sun, when three consecutive months average 32°C (90°F). Daytime maximum air temperatures are frequently between 43° and 48°C (about 110° to 120°F) in the warmer months. There is a comparatively cool season at the time of low Sun, but the coolest month averages a mild 16°C (61°F), and freezing temperatures are rarely recorded. No rainfall bars are shown on the climograph because precipitation averages less than 0.25 cm (0.1 in.) in all months. Over a 39-year period, the maximum rainfall recorded in a 24-hour period at Wadi Halfa was only 0.75 cm (0.3 in.).

Although the world's dry climates consist largely of extremely arid deserts, there are in addition broad zones at the margins of the desert that are best described as *semiarid.* These zones have a short wet season that supports the growth of grasses on which animals (both wild and domestic) graze. Geographers also call these semiarid regions **steppes.** Nomadic tribes and their herds of animals visit these areas during and after the brief moist period. In Figures 7.6 (world climate map) and 7.16 (world map of dry climates), the two subdivisions of dry climates are distinguished with the letters *a* (arid) and *s* (semiarid).

> The dry tropical climate ④ lies in the belt of persistent subtropical high pressure, so rainfall is rare. Temperatures are very hot during the high-Sun season but are significantly cooler during the low-Sun season.

An example of the semiarid dry tropical climate ④ is that of Kayes, Mali, which we presented earlier as a sample climograph (Figure 7.5). Located in the Sahel region of Africa, this station has a distinct rainy season that occurs when the intertropical convergence zone moves north in the high-Sun season. This precipitation pattern shows the semiarid subtype as a transition between the arid dry tropical climate ④ and the wet-dry tropical climate ③.

The Earth's desert landscapes are actually quite varied (Figure 7.18). Much of the arid desert consists of barren areas of drifting sand or sterile salt flats. However, in semiarid regions, thorny trees and shrubs are often abundant, since the climate includes a small amount of regular rainfall. Figure 7.18*a* shows a scene from the semiarid part of the Kalahari desert in southwest Africa (Figure 7.16), featuring the strange-looking baobab tree. Baja California also supports a sparse collection of plants especially adapted to semiarid desert conditions.

An important variation of the dry tropical climate ④ occurs in narrow coastal zones along the western edge of continents. These regions are strongly influenced by cold ocean currents and the upwelling of deep, cold water, which occurs just offshore. The cool water moderates coastal zone temperatures and reduces the seasonality of the temperature cycle. Figure 7.19 shows a climograph for Walvis Bay, a port city on the west coast of Namibia (South-West Africa), at lat. 23° S (Figure 7.16). (In the figure, the yearly cycle begins with July because this is a southern hemisphere station.) For a location nearly on the tropic of capricorn (23½° S), the monthly temperatures are remarkably cool, with the

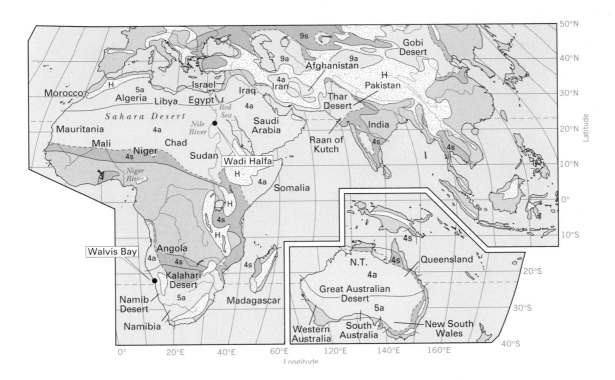

warmest monthly mean only 20°C (68°F) and the coolest monthly mean 14°C (57°F). This provides an annual range of only 5°C (9°F). Coastal fog is a persistent feature of this climate. Another important occurrence of this western coastal desert subtype is along the western coast of South America in Peru and Chile, where it is known as the Atacama desert.

MIDLATITUDE CLIMATES

The *midlatitude climates* almost fully occupy the land areas of the midlatitude zone and a large proportion of the subtropical latitude zone. Along the western fringe of Europe, they extend into the

The midlatitude climates lie in a zone of interaction between tropical and polar air masses that is marked by traveling cyclones, traveling anticyclones, and frontal boundaries. They range from very wet to very dry and usually show a strong variation in temperature and/or precipitation through the year.

subarctic latitude zone as well, reaching to the 60th parallel. Unlike the low-latitude climates, which are about equally distributed between northern and southern hemispheres, nearly all of the midlatitude climate area is in the northern hemisphere. In the southern hemisphere, the land area poleward of the 40th parallel is so small that the climates are dominated by a great southern ocean and do not develop the continental characteristics of their counterparts in the northern hemisphere.

The midlatitude climates of the northern hemisphere lie in a broad zone of intense interaction between two groups of very unlike air masses (Figure 7.4). From the subtropical zone, tongues of

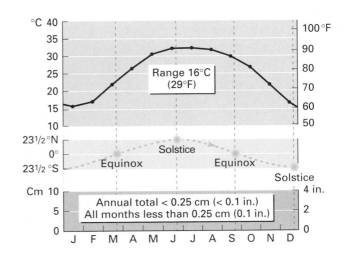

7.17 Dry tropical climate ④, dry desert *Wadi Halfa is a city on the Nile River in Sudan at lat. 22° N, close to the Egyptian border. Too little rain falls to be shown on the graph. Air temperatures are very high during the high-Sun months.*

7.18 Desert Landscapes

a...*Eye on the Landscape* *The baobab* This strange-looking baobab tree is a common inhabitant of the thorntree semidesert of Botswana, in the Kalahari region of southern Africa. **What else would the geographer see?** ... Answers at the end of the chapter.

b...*Great Australian desert* Red colors dominate this desert scene from the Rainbow Valley, south of Alice Springs.

c...*Sahara desert* This sandy plain in Algeria is dotted with date palms that tap ground water near the surface.

d...*Eye on the Landscape Gobi desert* *Dry, windswept basins alternate with rock outcrops and ranges in the high Gobi Desert of Mongolia.* **What else would the geographer see? ... Answers at the end of the chapter.**

e...*Baja California desert* *Rounded granite boulders and many plants adapted to dry desert conditions are visible in this scene from the Catavina Desert of the northern Baja California Pennisula, Mexico.*

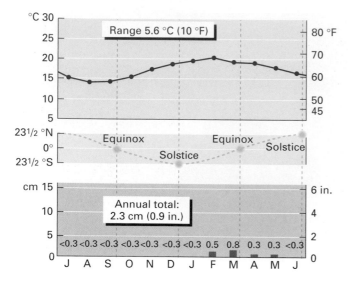

7.19 Dry tropical climate ④, western coastal desert subtype *Walvis Bay, Namibia (southwest Africa), is a desert station on the west coast of Africa at lat. 23° S. Air temperatures are cool and remarkably uniform throughout the year.*

maritime tropical (mT) air masses enter the midlatitude zone. There, they meet and conflict with tongues of maritime polar (mP) and continental polar (cP) air masses along the discontinuous and shifting polar-front zone.

In terms of prevailing pressure and wind systems, the midlatitude climates include the poleward halves of the great subtropical high-pressure systems and much of the belt of prevailing westerly winds (see Figure 5.16). As a result, weather systems, such as traveling cyclones and their fronts, characteristically move from west to east. This dominant global eastward airflow influences the distribution of climates from west to east across the North American and Eurasian continents.

The six midlatitude climate types range from two that are very dry to three that are extremely moist (Figure 7.20). The midlatitude climates span the range from those with strong wet and dry seasons—the Mediterranean climate ⑦—to those with precipitation that is more or less uniformly distributed through the year. Temperature cycles are also quite varied. Low annual ranges are seen along the windward west coasts. In contrast, annual ranges are large in the continental interiors. Table 7.4 summarizes the important features of these climates.

7.20 Climographs for the six midlatitude climates

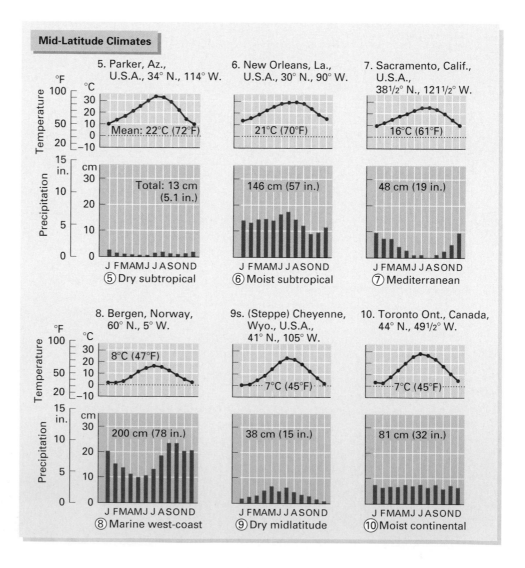

Table 7.4 | **Midlatitude Climates**

Climate	Temperature	Precipitation	Explanation
Dry subtropical ⑤	Distinct cool or cold season at low-Sun period.	Precipitation is low in nearly all months.	This climate lies poleward of the subtropical high-pressure cells and is dominated by dry cT air most of the year. Rainfall occurs when moist mT air reaches the region, either in summer monsoon flows or in winter frontal movements.
Moist subtropical ⑥	Temperatures show strong annual cycle, but with no winter month below freezing.	Abundant rainfall, cyclonic in winter and convectional in summer. Humidity generally high.	The flow of mT air from the west sides of subtropical high-pressure cells provides moist air most of the year. cP air may reach this region during the winter.
Mediterranean ⑦	Temperature range is moderate, with warm to hot summers and mild winters.	Unusual pattern of wet winter and dry summer. Overall, drier when nearer to subtropical high pressure.	The poleward migration of subtropical high-pressure cells moves clear, stable cT air into this region in the summer. In winter, cyclonic storms and polar frontal precipitation reach the area.
Marine west-coast ⑧	Temperature cycle is moderated by marine influence.	Abundant precipitation but with a winter maximum.	Moist mP air, moving inland from the ocean to the west, dominates this climate most of the year. In the summer, subtropical high pressure reaches these regions, reducing precipitation.
Dry midlatitude ⑨	Strong temperature cycle with large annual range. Summers warm to hot, winters cold to very cold.	Precipitation is low in all months but usually shows a summer maximum.	This climate is dry because of its interior location, far from mP source regions. In winter, cP dominates. In summer, a local dry continental air mass develops.
Moist continental ⑩	Summers warm, winters cold with three months below freezing. Very large annual temperature range.	Ample precipitation, with a summer maximum.	This climate lies in the polar-front zone. In winter, cP air dominates, while mT invades frequently in summer. Precipitation is abundant, cyclonic in winter and convectional in summer.

The Dry Subtropical Climate ⑤
(Köppen: *BWh, BWk, BSh, BSk*)

The **dry subtropical climate** ⑤ is simply a poleward extension of the dry tropical climate ④, caused by somewhat similar air mass patterns. A point of difference is in the annual temperature range, which is greater for the dry subtropical climate ⑤. The lower latitude portions have a distinct cool season, and the higher latitude portions, a cold season. The cold season, which occurs at a time of low Sun, is due in part to invasions of cold continental polar (cP) air masses from higher latitudes. Precipitation occurring in the low-Sun season is produced by midlatitude cyclones that occasionally move into the subtropical zone. As in the dry tropical climate ④, both arid and semiarid subtypes are recognized.

Figure 7.16 shows the global distribution of the dry subtropical climate ⑤. A broad band of this climate type is found in North Africa, connecting with the Near East. Southern Africa and southern Australia also contain regions of dry subtropical climate ⑤ poleward of the dry tropical climate ④. In South America, a band of dry subtropical climate ⑤ occupies Patagonia, a region east of the Andes in Argentina. In North America, the Mojave and Sonoran

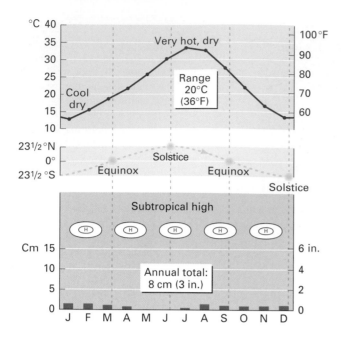

7.21 *Dry subtropical climate* ⑤ *Yuma, Arizona, lat. 33° N, has a strong seasonal temperature cycle. Compare with Wadi Halfa (Figure 7.17).*

deserts of the American Southwest and northwest Mexico are of the dry subtropical type.

Figure 7.21 is a climograph for Yuma, Arizona, a city within the arid subtype of the dry subtropical climate ⑤, close to the Mexican border at lat. 33° N. The pattern of monthly temperatures shows a strong seasonal cycle with a dry, hot summer. A cold season brings monthly means as low as 13°C (55°F). Freezing temperatures—0°C (32°F) and below—can be expected at night in December and January. The annual range is 20°C (36°F). Precipitation, which totals about 8 cm (3 in.), is small in all months but has peaks in late winter and late summer. The August maximum is caused by the invasion of maritime tropical (mT) air masses, which bring thunderstorms to the region. Higher rainfalls from December through March are produced by midlatitude wave cyclones following a southerly path. Two months, May and June, are nearly rainless.

The environment of the dry subtropical climate ⑤ is similar to that of the dry tropical climate ④ in that both are very dry. The boundary between these two climate types is gradational. But if we were to travel northward in the subtropical climate zone of North America, arriving at about 34° N in the interior Mojave desert of southeastern California, we would encounter environmental features significantly different from those of the low-latitude deserts of tropical Africa, Arabia, and northern Australia. Although

---

The dry subtropical climate ⑤ resembles the dry tropical climate ④ but has cooler temperatures during the low-Sun season, when continental polar air masses invade the region.

---

the great summer heat of the low-elevation regions of the Mojave desert is comparable to that experienced in the Sahara desert, the low Sun brings a winter season that is not found in the tropical deserts. Here, cyclonic precipitation can occur in most months, including the cool low-Sun months.

In the Mojave desert and adjacent Sonoran desert, plants are often large and numerous, in some places giving the appearance of an open woodland. One example is the occurrence of forest-like stands of the tall, cylindrical saguaro cactus. Another is the woodland of Joshua trees found in higher parts of the Mojave desert (Figure 7.22). Other distinctive plants include the prickly pear cactus, the ocotillo plant, and the creosote bush.

Both plants and animals of deserts are adapted to the dry environment. As in the dry tropical environment, many annual plants remain dormant as seeds during long dry periods, then spring to life, flower, and bloom very quickly when rain falls. Certain invertebrate animals adopt the same life pattern. For example, the tiny brine shrimp of the North American desert may wait many years in dormancy until normally dry lakebeds fill with water, an event that occurs perhaps three or four times per century. The shrimp then emerge and complete their life cycles before the lake evaporates.

The Moist Subtropical Climate ⑥ (Köppen: *Cfa*)

Recall that circulation around the subtropical high-pressure cells provides a flow of warm, moist air onto the eastern side of continents (see Figure 5.18). This flow of maritime tropical (mT) air dominates the **moist subtropical climate** ⑥. Summer in this climate sees abundant rainfall, much of it convectional. Occasional tropical cyclones further enhance summer precipitation. In Southeast Asia, this climate is characterized by a strong monsoon effect, with summer rainfall much increased above winter rainfall. Summer temperatures are warm, with persistent high humidity.

Winter precipitation in the moist subtropical climate ⑥ is also plentiful, produced in midlatitude cyclones. Invasions of continental polar (cP) air masses are frequent in winter, bringing spells of subfreezing weather. No winter month has a mean temperature below 0°C (32°F).

Figure 7.23 presents a global map of the moist subtropical climate ⑥ It is found on the eastern sides of continents in the latitude range 20° to 35° N and S. In South America, it includes parts of Uruguay, Brazil, and Argentina. In Australia, it consists of a narrow band between the eastern coastline and the eastern interior ranges. Southern China, Taiwan, and southernmost Japan are regions of the moist subtropical climate ⑥ in Asia. In the United States, the moist subtropical climate ⑥ covers most of the Southeast, from the Carolinas to east Texas.

7.22   A Mojave desert landscape *The strange-looking Joshua tree, shown in the foreground, is abundant at higher elevations in the Mojave desert.*

Figure 7.24 is a climograph for Charleston, South Carolina, located on the eastern seaboard at lat. 33° N. In this region, a marked summer maximum of precipitation is typical. Total annual rainfall is abundant—120 cm (47 in.)—and ample precipitation falls in every month. The annual temperature cycle is strongly developed, with a large annual range of 17°C (31°F). Winters are mild, with the January mean temperature well above the freezing mark.

Much of the natural vegetation in the North American area of this moist climate type consists of *broadleaf deciduous forest.* (In a deciduous forest, leaf shedding occurs annually, and the trees are bare throughout the cold or dry season.) Broadleaf deciduous forest can be found on the interior

> The moist subtropical climate ⑥, found on the eastern sides of continents in the midlatitudes, has abundant precipitation. In summer, warm, moist maritime tropical air masses provide convectional showers, while in winter, wave cyclones provide rain and occasional snow.

uplands of the Carolinas and across Tennessee. An entirely different forest type occurs farther south and east on the low, sandy coastal plain of the Gulf states, on the Florida Peninsula, and on the Atlantic coastal plain of Georgia and the Carolinas. It is the *southern pine forest,* which is well adapted to sandy soils. Over a large part of southern China and the south island of Japan (Kyushu), the native vegetation was formerly a *broadleaf evergreen* forest (Chapter 9). Today this forest is gone from China, but some small areas in Japan remain. On the North American continent, in Louisiana and farther east on the Gulf coast, the evergreen broadleaf forest is represented by a few small areas of Evangeline oak and magnolia (Figure 7.25).

7.23 World map of the moist subtropical climate *(Based on Goode Base Map.)*

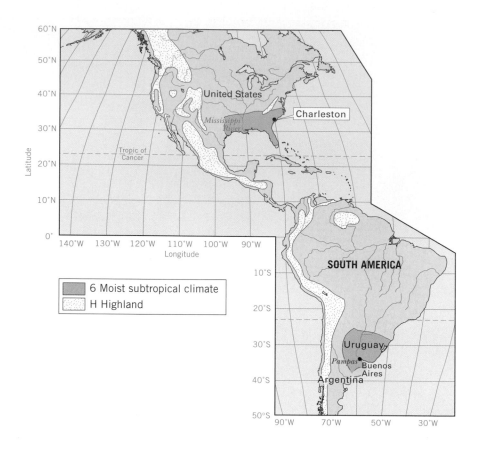

6 Moist subtropical climate
H Highland

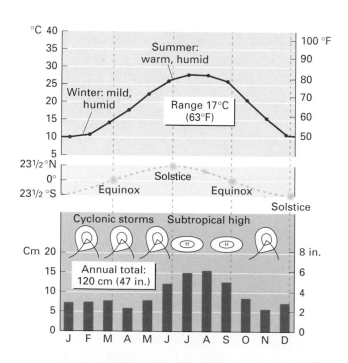

7.24 Moist subtropical climate ⑥ *Charleston, South Carolina, lat. 33° N, has a mild winter and a warm summer. There is ample precipitation in all months but a definite summer maximum.*

7.25 Broadleaf evergreen forest of the Gulf coast
A typical species of the broadleaf evergreen forest is the Evangeline oak, here bearing Spanish "moss"—an epiphyte that forms long beard-like streamers. The ground beneath is maintained as a lawn. Evangeline State Park, Bayou Teche, Louisiana. (A. N. Strahler.)

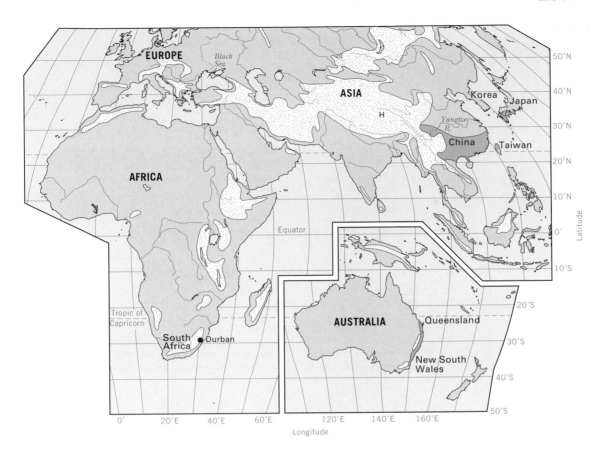

The Mediterranean Climate ⑦ (Köppen: *Csa, Csb*)

The **Mediterranean climate** ⑦ is unique among the climate types because its annual precipitation cycle has a wet winter and a very dry summer. The reason for this precipitation cycle lies in the poleward movement of the subtropical high-pressure cells during the summer season. The Mediterranean climate ⑦ is located along the west coasts of continents, just poleward of the dry, eastern side of the subtropical high-pressure cells (see Figure 5.18). When the subtropical high-pressure cells move poleward in summer, they enter the region of this climate. Dry continental tropical (cT) air then dominates, producing the dry summer season. In winter, the moist mP air mass invades with cyclonic storms and generates ample rainfall.

In terms of total annual rainfall, the Mediterranean climate ⑦ spans a wide range from arid to humid, depending on location. Generally, the closer an area is to the tropics, the stronger the influence of subtropical high pressure will be, and thus the drier the climate. The temperature range is moderate, with warm to hot summers and mild winters. Coastal zones between lat. 30° and 35° N and S, such as southern California, show a smaller annual range, with very mild winters.

Figure 7.26 is a climograph for Monterey, California, a Pacific coastal city at lat. 36° N. The annual temperature cycle is very weak. The small annual range and cool summer

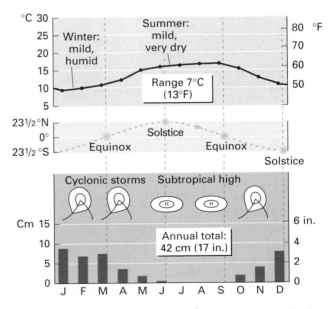

7.26 Mediterranean climate ⑦ *Monterey, California, lat. 36° N, has a very weak annual temperature cycle because of its closeness to the Pacific Ocean. The summer is very dry.*

7.27 *World map of the Mediterranean ⑦ and marine west-coast ⑧ climates* (Based on Goode Base Map.)

7 Mediterranean climate
8 Marine west-coast climate
H Highland

reflect the strong control of the cold California current and its cool, marine air layer. Fogs are frequent. This temperature regime is found only in a narrow coastal zone. Rainfall drops to nearly zero for four consecutive summer months but rises to substantial amounts in the rainy winter season. In California's Central Valley, the dry summers persist, but the annual temperature range is greater, so that daily high temperatures match those of the adjacent dry climates.

A global map of the Mediterranean climate ⑦ is shown in Figure 7.27. It is found in the latitude range 30° to 45° N and S. In the southern hemisphere, it occurs along the coast of Chile, in the Cape Town region of South Africa, and along the southern and western coasts of Australia. In North America, it is found in central and southern California. In Europe, this climate type surrounds the Mediterranean Sea, which gives the climate its distinctive name.

The native vegetation of the Mediterranean climate environment is adapted to survival through the long summer drought. Shrubs and trees are typically equipped with small, hard or thick leaves that resist water loss through transpiration. These plants are called *sclerophylls;* the prefix scler, from the Greek for "hard," is combined with phyllo, which is Greek for "leaf." Sclerophylls of the

---

The Mediterranean climate ⑦, found along midlatitude west coasts, is distinguished by its dry summer and wet winter. In summer, dry subtropical high pressure blocks rainfall, while in winter, wave cyclones produce ample precipitation.

Mediterranean environment are typically evergreen, retaining their leaves through the entire yearly cycle. Examples are the evergreen oaks, of which there are several common species in California, and the cork oak of the Mediterranean lands (Figure 7.28a). Another example is the olive tree, native to the Mediterranean lands. In Australia, the thick-leafed eucalyptus tree is the dominant sclerophyll. Oak woodland of California bears a ground cover of grasses that turn to straw in the summer (Figure 7.28b). At higher elevations, drought-resistant conifers often occur.

Another form of native vegetation in this environment is a cover of drought-resistant shrubs, including sclerophylls and spiny-leafed species. In the Mediterranean lands, this scrub vegetation goes under the name of maquis or garrigue. In California, where it is called *chaparral,* it clothes steep hill and mountain slopes too dry to support oak woodland or oak forest (Figure 7.28c).

Wildfire is an integral part of the Mediterranean environment of California. Chaparral is extremely flammable during the long summer fire season (Figure 5.10). Brushfires rage through chaparral and oak forests and leave the soil surface bare and unprotected. When torrential rains occur in winter, large quantities of coarse mineral debris are swept

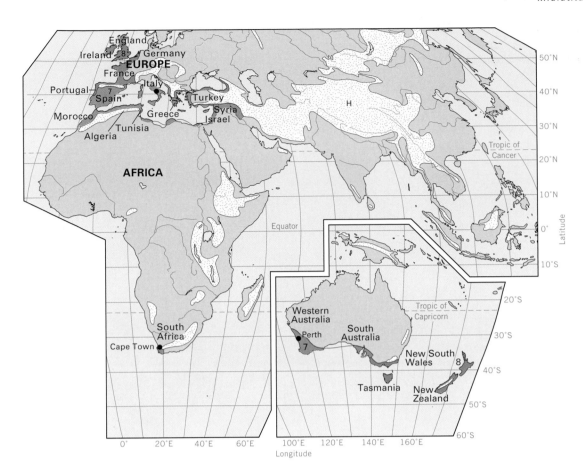

downslope and carried long distances by streams in flood. Mudflows and debris floods (usually called "mudslides" in the news media) are particularly destructive to communities on canyon floors (see Chapter 14).

The Marine West-Coast Climate ⑧ (Köppen: *Cfb, Cfc*)

The **marine west-coast climate** ⑧ occupies midlatitude west coasts. These locations receive the prevailing westerlies from over a large ocean and experience frequent cyclonic storms involving cool, moist mP air masses. Where the coast is mountainous, the orographic effect causes a very large annual precipitation. In this moist climate, precipitation is plentiful in all months, but there is often a distinct winter maximum. In summer, subtropical high pressure extends poleward into the region, reducing rainfall. The annual temperature range is comparatively small for midlatitudes. The marine influence keeps winter temperatures mild, as compared with inland locations at equivalent latitudes.

The global map of the marine west-coast climate ⑧ (Figure 7.27) shows the areas in which this climate occurs.

> The marine west-coast climate ⑧ features frequent cyclonic storms that provide abundant precipitation, especially when enhanced by an orographic effect. Summers are normally drier as subtropical high pressure moves poleward, blocking storm tracks.

In North America, the climate occupies the western coast from Oregon to northern British Columbia. In Western Europe, the British Isles, Portugal, and much of France fall into the marine west-coast climate. New Zealand and the southern tip of Australia, as well as the island of Tasmania, are marine west-coast climate regions found in the southern hemisphere, as is the Chilean coast south of 35° S. The general latitude range of this climate is 35° to 60° N and S.

Figure 7.29 is a climograph for Vancouver, British Columbia, just north of the U.S.–Canadian border. The annual precipitation is very great, and most of it falls during the winter months. Notice the greatly reduced rainfall in the summer months. The temperature cycle shows a remarkably small range for this latitude. Even the winter months have averages above the freezing mark.

Forest is the native vegetation of this climate. Dense needleleaf forests of redwood, fir, cedar, hemlock, and spruce (Figure 7.30) flourish in the wet mountainous areas of the northern Pacific coast. Under the lower precipitation regime of Ireland, southern England, France, and the Low Countries, a broadleaf deciduous forest was the native vegetation, but much of it disappeared many centuries ago under cultivation. Only scattered forest plots or groves

a...Cork oak   *The cork oak, Quercus suber, has tough, thick outer bark that is harvested for wine corks. The underlying live bark is reddish in color. Algarve Province, Portugal.*

b...California oak woodland in summer *Blue oaks (Quercus douglasii) are scattered over a cover of dry grasses in the inner Coast Ranges, near Williams, California.*

c...California chaparral
Wiry shrubs cloak the
steep slopes of a coast
range near Acton,
California.

d...Orchard agriculture
Groves of lemon, orange,
and avocado trees
surround these homes and
stables in Montecito,
California. Chaparral
covers the steep slopes of
the Santa Ynez Mountains
in the background. (A. N.
Strahler.)

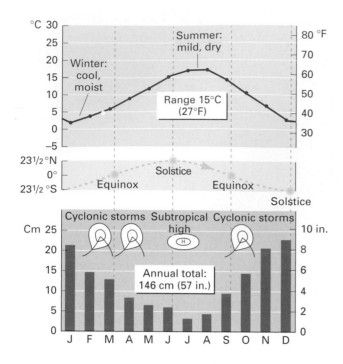

7.29 Marine west-coast climate ⑧ *Vancouver, British Columbia, lat. 49° N, has a large annual total precipitation but with greatly reduced amounts in the summer. The annual temperature range is small, and winters are very mild for this latitude.*

remain (see Figure 7.31). Sometimes called "summer-green" deciduous forest, it is dominated by tall broadleaf trees that provide a continuous and dense canopy in summer but shed their leaves completely in winter.

The Dry Midlatitude Climate ⑨ (Köppen: *BWk, BSk*)

The **dry midlatitude climate** ⑨ is limited almost exclusively to interior regions of North America and Eurasia, where it lies within the rain shadow of mountain ranges on the west or south. Maritime air masses are effectively blocked out much of the time, so that the continental polar (cP) air mass dominates the climate in winter. In summer, a dry continental air mass of local origin is dominant. Summer rainfall is mostly convectional and is caused by occasional invasions of maritime air masses. The annual temperature cycle is strongly developed, with a large annual range. Summers are warm to hot, but winters are cold to very cold.

The largest expanse of the dry midlatitude climate ⑨ is in Eurasia, stretching from the southern republics of the former Soviet Union to the Gobi Desert and northern China (Figure 7.16). In the central portions of this region lie true deserts of the arid climate subtype, with very low precipitation. Extensive areas of highlands occur here as well. In North America, the dry western interior regions, including the Great Basin, Columbia Plateau, and the Great Plains, are of the semiarid subtype. A small area of dry midlatitude climate ⑨

7.30 Needleleaf forest *Sitka spruce and hemlock populate the Hoh rainforest, Olympic National Park, Washington. Ferns and mosses provide a lush ground cover in this very wet environment.*

7.31 Marine west-coast landscape *This lush landscape near Devon, England, is located in the domain of the summer-green deciduous forest. After many centuries of human occupation and cultivation, the forest is now reduced to small patches and scattered individual trees in hollows and along fence rows.*

---

is found in southern Patagonia, near the tip of South America. The latitude range of this climate is 35° to 55° N.

Figure 7.32 is a climograph for Pueblo, Colorado, a semiarid station located at lat. 38° N, just east of the

---

The dry midlatitude climate ⑨ occupies continental interiors in rain shadows or far from oceanic moisture sources. Precipitation is low and the annual temperature variation is large.

Rocky Mountains. Total annual precipitation is 31 cm (12 in.). Most of this precipitation is in the form of convectional summer rainfall, which occurs when moist maritime tropical (mT) air masses invade from the south and produce thunderstorms. In winter, snowfall is light and yields only small monthly precipitation averages. The temperature cycle has a large annual range, with warm summers and cold winters. January, the coldest winter month, has a mean temperature just below freezing.

The low precipitation and cold winters of this semiarid climate produce a steppe landscape dominated by hardy perennial short grasses. In North America, this cover is termed *short-grass prairie* rather than steppe. Wheat is a major crop of the semiarid, dry midlatitude steppelands, but wheat harvests are at the mercy of rainfall variations from year to year. With good spring rains, there is a good crop, but if spring rains fail, so does the wheat crop.

The Moist Continental Climate ⑩ (Köppen: *Dfa, Dfb, Dwa, Dwb*)

The **moist continental climate** ⑩ is located in central and eastern parts of North America and Eurasia in the midlatitudes. This climate lies in the polar-front zone—the battleground of polar and tropical air masses. Seasonal temperature contrasts are strong, and day-to-day weather is highly variable. Ample precipitation throughout the year is increased in summer by invading maritime tropical (mT) air masses. Cold winters are dominated by continental polar (cP) and continental arctic (cA) air masses from subarctic source regions.

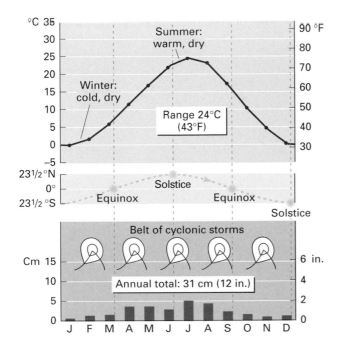

7.32 Dry midlatitude climate ⑨ *Pueblo, Colorado, lat. 38° N, shows a marked summer maximum of rainfall in the summer months. Note also the cold, dry winter season. Figure 7.16 shows the location of this station.*

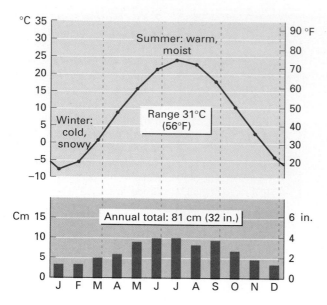

7.33   Moist continental climate ⑩ *Madison, Wisconsin, lat. 43° N, has cold winters and warm summers, making the annual temperature range very large.*

⑩ lies in a higher latitude belt (45° to 60° N) and receives precipitation from mP air masses coming from the North Atlantic.

Madison, Wisconsin, lat. 43° N, in the American Midwest (Figure 7.33), provides an example of the moist continental climate ⑩. The annual temperature range is very large. Summers are warm, but winters are cold, with three consecutive monthly means well below freezing. Precipitation is ample in all months, and the annual total is large. There is a summer maximum of precipitation when the maritime tropical (mT) air mass invades, and thunderstorms are formed along moving cold fronts and squall lines. Much of the winter precipitation is in the form of snow, which remains on the ground for long periods.

Figure 7.34 shows the global locations of the moist continental climate ⑩. It is restricted to the northern hemisphere, occurring in latitudes 30° to 55° N in North America and Asia, and in latitudes 45° to 60° N in Europe. In Asia, it is found in northern China, Korea, and Japan. Most of central and eastern Europe has a moist continental climate, as does most of the eastern half of the United States from Tennessee to the north, as well as the southernmost strip of eastern Canada.

Throughout most of the moist continental climate ⑩, forests are the dominant natural vegetation cover. However, where the climate grades into drier climates, such as the dry midlatitude climate ⑨, tall, dense grasses may be the natural cover. The *tall-grass prairie* of Illinois, Iowa, and Nebraska is an example. These lands are now the heart of the American corn belt. In Europe, lands of the moist continental climate ⑩ have been in cultivation for many centuries, providing a multitude of crops. Forests are planted and managed for timber yield. The result is a landscape that shows human influence everywhere (Figure 7.35).

In eastern Asia—China, Korea, and Japan—the seasonal precipitation pattern shows more summer rainfall and a drier winter than in North America. This is an effect of the monsoon circulation, which moves moist maritime tropical (mT) air across the eastern side of the continent in summer and dry continental polar southward through the region in winter. In Europe, the moist continental climate

---

The moist continental climate ⑩ lies in the polar-front zone where day-to-day weather is highly variable. Ample frontal precipitation is enhanced in summer by maritime tropical air masses. Winter temperatures fall well below freezing.

7.34   World map of the moist continental climate ⑩ *(Based on Goode Base Map.)*

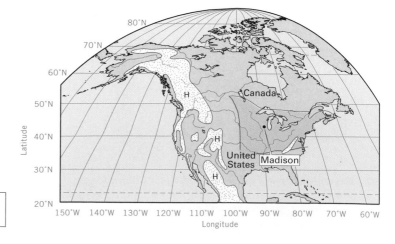

7.35 Eye on the Landscape Moist continental landscape *The Mosel River in its entrenched, meandering gorge through the Rhineland-Pfalz province of western Germany. On the steep, undercut valley wall at the right are vineyards and forested land. Abundant rainfall, fertile soils, and mild summer temperatures provide an environment well suited to agriculture.* **What else would the geographer see? … Answers at the end of the chapter.**

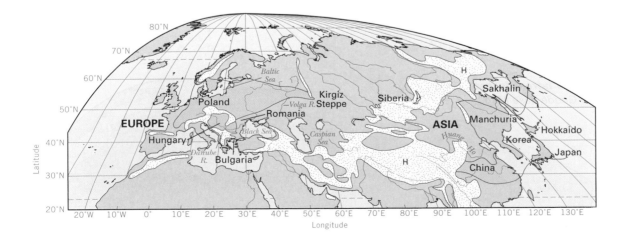

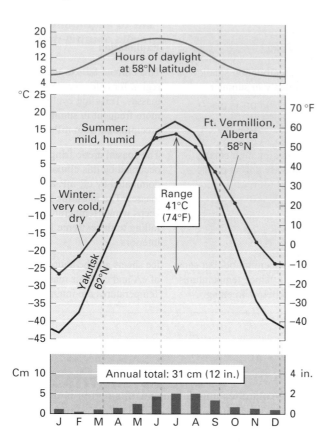

7.38 Boreal forest climate ⑪ *Extreme winter cold and a very great annual range in temperature characterize the climate of Fort Vermilion, Alberta. The temperature range of Yakutsk, Siberia, is even greater.*

7.39 Boreal forest *Lichen woodland near Fort McKenzie, lat. 57° N, in northern Quebec. The trees are black spruce. Between the trees is a carpet of lichen. (R. N. Drummond.)*

tree. Associated with the needleleaf trees are stands of aspen, balsam poplar, willow, and birch. Along the northern fringe of boreal forest lies a zone of woodland in which low trees, such as black spruce, are spaced widely apart. The open areas are covered by a surface layer of lichens and mosses (Figure 7.39). This cold woodland is referred to as *taiga*.

Although the growing season in the boreal forest climate ⑪ is short, crop farming is still possible. It is largely limited to lands surrounding the Baltic Sea, bordering Finland and Sweden. Crops grown in this area include barley, oats, rye, and wheat. Along with dairying, these crops primarily supply food for subsistence. The needleleaf forests provide paper, pulp, cellulose, and construction lumber.

The Tundra Climate ⑫ (Köppen: *ET*)

The **tundra climate** ⑫ occupies arctic coastal fringes and is dominated by polar (cP, mP) and arctic (cA) air masses. Winters are long and severe. A moderating influence of the nearby ocean water prevents winter temperatures from falling to the extreme lows

The tundra climate ⑫ occupies arctic coastal fringes. Although the climate is very cold, the maritime influence keeps winter temperatures from falling to the levels of the boreal forest climate ⑪. A mild season provides a few months of thaw.

found in the continental interior. There is a very short mild season, which many climatologists do not recognize as a true summer.

The world map of the tundra climate ⑫ (Figure 7.40) shows the tundra ringing the Arctic Ocean and extending across the island region of northern Canada. It includes the Alaskan north slope, the Hudson Bay region, and the Greenland coast in North America. In Eurasia, this climate type occupies the Siberian arctic coast. The Antarctic Peninsula (not shown in Figure 7.40) belongs to the tundra climate ⑫. The latitude range for this climate is 60° to 75° N and S, except for the northern coast of Greenland, where tundra occurs at latitudes greater than 80° N.

Figure 7.41 is a climograph for Upernavik, located on the west coast of Greenland at lat. 73° N. A short mild period, with above-freezing temperatures, is equivalent to a summer season in lower latitudes. The long winter is very cold, but the annual temperature

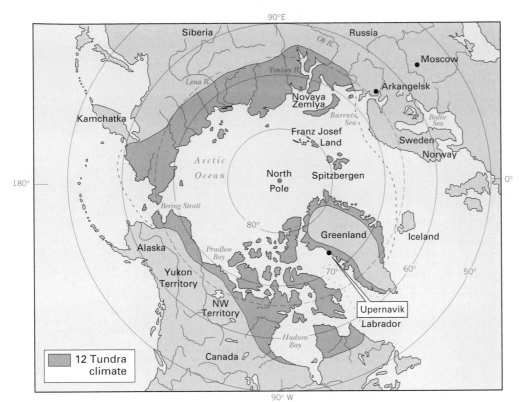

7.40 *World map of the tundra climate* ⑫

12 Tundra climate

7.41 *Tundra climate* ⑫ *Upernavik, Greenland, lat. 73°N, shows a smaller annual range than Fort Vermilion (Figure 7.38).*

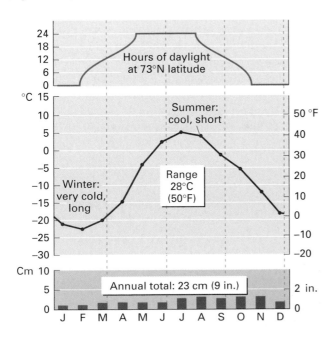

range is not as large as that for the boreal forest climate to the south. Total annual precipitation is small. Increased precipitation beginning in July is explained by the melting of the sea-ice cover and a warming of ocean water temperatures. This increases the moisture content of the local air mass, allowing more precipitation.

The term *tundra* describes both an environmental region and a major class of vegetation (Figure 7.42). (An equivalent climatic environment—called *alpine tundra*—prevails in many global locations in high mountains above the timberline.) Soils of the arctic tundra are poorly developed and consist of freshly broken mineral particles and varying amounts of humus (finely divided, partially decomposed plant matter). Peat bogs are numerous. Because soil water is solidly and permanently frozen not far below the surface, the summer thaw brings a condition of water saturation to the soil.

Vegetation of the tundra consists of a cover of scattered grasses, sedges, and lichens, along with shrubs of willow. Vegetation is scarce on dry, exposed slopes and summits. Here the surface cover is often a rocky pavement of angular rock fragments. Trees exist in the tundra only as small, shrub-like plants. They are stunted because of the seasonal damage to roots by freeze and thaw of the soil layer and to branches exposed to the abrading action of wind-driven snow. In some places, a distinct tree line separates the forest and tundra. It coincides approximately with the 10°C (50°F)

7.42   *Tundra landscape* *Caribou migration across the arctic tundra of northern Alaska.*

isotherm of the warmest month and has been used by geographers as a boundary between boreal forest and tundra.

Because of the cold temperatures experienced in the tundra and northern boreal forest climate zones, the ground is typically frozen to great depth. This perennially frozen ground, or **permafrost,** prevails over the tundra region and a wide bordering area of boreal forest climate. Normally, a top layer of the ground will thaw each year during the mild season. This active layer of seasonal thaw is from 0.6 to 4 m (2 to 13 ft) thick, depending on latitude and the nature of the ground.

Continuous permafrost, which extends without gaps or interruptions under all surface features, coincides largely with the tundra climate, but also includes a large part of the boreal forest climate in Siberia. *Discontinuous permafrost,* which occurs in patches separated by frost-free zones under lakes and rivers, occupies much of the boreal forest climate zone of North America and Eurasia. Sporadic occurrence of permafrost in small patches extends into the southern limits of the boreal forest climate. Chapter 14 provides more detail on permafrost in arctic and boreal regions.

The ice sheet climate ⑬ has the lowest temperatures found on Earth. No month shows mean temperatures above freezing, and winter mean monthly temperatures can fall to 40°C (−40°F) and below.

The Ice Sheet Climate ⑬ (Köppen: *EF*)

The **ice sheet climate** ⑬ coincides with the source regions of arctic (A) and antarctic (AA) air masses, situated on the vast, high ice sheets of Greenland and Antarctica and over polar sea ice of the Arctic Ocean. Mean annual temperature is much lower than that of any other climate, with no monthly mean above freezing. Strong temperature inversions, caused by radiation loss from the surface, develop over the ice sheets. In Antarctica and Greenland, the high surface altitude of the ice sheets intensifies the cold. Strong cyclones with blizzard winds are frequent. Precipitation, almost all occurring as snow, is very low but accumulates because of the continuous cold. The latitude range for this climate is 65° to 90° N and S.

Figure 7.43 shows temperature graphs for several representative ice sheet stations. The graph for Eismitte, a research station on the Greenland ice cap, shows the northern hemisphere temperature cycle, whereas the other four examples are all from Antarctica. Temperatures in the interior of Antarctica have proved to be far lower than those at any other place on Earth. A Russian meteorological

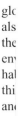

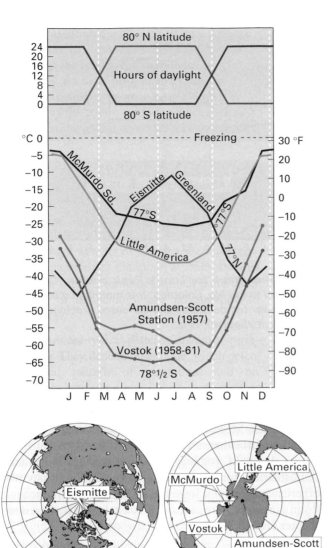

7.43 Ice sheet climate ⑬ *Temperature graphs for five ice sheet stations.*

station at Vostok, located about 1300 km (about 800 mi) from the south pole at an altitude of about 3500 m (11,500 ft), may be the world's coldest spot. Here a low of –88.3°C (–127°F) was observed in 1958. At the pole itself (Amundsen-Scott Station), July, August, and September of 1957 had averages of about –60°C (–76°F). Temperatures are considerably higher, month for month, at Little America in Antarctica because it is located close to the Ross Sea and is at a low altitude.

HIGHLAND CLIMATES

Highland climates, shown in a white pattern on the world climate map, are cool to cold, usually moist, climates that occupy mountains and high plateaus. Generally, the higher the location, the colder and wetter is its climate. Tempera-

tures are lower since air temperatures in the atmosphere normally decrease with altitude (see Chapter 3). Rainfall increases because orographic precipitation tends to be induced when air masses ascend to higher elevations (Chapter 4). Highland climates are not usually included in the broad schemes of climate classification. Many small highland areas are simply not shown on a world map.

The character of the climate of a given highland area is usually closely related to that of the climate of the surrounding lowland, particularly the form of the annual temperature cycle and the times of occurrence of wet and dry seasons. An example of this effect in the tropical zone is shown by climographs for two Indian stations in close geographical proximity (Figure 7.44). New Delhi, the capital city, lies in the Ganges lowland. Simla, a mountain refuge from the hot weather, is located nearby at about 2200 m (about 7200 ft) in the foothills of the Himalayas. When the hot-season temperature averages over 32°C (90°F) in New Delhi, Simla is enjoying a pleasant 18°C (64°F), which is a full 14°C (25°F) cooler. Notice, however, that the two temperature cycles are quite similar in shape, with January as the minimum month for both. The annual rainfall cycles are also similar. New Delhi shows the typical rainfall pattern of the wet-dry tropical climate ③ of Southeast Asia, with monsoon rains peaking in July and August. Simla has the same pattern, but the amounts are larger in every month, and the monsoon peak is very strong. Simla's annual total rainfall is well over twice that of New Delhi.

At higher latitudes, similar effects are encountered. Figure 7.45 shows a climograph from a station at 2730 m (8956 ft) near Long's Peak, Colorado. Pueblo (Figure 7.32), which is located just east of the Colorado Front Range at an elevation of 1417 m (4658 ft), shows a similar annual cycle of temperature and precipitation, but temperatures are 5 to 10°C (9 to 18°F) cooler and precipitation is nearly doubled.

OUR CHANGING CLIMATE

Earlier in this chapter, we defined climate as the average weather of a region, described by the average values of monthly temperature and precipitation observed at weather stations. These average values are obtained over significant periods of time—typically decades. However, it is important to realize that human activities have now modified the weather we experience. Moreover, that modification will continue into the future, with increasingly stronger effects. In this way, the climate of every location is changing, and changing because of human modification of the atmosphere, land, and oceans.

As we noted in our interchapter feature, *A Closer Look: Eye on Global Change 3.2 • The IPCC Report of 2001*, recent human activity has raised global temperatures, which in turn have reduced global snow and ice cover and raised sea levels. Precipitation, enhanced by greater evaporation, has increased in mid- and high-latitude regions, but

Table E7.1 | **Impact of Global Climate Change on Regions of the United States and Canada**

Region	Observed Climate Trends, Past Century	Future Climate Trends, Next Century	Agriculture	Forests and Ecosystems
Alaska, British Columbia, and Yukon	• Substantial warming—2°C (4°F) since 1950s; especially interior in winter, 4°C (7°F). • Growing season lengthened 14 days since 1950s • Precipitation increased 30% since 1968	• Warming to continue, 3–10°C (7–18°F) • Precipitation to increase 20–25% with 10% decrease along south coast	• Lengthened growing season will enhance productivity • Summer drought on south coast may reduce productivity	• Warming will increase forest productivity on moist southern coast but reduce productivity in dry interior • Increased disturbance, including insects, blowdowns, and fire will reduce forest productivity • Warming will enhance decay of soil organic matter, adding CO_2 to carbon cycle • Potential shift of boreal forest northward into tundra zone
Canadian Arctic	• Mackenzie River district has warmed by 1.5°C (3°F); arctic tundra by 0.5°C (1°F) over last 100 years • Arctic mountains and fiords of eastern Arctic have cooled slightly	• Future winter temperature increases of 5–7°C (9–13°F) predicted over mainland and arctic islands • Modest cooling in extreme eastern arctic • Summer temperatures to increase up to 5°C (9°F) on mainland, 1–2°C (2–4°F) over marine areas • Annual precipitation to increase up to 25%	• Agricultural opportunities (e.g., irrigated wheat) will arise in central and upper Mackenzie River basin, but will be restricted by availability of suitable soils	• Tundra and taiga/tundra ecosystems reduced by as much as 2/3 in size • Freshwater species to migrate northward about 150 km (50 mi) per °C (°F) increase in temperature • Seal, sea lion, and walrus populations will decline through pack ice recession • Muskoxen and high-arctic Peary caribou may become extinct
Pacific Northwest	• Average annual temperature has increased 0.5–1.5°C (1–3°F) over most of the region • Annual precipitation has increased by 10%; to 30–40% east of the Cascades • Warm-dry and cool-wet years correlate with ENSO and Pacific Decadal oscillation cycles	• Annual temperatures to increase steadily, reaching +4–4.5°C (+7–8°F) by 2090 • Winter temperatures to rise by 4.5–6°C (8–11°F) • Precipitation to rise, possibly as much as 50% by 2090, with summer precipitation unchanged or slightly decreasing • Extreme precipitation events increase substantially	• Dry-land farming cycle shifted by wetter and warmer winters • Summer droughts will impact irrigated agriculture in conflict with urban usage	• Salmon populations reduced by increased winter flooding, reduced summer and fall flows, rising stream and estuary temperatures • Conifer forest will be stressed by warm, dry summers leading to pest infestations and fires • Conifer recruitment reduced by summer stress on seedlings

Water Cycle	Urban/Human Impact	Transportation and Infrastructure	Coastal/Marine Environments	Natural Hazards
• Spring flooding enhanced by warm temperatures and rainfall • Flood protection works on south coast rivers and streams may not be adequate	• Summer drought along south coast and southern interior will place water supplies for urban areas in contention with agriculture • Possible urban air quality impacts of summer drought	• Melting permafrost will damage roads, pipelines, and structures • Sea-level rise will increase coastal flooding, placing docks and port facilities at risk	• Sea-level rise could be as much as 30–50 cm (12–20 in.) • Marine ecosystems of Gulf of Alaska and Bering Sea already show large fluctuations with causes unknown; climate change effect likely to be large and unpredictable	• Retreat of glaciers will cause local flooding and enable landslides and mudflows, causing loss of life and infrastructure • Permafrost will thaw in discontinuous permafrost regions, causing erosion, landslides, sinking of ground surface, damage to forests, buildings, infrastructure • Sea ice will retreat, allowing coastal erosion and storm surges
• Increased evaporation in arctic regions from warmer atmosphere and longer thaw period will decrease flows and levels of northward-flowing rivers • River ice season reduced by 1 month by 2050; ice season for large lakes by 2 weeks	• Subsistence of native peoples likely to be made more difficult as populations of mammals, fish, and sea birds fluctuate, and lack of snow and ice makes hunting more difficult	• Reduced sea ice will benefit offshore oil and gas operations • Melting permafrost will negatively affect pipelines • Shipping season extended, with easy transit through northwest passage at times	• Flooding of coastal ecosystems, e.g. Mackenzie Delta, from sea-level rise • Reduced sea ice and increased water temperatures with unknown effects on marine biota	• Melting of permafrost will cause land subsidence, forest loss, damage to structures • Retreat of eastern mountain glaciers will produce soil instability with landslides and mudflows
• Warmer, wetter winters will increase flooding in rainfed rivers and trade snow pack for runoff; snow pack reduced by 75–125 cm (30–50 in.) • Summer shortages will be more severe because of reduced snow pack and earlier melting; summer soil moisture reduced 10–25% • Allocation conflicts and conflicting authorities may enhance vulnerability to drought	• Sea-level rise to require substantial investments to control coastal flooding, especially in southern Puget Sound where subsidence is occurring • Summer drought to impact urban areas through water supply, air quality	• New investments needed for water resource management for winter floods and summer droughts	• Increased frequency of severe storms will enhance storm surge flooding and coastal erosion, especially during El Niño events	• Higher precipitation and more extreme events will increase soil saturation, mudflows and mass movements • Winter flooding enhanced, with large populations at risk

(table continues)

Table E7.1 | (continued)

Region	Observed Climate Trends, Past Century	Future Climate Trends, Next Century	Agriculture	Forests and Ecosystems
Southeast	• Temperatures were warm during the 1920s-1940s; cooled through the 1960s; warmed again starting in 1970s to levels of the 1920s and 1930s • Coastal regions warmed by 2°C (4°F) • Rainfall increased 20–30% or more over much of the region • Strong El Niño and La Niña effects provide large seasonal and interannual variation in temperature and precipitation, with hurricanes more frequent in La Niñas	• Models predict warming from about 3–6°C (5–10°F), depending on model and region • Models disagree on precipitation predictions, ranging from neutral or slight increase to 25% increase • El Niño rainfall and La Niña droughts may intensify as atmospheric CO_2 increases • Heat indexes rise dramatically	• Models disagree on soil moisture trends; could increase or decrease depending on amount of warming and change in precipitation • Models predict different crop yield scenarios ranging from increases in interior regions to decreases for dryland crops • Significant decreases in yields of corn, peanuts, sorghum along Gulf Coast	• Models disagree on forest productivity; generally it increases, but decreases in some places for some ecosystems in some scenarios • If soil moisture drops, pine forests are replaced by savannas and grasslands
Northeast and Southern Quebec	• Temperatures have increased as much as 2°C (4°F) in last 100 years along coastal margins • Precipitation has increased greater than 20% over much of the region • Precipitation extremes are increasing, drought decreasing • Period between first and last dates of snow on the ground has decreased by 7 days in the last 50 years	• Temperatures will increase 3–5°C (5–9°F) depending on area and model • Winter minimum temperatures show greatest increases • Precipitation projections range from neutral or modest increases to nearly 25% • Winter snowfalls and periods of extreme cold will decrease • Ice storms, rains over frozen ground, and rapid snow melting events will increase • Heavy precipitation events will increase; hurricane frequency could increase	• Temperature and rainfall increases may enhance crop productivity • Earlier greenup will extend growing season • More frequent extreme rainfalls and storms will affect local agriculture	• Forest composition will change; northern hardwoods move north as oak-hickory forests replace them; sugar maple to migrate out of New England • Lobster populations will move northward • Migratory bird habitat will be reduced by sea-level rise • Trout populations reduced in Pennsylvania • Muting of fall foliage as species composition changes with added warmth • Milder winters will favor insect vectors for human and animal disease
Canadian Atlantic Provinces	• Slight cooling experienced in past 50 years • Higher frequency of extreme events observed	• No strong evidence for significant warming • Increased intensity and/or frequency of storms anticipated • More temperature extremes, leading to milder winters, early extended thaws, late springs, early frosts	• Increased frequency of storms could impact crop productivity	• Fish habitat could be lost; distribution of fish species and migration patterns altered, with life cycles interrupted • Winter ranges of terrestrial birds could shift; seabirds could change in range, distribution, and breeding success • Reduced snow cover could increase deer populations but reduce forest regeneration and species diversity • Increased forest blow-downs and mortality with increased storms and insect outbreaks

Water Cycle	Urban/Human Impact	Transportation and Infrastructure	Coastal/Marine Environments	Natural Hazards
• Stresses on water quality are associated with intensive agricultural practices, urban development, coastal processes, and mining activities • Water quality is impacted by higher temperatures that reduce dissolved oxygen and by contamination from agricultural runoff, untreated sewage, and chemical releases in catastrophic rainfall events	• Hurricanes, floods, and heat waves have major impacts on human population; climate change could enhance their frequency and severity • Low air quality episodes from increased temperatures and pollution releases accompany heat waves	• Flooding from extreme events may create transportation difficulties on roads and rivers	• Rising sea level, coupled with subsidence due to ground water withdrawal, sediment compaction, wetland drainage, and levee construction, will cause continued loss of coastal wetlands • Salt water intrusion of ground water from rising sea level will continue to kill coastal forests • Rising sea level increases frequency of storm surge and flooding of low-lying areas by storms and causes retreat of barrier beaches	• Coastal flooding in hurricanes can produce catastrophic loss of life
• Variations in water supply in Quebec may adversely affect power generation	• Climate change will add significantly to stresses on major urban areas, such as electric power consumption, summer air quality, heat waves, etc. • Summer recreation season to increase, but winter ski season to be shorter • Loss of beachfront property and recreation areas from sea level rise	• Low water levels in the St. Lawrence River will impact shipping and the marine environment • Sea-level rise may require engineering structures for coastal protection	• Estuarine water quality will fall as increased temperatures reduce dissolved oxygen and extreme rainfall events provide more polluted runoff and reduce salinity • Sea-level rise will substantially increase loss of wetlands and marshes	• Enhanced coastal flooding in hurricanes and northeasters from sea-level rise
• Less winter snow cover is predicted • More extremes of excessive moisture and drought • Declining runoff would reduce hydroelectric power generation	• Sea-level rise will increase danger of flooding of urban areas	• Changes in ice-free days would affect marine transportation and offshore oil and gas industry.	• Sea-level rise will affect coastlines from Bay of Fundy to Newfoundland; threaten Acadian dykeland agriculture in Nova Scotia	• Sea-level rise will enhance coastal flooding during severe storms

EYE ON THE LANDSCAPE

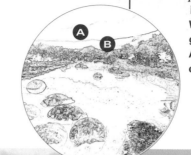

Giant tortoises of the Galápagos Islands wallowing in a seasonal pool in the crater of Alcedo Volcano, Isabela Island. **What else would the geographer see? … Answers at the end of the chapter.**

8 | BIOGEOGRAPHIC PROCESSES

. . . .
PUTTING YOU IN THE PICTURE

The Earth's biological realm is large and diverse, including millions of species of organisms found from the ocean's abyssal depths to the land's highest peaks. This diversity has arisen through evolution, a biogeographic process in which natural selection acts on variation that occurs in reproducing populations of species to permute and transform strains of organisms, creating new species even as old strains die out.

The observation that natural selection might be responsible for evolution is credited to Charles Darwin, who published his ideas on *The Origin of Species by Means of Natural Selection* in 1859. One of Darwin's pivotal experiences in developing his theory of evolution was a visit to the Galápagos Islands, made in 1835 as the naturalist aboard the British survey vessel *HMS Beagle*. Impressed by "the amount of creative force displayed

on these small, barren and rocky islands," he documented a variety of life-forms that he would later hypothesize to have evolved from common ancestors and become specialized and adjusted to the habitats of each island. Although human activity has influenced the islands in the many years since his visit, much of the striking character of these islands remains. Imagine yourself on a modern-day visit to the Galápagos…

The guide cuts the motor, and the rubber boat runs aground on the small crescent of beach in Shipton Cove, on the eastern shore of Isla Isabela, largest of the Galápagos Islands. Your small group steps neatly to the sand, having practiced this landing before on the many earlier stops of your two-week-long boat tour of the islands. This is the high point of your trip—a two-day round-trip trek to the summit of Alcedo Volcano, one of five volcanoes on this nearly uninhabited island. You'll climb from sea level to nearly 1100 m (3600 ft) in about 12 km (7.5 mi), reaching the summit camp by midafternoon. The views are supposed to be truly spectacular. And you are sure to see many of the famous Galápagos tortoises in their natural habitat.

"Look, a flightless cormorant!" The guide alerts your to one of the rarer and more unusual birds of the Galápagos. Swimming through the water with only its brown head and neck visible, the bird flashes its turquoise eyes in your direction. Leaping upward and then diving downward in a single motion, it heads off in search of its favorite bottom-living prey, the octopus.

You clamber up the steep path around the ocean cliff, barely noticing the basking marine iquanas that at first seemed so strange and by now are routine. These land reptiles have acquired the habit of grazing on underwater algae and seaweed. Like nearly all the other native animals of the Galápagos, they have no fear of humans and regard you with their typical disdain.

At first, the trail winds through an arid zone of prickly-pear and candelabra cacti alternating with stands of spindly palo santo trees and acacias. Suddenly you come upon several land iguanas chewing away on the pads of a prickly pear. Although resembling their marine cousins, they are tan to brownish in color, with shorter spines along their backbones, and are considerably rarer. Both species are descended from a common ancestor, probably the green iquana now common in mainland Ecuador.

As you climb, the vegetation becomes more and more lush, and you enter a cloud forest of odd-looking trees festooned with mosses, ferns, and even orchids. Your guide points out a woodpecker finch, a small gray-green bird perched on a dead shrub near the trail. Holding a cactus spine in its stout beak, it probes holes in the dead wood for insects. According to your guide, it is one of the 13 finch species unique to the Galápagos that were studied by Darwin and used as evidence for his theory of evolution by means of natural selection.

Some hours later, you reach the rim of Alcedo Volcano's crater. The view is indeed spectacular. A vast expanse of green shrub forest sprawls below you, with a brown network of seasonal pools on the crater floor. In the far distance, the peaks of the other four volcanoes on Isabela are visible, two to the left and two to the right.

The next morning, you arise early in camp and set off for the crater, anxious to see the famous giant tortoises in their natural habitat. By ones and twos, the giant tortoises appear near the trail, extending their long necks to graze on the lower branches of the shrubs. As your guide reports, these are members of the *vandenberghi* subspecies, which is restricted to this volcano. In fact, each of the five volcanoes on Isabela has its own unique subspecies of giant tortoise. Finally, you reach a large group of tortoises wallowing in a seasonal pool. To the clicking of cameras, you watch as they frolic in their communal mud bath. What an odd and curious place this is, for reptiles such as tortoises and iguanas to be so common! No wonder the Galápagos Islands have captured the imagination of naturalists like Charles Darwin for almost two centuries. ■

BIOGEOGRAPHIC PROCESSES

This chapter is the first of two chapters that are concerned with biogeography. **Biogeography** is a branch of geography that focuses on the distribution of plants and animals—the *biota*—over the Earth. It attempts to identify and describe the processes that influence plant and animal distribution patterns at varying scales of space and time. We can think of biogeography as encompassing two major views or themes. *Ecological biogeography* is concerned with how the distribution patterns of organisms are affected by the environment, including both the physical environment experienced by organisms and the biological environment created by interaction with other organisms. *Historical biogeography* focuses on how spatial distribution patterns of organisms arise over time and space. Evolution of species, migration of organisms and their methods of dispersal, and extinction of species are processes of interest in historical biogeography.

In this chapter, we identify the key processes of ecological and historical biogeography that determine how the distribution patterns of plants and animals have arisen and how they change with time. Our next chapter inventories the global pattern of vegetation and animal life, stressing how climate influences that pattern.

ENERGY AND MATTER FLOW IN ECOSYSTEMS

We begin our first chapter by examining some ideas from the domain of **ecology**, which is the study of the interactions between life-forms and their environment. These ideas focus on how organisms live and interact as ecosystems and how energy and matter are cycled by ecosystems.

We can define an **ecosystem** as a group of organisms and the environment with which they interact. Ecosystems have inputs of matter and energy that plants and animals use to grow, reproduce, and maintain life. Matter and energy are also exported from ecosystems. Figure 8.1 presents three distinctive ecosystems—tundra, salt marsh, and savanna.

The Food Web

A salt marsh provides a good example of an ecosystem (Figure 8.2). A variety of organisms are present—algae and aquatic plants, microorganisms, insects, snails, and crayfish, as well as such larger organisms as fishes, birds, shrews, mice, and rats. Inorganic components will be found as well—water, air, clay particles and organic sediment, inorganic nutrients, trace elements, and light energy. Energy transformations in the ecosystem occur by means of a series of steps or levels, referred to a **food chain** or **food web**.

The plants and algae in the food web are the **primary producers.** They use light energy to convert carbon dioxide and water into carbohydrates (long chains of sugar molecules) and eventually into other biochemical molecules needed for the support of life. This process of energy conversion is called *photosynthesis,* and we will return to it in more detail shortly. Organisms engaged in photosynthesis form the base of the food web.

The primary producers support the **consumers**—organisms that ingest other organisms as their food source. At the lowest level of consumers are the *primary consumers* (the snails, insects, and fishes). At the next level are the *secondary consumers* (the mammals, birds, and larger fishes), which feed on the primary consumers. Still higher levels of feeding occur in the salt-marsh ecosystem as marsh hawks and owls consume the smaller animals below them in the food web. The **decomposers** feed on *detritus,* or decaying organic matter, derived from all levels. They are largely microscopic organisms (microorganisms) and bacteria.

The food web is really an energy flow system, tracing the path of solar energy through the ecosystem. Solar energy is absorbed by the primary producers and stored in the chemical products of photosynthesis. As these organisms are eaten and digested by consumers, chemical energy is released. This chemical energy is used to power new biochemical reactions, which again produce stored chemical energy in the bodies of the consumers.

> The food web describes how food energy flows from organism to organism within an ecosystem. Primary producers support primary, secondary, and higher-level consumers. Decomposers feed on dead plant and animal matter from all levels.

At each level of energy flow in the food web, energy is lost to *respiration.* Respiration can be thought of as the burning of fuel to keep the organism operating. It will be discussed in more detail in the next section. Energy expended in respiration is ultimately lost as waste heat and cannot be stored for use by other organisms higher up in the food chain. This means that, generally, both the numbers of organisms and their total amount of living tissue must decrease greatly up the food chain. In general, only 10 to 50 percent of the energy stored in organic matter at one level can be passed up the chain to the next level. Normally, there are about four levels of consumers.

Figure 8.3 is a bar graph showing the percentage of energy passed up the chain when only 10 percent moves from one level to the next. The horizontal scale is in powers of 10. In ecosystems of the lands, the mass of organic matter and the number of individuals of the consuming animals decrease with each upward step. In the food chain shown in Figure 8.2, there are only a few marsh hawks and owls in the third level of consumers, while countless individuals are found in the primary level.

For individual species, the number of individuals of a species present in an ecosystem ultimately depends on the level of resources available to support the species population. If these resources provide a steady supply of energy, the population size will normally attain a steady level. In some cases, however, resources vary with time, for example, in an annual cycle. The population size of a species depending on these resources may then also fluctuate in a corresponding cycle.

Photosynthesis and Respiration

Stated in the simplest possible terms, **photosynthesis** is the production of carbohydrate. *Carbohydrate* is a general term for a class of organic compounds consisting of the elements carbon, hydrogen, and oxygen. Carbohydrate molecules are composed of short chains of carbon bonded to one another. Also bonded to each carbon are hydrogen (H) atoms and hydroxyl (OH) molecules. We can symbolize a single carbon atom with its attached hydrogen atom and hydroxyl molecule as –CHOH–. The leading and trailing dashes indicate that the unit is just one portion of a longer chain of connected carbon atoms.

> Photosynthesis is the process in which plants combine water, carbon dioxide, and solar energy to form carbohydrate. Respiration is the reverse process, in which carbohydrate is oxidized in living tissues to yield the energy that sustains life.

Photosynthesis of carbohydrate requires a series of complex biochemical reactions using water (H_2O) and carbon dioxide (CO_2) as well as light energy. A simplified chemical reaction for photosynthesis can be written as follows:

$$H_2O + CO_2 + \text{light energy} \rightarrow -CHOH- + O_2$$

a...*Eye on the Landscape* *Caribou in the foothills of the Brooks Range* The caribou, a large grazing mammal, is one of the important primary consumers of the tundra ecosystem. **What else would the geographer see?...Answers at the end of the chapter.**

b...*Salt marsh* The salt marsh ecosystem supports a wide variety of life forms, both plant and animal. Here, the white ibis, great egret, and other wading bird species forage at the Merritt Island National Wildlife Refuge, Florida.

c...*Savanna* The savanna ecosystem, with its abundance of grazing mammals, has a rich and complex food web. Here a top predator, a lioness, preys on a herd of zebra. Maasai Mara, Kenya.

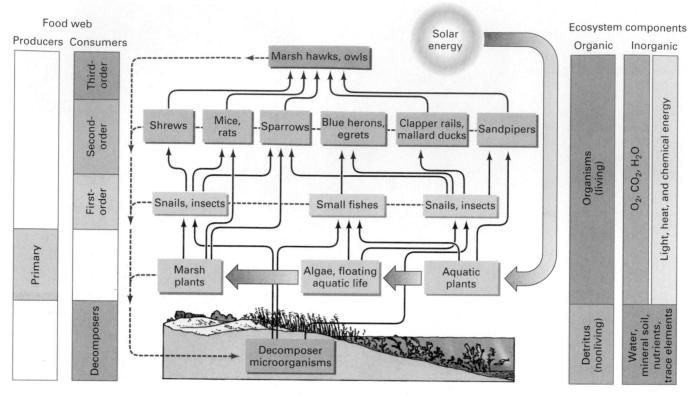

8.2 Energy flow diagram of a salt-marsh ecosystem in winter *The arrows show how energy flows from the Sun to producers, consumers, and decomposers. (Food chain after R. L. Smith, Ecology and Field Biology, Harper and Row, New York.)*

Oxygen in the form of gas molecules (O_2) is a byproduct of photosynthesis. Photosynthesis is also referred to as *carbon fixation,* since in the process gaseous carbon as CO_2 is "fixed" to a solid form in carbohydrate.

Respiration is the process opposite to photosynthesis in which carbohydrate is broken down and combined with oxygen to yield carbon dioxide and water. The overall reaction is as follows:

$$-CHOH- + O_2 \rightarrow CO_2 + H_2O + \text{chemical energy}$$

8.3 Energy loss *Percentage of energy passed up the steps of the food chain, assuming 90 percent is lost energy at each step.*

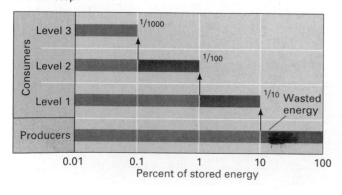

As in the case of photosynthesis, the actual reactions are far from simple. The chemical energy released is stored in several types of energy-carrying molecules in living cells and used later to synthesize all the biological molecules necessary to sustain life.

Because both photosynthesis and respiration occur simultaneously in a plant, the amount of new carbohydrate placed in storage is less than the total carbohydrate being synthesized. We must thus distinguish between gross photosynthesis and net photosynthesis. **Gross photosynthesis** is the total amount of carbohydrate produced by photosynthesis. **Net photosynthesis** is the amount of carbohydrate remaining after respiration has broken down sufficient carbohydrate to power the plant. Stated as an equation,

Net photosynthesis = Gross photosynthesis – Respiration

Because both photosynthesis and respiration occur in the same cell, gross photosynthesis cannot be measured readily. Instead, we will deal with net photosynthesis. In most cases, respiration will be held constant, so use of the net instead of the gross will show the same trends.

The rate of net photosynthesis is strongly dependent on the intensity of light energy available, up to a limit. Figure 8.4 shows this principle. The rate of net photosynthesis is indicated on the vertical axis by the rate at which a plant takes up carbon dioxide. On the horizontal axis, light intensity increases from left to right. At first, net photosynthesis

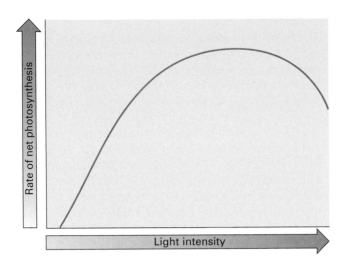

8.4 Net photosynthesis *The curve of net photosynthesis shows a steep initial rise, then levels off as light intensity rises.*

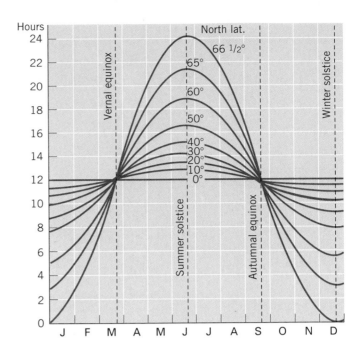

8.5 Day length variation *Duration of the daylight period (sunrise to sunset) at various latitudes throughout the year. The vertical scale gives the number of hours the Sun is above the horizon.*

rises rapidly as light intensity increases. The rate then slows and reaches a maximum value, shown by the plateau in the curve. Above this maximum, the rate falls off because the incoming light is also causing heating. This heating increases the rate of respiration, which offsets gross production by photosynthesis and decreases the net.

Light intensity sufficient to allow maximum net photosynthesis is only 10 to 30 percent of full summer sunlight for most green plants. Additional light energy is simply ineffective. Duration of daylight then becomes the important factor in the rate at which products of photosynthesis accumulate as plant tissues. On this subject, you can draw on your knowledge of the seasons and the changing angle of the Sun's rays with latitude. Figure 8.5 shows the duration of the daylight period with changing seasons for a wide range of latitudes in the northern hemisphere. At low latitudes, days are not far from the average 12-hour length throughout the year. At high latitudes, days are short in winter but long in summer. The seasonal contrast in day length increases with latitude. In subarctic latitudes, photosynthesis can go on in summer during most of the 24-hour day, a factor that can compensate significantly for the shortness of the growing season.

The rate of photosynthesis also increases as air temperature increases, up to a limit. Figure 8.6 shows the results of a laboratory experiment in which sphagnum moss was grown under constant illumination. Gross photosynthesis increased rapidly to a maximum at about 20°C (68°F), then leveled off. Respiration increased quite steadily to the limit of the experiment. Net photosynthesis, which is the difference (sunrise to sunset) between the values in the two curves, peaked at about 18°C (64°F), then fell off rapidly.

Net Primary Production

Plant ecologists measure the accumulated net production by photosynthesis in terms of the **biomass**, which is the dry weight of organic matter. This quantity could, of course, be

stated for a single plant or animal, but a more useful measurement is the biomass per unit of surface area within the ecosystem—that is, grams of biomass per square meter or (metric) tons of biomass per hectare (1 hectare = 10^4 m²). Of all ecosystems, forests have the greatest biomass because of the large amount of wood that the trees accumulate through time. The biomass of grasslands and croplands is much

8.6 Temperature and energy flow *Respiration and gross and net photosynthesis vary with temperature. (Data of Stofelt, in A. C. Leopold, Plant Growth and Development, McGraw-Hill, New York.)*

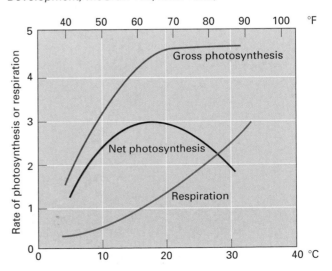

Table 8.1 | **Net Primary Production for Various Ecosystems**

	Grams per Square Meter per Year	
	Average	**Typical Range**
Lands		
Rainforest of the equatorial zone	2000	1000–5000
Freshwater swamps and marshes	2500	800–4000
Midlatitude forest	1300	600–2500
Midlatitude grassland	500	150–1500
Agricultural land	650	100–4000
Lakes and streams	500	100–1500
Extreme desert	3	0–10
Oceans		
Algal beds and reefs	2000	1000–3000
Estuaries (tidal)	1800	500–4000
Continental shelf	360	300–600
Open ocean	125	1–400

thetic activity, it can be misleading. In some ecosystems, biomass is broken down very quickly by consumers and decomposers, so the amount maintained is less. From the viewpoint of ecosystem productivity, what is important is the annual yield of useful energy produced by the ecosystem, or the *net primary production.*

Table 8.1 provides the net primary production of various ecosystems in units of grams of dry organic matter produced annually from one square meter of surface. The figures are rough estimates, but they are nevertheless highly meaningful. Note that the highest values are in two quite unlike environments: forests and wetlands (estuaries). Agricultural land compares favorably with grassland, but the range is very large in agricultural land, reflecting many factors such as availability of soil water, soil fertility, and use of fertilizers and machinery.

Productivity of the oceans is generally low. The deep water oceanic zone, which comprises about 90 percent of the world ocean area, is the least productive of the marine ecosystems. Continental shelf areas are a good deal more productive and support much of the world's fishing industry (Figure 8.7).

Upwelling zones are also highly productive. Upwelling of cold water from ocean depths brings nutrients to the surface and greatly increases the growth of microscopic floating plants known as *phytoplankton.* These, in turn, serve as food sources for marine animals in the food chain. Consequently, zones of upwelling near habitable coastlines are highly productive fisheries. An example is the Peru Current off the west coast of South America. Here, countless individuals of a single species of small fish, the

smaller in comparison. For freshwater bodies and the oceans, the biomass is even smaller—on the order of one-hundredth that of the grasslands and croplands.

Although the amount of biomass present per unit area is an important indicator of the amount of photosyn-

---

Net primary production measures the rate of accumulation of carbohydrate by primary producers. Equatorial rainforests and freshwater swamps and marshes are among the most productive ecosystems, while deserts are least productive.

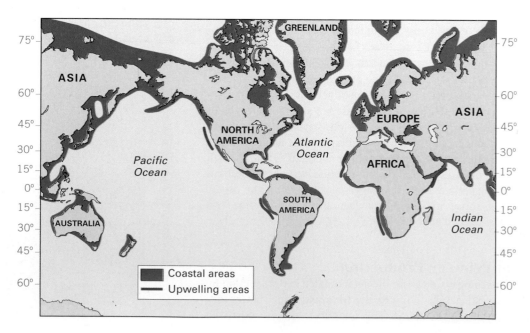

8.7 Distribution of World fisheries *Coastal areas and upwelling areas together supply over 99 percent of world production. (Compiled by the National Science Board, National Science Foundation.)*

anchoveta, provide food for larger fish and for birds. The birds, in turn, excrete their wastes on the mainland coast of Peru. The accumulated deposit, called guano, is a rich source of nitrate fertilizer that is now severely depleted.

GEODISCOVERIES Remote Sensing and Biosphere Interactivity. Explore satellite images from local to global scales to examine land and ocean productivity. Identify ocean algae blooms.

Net Production and Climate

What climatic factors control net primary productivity? We have already identified light intensity and duration, as well as temperature, as influencing net photosynthesis. Another important factor is the availability of water. A shortage or surplus of soil water might be the best climatic factor to examine, but data are not available. Ecologists have related net annual primary production to mean annual precipitation, as shown in Figure 8.8. The production values are for plant structures above the ground surface. Although the productivity increases rapidly with precipitation in the lower range from desert through semiarid to subhumid climates, it levels off in the humid range.

> Day length, air and soil temperature, and water availability are the most important climatic factors that control net primary productivity.

Combining the effects of light intensity, temperature, and precipitation, we can assign rough values of productivity to each of the climates as follows (units are grams of carbon per square meter per year):

Highest (over 800)	Wet equatorial ①
Very high (600–800)	Monsoon and trade-wind coastal ② Wet-dry tropical ③
High (400–600)	Wet-dry tropical ③ (Southeast Asia) Moist subtropical ⑥ Marine west coast ⑧
Moderate (200–400)	Mediterranean ⑦ Moist continental ⑩
Low (100–200)	Dry tropical, semiarid ④s Dry midlatitude, semiarid ⑨s Boreal forest ⑩
Very low (0–100)	Dry tropical, desert ④d Dry midlatitude, desert ⑨d Boreal forest ⑩ Tundra ⑫

Within the past decade or so, remote sensing has come into use as a tool for mapping primary productivity on a global scale. Our interchapter feature, *A Closer Look: Eye on Global Change 8.4 • Monitoring Global Productivity from Space* provides more information on how this is done. Using remote sensing, scientists have concluded that terrestrial productivity has increased since about 1980, while ocean productivity has decreased. These changes are most likely linked to global climate changes, including global warming at higher latitudes, reductions in cloud cover in equatorial regions, and decreasing winds over oceans.

Biomass as an Energy Source

Net primary production represents a source of renewable energy derived from the Sun that can be exploited to fill human energy needs. The use of biomass as an energy source involves releasing solar energy that has been fixed in plant tissues through photosynthesis. This process can take place in a number of ways—the simplest is direct burning of plant matter as fuel, as in a campfire or a wood-burning stove. Other approaches involve the generation of intermediate fuels from plant matter—methane gas, charcoal, and alcohol, for example. Biomass energy conversion is not highly energy efficient. Typical values of net annual primary production of plant communities range from 1 to 3 percent of available solar energy. However, the abundance of terrestrial biomass is so great that biomass utilization could provide the energy equivalent to 3 million barrels of oil per day for the United States with proper development.

One important use of biomass energy is the burning of firewood for cooking (and some space heating) in developing nations. The annual growth of wood in the forest of developing countries totals about half the world's energy production—plenty of firewood is thus available. However, fuelwood use exceeds production in many areas, creating local shortages and severe strains on some forest ecosystems. The forest–desert transition areas of thorntree, savanna, and desert scrub in central Africa south of the Sahara Desert are examples.

8.8 Precipitation and net production *Net primary production increases rapidly with increasing precipitation but levels off in the higher values. Observed values fall mostly within the shaded zone. (Data of Whittaker, 1970.)*

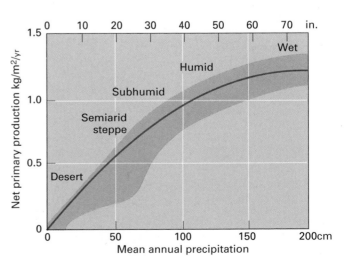

Even in closed stoves, wood burning is not very efficient, ranging from 10 to 15 percent for cooking. However, the conversion of wood to charcoal or gas can boost efficiencies to values as high as 70 to 80 percent with appropriate technology. In this process, termed *pyrolysis,* controlled partial burning in an oxygen-deficient environment reduces carbohydrate to free carbon (charcoal) and yields flammable gases such as carbon monoxide and hydrogen. Charcoal is more energy efficient than wood, burns more cleanly, and is easier to transport. As an added advantage, charcoal can be made from waste fibers and agricultural residues that would normally be discarded. Thus, charcoal is an efficient fuel that can help extend the firewood supply in areas where wood is in high demand.

A second method of extracting energy from biomass uses anaerobic digestion to produce *biogas.* In this process, animal and human wastes are fed into a closed digesting chamber, where anaerobic bacteria break down the waste to produce a gas that is a mixture of methane and carbon dioxide. The biogas can be easily burned for cooking or heating, or it may be used to generate electric power. The digested residue is a sweet-smelling fertilizer. China now maintains a vigorous program of construction of biogas digesters for the use of small family units. The benefits include better sanitation and reduced air pollution, as well as more efficient fuel usage.

Another use of biomass that is increasing in importance is the conversion of agricultural wastes to alcohol. In this process, yeast microorganisms are used to convert the carbohydrate to alcohol through fermentation. An advantage of alcohol is that it can serve as a substitute and extender for gasoline. Gasohol, a mixture of up to 10 percent alcohol in gasoline, can be burned in conventional engines without adjustment.

Brazil, a country without adequate petroleum production, has relied heavily on alcohol fuel derived from sugarcane. In a recent year, for example, alcohol provided 63 percent of Brazil's automotive fuel needs. Distillation of alcohol, however, requires heating, thus greatly reducing the net energy yield. Alcohol, charcoal, and firewood are all alternatives to fossil fuels that will become increasingly important as petroleum becomes scarcer and more costly in the coming decades.

Relying on biomass energy can also yield important benefits in reducing carbon dioxide emissions. However, burning biomass does not reduce the CO_2 flow to the atmosphere directly. The burning of biomass quickly releases CO_2 that would normally be released more slowly, as the biomass decays. But the energy obtained in the biomass burning will in all likelihood substitute for some fossil fuel burning. Because this fossil fuel is not burned, its CO_2 is not released to the atmosphere, thus reducing overall carbon dioxide emissions.

Biomass burning is not always controlled. In some ecosystems, such as grasslands, savannas, and woodlands, wildfires are frequent, and ecosystems are well-adjusted to burning. In others, such as forest, wildfires may be infrequent but severe and damaging. We will return to the subject of fires in a following section.

The Carbon Cycle

We have seen how energy of solar origin flows through ecosystems, passing from one part of the food chain to the next, until it is ultimately lost from the biosphere as energy radiated to space. Matter also moves through ecosystems, but because gravity keeps surface material Earthbound, matter cannot be lost in the global ecosystem. As molecules are formed and reformed by chemical and biochemical reactions within an ecosystem, the atoms that compose them are not changed or lost. Thus, matter is conserved within an ecosystem, and atoms and molecules can be used and reused, or cycled, within ecosystems.

Atoms and molecules move through ecosystems under the influence of both physical and biological processes. The pathways of a particular type of matter through the Earth's ecosystem comprise a **biogeochemical cycle** (sometimes referred to as a *material cycle* or *nutrient cycle*).

The major features of a biogeochemical cycle are diagrammed in Figure 8.9. Any area or location of concentration of a material is a **pool**. There are two types of pools: *active pools,* where materials are in forms and places easily accessible to life processes, and *storage pools,* where materials are more or less inaccessible to life. A system of pathways of material flows connects the various active and storage pools within the cycle. Pathways can involve the movement of material in all three states of matter—gas, liquid, and solid. For example, carbon moves freely in the atmosphere as carbon dioxide gas and freely in water as dissolved CO_2 and as carbonate ion (CO_3^-). It also takes the form of a solid in deposits of limestone and dolomite (calcium and magnesium carbonate).

Ecologists have studied and documented biogeochemical cycles for many elements, including carbon, oxygen, nitrogen, sulfur, and phosphorus. Of these, the **carbon cycle** is probably the most important for two reasons. First, all life is composed of carbon compounds of one form or another. Second, human activities are modifying the carbon cycle in important ways.

Some details of the *carbon cycle* are shown in a schematic diagram, Figure 8.10. In the gaseous portion of the cycle, carbon moves largely as carbon dioxide (CO_2), which is a free gas in the atmosphere and a dissolved gas in fresh and saltwater. In the sedimentary portion of its cycle, carbon resides in carbohydrate molecules in organic matter, as hydrocarbon compounds in rock (petroleum, coal), and as mineral carbonate compounds such as calcium carbonate ($CaCO_3$). The world supply of atmospheric carbon dioxide is represented in Figure 8.10

The carbon cycle is a biogeochemical cycle in which carbon flows among storage pools in the atmosphere, ocean, and on the land. Human activity has affected the carbon cycle, causing carbon dioxide concentrations in the atmospheric storage pool to increase.

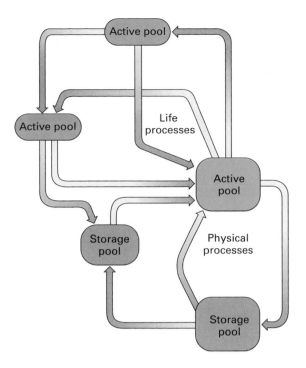

8.9 *General features of a biogeochemical cycle*

by a box. It is a small portion of the carbon in active pools, constituting less than 2 percent. This atmospheric pool is supplied by plant and animal respiration in the oceans and on the lands. Under natural conditions, some new carbon

enters the atmosphere each year from volcanoes by outgassing in the form of CO_2 and carbon monoxide (CO). Industry injects substantial amounts of carbon into the atmosphere through combustion of fossil fuels. This increment from fuel combustion and its probable effects on global air temperatures were discussed in Chapter 3.

Carbon dioxide leaves the atmospheric pool to enter the oceans, where it is used in photosynthesis by phytoplankton. These organisms are primary producers in the ocean ecosystem and are consumed by marine animals in the food chain. Phytoplankton also build skeletal structures of calcium carbonate. This mineral matter settles to the ocean floor to accumulate as sedimentary strata, an enormous storage pool not available to organisms until released later by rock weathering. Organic compounds synthesized by phytoplankton also settle to the ocean floor and eventually are transformed into the hydrocarbon compounds making up petroleum and natural gas. On the lands, plant matter accumulating over geologic time forms layers of peat that are ultimately transformed into coal. Petroleum, natural gas, and coal comprise the fossil fuels, and these represent huge storage pools of carbon.

Human activity is presently affecting the carbon cycle very significantly. Through the burning of fossil fuels, CO_2 is being released to the atmosphere at a rate far beyond that of any natural process. *Eye on Global Change 8.1 • Human Impact on the Carbon Cycle* documents how human activity has influenced the major flows within the carbon cycle.

8.10 *The carbon cycle* (Copyright © A. N. Strahler.)

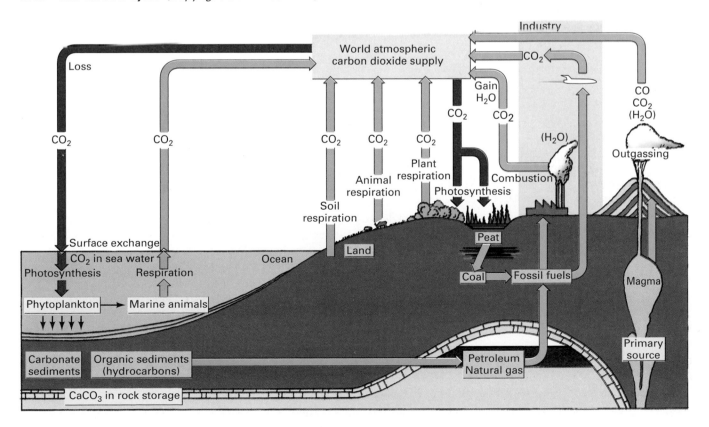

Eye on Global Change | 8.1

Human Impact on the Carbon Cycle

Carbon is an element that is abundant at the Earth's surface and is also essential for life. As noted earlier in this chapter, carbon cycles continuously among the land surface, atmosphere, and ocean in many complex pathways. However, these flows are now strongly influenced by human activity. The most important human impact on the carbon cycle is the burning of fossil fuels. Another important human impact lies in changing the Earth's land covers— for example, in clearing forests or abandoning agricultural areas. Let's look at these impacts in more detail.

The figure below shows a simple diagram of the major flows within the carbon cycle for the period 1989–1998. The magnitudes of the annual flows are shown in gigatons (Gt) of carbon per year (1

gigaton = 10^9 metric tons = 10^{12} kg = 1.1×10^9 English tons = 1.1 English gigatons). These flows are estimates, and a second value after each value indicates its uncertainty. For example, fossil fuel burning liberates 6.3 ± 0.6 Gt/yr, which we can interpret as a flow that is most likely to be in the range $6.3 - 0.6 = 5.7$ to $6.3 + 0.6 = 6.9$ Gt/yr.

By comparing the flows, we see that about half of the output of carbon by fossil fuel burning is taken up by the atmosphere (3.3 ± 0.2 Gt/yr). Of the remaining amount, about 2/3 (2.3 ± 0.8 Gt/yr) is absorbed by the oceans. This leaves unaccounted an amount of about $6.3 - 3.3 - 2.3 = 0.7$ Gt/yr. Since there are no other significant pathways, this carbon must be flowing into the biosphere. In other words, ecosystems are a *sink* for

CO_2, accepting about 0.7 Gt/yr of carbon.

Ecosystems cycle carbon in photosynthesis, respiration, decomposition, and combustion. Photosynthesis and respiration are basic physiological processes that fix and release CO_2. Decomposition is the process in which bacteria and fungi digest dead organic matter, and is actually a form of respiration. Combustion refers to uncontrolled combustion, as when an ecosystem burns. It is very hard to account for these processes globally in such a way as to know their net effect, but by applying the logic of budgeting, we know that they must sum to the value of 0.7 Gt/yr of carbon buildup in land ecosystems mentioned above.

If the value of 0.7 Gt/yr in carbon uptake is correct, the amount

The global carbon cycle *Values are in gigatons of carbon per year. (Data from UN/IPCC.)*

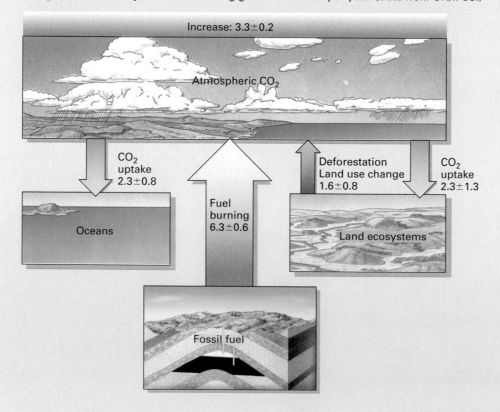

Increase: 3.3 ± 0.2

Atmospheric CO_2

CO_2 uptake 2.3 ± 0.8

Oceans

Fuel burning 6.3 ± 0.6

Deforestation Land use change 1.6 ± 0.8

CO_2 uptake 2.3 ± 1.3

Land ecosystems

Fossil fuel

of terrestrial biomass must be increasing at that rate. However, forests are presently diminishing in area as they are logged or converted to farmland or grazing land. This conversion is primarily occurring in tropical and equatorial regions, and it is estimated to release about 1.6 ± 0.8 Gt/yr of carbon to the atmosphere. Since this release is included in the net land ecosystem uptake of 0.7 Gt/yr, the remainder of the world's forests must be taking up the 1.6 Gt/yr loss from deforestation as well as an additional 0.7 Gt/yr. So we can estimate that mid- and high-latitude forests are increasing in area or biomass to fix carbon at a rate of $1.6 + 0.7 = 2.3$ Gt/yr.

Independent evidence seems to confirm this conclusion. In Europe, for example, forest statistics show an increase of growing stock—the volume of living trees—of about 25 percent from 1970 to 1990. This increase has been sustained in spite of damage to forests by air pollution, especially in eastern Europe. In North America, forest areas are increasing in many regions as agricultural production has abandoned marginal areas to natural forest growth. New England is a good example of this trend. A century ago, only a small portion of New England was forested. Now only a small portion is cleared.

Some of the increase in global biomass may also be the effect of enhancement of photosynthesis by warmer temperatures and increased CO_2 concentrations (discussed in more detail shortly). Another factor proposed to account for increased ecosystem productivity is nitrogen fertilization of soils by washout of nitrogen pollutant gases in the atmosphere.

Some foresters have observed that harvesting mature forests and replacing them with young, fast-growing timber should increase the rate of withdrawal of CO_2 from the atmosphere. Since the lumber of the mature forests goes into semipermanent storage in dwellings and structures where it is protected from decay and oxidation to CO_2, it represents a withdrawal of CO_2 from the atmosphere. The young forests that replace the mature ones grow quickly, fixing carbon at a much faster rate than the older, mature forest, in which annual growth has slowed.

A report of research scientists at the College of Forestry of Oregon State University showed, however, that the conversion of old-growth forests to young, fast-growing forests will not significantly decrease atmospheric CO_2. They calculated that while 42 percent of the harvested timber goes into comparatively long-term storage (greater than five years) in building structures, much of the remainder is directly discarded on the logging site where it is burned or rapidly decomposes. In addition, some biomass becomes waste in factory processing of the lumber, where sawdust and scrap are burned as fuel. Similarly, the manufacture of paper also results in short-term conversion of a large proportion of the harvested trees to CO_2. In sum, harvesting of old-growth forests as now practiced actually contributes substantially to atmospheric CO_2.

Some environmentalists have advocated increased tree planting as a way of enhancing CO_2 fixation. To take up the quantity of carbon now being released by fossil fuel burning would require some 7 million square kilometers of new closed-crown broadleaved deciduous forest—an area about the size of Australia. To absorb the net increase in atmospheric carbon would require about half that area. This would be a daunting task at best.

Another factor is that increased CO_2 concentration in the atmosphere might enhance photosynthesis and thus increase the rate of carbon fixation. The enhancement of photosynthesis by increased CO_2 concentrations has been observed for many plants and demonstrated as a way of increasing yields of some crops. However, CO_2 is only one factor in photosynthesis—light, temperature, nutrients, and water are also needed, and restrictions in any of these will reduce photosynthesis. In one research study, forest photosynthesis under enriched CO_2 conditions was stimulated, but no net increase in carbon storage was observed. On the other hand, the CO_2 enrichment seemed to enhance root growth and nitrogen fixation by root nodules, thus making the trees more able to withstand stress.

While the dynamics of forests are important in the global carbon cycle, soils may be even more important. Recent inventories estimate that about four times as much carbon resides in soils than in above-ground biomass. The largest reservoir of soil carbon is in the boreal forest. In fact, there is about as much carbon in boreal forest soils as in all above-ground vegetation. This soil carbon has accumulated over thousands of years under cold conditions that have retarded its decay. However, there is now great concern that global warming, which is acting more strongly at high latitudes, will increase the rate of decay of this vast carbon pool and that boreal forests, which are presently a sink for CO_2, will become a source.

Reducing the rate of carbon dioxide buildup in the atmosphere is a matter of great international concern. As we noted in Chapter 3, an international treaty limiting emissions of CO_2 and other greenhouse gases was signed at the Rio de Janeiro Earth Summit in 1992 by nearly 150 nations. Since that time, the world's nations have been struggling with the implementation of a plan to control these emissions. While much good progress has been made, more work is needed. An effective global commitment to reduction of CO_2 releases and control of global warming still awaits us.

The Nitrogen Cycle

A second important biogeochemical cycle is the *nitrogen cycle,* diagrammed in Figure 8.11. In this cycle, the atmosphere, containing 78 percent nitrogen as N_2 by volume, is a vast storage pool. Nitrogen in the atmosphere in the form of N_2 cannot be assimilated directly by plants or animals. Only certain microorganisms possess the ability to utilize N_2 directly, a process termed *nitrogen fixation.* One class of such microorganisms consists of certain species of free-living soil bacteria. Some blue-green algae can also fix nitrogen.

Another class consists of the symbiotic nitrogen fixers. In a symbiotic relationship, two species of organisms live in close physical contact, each contributing to the life processes or structures of the other. Symbiotic nitrogen fixers are bacteria of the genus *Rhizobium.* These bacteria are associated with some 190 species of trees and shrubs as well as almost all members of the legume family. Legumes important as agricultural crops are clover, alfalfa, soybeans, peas, beans, and peanuts. *Rhizobium* bacteria infect the root cells of these plants in root nodules produced jointly by action of the plant and the bacteria. The bacteria supply the nitrogen to the plant through nitrogen fixation, while the plant supplies nutrients and organic compounds needed by the bacteria. Crops of legumes are often planted in seasonal rotation with other food crops to ensure an adequate nitrogen supply in the soil. Both the action of nitrogen-fixing crops and that of soil bacteria are shown in the nitrogen cycle diagram (Figure 8.11).

Nitrogen is lost to the biosphere by *denitrification,* a process in which certain soil bacteria convert nitrogen from usable forms back to N_2. This process is also shown in the diagram. Denitrification completes the organic portion of the nitrogen cycle, as nitrogen returns to the atmosphere.

At the present time, nitrogen fixation far exceeds denitrification, and usable nitrogen is accumulating in the life layer. This excess of fixation is produced almost entirely by human activities. Human activity fixes nitrogen in the manufacture of nitrogen fertilizers and by oxidizing nitrogen in the combustion of fossil fuels. Widespread cultivation of legumes has also greatly increased worldwide nitrogen fixation. At present rates, nitrogen fixation attributable to human activity nearly equals all natural biological fixation.

Much of the nitrogen fixed by human activities is carried from the soil into rivers and lakes and ultimately reaches the ocean. Major water pollution problems can arise when nitrogen stimulates the growth of algae and phytoplankton. The respiration of these organisms can then reduce quantities of dissolved oxygen to levels that are detrimental to desirable forms of aquatic life. These problems will be accentuated in years to come because industrial fixation of nitrogen in fertilizer manufacture is doubling about every six years at present. The global impact of such large amounts of nitrogen reaching rivers, lakes, and oceans on the Earth's global ecosystem remains uncertain.

The carbon and nitrogen cycles are linked in the process of plant growth. Synthesis of plant matter requires both carbon and nitrogen, which are taken up from the atmosphere

8.11 *The nitrogen cycle* (Copyright © A. N. Strahler.)

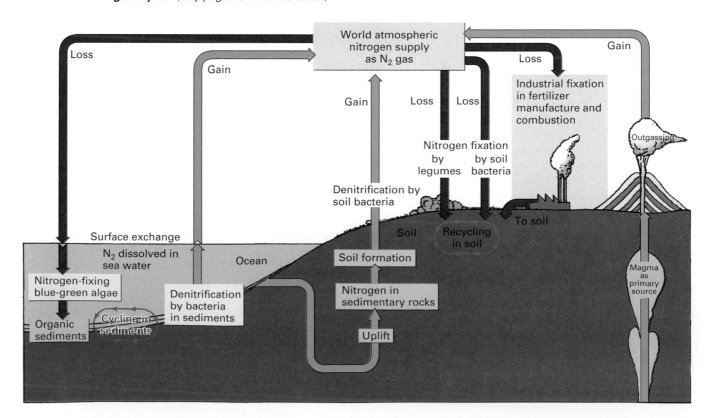

and soil, respectively. When the plant matter decays, it releases the carbon and nitrogen. Carbon and nitrogen can be limiting factors to plant growth. For example, if fertilizer is applied to crops, they will typically grow more vigorously, causing more carbon fixation. If CO_2 concentrations increase as predicted (see *Eye on Global Change 3.1 • Carbon Dioxide—On the Increase*), plants will tend to fix more nitrogen, an effect that will favor legumes and could cause ecosystems to change.

The carbon and nitrogen cycles are also linked through biomass burning. Hot combustion oxidizes atmospheric N_2 to such compounds as NO and NO_2, serving to fix nitrogen that then cycles through the biosphere.

ECOLOGICAL BIOGEOGRAPHY

In the preceding section, we viewed ecosystems from the perspective of energy and showed how the biosphere fixes sunlight to power global cycles of elements. But ecosystems are composed of individual organisms that utilize and interact with their environment in different ways. From fungi digesting organic matter on a forest floor to ospreys fishing in a coastal estuary, each organism has a range of environmental conditions that limits its survival as well as a set of characteristic adaptations that it exploits to obtain the energy it needs to live. **Ecological biogeography** examines the distribution patterns of plants and animals from the viewpoint of ecological factors and interrelationships between species.

We begin our discussion of ecological biogeography with the relationship between organisms and their physical environment. As we travel through a hilly, wooded area, it is easy to see that the ecosystems we encounter are strongly influenced by landform and soil. For example, the upland forest of oak and hickory on the Blue Ridge Mountains of Virginia gives way to hemlock, birch, and maple in small valleys and low places. Upland soils are thick, stony, and well-drained, while the soils of the valleys and swales are finer, richer in organic matter, and wetter more of the time. Forest communities are

The *habitat* of a species describes the physical environment that harbors its activities. The *ecological niche* of a species describes how it obtains its energy and how it influences other species and its own environment. The *community* is a group of interacting organisms that occupy a particular habitat.

also strikingly different in form on rocky ridges and on steep cliffs, where pines and scrubby oaks abound. Here water drains away rapidly, and soil is thin or largely absent. These variations illustrate the concept of the **habitat**—a subdivision of the environment according to the needs and preferences of organisms or groups of organisms. Figure 8.12 presents an example taken from a Canadian boreal forest. Here, there are six distinctive habitats: upland, bog, bottomland, ridge, cliff, and active sand dune. Each habitat supports a different type of ecosystem.

A concept related to the habitat, the *ecological niche*, includes the functional role played by an organism as well as the physical space it inhabits. If the habitat is the individual's "address," then the niche is its "profession," including how and where it obtains its energy and how it influences other species and the environment around it. Included in the ecological niche are the organism's tolerances and responses to changes in moisture, temperature, soil chemistry, illumination, and other factors. Although many different species may occupy the same habitat, only a few of these species will ever share the same ecological niche, for, as we'll see shortly, evolution will tend to separate them.

As we move from habitat to habitat, we find that each is the home of a group of organisms, each occupying different but interrelated ecological niches. We can define a *community* as an assemblage of organisms that live in a particular habitat and interact with one another. Although every organism must adjust to variations in the environment on its own, we find that similar habitats often contain similar assemblages of organisms. Biogeographers and ecologists recognize specific types of communities, called *associations,* in which typical organisms are likely to be found together. Sometimes these associations are defined by species, as in the beech-birch-maple forest that is found in the Great Lakes region and that stretches to New England. Other times they are defined more generally by the life-form of the vegetation cover, as in the boreal forest biome (sometimes facetiously termed the "spruce-moose" biome), which consists of the broad circumpolar band of coniferous forest found in the northern hemisphere and

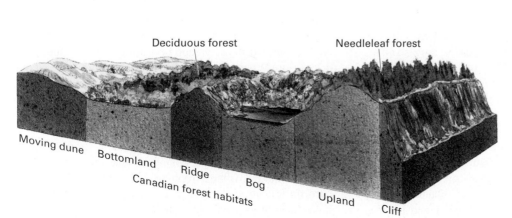

Deciduous forest   Needleleaf forest

Moving dune   Bottomland   Ridge   Bog   Upland   Cliff
Canadian forest habitats

8.12 Habitats within the Canadian boreal forest
Habitats of the Canadian boreal forest are quite varied and include moving dune, bottomland, ridge, bog, and upland. (After P. Dansereau.)

includes many similar and related species of plants, animals, and microbes. (The *biome* is the largest division of ecosystems. (We'll say more about biomes in Chapter 9.)

What physical environmental factors are most important in determining where organisms, as individuals and species, are found? In general, moisture and temperature are most important. Although organisms are sometimes present under conditions of extreme temperatures or dryness as spores or cysts, nearly all organisms have limits that are exceeded at least somewhere on Earth at some time. At the global scale, temperature and moisture patterns translate into climate. For this reason, as we will see in Chapter 9, there is a very strong relationship between climate and vegetation.

Other environmental factors that influence plant and animal distribution patterns and life cycles are light and wind. Light varies within communities, as, for example, between the top and bottom of a forest canopy, as well as with time, as in the changes in daylight length that occur with the seasons. Wind exposes plants to drying and can cause plants to be stunted on the windward side. Let's look at environmental factors in more detail.

Water Need

Both plants and animals show a variety of adaptations that enable them to cope with the abundance or scarcity of water. In plants, many of these adaptations affect the transpiration mechanism. Evaporation at the leaf is controlled by specialized leaf pores, which provide openings in the outer layer of cells. When soil water is depleted, the pores close and evaporation is greatly reduced. Plants that are adapted to drought conditions are termed **xerophytes.** The word "xerophyte" comes from the Greek roots *xero-,* meaning "dry," and *phyton,* meaning "plant." Some xerophytes are adapted to habitats that dry quickly following rapid drainage of precipitation—for example, sand dunes, beaches, and bare rock surfaces. Others are adapted to habitats in which rainfall is simply scarce, such as deserts.

In some xerophytes, water loss is reduced by a thick layer of wax or wax-like material on leaves and stems. The wax helps to seal water vapor inside the leaf or stem. Still other xerophytes adapt to a desert environment by greatly reducing their leaf area or by bearing no leaves at all. Needlelike leaves, or spines in place of leaves, are also adaptations of plants to conserve water. In cactus plants, the foliage leaf is not present, and transpiration is limited to thickened, water-filled stems that store water for use during long, dry periods (Figure 8.13).

Adaptations of plants to water-scarce environments also include improved abilities to obtain and store water. Roots may extend deeply to reach soil moisture far from the surface. In cases where the roots reach to the ground water zone, a steady supply of water is assured. Plants drawing from ground water are termed *phreatophytes* and may be

8.13 Prickly pear cactus (Opuntia) *The prickly pear cactus is widely distributed in the western hemisphere. This clump of cactus is in the Sonoran desert, Arizona.*

found along dry stream channels and valley floors in desert regions. In these environments, ground water is usually near the surface. Other desert plants produce a widespread, but shallow, root system. This system enables them to absorb water from short desert downpours that saturate only the uppermost soil layer. Commonly, leaves and stems of desert plants are greatly thickened by a spongy tissue in which much water can be stored. Plants employing this adaptation are called *succulents.*

Another adaptation to extreme aridity is a very short life cycle. Many small desert plants will germinate from seed, then leaf out, bear flowers, and produce seed in the few weeks immediately following a heavy rain shower. In this way, they complete their life cycle when soil moisture is available, and they survive the dry period as dormant seeds that require no moisture.

Certain climates, such as the wet-dry tropical climate ③ and the moist continental climate ⑩, have a yearly cycle with one season in which water is unavailable to plants because of lack of precipitation or because the soil water is frozen. This season alternates with one in which there is abundant water. Plants adapted to such regimes are called *tropophytes,* from the Greek word *trophos,* meaning "change" or "turn." Tropophytes respond to this pattern by dropping their leaves at the close of the moist season and becoming dormant during the dry season. When water is again available, they leaf out and grow at a rapid rate. Trees and shrubs that shed their leaves seasonally are termed *deciduous,* while *evergreen* plants retain most of their leaves in a green state through one or more years.

The Mediterranean climate ⑦ also has a strong seasonal wet-dry alternation, with dry summers and wet winters. Plants in this climate are often xerophytic and characteristically have hard, thick, leathery leaves. An example is the live oak, which holds most of its leaves through the dry season (Figure 8.14).

> Xerophytes are plants that are adapted to a dry and sometimes hot environment. Examples are phreatophytes, which have deep roots, succulents, which store water internally in spongy tissues, and a deciduous habit, in which leaf drop limits water loss from transpiration.

8.14 Live oak *This California live oak is an example of a sclerophyll—a plant with thick, leathery leaves that is adapted to an environment with a very dry season.*

As we saw in Chapter 7, such hard-leaved evergreen trees and woody shrubs are called *sclerophylls.* (The prefix *scler-* is from the Greek root for "hard" and is combined with the Greek word for leaf, *phyllon.*) Plants that hold their leaves through a dry or cold season have the advantage of being able to resume photosynthesis immediately when growing conditions become favorable, whereas the deciduous plants must grow a new set of leaves.

To cope with water shortages, **xeric animals** have evolved methods that are somewhat similar to those used by the plants. Many of the invertebrates exhibit the same pattern as ephemeral annuals—evading the dry period in dormant states. When rain falls, they emerge to take advantage of the new and short-lived vegetation that often results. For example, many species of birds regulate their behavior to nest only when the rains occur, the time of most abundant food for their offspring. The tiny brine shrimp of the Great Basin may wait many years in dormancy until normally dry lakebeds fill with water, an event that occurs perhaps three or four times a century. The shrimp then emerge and complete their life cycles before the lake evaporates.

Mammals are by nature poorly adapted to desert environments, but many survive through a variety of mechanisms that enable them to avoid water loss. Just as plants reduce transpiration to conserve water, so many desert mammals do not sweat through skin glands. Instead they rely on other methods of cooling, such as avoiding the Sun and becoming active only at night. In this respect, they are joined by most of the rest of the desert fauna, spending their days in cool burrows in the soil and their nights foraging for food (Figure 8.15).

Temperature

The temperature of the air and soil, the second of the important climatic factors in ecology, acts directly on organisms through its influence on the rates at which physiological processes take place in plant and animal tissues. In general,

each plant species has an optimum temperature associated with each of its functions, such as photosynthesis, flowering, fruiting, or seed germination. There are also limiting lower and upper temperatures for these individual functions and for the total survival of the plant itself.

Temperature can also act indirectly on plants and animals. For example, higher air temperatures reduce the relative humidity of the air (Chapter 4), thus enhancing transpiration from plant leaves as well as increasing direct evaporation of soil water.

In general, the colder the climate, the fewer the species that are capable of surviving. A large number of tropical plant species cannot survive below-freezing temperatures for more than a few hours. In the severely cold arctic and alpine environments of high latitudes and high altitudes, only a few plant and animal species are found. This principle explains why an equatorial rainforest contains such a diverse array of plants and animals, whereas a forest of the

8.15 Desert reptile *The noctural activity of the night snake, Hypsiglena torquata, is captured in this flash photo from Baja, Mexico.*

subarctic zone will be dominated by only a few. Tolerance to cold in plants is closely tied to the physical disruption that accompanies the growth of ice crystals inside cells. Cold-tolerant plant species can expel excess water from cells to spaces between cells, where freezing does no damage.

The effects of temperature variations on animals are moderated by their physiology and by their ability to seek sheltered environments. Most animals lack a physiological mechanism for internal temperature regulation. These animals, including reptiles, invertebrates, fish, and amphibians, are *cold-blooded animals*—their body temperature passively follows the environment. With a few exceptions (notably fish and some social insects), these animals are active only during the warmer parts of the year. They survive the cold weather of the midlatitude zone winter by becoming dormant. Some vertebrates enter a dormant state termed *hibernation* in which metabolic processes virtually stop and body temperatures closely parallel those of the surroundings. Most hibernators seek out burrows, nests, or other environments where winter temperatures do not reach extremes or fluctuate rapidly. Because the annual range of soil temperatures is greatly reduced below the uppermost layers, soil burrows are particularly suited to hibernation.

Other animals maintain their tissues at a constant temperature by internal metabolism. This group includes the birds and mammals. These *warm-blooded animals* possess a variety of adaptations to maintain a constant internal temperature. Fur, hair, and feathers act as insulation by trapping dead air spaces next to the skin surface, reducing heat loss to the surrounding air or water. A thick layer of fat will also provide excellent insulation (Figure 8.16). Other adaptations are for cooling—for example, sweating or panting uses the high latent heat of vaporization of water

---

Temperature affects physiological processes occurring in plant and animal tissues. In general, colder climates have fewer plant and animal species.

In addition to temperature and moisture, ecological factors of light intensity, length of the daylight period, length of the growing season, and wind duration and intensity act to determine plant and animal distribution patterns.

---

to remove heat. Heat loss is also facilitated by exposing blood-circulating tissues to the cooler surroundings. The seal's flippers and bird's feet serve this function.

Adaptations to temperature extremes can allow a species to exploit a potentially harsh environment. The caribou (Figure 8.1*a*) is but one of several species of large grazing mammals that can endure very cold temperatures. During the mild season, caribou graze the far northern tundra, then migrate southward to pass the winter in a less hostile environment.

Other Climatic Factors

The factor of light is also important in determining local plant distribution patterns. Some plants are adapted to bright sunlight, while others require shade (Figure 8.17). The amount of light available to a plant will depend in large part on the plant's position. Tree crowns in the upper layer of a forest receive maximum light but correspondingly reduce the amount available to lower layers. In extreme cases, forest trees so effectively cut off light that the forest floor is almost free of shrubs and smaller plants. In certain deciduous forests of midlatitudes, the period of early spring, before the trees are in leaf, is one of high light intensity at ground level, permitting the smaller plants to go through a rapid growth cycle. In summer these plants will largely disappear as the leaf canopy is completed. Other low plants in the same habitat require shade and do not appear until the leaf canopy is well developed.

Treated on a global basis, the factor of light available for plant growth varies by latitude. Duration of daylight in summer increases rapidly with higher latitude and reaches its maximum poleward of the arctic and antarctic circles, where the Sun may be above the horizon for 24 hours (see Figure 8.5). Although the

8.16 Alaskan brown bear
This brown bear, snacking on a salmon, is well-insulated against winter cold by a heavy coat and a layer of fat.

8.17 Sun-loving and shade-loving plants *Sun-loving spring flowers, including baby blue-eyes and California poppies, bloom in this open field near San Luis Opisbo, California (left). In contrast, the forest floor in this scene in the Great Smoky Mountains National Park is carpeted with shade-loving trillium flowers (right).*

growing season for plants is greatly shortened at high latitudes by frost, the rate of plant growth in the short frost-free summer is greatly accelerated by the prolonged daylight.

In midlatitudes, where vegetation is of a deciduous type, the annual rhythm of increasing and decreasing periods of daylight determines the timing of budding, flowering, fruiting, leaf shedding, and other vegetation activities. As to the importance of light intensity itself, even on overcast days there is sufficient light to permit most plants to carry out photosynthesis at their maximum rates.

Light also influences animal behavior. The day–night cycle controls the activity patterns of many animals. Birds, for example, are generally active during the day, whereas small foraging mammals, such as weasels, skunks, and chipmunks, are more active at night. Light also controls seasonal activity through *photoperiod,* or daylight length, in midlatitudes. As autumn days grow shorter and shorter, squirrels and other rodents hoard food for the coming winter season. Later, increasing photoperiod will trigger such activities as mating and reproduction in the spring.

Wind is also an important environmental factor in the structure of vegetation in highly exposed positions. Close to the timberline in high mountains and along the northern limits of tree growth in the arctic zone, trees are deformed by wind in such a way that the branches project from the lee side of the trunk only (flag shape) (see Figure 9.22). Some

trees may show trunks and branches bent to near-horizontal attitude, facing away from the prevailing wind direction. The effect of wind is to cause excessive drying, damaging the exposed side of the plant. The tree limit on mountainsides thus varies in elevation with degree of exposure of the slope to strong prevailing winds and will extend higher on lee slopes and in sheltered pockets.

Bioclimatic Frontiers

Taken separately or together, climatic factors of moisture, temperature, light, and wind can act to limit the distribution of plant and animal species. Biogeographers recognize that there is a critical level of climatic stress beyond which a species cannot survive and that there will be a geographic boundary marking the limits of the potential distribution of a species. Such a boundary is sometimes referred to as a **bioclimatic frontier.** Although the frontier is usually marked by a complex of climatic elements, it is sometimes possible to single out one climatic element related to soil water or temperature that coincides with it.

The distribution of ponderosa pine *(Pinus ponderosa)* in western North America provides an example (Figure 8.18). In this mountainous region, annual rainfall varies sharply with elevation. The 50 cm (20 in.) isohyet (rainfall contour) of annual total precipitation encloses most of the upland

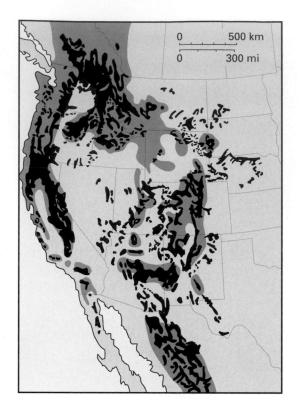

8.18   Distribution of ponderosa pine in western North America *Areas of ponderosa pine (Pinus ponderosa) are shown in black. The edge of the shaded area marks the rainfall contour (isohyet) of 50 cm (20 in.).*

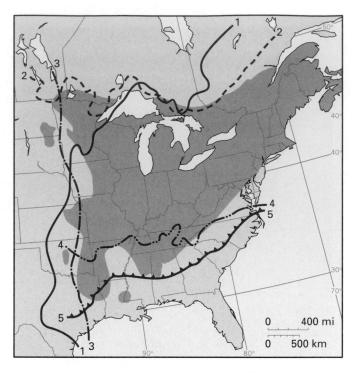

8.19   Bioclimatic limits of sugar maple *The shaded area shows the distribution of sugar maple (Acer saccharum) in eastern North America. Line 1, 75 cm (30 in.) annual precipitation. Line 2, –40°C (–40°F) mean annual minimum temperature. Line 3, eastern limit of yearly boundary between arid and humid climates. Line 4, 25 cm (10 in.) mean annual snowfall. Line 5, –10°C (16°F) mean annual minimum temperature.*

areas having the yellow pine. It is the parallelism of the isohyet with forest boundary, rather than actual degree of coincidence, that is significant. The sugar maple *(Acer saccharum)* is a somewhat more complex case (Figure 8.19). Here the boundaries on the north, west, and south coincide roughly with selected values of annual precipitation, mean annual minimum temperature, and mean annual snowfall.

Although bioclimatic limits must exist for all species, no plant or animal need necessarily be found at its frontier. Many other factors may act to keep the spread of a species in check. A species may be limited by diseases or predators found in adjacent regions. In another example, a species (especially a plant species) may migrate slowly and may still be radiating outward from the location in which it evolved. (More details will be given later.) Or a species may be dependent on another species and therefore be limited by the latter's distribution.

Geomorphic Factors

Geomorphic factors (landform factors) influencing ecosystems include such elements as slope steepness (the angle that the ground surface makes with respect to the horizontal), slope aspect (the orientation of a sloping ground surface with respect to geographic north), and relief (the differ-

---

Geomorphic (landform) factors influencing plant and animal distributions include slope angle, slope aspect, and relief. Edaphic (soil) factors include soil particle size (e.g., coarse sand or fine clay) and amount and nature of organic matter in the soil.

---

ence in elevation of divides and adjacent valley bottoms). In a much broader sense, geomorphic factors include the entire sculpturing of the landforms of a region by processes of erosion, transportation, and deposition via streams, waves, wind, and ice, and by forces of volcanism and mountain building. These are topics covered in detail in Chapters 13 through 19.

Slope steepness acts indirectly by influencing the rate at which precipitation is drained from the surface. On steep slopes, surface runoff is rapid. On gentle slopes, much of the precipitation can penetrate the soil and be retained. More rapid erosion on steep slopes may result in thin soil, whereas that on gentler slopes is thicker. Slope aspect has a direct influence on plants by increasing or decreasing the exposure to sunlight and prevailing winds. Slopes facing the Sun have a warmer, drier environment than slopes that face away from the Sun and therefore lie in shade for much longer periods of the day. In midlatitudes, these slope-aspect contrasts may be so strong as to produce quite different biotic communities on north-facing and south-facing slopes (Figure 8.20).

Geomorphic factors are in part responsible for the dryness or wetness of the habitat within a region that has

8.20 Eye on the Landscape Slope orientation and habitat *In this scene from the Chisos Mountains of Big Bend National Park, dry south-facing slopes on the left support a community of low, xerophytic shrubs, while moister north-facing slopes on the right support an open forest cover of piñon pine and juniper.* **What else would the geographer see? ... Answers at the end of the chapter.**

essentially the same overall climate. Each community has its own microclimate. On divides, peaks, and ridge crests, the soil tends to dryness because of rapid drainage and because the surfaces are more exposed to sunlight and drying winds. By contrast, the valley floors are wetter because surface runoff over the ground and into streams causes water to converge there. In humid climates, the ground water table in the valley floors may lie close to or at the ground surface to produce marshes, swamps, ponds, and bogs (see Chapter 15).

Edaphic Factors

Edaphic factors are those related to the soil. In terms of biogeography, we can look at soils from two perspectives. First, the broad pattern of soil types that we will recognize in Chapter 10 is largely related to climate, as is the broad pattern of distribution of plants and animals that we will see in Chapter 9. Thus, there is a strong coincidence between climate, soil, and biota at the global level. We'll return to this topic in those chapters.

A second viewpoint is in terms of habitats—the fine-scale mosaic of place-to-place variations of the Earth's sur-

face. Soils can vary widely from one small area to the next, thus influencing the local distribution of plants and animals. For example, sandy soils store less water than soils with abundant silt and clay, and thus often display a vegetation cover with xeric adaptations. A high content of organic matter in the soil often means nutrients are abundant rather than scarce. Such a rich soil usually harbors more plant species and allows them to grow more rapidly. We will return to some of the soil factors that are important to plants and animals in Chapter 10.

While soil conditions often affect the types of plants and animals found at a locality, the biota can also act to change the soil conditions. Given a barren habitat recently formed by some geologic event, such as the outpouring of lava or the emergence of a coastal zone from beneath the sea, the soil undergoes a gradual evolution with the occupance of the habitat by a succession of biotic communities. The plants alter the soil by such processes as contributing organic matter or producing acids that act on the mineral matter. Animal life, feeding on the plant life, also makes its contribution to the physical and chemical processes of soil evolution.

Disturbance

Another environmental factor affecting ecosystems is *disturbance,* which includes fire, flood, volcanic eruption, storm waves, high winds, and other infrequent catastrophic events that damage or destroy ecosystems and modify habitats. Although disturbance can greatly alter the nature of an ecosystem, it is often part of a natural cycle of regeneration that provides opportunities for short-lived or specialized species to grow and reproduce. In this way, disturbance is often a natural process to which many ecosystems are adapted.

> Disturbance, by such factors as fire, flooding, or high winds, is a natural process to which many ecosystems are adapted. In semiarid regions, fires act to maintain grasslands and open forests.

For example, *fire* is a phenomenon that strikes most forests sooner or later. In many cases, the fire is beneficial. It cleans out the understory and consumes dead and decaying organic matter while leaving most of the overstory trees untouched. On the forest floor, mineral soil is exposed and fertilized with new ash, providing a productive environment for dormant seeds. Sunlight is also abundant, with shrubs and forbs no longer shading the soil. Among tree species, pines are typically well adapted to germinating under such conditions. In fact, the jack pine of eastern North America and the lodgepole pine of the intermountain West have cones that remain tightly closed until the heat of a fire opens them, allowing the seeds to be released. These species are thus directly dependent on fire to maintain their geographic range and importance in the ecosystem. In the Rockies and boreal forests, there are many patches, large and small, of jack pine and lodgepole pine of different ages that document a long history of burns. These stands also serve as specialized habitats for particular insects, birds, and mammals.

Fires are also important to the preservation of grasslands. Grasses have extensive root systems below ground and germinal buds located at or just below the surface, making them quite fire-resistant. However, woody plants are not so resistant and are usually killed by grassfires. Most grasslands are dependent to some degree on fire for their maintenance. In Mediterranean climates, chaparral vegetation is also adapted to regular burning.

In many regions, active fire suppression has reduced the frequency of burning to well below natural levels. In forests, this causes dead wood to build up on the forest floor. When a fire does start, it burns hotter and more rapidly and consumes the crowns of many overstory trees. Once beneficial, fire is now destructive, leaving only a charred landscape of blackened soil at the mercy of erosion. In most cases, the forest comes back to health, but it may take many years.

Fires, both natural and human-induced, have effects well beyond the area burned. Smoke released from fires is a major source of air pollution in areas where there is a dry season of frequent fires. Gases released by combustion, including sulfur and nitrogen oxides, enhance the greenhouse effect and thus add to global climate warming. *Focus on Remote Sensing 8.2 • Remote Sensing of Fires* shows how remote sensing is used to monitor the global occurrence of fires.

Although fire is an obvious and frequent type of disturbance, other types are also important. Flooding, in addition to displacing animal communities, deprives plant roots of oxygen. Where flooding brings a swift current, mechanical damage rips limbs from trees and scours out roots. Frequent flooding, for example, along the banks of major rivers, often limits the vegetation cover to species that are resistant to such effects.

High winds can blow down large areas of forest, uprooting trees and setting up conditions for large fires after a few years of decay of the fallen trees. High winds also bring destructive waves to coral reefs, as well as sand and scouring to bays and coastal marshes. At a fine spatial scale, disturbance includes the fall of individual trees or large limbs within forests, creating light openings for shaded species in the understory to fill. Even animal wallows can provide unique habitats of disturbance.

GEODISCOVERIES **Remote Sensing and Biosphere Interactivity.** See disturbance at work by analyzing satellite images of fires and deforestation from Los Alamos to Madagascar.

Interactions among Species

Species interactions can also be important factors in determining the distribution patterns of plants and animals. Two species that are part of the same ecosystem can interact with one another in three ways: interaction may be negative to one or both species; or the two species may be neutral, not affecting each other; or interaction may be positive, benefiting at least one of the species.

Competition between species, a negative interaction, occurs whenever two species require a common resource that is in short supply. Because neither species has full use of the resource, both populations suffer, showing growth rates lower than those when only one of the species is present. Sometimes one species will win the competition and crowd out its competitor. At other times, the two species may remain in competition indefinitely.

Competition between species is an unstable situation. If a genetic strain within one of the populations emerges that uses a substitute resource for which there is no competition, its survival rate will be higher than that of the remaining strain, which still competes. The original strain may become extinct. In this way, evolutionary mechanisms tend to reduce competition among species.

Predation and parasitism are other negative interactions between species. *Predation* occurs when one species feeds on another (Figure 8.21). The benefits are obviously positive to the predator species, which obtains energy for survival, and negative to the prey species. *Parasitism* occurs when one species gains nutrition from another, typically when the parasite organism invades or attaches to the body of the host in some way.

Although we tend to think of predation and parasitism as negative processes that benefit one species at the expense of the other, it may well be that these interactions are really

8.21 Predation *This giant anteater enjoys a lunch of Brazilian termites.*

beneficial in the long term to the host or prey populations. A classic example is the growth of the deer herd on the Kaibab Plateau north of the Grand Canyon in Arizona (Figure 8.22). Initially at a population of about 4000, in an area of 283,000 hectares (700,000 acres), the herd grew to nearly 100,000 in the short span of 1907–1924 in direct proportion to a government predator control and game protection program. Wolves became extinct in the area, and populations of coyotes and mountain lions were greatly reduced. The huge deer population, however, proved too much for the land, and overgrazing led to a population crash. In one year, half the animals starved to death; by the late 1930s, the population had declined to a stable level near 10,000. Thus, predation maintained the deer population at levels that were in harmony with the supportive ability of the environment. In addition to maintenance of equilibrium population levels, predation and parasitism differentially remove the weaker individuals and can improve the genetic composition of the species.

A third type of predation is *herbivory,* in which grazing of plants by animals reduces the viability of the plant species population. Some species are well-adapted to grazing and can maintain themselves well in the face of grazing pressure. Others may be quite sensitive to this process. When overgrazing occurs, these differing sensitivities can produce significant changes in the structure and composition of plant communities.

A fourth type of negative interaction is *allelopathy,* a phenomenon of the plant kingdom in which chemical toxins produced by one species serve to inhibit the growth of others. As an example, sage, a common shrub species in the California chaparral, produces leaves rich in volatile toxins (cineole and camphor). As the leaves fall and accumulate in the soil, the

> Negative interactions among species include competition, predation, parasitism, herbivory, and allelopathy. Positive interaction includes commensalism, protocooperation, and mutualism, which are three forms of symbiosis.

allelopathic toxins build to a level sufficient to inhibit the growth of herbaceous plants, such as grasses, which are thus only found in adjacent areas. Still other chaparral shrubs produce water-soluble antibiotics that also inhibit the growth of nearby grasses. These chemical defenses, however, are broken down by periodic fires, which are events essential to maintenance of the chaparral ecosystem. The fires destroy the toxins and also trigger the germination of seeds of many species of annual herbaceous plants by breaking their seed coats. The annuals then dominate the area until the shrubs grow and force them out by allelopathy, beginning the cycle anew.

The term **symbiosis** includes three types of positive interactions between species: commensalism, protocooperation,

8.22 Rise and fall of the Kaibab deer herd *This graph plots the population size of the deer herd in the Kaibab National Forest, Arizona, as it rose in response to the abolition of predators and then crashed when the population ran out of food. (After D. I. Rasmussen, Ecological Monographs, vol. 11, 1941, p. 237.)*

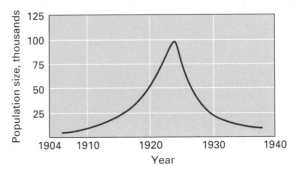

Focus on Remote Sensing | **8.2**

Remote Sensing of Fires

Wildfires occur frequently on the Earth's land surface, and biomass burning has important effects on both local and global ecosystems. Biomass burns inefficiently, releasing not only carbon dioxide and water, but also a number of other greenhouse gases that absorb outgoing longwave radiation and enhance the greenhouse effect. Aerosols are another byproduct of inefficient combustion that can effect atmospheric processes. Burning mobilizes such nutrients as nitrogen, phosphorus, and sulfur in ash so that they become available for a new generation of plants, but it also carries them upward in smoke and as gases. Fire affects ecosystems by changing species composition and creating a patchy structure of diversity on the landscape. It can also stimulate runoff and soil erosion where a significant layer of vegetation is lost to fire. For these reasons and more, monitoring of fires by remote sensing is a topic of intense interest to global change researchers.

Fires can be remotely sensed in several ways. Thermal imagers detect active fires as bright spots because they emit more heat energy than normal surfaces. However, fires may be obscured under clouds. Smoke plumes can also identify the location of fires but are hard to distinguish from clouds in some images. Fire scars can also be detected, especially using mid-infrared bands.

Image (*a*) shows the Earth as imaged by NASA's Moderate Resolution Imaging Spectroradiometer (MODIS) in true color on August 23, 2000. Superimposed on the true color browse image are red squares indicating high temperatures as sensed by MODIS thermal bands. The inset images highlight fires in the Amazon basin, southern Africa, and Australia. Image (*b*) is a MODIS image of bush fires in northern Australia on October 2, 2000. Inset into the Gulf of Carpentaria is a closeup of one of the

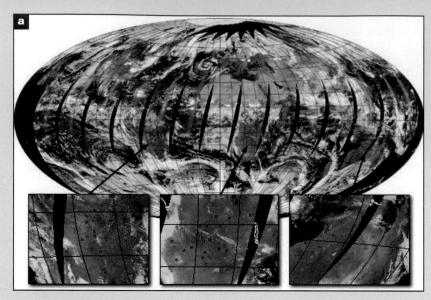

MODIS fire browse image *Global MODIS coverage for August 23, 2000, displayed in true color. (MODIS Land Team/C. Justice/L. Giglio/J. Descloitres/NASA.)*

larger ones. The red outlines identify pixels where fire has been detected. The dark burn scar and smoke plumes are readily visible.

Images (*c*) and (*d*) show Los Alamos, New Mexico, from Landsat-7 before and after the Cerro Grande Fire of May, 2000. Over

Australian bush fires from MODIS *Fires in north-central Australia, shown in true color. Red outlines identify pixels flagged as burning by thermal bands. (MODIS Land Team/C. Justice/L. Giglio/J. Descloitres/NASA)*

Los Alamos on April 14, 2000 *(Robert Simmon, NASA GSFC.)*

Los Alamos on June 17, 2000, after the fire *(Robert Simmon, NASA GSFC.)*

20,000 people were forced to flee their homes as this disastrous fire progressed, and more than 200 homes were consumed by the flames. The images are composites of mid-infrared, near-infrared, and green Landsat bands assigned colors of red, green, and blue, respectively. Green colors show vegetation, with the brightest green identifying the dense grass of golf courses. Blue and purplish tones are developed areas. The strong red color in the June image identifies the burned area, which is very dark in green and near-infrared bands, but bright in the mid-infrared. The blue stripes on the left edge of the April image (*c*) are ski runs covered with snow. They appear bright green due to their grass cover in June.

Like MODIS, the SeaWiFS instrument produces a wide view of the Earth's surface that can detect the smoke from fires. Image (*e*) is a true color image of the southeastern United States acquired by the instrument from a track over west Texas on February 5, 2001. The view is to the east, along the Gulf coast from Texas to Florida. Dozens of smoke plumes are clearly visible. The Mississippi River valley crosses the center of the image from left to right as an area of light-colored fallow soils. Louisiana's Mississippi Delta is an obvious coastal feature, with a plume of fresh sediment extending out into the Gulf of Mexico.

Southeastern U.S. from SeaWiFS
This oblique view of the Gulf Coast from the SeaWiFS imager aboard the OrbView-2 satellite shows numerous smoke plumes. (Image courtesy SeaWiFS Project, NASA/Goddard Space Flight Center, and ORBIMAGE.)

and mutualism. In commensalism, one of the species is benefited and the other is unaffected. Examples of commensals include the epiphytic plants—such as orchids or Spanish moss—which live on the branches of larger plants (Figure 9.4c). These *epiphytes* depend on their hosts for physical support only. In the animal kingdom, small commensal crabs or fishes seek shelter in the burrows of sea worms; or the commensal remora fish attaches itself to a shark, feeding on bits of leftover food as its host dines.

When the relationship benefits both parties but is not essential to their existence, it is termed protocooperation. The attachment of a stinging coelenterate to a crab is an example of protocooperation. The crab gains camouflage and an additional measure of defense, while the coelenterate eats bits of stray food which the crab misses.

Where protocooperation has progressed to the point that one or both species cannot survive alone, the result is mutualism. A classic example is the association of the nitrogen-fixing bacterium *Rhizobium* with the root tissue of certain types of plants (legumes), in which the action of the bacteria converts nitrogen gas to a form directly usable by the plant. The association is mutualistic because *Rhizobium* cannot survive alone.

ECOLOGICAL SUCCESSION

The phenomenon of change in plant and animal communities through time is a familiar one. A drive in the country reveals patches of vegetation in many stages of development—from open, cultivated fields through grassy shrublands to forests. Clear lakes, gradually filled with sediment from the rivers that drain into them, become bogs. These kinds of changes, in which biotic communities succeed one another are referred to as **ecological succession.**

GEODISCOVERIES **Succession.** View this animation to see the sequence of successional changes that occur when a beaver dam turns a low valley in the boreal forest into a bog.

In general, succession leads to formation of the most complex community of organisms possible in an area, given its physical controlling factors of climate, soil, and water. The series of communities that follow one another on the way to the stable stage is called a *sere*. Each of the temporary communities is referred to as a *seral stage*. The stable community, which is the end point of succession, is the **climax.** If succession begins on a newly constructed deposit of mineral sediment, it is termed *primary succession*. If succession occurs on a previously vegetated area that has been recently disturbed by such agents as fire, flood, windstorm, or humans, it is referred to as *secondary succession*.

A new site on which primary succession occurs may have one of several origins—for example, a sand dune, a sand beach, the surface of a new lava flow or freshly fallen layer of volcanic ash, or

the deposits of silt on the inside of a river bend that is gradually shifting. Such a site will not have a well-developed soil. Rather, it may perhaps be little more than a deposit of coarse mineral fragments. In other cases, such as that of floodplain silt deposits, the surface layer may represent redeposited soil endowed with substantial amounts of organic matter and nutrients.

The first stage of a succession is a *pioneer stage*. It includes a few plant and animal species unusually well adapted to adverse conditions of rapid water drainage and drying of soil and to excessive exposure to sunlight, wind, and extreme ground and lower-air temperatures. As pioneer plants grow, their roots penetrate the soil, and their subsequent decay adds organic matter directly to the soil. Fallen leaves and stems add an organic layer to the ground surface. Bacteria and animals begin to live in the soil in large numbers. Grazing mammals feed on the small plants. Birds forage the newly vegetated area for seeds and grubs.

Soon conditions are favorable for other species that invade the area and displace the pioneers. The new arrivals may be larger plant forms providing more extensive cover of foliage over the ground. In this case the climate near the ground is considerably altered toward one of less extreme air and soil temperatures, high humidities, and less intense insolation. Still other species now invade and thrive in the modified environment. When the succession has finally run its course, a climax community of plant and animal species in a more or less stable composition will exist.

The colonization of a sand dune provides an example of primary succession. Growing foredunes bordering the ocean or lake shore present a sterile habitat. The dune sand—usually largely quartz, feldspar, and other common rock-forming minerals—lacks such important nutrients as nitrogen, calcium, and phosphorus, and its water-holding ability is very low. Under the intense solar radiation of the day, the dune surface is a hot, drying environment. At night, radiation cooling in the absence of moisture produces low surface temperatures.

One of the first pioneers of this extreme environment is beachgrass (Figure 8.23, left). This plant reproduces by sending out rhizomes (creeping underground stems), and the plant thus slowly spreads over the dune. Beachgrass is well adapted to the eolian environment; it does not die when buried by moving sand, but instead puts up shoots to reach the new surface.

After colonization, the shoots of beachgrass act to form a baffle that suppresses movement of sand, and thus the dune becomes more stable. With increasing stabilization, plants that are more adapted to the dry, extreme environment but cannot withstand much burial begin to colonize the dune. Typically, these are low, matlike woody shrubs, such as beach wormwood or false heather.

On older beach and dune ridges of the central Atlantic coastal plain, the species that follow matlike shrubs are typically larger woody plants and such

---

In the process of ecological succession, an ecosystem proceeds through seral stages to reach a climax. Primary succession occurs on new soil, while secondary succession occurs where disturbance has removed or altered existing communities.

8.23 Dune succession at Sandy Hook, New Jersey *(left) Beachgrass is a pioneer on beach dunes and helps stabilize the dune against wind erosion. (right) The climax forest on dunes. Holly (Ilex opaca), seen on the left, is an important constituent of the climax forest. Note the leaves and decaying organic matter on the forest floor. (Alan Strahler)*

trees as beach plum, bayberry, poison ivy, and choke cherry. These species all have one thing in common—their fruits are eaten by birds. The seeds are excreted as the birds forage among the low dune shrubs, thereby sowing the next stage of succession. As the scrubby bushes and small trees spread, they shade out the mat-like shrubs and any remaining beachgrass. Pines may also enter at this stage.

At this point, the soil begins to accumulate a significant amount of organic matter. No longer dry and sterile, it now possesses organic compounds and nutrients, and it has accumulated enough fine particles to hold water for longer intervals. These soil conditions encourage the growth of such

broadleaf species as red maple, hackberry, holly, and oaks, which shade out the existing shrubs and small trees (Figure 8.23, right). Once the forest is established, it tends to reproduce itself; the species of which it is composed are tolerant to shade, and their seeds can germinate on the organic forest floor. Thus, the climax is reached. The stages through which the ecosystem has developed constitute the sere, progressing from beachgrass to low shrubs to higher shrubs and small trees to forest.

Although this example has stressed the changes in plant cover, animal species are also changing as succession proceeds. Table 8.2 shows how some typical invertebrates

Table 8.2 | Invertebrate Succession on the Lake Michigan Dunes

Invertebrate	Beachgrass–Cottonwood	Jack Pine Forest	Black Oak Dry Forest	Oak and Oak–Hickory Moist Forest	Beech–Maple Forest Climax
White tiger beetle	x				
Sand spider	x				
Long-horn grasshopper	x	x			
Burrowing spider	x	x			
Bronze tiger beetle		x			
Migratory locust		x			
Ant lion			x		
Flatbug			x		
Wireworms			x	x	x
Snail			x	x	x
Green tiger beetle				x	x
Camel cricket				x	x
Sowbugs				x	x
Earthworms				x	x
Woodroaches				x	x
Grouse locust					x

Source: V. E. Shelford, as presented in E. P. Odum, *Fundamentals of Ecology* (Philadelphia: W. B Saunders Co.), p. 259.

appear and disappear through succession on the Lake Michigan dunes. Note that the seral stages shown in the table for these inland dunes are somewhat different from those described for the coastal environment.

Where disturbance alters an existing community, secondary succession can occur. *Old-field succession,* taking place on abandoned farmland, is a good example of secondary succession. In the eastern United States, the first stages of the sere often depend on the last use of the land before abandonment. If row crops were last cultivated, one set of pioneers, usually annuals and biennials, will appear. If small grain crops were cultivated, the pioneers are often perennial herbs and grasses. If pasture is abandoned, those pioneers that were not grazed will have a head start. Where mineral soil was freshly exposed by plowing, pines are often important following the first stages of succession because pine seeds favor disturbed soil and strong sunlight for germination. Although slower-growing than other pioneers, the pines will eventually shade the others out and become dominant. Their dominance is only temporary, however, because their seeds cannot germinate in shade and litter on the forest floor. Seeds of hardwoods such as maples and oaks can germinate under these conditions, and as the pines die, hardwood seedlings grow quickly to fill the holes produced in the canopy. The climax, then, is the hardwood forest. Figure 8.24 is a schematic diagram showing this example of old-field succession. Figure 8.25 presents photos of old-field succession in eastern Pennsylvania. Here, pines are less prominent in the succession process.

Succession, Change, and Equilibrium

The successional changes we have described result from the actions of the plants and animals themselves. One set of inhabitants paves the way for the next. As long as nearby populations of species provide colonizers, the changes lead automatically from bare soil or fallow field to climax forest. This type of succession is often termed *autogenic* (self-producing) *succession.*

In many cases, however, autogenic succession does not run its full course. Environmental disturbances, such as wind, fire, flood, or renewed clearing for agriculture, may occur, diverting the course of succession temporarily or even permanently. For example, autogenic succession on seaside dunes may proceed for some years, but sooner or later a severe storm will generate waves and wind that reduce the developing community to a sand bar once again. Or a mature forest may be destroyed by fire, inviting the succession of plants and animals that are specifically adapted to burned environments. *Eye on the Environment 8.3 • The Great Yellowstone Fire* describes the fires that swept the forests of Yellowstone National Park in 1988 and explains the role of fire in the dynamics of the western forest ecosystem. In addition, habitat conditions such as site exposure, unusual bedrock, or impeded drainage can hold back or divert the course of succession so successfully that the climax is never reached.

Introduction of new species can also greatly alter existing ecosystems and successional pathways. The parasitic chestnut blight, introduced from Europe to New York in about 1910, decimated populations of the American chestnut tree within a period of about 40 years. This tree species, which may have accounted for as many as one-fourth of the mature trees in eastern forests, is now found only as small blighted stems sprouting from old root systems.

These examples show that while succession is a reasonable model to explain many of the changes that we see in ecosystems with time, it may be more realistic to view the pattern of ecosystems on the landscape as reflecting a spatial dynamic equilibrium between autogenic forces of self-

8.24 Old-field succession *A typical old-field succession sequence for the southeastern United States, following abandonment of cultivated fields. This is a pictorial graph of continuously changing plant composition spanning about 150 years.*

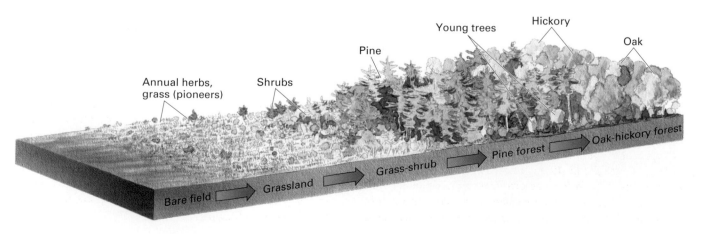

induced change and external forces that reverse or rechannel autogenic change temporarily or permanently. From this viewpoint, the biotic landscape is thus a mosaic of patches of distinctive biotic communities with different biological potentials and different histories.

This view of the landscape assumes that all successional species are always available to colonize new space or invade seral communities. The nature of the biotic communities that we see will then be determined by varying environmental and ecological factors as they act within new space created by physical and human processes. But what about the continental and global scale, taken over longer spans of time? Here, not all species are available to colonize new space. On this scale, the processes of migration, dispersal, evolution, and extinction are more important in determining the spatial patterns we observe. These processes are within the realm of historical biogeography, to which we turn next.

We can view the pattern of plant and animal communities on the landscape as a dynamic equilibrium between succession, in which the community modifies its own habitat and composition, and environmental disturbance, such as wind, flood, fire, or logging.

HISTORICAL BIOGEOGRAPHY

Historical biogeography focuses on how spatial distribution patterns of organisms arise over space and time. It examines four key processes: evolution, speciation, extinction, and dispersal. Let's look at each of these in turn, beginning with evolution.

Evolution

An astonishing number of organisms exist on Earth, each adapted to the ecosystem in which it carries out its life cycle. About 40,000 species of microorganisms, 350,000 species of plants, and 2.2 million species of animals, including some 800,000 insect species, have been described and identified. However, many organisms remain unclassified. Estimates suggest that species of plants will ultimately number about 540,000. Of an estimated 2 million insect species, only slightly more than one-third have been classified.

How has life gained this astonishing diversity? Through the process of **evolution,** the environment itself has acted on organisms to create this diversity of life-forms, even as organic processes have been a prime factor in shaping the environment. You are probably familiar with the name of Sir Charles Darwin, whose monumental work, *The Origin of Species by Means of Natural Selection,* was published in 1859. Through exhaustive studies, Darwin showed that all life possessed *variation,* the differences that arise between parent and offspring. The environment acts on variation in organisms, Darwin observed, in much the same way that a

---

Natural selection acts on the variation that occurs within populations of species to produce evolution. Variation is produced by mutation, in which genetic material is altered, and recombination, in which new combinations of existing genetic material arise.

---

plant or animal breeder does, selecting for propagation only those individuals with the best qualities, those best suited to their environment. Darwin termed this survival and reproduction of the fittest **natural selection.** He saw that variation could, when acted upon by natural selection through time, bring about the formation of new species whose individuals differed greatly from their ancestors. Thus, Darwin viewed the formation of new species as a product of variation acted upon by natural selection.

The weakness in Darwin's theory lay not in the origin of species as products of natural selection, but in the process of variation. He was at a loss to explain why variation occurred, and he simply accepted it as a natural and an automatic property of life. We know now that variation results from the interaction of two sources: *mutation,* which alters the genetic material and consequently the physical characteristics of organisms; and *recombination,* the pairing of parental genetic material in offspring in unique assortments.

Mutation results when the genetic material (DNA, or deoxyribonucleic acid) of a reproductive cell is changed. This requires breaking and reassembling chemical bonds in the DNA of chromosomes, which can come about when the cell is exposed to heat, ionizing radiation, or to certain types of chemical agents. Most mutations either have no effect or are deleterious, but a small proportion may have a positive effect on the genetic makeup of the individual. If that positive effect makes the individual organism more likely to survive and reproduce, then the altered gene is likely to survive as well and be passed on to offspring.

Recombination describes the process by which an offspring receives two slightly different copies, or *alleles,* of each gene from its parents. One allele may be dominant and suppress the other, or the two alleles may act simultaneously. Because each individual receives two alleles of each gene, and there are typically tens of thousands of genes in an organism, the possible number of genetic combinations is very large. Thus, recombination provides a constant source of variation that acts to make every offspring slightly different from the next.

Mutations act to change the nature of species through time. But just what is a species? For our purposes here, we can define a **species** (plural, *species*) as all individuals capable of interbreeding to produce fertile offspring. A *genus* (plural, *genera*) is a collection of closely related species that share a similar genetic evolutionary history. Note that each species has a scientific name, composed of a generic name and a specific name in combination. Thus, red oak, a common deciduous tree of eastern North America, is *Quercus rubra.* The related white oak is *Quercus alba* (Figure 8.26).

a...*Early stage* When cultivation ceases, grasses and forbs colonize the bare soil. Invading tree and shrub species begin acquiring a foothold. This scene is about 10 years or more after abandonment, Pocono Mountains, Pennsylvania.

b...*Woody pioneers* In this scene from northeastern Pennsylvania, red cedar, locust, and pine are now established. About 20 years or more after abandonment.

c...Advance of the forest A decade or two later, the cedars are larger and broadleaf deciduous species (wild cherry, red maple) are becoming more prominent. Delaware Water Gap National Recreation Area, Pennsylvania.

d...Mature second growth forest After several more decades, the deciduous hardwoods shade out the conifers. Maple and birch, which are well adapted to a dense forest environment, increase, and the forest canopy becomes nearly closed. The old stone fence marks the boundary between former fields. Pennsylvania.

Eye on the Environment | 8.3

The Great Yellowstone Fire

Yellowstone is the largest and oldest American national park. Thanks in part to the magnificent photographs of its wondrous geysers and travertine terraces, taken by the pioneer photographer, William Henry Jackson, and brought back to Congress in Washington, it was declared a park in 1872. Almost a square in outline, its 900,000 hectares (2.2 million acres) occupy the northwest corner of Wyoming within the Rocky Mountain region. Volcanic rocks dominate the geology, and lava flows occupy much of the area, forming a high plateau. Because an ancient caldera underwent collapse here, geothermal activity continues to this day in many localities in the park. (See Chapter 13 and Figures 13.10 and 13.11.) Its rich, well-watered forests and parks support populations of bison, elk, and grizzly bear, along with many other mammal and bird species—a powerful attraction for millions of tourists. All in all, we have here a priceless forest ecosystem, little disturbed by natural catastrophe or human interference for at least the past two centuries.

Through August and September of 1988, many forest fires burned out of control in Yellowstone Park,

casting a smoke pall over large areas of surrounding states. Of the 45 fires, most were started by lightning strikes, and this number was not unusual for the area. It had, however, been the driest summer for more than a century of record, and temperatures were persistently high. Once started, the fires spread rapidly and uncontrollably under the driving force of strong winds that in one fire reached 160 km (100 mi) per hour. Firefighters were powerless to check the spread of the flames. Dense forests of lodgepole pine that had not burned for 250 years were killed by flames that raced through the forest canopy. Fires at ground level spread rapidly through areas of older forest with ample fuel supplies accumulated as fallen trees and branches. The fires also consumed patches of young forest that rarely ignite and have typically served well as natural firebreaks.

Contrary to greatly exaggerated stories in the news media, a later study of air photographs showed that only 20 percent of the park land had been burned over in some degree. Fears of massive extermination of wildlife were also unfounded. Most of the large ani-

mals survived: only 9 bison of the herd of 2500 and 350 elk of the herd of 30,000 perished in the fires. Mammals large and small, along with insects and birds, returned quickly to the burned areas, with the herbivores taking advantage of grasses that grew vigorously among the ashes of the forest floor.

For a full century since the establishment of Yellowstone Park in 1872, the National Park Service had practiced its "no-burn" policy of not allowing any fire to spread unchecked. This policy was based on the concept that national parks must be maintained in a pristine condition, their plants being permitted to grow and die unaffected by any human activity or by fires. In 1972, this practice was reversed to a "let-burn" policy under which naturally occurring fires were to be allowed to spread unchecked. As expected, the Park Service immediately came under strong criticism for having practiced their let-burn policy by standing aside and allowing the July blazes to spread to mammoth proportions. By late July, park officials decided to suppress all fires, but a massive effort with national support was to no avail. In retrospect, however, it is question-

8.26 Red and white oaks *Although similar in general appearance, these two species of oak are easily separated. Red oak acorns have a flat cap and stubby nut, with pointed, bristle tips on the leaf lobes (left). White oak acorns have a deeper cap and a pointed nut, with rounded leaf-lobe tips (right).*

Yellowstone fire and recovery   *The fires that ravaged Yellowstone National Park in 1988 completely destroyed many stands of trees (left). After 10 years, however, natural regeneration had started new forests to take their place (right).*

able whether immediate action to put out the first fires could have made much difference over the vast area of the park. Another carefully drawn conclusion following study of the fire by forest ecologists was that the additional fuel accumulated in the 100-year "no-burn" period made only a minor difference in the extent and intensity of the 1988 fire.

Ecologists view the occurrence of a season of great fires in Yellowstone Park about every 250 to 300 years as part of a natural cycle of fire-driven ecological succession. Following such a fire, saplings of lodgepole pine occupy the burned area, growing tall and closely set to form a dense crown canopy, enduring between 150 and 250 years after the initial fire. During this phase, large canopy burns can occur, restarting the succession. If no fire occurs, the succession continues with a dying out of the pines and the growth of a new generation of other tree species, such as the spruce and fir. By this time—more than 300 years from the start—the forest floor becomes highly flammable and can be readily swept by fire to restart the succession.

Recent studies have established that the natural succession described above affects isolated patches of the entire forested region, resulting in a mosaic of patches in different stages of succession. In this mosaic, the younger patches serve as natural firebreaks to limit the spread of a fire occurring in adjacent older patches. Wildlife is thus able to escape the fires and then reinhabits the burned area, where a new ground cover of grasses and shrubs provides food for the grazing herbivores. This natural process of fire and renewal is important to the maintenance of other types of ecosystems as well, including the tall-grass prairies of Kansas, the pine forests of the southeastern United States, and much of the Canadian boreal forest.

Although the true test of the species is the ability of all of its individuals to reproduce successfully with one another, this criterion is not always easily applied. Instead, the species is usually defined by *morphology*—the outward form and appearance of its individuals. The *phenotype* of an individual is the morphological expression of its gene set, or *genotype,* and includes all the physical aspects of its structure that are readily perceivable. Species, then, are usually defined by a characteristic phenotype or range of phenotypes.

Speciation

Biogeographers use the term **speciation** to refer to the process by which species are differentiated and maintained. Actually, speciation is not the result of a single process but arises from a number of component processes acting together through time. One of these component processes is mutation, which we have already described. The rate of mutation depends on the organism's exposure to mutagenic agents as well as the organism's sensitivity to those agents. Another process is natural selection, which as we have seen acts to favor individuals with genotypes that produce successful traits for a particular environment.

A third speciation process is *genetic drift*. In this process, chance mutations without any particular beneficial effect change the genetic composition of a breeding population until it diverges from other populations. Genetic drift is a weak factor in large populations, but in small populations, such as a colony of a few pioneers in a new habitat, random mutations are more likely to be preserved. *Gene flow* is an opposite process in which evolving populations exchange alleles as individuals move among populations. This process helps maintain the uniformity of the gene pool of the species by moving new alleles into all populations.

Speciation often occurs when populations become isolated from one another. This **geographic isolation** can happen in several ways. For example, plate tectonics may uplift a mountain range that separates a population into two different subpopulations by a climatic barrier. Or a chance long-distance dispersal may establish a new population far from the main one. These are examples of *allopatric speciation,* in which populations are geographically isolated and gene flow between the populations does not take place. As genetic drift and natural selection proceed, the populations gradually diverge and eventually lose the ability to interbreed successfully.

> **Speciation is the process by which species are differentiated and maintained. Component processes affecting speciation include mutation, natural selection, genetic drift, and gene flow. Isolation, in which breeding populations are separated, enhances speciation.**

The evolution of finch species on the Galápagos Islands is an example of allopatric speciation created by isolation and natural selection (Figure 8.27). This cluster of five major volcanic islands and nine lesser ones, located about 800 km (500 mi) from the coast of Ecuador, was visited by Charles Darwin and provided much raw material for his ideas about evolution. As the story has been reconstructed, the islands were first colonized by a single original finch species, the blue-black grassquit. Over time, individual populations became adapted to conditions on particular islands through natural selection, and, enhanced by their isolation on different islands, evolved into different species. Later, some of these species successfully reinvaded other islands, continuing the

8.27 Adaptive radiation of finch species of the Galápagos Islands
Five genera and 13 species of finch evolved from a single ancestral population of the blue-black grassquit. Beak shapes are adapted to the primary food source: seeds, buds, and insects. (From J. H. Brown and M. V. Lomolino, Biogeography, second ed., 1998, Sinauer, Sunderland, Massachusetts, used by permission.)

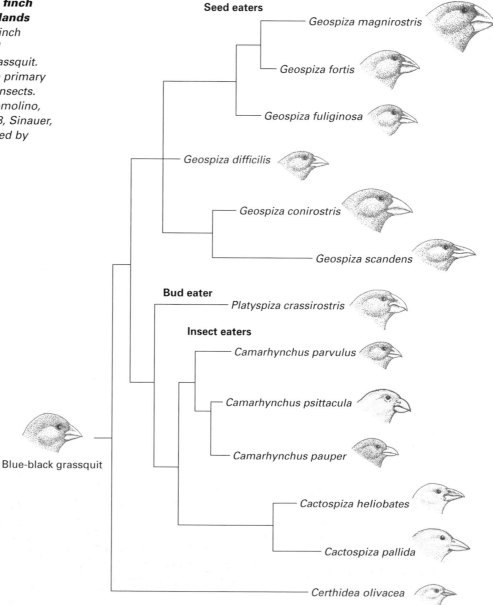

speciation and evolution process. Today 5 genera and 13 species of finches are found on the Galápagos, specializing in diets of seeds, buds, and insects.

Another example of allopatric speciation from the Galápagos is the giant tortoise (see chapter opener photo). Each of the larger islands bears at least one distinctly different population of these large reptiles. Like the finches, they are believed to be evolved from a single ancestral stock that colonized the island chain and then diverged into unique types.

In contrast to allopatric speciation is *sympatric speciation,* in which speciation occurs within a larger population. Imagine a species that has two different primary food sources. Eventually, mutations will arise that favor each food source at the expense of the other—for example, two different lengths or shapes of a bird's beak that facilitate feeding on two different types of fruit or seeds. As these mutations are exposed to natural selection, they will produce two different populations, each adapted to its own food source. Eventually, the populations may become separate species. For example, hundreds of species of cichlid fishes have evolved from a few founding stocks in the lakes of the African Rift Valley. Lake Victoria alone, which was dry as recently as about 12,000 years before present, supports more than 300 of these species. Although these populations have all been in contact in the same shallow lake, they have specialized and diverged through natural selection to the point of becoming individual species. This type of evolution, in which a new environment provides the opportunity for the formation of many new species adjusted to different habitats is termed *adaptive radiation.*

Another mechanism of sympatric speciation that is quite important in plants is **polyploidy.** Normal organisms have two sets of genes and chromosomes that is, they are *diploid.* Through accidents in the reproduction process, two closely related species can cross in such a way that the offspring has both sets of genes from both parents. These *tetraploids* are fertile but cannot reproduce with the populations from which they arose, and so they are instantly isolated as new species. By some estimates, 70 to 80 percent of higher plant species have arisen in this fashion.

Extinction

Over geologic time, the fate of all species is **extinction.** When conditions change more quickly than populations can evolve new adaptations, population size falls. When that occurs, the population becomes increasingly more vulnerable to chance occurrences, such as a fire, a rare climatic event, or an outbreak of disease. Ultimately, the population succumbs, and the species becomes extinct.

> **Extinction occurs when all individuals of a species die. If the environment changes too rapidly for a population to adjust by evolution, it dies out. Extreme events, such as the collision of an asteroid with the Earth about 65 million years ago, can cause mass extinctions.**

Some extinctions are very rapid, particularly those induced by human activity. A classic example is that of the passenger pigeon, which was a dominant bird of eastern North America in the late nineteenth century. Flying in huge flocks and feeding on seeds and fruits such as beechnuts and acorns, these birds were easily captured in nets and shipped to markets for food. By 1890, they were virtually gone, and the last known passenger pigeon died in the Cincinnati Zoo in 1914.

Rare but extreme events can also cause extinctions. Many lines of evidence have converged to document that the Earth was struck by an asteroid about 65 million years ago. The impact, which occurred on the continental shelf near the Yucatan Peninsula, raised a global dust cloud that blocked sunlight from the surface, cooling the Earth's climate intensely for a period of perhaps several years. Dinosaurs and many other groups of terrestrial and marine organisms were wiped out. Less affected were organisms that were less sensitive to a brief, but intense, period of cold. These included birds and mammals, which have internal metabolic temperature regulation, as well as seed plants and insects that pass part of their life cycle in a dormant state.

Dispersal

Nearly all types of organisms have some mechanism of **dispersal**—that is, a capacity of an individual to move from a location of origin to a new site. Often dispersal is confined to one life stage, as in the dispersal of higher plants as seeds. Even in animals that are inherently mobile, there is often a developmental stage when movement from one site to the next is more likely to occur.

> **Dispersal is the capacity to move from a location of origin to new sites. In diffusion, species extend their range slowly from year to year. In long-distance dispersal, unlikely events establish breeding populations at remote locations.**

Normally, dispersal does not change the geographic range of a species. Seeds fall near their sources, and animals seek out nearby habitats to which they are adjusted. Dispersal is thus largely a method for gene flow that helps to encourage the cross-breeding of organisms throughout a population. When land is cleared or new land is formed, dispersal moves colonists into the new environment. We documented this role of dispersal earlier in this chapter as part of succession. Species also disperse by *diffusion,* the slow extension of range from year to year.

A rare, long-distance dispersal event can be very significant in establishing biogeographic patterns. We have already noted how a single ancestral colony of finches invaded the Galápagos Islands and underwent adaptive radiation to populate all of the islands successfully.

Some species have modes of propagation that are especially well-adapted to long-distance dispersal. Mangrove species, which line coastal estuaries in equatorial and tropical regions, have

8.28 Red-footed falcon *In August of 2004, This small falcon was sighted for the first time in the western hemisphere at a grassy meadow airstrip on Martha's Vineyard Island, Massachusetts. Munching happily on butterflies, grasshoppers, and small voles, it remained at the airstrip for about two weeks before heading for parts unknown. The species normally winters in Africa and summers in eastern Europe.*

seeds that are carried thousands of miles on winds and ocean currents to populate far distant shores. Another example of a plant well adapted to oceanic dispersal is the coconut palm. Its large seed, housed in a floating husk, has made it a universal occupant of island beaches. Among the animals, birds, bats, and insects are frequent long-distance travelers (Figure 8.28). Generally, nonflying mammals, freshwater fishes, and amphibians are less likely to make long leaps, with rats and tortoises the exceptions.

The case of the cattle egret demonstrates both long-distance dispersal and diffusion (Figure 8.29). This small heron crossed the Atlantic, arriving in northeastern South America from Africa in the late 1880s. A hundred years later, it had become one of the most abundant herons of the Americas. Figure 8.30 maps its range extension over much of this period. Another example of diffusion is the northward colonization of the British Isles by oaks following the retreat of continental glaciers after the close of the Ice Age. As shown in Figure 8.31, oaks required about 3500 years, from about 9500 years before present to 6000 years before present, to reach their northern limit.

Dispersal often means surmounting *barriers*—that is, regions a species is unable to colonize or perhaps even occupy for a short period of time. Long-distance dispersal can mean bridging such obvious barriers as an ocean of salt water or an ice sheet by an unlikely accident. But other barriers are not so obvious. For example, the basin and range country of Utah, Nevada, and California presents a sea of desert with islands of forest to some diffusing species. While birds and bats may have no difficulty moving from one island to the next, a small mammal may never cross the desert sea, at least under its own power. In this case, the barrier is one in which the physiological limits of the species are exceeded. But there may be ecological barriers as well—for example, a zone of intense predation or a region occupied by strongly and successfully competing species.

8.29 Cattle egret *This small, white heron migrated from Africa to South America in the late 1880s. It follows grazing animals, such as this Texas steer, and feeds on insects and small invertebrates flushed by the grazing action.*

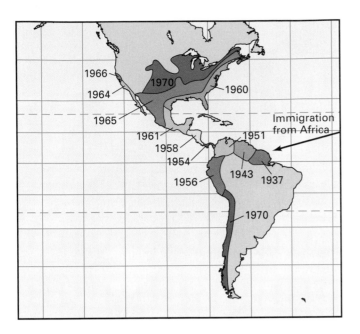

8.30 *Diffusion of the cattle egret* *After long-distance dispersal to northeastern South America, the cattle egret spread to Central and North America as well as to coastal regions of western South America. (From J. H. Brown and M. V. Lomolino, Biogeography, second ed., 1998, Sinauer, Sunderland, Massachusetts, used by permission.)*

Just as there are barriers to dispersal, so there are corridors that facilitate dispersal. Central America forms a present-day land bridge connecting North and South America, for example. It has been in place for about 3.5 million years. Other corridors of great importance to present-day species distribution patterns have existed in the recent past. For example, the Bering Strait region between Alaska and easternmost Siberia was dry land during the early Cenozoic Era (about 60 million years ago) and during the Ice Age, when sea level dropped by more than 100 m (325 ft). Many plant and animal species of Asia are known to have crossed this bridge and then spread southward into the Americas. One notable migrant species of the last continental glaciation was the aboriginal human, and there is substantial evidence to support the hypothesis that the skilled hunters who crossed the Bering land bridge were responsible for the extinction of many of the large animals, including wooly mammoths and ground sloths, that disappeared from the Americas about 10,000 years ago (Figure 8.32).

8.31 *Diffusion of oaks* *Following the retreat and melting of continental glaciers at the close of the Ice Age, oak species diffused northward across the British Isles. Contours indicate northern border at times in years before present. Dashed lines are less certain. (From H. J. B. Birks, J. Biogeography, vol. 16, pp. 503–540. Used by permission.)*

8.32 *Wooly mammoth* *A reconstruction of the wooly mammoth, a huge tusked mammal that inhabited North America throughout the Ice Age and became extinct about 10,000 years ago, most likely from hunting by prehistoric humans.*

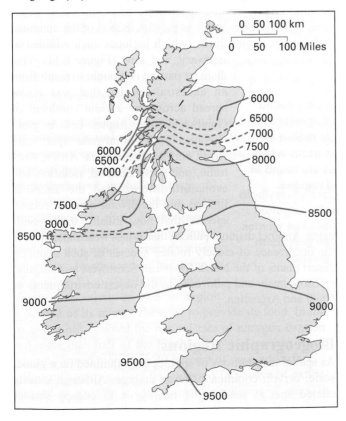

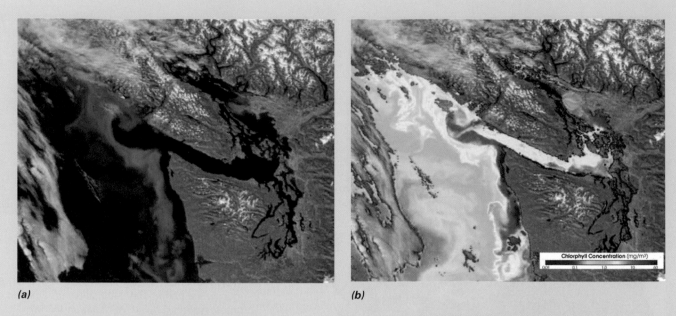

(a)

(b)

Figure 2   SeaWiFS views Puget Sound *(a) A true-color image of Puget Sound, Washington, and British Columbia, acquired on July 9, 2003. (b) Chlorophyll concentration on the same day. (SeaWiFS Project, NASA/GSFC/ORBIMAGE.)*

Global Productivity

Figure 3 shows a global map of net primary production of both land and oceans for 2002. The first thing to note is that net primary production is generally higher on land than in oceans. However, there is a lot more ocean surface than land surface. When this fact is taken into account, terrestrial and oceanic net primary production are about equal.

Looking at the ocean pattern, we see that large central areas of ocean are unproductive (dark purple). This is largely due to lack of essential nutrients in surface waters. Near land, and along

Figure 3   Global net primary productivity from MODIS for 2002 *This image maps global productivity, including both land and oceans, as viewed by the MODIS instruments on NASA's Terra and Aqua satellite platforms. (MODIS Science Team/NASA.)*

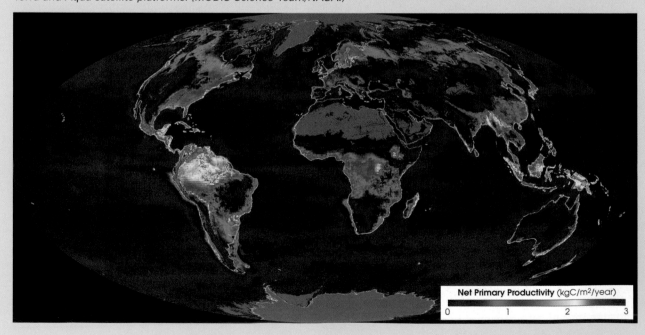

coasts where nutrient-rich deep water upwells from below, nutrients are in greater supply and oceans are more productive. As shown in Figure 22.8, upwelling is particularly important along west coasts—for example, the west coast of South America from Peru southward shows the dark and light blue tones that are more characteristic of land than ocean. Higher levels are also seen at high latitudes. In these regions, the thermocline (Chapter 7) that inhibits mixing of surface and deep waters is absent for much of the year, so nutrients are more abundant and net primary production is enhanced.

On land, the highest values of net primary production are shown by the yellow and red tones of the Amazon Basin and equatorial Asia. Lesser, but still high, values are encountered in eastern North America, central Africa, eastern Asia, and Scandinavia. Low values characterize arid and semiarid regions, such as the Kalahari Desert of southern Africa, the interior deserts of Australia, semiarid western North America, the Sahara, and the interior steppelands of Asia. (Gray areas show regions for which data are not available.)

Figure 4 shows net primary productivity for June 2002 *(a)* and December 2002 *(b)*. Comparing the two images, we see that ocean productivity patterns are much the same at low and midlatitudes, but quite different at high latitudes. Here, waters are significantly more productive in summer in each hemisphere. Over land, the June pattern shows the highest values of net primary productivity in the boreal and eastern continental zones of the northern hemisphere. These values are produced by the long days and warm temperatures of June. Productivity remains high in the Amazon and equatorial regions. In December, net primary production is high in South America and sub-Saharan Africa. Australia shows a significant green-up as equatorial Asia maintains high values. Meanwhile, most of northern North America and Eurasia are dormant.

Figure 4   *Global net primary productivity with the seasons* (a) Net primary productivity for June 2002 as derived from MODIS. (b) Net primary productivity for December 2002. (MODIS Science Team/NASA.)

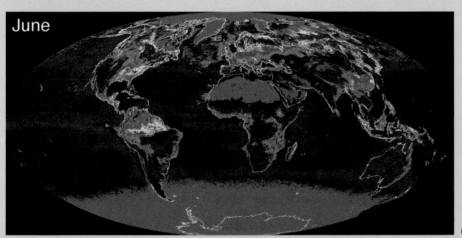

(a)

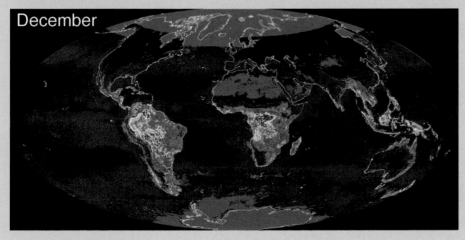

(b)

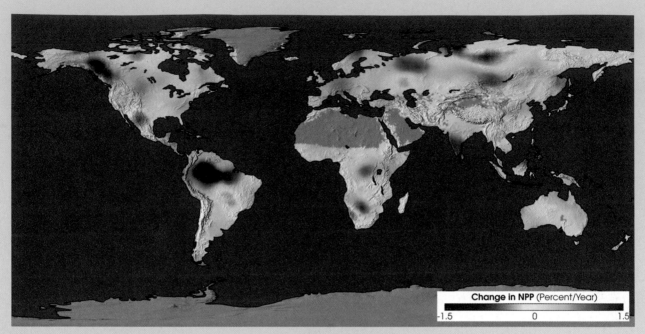

Figure 5 *Change in net primary productivity for land, 1982–1999* This image, constructed from images of NOAA's AVHRR instruments acquired from 1982 to 1999, shows the change in net primary productivity in units of percent per year. (R. Nemani and S. W. Running, University of Montana NTSG/NASA.)

Recent Changes in Global Productivity

In a recent study analyzing satellite images acquired by NOAA's Advanced Very High Resolution Radiometer (AVHRR) between 1982 and 1999, a team of scientists were able to map changes in land net primary productivity over the past two decades (Figure 5).[1] Overall, they showed that land productivity increased by about 6 percent during the two decades. As shown in the figure, the greatest increases occurred in equatorial and subtropical South America, Africa, and India. Large increases were also noted in northwestern North America and northern Russia, west of the Ural Mountains. By comparing these results with meteorological data, the scientists also showed that the increase at low latitudes was due to reduced cloud cover, which allowed more light for photosynthesis. At high latitudes, the causes were increased temperature, and, to some extent, increased water availability.

Over about the same time period, large changes in ocean phytoplankton concentration took place as well. Remote sensing scientists recently compared average chlorophyll concentrations during the months of July through September for the years 1979–1986 with years 1997–2000.[2] Although the data from the two periods were acquired by different satellite instruments, the researchers blended both sets of data with observations from ocean buoys and research vessels to make them comparable. Figure 6 shows an image of changes in chlorophyll concentration that they observed. Note that the color scale is logarithmic, with deeper tones of blue and red showing much larger changes than their lighter tones. The most striking feature the scientists observed was the decline in phytoplankton in northern oceans (blue), which amounted to about 30 percent in the North Pacific and 14 percent in the North Atlantic. In the equatorial zones, the researchers observed increases of up to 50 percent (red tones) at some locations, but the increases were not large enough to account for the high-latitude decreases. The scientists concluded that global concentrations of phytoplankton had decreased overall.

What could be the cause of such a decline? One possibility is that increasing sea-surface temperature

[1]Nemani, R. R., Keeling, C. D., Hashimoto, H., Jolly, W. M., Piper, S. C., Tucker, C. J., Myneni, R. B. and Running, S. W., 2003, Climate-driven increases in global terrestrial net primary production from 1982 to 1999. *Science* (June 6, 2003).

[2]Gregg, W. W. and Conkright, M. E., 2002, Decadal changes in global ocean chlorophyll, *Geophys. Res. Lett.*, 29 (15), doi:10.1029/2002GL014689, 2002; Gregg, W. W., Conkright, M. E., Ginoux, P., O'Reilly, J. E., and Casey, N. W., 2003, Ocean primary production and climate: Global decadal changes, *Geophys. Res. Lett.*, 30 (15), 1809, doi:10.1029/2003GL016889, 2003.

Figure 6   Change in ocean chlorophyll concentration from 1979–1986 to 1997–2000 *This image shows how summer ocean chlorophyll concentrations have changed over the past two decades. Data are for July–September as acquired by NOAA's Coastal Zone Color Scanner (1979–1986) and SeaWiFs instrument (1997–2000). (NASA/NOAA.)*

is increasing the duration and strength of the thermocline at high latitudes, which inhibits the mixing of nutrient-rich deep water with nutrient-poor surface water and thus keeps the phytoplankton population in a nutrient-limited condition. Another possibility is that wind speeds are decreasing, which will also reduce mixing. Actually, both of these changes have already been observed. Summer sea-surface temperatures in northern regions increased by 0.4°C (0.7°F) from the early 1980s to 2000, and average spring wind stresses on the sea surface have decreased by about 8 percent. However, it is not certain that these changes are the result of global warming rather than a multiyear ocean cycle yet to be discovered.

Implications for the Global Carbon Budget

What are the implications of these changes in global productivity for the global carbon budget? First, it would seem that the balance in global productivity between land and ocean is shifting toward land. Although this may increase the amount of terrestrial biomass and decrease the rate of CO_2 buildup, it also means that ocean productivity is probably declining at the cost of damage to oceanic ecosystems.

Second, it is important to keep in mind that net primary productivity isn't the whole story, at least on land. It doesn't include soil respiration, which could be very important. By soil respiration, we mean the decay of organic matter in soils, which releases CO_2 to the atmosphere. Soil respiration is quite temperature-dependent, and small increases in temperature can stimulate large increases in respiration. Considering that boreal forest soils are very rich in organic matter and that global temperatures are increasing most rapidly at high latitudes, increased release of CO_2 by soil respiration could well overwhelm increasing fixation due to higher temperatures.

Third, we don't know if the increase in land productivity will continue. For example, with more sunlight and higher temperatures, moisture may become limiting in equatorial and tropical forests, causing net primary productivity to plateau or even decrease. Moreover, the large changes in temperature forecast for high-latitude regions will ultimately lead to reduced productivity as boreal forests come under increasing stress and trees at their southern limits die.

All these uncertainties emphasize the importance of being able to map and monitor global productivity using remote sensing. While we may not yet be able to predict exactly how the carbon cycle will behave in the future, at least we can track the changes that are occurring. With time, that will allow us to refine carbon cycle models so that we will indeed come to understand the full impact of human activity on the global carbon cycle.

EYE ON THE LANDSCAPE

*A train streaks across the
Mojave Desert at sunset.*
**What else would the
geographer see? … Answers
at the end of the chapter.**

9 | GLOBAL BIOGEOGRAPHY

PUTTING YOU IN THE PICTURE

We've seen how the processes of ecological and historical biogeography can influence the patterns of plant and animal species on the landscape. But how do these processes actually play out at the global scale? This chapter surveys the characteristics and distribution patterns of the major units of biotic life on land.

As an introduction to the scale of these patterns, imagine yourself on a train trip across the American West, sampling a transect of the many diverse biogeographic landscapes of this unique region…

All aboard! The conductor's cry resounds through Union Station, Los Angeles, and at precisely 11:50 A.M., your train begins to move. At last your journey is underway! You're headed for Chicago on a three-day train ride that will take you through some of the most breathtaking scenery in America.

An hour later, you are relaxing in the comfortable armchair of your roomette, gazing out the large picture window. The Mojave Desert flashes by. The strange forms of Joshua trees contrast against the gray and tan colors of the desert earth. Overhead a bird with a large wingspan glides effortlessly. You wonder if it could be a California condor, far from its coastal habitat. The coach rushes across a dry lakebed of white salt sparkling in the Sun. Sharp peaks loom in the far distance, their angular foothills terminating the broad plains of grayish creosote bush that sweep toward the mountain fronts.

Early that evening, the train pulls out of Las Vegas, headed up toward the high desert of the Colorado Plateau. As the Sun slowly sets, the reds and browns of the rocks and soils intensify. Soon the desert sky darkens to a blue-black. Sagebrush carpets the landscape, looking soft and inviting in the moonlight. Reluctantly, you draw the shade and turn in for the night.

"More coffee?" The steward expertly refills your breakfast coffee cup, swaying with the motion of the dining car. During the night, the train has slowly gained elevation to enter the rugged upper reaches of the Colorado Basin. Twisted crowns of piñon pines and junipers dot the hills. A frightened squirrel gathering pine nuts leaps away quickly. Gray-green sagebrush blankets the lowlands, with green, willowy salt-bush lining the dry creek beds.

By early afternoon, you are well into your crossing of the Rocky Mountains. The track follows the narrow canyon of the upper Colorado. Steep, conifer-clad slopes enclose the rushing train. Soon you are in the high country. Ragged, windswept peaks jut skyward, spread with a green and white quilt of snowfields, conifer forests, and aspen groves. You glimpse a pair of mule deer, half hidden in a small stand of firs. Suddenly the train plunges into the Moffat Tunnel for the long passage under the continental divide. Emerging on the east side, you descend steeply toward the high plains and the skyscrapers of Denver.

Later that evening, you sit alone in your darkened compartment, gazing out the window. The short-grass prairie sweeps by, its moonlit surface like a table spread with faded lace. A prairie dog town flashes past, with burrows like blisters on the brown soil. Soon, the rocking motion of the train lulls you to sleep.

Noises in the station at Omaha awaken you early in the morning. After breakfast, you watch Iowa roll by. Maturing corn and soybean crops form a dense, green blanket on the Earth. Cattle graze stubbly green fields where hay was harvested earlier in the season. As the train heads eastward, the density of settlement increases. By late afternoon, you reach the Chicago area, and precisely at 4:15 P.M., your train pulls into the station. Regretfully, you hoist your suitcase and step off the train. Your trip is over, but you will long remember the magnificent landscapes and scenic vistas of the American West. ∎

GLOBAL BIOGEOGRAPHY

Our last chapter focused on biogeography, examining the principles and processes that determine the distribution of plants and animals on the Earth's land surface. In this chapter, we survey the broad global distribution patterns of ecosystems, emphasizing the characteristics of the vegetation cover. We emphasize the vegetation because it is a visible and obvious part of the landscape and because humans depend on plants for many life essentials, including food, medicines, fuel, clothing, and shelter. Also, the largest division of ecosystems—the biome—is defined primarily on the characteristics of the vegetation cover. Note that vegetation is often strongly related to climate, so we will find that the occurrence of major biomes coincides in many cases with broad climate types. Thus, your knowledge of climate from Chapter 7 will come in handy as you study the world's vegetation.

GEODISCOVERIES **Interaction of Climate, Vegetation and Soil.** Return to the animations for Chapter 7 to view climate, vegetation, and soils maps superimposed to see common patterns. One animation for each of five global regions.

NATURAL VEGETATION

Over the last few thousand years, human societies have come to dominate much of the land area of our planet. In many regions, humans have changed the natural vegetation—sometimes drastically, other times subtly.

Most areas of the Earth's land surface are influenced subtly or strongly by human activity. Human influence includes such factors as clearing for agriculture and grazing, fire suppression, and introduction of alien plants and animals.

What do we mean by natural vegetation? **Natural vegetation** is a plant cover that develops with little or no human interference. It is subject to natural forces of modification and destruction, such as storms or fires. Natural vegetation can still be seen over vast areas of the wet equatorial climate, although the rainforests there are being rapidly cleared. Much of the arctic tundra and the boreal forest of the subarctic zones is in a natural state.

In contrast to natural vegetation is *human-influenced vegetation,* which is modified by human activities. Much of the land surface in midlatitudes is totally under human control, through intensive agriculture, grazing, or urbanization. Some areas of natural vegetation appear to be untouched but are actually dominated by human activity in a subtle manner. For example, most national parks and national forests have been protected from fire for many decades. When lightning starts a forest fire, the firefighters put out the flames as fast as possible. However, periodic burning is part of the natural cycle in many regions. One vital function of fire is to release nutrients that are stored in plant tissues. When the vegetation burns, the ashes containing the nutrients remain. These enrich the soil for the next cycle of vegetation cover. In recent years, managers of some parks and forests have stopped suppressing wildfires, allowing the return of more natural periodic burning. *(See Eye on the Environment 8.3 • The Great Yellowstone Fire.)*

Our species has influenced vegetation in yet another way—by moving plant species from their original habitats to foreign lands and foreign environments. The eucalyptus tree is a striking example. From Australia, various species of eucalyptus have been transplanted to such far-off lands as California, North Africa, and India. Sometimes exported plants thrive like weeds, forcing out natural species and becoming a major nuisance. Few of the grasses that clothe the coastal ranges of California are native species, yet a casual observer might think that these represent native vegetation.

Even so, all plants have limited tolerance to the environmental conditions of soil water, heat and cold, and soil nutrients. Consequently, the structure and outward appearance of the plant cover conforms to basic environmental controls, and each vegetation type is associated with a characteristic geographical region—whether forest, grassland, or desert.

STRUCTURE AND LIFE-FORM OF PLANTS

Plants come in many types, shapes, and sizes. Botanists recognize and classify plants by species. However, the plant geographer is less concerned with individual species and more concerned with the plant cover as a whole. In describing the plant cover, plant geographers refer to the **life-form** of the plant—its physical structure, size, and shape. Although the life-forms go by common names and are well understood by almost everyone, we will review them to establish a uniform set of meanings.

Both trees and shrubs are erect, woody plants (Figure 9.1). They are *perennial,* meaning that their woody tissues endure from year to year. Most have life spans of many years. *Trees* are large, woody perennial plants having a single upright main trunk, often with few branches in the lower part but branching in the upper part to form a crown. *Shrubs* are woody perennial plants that have several stems branching from a base near the soil surface, so as to place the mass of foliage close to ground level.

Lianas are also woody plants, but they take the form of vines supported on trees and shrubs. Lianas include not only the tall, heavy vines of the wet equatorial and tropical rainforests, but also some woody vines of midlatitude forests. Poison ivy and the tree-climbing form of poison oak are familiar North American examples of lianas.

Herbs comprise a major class of plant life-forms. They lack woody stems and so are usually small, tender plants. They occur in a wide range of shapes and leaf types. Some are *annuals,* living only for a single season—while others are perennials—living for multiple seasons. Some herbs are broad-leaved, and others are narrow-leaved, such as grasses. Herbs as a class share few characteristics in common except that they usually form a low layer as compared with shrubs and trees.

Forest is a vegetation structure in which trees grow close together. Crowns are in contact, so that the foliage largely shades the ground. Many forests in moist climates show at least three layers of life-forms (Figure 9.1). Tree crowns form the uppermost layer, shrubs an intermediate layer, and herbs a lower layer. There is sometimes a fourth, lowermost layer that consists of mosses and related very small plants. In **woodland,** crowns of trees are mostly separated by open areas that usually have a low herb or shrub layer.

Lichens are another life-form seen in a layer close to the ground. They are plant forms in which algae and fungi live together to form a single plant structure. In some alpine and arctic environments, lichens grow in profusion and dominate the vegetation (Figure 9.2).

TERRESTRIAL ECOSYSTEMS— THE BIOMES

From the viewpoint of human use, ecosystems are natural resource systems. Food, fiber, fuel, and structural material are products of ecosystems and are manufactured by organisms using energy derived from the Sun. Humans harvest that energy by using ecosystem products. The products and

9.1 Layers of a beech-maple-hemlock forest *In this schematic diagram, the vertical dimensions of the lower layers are greatly exaggerated. (After P. Dansereau.)*

Sugar maples   Hemlock   Beech   Ash   Sugar maples

Liana

Tree layer

Dogwood

Shrub layer

Herb layer

Moss layer

9.2 Lichen *Reindeer moss, a white variety of lichen, seen here on rocky tundra of Alaska.*

productivity of ecosystems depend to a large degree on climate. Where temperature and rainfall cycles permit, ecosystems provide a rich bounty for human use. Where temperature or rainfall cycles restrict ecosystems, human activities can also be limited. Of course, humans, too, are part of the ecosystem. A persistent theme of human geography is the study of how human societies function within ecosystems, utilizing ecosystem resources and modifying ecosystems for human benefit.

Ecosystems fall into two major groups—aquatic and terrestrial. *Aquatic ecosystems* include marine environments and the freshwater environments of the lands. Marine ecosystems include the open ocean, coastal estuaries, and coral reefs. Freshwater ecosystems include lakes, ponds, streams, marshes, and bogs. Our survey of physical geography will not include these aquatic environments. Instead, we will focus on the **terrestrial ecosystems,** which are dominated by land plants spread widely over the upland surfaces of the continents. The terrestrial ecosystems are directly influenced by climate and interact with the soil. In this way, they are closely woven into the fabric of physical geography.

Within terrestrial ecosystems, the largest recognizable subdivision is the **biome.** Although the biome includes the total assemblage of plant and animal life interacting within the life layer, the green plants dominate the biome physically because of their enormous biomass, as compared with that of other organisms. Plant geographers concentrate on the characteristic life-form of the green plants within the biome. These life-forms are principally trees, shrubs, lianas, and herbs, but other life-forms are important in certain biomes.

There are five principal biomes. The **forest biome** is dominated by trees, which form a closed or nearly closed canopy. Forest requires an abundance of soil water, so

> Biogeographers recognize five principal biomes: forest, grassland, savanna, desert, and tundra. Formation classes are subdivisions of biomes based on vegetation structure and life-form.

forests are found in moist climates. Temperatures must also be suitable, requiring at least a warm season, if not warm temperatures the year round. The **savanna biome** is transitional between forest and grassland. It exhibits an open cover of trees with grasses and herbs underneath. The **grassland biome** develops in regions with moderate shortages of soil water. The semiarid regions of the dry tropical, dry subtropical, and dry midlatitude climates are the home of the grassland biome. Temperatures must also provide adequate warmth during the growing season. The **desert biome** includes organisms that can survive a moderate to severe water shortage for most, if not all, of the year. Temperatures can range from very hot to cool. Plants are often xerophytes, showing adaptations to the dry environment. The **tundra biome** is limited by cold temperatures. Only small plants that can grow quickly when temperatures warm above freezing in the warmest month or two can survive.

Biogeographers break the biomes down further into smaller vegetation units, called *formation classes,* using the life-form of the plants. For example, at least four and perhaps as many as six kinds of forests are easily distinguished within the forest biome. At least three kinds of grasslands are easily recognizable. Deserts, too, span a wide range in terms of the abundance and life-form of plants. The formation classes described in the remaining portion of this chapter are major, widespread types that are clearly associated with specific climate types. Figure 9.3 is a generalized world map of the formation classes. It simplifies the very complex patterns of natural vegetation to show large uniform regions in which a given formation class might be expected to occur.

With the advent of remote sensing, it is possible to map global land cover more accurately and at a finer scale. *Focus on Remote Sensing 9.1 • Mapping Global Land Cover by*

Satellite describes how satellite image data are used for this purpose.

Forest Biome

Within the forest biome, we can recognize six major formations: low-latitude rainforest, monsoon forest, subtropical evergreen forest, midlatitude deciduous forest, needleleaf forest, and sclerophyll forest.

LOW-LATITUDE RAINFOREST *Low-latitude rainforest,* found in the equatorial and tropical latitude zones, consists of tall, closely set trees. Crowns form a continuous canopy of foliage and provide dense shade for the ground and lower layers (Figure 9.4a). The trees are characteristically smooth-barked and unbranched in the lower two-thirds. Tree leaves are large and evergreen—thus, the equatorial rainforest is often described as *broadleaf evergreen forest.*

Crowns of the trees of the low-latitude rainforest tend to form two or three layers (Figure 9.4b). The highest layer consists of scattered "emergent" crowns that protrude from the closed canopy below, often rising to 40 m (130 ft). Some emergent species develop wide buttress roots, which aid in their physical support (Figure 9.6). Below the layer of emergents is a second, continuous layer, which is 15 to 30 m (about 50 to 100 ft) high. A third, lower layer consists of small, slender trees 5 to 15 m (about 15 to 50 ft) high with narrow crowns.

Typical of the low-latitude rainforest are thick, woody lianas supported by the trunks and branches of trees. Some are slender, like ropes, while others reach thicknesses of 20 cm (8 in.). They climb high into the trees to the upper canopy, where light is available, and develop numerous branches of their own. *Epiphytes* ("air plants") are also common in low-latitude rainforest. These plants attach themselves to the trunk, branches, or foliage of trees and lianas. Their host is used solely as a means of physical support. Epiphytes include plants of many different types—ferns, orchids, mosses, and lichens (Figure 9.4c).

A particularly important characteristic of the low-latitude rainforest is the large number of species of trees that coexist. In equatorial regions of rainforest, as many as 3000 species may be found in a few square kilometers. Individuals of a given species are often widely separated. Many species of plants and animals in this very diverse ecosystem still have not been identified or named by biologists.

Equatorial and tropical rainforests are not jungles of impenetrable plants thickets. Rather, the floor of the low-latitude rainforest is usually so densely shaded that plant

foliage is sparse close to the ground. This gives the forest an open aspect, making it easy to travel within its interior. The ground surface is covered only by a thin litter of leaves. Dead plant matter rapidly decomposes because the warm temperatures and abundant moisture promote its breakdown by bacteria. Nutrients released by decay are quickly absorbed by roots. As a result, the soil is low in organic matter.

Large herbivores are uncommon in the low-latitude rainforest. They include the African okapi and the tapir of South America and Asia. Most herbivores are climbers, and they include many primates—monkeys and apes. Toucans, parrots, and tinamous join fruit-eating bats as flying grazers of the forest. Tree sloths spend their lifetimes hanging upside down as they browse the forest canopy. There are few large predators. Notable are the leopards of African and Asian forests and the jaguars and ocelots of the South American forests.

Low-latitude rainforest develops in a climate that is continuously warm, frost-free, and has abundant precipitation in all months of the year (or, at most, has only one or two dry months). These conditions occur in the wet equatorial climate ① and the monsoon and trade-wind coastal climate ②. In the absence of a cold or dry season, plant growth goes on continuously throughout the year. In this uniform environment, some plant species grow new leaves continuously, shedding old ones continuously as well. Still other plant species shed their leaves according to their own seasons, responding to the slight changes in daylight length that occur with the seasons.

World distribution of the low-latitude rainforest is shown in Figure 9.6. A large area of rainforest lies astride the equator. In South America, this equatorial rainforest includes the Amazon lowland. In Africa, the *equatorial rainforest* is found in the Congo lowland and in a coastal zone extending westward from Nigeria to Guinea. In Indonesia, the island of Sumatra, on the west, bounds a region of equatorial rainforest that stretches eastward to the islands of the western Pacific.

> Low-latitude rainforests are very diverse, containing large numbers of plant and animal species. Broadleaf evergreen trees dominate the vegetation cover. The rainforest climate is wet year round or has a short dry season.

The low-latitude rainforest extends poleward through the tropical zone (lat. 10° to 25° N and S) along monsoon and trade-wind coasts. The monsoon and trade-wind coastal climate in which this *tropical-zone rainforest* thrives has a short dry season. However, the dry season is not intense enough to deplete soil water.

In the northern hemisphere, trade-wind coasts that have rainforests are found in the Philippine Islands and also along the eastern coasts of Central America and the West Indies. These highlands receive abundant orographic rainfall in the belt of the trade winds. A good example of tropical-zone rainforest is the rainforest of the eastern mountains of Puerto Rico. In Southeast Asia, tropical-zone rainforest is extensive in monsoon coastal zones and highlands that have heavy rainfall and a very short dry season.

Focus on Remote Sensing | 9.1

Mapping Global Land Cover by Satellite

Imagine yourself as an astronaut living on an orbiting space station, watching the Earth turn underneath you. One of the first things that would strike you about the land surface is its color and how it changes from place to place and time to time. Deserts are in shades of brown, dotted with white salty playas and the black spots and streaks of recent volcanic activity. Equatorial forests are green and lush, dissected by branching lines of dark rivers. Shrublands are marked by earth colors, but with a greenish tinge. Some regions show substantial change throughout the year. In the midlatitude zone, forests and agricultural lands go from intense green in the summer

to brown as leaves drop and crops are harvested. Snow expands equatorward in the fall and winter and retreats poleward in the spring and summer. In the tropical zones, grasslands and savannas go from brown to green to brown again as the rainy season comes and goes. Some features, such as lakes, remain nearly unchanged throughout the year. Thus, the color of the land surface and the change in color through time, as viewed from an orbiting Earth satellite, can provide information about the type of land cover present at a location.

Ever since the first satellite images of the Earth were received, scientists have used color—that is, the spectral reflectance of the sur-

face—as an indicator of land cover type. For example, there is a thirty-year history of producing land cover maps for local areas using individual Landsat images from cloud-free dates. But global mapping of land cover requires instruments that can observe the surface on a daily or near-daily basis, thus maximizing the opportunity to image the land surface in parts of the globe that are frequently cloud-covered. These instruments have a coarser ground resolution than Landsat, with pixels in the range of 500 to 1100 meters on a side, but that is not a deficiency when working at a global scale.

Shown below is a map of global land cover produced from MODIS

Global land cover from MODIS   This map of global land cover types was constructed from MODIS data acquired largely during 2001. The map has a spatial resolution of 1 km^2—that is, each square kilometer of the Earth's land surface is independently assigned a land cover type label. Goode's homolosine projection. (A. H. Strahler, Boston University/NASA.)

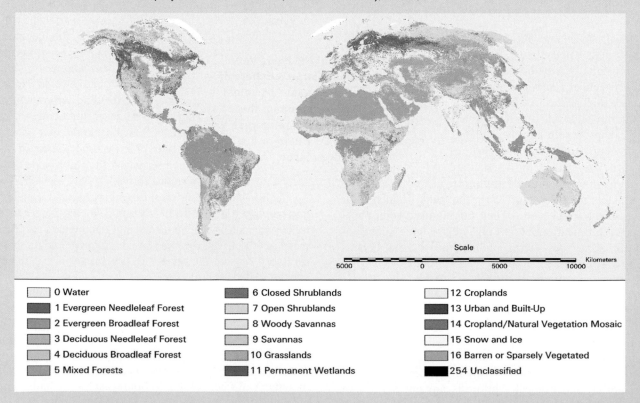

Scale
Kilometers
5000   0   5000   10000

0 Water	6 Closed Shrublands	12 Croplands
1 Evergreen Needleleaf Forest	7 Open Shrublands	13 Urban and Built-Up
2 Evergreen Broadleaf Forest	8 Woody Savannas	14 Cropland/Natural Vegetation Mosaic
3 Deciduous Needleleaf Forest	9 Savannas	15 Snow and Ice
4 Deciduous Broadleaf Forest	10 Grasslands	16 Barren or Sparsely Vegetated
5 Mixed Forests	11 Permanent Wetlands	254 Unclassified

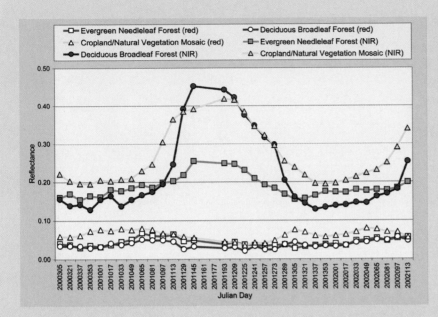

Legend:
- □ Evergreen Needleleaf Forest (red)
- ○ Deciduous Broadleaf Forest (red)
- △ Cropland/Natural Vegetation Mosaic (red)
- ■ Evergreen Needleleaf Forest (NIR)
- ● Deciduous Broadleaf Forest (NIR)
- △ Cropland/Natural Vegetation Mosaic (NIR)

Spectral and temporal reflectance patterns The plot shows how the spectral reflectance of three land cover types in the southeastern United States varies during the period 31 October 2000 to 23 April 2002. Dates are shown in Julian date format: the first four digits indicate the year, and the remaining three indicate the day of the year with 1 January taken as 001. (A. H. Strahler, Boston University/NASA.)

images acquired largely in 2001. The legend recognizes 17 types of land covers, including forests, shrublands, savannas, grasslands, and wetlands.

The global pattern of land cover types is rather similar to that shown in Figure 9.3. Evergreen broadleaf forest dominates the equatorial belt, stretching from South America, through Central Africa, to south Asia. Adjoining the equatorial forest belt are regions of savannas and grasslands, which have strong wet-dry climates. The vast desert region running from the Sahara to the Gobi is barren or sparsely vegetated. It is flanked by grasslands on the west, north, and east. Broadleaf deciduous forests are prominent in eastern North America, western Europe, and eastern Asia. Evergreen needleleaf forests span the boreal zone from Alaska and northwest Canada to Siberia. Croplands are found throughout most regions of human habitation, except for dry desert regions and cold boreal zones.

The map was constructed using both spectral and temporal information. The graph above shows how these information sources are used. It depicts reflectance values in red and near-infrared (NIR) spectral bands for three land cover types as observed in the southeastern United States—evergreen needleleaf forest, cropland/natural vegetation mosaic, and deciduous broadleaf forest. The reflectances are shown as they change over the course of about a year and a half, from 31 October 2000 (2000305) to 23 April 2002 (2002113).

The top three curves, which are near-infrared values, show the patterns of the three types most clearly. During the winter, values are generally low, with deciduous broadleaf forest, evergreen needleleaf forest, and cropland in increasing order of reflectance. As spring begins, cropland reflectance rises before deciduous broadleaf forest but deciduous broadleaf forest reaches a higher peak. Evergreen needleleaf forest also shows a spring green-up, but it is later than the others and peaks at a lower value. Reflectance gradually drops during the fall, and the three types reach about the same reflectance levels as in the prior year. The three lower curves, which display the red band, also have distinctive features, but they are less obvious on this plot.

Given spectral and temporal information, how is the global map made? The process by which each global pixel is given a label is referred to as *classification*. In short, a computer program is presented with many examples of each land cover type. It then "learns" the examples and uses them to classify pixels depending on their spectral and temporal pattern. The MODIS global land cover map shown was prepared with more than 1500 examples of the 17 land cover types. It is estimated to be about 75-80 percent accurate.

Land cover mapping is a common application of remote sensing. Given the ability of spaceborne instruments to image the Earth consistently and repeatedly, classification of remotely sensed data is a natural way of extending our knowledge from the specific to the general to provide valuable new geographic information.

9.3 *Natural vegetation of the world*

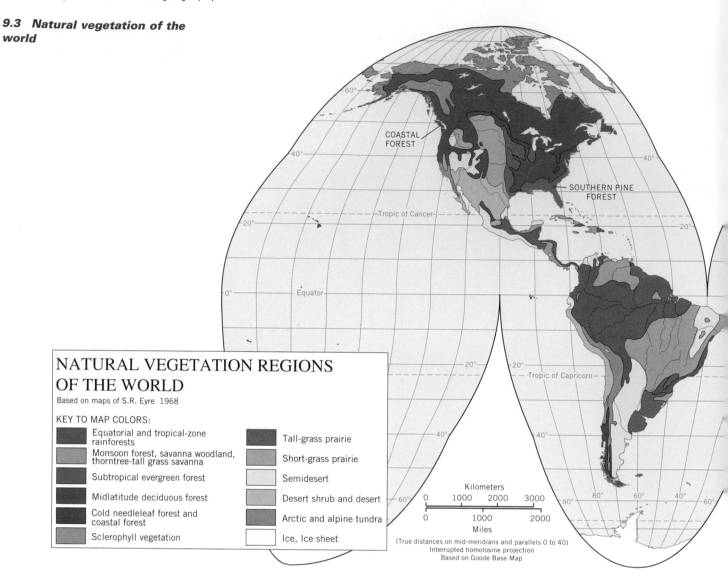

NATURAL VEGETATION REGIONS OF THE WORLD

Based on maps of S.R. Eyre 1968

KEY TO MAP COLORS:

- Equatorial and tropical-zone rainforests
- Monsoon forest, savanna woodland, thorntree-tall grass savanna
- Subtropical evergreen forest
- Midlatitude deciduous forest
- Cold needleleaf forest and coastal forest
- Sclerophyll vegetation
- Tall-grass prairie
- Short-grass prairie
- Semidesert
- Desert shrub and desert
- Arctic and alpine tundra
- Ice, Ice sheet

Kilometers
0   1000   2000   3000

0   1000   2000
Miles

(True distances on mid-meridians and parallels 0 to 40)
Interrupted homolosine projection
Based on Goode Base Map

These occur in Vietnam and Laos, southeastern China, and on the western coasts of India and Myanmar. In the southern hemisphere, belts of tropical-zone rainforest extend down the eastern Brazilian coast, the Madagascar coast, and the coast of northeastern Australia.

Within the regions of low-latitude rainforest are many island-like highland regions where climate is cooler and rainfall is increased by the orographic effect. Here, rainforest extends upward on the rising mountain slopes. Between 1000 and 2000 m (about 3300 and 6500 ft), the rainforest gradually changes in structure and becomes *montane forest* (Figure 9.6). The canopy of montane forest is more open, and tree heights are lower, than in the rainforest. With increasing elevation, the forest canopy height becomes even lower. Tree ferns and bamboos are numerous, and epiphytes are particularly abundant. As elevation increases, mist and fog become persistent, giving high-elevation montane forest the name *cloud forest.*

Low-latitude rainforest is under increasing human pressure. Slowly but surely, the rainforest is being conquered by logging, clearcutting, and conversion to grazing and farming. *Eye on the Environment 9.2 ● Exploitation of the Low-Latitude Rainforest Ecosystem* describes this process in more detail.

MONSOON FOREST   *Monsoon forest* of the tropical latitude zone differs from tropical rainforest because it is deciduous, with most of the trees of the monsoon forest shedding their leaves during the dry season. Shedding of leaves results from the stress of a long dry season that occurs at the time of low sun and cooler temperatures. In the dry season, the forest resembles the deciduous forests of the midlatitudes during their leafless winter season.

Monsoon forest consists of an open cover of deciduous trees that shed their leaves during the pronounced dry season. It is found in regions of wet-dry tropical climate ③ and ranges from South America to Africa and southern Asia.

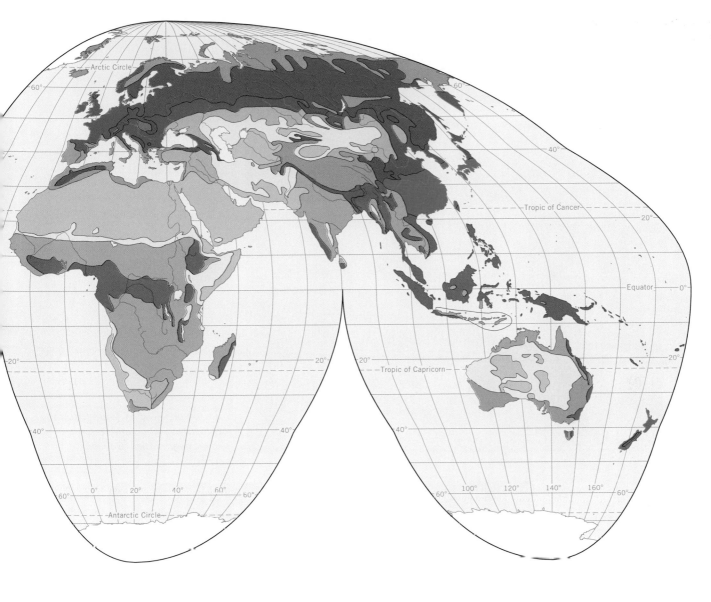

9.5 Rainforest layers

This diagram shows the typical structure of equatorial rainforest. (After J. S. Beard, The Natural Vegetation of Trinidad, Clarendon Press, Oxford.)

a...Aerial view of low-latitude rainforest *Middle Mazaruni River near Bartica, Guyana.*

b...Buttress roots at the base of a large rainforest tree *From Daintree National Park, Queensland, Australia.*

c...Epiphytes *In this photo from the El Yunque rainforest, Caribbean National Forest, Puerto Rico, red-flowering epiphytes adorn the trunks of sierra palms.*

d...Three-toed tree sloth *This slow-moving, amiable denizen of the low-latitude rainforest, here photographed in French Guyana, lives in the trees, foraging on the leaves and fruits of the many rainforest tree species. Once more widespread, the tree sloth is now endangered.*

9.6 *Low-latitude rainforest* *World map of low-latitude rainforest, showing equatorial and tropical rainforest types. (Data source same as Figure 9.3. Based on Goode Base Map.)*

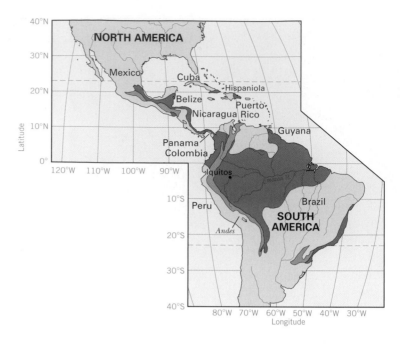

Eye on Global Change | 9.2

Exploitation of the Low-Latitude Rainforest Ecosystem

Many of the world's equatorial and tropical regions are home to the rainforest ecosystem. This ecosystem is perhaps the most diverse on Earth. That is, it possesses more species of plants and animals than any other. Very large tracts of rainforest still exist in South America, south Asia, and some parts of Africa. Ecologists regard this ecosystem as a genetic reservoir of many species of plants and animals. But as human populations expand and the quest for agricultural land continues, low-latitude rainforests are being threatened with clearing, logging, cultivation of cash crops, and animal grazing.

In the past, low-latitude rainforests were farmed by native peoples using the *slash-and-burn* method—cutting down all the vegetation in a small area, then burning it (see photo at right). In a rainforest ecosystem, most of the nutrients are held within living plants rather than in the soil. Burning the vegetation on the site releases the trapped nutrients, returning a portion of them to the soil. Here, the nutrients are available to growing crops. The supply

of nutrients derived from the original vegetation cover is small, however, and the harvesting of crops rapidly depletes the nutrients. After a few seasons of cultivation, a new field is cleared, and the old field is abandoned. Rainforest plants reestablish their hold on the abandoned area. Eventually, the rainforest returns to its original state. This cycle shows that primitive, slash-and-burn agriculture is fully compatible with maintenance of the rainforest ecosystem.

On the other hand, modern intensive agriculture uses large areas of land and is not compatible with the rainforest ecosystem. When large areas are abandoned, seed sources are so far away that the original forest species cannot take hold. Instead, secondary species dominate, often accompanied by species from other vegetation types. These species are good invaders, and once they enter an area, they tend to stay. The dominance of these secondary species is permanent, at least on the human time scale. Thus, we can regard the rainforest ecosystem as a resource that, once cleared, will

never return. The loss of low-latitude rainforest will result in the disappearance of thousands of species of organisms from the rainforest environment—a loss of millions of years of evolution, together with the destruction of the most complex ecosystem on Earth.

In Amazonia, transformation of large areas of rainforest into agricultural land uses heavy machinery to carve out major highways, such as the Trans-Amazon Highway in Brazil, and innumerable secondary roads and trails. Large fields for cattle pasture or commercial crops are created by cutting, bulldozing, clearing, and burning the vegetation. In some regions, the great broadleaved rainforest trees are removed for commercial lumber.

What are the effects of large-scale clearing? A recent study using a computer model by scientists of the University of Maryland and the Brazilian Space Research Institute indicated that when the Amazon rainforest is entirely removed and replaced with pasture, surface and soil temperatures will be increased 1 to 3°C (2 to 5°F).

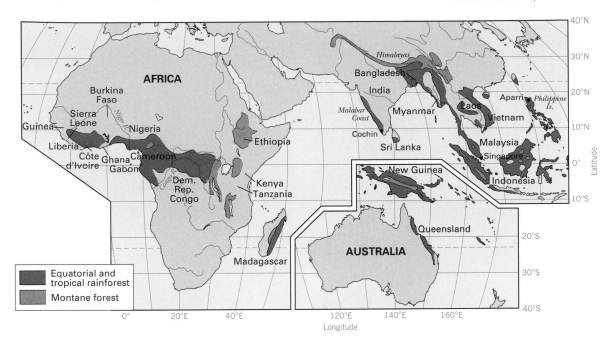

Legend:
- Equatorial and tropical rainforest
- Montane forest

Slash-and-burn clearing *This rainforest in Maranhão, Brazil, has been felled and burned in preparation for cultivation.*

Precipitation in the region will decline by 26 percent and evaporation by 30 percent. The deforestation will change weather and wind patterns so that less water vapor enters the Amazon Basin from outside sources, making the basin even drier. In areas where a marked dry season occurs, that season will be lengthened. Although such models contain simplifications and are subject to error, the results confirm the pessimistic conclusion that once large-scale deforestation has occurred, artificial restoration of a rainforest comparable to the original one may be impossible to achieve.

According to a report issued by the United Nations Food and Agriculture Organization, about 0.6 percent of the world's rainforest is lost annually by conversion to other uses. More rainforest land, 2.2 million hectares (about 8500 mi²), is lost annually in Asia than in Latin America and the Caribbean, where 1.9 million hectares (about 7300 mi²) are converted every year. Africa's loss of rainforest was estimated at about 470,000 hectares per year (1800 mi²). Among individual countries, Brazil and Indonesia are the loss leaders, accounting for nearly half of the rainforest area converted to other uses. Note that these values do not include even larger losses of moist deciduous forests in these regions. Deforestation in low-latitude dry deciduous forests and hill and montane forests is also very serious.

Although deforestation rates are very rapid in some regions, many nations are now working to reduce the rate of loss of rainforest environment. However, because the rainforest can provide agricultural land, minerals, and timber, the pressure to allow deforestation continues.

9.7 Monsoon woodland
This woodland is in the Bandipur Wild Animal Sanctuary in the Nilgiri Hills of southern India. The scene is taken in the rainy season, with trees in full leaf.

Monsoon forest is typically open. It grades into woodland, with open areas occupied by shrubs and grasses (Figure 9.7). Because of its open nature, light easily reaches the lower layers of the monsoon forest. As a result, these lower layers are better developed than in the rainforest. Tree heights are also lower. Typically, many tree species are present—as many as 30 to 40 species in a small tract—although the rainforest has many more. Tree trunks are massive, often with thick, rough bark. Branching starts at a comparatively low level and produces large, round crowns.

Figure 9.8 is a world map of the monsoon forest and closely related formation classes. Monsoon forest develops in the wet-dry tropical climate ③ in which a long rainy season alternates with a dry, rather cool season. These conditions, though most strongly developed in the Asiatic monsoon climate, are not limited to that area. The typical regions of monsoon forest are in Myanmar, Thailand, and Cambodia. In the monsoon forest of southern Asia, the teakwood tree was once abundant and was widely exported to the Western world to make furniture, paneling, and decking. Now this great tree is logged out, and the Indian elephant, once trained to carry out this logging work, is unemployed. Large areas of monsoon forest also occur in south-central Africa and in Central and South America, bordering the equatorial and tropical rainforests.

9.8 Monsoon forest *World map of monsoon forest and related types—savanna woodland and thorntree-tall grass savanna. (Data source same as Figure 9.3. Based on Goode Base Map.)*

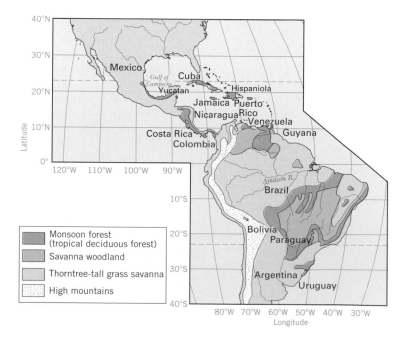

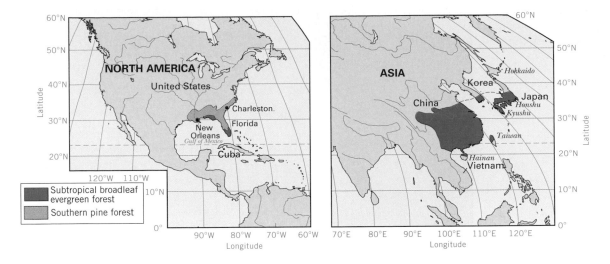

9.9 *Subtropical evergreen forest* *Northern hemisphere map of subtropical evergreen forests, including the southern pine forest. (Data source same as Figure 9.3. Based on Goode Base Map.)*

SUBTROPICAL EVERGREEN FOREST *Subtropical evergreen forest* is generally found in regions of moist subtropical climate ⑥, where winters are mild and there is ample rainfall throughout the year. This forest occurs in two forms: broadleaf and needleleaf. The *subtropical broadleaf evergreen forest* differs from the low-latitude rainforests, which are also broadleaf evergreen types, in having relatively few species of trees. Trees are not as tall as in the low-latitude rainforests. Their leaves tend to be smaller and more leathery, and the leaf

> The subtropical evergreen forest includes both broadleaf and needleleaf evergreen trees and is found in moist subtropical climate ⑥ regions of southeastern North America and Southeast Asia. Most of this formation class has been lost to cultivation.

canopy less dense. The subtropical broadleaf evergreen forest often has a well-developed lower layer of vegetation. Depending on the location, this layer may include tree ferns, small palms, bamboos, shrubs, and herbaceous plants. Lianas and epiphytes are abundant.

Figure 9.9 is a map of the subtropical evergreen forests of the northern hemisphere. Here subtropical evergreen forest consists of broad-leaved trees such as evergreen oaks and trees of the laurel and magnolia families. The name "laurel forest" is applied to these forests,

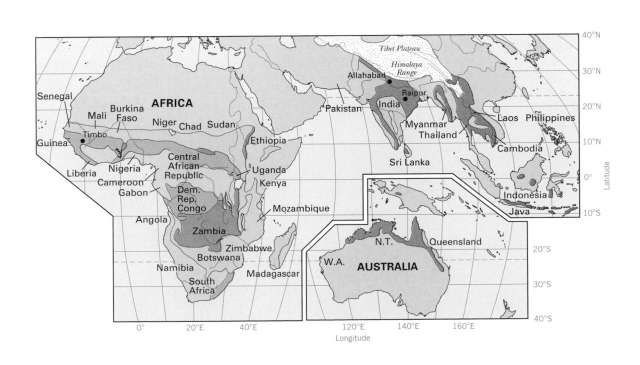

9.10 Pine plantation *This plantation of longleaf pine grows on the sandy soil of the southeastern coastal plain. Near Waycross, Georgia.*

which are associated with the moist subtropical climate ⑥ in the southeastern United States, southern China, and southern Japan. However, these regions are under intense crop cultivation because of their favorable climate. In these areas, the land has been cleared of natural vegetation for centuries, and little natural laurel forest remains.

The *subtropical needleleaf evergreen forest* occurs only in the southeastern United States (Figure 9.9). Here it is referred to as the southern pine forest, since it is dominated by species of pine. It is found on the wide belt of sandy soils that fringes the Atlantic and Gulf coasts. Because the soils are sandy, water drains away quickly, leaving the soils quite dry. In infrequent drought years, these forests may burn. Since pines are well adapted to droughts and fires, they form a stable vegetation cover for large areas of the region. Timber companies

have taken advantage of this natural preference for pines, creating many plantations yielding valuable lumber and pulp (Figure 9.10).

MIDLATITUDE DECIDUOUS FOREST *Midlatitude deciduous forest* is the native forest type of eastern North America and Western Europe. It is dominated by tall, broadleaf trees that provide a continuous and dense canopy in summer but shed their leaves completely in the winter. Lower layers of small trees and shrubs are weakly developed. In the spring, a lush layer of lowermost herbs quickly develops but soon fades after the trees reach full foliage and shade the ground.

Figure 9.11 is a map of midlatitude deciduous forests, which are found almost entirely in the northern hemisphere.

9.11 Midlatitude deciduous forest *Northern hemisphere map of midlatitude deciduous forests. (Data source same as Figure 9.3. Based on Goode Base Map.)*

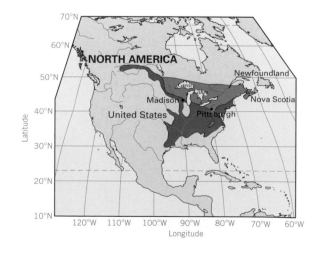

Throughout much of its range, this forest type is associated with the moist continental climate ⑩. Recall from Chapter 7 that this climate receives adequate precipitation in all months, normally with a summer maximum. There is a strong annual temperature cycle with a cold winter season and a warm summer.

Common trees of the deciduous forest of eastern North America, southeastern Europe, and eastern Asia are oak, beech, birch, hickory, walnut, maple, elm, and ash. A few needleleaf trees are often present as well—hemlock, for example (Figure 9.12). Where the deciduous forests have been cleared by lumbering, pines readily develop as second-growth forest.

In Western Europe, the midlatitude deciduous forest is associated with the marine west-coast climate ⑧. Here the dominant trees are mostly oak and ash, with beech in cooler and moister areas. In Asia, the midlatitude deciduous forest occurs as a belt between the boreal forest to the north and steppelands to the south. A small area of deciduous forest is found in Patagonia, near the southern tip of South America.

The deciduous forest includes a great variety of animal life, much of it stratified according to canopy layers. As many as five layers can be distinguished: the upper canopy, lower canopy, understory, shrub layer, and ground layer. Because the ground layer presents a more uniform environment in terms of humidity and temperature, it contains the largest concentration of organisms and the greatest diversity of species. Many small mammals burrow in the soil for shelter or food in the form of soil invertebrates. Among this burrowing group are ground squirrels, mice, and shrews, as well as some larger animals—foxes, woodchucks, and rabbits. Most of the larger mammals feed on ground and shrub layer vegetation, except for some, such as the brown bear, which are omnivorous and prey upon the small animals as well.

Even though birds possess the ability to move through the layers at will, most actually restrict themselves to one or more layers. For example, the wood peewee is found in the lower canopy, and the red-eyed vireo is found in the

9.12 Deciduous forest *In this deciduous forest of the Catskill Mountains, New York, some needleleaf trees—pine and hemlock—are also present.*

understory. Above them are the scarlet tanagers and blackburnian warblers, which are upper canopy dwellers. Below are the ground dwellers, such as grouse, warblers, and ovenbirds. Flying insects often show similar stratification patterns.

Among the large herbivores that graze in the deciduous forest are the red deer and roe deer of Eurasia and the white-tailed deer of North America. Smaller herbivores include voles, mice, and squirrels. Predators include bears, wildcats, lynx, wolves, foxes, weasels, and, among birds, owl species.

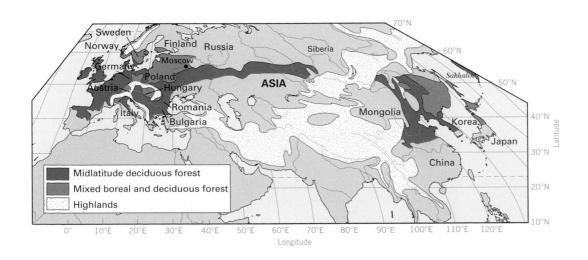

9.13 **Needleleaf forest** *Northern hemisphere map of cold-climate needleleaf forests, including coastal forest. (Data source same as Figure 9.3. Based on Goode Base Map.)*

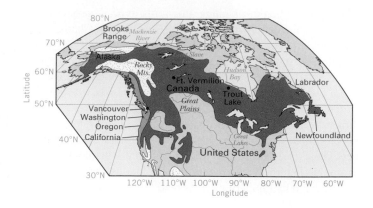

NEEDLELEAF FOREST *Needleleaf forest* refers to a forest composed largely of straight-trunked, cone-shaped trees with relatively short branches and small, narrow, needle-like leaves. These trees are conifers. Most are evergreen, retaining their needles for several years before shedding them. When the needleleaf forest is dense, it provides continuous and deep shade to the ground. Lower layers of vegetation are sparse or absent, except for a thick carpet of mosses that may occur. Species are few—in fact, large tracts of needleleaf forest consist almost entirely of only one or two species.

Needleleaf forest includes boreal and coastal forest. Boreal forest stretches across the northern reaches of North America and Eurasia. Coastal forest is restricted to the steep slopes of the coast ranges in the Pacific Northwest region.

Boreal forest is the cold-climate needleleaf forest of high latitudes. It occurs in two great continental belts, one in North America and one in Eurasia (Figure 9.13). These belts span their land masses from west to east in latitudes 45° N to 75° N, and they closely correspond to the region of boreal forest climate ⑪. The boreal forest of North America, Europe, and western Siberia is composed of such evergreen conifers as spruce and fir (Figure 9.14). The boreal forest of north-central and eastern Siberia is dominated by larch. The larch tree sheds its needles in winter and is thus a deciduous needleleaf tree.

9.14 **Boreal forest** *A view of the boreal forest, Denali National Park, Alaska, pictured here just after the first snowfall of the season. At this location near the northern limits of the boreal forest, the tree cover is sparse. The golden leaves of aspen mark the presence of this deciduous species.*

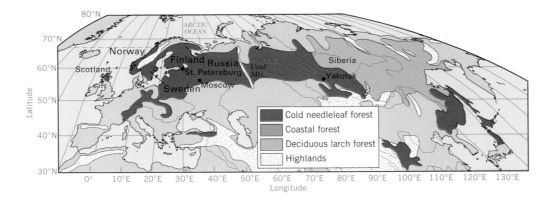

Broadleaf deciduous trees, such as aspen, balsam poplar, willow, and birch, tend to take over rapidly in areas of needleleaf forest that have been burned over. These species can also be found bordering streams and in open places. Between the boreal forest and the midlatitude deciduous forest lies a broad transition zone of mixed boreal and deciduous forest.

Needleleaf evergreen forest extends into lower latitudes wherever mountain ranges and high plateaus exist. For example, in western North America this formation class extends southward into the United States on the Sierra Nevada and Rocky Mountain Ranges and over parts of the higher plateaus of the southwestern states (Figure 9.15, *left*). In Europe, needleleaf evergreen forests flourish on all the higher mountain ranges.

In its northernmost range, the boreal needleleaf forest grades into cold woodland. This form of vegetation is limited to the northern portions of the boreal forest climate ⑪ and the southern portions of the tundra climate ⑫. Trees are low in height and spaced well apart. A shrub layer may be well developed. The ground cover of lichens and mosses is distinctive. Cold woodland is often referred to as *taiga*. It is transitional into the treeless tundra at its northern fringe.

Mammals of the boreal needleleaf forest in North America include deer, moose, elk, black bear, marten, mink, wolf, wolverine, and fisher. Common birds include jays, ravens, chickadees, nuthatches, and a number of warblers. The caribou, lemming, and snowshoe rabbit inhabit both needleleaf forest and the adjacent tundra biome. The boreal forest often experiences large fluctuations in animal species populations, a result of the low diversity and highly variable environment.

Coastal forest is a distinctive needleleaf evergreen forest of the Pacific Northwest coastal belt, ranging in latitude from northern California to southern Alaska (Figure 9.13). Here, in a band of heavy orographic precipitation, mild temperatures, and high humidity, are perhaps the densest of all conifer forests, with magnificent specimens of cedar, spruce, and Douglas fir. At the extreme southern end, coastal forest includes the world's largest trees—redwoods (Figure 9.15, *right*). Individual redwood trees attain heights of over 100 m (about 330 ft) and girths of over 20 m (about 65 ft).

SCLEROPHYLL FOREST   The native vegetation of the Mediterranean climate ⑦ is adapted to survival through the long summer drought. Shrubs and trees that can survive such drought are characteristically equipped with small, hard, or thick leaves that resist water loss through transpiration. As we noted earlier in the chapter, these plants are called sclerophylls.

Sclerophyll forest consists of trees with small, hard, leathery leaves. The trees are often low-branched and gnarled, with thick bark. The formation class includes *sclerophyll woodland,* an open forest in which only 25 to 60 percent of the ground is covered by trees. Also included are extensive areas of *scrub*, a plant formation type consisting of shrubs covering somewhat less than half of the ground area. The trees and shrubs are evergreen, retaining their thickened leaves despite a severe annual drought.

> Sclerophyll forest is dominated by low trees with thick, leathery leaves that are well-adapted to the long summer drought of the Mediterranean climate ⑦. Southern California's chaparral, found on coast-range slopes, is a form of sclerophyll scrub.

Our map of sclerophyll vegetation, Figure 9.16, includes forest, woodland, and scrub types. Sclerophyll forest is closely associated with the Mediterranean climate ⑦ and is narrowly limited to west coasts between 30° and 40° or 45° N and S latitude. In the Mediterranean lands, the sclerophyll forest forms a narrow, coastal belt ringing the Mediterranean Sea. Here, the Mediterranean forest consists of such trees as cork oak, live oak, Aleppo pine, stone pine, and olive. Over the centuries, human activity has reduced the sclerophyll forest to woodland or destroyed it entirely. Today, large areas of this former forest consist of dense scrub.

The other northern hemisphere region of sclerophyll vegetation is the California coast ranges. Here, the sclerophyll forest or woodland is typically dominated by live oak and white oak. Grassland occupies the open ground between the scattered oaks (see Figure 7.28b). Much of the remaining vegetation is sclerophyll scrub or "dwarf forest," known as *chaparral*. It varies in composition with elevation and expo-

9.15 Two kinds of needleleaf forest of the western United States *(left) Open forest of western yellow pine (ponderosa pine), in the Kaibab National Forest, Arizona. (right) A grove of great redwood trees in Humboldt State Park, California.*

sure. Chaparral may contain wild lilac, manzanita, mountain mahogany, poison oak, and live oak.

In central Chile and in the Cape region of South Africa, sclerophyll vegetation has a similar appearance, but the dominant species are quite different. Important areas of sclerophyll forest, woodland, and scrub are also found in southeast, south-central, and southwest Australia, including many species of eucalyptus and acacia.

Savanna Biome

The savanna biome is usually associated with the tropical wet-dry climate ③ of Africa and South America. It includes vegetation formation classes ranging from woodland to grassland. In *savanna woodland,* the trees are spaced rather

widely apart because soil moisture during the dry season is not sufficient to support a full tree cover. The open spacing permits development of a dense lower layer, which usually consists of grasses. The woodland has an open, park-like appearance. Savanna woodland usually lies in a broad belt adjacent to equatorial rainforest.

In the tropical savanna woodland of Africa, the trees are of medium height. Tree crowns are flattened or umbrella-shaped, and the trunks have thick, rough bark (see Figure 7.15). Some species of trees are xerophytic forms with small leaves and thorns. Others are broad-leaved deciduous species that shed their leaves in the dry season. In this respect, savanna woodland resembles monsoon forest.

Fire is a frequent occurrence in the savanna woodland during the dry season, but the tree species of the savanna

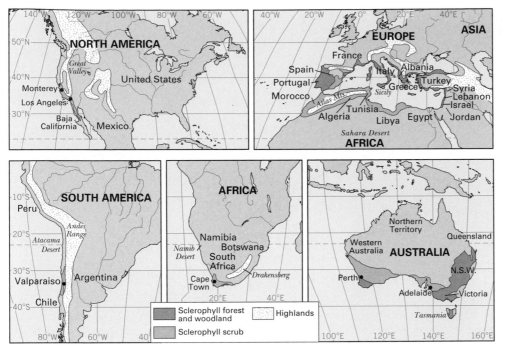

are particularly resistant to fire. Many geographers hold the view that periodic burning of the savanna grasses maintains the grassland against the invasion of forest. Fire does not kill the underground parts of grass plants, but it limits tree growth to individuals of fire-resistant species. Many rainforest tree species that might otherwise grow in the wet-dry climate regime are prevented by fires from invading. The browsing of animals, which kills many young trees, is also a factor in maintaining grassland at the expense of forest.

The regions of savanna woodland are shown in Figure 9.8, along with monsoon forest (discussed earlier). In Africa, the savanna woodland grades into a belt of *thorn-tree-tall-grass savanna,* a formation class transitional to the desert biome. The trees are largely of thorny species. Trees are more widely scattered, and the open grassland is more extensive than in the savanna woodland. One characteristic tree is the flat-topped acacia, seen in Figure 7.15. Elephant grass is a common species. It can grow to a height of 5 m (16 ft) to form an impenetrable thicket.

The thorntree-tall-grass savanna is closely identified with the semiarid subtype of the dry tropical and subtropical climates (④s, ⑤s). In the semiarid climate, soil water storage is adequate for the needs of plants only during the brief rainy season. The onset of the rains is quickly followed by the greening of the trees and grasses. For this reason, vegetation of the savanna biome is described as rain-green, an

> **The savanna biome is adapted to a strong wet-dry annual cycle. Grazing by large mammals and periodic burning in the dry season help to maintain the openness of the savanna by suppressing tree seedlings.**

adjective that also applies to the monsoon forest.

The African savanna is widely known for the diversity of its large grazing mammals, which include more than a dozen antelopes. Careful studies have shown that each species has a particular preference for different parts of the grasses it consumes—blade, sheath, and stem. Grazing stimulates the grasses to continue to grow, and so the ecosystem is more productive when grazed than when left alone. With these grazers comes a large variety of predators—lions, leopards, cheetahs, hyenas, and jackals. Elephants are the largest animals of the savanna and adjacent woodland regions.

Grassland Biome

The grassland biome includes two major formation classes that we will discuss here—tall-grass prairie and steppe (Figure 9.17). *Tall-grass prairie* consists largely of tall grasses. *Forbs,* which are broad-leaved herbs, are also present. Trees and shrubs are absent from the prairie but may occur in the same region as narrow patches of forest in stream valleys. The grasses are deeply rooted and form a thick and continuous turf (Figure 9.18).

Prairie grasslands are best developed in regions of the midlatitude and subtropical zones with well-developed winter and summer seasons. The grasses flower in spring and early summer, and the forbs flower in late summer. Tall-grass prairies are closely associated with

> **The grassland biome includes tall-grass prairie and short-grass prairie (steppe). Tall-grass prairie provides rich agricultural land suited to cultivation and cropping. Short-grass prairie occupies vast regions of semidesert and is suited to grazing.**

9.17 *Grassland* *World map of the grassland biome in subtropical and midlatitude zones. (Data source same as Figure 9.3. Based on Goode Base Map.)*

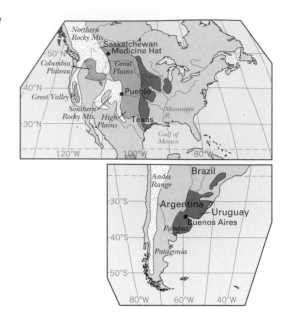

the drier areas of moist continental climate ⑩. Here, soil water is in short supply during the summer months.

When European settlers first arrived in North America, the tall-grass prairies were found in a belt extending from the Texas Gulf coast northward to southern Saskatchewan (Figure 9.17). A broad peninsula of tall-grass prairie extended eastward into Illinois, where conditions are somewhat more moist. Since the time of settlement, these prairies have been converted almost entirely to agricultural land. Another major area of tall-grass prairie is the Pampa

9.18 *Tall-grass prairie, Iowa*
In addition to grasses, tall-grass prairie vegetation includes many forbs, such as the flowering species shown in this photo.

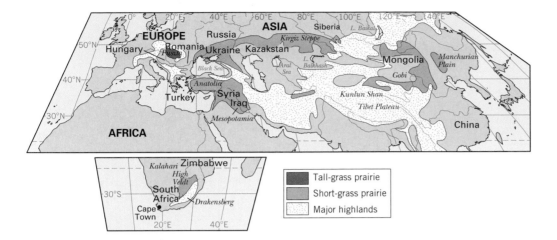

region of South America, which occupies parts of Uruguay and eastern Argentina. The Pampa region falls into the moist subtropical climate ⑥, with mild winters and abundant precipitation.

Recall from Chapter 7 that **steppe,** also called *short-grass prairie,* is a vegetation type consisting of short grasses occurring in sparse clumps or bunches. Scattered shrubs and low trees may also be found in the steppe. The plant cover is poor, and much bare soil is exposed. Many species of grasses and forbs occur. A typical grass of the American steppe is buffalo grass. Other typical plants are the sunflower and loco weed. Steppe grades into semidesert in dry environments and into prairie where rainfall is higher.

Our map of the grassland biome (Figure 9.17) shows that steppe grassland is concentrated largely in the midlatitude areas of North America and Eurasia. The only southern hemisphere occurrence shown on the map is the "veldt" region of South Africa, a highland steppe surface in Orange Free State and Transvaal.

Steppe grasslands correspond well with the semiarid subtype of the dry continental climate ⑨. Spring rains nourish the grasses, which grow rapidly until early summer. By midsummer, the grasses are usually dormant. Occasional summer rainstorms cause periods of revived growth.

The animals of the grassland are distinctive. Before the exploitation of the North American grassland for cattle ranching, large grazing mammals were abundant. These included the pronghorn antelope, the elk, and the buffalo, which ranged widely from tall-grass prairie to steppe. Now nearly extinct, the buffalo *(Bison)* once numbered 60 million and roamed the grasslands from the Rockies to the Shenandoah Valley of Virginia. By 1889, however, this herd had been reduced to 800 individuals. Most of the present buffalo population is confined to Yellowstone National Park.

Today, rodents and rabbits join cattle as the major grazers in the grasslands ecosystem.

The grassland ecosystem supports some rather unique adaptations to life. A common adaptive mechanism is jumping or leaping locomotion, assuring an unimpeded view of the surroundings. Jackrabbits and jumping mice are examples of jumping rodents. The pronghorn combines the leap with great speed, which allows it to avoid predators and fire. Burrowing is also another common life habit, for the soil provides the only shelter in the exposed grasslands. Examples are burrowing rodents, including prairie dogs, gophers, and field mice. Rabbits exploit old burrows, using them for nesting or shelter. Invertebrates also seek shelter in the soil, and many are adapted to living with the burrows of rodents, where extremes of moisture and temperature are substantially moderated.

Desert Biome

The desert biome includes several formation classes that are transitional from grassland and savanna biomes into vegetation of the arid desert. Here we recognize two basic formation classes: semidesert and dry desert. Figure 9.19 is a world map of the desert biome.

Semidesert is a transitional formation class found in a wide latitude range—from the tropical zone to the midlatitude zone. It is identified primarily with the arid subtypes of all three dry climates. Semidesert consists of sparse xerophytic shrubs. One example is the sage-brush vegetation of the middle and southern Rocky Mountain region and Colorado Plateau (Figure 9.20). Recently, as a result of overgrazing and trampling by livestock, semidesert shrub vegetation seems to have expanded widely into areas of the western United States that were formerly steppe grasslands.

The desert biome includes semidesert and dry desert and occupies the dry tropical ④, dry subtropical ⑤, and dry midlatitude ⑨ climate zones. Desert plants vary widely in appearance and in adaptation to the dry environment.

9.19 **Desert** *World map of the desert biome, including desert and semidesert formation classes. (Data source same as Figure 9.3. Based on Goode Base Map.)*

9.20 *Eye on the Landscape* **Sagebrush semidesert** *Sagebrush dominates the landscape near Monument Valley, Utah—a region of mesas, buttes, and pinnacles on the Colorado Plateau.* **What else would the geographer see? ... Answers at the end of the chapter.**

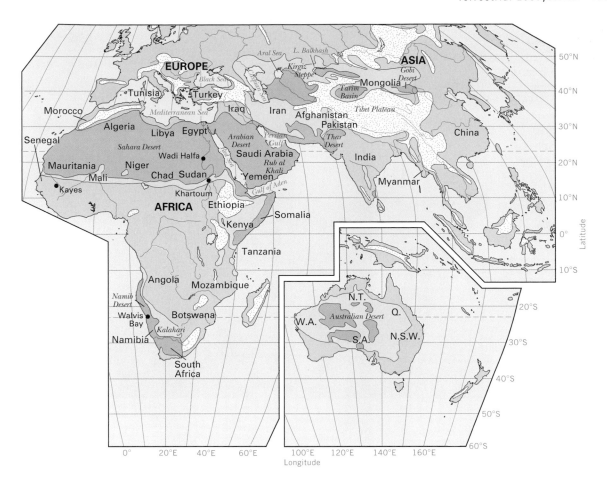

Thorntree semidesert of the tropical zone consists of xerophytic trees and shrubs that are adapted to a climate with a very long, hot dry season and only a very brief, but intense, rainy season. These conditions are found in the semiarid and arid subtypes of the dry tropical ④ and dry subtropical ⑤ climates. The thorny trees and shrubs are known locally as thorn forest, thornbush, or thornwoods (see Figure 7.18a). Many of these are deciduous plants that shed their leaves in the dry season. The shrubs may be closely intergrown to form dense thickets. Cactus plants are present in some localities.

Dry desert is a formation class of xerophytic plants that are widely dispersed over only a very small proportion of the ground. The visible vegetation of dry desert consists of small, hard-leaved, or spiny shrubs, succulent plants (such as cactus), or hard grasses. Many species of small annual plants may be present but appear only after a rare, but heavy, desert downpour. Much of the world map area assigned to desert vegetation has no plant cover at all because the surface consists of shifting dune sands or sterile salt flats.

Desert plants differ greatly in appearance from one part of the world to another. In the Mojave and Sonoran deserts of the southwestern United States, plants are often large, giving the

appearance of a woodland (Figure 9.21). Examples are the tree-like saguaro cactus, the prickly pear cactus, the ocotillo, creosote bush, and smoke tree.

Desert animals, like the plants, are typically adapted to the dry conditions of the desert. We have already mentioned some adaptations of xeric animals to the water scarcity of the desert. Important herbivores in American deserts include kangaroo rats, jackrabbits, and grasshopper mice. Insects are abundant, as are insect-eating bats and birds such as the cactus wren. Reptiles, especially lizards, are also common.

Tundra Biome

Arctic tundra is a formation class of the tundra climate ⑫. (See Figure 7.40 for a polar map of the arctic tundra.) In this climate, plants grow during the brief summer of long days and short (or absent) nights. At this time, air temperatures rise above freezing, and a shallow surface layer of ground ice thaws. The permafrost beneath, however, remains frozen, keeping the meltwater at the surface. These conditions create a marshy environment for at least a short time over wide areas. Because plant remains decay very slowly within the cold meltwater, layers of organic matter can build up in the marshy ground. Frost action in

The tundra biome includes low plants that are adapted to survival through a harsh, cold winter. They grow, bloom and set seed during a short summer thaw.

9.21 *Eye on the Landscape*
Desert plants *A desert scene near Phoenix, Arizona. The tall, columnar plant is saguaro cactus; the delicate wand-like plant is ocotillo. Small clumps of prickly pear cactus are seen between groups of hard-leaved shrubs.* **What else would the geographer see? ... Answers at the end of the chapter.**

the soil fractures and breaks large roots, keeping tundra plants small. In winter, wind-driven snow and extreme cold also injure plant parts that project above the snow.

Plants of the arctic tundra are mostly low herbs, although dwarf willow, a small woody plant, occurs in places. Sedges, grasses, mosses, and lichens dominate the tundra in a low layer (Figure 7.42). Typical plant species are ridge sedge, arctic meadow grass, cotton grasses, and snow lichen. There are also many species of forbs that flower brightly in the summer. Tundra composition varies greatly as soils range from wet to well drained. One form of tundra consists of sturdy hummocks of plants with low, water-covered ground between. Some areas of arctic scrub vegetation composed of willows and birches are also found in tundra.

Tundra vegetation is also found at high elevations. This *alpine tundra* develops above the limit of tree growth and below the vegetation-free zone of bare rock and perpetual snow (Figure 9.22). Alpine tundra resembles arctic tundra in many physical respects.

As is most often true in particularly dynamic environments, species diversity in the tundra is low, but the abundance of individuals is high. Among the animals, vast herds of caribou in North America and reindeer (their Eurasian relatives) roam the tundra, lightly grazing the lichens and plants and moving constantly. A smaller number of musk-oxen are also primary consumers of the tundra vegetation. Wolves and wolverines, as well as arctic foxes and polar bears, are predators. Among the smaller mammals, snowshoe rabbits and lemmings are important herbivores. Invertebrates are scarce in the tundra, except for a small number of insect species. Black flies, deerflies, mosquitoes, and "no-see-ums" (tiny biting midges) are all

9.22 **Alpine tundra** *Flag-shaped spruce trees (on left side of photo), shaped by prevailing winds, mark the upper limit of tree growth. Near the summit of the Snowy Range, Wyoming.*

abundant and can make July on the tundra most uncomfortable. Reptiles and amphibians are also rare. The boggy tundra, however, presents an ideal summer environment for many migratory birds such as waterfowl, sandpipers, and plovers.

The food web of the tundra ecosystem is simple and direct. The important producer is reindeer moss, the lichen *Cladonia rangifera.* In addition to the caribou and reindeer, lemmings, ptarmigan (arctic grouse), and snowshoe rabbits are important lichen grazers. The important predators are the fox, wolf, and lynx, although all these animals may feed directly on plants as well. During the summer, the abundant insects help support the migratory waterfowl populations.

Altitude Zones of Vegetation

In earlier chapters, we described the effects of increasing elevation on climatic factors, particularly air temperature and precipitation. We noted that, with elevation, temperatures decrease and precipitation generally increases. These changes produce systematic changes in the vegetation cover as well, yielding a sequence of vegetation zones related to altitude.

The vegetation zones of the Colorado Plateau region in northern Arizona and adjacent states provide a striking example of this altitude zonation. Figure 9.23 is a diagram showing a cross section of the land surface in this region. Elevations range from about 700 m (about 2300 ft) at the bottom of the Grand Canyon to 3844 m (12,608 ft) at the top of San Francisco Peak. The vegetation cover and rainfall range are shown on the left. The vegetation zonation includes desert shrub, grassland, woodland, pine forest, Douglas fir forest, Engelmann spruce forest, and alpine meadow. Annual rainfall ranges from 12 to 25 cm (about 5 to 10 in.) in the desert shrub vegetation type to 80–90 cm (about 30–35 in.) in the Engelmann spruce forest.

Biogeographers have used the vegetation zonation to set up a series of *life zones,* which are also shown on the figure. These range from the lower Sonoran life zone, which includes the desert shrubs typical of the Sonoran desert, to the arctic-alpine life zone, which includes the alpine meadows at the top of San Francisco Peak. Other life zones take their names from typical regions of vegetation cover. For example, the Hudsonian zone, 2900 to 3500 m (about 9500 to 11,500 ft), bears a needleleaf forest quite similar to needleleaf boreal forest of the subarctic zone near Hudson's Bay, Canada.

Climatic Gradients and Vegetation Types

In discussing the major formation classes of vegetation, we have emphasized the importance of climate. As climate changes with latitude or longitude, vegetation will also change. Figure 9.24 shows three transects across portions of continents that illustrate this principle. (For these transects, we will ignore the effects of mountains or highland regions on climate and vegetation.)

The upper transect stretches from the equator to the tropic of cancer in Africa. Across this region, climate ranges through all four low-latitude climates: wet equatorial ①, monsoon and tradewind coastal ②, wet-dry tropical ③, and dry tropical ④. Vegetation grades from equatorial rainforest, savanna wood-

---

Because climate factors of temperature and precipitation vary with elevation and over space, vegetation patterns often show zonation with altitude and systematic variation on long transects.

9.23   Altitude zone of vegetation in the arid southwestern United States *The profile shows the Grand Canyon-San Francisco Mountain district of northern Arizona. (Based on data of G. A. Pearson, C. H. Merriam, and A. N. Strahler.)*

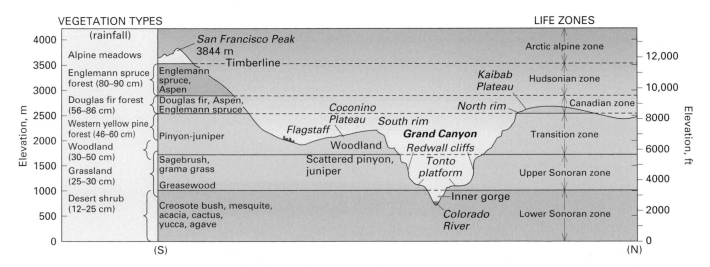

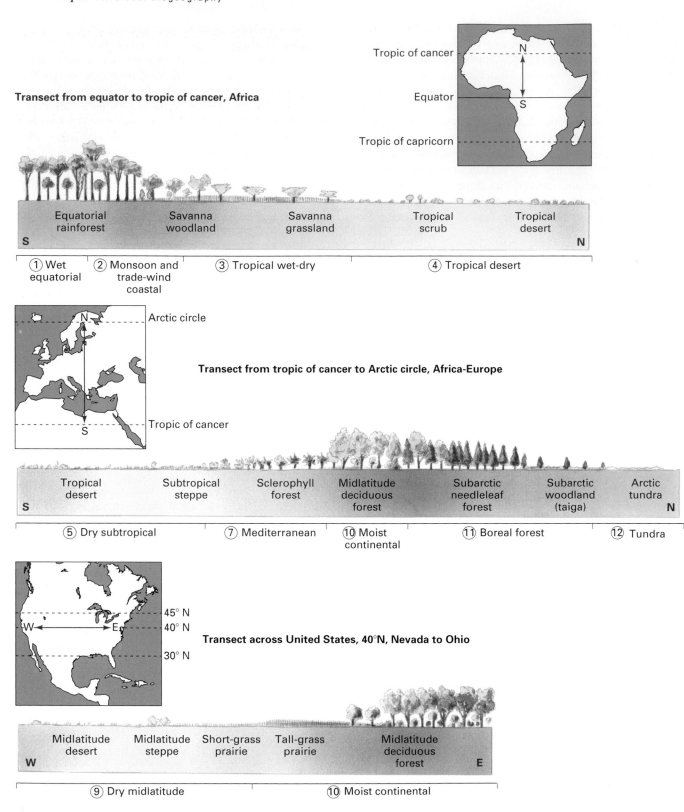

Transect from equator to tropic of cancer, Africa

Tropic of cancer

Equator

Tropic of capricorn

| Equatorial rainforest | Savanna woodland | Savanna grassland | Tropical scrub | Tropical desert |

S   N

① Wet equatorial ② Monsoon and trade-wind coastal ③ Tropical wet-dry ④ Tropical desert

Arctic circle

Transect from tropic of cancer to Arctic circle, Africa-Europe

Tropic of cancer

| Tropical desert | Subtropical steppe | Sclerophyll forest | Midlatitude deciduous forest | Subarctic needleleaf forest | Subarctic woodland (taiga) | Arctic tundra |

S   N

⑤ Dry subtropical ⑦ Mediterranean ⑩ Moist continental ⑪ Boreal forest ⑫ Tundra

45° N
40° N
30° N

Transect across United States, 40°N, Nevada to Ohio

W → E

| Midlatitude desert | Midlatitude steppe | Short-grass prairie | Tall-grass prairie | Midlatitude deciduous forest |

W   E

⑨ Dry midlatitude ⑩ Moist continental

9.24 Vegetation transects *Three continental transects showing the sequence of plant formation classes across climatic gradients.*

land, and savanna grassland to tropical scrub and tropical desert.

The middle transect is a composite from the tropic of cancer to the arctic circle in Africa and Eurasia. Climates include many of the mid- and high-latitude types: dry subtropical ⑤, Mediterranean ⑦, moist continental ⑩, boreal forest ⑪, and tundra ⑫. The vegetation cover grades from tropical desert through subtropical steppe to sclerophyll forest in the Mediterranean. Further north is the midlatitude deciduous forest in the region of moist continental climate ⑩, which grades into boreal needleleaf forest, subarctic woodland, and finally tundra.

The lower transect ranges across the United States, from Nevada to Ohio. On this transect, the climate begins as dry midlatitude ⑨. Precipitation gradually increases eastward, reaching moist continental ⑩ near the Mississippi River. The vegetation changes from midlatitude desert and steppe to short-grass prairie, tall-grass prairie, and midlatitude deciduous forest.

The changes on these transects are largely gradational rather than abrupt. Yet, the global maps of both vegetation and climate show distinct boundaries from one region to the next. Which is correct? The true situation is gradational rather than abrupt. Maps must necessarily have boundaries to communicate information. But climate and vegetation know no specific boundaries. Instead, they are classified into specific types for convenience in studying their spatial patterns. When studying any map of natural features, keep in mind that boundaries are always approximate and gradational.

GEODISCOVERIES **Web Quiz.** Take a quick quiz on the key concepts of this chapter.

A LOOK AHEAD

As we have seen in this chapter, climate has an important influence on the Earth's biomes, and the global pattern of biomes and formation classes is strongly related to the global pattern of climate. This pattern is also evident at the continental scale, as shown by transects that close the chapter. The pattern is provided by the biogeographic processes discussed in Chapter 8 that act individually on plants and animals to limit them to particular environments and locations depending primarily on climatic factors.

The key ingredients of climate are temperature, moisture, and the variation of temperature and moisture through the year. These same factors are important in the formation of soils, which is the subject of the next chapter. The vegetation cover also influences soil formation. For example, soils developed on grasslands are very different from those developed under conifer forests. Other important determinants of soil formation are the nature of the soil's parent material as it is derived from weathered rock and the time allowed for soil formation to proceed.

GEODISCOVERIES **Web Links.** Trek through the world's biomes on photo safaris. Take field trips from Colorado to the Amazon basin, Madagascar, and the Sea of Cortez. It's all in this chapter's web links.

In Review | Global Biogeography

- **Natural vegetation** is a plant cover that develops with little or no human interference. Although much vegetation appears to be in a natural state, humans influence the vegetation cover by fire suppression and introduction of new species.

- The **life-form** of a plant refers to its physical structure, size, and shape. Life-forms include *trees, shrubs, lianas, herbs,* and *lichens.*

- The largest unit of terrestrial ecosystems is the **biome:** forest, grassland, savanna, desert, and tundra. The **forest biome** includes a number of important forest formation classes. The *low-latitude rainforest* exhibits a dense canopy and open floor with a very large number of species. *Subtropical evergreen forest* occurs in *broadleaf* and *needleleaf* forms in the moist subtropical climate ⑥. *Monsoon forest* is largely deciduous, with most species shedding their leaves after the wet season.

- *Midlatitude deciduous forest* is associated with the moist continental climate ⑩. Its species shed their leaves before the cold season. *Needleleaf forest* consists largely of evergreen conifers. It includes the *coastal forest* of the Pacific Northwest, the *boreal forest* of high latitudes, and needle-leaved mountain forests. *Sclerophyll forest* is comprised of trees with small, hard, leathery leaves and is found in the Mediterranean climate ⑦ region.

- The **savanna biome** consists of widely spaced trees with an understory, often of grasses. Dry-season fire is frequent in the savanna biome, limiting the number of trees and encouraging the growth of grasses.

- The **grassland biome** of midlatitude regions includes *tall-grass prairie* in moister environments and *short-grass prairie,* or **steppe,** in semiarid areas.

- Vegetation of the **desert biome** ranges from thorny shrubs and small trees to dry desert vegetation comprised of drought-adapted species.

- **Tundra biome** vegetation is limited largely to low herbs that are adapted to the severe drying cold experienced on the fringes of the Arctic Ocean.

- Since climate changes with altitude, vegetation typically occurs in altitudinal zones. Climate also changes gradually with latitude, and so biome changes are typically gradual, without abrupt boundaries.

Key Terms

natural vegetation,
   p. 332
life form, p. 333
forest, p. 333

woodland, p. 333
terrestrial ecosystems,
   p. 334
biome, p. 334

forest biome, p. 334
savanna biome, p. 334
grassland biome, p. 334
desert biome, p. 334

tundra biome, p. 334
steppe, p. 353

Review Questions

1. What is natural vegetation? How do humans influence vegetation?

2. Plant geographers describe vegetation by its overall structure and by the life-forms of individual plants. Define and differentiate the following terms: forest, woodland, tree, shrub, herb, liana, perennial, deciduous, evergreen, broadleaf, and needleleaf.

3. What are the five main biome types that ecologists and biogeographers recognize? Describe each briefly.

4. Low-latitude rainforests occupy a large region of the Earth's land surface. What are the characteristics of these forests? Include forest structure, types of plants, diversity, and climate in your answer.

5. Monsoon forest and midlatitude deciduous forest are both deciduous but for different reasons. Compare the characteristics of these two formation classes and their climates.

6. Subtropical broadleaf evergreen forest and tall-grass prairie are two vegetation formation classes that have been greatly altered by human activities. How was this done and why?

7. Distinguish among the types of needleleaf forest. What characteristics do they share? How are they different? How do their climates compare?

8. Which type of forest, with related woodland and scrub types, is associated with the Mediterranean climate? What are the features of these vegetation types? How are they adapted to the Mediterranean climate?

9. How do traditional agricultural practices in the low-latitude rainforest compare to present-day practices? What are the implications for the rainforest environment?

10. What are the effects of large-scale clearing on the rainforest environment?

11. Describe the formation classes of the savanna biome. Where is this biome found and in what climate types? What role does fire play in the savanna biome?

12. Compare the two formation classes of the grassland biome. How do their climates differ?

13. Describe the vegetation types of the desert biome.

14. What are the features of arctic and alpine tundra? How does the cold tundra climate influence the vegetation cover?

15. How does elevation influence vegetation? Provide an example of how vegetation zonation is related to elevation.

Visualizing Exercises

1. Forests often contain plants of many different life-forms. Sketch a cross section of a forest including typical life-forms, and identify them with labels.

2. How does elevation influence vegetation? Sketch a hypothetical mountain peak in the southwestern U.S. desert that rises from a plain at about 500 m (about 1600 ft) elevation to a summit at about 4000 m (about 13,000 ft) and label the vegetation zones you might expect to find on its flanks.

Essay Questions

1. Figure 9.24 presents a vegetation transect from Nevada to Ohio. Expand the transect on the west so that it begins in Los Angeles. On the east, extend it northeast from Ohio through Pennsylvania, New York, western Massachusetts, and New Hampshire, to end in Maine. Sketch the vegetation types in your additions and label them, as in the diagram. Below your vegetation transect, draw a long bar subdivided to show the climate types.

2. Construct a similar transect of climate and vegetation from Miami to St. Louis, Minneapolis, and Winnipeg.

Eye on the Landscape

Chapter Opener A train streaks across the Mojave Desert Angular mountains **(A)** ascend from gravel-covered plains **(B)** in this sunset view of the Mojave Desert. The steep-sided mountain slopes are carved by running water from desert storms. Although such storms are infrequent, their effects are intense because of the lack of vegetation cover to hold the soil in place. As debris-laden streams drain into the lowlands, they deposit gravelly sediment in fans and plane off the underlying rock to form pediments. Stream erosion is the subject of Chapter 16, and it includes a section on landforms of mountainous deserts.

9.20 Sagebrush semidesert These tall columnar landforms are buttes **(A)**. Mesas are larger, isolated rock platforms **(B)**. Here in Monument Valley they are formed by a thick and uniform rock layer that weathers into rectangular blocks along joint planes. The blocks fall away, leaving a vertical cliff face behind. Buttes and mesas are discussed in Chapter 17, and joints are covered in Chapter 14.

9.21 Desert plants This sky of puffy altocumulus clouds and layered altostratus **(A)** indicates moisture at higher levels in the troposphere. The photo, taken in July, reflects conditions of the local "monsoon" season, in which moist air from the Gulf of California moves into southern Arizona, often generating intense thunderstorms and flash floods. The gravel-covered ground surface **(B)** is characteristic of deserts, where wind and storm runoff remove fine particles and leave coarser rock fragments behind. Clouds are covered in Chapter 4, and the Arizona monsoon is mentioned in Chapter 5. Erosion by runoff and wind are treated in Chapters 16 and 18.

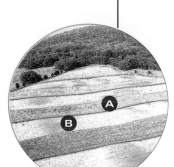

10 | GLOBAL SOILS

• • • • • • • • • • • • • • • •
PUTTING YOU IN THE PICTURE

This chapter is about soil—the loose surface layer of Earth that supports the growth of vegetation. North American soils provide the base for the most efficient and productive agriculture in the world. But this has not always been the case.

At the close of the eighteenth century, the fertility of the agricultural lands of the Southeast was declining rapidly. Romantically, we picture George Washington, happily retired on his Virginia estate, Mount Vernon, reaping a richly deserved bounty from expansive farmlands under his personal supervision. This vision is far from the truth. In fact, agricultural yields at Mount Vernon, and elsewhere in the Southeast, were dropping. In 1834, 35 years after Washington's death, a visitor to Mount Vernon declared that "a more widespread and perfect agricultural ruin could not be imagined."

The mystery of failing agricultural fertility was solved by Edmund Ruffin (1794–1865), who owned lands on the coastal plain of Virginia that were rapidly declining in the early 1800s. Quite by chance, Ruffin obtained a copy of Sir Humphry Davy's *Agricultural Chemistry,* published in 1813. Despite Ruffin's lack of formal education in science, he was quick to grasp the significance of one statement: "any acid matter … may be ameliorated by application of quicklime."

So it came about that on a February morning in 1818, Ruffin directed his fieldhands to haul marl from pits in low areas of his lands. Marl is a soft, lime-rich mud that occurs widely on the eastern coastal plain. The workers spread 200 bushels of marl over several acres of newly cleared ridge land of poor quality. In the spring, Ruffin planted this

area in corn to test the effect of the marl. In the words of historian Avery Craven, this is what happened: "Eagerly he waited. As the season advanced, he found reason for joy. From the very start the plants on marled ground showed marked superiority, and at harvest time they yielded an advantage of fully forty per cent. The carts went back to the pits. Fields took on fresh life. A new era in agricultural history of the region had dawned."*

Why did the application of lime enhance soil fertility so dramatically? As we will see in this chapter, nutrients are held in soils on the surfaces of fine particles. In an acid environment, these surfaces do not hold nutrients well, and so downward-moving water from precipitation washes nutrients out of the reach of plant roots. Lime reduces acidity and restores the ability of soil particles to hold nutrients, so that they remain available to plants.

Why didn't American farmers understand the importance of liming their fields? The colonists who settled this region were largely from England, where soils are formed on freshly ground mineral matter left by the great ice sheets. The breakdown products of this fresh mineral matter act like lime to reduce soil acidity, so that liming is not needed. In contrast, upland soils of the eastern seaboard from Virginia to Georgia have been continuously exposed to a mild, moist climate for tens of thousands of years. Fresh mineral matter in these soils has long been broken down, and the residual mineral matter that remains is highly acid. Thus, the colonists had no experience with these fundamentally different southeastern soils.

Soils are influenced by the rock material from which they develop, by the climate of the region (especially precipitation and temperature), by the vegetation cover that develops on them, and by the length of time that the soil has been in place. Your new knowledge of global climate and vegetation, acquired in the last two chapters, will be quite helpful in understanding soils and the processes that form them. ■

* Avery Craven, *Edmund Ruffin, Southerner* (New York; Appleton, 1932), p. 55.

GLOBAL SOILS

This chapter is devoted to soil systems, including the processes that form soils and give them their distinctive characteristics, to soil classification, and to global distribution of soil types. **Soil** is the uppermost layer of the land surface that plants use and depend on for nutrients, water, and physical support. Soils can vary greatly from continent to continent, region to region, and even from field to field. This is because they are influenced by factors and processes that can vary widely from place to place. For example, a field near a large river that floods regularly may acquire a layer of nutrient-rich silt, making its soil very productive. A nearby field at a higher elevation, without the benefit of silt enrichment, may be sandy or stony and require the addition of fertilizers to grow crops productively.

Vegetation is an important factor in determining soil qualities. For example, some of America's richest soils developed in the Middle West under a cover of thick grass sod. The deep roots of the grass, in a cycle of growth and decay, deposited nutrients and organic matter throughout the thick soil layer. In the Northeast, conifer forests provided a surface layer of decaying needles that kept the soil quite acid. This acidity allowed nutrients to be washed below root depth, out of the reach of plants. When farmed today, these soils need applications of lime to reduce their acidity and enhance their fertility.

> Soil is the uppermost layer of the land surface. Plants depend on soil for nutrients, water, and physical support. Vegetation, climate, and time are important factors in soil development.

Climate, measured by precipitation and temperature, is also an important determinant of soil properties. Precipitation controls the downward movement of nutrients and other chemical compounds in soils. If precipitation is abundant, water tends to wash soluble compounds, including nutrients, deeper into the soil and out of reach of plant roots.

Temperature acts to control the rate of decay of organic matter that falls to the soil from the plant cover or that is provided to the soil by the death of roots. When conditions are warm and moist, decay organisms work efficiently, consuming organic matter readily. Thus, organic matter and nutrients in soils of the tropical and equatorial zones are generally low. Where conditions are cooler, decay proceeds more slowly, and organic matter is more abundant in the soil. Of course, if the climate is very dry or desert-like, then vegetation growth is slow or absent. No matter what desert temperatures are like, organic matter will be low.

Time is also an important factor. The characteristics and properties of soils require time for development. For example, a fresh deposit of mineral matter, like the clean, sorted sand of a dune, may require hundreds to thousands of years to acquire the structure and properties of a sandy soil.

Geographers are keenly interested in the differences in soils from place to place over the globe. The ability of the soils and climate of a region to produce food largely determines the size of the population it will support. In spite of the growth of cities, most of the world's inhabitants still live close to the soil that furnishes their food. And many of those same inhabitants die prematurely when the soil does not furnish enough food for all.

THE NATURE OF THE SOIL

Soil, as the term is used in soil science, is a natural surface layer that contains living matter and can support plants. The soil consists of matter in all three states—solid, liquid, and gas. It includes both *mineral matter* and *organic matter.* Mineral matter is largely derived from rock material, whereas organic matter is of biological origin and may be living or dead. Living matter in the soil consists not only of plant roots, but also of many kinds of organisms, including microorganisms.

Soil scientists use the term *humus* to describe finely divided, partially decomposed organic matter in soils. Some humus rests on the soil surface, and some is mixed through the soil. Humus particles of the finest size are gradually carried downward to lower soil layers by rainfall that sinks in and moves through the soil. When abundant, humus particles can give the soil a brown or black coloration.

Both air and water are found in soil. Water may tend to contain high levels of dissolved substances, such as nutrients. Air in soils may have high levels of such gases as carbon dioxide or methane, and low levels of oxygen.

The solid, liquid, and gaseous matter of the soil are constantly changing and interacting through chemical and physical processes. This makes the soil a very dynamic layer. Because of these processes, soil science, often called *pedology,* is a highly complex body of knowledge.

Although we may think of soil as occurring everywhere, large expanses of continents possess a surface layer that cannot be called soil. For example, dunes of moving sand, bare rock surfaces of deserts and high mountains, and surfaces of fresh lava near active volcanoes do not have a soil layer.

The characteristics of soils are developed over a long period of time through a combination of many processes acting together. Physical processes act to break down rock fragments of regolith into smaller and smaller pieces. Chemical processes alter the mineral composition of the original rock, producing new minerals. Taken together, these physical and chemical processes are referred to as *weathering,* which we will describe in Chapter 14. Weathering occurs in soils and is part of the process by which soils develop their properties and characteristics.

In most soils, the inorganic material of the soil consists of fine particles of mineral matter. The term **parent material** describes all forms of mineral matter that are suitable for transformation into soil. Parent material may be derived

Soil is a complex mixture of solids, liquids, and gases. Solid matter includes both mineral and organic matter. Watery solutions and atmospheric gases are also found in soils.

10.1 A cross section through the land surface *In this cross section, vegetation and forest litter lie atop the soil. Below is regolith, produced by the breakup of the underlying bedrock.*

from the underlying *bedrock,* which is solid rock below the soil layer (Figure 10.1). Over time, weathering processes soften, disintegrate, and break bedrock apart, forming a layer of *regolith,* or residual mineral matter. Regolith is one of the common forms of parent material. Other kinds of regolith consist of mineral particles transported to a place of rest by the action of streams, glaciers, waves and water currents, or winds. For example, dunes formed of sand transported by wind are a type of regolith on which soil may be formed.

Soil Color and Texture

The most obvious feature of a soil or soil layer is probably its color. Some color relationships are quite simple. For example, the soils of the Midwest prairies have a black or dark brown color because they contain abundant particles of humus. Red or yellow colors often mark the soils of the Southeast. These colors are created by the presence of iron-containing oxides.

In some areas, soil color may be inherited from the mineral parent material, but, more generally, soil color is generated by soil-forming processes. For example, a white surface layer in soils of dry climates often indicates the presence of mineral salts brought upward by evaporation. A pale, ashgray layer near the top of soils of the boreal forest climate results when organic matter and various colored minerals are washed downward, leaving only pure, light-colored mineral matter behind. As we explain soil-forming processes and describe the various classes of soils, soil color will take on more meaning.

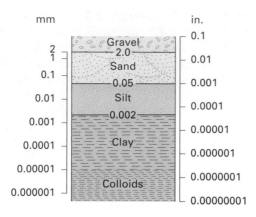

10.2 Mineral particle sizes *Size grades, which are names like sand, silt, and clay, refer to mineral particles within a specific size range. They are defined using the metric system. English equivalents are also shown.*

The mineral matter of the soil consists of individual mineral particles that vary widely in size. The term **soil texture** refers to the proportion of particles that fall into each of three size grades—*sand, silt,* and *clay.* The diameter range of each of these grades is shown in Figure 10.2. Millimeters are the standard units. Each unit on the scale represents a power of ten, so that clay particles of 0.000,001 millimeter diameter are one-millionth the size of sand grains 1 mm in diameter. The finest of all soil particles are termed *colloids.* In measuring soil texture, gravel and larger particles are eliminated, since these play no important role in soil processes.

Soil texture is described by a series of names that emphasize the dominant particle size, whether sand, silt, or clay (including colloids). Figure 10.3 gives examples of five soil textures with typical percentage compositions. A *loam* is a

---

Soil texture refers to the proportions of sand, silt, and clay found in a soil. Soil color is usually determined by soil-forming processes and varies widely.

---

mixture containing a substantial proportion of each of the three grades. Loams are classified as sandy, silty, or clayrich when one of these grades is dominant.

Why is soil texture important? Texture largely determines the ability of the soil to retain water. Coarse-textured (sandy) soils have many small passages between touching mineral grains that quickly conduct water through to deeper layers. If the soil consists of fine particles, passages and spaces are much smaller. Thus, water will penetrate more slowly and also tend to be retained. We will return to the important topic of the water-holding ability of soils in a later section.

Soil Colloids

Soil colloids consist of particles smaller than one hundred-thousandth of a millimeter (0.000,01 mm, 0.000,000,4 in.). Like other soil particles, some colloids are mineral, while others are organic. Mineral colloids are usually very fine particles of clay minerals. If you examine mineral colloids under a microscope, you will find that they consist of thin, plate-like bodies (Figure 10.4). When well mixed in water, particles this small remain suspended indefinitely, giving the water a murky appearance. Organic colloids are tiny bits of organic matter that are resistant to decay.

Soil colloids are important because their surfaces attract soil nutrients, which are in the form of ions dissolved in soil water. Figure 10.5 diagrams a colloidal particle, showing this effect. Colloid surfaces tend to be negatively

10.4 Mineral colloids *Seen here enlarged about 20,000 times are tiny flakes of clay minerals of colloidal dimensions. These particles have settled from suspension in San Francisco Bay.*

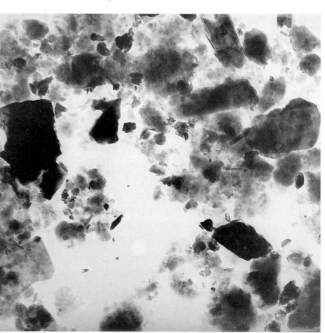

10.3 Soil textures *These diagrams show the proportion of sand, silt, and clay in five different soil texture classes. For description of soil texture, clay includes colloids.*

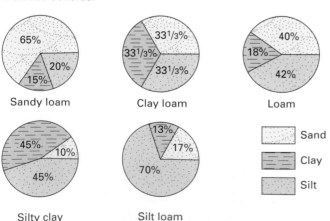

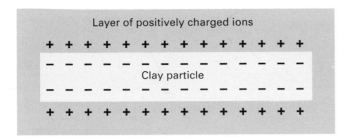

10.5 Schematic diagram of a colloid particle *The thin, flat colloidal particle has negative surface charges and a layer of positively charged ions held to the surface.*

charged because of their molecular structure, and thus attract and hold positively charged ions. Among the many ions in soil water, one important group consists of **bases,** which are ions of four elements: calcium (Ca^{++}), magnesium (Mg^{++}), potassium (K^+), and sodium (Na^+). Because plants require these elements, they are among the *plant nutrients*—ions or chemical compounds that are needed for plant growth. Colloids hold these ions, but also give them up to plants when in close contact with root membranes. Without this ion-holding ability of soil colloids, most of the vital nutrients would be carried out of the soil by percolating water and would be taken out of the region in streams, eventually reaching the sea. This leaching process goes on continually in moist climates, but loss is greatly retarded by the ion-holding capacity of soil colloids.

> Colloids are the finest particles in the soil. The surfaces of colloids attract base ions, which plants use as nutrients.

> Soil acidity, as measured by pH, varies widely. Soils of cool, moist regions are generally acid, while soils of arid climates are alkaline. Acid soils often have a low base status.

Soil Acidity and Alkalinity

The soil solution also contains hydrogen (H^+) and aluminum (Al^{+++}) ions. But unlike the bases, they are not considered to

be plant nutrients. The presence of these acid ions in the soil solution tends to make the solution acid in chemical balance.

An important principle of soil chemistry is that the acid ions have the power to replace the nutrient bases clinging to the surfaces of the soil colloids. As acid ions accumulate, the bases are released to the soil solution. They are gradually washed downward below rooting level, reducing soil fertility. When this happens, the soil acidity is increased.

The degree of acidity or alkalinity of a solution is designated by the *pH value*. The lower the pH value, the greater the degree of acidity. A pH value of 7 represents a neutral state—for example, pure water has a pH of 7. Lower values are in the acid range, while higher values are in the alkaline range.

Table 10.1 shows the natural range of acidity and alkalinity found in soils. High soil acidity is typical of cold, humid climates. In arid climates, soils are typically alkaline. Acidity can be corrected by the application of lime, a compound of calcium, carbon, and oxygen ($CaCO_3$), which removes acid ions and replaces them with the base calcium.

Soil Structure

Soil structure refers to the way in which soil grains are grouped together into larger masses, called *peds*. Peds range in size from small grains to large blocks. They are bound together by soil colloids. Small peds, roughly shaped like spheres, give the soil a granular structure or crumb structure (see Figure 10.6). Larger peds provide an angular, blocky structure. Peds form when colloid-rich clays shrink in volume as they dry out. Shrinkage results in formation of soil cracks, which define the surfaces of the peds.

Soils with a well-developed granular or blocky structure are easy to cultivate. This is an important agricultural factor

Table 10.1	Soil Acidity and Alkalinity											
pH	**4.0**	**4.5**	**5.0**	**5.5**	**6.0**	**6.5**	**6.7**	**7.0**	**8.0**	**9.0**	**10.0**	**11.0**
Acidity	Very strongly acid		Strongly acid	Moderately acid	Slightly acid			Neutral	Weakly alkaline	Alkaline	Strongly alkaline	Excessively alkaline
Lime requirements	Lime needed except for crops requiring acid soil		Lime needed for all but acid-tolerant crops		Lime generally not required			No lime needed				
Occurrence	Rare	Frequent	Very common in cultivated soils of humid climates					Common in subhumid and arid climates			Limited areas in deserts	

Source: Based on data of C. E. Millar, L. M. Turk, and H. D. Foth, *Fundamentals of Soil Science,* John Wiley & Sons, New York.

10.6 Soil structure *This soil shows a granular structure. The grains are referred to as peds.*

in lands where primitive plows, drawn by animals, are still widely used. Soils with a high clay content can lack peds. These soils are sticky and heavy when wet and are difficult to cultivate. When dry, they become too hard to be worked.

Minerals of the Soil

Soil scientists recognize two classes of minerals abundant in soils: primary minerals and secondary minerals. The *primary minerals* are compounds present in unaltered rock. These are mostly silicate minerals—compounds of silicon and oxygen, with varying proportions of aluminum, calcium, sodium, iron, and magnesium. (The silicate minerals are described more fully in Chapter 11.) Primary minerals form a large fraction of the solid matter of many kinds of soils, but they play no important role in sustaining plant or animal life.

When primary minerals are exposed to air and water at or near the Earth's surface, they are slowly altered in chemical composition. This process is part of *mineral alteration,* a chemical weathering process that is explained in more detail in Chapter 11. The primary minerals are altered into **secondary minerals,** which are essential to soil development and to soil fertility.

In terms of the properties of soils, the most important secondary minerals are the *clay minerals.* They form the majority of fine mineral particles in soils. From the viewpoint of soil fertility, the ability of a clay mineral to hold base ions is its most important property. This ability varies with the particular type of clay mineral; some hold bases tightly, and others loosely.

The nature of the clay minerals in a soil determines its *base status.* If the clay minerals can hold abundant base ions, the soil is of *high base status* and generally will be highly fertile. If the clay minerals hold a smaller supply of

---

Primary minerals in soils are minerals that remain from unaltered rock. Secondary minerals are formed by mineral alteration. Clay minerals and sesquioxides are important secondary minerals.

---

bases, the soil is of *low base status* and is generally less fertile. Humus colloids have a high capacity to hold bases so that the presence of humus is usually associated with potentially high soil fertility.

Mineral oxides are secondary minerals of importance in soils. They occur in many kinds of soils, particularly those that remain in place in areas of warm, moist climates over very long periods of time (hundreds of thousands of years). Under these conditions, minerals are ultimately broken down chemically into simple oxides, compounds in which a single element is combined with oxygen.

Oxides of aluminum and iron are the most important oxides in soils. Two atoms of aluminum are combined with three atoms of oxygen to form the *sesquioxide* of aluminum (Al_2O_3). (The prefix *sesqui-* means "one and a half" and refers to the chemical composition of one and one-half atoms of oxygen for every atom of aluminum.) In soils, aluminum oxide forms the mineral *bauxite,* which is a combination of aluminum sesquioxide and water molecules bound together. It occurs as hard, rock-like lumps and layers below the soil surface. Where bauxite layers are thick and uniform, they are sometimes strip-mined as aluminum ore.

Sesquioxide of iron (Fe_2O_3), again held in combination with water molecules, is *limonite,* a yellowish to reddish mineral that supplies the typical reddish to chocolate-brown colors of soils and rocks. Some shallow accumulations of limonite were formerly mined as a source of iron. Limonite and bauxite occur in close association in soils of warm, moist climates in low latitudes.

Soil Moisture

Besides providing nutrients for plant growth, the soil layer serves as a reservoir for the moisture that plants require. Soil moisture is a key factor in determining how the soils of a region support vegetation and crops.

The soil receives water from rain and from melting snow. Where does this water go? First, some of the water can run off the soil surface and not sink in. Instead, it flows into brooks, streams, and rivers, eventually reaching the sea. What of the water that sinks into the soil? Some of this water is returned to the atmosphere as water vapor. This happens when soil water evaporates and when transpiration by plants lifts soil water from roots to leaves, where it evaporates. Taken together, we can term these last two losses *evapotranspiration*. Some water can also flow completely through the soil layer to recharge supplies of ground water at depths below the reach of plant roots.

When precipitation infiltrates the soil, the water wets the soil layer. This process is called *soil water recharge*. Eventually, the soil layer holds the maximum possible quantity of water, even though the larger pores may remain filled with air. Water movement then continues downward.

Suppose now that no further water enters the soil for a time. Excess soil water continues to drain downward, but some water clings to the soil particles. This water resists the pull of gravity because of the force of *capillary tension*. To understand this force, think about a droplet of condensation that has formed on the cold surface of a glass of ice water. The water droplet seems to be enclosed in a "skin" of surface molecules, drawing the droplet together into a rounded shape. The "skin" is produced by capillary tension. This force keeps the drop clinging to the side of the glass indefinitely, defying the force of gravity. Similarly, tiny films of water adhere to soil grains, particularly at the points of grain contacts. They remain until they evaporate or are absorbed by plant rootlets.

When a soil has first been saturated by water and then allowed to drain under gravity until no more water moves downward, the soil is said to be holding its *storage capacity* of water. For most soils, drainage takes no more than two or three days. Most excess water is drained out within one day.

Storage capacity is measured in units of depth, usually centimeters or inches, as with precipitation. It depends largely on the texture of the soil, as shown in Figure 10.7. Finer textures hold more water than coarser textures. This occurs because fine particles have a much larger surface area in a unit of volume than coarse particles. Thus, a sandy soil has a small storage capacity, while a clay soil has a large storage capacity.

The figure also shows the *wilting point*, which is the water storage level below which plants will wilt. The wilting point depends on soil texture. Because fine particles hold water more tightly, it is more difficult for plants to extract moisture from fine soils. Thus, plants can wilt in fine-textured soils even though more soil water is present than in coarse-textured soils. The difference between the storage capacity of a soil and its wilting point is the *available water capacity*—that is, the maximum amount of water available

> Soil moisture clings to soil particles by capillary action. Soil storage capacity, which depends on soil texture, measures the ability of a soil to hold moisture after excess water has drained away.

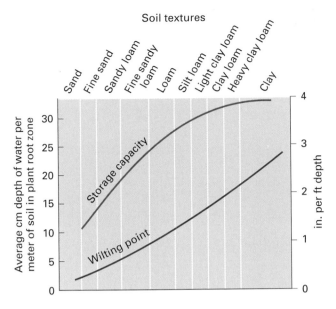

10.7 Storage capacity and wilting point according to soil texture *Finer textured soils hold more water. They also hold water more tightly, so that plants wilt more quickly.*

to plants when the soil is at storage capacity. The available water capacity is greatest in loamy soils.

THE SOIL WATER BALANCE

Water in the soil is a critical resource needed for plant growth. The amount of water available at any given time is determined by the *soil water balance,* which includes the gain, loss, and storage of soil water. Figure 10.8 is a pictorial flow diagram that illustrates the components of the balance. Water held in storage in the soil water zone is increased by recharge during precipitation but decreased by use through evapotranspiration. Surplus water is disposed of by downward percolation to the ground water zone or by overland flow.

To proceed, we must recognize two ways to define evapotranspiration. First is *actual evapotranspiration (Ea),* which is the true or real rate of water vapor return to the atmosphere from the ground and its plant cover. Second is *potential evapotranspiration (Ep),* representing the water vapor loss under an ideal set of conditions. One condition is that there is present a complete (or closed) cover of uniform vegetation consisting of fresh green leaves and no bare ground exposed through that cover. A second condition is that there is an adequate water supply, so that the storage capacity of the soil is maintained at all times. This condition can be fulfilled naturally by abundant and frequent precipitation, or artificially by irrigation.

To simplify the ponderous terms we have just defined, they may be transformed as follows:

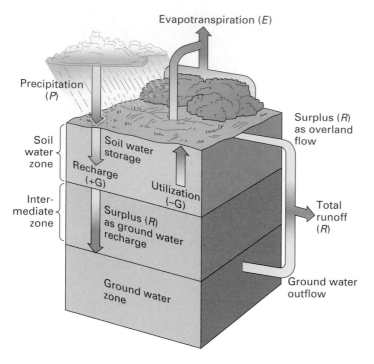

10.8 Schematic diagram of the soil water balance in a soil column (Copyright © A. N. Strahler.)

- Actual evapotranspiration *(Ea)* is **water use.**
- Potential evapotranspiration *(Ep)* is **water need.**

The word "need" signifies the quantity of soil water needed if plant growth is to be maximized for the given conditions of solar radiation and air temperature and the available supply of nutrients. The most important factor in determining water need is temperature. In warmer months, water need will be greater, while in cooler months, it will be less.

The difference between water use and water need is the *soil water shortage,* or *deficit.* This is the quantity of water that must be furnished by irrigation to achieve maximum crop growth within an agricultural system.

A Simple Soil Water Budget

We now turn to a simple accounting of the monthly and annual quantities of the components of the soil water balance. The numerical accounting is called a *soil water budget,* and it involves only simple addition and subtraction of monthly mean values for a given observing station. All terms of the soil water budget are stated in centimeters of water depth, the same as for precipitation.

A simplified soil water budget is shown in Figure 10.9. The seven terms we need for a complete budget are listed as follows, along with abbreviations used on the graph:

Precipitation, *P*
Water need, *Ep*

The soil water budget measures the balance between water need, water use, and precipitation for each month. Depending on the balance, soil moisture may be lowered or recharged.

Water use, *Ea*
Storage withdrawal, *−G*
Storage recharge, *+G*
Soil water shortage, *D*
Water surplus, *R*

Points on the graph represent average monthly values of precipitation and water need. They are connected by smooth curves to enhance annual cycles of change. In our example, precipitation *(P)* is much the same in all months, with no strong annual cycle. In contrast, water need *(Ep)* shows a strong seasonal cycle, with low values in winter and a high summer peak. This example would fit a typical moist mid-latitude climate with mild winters.

At the start of the year, precipitation greatly exceeds water use and a large water surplus *(R)* exists. This surplus is disposed of by runoff. By May, water use exceeds precipitation, and a water deficit occurs. In this month plants begin to withdraw soil water from storage.

Storage withdrawal (−G) is represented by the difference between the water-use curve and the precipitation curve. As storage withdrawal continues, however, plants draw soil water only with increasing difficulty. Thus, water use *(Ea)* is less than water need *(Ep)* during this period. Storage withdrawal continues throughout the summer. The deficit period lasts through September. The area labeled soil water shortage *(D)* is the difference between water need and water use. It represents the total quantity of water needed by irrigation to ensure maximum growth throughout the deficit period.

In October, precipitation *(P)* again begins to exceed water need *(Ep),* but the soil must first absorb an amount equal to the summer storage withdrawal. So there follows a period of *storage recharge (+G)* that lasts through November. In December

10.9 A simplified soil water budget *This soil water budget is typical of a moist climate in middle latitudes.*

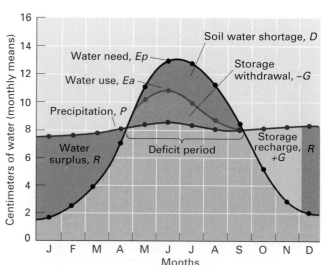

the soil reaches its full storage capacity, arbitrarily fixed at 30 cm (11.8 in.). Now, a water surplus *(R)* again sets in, lasting through the winter.

The soil water budget was developed by C. Warren Thornthwaite, a distinguished climatologist and geographer who was concerned with practical problems of crop irrigation. He developed the calculation of the soil water budget in order to place irrigation on a precise, accurate basis. Only in the equatorial zone and in a few parts of the tropical and midlatitude zones is precipitation ample to fulfill the water need during the growing season. In a world beset by severe and prolonged food shortages, the Thornthwaite concepts and calculations are of great value in assessing the benefits to be gained by increased irrigation.

SOIL DEVELOPMENT

How do soils develop their distinctive characteristics? There are a number of important processes that act to form soils. But before we describe them, you will need to know something about soil horizons.

Soil Horizons

Most soils possess **soil horizons**—distinctive horizontal layers that differ in

___

Soil horizons are distinctive layers found in soils that differ in physical or chemical composition, organic content, or structure. The soil profile refers to the display of horizons on a cross section through the soil.

___

physical composition, chemical composition, or organic content or structure (Figure 10.10). Soil horizons are developed by the interactions through time of climate, living organisms, and the configuration of the land surface. Horizons usually develop by either selective removal or accumulation of certain ions, colloids, and chemical compounds. The removal or accumulation is normally produced by water seeping down through the soil profile from the surface to deeper layers. Horizons are often distinguished by their color. The display of horizons on a cross section through the soil is termed a **soil profile.**

Figure 10.10 also illustrates the idea of the *pedon*—a soil column, extending down from the surface to a lower limit in regolith or bedrock, which is taken as the smallest distinctive division of the soil of a given area. The pedon has all the distinctive features needed to properly classify and describe the soil at a location. Soil scientists often visualize the pedon as a six-sided column, as shown in the figure. A patch of soil of the same type, which is made up of many pedons, is termed a *polypedon*.

Let's review briefly the main types of horizons and their characteristics. For now, this discussion will apply to the types of horizons and processes that are found in moist forest climates. These are shown in Figure 10.11. Soil horizons are of two types: organic and mineral. Organic horizons, designated by the capital letter *O*, overlie the mineral horizons and are formed from accumulations of organic matter derived from plants and animals. Soil scientists recognize two possible layers. The upper O_i horizon contains decomposing organic matter that is recognizable as leaves or twigs. The lower O_a horizon contains material that is broken down beyond recognition by eye. This material is humus, which we mentioned earlier.

Mineral horizons lie below the organic horizons. Four main horizons are important—*A, E, B,* and *C*. Plant roots readily penetrate *A, E,* and *B* horizons and influence soil development within them. Soil scientists limit the term *soil* to refer to the *A, E,* and *B* horizons. The *A horizon* is the uppermost mineral horizon. It is rich in organic matter, consisting of numerous plant roots and downwashed humus from the organic horizons above. Next is the *E horizon*. Clay particles and oxides of aluminum and iron are removed from the *E horizon* by downward-seeping water, leaving behind pure grains of sand or coarse silt.

The *B horizon* receives the clay particles, aluminum, and iron oxides, as well as organic matter washed down from the *A* and *E* horizons. It is made dense and tough by the filling of natural spaces with clays and oxides. Transitional horizons are present at some locations.

Beneath the *B horizon* is the *C horizon*. It consists of the parent mineral matter of the soil and has been described earlier in this chapter as regolith (see Figure 10.1). Below the regolith lies bedrock or sediments of much older age than the soil.

10.10 Soil horizons *A column of soil will normally show a series of horizons, which are horizontal layers with different properties.*

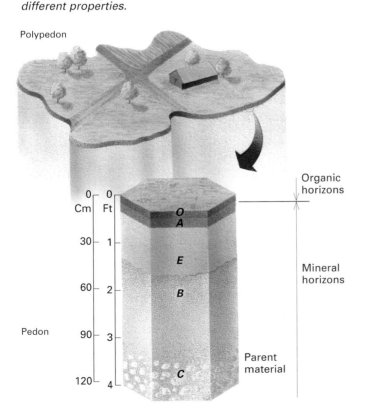

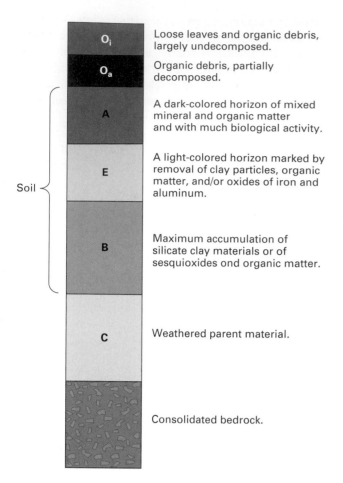

10.11 Soil horizons of moist forest climates *A sequence of horizons that might appear in a forest soil developed under a cool, moist climate. (Natural Resources Conservation Service, U.S. Department of Agriculture.)*

Table 10.2 | Soil-Forming Processes

Enrichment	Addition of material to the soil, for example, by deposition of mineral matter by water or wind action.
Removal	Removal of material from the soil, for example, by erosion of uppermost layers or by leaching of dissolved matter to lower layers or to ground water.
Decalcification	Leaching of calcium carbonate from the soil to the ground water below, carried by large amounts of infiltrating precipitation in moist climates.
Translocation	Movement of materials upward or downward within the soil body.
Eluviation	Downward transport of fine materials from the upper part of the soil.
Illuviation	Accumulation of fine materials in a lower part of the soil.
Calcification	Accumulation of calcium carbonate by dissolution in upper layers and precipitation in the *B* horizon.
Salinization	Upward wicking of salt-laden ground water toward the soil surface with evaporation to produce a layer of salt accumulation.
Transformation	Transformation of material in the soil body, for example conversion of primary to secondary minerals.
Humification	Decomposition of organic matter to produce humus.

Soil-Forming Processes

There are four classes of soil-forming processes (Table 10.2). The first includes processes of *soil enrichment,* which add material to the soil body. For example, inorganic enrichment occurs when sediment is brought from higher to lower areas by overland flow. Stream flooding also deposits fine mineral particles on low-lying soil surfaces. Wind is another source of fine material that can accumulate on the soil surface. Organic enrichment occurs when humus accumulating in *O* horizons is carried downward to enrich the *A* horizon below.

The second class includes processes that remove material from the soil body. This *removal* occurs when surface erosion carries sediment away from the uppermost layer of soil. Another important process of loss is *leaching,* in which seeping water dissolves soil materials and moves them to deep levels or to ground water.

In moist climates, a large amount of surplus soil water moves downward to the ground water zone. This water movement leaches calcium carbonate from the entire soil in a process called *decalcification.* Soils that have lost most of their calcium are also usually acid in chemical balance and so are low in bases. Addition of lime or pulverized limestone not only corrects the acid condition, but also restores the calcium, which is used as a plant nutrient.

The third class of soil-forming processes involves *translocation,* in which materials are moved within the soil body, usually from one horizon to another. Two processes of translocation that operate simultaneously are eluviation and illuviation. **Eluviation** consists of the downward transport of fine particles, particularly the clays and colloids, from the uppermost part of the soil. Eluviation leaves behind grains of sand or coarse silt, forming the *E* horizon. **Illuviation** is the accumulation of materials that are brought down downward, normally from the *E* horizon to the *B* horizon. The materials that accumulate may be clay particles, humus, or sesquioxides of iron and aluminum.

> The four classes of soil-forming processes are enrichment, removal, translocation, and transformation. In translocation, fine particles are transported downward by eluviation and accumulate in lower horizons by illuviation.

GEODISCOVERIES **Soil Horizons.** Watch an animation demonstrating eluvation and illuviation through the soil profile.

10.12   A forest soil profile on outer Cape Cod *The pale grayish E horizon overlies a reddish B horizon. A thin layer of wind-deposited silt and dune sand (pale brown layer) has been deposited on top.*

Figure 10.12 is a soil profile developed under a cool, humid forest climate. It shows the effects of both soil enrichment and translocation processes. The topmost layer of the soil is a thin deposit of wind-blown silt and dune sand, which has enriched the soil profile. In translocation processes, eluviation has removed colloids and sesquioxides from the whitened *E* horizon. Illuviation has added them to the *B* horizon, which displays the orange-red colors of iron sesquioxide.

The translocation of calcium carbonate is another important process. In pure form, this secondary mineral is calcite ($CaCO_3$). In many areas, the parent material of the soil contains a substantial proportion of calcium carbonate derived from the disintegration of limestone, a common variety of bedrock. Carbonic acid, which forms when carbon dioxide gas dissolves in rainwater or soil water, readily reacts with calcium carbonate. The products of this reaction remain dissolved in solution as ions.

In dry climates, calcium carbonate is dissolved in the upper layers of the soil during periods of rain or snowmelt

when soil water recharge is taking place. The dissolved carbonate matter is carried down to the *B* horizon, where water penetration reaches its limits. Here, the carbonate matter is precipitated (deposited in crystalline form) in the *B* horizon, a process called *calcification.* Calcium carbonate deposition takes the form of white or pale-colored grains, nodules, or plates in the *B* or *C* horizons.

Translocation also occurs in desert climates. In some low areas, a layer of ground water lies close to the surface, producing a flat, poorly drained area. Evaporation of water at or near the soil surface draws up a continual flow of ground water by capillary tension, much like a cotton wick draws oil upward in an oil lamp. Moreover, the ground water is often rich in dissolved salts. When evaporation occurs, the salts precipitate and accumulate as a distinctive *salic horizon.* This process is called *salinization.* Most of the salts are compounds of sodium, of which ordinary table salt (sodium chloride, or halite, NaCl) is a familiar example. Sodium in large amounts is associated with highly alkaline conditions and is toxic to many kinds of plants. When salinization occurs in irrigated lands in a desert climate, the soil can be ruined for further agricultural use. *Eye on the Environment 10.1 ● Death of a Civilization* shows how the ancient cultures of Babylon and Sumer declined as their irrigated desert soils deteriorated from salinization and waterlogging.

The last class of soil-forming processes involves the *transformation* of material within the soil body. An example is the conversion of minerals from primary to secondary types, which we have already described. Another example is decomposition of organic matter to produce humus, a process termed *humification.* In warm, moist climates, humification can decompose organic matter completely to yield carbon dioxide and water, leaving virtually no organic matter in the soil.

Soil Temperature and Other Factors

Soil temperature is another important factor in determining the chemical development of soils and the formation of horizons. Temperature acts as a control over biologic activity and also influences the intensity of chemical processes affecting soil minerals. Below 10°C (50°F), biological activity is slowed, and at or below the freezing point (0°C, 32°F), biological activity stops. Chemical processes affecting minerals are inactive. The root growth of most plants and germination of their seeds require soil temperatures above 5°C (41°F). For plants of the warm, wet low-latitude climates, germination of seeds may require a soil temperature of at least 24°C (75°F).

The temperature of the uppermost soil layer and the soil surface strongly affects the rate at which organic matter is decomposed by microorganisms. Thus, in cold climates, where decomposition is slow, organic matter in the form of fallen leaves and stems tends to accumulate to form a thick *O* horizon. As we have

> **Temperature has an important influence on soil development. In cold climates, decomposition of organic matter is slow and organic matter accumulates. In warm climates, organic matter decomposes rapidly and soil organic matter is scarce.**

composition of these agricultural soils have undergone great changes. These altered soils are often recognized as distinct soil classes that are just as important as natural soils.

THE GLOBAL SCOPE OF SOILS

An important aspect of soil science for physical geography is the classification of soils into major types and subtypes that are recognized in terms of their distribution over the Earth's land surfaces. Geographers are particularly interested in the linkage of climate, parent material, time, biologic process, and landform with the distribution of types of soils. Geographers are also interested in the kinds of natural vegetation associated with each of the major soil classes. The geography of soils is thus essential in determining the quality of environments of the globe. It is important because soil fertility, along with availability of fresh water, is a basic measure of the ability of an environmental region to produce food for human consumption.

> Soils are classified by soil order and suborder. These divisions are largely distinguished by the presence of diagnostic horizons with unique physical or chemical properties.

The soils of the world have been classified according to a system developed by scientists of the U.S. Soil Conservation Service, in cooperation with soil scientists of many other nations. Here we are concerned only with the two highest levels of this classification system. The top level contains 11 **soil orders** summarized in Table 10.3. The second level consists of *suborders,* of which we need to mention only a few.

Soil orders and suborders are often distinguished by the presence of a diagnostic horizon. Each diagnostic horizon has some unique combination of physical properties (color, structure, texture) or chemical properties (minerals present or absent). The two basic kinds of diagnostic horizons are (1) a horizon formed at the surface and called an *epipedon* (from the Greek, word *epi,* meaning "over" or "upon") and (2) a subsurface horizon formed by the removal or accumulation of matter. In our descriptions of soil orders, we will refer to a number of diagnostic horizons.

We can recognize three groups of soil orders. The largest group includes seven orders with well-developed hori-

Table 10.3 | **Soil Orders**

Group I	
Soils with well-developed horizons or with fully weathered minerals, resulting from long-continued adjustment to prevailing soil temperature and soil water conditions.	
Oxisols	Very old, highly weathered soils of low latitudes, with a subsurface horizon of accumulation of mineral oxides and very low base status.
Ultisols	Soils of equatorial, tropical, and subtropical latitude zones, with a subsurface horizon of clay accumulation and low base status.
Vertisols	Soils of subtropical and tropical zones with high clay content and high base status. Vertisols develop deep, wide cracks when dry, and the soil blocks formed by cracking move with respect to each other.
Alfisols	Soils of humid and subhumid climates with a subsurface horizon of clay accumulation and high base status. Alfisols range from equatorial to subarctic latitude zones.
Spodosols	Soils of cold, moist climates, with a well-developed *B* horizon of illuviation and low base status.
Mollisols	Soils of semiarid and subhumid midlatitude grasslands, with a dark, humus-rich epipedon and very high base status.
Aridisols	Soils of dry climates, low in organic matter, and often having subsurface horizons of accumulation of carbonate minerals or soluble salts.
Group II	
Soils with a large proportion of organic matter.	
Histosols	Soils with a thick upper layer very rich in organic matter.
Group III	
Soils with poorly developed horizons or no horizons, and capable of further mineral alteration.	
Entisols	Soils lacking horizons, usually because their parent material has accumulated only recently.
Inceptisols	Soils with weakly developed horizons, having minerals capable of further alteration by weathering processes.
Andisols	Soils with weakly developed horizons, having a high proportion of glassy volcanic parent material produced by erupting volcanoes.

zons or fully weathered minerals. A second group includes a single soil order that is very rich in organic matter. The last group includes three soil orders with poorly developed horizons or no horizons.

The world soils map presented in Figure 10.13 shows the major areas of occurrence of the soil orders. The Alfisols (Table 10.3) have been subdivided into four important suborders that correspond well to four basic climate zones. The map is quite general, indicating those areas where a given soil order is likely to be found. The map does not show many important areas of Entisols, Inceptisols, Histosols, and Andisols (Table 10.3). These orders are largely of local occurrence, since they are found on recent deposits such as floodplains, glacial landforms, sand dunes, marshlands, bogs, or volcanic ash deposits. The map also shows areas of highlands. In these regions, the soil patterns are too complex to show at a global scale.

....
GEODISCOVERIES **Soils of the World**. Take a second look at the world map of soils and click on a soil type to see a photo of the soil profile. An animation.
....

Soil Orders

Table 10.4 explains the names of the soil orders. The formative element is a syllable used in the names of suborders and lower groups. Although each order has several suborders, we will refer to only a few.

Three soil orders dominate the vast land areas of low latitudes: Oxisols, Ultisols, and Vertisols. Soils of these orders have developed over long time spans in an environment of warm soil temperatures and soil water that is abundant in a wet season or lasts throughout the year. We will discuss these orders first.

OXISOLS   Oxisols have developed in equatorial, tropical, and subtropical zones on land surfaces that have been stable over long periods of time. During soil development, the climate has been moist, with a large water surplus. Oxisols have developed over vast areas of South America and Africa in the wet equatorial climate ①. Here the native vegetation is rainforest. The wet-dry tropical climate ③ with its large seasonal water surplus is also associated with Oxisols in South America and Africa.

Oxisols usually lack distinct horizons, except for darkened surface layers. Soil minerals are weathered to an extreme degree and are dominated by stable sesquioxides of aluminum and iron. Red, yellow, and yellowish-brown colors are normal (Figures 10.14a and 10.15a). The base status of the Oxisols is very low, since nearly all the bases required by plants have been removed from the soil profile. A small store of nutrient bases occurs very close to the soil surface. The soil is quite easily broken apart and allows easy penetration by rainwater and plant roots.

> Oxisols and Ultisols develop over long time periods in warm, moist climates. Oxisols have substantial accumulations of iron and aluminum sesquioxides. Ultisols have a horizon of clay accumulation.

ULTISOLS   Ultisols are quite closely related to the Oxisols in outward appearance and environment of origin. Ultisols are reddish to yellowish in color (Figures 10.14b and 10.15b). They have a subsurface horizon of clay accumulation, called an *argillic horizon*, which is not found in the Oxisols. It is a B horizon and has developed through accumulation of clay in the process of illuviation. Although forest is the characteristic native vegetation, the base status of the Ultisols is low. As in the Oxisols, most of the bases are found in a shallow surface where they are released by the decay of plant matter. They are quickly taken up and recycled by the shallow roots of trees and shrubs.

In a few areas, the Ultisol profile contains a subsurface horizon of sesquioxides. This horizon is capable of hardening to a rock-like material if it becomes exposed at the surface and is subjected to repeated wetting and drying. This material is referred to as *plinthite* (from the Greek word *plinthos,* meaning "brick"). In the hardened state, plinthite is referred to as *laterite* (from the Latin *later,* or brick). In Southeast Asia, plinthite is quarried and cut into building blocks (Figure 10.15c). These blocks harden into laterite blocks when they are exposed to the air.

Ultisols are widespread throughout Southeast Asia and the East Indies. Other important areas are in eastern Australia, Central America, South America, and the southeastern United States. Ultisols extend into the lower midlatitude zone in the United States, where they correspond quite closely in extent with the area of moist subtropical climate ⑥. In lower latitudes, Ultisols are identified with the wet-dry tropical climate ③ and the monsoon and trade-wind coastal climate ②. Note that all these climates have a dry season, even though it may be short.

Both Oxisols and Ultisols of low latitudes were used for centuries under shifting agriculture prior to the advent of modern agricultural technology. This primitive agricultural method, known as slash-and-burn, is still widely practiced. Without fertilizers, these soils can sustain crops on freshly cleared areas for only two or three years, at most, before the nutrient bases are exhausted and the garden plot must be abandoned. Substantial use of lime, fertilizers, and other industrial inputs is necessary for high, sustained crop yields. Furthermore, the exposed soil surface of the Ultisols is vulnerable to devastating soil erosion, particularly on steep hill slopes.

VERTISOLS   Vertisols have a unique set of properties that stand in sharp contrast to the Oxisols and Ultisols. Vertisols are black in color and have a high clay content (Figures 10.14c and 10.15d). Much of the clay consists of a particular mineral that shrinks and swells greatly with seasonal changes in soil water content. Wide, deep vertical cracks develop in the soil during the dry season. As the dry soil blocks are wetted and softened by rain, some fragments of surface soil drop into the cracks before they close, so that the soil "swallows itself" and is constantly being mixed.

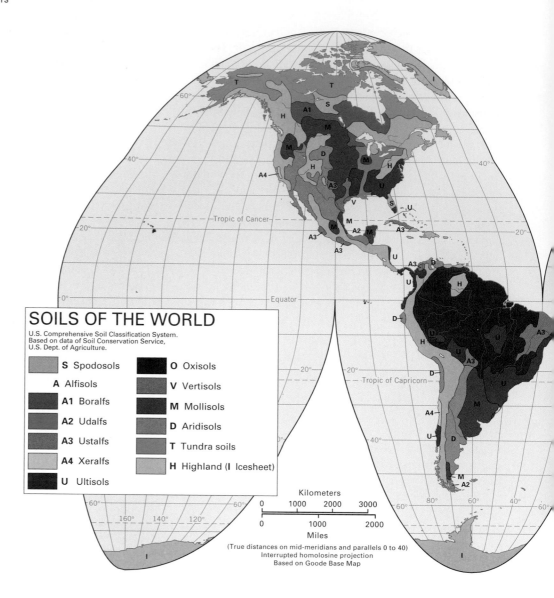

SOILS OF THE WORLD

U.S. Comprehensive Soil Classification System.
Based on data of Soil Conservation Service,
U.S. Dept. of Agriculture.

- **S** Spodosols
- **A** Alfisols
- **A1** Boralfs
- **A2** Udalfs
- **A3** Ustalfs
- **A4** Xeralfs
- **U** Ultisols
- **O** Oxisols
- **V** Vertisols
- **M** Mollisols
- **D** Aridisols
- **T** Tundra soils
- **H** Highland (**I** Icesheet)

Kilometers
0 1000 2000 3000

0 1000 2000
Miles

(True distances on mid-meridians and parallels 0 to 40)
Interrupted homolosine projection
Based on Goode Base Map

Table 10.4 | **Formative Elements in Names of Soil Orders**

Name of Order	Formative Element	Derivation of Formative Element	Pronunciation of Formative Element
Entisol	ent	Meaningless syllable	recent
Inceptisol	ept	L. *inceptum*, beginning	inept
Histosol	ist	Gr. *histos*, tissue	histology
Oxisol	ox	F. *oxide*, oxide	ox
Ultisol	ult	L. *ultimus*, last	ultimate
Vertisol	ert	L. *verto*, turn	invert
Alfisol	alf	Meaningless syllable	alfalfa
Spodosol	od	Gr. *spodos*, wood ash	odd
Mollisol	oll	L. *mollis*, soft	mollify
Aridisol	id	L. *aridus*, dry	arid
Andisol	and	Eng. *andesite*, a volcanic rock type	and

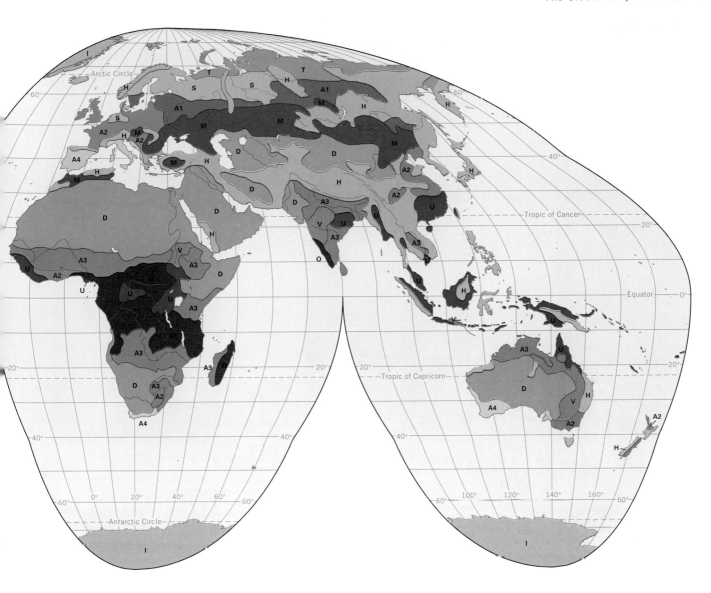

Vertisols typically form under grass and savanna vegetation in subtropical and tropical climates with a pronounced dry season. These climates include the semiarid subtype of the dry tropical steppe climate ④ and the wet-dry tropical climate ③. Because Vertisols require a particular clay mineral as a parent material, the major areas of occurrence are scattered and show no distinctive pattern on the world map. An important region of Vertisols is the Deccan Plateau of western India, where basalt, a dark variety of igneous rock, supplies the silicate minerals that are altered into the necessary clay minerals.

Vertisols are high in base status and are particularly rich in such nutrient bases as calcium and magnesium. The soil solution is nearly neutral in pH, and a moderate content of organic matter is distributed through the soil. The soil retains large amounts of water because of its fine texture, but much of this water is held tightly by the clay particles and is not

Vertisols develop on certain rock types in wet-dry climates under grassland and savanna vegetation. They expand and contract strongly on wetting and drying, creating deep cracks that allow the soil to "swallow itself" and remain constantly mixed.

available to plants. Where soil cultivation depends on human or animal power, as it does in most of the developing nations where the soil occurs, agricultural yields are low. This is because the moist soil becomes highly plastic and is difficult to till with primitive tools. For this reason, many areas of Vertisols have been left in grass or shrub cover, providing grazing for cattle. Soil scientists think that the use of modern technology, including heavy farm machinery, could result in substantial production of food and fiber from Vertisols that are not now in production.

ALFISOLS The **Alfisols** are soils characterized by an argillic horizon, produced by illuviation. Unlike the argillic horizon of the Ultisols, this *B* horizon is enriched by silicate clay minerals that have an adequate capacity to hold bases such as calcium and magnesium. The base status of the Alfisols is therefore generally quite high.

OXISOLS

A   Torrox, Hawaii

ULTISOLS

B   Udult, Virginia

VERTISOLS

C   Ustert, India

ALFISOLS

D   Udalf, Michigan

ALFISOLS

E   Ustalf, Texas

SPODOSOLS

F   Orthod, France

10.14 Soil profiles of several soil orders

MOLLISOLS

G   Boroll, USSR

MOLLISOLS

H   Udoll, Argentina

MOLLISOLS

I   Ustoll, Colorado

MOLLISOLS

J   Rendoll, Argentina

ARIDISOLS

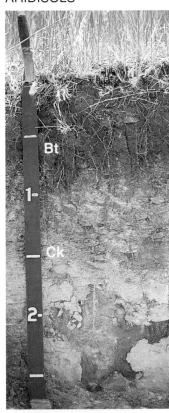

K   Argid, Colorado

HISTOSOLS

L   Fibrist, Minnesota

a...*An Oxisol in Hawaii*
Sugarcane is being cultivated here.

b...*Ultisol profile in North Carolina* *The thin, pale layer at the top is an E horizon, showing the effects of removal of materials by eluviation. Below the base of the thick, reddish B horizon is a blotchy-colored zone of plinthite.*

c...*Laterite in India* *Laterite, formed by hardening of plinthite, is being quarried for building stone in this scene from India.*

d...*A Vertisol in Texas* *The clay minerals that are abundant in Vertisols shrink when they dry out, producing deep cracks in the soil surface.*

Above the *B* horizon of clay accumulation is a horizon of pale color, the *E* horizon, that has lost some of the original bases, clay minerals, and sesquioxides by the process of eluviation. These materials have become concentrated by illuviation in the *B* horizon. Alfisols also have a gray, brownish, or reddish surface horizon.

The world distribution of Alfisols is extremely wide in latitude (see Figure 10.13). Alfisols range from latitudes as high as 60° N in North America and Eurasia to the equatorial zone in South America and Africa. Obviously, the Alfisols span an enormous range in climate types. For this reason, we need to recognize four of the important suborders of Alfisols, each with its own climate affiliation.

Boralfs are Alfisols of cold (boreal) forest lands of North America and Eurasia. They have a gray surface horizon and a brownish subsoil. *Udalfs* are brownish Alfisols of the midlatitude zone. They are closely associated with the moist continental climate ⑩ in North America, Europe, and eastern Asia (Figure 10.14*d*).

Ustalfs are brownish to reddish Alfisols of the warmer climates (Figure 10.14*e*). They range from the subtropical zone to the equator and are associated with the wet-dry tropical climate ③ in Southeast Asia, Africa, Australia, and South America. *Xeralfs* are Alfisols of the Mediterranean climate ⑦, with its cool moist winter and dry summer. The Xeralfs are typically brownish or reddish in color.

SPODOSOLS Poleward of the Alfisols in North America and Eurasia lies a great belt of soils of the order *Spodosols,* formed in the cold boreal forest climate ⑪ beneath a needleleaf forest. Spodosols have a unique property—a *B* horizon of accumulation of reddish mineral matter with a low capacity to hold bases (Figure 10.14*f*). This horizon is called the spodic horizon (Figure 10.16). It is made up of a dense mixture of organic matter and compounds of aluminum and iron, all brought downward by eluviation from an overlying *E* horizon. Because of the intensive removal of matter from the *E* horizon, it has a bleached, pale gray to white appearance (Figure 10.12). This conspicuous feature led to the naming of the soil as *podzol* (ash-soil) by Russian peasants. In modern terminology, this pale layer is an *albic horizon.* The *O* horizon, a thin, very dark layer of organic matter, overlies the *A* horizon.

Spodosols are strongly acid and are low in plant nutrients such as calcium and magnesium. They are also low in humus. Although the base status of the Spodosols is low, forests of pine and spruce are supported through the process of recycling of the bases.

Spodosols are closely associated with regions recently covered by the great ice sheets of the Pleistocene Epoch. These soils are therefore very young. Typically, the parent material is

10.16 Diagram of a Spodosol profile *The spodic horizon, a dense mixture of organic matter, aluminum, and iron oxides, and the gray to white albic horizon, are diagnostic features of a Spodosol profile.*

Alfisols have horizons of eluviation and illuviation of clays. They have a high base status and can be very productive.

Spodisols have a light-colored (albic) horizon of eluviation and a dense horizon of illuvation (spodic horizon). They develop under cold needleleaf forests.

Histosols are organic soils, often termed peats or mucks. They are typically formed in cool or cold climates in areas of poor drainage.

coarse sand consisting largely of the mineral quartz. This mineral cannot weather to form clay minerals.

Spodosols are naturally poor soils in terms of agricultural productivity. Because they are acid, application of lime is essential. Heavy applications of fertilizers are also required. With proper management and the input of the required industrial products, Spodosols can be highly productive, if the soil texture is favorable. High yields of potatoes from Spodosols in Maine and New Brunswick are examples. Another factor unfavorable to agriculture is the shortness of the growing season in the more northerly parts of the Spodosol belt.

HISTOSOLS Throughout the northern regions of Spodosols are countless patches of **Histosols.** This unique soil order has a very high content of organic matter in a thick, dark upper layer (Figure 10.14*l*). Most Histosols go by such common names as peats or mucks. They have formed in shallow lakes and ponds by accumulation of partially decayed plant matter. In time, the water is replaced by a layer of organic matter, or *peat,* and becomes a *bog* (Figure 10.17). Peat bogs are used extensively for cultivation of cranberries (cranberry bogs). Sphagnum peat from bogs is dried and baled for sale as a mulch for use on suburban lawns and shrubbery beds. For centuries, Europe has used dried peat from bogs of glacial origin as a low-grade fuel.

10.17   Eye on the Landscape Peat bog *This peat bog in Galway, Ireland, has been trenched to reveal a Histosol profile. Peat blocks, seen to the sides of the trench, are drying for use as fuel.*   **What else would the geographer see? ... Answers at the end of the chapter.**

Some Histosols are *mucks*—organic soils composed of fine black materials of sticky consistency. These are agriculturally valuable in midlatitudes, where they occur as beds of former lakes in glaciated regions. After appropriate drainage and application of lime and fertilizers, these mucks are remarkably productive for garden vegetables (Figure 10.18). Histosols are also found in low latitudes, where conditions of poor drainage have favored thick accumulations of plant matter.

ENTISOLS   Entisols have in common the combination of a mineral soil and the absence of distinct horizons. Entisols are soils in the sense that they support plants, but they may be found in any climate and under any vegetation. Entisols lack distinct horizons for two reasons. It may be the result of a parent material, such as quartz sand, in which horizons do not readily form. Or it may be the result of lack of time for horizons to form in recent deposits of alluvium or on actively eroding slopes.

Entisols occur from equatorial to arctic latitude zones. From the stand-

> Entisols lack horizons, often because they are only recently deposited. They may occur in any climate or region.

> Inceptisols have only weakly developed horizons. Inceptisols of river floodplains and deltas are often very productive where they are regularly enriched by flood borne silt.

point of agricultural productivity, Entisols of the subarctic zone and tropical deserts (along with arctic areas of Inceptisols) are the poorest of all soils. In contrast, Entisols and Inceptisols of floodplains and delta plains in warm and moist climates are among the most highly productive agricultural soils in the world because of their favorable texture, ample nutrient content, and large soil water storage.

INCEPTISOLS   Inceptisols are soils with horizons that are weakly developed, usually because the soil is quite young. These areas occur within some of the regions shown on the world map as Ultisols and Oxisols. Especially important are the Inceptisols of river floodplains and delta plains in South-east Asia that support dense populations of rice farmers.

In these regions, annual river floods cover low-lying plains and deposit layers of fine silt. This sediment is rich in primary minerals that yield bases as they weather chemically over time. The constant enrichment of the soil explains the high soil fertility in a region where uplands develop only

10.18 A Histosol in cultivation *Garden crops cultivated on a Histosol of a former glacial lakebed, Southern Ontario, Canada.*

Ultisols of low fertility. Inceptisols of these floodplain and delta lands are of a suborder called *Aquepts*—Inceptisols of wet places. Much closer to home is another prime example of Aquepts within the domain of the Ultisols—the lower Mississippi River floodplain and delta plain.

> **Andisols are unique soils that form on volcanic ash of relatively recent origin. They are dark in color and typically fertile.**

horizon and is always more than 25 cm (9.8 in.) thick. The soil has a loose, granular structure (Figure 10.6) or a soft consistency when dry. Other important qualities of the Mollisols are the dominance of calcium among the

ANDISOLS **Andisols** are soils in which more than half of the parent mineral matter is volcanic ash, spewed high into the air from the craters of active volcanoes and coming to rest in layers over the surrounding landscape. The fine ash particles are glass-like shards. A high proportion of carbon, formed by the decay of plant matter, is also typical, so that the soil usually appears very dark in color. Andisols form over a wide range of latitudes and climates. They are for the most part fertile soils, and in moist climates they support a dense natural vegetation cover.

Andisols do not appear on our world map because they are found in small patches associated with individual volcanoes that are located mostly in the "Ring of Fire"—the chain of volcanic mountains and islands that surrounds the great Pacific Ocean. Andisols are also found on the island of Hawaii, where volcanoes are presently active.

MOLLISOLS **Mollisols** are soils of grasslands that occupy vast areas of semiarid and subhumid climates in midlatitudes. Mollisols are unique in having a very thick, dark brown to black surface horizon called the *mollic epipedon* (Figures 10.14*g* to *j* and 10.19). This layer lies within the *A*

10.19 Schematic diagram of a Mollisol profile *The thick, dark brown to black mollic epipedon is a diagnostic feature of the Mollisol.*

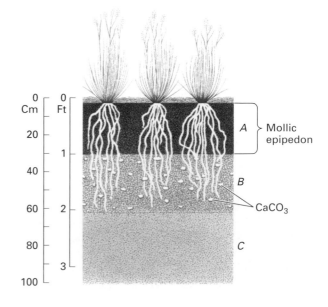

bases of the *A* and *B* horizons and the very high base status of the soil.

Most areas of Mollisols are closely associated with the semiarid subtype of the dry midlatitude climate ⑨ and the adjacent portion of the moist continental climate ⑩. In North America, Mollisols dominate the Great Plains region, the Columbia Plateau, and the northern Great Basin. In South America, a large area of Mollisols covers the Pampa region of Argentina and Uruguay. In Eurasia, a great belt of Mollisols stretches from Romania eastward across the steppes of Russia, Siberia, and Mongolia. Russians refer to the Mollisols as *chernozems,* a term that has gained widespread use throughout the Western world as well.

Because of their loose texture and very high base status, Mollisols are among the most naturally fertile soils in the world. They now produce most of the world's commercial grain crop. Most of these soils have been used for crop production only in the last century. Prior to that time, they were used mainly for grazing by nomadic herds. The Mollisols have favorable properties for growing cereals in large-scale mechanized farming and are relatively easy to manage. Production of grain varies considerably from one year to the next because seasonal rainfall is highly variable.

A brief mention of four suborders of the Mollisols as they occur in the United States and Canada will help you to understand important regional soil differences related to climate. *Borolls,* the cold climate suborder of the Mollisols, are found in a large area extending on both sides of the U.S.-Canadian border east of the Rocky Mountains (Figure 10.14*g*). *Udolls* are Mollisols of a relatively moist climate, as compared with the other suborders. Formerly, the Udolls supported tall-grass prairie, but today they are closely identified with the corn belt in the American Midwest (Figure 10.14*h*).

Ustolls are Mollisols of the semiarid subtype of the dry midlatitude climate ⑨, with a substantial soil water shortage in the summer months (Figure 10.14*i*). The Ustolls underlie much of the short-grass prairie region east of the Rockies (Figure 10.20). *Xerolls* are Mollisols of the Mediterranean climate ⑦, with its tendency to cool, moist winters and rainless summers.

Desert and Tundra Soils

Desert and tundra soils are soils of extreme environments. Aridisols characterize the desert climate. As might be expected, they are low in organic matter and high in salts. Tundra soils are poorly developed because they are formed on very recent parent material, left in place by glacial activity during the Ice Age. Cold temperatures have also restricted soil development in tundra regions.

Mollisols are soils of grasslands in subhumid to semiarid climates. They have a thick, dark brown surface layer termed a mollic epipedon. Their loose texture and high base status place them among the most productive soil types in the world.

Aridisols are desert soils with weakly developed horizons. They often exhibit subsurface layers of accumulation of calcium carbonate or soluble salts. With irrigation and proper management, they are quite fertile.

ARIDISOLS Aridisols, soils of the desert climate, are dry for long periods of time. Because the climate supports only a very sparse vegetation, humus is lacking and the soil color ranges from pale gray to pale red (Figure 10.14*k*). Soil horizons are weakly developed, but there may be important subsurface horizons of accumulated calcium carbonate (petrocalcic horizon) or soluble salts (salic horizon) (Figure 10.21). The salts, of which sodium is a dominant constituent, give the soil a very high degree of alkalinity. The Aridisols are closely correlated with the arid subtype of the dry tropical ④, dry subtropical ⑤, and dry midlatitude ⑨ climates.

Most Aridisols are used for nomadic grazing, as they have been through the ages. This use is dictated by the limited rainfall, which is inadequate for crops without irrigation.

10.20 A Mollisol developed on loess *Dry prairie grasses are seen on the surface.*

10.21 Salic horizon *Appearing as a white layer, a salic horizon lies close to the surface in this Aridisol profile in the Nevada desert. The scale is marked in feet (1 ft = 30.5 cm).*

Locally, where water supplies from mountain streams or ground water permit, Aridisols can be highly productive for a wide variety of crops under irrigation (Figure 10.22). Great irrigation systems, such as those of the Imperial Valley of the United States, the Nile Valley of Egypt, and the Indus Valley of Pakistan, have made Aridisols highly productive, but not without problems of salt buildup and waterlogging.

TUNDRA SOILS Soils of the arctic tundra fall largely into the order of Inceptisols, soils with weakly developed horizons that are usually associated with a moist climate. Inceptisols of the tundra climate belong to the suborder of Aquepts, which as we noted earlier are Inceptisols of wet places. More specifically, the tundra soils can be assigned to the *Cryaquepts,* a subdivision within the Aquepts. The prefix *cry* is derived from the Greek word *kryos,* meaning "icy cold." We may refer to these soils simply as **tundra soils**.

Tundra soils are formed largely of primary minerals ranging in size from silt to clay that are broken down by frost action and glacial grinding. Layers of peat are often present between mineral layers. Beneath the tundra soil lies perennially frozen ground (permafrost), described in Chapter 14.

10.22 Eye on the Landscape Irrigated Aridisols *Cotton farming along the Colorado River, near Parker, Arizona, is shown in this oblique air photo.* **What else would the geographer see? ... Answers at the end of the chapter.**

Because the annual summer thaw affects only a shallow surface layer, soil water cannot easily drain away. Thus, the soil is saturated with water over large areas. Repeated freezing and thawing of this shallow surface layer disrupts plant roots, so that only small, shallow-rooted plants can maintain a hold.

Tundra soils are wet and cold Inceptisols. They are often underlain by permafrost.

GEO*DISCOVERIES* **Interaction of Climate, Vegetation and Soil.** Return to the animations for Chapter 7 to view climate, vegetation, and soils maps superimposed to see common patterns. One animation for each of five global regions.

A Midcontinental Transect from Aridisols to Alfisols

Figure 10.23 provides a diagram showing generalized changes in soil profile and soil type as they might occur on a transect from a cool, dry desert to a cool moist climate, starting in the northern desert of the Great Basin and crossing the midwest. Starting with the Aridisols in the west, horizons are thin but show an accumulation of clay minerals in the *B* horizon. As precipitation increases, grasses dominate and Mollisols are formed. The *B* horizon thickens and includes calcium accumulation. In the east, where alfisols occur, enhanced precipitation generates an *E* horizon that takes its place between the *A* and *B* horizons.

GLOBAL CLIMATE CHANGE AND AGRICULTURE

Soils are the foundation of agriculture, supporting and nourishing crops as well as native plants that yield food for humans and animals alike. However, our food supply is also dependent on the weather and climate that crops and plants experience during their growing seasons. As we saw earlier, global climate change is predicted to increase global temperatures and summer droughts, change rainfall patterns, and produce more extreme events. All of these changes will have impacts on agriculture.

In general, the impacts on crop yields are expected to be at first positive, but, as temperatures rise, then negative. An important factor is that CO_2 rises will act to fertilize plants, somewhat offsetting the effects of higher temperatures and drought stresses. According to crop growth models linked to climate models and economic models, food costs will rise as increases in agricultural outputs fall behind increases in demand. However, widespread adaptation by farmers and farm managers to new and changing climate conditions may be effective enough to compensate for the changes. Our interchapter feature, *A Closer Look: Eye on Global Change 10.2 • Global Climate Change and Agriculture*, at the end of this chapter, presents more details.

GEO*DISCOVERIES* **Web Quiz.** Take a quick quiz on the key concepts of this chapter.

A LOOK AHEAD Our chapter began with an examination of the processes that create and differentiate soils. Using these processes, we described a number of important soil types that are of wide occurrence. As in the case of vegetation, we saw that the global pattern of soils is strongly related to global patterns of climate and vegetation.

An important message of these last three chapters is that climate, vegetation, and soils are closely interrelated. The nature of the vegetation cover depends largely on the climate, varying from desert to tundra biomes. Soils depend on both climate and vegetation to develop their unique characteristics. But soils can also influence vegetation development. Similarly, the climate at a location can be influenced by its vegetation cover.

10.23 Soil profile transect *A schematic diagram of the changing soil profile from a cool dry desert on the west to a cool moist climate on the East. (After C. E. Millar, L. M. Turk, and H. D. Foth, Fundamentals of Soil Science, John Wiley and Sons, New York.)*

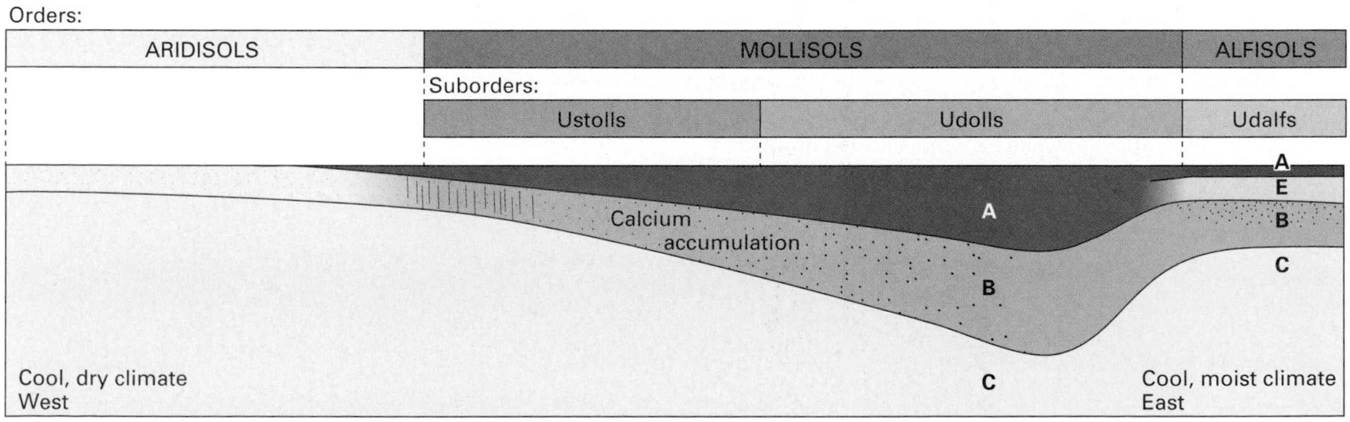

The next three chapters also comprise a set of topics that are strongly related. They deal with the lithosphere—the realm of the solid Earth, as we described in the Prologue. Our survey of the lithosphere will begin with the nature of Earth materials, then move to a discussion of how continents and ocean basins are formed and how they are continually changing, even today. Finally, we will discuss landforms occurring within continents that are produced by such lithospheric processes as volcanic activity and earthquake faulting.

GEO**DISCOVERIES** **Web Links.** An underground adventure, surviving the Dust Bowl, and a worldwide gallery of soils photos—see all these and more at this chapter's web links. Lots of good reference information on soils as well.

In Review | Global Soils

- The **soil** layer is a complex mixture of solid, liquid, and gaseous components. It is derived from **parent material,** or *regolith,* that is produced from rock by *weathering.* The major factors influencing soil and soil development are parent material, climate, vegetation, and time.

- **Soil texture** refers to the proportions of *sand, silt,* and *clay* that are present. *Colloids* are the finest particles in soils and are important because they help retain nutrient ions, or **bases,** that are used by plants. Soils show a wide range of *pH values,* from acid to alkaline. Soils with granular or blocky structures are most easily cultivated.

- In soils, *primary minerals* are chemically altered to **secondary minerals,** which include oxides and *clay minerals.* The nature of the clay minerals determines the soil's base status. If *base status* is *high,* the soil retains nutrients. If *low,* the soil can lack fertility. When a soil is fully wetted by heavy rainfall or snowmelt and allowed to drain, it reaches its *storage capacity.* Evaporation from the surface and transpiration from plants draws down the soil water store until precipitation occurs again to recharge it.

- The *soil water balance* describes the gain, loss, and storage of soil water. It depends on **water need** *(potential evapotranspiration),* **water use** *(actual evapotranspiration),* and precipitation. Monitoring these values on a monthly basis provides a *soil water budget* for the year.

- Most soils possess distinctive horizontal layers called **horizons.** These layers are developed by processes of *enrichment, removal, translocation,* and *transformation.* In downward translocation, materials such as humus, clay particles, and mineral oxides are removed by **eluviation** from an upper horizon and accumulate by **illuviation** in a lower one. In *salinization,* salts are translocated upward by evaporating water to form a *salic horizon.* In *humification,* a transformation process, organic matter is broken down by bacterial decay. Where soil temperatures are warm, this process can be highly effective, leaving a soil low in organic content. Animals, such as earthworms, can be very important in soil formation where they are abundant.

- Global soils are classified into 11 **soil orders,** often by the presence of one of more diagnostic horizons. **Oxisols** are old, highly weathered soils of low latitudes. They have a horizon of mineral oxide accumulation and a low base status. **Ultisols** are also found in low latitudes. They have a horizon of clay accumulation and are also of low base status. **Vertisols** are rich in a type of clay mineral that expands and contracts with wetting and drying, and has a high base status. **Alfisols** have a horizon of clay accumulation like Ultisols, but they are of high base status. They are found in moist climates from equatorial to subarctic zones. **Spodosols,** found in cold, moist climates, exhibit a horizon of illuviation and low base status. **Histosols** have a thick upper layer formed almost entirely of organic matter.

- Three soil orders have poorly developed horizons or no horizons—**Entisols, Inceptisols,** and **Andisols.** Entisols are composed of fresh parent material and have no horizons. The horizons of Inceptisols are only weakly developed. Andisols are weakly developed soils occurring on young volcanic deposits.

- **Mollisols** have a thick upper layer rich in humus. They are soils of midlatitude grasslands. **Aridisols** are soils of arid regions, marked by horizons of accumulation of carbonate minerals or salts.

- **Tundra soils** are largely wet, cold Inceptisols.

- Global climate change will eventually reduce crop yields as temperatures and drought stress increase. Food prices will probably rise, but adjustments in farming practices may compensate.

Key Terms

soil, p. 364
parent material, p. 365
soil texture, p. 366
soil colloids, p. 366
bases, p. 367
secondary minerals,
  p. 368

water use, p. 370
water need, p. 370
soil horizons, p. 371
soil profile, p. 371
eluviation, p. 372
illuviation, p. 372
soil orders, p. 376

Oxisols, p. 377
Ultisols, p. 377
Vertisols, p. 377
Alfisols, p. 379
Spodosols, p. 384
Histosols, p. 384
Entisols, p. 385

Inceptisols, p. 385
Andisols, p. 386
Mollisols, p. 386
Aridisols, p. 387
tundra soils, p. 388

Review Questions

1. Which important factors condition the nature and development of the soil?
2. Soil color, soil texture, and soil structure are used to describe soils and soil horizons. Identify each of these three terms, showing how they are applied.
3. Explain the concepts of acidity and alkalinity as they apply to soils.
4. Identify two important classes of secondary minerals in soils and provide examples of each class.
5. How does the ability of soils to hold water vary, and how does this ability relate to soil texture?
6. Define water need (potential evapotranspiration) and water use (actual evapotranspiration). How are they used in the soil water balance?
7. Identify the following terms as used in the soil water budget: storage, withdrawal, storage recharge, soil water shortage, water surplus.
8. What is a soil horizon? How are soil horizons named? Provide two examples.
9. Identify four classes of soil-forming processes and describe each.
10. What are translocation processes? Identify and describe four translocation processes.
11. How many soil orders are there? Try to name them all.
12. Name three soil orders that are especially associated with low latitudes. For each order, provide at least one distinguishing characteristic and explain it.
13. Compare Alfisols and Spodosols. What features do they share? What features differentiate them? Where are they found?
14. Where are Mollisols found? How are the properties of Mollisols related to climate and vegetation cover? Name four suborders within the Mollisols.

15. Desert and tundra are extreme environments. Which soil order is characteristic of each environment? Briefly describe desert and tundra soils.

Eye on the Environment 10.1 • Death of a Civilization

1. Describe the processes of salinization, waterlogging, and siltation and their impact on agriculture.
2. A technological "fix" for siltation is to build a dam upstream of an irrigation canal complex, so that silt will be trapped behind the dam. What other effects might building such a dam produce, both desirable and undesirable?

A Closer Look:
Eye on Global Change 10.2 • Global Climate Change and Agriculture

1. How will increasing temperature affect agricultural crop yields? What will be the effect of increasing atmospheric CO_2 concentrations?
2. What actions can farmers and farm managers take to mitigate the effects of climate change?
3. How will climate change influence the quality of the agricultural environment?
4. What is the predicted impact of global climate change on food prices? Who will be most affected?

Visualizing Exercises

1. Sketch the profile of a Spodosol, labeling *O, A, E, B,* and *C* horizons. Diagram the movement of materials from the zone of eluviation to the zone of illuviation.

2. Examine the world soils map (Figure 10.13) and identify three soil types that are found near your location. Develop a short list of characteristics that would help you tell them apart.

Essay Questions

1. Document the important role of clay particles and clay mineral colloids in soils. What is meant by the term *clay?* What are colloids? What are their properties? How does the type of clay mineral influence soil fertility? How does the amount of clay influence the water-holding capacity of the soil? What is the role of clay minerals in horizon development?

2. Using the world maps of global soils and global climate, compare the pattern of soils on a transect along the 20° E longitude meridian with the patterns of climate encountered along the same meridian. What conclusions can you draw about the relationship between soils and climate? Be specific.

Eye on the Landscape

Chapter Opener Fields, Cedar Mountain, Virginia Note the strip-fallow pattern of cultivation, in which crops are planted in strips alternating with fallow ground **(A)**. This practice aids in maintaining soil fertility and protects against soil erosion. Within the fallow strips, soil color goes from light to dark **(B),** with the darker colors indicating more soil moisture at the time of the photo.

10.17 Peat bog Peat bogs are typical of glacial terrain. Moving ice sheets remove and take up loose soil and rock, then leave sediment behind as they melt. The low, hummocky terrain **(A)** at the edge of this bog may be part of a moraine, a landform that occurs at the melting edge of an ice sheet as wasting ice leaves piles of sediment behind in a chaotic and disorganized fashion. The isolated angular boulders **(B)** may be erratics—large rocks that are carried in the ice and moved long distances from their sources. Landforms of glacial ice sheets are described in Chapter 19.

10.22 Irrigated Aridisols The broad floodplain of the Colorado River (right) shows how productive Aridisols can be when properly managed and irrigated. A consistent climate with abundant sunlight, coupled with abundant river water, makes for high productivity and crop yields. Fallow fields **(A)** show typical Aridisol colors of gray to brown, while cotton fields are vibrant green **(B)**. Note the network of canals **(C)** serving the fields. Aridisols are covered in this chapter.

A CLOSER LOOK

Eye on Global Change 10.2 | Global Climate Change and Agriculture

For the remainder of the century, and probably well beyond, our global climate will change. The Earth will become warmer, especially in mid- and high latitudes. Most areas will have more precipitation, although higher temperatures will often bring more summer drought stress. Extreme events—heavy rainfalls and high winds—will be more frequent. How will global climate change impact agriculture?

Warming Temperatures and CO$_2$ Fertilization

Let's look first at the effects of warmer temperatures. In general, higher temperatures will increase the productivity of most mid- and high-latitude crops by shortening the growing season. But as you might imagine, once temperatures get too high, the effects will be negative. For crops on the edge of their high-temperature range, any warming will reduce productivity. Recall also that global warming is expected to reduce minimum temperatures. This will be beneficial for most mid- and high-latitude crops but detrimental to some tropical and equatorial crops.

On the other hand, a significant CO$_2$ fertilization effect is expected to occur as atmospheric CO$_2$ concentrations double. Recall that plants take in atmospheric CO$_2$ for photosynthesis and that because CO$_2$ is present in the atmosphere only in low concentrations, CO$_2$ limits the photosynthetic process in many cases. With higher concentrations, plants will be able to photosynthesize more rapidly and become more productive. This fertilization effect is well documented in many studies, both in greenhouses and by free-air release of CO$_2$ gas upwind from agricultural fields. The fertilization effect appears to be greater when plants are under greater stress, for example, from warmer temperatures and drought.

Young corn field, Iowa *Climate change will impact how crops grow. In midlatitudes, earlier seasonal warming will allow a longer growing season, but hotter summers with higher drought potential may reduce later growth. However, increasing atmospheric CO$_2$ will tend to increase growth.*

Crop Yields and Adaptation

What are the combined effects of changing temperatures and increasing CO$_2$ on crop yields? In general, if warming is less than about 2.5°C (4.5°F), yields increase, but if greater than that amount, yields decrease.[1] However, the predicted changes for different crops and regions vary significantly. For example, studies cited in the IPCC Global Change Report predict decreasing yields for corn, wheat, and rice in Egypt; a slight decrease for corn in

Romania; increasing yields for wheat in Australia; and increasing yields for rice in temperate Asia.

An important factor affecting yields is *adaptation*. Adaptation describes actions taken by farmers to respond to climate change, such as changing planting and harvesting dates or selecting different strains of crops that are better adapted to changed conditions. Higher levels of adaptation include changing the crops that are planted, adding or modifying irrigation, using more or different fertilizers and pesticides, and other actions.

Studies show that adaptation can mitigate many of the negative effects of global change. For example, the U.S. Global Change Research Program Climate Change Report,[2] which includes adaptation

---

[1]See *Climate Change 2001: The Scientific Basis, Contribution of Working Group I to the Third Assessment Report of the Intergovernmental Panel on Climate Change*, IPCC Cambridge University Press, 2001, and *Climate Change 2001: Impacts, Adaptation, and Vulnerability, Contribution of Working Group II to the Third Assessment Report of the Intergovernmental Panel on Climate Change*, IPCC, Cambridge University Press, 2001, which are used as the basis for this discussion.

---

[2]*Climate Change Impacts on the United States: The Potential Consequences of Climate Variability and Change*, National Assessment Synthesis Team, U.S. Global Change Research Program, Washington, DC, 2000.

Cereal crop harvest, Novosibirsk region, Russia *With a changing climate, crop yields will change, but how they change will depend on the crop, the region, and the degree of adaptation employed by growers.*

also increase if global warming enhances wind speeds.

Insect pests will be affected by climate change, but the exact effects seem to depend on the pest, crop, and type of climate change. For example, the IPCC report cites a study showing that warmer temperatures increase the severity of rice leaf blast in cool subtropical regions, while reducing the severity in warm and humid subtropics. In the United States, the ranges of several important crop pests have been shown to expand in patterns that follow climate changes noted since the 1970s. Studies have also shown that weeds are stimulated by warm temperatures and higher levels of CO_2, and in some cases, they become more effective competitors, thus reducing yields.

Livestock are affected by climate change both directly and indirectly. Higher temperatures produce more stress in animals, which can impact growth, reproduction, and yield of milk or wool. Dairy cows will be less productive during the hotter summer months,

as well as temperature change and CO_2 fertilization in its study, predicts that the productivity of American cotton, corn, soybeans, sorghum, barley, sugar beets, and citrus fruits will increase over the next century. However, yields for wheat, rice, oats, hay, sugar cane, potatoes, and tomatoes will increase under some conditions and decrease under others.

expected to increase as well, as more frequent high-rainfall events induce rilling and gullying. Wind deflation of productive soils will

Other Factors

Although global climate change will affect future agricultural yields, other factors may be important as well. Soil degradation, which includes erosion of productive soil layers, chemical depletion of nutrients, waterlogging, and salinization, is a major challenge. A United Nations report estimated that 23 percent of the world's agricultural lands, pastures, forests, and woodlands have been degraded to a least some extent since World War II. Irrigated land, which provides about 40 percent of the world's food from 16 percent of the world's cropland, is increasing, but so is irrigated land that is degraded by salinization and waterlogging. Erosion can be

Soil erosion *Soil erosion, which strips off the most fertile part of the soil, presents an important challenge to increasing crop production and yield. More frequent and more intense rainfall events, which are predicted for midlatitude summers, will enhance soil loss by rilling and gullying of unprotected surfaces.*

Thus, the question is not simply whether production will increase in the future, but whether it will keep pace with demand. Most studies seem to predict that under scenarios of global climate change greater that 2.5°C (4.5°F), demand will exceed supply and food prices will rise. Associated with this change will be small positive changes in income for developed regions, with small negative changes in income for developing regions. Vulnerable populations, such as marginal farmers and poor urban dwellers, will be placed at greater risk of hunger. However, if adaptation to climate change is more effective, these consequences may not occur.

Agriculture is a human activity that is essential to us all, and from the discussion above, it is obvious that the effects of global change on agriculture will be significant as our climate warms and CO_2 levels rise. Let's hope that our species is smart enough to adapt to the changes and provide an abundance of food for all.

Grazing in Burkina Faso *Livestock will be affected by climate change. Higher temperatures will produce more summer stress on grazing animals, but less winter stress. The quality and availability of forage will also be affected.*

and enhanced heat waves or winter storms will increase death rates in vulnerable animals. Indirectly, climate change will change the nature and availability of forage, grain, diseases, and parasites affecting livestock.

Food Prices and Hunger Risks

What are the likely effects of global climate change on food availability and food prices? Keep in mind that, so far, agricultural production has expanded to meet the expanding needs of the world's population.

Vegetable vendor, Cairo, Egypt *Climate change will affect the price and availability of food from region to region. With global warming greater than 2.5°C (4.5°F), most studies predict that future supply will not meet future demand at present levels and prices will rise.*

A lava flow on the lower flanks of Kilauea Volcano, Volcanoes National Park, Hawaii.

11 | EARTH MATERIALS

PUTTING YOU IN THE PICTURE

Perhaps from observing pebbles on a beach or stones in the bed of a stream, you may be aware that there are many different kinds of rocks. The primary objective of this chapter is to describe the more important types of rocks and minerals and how they are formed. Although most processes of rock formation are slow and steady, some are rapid and even a bit dangerous to witness. Imagine yourself on a journey to a pit crater on the Hawaiian volcano of Kilauea to watch the formation of new rock from molten lava…

The "Visitor Parking" sign emerges quickly from the fog, and you nose the car to the left, pulling into a vacant space in the parking lot. You expected better weather, but the whole eastern half of the "Big Island"—Hawaii—is covered by trade-wind clouds. At this elevation, about 1200 m (4000 ft), you are in the middle of the wet, gray, cloud layer. You open the trunk to get the sweatshirt from your backpack and then change into your sturdy hiking boots. Your destination is Mauna Ulu, a nearly circular pit crater that contains a pool of molten lava.

At first, the trail winds through a scrubby forest of low trees and shrubs. The tough rock underfoot is broken into angular blocks, separated by cracks and fissures. The footing is difficult. Each step requires attention to keep your boot from becoming wedged into a crevice. Soon you emerge from the woodland onto a surface of fresh lava. The trail is marked by small flags every 20 feet or so. The fog thickens a bit. As you walk carefully from one flag to the next, you seem to be inside a dim, gray bubble on a strange planet. There are no landmarks—nothing familiar is within sight—as you pick your way across the rough terrain.

You gradually become aware of a noise, fall. As you con... l, it gets louder and ...e ground shaking beneath your feet. The fog takes on a redish glow. The acrid scent of sulfur catches in your nose and tightens your throat. Dimly, something emerges ahead. You are nearing the rim of the crater. You make out a wooden platform on the edge, with perhaps a half-dozen people clustered toward the back. As you reach the platform, the noise builds to a great, lowpitched roar. You mount the trembling platform and approach the edge. The heat from the lava strikes your face with an unexpected intensity.

The sides of the crater drop away steeply. At the bottom of the great pit is a black surface crust of congealed lava, covering the hot magma. Long cracks gash the crust, glowing red from deep within. Suddenly, a huge rock mass falls from the side of the crater into the pit, fracturing the black surface into jagged pieces that are tossed outward by the impact. Molten rock splashes slowly upward, spattering the rock wall with red and white spray. The heat of the fresh molten rock is unbearable, and you turn away.

After watching the incredible spectacle for as long as you can endure the heat, you leave the platform and head back. As you walk, the roaring fades, and the fog loses its red glow. The lava landscape seems mysterious rather than ominous and threatening. The scrubby

woods seems somehow welcoming, its twisted trees beckoning as outposts of Earthly life on your return journey to familiar ground. You feel small and insignificant, humbled by the immense physical power of the Earth.

The cooling of molten lava that is released at the Earth's surface is one way in which new rock is formed. This chapter explores other ways that are perhaps not so dramatic, but equally important. Our objective will be to lay the groundwork necessary for understanding how the Earth's crustal processes control landforms and landscapes, as well as provide the raw materials for the land-forming agents of water, wind, and glacial ice that we discuss in later chapters. ∎

EARTH MATERIALS

This chapter is the first in a sequence of three chapters that focus on the solid mineral realm of our planet. The first chapter deals with the materials that compose the Earth's outer rock layer—minerals and rocks that are formed in various ways both deep within the Earth and near or at its surface. In the second chapter, we will see that the outermost layer of the solid Earth is a hardened crust of rock that is fractured, broken into large plates, and moved by forces deep within the Earth. In the third chapter, we will show how surface features reveal the history of the crust and the forces that have shaped it. The topics in these three chapters are drawn from *geology,* the science of the solid Earth and its history.

Why are physical geographers concerned with the solid Earth? The Earth's outer layer serves as a platform, or base, for life on the lands. It provides the continental surfaces that are carved into landforms by moving water, wind, and glacial ice. Landforms, in turn, influence the distribution of ecosystems and exert strong controls over human occupation of the lands. Landforms made by water, wind, and ice are the subject of the closing chapters of this book.

We begin our study of the solid Earth by examining the minerals and rocks that are found at or near the Earth's surface. There are a great number of minerals and rocks, but we will focus only on the few that are most important for a

broad understanding of the continents, ocean basins, and their varied features. We will also examine the rock cycle, in which Earth materials are constantly formed and reformed over geologic time in a cycle powered largely by heat from the Earth's interior.

THE CRUST AND ITS COMPOSITION

The thin, outermost layer of our planet is the *Earth's crust.* This skin of varied rocks and minerals ranges from about 8 to 40 km (about 5 to 25 mi) thick and contains the continents and ocean basins. It is the source of soil on the lands, of salts of the sea, of gases of the atmosphere, and of all the water of the oceans, atmosphere, and lands.

Figure 11.1 displays the eight most abundant elements of the Earth's crust in terms of percentage by weight. Oxygen, the predominant element, accounts for a little less than half the total weight. Second is silicon, which accounts for a little more than a quarter. Together they account for 75 percent of the crust, by weight.

Aluminum accounts for approximately 8 percent and iron for about 5 percent of the Earth's crust. These metals are very important to our industrial civilization, and, fortunately, they are relatively abundant. Four other metallic elements—calcium, sodium, potassium, and magnesium—

The Earth's crust is the outermost layer of the solid Earth. It contains the rocks of the continents and ocean basins, and is largely composed of oxygen, silicon, aluminum, and iron.

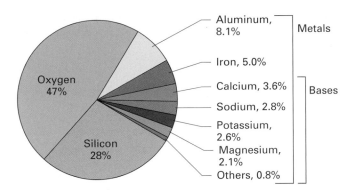

11.1 Crustal composition *The eight most abundant elements in the Earth's crust, measured by percentage of weight. Oxygen and silicon dominate, with aluminum and iron following.*

make up the remaining 12 percent. All four occur at about the same order of abundance (2 to 4 percent). These elements are essential nutrients for plant and animal life and are described in Chapter 8 as plant nutrients. Because of this role, they are also important determiners of soil fertility (Chapter 10).

Of the remaining chemical elements composing the Earth's crust, a few are very important from the viewpoint of powering the cycles of the solid Earth. These are the radioactive forms of elements that, through slow radioactive decay, provide a nearly infinite source of heat that seeps slowly outward from the Earth's interior. We will return to the topic of radioactive decay and radiogenic heating in Chapter 12.

Rocks and Minerals

The elements of the Earth's crust are usually bonded with other elements to form chemical compounds. We recognize these compounds as minerals. A **mineral** is a naturally occurring, inorganic substance that usually possesses a definite chemical composition and characteristic atomic structure. Most minerals have a crystalline structure—gemstones such as diamonds or rubies are examples, although their crystalline shape is enhanced by the stonecutter. Quartz is an example of a very common crystalline mineral. It usually occurs as a clear, six-sided prism (Figure 11.2).

Minerals are combined into **rock,** which we can broadly define as an assemblage of minerals in the solid state. Rock comes in a very wide range of compositions, physical characteristics, and ages. A given variety of rock is usually composed of two or more minerals, and often many different minerals are present. However, a few rock varieties consist almost entirely of one mineral. Most rock of the Earth's crust is extremely old by human standards, with the age of

Rocks are composed of minerals, which are naturally occurring inorganic substances. The three major classes of rocks are igneous, sedimentary, and metamorphic. Earth processes transform rocks from one class to another.

11.2 Quartz crystals *These large crystals of quartz form six-sided, translucent columns.*

formation often ranging back many millions of years. But rock is also being formed at this very hour as active volcanoes emit lava that solidifies on contact with the atmosphere or ocean.

Rocks of the Earth's crust fall into three major classes. (1) **Igneous rocks** are solidified from mineral matter in a high-temperature molten state. (2) **Sedimentary rocks** are formed from layered accumulations of mineral particles derived mostly by weathering and erosion of preexisting rocks. (3) **Metamorphic rocks** are formed from igneous or sedimentary rocks that have been physically or chemically changed, usually by application of heat and pressure during crustal mountain-making.

The three classes of rocks are constantly being transformed from one to another in a continuous process through which the crustal minerals have been recycled during many millions of years of geologic time. Figure 11.3 diagrams these transformations. In the process of melting, preexisting rock of any class is melted and then later cools to form igneous rock. In weathering and erosion, preexisting rock is broken down and accumulated in layers that become sedimentary rock. Heat and pressure convert igneous and sedimentary rocks to metamorphic rock. We will return to this cycle at the end of the chapter, after we have taken a more detailed look at rocks, minerals, and their formation processes.

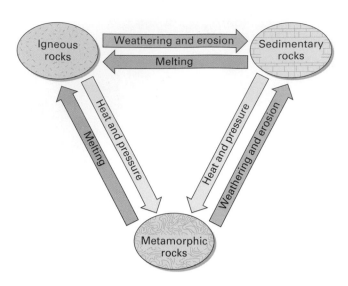

11.3 Rock transformation *The three classes of rock are transformed into one another by weathering and erosion, melting, and exposure to heat and pressure.*

IGNEOUS ROCKS

Igneous rocks are formed when molten material moves from deep within the Earth to a position within or atop the crust. There the molten material cools, forming rocks composed of mineral crystals. Table 11.1 presents the more important igneous rock types that we will refer to in this chapter.

Most igneous rock consists of *silicate minerals,* chemical compounds that contain silicon and oxygen atoms. Most of the silicate minerals also have one, two, or more of the metallic elements listed in Figure 11.1—that is, aluminum, iron, calcium, sodium, potassium, and magnesium. Although there are many silicate minerals, we will only be concerned with seven of them, which are shown in Figure 11.4.

Among the most common minerals of all rock classes is **quartz,** mentioned earlier, which is silicon dioxide (SiO_2) (Figure 11.2). It is quite hard and resists chemical breakdown. Two silicate-aluminum minerals called *feldspars* follow. One type, *potash*

feldspar, contains potassium as the dominant metal besides aluminum. A second type, *plagioclase feldspar,* is rich in sodium, calcium, or both. Quartz and feldspar form a silicate mineral group described as **felsic** ("fel" for feldspar; "si" for silicate).

Quartz and the feldspars are light in color (white, pink, or grayish) and lower in density than the other silicate minerals. By *density,* we mean the mass of matter contained in a unit volume. Figure 11.5 shows the density of four Earth materials: water, quartz, the mineral olivine (discussed below), and pure iron.

The next three silicate minerals are actually groups of minerals, with a number of mineral varieties in each group. They are the *mica, amphibole,* and *pyroxene* groups. All three are silicates containing aluminum, magnesium, iron, and potassium or calcium. The seventh mineral, *olivine,* is a silicate of only magnesium and iron that lacks aluminum. Altogether, these minerals are described as **mafic** ("ma" for magnesium; "f" from the chemical symbol for iron, Fe). The mafic minerals are dark in color (usually black) and are denser than the felsic minerals.

······················
GEODISCOVERIES **Igneous Rock Animation.** Take another look at our diagram of silicate minerals and igneous rocks. Click on the diagram to see photos of the minerals and rocks and learn more about their characteristics.
···

Common Igneous Rocks

Igneous rocks solidify from rock in a hot, molten state, known as **magma.** From pockets a few kilometers below the Earth's surface, magma makes its way upward through fractures in older solid rock and eventually solidifies as igneous rock. No single igneous rock is made up of all seven silicate minerals listed in Figure 11.4. Instead, a given rock variety contains three or four of those minerals as the major ingredients. The mineral grains in igneous rocks are very tightly interlocked, and the rock is normally very strong.

The column in the center of Figure 11.4 shows four common igneous rocks. Each rock is connected by arrows to the principal minerals it contains. These

> Igneous rocks form when molten rock cools, forming mineral crystals. Silicate minerals in igneous rocks are classed as felsic (light colored, less dense) and mafic (dark colored, more dense). The felsic mineral quartz is very common.

Table 11.1 | Some Common Igneous Rock Types

Subclass	Rock Type	Composition
Intrusive (cooling at depth, producing coarse crystal texture)	Granite	Felsic minerals, typically quartz, feldspars, and mica
	Diorite	Felsic minerals without quartz, usually including plagioclase feldspar and amphibole
	Gabbro	Mafic minerals, typically plagioclase feldspar, pyroxene, and olivine
	Peridotite	An ultramafic rock of pyroxene and olivine
Extrusive (cooling at the surface, producing fine crystal texture)	Rhyolite	Same as granite
	Andesite	Same as diorite
	Basalt	Same as gabbro

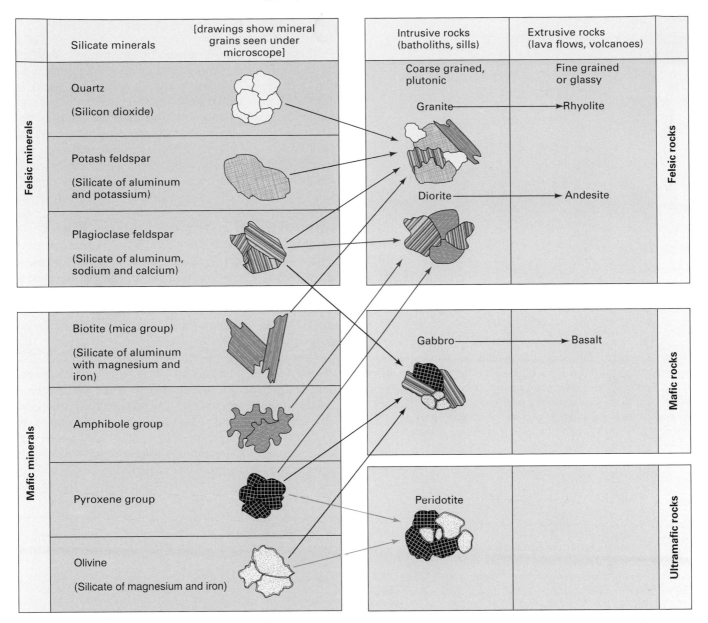

11.4   *Silicate minerals and igneous rocks* *Only the most important silicate mineral groups are listed, along with four common igneous rock types. The patterns shown for mineral grains indicate their general appearance through a microscope, and do not necessarily indicate the relative amounts of the minerals within the rocks.*

four rocks are carefully selected to be used in our later explanation of features of the Earth's crust.

The first igneous rock is **granite**. The bulk of granite consists of quartz (27 percent), potash feldspar (40 percent), and plagioclase feldspar (15 percent). The remainder is mostly biotite and amphibole. Because most of the volume of granite is of felsic minerals, we classify granite as a *felsic igneous rock*. Granite is a mixture of white, grayish or pinkish, and black grains, but the overall appearance is a light gray or pink color (Figure 11.6*a*).

Diorite, the second igneous rock on the list, lacks quartz. It consists largely of plagioclase feldspar (60 percent) and sec-

> Granite, diorite, gabbro, and peridotite are igneous rocks ranging from felsic to mafic and ultramafic in composition.

ondary amounts of amphibole and pyroxene. Diorite is a light-colored felsic rock that is only slightly denser than granite. When its grains are coarse, it may have a speckled appearance (Figure 11.6*b*).

The third igneous rock is *gabbro,* in which the major mineral is pyroxene (60 percent). A substantial amount of plagioclase feldspar (20 to 40 percent) is present, and, in addition, there may be some olivine (0 to 20 percent). Since the mafic minerals pyroxene and olivine are dominant, gabbro is classed as a *mafic igneous rock.* It is dark in color and denser than the felsic rocks.

The fourth igneous rock, *peridotite,* is dominated by olivine (60 percent). The rest is mostly pyroxene (40 per-

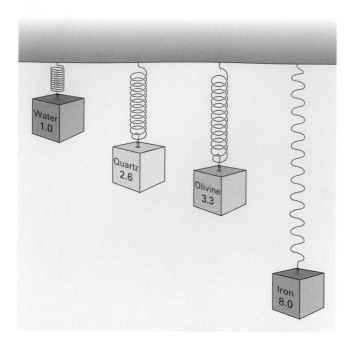

11.5 Density *The concept of density is illustrated by several cubes of the same size, but of different materials, hung from coil springs under the influence of gravity. The stretching of the coil spring is proportional to the density of each material, shown in thousands of kilograms per cubic meter. Quartz and olivine are common minerals. (Copyright © A. N. Strahler.)*

cent). Peridotite is classed as an *ultramafic igneous rock,* denser even than the mafic types.

These four common varieties of igneous rock show an increasing range of density, from felsic, through mafic, to ultramafic types. This arrangement according to density is duplicated on a grand scale in the principal rock layers that comprise the solid Earth, with the least dense layer (mostly felsic rocks) near the surface and the densest layer (ultramafic rocks) deep in the Earth's interior. We will stress this layered arrangement again in describing the Earth's crust and the deeper interior zones in Chapter 12.

Intrusive and Extrusive Igneous Rocks

Magma that solidifies below the Earth's surface and remains surrounded by older, preexisting rock is called **intrusive igneous rock.** The process of injection into existing rock is *intrusion.* Where magma reaches the surface, it emerges as **lava,** which solidifies to form **extrusive igneous rock** (Figure 11.7). The process of release at the surface is called *extrusion.*

Although both intrusive rock and extrusive rock can solidify from the same original body of magma, their outward appearances are quite different when you compare freshly broken samples of each. Intrusive igneous rocks cool very slowly—over hundreds or thousands of years—and, as a result, develop large mineral crystals—that is, they are *coarse-textured.* The granite and diorite samples in Figure 11.6 are good examples of coarse texture.

11.6 Intrusive igneous rock samples *(a) A coarse-grained granite. Dark grains are amphibole and biotite; light grains are feldspars; clear grains are quartz. (b) A coarse-grained diorite. Feldspar grains are light; amphibole and pyroxene grains are dark. Compare with granite in (a)—clear quartz grains are lacking.*

(a)

(b)

11.7 Fresh lava *This fresh black lava shows a glassy surface and flow structures. Chain of Craters Road, Hawaii Volcanoes National Park, Hawaii.*

seen through a microscope. Rocks with such small crystals are termed *fine-textured*. If the lava contains dissolved gases, the gases expand as the lava cools, forming a rock with a frothy, bubble-filled texture, called *scoria* (Figure 11.8*b*). Sometimes a lava cools to form a shiny natural volcanic glass (Figure 11.8*a*). Most lava solidifies simply as a dense, uniform rock with a dark, dull surface.

Since the outward appearance of intrusive and extrusive rocks formed from the same magma are so different, they are named differently. The igneous rock types we have discussed so far—granite, diorite, gabbro, and peridotite—are intrusive rocks. Except for peridotite, all have counterparts as extrusive rocks. They are named in the right column of Figure 11.4. Each one has the same mineral composition as the intrusive rock named at the left. *Rhyolite* is the name for lava of the same composition as granite; **andesite** is lava with the mineral composition of diorite; and **basalt** is lava of the composition of gabbro. Andesite and basalt are the two most common types of lavas. Rhyolite and andesite are pale grayish or pink in color, whereas basalt is black. Lava flows, along with particles of solidified lava blown explosively from narrow vents, often accumulate as isolated hills or mountains that we recognize as volcanoes. They are described in Chapter 13.

A body of intrusive igneous rock is called a **pluton.** Granite typically accumulates in enormous plutons, called *batholiths.* Figure 11.9 shows the relationship of a batholith to the overlying rock. As the hot fluid magma rises, it melts and incorporates the older rock lying above it. A single batholith extends down several kilometers and may occupy an area of several thousand square kilometers.

Figure 11.9 shows other common forms of plutons. One is a *sill,* a plate-like layer formed when magma forces its way between two preexisting rock layers. In the example shown, the sill has lifted the overlying rock layers to make

In an intrusive igneous rock, individual mineral crystals are visible with the unaided eye or with the help of a simple magnifying lens. In an extrusive rock, which cools very rapidly, the individual crystals are very small. They can only be

11.8 Extrusive igneous rock samples *(a) Obsidian, or volcanic glass. The smooth, glassy appearance is acquired when a gas-free lava cools very rapidly. This sample shows red and black streaks caused by minor variations in composition. (b) A specimen of scoria, a form of lava containing many small holes and cavities produced by gas bubbles.*

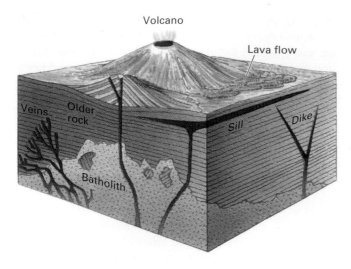

11.9 Volcanic rock formations *This block diagram illustrates various forms of intrusive igneous rock plutons as well as an extrusive lava flow.*

room. A second kind of pluton is the *dike,* a wall-like body formed when a vertical rock fracture is forced open by magma. Commonly, these vertical fractures conduct magma to the land surface in the process of extrusion. Figure 11.10 shows a dike of mafic rock cutting across layers of older rock. The dike rock is fine-textured because of its rapid cooling. Magma entering small, irregular, branching fractures in the surrounding rock solidifies in a branching network of thin *veins.*

Intrusive igneous rocks solidify below the Earth's surface. Because they cool slowly, they develop mineral crystals visible to the eye. Extrusive igneous rocks cool very rapidly on the land surface or ocean bottom and thus show crystals of only microscopic size.

11.10 Exposure of a dike *A dike of mafic igneous rock with nearly vertical parallel sides, cutting across flat-lying sedimentary rock layers. Arrows mark the contact between igneous rock and sedimentary rock. Spanish Peaks region, Colorado.*

The formation of extrusive igneous rock can be witnessed today where volcanic processes are active. *Eye on the Environment 11.1 • Battling Iceland's Heimaey Volcano* describes the struggle of courageous Icelanders to save their volcanic island village and harbor from the onslaught of a volcanic eruption.

Chemical Alteration of Igneous Rocks

The minerals in igneous rocks are formed at high temperatures, and often at high pressures, as magma cools. When igneous rocks are exposed at or near the Earth's surface, the conditions are quite different. Temperatures and pressures are low. Also, the rocks are exposed to soil water and ground water solutions that contain dissolved oxygen and carbon dioxide. In this new environment, the minerals within an igneous rock may no longer be stable. Instead, most of these minerals undergo a slow chemical change that weakens their structure. Chemical change in response to this alien environment is called **mineral alteration.** It is a process of *weathering,* which we will discuss further in Chapter 15.

Weathering also includes the physical forces of disintegration that break up igneous rock into small fragments and separate the component minerals, grain by grain. This breakup, or fragmentation, is essential for the chemical reactions of mineral alteration. The reason is that fragmentation results in a great increase in the mineral surface area that is exposed to chemically active solutions in soils. (We will take up the processes of physical disintegration of rocks in Chapter 14.)

Another chemical alteration process is *oxidation.* This process occurs when oxygen dissolved in soil or ground water reacts with minerals. Oxidation is the normal fate of most silicate minerals exposed at the surface. With oxidation, the silicate minerals are converted to *oxides,* in which silicon and the metallic elements—such as calcium, magnesium, and iron—each bond completely with oxygen. Oxides are very stable. Quartz, with the composition silicon dioxide (SiO_2), is a common mineral oxide. It is very long-lasting and is found abundantly in many types of rocks and sediments. As we will see shortly, quartz is a major constituent of sedimentary rocks.

Silicate minerals do not generally dissolve in water, but some react chemically with water in a chemical alteration process called *hydrolysis.* This process is not merely a soaking or wetting of the mineral, but a true chemical change that produces a different mineral compound. The products of hydrolysis are stable and long-lasting, as are the products of oxidation.

Some of the alteration products of silicate minerals are clay minerals, described in Chapter 10. These minerals are produced by a combination of oxidation and hydrolysis acting on silicates. A **clay mineral** is one that has plastic properties when moist, because it consists of very small, thin flakes that become lubricated by layers of water molecules. Clay minerals formed by mineral alteration are abundant in common types of sedimentary rocks.

Solution is another mechanism by which minerals are altered. Most minerals do not dissolve directly in water. One important exception is rock salt (sodium chloride), which is a constituent of sea water. When carbon dioxide dissolves in water, a weak acid—*carbonic acid*—is formed. Carbonic acid can dissolve certain minerals, especially calcium carbonate. In addition, where decaying vegetation is present, soil water contains many complex organic acids that are capable of reacting with minerals.

Mineral alteration occurs when the minerals in igneous rocks are transformed chemically into new minerals that are more stable at or near the Earth's surface. Processes of mineral alteration include oxidation, hydrolysis, and solution.

SEDIMENTS AND SEDIMENTARY ROCKS

We can now turn to the second great rock class, the *sedimentary rocks*. The mineral particles in sedimentary rocks can be derived from preexisting rock of any of the three rock classes as well as from newly formed organic matter. However, igneous rock is the most important original source of the inorganic mineral matter that makes up sedimentary rock. For example, a granite can weather to yield grains of quartz and particles of clay minerals derived from feldspars, thus contributing sand and clay to a sedimentary rock. Sedimentary rocks include rock types with a wide range of physical and chemical properties. We will only touch on a few of the most important kinds of sedimentary rocks, which are shown in Table 11.2.

In the process of mineral alteration, solid rock is weakened, softened, and fragmented, yielding particles of many sizes and mineral compositions. When transported by a fluid medium—air, water, or glacial ice—these particles are known collectively as **sediment.** Used in its broadest sense, sediment includes both inorganic and organic matter. Dissolved mineral matter in solution must also be included.

Streams and rivers carry sediment to lower land levels, where sediment can accumulate. The most favorable sites of sediment accumulation are shallow seafloors bordering continents. But sediments also accumulate in inland valleys, lakes, and marshes. Thick accumulations of sediment may become deeply buried under newer (younger) sediments. Wind and glacial ice also transport sediment but not necessarily to lower elevations or to places suitable for accumulation. Over long spans of time, the sediments can undergo physical or chemical changes, becoming compacted and hardened to form sedimentary rock.

There are three major classes of sediment. First is **clastic sediment,** which consists of inorganic rock and mineral fragments, called *clasts*. Examples are the materials in a sand bar of a river bed or on a ocean beach. Second is **chemically precipitated sediment,** which consists of inorganic mineral compounds precipitated from a saltwater solution or as hard parts of organisms. In the process of chemical precipitation, ions in solution combine to form

Table 11.2 | Some Common Sedimentary Rock Types

Subclass	Rock Type	Composition
Clastic (composed of rock and/or mineral fragments)	Sandstone	Cemented sand grains
	Siltstone	Cemented silt particles
	Conglomerate	Sandstone containing pebbles of hard rock
	Mudstone	Silt and clay, with some sand
	Claystone	Clay
	Shale	Clay, breaking easily into flat flakes and plates
Chemically precipitated (formed by chemical precipitation from sea water or salty inland lakes)	Limestone	Calcium carbonate, formed by precipitation on sea or lake floors
	Dolomite	Magnesium and calcium carbonates, similar to limestone
	Chert	Silica, a microcrystalline form of quartz
	Evaporites	Minerals formed by evaporation of salty solutions in shallow inland lakes or coastal lagoons
Organic (formed from organic material)	Coal	Rock formed from peat or other organic deposits; may be burned as a mineral fuel
	Petroleum (mineral fuel)	Liquid hydrocarbon found in sedimentary deposits; not a true rock but a mineral fuel
	Natural gas (mineral fuel)	Gaseous hydrocarbon found in sedimentary deposits; not a true rock but a mineral fuel

Eye on the Environment | 11.1

Battling Iceland's Heimaey Volcano

Normally the processes of rock formation are very slow, but when a volcanic eruption occurs, large volumes of fresh rock can be created very quickly. In 1973, inhabitants of Heimaey, a small island very near the southern coast of Iceland, found themselves witnessing the birth of new rock from a vantage point that was a little too close.

It was around 2:00 A.M., early on a January morning, that the eruption began. First, a fissure split the eastern side of the island from one coast to the other, sending up a curtain of fire in a pyrotechnical display nearly 2 km (1.2 mi) long. Soon, however, the spraying fountains of volcanic debris became restricted to a small area not far from Helgafell, an older volcanic

cone. The lava and lava fragments of ash and cinders, called *tephra*, poured out at a rate of 100 m³/sec (about 3500 ft³/sec), building a cone that soon reached a height of about 100 m (about 300 ft) above sea level. It was dubbed Kirkjufell after a farmstead, Kirkjubaer, which lay beneath the debris.

It wasn't long before strong easterly winds set in, and Iceland's

Vestmannaeyjar after the eruption Lava (right) invaded the village of Vestmannaeyjar, while fine black cinders (now swept from roofs and roads) covered the town.

main fishing port, Vestmannaeyjar, located within a kilometer (about a half-mile) from the eruption, began to receive a "snowfall" of fine, black cinders. Houses on the east side of the town were buried under the tephra. Many of the houses collapsed under the weight of the hot ash, while others were set afire. Lava flows soon reached the village, burying and burning still other buildings (see photo).

Over the passing weeks, the emissions of tephra ceased, but lava continued to flow from the cone, which soon reached 200 m (about 600 ft) in height. Unfortunately, the lava began to flow northward, narrowing the harbor and threatening the future livelihood of the town and its evacuated inhabitants. Fishing is a major industry in Iceland, accounting for nearly 80 percent of Iceland's foreign exchange. Vestmannaeyjar normally lands and processes 20 percent of the nation's fish catch.

Because the harbor and fishing port are important to the nation's economy, Icelanders embarked on a bold plan to save the harbor by altering the course of the lava, diverting the flow eastward. This was to be accomplished by cooling the flow on its north edge with water streams, creating a natural wall to channel the flow alongside the harbor instead of across it. Within a few weeks, the first pumping of water onto the flowing lava began. By early March, a pump ship came into operation in the harbor, providing a steady flow of sea water to cool the slowly moving flows. It was joined in April by as many as 47 high-capacity pumps floating on barges, delivering in total as much as 1 cu m of sea water per second (35 ft^3/sec).

The most effective technique for slowing the lava at a particular location began with cooling the edge

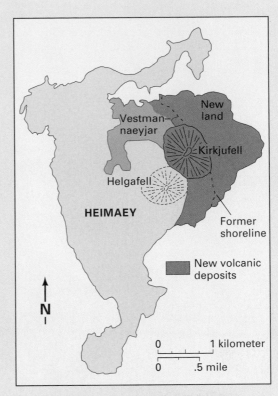

Map of Heimaey Island, Iceland *The map shows the extent of lava flows from the eruptions of the Kirkjufell crater. (Modified from U.S. Geological Survey.)*

and nearby surface of the flow with water from hoses. This allowed bulldozers to build a crude road up and over the slowly moving flow, using nearby tephra as the road material. Large plastic pipes were then laid along the road and across the flow, with small holes spraying water on hotspots. As long as sea water was flowing in the plastic pipes, they remained cool enough not to melt. After a day or so, the flow typically began to slow. Pumping usually continued for about two weeks, until the lava stopped steaming at spray points. The result of the water applications was to build a broad wall of cool, lava rubble with thickening lava behind it.

The huge undertaking successfully stabilized the northern front of the lava flow, keeping the harbor

from becoming closed (see map). Although the lava had indeed reached the harbor, it had merely narrowed its entrance. In fact, the new flow improved the harbor's ability to shelter the boats within it (see map). Within about five months, the eruption was over, and the digging out began in earnest. Within a year, life was back to normal on Heimaey.

The diversion of the lava and reconstruction of the village of Vestmannaeyjar were extremely costly. To pay for the cost, Iceland passed a special tax increase, requiring the average Icelandic family to pay about 10 percent of its annual income for one year. Generous foreign aid also helped cover the enormous expenses borne by the tiny nation.

11.11 Eye on the Landscape Sandstone strata *This photo of an eroded sandstone formation on the Colorado Plateau shows individual layers, or strata, that make up the rock. The layers were originally deposited within a field of moving sand dunes.* **What else would the geographer see? ... Answers at the end of the chapter.**

solid mineral matter separate from the solution. A layer of rock salt, such as that found in dry lakebeds in arid regions, is an example. A third class is **organic sediment** which consists of the tissues of plants and animals, accumulated and preserved after the death of the organism. An example is a layer of peat in a bog or marsh.

Sediment accumulates in more-or-less horizontal layers, called **strata,** or simply "beds" (Figure 11.11). Individual strata are separated from those below and above by surfaces called stratification planes or bedding planes. These separation surfaces allow one layer to be easily removed from the next. Strata of widely different compositions can occur alternately, one above the next.

> Sedimentary rocks are composed of sediment, which may be clastic, chemically precipitated, or organic. Layers of sediment are termed strata.

Clastic Sedimentary Rocks

Clastic sediments are derived from clasts of any and all of the rock groups—igneous, sedimentary, metamorphic—and thus may include a very wide range of minerals for sedimentary rock formation. Silicate minerals are the most important, both in original form and as altered by oxidation and hydrolysis. Quartz and feldspar usually dominate. Because quartz is hard and is immune to alteration, it is the most important single component of the clastic sediments (Figure 11.12). Second in abundance are fragments of unaltered fine-grained parent rocks, such as tiny pieces of lava rock. Feldspar and mica are also commonly present. Clay minerals are major constituents of the finest clastic sediments.

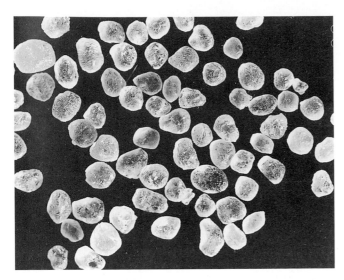

11.12 Rounded quartz grains from an ancient sandstone *The grains average about 1 mm (0.039 in.) in diameter.*

The range of particle sizes in a clastic sediment determines how easily and how far the particles are transported by water currents. The finer the particles, the more easily they are held suspended in the fluid. On the other hand, the coarser particles tend to settle to the bottom of the fluid layer. In this way, a separation of size grades, called *sorting,* occurs. Sorting determines the texture of the sediment deposit and of the sedimentary rock derived from that sediment. The finest clay particles do not settle out unless they are made to clot together into larger clumps. This clotting process, called *flocculation,* normally occurs when river water carrying clay mixes with the saltwater of the ocean.

> **Important varieties of clastic sedimentary rocks include sandstone, conglomerate, mudstone, claystone, and shale. They are formed when sediments are compressed and cemented by solutions containing silica or calcium carbonate.**

When sediments accumulate in thick sequences, the lower strata are exposed to the pressure produced by the weight of the sediments above them. This pressure compacts the sediments, squeezing out excess water. Cementation occurs as dissolved minerals recrystallize where grains touch and in the spaces between mineral particles. Silicon dioxide (quartz, SiO_2) is very slightly soluble in water, and so the cement is often a form of quartz, called *silica,* which lacks a true crystalline form. Calcium carbonate ($CaCO_3$) is another common material that cements clastic sedimentary rocks. Compaction and cementation produce sedimentary rock.

The important varieties of clastic sedimentary rock are distinguished by the size of their particles. They include sandstone, conglomerate, mudstone, claystone, and shale. **Sandstone** is formed from fine to coarse sand (Figure 11.13). The cement may be silica or calcium carbonate. The sand grains are commonly of quartz, such as those shown in Figure 11.12. (Refer to Figure 10.2 for the names and diameters of the various grades of sediment particles.) Sandstone containing numerous rounded pebbles of hard rock is called *conglomerate* (Figure 11.14).

A mixture of water with particles of silt and clay, along with some sand grains, is called *mud.* The sedimentary rock hardened from such a mixture is called *mudstone.* Compacted and hardened clay layers become *claystone.* Sedimentary rocks of mud composition are commonly layered in such a way that they easily break apart into small flakes and plates. The rock is then described as being *fissile* and is given the name **shale.** Shale, the most abundant of all sedimentary rocks, is formed largely of clay minerals. The compaction of the mud to form mudstone and shale involves a considerable loss of volume as water is driven out of the clay. Figure 11.15 shows an eroded

11.13 Eye on the Landscape Massive sandstone *A thick formation of massive sandstone forms the sheer cliff in this view of rock formations on the North Rim of the Grand Canyon, Arizona. Termed the Coconino Formation, the sandstone is an ancient dune deposit.* **What else would the geographer see? ... Answers at the end of the chapter.**

11.14 Conglomerate section *A piece of quartzitic conglomerate, cut through and polished, reveals rounded pebbles of quartz (clear and milky colors) and chert (grayish). It is about 12 cm (4.7 in.) in diameter.*

shale formation in southern Utah. Here some of the shale beds have distinctive colors, so the bedding is especially prominent.

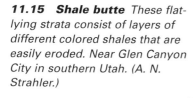 **Clastic Rocks Animation.** Learn the terms used for clasts of different sizes and examine several different types of clastic rocks.

Chemically Precipitated Sedimentary Rocks

Under favorable conditions, mineral compounds are deposited from the salt solutions of sea water and of salty inland lakes in desert climates. One of the most common sedimentary rocks formed by chemical precipitation is

limestone, composed largely of the mineral calcite. *Calcite* is calcium carbonate ($CaCO_3$). Marine limestones—limestone strata formed on the seafloor—accumulated in thick layers in many ancient seaways in past geologic eras (Figure 11.16). A closely related rock, also formed by chemical precipitation, is *dolomite,* composed of calcium-magnesium carbonate. Limestone and dolomite are grouped together as the *carbonate rocks.* They are dense rocks with white, pale gray, or even black color.

Sea water also yields sedimentary layers of silica in a hard, noncrystalline form called *chert.* Chert is a variety of sedimentary rock, but it also commonly occurs combined with limestone (cherty limestone).

Shallow water bodies acquire a very high level of salinity where evaporation is sustained and intense. One type of shallow water body is a bay or estuary in a coastal desert region. Another type is the salty lake of inland desert basins (see Figure 16.32). Sedimentary minerals and rocks deposited from such concentrated solutions are called **evaporites.** Ordinary rock salt, the mineral halite (sodium chloride), has accumulated in this way in thick sedimentary rock layers. These layers are mined as major commercial sources of halite.

Limestone, dolomite, and chert are rocks formed by chemical precipitation in a marine environment. Evaporites form when salty water evaporates, leaving layers of soluble minerals behind.

Hydrocarbon Compounds in Sedimentary Rocks

Hydrocarbon compounds (compounds of carbon, hydrogen, and oxygen) form a most important type of organic sediment—one on which human society increasingly depends for fuel. These substances occur both as solids (peat and coal) and as liquids and gases (petroleum and natural gas). Only coal qualifies physically as a rock. *Peat* is a soft, fibrous substance of brown to black color. (See Figure 10.20.) It accumulates in a bog environment where the continual presence of water inhibits the decay of plant remains.

11.15 Shale butte *These flat-lying strata consist of layers of different colored shales that are easily eroded. Near Glen Canyon City in southern Utah. (A. N. Strahler.)*

11.16   Eye on the Landscape   Chalk cliffs *The Etretât cliffs of Normandy, France, are composed of soft limestone, known as chalk.* **What else would the geographer see? ... Answers at the end of the chapter.**

At various times and places in the geologic past, plant remains accumulated on a large scale, accompanied by sinking of the area and burial of the compacted organic matter under thick layers of inorganic clastic sediments. *Coal* is the end result of this process (Figure 11.17). Individual coal seams are interbedded with shale, sandstone, and limestone strata. *Petroleum* (or *crude oil,* as the liquid form is often called) includes many hydrocarbon compounds. *Natural gas,* which is found in close association

with accumulations of liquid petroleum, is a mixture of gases. The principal gas is methane (marsh gas, CH_4). Geologists generally agree that petroleum and natural gas are of organic origin, but the nature of their formation is not fully understood. They are classed not as minerals but rather separately as mineral fuels.

Natural gas and petroleum commonly occupy open interconnected pores in a thick sedimentary rock layer—a porous sandstone, for example. The simplest arrangement of strata

11.17   Strip mine *A coal seam near Sheridan, Wyoming, being strip mined by heavy equipment.*

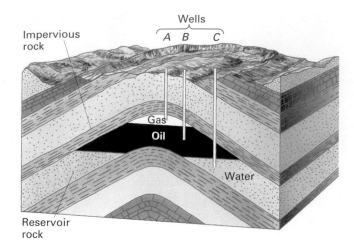

Impervious rock

Wells
A B C

Gas
Oil

Water

Reservoir rock

11.18 **Trapping of oil and gas** *Idealized cross section of an oil pool on a dome structure in sedimentary strata. Well A will draw gas; well B will draw oil; and well C will draw water. The cap rock is shale; the reservoir rock is sandstone. (Copyright © A. N. Strahler.)*

favorable to trapping petroleum and natural gas is an uparching of the type shown in Figure 11.18. Shale forms an impervious cap rock. A porous sandstone beneath the cap rock serves as a reservoir. Natural gas occupies the highest position, with the oil below it, and then water, in increasing order of density.

Yet another form of occurrence of hydrocarbon fuels is *bitumen,* a variety of petroleum that behaves much as a solid, although it is actually a highly viscous liquid. Bitumen goes by other common names, such as tar, asphalt, or pitch. In some localities, bitumen occupies pore spaces in layers of sand or porous sandstone. It remains immobile in the enclosing sand and will flow only when heated. Outcrops of *bituminous sand (oil sand)* exposed to the Sun will show bleeding of the bitumen. Perhaps the best known of the great bituminous sand deposits are those occurring in Alberta, Canada. Where exposed along the banks of the Athabasca River, the oil sand is extracted from surface mines.

Hydrocarbon compounds in sedimentary rocks are important because they provide an energy resource on which modern human civilization depends. These **fossil fuels,** as they are called collectively, have required millions of years to accumulate. However, they are being consumed at a very rapid rate by our industrial society. These fuels are nonrenewable resources. Once they are gone, there will be no more because the quantity produced by geologic processes even in a thousand years is scarcely measurable in comparison to the quantity stored through geologic time.

GEODISCOVERIES **Hydrocarbons in Sedimentary Rocks.** Watch this animation to see how ocean floor sediment accumulates and ultimately provides deposits of oil and gas.

Hydrocarbons in sedimentary rocks include coal, petroleum, natural gas, and peat. These mineral fuels power modern industrial society.

Table 11.3	Some Common Metamorphic Rock Types
Rock Type	**Description**
Slate	Shale exposed to heat and pressure that splits into hard flat plates
Schist	Shale exposed to intense heat and pressure that shows evidence of shearing
Quartzite	Sandstone that is "welded" by a silica cement into a very hard rock of solid quartz
Marble	Limestone exposed to heat and pressure, resulting in larger, more uniform crystals
Gneiss	Rock resulting from the exposure of clastic sedimentary or intrusive igneous rocks to heat and pressure

METAMORPHIC ROCKS

Any type of igneous or sedimentary rock may be altered by the tremendous pressures and high temperatures that accompany the mountain-building processes of the Earth's crust. The result is a rock so changed in texture and structure as to be reclassified as **metamorphic rock.** Mineral components of the parent rock are, in many cases, reconstituted into different mineral varieties. Recrystallization of the original minerals can also occur. Our discussion of metamorphic rocks will mention only five common types—slate, schist, quartzite, marble, and gneiss (Table 11.3).

Slate is formed from shale that is heated and compressed by mountain-making forces. This fine-textured rock splits neatly into thin plates, which are familiar as roofing shingles and as patio flagstones. With application of increased heat and pressure, slate changes into **schist,** representing the most advanced stage of metamorphism. Schist has a structure called foliation, consisting of thin but rough, irregularly curved planes of parting in the rock (Figure 11.19). These

11.19 **Schist sample** *A specimen of foliated schist.*

11.20 Banded gneiss *This surf-washed rock surface exposes banded gneiss, Pemaquid Point, Maine.*

are evidence of *shearing*—a stress that pushes the layers sideways, like a deck of cards pushed into a fan with the sweep of a palm. Schist is set apart from slate by the coarse texture of the mineral grains, the abundance of mica, and occasionally the presence of scattered large crystals of newly formed minerals, such as garnet.

The metamorphic equivalent of conglomerate, sandstone, and siltstone is **quartzite,** which is formed by the addition of silica to fill completely the open spaces between grains. This process is carried out by the slow movement of underground waters carrying silicate into the rock, where it is deposited.

Limestone, after undergoing metamorphism, becomes *marble,* a rock of sugary texture when freshly broken. During the process of internal shearing, calcite in the limestone re-forms into larger, more uniform crystals than before. Bedding planes are obscured, and masses of mineral impurities are drawn out into swirling bands.

Finally, the important metamorphic rock **gneiss** may be formed either from intrusive igneous rocks or from clastic sedimentary rocks that have been in close contact with intrusive magmas. A single description will not fit all gneisses because they vary considerably in appearance, mineral composition, and structure. One variety of gneiss is strongly banded into light and dark layers or lenses (Figure 11.20), which may be bent into wavy folds. These bands have differing mineral compositions. They are

> **Metamorphic rocks are formed from preexisting rocks by intense heat and pressure, which alter rock structure and chemical composition. Shale is transformed to slate or schist, sandstone to quartzite, and limestone to marble. Gneiss forms when an intrusive magma cools next to igneous or sedimentary rocks.**

thought to be relics of sedimentary strata, such as shale and sandstone, to which new mineral matter has been added from nearby intrusive magmas.

One of the more exciting developments in remote sensing in the past few years has been the launch of the ASTER instrument (Advanced Spaceborne Thermal Emission and Reflection Spectroradiometer) on NASA's Terra satellite platform. It has a unique ability to aid in geologic mapping and in identification of areas with potentially valuable ore deposits. *Focus on Remote Sensing 11.2 • Geologic Mapping with ASTER* tells this interesting story.

GEODISCOVERIES **Virtual Rock Lab Interactivity.** How are minerals and rocks identified? Learn the characteristics of common minerals and rocks and test the knowledge you've gained in the chapter with this interactivity.

THE CYCLE OF ROCK CHANGE

The processes that form rocks, when taken together, constitute a single system that cycles and recycles Earth materials over geologic time from one form to another. The **cycle of rock change,** shown in Figure 11.21, describes this system. There are two environments—a surface environment of low pressures and temperatures and a deep environment of high pressures and temperatures. The sur-

Focus on Remote Sensing | 11.2

Geologic Mapping with ASTER

A unique imaging instrument built by Japan that is of special interest to geologists is aboard NASA's Terra satellite platform, launched in December 1999. ASTER, the Advanced Spaceborne Thermal Emission and Reflection Spectroradiometer, acquires multispectral images in three different waveband regions—visible and near-infrared, shortwave infrared, and thermal infrared. Recall from *Geographer's Tools 2.4 • Remote Sensing for Physical Geography* that human eyes are sensitive only to the visible light portion of the spectrum, from about 0.4 to 0.65 μm, while the Sun provides enough energy for good imaging from about 0.3 to 3.0 μm. This means that surface substances can be imaged in these wavelengths and have "colors" that are unknown in human experience. We refer to these colors as spectral signatures. As it happens, minerals and rocks often have distinctive spectral signatures in near- and shortwave infrared domains, and so near- and shortwave infrared images are particularly useful for geologic mapping.

Another spectral region of particular interest is the thermal infrared, especially the wavelengths from 8.0 to 12.0 μm. Here the energy for sensing is the radiant energy emitted by substances as a function of their temperature. However, some types of rocks and minerals emit more energy of a given wavelength at a given temperature than others. In this way, we can think of these substances as having spectral signatures in the thermal infrared, too.

The two graphs below illustrate this principle. They show reflectance plotted against wavelength for two common minerals—quartz and calcite. Also shown are the spectral locations of the ASTER wavebands. In the left graph, we can see that both quartz and calcite are quite bright in ASTER's two visible bands (bands 1 and 2, green and red). They appear white to the eye, with calcite, which is slightly brighter in the red band, appearing to be a "warmer" white. In the shortwave infrared, however, calcite is significantly darker in ASTER band 8 than in surrounding bands 7 and 9. The right graph shows spectral reflectance in the thermal infrared spectral region. Calcite is brightest in ASTER band 13 while

being darkest in the adjacent band 14. Quartz has a distinctive signature as well, being about 40 percent brighter in bands 10–12 than in 13–14. Thus, both minerals have unique spectral signatures in this spectral region, too.

Color images in the three waveband regions, shown at right, illustrate how ASTER can help identify different types of rocks and minerals by their spectral signatures. The images are from the Saline Valley, a dry semidesert region in southeastern California near Death Valley, and were acquired on March 30, 2000. Trending diagonally across the center of the image is the valley itself, which is the now-nearly-dry bed of a lake that was filled with water during the Ice Age. Lying to the southwest is the Inyo mountain chain, with a number of steep valleys cutting into its flanks. In the lower left corner, we see a small part of the Owens Valley. To the northeast of Saline Valley lies a complex geologic region at the northern end of the Panamint Range.

Image *(a)* is a color infrared display in which true colors of green, red, and near-infrared are shown

Reflectance spectra for quartz and calcite *Wavebands in which ASTER acquires images are identified as numbered bands. Left, the visible and near-infrared spectral region; right, the thermal infrared spectral region.*

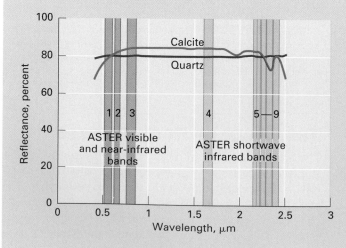

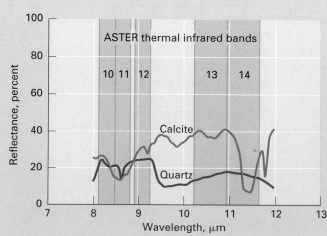

***Multispectral ASTER images of Saline Valley,
California** (a) visible and near-infrared image; (b)
shortwave infrared image; (c) thermal infrared image.
(NASA/GSFC/MITI/ERSDAC/JAROS and U.S./Japan ASTER
Science Team.)*

as blue, green, and red in the
image. The forests of the Inyos
appear in a distinctive red color
because vegetation is very bright
in the near-infrared region. Snow
along the summit of the Inyos is
white, as are the salty dry basins of
the valleys. Many different rock
types appear, in tones ranging
from brown, gray, and yellow to
blue. Image *(b)* displays ASTER
shortwave infrared bands 8, 6, and

4 as blue, green and red. These
bands distinguish carbonate, sulfate, and clay minerals. Limestones
are yellow-green, while the clay
mineral kaolinite appears in purplish tones. In *(c)*, ASTER bands 10,
12, and 13 are shown in blue,
green, and red, respectively. Here,
rocks rich in quartz appear in red
tones, while carbonate rocks are
green. Mafic volcanic rocks are visible in purple tones.

By comparing the three images,
it is easy to see how the spectral
information acquired by ASTER
has the ability to make geologic
mapping faster and easier. By
using ASTER data, geologists can
not only come to understand better
the geologic history of a region,
but also identify the geologic settings in which valuable mineral
ores may be found.

11.21 The cycle of rock change
This cycle links sediment with sedimentary, metamorphic, intrusive igneous, and extrusive igneous rocks in processes of rock formation and destruction.

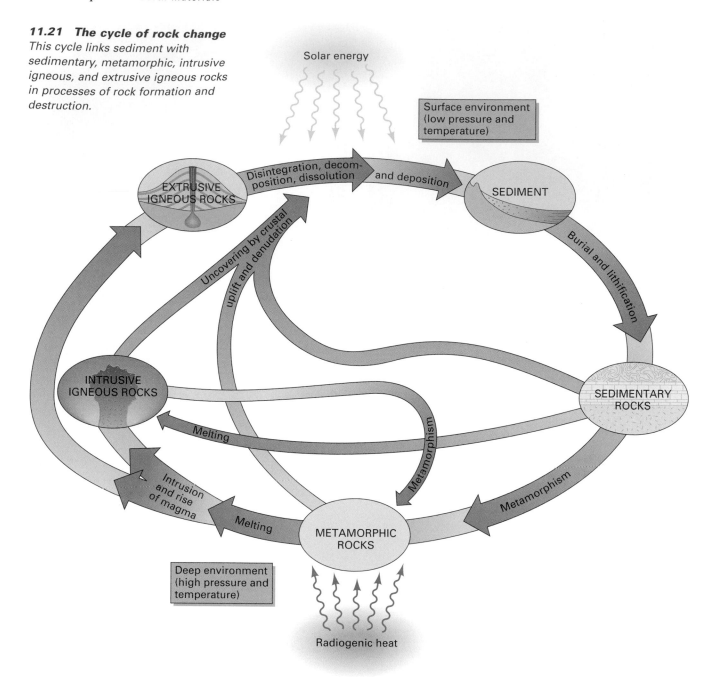

---

face environment is the site of rock alteration and sediment deposition. In this environment, igneous, sedimentary, and metamorphic rocks are uplifted and exposed to air and water. Their minerals are altered chemically and broken free from the parent rock, yielding sediment. The sediment accumulates in basins, where deeply buried sediment layers are compressed and cemented into sedimentary rock.

Sedimentary rock, entering the deep environment, is heated by the slow radioactive decay of elements and comes into a zone of high confining pressure. Here, it is trans-

The cycle of rock change describes how Earth materials are cycled and recycled by Earth processes over geologic time. In the surface environment, rocks weather into sediment. In the deep environment, heat and pressure transform sediment into rock that is eventually exposed at the surface.

formed into metamorphic rock. Pockets of magma are formed in the deep environment and move upward, melting and incorporating surrounding rock as they rise. Upon reaching a higher level, magma cools and solidifies, becoming intrusive igneous rock. Or it may emerge at the surface to form extrusive igneous rock. Either way, the cycle is completed.

The cycle of rock change has been active since our planet became solid and internally stable, continuously forming and re-forming rocks of all three major classes. Not even the oldest igneous and metamorphic rocks found thus far are the "original" rocks of the Earth's crust, for they were recycled eons ago.

GEO**DISCOVERIES** **Web Quiz.** Take a quick quiz on the key concepts of this chapter.

A LOOK AHEAD This chapter has focused on the processes by which the minerals and rocks of the Earth's surface are formed. As we look further into the Earth's outermost layers in the next chapter, we will see that these processes do not occur everywhere. Instead, there is a grand plan that organizes the formation and destruction of rocks and distributes the processes of the cycle of rock change in a geographic pattern. This pattern is controlled by the pattern in which the solid Earth's brittle outer layer is fractured into great plates that split and separate and also converge and collide. The grand plan is plate tectonics, the scheme for understanding the dynamics of the Earth's crust over millions of years of geologic time.

GEO**DISCOVERIES** **Web Links.** View more rocks and minerals, learn more about the Heimaey volcanic eruption, examine the formation of petroleum—all in this chapter's web links.

In Review | Earth Materials

- The elements oxygen and silicon dominate the *Earth's crust.* Metallic elements, which include aluminum, iron, and the base elements, account for nearly all the remainder.

- **Minerals** are naturally occurring, inorganic substances. Each has an individual chemical composition and atomic structure. **Rocks** are naturally-occurring assemblages of minerals.

- *Silicate minerals* make up the bulk of **igneous rocks.** They contain silicon and oxygen together with some of the metallic elements.

- There are three broad classes of igneous rocks, depending on their mineral content. **Felsic** rocks contain mostly felsic minerals and are least dense; **mafic** rocks, containing mostly mafic minerals, are denser; and *ultramafic* rocks are most dense. Because felsic rocks are least dense, they are generally found in the upper layers of the Earth's crust. Mafic and ultramafic rocks are more abundant in the layers below.

- If **magma** erupts on the surface to cool rapidly as lava, the rocks formed are **extrusive** and have a fine crystal texture. If the magma cools slowly below the surface as a **pluton,** the rocks are **intrusive** and the crystals are larger. **Granite** (felsic, intrusive), **andesite** (felsic, extrusive), and **basalt** (mafic, extrusive) are three very common igneous rock types.

- Most silicate minerals found in igneous rocks undergo **mineral alteration** when exposed to air and moisture at the Earth's surface. Mineral alteration occurs through *oxidation, hydrolysis,* or *solution.* **Clay minerals** are commonly produced by mineral alteration.

- **Sedimentary rocks** are formed in layers, or **strata. Clastic sedimentary** rocks are composed of fragments of rocks and minerals that usually accumulate on ocean floors. As the layers are buried more and more deeply, water is pressed out and particles are cemented together. **Sandstone** and **shale** are common examples.

- **Chemical precipitation** also produces sedimentary rocks, such as **limestone.** Coal, petroleum, and natural gas are hydrocarbon compounds occurring in sedimentary rocks that are used as mineral fuels.

- **Metamorphic rocks** are formed when igneous or sedimentary rocks are exposed to heat and pressure. Shale is altered to *slate* or **schist,** sandstones become **quartzite,** and intrusive igneous rocks or clastic sediments are metamorphosed into **gneiss.**

- In the **cycle of rock change,** rocks are exposed at the Earth's surface, and their minerals are broken free and altered to form sediment. The sediment accumulates in basins, where the layers are compressed and cemented into sedimentary rock. Deep within the Earth, the heat of radioactive decay melts preexisting rock into magma, which can move upward into the crust to form igneous rocks that cool at or below the surface. Rocks deep in the crust are exposed to the heat and pressure, forming metamorphic rock. Mountain-building forces move deep igneous, sedimentary, and metamorphic rocks upward to the surface, providing new material for surface alteration and breakup and completing the cycle.

Key Terms

mineral, p. 399
rock, p. 399
igneous rocks, p. 399
sedimentary rocks, p. 399
metamorphic rocks,
    p. 399
quartz, p. 400
felsic, p. 400
mafic, p. 400
magma, p. 400

granite, p. 401
intrusive igneous rock,
    p. 402
lava, p. 402
extrusive igneous rock,
    p. 402
andesite, p. 403
basalt, p. 403
pluton, p. 403
mineral alteration, p. 404

clay mineral, p. 405
sediment, p. 405
clastic sediment, p. 405
chemically precipitated
    sediment, p. 405
organic sediment, p. 408
strata, p. 408
sandstone, p. 409
shale, p. 409
limestone, p. 410

evaporites, p. 410
fossil fuels, p. 412
metamorphic rock,
    p. 412
schist, p. 412
quartzite, p. 413
gneiss, p. 413
cycle of rock change,
    p. 413

Review Questions

1. What is the Earth's crust? What elements are most abundant in the crust?

2. Define the terms *mineral* and *rock.* Name the three major classes of rocks.

3. What are silicate minerals? Describe two classes of silicate minerals.

4. Name four types of igneous rocks and arrange them in order of density.

5. How do igneous rocks differ when magma cools (a) at depth and (b) at the surface?

6. How are igneous rocks chemically altered? Identify and describe three processes of chemical alteration.

7. What is sediment? Define and describe three types of sediments.

8. Describe two processes that produce sedimentary rocks, and identify at least three important varieties of clastic sedimentary rocks.

9. How are sedimentary rocks formed by chemical precipitation?

10. What types of sedimentary deposits consist of hydrocarbon compounds? How are they formed?

11. What are metamorphic rocks? Describe at least three types of metamorphic rocks and how they are formed.

Eye on the Environment 11.1 • Battling Iceland's
Heimaey Volcano

1. What were the initial effects of the eruption of Heimaey's volcano?

2. What important industry was threatened by the volcanic activity and why?

3. How was sea water used to keep lava from blocking the harbor?

Visualizing Exercises

1. Sketch a cross section of the Earth showing the following features: batholith, sill, dike, veins, lava, and volcano.

2. Sketch the cycle of rock change and describe the processes that act within it to form igneous, sedimentary, and metamorphic rocks.

Essay Question

1. A granite is exposed at the Earth's surface, high in the Sierra Nevada mountain range. Describe how mineral grains from this granite might be released, altered, and eventually become incorporated in a sedimentary rock. Trace the route and processes that would incorporate the same grains in a metamorphic rock.

Eye on the Landscape

11.11 Sandstone strata Note how these fine sedimentary beds **(A)** are crossed at angles by other beds. This cross-bedding is characteristic of dune sands. As the sand dune moves forward, sand layers accumulate on its sloping forward surface. Later, the wind erodes the dune, forming a new surface across the beds that cuts them at an angle. That surface is then covered by more sand layers. The result is the distinctive pattern of sloping sand beds cut by other beds at low angles that we see in this rock formation. Sand dune formation and movement is covered in Chapter 18.

11.13 Massive sandstone The "stairstep" topography of the Grand Canyon is a unique product of uplift of the Colorado Plateau and deep downcutting by the through-flowing Colorado River. The steep canyon walls carved by this process form vertical faces ("risers") **(A)** where massive, hard, rock formations, such as the Coconino Formation, are exposed. Weaker beds of sandstone and shale form sloping surfaces ("steps") **(B)** with a cover of rock fragments and sediment. Although the region is very dry, there is enough rainfall at higher elevations to support an open stand of pinyon pine and juniper forest atop the plateau **(C)** as well as a sparse cover on the slopes of the canyon walls. You can read more about landforms of horizontal rock strata in Chapter 17. Altitudinal zonation of vegetation in the Grand Canyon region was discussed in Chapter 9.

11.16 Chalk cliffs Note the hazy air **(A)** that is apparent in this photo. Marine aerosols are particularly rich in tiny particles of sea salt. Like ordinary table salt during humid weather, these particles attract water vapor. The vapor accumulates around the salt particles until tiny droplets are formed. These droplets absorb and scatter sunlight, creating the marine haze that is so evident in this photo. Recall that haze was covered in Chapter 4 in *Eye on the Environment 4.2 • Air Pollution.*

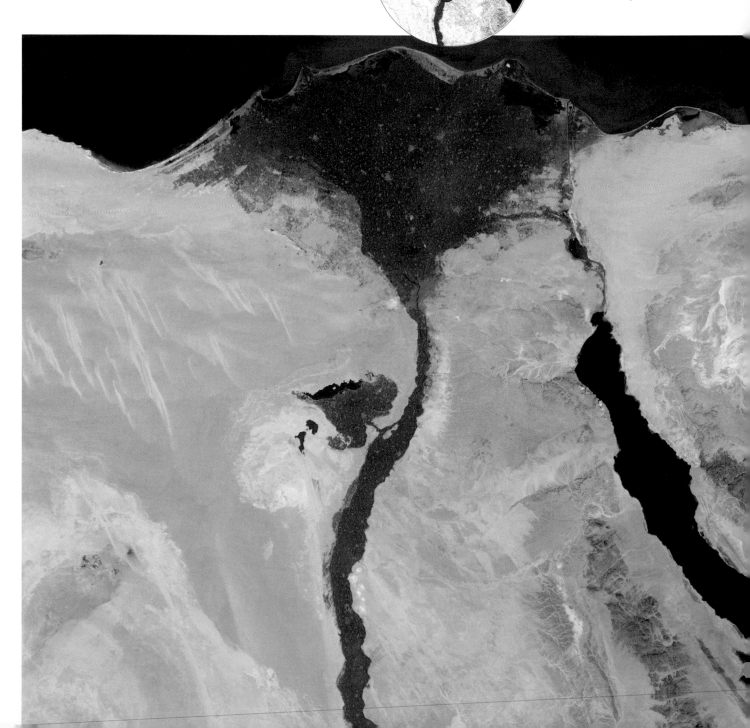

EYE ON THE LANDSCAPE

Egypt, the Nile Delta, and the Sinai Peninsula imaged by the MODIS satellite sensor in February, 2003. The arms of the Red Sea embracing the peninsula are rift valleys caused by crustal spreading. **What else would the geographer see? … Answers at the end of the chapter.**

12 | THE LITHOSPHERE AND PLATE TECTONICS

• •

PUTTING YOU IN THE PICTURE

Perhaps it was in that middle school geography class when you began to stare at the wall map of the world that hung in the front of the room, and you noticed that some parts of the map looked like a puzzle coming apart. The upper right corner of Africa was particularly suspect. Twisting the continent toward the northeast would close the Red Sea and Persian Gulf, making the Arabian Peninsula join Africa and the Middle East in a continuous broad land bridge.

Then you noticed the Mediterranean. With a little squeezing, it could shut quite nicely, uniting Europe and Africa. Greece would have to tuck in under Turkey, which would move northward to fill in the Black Sea. Italy and its islands would have to move south, filling in the obvious gap in the African coast of Libya and Tunisia. And then there was that funny bulge on the east coast of South America that would lie rather nicely along the west coast of Africa, with the Guianas butting against the west African republics from Liberia to Nigeria.

North America was a lot tougher, with those messy Caribbean islands and Central America to worry about. Could North and South America have been closer? If the Yucatan and Honduran-Nicaraguan peninsulas curled north and west, they would tuck in along the Gulf coast. Then Florida would nestle up against Panama, with Cuba, Jamaica, and Hispaniola lying along the Venezuelan coast. Now, with North America closer to South America, the east coast would fit against the bulge of western Africa rather nicely.

Perhaps, you wondered, all these lands actually did once fit together in a single world continent. Fun to think about but utterly fantastic.

Or was it? The idea that the continents were once united and then broken apart is an old one. In fact, in 1668, a Frenchman interpreted the matching coastlines of eastern

421

South America and western Africa as proof that the two continents were separated during the biblical flood!

Within the last 30 years, the slow movement of continents over long spans of geologic time has become widely accepted by geologists and physical geographers. Evidence for the fracturing of the Earth's outer rock layer and movement of the resulting rock plates has come from many sources—earthquake analysis, studies of ancient collections of plants and animals as they may have existed on united continents, and the matching of geologic structures, such as mountain chains and rock sequences, from conti-

nent to continent. Most recently, the rates of movement of continents have actually been measured using laser beams bounced from continents to orbiting satellites and back. Thus, many lines of evidence now converge on *plate tectonics*—the body of knowledge describing the movements and changes through time of lithospheric plates carrying continents and ocean basins.

Plate tectonics provides the plan of the Earth's major relief features, from the locations of mountain ranges and basins to the positions of oceans and inland seas. An understanding of plate tectonics is thus important to the understanding of the global patterns of the Earth's landscapes—including climate, soils, vegetation, landforms,

and, ultimately, human activity. In other words, the processes of physical geography are superimposed on a global geography given by plate tectonics. For this reason, the motions and histories of continental plates—splitting and separating to form ocean basins, closing and colliding to form mountain ranges—can be taken as a grand plan to organize a vast body of geographic and geologic knowledge. That grand plan—and the forces that have shaped it—are the subjects of this chapter. ∎

THE LITHOSPHERE AND PLATE TECTONICS

On the globes and maps we've seen since early childhood, the outline of each continent is so unique that we would never mistake one continent for another. But why are no two continents even closely alike? As we will see in this chapter, the continents have had a long history. In fact, in each of the continents some regions of metamorphic rocks date back more than 2 billion years. As part of that history, the continents have been fractured and split apart, as well as pushed together and joined.

Perhaps you've visited an old New England farmhouse that was constructed over hundreds of years—first the small two-room house, to which the kitchen shed was added at the back, and then the parlor wing at the side. Later the roof was raised for a second story, the tool house and barn were joined to the main house, the carriage house was built, and so it went. The Earth's continents have that kind of history. They are composed of huge masses of continental crust that have been assembled at different times in each continent's history. The theory describing the motions and changes through time of the continents and ocean basins, and the processes that fracture and fuse them, is called *plate tectonics*.

Briefly stated, plate tectonic theory maintains that the Earth's outermost solid layer consists of huge plates that are in constant but slow motion, powered by energy sources deep within the Earth. Floating on a layer of plastic rock below, these rigid plates can both collide with other plates and split apart to form new plates. When crustal plates collide, one plate may be forced under the other in a process called *subduction*. In this case, part of the subducted plate can melt, creating pockets of magma that move upward to

the surface and create volcanic mountain chains and island arcs. Plates can also collide without subduction, forming mountain chains of rocks that are fractured, folded, and compressed into complex mountain structures. Where crustal plates split apart, creating rift valleys and ultimately ocean basins, lava moves upward to fill the gap. Thus, the Earth's surface arrangement of continents and oceans is constantly but slowly changing. Ocean basins expand with rifting and contract with subduction, while continents grow by collision and lose parts by splitting.

Because plate motions are powered by internal Earth forces, they are independent of surface conditions. So we find volcanoes erupting in the cold desert of Antarctica as well as near the equator in African savannas. An alpine mountain range has been pushed up in the cold subarctic zone of Alaska, where it runs east-west. Yet another range lies astride the equator in South America and runs north-south. Both ranges lie in belts of crustal collision, where many strong earthquakes occur.

Although internal tectonic processes operate independently, the processes that determine climate, vegetation, and soils are dependent on the major relief features and Earth materials provided by the tectonic setting. Thus, an understanding of plate tectonics is important to our understanding of the global patterns of the Earth's landscapes—including its climate, soils, vegetation, and, ultimately, human activity.

In this chapter we will survey the major geologic features of our planet, starting with the layered structure of its deep interior. We will then examine the crust and compare the crust of the continents with the crust of the ocean basins. Lastly, we will turn to plate tectonics and describe how plate movements have created broad regions of igneous, sedimentary, and metamorphic rocks. The motions and histories of these vast rock plates, splitting and separating to form ocean basins, closing and colliding to form mountain ranges, can be taken as an overarching framework to organize a great body of geologic and geographic knowledge. That is why this revolutionary framework—plate tectonic theory—ranks with the theory of evolution as one of the great milestones in scientific study of the Earth.

THE STRUCTURE OF THE EARTH

What lies deep within the Earth? From studies of earthquake waves, reflected from deep Earth layers, scientists have discovered that our Earth is far from uniform from its outer crust to its center. Instead, it consists of a central core with several layers, or shells, surrounding it. The densest matter is at the center, and each layer above it is increasingly less dense. This structure is inherited from the Earth's earliest history as it was formed by accretion from a mass of gas and dust orbiting the Sun. We will begin our examination of the Earth's inner structure at the center and then work outward.

The Earth's Interior

Figure 12.1 is a cutaway diagram of the Earth showing its interior. The Earth as a whole is an almost spherical body

---

The layers of the Earth's interior include the crust, mantle, liquid outer core, and solid inner core. Continental crust has both felsic and mafic rock zones, while oceanic crust has only mafic rock.

---

approximately 6400 km (about 4000 mi) in radius. The center is occupied by the **core,** which is about 3500 km (about 2200 mi) in radius. Because earthquake waves suddenly change behavior upon reaching the core, scientists have concluded that the outer core has the properties of a liquid. However, the innermost part of the core is in the solid state. Based on earthquake waves (and other kinds of data), it has long been inferred that the core consists mostly of iron, with some nickel. The core is very hot, but its temperature is not known very well. It is estimated to lie somewhere between 3000°C and 5000°C (about 5400°F to 9000°F).

Enclosing the metallic core is the **mantle,** a rock shell about 2900 km (about 1800 mi) thick. Earthquake waves indicate that mantle rock is composed of mafic minerals similar to olivine (a silicate of magnesium and iron) and may resemble the ultramafic igneous rock peridotite, which is found exposed here and there on the continental surface (see Figure 11.4 and Table 11.1). Temperatures in the mantle range from about 2800°C (about 5100°F) near the core to about 1800°C (about 3300°F) near the crust.

The outermost and thinnest of the Earth shells is the **crust,** a layer normally about 8 to 40 km (about 5 to 25 mi) thick (Figure 12.2). It is formed largely of igneous rock, but it also contains substantial proportions of metamorphic rock and a comparatively thin upper layer of sedimentary rock. The base of the crust is sharply defined where it contacts the mantle. This contact is detected by the way in which earth-

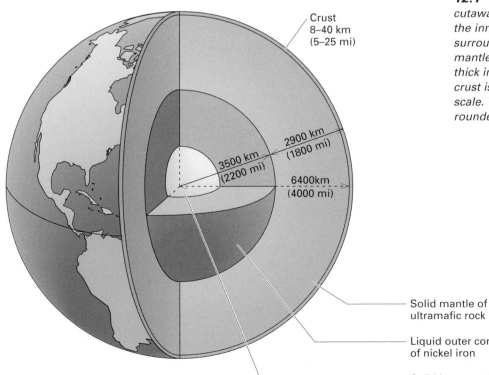

Crust
8–40 km
(5–25 mi)

3500 km
(2200 mi)

2900 km
(1800 mi)

6400km
(4000 mi)

Solid mantle of
ultramafic rock

Liquid outer core
of nickel iron

Solid inner core

12.1 The Earth's interior *This cutaway diagram of the Earth shows the inner core of iron, which is solid, surrounded by a liquid outer core. The mantle, which surrounds the core, is a thick inner layer of ultramafic rock. The crust is too thin to show to correct scale. Thicknesses of layers are rounded to the nearest 100 units.*

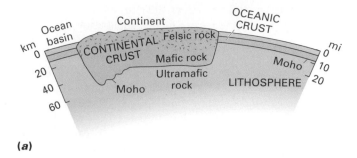

(a)

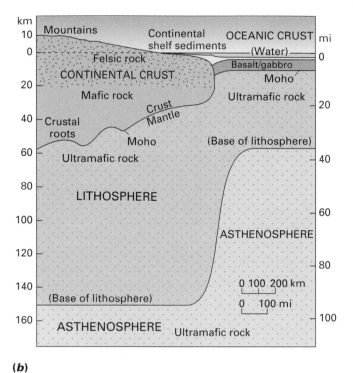

(b)

12.2   *Outer layers of the Earth* *(a) Idealized cross section of the Earth's crust and upper mantle. (b) Details of the crust and mantle at the edge of a continent, including the types of rocks found there. Also shown are the lithosphere and asthenosphere. (Copyright © A. N. Strahler.)*

has a chemical composition similar to that of granite, it is commonly described as being *granitic rock.* Much of the granitic rock is metamorphic rock. There is no sharply defined separation between the felsic and mafic zones.

While continental crust typically has two layers of different composition, **oceanic crust** has only one. It consists almost entirely of mafic rocks with the composition of basalt and gabbro. Basalt, as lava, forms an upper zone, whereas gabbro, an intrusive rock of the same composition, lies beneath the basalt.

Another key distinction between continental and oceanic crust is that the crust is much thicker beneath the continents than beneath the ocean floors (Figure 12.2). While 35 km (22 mi) is a good average figure for crustal thickness beneath the continents, 7 km (4 mi) is a typical figure for thickness of the basalt and gabbro crust beneath the deep ocean floors. Later in this chapter we will relate this difference in thickness to the processes that form the two types of crust.

The Lithosphere and Asthenosphere

Geologists use the term **lithosphere** to mean an outer Earth zone, or shell, of rigid, brittle rock. The lithosphere includes not only the crust, but also the cooler, upper part of the mantle that is composed of brittle rock. The lithosphere ranges in thickness from 60 to 150 km (40 to 95 mi). It is thickest under the continents and thinnest under the ocean basins.

Some tens of kilometers deep in the Earth, the brittle condition of the lithospheric rock gives way gradually to a plastic, or "soft," layer named the **asthenosphere** (Figure 12.2). (This word is derived from the Greek root *asthenes,* meaning "weak.") However, at still greater depth in the mantle, the strength of the rock material again increases. Thus, the asthenosphere is a soft layer sandwiched between the "hard" lithosphere above and a "strong" mantle rock layer below. In terms of states of matter, the asthenosphere is not a liquid, even though its temperature reaches 1400°C (about 2600°F).

The lithosphere resting atop the asthenosphere can be thought of as a hard, brittle shell resting on a soft, plastic underlayer. Because the asthenosphere is soft and plastic, the rigid lithosphere can easily move over it. The lithospheric shell consists of large pieces called **lithospheric plates.** A single plate can be as large as a continent and can move independently of the plates that surround it. Like great slabs of floating ice on the polar sea, lithospheric plates can separate from one another at one location, while elsewhere they may collide in crushing impacts that raise great ridges. Along these collision ridges, one plate can be found diving down beneath the edge of its neighbor. These varied sorts of plate movements will be described shortly.

quake waves abruptly change velocity at that level. The boundary surface between crust and mantle is called the *Moho,* a simplification of the name of the scientist, Andrija Mohorovicic, who discovered it in 1909.

The continental crust is quite different from the crust beneath the oceans. From studies of earthquake waves, geologists have concluded that the **continental crust** consists of two continuous zones—a lower, continuous rock zone of mafic composition, which is more dense, and an upper, continuous zone of felsic rock, which is less dense (Figure 12.2). Because the felsic portion

The lithosphere is the solid, brittle outermost layer of the Earth. It includes the crust and the cooler, brittle upper part of the mantle. The asthenosphere, which lies below the lithosphere, is plastic.

THE GEOLOGIC TIME SCALE

To place the great movements of lithospheric plates in their correct positions in historical sequence, we will need to refer to some major units in the scale of geologic time. Table 12.1 lists the major geologic time divisions. All time older than 570 million years (m.y.) before the present is *Precambrian time*. Three *eras* of time follow: *Paleozoic, Mesozoic,* and *Cenozoic*. These eras saw the evolution of life-forms in the oceans and on the lands. The geologic eras are subdivided into *periods*. Their names, ages, and durations are also given in Table 12.1.

The Cenozoic Era is particularly important in terms of the continental surfaces because nearly all landscape features seen today have been produced in the 65 million years since that era began. The Cenozoic Era is comparatively short in duration, scarcely more than the average duration of a single period in older

> The geologic time scale includes the Paleozoic, Mesozoic, and Cenozoic Eras. The Cenozoic Era is most recent, and nearly all the landscape features visible today have been formed within that era.

eras. It is subdivided directly into seven lesser time units called *epochs*. (Note that the terms *Tertiary Period* and *Quaternary Period* are sometimes applied to the Cenozoic Epochs Paleocene through Pliocene, and Pleistocene, respectively.) Details of the Pleistocene and Holocene epochs are given in Chapter 19.

Geologic time is often difficult to comprehend on a human scale. If we think of the history of the Earth since its formation as spanning a single 24-hour day, we can place the age of each geologic time division on a 24-hour clock time scale. As shown in Table 12.1, Precambrian time would end at about 23:42. Thus, only during the last 18 minutes of this day would life proliferate on the surface of the Earth. The human genus itself would arise at about 4 seconds before midnight and the last 5000 years of human civilization would occupy about 9 milliseconds—truly a fleeting moment in our planet's vast history.

Table 12.1 | **Geologic Time Scale**

Era	Period	Epoch	Duration (millions of years)	Age (millions of years)	24-hour clock time	Orogenies	Evolution of Life-Forms
Cenozoic		Holocene	(10,000 yr)				
		Pleistocene	2	2	23:59:56		Human genus
		Pliocene	3	5	23:59:51		
		Miocene	19	24	23:59:15		Hominoids
		Oligocene	13	37	23:58:51		Whales
		Eocene	21	58	23:58:12		Bats
		Paleocene	8	66	23:57:57	Cordilleran	Mammals
Mesozoic	Cretaceous		78	144	23:55:32		Flowering plants
	Jurassic		64	208	23:53:34	Allegheny, or Hercynian	Dinosaurs (extinct)
	Triassic		37	245	23:52:25		Turtles
Paleozoic	Permian		41	286	23:51:09		Frogs
	Carboniferous		74	360	23:48:51		Conifers; higher fishes
	Devonian		48	408	23:47:22	Caledonian	Vascular plants; primitive fishes
	Silurian		30	438	23:46:26		
	Ordovician		67	505	23:44:22		
	Cambrian		65	570	23:42:21		Invertebrates

Precambrian Time (Extends to oldest known rocks, about 4 billion years)
Age of Earth as a planet: 4.6 to 4.7 billion years.
Age of universe: 17 to 18 billion years.

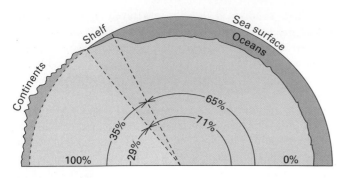

12.3 *Continent and ocean areas compared* *Actual global percentages of land and ocean areas compared with percentages if sea level were to drop 180 m (about 600 ft), exposing the continental shelves.*

MAJOR RELIEF FEATURES OF THE EARTH'S SURFACE

Before we begin our discussion of plate tectonics, it is important to examine the major relief features of the Earth—its continents and ocean basins—since they are produced by plate tectonic processes. Detailed global maps show that about 29 percent of the Earth's surface is land and 71 percent oceans (Figure 12.3). If the seas were to drain away, however, we would see that broad sloping areas lie close to the continental shores. These continental shelves are covered by shallow water, less than 150 m (500 ft) deep. From these relatively shallow continental shelves, the ocean floor drops rapidly to depths of thousands of meters. In other words, the ocean basins seem to be more than "brim full" of water—the oceans have spread over the margins of ground that would otherwise be assigned to the continents. If the ocean level were to drop by 150 m (about 500 ft), the shelves would be exposed, adding about 6 percent to the area of the continents. The surface area of continents would then be increased to 35 percent, and the ocean basin area decreased to 65 percent. These revised figures represent the true relative proportions of continents and oceans.

Figure 12.4 is a map showing some of the major relief features of continents and oceans, including mountain arcs, island arcs, ocean trenches, and the midoceanic ridge. We will refer to this map as we discuss the relief features of continents and oceans in turn.

Relief Features of the Continents

Broadly viewed, the continents consist of two basic subdivisions: active belts of mountain-making and inactive regions of old, stable rock. The mountain ranges in the active belts grow through one of two very different geologic processes. First is *volcanism,* the formation of massive accumulations of volcanic rock by extrusion of magma. Many lofty moun-

12.4 *Tectonic features of the world* *Principal mountain arcs, island arcs, and trenches of the world and the midoceanic ridge. (Midoceanic ridge map copyright © A. N. Strahler.)*

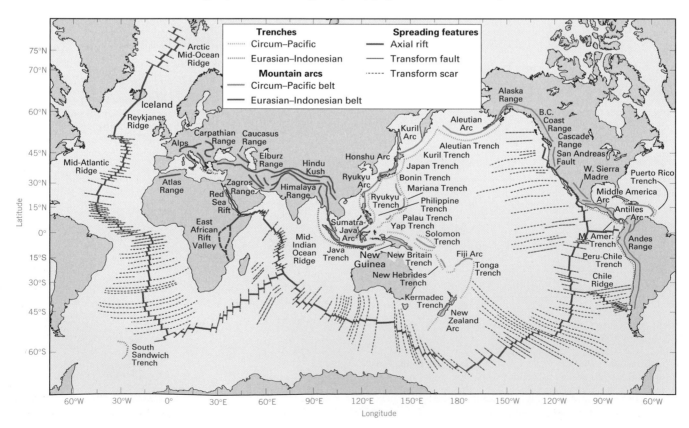

tain ranges consist of chains of volcanoes built of extrusive igneous rocks.

The second mountain-building process is *tectonic activity,* the breaking and bending of the Earth's crust under internal Earth forces. This tectonic activity usually occurs when great lithospheric plates come together in titanic collisions. (We will return to this topic later in this chapter.) Crustal masses that are raised by tectonic activity form mountains and plateaus. In some instances, both volcanism and tectonic activity have combined to produce a mountain range. Tectonic activity can also lower crustal masses to form depressions that may be occupied by ocean embayments or inland seas. Landforms produced by volcanic and tectonic activity are the subject of Chapter 13.

ALPINE CHAINS Active mountain-making belts are narrow zones that are usually found along the margins of lithospheric plates. These belts are sometimes referred to as *alpine chains* because they are characterized by high, rugged mountains, such as the Alps of Central Europe. These mountain belts were formed in the Cenozoic Era by volcanism or tectonic activity or a combination of both. Alpine mountain-building continues even today in many places.

The alpine chains are characterized by broadly curved lines on the world map (Figure 12.4). Each curved section of an alpine chain is referred to as a **mountain arc.** The arcs are linked in sequence to form two principal mountain belts. One is the *circum-Pacific belt* (shown in green), which rings the Pacific Ocean Basin. In North and South America, this belt is largely on the continents and includes the Andes and Cordilleran Ranges. In the western part of the Pacific Basin, the mountain arcs lie well offshore from the continents and take the form of **island arcs.** Partly submerged, they join the Aleutians, Kurils, Japan, the Philippines, and other smaller islands. These island arcs are the result of volcanic activity. Between the larger islands, the arcs are represented by volcanoes rising above the sea as small, isolated islands.

The second chain of major mountain arcs forms the *Eurasian-Indonesian belt,* shown in blue in Figure 12.4. It starts in the west at the Atlas Mountains of North Africa and continues through the European Alps and the ranges of the Near East and Iran to join the Himalayas. The belt then continues through Southeast Asia into Indonesia, where it abruptly meets the circum-Pacific belt. Later, we will return to these active belts of mountain-making and explain them in terms of subduction of lithospheric plates.

The two basic subdivisions of continental masses are active belts of mountain-making and inactive regions of old, stable rock. Mountains are built by volcanism and tectonic activity.

Alpine chains include mountain arcs and island arcs. They occur in two prominent belts—the circum-Pacific belt and the Eurasian-Indonesian belt.

Inactive continental regions of stable rocks include continental shields and ancient mountain roots. Continental shields are low-lying areas of old igneous and metamorphic rock and may be exposed or covered by sediments.

Mountain roots mark ancient collisions of lithospheric plates. They are now eroded into regions of low highlands and ridges.

CONTINENTAL SHIELDS Belts of recent and active mountain-making account for only a small portion of the continental crust. The remainder consists of comparatively inactive regions of much older rock. Within these stable regions we can recognize two types of crustal structure—continental shields and mountain roots. **Continental shields** are low-lying continental surfaces beneath which lie igneous and metamorphic rocks in a complex arrangement. Figure 12.5 is a generalized map showing the shield areas of the continents. Two classes of shields are shown: exposed shields and covered shields.

Exposed shields include very old rocks, mostly from Precambrian time, and have had a very complex geologic history. An example of an exposed shield is the Canadian Shield of North America. Exposed shields are also extensive in Scandinavia, South America, Africa, Asia, peninsular India, and Australia. The exposed shields are largely regions of low hills and low plateaus, although there are some exceptions where large crustal blocks have been recently uplifted. Many thousands of meters of rock have been eroded from these shields throughout the past half-billion or more years.

Covered shields are areas of the continental shields that are covered by younger sedimentary layers, ranging in age from Paleozoic through Cenozoic eras. These strata accumulated at times when the shields were inundated by shallow seas. Marine sediments were laid down on the ancient shield rocks in thicknesses ranging from hundreds to thousands of meters. These shield areas were then broadly arched upward to become land surfaces again. Erosion has since removed large sections of their sedimentary cover, but it still remains intact over vast areas. The covered shields are shown in Figure 12.5.

Some core areas of the shields are composed of rock as old as early Precambrian time, dating back to a time period called the Archean Eon, 2.5 to 3.5 billion years ago. On our map, these ancient areas are shown encircled by bold lines. The ancient cores are exposed in some areas but covered in others.

ANCIENT MOUNTAIN ROOTS Remains of older mountain belts lie within the shields in many places. These *mountain roots* are mostly formed of Paleozoic and early Mesozoic sedimentary rocks that have been intensely bent and folded, and in some locations changed into metamorphic rocks—slate, schist, and quartzite, for example. Thousands of meters of overlying rocks have been removed from these old tectonic belts, so that only the lowermost structures

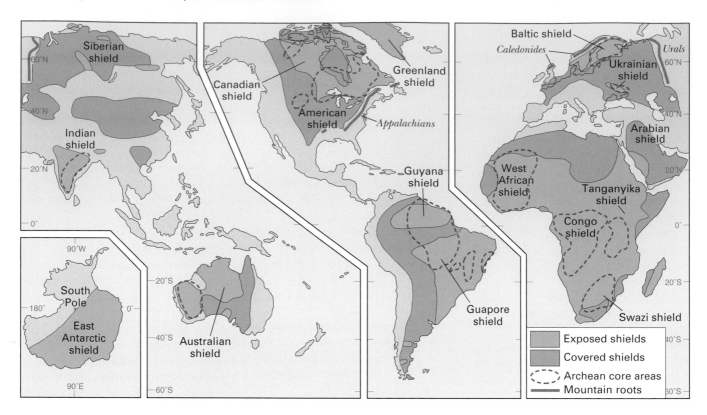

12.5 Continental shields *Generalized world map of continental shields, exposed and covered. Continental centers of early Precambrian age (Archean) lie with the areas encircled by a broken red line. Heavy brown lines show mountain roots of Caledonian and Hercynian (Appalachian) orogenies. (Based in part on data of R. E. Murphy, P. M. Hurley, and others. Copyright © A. N. Strahler.)*

remain. Roots appear as chains of long, narrow ridges, rarely rising over a thousand meters above sea level.

One important system of mountain roots was formed in the Paleozoic Era, during a great collision between two enormous lithospheric plates that took place about 400 million years ago. This collision created high alpine mountain chains that have since been worn down to belts of subdued mountains and hills. Today these roots, called Caledonides, form a highland belt across the northern British Isles and Scandinavia. They are also present in the Maritime Provinces of eastern Canada and in New England. A second, but younger, root system was formed during another great collision of plates near the close of the Paleozoic Era, about 250 million years ago. In North America, this highland system is represented by the Appalachian Mountains. The Caledonides and Appalachians are shown as mountain roots in Figure 12.5.

Relief Features of the Ocean Basins

The relief features of ocean basins are quite different from those of the continents. Crustal rock of the ocean floors consists almost entirely of basalt, which is covered over large areas by a comparatively thin accumulation of sediments. Age determinations of the basalt and its sediment cover show that the oceanic crust is quite young, geologically speaking. Much of the oceanic crust is less than 60 million years old, although some large areas have ages of

about 65 to 135 million years. When we consider that the great bulk of the continental crust is of Precambrian age—mostly over 1 billion years old—the young age of the oceanic crust is quite remarkable. However, we will soon see how plate tectonic theory explains this young age.

THE MIDOCEANIC RIDGE AND OCEAN BASIN FLOOR Figure 12.6 shows the important relief features of ocean basins. The ocean basins are characterized by a central ridge structure that divides the basin about in half. This *midoceanic ridge* consists of submarine hills that rise gradually to a rugged central zone. Precisely in the center of the ridge, at its highest point, is the *axial rift,* which is a narrow, trench-like feature. The location and form of this rift suggest that the crust is being pulled apart along the line of the rift.

The midoceanic ridge and its principal branches can be traced through the ocean basins for a total distance of about 60,000 km (about 37,000 mi). Figure 12.4 shows the extent of the ridge. Beginning in the Arctic Ocean, it then divides the Atlantic Ocean Basin from Iceland to the South Atlantic. Turning east, it enters the Indian Ocean, where one branch penetrates Africa. The other branch continues east between Australia and Antarctica, and then swings across the South Pacific. Nearing South America, it turns north and reaches North America at the head of the Gulf of California.

On either side of the midoceanic ridge are broad, deep plains that belong to the *ocean basin floor* (Figure 12.6). Their

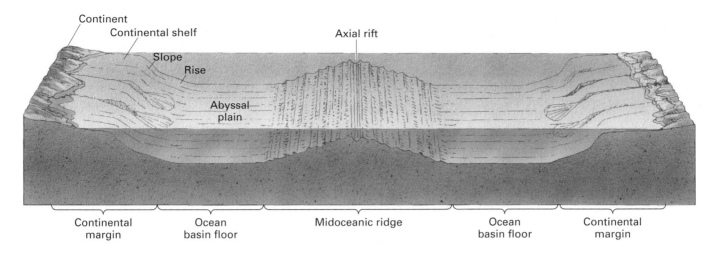

12.6 *Ocean basins* This schematic block diagram shows the main features of ocean basins. It applies particularly well to the North and South Atlantic oceans.

average depth below sea level is about 5000 m (about 16,000 ft). These large, flat expanses of ocean floor are called *abyssal plains.* They are extremely smooth because they have been built up of fine sediment that has settled slowly and evenly from ocean water above. Some abyssal regions include *abyssal hills,* small hills rising to heights from a few tens of meters to a few hundred meters above the ocean floor.

Many details of the ocean basins and their submarine landforms are shown in Figure 12.7. This image of the ocean floor was constructed from data of a U.S. Navy satellite that measured the surface height of the ocean very precisely using radar. Because small variations in gravity caused by undersea ridges and valleys produce corresponding small variations in the ocean height, it is possible to infer the undersea topography from ocean height measurement. For example, the mass of a submerged seamount may attract enough sea water to raise sea levels above it by 1 to 2 m (3 to 6 ft), depending on its bulk. Similarly, the ocean surface level drops over a deep ocean trench, where there is less mass to attract sea water. The right page of the figure shows the North Atlantic Basin. The prominent central feature is the Mid-Atlantic Ridge. The left page shows the deep trenches of the western Pacific that mark the positions of subduction arcs—features of plate motion that we will discuss shortly.

CONTINENTAL MARGINS The *continental margin,* shown on the left and right sides of Figure 12.6, is the narrow zone in which oceanic lithosphere is in contact with continental lithosphere (see Figure 12.2*b.*) As the continental margin is approached from deep ocean, the ocean floor begins to slope gradually upward, forming the *continental rise*

Relief features of ocean basins include a midoceanic ridge with a central axial rift where crust is being pulled apart. Abyssal plains, with some abyssal hills, stretch to continental margins.

Continental lithosphere contacts oceanic lithosphere at a continental margin. Passive continental margins accumulate thick deposits of continental sediments. Active continental margins have oceanic trenches where oceanic crust is sliding beneath continental crust.

(Figure 12.6). The floor then steepens greatly on the *continental slope.* At the top of this slope we arrive at the edge of the *continental shelf,* a gently sloping platform that is about 120 to 160 km (about 75 to 100 mi) wide along the eastern margin of North America. Water depth is about 150 m (about 500 ft) at the outer edge of the shelf. These three features—rise, slope, and shelf—form the continental margin.

Figure 12.6 illustrates a symmetrical ocean floor model—a midoceanic ridge with ocean basin floors on either side. This model nicely fits the North Atlantic and South Atlantic Ocean basins. It also applies rather well to the Indian Ocean and Arctic Ocean basins. The margins of these symmetrical basins are described as *passive continental margins* because they have not been subjected to strong tectonic and volcanic activity during the last 50 million years. This is because the continental and oceanic lithosphere that join at a passive continental margin are part of the same lithospheric plate and move together, away from the axial rift.

Many passive continental margins have accumulated great thicknesses of continental sediments. Near the continent, the strata of the shelf form a wedge-shaped deposit, thickening oceanward. A block diagram, Figure 12.8, shows details of this deposit. The river-borne sediments brought from the land are spread over the shallow seafloor by currents. Beneath the continental rise and its adjacent abyssal plain is another thick sediment deposit. It is formed from deep-sea sediments carried down the continental slope by swift muddy currents. The weight of these accumulated sediments causes them to sink, depressing the oceanic crust at its margin with the continental crust.

Deltas built by rivers contribute a great deal of the shelf sediment. Tongue-like turbid currents thickened

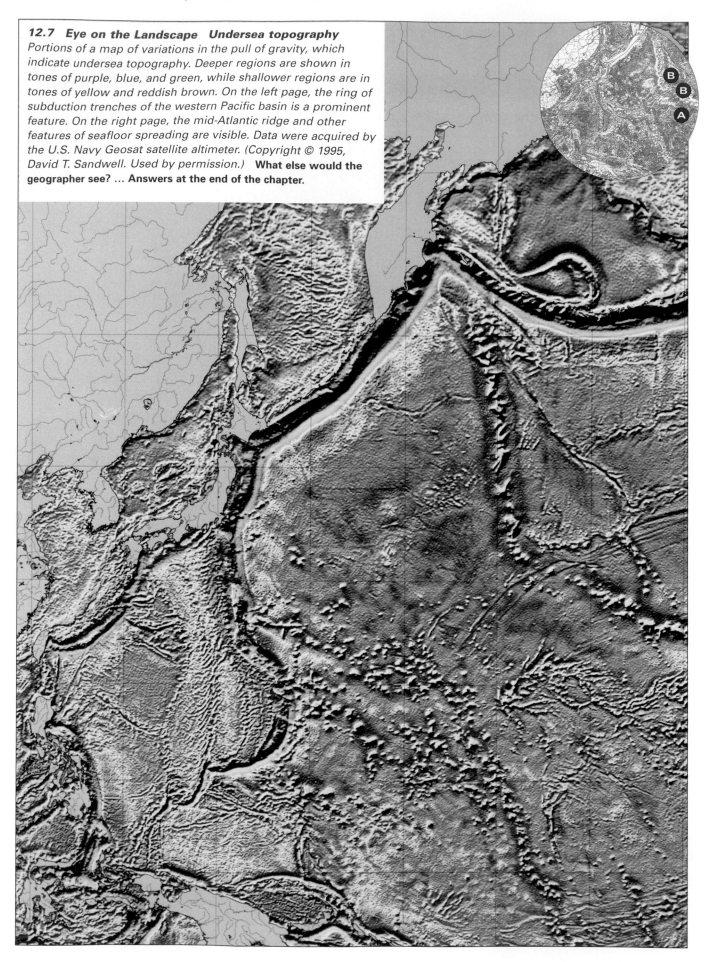

12.7 Eye on the Landscape Undersea topography
Portions of a map of variations in the pull of gravity, which indicate undersea topography. Deeper regions are shown in tones of purple, blue, and green, while shallower regions are in tones of yellow and reddish brown. On the left page, the ring of subduction trenches of the western Pacific basin is a prominent feature. On the right page, the mid-Atlantic ridge and other features of seafloor spreading are visible. Data were acquired by the U.S. Navy Geosat satellite altimeter. (Copyright © 1995, David T. Sandwell. Used by permission.) **What else would the geographer see? ... Answers at the end of the chapter.**

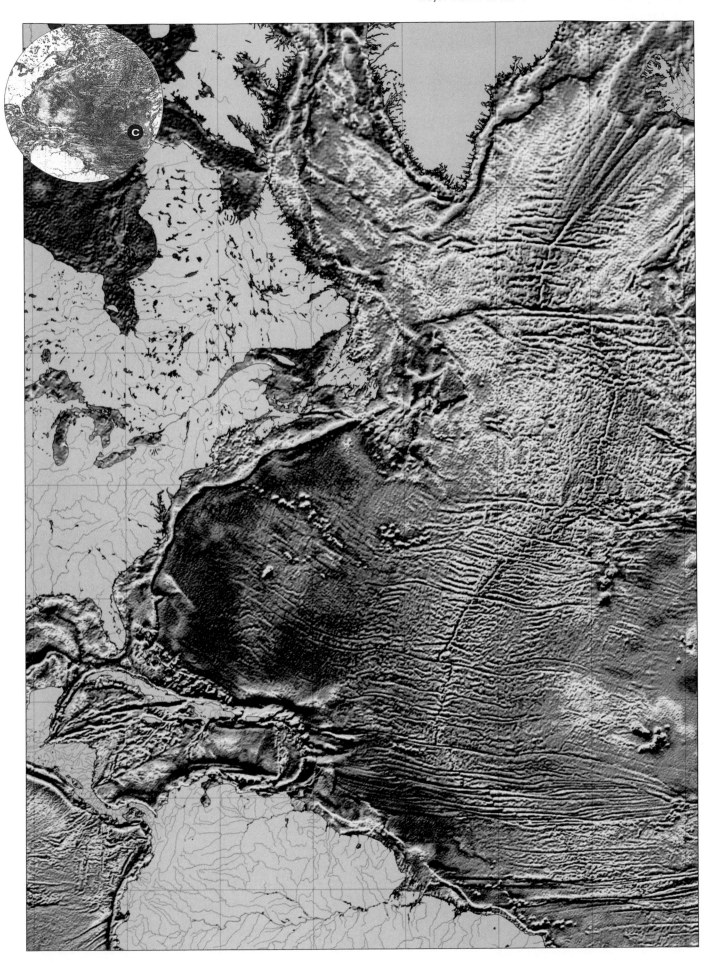

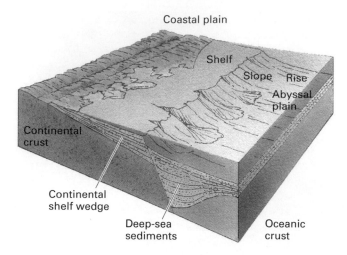

12.8 Structure of the continental shelf *This block diagram shows an inner wedge of sediments beneath the continental shelf and an outer wedge of deep-sea sediments beneath the continental rise and abyssal plain.*

with fine silt and clay from these deltas carve submarine canyons into the continental shelf. Where these currents emerge from the canyons, they deposit their sediment and build *deep-sea cones* (Figure 12.9).

The margins of the Pacific Ocean Basin are very different from those of the Atlantic. Although the Pacific has a midoceanic ridge with ocean basin floors on either side, its margins are characterized by mountain arcs or island arcs with deep offshore *oceanic trenches* (see Figure 12.7). Geologists refer to these trenched ocean-basin edges as *active continental margins*. As we will describe in more detail in the next section, oceanic crust is here being bent downward and forced under continental crust, creating trenches and inducing volcanic activity. The locations of the major trenches are shown in Figure 12.4. Trench floors can reach depths of nearly 11,000 m (about 36,000 ft), although most range from 7000 to 10,000 m (about 23,000 to 33,000 ft).

12.9 Deep-sea cone *A deep-sea cone of sediment forms at the base of a submarine canyon cut into the continental shelf. (Copyright © A. N. Strahler.)*

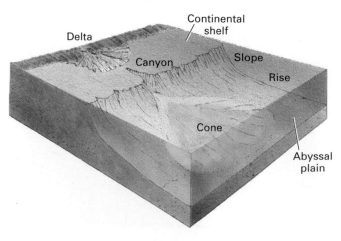

PLATE TECTONICS

With the structures and features of continents and ocean basins as a background, we can now turn to the motion of lithospheric plates and their interactions at boundaries—that is, to **plate tectonics. Tectonics** is a noun meaning "the study of tectonic activity." It refers here to all forms of breaking and bending of the entire lithosphere, including the crust. Breaking and bending occur on a very large scale when lithospheric plates collide. Sedimentary strata that lay flat and undisturbed for tens of millions of years on ocean floors and continental margins are crumpled and sheared into fragments by such collisions. The collision process itself may take millions of years to complete, but in the perspective of geologic time, it's only a brief episode.

Tectonic Processes

Generally speaking, prominent mountain masses and mountain chains (other than volcanic mountains) are elevated by one of two basic tectonic processes: *extension* and *compression* (Figure 12.10). Extensional tectonic activity—"pulling apart"—occurs where oceanic plates are separating or where a continental plate is undergoing breakup into fragments. As the crust thins, it is fractured and pushed upward, producing block mountains. We will return to a more detailed description of this process in a later section on continental rupture.

Compressional tectonic activity—"squeezing together" or "crushing"—acts at converging plate boundaries. The result is often an alpine mountain chain consisting of intensely deformed strata of marine origin. The strata are tightly compressed into wave-like structures called *folds*.

12.10 Two basic forms of tectonic activity *Flat-lying rock layers may be compressed to form folds or pulled apart to form faults by rifting.*

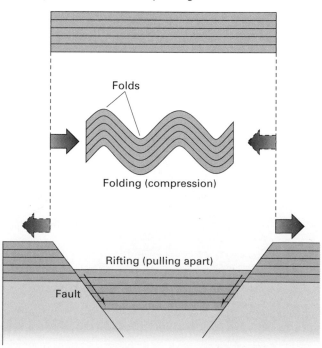

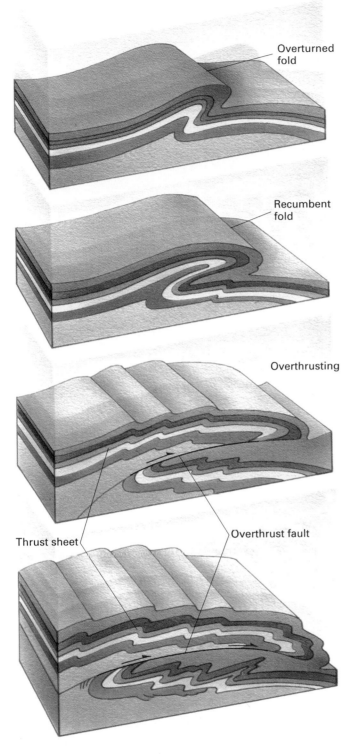

Overturned fold

Recumbent fold

Overthrusting

Thrust sheet

Overthrust fault

12.11 Folding in compressional tectonic activity
These schematic diagrams show the development of a recumbent fold, broken by a low-angle overthrust fault to produce a thrust sheet, or nappe, in alpine structure. (Based on diagrams by A. Heim, 1922, Geologie der Schweiz, vol. II-1, Tauschnitz, Leipzig.)

Typically, alpine folds can be traced through a history. First, they are overturned, and then they become *recumbent* as they are further overturned upon themselves (Figure 12.11). Accompanying the folding is a form of faulting in which slices of rock move over the underlying rock on fault surfaces with gentle inclination angles. These are called *overthrust faults.* The individual rock slices, called *thrust sheets,* are carried many tens of kilometers over the underlying rock. In the European Alps, thrust sheets of this kind were named *nappes* (from the French word meaning "cover sheet" or "tablecloth"). Nappes may be thrust one over the other to form a great pile. The entire deformed rock mass produced by such compressional mountain-making is called an *orogen,* and the event that produced it is an *orogeny.*

Plate Motions and Interactions

Figure 12.12 shows the major features of plate interactions. The vertical dimension of the block diagram (*a*) is greatly exaggerated, as are the landforms. A true-scale cross section (*b*) shows the correct relationships between crust and lithosphere, but surface relief features are too small to be shown. Diagram (*c*) is a sketch of plate motions on a spherical Earth.

Note that the figure shows two different kinds of lithospheric plates (see Figure 12.12*b*). Plates that lie beneath the ocean basins consist of *oceanic lithosphere.* This form of lithosphere is comparatively thin (about 50 km or 30 mi thick). The diagrams show two plates, X and Y, both made up of oceanic lithosphere. Plate Z bears continental crust and is made up of *continental lithosphere,* which is much thicker (about 150 km or 95 mi).

The lithosphere can be thought of as "floating" on the soft asthenosphere, but there is a difference in the relative surface heights of the two kinds of floating lithosphere. Consider two blocks of wood, one thicker than the other, floating in a pan of water. The surface of the thick block will ride higher above the water surface than that of the thin block. This principle explains why the continental surfaces rise high above the ocean floors.

As shown in Figure 12.12, plates X and Y are pulling apart along their common boundary, which lies along the axis of a midoceanic ridge. This pulling apart tends to create a gaping crack in the crust, but magma continually rises from the mantle beneath to fill it. The magma appears as basaltic lava in the floor of the rift and quickly congeals. At greater depth under the rift, magma solidifies into *gabbro,* an intrusive rock of the same

A simple experiment you can do will demonstrate how folding occurs in mountain-building. Take an ordinary towel of thick, limp cloth and lay it out on a smooth table top. Using both hands, palms down, bring the ends of the cloth slowly together. First, a simple up-fold will develop and grow, until it overturns to one side or the other. Then more folds will form, grow, and overturn, giving you a simple model of a new mountain range.

Tectonic processes include extension and compression. Extension causes fracturing and faulting of the crust, while compression produces folds and overthrust faults.

12.12 Schematic cross sections showing some of the important elements of plate tectonics Diagram (a) is greatly exaggerated in vertical scale, and emphasizes surface and crustal features. Only the uppermost 30 km (20 mi) is shown. Diagram (b) is drawn to true scale and shows conditions to a depth of 250 km (155 mi). Here the actual relationships between lithospheric plates can be examined, but surface features are too small to be shown. Diagram (c) is a pictorial rendition of plates on a spherical Earth and is not to scale. (Copyright © A. N. Strahler.)

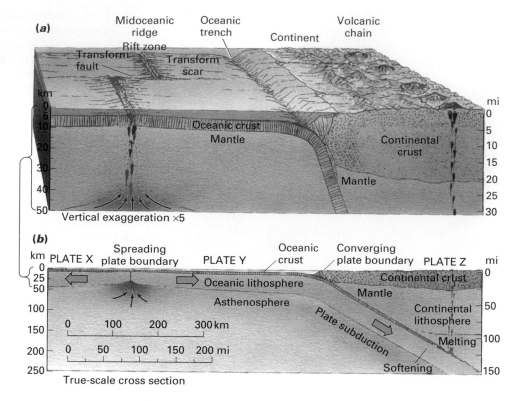

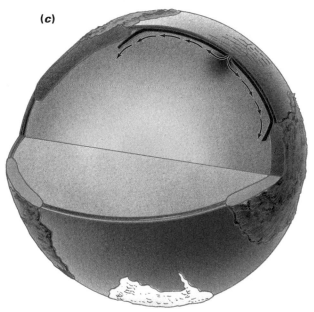

composition as basalt. Together, the basalt and gabbro continually form new oceanic crust. This type of boundary between plates is termed a *spreading boundary.*

At the right, the oceanic lithosphere of plate Y is moving toward the thick mass of continental lithosphere that comprises plate Z. Where these two plates collide, they form a *converging boundary.* Because the oceanic plate is comparatively thin and dense, in contrast to the thick, buoyant continental plate, the oceanic lithosphere bends down and plunges into the soft layer, or asthenosphere. The process in which one plate is carried beneath another is called **subduction.**

The leading edge of the descending plate is cooler and therefore denser than the surrounding hot, soft asthenos-

phere. As a result, the slab "sinks under its own weight," once subduction has begun. However, the slab is gradually heated by the surrounding hot rock and thus eventually softens. The underportion, which is mantle rock in composition, simply reverts to mantle rock as it softens.

The descending plate is covered by a thin upper layer of less dense mineral matter derived from oceanic and continental sediments. This material can melt and become magma. The magma tends to rise because it is less dense than the surrounding material. Figure 12.12b shows some magma pockets formed from the upper edge of the slab. They are pictured as rising like hot-air balloons through the overlying continental lithosphere. When they reach the

Earth's surface, they form a chain of volcanoes lying about parallel with the deep oceanic trench that marks the line of descent of the oceanic plate.

Viewing plate Y as a unit in Figure 12.12, we see that this single lithospheric plate is simultaneously undergoing both *accretion* (growth by addition) and *consumption* (loss by softening and melting in subduction zones). If rates of accretion and consumption are equal, the plate will maintain its overall size. If consumption is greater, the area of the plate will decrease. If accretion is greater, the area of the plate will expand.

We have yet to consider a third type of lithospheric plate boundary. Two lithospheric plates may be in contact along a common boundary on which one plate merely slides past the other with no motion that would cause the plates either to separate or to converge (Figure 12.13). This is a *transform boundary*. The plane along which motion occurs is a nearly vertical fracture extending down through the entire lithosphere, and it is called a *transform fault*. A *fault* is a rock plane along which there is motion of the rock mass on one side with respect to that on the other. (More about faults will appear in Chapter 13.) Transform boundaries are often associated with midoceanic ridges and are shown in Figures 12.7 and 12.12.

GEODISCOVERIES **Plate Tectonics.** See the structure of active and passive plate margins in this animation. Watch as sea floor spreads, forming oceanic crust that collides with a continent and is subducted.

PLATE BOUNDARIES SUMMARIZED In summary, there are three major kinds of active plate boundaries:

- *Spreading boundaries.* New lithosphere is being formed by accretion. Example: Seafloor spreading along the axial rift.

Boundaries between lithospheric plates may be of spreading, converging, or transform types. At a spreading boundary, crust is being pulled apart. At a converging boundary, plates are in collision and one plate may be subducted beneath another. At a transform boundary, two plates glide past each other.

- *Converging boundaries.* Subduction is in progress, and lithosphere is being consumed. Example: Active continental margin.
- *Transform boundaries.* Plates are gliding past one another on a transform fault. Example: Transform boundary associated with midoceanic ridge.

Let us put these three boundaries into a pattern to include an entire lithospheric plate (Figure 12.14). Visualize the sunroof of an automobile, in which a portion of the roof slides to open. Just as the sunroof can move by sliding past the fixed portion of the roof at its sides, so a lithospheric plate can move by sliding past other plates on transform faults. Where the sunroof opens, the situation is similar to a spreading boundary. Where the sunroof slides under the rear part of the roof, the situation is similar to a converging boundary. Boundaries of lithospheric plates can be curved as well as straight, and individual plates can pivot as they move. There are many geometric variations in the shapes and motions of individual plates.

GEODISCOVERIES **Tectonic Plate Boundary Relationships.** Play this movie to see the landscapes of spreading, converging, and transform boundaries between lithospheric plates. Iceland, the Cascades, Himalayas, Alps, and the San Andreas fault are featured.

The motions of lithospheric plates follow a time cycle in which a single supercontinent is split apart, then joined back together, and then split apart again. Named the Wilson Cycle, it is described in more detail in *Eye on the Environment 12.1 • The Wilson Cycle and Supercontinents.*

12.14 A simple lithospheric plate *A schematic diagram of a single rectangular lithospheric plate with two transform boundaries. (Copyright © A. N. Strahler.)*

12.13 Transform fault *A transform fault involves the horizontal motion of two adjacent lithospheric plates, one sliding past the other. (Copyright © A. N. Strahler.)*

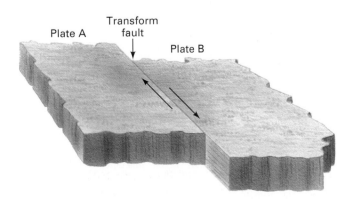

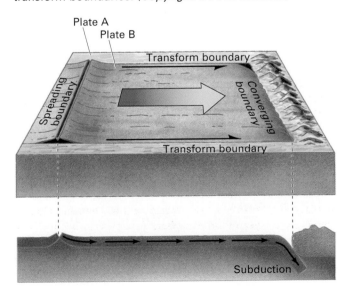

Eye on the Environment | 12.1

The Wilson Cycle and Supercontinents

As you have learned in this chapter, the geography of the Earth and its varied environments has been changing slowly but continuously for hundreds of millions of years. The driving force for that slow change is the motion of the Earth's lithospheric plates. While it seems remarkable that the continents are actually in constant motion, what is more remarkable is the strong evidence suggesting that all continents were once joined in a single land mass that subsequently broke apart. Not only that, but over the billions of years of the Earth's geologic history, the union of the continents and their breakup is actually a repeating process—the *Wilson cycle*—that has occurred half a dozen times or more.

The Wilson cycle bears the name of the distinguished Canadian geophysicist Professor J. Tuzo Wilson of the University of Toronto. He made important new discoveries and interpretations that helped lead to a full-blown theory of plate tectonics. By the time he formulated his theory, all of the parts were known—continental rupture to start the opening of a new ocean basin, plate subduction to generate island arcs, and collisions to weld continents together. Using all of these separate lithospheric activities, Wilson forged a logical time chain of plate tectonic events, and it quickly gained wide acceptance as the *Wilson cycle.*

The Wilson cycle can best be appreciated by use of a cartoon-like presentation of the essential elements of plate tectonics. In our illustration at left, these elements are shown arranged throughout six stages and are listed with references to our text diagrams and examples found on the planet today. This ideal cycle requires some 300 to 500 million years to complete.

The Wilson cycle *Schematic diagram depicting the six stages of the Wilson cycle. The diagrams are not to true scale. (From Plate Tectonics, copyright © 1998 by Arthur N. Strahler. Used by permission.)*

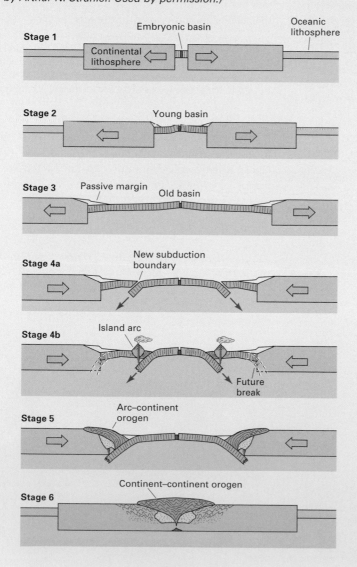

- *Stage 1.* Embryonic ocean basin. (See also Figure 12.19*b.*) The Red Sea separating the Arabian Peninsula from Africa is an active example.
- *Stage 2.* Young ocean basin. The Labrador Basin, a branch of the North Atlantic lying between Labrador and Greenland, is a fair example of this stage.
- *Stage 3.* Old ocean basin. (Figure 12.19*c.*) Includes all of the vast expanse of the North and South Atlantic oceans and the Antarctic Ocean. Passive margin sedimentary wedges have become wide and thick.
- *Stage 4a.* The ocean basin begins to close as continental plates collide with it. New subduction boundaries begin to form.
- *Stage 4b.* Island arcs have risen and grown into great volcanic island chains. (Figure 12.18*a.*) These are found surrounding the Pacific plate, with the Aleutian arc as a fine example.
- *Stage 5.* Closing continues. Formation of new subduction margins close to the continents is

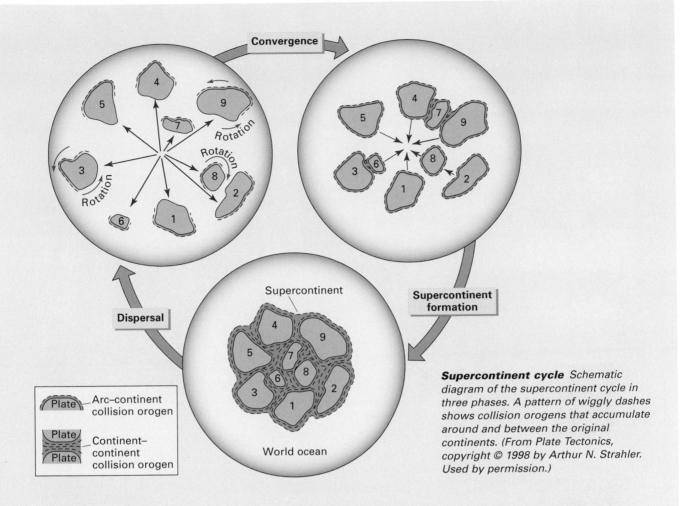

Plate — Arc–continent collision orogen

Plate / Plate — Continent–continent collision orogen

Supercontinent cycle *Schematic diagram of the supercontinent cycle in three phases. A pattern of wiggly dashes shows collision orogens that accumulate around and between the original continents. (From Plate Tectonics, copyright © 1998 by Arthur N. Strahler. Used by permission.)*

followed by arc-continent collisions. The Japanese Islands represent this stage.

- *Stage 6*. The ocean basin has finally closed with a collision orogen, forming a continental suture (Figure 12.18c). The Himalayan orogen is a fine recent example, with activity continuing today.

Note that the continent of the final stage is wider than the continent of the first stage because of the additional continental lithosphere formed during the intervening collisions. This is how continents can grow over geologic time.

Our stage diagrams show a single continent splitting into two continents, then rejoining to form one. Suppose that over the entire globe several continents are splitting apart and reclosing at about the same time. Expanding on this idea, imagine that these fragments

become detached from a single world continent that can be called a *supercontinent*.

Several powerful lines of evidence show that a supercontinent actually came into existence, starting about 200 million years ago. Called *Pangea,* it is described in our chapter text. Good evidence has now been found that an earlier supercontinent, dubbed *Rodinia,* was fully formed about 700 million years ago. It consisted of early representatives of the same continents that later made up Pangea. Rodinia broke apart, and its fragments were carried away in different directions. Then they reversed their motions and headed back toward a common center, where many continent–continent collisions bonded them together by sutures to comprise Pangea. Some interesting evidence has also pointed to the former existence of a supercontinent even older than Rodinia.

The illustration above presents the supercontinent cycle as a loop with three stages. Analogous to Stages 1–3 of the Wilson cycle is the dispersal phase, followed by a convergence phase that corresponds to Wilson stages 4 through 6. The cycle ends in a complete new supercontinent. Many new collision orogens are formed between the original continental fragments. Given, say, 3000 million years ago (Middle Archean time) as the first occurrence of a full-blown supercontinent cycle, there could have been some 6 to 10 such cycles. The hypothesis of a time cycle of supercontinents, repeating the Wilson cycle over and over again, now holds its place as the basic theme of the geologic evolution of our planet.

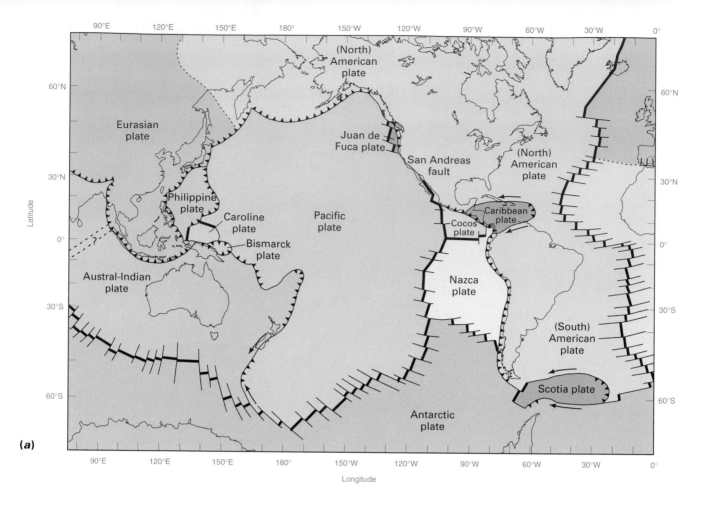

(a)

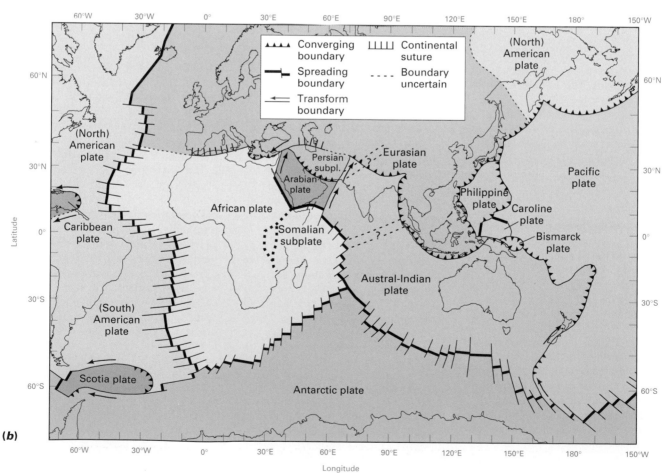

(b)

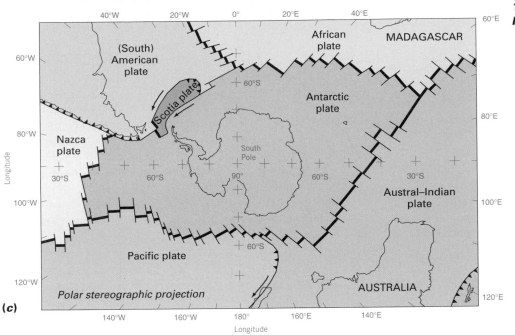

(c)

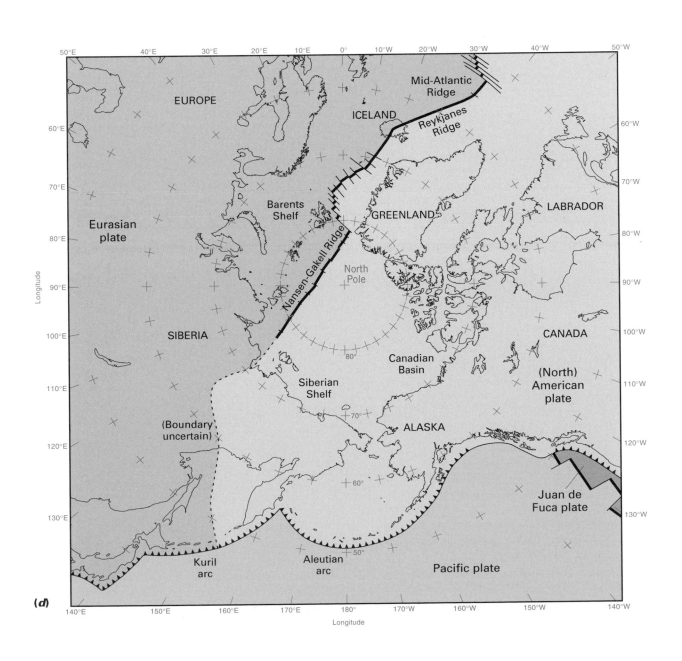

(d)

Table 12.2 | The Lithospheric Plates

Great plates	Lesser plates
Pacific	Nazca
American (North, South)	Cocos
Eurasian	Philippine
Persian subplate	Caribbean
African	Arabian
Somalian subplate	Juan de Fuca
Austal-Indian	Caroline
Antarctic	Bismark
	Scotia

The Global System of Lithospheric Plates

The global system of lithospheric plates consists of six great plates. These are listed in Table 12.2 and are shown on a world map in Figure 12.15. Several lesser plates and subplates are also recognized. They range in size from intermediate to comparatively small. Plate boundaries are shown by symbols, explained in the key accompanying the map.

The Earth's lithospheric shell is divided into six great lithospheric plates and at least nine lesser plates.

The great Pacific plate (Figure 12.15*a*) occupies much of the Pacific Ocean Basin and consists almost entirely of oceanic lithosphere. Its relative motion is northwesterly, so that it has a subduction boundary along most of the western and northern edge. The eastern and southern edge is mostly a spreading boundary. A sliver of continental lithosphere is included and makes up the coastal portion of California and all of Baja California. The California portion is bounded by an active transform fault (the San Andreas fault).

The American plate (Figure 12.15*a*) includes most of the continental lithosphere of North and South America as well as the entire oceanic lithosphere lying west of the midoceanic ridge that divides the Atlantic Ocean Basin down the middle. For the most part, the western edge of the American plate is a subduction boundary, with oceanic lithosphere diving beneath the continental lithosphere. The eastern edge is a spreading boundary. (Some classifications recognize separate North American and South American plates.)

The Eurasian plate (Figure 12.15*b*) is mostly continental lithosphere, but it is fringed on the west and north by a belt of oceanic lithosphere. The African plate has a central core of continental lithosphere nearly surrounded by oceanic lithosphere.

The Austral-Indian plate takes the form of a long rectangle. It is mostly oceanic lithosphere but contains two cores of continental lithosphere—Australia and peninsular India. Recent evidence shows that these two continental masses are moving independently and may actually be considered to be parts of separate plates. The Antarctic plate (Figure 12.15*c*) has an elliptical shape and is almost completely enclosed by a spreading plate boundary. This means that the other plates are moving away from the pole. The continent of Antarctica forms a central core of continental lithosphere completely surrounded by oceanic lithosphere.

Of the nine lesser plates, the Nazca and Cocos plates of the eastern Pacific are rather simple fragments of oceanic lithosphere bounded by the Pacific midoceanic spreading boundary on the west and by a subduction boundary on the east. The Philippine plate is noteworthy as having subduction boundaries on both east and west edges. Two small but distinct lesser plates—Caroline and Bismark—lie to the southeast of the Philippine plate. The Arabian plate has two transform fault boundaries, and its relative motion is northeasterly. The Caribbean plate also has important transform fault boundaries. The tiny Juan de Fuca plate is steadily diminishing in size and will eventually disappear by subduction beneath the American plate. Similarly, the Scotia plate is being consumed by the American and Antarctic plates.

Figure 12.16 is a schematic circular cross section of the lithosphere along a great circle in low latitudes. It shows several of the great plates and their boundaries. The great circle is tilted by about 30° with respect to the equator. The section crosses the African plate, heads northeast across the Eurasian plate through the Himalayas to Japan and Korea, then dips southeast across the Pacific plate, cutting across the South American plate, and finally returns to Africa. Three spreading boundaries at midoceanic ridges are encountered, with two subduction zones (the Japan and Peru trenches) and a continent-to-continent collision where the Austral-Indian plate dives under the Eurasian plate.

GEODISCOVERIES **Remote Sensing and Tectonic Landforms Interactivity.** Select "tectonics" to review the names and locations of tectonic plates as well as examine a famous transform fault—the San Andreas.

12.16 Arrangement of lithospheric plates *Schematic circular cross section of the major plates on a great circle tilted about 30 degrees with respect to the equator. (A. N. Strahler.)*

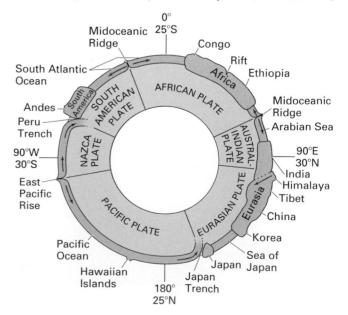

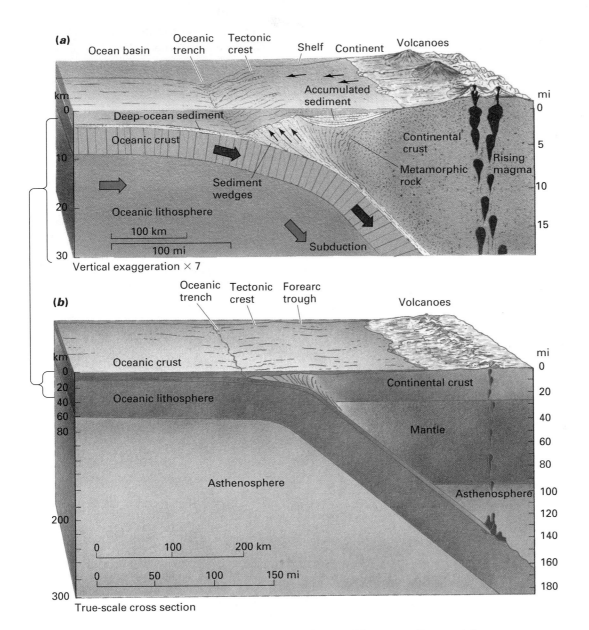

(a) Ocean basin · Oceanic trench · Tectonic crest · Shelf · Continent · Volcanoes

Ocean basin
Oceanic trench
Tectonic crest
Shelf
Continent
Volcanoes

km
Accumulated sediment
mi
0
Deep-ocean sediment
0
Oceanic crust
Continental crust
5
10
Metamorphic rock
Rising magma
Sediment wedges
10
20
15
Oceanic lithosphere
100 km
100 mi
30
Subduction
Vertical exaggeration × 7

(b)
Oceanic trench · Tectonic crest · Forearc trough · Volcanoes

km
mi
0
Oceanic crust
0
20
Continental crust
40
Oceanic lithosphere
20
60
80
40
Mantle
60
80
Asthenosphere
100
Asthenosphere
200
120
140
100
200 km
160
0
50
100
150 mi
180
300
True-scale cross section

12.17   Typical features of an active subduction zone *The upper diagram (a) uses vertical exaggeration to show surface and crustal details. Sediments scraped off the moving plate form tilted wedges that accumulate in a rising tectonic mass. Near the mainland is a shallow trough in which sediment brought from the land accumulates. Metamorphic rock forms above the descending plate. Magma rising from the top of the descending plate reaches the surface to build a chain of volcanoes. Diagram (b) is a true-scale cross section showing the entire thickness of the lithospheric plates. (Copyright © A. N. Strahler.)*

Subduction Tectonics

Converging plate boundaries, with subduction in progress, are zones of intense tectonic and volcanic activity. The narrow zone of a continent that lies above a plate undergoing subduction is therefore an active continental margin. (See plates Y and Z in Figure 12.12.) Figure 12.17 shows some details of the geologic processes that are associated with plate subduction. Two diagrams are used. Part *a* is

When oceanic crust collides with continental crust, deep ocean sediment accumulates in an accretionary prism. Subducted oceanic crust melts and rises as andesite magma, creating a mountain arc.

exaggerated to show crustal and surface details, and part *b* is drawn to true scale to show the lithospheric plates.

The oceanic trench receives sediment coming from two sources. Carried along on the moving oceanic plate is deep-ocean sediment—fine clay and ooze—that has settled to the ocean floor. From the continent comes terrestrial sediment in the form of sand and mud brought by streams to the shore and then swept into deep water by currents. In the bottom of the trench, both types of sediment are intensely deformed and are dragged down with the moving plate. The deformed sediment is then scraped off the plate and shaped into wedges that ride up, one over the other, on steep fault planes. The wedges accumulate at the plate boundary, forming an *accretionary prism* in which metamorphism takes place. In this way, new continental crust of metamorphic rock is formed, and the continental plate is built outward.

The accretionary prism is of relatively low density and tends to rise, forming a *tectonic crest.* The tectonic crest is shown to be submerged in the figure, but in some cases it forms an island chain paralleling the coast—that is, a *tectonic arc.* Between the tectonic crest and the mainland is a shallow trough, the *forearc trough* (Figure 12.17b). This trough traps a great deal of terrestrial sediment, which accumulates in a basin-like structure. The bottom of the forearc trough continually subsides under the load of the added sediment. In some cases, the seafloor of the trough is flat and shallow, forming a type of continental shelf. Sediment carried across the shelf moves down the steep outer slope of the accretionary prism in tongue-like flows of turbidity currents.

The lower diagram of Figure 12.17 shows the descending lithospheric plate entering the asthenosphere. Intense heating of the upper surface of the plate melts the oceanic crust, forming basaltic magma. As this magma rises, it is changed in chemical composition at the base of the crust and becomes andesite magma. The rising andesite magma reaches the surface to form volcanoes of andesite lava, such as those we see in the Andes of South America.

Orogens and Collisions

Visualize, now, a situation in which two continental lithospheric plates converge along a subduction boundary. Ultimately, the two masses must collide because the impacting masses are too thick and too buoyant to allow either plate to slip under the other. The result is an orogeny in which various kinds of crustal rocks are crumpled into folds and sliced into nappes. This process has been called "telescoping" after the behavior of a folding telescope that collapses from a long tube into a short cylinder. Collision permanently unites the two plates, terminating further tectonic activity along that collision zone. Appropriately, the collision zone is named a **continental suture.** Our world map of plates, Figure 12.15, uses a special symbol for these sutures, shown in northern Africa and near the Aral Sea.

Continent–continent collisions occurred in the Cenozoic Era along a great tectonic line that marks the southern boundary of the Eurasian plate. (See Figure 12.15, map *b.*) The line begins with the Atlas Mountains of North Africa, and it runs across the Aegean Sea region into western Turkey. Beyond a major gap in Turkey, the line takes up again in the Zagros Mountains of Iran. Jumping another gap

When two continental lithospheric plates collide in an orogeny, continental rocks are crumpled and overthrust. The plates eventually become joined in a continental suture.

in southeastern Iran and Pakistan, the collision line sets in again in the great Himalayan Range, where it is still active.

Each segment of this collision zone represents the collision of a different north-moving plate against the single and relatively immobile Eurasian plate. A European segment containing the Alps was formed when the African plate collided with the Eurasian plate in the Mediterranean region. A Persian segment resulted from the collision of the Arabian plate with the Eurasian plate. A Himalayan segment represents the collision of the Indian continental portion of the Austral-Indian plate with the Eurasian plate.

Figure 12.18 is a series of cross sections in which the tectonic events of a typical continent–continent collision are reconstructed. Diagram *a* shows a passive margin at the left and an active subduction margin at the right. As the ocean between the converging continents is eliminated, a succession of overlapping thrust faults cuts through the oceanic crust in diagram *b.* The thrust slices ride up, one over the other, telescoping the oceanic crust and the sediments above it. As the slices become more and more tightly squeezed, they are forced upward. The upper part of each thrust sheet assumes a horizontal attitude to form a nappe in diagram *c,* which then glides forward under gravity on a low downgrade. A mass of metamorphic rock is formed between the joined continental plates, welding them together. This new rock mass is the continental suture. It is a distinctive type of orogen.

Continent–continent collisions have occurred many times since the late Precambrian time. Several ancient sutures have been identified in the continental shields. The Ural Mountains, which divide Europe from Asia, are one such suture, formed near the end of the Paleozoic Era.

Another type of collision is the arc–continent collision. Recall that island arcs often form in subduction zones as sediments of lesser density are carried into the mantle, then melt and rise as magma. In some situations, an ancient island arc can be carried toward a continent and collide with a passive continental margin. This creates a complex orogen that includes folded, faulted, and metamorphosed rocks derived from both the island arc and the sediments of the forearc trough (Figure 12.17b). Examples of orogens resulting from arc–continent collisions can be found on both eastern and western sides of North America. They include the ancient Appalachian and Ouachita Mountain belts as well as the younger Cordilleran Ranges of western North America.

Continental Rupture and New Ocean Basins

We have already noted that the continental margins bordering the Atlantic Ocean Basin on both its eastern and western sides are very different from the active margin of a subduction zone. At present, the Atlantic margins have no important tectonic activity and are passive continental margins.

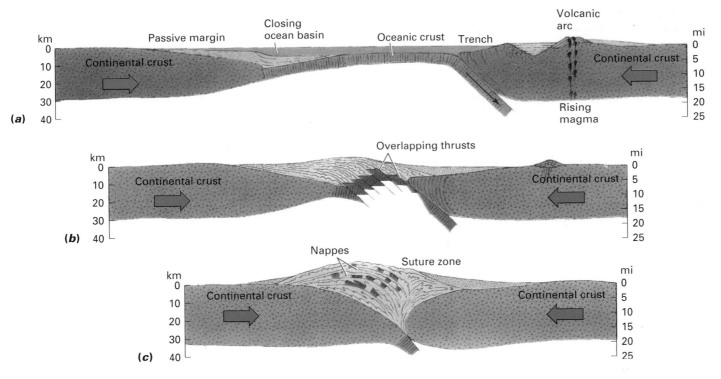

12.18   Continent–continent collision *Schematic cross sections showing continent–continent collision and the formation of a suture zone with nappes. (Copyright © A. N. Strahler.)*

Even so, they represent the contact between continental lithosphere and oceanic lithosphere, with continental crust meeting oceanic crust, as shown in Figure 12.8. The formation of passive margins begins when a single plate of continental lithosphere is rifted apart. This process is called *continental rupture.*

Figure 12.19 uses three schematic block diagrams to show how continental rupture takes place and leads to the development of passive continental margins. At first, the crust is both lifted and stretched apart as the lithospheric plate is arched upward. The crust fractures and moves along faults—upthrown blocks form mountains, while down-dropped blocks form basins.

Eventually a long narrow valley, called a *rift valley* appears (block *a*). The widening crack in its center is continually filled in with magma rising from the mantle below. The magma solidifies to form new crust in the floor of the

12.19   Continental rupture and spreading *Schematic block diagrams showing stages in continental rupture and the opening of a new ocean basin. The vertical scale is greatly exaggerated to emphasize surface features. (a) The crust is uplifted and stretched apart, causing it to break into blocks that become tilted on faults. (b) A narrow ocean is formed, floored by new oceanic crust. (c) The ocean basin widens, while the passive continental margins subside and receive sediments from the continents. (Copyright © A. N. Strahler.)*

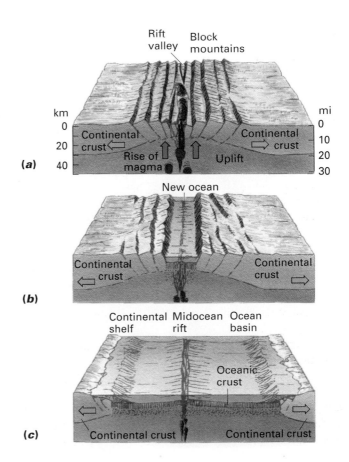

rift valley. Crustal blocks on either side slip down along a succession of steep faults, creating a mountainous landscape. The Rift Valley system of East Africa—described in more detail in Chapter 13—is a notable example of this stage of continental rupture. As separation continues, the rift valley widens and opens to the ocean. The ocean enters the narrow valley with a spreading plate boundary running down its center (block *b*). Rising magma in the central rift produces new oceanic crust and lithosphere.

The Red Sea is a narrow ocean formed by a continental rupture. Its straight coasts mark the edges of the rupture. The widening of such an ocean basin can continue until a large ocean has formed and the continents are widely separated (Figure 12.19, block *c*).

Figure 12.20 is an astronaut photo of the Red Sea where it joins the Gulf of Aden. As shown in the inset map, this is a triple junction of three spreading boundaries created by the motion of the Arabian plate pulling away from the African plate. It is easy to visualize how the two plates have split apart, allowing the ocean to enter.

Continental rupture begins with the formation of a rift valley and tilted block mountains. Ocean soon invades the rift. As the continental crust recedes, oceanic crust fills the gap.

During the process of opening of an ocean basin, the spreading boundary develops a series of offset breaks, one of which is shown in the upper left-hand part of diagram *a* of Figure 12.12. The offset ends of the axial rift are connected by an active transform fault. As spreading continues, the offsets slide past each other, and a scar-like feature is formed on the ocean floor as an extension of the transform fault. These *transform scars* take the form of narrow ridges or cliff-like features and may extend for hundreds of kilometers across the ocean floors. Before the true nature of these scars was understood, they were called "fracture zones." That name still persists and can be seen on maps of the ocean floor. The scars are not, for the most part, associated with active faults.

The Power Source for Plate Movements

The system of lithospheric plates in motion represents a huge flow system of dense mineral matter. Its operation requires enormous power. It is generally agreed that the source of this power lies in the heat released by radioactivity. You may recall

12.20   Eye on the Landscape   The Red Sea and Gulf of Aden from orbit *This spectacular photo, taken by astronauts on the Gemini XI mission, shows the southern end of the Red Sea and the southern tip of the Arabian Peninsula.* **What else would the geographer see?... Answers at the end of the chapter.**

from basic chemistry that some elements are found in forms that differ with respect to their atomic mass. These forms are known as *isotopes*. For example, the most common isotope of uranium (U) is uranium-238, a form with an atomic mass of 238. Another form is uranium-235, which has an atomic mass number of 235. Chemists distinguish these two forms by writing them as ^{238}U and ^{235}U.

A key to understanding radioactivity is that certain isotopes are unstable, meaning that the composition of the atomic nucleus of the isotope can experience an irreversible change. This change process is known as *radioactive decay.* When a nucleus decays, it emits matter and energy. The energy is absorbed by the surrounding matter and thus ultimately takes the form of sensible heat. The flow of heat from radioactive decay is termed *radiogenic heat.* Nearly all of this heat is generated by the decay of isotopes of uranium (^{238}U, ^{235}U), thorium (^{232}Th), and potassium (^{40}K). Most of the radiogenic heat is liberated in the rock beneath the continents, within the uppermost 100 km or so (about 60 mi). Radiogenic heat is sufficient to keep Earth layers below the crust close to the melting point and thus provides the power source for the formation of magma.

How does radiogenic heating produce plate motions? The answer is not completely known, but one theory is that plate motions are produced by *convection currents* in hot mantle rock. Recall that in the case of the atmosphere, upward motion of warmer, less dense air takes place by convection. It is thought that, in a somewhat similar type of convection, unequal heating produces streams of upwelling mantle rock that rise steadily beneath spreading plate boundaries. Geologists do not yet have a full understanding of how this rise of heated rock causes plates to move. One hypothesis states that, as the rising mantle lifts the lithospheric plate to a higher elevation, the lithospheric plate tends to move horizontally away from the spreading axis under the influence of gravity.

At the opposite edge of the plate, subduction occurs because the oceanic plate is colder and denser than the asthenosphere through which it is sinking. The motion of the oceanic plate exerts a drag on the underlying asthenosphere, setting in motion flow currents in the upper mantle. Thus, slow convection currents probably exist in the asthenosphere beneath the moving plates, but their pathways and depths of operation are not well understood.

CONTINENTS OF THE PAST

Although modern plate tectonic theory is only a few decades old, the concept of a breakup of an early supercontinent into fragments that drifted apart dates back into the nineteenth century and beyond. Almost as soon as good

> The motion of lithospheric plates is thought to result from convection currents of upwelling plastic mantle rock that lift the plates and cause them to split apart.

> A single great continent, Pangea, surrounded by a single great ocean, Panthalassa, broke apart over hundreds of millions of years to form the present-day pattern of continents, islands, and oceans.

navigational charts became available to show the continental outlines, geographers became intrigued with the close correspondence in outline between the eastern coast of South America and the western coastline of Africa. Credit for the first full-scale scientific hypothesis of the breakup of a single large continent belongs to Alfred Wegener, a German meteorologist and geophysicist, who offered geologic evidence as early as 1915 that the continents had once been united and had drifted apart (Figure 12.21). He reconstructed a supercontinent named *Pangea,* which existed intact as early as about 300 million years ago, in the Carboniferous Period.

A storm of controversy followed, and many American geologists denounced Wegener's "continental drift" hypothesis. However, he had some loyal supporters in Europe, South Africa, and Australia. Several lines of hard scientific evidence presented by Wegener strongly favored the former existence of Pangea. The prominent geographer and climatologist, Vladimir Köppen collab-

12.21 Wegener's Pangea *Alfred Wegener's 1915 map fits together the continents that today border the Atlantic Ocean basin. The sets of dashed lines show the fit of Paleozoic tectonic structures between Europe and North America and between southernmost Africa and South America. (From A. Wegener, 1915, Die Entstehung der Kontinente und Ozeane, F. Vieweg, Braunschweig.)*

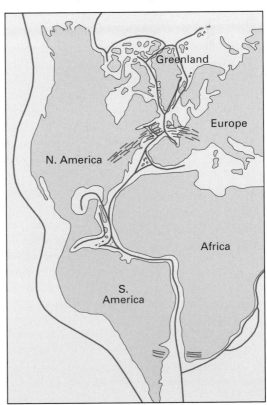

orated with Wegener in introducing favorable evidence from distribution patterns of fossil and present-day plant species. But Wegener's explanation of the physical process that separated the continents was weak and was strongly criticized on valid physical grounds. He had proposed that a continental layer of less dense rock had moved like a great floating "raft" through a "sea" of denser oceanic crustal rock. Geologists could show by use of established principles of physics that this proposed mechanism was impossible. In 1930, Wegener perished of cold and exhaustion while on an expedition to the Greenland ice sheet. There followed three decades in which only a small minority of scientists promoted his hypothesis.

In the 1960s, however, seismologists showed beyond doubt that thick lithospheric plates are in motion, both along the midoceanic ridge and beneath the deep offshore trenches of the continents. Other geophysicists used magnetic data "frozen" into crustal rock to conclude that the continents had moved great distances apart. Within only a few years, Wegener's scenario was validated, but only by applying a mechanism for the process that was never dreamed of in his time.

The continents are moving today. Data from orbiting satellites have shown that rates of separation, or of convergence, between two plates are on the order of 5 to 10 cm (about 2 to 4 in.) per year, or 50 to 100 km (about 30 to 60 mi) per million years. At that rate, global geography must have been very different in past geologic eras than it is today. Many continental riftings and many plate collisions have taken place over the past two billion years. Single continents have fragmented into smaller ones, while at other times, small continents have merged to form large ones. (See *Eye on the Environment 12.1* • *The Wilson Cycle and Supercontinents.*)

A brief look at the changing continental arrangements and locations over the past 250 m.y. is worthwhile in our study of physical geography because those changes brought with them changes in climate, soils, and vegetation on each continent as the continents moved across the parallels of latitude. Geography of the geologic past bears the name "paleogeography." If you decide to become a paleogeographer, you will need to carry with you into the past all you have learned about the physical geography of the present.

Wegener had made a crude map showing stages in the breakup of Pangea, but his timetable had been in part incorrect. Modern reconstructions of the global arrangements of past continents have been available since the mid-1960s. Global maps drawn for each geologic period have been repeatedly revised in the light of new evidence, but differences of interpretation affect only the minor details.

Figure 12.22 shows stages in the separations and travels of our continents, starting in the Permian Period of the Mesozoic Era, about 250 m.y. ago. In the first map, Pangea lies astride the equator and extends nearly to the two poles. Regions that are now North America and western Eurasia lie in the northern hemisphere. Jointly they are called *Laurasia.*

Regions that are now South America, Africa, Antarctica, Australia, New Zealand, Madagascar, and peninsular India lie south of the equator. Jointly, they go by the name *Gondwana.* Subsequent maps (*b* through *d*) show the breaking apart and dispersal of the Laurasia and Gondwana plates to yield their modern components and locations, as seen in map *e*.

Note in particular that North America traveled from a low-latitude location into high latitudes, finally closing off the Arctic Ocean as a largely landlocked sea. This change may have been a major factor in bringing on the Ice Age in late Cenozoic time, about two million years ago. (See Chapter 19.) Another traveler was the Indian Peninsula, which started out from a near-subarctic southerly location in Permian time and streaked northeast across the Thethys Sea to collide with Asia in the northern tropical savanna zone. India's bedrock still bears the grooves and scratches of a great glaciation in Permian time, when it was nearer to the south pole. For the future, we may safely predict that the Atlantic Ocean basins will become much wider, and the westward motion of the Americas will cause a reduction in the width of the Pacific Basin.

GEODISCOVERIES **Continents of the Past.** Follow today's continents from Precambrian to the present as they converge into a supercontinent and then split apart. An animation.

GEODISCOVERIES **Web Quiz.** Take a quick quiz on the key concepts of this chapter.

A LOOK AHEAD

Over the long spans of geologic time, our planet's surface is shaped and reshaped endlessly. Oceans open and close, mountains rise and fall. Rocks are folded, faulted, and fractured. Arcs of volcanoes spew lava to build chains of lofty peaks. Deep trenches consume sediments that are carried beneath adjacent continents. These activities are byproducts of the motions of lithospheric plates and are described by plate tectonics.

For geographers, the great value of plate tectonics is that it provides a grand scheme for understanding the pattern of the largest and most obvious features of our planet's surface. These include its continents and ocean basins at the global scale, as well as its mountain ranges and oceanic trenches at a continental scale. However, large landforms such as mountain ranges are made up of many smaller landforms—individual peaks, for example. In the next chapter, we will look at the continental surface in more detail, examining the processes that produce the regional- or local-scale volcanic and tectonic landforms that result when volcanoes erupt and rock layers are folded and faulted.

GEODISCOVERIES **Web Links.** Dive to the ocean floor and explore undersea tectonic landforms. Watch the continents move through the eons. Chart geologic time and discover ancient environments. It's all in this chapter's web links.

12.22 Pangea's breakup *The breakup of Pangea is shown in five stages. Inferred motion of lithospheric plates is indicated by arrows. (Redrawn and simplified from maps by R. S. Dietz and J. C. Holden, Jour. Geophysical Research, vol. 75, pp. 4943–4951, Figures 2 to 6. Copyrighted by the American Geophysical Union. Used by permission.)*

In Review | The Lithosphere and Plate Tectonics

- At the center of the Earth lies the **core**—a dense mass of liquid iron and nickel that is solid at the very center. Enclosing the metallic core is the **mantle,** composed of ultramafic rock. The outermost layer is the **crust. Continental crust** consists of two zones—a lighter zone of felsic rocks atop a denser zone of mafic rocks. **Oceanic crust** consists only of denser, mafic rocks.

- The **lithosphere,** the outermost shell of rigid, brittle rock, includes the crust and an upper layer of the mantle. Below the lithosphere is the **asthenosphere,** a region of the mantle in which mantle rock is soft or plastic.

- Geologists trace the history of the Earth through the geologic time scale. *Precambrian time* includes the Earth's earliest history. It is followed by three major divisions—the *Paleozoic, Mesozoic,* and *Cenozoic* eras.

- Continental masses consist of active belts of mountain-making and inactive regions of old, stable rock. Mountain-building occurs by *volcanism* and *tectonic activity.*

Alpine chains include **mountain arcs** and **island arcs.** They occur in two principal mountain belts—the circum-Pacific and Eurasian-Indonesian belts.

- **Continental shields** are regions of low-lying igneous and metamorphic rocks. They may be *exposed* or *covered* by layers of sedimentary rocks. Ancient *mountain roots* lie within some shield regions.

- The ocean basins are marked by a *midoceanic ridge* with its central *axial rift.* This ridge occurs at the site of crustal spreading. Most of the *ocean basin floor* is *abyssal plain,* covered by fine sediment. As *passive continental margins* are approached, the *continental rise, slope,* and *shelf* are encountered. At *active continental margins,* deep *oceanic trenches* lie offshore.

- The two basic tectonic processes are extension and compression. Both processes can lead to the formation of mountains. *Extension* occurs in the splitting of plates, when the crust thins, is fractured, and then pushed upward to produce block mountains. When lithospheric plates collide, *compression* occurs, shaping rock layers into *folds* that then break and move atop one another along *overthrust faults.*

- *Continental lithosphere* includes the thicker, lighter continental crust and a rigid layer of mantle rock beneath. *Oceanic lithosphere* is comprised of the thinner, denser oceanic crust and rigid mantle below. The lithosphere is fractured and broken into a set of **lithospheric plates,** large and small, that move with respect to each other.

- Where plates move apart, a *spreading boundary* occurs. At *converging boundaries,* plates collide. At *transform boundaries,* plates move past one another on a *transform fault.* There are six major lithospheric plates.

- When oceanic lithosphere and continental lithosphere collide, the denser oceanic lithosphere plunges beneath the continental lithospheric plate, a process called **subduction.** A trench marks the site of downplunging. Some subducted oceanic crust melts and rises to the surface, producing volcanoes. Under the severe compression that occurs with continent–continent collision, the two continental plates are welded together in a zone of metamorphic rock named a **continental suture.**

- In *continental rupture,* extensional tectonic forces move a continental plate in opposite directions, creating a *rift valley.* Eventually, the rift valley widens and opens to the ocean, and new oceanic crust forms as spreading continues.

- Plate movements are thought to be powered by *convection currents* in the plastic mantle rock of the asthenosphere.

- During the Permian Period, the continents were joined in a single, large supercontinent—Pangea—that broke apart, leading eventually to the present arrangement of continents and ocean basins.

Key Terms

core, p. 423	oceanic crust, p. 424	mountain arc, p. 427	tectonics, p. 432
mantle, p. 423	lithosphere, p. 424	island arcs, p. 427	subduction, p. 434
crust, p. 423	asthenosphere, p. 424	continental shields, p. 427	continental suture, p. 442
continental crust, p. 424	lithospheric plates, p. 424	plate tectonics, p. 432	

Review Questions

1. Describe the Earth's inner structure, from the center outward. What types of crust are present? How are they different?

2. How do geologists use the term *lithosphere?* What layer underlies the lithosphere, and what are its properties? Define the term *lithospheric plate.*

3. More recent geologic time is divided into three eras. Name them in order from oldest to youngest. How do geologists use the terms *period* and *epoch?* What age is applied to time before the earliest era?

4. What proportion of the Earth's surface is in ocean? in land? Do these proportions reflect the true proportions of continents and oceans? If not, why not?

5. What are the two basic subdivisions of continental masses?

6. What term is attached to belts of active mountain-making? What are the two basic processes by which mountain belts are constructed? Provide examples of mountain arcs and island arcs.

7. What is a continental shield? How old are continental shields? What two types of shields are recognized?

8. Describe how compressional mountain-building produces folds, faults, overthrust faults, and thrust sheets (nappes).

9. Name the six great lithospheric plates. Identify an example of a spreading boundary by general geographic location and the plates involved. Do the same for a converging boundary.

10. Describe the process of subduction as it occurs at a converging boundary of continental and oceanic lithospheric plates. How is the continental margin extended? How is subduction related to volcanic activity?

11. How does continental rupture produce passive continental margins? Describe the process of rupturing and its various stages.

12. What are transform faults? Where do they occur?

13. How is the principle of convection thought to be related to the power source for plate tectonic motions? What role does gravity play in the motion of lithospheric plates?

14. Provide a brief history of the idea of "drifting continents."

15. What was Wegener's theory about "continental drift?" Why was it opposed at the time?

16. Briefly summarize the history of our continents that geologists have reconstructed beginning with the Permian period.

Visualizing Exercises

1. Sketch a cross section of an ocean basin with passive continental margins. Label the following features: midoceanic ridge, axial rift, abyssal plain, continental rise, continental slope, and continental shelf.

2. Identify and describe two types of lithospheric plates. Sketch a cross section showing a collision between the two types. Label the following features: oceanic crust, continental crust, mantle, oceanic trench, and rising magma. Indicate where subduction is occurring.

3. Sketch a continent–continent collision and describe the formation process of a continental suture. Provide a pres-

ent-day example where a continental suture is being formed, and give an example of an ancient continental suture.

4. Figure 12.15 is a Mercator map of lithospheric plates, whereas Figure 12.16 presents a cross section of plates on a great circle. Construct a similar cross section of plates on the 30° S parallel of latitude. As in Figure 12.16, label the plates and major geographic features. Refer to Figure 12.4 for arcs, trenches, and midocean ridges.

Eye on the Environment 12.1 ● The Wilson Cycle and Supercontinents

1. What is the Wilson cycle of plate tectonics? What is the net effect of a Wilson cycle on the continental mass?

2. Using a sketch, describe the cycle by which supercontinents are formed and reformed.

Essay Question

1. Suppose astronomers discover a new planet that, like Earth, has continents and oceans. They dispatch a reconnaissance satellite to photograph the new planet. What features would you look for, and why, to detect past and present plate tectonic activity on the new planet?

Eye on the Landscape

Chapter Opener Egypt, Nile Delta, and Sinai Peninsula The Nile valley (**A**) and delta (**B**) are intensively farmed, as indicated by the deep green color in this image. Brown spots in the green are urbanized areas—cities and towns—of Egypt. Irrigation and agriculture are discussed in Chapter 10. Note also the elongated sand dune fields of the Egyptian Sahara, shown as light streaks (**C**) drawn out by prevailing northwesterly winds. Dune are covered in Chapter 18.

12.7 Undersea topography Notice the Hawaiian Islands (**A**) and the trail of seamounts (**B**) leading up to them. The islands are outpourings of lava from a "hotspot" in the mantle. The hotspot has remained fixed, however, as the Pacific lithospheric plate has moved across it. The seamounts thus mark the path of motion of the

Pacific plate. Note that the direction of motion changed abruptly at one point in time. Some hotspots are relatively recent and don't show a trail of ancient eruptions. The Cape Verde Islands (**C**) are an example. Hotspot volcanoes are described in Chapter 13.

12.20 Red Sea and Gulf of Aden from orbit The pinkish tones of the interior Arabian desert (**A**) are caused by iron oxides in the desert rocks and soils; note the absence of any dark vegetation (see Chapter 14 for weathering and oxide formation). At (**B**), a dark plateau has been dissected by a stream system leading down to the low, central desert; fluvial dissection is covered in Chapter 16. The cumulus clouds at (**C**) are the result of the lifting of moist air over the coastal mountain ranges. Recall that we covered orographic precipitation in Chapter 4.

13 | VOLCANIC AND TECTONIC LANDFORMS

PUTTING YOU IN THE PICTURE

Some of the most devastating natural phenomena are eruptions of volcanoes and great earthquakes, both of which are subjects of this chapter. Another related hazard is the seismic sea wave, or tsunami, created when an undersea earthquake rapidly raises or lowers a large area of ocean bottom or triggers an underwater landslide. Although tsunamis are less frequent than damaging earthquakes, a single tsunami has the power to devastate thousands of kilometers of low-lying coast. What would it be like to live through a tsunami?

Imagine yourself on the balcony of an ocean-view room at an exclusive beach hotel at Waikiki, taking in a view that is postcard-perfect. The arc of hotels stretches to your right and left, fringed with palms and pools. In front of you lies the beach, lined with sun worshipers. Heads and arms of swimmers bob and dunk in the surf zone just beyond. Sailboats glide lazily back and forth in the lagoon, while outrigger canoes move more deliberately under paddle power. Beyond the lagoon, the green waters of the sheltering reef complete the tropical scene.

    Suddenly you are aware of a roaring noise, building in intensity. On the horizon, a low, dark line appears. Beyond the sailors and surfriders, the reef begins to foam and rapidly becomes a white crescent of churning, seething water. Something very wrong is happening—a wall of water is moving inland toward the beach! It sweeps relentlessly forward, rolling and pushing sailboats, canoes, and swimmers into a chaotic cascade of foam. As the wave hits the beach, bathers running landward are overtaken and tumbled among the tables and chairs swept from beachside terraces. Palm trees bend and fall under the onslaught.

PUTTING YOU IN THE PICTURE

The beach has completely disappeared, and the giant wave now crashes full-force against the hotel, shattering glass windows and doors and breaking interior partitions. The building shakes and sways from the impact, and you cling to the terrace rail for support. Although the wave crest has passed, the water remains high and ocean surf is now attacking the hotel. You can feel the thumping and tearing of steel and concrete as the building shudders with the blows.

Just as you are beginning to think about what to do, the water begins to retreat, first slowly, then as a great outgoing flood. Splintered woodwork, uprooted plants, and even floating cars flash past as the ebbing waters carry them seaward. The beach is visible once again, now gullied by the ocean-bound water. The surf withdraws far out in the lagoon, leaving a vast sandy plain littered with debris and shallow water pools, glistening in the Sun. Awestruck by the devastation spread in front of you, you thank your lucky stars that you were not a casualty of the great tsunami. But then you glance seaward, and stare with horror. The reef is awash with foam once more. Another great sea wave is headed for the beach!

Tsunamis present a major hazard for low-lying coasts, even when they are far from regions of volcanic activity. The Indian Ocean tsunami of December 26, 2004, was triggered by a major earthquake off the west coast of the Indonesian island of Sumatra, and its devastating effects were felt as far away as Somalia on the eastern coast of Africa. Coastal regions of Indonesia, Thailand, India, and Sri Lanka were overrun by waves with heights of tens of meters that destroyed everything within their reach. Islands in the Bay of Bengal and Indian Ocean to the southwest of southern India were also hard hit. Casualty estimates reached the 220,000 mark a few weeks after the tragedy. *Eye on the Environment 13.3 • The Indian Ocean Tsunami of 2004* provides more information about this major environmental disaster.

A tsunami is a very dramatic example of Earth forces at work—in this case, a secondary effect of a huge, submarine earthquake. This chapter focuses on how Earth forces act to shape the landscape, from the building of steep-sided volcanoes by volcanic eruptions to the lifting of huge masses of rock by motions along earthquake faults. As we will see, the power of the Earth in building these landforms can be awesome indeed. ∎

VOLCANIC AND TECTONIC LANDFORMS

The two previous chapters have now set the stage for the study of volcanic and tectonic landforms, which is the subject of this chapter. These features of the landscape are created by internal Earth forces. Upwelling magma spews forth explosively from vents and fissures, creating steep-sided volcanoes or flooding vast areas with molten rock. Compressional stresses generated by plate motions fold flat-lying rocks into wavelike forms, producing long ridges from upfolds and long valleys from downfolds. Earthquake faults mark the lines on which rock layers break and move past one other, producing huge uplifted mountain blocks next to deep, downdropped valleys.

By looking in detail at landforms created by volcanic and tectonic activity, we are moving down from the global scale of enormous lithospheric plates that collide to form vast mountain arcs or separate to form yawning ocean basins. We are now "zooming in" to examine individual landscape features that are actually small enough to view from a single vantage point. As we will see, the global perspective of plate tectonics, coupled with the processes that create individual landforms, will help explain the pattern of landscape features we observe at continental and regional scales.

LANDFORMS

Landforms are the surface features of the land—for example, mountain peaks, cliffs, canyons, plains, beaches, and sand dunes. Landforms are created by many processes, and much of the remainder of this book describes landforms and how they are produced. **Geomorphology** is the scientific study of the processes that shape landforms. In this chapter, we will examine landforms produced directly by volcanic and tectonic processes.

The shapes of continental surfaces reflect the "balance of power," so to speak, between two opposing sets of processes. **Endogenic processes** act from inside the Earth to move crustal materials upward through volcanic and tectonic processes, thus bringing fresh rock to the Earth's surface. In opposition are **exogenic processes** that act to lower continental surfaces by removing and transporting mineral matter through the action of running water, waves and currents, glacial ice, and wind. We can refer to these processes of land sculpture collectively as **denudation.**

Seen in this perspective, landforms in general fall into two basic groups—initial landforms, created by endogenic processes, and sequential landforms, created by exogenic processes. *Initial landforms* are produced directly by volcanic and tectonic activity. They include volcanoes and lava flows, as well as downdropped rift valleys and elevated mountain blocks in zones of recent crustal deformation. Figure 13.1a shows a mountain block uplifted by crustal activity. The energy for lifting molten rock and rigid crustal masses to produce the initial landforms comes from an inter-

> Landforms reflect a "balance of power" between endogenic internal Earth forces that bring fresh rock to the surface and exogenic denudation processes that remove and transport mineral matter from fresh rock masses.

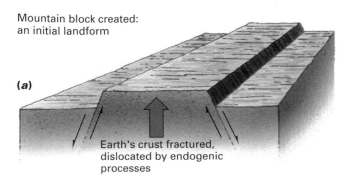

Mountain block created: an initial landform

(a)

Earth's crust fractured, dislocated by endogenic processes

Mountain block carved into sequential landforms by exogenic processes

(a) Erosional:
Canyon
Divide

(b)

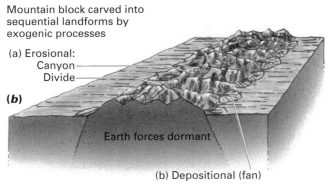

Earth forces dormant

(b) Depositional (fan)

13.1 Initial and sequential landforms *An initial landform is created, here by tectonic activity, then carved into sequential landforms. (Drawn by A. N. Strahler.)*

nal heat source. As we explained in Chapter 12, this heat energy is generated largely by natural radioactivity in rock of the Earth's crust and mantle. It is the fundamental energy source for the motions of lithospheric plates.

Landforms shaped by exogenic processes of denudation belong to the group of *sequential landforms.* The word "sequential" means that they follow in sequence after the initial landforms have been created, and a crustal mass has been raised to an elevated position. Figure 13.1*b* shows an uplifted crustal block (an initial landform) that has been attacked by agents of denudation and carved up into a large number of sequential landforms.

You can think of any landscape as representing the existing stage in a great contest of opposing endogenic and exogenic forces. As lithospheric plates collide or pull apart, internal Earth forces periodically elevate parts of the crust to create initial landforms. The external agents of denudation—running water, waves, wind, and glacial ice—persistently wear these masses down and carve them into vast numbers of smaller sequential landforms.

Today we can observe the many stages of this endless struggle between endogenic and exogenic forces by traveling to different parts of the globe. Where we find high alpine mountains and volcanic chains, internal Earth forces have recently dominated the contest. In the rolling low plains of the continental interiors, the agents of denudation have won a temporary victory. At other locations, we can find many intermediate stages. Because the internal Earth forces act

repeatedly and violently, new initial landforms keep coming into existence as old ones are subdued.

This chapter focuses on initial landforms that are created directly by volcanic activity and tectonic activity. After we have described the most important agents of denudation in Chapters 14 and 16, we will return in Chapter 17 to the sequential landforms that develop on volcanic and tectonic landforms.

VOLCANIC ACTIVITY

We have already identified *volcanism,* or volcanic activity, as one of the forms of mountain-building. The extrusion of magma builds landforms, and these landforms can accumulate in a single area both as volcanoes and as thick lava flows. Through these volcanic activities, imposing mountain ranges are constructed.

A **volcano** is a conical or dome-shaped initial landform built by the emission of lava and its contained gases from a constricted vent in the Earth's surface (Figure 13.2). The magma rises in a narrow, pipe-like conduit from a magma reservoir lying beneath. Upon reaching the surface, igneous material may pour out in sluggish, tongue-like lava flows. Magma may also be violently ejected in the form of solid fragments driven skyward under pressure of confined gases. Ejected fragments, ranging in size from boulders to fine dust, are collectively called *tephra.* Forms and dimensions of a volcano are quite varied, depending on the type of lava and the presence or absence of tephra.

GEODISCOVERIES **Volcanoes.** Watch and compare the eruptions of shield volcanoes and stratovolcanoes in this video. Concludes with footage of the fiery, explosive eruption of Mount St. Helens.

13.2 Anatomy of a stratovolcano *Idealized cross section of a stratovolcano with feeders from magma chamber beneath. The steep-sided cone is built up from layers of lava and tephra. (Copyright © A. N. Strahler.)*

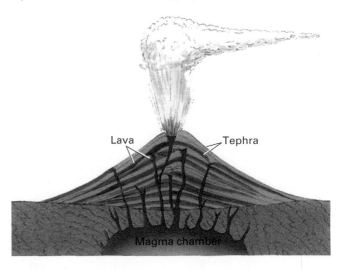

Lava

Tephra

Magma chamber

a...Mount St. Helens This stratovolcano of the Cascade Range in southwestern Washington erupted violently on the morning of May 18, 1980, emitting a great cloud of condensed steam, heated gases, and ash from the summit crater. Within a few minutes, the plume had risen to a height of 20 km (12 mi), and its contents were being carried eastward by stratospheric winds. The eruption was initiated when an explosion demolished the northern portion of the cone, which is concealed from this viewpoint.

b...Mount Mayon *Located in southeastern Luzon, the Philippines, Mount Mayon is often considered the world's most nearly perfect stratovolcanic cone. Its summit rises to an altitude of nearly 2400 m (about 8000 ft). Mount Mayon has erupted at least 40 times since 1616. Its most recent eruption was in March 2000, causing the evacuation of a local population of about 55,000 people.*

c...Crater Lake *Crater Lake, Oregon, is a water-filled caldera marking the remains of the summit of Mount Mazama, which exploded about 6600 years ago. Wizard Island (center foreground) was built on the floor of the caldera after the major explosive activity had ceased. It is an almost perfectly shaped cone of cinders capping small lava flows.*

Stratovolcanoes

The nature of volcanic eruption, whether explosive or quiet, depends on the type of magma. Recall from Chapter 11 that there are two main types of igneous rocks: felsic and mafic. The felsic lavas (rhyolite and andesite) have a high degree of viscosity—that is, they are thick and gummy, and resist flow. So, volcanoes of felsic composition typically have steep slopes, and lava usually does not flow long distances from the volcano's vent. When the volcano erupts, tephra falls on the area surrounding the crater and contributes to the structure of the cone. Volcanic bombs are also included in the tephra. These solidified masses of lava range up to the size of large boulders and fall close to the crater.

The interlayering of sluggish streams of felsic lava and falls of tephra produces a **stratovolcano.** This tall, steep-sided cone usually steepens toward the summit, where a bowl-shaped depression—the *crater*—is located. The crater is the principal vent of the volcano. Felsic lavas usually hold large amounts of gas under high pressure. As a result, these lavas can produce explosive eruptions. The eruption of Mount St. Helens in 1980 is an example of an explosive eruption of felsic lavas (Figure 13.3). Very fine volcanic dust from such eruptions can rise high into the troposphere and stratosphere, traveling hundreds or thousands of kilometers before settling to the Earth's surface.

Lofty, conical stratovolcanoes are well known for their scenic beauty. Fine examples are Mount Hood and Mount St. Helens in the Cascade Range, Mount Fuji in Japan, Mount Mayon in the Philippines (Figure 13.3), and Mount Shishaldin in the Aleutian Islands. Stratovolcanoes are sometimes referred to as *composite volcanoes,* or composite cones, since they are composed of composites of ash and lava.

Another important form of emission from explosive stratovolcanoes is a cloud of white-hot gases and fine ash. This intensely hot cloud, or "glowing avalanche," travels rapidly down the flank of the volcanic cone, searing everything in its path. On the Caribbean island of Martinique, in 1902, a glowing cloud issued without warning from Mount Pelée. It swept down on the city of St. Pierre, destroying the city and killing all but two of its 30,000 inhabitants. More recently, glowing avalanches spawned by a 1997 eruption of the Soufrière Hills volcano on Montserrat, another island of the Lesser Antilles, killed about 20 people in small villages. Plymouth, the island's capital, was flooded with hot ash and debris, causing extensive fires that devastated the evacuated city (Figure 13.4). The southern two-thirds of the small island was left uninhabitable.

CALDERAS   One of the most catastrophic of natural phenomena is a volcanic explosion so violent that it destroys the entire central portion of the volcano. Vast quantities of ash and dust are emitted and fill the atmosphere for many hundreds of square kilometers around the volcano. Only a great central depression, named a *caldera,* remains after the explosion. Although some of the upper part of the volcano is blown outward in fragments, most of it settles back into the cavity formed beneath the former volcano by the explosion.

Krakatoa, a volcanic island in Indonesia, exploded in 1883, leaving a huge caldera. Great seismic sea waves generated by the explosion killed many thousands of persons living in low coastal areas of Sumatra and Java. About 75 km³ (18 mi³) of rock was blown out of the crater during the explosion. Vast quantities of gas and fine particles of dust were carried into the stratosphere, where they contributed to a rosy glow of sunrises and sunsets that was seen around the world for several years afterward.

A classic example of a caldera produced in prehistoric times is Crater Lake, Oregon (Figure 13.3). The former volcano, named Mount Mazama, is estimated to have risen 1200 m (about 4000 ft) higher than the present caldera rim. The great explosion and collapse occurred about 6600 years ago.

STRATOVOLCANOES AND SUBDUCTION ARCS   Most of the world's active stratovolcanoes lie within the circum-Pacific mountain belt. Here, subduction of the Pacific, Nazca, Cocos, and Juan de Fuca plates is active. In Chapter 12, we explained how andesitic magmas rise beneath volcanic arcs of active continental margins and island arcs (see Figure 12.12). One good example is the volcanic arc of Sumatra and Java, lying over the subduction zone between the Australian plate and the Eurasian plate. Another is the Aleutian volcanic arc, located where the Pacific plate dives beneath the North American plate. The Cascade Mountains of northern California, Oregon, and Washington form a similar chain that continues into the Garibaldi volcanic belt of southern British Columbia. Important segments of the Andes Mountains in South America consist of stratovolcanoes.

> Stratovolcanoes are built of layers of felsic lava and volcanic ash. Because felsic lava is viscous, it builds a tall, steep conical form. Felsic magma can contain gases under high pressure, so felsic eruptions are often explosive.

Shield Volcanoes

In contrast to thick, gassy felsic lava, mafic lava (basalt) is often highly fluid. It typically has a low viscosity and holds little gas. As a result, eruptions of basaltic lava are usually quiet, and the lava can travel long distances to spread out in thin layers. Typically, then, large basaltic volcanoes are broadly rounded domes with gentle slopes. They are referred to as **shield volcanoes.** Hawaiian volcanoes are of this type.

The shield volcanoes of the Hawaiian Islands are characterized by gently rising, smooth slopes that flatten near the top, producing a broad-topped volcano (Figure 13.5). Domes on the island of Hawaii rise to summit elevations of about 4000 m (about 13,000 ft) above sea level. Including the basal portion lying below sea level, they are more than twice that high. In width they range from 16 to 80 km (10 to 50 mi) at sea level and up to 160 km (about 100 mi) at the

13.4 **Ash cloud** *A cloud of hot, dense volcanic ash, emitted by the Soufrière Hills volcano, courses down this narrow valley on the island of Monserrat in the Lesser Antilles.*

13.5 **Basaltic shield volcanoes of Hawaii** *At lower left is the now-cold Halemaumau pit crater, formed in the floor of the central depression of Kilauea volcano. On the distant skyline is the snow-capped summit of Mauna Kea volcano, its elevation over 4000 m (about 13,000 ft).*

submerged base. The basalt lava of the Hawaiian volcanoes is highly fluid and travels far down the gentle slopes. Most of the lava flows issue from fissures (long, gaping cracks) on the flanks of the volcano.

Hawaiian lava domes have a wide, steep-sided central depression that may be 3 km (2 mi) or more wide and several hundred meters deep. These large depressions are a type of collapsed caldera. Molten basalt is sometimes seen in the floors of deep pit craters that occur on the floor of the central depression or elsewhere over the surface of the lava dome.

HOTSPOTS, SEAFLOOR SPREADING, AND SHIELD VOLCANOES

The chain of Hawaiian volcanoes was created by the motion of the Pacific plate over a *hotspot*—a plume of upwelling basaltic magma deep within the mantle, arising far down in the asthenosphere. Figure 13.6 diagrams this process. As the hot mantle rock rises, magma forms in bodies that melt their way through the lithosphere and reach the seafloor. Each major pulse of the plume sets off a cycle of volcano formation. However, the motion of the oceanic lithosphere eventually carries the volcano away from the location of the deep plume, and so it becomes extinct. Erosion processes wear the volcano away, and ultimately it becomes a low island. Continued attack by waves and slow settling of the island reduce it to a coral-covered platform. Eventually only a sunken island, or *guyot*, exists.

The process of crustal motion over a hotspot thus produces a long trail of islands and guyots. The Hawaiian trail,

---

> Hotspots are plumes of rising basaltic magma that generate volcanic activity. When they occur beneath moving plates of oceanic crust, they create chains of islands and seamounts. On land, they cover large regions with flood basalts.

---

shown in Figure 13.7, trends northwestward. It is 2400 km (about 1500 mi) long and includes a sharp bend to the north caused by a sudden change of direction of the Pacific plate. This distant leg consists of the Emperor Seamounts. Several other long trails of volcanic seamounts cross the Pacific Ocean basin. They, too, follow parallel paths that reveal the plate motion.

A few basaltic volcanoes also occur along the midoceanic ridge, where seafloor spreading is in progress. Perhaps the outstanding example is Iceland, in the North Atlantic Ocean. Iceland is constructed entirely of basalt. Basaltic flows are superimposed on older basaltic rocks as dikes and sills formed by magma emerging from deep within the spreading rift. Mount Hekla, an active volcano on Iceland, is a shield volcano somewhat similar to those of Hawaii. In Chapter 11, *Eye on the Environment 11.1 ● Battling Iceland's Heimaey Volcano* documents how valiant Icelanders coped with a recent eruption. Other islands consisting of basaltic volcanoes located along or close to the axis of the Mid-Atlantic Ridge are the Azores, Ascension, and Tristan da Cunha.

Where a mantle plume lies beneath a continental lithospheric plate, the hotspot may generate enormous volumes of basaltic lava that emerge from numerous vents and fissures and accumulate layer upon layer. The basalt may ultimately attain a thickness of thousands of meters and cover thousands of square kilometers. These accumulations are called *flood basalts*.

An important American example is found in the Columbia Plateau region of southeastern Washington, northeast-

---

13.6 Hotspot volcano chain

A chain of volcanic islands is formed as oceanic crust moves across a hotspot of rising magma. (Copyright © A. N. Strahler.)

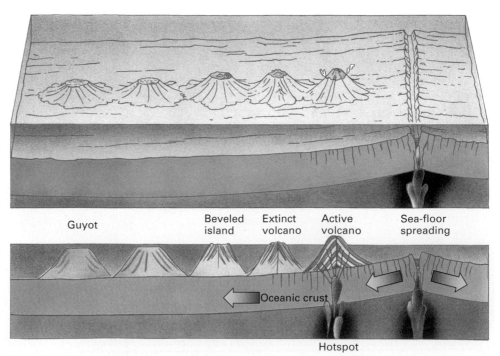

Guyot   Beveled island   Extinct volcano   Active volcano   Sea-floor spreading

Oceanic crust

Hotspot

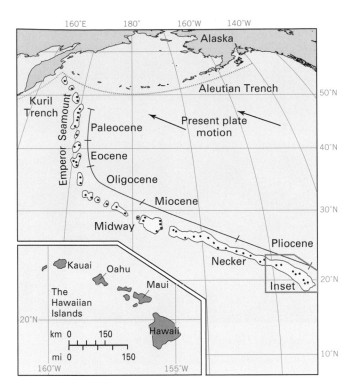

13.7 *Hawaiian seamount chain* *This sketch map locates the Hawaiian seamount chain in the northwest Pacific Ocean basin. Dots are summits. The enclosing colored area marks the base of the volcano at the ocean floor. (Copyright © A. N. Strahler.)*

ern Oregon, and westernmost Idaho. Here, basalts of Cenozoic age cover an area of about 130,000 km² (about 50,000 mi²)—nearly the same area as the state of New York. Individual basalt flows are exposed along the walls of river gorges as cliffs in which vertical joint columns are conspicuous (Figure 13.8).

Associated with flood basalts, shield volcanoes, and scattered occurrences of basaltic lava flows is a small volcano known as a *cinder cone* (Figure 13.9). Cinder cones form when frothy basalt magma is ejected under high pressure from a narrow vent, producing tephra. The rain of tephra accumulates around the vent to form a roughly circular hill with a central crater. Cinder cones rarely grow to heights of more than a few hundred meters. An exceptionally fine example of a cinder cone is Wizard Island, built on the floor of Crater Lake long after the caldera was formed (Figure 13.3).

HOT SPRINGS AND GEYSERS   Where hot rock material is near the Earth's surface, it can heat nearby ground water to high temperatures. When the ground water reaches the surface, it provides *hot springs* at temperatures not far below the boiling point of water (Figure 13.10). At some places, jet-like emissions of steam and hot water occur at intervals from small vents—producing *geysers* (Figure 13.11). Since the water that emerges from hot springs and geysers is largely ground water that has been heated in contact with hot rock, this water is

13.8 *Eye on the Landscape*   Flood basalts *Basalt lava flows exposed in cliffs bordering the Columbia River in Washington. Each set of cliffs is a major lava flow. In cooling, vertical cracks form in the lava, creating tall columns.* **What else would the geographer see? ... Answers at the end of the chapter.**

13.9 **Cinder cone** *This young cinder cone is built atop rough-surfaced basalt lava flows. Lava Beds National Monument, northern California.*

13.10 **Mammoth Hot Springs** *Small terraces ringed by mineral deposits hold steaming pools of hot water as the spring cascades down the slope. This example of geothermal activity is from Yellowstone National Park, Wyoming.*

13.11 **Old Faithful Geyser** *An eruption of Old Faithful Geyser in Yellowstone National Park, Wyoming.*

recycled surface water. Little, if any, is water that was originally held in rising bodies of magma.

The heat from masses of lava close to the surface in areas of hot springs and geysers provides a source of energy for electric power generation. *Eye on the Environment 13.1 • Geothermal Energy Sources* provides more information about this application.

Volcanic Activity over the Globe

Figure 13.12 shows the locations of volcanoes that have been active within the last 12,000 years. By comparing this map with that of Figure 12.4, it is easy to see that many volcanoes are located along subduction boundaries. In fact, the "ring of fire" around the Pacific Rim is the most obvious feature on the map. Other volcanoes are located on or near oceanic spreading centers. Iceland is an example. In continental regions, spreading in East Africa has also produced volcanoes. (We'll return to the East African rift later in this chapter.) Hotspot activity, as in the location of the Hawaiian Islands, is also present.

Volcanic activity is frequent along subduction boundaries, which accounts for the "ring of fire" around the Pacific Rim. Midocean spreading centers and continental rifts are also locations of volcanic activity.

GEODISCOVERIES **Remote Sensing and Tectonic Landforms Interactivity.** Choose the "volcanoes" option to inspect some of the Earth's major volcanoes located in developed areas. Identify craters, lava flows, and fly over Mount St. Helens.

Volcanic Eruptions as Environmental Hazards

The eruptions of volcanoes and lava flows are environmental hazards of the severest sort, often taking a heavy toll of plant and animal life and devastating human habitations. What natural phenomenon can compare with the Mount Pelée disaster in which thousands of lives were snuffed out in seconds? Perhaps only an earthquake or storm surge of a tropical cyclone is equally disastrous.

Wholesale loss of life and destruction of towns and cities are frequent in the history of peoples who live near active volcanoes. Loss occurs principally from sweeping clouds of incandescent gases that descend the volcano slopes like great avalanches, from lava flows whose relentless advance engulfs whole cities, from showers of ash, cinders, and bombs, and from violent earthquakes associated with volcanic activity. For habitations along low-lying coasts, there is the additional peril of great seismic sea waves, generated elsewhere by explosive destruction of undersea or island volcanoes.

In 1985, an explosive eruption of Ruiz Volcano in the Colombian Andes caused the rapid melting of ice and

Volcanic eruptions can have extreme environmental impacts. Flows of hot gas, showers of ash, cinders, and bombs, violent earthquakes, and accompanying seismic sea waves can cause great loss of life.

There are two basic forms of tectonic activity: compression and extension. Compression occurs at converging lithospheric plate margins, while extension occurs along continental and oceanic rifting.

snow in the summit area. Mixing with volcanic ash, the water formed a variety of mudflow known as a *lahar*. Rushing downslope at speeds up to 145 km (90 mi) per hour, the lahar became channeled into a valley on the lower slopes, where it engulfed a town and killed more than 20,000 persons.

Scientific monitoring techniques are reducing the toll of death and destruction from volcanoes. By analyzing the gases emitted from the vent of an active volcano, as well as the minor earthquakes and local land tilting that precede a major quake, scientists have successfully predicted periods of volcanic activity. Extensive monitoring of Mount Mayon and the Mexican volcano Popocatepetl to predict recent eruptions has led to evacuations that saved hundreds or thousands of lives. However, not every volcano is well monitored or predictable.

Despite their potential for destructive activity, volcanoes are a valuable natural resource in terms of recreation and tourism. Few landscapes can rival in beauty the mountainous landscapes of volcanic origin. National parks have been made of Mount Rainier, Mount Lassen, and Crater Lake in the Cascade Range, a mountain mass largely of volcanic construction. British Columbia's Garibaldi Provincial Park preserves volcanic mountain vistas in a vast wilderness area of snow-covered peaks and swift rivers. Hawaii Volcanoes National Park recognizes the natural beauty of Mauna Loa and Kilauea—their breathtaking displays of molten lava are a living textbook of igneous processes. *Focus on Remote Sensing 13.2 • Remote Sensing of Volcanoes* shows Mount Vesuvius, Mount Fuji, and Popocatepetl as imaged by several different remote sensing systems.

LANDFORMS OF TECTONIC ACTIVITY

Recall from Chapter 12, our introduction to global plate tectonics, that there are two basic forms of tectonic activity: compression and extension (see Figure 12.10). Along converging lithospheric plate boundaries, tectonic activity is primarily compression. In subduction zones, sedimentary layers of the ocean floor are compressed within a trench as the descending plate forces them against the overlying plate.

In continental collision, compression is of the severest kind. In zones of rifting of continental plates, however, the brittle continental crust is pulled apart and yields by faulting. This motion is extensional and produces faults. We begin our examination of landforms of tectonic activity with folding produced by compression.

Eye on the Environment | 13.1

Geothermal Energy Sources

Geothermal energy is energy in the form of sensible heat that originates within the Earth's crust and makes its way to the surface by conduction. Heat may be conducted upward through solid rock or carried up by circulating ground water that is heated at depth and returns to the surface. Concentrated geothermal heat sources are usually associated with igneous activity, but there also exist deep zones of heated rock and ground water that are not directly related to igneous activity.

Observations made in deep mines and bore holes show that the temperature of rock increases steadily with depth. Although the rate of increase falls off quite rapidly with increasing depth, temperatures attain very high values in the upper mantle, where rock is close to its melting point. Heat within the Earth's crust and mantle is produced largely by radioactive decay. Slow as this internal heat production is, it scarcely diminishes with time, and the basic energy resource it provides can be regarded as limitless on a human scale.

It might seem simple enough to obtain all our energy needs by drilling deep holes at any desired location into the crust and letting the hot rock turn injected fresh water into steam, which we could use to generate electricity as our primary energy resource. Unfortunately, at the depths usually required to furnish the needed heat intensity, crustal rock tends to close any cavity or opening by rupture and slow flowage. This phenomenon would either prevent the holes from being drilled or would close them in short order. Generally, then, we must look for geothermal localities, where special conditions have caused hot rock and hot ground water to lie within striking distance of conventional drilling methods. Areas of hot springs and geysers are primary candidates.

Natural hot-water and steam localities were the first type of geothermal energy source to be developed and at present account for nearly all production of geothermal electrical power. Wells are drilled to tap the hot water. When it reaches the surface, the water flashes into steam under the reduced pressure of the atmosphere. The steam is fed into generating turbines to produce electricity, then condensed in large cooling towers (see photo below). The resulting hot water is usually released into surface stream flow, where it may create a thermal pollution problem. The larger steam fields have sufficient energy to generate at least 15 megawatts of electric power, and a few can generate 200 megawatts or more.

In certain areas, the intrusion of magma has been sufficiently recent that solid igneous rock of a batholith is still very hot in a depth range of perhaps 2 to 5 km (about 1 to 3 mi). At this depth, the rock is strongly compressed and contains little, if any, ground water. Rock in this zone may be as hot as 300°C (about 575°F) and could supply an enormous quantity of heat energy. The planned development of this resource includes drilling into the hot zone and then shattering the surrounding rock by hydrofracture—a method using water under pressure that is widely used in petroleum development. Surface water would then be pumped down one well into the fracture zone and heated water pumped up another well. Although some experiments have been conducted, this heat source has not yet been exploited in any practical way.

Geothermal power plant This electricity-generating power plant at the Geysers, California, runs on steam produced by superheated ground water. Steam pipes in the foreground lead to the plant. After use in generating turbines, the steam is condensed in large cylindrical towers.

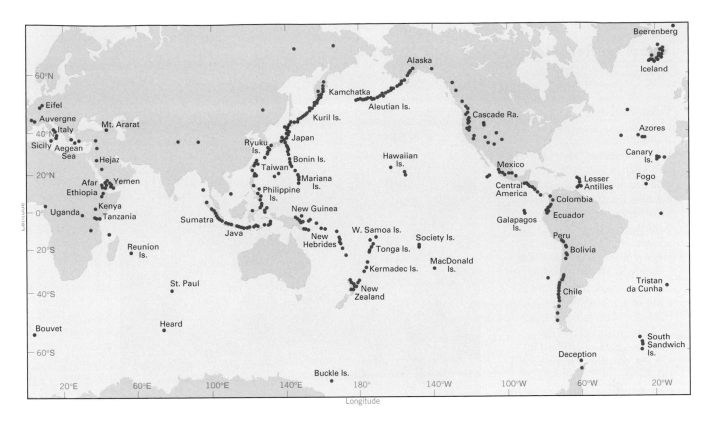

13.12 *Volcanic activity of the Earth* Dots show the locations of volcanoes known or believed to have erupted within the past 12,000 years. Each dot represents a single volcano or cluster of volcanoes. (After data of NOAA. Copyright © A. N. Strahler)

Fold Belts

In Chapter 12, we saw that two plates of continental lithosphere can collide, causing severe compressional stress. When flat-lying strata from a continental shelf or margin are caught in the collision, they can experience **folding** (see Figure 12.10). The wave-like shapes imposed on the strata consist of alternating arch-like upfolds, called *anticlines,* and through-like downfolds, called *synclines.* Thus, the initial landform associated with an anticline is a broadly rounded mountain ridge, and the landform corresponding to a syncline is an elongate, open valley.

GEO**DISCOVERIES** **Folding.** This animation shows how layers of sedimentary rocks are folded into anticlines and synclines. Erosion of fold belts creates lines of narrow ridges and valleys.

An example of open folds of comparatively young geologic age that has long attracted the interest of geographers is the Jura Mountains of France and Switzerland. Figure 13.13 is a block diagram of a small portion of that fold belt. The rock strata are mostly limestone layers and were capable of being deformed by bending with little brittle fracturing. Folding occurred in late Cenozoic (Miocene) time. Notice that each mountain crest is associated with the axis of an anticline, while each valley lies over the axis of a syncline. Some of the anticlinal arches have been partially removed by erosion processes. The rock structure can be seen clearly in the walls of the winding gorge of a major river that crosses the area. The

Jura folds lie just to the north of the main collision orogen of the Alps. Because of their location near a mountain mass, they are called *foreland folds.* The ridge and valley region of Pennsylvania, Maryland, and Virginia is another example but of much greater age.

GEO**DISCOVERIES** **Folding.** A video focusing on the Appalachian mountains shows a landscape of ridges and valleys created by folding.

Faults and Fault Landforms

A **fault** in the brittle rocks of the Earth's crust occurs when rocks suddenly yield to unequal stresses by fracturing. Faulting is accompanied by a displacement—a slipping motion—along the plane of breakage, or *fault plane.* Faults are often of great horizontal extent, so that the surface trace, or fault line, can sometimes be followed along the ground for many kilometers. Most major faults extend down into the crust for at least several kilometers.

Faulting occurs in sudden slippage movements that generate earthquakes. A single fault movement may result in slippage of as little as a centimeter or as much as 15 m (about 50 ft). Successive movements may occur many years or decades apart, even several centuries apart. Over long time spans, the accumulated displacements can amount to tens or hundreds of kilometers. In some places, clearly recognizable sedimentary rock layers are offset on opposite

13.13 Anticlines and synclines Structural diagrams for the Jura Mountains, France and Switzerland. A cross section shows the folds and ground surface (a). The landscape developed on the folds is shown in the block diagram (b). (After E. Raisz.)

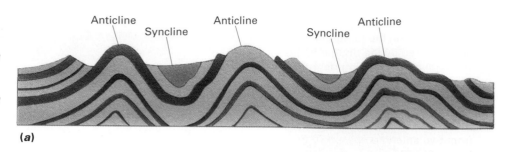

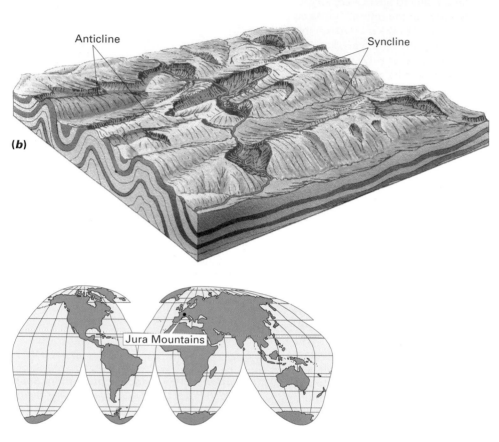

sides of a fault, allowing the total amount of displacement to be measured accurately.

NORMAL FAULTS One common type of fault associated with crustal rifting is the **normal fault** (Figure 13.14a). The plane of slippage, or fault plane, is steeply inclined. The crust on one side is raised, or upthrown, relative to the other, which is downthrown. A normal fault results in a steep, straight, cliff-like feature called a *fault scarp* (Figure 13.14). Fault scarps range in height from a few meters to a few hundred meters (Figure 13.15). Their length is usually measurable in kilometers. In some cases, they attain lengths as great as 300 km (about 200 mi).

Normal faults are not usually isolated features. Commonly, they occur in multiple arrangements, often as a set of parallel faults. These arrangements give rise to a grain or pattern of rock structure and topography. A narrow block

---
In a fault, rocks break apart and move along a fault plane. Normal faults are caused by extension and produce downdropped blocks (grabens) and upthrown blocks (horsts).

---

dropped down between two normal faults is a *graben* (Figure 13.16). A narrow block elevated between two normal faults is a *horst*. Grabens make conspicuous topographic trenches, with straight, parallel walls. Horsts make block-like plateaus or mountains, often with a flat top but steep, straight sides.

In rifted zones of the continents, regions where normal faulting occurs on a grand scale, mountain masses called *block mountains* are produced. The up-faulted mountain blocks can be described as either tilted or lifted (Figure 13.17). A tilted block has one steep face—the fault scarp—and one gently sloping side. A lifted block, which is a type of horst, is bounded by steep fault scarps on both sides.

TRANSCURRENT FAULTS Recall that lithospheric plates also slide past one another horizontally along major transform faults and that these features comprise one type of lithos-

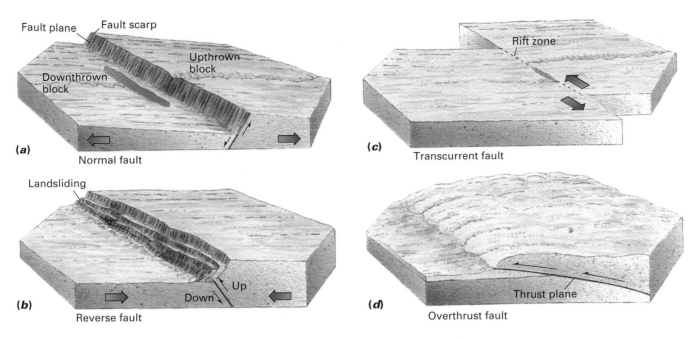

(a) Normal fault

(b) Reverse fault

(c) Transcurrent fault

(d) Overthrust fault

13.14 Four types of faults

pheric plate boundary. Long before the principles of plate tectonics became known, geologists referred to such faults as **transcurrent faults** (Figure 13.14c), or sometimes as *strike-slip faults*. In a transcurrent fault, the movement is predominantly horizontal. Where the land surface is nearly flat, no scarp, or a very low one at most, results. Only a thin fault

Transcurrent faults occur where lithospheric plates slide past each other. Movement is predominantly horizontal. The San Andreas fault of California is a famous transcurrent fault.

line is traceable across the surface. In some places a narrow trench, or rift, marks the fault.

The best known of the active transcurrent faults is the great San Andreas fault, which can be followed for a distance of about 1000 km (about 600 mi) from the Gulf of California to Cape Mendocino, a location well north of the San Francisco area, where it heads out to sea. It is a transform fault that marks the active boundary between the Pacific plate and the North American plate (see Figure 12.4). The Pacific plate is moving toward the northwest, which means that a great portion of the state of California and all of Lower (Baja) California

13.15 Fault scarp *This fault scarp was formed during the Hebgen Lake, Montana, earthquake of 1959. In a few moments, a displacement of 6 m (20 ft) took place on a normal fault.*

13.16 Initial landforms of normal faulting *A graben is a downdropped block, often forming a long, narrow valley. A horst is an upthrown block, forming a plateau, mesa, or mountain. (A. N. Strahler)*

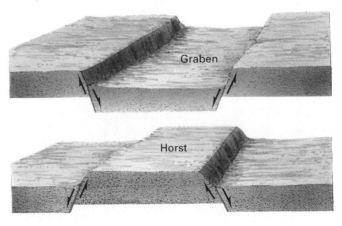

Graben

Horst

13.17   Fault block mountains *Fault block mountains may be of tilted type (left) or lifted type (right). (After W. M. Davis.)*

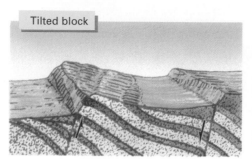

Tilted block

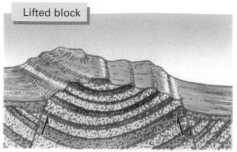

Lifted block

is moving bodily northwest with respect to the North American mainland.

Throughout many kilometers of its length, the San Andreas fault appears as a straight, narrow scar. In some places this scar is a trench-like feature, and elsewhere it is a low scarp (Figure 13.18). Frequently, a stream valley takes

> Reverse and overthrust faults are caused by compression. In a reverse fault, an overhanging scarp that slumps downward is formed. In an overthrust fault, one rock mass slides up and over another.

an abrupt jog—for example, first right, then left—when crossing the fault line. This offset in the stream's course shows that many meters of movement have occurred in fairly recent time.

REVERSE AND OVERTHRUST FAULTS   In a *reverse fault,* the inclination of the fault plane is such that one side rides up over the other and a crustal shortening occurs (Figure 13.14*b*). Reverse faults produce fault scarps similar to those of normal faults, but the possibility of landsliding is greater because an overhanging scarp tends to be formed. The San Fernando, California, earthquake of 1971 was generated by slippage on a reverse fault.

The *low-angle overthrust fault* (Figure 13.14*d*) involves predominantly horizontal movement. One slice of rock rides over the adjacent ground surface. A thrust slice may be up to 50 km (30 mi) wide. The evolution of low-angle thrust faults was explained in Chapter 12 and illustrated in Figure 12.11.

GEODISCOVERIES   **Major Types of Faulting.** See how crustal extension and compression create normal, reverse, and overthrust faults in this animation. Watch a transcurrent fault form at the boundary of two lithospheric plates moving in opposite directions.

The Rift Valley System of East Africa

Rifting of continental lithosphere is the very first stage in the splitting apart of a continent to form a new ocean basin. The process is beautifully illustrated by the East African Rift Valley system. This region has attracted the attention of geologists since the early 1900s. They gave the name *rift valley* to what is basically a graben but with a more complex history that includes the building of volcanoes on the graben floor.

Figure 13.19 is a sketch map of the East African Rift Valley system. It is about 3000 km (1900 mi) long and extends from the Red Sea southward to the Zambezi River. Along this axis, the Earth's crust is being lifted and spread apart in a long, ridge-like swell. The Rift Valley system consists of a number of graben-like troughs. Each is a separate rift valley

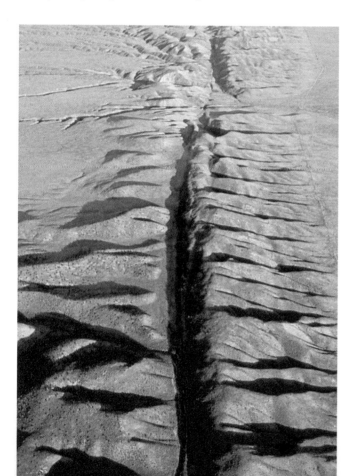

13.18   The San Andreas fault in southern California *The fault is marked by a narrow trough. The fault is slightly offset in the middle distance.*

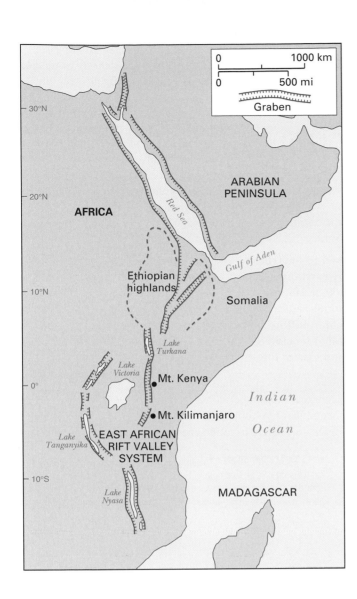

13.19 East African Rift Valley *This sketch map shows the East African Rift Valley system and the Red Sea to the north.*

ranging in width from about 30 to 60 km (20 to 40 mi). As geologists noted in early field surveys of this system, the rift valleys are like keystone blocks of a masonry arch that have slipped down between neighboring blocks because the arch has spread apart somewhat. Thus, the floors of the rift valleys are above the elevation of most of the African continental surface. Major rivers and several long, deep lakes—Lake Nyasa and Lake Rudolph, for example—occupy some of the valley floors.

The sides of the rift valleys typically consist of multiple fault steps (Figure 13.20). Sediments, derived from the high plateaus that form the flanks of troughs, make thick fills in the floors of the valleys. Two great stratovolcanoes have been built close to the Rift Valley east of Lake Victoria. One is Mount Kilimanjaro, whose summit rises to over 6000 m (about 19,000 ft). The other, Mount Kenya, is only a little lower and lies right on the equator.

EARTHQUAKES

You have probably seen television news accounts of disastrous earthquakes and their destructive effects (Figure 13.21). Californians know about severe earthquakes from first-hand experience, but several other areas in North America have also experienced strong earthquakes, and a few of these have been very severe. An **earthquake** is a motion of the ground surface, ranging from a faint tremor to a wild motion capable of shaking buildings apart.

13.20 Eye on the Landscape   The Rift Valley wall in Ethiopia *Multiple fault scarps give the landscape a stepped appearance.*   **What else would the geographer see? ... Answers at the end of the chapter.**

The earthquake is a form of energy of wave motion transmitted through the surface layer of the Earth. Waves move outward in widening circles from a point of sudden energy release, called the *focus*. Like ripples produced when a pebble is thrown into a quiet pond, these seismic waves gradually lose energy as they travel outward in all directions. (The term *seismic* means "pertaining to earthquakes.")

Most earthquakes are produced by sudden slip movements along faults. They occur when rock on both sides of the fault is slowly bent over many years by tectonic forces. Energy accumulates in the bent rock, just as it does in a bent archer's bow. When a critical point is reached, the strain is relieved by slippage on the fault, and the rocks on opposite sides of the fault move in different directions. A large quantity of energy is instantaneously released in the form of seismic waves, which shake the ground. In the case of a transcurrent fault, on which movement is in a horizontal direction, slow bending of the rock that precedes the shock takes place over many decades. Sometimes a slow, steady displacement known as *fault creep* occurs, which tends to reduce the accumulation of stored energy.

The devastating San Francisco earthquake of 1906 resulted from slippage along the San Andreas fault, which is dominantly a transcurrent fault. This fault also passes about

---

An earthquake is a wave motion transmitted through the surface layer of the Earth. It is usually produced by sudden slippage on a fault.

The Richter scale is used to measure the energy released by earthquakes. It ranges from 0 to 9 or more. Earthquakes in populous regions measuring 7 or greater on the Richter scale are usually associated with major damage and loss of life.

---

60 km (about 40 mi) inland of Los Angeles, placing the densely populated metropolitan Los Angeles region in great jeopardy. Associated with the San Andreas fault are several important parallel and branching transcurrent faults, all of which are capable of generating severe earthquakes.

Earthquakes can also be produced by volcanic activity, as when magma rises or recedes within a volcanic chamber.

A scale of earthquake magnitudes was devised in 1935 by the distinguished seismologist Charles F. Richter. Now called the *Richter scale* it describes the quantity of energy released by a single earthquake. Scale numbers range from 0 to 9, but there is really no upper limit other than nature's own energy release limit. For each whole unit of increase (say, from 5.0 to 6.0), the quantity of energy released increases by a factor of 32. A value of 9.5 is the largest observed to date—the Chilean earthquake of 1960. The great San Francisco earthquake of 1906 is now rated as magnitude 7.9. Table 13.1 and Figure 13.22 show how the Richter scale relates to the energy released by earthquakes.

GEODISCOVERIES **The Impact of Earthquakes.** The Hebgen Lake disaster is an example of the awesome power of earthquakes. Tour the disaster site in this video to see how the earthquake triggered a landslide that dammed the Madison River canyon, forming an instant lake.

13.21 Earthquake devastation *This building did not survive the Mexico City earthquake of September 1985.*

Table 13.1 | Richter Magnitude and Energy Release

Magnitude, Richter Scale*	Energy Release (joules)	Comment
2.0	6×10^7	Smallest quake normally detected by humans.
2.5–3.0	10^8–10^9	Quake can be felt if it is nearby. About 100,000 shallow quakes of this magnitude per year.
4.5	4×10^{11}	Can cause local damage.
5.7	2×10^{13}	Energy released by Hiroshima atom bomb.
6.0	6×10^{13}	Destructive in a limited area. About 100 shallow quakes per year of this magnitude.
6.7	7×10^{14}	Northridge earthquake of 1994.
7.0	2×10^{15}	Rated a major earthquake above this magnitude. Quake can be recorded over whole Earth. About 14 per year this great or greater.
7.1	3×10^{15}	Loma Prieta earthquake of 1989.
8.25 (7.9)	4.5×10^{16}	San Francisco earthquake of 1906.
8.1	10^{17}	Mexican earthquake of 1986.
8.4 (9.2)	4×10^{18}	Alaskan earthquake of 1964.
8.3 (9.5)	10^{19}	Chilean earthquake of 1960, near the border of Equador.

* ( ) indicates magnitude as adjusted by Kanamori.

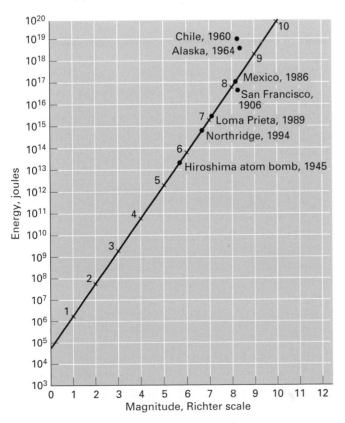

13.22 Great earthquakes on the Richter scale *This graph plots the energy released and the Richter scale rating for some great earthquakes mentioned in this chapter. Note that the energy scale is logarithmic and increases by powers of ten.*

Earthquakes and Plate Tectonics

Seismic activity—the repeated occurrence of earthquakes—occurs primarily near lithospheric plate boundaries. Figure 13.23, which shows the location of all earthquake centers during a typical seven-year period, clearly reveals this pattern. The greatest intensity of seismic activity is found along converging plate boundaries where oceanic plates are undergoing subduction. Strong pressures build up at the downward-slanting contact of the two plates, and these are relieved by sudden fault slippages that generate earthquakes of large magnitude. This mechanism explains the great earthquakes experienced in Japan, Alaska, Central America, Chile, and other narrow zones close to trenches and volcanic arcs of the Pacific Ocean Basin.

Good examples can be cited from the Pacific coast of Mexico and Central America, where the subduction boundary of the Cocos plate lies close to the shoreline. The great earthquake that devastated Mexico City in 1986 was centered in the deep trench offshore. Two great shocks in close succession, the first of magnitude 8.1 and the second of 7.5, damaged cities along the coasts of the Mexican states of Michocoan and Guerrero. Although Mexico City lies inland about 300 km (about 185 mi) distant from the earthquake epicenters, it experienced intense ground shaking of underlying saturated clay formations, with the resulting death toll of some 10,000 persons (Figure 13.21).

Transcurrent faults on transform boundaries that cut through the continental lithosphere are also sites of intense seismic activity, with moderate to strong earthquakes. The most familiar example is the San Andreas fault, discussed in a following section.

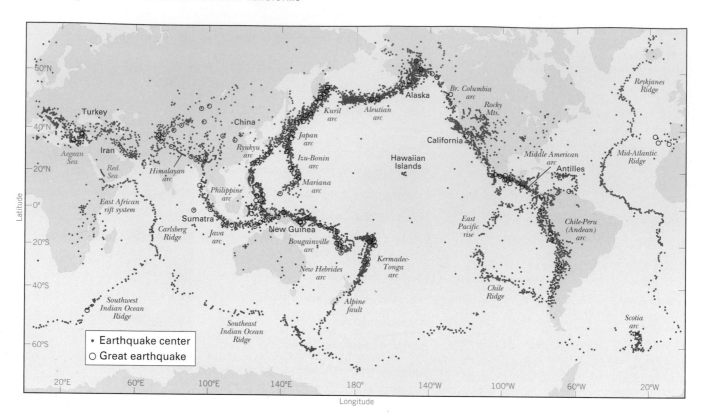

13.23 Earthquake locations *This world map plots earthquake center locations and centers of great earthquakes. Center locations of all earthquakes originating at depths of 0 to 100 km (62 mi) during a six-year period are shown by red dots. Each dot represents a single location or a cluster of centers. Black circles identify centers of earthquakes of Richter magnitude 8.0 or greater during an 80-year period. The map clearly shows the pattern of earthquakes occurring at subduction boundaries. (Compiled by A. N. Strahler from data of U.S. government. Copyright @ A. N. Strahler.)*

Another transcurrent fault often in the news is the North Anatolian Fault in Turkey, where the Persian subplate is moving westward at its boundary with the European plate. The year 1999 saw a major earthquake there on August 17, centered near the city of Izmit, which measured 7.4 on the Richter scale and killed more than 15,000. A few months later, a quake of magnitude 7.2 occurred not far away on the same fault, killing hundreds more. Central and southeast Turkey shook again on related faults in 2002 and 2003, with death tolls in the hundreds.

Spreading boundaries are the locations of a third class of narrow zones of seismic activity related to lithospheric plates. Most of these boundaries are identified with the midoceanic ridge and its branches. For the most part, earthquakes in this class are limited to moderate intensities.

Earthquakes also occur at scattered locations over the continental plates, far from active plate boundaries. In many cases, no active fault is visible, and the geologic cause of the earthquake is uncertain. For example, the great New Madrid earthquake of 1811 was cen-

tered in the Mississippi River floodplain in Missouri. It produced three great shocks in close succession, rated from 8.1 to 8.3 on the Richter scale. In southeastern Canada, significant earthquakes occur from time to time in southern Quebec and along the St. Lawrence River valley. The most recent of these is the Saguenay earthquake of 1988, which rated 5.9 on the Richter scale.

Seismic Sea Waves

An important environmental hazard often associated with a major earthquake centered on a subduction plate boundary is the *seismic sea wave,* or **tsunami,** as it is known to the Japanese. A train of these water waves is often generated in the ocean by a sudden movement of the sea floor at a point near the earthquake source. The waves travel over the ocean in ever-widening circles, but they are not perceptible at sea in deep water. Seismic sea waves are sometimes referred to as "tidal waves," but since they have nothing to do with tides, the name is quite misleading.

> **Earthquakes are frequent at spreading and converging boundaries of lithospheric plates. Transcurrent faults on transform boundaries are also sites of earthquake occurrence.**

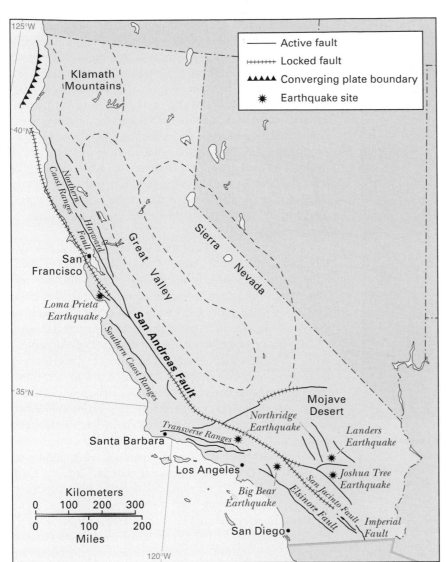

13.24 San Andreas fault system in California *A sketch map of the San Andreas fault and Transverse Ranges showing the locked sections of the fault alternating with active sections. (Based on data of the U.S. Geological Survey.)*

When a tsunami arrives at a distant coastline, the effect is to cause a temporary and rapid rise of sea level. Ocean waters rush landward and surge far inland, destroying coastal structures and killing inhabitants. After some minutes, the waters retreat, continuing the devastation. Several surging waves may occur, one after the other. The most damaging tsunami thus far recorded struck the Indian Ocean region in December of 2004 following a massive undersea earthquake in the Java Trench, west of Sumatra. *Eye on the Environment 13.3 • The Indian Ocean Tsunami of 2004,* at the close of this chapter, provides more details.

Earthquakes along the San Andreas Fault

Almost a hundred years have passed since the great San Francisco earthquake of 1906 was generated by movement on the San Andreas fault. The maximum horizontal displacement of

The San Andreas fault and related faults in southern and central California are potential sources of great earthquakes occurring in densely populated regions. The Loma Prieta, Landers, San Fernando, Whittier Narrows, and Northridge earthquakes are recent examples.

the ground was about 6 m (20 ft). Since then, this sector of the fault has been locked—that is, the rocks on the two sides of the fault have been held together without sudden slippage (Figure 13.24). In the meantime, the two lithospheric plates that meet along the fault have been moving steadily with respect to one another. This means that a huge amount of unrelieved strain energy has already accumulated in the crustal rock on either side of the fault.

On October 17, 1989, the San Francisco Bay area was severely jolted by an earthquake with a Richter magnitude of 7.1. The earthquake's epicenter was located near Loma Prieta peak, about 80 km (50 mi) southeast of San Francisco, at a point only 12 km (7 mi) from the city of Santa Cruz, on Monterey Bay. The city of Santa Cruz suffered severe structural damage to older buildings. In the distant San Francisco Bay area, destructive ground shaking proved surprisingly severe. Buildings, bridges, and

13.25 Earthquake damage in Oakland, California
This section of the double-decked Nimitz Freeway (Interstate 880) in Oakland, California, collapsed during the Loma Prieta earthquake, crushing at least 39 people in their cars.

viaducts on landfills were particularly hard hit (Figure 13.25). Altogether, 62 lives were lost in this earthquake, and the damage was estimated to be about $6 billion. In comparison, the 1906 earthquake took a toll of 700 lives and property damage equivalent to about 30 billion present-day dollars.

The displacement that caused the Loma Prieta earthquake occurred deep beneath the surface not far from the San Andreas fault, which has not slipped since the great San Francisco earthquake of 1906. The slippage on the Loma Prieta fault amounted to about 1.8 m (6 ft) horizontally and 1.2 m (4 ft) vertically, but did not break the ground surface above it. Geologists state that the Loma Prieta slippage, though near the San Andreas fault, probably has not relieved more than a small portion of the strain on the San Andreas. While the occurrence of another major earthquake in the San Francisco region cannot be predicted with precision, it is inevitable. As each decade passes, the probability of that event becomes greater.

We may need only to look to Japan for a scenario of what the citizens of the San Francisco Bay area could experience when a branch of the San Andreas fault lets go. The Hyogo-ken Nanbu earthquake that devastated the city of Kobe in January of 1995 (Figure 13.26) occurred on a short side branch of a major transcurrent fault quite similar tectonically to the San Andreas. A similar side branch of the main San Andreas fault, called the Hayward fault, runs through the East Bay region of San Francisco. Seismologists estimate that a slip on the Hayward fault would generate a quake of magnitude 7.0—about the same as the Kobe quake—and has a 28 percent probability of occurring by the year 2018. Although the nation of Japan prides itself on its earthquake preparedness, the Kobe catastrophe left 5000 dead and 300,000 homeless, and did property damage estimated at 10 times that of the Northridge earthquake of 1994, which was the most costly earthquake in American history.

Along the southern California portion of the San Andreas fault, a recent estimate placed at about 50 percent the likelihood that a very large earthquake will occur within the next 30 years. In 1992 three severe earthquakes occurred in close succession along active local faults a short distance north of the San Andreas fault in the southern Mojave desert (Figure 13.24). The second of these, the Landers earthquake, a powerful 7.5 on the Richter scale, occurred on a transcurrent fault trending north-northwest. It caused a 80-km (50-mi) rupture across the desert landscape. These three events have led to speculation that the likelihood of a major slip on the nearby San Andreas fault in the near future has substantially increased.

For residents of the Los Angeles area, an additional serious threat lies in the large number of active faults close at hand. Movements on these local faults have produced more than 40 damaging earthquakes since 1800, including the Long Beach earthquakes of the 1930s and the San Fernando earthquake of 1971. The San Fernando earthquake measured 6.6 on the Richter scale and produced severe structural damage near the earthquake center. In 1987 an earthquake of magnitude 6.1 struck the vicinity of Pasadena and Whittier, located within about 20 km (12 mi) of downtown Los Angeles. Known as the Whittier Narrows earthquake, it was generated along a local fault system that had not previously shown significant seismic activity. The Northridge earthquake of 1994, at 6.7 on the Richter scale, produced the strongest ground motions ever recorded in an urban setting in North America and the greatest financial losses from an earthquake in the United States since the San Francisco earthquake of 1906. Sections of three freeways were closed, including the busiest highway in the country, I-5.

A slip along the San Andreas fault, some 50 km (31 mi) to the north of the densely populated region of Los Angeles, will release an enormously larger quantity of energy than local earthquakes, such as the Northridge or San Fernando earthquakes. On the other hand, the destructive effects of a San Andreas earthquake in downtown Los Angeles will be somewhat moderated by the greater travel distance. Although the intensity of ground shaking might not be much different from that of the San Fernando earthquake, for

13.26 Kobe earthquake *This area within the city of Kobe, Japan, was reduced to rubble by the earthquake of January 1995 and the fires that followed in its aftermath.*

example, it will last much longer and cover a much wider area of the Los Angeles region. The potential for damage and loss of life is enormous.

GEODISCOVERIES **Web Quiz.** Take a quick quiz on the key concepts of this chapter.

A LOOK AHEAD In the last three chapters, we have surveyed the composition, structure, geologic activity, and initial landforms of the Earth's crust. We began with a study of the rocks and minerals that make up the Earth's crust and core. We saw how the cycle of rock transformation involves a continuous cycling and recycling of rocks and minerals that has occurred over some 3 billion years or more of geologic time. In the second chapter, we developed plate tectonics as the mechanism powering the rock cycle. The global pattern of plate tectonics also explains the geographical pattern of mountain ranges, ocean basins, and continental shields occurring on the Earth's surface. In this

chapter, we described the initial landforms that result directly from endogenic volcanic and tectonic activity, occurring primarily at the boundaries of spreading or colliding lithospheric plates.

With this survey of the Earth's crust and the geologic processes that shape it now completed, we can turn to exogenic landform-creating processes in the following chapters. First will be the processes of weathering, which breaks rock into small particles, and mass wasting, which moves them downhill as large and small masses under the influence of gravity. Then we will turn to running water in three chapters that describe the behavior of rivers and streams, their work in shaping landforms, and how running water dissects rock layers to reveal their inner structures. In our two concluding chapters, we will examine landforms created by waves, wind, and glacial ice.

GEODISCOVERIES **Web Links.** Tour volcanoes, from Vesuvius to Kilauea, at this chapter's web links. Spot new earthquakes and find out more about earthquake and tsunami hazards.

The Indian Ocean Tsunami of 2004

It was 7:59 AM local time on a Sunday morning, December 26, 2004, when the great undersea earthquake struck. Centered about 85 km (50 mi) off the west coast of northern Sumatra—the western-most of Indonesia's three major islands—its magnitude registered 9.0 on the Richter scale. It was the fourth largest earthquake since 1900 and the largest since the Alaskan earthquake of 1964. In Banda Aceh, a provincial capital about 230 km (140 mi) north of the epicenter, buildings toppled as residents ran into the streets. Hundreds died in the rubble. But it wasn't more than a few minutes before a giant tsunami washed over the city (see photos at right), killing thousands. As the wave moved down the Sumatran coastline, it killed many more, ultimately yielding an Indonesian death toll in excess of 166,000.

The earthquake arose in the Java Trench, a subduction zone where the Australia tectonic plate plunges beneath the Eurasia plate. About 1000 km (600 mi) of fault ruptured, causing the sea floor nearby to move upward about 5 m (16 ft). It was this rapid motion of a vast area of ocean bottom that generated the tsunami.

Undersea earthquakes and their tsunamis are no strangers to this subduction boundary. In fact, Indonesia had seen more than 50,000 deaths in 30 tsunamis of recorded history prior to the great calamity of 2004. Most notable were the tsunamis generated by the eruptions and final explosion of the Krakatau volcano on August 26, 1883, which produced waves reaching heights of nearly 40 m (130 ft) above sea level and killed at least 36,000 people.

In deep ocean waters, a tsunami takes the form of a gentle rise and fall of the ocean surface of a meter or less during a period of several minutes to an hour or more. This motion is normally unnoticed by ships, making tsunamis hard to detect in the open ocean. Tsunamis move much more rapidly than wind waves, reaching velocities of 200 m/s (440 mi/hr) in deep water (4 km, 2.5 mi). As the wave approaches land, however, it "feels the bottom" and slows, causing the wave to steepen and shorten. It approaches with a steep breaking front, but then keeps coming. It acts like a temporary change of sea level, and ocean water flows inland at speeds of up to 15 m/s (34 mi/hr) for several minutes. Considering that each cubic meter of water weighs about 1000 kg (65 lb/ft³), the power of the water surge is enormous. Trees are broken off at the roots, buildings are smashed, and cars become battering rams impelled by the force of the moving water. As the wave retreats, even more debris is carried seaward, doing still more damage. The height and force of a tsunami can vary from location to location. Undersea topography can funnel the wave into a bay, accentuating its height and focusing its energy. Often multiple waves occur, with two or three large inundations several minutes apart. The tsunami can start either as a surge of water or as a dramatic but puzzling retreat of the ocean lasting several minutes.

Although the effects of the tsunami were felt most directly and immediately along the Sumatran coast, it wasn't long before the giant wave began attacking other coastlines. The west coast of the Indochina peninsula, including Thailand and Myanmar, was one of the first regions beyond Indonesia to feel its effects. Thai beach resorts were packed with holiday vacationers and casualties were heavy, especially on the resort island of Phuket. The Thai death toll exceeded 5000. The expanding wave, now traveling for two hours, then hit the eastern coast of Sri Lanka, devastating the entire coastal strip and killing at least 30,000 more. Soon after, India experienced the wave's wrath, reporting about 4000 dead in coastal cities and towns from Calcutta to Kerala. About 6000 more deaths were recorded on the low islands of the Bay of Bengal.

It took three hours for the tsunami to reach the Maldives, a nation of low coral islands southwest of India, where about 100 lives were lost. After about six hours of travel time, the wave struck the coast of Africa. Damage was not as severe as in Asia, but deaths were still recorded in Somalia, Kenya, and Tanzania. The wave was so powerful that it was still detectable with tide gages as much as 36 hours later on reaching the Atlantic coasts of eastern North America and the Pacific islands of far eastern Russia.

Although no warning network was in place in the Indian Ocean to alert nations and their citizens of the impending disaster, one of the first efforts following the catastrophe was to start building such a network. With luck, the next great earthquake in the Java Trench will find the world better prepared for its aftermath—another giant, deadly tsunami.

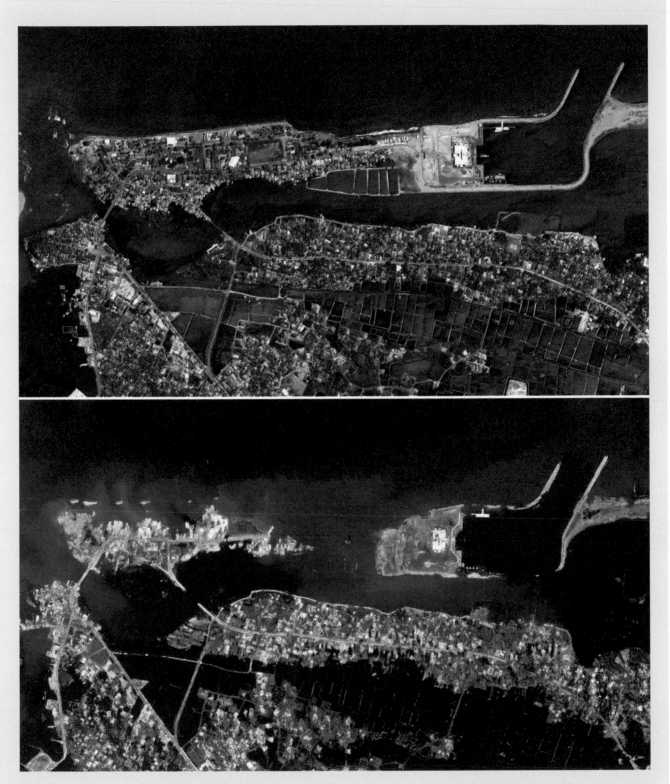

These two satellite images show a portion of the city of Banda Aceh on June 23 and December 28, 2004. The devastation caused by the earthquake and tsunami is complete.

In Review | Volcanic and Tectonic Landforms

- **Landforms** are the surface features of the land, and **geomorphology** is the scientific study of landforms. **Endogenic processes** of volcanic and tectonic activity shape *initial landforms*, while **exogenic processes** of denudation, such as erosion and deposition by running water, waves, wind, and glacial ice, sculpt *sequential landforms*.

- **Volcanoes** are landforms marking the eruption of lava at the Earth's surface. **Stratovolcanoes,** formed by the emission of thick, gassy, felsic lavas, have steep slopes and tend toward explosive eruptions that can form *calderas*. Most active stratovolcanoes lie along the Pacific rim, where subduction of oceanic lithospheric plates is occurring.

- At *hotspots,* rising mantle material provides mafic magma that erupts as basaltic lavas. Because these lavas are more fluid and contain little gas, they form broadly rounded **shield volcanoes.** Hotspots occurring beneath continental crust can also provide vast areas of *flood basalts*. Some basaltic volcanoes occur along the midoceanic ridge.

- The two forms of tectonic activity are compression and extension. Compression occurs at lithospheric plate collisions. At first, the compression produces **folding**—anticlines (upfolds) and synclines (downfolds). If compression continues, folds may be overturned and eventually overthrust faulting can occur.

- Extension occurs where lithospheric plates are spreading apart, generating **normal faults.** These can produce upthrown and downdropped blocks that are sometimes as large as mountain ranges or *rift valleys*. **Transcurrent faults** occur where two rock masses move horizontally past each other.

- **Earthquakes** occur when rock layers, bent by tectonic activity, suddenly fracture and move. The sudden motion at the fault produces earthquake waves that shake and move the ground surface in the adjacent region. The energy released by an earthquake is measured by the *Richter scale.* Large earthquakes occurring near developed areas can cause great damage. Most severe earthquakes occur near plate collision boundaries.

- The San Andreas fault is a major transcurrent fault located near two great urban areas—Los Angeles and San Francisco. The potential for a severe earthquake on this fault is high, and the probability of a major Earth movement increases every year.

Key Terms

landforms, p. 452
geomorphology, p. 452
endogenic processes, p. 452

exogenic processes, p. 452
denudation, p. 452
volcano, p. 453

stratovolcano, p. 456
shield volcano, p. 456
folding, p. 463
fault, p. 463

normal fault, p. 466
transcurrent fault, p. 467
earthquake, p. 469
tsunami, p. 472

Review Questions

1. Distinguish between initial and sequential landforms. How do they represent the balance of power between endogenic and exogenic processes?

2. What is a stratovolcano? What is its characteristic shape, and why does that shape occur? Where do stratovolcanoes generally occur and why?

3. What is a shield volcano? How is it distinguished from a stratovolcano? Where are shield volcanoes found, and why? Give an example of a shield volcano. How are flood basalts related to shield volcanoes?

4. Describe the stages in the life cycle of a basaltic shield volcano of the Hawaiian type.

5. What is a hotspot? What produces it? How is it related to the life cycle?

6. How can volcanic eruptions become natural disasters? Be specific about the types of volcanic events that can devastate habitations and extinguish nearby populations.

7. Briefly describe the Rift Valley system of East Africa as an example of normal faulting.

8. How does a transcurrent fault differ from a normal fault? What landforms are expected along a transcurrent fault? How are transcurrent faults related to plate tectonic movements?

9. What is an earthquake, and how does it arise? How are the locations of earthquakes related to plate tectonics?

10. Describe the tsunami, including its origin and effects.

11. Briefly summarize the geography and recent history of the San Andreas fault system in California. What are the prospects for future earthquakes along the San Andreas fault?

Eye on the Environment 13.1 • Geothermal Energy Sources

1. What is the ultimate source of geothermal power? Where would you go, and why, to find a geothermal power source?

2. How is geothermal energy extracted? What environmental concerns arise in this process?

Eye on the Environment 13.3 ● The Indian Ocean Tsunami of 2004

1. What was the plate tectonic setting of the Java Trench earthquake of December 26, 2004?

2. Describe how a tsunami travels in deep ocean and what happens when it arrives at a coastline.

Visualizing Exercises

1. Sketch a cross section through a normal fault, labeling the fault plane, upthrown side, downthrown side, and fault scarp.

2. Sketch a cross section through a foreland fold belt showing rock layers in different colors or patterns. Label anticlines and synclines.

Essay Questions

1. Write a fictional news account of a volcanic eruption. Select a type of volcano—composite or shield—and a plausible location. Describe the eruption and its effects as it was witnessed by observers. Make up any details you need, but be sure they are scientifically correct.

2. How are mountains formed? Provide the setting for mountain formation by plate tectonics, and then describe now specific types of mountain landforms arise.

Eye on the Landscape

Chapter Opener Diamond Head and Waikiki Beach Diamond Head **(A)** is a peak on the rim of a crater **(B)** of a now-extinct volcano. Erosion of the volcano's slopes has revealed the traces of gently sloping individual lava flows that once built the volcano **(C)**. Coral reef **(D)** is visible in near-shore waters as a collection of dark masses marked by breaking waves. Volcanoes are one of the main subjects of this chapter, while coral reef coasts are examined in Chapter 18.

13.8 Flood basalts The Columbia River and its tributaries drain a large mountainous area reaching as far east as the Bitterroot Mountains of Idaho and as far north as Jasper National Park in Alberta. The river has been extensively developed for hydropower generation with the building of many large dams. Here we see the still waters **(A)** of a reservoir and a narrow lake shore **(B)** at the water's edge. Note also the sparse vegetation **(C)** characteristic of this location in the rain shadow of the Cascades. Lakes and dams are discussed in Chapters 15 and 16. Rain shadow effects on precipitation were covered in Chapter 4.

13.20 Ethopian Rift Valley The local agriculture exploits the stepped landscape at the edge of the Rift Valley with cultivated fields **(A)** laid out on the flat tops of terraces. Given the mix of fallow and still-green fields, this photo is probably from the end of the growing season. Note also the flat faces of the slopes on the fault scarps between gullies **(B)**. These are likely to be remnants of the original planes of motion, given the recent geologic age of the Rift Valley. Chapter 9 shows the natural vegetation of the Ethiopean highlands as rainforest; precipitation is over 100 cm (40 in.) per year (Chapter 7). Fault planes and scarps are covered in this chapter.

These debris avalanches descended on the town of San Ricardo, Leyte Province, Philippines, in December of 2003, following six days of intense rainfall.

14 | WEATHERING AND MASS WASTING

PUTTING YOU IN THE PICTURE

The pull of gravity is relentless and unforgiving. It acts to move all things closer to the Earth's center, and for objects on the Earth's surface, that generally means downhill. If you are a skier, you may be grateful for that downhill pull (providing the ski lift is working to handle the uphill part of skiing). As a hiker, the downhill force makes the trek home from the summit a lot easier (if your knees and leg muscles are in good shape). But if you are an inhabitant of a peaceful valley below a steep mountain slope that suddenly gives way, you may not be so grateful for the force that has buried your home under tons of rocky debris.

Landslide, earthflow, mudflow, soil creep—these words describe the different ways that Earth materials move downhill under the force of gravity. Sometimes the materials move very quickly, other times very slowly. Perhaps you've walked the sidewalks of a town or city built on a steep slope and seen retaining walls leaning over or even toppled by the slow downhill creep of soil. While annoying and expensive for a homeowner, a failing retaining wall is not likely to result in death or destruction. But a landslide, earthflow, or mudflow can easily take lives and destroy property.

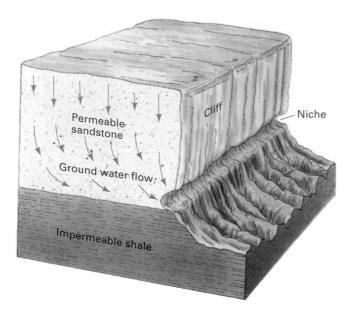

14.6 **Niche formation** *In dry climates there is a slow seepage of water from the cliff base. Salt-crystal growth separates the grains of permeable sandstone, breaking them loose and creating a niche.*

14.7 **The White House Ruin** *A former habitation of Native Americans occupies a large niche in sandstone in the lower wall of Canyon de Chelly, Arizona.*

way were occupied by Native Americans. Their cliff dwellings gave them protection from the elements and safety from armed attack (Figure 14.7).

Salt crystallization also damages masonry buildings, as well as concrete sidewalks and streets. Brick and concrete in contact with moist soil are highly susceptible to grain-by-grain disintegration from salt crystallization. On damp basement floors and walls, the salt crystals can be seen as a soft, white, fibrous layer. The deicing salts spread on streets and highways can be quite destructive. Sodium chloride (rock salt), widely used for this purpose, is particularly damaging to concrete pavements and walks, curb-stones, and other exposed masonry structures.

Salt-crystal growth occurs naturally in arid and semiarid regions. In humid climates, abundant rainfall dissolves salts and carries them downward to ground water. (Chapter 15 describes how rainwater infiltrates soils and moves to ground water below).

> In arid climates, slow evaporation of ground water from outcropping sandstone surfaces causes the growth of salt crystals. Crystal growth breaks the rock apart grain by grain, producing niches, shallow caves, and rock arches.

Unloading

A widespread process of rock disruption related to physical weathering results from *unloading,* a process that relieves the confining pressure on underlying rock. *Exfoliation* is another term used for unloading. Unloading occurs as rock is brought near the surface by erosion of overlying layers. Rock formed at great depth beneath the Earth's surface (particularly igneous and metamorphic rock) is in a slightly compressed state because of the confining pressure of overlying rock. As the rock above is slowly worn away, the pressure is reduced, and the rock expands slightly in volume.

This causes the rock to crack in layers that are more or less parallel to the surface, creating a type of jointing called *sheeting structure.* In massive rocks like granite or marble, thick curved layers or shells of rock break free in succession from the parent mass below, much as you might peel the layers of an onion.

Where sheeting structure has formed over the top of a single large knob or hill of massive rock, an *exfoliation dome* is produced (Figure 14.8). Domes are among the largest of the landforms shaped primarily by weathering. In Yosemite Valley, California, where domes are spectacularly displayed, the individual rock sheets may be as thick as 15 m (50 ft).

Other Physical Weathering Processes

Most rock-forming minerals expand when heated and contract when cooled. Where rock surfaces are exposed daily to the intense heating of the Sun alternating with nightly cooling, the resulting expansion and contraction exert powerful disruptive forces on the rock. Although first-hand evidence

14.8 Exfoliation domes *The sheeting structure of these exfoliation domes is visible in the lower part of the photo, where successive shells of rock have fallen away. North Dome and Royal Arches, Yosemite National Park, California.*

is lacking, it seems likely that daily temperature changes can cause the breakup of a surface layer of rock already weakened by other agents of weathering.

Another mechanism of rock breakup is the growth of plant roots, which can wedge joint blocks apart. You have probably observed concrete sidewalk blocks uplifted and fractured by the growth of tree roots. This process is also active when roots grow between rock layers or joint blocks. Even fine rootlets in joint fractures can cause the loosening of small rock fragments and grains.

In chemical weathering, the minerals that make up rocks are chemically altered or dissolved. The end products are often softer and bulkier forms that are more susceptible to erosion and mass movement.

CHEMICAL WEATHERING AND ITS LANDFORMS

We investigated **chemical weathering** processes in Chapter 11 under the heading of mineral alteration. Recall that the dominant processes of chemical change affecting silicate minerals are oxidation, hydrolysis, and carbonic acid action. *Oxidation* and *hydrolysis* change the chemical structure of minerals, turning them into new minerals that are typically softer and bulkier and therefore more susceptible to erosion and mass movement. *Carbonic acid action* dissolves minerals, washing them away in runoff. Note also that chemical reactions proceed more rapidly at warmer temperatures. Thus, chemical weathering is most effective in warm, moist climates.

Hydrolysis and Oxidation

Decomposition by hydrolysis and oxidation changes the minerals of strong rock into weaker forms that are rich in clay minerals and oxides. In warm, humid climates of the equatorial, tropical, and subtropical zones, hydrolysis and oxidation over thousands of years have resulted in the decay of igneous and metamorphic rocks to depths as great as 100 m (about 300 ft). The decayed rock material is soft, clay-rich, and easily eroded. To the construction engineer, deeply weathered rock is of major concern in the building of highways, dams, or other heavy structures. Although the weathered rock is soft and easy to move, its high clay content reduces its strength, and foundations built on the weathered rock can fail under heavy loads.

In dry climates, exposed granite weathers by hydrolysis to produce many interesting boulder and pinnacle forms (Figure 14.9). Although rainfall is infrequent, water penetrates the granite along planes between crystals of quartz and feldspar. Chemical weathering of these surfaces then breaks individual crystal grains away from the main mass of rock, leaving the rounded forms shown in the photo. The grain-by-grain breakup forms a fine desert gravel consisting largely of quartz and partially decomposed feldspar crystals.

Acid Action

Chemical weathering is also produced by *acid action*, largely that of *carbonic acid*. This weak acid is formed when carbon dioxide dissolves in water. Rainwater, soil water, and stream water all normally contain dissolved carbon dioxide. Carbonic acid slowly dissolves some types of minerals. Carbonate sedimentary rocks, such as limestone and marble, are particularly susceptible to the acid action. In this process, the mineral calcium carbonate is dissolved and carried away in solution in stream water.

Carbonic acid reaction with limestone produces many interesting surface forms, mostly of small dimensions. Outcrops of limestone typically show cupping (formation of rounded cavities), rilling (formation of surface valleys), grooving, and fluting in intricate designs (Figure 14.10). In a few places, the scale of deep grooves and high wall-like rock fins reaches proportions that keep people and animals

14.9 Granular disintegration
Large joint blocks of granite are gradually rounded into smooth forms by grain-by-grain disintegration in a desert environment. Alabama Hills, Owens Valley, California.

from passing through. Carbonic acid in ground water can dissolve limestone to produce underground caverns as well as distinctive landscapes that form when underground caverns collapse. These landforms and landscapes will be described in Chapter 15.

14.10 Solution features in limestone *This outcrop of pure limestone shows grooves and cavities formed by carbonic acid action. County Clare, Ireland.*

In urban areas, air is commonly polluted by sulfur and nitrogen oxides. When these gases dissolve in rainwater, the result is acid precipitation (see Chapter 4). The acids rapidly dissolve limestone and chemically weather other types of building stones. The result can be very damaging to stone sculptures, building decorations, and tombstones (Figure 14.11).

In the wet low-latitude climates, mafic rock, particularly basaltic lava, dissolves rapidly under attack by soil acids. The effects of solution removal of basaltic lava are displayed in spectacular grooves, fins, and spires on the walls of deep alcoves in part of the Hawaiian Islands (Figure 14.12). The landforms produced are quite similar to those formed by carbonic acid action on massive limestones in the moist climates of the midlatitudes.

MASS WASTING

With our discussion of weathering, we have described an array of processes that act to alter rock chemically and break up rock into fragments. These rock fragments are subjected to gravity, running water, waves, wind, and the flow of glacial ice in landform-making processes. In the remainder of this chapter, we consider the first of these landform agents—gravity. We will return to the others in the following chapters.

Everywhere on the Earth's surface, gravity pulls continuously downward on all materials. Bedrock is usually so strong and well supported that it remains fixed in place. However, when a mountain slope becomes too steep, bedrock masses can break free and fall or slide to new positions of rest. In cases where huge masses of bedrock are involved, the result can be catastrophic to towns and villages

14.11 Chemical weathering of tombstones *These weathered tombstones are from a burying ground in Boston, Massachusetts. The marker on the left, carved in marble, has been strongly weathered, weakening the lettering. The marker on the right, made of slate, is much more resistant to erosion.*

14.12 Eye on the Landscape Solution weathering of basalt *The steep walls of many narrow coastal ravines are deeply grooved by chemical weathering of the basaltic lava on the Napali Coast, Kauai, Hawaii.* **What else would the geographer see? ... Answers at the end of the chapter.**

14.34 Stone circles *Sorted circles of gravel abound on this low, wet plain underlain by permafrost. The circles in the foreground are 3 to 4 m (10 to 13 ft) across; the gravel ridges are 20 to 30 cm (8 to 12 in.) high. Broggerhalvoya, western Spitsbergen, latitude 78° N.*

single mass, typically at an annual rate of a few millimeters. The process creates *solifluction terraces* and *solifluction lobes* that give the tundra slope a stepped appearance (Figure 14.36).

14.35 Stone stripes *This diagram shows how stone rings are often drawn out downslope into stone stripes. (Adapted from C. F. S. Sharpe, Landslides and Related Phenomena, p. 37, Figure 5. New York, Columbia Univ. Press. Used by permission of the publisher.)*

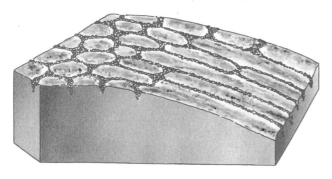

Alpine Tundra

Most of the periglacial processes and forms of the low arctic tundra are also found in the alpine tundra of high mountains at middle and high latitudes. Major regions of *alpine permafrost* in the northern hemisphere are shown on our map, Figure 14.26. In alpine tundra, there is a dominance of steep mountainsides with large exposures of hard bedrock that has been strongly abraded by glacial ice. Post-glacial talus slopes and cones formed of large angular blocks are conspicuously developed (Figure 14.4). Patterned ground and solifluction terraces occupy relatively small valley floors where slopes are low and finer sediment tends to accumulate.

Alpine permafrost is restricted to elevations at which the mean annual temperature is below freezing. The general elevation at which mean annual temperatures fall to 0°C (32°F) will, of course, be related to latitude. In subtropical latitudes, elevations of 4,000 m (about 13,000 ft) or greater are required, while at latitudes above 70° permafrost can be encountered at sea level. Figure 14.37 is a schematic graph showing the boundary between continuous and discontinuous permafrost as it varies with elevation and latitude. While the boundary at lat. 40° lies at

14.36 *Solifluction* *Solifluction has created this landscape of soil mounds in the Richardson Mountains, Northwest Territories, Canada. Bulging masses of water-saturated regolith have slowly moved downslope, lubricated by a water-rich layer of sediment at the top of the permafrost.*

14.37 Boundary between continuous and discontinuous permafrost *This graph shows how the elevation of the boundary between continuous and discontinuous alpine permafrost changes with latitude.*

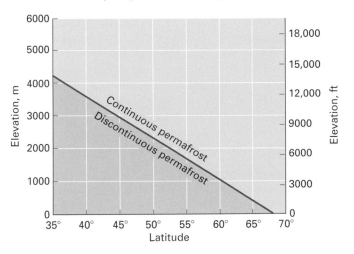

about 3500 m (about 11,500 ft), it has fallen to 2200 m (about 6600 ft) at lat. 50°, and by lat. 68° has descended to sea level.

Environmental Problems of Permafrost

Environmental degradation of permafrost regions arises from surface changes produced by human activity. One such activity is the destruction or removal of insulating surface cover that typically consists of a layer of decaying organic matter in combination with living plants of the tundra or arctic forest. When this layer is scraped off or burned away, the summer thaw is extended to a greater depth, with the result that ice lenses near the permafrost table melt and the soil sinks. The meltwater mixes with silt and clay to form mud, which is then eroded and transported by water streams, leaving trench-like morasses. This total activity is called *thermal erosion*.

Over large expanses of nearly flat arctic tundra, removal of the natural surface cover is followed by widespread subsidence of the ground and the formation of water-filled depressions. As the shallow water thaws ground ice at the edges of these depressions, they spread outward to form *thermokarst lakes.* (The word "karst," to be explained in Chapter 15, means a hummocky terrain developed by uneven solution removal of limestone bedrock.)

The consequences of disturbance of permafrost terrain became evident in World War II, when military bases, airfields, and highways were constructed hurriedly without regard for protection of permafrost. Thawing led to rapid formation of thermokarst depressions and lakes, which tilted roads and runways and swamped buildings as they cracked and settled irregularly.

Modern building practices place structures on insulated pilings with air space underneath, allowing cold winter air to maintain low soil temperatures. Water, steam, and electric lines are not buried below ground, but are carried in above-ground conduits. Roadways and runways crossing wet permafrost are built on thick pads of insulating gravel. Pipelines are carried on pilings over ice-rich permafrost and routed underground through taliks for stream crossings. Structures such as dams are carefully engineered and often designed with a frozen core that is maintained by *thermosiphons*—devices that pump heat from the ground.

Oil exploration and development, coupled with mining, pose major challenges to engineering in high arctic regions. Development of petroleum resources requires building structures, roads, and pipelines. Contaminated water is often a byproduct of drilling that is difficult to dispose of. Mining usually requires keeping large amounts of tailings in a stable condition, as well as managing the movement of large volumes of ground water when mining takes place in a talik.

Another serious engineering problem of arctic regions is the behavior of streams in winter. As the surfaces of streams and springs freeze over, the water beneath bursts out from place to place, freezing into huge accumulations of ice. If this phenomenon occurs at a highway bridge or culvert, the roadway may become impassable.

The lessons of superimposing our technology on a highly sensitive natural environment were learned the hard way—by encountering undesirable and costly effects that were not anticipated. Continued economic development of arctic regions is likely to teach additional hard lessons.

Climate Change in the Arctic

As we saw in Chapter 7 and in our interchapter feature *A Closer Look: Eye on Global Change 7.3 • Regional Impacts of Climate Change on North America*, climate warming is expected to bring warmer temperatures and increased precipitation to much of the North American arctic region. Substantial warming has already occurred, and predictions are that by the end of the present century winter temperatures will have increased by 3 to 10°C (7 to 18°F). Annual precipitation will increase by as much as 25 percent. What are the impacts of these changes on the arctic and boreal environment?

Clearing of natural surface layers can induce rapid thawing of ice masses in permafrost, leading to thermal erosion and the growth of shallow thermokarst lakes.

First, it seems certain that warming temperatures and increasing precipitation, especially in the form of snow, will deepen the active layer over broad areas of continuous permafrost. This is likely to be accompanied by extensive development of thermokarst terrain where the ice-rich upper layers of permafrost melt and subside. Roads and pipelines will be disrupted. Northward-flowing rivers will show flow reductions due to increased summer evaporation. Subsistence of native peoples will become more difficult as populations of mammals, fish, and sea birds fluctuate and the winter hunting season becomes shorter.

The boreal forest will migrate poleward, carrying along the border between continuous and discontinuous permafrost as increased snowfall warms the ground under new forest. Discontinuous permafrost will be reduced at the southern boundary and the isolated permafrost to the south will largely disappear. Warmer soil temperatures will increase the decay of soil organic matter, releasing CO_2 to further boost warming, while forest productivity declines from summer drought stress, increased disease and insect damage, and more frequent burns. In short, major changes in the arctic environment seem to be in store.

GEODISCOVERIES Web Quiz. Take a quick quiz on the key concepts of this chapter.

A LOOK AHEAD

In this chapter, we have examined the processes of weathering and mass wasting. In the weathering process, rock near the surface is broken up into smaller fragments and often altered in chemical composition. In the mass wasting process, weathered rock and soil move downhill in slow to sudden mass movements. Mass wasting acts at local and individual scales to create a pattern of landscape features that is readily visible from a roadside or hilltop vantage point. However, a regional- or continental-scale setting for these processes is provided by climate, which through temperature and precipitation affects both the nature of weathering and the mass wasting processes that will be active.

Note that the landforms of mass wasting are produced by gravity acting directly on soil and regolith. Gravity also powers another landform-producing agent—running water—which we take up in the next three chapters. The first deals with water in the hydrologic cycle, in soil, and in streams. The second deals specifically with how streams and rivers erode regolith and deposit sediment to create landforms. The third describes how stream erosion strips away rock layers of different resistance, providing large landforms that reveal underlying rock structures.

GEODISCOVERIES Web Links. Examine gravestone weathering, tour earthflows and landslides, and view the periglacial environment, all by visiting the web links for this chapter.

In Review | Weathering and Mass Wasting

- **Weathering** is the action of processes that cause rock near the surface to disintegrate and decompose into **regolith**. **Mass wasting** is the spontaneous downhill motion of soil, regolith, or rock under gravity.

- **Physical weathering** produces regolith from solid rock by breaking bedrock into pieces. *Frost action* breaks rock apart by the repeated growth and melting of ice crystals in rock fractures and *joints,* as well as between individual mineral grains. In mountainous regions of vigorous frost, fields of angular blocks accumulate as *felsenmeers.* Slopes of rock fragments form *talus cones.* In soils and sediments, needle ice and ice lenses push rock and soil fragments upward. *Salt-crystal growth* in dry climates breaks individual grains of rock free, and can damage brick and concrete. *Unloading* of the weight of overlying rock layers can cause some types of rock to expand and break loose into thick shells, producing *exfoliation domes.* Daily temperature cycles in arid environments are thought to cause rock breakup. Wedging by plant roots also forces rock masses apart.

- **Chemical weathering** results from mineral alteration. Igneous and metamorphic rocks can decay to great depths through *hydrolysis* and *oxidation,* producing a regolith that is often rich in clay minerals. *Carbonic acid* action dissolves limestone. In warm, humid environments, basaltic lavas can also show features of solution weathering produced by acid action.

- Mass wasting occurs on slopes that are mantled with regolith. **Soil creep** is a process of mass wasting in which regolith moves down slopes almost imperceptibly under the influence of gravity. In an **earthflow,** water-saturated soil or regolith slowly flows downhill. Quick clays, which are unstable and can liquefy when exposed to a shock, have produced earthflows in previously glaciated regions. A **mudflow** is much swifter than an earthflow. It follows stream courses, becoming thicker as it descends and picks up sediment. A watery mudflow with debris ranging from fine particles to boulders to tree trunks and limbs is called a *debris flow.* A **landslide** is a rapid sliding of large masses of bedrock, sometimes triggered by an earthquake.

- The **scarification** of land by human activities, such as mining of coal or ores, can heap up soil and regolith into unstable masses that produce earthflows or mudflows. Mass wasting can also be caused by removal of supporting layers, undermining the natural support of soil and regolith. These actions are termed *induced mass wasting.*

- The tundra environment is dominated by the **periglacial** *system* of distinctive landforms and processes related to freezing and thawing of water in the active layer of **permafrost.** *Continuous permafrost* and *sub-sea permafrost* occur at the highest latitudes, flanked by a band of *discontinuous permafrost* that is transitional to warmer regions. Permafrost is deepest toward the pole and under regions not covered by the ice sheets of the last Ice Age.

- Ground temperature is influenced by a number of factors besides simple mean annual air temperature. Snow insulates the ground from winter heat loss, so a thicker snow layer keeps ground temperatures warmer. Water in the soil layer tends to make ground temperatures colder. A vegetation layer will tend to reduce ground temperatures. Ground doesn't freeze under lakes or rivers, so these water bodies are underlain by *taliks*—pockets of ground with temperatures above 0°C.

- The *active layer* overlies permafrost and thaws each year during the warm season. It contains the roots of plants as well as the water and nutrients needed to support them. The active layer is thinner in colder regions and where water is more abundant.

- *Segregated ice* includes ice lenses, ice wedges, and veins of nearly pure ice. **Ice lenses** often accumulate at the base of the active layer and top of the permafrost layer. **Ice wedges** form when water fills cracks in the active layer caused by shrinkage due to extreme winter cold. Ice wedges occur in systems of *ice-wedge polygons. Pingos* are distinctive domed hills of ice that form when shallow lakes are drained and permafrost invades the water-rich talik below, creating pressure as the water freezes and expands. The pressurized water breaks through the permafrost and wells upward to freeze near the surface.

- **Patterned ground** includes circles, polygons and nets that cover large areas of tundra and are the result of *cryoturbation.*

- **Solifluction** (soil flowage) occurs in late summer, when the bottom of the active layer thaws, releasing water that lubricates downhill movement of the active layer.

- Alpine tundra shows many of the same landforms and processes of arctic tundra, but is restricted to higher elevations where mean annual ground temperatures are below freezing. The elevation at which alpine tundra begins increases toward the equator.

- Disturbance of the surface layer in permafrost terrain by human activity can induce the formation of *thermokarst.* Structures, roads, and pipelines must be constructed so as not to thaw ice-rich permafrost.

- Climate warming will thaw vast areas of permafrost, producing extensive regions of *thermokarst lakes* and subsiding terrain. The boreal forest will migrate poleward, extending discontinuous permafrost far to the north as it disappears from the south.

Key Terms

weathering, p. 482	bedrock, p. 490	landslide, p. 494	ice wedge, p. 501
regolith, p. 482	sediment, p. 490	scarification, p. 496	patterned ground, p. 502
mass wasting, p. 482	alluvium, p. 491	periglacial, p. 498	solifluction, p. 503
physical weathering, p. 483	soil creep, p. 491	permafrost, p. 499	
chemical weathering,	earthflow, p. 491	ground ice, p. 499	
p. 487	mudflow, p. 493	ice lenses, p. 501	

Review Questions

1. What is meant by the term *weathering?* What types of weathering are recognized?
2. Define the terms *regolith, bedrock, sediment,* and *alluvium.*
3. How does frost action break up rock? Describe some landforms created by frost action and how they are formed.
4. How does salt-crystal growth break up rock? Give an example of a landform that arises from salt-crystal growth.
5. What is an exfoliation dome, and how does it arise? Provide an example.
6. Name three types of chemical weathering. Describe how limestone is often altered by a chemical weathering process.
7. Define mass wasting and identify the processes it includes.
8. What is soil creep, and how does it arise?
9. What is an earthflow? What features distinguish it as a landform?
10. Contrast earthflows and mudflows, providing an example of each.
11. Define the term *landslide.* How does a landslide differ from an earthflow?
12. Define and describe induced mass wasting. Provide some examples.
13. Explain the term *scarification.* Provide an example of an activity that produces scarification.
14. What is meant by the term *periglacial?*
15. Define and describe permafrost and some of its features, including ground ice, active layer, and permafrost table.

16. Identify the zones of permafrost and describe their general location.
17. Identify the factors that affect the temperature of permafrost. Describe how and why each factor acts to create warmer or cooler ground temperatures.
18. What is a *talik?* How does the size of a talik under a lake depend on the width of the lake?
19. What is the *active layer?* Why is it important to plants? What factors influence the thickness of the active layer and how?
20. What are ice lenses? Where do they form?
21. Describe the formation of an ice wedge.
22. What is a *pingo?* How does it form?
23. Identify five major categories of patterned ground.
24. What is meant by *solifluction?* How and when does it occur?
25. Does alpine permafrost differ from arctic permafrost? How does the domain of alpine permafrost change with latitude?
26. Define *thermal erosion* and describe the formation of a thermokarst lake.
27. What techniques are used to safely build structures, roads and pipelines in permafrost terrains?
28. How will global climate warming affect boreal and arctic regions?

Eye on the Environment 14.1 ● The Great Hebgen Lake Earthquake

1. Describe the formation of Earthquake Lake. What four forms of natural environmental disaster were involved?

Visualizing Exercises

1. Define the terms *regolith, bedrock, sediment,* and *alluvium.* Sketch a cross section through a part of the landscape showing these features and label them on the sketch.
2. Copy or trace Figure 14.13; then identify and plot on the diagram the mass movement associated with each of the following locations: Turtle Mountain, Palos Verdes Hills, Nicolet, Mount St. Helens, Madison River, and Herculaneum.
3. Diagram the formation of a pingo, adding explanatory text as needed to document the process.

Essay Questions

1. A landscape includes a range of lofty mountains elevated above a dry desert plain. Describe the processes of weathering and mass wasting that might be found on this landscape and identify their location.

2. Identify and describe the unique processes of mass wasting that characterize arctic environments. Explain how permafrost plays a central role. How has human activity affected the arctic environment in the past and what impact is predicted for the future?

3. Imagine yourself as the newly appointed director of public safety and disaster planning for your state or province. One of your first jobs is to identify locations where human populations are threatened by potential disasters, including those of mass wasting. Where would you look for mass wasting hazards and why? In preparing your answer, you may want to consult maps of your state or province.

Eye on the Landscape

14.4 Talus cones Individual rock strata **(A)** are readily visible in this photo. They are ancient sedimentary rocks that were thrust over and above younger rocks of the plains during an arc-continent collision. Strong and resistant to erosion, they now form the magnificent peaks of the northern Rockies in Alberta. At **(B)** are the remains of a small glacier, coated with gray blocks of talus. Chapter 12, on plate tectonics, describes overthrust faults and arc-continent collisions. Alpine glaciers are covered in Chapter 19.

14.12 Solution weathering of basalt Kauai is the oldest of the Hawaiian Islands. Note the rounded dome shape of its outline **(A)**, which is characteristic of shield volcanoes (Chapter 13). The red-brown colors of soil, exposed on lower slopes **(B)**, are those of iron oxides and indicate Oxisols (Chapter 10). Pocket beaches and an arch at **(C)** are products of wave action (Chapter 18).

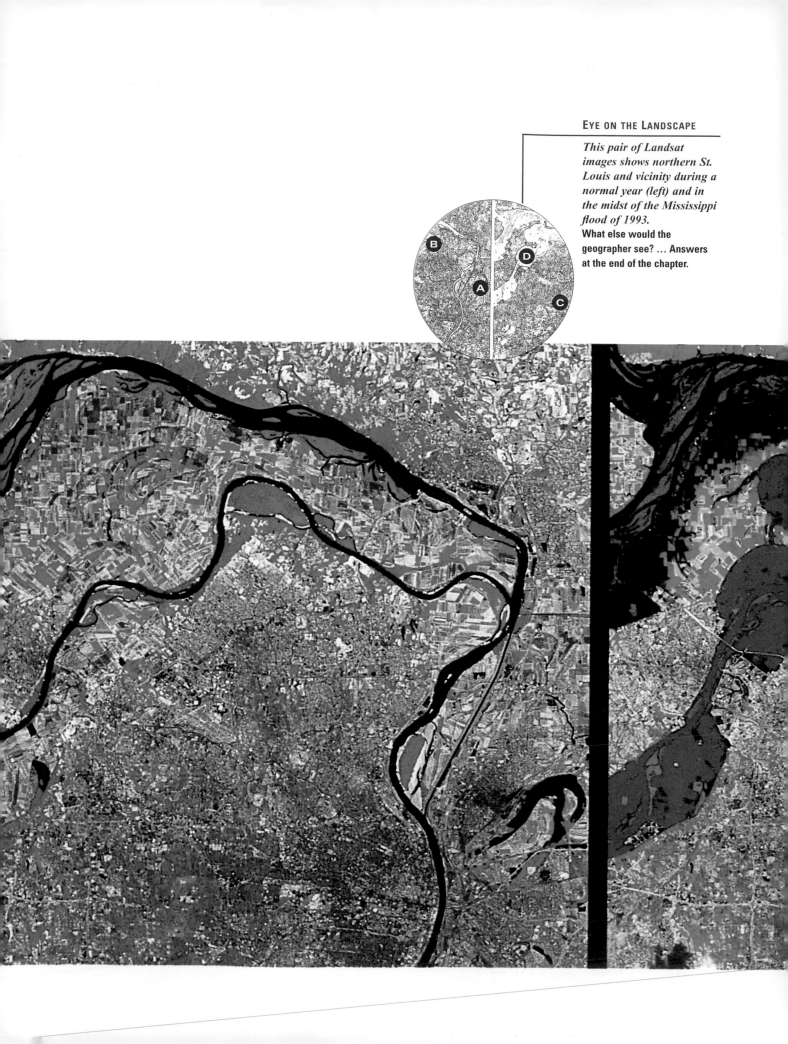

EYE ON THE LANDSCAPE

This pair of Landsat images shows northern St. Louis and vicinity during a normal year (left) and in the midst of the Mississippi flood of 1993. What else would the geographer see? … Answers at the end of the chapter.

15 | FRESH WATER OF THE CONTINENTS

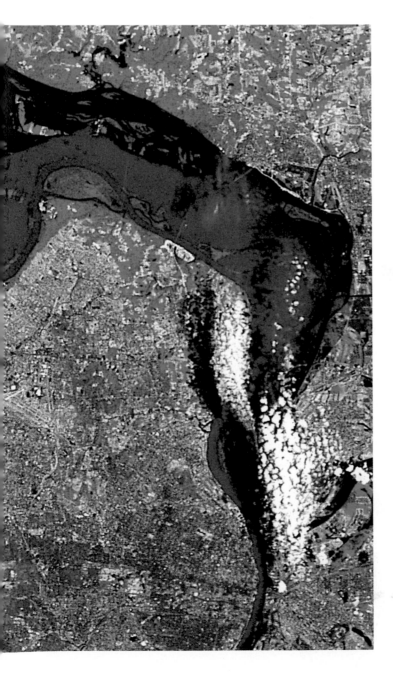

● ● ● ● ● ● ● ● ● ● ● ● ● ● ● ● ● ●
PUTTING YOU IN THE PICTURE

The violent blast cut the still night air with a force that broke windows and set off car alarms on the far side of the mile-wide river. The muddy waters of the mighty Mississippi, thrown back at first by the force of the dynamite, surged forward through a new gap in the levee just upstream from Prairie du Rocher, Illinois. Fifteen minutes later, a second thundering explosion resounded across the width of the seething river, and floodwaters spilled through another new gash.

At 3:30 that morning, August 4, 1993, the commissioners of the Fort Chartres–Ivy Landing Drainage and Levee District had approved a risky plan to dynamite two new crevasses in the levee upstream from the historic village of Prairie du Rocher. They hoped that the new breaches would skim the top off the crest of high waters approaching the main levee that had so far held the town secure from flooding. The waters from the breached levee would take hostage the fields and farms of a large area of upriver floodplain in return for sparing the village. It wasn't long before their vote was affirmed by the two blasts that echoed for miles up and down the river.

In the eyes of the commissioners, Prairie du Rocher was a prize worth saving. The town traces its roots back to its founding as a French trading post in 1722 and considers

itself to be the birthplace of Illinois. Its quaint, turn-of-the-century architecture and its reputation for bed-and-breakfast inns and fine French food made the small town famous in the region as an upscale tourist mecca.

The vote of the commissioners to dynamite the levee was against the advice of the U.S. Army Corps of Engineers, the agency charged with building and maintaining the levees, dams, reservoirs, and other flood control structures that normally keep the powerful Mississippi River shackled and controlled. The Corps's engineers were afraid that the shock wave from the blast, transmitted through the river, would damage the levee near the town, flooding the village instead of protecting it. The pressure wave might also cause the levee at the site to lose its strength, turning rapidly into a mixture of sediment and water in a process called liquefaction. The resulting break would be vast enough to send a huge

volume of water through the levee that could swamp other levees and dikes and eventually attack the town from the rear. Even without liquefaction, the flooding could be severe enough to engulf areas that would have otherwise remained dry.

On August 3, one day earlier, the Corps had created its own breach in the upstream levee, dispatching a crane shovel on a barge to remove the top 1.2 m (4 ft) of a 120-m (400 ft) section of the levee. According to plan, an area of about 50 km^2 (20 mi^2) was flooded sooner rather than later, thus helping to blunt the rapidly approaching flood crest. But the water continued to rise, relentlessly threatening the historic village and leading to the late-night meeting and vote by the district commissioners.

Fortunately, none of the catastrophes foretold by the Corps' engineers came about. Prairie du Rocher was saved from flooding, but whether the extreme measures adopted by the desperate commissioners made the difference in keeping

the floodwaters from overtopping the levees is not really known.

The summer of 1993 was a time of extreme measures all along the upper reaches of the Mississippi. In June and July, unprecedented rainfall deluged the upper Mississippi Basin, including southern Minnesota, western Wisconsin, Iowa, Illinois, and Missouri. The result was a flood of a magnitude estimated to recur only once in 500 years. Devastation was widespread, and costs of the flood control, damage, and cleanup exceeded $12 billion.

Rivers are but one part of the hydrologic cycle—the set of complex flow pathways by which water moves as vapor over the land, condenses as precipitation and falls to Earth, then runs off as surface water and sinks in as ground water. This chapter focuses on these latter parts of the hydrologic cycle because they provide the fresh water that supports not only human activities, but nearly all biological activity on land. ■

FRESH WATER OF THE CONTINENTS

Water is essential to life. Nearly all organisms require a constant flux of water or at least a water-rich environment for survival. Humans are no exception. Our activity depends on a constant supply of fresh water that is provided by precipitation over the lands. Some of this water infiltrates the land surface and is stored in soils, regolith, and pores in bedrock. An even smaller portion is in motion as flowing fresh water in streams and rivers. In this chapter, we focus on these two parts of the hydrologic cycle—water at the land surface and water that lies within the ground.

Recall from Chapter 4 that fresh water on the continents in surface and subsurface water is only a very small part—about 3 percent—of the hydrosphere's total water. Most of this fresh water is locked into ice sheets and mountain glaciers. Ground water accounts for a little more than half of 1 percent. Although this is a very small fraction of global water, it is still many times larger than the amount of fresh water in lakes, streams, and rivers, which account for only three-hundredths of 1 percent of the total water. Note also that ground water can be found at almost every location on

land that receives rainfall. In contrast, fresh surface water varies widely in abundance. In many arid regions, streams and rivers are nonexistent for most or all of the year.

Let's review the hydrologic cycle, focusing on surface and ground water. In Chapter 4, we discussed atmospheric moisture and precipitation, describing the part of the hydrologic cycle in which water evaporates from ocean and land surfaces and then precipitates, falling to Earth as rain or snow. What happens then to this precipitation? Figure 15.1 provides the answer. As the diagram shows, a portion of the precipitation returns directly to the atmosphere through evaporation from the soil. Another portion travels downward, moving through the soil under the force of gravity to become part of the underlying ground water. Following underground flow paths, this subsurface water eventually emerges to become surface water, or it may emerge directly in the shore zone of the ocean. A third portion flows over the ground surface as runoff to lower levels. As it travels, the water flow becomes collected into streams, which eventually conduct the running water to the ocean.

When precipitation reaches the ground, it either runs off or infiltrates into the soil. As runoff, it flows into streams. As infiltration, it either returns to the air through evapotranspiration or seeps downward to become ground water.

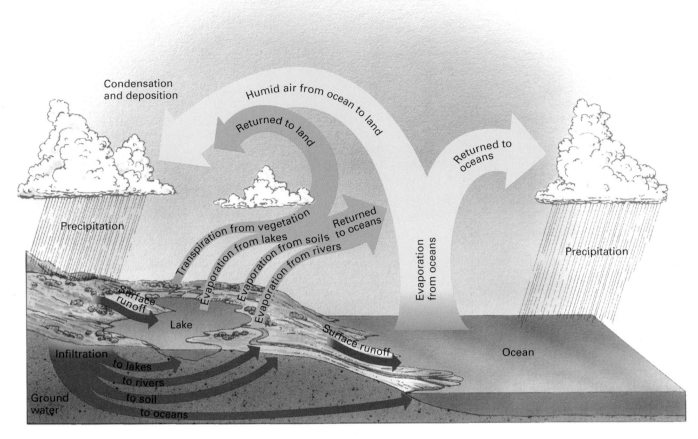

15.1   *The hydrologic cycle* *The hydrologic cycle traces the various paths of water from oceans, through the atmosphere, to land, and its return to oceans.*

In this chapter, we will trace the parts of the hydrologic cycle that include both the subsurface and surface pathways of water flow. The study of these flows is part of the science of *hydrology,* which is the study of water as a complex but unified system on the Earth.

Figure 15.2 shows what happens to water from precipitation as it first reaches the land surface. Most soil surfaces in their undisturbed, natural states are capable of absorbing the water from light or moderate rains by **infiltration.** In this process, water enters the small natural passageways between irregularly shaped soil particles, as well as the larger openings in the soil surface. These openings are formed by the borings of worms and animals, earth cracks produced by soil drying, cavities left from decay of plant roots, or spaces made by the growth and melting of frost crystals. A mat of decaying leaves and stems breaks the force of falling water drops and helps to keep these openings clear.

The precipitation that infiltrates the soil is temporarily held in the soil layer as soil water, occupying the *soil water belt* (Figure 15.2). Water within this belt can be returned to the surface and then to the atmosphere through a process

that combines two components—direct evaporation from soil and transpiration by vegetation. As we explained in Chapter 3, these two forms of water vapor transport are combined in the term *evapotranspiration.*

When rain falls too rapidly to be passed downward through soil openings, **runoff** occurs and a surface water layer runs over the surface and down the direction of ground slope. This surface runoff is called **overland flow.** In periods of heavy, prolonged rain or rapid snowmelt, overland flow feeds directly to streams.

Overland flow also occurs when soil that is already saturated receives rainfall or snowmelt. Since soil openings and pores are already filled, water cannot infiltrate the soil and drain down to deeper layers. Under these conditions, nearly all of the precipitation or snowmelt will run off.

Runoff as overland flow moves surface particles from hills to valleys, and so it is an agent that shapes landforms. Because runoff supplies water to streams and rivers, it also allows rivers to cut canyons and gorges, and carry sediment to the ocean—but we are getting ahead of our story. We'll return to landforms carved by running water in Chapter 16.

15.2 Paths of precipitation Precipitation falling on the land follows three primary paths. Some precipitation is returned to the atmosphere through evapotranspiration, while some runs off the soil surface. The remainder sinks into the soil water belt, where it is accessible to plants. A portion of the infiltrating water passes through the soil water belt and percolates down to the ground water zone. (A. H. Strahler.)

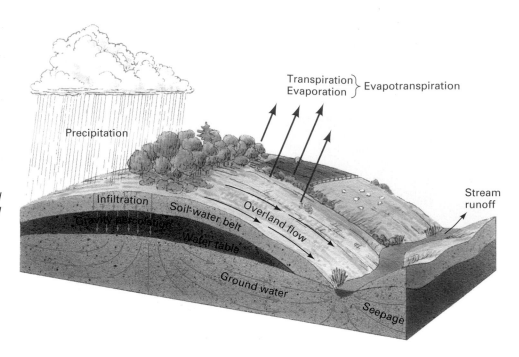

GROUND WATER

As shown in Figure 15.2, water derived from precipitation can continue to flow downward beyond the soil water belt. This slow downward flow under the influence of gravity is termed *percolation*. Eventually, the percolating water reaches ground water. **Ground water** is the part of the subsurface water that fully saturates the pore spaces in bedrock, regolith, or soil, and so occupies the *saturated zone* (Figure 15.3). The **water table** marks the top of this zone. Above it is the *unsaturated zone* in which water does not fully saturate the pores. Here, water is held in thin films adhering to mineral surfaces. This zone also includes the soil water belt.

Ground water moves slowly along deep flow paths, eventually emerging by seepage into streams, ponds, lakes, and marshes. In these places the land surface dips below the water table. Streams that flow throughout the year—perennial streams—derive much of their water from ground water seepage. As we will see on later pages, this seepage is termed *base flow*.

GEODISCOVERIES **Ground Water.** Watch an animation of the hydrologic cycle and trace the path of ground water as it infiltrates the soil, percolates to the water table, and flows to streams.

The Water Table Surface

Where there are many wells in an area, the position of the water table can be mapped in detail (Figure 15.4). This is done by plotting the water heights in the wells and noting the trend of change in elevation from one well to the other. The water table is highest under the highest areas of land sur-

15.3 Zones of subsurface water Water in the soil water belt is available to plants. Water in the unsaturated zone percolates downward to the saturated zone of ground water, where all pores and spaces are filled with water.

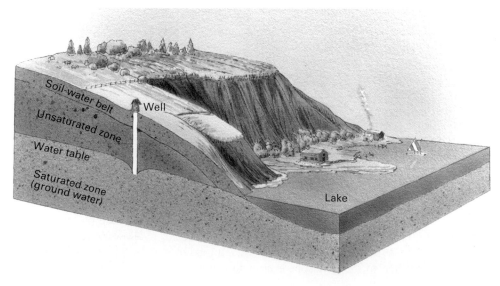

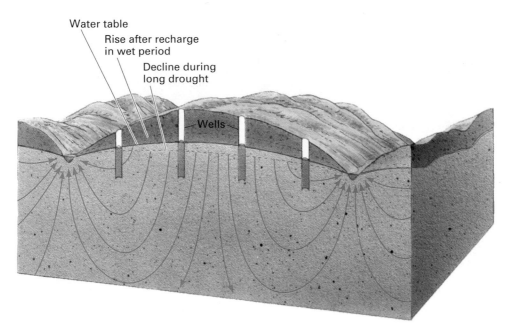

Water table
Rise after recharge
in wet period
Decline during
long drought
Wells

15.4 Water table surface
The configuration of the water table surface conforms broadly with the land surface above it. It varies in response to prolonged wet and dry periods. Ground water flow paths circulate water to deep levels in a very slow motion and eventually feed streams by seepage.

face—hilltops and divides. The water table declines in elevation toward the valleys, where it appears at the surface close to streams, lakes, or marshes.

The reason for this water table configuration is that water percolating down through the unsaturated zone tends to raise the water table, while seepage into lakes, streams, and marshes tends to draw off ground water and to lower its level. These differences in water table level are built up and maintained because ground water moves extremely slowly through the fine chinks and pores of bedrock and regolith. In periods of high precipitation, the water table rises under hilltops or divide areas. In periods of water deficit, or during a drought, the water table falls (Figure 15.4).

Figure 15.4 also shows paths of ground water flow. The direction of flow at any point depends on the direction of pressure at that point. Gravity always exerts a downward pressure, while the difference in the height of the water table between hilltop and streambed produces a sideward pressure force. In the presence of resistance to flow, the result of these downward and sideward pressures causes ground water to flow in curving paths. Water that enters the hillside midway between the hilltop and the stream flows rather directly toward the stream. Water reaching the water table midway between the two streams, however, flows almost straight down to great depths before recurving and rising upward again. Progress along these deep paths is incredibly slow, while flow near the surface is much faster. The most rapid flow is close to the stream, where the arrows converge. Over time, the level of the water table tends to remain stable, and the flow of water released to streams and lakes must balance the flow of water percolating down into the water table.

> The water table marks the top of the saturated zone of ground water. It is highest under hilltops and divides, and it slopes to intersect the surface at lakes, marshes, and streams.

Aquifers

Sedimentary layers often exert a strong control over the storage and movement of ground water. For example, clean, well-sorted sand—such as that found in beaches, dunes, or stream alluvium—can hold an amount of ground water about equal to about one-third of its bulk volume. A bed of sand or sandstone is thus often a good *aquifer*—that is, a layer of rock or sediment that contains abundant, freely flowing ground water. In contrast, beds of clay and shale are relatively impermeable and hold little free water. They are known as *aquicludes*. Figure 15.5 shows a situation in which a shale bed is overlain by a bed

15.5 Ground water in horizontal strata *Water flows freely within the sandstone aquifer but only very slowly in the shale aquiclude. A lens of shale creates a perched water table above the main water table. (Copyright © A.N. Strahler.)*

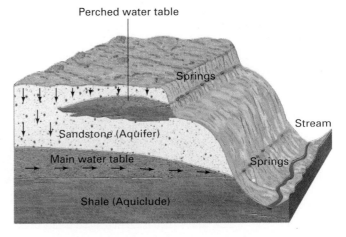

Perched water table
Springs
Sandstone (Aquifer)
Main water table
Springs
Stream
Shale (Aquiclude)

15.6 Artesian well A dipping sandstone layer interleaved between impervious layers provides a source of water under pressure that flows naturally to the surface. (Drawn by Erwin Raisz. Copyright © A.N. Strahler.)

of sandstone. Ground water moves freely through the sandstone aquifer and across the top of the shale aquiclude, emerging in springs along the canyon shown at the right. Also shown is a small lens of shale, which accumulates a shallow *perched water table* above it.

When an aquifer is situated between two aquicludes, ground water in the aquifer may be under pressure and thus flow freely from a well. This type of self-flowing well is an **artesian well.** Figure 15.6 illustrates this situation, in which a porous sandstone bed (aquifer) is sandwiched between two impervious rock layers (aquicludes). Precipitation on the hills where the sandstone outcrops provides water that saturates the sandstone layer, filling it to that elevation. Since the elevation of the well that taps the aquifer is below that of the range of hills feeding the aquifer, hydrostatic pressure causes water to rise in the well.

LIMESTONE SOLUTION BY GROUND WATER

We saw in Chapter 14 that in moist climates limestone at the surface is slowly dissolved by carbonic acid action, produc-

ing lowland areas. The slow flow of ground water in the saturated zone can also dissolve limestone below the surface, producing deep underground caverns. These features can then collapse, producing a sinking of the ground above and the development of a unique type of landscape.

Limestone Caverns

You are probably familiar with such famous caverns as Mammoth Cave or Carlsbad Caverns. *Limestone caverns* are interconnected subterranean cavities in bedrock formed by the corrosive action of circulating ground water on limestone. Figure 15.7 shows how caverns develop. As shown in the left diagram, the action of carbonic acid is particularly concentrated in the saturated zone just below the water table. This removal process forms many kinds of underground "landforms," such as tortuous tubes and tunnels, great open chambers, and tall chimneys. Subterranean streams can be found flowing in the lowermost tunnels, and these carry the products of solution to emerge along the banks of surface streams and rivers.

In a later stage, shown in the right diagram, the stream has deepened its valley, and the water table has been corre-

15.7 Cavern development Limestone dissolves at the top of the ground water zone. When rapid erosion of streams lowers the water table, caverns result in the unsaturated zone. Water flow through the caverns results in travertine deposition. (Copyright © A.N. Strahler.)

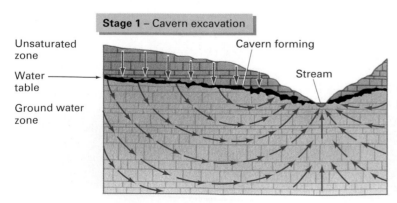

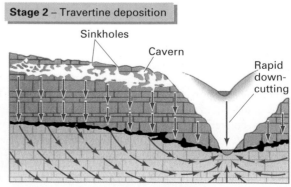

15.8 *Inside a cavern*
Travertine deposits in the Papoose Room of Carlsbad Caverns in New Mexico. Deposits include stalactites (slender rods hanging from the ceiling), stalagmites (upward pointing rods), and sturdy columns, all formed when dripping ground water evaporates, leaving travertine deposits of calcium carbonate behind.

spondingly lowered to a new position. The cavern system previously formed is now in the unsaturated zone. Deposition of carbonate matter, known as *travertine,* takes place on exposed rock surfaces in the caverns. Encrustations of travertine take many beautiful forms—stalactites (hanging rods), stalagmites (upward pointing rods), columns, and drip curtains (Figure 15.8).

Karst Landscapes

Where limestone solution is very active, we find a landscape with many unique landforms. This is especially true along the Dalmatian coastal area of Croatia, where the landscape is called *karst.* Geographers apply that term to the topography of any limestone area where sinkholes are numerous and small surface streams are nonexistent. A *sinkhole* is a surface depression in a region of cavernous limestone (Figure 15.9). Some

> Carbonic acid action dissolves limestone, producing caverns. Cavern collapse creates sinkholes and a karst landscape.

sinkholes are filled with soil washed from nearby hillsides, while others are steep-sided, deep holes. They develop where the limestone is more susceptible to solution weathering, or where an underground cavern near the surface has collapsed.

Development of a karst landscape is shown in Figure 15.10. In an early stage, funnel-like sinkholes are numerous. Later, the caverns collapse, leaving open, flat-floored valleys. Examples of some important regions of karst or karst-like topography are the Mammoth Cave region of Kentucky, the Yucatan Peninsula, and parts of Cuba and Puerto Rico. In regions such as southern China and west Malaysia, the karst landscape is dominated by steep-sided, conical limestone hills or towers, 100 to 500 m (about 300 to 1500 ft) high (Figure 15.11). The towers are sometimes capped by beds of more resistant rock or by impure limestones that dissolve more slowly. They are often riddled with caverns and passageways.

15.9 Eye on the Landscape Sinkholes *Sinkholes in limestone are created by solution. These sinkholes are near Roswell, New Mexico.* **What else would the geographer see? ... Answers at the end of the chapter.**

15.10 Evolution of a karst landscape *(a) Rainfall enters the cavern system through sinkholes in the limestone. (b) Extensive collapse of caverns reveals surface streams flowing on shale beds beneath the limestone. Some parts of the flat-floored valleys can be cultivated. (Drawn by Erwin Raisz. Copyright © A. N. Strahler.)*

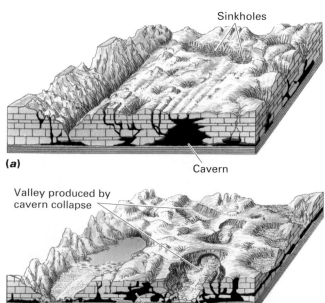

Sinkholes

(a)

Cavern

Valley produced by cavern collapse

Cavern

(b)

PROBLEMS OF GROUND WATER MANAGEMENT

Rapid withdrawal of ground water has seriously impacted the environment in many places. Increased urban populations and industrial developments require larger water supplies—needs that cannot always be met by constructing new surface water reservoirs. To fill these needs, vast numbers of wells using powerful pumps draw huge volumes of ground water to the surface, greatly altering nature's balance of ground water discharge and recharge.

In dry climates, agriculture is often heavily dependent on irrigation water from pumped wells—especially since major river systems are likely to be already fully utilized for irrigation. Wells are also convenient water sources. They can be drilled within the limits of a given agricultural or industrial property and can provide immediate supplies of water without any need to construct expensive canals or aqueducts.

In earlier times, the small well that supplied the domestic and livestock needs of a home or farmstead was actually dug by hand and sometimes lined with masonry. By contrast, a modern well supplying irrigation and industrial water is drilled by powerful machinery that can bore a hole 40 cm (16 in.) or more in diameter to depths of 300 m (about 1000 ft) or more. Drilled wells are lined with metal casings that exclude impure near-surface water and prevent the walls from caving in and clogging the tube. Near the lower end of

15.11 Eye on the Landscape Tower karst *White limestone can be seen exposed in the nearly vertical sides of these towers. Near Guilin (Kweilin), Guanxi Province, southern China at lat. 25° N.* **What else would the geographer see? ... Answers at the end of the chapter.**

the hole, in the ground water zone, the casing is perforated to admit the water. The yield of a single drilled well ranges from as low as a few hundred liters or gallons per day in a domestic well to many millions of liters or gallons per day for a large industrial or irrigation well.

Water Table Depletion

As water is pumped from a well, the level of water in the well drops. At the same time, the surrounding water table is lowered in the shape of a downward-pointing cone, termed the *cone of depression* (Figure 15.12). The difference in height between the cone tip and the original water table is the *drawdown*. The cone of depression may extend out as far as 16 km

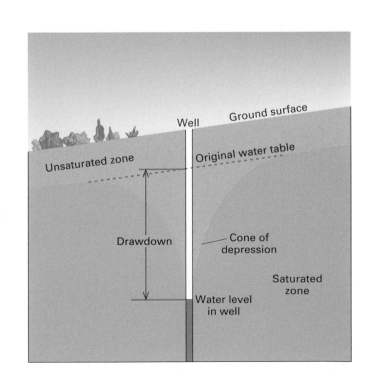

15.12 Drawdown and cone of depression in a pumped well *As the well draws water, the water table is depressed in a cone shape centered on the well. (A. H. Strahler.)*

(10 mi) or more from a well where heavy pumping is continued. Where many well are in operation, their intersecting cones will produce a general lowering of the water table.

Water table depletion often greatly exceeds recharge—the rate at which infiltrating water moves downward to the saturated zone. In arid regions, much of the ground water for irrigation is drawn from wells driven into thick aquifers of sand and gravel. These deposits are often recharged by the seasonal flow of streams that originate high in adjacent mountains. Fanning out across the dry lowlands, the streams lose water, which sinks into the sands and gravels and eventually percolates to the water table below. The extraction of ground water by pumping can greatly exceed this recharge by stream flow, lowering the water table. Deeper wells and more powerful pumps are then required. The result is exhaustion of a natural resource that is not renewable except over very long periods of time.

Another byproduct of water table depletion is subsidence—a sinking of the land in response to the removal of water from underlying sediments. This problem has plagued a number of major cities that rely heavily on ground water wells for their water supplies. *Eye on Global Change 15.1 • Sinking Cities* provides more information on this topic.

Contamination of Ground Water

Another major environmental problem related to ground water withdrawal is contamination of wells by pollutants that infiltrate the ground and reach the water table. Both solid and liquid wastes are responsible. Disposal of solid wastes poses a major environmental problem in developed countries because their advanced industrial economies provide an endless source of garbage and trash. Traditionally, these waste products were trucked to the town dump and burned there in continually smoldering fires that emitted foul smoke and gases. The partially consumed residual waste was then buried under earth.

In recent decades, a major effort has been made to improve solid-waste disposal methods. One method is high-

---

Wells draw down the water table at a point, creating a cone of depression. As many wells exploit an aquifer, their cones of depression merge to create a general lowering of the water table.

Sanitary landfills can release pollutants and toxic compounds that infiltrate to the water table, causing ground water contamination that renders adjacent well waters unfit for consumption.

---

temperature incineration, but it often leads to air pollution. Another is the sanitary landfill method in which waste is not allowed to burn. Instead, layers of waste are continually buried, usually by sand or clay available on the landfill site. The waste is thus situated in the unsaturated zone. Here it can react with rainwater that infiltrates the ground surface. This water picks up a wide variety of chemical compounds from the waste body and carries them down to the water table (Figure 15.13).

Once in the water table, the pollutants follow the flow paths of the ground water. As the arrows in the figure indicate, the polluted water may flow toward a supply well that draws in ground water from a large radius. Once the polluted water has reached the well, the water becomes unfit for human consumption. Polluted water may also move toward a nearby valley, causing pollution of the stream flowing there (left side of Figure 15.13).

Another source of contamination in coastal wells is *saltwater intrusion*. Since fresh water is less dense than saltwater, a coastal aquifer can be underlain by a layer of saltwater from the ocean. When the aquifer is depleted, the level of saltwater rises and eventually reaches the well from below, rendering the well unusable.

SURFACE WATER

So far, we have examined how water moves below the land surface. Now, we turn to tracing the flow paths of surplus water that runs off the land surface and ultimately reaches the sea. Here, we will be concerned primarily with rivers and streams. (In general usage, we speak of "rivers" as large watercourses and "streams" as smaller ones. However, the word "stream" is also used as a scientific term designating the channeled flow of surface water of any amount.)

GEODISCOVERIES **Surface Water.** Take a journey down the Rhine River through the heart of Europe, starting high in the Alps and ending at the Atlantic Coast of The Netherlands. A video.

15.13 Movement of polluted ground water
Polluted water, leached from a waste disposal site, moves toward a supply well (right) and a stream (left). (Copyright © A. N. Strahler.)

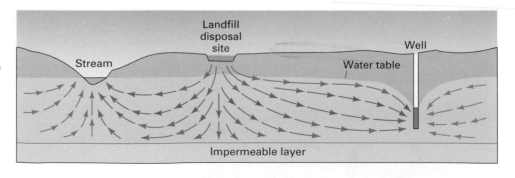

15.14 Overland flow
Following a downpour, a thin sheet of water flows across this semiarid grassland near Holbrook, Arizona.

Overland Flow and Stream Flow

As we saw earlier in this chapter, runoff that flows down the slopes of the land in broadly distributed sheets is overland flow. We can distinguish overland flow from *stream flow,* in which the water occupies a narrow channel confined by lateral banks. Overland flow can take several forms. Where the soil or rock surface is smooth, the flow may be a continuous thin film, called *sheet flow* (Figure 15.14). Where the ground is rough or pitted, flow may take the form of a series of tiny rivulets connecting one water-filled hollow with another. On a grass-covered slope, overland flow is subdivided into countless tiny threads of water, passing around the stems. Even in a heavy and prolonged rain, you might not notice overland flow in progress on a sloping lawn. On heavily forested slopes, overland flow may pass entirely concealed beneath a thick mat of decaying leaves.

Overland flow eventually contributes to a stream, which is a much deeper, more concentrated form of runoff. We can define a **stream** as a long, narrow body of flowing water occupying a trench-like depression, or channel, and moving to lower levels under the force of gravity. The **channel** of a stream is a narrow trough. The forces of flowing water shape the trough to its most effective form for moving the quantities of water and sediment supplied to the stream (Figure 15.15). A channel may be so narrow that you can easily jump across it, or, in the case of the Mississippi River, as wide as 1.5 km (about 1 mi) or more.

As a stream flows under the influence of gravity, the water encounters resistance—a form of friction—with the channel walls. As a result, water close to the bed and banks moves slowly, while water in the central part of the flow moves faster. If the channel is straight and symmetrical, the single line of maximum velocity is located in midstream. If the stream curves, the maximum velocity shifts toward the bank on the outside of the curve.

Actually, the arrows in Figure 15.15 only show average velocity. In all but the most sluggish streams, the water is

15.15 Characteristics of stream flow The velocity of flow is greatest in the middle (a) and at the top (b) of the stream. (c) Mean velocity, cross-sectional area and slope change in the pools and rapids of a stream section of uniform discharge. (b, Copyright © A. N. Strahler.)

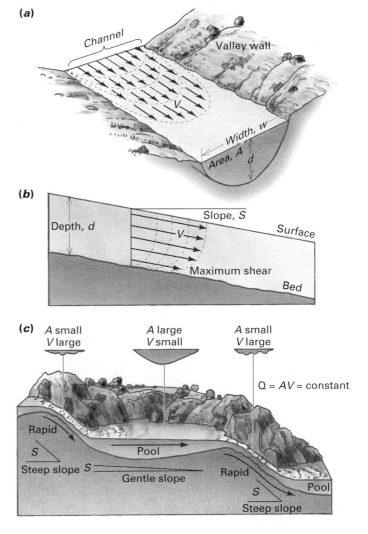

Eye on Global Change | 15.1

Sinking Cities

Ground water is a resource on which human civilization now depends to meet much of its demand for fresh water. However, it may take thousands of years to accumulate large reservoirs of underground water. When this water is removed rapidly by pumping, the rate of removal far exceeds the rate of recharge. The volume of water in the reservoir is reduced, and the water table falls. What are the effects of this change?

One important environmental effect of excessive ground water withdrawal is subsidence of the ground surface. Venice, Italy, provides a dramatic example of this side effect. Venice was built in the eleventh century A.D. on low-lying islands in a coastal lagoon, sheltered from the ocean by a barrier beach. Underlying the area are some 1000 m (about 3300 ft) of layers of sand, gravel, clay, and silt, with some layers of peat. Compaction of these soft layers has been going on gradually for centuries under the heavy load of city buildings. However, ground water withdrawal, which has been greatly accelerated in recent decades, has aggravated the condition.

Many ancient buildings in Venice now rest at lower levels and have suffered severe damage as a result of flooding during winter storms on the adjacent Adriatic Sea. Coastal storms normally raise sea level, and when high tides occur at the same time, water rises even higher. The problem of flooding during storms is aggravated by the fact that many of the canals of Venice receive raw sewage, so that the floodwater is contaminated.

Most of the subsidence in recent decades has been attributed to withdrawals of large amounts of ground water from industrial wells at Porto Marghere, the modern port of Venice, located a few kilometers distant on the mainland shore. This pumping has now been greatly curtailed, reducing the rate of subsidence to a very small natural rate (about 1 mm per year). However, the threat of flooding and damage to churches and other buildings of great historical value remains. Flood control now depends on the construction of seawalls and floodgates on the barrier beach that lies between Venice and the open ocean.

By the early 1980s, the port city of Bangkok, located on the Chao

Phraya River a short distance from the Gulf of Thailand, had become the world's most rapidly sinking city as a result of massive ground water withdrawals from soft marine sediments beneath the city. During the 1980s the rate of subsidence reached 14 cm (6 in.) per year, and major floods were frequent. Some reduction in the rate of ground water withdrawal has produced a modest decrease in the rate of subsidence, but as in the case of Venice, the flood danger remains.

Ground water withdrawal has affected several regions in California, where ground water for irrigation has been pumped from basins filled with alluvial sediments. Water table levels in these basins have dropped over 30 m (98 ft), with a maximum drop of 120 to 150 m (394 to 492 ft) being recorded in one locality of California's San Joaquin Valley. In the Los Bannos–Kettleman City area, ground subsidence of as much as 4.2 to 4.8 m (14 to 16 ft) was measured at some locations in a 35-year period.

Another important area of ground subsidence accompanying water withdrawal is beneath Hous-

---

affected by *turbulence,* a system of countless eddies that are continually forming and dissolving. If we follow a particular water molecule, it will travel a highly irregular, corkscrew path as it is swept downstream. Motions include upward, downward, and sideward directions. Only if we measure the water velocity at a certain fixed point for a long period of time, say, several minutes, will the average motion at that point be downstream and in a line parallel with the surface and bed.

Stream Discharge

Stream flow at a given location is measured by its **discharge,** which is defined as the volume of water per unit time passing through a cross section of the stream at that location. It is measured in cubic meters (cubic feet) per second. The cross-sectional area and average velocity of a stream can change within a short distance, even though the stream discharge does not change. These changes occur because of changes in the *gradient* of the stream channel. The gradient is the rate of fall in elevation of the stream surface in the downstream direction (Figure 15.15).

When the gradient is steep, the force of gravity will act more strongly and flow velocity will be greater. When the stream channel has a gentle gradient, the velocity will be slower. However, in a short stretch of stream, the discharge will remain constant. As shown in Figure 15.15, this means that in stretches of rapids, where the stream flows swiftly, the stream channel will be shallow and narrow. In pools,

Flooding in Venice Land subsidence has subjected Venice to episodes of flooding by waters of the Adriatic Sea. Here, high water has flooded the Piazza San Marco and an outdoor café.

ton, Texas, where the ground surface has subsided from 0.3 to 1 m (1 to 3 ft) in a metropolitan area 50 km (31 mi) across. Damage to buildings, pavements, airport runways, and other structures has resulted.

Perhaps the most celebrated case of ground subsidence is that affecting Mexico City. Carefully measured ground subsidence has ranged from about 4 to 7 m (13 to 23 ft). The subsidence has resulted from the withdrawal of ground water from an aquifer system beneath the city and has caused many serious engineering problems. As water has been drained out, the volume of clay beds overlying the aquifer has contracted greatly. To combat the ground subsidence, recharge wells were drilled to inject water into the aquifer. In addition, new water supplies from sources outside the city area were developed to replace local ground water use.

where the stream flows more slowly, the stream channel will be wider and deeper to maintain the same discharge. Sequences of pools and rapids can be found along streams of all sizes.

Stream discharge at a location on a stream is determined by noting the height, or *stage,* of the surface of the stream with respect to a fixed level nearby, such as a marker on a bridge abutment. Stage is measured by a *stream gage,* which uses a float inside a stilling well to record the height of the water surface (Figure 15.16). Stage is then converted to discharge by consulting a table made from flow measurements acquired at that location at various stages in the past.

The discharge of a stream measures its volume rate of flow. Discharge is measured by recording the height of the water surface, or stage, at a gaging station where the relation between height and discharge is known.

The discharges of streams and rivers change from day to day, and records of daily and flood discharges of major streams and rivers are important information. They are used in planning the development and distribution of surface waters, as well as in designing flood-protection structures and generating models of how floods progress down a particular river system. An important activity of the U.S. Geological Survey is the measurement, or gaging, of stream discharge in the United States. In cooperation with states and municipalities, this organization maintains over 6000 gaging stations on principal streams and their tributaries. In Canada, the Water Survey

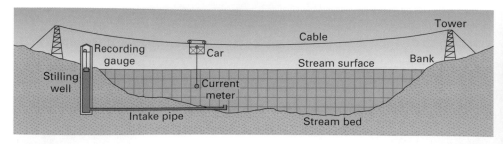

15.16 *Current meter* A hydrologist sits in a cable car, lowering a current meter into a large river. At the bottom of the tether is a streamlined weight with a vertical fin. The current meter, located just above the weight, has a set of three cups that are propelled in a circular motion by the force of the flowing water. Each revolution of the cup set closes and opens an electrical connection, providing a series of "clicks" that can be counted manually or automatically. The rate of clicking determines the velocity of the water flow.

of Canada monitors water levels in rivers and lakes using a network of about 2500 gages, many of which are operated in cooperation with individual provinces.

Figure 15.17 is a map showing the relative discharge of major rivers of the United States. The mighty Mississippi with its tributaries dwarfs all other North American rivers. Two other discharges are of major proportions—the Columbia River, draining a large segment of the Rocky Mountains in southwestern Canada and the northwestern United States, and the Great Lakes, discharging through the St. Lawrence River.

The Colorado River, a much smaller stream, has its origin in the snowmelt of the Rocky Mountains and then crosses a vast semiarid and arid region that adds little tributary flow.

As the figure shows, the discharge of major rivers increases downstream as a natural consequence of the way streams and rivers combine to deliver runoff and sediment to the oceans. The gradient also changes in a downstream direction. The general rule is the larger the cross-sectional area of the stream, the lower the gradient. Great rivers, such as the Mississippi and Amazon, have gradients so low that they can

15.17 *River discharge* This schematic map shows the relative magnitude of the discharge of U.S. rivers. Width of the river as drawn is proportional to mean annual discharge. (After U.S. Geological Survey.)

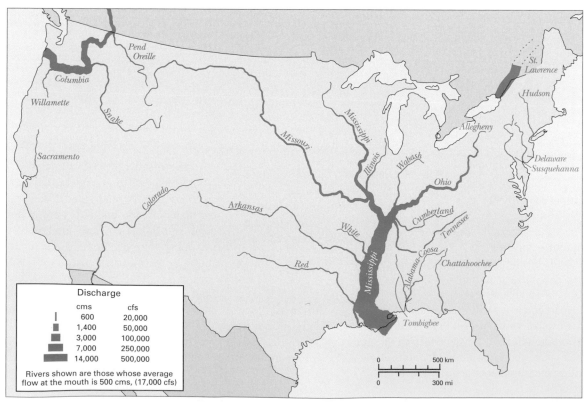

be described as "flat." For example, the water surface of the lower Mississippi River falls in elevation about 3 cm for each kilometer of downstream distance (1.9 in. per mi).

Rivers with headwaters in high mountains have characteristics that are especially desirable for utilizing river flow for irrigation and for preventing floods. The higher ranges serve as snow storage areas, slowly releasing winter and spring precipitation through early or midsummer. As summer progresses, melting proceeds to successively higher levels. In this way, a continuous, sustained river flow is maintained. Among the snow-fed rivers of the western United States and Canada are the Columbia, Fraser, Mackenzie, Snake, Missouri, Arkansas, and Colorado.

Drainage Systems

As runoff moves to lower and lower levels and eventually to the sea, it becomes organized into a **drainage system.** The system consists of a branched network of stream channels, as well as the adjacent sloping ground surfaces that contribute overland flow to those channels. Between the channels on the crests of ridges are *drainage divides,* which mark the boundary between slopes that contribute water to different streams or drainage systems. The entire system is bounded by an outer drainage divide that outlines a more-or-less pear-shaped **drainage basin** or **watershed** (Figure 15.18).

A typical stream network within a drainage basin is shown in Figure 15.18. Each fingertip tributary receives runoff from a small area of land surface surrounding the channel. This runoff is carried downstream and merged with runoff from other small tributaries as they join the main

---

A drainage basin consists of a branched network of stream channels and adjacent slopes that feed the channels. It is bounded by a drainage divide.

---

stream. The drainage system thus provides a converging mechanism that funnels overland flow into streams and smaller streams into larger ones.

STREAM FLOW

The discharge of a stream will increase in response to a period of heavy rainfall or snowmelt. However, the response is delayed, as the movement of water into stream channels takes time. The length of delay depends on a number of factors. The most important factor is the size of the drainage basin feeding the stream. Larger drainage basins show a longer delay.

The relationship between stream discharge and precipitation is best studied by means of a simple graph, called a *hydrograph,* which plots the discharge of a stream with time at a particular stream gage. Figure 15.19 is a hydrograph for a drainage basin of about 800 km² (300 mi²) in area located in Ohio within the moist continental climate ⑩. The graph shows the discharge of Sugar Creek (smooth line), the main stream of the drainage basin, during a four-day period that included a rainstorm. Rainfall for the 12-hour storm is shown by a bar graph giving the number of centimeters of precipitation in each two-hour period. The average total rainfall over the watershed of Sugar Creek was about 15 cm (6 in.). About half of this amount passed down the stream within three days' time. Some rainfall was held in the soil as soil water, some evaporated, and some infiltrated to the water table to be held in long-term storage as ground water.

Studying the rainfall and runoff graphs in Figure 15.19, we see that prior to the onset of the storm, Sugar Creek was carrying a small discharge. This flow, which is supplied by

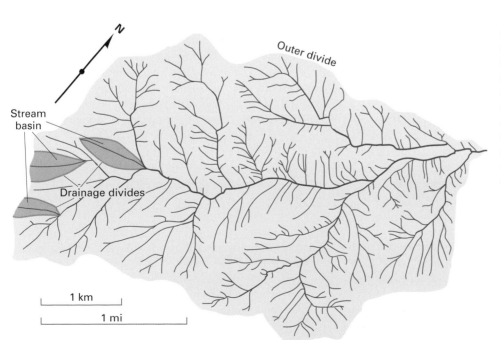

15.18 Channel network of a stream Smaller and larger streams merge in a network that carries runoff downstream. Each small tributary has its own small drainage basin, bounded by drainage divides. An outer drainage divide delineates the stream's watershed at any point on the stream. (Data of U.S. Geological Survey and Mark A. Melton.)

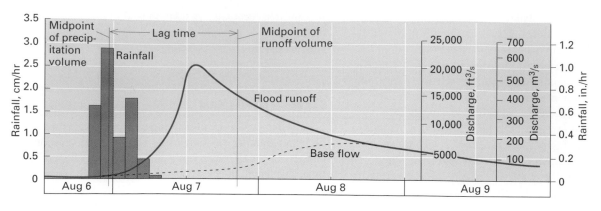

15.19 Sugar Creek hydrograph *Four days of precipitation and stream flow at Sugar Creek, Ohio, following a heavy rainstorm in August. (After Hoyt and Langbein, Floods, copyright © Princeton University Press. Used by permission.)*

the seepage of ground water into the channel, is termed *base flow.* After the heavy rainfall began, several hours elapsed before the stream gage began to show a rise in discharge. This interval, called the *lag time,* indicates that the branching system of channels was acting as a temporary reservoir. The channels were at first receiving inflow more rapidly than it could be passed down the channel system to the stream gage.

Lag time is measured as the difference between the time at which half of the precipitation has occurred and that at which half the runoff has passed downstream. In the Sugar Creek example, the lag time was about 18 hours, with the peak flow reached almost 24 hours after the rainfall began. Note also that the stream's discharge rose much more abruptly than it fell. In general, the larger a watershed, the longer is the lag time between peak rainfall and peak discharge, and the more gradual is the rate of decline of discharge after the peak has passed. Another typical feature of a flood hydrograph is the slow but distinct rise in the amount of discharge contributed by base flow.

How Urbanization Affects Stream Flow

The growth of cities and suburbs affects the flow of small streams in two ways. First, an increasing percentage of the surface becomes impervious to infiltration as it is covered by buildings, driveways, walks, pavements, and parking lots. In a closely built-up residential area with small lot sizes, the percentage of impervious surface may run as high as 80 percent.

As the proportion of impervious surface increases, overland flow from the urbanized area generally increases. This change acts to increase the frequency and height of flood peaks during heavy storms for small watersheds lying largely within the urbanized area. Recharge to the ground water body beneath is also reduced, and this reduction, in turn, decreases the base flow contribution to channels in the same area. Thus, the full range of stream discharges, from

> A hydrograph plots stream flow with time. Peaks in the hydrograph occur after rainfall events. Between rains, stream flow falls to base flow, which is fed by ground water seepage into the stream's channels.

low stages in dry periods to flood stages in wet periods, is made greater by urbanization.

A second change caused by urbanization is the introduction of storm sewers that quickly carry storm runoff from paved areas directly to stream channels for discharge. Thus, runoff travel time to channels is shortened, while the proportion of runoff is increased by the expansion in impervious surfaces. The two changes together act to reduce the lag time of urban streams and increase their peak discharge levels. Many rapidly expanding suburban communities are finding that low-lying, formerly flood-free, residential areas now experience periodic flooding as a result of urbanization.

The Annual Flow Cycle of a Large River

In regions of humid climates, where the water table is high and normally intersects the important stream channels, the hydrographs of larger streams will show clearly the effects of two sources of water—base flow and overland flow. Figure 15.20 is a hydrograph of the Chattahoochee River in Georgia, a fairly large river draining a watershed of 8700 km² (3350 mi²), much of it in the southern Appalachian Mountains. The sharp, abrupt fluctuations in discharge are produced by overland flow following rain periods of one to three days' duration. These are each similar to the hydrograph of Figure 15.19, except that here they are shown much compressed by the time scale.

After each rain period the discharge falls off rapidly, but if another storm occurs within a few days, the discharge rises to another peak. The enlarged inset graph in Figure 15.20 shows details for the month of January. Here, three storms occur in rapid succession. Runoff drops between each storm but not completely to the level of base flow. When a long period intervenes between storms, the discharge falls to a low value, the base flow, at which it levels off.

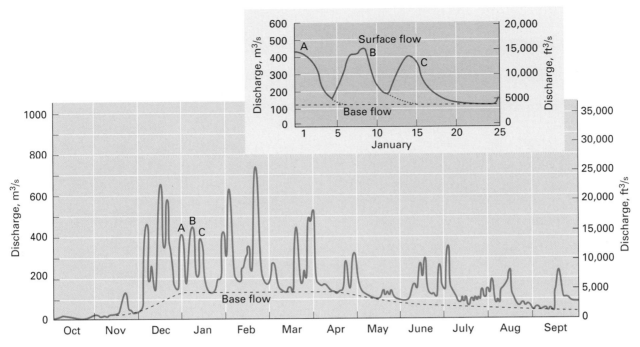

15.20 *Chattahoochee River hydrograph* This hydrograph shows the fluctuating discharge of the Chattahoochee River, Georgia, throughout a typical year. The high peaks are caused by runoff from streams that produced heavy overland flow. The inset graph expands the graph for the month of January. (Data of U.S. Geological Survey.)

Throughout the year the base flow, which represents ground water inflow into the stream, undergoes a marked annual cycle. During winter and early spring, water table levels are raised, and the rate of inflow into streams is increased. For the Chattahoochee River, the rate of base flow during January, February, March, and April holds uniform at about 100 m³/s (about 3500 ft³/s). The base flow begins to decline in spring, as heavy evapotranspiration losses reduce soil water and therefore cut off the recharge of ground water. The decline continues through the summer, reaching a low of about 30 m³/s (about 1000 ft³/s) by the end of October.

River Floods

You've probably seen enough media coverage of river floods to have a good idea of the appearance of floodwaters and the damage caused by flood erosion and deposition of silt and clay. We can define the term **flood** as the condition that exists when the discharge of a river cannot be accommodated within its normal channel. As a result, the water spreads over the adjoining ground, which is normally cropland or forest. Sometimes, however, the ground is occupied by houses, factories, or transportation corridors.

Most rivers of humid climates have a *floodplain* a broad belt of low, flat ground bordering the channel on one or both sides that is flooded by stream waters about once a year (Figure 15.21). This flood usually occurs in the season when abundant surface runoff combines with the

_____

A flood occurs when a river rises to leave its bed and cover adjacent lands. Flood forecasts rely on precipitation patterns, past history, and present river levels to predict when and how high a flood will crest.

_____

effects of a high water table to supply more runoff than can be carried in the channel. Annual inundation is considered a flood, even though its occurrence is expected and does not prevent the cultivation of crops after the flood has subsided. Annual flooding does not interfere with the growth of dense forests, which are widely distributed over low, marshy floodplains in all humid regions of the world. The National Weather Service, which provides a flood-warning service, designates a particular river stage at a given place as the *flood stage*. Above this critical level, inundation of the floodplain will occur. Still higher discharges of water, the rare and disastrous floods that may occur as seldom as once in 30 or 50 years, inundate ground lying well above the floodplain. Figure 15.22 shows some views of rivers in flood.

Flash floods are characteristic of streams draining small watersheds with steep slopes. These streams have short lag times—perhaps only an hour or two—so when an intense rainfall event occurs, the stream rises very quickly to a high level. The flood arrives as a swiftly moving wall of turbulent water, sweeping away buildings and vehicles in its path. In arid western watersheds, great quantities of coarse rock debris are swept into the main channel and travel with the floodwater, producing debris floods (Chapter 14). In forested landscapes, tree limbs and trunks, soil, rocks, and boulders are swept downstream in the floodwaters. Because flash floods often occur too quickly to warn affected populations, they can cause significant loss of life.

15.21 **Floodplain** *This aerial view shows the floodplain of the vast Amazon River in the foreground and far distance.*

Flood Prediction

The magnitude of a flood is usually measured by the peak discharge or highest stage of a river during the period of flooding. As the flood history of any river shows, large floods occur less frequently than smaller ones—that is, the greater the discharge or higher the stage, the less likely is the flood. A tool used by hydrologists to present the flood history of a river is the flood expectancy graph. Figure 15.23 shows expectancy graphs for two rivers. The meaning of the bar symbols is explained in the key. The Mississippi River at Vicksburg illustrates a great river responding largely to spring floods, with high waters in April and May and low flows in September and October. The Sacramento River shows the effects of the Mediterranean climate, with its winter wet season and long severe summer drought. Winter floods in January and February are caused by torrential rainstorms and snowmelt in the mountain watersheds of the Sierra Nevada and southern Cascades. By midsummer, river flow has shrunk to a very low stage.

The National Weather Service operates a River and Flood Forecasting Service through 85 offices located at strategic points along major river systems of the United States. When a flood threatens, forecasters analyze precipitation patterns and the progress of high waters moving downstream. Examining the flood history of the rivers and streams concerned, they develop specific flood forecasts. These are delivered to communities within the associated district, which usually covers one or more large watersheds. Flood warnings are publicized by every possible means, and various agencies cooperate closely to plan the evacuation of threatened areas and the removal or protection of property.

The Mississippi Flood of 1993

The Mississippi River Flood of 1993 provides an example of one of the most serious and damaging floods to strike the United States in recent years. (See chapter opener photo and *Putting You in the Picture.*) Although the usual time for the flooding of the Mississippi is in spring (Figure 15.23), this extreme event occurred in midsummer. The 1993 flood was triggered by a succession of unprecedented rainfalls in the upper Mississippi Basin. In June of that year, rainfall totaled over 30 cm (12 in.) for large areas of the region. Southern Minnesota and western Wisconsin received even larger amounts. Monthly rainfall totals were the highest on many records dating back more than 100 years. The heavy rainfall continued into July, concentrated in Iowa, Illinois, and Missouri. Inundated by huge volumes of rain, the vast wet landscape of the upper Midwest came to resemble a sixth Great Lake when viewed from the air.

As the water drained from the landscape, so the Mississippi and its tributaries rose, creating a flood crest of swiftly moving turbid water that worked its way slowly downstream through July and early August. At nearly every community along the length of the Mississippi and Missouri rivers, citizens fought to raise and reinforce the levees that protected their lands, homes, and businesses from the ravages of the flood. Where levees failed to keep them in check, the rivers filled their broad floodplains from bluff to bluff, as shown in the two Landsat images of our chapter opener photo. By the time it was over, the waters had crested at 16.8 m (49.4 ft) at St. Louis, nearly 6 m (20 ft) above flood stage.

The Mississippi River Flood of 1993 was an environmental disaster of the first magnitude. An area twice the size of New Jersey was flooded, taking 50 lives and driving nearly 70,000 people from their homes. Property damage, including loss of agricultural crops, was estimated at $12 billion. Of the region's 1400 levees, at least 800 were breached or overtopped. Some flood engineers classed the event as a 500-year flood, meaning that only once in a 500-year interval is a flood of this magnitude likely to occur. However, this does not mean that a similar flood, or an even larger one, could not occur in the near future. For the people living on its banks and bottomlands, the mighty Mississippi is a sleeping giant that awakens with devastating consequences.

LAKES

A **lake** is a body of standing water found within continental margins that is enclosed on all sides by land. The term *lake* includes a wide range of water bodies. Ponds (which are small, usually shallow water bodies), marshes, and swamps with standing water can all be included under the definition of a lake. Lakes receive water input from streams, overland flow, and ground water, and so are included as parts of drainage systems. Many lakes lose water at an outlet, where water drains over a dam (natural or constructed) to become an outflowing stream. Lakes also lose water by evaporation. Lakes, like streams, are landscape features but are not usually considered to be landforms.

Lakes are quite important from the human viewpoint. They are frequently used as sources of fresh water and food, such as fish. Where dammed to a high level above the outlet stream, they can provide hydroelectric power as well. Lakes and ponds are also important recreation sites and sources of natural beauty. In North America, the Great Lakes form a vast network of inland waters of great economic and recre-

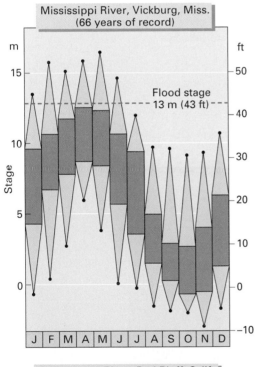

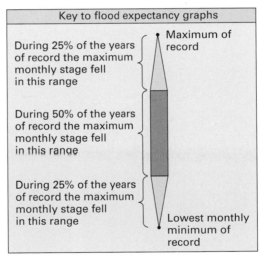

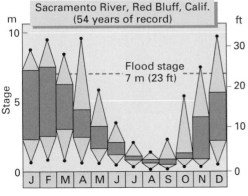

15.23 Flood expectancy graphs *Maximum and minimum monthly stages of the Mississippi River at Vicksburg, Mississippi, and the Sacramento River at Red Bluff, California.*

15.22 Rivers in Flood

a...Red River in flood
This photo shows the Red River, near Fargo, North Dakota, in flood in April 1997. The normal channel is marked by the sinuous bands of trees running across the lower part of the photo. Dikes have kept the water from flooding the town in the center of the image.

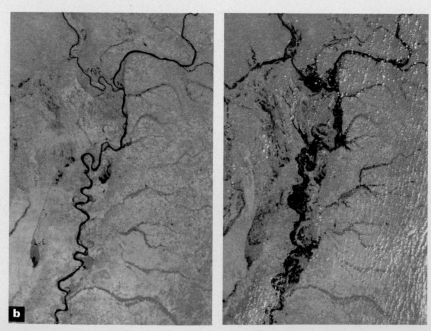

b...Mississippi Flood of 2002 These two false color images show flooding on the Mississippi River as it is joined by the Ohio River at the junction of Missouri, Illinois, and Kentucky (top center). The left image shows the region on April 25, and the right image shows it on May 18. The river, rising to levels 4m (12 ft) above its flood stage, has left its banks to inundate much of its natural valley.

c...River Power A river in flood possesses enormous power to erode and move sediment. Here the Tuolumne River careens down a steep slope in Yosemite National Park. Over time, rivers like this can carve deep canyons, even in very resistant rock.

d...Local flooding These houses in Lakeview, Ohio, are partially submerged following heavy rains in July 2003. Up to 38 cm (15 in.) of rain was reported in the region during this event.

ational value. *Eye on the Environment 15.2 • The Great Lakes* provides more information about the lakes, how they formed, and their present environmental problems.

Where lakes are not naturally present in the valley bottoms of drainage systems, we create lakes as needed by placing dams across the stream channels. Many regions that formerly had almost no natural lakes are now abundantly supplied. Some are small ponds built to serve ranches and farms, while others cover hundreds of square kilometers. In some areas, the number of artificial lakes is large enough to have significant effects on the region's hydrologic cycle.

Basins occupied by lakes show a wide range of origins as well as a vast range in dimensions. Lake basins, like stream channels, are true landforms. Basins are created by a number of processes. Tectonism creates rift valleys where the deepest lakes on Earth are found. Meteorite impact and volcanic eruptions form craters that can contain lakes. Lakes are created on the floodplains of rivers by fluvial erosion and deposition as well as by the solution of limestone in karst regions. Landslides can block rivers to create lakes in river valleys (see *Eye on the Environment 14.1 • The Great Hebgen Lake Disaster*).

In Canada and the northern United States, many lakes originated during the Ice Ages when moving continental ice sheets eroded bedrock, carving depressions in areas of low-lying weak rock. Lakes were also formed in the sedimentary deposits left behind by the melting ice. Western Siberia is another region rich in lakes created by glacial activity.

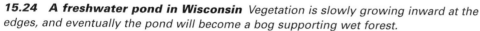

Lakes serve as vital reservoirs of fresh water on the land. They are formed in many different ways but are generally short-lived over geologic time.

An important point about lakes in general is that they are short-lived features on the geologic time scale. Lakes disappear by one of two processes, or a combination of both. First, lakes that have stream outlets will be gradually drained as the outlets are eroded to lower levels. Where a strong bedrock threshold underlies the outlet, erosion will be slow but nevertheless certain. Second, lakes accumulate inorganic sediment carried by streams entering the lake and organic matter produced by plants and animals within the lake. Eventually, they fill up, forming a boggy wetland with little or no free water surface (Figure 15.24).

Lakes can also disappear when climate changes. If precipitation is reduced within a region, or temperatures and net radiation increase, evaporation can exceed input and the lake will dry up. Many former lakes of the southwestern United States flourished in moister periods of glacial advance during the Ice Age. Today, they have shrunk greatly or have disappeared entirely under the present arid regime.

In moist climates, the water level of lakes and ponds coincides closely with the water table in the surrounding area. Seepage of ground water into the lake, as well as direct runoff of precipitation, maintains these water surfaces permanently throughout the year. Examples of such freshwater ponds are found widely distributed in glaciated regions of North America and Europe. Here, plains of glacial sand and gravel contain natural pits and hollows left by the melting of stagnant ice masses that were buried in the sand and gravel

15.24 A freshwater pond in Wisconsin *Vegetation is slowly growing inward at the edges, and eventually the pond will become a bog supporting wet forest.*

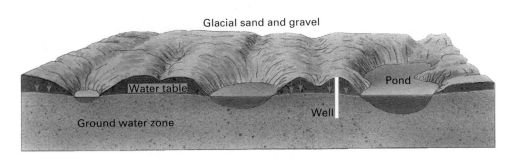

Glacial sand and gravel

Water table

Ground water zone

Well

Pond

15.25 Freshwater ponds *A sketch of freshwater ponds in sandy glacial deposits on Cape Cod, Massachusetts. The water level of the ponds corresponds closely to the water table. (Redrawn from A Geologist's View of Cape Cod, copyright © A. N. Strahler, 1966. Used by permission of Doubleday, a division of Bantam Doubleday Dell Publishing Group, Inc.)*

deposits (see Chapter 19). Figure 15.25 is a block diagram showing small freshwater ponds on Cape Cod. The surface elevation of these ponds coincides closely with the level of the surrounding water table.

Many former freshwater water table ponds have become partially or entirely filled by organic matter from the growth and decay of water-loving plants (Figure 15.24). The ultimate result is a bog with its surface close to the water table. Freshwater marshes and swamps, in which water stands at or close to the ground surface over a broad area, also represent the appearance of the water table at the surface. Such areas of poor surface drainage are included under the name of *wetlands.*

Saline Lakes and Salt Flats

Lakes with no surface outlet are characteristic of arid regions. Here, the average rate of water loss by evaporation balances the average rate of stream inflow. If the rate of inflow increases, the lake level will rise. At the same time, the lake surface will increase in area, allowing a greater rate of evaporation. A new balance can then be achieved. Similarly, if the region becomes more arid, reducing input and increasing evaporation, the water level will fall to a lower level.

Lakes without outlets often show salt buildup. Dissolved solids are brought into the lake by streams—usually streams that head in distant highlands where a water surplus exists. Since evaporation removes only pure water, the salts remain behind and the salinity of the water slowly increases. Salinity, or degree of "saltiness," refers to the abundance of certain common ions in the water. Eventually, salinity level reach a point where salts are precipitated as solids (Figure 15.26).

Sometimes the surfaces of such lakes lie below sea level. An example is the Dead Sea, with a surface elevation of −396 m (−1299 ft). The largest of all lakes, the Caspian Sea, has a surface elevation of −25 m (82 ft). Both of these large lakes are saline.

In regions where climatic conditions consistently favor evaporation over input, the lake may be absent. Instead, a shallow basin covered with salt deposits (see Figure 16.32), otherwise known as a *salt flat* or dry lake, will occur. In Chapter 16 we will describe dry lakebeds as landforms. On rare occasions, these flats are covered by a shallow layer of water, brought by flooding streams heading in adjacent highlands.

A number of desert salts are of economic value and have been profitably extracted from salt flats. In shallow coastal estuaries in the desert climate, sea salt for human consumption is commercially harvested by allowing it to evaporate in shallow basins. One well-known source of this salt is the Rann of Kutch, a coastal lowland in the tropical desert of westernmost India, close to Pakistan. Here the evaporation of shallow water of the Arabian Sea has long provided a major source of salt for inhabitants of the interior.

The Aral Sea is an inland lake that is rapidly becoming saline through human activity. The two major rivers that feed this vast central Asian water body have been largely diverted into irrigation of agricultural lands, and with its inflow greatly reduced, the lake has shrunk and become increasingly salty. Our interchapter feature *A Closer Look: Eye on Global Change 15.3 • The Aral Sea—A Dying Saline Lake* tells the story of this environmental disaster.

Desert Irrigation

Human interaction with the tropical desert environment is as old as civilization itself. Two of the earliest sites of civilization—Egypt and Mesopotamia—lie in the tropical deserts. Successful occupation of these deserts requires irrigation with large supplies of water from nondesert sources. For Egypt and Mesopotamia, the water sources of ancient times were the rivers that cross the desert but derive their flow from regions that have a water surplus. These are referred to as *exotic rivers* because their flows are derived from an outside region.

Irrigation systems in arid lands divert the discharge of an exotic river such as the Nile, Indus, Jordan, or Colorado into a distribution system that allows the water to infiltrate the soil of areas under crop cultivation. Ultimately, such irrigation projects can suffer from two undesirable side effects: salinization and waterlogging of the soil.

Salinization occurs when salts build up in the soil to levels that inhibit plant growth. This happens because an irrigated area within a desert loses large amounts of soil water through evapotranspiration. Salts contained in the irrigation water remain in the soil and increase to high concentrations. Salinization may be prevented or cured by flushing the soil salts downward to lower levels by the use of more water. This remedy requires greater water use than for crop growth alone. In addition, new drainage systems must be installed to dispose of the excess saltwater.

Eye on the Environment | 15.2

The Great Lakes[1]

The Great Lakes—Superior, Huron, Michigan, Erie, and Ontario—along with their smaller bays and connecting lakes form a vast network of inland waters in the heart of North America. They contain 23,000 km^3 (5500 mi^3) of water—about 18 percent of all the fresh, surface water on Earth. Only the polar ice caps and Lake Baikal in Siberia have a larger volume. Of the Great Lakes, Lake Superior is by far the largest. In fact, the volume of the other Great Lakes combined would not fill its basin. The Great Lakes watershed contains a population of about 33 million people—22.8 million Americans and 9.2 million Canadians. The lakes are an essential resource for drinking water, fishing, agriculture, manufacturing, transportation, and power generation.

The Great Lakes are largely the legacy of Ice Age glaciation, formed in a low interior basin of old, largely sedimentary rock. During at least four major periods in the last two million years, ice sheets advanced over this basin, scouring the rocks and lowering the surface by as much as 500 m (1600 ft) below the surrounding terrain. As the continental ice sheets of the last glacial advance retreated, water filled these depressions, creating lakes dammed by glacial deposits and melting ice. With the final melting of the ice and a slow, gentle uplift of the terrain, the lakes eventually acquired their present shapes and configurations as the Great Lakes.

The Great Lakes play an important role in moderating the climate

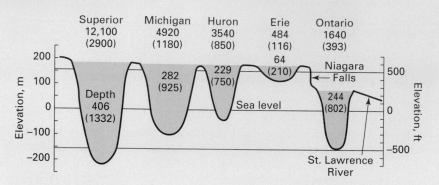

Volumes, elevations, and depths of the five Great Lakes *Volumes are shown below the name of each lake in km3 (mi3). Depths are shown in m (ft). (Modified from A. N. Strahler, The Earth Sciences. Used by permission.)*

The Great Lakes and their watersheds
The Great Lakes constitute a vast water resource lying astride the boundary between Canada and the United States. (© A. N. Strahler.)

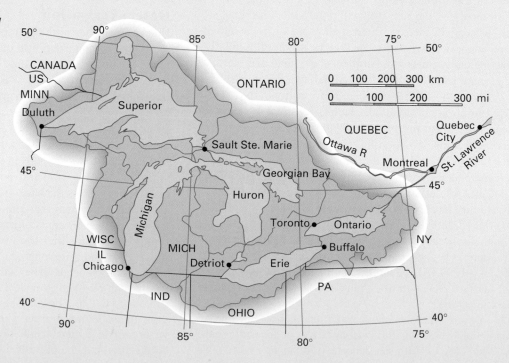

[1]We are indebted to Professor R. Gilbert, of Queens University, Ontario, Canada, for providing much of the text of this feature.

of their region. Because water bodies heat and cool more slowly than adjacent land, autumn and winter temperatures near large lakes are warmer, while spring and summer temperatures are cooler. For the Great Lakes, the difference may be as much as 5 to 10°C (9 to 18°F), depending on wind pattern over the lake. The frost-free period near the lakes is up to 50 days longer each year. To the east of each of the lakes are snow belts where average snowfall ranges from 200 to 350 cm (about 80 to 140 in.) per year, approaching twice the amount that would occur otherwise. The extra snow arises by evaporation from the relatively warm, free-water surface of the lake followed by condensation in cold, winter air.

Ice forms on the Great Lakes each winter. Although Lake Erie is the southernmost of the Great Lakes, it is normally more than 90 percent ice-covered in February because its volume is small and it has a limited ability to store heat. Lake Superior (75%), Lake Huron (70%), Lake Michigan (50%) and Lake Ontario (25%) all are less ice-covered on average, although the amounts vary greatly from year to year as the climate fluctuates. As we experience global climate warming, the ice cover on the lakes will decrease, and by the last decades of this century ice may not form at all on some of the lakes.

Because of their position close to centers of population and agricultural development, the Great Lakes have suffered significant water pollution. Lake Erie, with the smallest water volume and its heavily developed coastal region, was hard hit in the 1960s and 1970s. Excess nutrients, especially phosphorous from fertilizer, sewage, and detergents, entered Lake Erie in amounts sufficient to cause a large increase in the biological productivity of the lake. The large amount of biomass produced by this "fertilization" depleted the available oxygen dissolved in the water as it decayed.

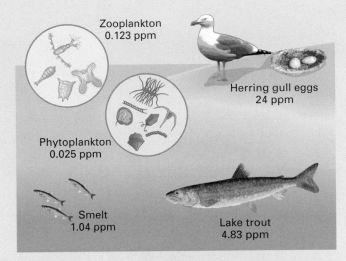

Concentration of PCBs in the Great Lakes food chain *The degree of concentration of PCBs in each level of the Great Lakes aquatic food chain increases from aquatic plants to top predators. The highest levels are reached in the eggs of fish-eating birds such as herring gulls. (After EPA.)*

Suffocation threatened much of the aquatic life in the lake. (See *eutrophication* under "Pollution of Surface Water" in this chapter for a fuller explanation of this process.) The Great Lakes Water Quality Agreement between Canada and the United States, first passed in 1972 and renewed in 1978, was the first step in remediation of pollution of the lakes and served as an important beginning of the recognition of their environmental degradation. Controls on pollution, especially phosphates, were put in place and water quality in Lake Erie has significantly improved.

Persistent organic compounds have also been a source of concern. These include organic substances largely of industrial origin that are long-lasting, highly mobile in the aquatic system, and toxic in very small amounts. Many of these compounds accumulate up the food chain as predators consume contaminated prey. For example, the concentration of polychlorinated biphenyls (PCBs) in the algae of Lake Ontario has been measured at 0.02 parts per million (ppm). This very small amount is equivalent to about half a cubic millimeter

(0.00003 in³) in the volume of a small room. However, this low concentration is magnified up the food chain until the eggs of herring gulls contain as much as 24 ppm. This amount is still small, but it is greater by ten million times than the concentrations in the lake water and is sufficient to cause deformities and high mortality in the chicks. The figure above diagrams this process.

Human impact on the Great Lakes varies significantly from place to place. In 1987 the International Joint Commission identified 43 "Areas of Concern," of which 28 are in the United States and 15 are in Canada. Most were located near major urban centers, or sources of industrial pollution, especially where enclosed harbors or bays prevented dispersion of pollutants. Remedial action plans were proposed and implemented and many of the sites have experienced much improvement. For those interested in up-to-date information on the Great Lakes and their water quality issues, the internet is an excellent source of information by governments and advocacy groups.

15.26 Salt encrustations
These salt encrustations at the edge of Great Salt Lake, Utah, were formed when the lake level dropped during a dry period.

Waterlogging occurs when irrigation with large volumes of water causes a rise in the water table, bringing the zone of saturation close to the surface. Most food crops cannot grow in perpetually saturated soils. When the water table rises to the point at which upward movement under capillary action can bring water to the surface, evaporation is increased and salinization is intensified.

Agricultural areas of major salinization include the Indus River valley in Pakistan, the Euphrates valley in Syria, the Nile delta of Egypt, and the wheat belt of western Australia. In the United States, extensive regions of heavily salinized agriculture are found in the San Joaquin and Imperial valleys of California. Other areas of salinization occur throughout the entire semiarid and arid regions of the western United States. *Eye on the Environment 10.1 • Death of a Civilization* documented the effects of salinization and waterlogging on the civilizations of ancient Mesopotamia.

Pollution of Surface Water

Streams, lakes, bogs, and marshes are specialized habitats of plants and animals. Their ecosystems are particularly sensitive to changes induced by human activity in the water balance and in water chemistry. Our industrial society not only makes radical physical changes in water flow by construction of engineering works (dams, irrigation systems, canals, dredged channels), but also pollutes and contaminates our surface waters with a large variety of wastes.

Salinization and waterlogging are undesirable side effects of long-continued irrigation. Arid regions watered by exotic rivers are most affected.

The sources of water pollutants are many and varied. Some industrial plants dispose of toxic metals and organic compounds by discharging them directly into streams and lakes. Many communities still discharge untreated or partly treated sewage wastes into surface waters. In urban and suburban areas, pollutant matter entering streams and lakes includes deicing salt and lawn conditioners (lime and fertilizers), which can also contaminate ground water. In agricultural regions, important sources of pollutants are fertilizers and livestock wastes. Mining and processing of mineral deposits are also major sources of water pollution. Even contamination by radioactive substances released from nuclear power and processing plants can occur.

Among the common chemical pollutants of both surface water and ground water are sulfate, chloride, sodium, nitrate, phosphate, and calcium ions. (Recall from Chapter 10 that an ion is the charged form of a molecule or an atom and that many chemical compounds dissolve in water by forming ions.) Sulfate ions enter runoff both by fallout from polluted urban air and as sewage effluent. Chloride and sodium ions are contributed both by fallout from polluted air and by deicing salts used on highways. In some locations with snowy winters, community water supplies located close to highways have become polluted from deicing salts. Important sources of nitrate ions are fertilizers and sewage effluent. Excessive concentrations of nitrate in freshwater supplies are highly toxic, and, at the same time, their removal is difficult and expensive. Phosphate ions are contributed in part by fertilizers and by detergents in sewage effluent.

Phosphate and nitrate are plant nutrients and can lead to excessive growth of algae and other aquatic plants in streams and lakes. Applied to lakes, this process is known as *eutrophication,* which is often described as the "aging" of a lake. In eutrophication, the accumulation of nutrients stimulates plant growth, producing a large supply of dead organic matter in the lake. Microorganisms break down this organic matter but require oxygen in the process. However, oxygen dissolves only slightly in water, and so it is normally present only in low concentrations. The added burden of oxygen use by the decomposers reduces the oxygen level to the point where other organisms, such as desirable types of fish, cannot survive. After a few years of nutrient pollution, the lake can take on the characteristics of a shallow pond that results when a lake is slowly filled with sediment and organic matter over thousands of years by natural "aging" processes.

A particular form of chemical pollution of surface water goes under the name of *acid mine drainage.* It is an important form of environmental degradation in parts of Appalachia where abandoned coal mines and strip-mine workings are concentrated (Figure 15.27). Ground water emerges from abandoned mines and as soil water percolating through strip-mine waste banks. This water contains sulfuric acid and various salts of metals, particularly of iron. Acid of this origin in stream waters can have adverse effects on animal life. In sufficient concentrations, it is lethal to certain species of fish and has at times caused massive fish kills.

Toxic metals, among them mercury, along with pesticides and a host of other industrial chemicals, are introduced into

Water pollutants include various types of common ions and salts, as well as heavy metals, organic compounds, and acids. Excessive plant nutrients in runoff feeding lakes can lead to eutrophication— the artificial "aging" of a lake.

streams and lakes in quantities that are locally damaging or lethal to plant and animal communities. In addition, sewage introduces live bacteria and viruses that are classed as biological pollutants. These pose a threat to the health of humans and animals alike.

Another form of pollution is *thermal pollution,* which refers to the discharge of heat into the environment from combustion of fuels and from the conversion of nuclear energy into electric power. Thermal pollution of water takes the form of discharges of heated water into streams, estuaries, and lakes, which can have drastic effects on local aquatic life. The impact may be quite large in a small area.

SURFACE WATER AS A NATURAL RESOURCE

Fresh surface water is a basic natural resource essential to human agricultural and industrial activities. Runoff held in reservoirs behind dams provides water supplies for great urban centers, such as New York City and Los Angeles. When diverted from large rivers, it provides irrigation water for highly productive lowlands in arid lands, such as the Sacramento and San Joaquin valleys of California and the Nile Valley of Egypt. To these uses of runoff are added hydroelectric power, where the gradient of a river is steep, or routes of inland navigation, where the gradient is gentle.

Our heavily industrialized society requires enormous supplies of fresh water for its sustained operation. Urban dwellers consume water in their homes at rates of 150 to 400 liters (50 to 100 gallons) per person per day (Figure 15.28). Large quan-

15.27 Strip-mine water pollution *This small stream is badly polluted by acid waters that have percolated through strip-mine waste.*

Visualizing Exercises

1. Sketch a cross section through the land surface showing the position of the water table and indicating flow directions of subsurface water motion with arrows. Include the flow paths of ground water. Be sure to provide a stream in your diagram. Label the saturated and unsaturated zones.

2. Why does water rise in an artesian well? Illustrate with a sketched cross-sectional diagram showing the aquifer, aquicludes, and the well.

Essay Questions

1. A thundershower causes heavy rain to fall in a small region near the headwaters of a major river system. Describe the flow paths of that water as it returns to the atmosphere and ocean. What human activities influence the flows? in what ways?

2. Imagine yourself a recently elected mayor of a small city located on the banks of a large river. What issues might you be concerned with that involve the river? In developing your answer, choose and specify some characteristics for this city—such as its population, its industries, its sewage systems, and the present uses of the river for water supply or recreation.

Eye on the Landscape

Chapter Opener Mississippi Flood of 1993 Note the former river channels that have been cut off by migration of the river channel **(A).** These are called ox-bow lakes and are described in Chapter 16. These images also demonstrate a type of false-color image in which the red color shows shortwave infrared reflectance, green shows near-infrared reflectance, and blue shows red reflectance. Recall from Chapter 3 that vegetation reflects very strongly in near-infrared wavelengths, and thus vegetation appears bright green **(B).** Urban surfaces are bright in the shortwave infrared and thus appear red **(C).** Sediment-laden river water is brown and so provides a strong red signal that translates as blue in the image **(D).**

15.9 Sinkholes Note the large amount of bare rock visible in many large patches on this arid plain **(A).** The lack of soil suggests that the limestone is so pure that its dissolution leaves little or no residual material behind. Also, look at the vegetation ringing the sinkholes **(B).** The plants are probably drawing on ground water. From this observation, we might conclude that ground water is not very far below the vegetated region between the two roads **(C).** Solution weathering of limestone was covered in Chapter 14. Phreatophytes, which are plants that survive in an arid environment by tapping the water table, are discussed in Chapter 8.

15.11 Tower karst As we saw in Chapter 14, solution weathering of certain types of bedrock in warm and wet environments can produce a landscape of steep, vertical slopes. Compare these towers **(A),** formed by solution of limestone, with the fins and grooves of Kauai in Figure 14.12, formed by solution of basaltic lava. Note also the flooded fields **(B).** They are probably rice paddies in the spring, just before planting with young rice stalks.

A CLOSER LOOK

Eye on Global Change 15.3 | The Aral Sea—A Dying Saline Lake

East of the Caspian Sea, astride the former Soviet republics of Kazakhstan and Uzbekistan, lies an immense saline lake—the Aral Sea. Fed by meltwaters of high glaciers and snowfields in the lofty Hindu Kush, Pamir, and Tien Shan Ranges, the lake endured through thousands of years as an oasis for terrestrial and aquatic wildlife deep in the heart of the central Asian desert.

But in the last 30 years, the Aral Sea, once larger than Lake Huron, has shrunk to a shadow of its former extent. The volume of its waters has decreased by 66 percent, and its salinity has increased from 1 percent to over 3 percent, making it more salty than sea water. Twenty of the 24 fish species native to the lake have disappeared. Its catch of commercial fish, which once supplied 10 percent of the total for the Soviet Union, has dwindled to zero. The deltas of the Amu Darya and Syr Darya rivers, which enter the south

and east sides of the lake, were islands of great ecological diversity, teeming with fingerling fishes, birds, and their predators. Now only about half of the species of nesting birds remain. Many species of aquatic plants, shrubs, and grasses have vanished. Commercial hunting and trapping have almost ceased.

What caused this ecological catastrophe? The answer is simple—the lake's water supply was cut off. As an inland lake with no outlet, the Aral Sea receives water from the Amu Darya and Syr Darya, as well as a small amount from direct precipitation, but it loses water by evaporation. Its gains balanced its losses, and, although these gains and losses varied from year to year, the area, depth, and volume of the lake remained nearly constant until about 1960.

In the late 1950s the Soviet government embarked on the first

phases of a vast irrigation program, using water from the Amu Darya and Syr Darya for cotton cropping on the region's desert plain. The diversion of water soon became significant as more and more land came under irrigation. As a result, the influx fell to nearly zero by the early 1980s. The surface level of the Aral was sharply lowered and its area reduced. The sea became divided into two separate parts.

As the lake's shoreline receded, the exposed lakebed became encrusted with salts. The once-flourishing fishing port of Muynak became a ghost town, 50 km (30 mi) from the new lake shoreline. Strong winds now blow salt particles and mineral dusts in great clouds southwestward over the irrigated cotton fields and westward over grazing pastures. These salts—particularly the sodium chloride and sodium sulfate components—are toxic to plants. The salt dust permanently poisons the soil and can only be flushed away with more irrigation water.

The dust also contains residues of pesticides and other agrochemical wastes. These airborne poisons have produced a high incidence of stillbirths, anemia, and eye and lung disease among Kazakhstan's 16 million people. In fact, some ecological journalists have called the lake a "liquid Chernobyl."

The future of the lake appears grim indeed. With the present fresh water inflow nearly zero, the salinity of the remaining lake has exceeded the level of the ocean. Without the sacrifice of agricultural production for

The Aral Sea shrinks *This pair of satellite images shows the Aral Sea in 1976 and 1997. About two-thirds of the sea's volume has been lost in the last 30 years.*

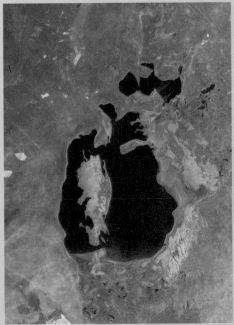

Graveyard of ships *As the Aral Sea shrank, it left behind the hulks of abandoned fishing vessels that were made useless by the loss of fish populations.*

water to fill the lake, or the importation of more water from vast distances to the north, there is little that can be done to save the lake.

However, a plan is now underway to rehabilitate at least a portion of this vast ecological ruin. The plan makes use of the fact that the flow of the Syr Darya

reaching the lake is still significant—in fact, it is enough to maintain the smaller northern section of the lake, called the Small Sea (see map), in a productive state. Simple in concept, the plan provides for a dike some 13 km (8 mi) long to separate the Small Sea from its larger brother, now

termed the Big Sea. The dike will trap the inflowing waters of the Syr Darya and raise the level of the Small Sea by some 4 m (13 ft), returning about 600 km² (230 mi²) of the surrounding salt plain to lake.

Salinity in the new Small Sea will drop from 35 parts per thou-

Blowing dust *Vast expanses of lake bottom, left high and dry by the shrinking of the Aral Sea, provide a source for wind-blown dust, here displayed along a road in the village of Kyzylkum.*

Salinization *Accumulation of salts in agricultural soils accompanies the shrinking of the Aral Sea. Salty windblown dust and saline ground water drawn to the surface concentrate salt in the top layer of soil.*

sand to a value between 4 and 17 parts per thousand. This will allow the 24 local species of fish to return and will revive the local fishing industry. In addition, the increased water surface area will increase local precipitation and humidity, expanding local pastures and cropping areas. The wetter soil will be less likely to blow in the chronic dust storms that have plagued the region. The expanded lake area should also reduce the problem of high salinity in local ground water.

The idea of a dike to separate the two arms of the Aral was first tested in the early 1990s. Desperate to improve the lives of the citizens of Aralsk, a seaport city of 35,000 now located 80 km (50 mi) from the lake shore, the mayor of Aralsk obtained a $2.5 million allocation from the central government to build a dike to enclose the flow of the Syr Darya within the Small Sea. The dike was built and at first worked well in containing the rising waters of the Small Sea. But since it was constructed of sand without a core of clay or a rock facing to protect it from erosion, it began to erode. Lacking a sluice-

way to release water to the Big Sea, it was overtopped and breached on several occasions.

The success of the dike did not go unnoticed, however. In 2001, a World Bank loan to Kazakhstan for $64.5 million to build a permanent dike was approved, and by 2002, the Kazakhstan government had ratified the loan. Construction began in 2003, with completion due in mid-2004. Added along the way were funds for improvements in the irrigation infrastructure of the Syr Darya that would enhance runoff to the Small Sea. The new dike will have a much more gentle slope on the Small Sea side and will also have a proper sluiceway to convey high waters to the Big Sea. In four years, the Small Sea will rise by 4 m (13 ft).

But what of the Big Sea? Unfortunately, its prospects are dim. Presently at a salinity level of 85 parts per thousand (more than twice as salty as ocean water), the last of its native fish species are dying. Still, there is some hope for the Big Sea's fishermen. When the salinity reaches 110 parts per thousand, conditions will be favorable for brine shrimp. These tiny crea-

tures are used as food for young fishes raised in fish farms worldwide and can provide a valuable cash crop. However, there will be no respite from the toxic dust storms of salt and pesticide residues that sweep over the region downwind from the Big Sea.

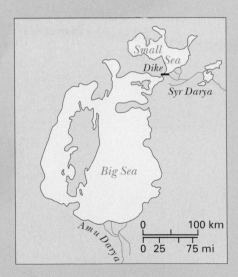

A dike for the Aral Sea *With the construction of the new dike, the Aral Sea will be divided into a relatively healthy Small Sea and a ruined Big Sea.*

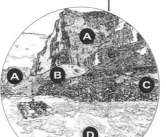

16.18 Braided stream The b[...]
Chitina River, Wrangell Mountain[...]
distinct channels separating and[...]
floodplain filled with glacial deb[...]

What processes cause allu[...]
floors and induce stream aggr[...]
vium to accumulate as a resu[...]
Other causes of aggradation a[...]
global climate, such as the on[...]
illustrates one natural cause[...]
ity—that has been of major i[...]
North America and Eurasia d[...]
photo example, a modern val[...]
quantity of coarse rock debr[...]
ley aggradation of a simila[...]
widespread in a broad zo[...]
edges of the great ice shee[...]
Age. The accumulated all[...]
most valleys to depths of s[...]
meters. Figure 16.19*a* sh[...]
filled in this manner by[...]
stream. The case could[...]
one of a large number of[...]
England or the Middle W[...]

Suppose, next, that th[...]
greatly diminished. In th[...]
the ice sheets have disap[...]

16.1 Erosional and[...]
Strahler.)

landforms made by w[...]
narrow contact zone b[...]
is why, in terms of are[...]
environment of terres[...]

Areas of fluvial lan[...]
ture. Except for areas[...]
formerly occupied by[...]
crop cultivation or for[...]
processes. For this rea[...]
tant to the support of t[...]

Erosional and D[...] Landforms

All agents of denudati[...]
of erosion, transporta[...]
there are two major gr[...]
forms and depositiona[...]
form, such as an upli[...]
attacked by the proces[...]
fluvial action. Valleys[...]
away by fluvial agent[...]
hills, or mountain su[...]
parts of the crustal blo[...]
ning water. These se[...]
forms, shaped by prog[...]
of the bedrock mass,[...]
landforms. Fragments[...]
and bedrock that are re[...]
parent rock mass are t[...]
deposited elsewhere[...]
entirely different set[...]
tures—the *depositional*[...]

Figure 16.1 illustr[...]
groups of landforms as[...]
ravine, canyon, peak, sp[...]
The fan, built of rock[...]

. . . .

PUTTING YOU IN THE PICTURE

Have you ever experienced the power of a river first-hand? One of the best ways to learn about rivers is to ride one for a while. Picture yourself on a rafting trip down the Colorado River as you follow the narrative below.

The rickety school bus turns off the pavement and bumps down the dirt road toward the riverbank. With a lurch, it stops on a wide, gravel-covered spot next to the river, and you clamber off. Behind you is the ancient truck carrying the rafts, paddles, and gear that you and your group will need for your 12-day rafting trip through the majestic Grand Canyon of the Colorado River.

Soon, you are afloat, seven to a raft, slowly drifting with the current down the wide river. "Left side, forward!" "Right side, back!" The river guide barks the orders as you practice paddling together as a team. Sitting on the outer tube of the raft, you twist sideways, dipping your canoe paddle deeply into the blue-green water and pushing hard. This is real work! The river guide explains that safe passage through the hundred or more rapids you'll encounter on the trip will depend on how well you and your raftmates can move your craft across the swift currents of the mighty river.

Then, almost too quickly, you are at the first riffle. The raft glides easily through the rough water, and you think that perhaps this won't be so difficult after all. Then your river guide tells you that before the day is done, you'll be shooting

PUTTING YOU IN THE PICTURE

Rapids, which have
lives over the years
exercises, this time

As the days pas
quite at home with
of wild white-wate
with the calm of sl
bright summer sun,
taken foot trips to e
canyons and histori
way, you've always
to continue your jo
a close bond with it
able feeling about th
change. Lava Falls—
obstacle on your riv
downriver. With its
is the highest in the

A booming noise
telling you that the r

LANDFORMS

Most of the world's l
ning water. Flowing
ning water picks up
into a stream channe
rivers swell, lifting la
them downstream. In
tains and hills, carves
chapter describes the
forms it creates.

Running water is
erode, transport, and
The other three are w
fluid agents carry out t
discussed in Chapter 1
action of exogenic pro
the continents are wo
resulting sediments a
the sea or closed inlan

Denudation is an ov
the land surface. If le
operate over geologic
will reduce a continen
tureless, sea-level su
recall that plate tecto
kept continental crust e
The result is that runnir
have always had plenty
the many landforms tha

16.16 Niagara River topographic setting

A bird's-eye view of the Niagara River with its falls and gorge carved in strata of the Niagara Escarpment. View is toward the southwest from a point over Lake Ontario. (After a sketch by G. K. Gilbert. Redrawn from A. N. Strahler. Copyright © A. N. Strahler.)

Aggradation and Allu

A graded stream, delicately ac
and rock waste from upstream
changes in those inputs. Cha
cover bring changes in disch
points, and these changes in
ments. One kind of change is
valley floors.

Consider first what happ
exceeding the transporting c
section of channel where th
coarse sediment accumulate
of bars of sand, gravel, and p
elevation of the stream bed
As more bed materials accu
dient is steepened and flow
enables bed materials to be
over the channel floor at m
sections. In this way, sedi
stream will be gradually s
the stream.

Aggradation typically
from a narrow and deep
Because bars are contin
divided into multiple th
repeatedly to give a typi
The coarse channel de
floodplain, burying fi
coarse material.

Focus on Remote Sensing	16.1

A Canyon Gallery

Deep canyons, carved by powerful rivers crossing high terrain, are among the most dramatic features of the landscape. They provide a stunning testament to the power of fluvial systems to shape the Earth. Who can forget the awesome spectacle of a yawning canyon, seen from a precarious perch on a high rim? Here's a gallery of satellite images of canyons as acquired by the MISR and ASTER instruments.

The Grand Canyon of the Colorado River is among the most famous in the world. Spanning a length of about 450 km (about 280 mi) with vertical drops up to about 1500 m (about 5000 ft), it is indeed spectacular. Image (*a*), in true color, was acquired by MISR on December 31, 2000. Trace the path of the Colorado from Lake Powell, at the upper right, through narrow Marble Canyon, until the canyon broadens to the southeast of the snow-covered Kaibab Plateau. Here the Grand Canyon begins, revealing a dissected landscape between the two canyon rims as the river curves around the plateau. Note the sharp black shadow at the south rim, indicating that the rim is steep indeed. The canyon continues as the river flows westward to the edge of the frame. To the south of the canyon are cloud streaks that have formed from condensation trails of jet aircraft. Looking closely, you can see the shadow of each cloud as a dark streak to the north of the cloud.

Image (*b*), acquired by ASTER on May 12, 2000, is a computer-generated perspective view of the Grand Canyon looking north up Bright Angel Canyon from the South Rim. In this false color image, vegetation appears green and water appears blue, but rocks are not shown in their true colors. The blue and black patches on the green Kaibab Plateau are burned areas from a fire that is still smoldering. A pall of smoke stretches to

the east. Compare this with Figure 17.5, which is a ground-level photo of Bright Angel Canyon.

Image (*c*), another MISR image, shows the coast of southern Peru in

the Ariquipa region. Here the Pacific coast runs nearly east-west. The coastline is obscured by low clouds and fog at the bottom of the picture. Note the two vast canyons reaching

Grand Canyon, Arizona, imaged by MISR *(Courtesy NASA/GSFC/LARC/JPL, MISR team.)*

Grand Canyon perspective view from ASTER *(Courtesy NASA/GSFC/MITI/ERSDAC/JAROS and U.S. Japan ASTER Science Team.)*

(c)

Canyons of the Andes as seen by MISR *(Courtesy NASA/GSFC/LARC/JPL, MISR team.)*

from the sea deep into the Andean Plateau. They are the canyons of the Rio Ocoña to the west and Rio Camaná to the east. Dwarfing the American Grand Canyon, they are far wider and deeper. In fact, the canyon of the middle branch of the Rio Ocoña (Rio Cotahuasi) reaches a depth of 3354 m (11,001 ft) below the plateau, which is more than twice as deep as the Grand Canyon. The white patch between the two canyon systems is the snow covered Nevado Coropuna, at 6425 m (21,074 ft) elevation. Peaks to the west and east are Nevado Solimana (6117 m, 20,064 ft) and Nevado Ampato (5795 m, 18,909 ft).

Our last image (*d*) is another ASTER scene, a color infrared image of the Yangtze River canyon in the Three Gorges region of the provinces of Hubei and Sichuan, China. Although not a candidate for the deepest canyon, it is among the most scenic of the world's canyons, with steep limestone cliffs and forest-covered slopes separating clusters of quaint villages where tributaries meet the main channel. The inset image shows the construction site for the Three Gorges Dam, which will create a reservoir 175 m (574 ft) deep and about 600 km (about 375 mi) long. The dam will provide vast amounts of hydroelectric power and sharply reduce extreme flooding of the Yangtze. However, two of the three gorges will be flooded, and many local residents will be displaced. The Chinese government is making a major effort to forecast and mitigate environmental problems that will be created by the huge project. Our book's cover provides a view of the Qutang Gorge as well as more information about the dam.

Three Gorges region of the Yangtze River imaged by ASTER *(Courtesy NASA/GSFC/MITI/ERSDAC/JAROS and U.S. Japan ASTER Science Team.)*

(*d*)

16.20 *Alluvial terraces* *These terraces line the Rakaia River gorge on the South Island of New Zealand. The flat terrace surface in the foreground is used as pasture for sheep. Two higher terrace levels can be seen at the left.*

obstructions prevent the cutting away of more alluvium. Consequently, as shown in (*c*) step-like alluvial surfaces remain on both sides of the valley. The treads of these steps are called *alluvial terraces.*

Alluvial terraces have always attracted human settlement because of the advantages over both the valley-bottom floodplain—which is subject to annual flooding—and the hill slopes beyond—which may be too steep and rocky to cultivate. Besides, terraces are easily tilled and make prime agricultural land (Figure 16.20). Towns are also easily laid out on the flat ground of a terrace. Roads and railroads can be constructed along the terrace surfaces with little difficulty.

Alluvial terraces form when an aggrading river loses its sediment input and begins degrading its bed, leaving terraces behind as it cuts deeper into its sediment-filled valley.

Alluvial Rivers and Their Floodplains

We turn now to the graded river with its floodplain. As time passes, the floodplain is widened, so that broad areas of floodplain lie on both sides of the river

---

An alluvial river, with its low gradient and broad floodplain, creates characteristic landforms including bluffs, meanders, cutoffs, ox-bow lakes, and natural levees.

---

channel. Civil engineers have given the name **alluvial river** to a large river of very low channel gradient. It flows on a thick floodplain accumulation of alluvium constructed by the river itself in earlier stages of its activity. Characteristically, an alluvial river experiences overbank floods each year or two. These floods occur during the season of large water surplus over the watershed. Overbank flooding of an alluvial river normally inundates part or all of a floodplain that is bounded on either side by rising steep slopes, called *bluffs.*

Typical landforms of an alluvial river and its floodplain are illustrated in Figure 16.21. Dominating the floodplain is the meandering river channel itself and abandoned stretches of former channels. Meanders develop narrow necks, which are cut through, thus shortening the river course and leaving a meander loop abandoned. This event is called a *cutoff.* It is quickly followed by deposition of silt and sand across the ends of the abandoned channel, producing an *ox-bow lake.* The ox-bow lake is gradu-

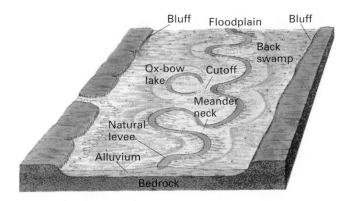

16.21 Floodplain landforms of an alluvial river *As meanders wander downriver, they create a variety of landforms, including ox-bow lakes, cutoffs, and natural levees. (Drawn by A. N. Strahler.)*

16.22 Ox-bow lakes *This aerial photo of the Mississippi River floodplain shows two ox-bow lakes— former river bends that were cut off as the river shifted its course. At the bottom is a thin former meander channel still receiving river water. If flood deposits seal it off from the river, it will become an ox-bow lake as well. Vegetation appears bright red in this color-infrared photo.*

ally filled in with fine sediment brought in during high floods and with organic matter produced by aquatic plants. Eventually, the ox-bows are converted into swamps, but their identity is retained indefinitely (Figure 16.22).

During periods of overbank flooding, when the entire floodplain is inundated, water spreads from the main channel over adjacent floodplain deposits (Figure 16.23). As the current slackens, sand and silt are deposited in a zone adjacent to the channel. The result is an accumulation of higher land on either side of the channel known as a **natural levee.** Because deposition is heavier closest to the channel and decreases away from the channel, the levee surface slopes away from the channel (Figure 16.21). Between the levees and the bluffs is lower ground, called the *backswamp.* In Figure 16.23, the small settlements are located on the higher ground of the levee, next to the river, while the agricultural fields occupy the backswamp area.

Overbank flooding not only results in the deposition of a thin layer of silt on the floodplain, but also brings an infusion of dissolved mineral substances that enter the soil. As a result of the resupply of nutrients, floodplain soils retain their remarkable fertility, even though they are located in regions of rainfall surplus from which these nutrients are normally leached away.

Entrenched Meanders

What happens when a broadly meandering river is uplifted by rapid tectonic activity? The uplift increases the river's gradient, so that it cuts downward into the bedrock below. This forms a steep-walled inner gorge. On either side lies the former floodplain, now a flat terrace high above river level. Any river deposits left on the terrace are rapidly stripped off by runoff because floods no longer reach the terraces to restore eroded sediment.

Where rapid uplift causes meandering rivers to cut deeply into bedrock, entrenched meanders are formed.

Uplift may cause the meanders to become impressed into the bedrock and give the inner gorge a meandering pattern (Figure 16.24). These sinuous bends are termed *entrenched meanders* to distinguish them from the floodplain meanders of an alluvial river (Figure 16.25). Although entrenched meanders are not free to shift about as floodplain meanders do, they can enlarge slowly so as to produce cutoffs. Cutoff of an entrenched meander leaves a high, round hill separated from the valley wall by the deep abandoned river channel and the shortened river course (Figure 16.24). As you might guess, such hills formed ideal natural fortifications. Many European fortresses of the Middle Ages were built on such cutoff meander spurs. Under unusual circumstances, where the bedrock includes a strong,

16.23   *Inundated floodplain* *This river floodplain in Bangladesh is largely under water during a flood. Villages occupy the higher ground of the natural levees bordering the river channel.*

16.24   *Block diagram of entrenched meanders* *Uplift of a meandering stream has produced entrenched meanders. One meander neck has been cut through, forming a natural bridge. (Drawn by E. Raisz. Copyright © A.N. Strahler.)*

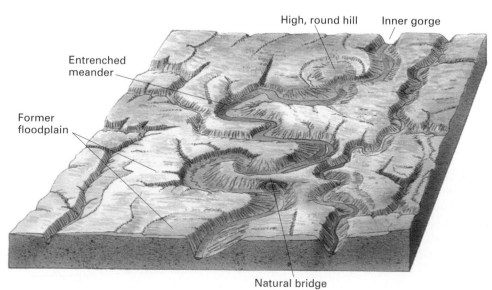

High, round hill   Inner gorge

Entrenched
meander

Former
floodplain

Natural bridge

16.25 Entrenched meanders *The Goosenecks of the San Juan River in Utah are deeply entrenched river meanders in horizontal sedimentary rock layers. The canyon, carved from sandstones and limestones, is about 370 m (1399 ft) deep.*

massive sandstone formation, meander cutoff leaves a *natural bridge* formed by the narrow meander neck.

The Geographic Cycle

The Earth's fluvial landscapes are quite diverse. They range from mountain regions of steep slopes and rugged peaks to regions of gentle hills and valleys to nearly flat plains that stretch from horizon to horizon. One way to view these landscapes is to consider them as stages of evolution in a cycle that begins with rapid uplift and follows with long erosion by streams in a graded condition. This cycle, called the *geographic cycle*, was first described by William Morris Davis, a prominent geographer and geomorphologist of the late nineteenth and early twentieth centuries. Let's look at this idea in more detail.

Consider a landscape made up of many drainage basins and their branching stream networks that has been rapidly uplifted by tectonic forces. The region is rugged, with steep mountainsides and high, narrow crests (Figure 16.26a). We refer to this landscape as being in a *youthful stage.*

After initial uplift, the main streams draining the region establish a graded condition. Rock debris is transported out of each drainage basin at the same average rate as the debris is being contributed from the land surfaces within the basin. Eventually, the export of debris lowers the land surface generally, and the average altitude of the land surface steadily declines. This decline must be accompanied by a reduction in the average gradients of all streams (b). As the sharp mountain peaks and gorges of the youthful stage give way to rounded hills and broad valleys, we reach the *mature stage* of the geographic cycle.

As time passes, the streams and valley-side slopes of the drainage basins undergo gradual change to lower gradients. In theory, the ultimate goal of the denudation process is to reduce the land mass to a featureless plain at sea level. In this process, a sea-level surface imagined to lie beneath

The geographic cycle traces the fate of rivers and fluvial landforms from an initial uplift creating steep slopes and canyons to a final low, gently rolling surface called a peneplain.

the entire land mass represents the lower limiting level, or *base level,* of the fluvial denudation (labeled in Figures 16.9 and 16.26). But because the rate of denudation becomes progressively slower, the land surface approaches the base-level surface of zero elevation at a slower and slower pace. Under this scenario, the ultimate goal can never be reached. Instead, after the passage of some millions of years, the land surface is reduced to a gently rolling surface of low elevation, called a *peneplain* (c). You can think of this strange term as meaning an "almost-plain." With the evolution of the peneplain, the landscape has reached *old age.*

Production of a peneplain requires a high degree of crustal and sea-level stability for a period of many millions of years. One region that has been cited as a possible example of a contemporary peneplain is the Amazon-Orinoco Basin of South America. This vast region is a stable continental shield of ancient rock with very low relief.

What happens if a peneplain is uplifted? Figure 16.26d shows the peneplain of (a) uplifted to an elevation of several hundred meters. The base level is now far below the land surface. Soon streams begin to trench the land mass and to carve deep, steep-walled valleys, shown in (e). This process is called *rejuvenation*. With the passage of many millions of years, the landscape will be carved into the rugged stage shown in (a), and the later stages of (b) and (c) will follow.

Equilibrium Approach to Landforms

While Davis's idealized geographic cycle is useful for understanding landscape evolution over very long periods of time, it does little to explain the diversity of the features observed in real landscapes. Most geomorphologists now approach landforms and landscapes from the viewpoint of *equilibrium*. This approach explains a fluvial landform as the product of forces acting upon it, including both forces of

(a)

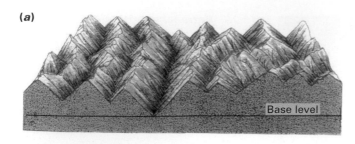

Base level

(b)

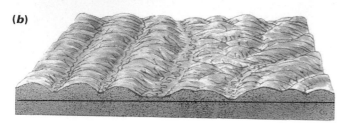

(c)

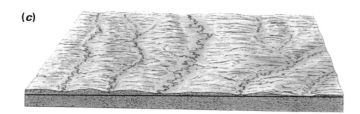

(d)

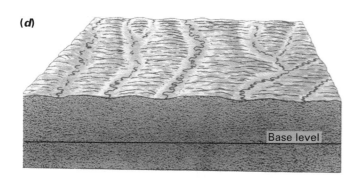

Base level

(e)

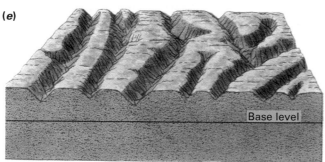

Base level

16.26 The geographic cycle *(a) In the youthful stage, relief is great, slopes are steep, and the rate of erosion is rapid. (b) In the mature stage, relief is greatly reduced, slopes are gentle, and rate of erosion is slow. Soils are thick over the broadly rounded hill summits. (c) In old age, after many millions of years of fluvial denudation, a peneplain is formed. Slopes are very gentle, and the landscape is an undulating plain. Floodplains are broad, and the stream gradients are extremely low. All of the land surface lies close to base level. (d) The peneplain is uplifted. (e) Streams trench a new system of deep valleys in the phase of land-mass rejuvenation. (Drawn by A.N. Strahler.)*

in which hill slopes and stream gradients remain steep in order to maintain a graded condition while eroding a strong rock like massive granite. In the next chapter, we will provide many examples of landforms that result from erosive processes acting on both strong and weak rock within the same region.

Another problem with Davis's geographic cycle is that it only applies where the land surface is stable over long periods of time. As we know from our study of plate tectonics in Chapter 12, crustal movements are frequent on the geologic time scale, and few regions of the land surface remain untouched by tectonic forces in the long run. Recall also that continental lithosphere floats on a soft asthenosphere. As layer upon layer of rock is stripped from a land mass by erosion, the land mass becomes lighter and is buoyed upward. The process of crustal rise in response to unloading is known as *isostatic compensation*. The proper model, then, is one of uplift as an ongoing process to which erosional processes are constantly adjusting rather than as a sudden event followed by denudation.

FLUVIAL PROCESSES IN AN ARID CLIMATE

Desert regions look strikingly different from humid regions in both vegetation and landforms. Obviously, the lower precipitation makes the difference. Vegetation is sparse or absent, and land surfaces are mantled with mineral material—sand, gravel, rock fragments, or bedrock itself.

Although deserts have low precipitation, rain falls in dry climates as well as in moist, and most landforms of desert regions are formed by running water. A particular locality in a dry desert may experience heavy rain only once in several years. But when rain does fall, stream channels carry water and perform important work as agents of erosion, transportation, and deposition. Fluvial processes are especially effective in shaping desert landforms because of the sparse vegetation cover. The few small

uplift and denudation, with the characteristics of the rock material playing an important role. Thus, we find steep slopes and high relief where the underlying rock is strong and highly resistant to erosion. Even a "youthful" landscape may be in a long-lived equilibrium state

The equilibrium approach sees fluvial landforms as reflecting a balance between processes of uplift and denudation acting on rocks of varying resistance to erosion.

16.27 Eye on the Landscape Flash flood *A flash flood has filled this desert channel in the Tucson Mountains of Arizona with raging, turbid waters. A distant thunderstorm produced the runoff.* **What else would the geographer see? ...Answers at the end of the chapter.**

plants that survive offer little or no protection to soil or bedrock. Without a thick vegetative cover to protect the ground and hold back the swift downslope flow of water, large quantities of coarse rock debris are swept into the streams. A dry channel is transformed in a few minutes into a raging flood of muddy water heavily charged with rock fragments (Figure 16.27).

An important contrast between regions of arid and humid climates lies in the way in which the water enters and leaves a stream channel (Figure 16.28). In a humid region (*a*) with a high water table sloping toward a stream channel, ground water moves steadily toward the channel and seeps into the stream bed, producing permanent (perennial) streams. In arid regions (*b*), the water table normally lies far below the channel floor. Where a stream flows across a plain of gravel and sand, water is lost from the channel by seepage. Loss of discharge by seepage and evaporation strongly depletes the flow of streams in alluvium-filled valleys of arid regions. As a result, aggradation occurs and braided channels are common. Streams of desert regions are often short and end in alluvial deposits or on the floors of shallow, dry lakes.

16.28 Stream water flow to ground water *In humid regions (a), a stream channel receives ground water through seepage. In arid regions (b), stream water seeps out of the channel and into the water table below. (Copyright © A.N. Strahler.)*

(a)

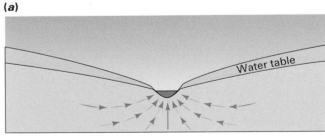

(b)

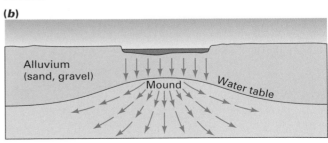

16.29 Features of an alluvial fan *A cross section shows mudflow layers interbedded with sand layers, providing water (arrows) for a well in the fan. (Copyright © A.N. Strahler.)*

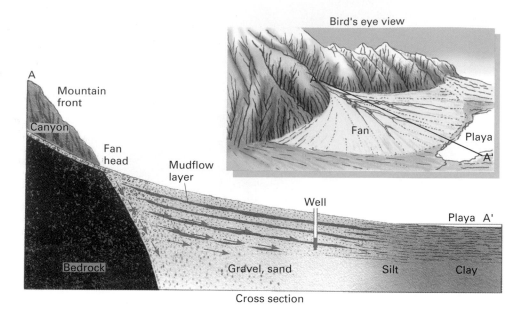

Alluvial Fans

One very common landform built by braided, aggrading streams is the **alluvial fan,** a low cone of alluvial sands and gravels resembling in outline an open Japanese fan (Figure 16.29). The apex, or central point of the fan, lies at the mouth of a canyon or ravine. The fan is built out on an adjacent plain. Alluvial fans are of many sizes. In fact, some desert fans are many kilometers across (Figure 16.30a).

Fans are built by streams carrying heavy loads of coarse rock waste from a mountain or an upland region. The braided channel shifts constantly, but its position is firmly fixed at the canyon mouth. The lower part of the channel, below the apex, sweeps back and forth. This activity accounts for the semicircular fan form and the downward slope in all radial directions away from the apex.

Large, complex alluvial fans also include mudflows (Figure 16.29). Mud layers are interbedded with sand and gravel layers. Water infiltrates the fan at its head, making its way to lower levels along sand layers. The mudflow layers serve as barriers to ground water movement. The trapped ground water is under pressure from water higher in the fan apex. When a well is drilled into the lower slopes of the fan, water rises spontaneously as artesian flow. (See Chapter 15 and Figure 15.6.)

Alluvial fans are the primary sites of ground water reservoirs in the southwestern United States. In many fan areas, sustained heavy pumping of these reserves for irrigation has lowered the water table severely. The rate of recharge is extremely slow in comparison. At some locations, recharge is increased by building water-spreading structures and infiltrating basins on the fan surfaces. A serious side effect of excessive ground water withdrawal is subsidence (sinking) of the land surface. (See *Eye on Global Change 15.1 • Sinking Cities.*)

> Although rain is infrequent in desert environments, running water shapes desert landforms with great effectiveness because of the lack of vegetation cover.

The Landscape of Mountainous Deserts

Where tectonic activity has recently produced block faulting in an area of continental desert, the assemblage of fluvial landforms is particularly diverse. The basin-and-range region of the western United States is such an area. It includes large parts of Nevada and Utah, southeastern California, southern Arizona and New Mexico, and adjacent parts of Mexico. The uplifted and tilted blocks, separated by downdropped tectonic basins, provide an environment for the development of spectacular erosional and depositional fluvial landforms.

Figure 16.31 demonstrates some landscape features of mountainous deserts. Figure 16.31a shows two uplifted fault blocks with a down dropped block between them. Although denudation acts on the uplifted blocks as they are being raised, we have shown them as very little modified at the time tectonic activity has ceased. At first, the faces of the fault block are extremely steep. They are scored with deep ravines, and talus blocks form cones at the bases of the blocks.

Figure 16.31b shows a later stage of denudation in which streams have carved up the mountain blocks into a rugged landscape of deep canyons and high divides. Rock waste furnished by these steep mountain slopes is carried from the mouths of canyons to form numerous large alluvial fans. The fan deposits form a continuous apron extending far out into the basins.

In the centers of desert basins lie the saline lakes and dry lake basins mentioned in Chapter 15. Accumulation of fine sediment and precipitated salts produces an extremely flat basin floor, called a **playa** in the southwestern United States and in Mexico. Salt flats are found where an evaporite layer forms the surface. In some playas, shallow water forms a salt lake.

Figure 16.30*b* is an air photograph of a mountainous desert landscape in the Death Valley region of eastern California. Three environmental zones can be seen in the photo. First is a region of rugged mountain masses dissected into canyons with steep rocky walls. At lower elevations, a zone of coalescing

Alluvial fans are common features of arid landscapes. They occur where streams discharge water and sediment from a narrow canyon or gorge onto an adjacent plain.

Landforms of mountainous deserts include alluvial fans, dry lakes or playas, and pediments—rock platforms veneered with alluvium.

alluvial fans lines the mountain front. Last is the white playa occupying the central part of the basin.

In this type of mountainous desert, fluvial processes are limited to local transport of rock particles from a mountain range to the nearest adjacent basin, which receives all the sediment. The basin gradually fills as the mountains diminish in elevation. Because there is no outflow to the sea, the concept of a base level of denudation has no meaning. Each arid basin becomes a closed system as far as transport of sediment is involved. Only the hydrologic system is open, with water entering as precipitation and leaving as evaporation.

As the desert mountain masses are lowered in height and reduced in extent, a gently sloping rock floor, called a *pediment* develops close to the receding mountain front (Figure 16.33). As the remaining mountains shrink further in size, the pediment surfaces expand to form wide rock platforms thinly veneered with alluvium. This advanced stage is shown in Figure 16.31*c*. The desert land surface produced in an advanced stage of fluvial activity is an undulating plain consisting largely of areas of pediment surrounded by areas of alluvial fan and playa surfaces.

GEODISCOVERIES **Web Quiz.** Take a quick quiz on the key concepts of this chapter.

16.31 Mountainous desert landforms *Idealized diagrams of landforms of the mountainous deserts of the southwestern United States. (a) Initial uplift of two blocks, with a downdropped valley between them. (b) Stage of rapid filling of tectonic basins with debris from high, rugged mountain blocks. (c) Advanced stage with small mountain remnants and broad playa and fan slopes. (Drawn by A. N. Strahler.)*

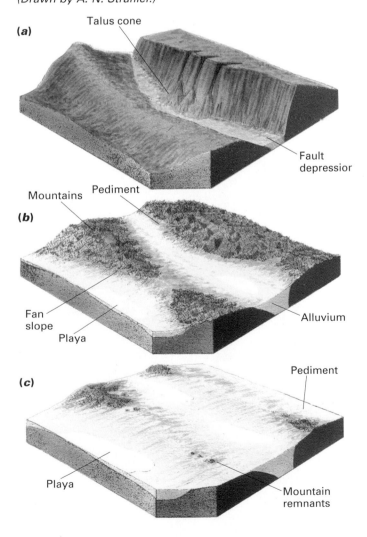

A Look Ahead In this chapter we have examined a number of geomorphic processes in which running water erodes, transports, and deposits sediment to create landforms. These processes are active at individual and local scales, but are organized at the regional level by large rivers that carve landscapes on their way to the sea. The downstream pattern is one of small streams eroding steep slopes at the river's headwaters, a river grading its course to smooth its profile in the middle reaches, and an alluvial river meandering across a broad floodplain to form terraces, natural levees, and oxbow lakes.

We should note, however, that running water, the primary agent of denudation, does not act equally on all types of rocks. Some rocks are more resistant to erosion, while others are less so. As a result, fluvial erosion can create unique and interesting landscapes that reveal rock structures of various kinds. This will be the subject of our next chapter.

GEODISCOVERIES **Web Links.** Visit this chapter's web sites to view awesome floods and dramatic waterfalls. Tour the spectacular Grand Canyon and the scenic Hudson River valley.

a...Alluvial fans *Great alluvial fans extend out upon the floor of Death Valley. The canyons from which they originate have carved deeply into a great uplifted fault block.*

c...Pediment *A pediment, gently sloping away from these hills in the Mojave Desert, is seen here in profile as a straight line of green vegetation.*

b...Desert playa *Racetrack Playa, a flat, white plain, is surrounded by alluvial fans and rugged mountains. This desert valley lies in the northern part of the Panamint Range, not far west of Death Valley, California. In the distance rises the steep eastern face of the Inyo Mountains, a great fault block.*

In Review | Landforms Made by Running Water

- This chapter has covered the landforms and land-forming processes of running water, one of the four active agents of *denudation.* Like the other agents, running water erodes, transports, and deposits rock material, forming both *erosional* and *depositional landforms.*

- The work of running water begins on slopes, producing *colluvium* where overland flow moves soil particles downslope, and producing **alluvium** when the particles enter stream channels and are later deposited. In most natural landscapes, *soil erosion* and soil formation rates are more or less equal, a condition known as the *geologic norm. Badlands* are an exception in which natural erosion rates are very high.

- The work of streams includes **stream erosion** and **stream transportation.** Where stream channels are carved into soft materials, large amounts of sediment can be obtained by *hydraulic action.* Where stream channels flow on bedrock, channels are deepened only by the abrasion of bed and banks by mineral particles, large and small. Both the *suspended load* and *bed load* of rivers increase greatly as velocity increases. Velocity, in turn, depends on gradient.

- Over time, streams tend to a **graded** condition, in which their gradients are adjusted to move the average amount of water and sediment supplied to them by slopes. Lakes and *waterfalls,* created by tectonic, volcanic, or glacial activity, are short-lived events, geologically speaking, that give way to a smooth, *graded* stream *profile.* Grade is maintained as landscapes are eroded toward base level.

- When provided with a sudden inflow of rock material, as, for example, by glacial action, streams build up their beds by *aggradation.* When that inflow ceases, streams resume downcutting, leaving behind *alluvial terraces.*

- Large rivers with low gradients that move large quantities of sediment are termed **alluvial rivers.** The **meandering** of these rivers forms *cutoff* meanders, *ox-bow lakes,* and other typical landforms. Alluvial rivers are sites of intense human activity. Their fertile floodplains yield agricultural crops and provide easy transportation paths. When a region containing a meandering alluvial river is uplifted, *entrenched meanders* can result.

- The *geographic cycle* organizes fluvial landscapes according to their age in a cycle of uplift that forms mountains and subsequent erosion to nearly flat surfaces called *peneplains.* In the *equilibrium* approach, landforms are viewed as products of uplift and erosion as continuous processes acting on rocks of varying resistance to erosion.

- Although rainfall is scarce in deserts, running water is very effective there in producing **fluvial landforms.** Desert streams, subject to flash flooding, build **alluvial fans** at the mouths of canyons. Water sinks into the fan deposits, creating local ground water reservoirs. Eventually, desert mountains are worn down into gently sloping *pediments.* Fine sediments and salts, carried by streams, accumulate in **playas,** from which water evaporates, leaving sediment and salt behind.

Key Terms

fluvial landforms, p. 546
fluvial processes, p. 546
alluvium, p. 549
stream erosion, p. 550

stream transportation, p. 550
stream deposition, p. 550
stream load, p. 551

graded stream, p. 553
alluvial meanders, p. 553
alluvial river, p. 562
natural levee, p. 563

alluvial fan, p. 568
playa, p. 569

Review Questions

1. List and briefly identify the four flowing substances that serve as agents of denudation.
2. Describe the process of slope erosion. What is meant by the geologic norm?
3. Contrast the two terms *colluvium* and *alluvium.* Where on a landscape would you look to find each one?
4. What special conditions are required for badlands to form?
5. When and how does sheet erosion occur? How does it lead to rill erosion and gullying?
6. In what ways do streams erode their bed and banks?
7. What is stream load? Identify its three components. In what form do large rivers carry most of their load?
8. How is velocity related to the ability of a stream to move sediment downstream?

9. How does stream degradation produce alluvial terraces?
10. Define the term *alluvial river.* Identify some characteristic landforms of alluvial rivers. Why are alluvial rivers important to human civilization?
11. Describe the evolution of a fluvial landscape according to the geographic cycle. What is meant by rejuvenation?
12. What is the equilibrium approach to landforms? How does it differ from interpretation using the geographic cycle?
13. Why is fluvial action so effective in arid climates, considering that rainfall is scarce? How do streams in arid climates differ from streams in moist climates?
14. Describe the evolution of the landscape in a mountainous desert. Use the terms *alluvial fan, playa,* and *pediment* in your answer.

Visualizing Exercises

1. Compare erosional and depositional landforms. Sketch an example of each type.
2. What is a graded stream? Sketch the profile of a graded stream and compare it with the profile of a stream draining a recently uplifted set of landforms.
3. Sketch the floodplain of a graded, meandering river. Identify key landforms on the sketch. How do they form?

Essay Questions

1. A river originates high in the Rocky Mountains, crosses the high plains, flows through the agricultural regions of the Midwest, and finally reaches the sea. Describe the fluvial processes and landforms you might expect to find on a journey along the river from its headwaters to the ocean.
2. What would be the effects of climate change on a fluvial system? Choose either the effects of cooler temperatures and higher precipitation in a mountainous desert, or warmer temperatures and lower precipitation in a humid agricultural region.

Eye on the Landscape

Chapter Opener White-water rafting on the Colorado Grand Canyon is an entrenched river gorge cutting through layers of flat-lying sandstone and shale **(A)**. Note the large accumulations of talus at the base of the cliffs **(B)**. Most of the canyon shows only sparse desert vegetation, but deep-rooted plants appear near the river and on sedimentary deposits of side streams **(C)**. Surprisingly, the river water in the canyon **(D)** is quite cold. Nearly all of it is released from the cold, deep waters of Lake Powell behind the Glen Canyon Dam, which is upstream. We will see more of landforms of the Grand Canyon in Chapter 17. Plants and water were covered in Chapter 8, and dams were discussed in the preceding chapter (15).

16.27 Flash flood One of the world's more vegetated deserts, the Sonoran Desert is known for its unique plants. At **(A)**, the distinctive spikes of the saguaro cactus are visible, projecting above the cover of streamside vegetation (probably ocotillo). Deserts were covered in Chapter 7; and vegetation of the Sonoran Desert is mentioned in Chapter 9. Note the sediment at **(B)**. It is probably not deposited by the stream, because it is unsorted and the rock fragments are quite angular. It appears to be desert pavement (Chapter 18), flooded by runoff from the left that is flowing toward the channel.

16.15 Victoria Falls A fault has shattered and broken rock layers, creating a zone of weakness that has been eroded by the Zambezi River to form the gorge of Victoria Falls **(A)**. Note the resistant rock layer that keeps the waterfall vertical **(B)**. Native vegetation here is thorntree-tall grass savanna, which is visible in the near distance **(C)**. Faults were covered in Chapter 13, while the vegetation of Africa is mapped and described in Chapter 9.

An aerial view of the Rapley Monocline, near Mexican Hat, Utah. What else would the geographer see? … Answers at the end of the chapter.

17 | LANDFORMS AND ROCK STRUCTURE

PUTTING YOU IN THE PICTURE

An aerial view of the Earth provides a unique perspective on the landscape. At the scale of a high-flying passenger aircraft, an overview emerges that brings out the broader patterns of landscape. In regions of diverse rock types, this big picture emphasizes the contrast between easily eroded rock formations and those that are more resistant. The central Rocky Mountains and Colorado Plateau are such regions. Imagine yourself on a flight from Denver to Las Vegas on a clear day in June. Here's what you might experience:

The force of the powerful jet engines pushes you deeply into your window seat as you roll down the runway. Quickly, the plane is airborne and heads westward toward the magnificent Rockies. The slope of the Front Range looms large, and as you head across the mountain barrier, the ground seems to rise up to meet you. Below is I-70, twisting and turning its way up the narrow valleys toward the summit. There's the entrance to the Eisenhower Tunnel! The tiny cars below disappear into the mountain slope for the long traverse beneath the mountain crest.

Looking south, you see the peaks of the Front Range spread out in a long line. The overlying sedimentary rocks have long been eroded away here in the center of this vast elongated dome, exposing the hard granite at the core. You easily identify Pikes Peak in the far distance, its summit silhouetted against the dark blue sky. Looking straight down, you see the gray of the ancient granite rock, mantling the slopes between the patches of snow still lying in the low places. Snowpacks in high valley heads below you hint at how the mountains must have looked when their glaciers slowly and majestically marched valleyward, carving broad, U-shaped valleys and leaving the ridges and piles of sediment

18.3 Shoaling waves *As waves approach the shore, wave length decreases and height increases until the wave becomes unstable and breaks.*

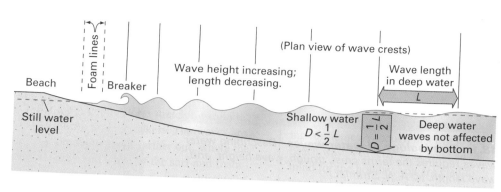

about 2.7 m (9 ft) on average, and the highest waves will reach 5.5 m (18 ft). For full development, a duration of 16 hours and a fetch of 300 km (160 mi) is required. Note that if we double the sustained wind speed to 50 knots (26 m/s, 58 mi/hr), wave heights are much more than doubled and can even reach peak heights of 30 m (99 ft). Couple this with the fact that the energy of a wave is proportional to the square of its height, and you can appreciate how hurricane winds can generate waves with enormous destructive power.

What happens when waves reach the shore? Most shore zones have a fairly smooth, sloping bottom extending offshore into deeper water. As a train of waves enters progressively shallower water depths, there comes a point at which the orbital motion of the waves encounters interference with the bottom. As a general rule, this critical depth is about equal to one-half the wave length (Figure 18.3).

As the waves continue to travel shoreward, the wave length decreases while the wave height increases, as shown in Figure 18.3. Consequently, the wave is steepened and becomes unstable. Rather suddenly the crest of the wave moves forward and the wave is transformed into a *breaker*, which then collapses (Figure 18.4). A foamy, turbulent sheet of water then rides up the beach. This *swash* is a powerful surge that causes a landward movement of sand and gravel on the beach. When the force of the swash has been spent against the slope of the beach, the return flow, or *backwash*, pours down the beach. This "undercurrent" or "undertow," as it is popularly called, can be strong enough to sweep unwary bathers off their feet and carry them seaward beneath the next oncoming breaker. The backwash carries sand and gravel seaward again to complete the wave cycle.

Marine Scarps and Cliffs

If you've ever visited a beach when waves are high, you can appreciate how the force of tons of water moving up and

down the beach can do enormous amounts of work. Where weak or soft materials—various kinds of regolith, such as alluvium—make up the coastline, the force of the forward-moving water alone easily cuts into the coastline. Here, erosion is rapid, and the shoreline may recede rapidly. Under these conditions, a steep bank—a *marine scarp*—is the typical coastal landform (Figure 18.5a). It retreats steadily under attack of storm waves.

GEODISCOVERIES **The Work of Waves.** Watch this video to see examples of breaking waves and to review the processes by which waves transport sediment.

Where a **marine cliff** lies within reach of the moving water, it is impacted with enormous force. Rock fragments of all sizes, from sand to cobbles, are carried by the surging water and thrust against the bedrock of the cliff. The impact breaks away new rock fragments, and the cliff is undercut at the base. In this way, the cliff erodes shoreward, maintaining its form as it retreats. The retreat of a marine cliff formed of hard bedrock is exceedingly slow, when judged in terms of a human life span.

Figure 18.6 illustrates some details of a typical marine cliff. A deep basal indentation, the *wave-cut notch,* marks the line of most intense wave erosion. The waves find points of weakness in the bedrock and penetrate deeply to form crevices and *sea caves*. Where a more resistant rock mass projects seaward, it may be cut through to form a picturesque *sea arch*. After an arch collapses, a rock column, known as a *stack,* remains (Figure 18.5b). Eventually, the stack is toppled by wave action and is leveled. As the sea cliff retreats landward, continued wave abrasion forms an *abrasion platform* (Figure 18.5c). This sloping rock floor continues to be eroded and widened by abrasion beneath the breakers. If a beach is present, it is little more than a thin layer of gravel and cobblestones atop the abrasion platform.

18.4 A breaking wave *As the wave approaches the beach (1–3), it steepens (4–5), and finally falls forward (6–7), rushing up the beach slope (8). (After W. M. Davis.)*

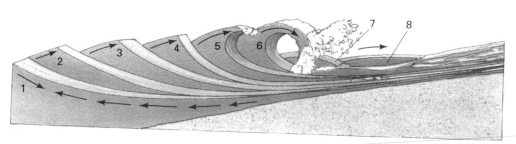

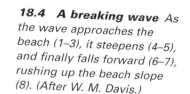

576

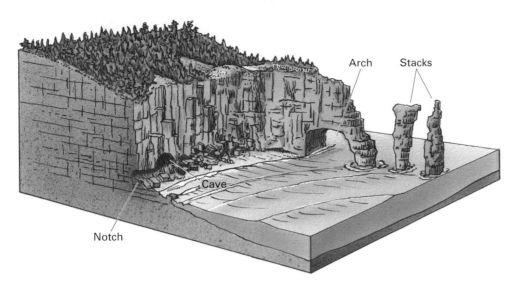

18.6 Landforms of sea cliffs *Wave action undercuts the marine cliff, maintaining its form. (Drawn by E. Raisz.)*

Arch

Stacks

Cave

Notch

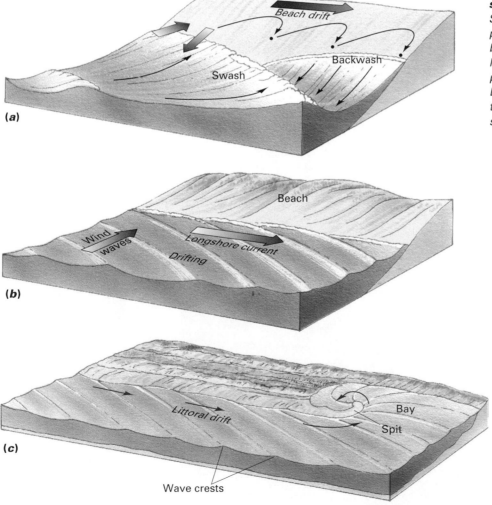

18.7 How waves move sediment by littoral drift *(a) Swash and backwash move particles along the beach in beach drift. (b) Waves set up a longshore current that move particles by longshore drift. (c) Littoral drift, produced by these two processes, creates a sandspit.*

Beach drift

Backwash

Swash

(a)

Beach

Wind waves

Longshore current

Drifting

(b)

Littoral drift

Bay

Spit

Wave crests

(c)

18.5 Landforms of Coastal Erosion

a...*Eye on the Landscape* ***Retreating shoreline*** *Mohegan Bluffs, Block Island, Rhode Island. This marine scarp of Ice Age sediments is being rapidly eroded, threatening historic Southeast Lighthouse. In 1993 the lighthouse was moved to a safer spot 73.5 m (245 ft) away.* **What else would the geographer see?...Answers at the end of the chapter.**

c...A wave-cut abrasion platform Continued wave abrasion formed this rock platform on the central coast of California, Montana d'Oro State Park.

b...Stacks on a shoreline of marine cliffs These rock stacks at Port Campbell National Park, Victoria, Australia, are dubbed the "Twelve Apostles." They are formed by the undercutting of marine cliffs by wave action. A promontory is first undercut from both sides, creating an arch and then a stack when the arch collapses.

Beaches

Where sand is in abundant supply, it accumulates as a thick, wedge-shaped deposit, or **beach.** Although beaches are most often formed of particles of fine to coarse quartz sand, some beaches are built from rounded pebbles or cobbles. Still others are formed from fragments of volcanic rock (Hawaii) or even shells (Florida).

Beaches absorb the energy of breaking waves. During short periods of storm activity, the beach is cut back, and sand is carried offshore a short distance by the heavy wave action. However, the sand is slowly returned to the beach during long periods when waves are weak. In this way, a beach may retain a fairly stable but alternating configuration over many years' time.

Littoral Drift

The unceasing shifting of beach materials with swash and backwash of breaking waves results in a sidewise movement known as *beach drift* (Figure 18.7a). Wave fronts usually approach the shore at less than a right angle, so that the swash and its burden of sand ride obliquely up the beach. After the wave has spent its energy, the backwash flows down the slope of the beach in the most direct downhill direction. The particles are dragged directly seaward and come to rest at a position to one side of the start-

---

Breakers attacking the shore at an angle produce littoral drift, which includes beach drift—a movement of sediment along the shoreline—as well as longshore drift—a sediment movement just offshore.

---

ing place. This movement is repeated many times, and individual rock particles travel long distances along the shore. Multiplied many thousands of times to include the numberless particles of the beach, beach drift becomes a very significant form of sediment transport.

Sediment in the shore zone is also moved along the beach in a related, but different, process. When waves approach a shoreline at an angle to the beach, a current is set up parallel to the shore in a direction away from the wind. This is known as a *longshore current* (Figure 18.7b). When wave and wind conditions are favorable, this current is capable of carrying sand along the sea bottom. The process is called *longshore drift.* Beach drift and longshore drift, acting together, move particles in the same direction for a given set of onshore winds. The total process is called **littoral drift** (Figure 18.7c. ("Littoral" means "pertaining to a coast or shore.")

Littoral drift operates to shape shorelines in two quite different situations. Where the shoreline is straight or broadly curved for many kilometers at a stretch, littoral drift moves the sand along the beach in one direction for a given set of prevailing winds. This situation is shown in Figure 18.7c. Where a bay exists, the sand is carried out into open water as a long finger, or *sandspit* (Figure 18.8). As the sandspit grows, it forms a barrier, called a *bar,* across the mouth of the bay.

18.8 Eye on the Landscape Sandspit This white sandspit is growing in a direction toward the observer. Monomoy Point, Cape Cod. Massachusetts. **What else would the geographer see? ... Answers at the end of the chapter.**

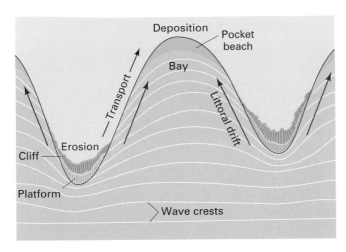

18.9 Pocket beaches *On an embayed coast, sediment is carried from eroding headlands to the bayheads, where pocket beaches are formed. (Copyright © A. N. Strahler.)*

A second situation is shown in Figure 18.9. Here the coastline consists of prominent headlands, projecting seaward, and deep bays. Approaching wave fronts slow when the water becomes shallow, and this slowing effect causes the wave front to wrap around the headland. High, wave-cut cliffs develop shoreward of an abrasion platform. Sediment from the eroding cliffs is carried by littoral drift along the sides of the bay, converging on the head of the bay. The result is a crescent-shaped beach, often called a *pocket beach.*

Littoral Drift and Shore Protection

When sand arrives at a particular section of the beach more rapidly than it is carried away, the beach is widened and built oceanward. This change is called **progradation** (building out). When sand leaves a section of beach more rapidly than it is brought in, the beach is narrowed and the shoreline moves landward. This change is called **retrogradation** (cutting back).

Along stretches of shoreline affected by retrogradation, the beach may be seriously depleted or even entirely disappear, destroying valuable shore property. In some circumstances, structures can be installed that will cause progradation, and so build a broad, protective beach. This is done by installing groins at close intervals along the beach. A *groin* is simply a wall or embankment built at right angles to the shoreline. It may be constructed of large rock masses, of concrete, or of wooden pilings. The groins act to trap sediment moving along the shore as littoral drift (Figure 18.10).

In some cases, the source of beach sand is sediment delivered to the coast by

> **Groins are walls or embankments built at right angles to the shoreline. They trap littoral drift and help prevent beach retrogradation.**

18.10 Breaching of a barrier beach *Erosion by severe storms during the winter of 1993 carved out an inlet in this barrier beach on the south shore of Long Island, New York. A system of groins has trapped sand, protecting the far stretch of beach. In the foreground, the beach has receded well inland of the houses that were once located on its edge. (© Vie De Lucia/NYT Pictures.)*

a river. Construction of dams far upstream on the river may drastically reduce the sediment load of the river, cutting off the source of sand for littoral drift. Retrogradation can then occur on a long stretch of shoreline.

•••••••••••••••••••••••••••••••
GEODISCOVERIES **Tides.** Watch this animation to see how the tides result from the Moon's gravity and the rotation of the Earth and Moon around their common center of mass.
•••

TIDAL CURRENTS

Most marine coastlines are influenced by the *ocean tide,* a rhythmic rise and fall of sea level under the influence of changing attractive forces of the Moon and Sun on the rotating Earth. Where tides are great, the effects of changing water level and the tidal currents thus set in motion are of major importance in shaping coastal landforms.

The tidal rise and fall of water level is graphically represented by the *tide curve.* Figure 18.11 is a tide curve for Boston Harbor covering a day's time. The water reached its maximum height, or high water, at 3.6 m (11.8 ft) on the tide staff and then fell to its minimum height, or low water, at 0.8 m (2.6 ft), occurring about $6\frac{1}{4}$ hours later. A second high water occurred about $12\frac{1}{2}$ hours after the previous high water, completing a single tidal cycle. In this example, the tidal range, or difference between heights of successive high and low waters, is 2.8 m (9.2 ft).

In bays and estuaries, the changing tide sets in motion currents of water known as *tidal currents.* The relationships between tidal currents and the tide curve are shown in Figure 18.12. When the tide begins to fall, an *ebb current* sets in. This flow ceases about the time when the tide is at its lowest point. As the tide begins to rise, a landward current, the *flood current,* begins to flow.

Ocean tides produce tidal currents at the shoreline. These currents scour inlets and distribute fine sediment in bays and estuaries.

Tidal Current Deposits

Ebb and flood currents generated by tides perform several important functions along a shoreline. First, the currents that flow in and out of bays through narrow inlets are very swift and can scour the inlet strongly. This keeps the inlet open, despite the tendency of shore-drifting processes to close the inlet with sand.

Second, tidal currents carry large amounts of fine silt and clay in suspension. This fine sediment is derived from streams that enter the bays or from bottom muds agitated by storm wave action. It settles to the floors of the bays and estuaries, where it accumulates in layers and gradually fills the bays. Much organic matter is present in this sediment.

In time, tidal sediments fill the bays and produce mud flats, which are barren expanses of silt and clay. They are exposed at low tide but covered at high tide. Next, a growth of salt-tolerant plants takes hold on the mud flat. The plant stems trap more sediment, and the flat is built up to approximately the level of high tide, becoming a *salt marsh* (Figure 18.13). A thick layer of peat is eventually formed at the surface. Tidal

18.11 **Tide curve** Height of water at Boston Harbor measured every half hour.

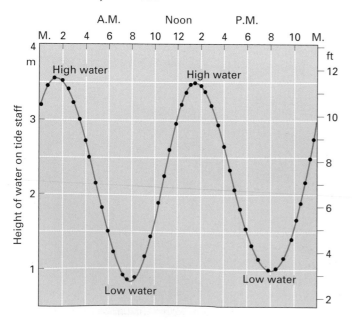

18.12 **Tidal currents** The ebb current flows seaward as the tide level falls. The flood current flows landward as the tide level rises. Tidal currents are strongest in the middle of the cycle when water level is changing most rapidly.

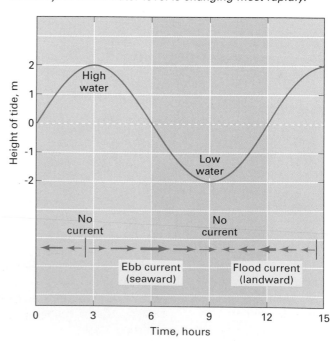

18.13 A tideland salt marsh At high tide, most of this salt marsh is flooded. Chincoteague National Wildlife Refuge, Virginia.

currents maintain their flow through the salt marsh by means of a highly complex network of winding tidal streams.

TYPES OF COASTLINES

The world's coastlines present a number of different coastline types. Each type is unique because of the distinctive land mass against which the ocean water has come to rest. One group of coastline types derives its qualities from **submergence,** the partial drowning of a coast by a rise of sea level or a sinking of the crust. Another group derives its qualities from **emergence,** the exposure of submarine landforms by a falling of sea level or a rising of the crust. Another group of coastline types results when new land is built out into the ocean by volcanoes and lava flows, by the growth of river deltas, or by the growth of coral reefs.

Several important types of coastlines are illustrated in Figure 18.14. The first two are the result of submergence. The *ria coast* is a deeply embayed coast resulting from submergence of a land mass dissected by streams. The *fiord coast* is deeply indented by steep-walled fiords, which are submerged glacial troughs (discussed further in Chapter 19). The *barrier-island coast* is associated with a recently emerged coastal plain. Here, the offshore slope is very gentle, and a barrier island of sand, lying a short distance from the coast, is created by wave action. large rivers build elaborate deltas, producing *delta coasts.* The *volcano coast* is formed by the eruption of volcanoes and lava flows, partly constructed below water level. Reef-building corals create new land and make a *coral-reef coast.* Downfaulting of the coastal margin of a continent can allow the shoreline to come to rest against a fault scarp, producing a *fault coast.*

Shorelines of Submergence

Shorelines of submergence include ria coasts and fiord coasts. The ria coast, which takes its name from the Spanish word for estuary, *ria,* has many offshore islands. A ria coast is formed when a rise of sea level or a crustal sinking (or both) brings the shoreline to rest against the sides of valleys previously carved by streams (Figure 18.15a). Wave attack forms cliffs on the exposed seaward sides of islands and headlands (*b*). Sediment produced by wave action accumulates in the form of beaches along the cliffed headlands and at the heads of bays. This sediment is carried by littoral drift and is often built into sandspits across bay mouths and as connecting links between islands and mainland (*c*). Eventually, the sandspits seal off the bays, forming estuaries (*d*). If sea level remains at the same height with respect to the land for a long time, the coast may evolve into a cliffed shoreline of narrow beaches (*e*).

The fiord coast is similar to the ria coast. However, the submerged valleys were carved by flowing glaciers instead of streams. As a result, the valleys are deep, with straight, steep sides. Because sediment rapidly sinks into the deep water, beaches are rare. Fiords are described further in Chapter 19 (see Figures 19.7 and 19.8).

Many glaciated coastlines, such as those of New England and the Canadian Maritime Provinces, are coastlines of submergence. During the Ice Age, the weight of ice sheets depressed the crust of these regions, and they are still slowly rising now that the ice sheets are gone. Meanwhile, ocean waves and currents are rapidly eroding their rocky shorelines, creating bays, bars, and estuaries, as shown in Figure 18.15.

GEO**DISCOVERIES** **Coastal Landforms Interactivity.** Review key concepts and terms of coastal landforms. Examine photos of shorelines from ground to satellite. Build spits and barrier islands, varying sand supply and wind direction.

Barrier-Island Coasts

In contrast to the bold relief and deeply embayed outlines of coastlines of submergence are low-lying coasts from which the land slopes gently beneath the sea. The coastal plain of the Atlantic and Gulf coasts of the United States presents a particularly fine example of such a gently sloping surface. As we explained in Chapter 17, this coastal plain is a belt of relatively young sedimentary strata, formerly accumulated beneath the sea

Ria coasts and fiord coasts result from submergence of a land mass. Islands, bars, estuaries, and deep bays are characteristic of these "drowned" coastlines.

Ria coast

Fiord coast

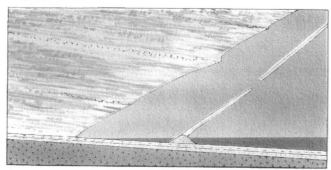

Barrier-island coast

Delta coast

Volcano coast (*left*)   Coral-reef coast (*right*)

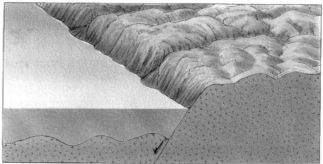

Fault coast

18.14   Seven types of coastlines *These sketches illustrate the important features of seven types of coastlines. (Drawn by A. N. Strahler.)*

as deposits on the continental shelf. During the latter part of the Cenozoic Era and into recent time, the coastal plain emerged from the ocean as a result of repeated crustal uplifts.

Along much of the Atlantic Gulf coast there exist *barrier islands,* low ridges of sand built by waves and further increased in height by the growth of sand dunes (Figure 18.16). Behind the barrier island lies a *lagoon.* It is a broad expanse of shallow water in places largely filled with tidal deposits.

A characteristic feature of barrier islands is the presence of gaps, known as *tidal inlets.* Strong currents flow alternately landward and seaward through these gaps as the tide rises and falls. In heavy storms, the barrier island may be breached by new inlets (Figure 18.10). After that occurs, tidal current scour will tend to keep a new inlet open. In some cases, the inlet is closed later by shore drifting of

Barrier island coasts are found where a coastal plain of gently sloping sediments emerges from the sea. Barrier island beaches protect a shallow lagoon that is serviced by tidal inlets in the barrier beach.

beach sand. Perhaps the finest example of a barrier-island coast is the Gulf coast of Texas (Figure 18.17).

Delta and Volcano Coasts

The deposit of clay, silt, and sand made by a stream or river where it flows into a body of standing water is known as a **delta.** Deposition is caused by rapid reduction in velocity of the current as it pushes out into the standing water. Typically, the river channel divides and subdivides into lesser channels called *distributaries.* The coarser sand and silt particles settle out first, while the fine clays continue out farthest and eventually come to rest in fairly deep water. Contact of fresh with saltwater causes the finest clay particles to clot together and form larger particles that settle to the seafloor.

Deltas show a wide variety of outlines. The Nile delta has the basic triangular shape of the Greek letter delta. In out-

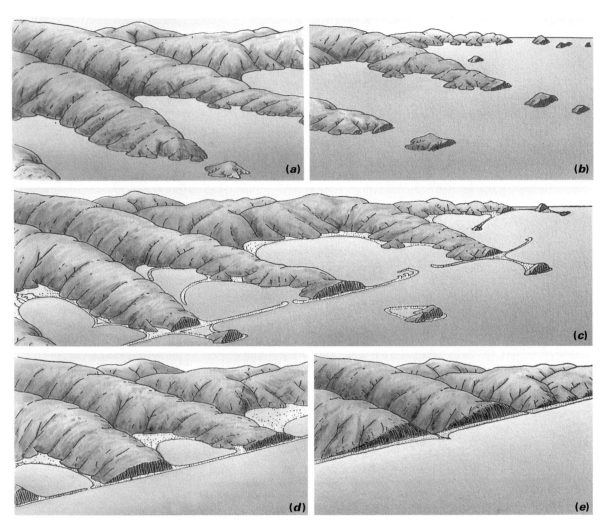

18.15   Stages in the evolution of a ria coastline *Wave action on a coastline of submergence creates many interesting coastal landforms. (Drawn by A. N. Strahler.)*

line, it resembles an alluvial fan. The Mississippi delta has a different shape. Long, branching fingers grow far out into the Gulf of Mexico at the ends of the distributaries, giving the impression of a bird's foot. A satellite image of the

A delta results when a river empties into the ocean. The Mississippi Delta has a bird's foot plan, with branching distributaries carrying river water and sediment to the ocean.

delta, Figure 18.18, shows the great quantity of suspended sediment—clay and fine silt—being discharged by the river into the Gulf. It amounts to about 1 million metric tons (about 1.1 million English tons) per day.

Delta growth is often rapid, ranging from 3 m (about 10 ft) per year for the Nile to 60 m (about 200 ft) per year for the Mississippi delta. Some cities and towns that were at river mouths several hundred years ago are today several kilometers inland.

Volcano coasts arise where volcanic deposits—lava and ash—flow from active volcanoes into the ocean. Low cliffs occur when wave action erodes the fresh deposits. Beaches

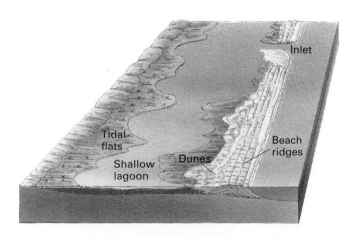

Inlet

Tidal flats

Shallow lagoon

Dunes

Beach ridges

18.16   Barrier island *A barrier island is separated from the mainland by a wide lagoon. Sediments fill the lagoon, while dune ridges advance over the tidal flats. An inlet allows tidal flows to pass in and out of the lagoon. (Drawn by A. N. Strahler.)*

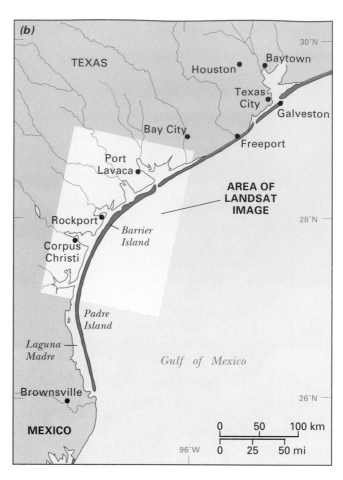

18.17 *Barrier-island coast* *(a) A Landsat image of the Texas barrier-island coast. Red colors on the Landsat image indicate vegetation. Bright white areas are dunes or beach sand. Lighter blue tones mark the presence of sediment in water inside of the barrier beach. (b) Index map of the location.*

18.18   *The Mississippi delta viewed by Landsat* *The natural levees of the bird-foot delta appear as lace-like filaments in a great pool of turbid river water. New Orleans can be seen at the upper left, occupying the region between the natural levees of the Mississippi River and the southern shore of Lake Pontchartrain.*

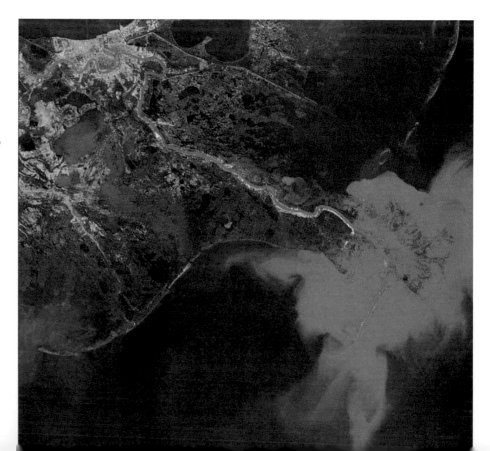

18.19 Fringing reefs *Coral reefs fringe the Island of Moorea, Society Islands, South Pacific Ocean. The island is a deeply dissected volcano with a history of submergence. Tahiti lies in the background.*

are typically narrow, steep, and composed of fine particles of the extrusive rock.

GEO*DISCOVERIES* **Satellite Imagery and the Earth's Rivers Interactivity.** View the deltas of the Earth's major rivers as seen from space. Includes Colorado, Nile, Yangtze, Ganges, Mississippi, Amazon, and Okavango rivers.

Coral-Reef Coasts

Coral-reef coasts are unique in that the addition of new land is made by organisms—corals and algae. Growing together, these organisms secrete rock-like deposits of mineral carbonate, called **coral reefs.** As coral colonies die, new ones are built on them, accumulating as limestone. Coral fragments are torn free by wave attack, and the pulverized fragments accumulate as sand beaches.

Coral-reef coasts occur in warm tropical and equatorial waters between the limits of lat. 30° N and 25° S. Water temperatures above 20°C (68°F) are necessary for dense growth of coral reefs. Reef corals live near the water

> **Coral reef coasts occur in warm oceans where corals build reefs at the land-sea margin. Volcano coasts are found where fresh volcanic deposits of lava and ash reach the ocean. Raised shorelines are marked by marine terraces.**

surface. The sea water must be free of suspended sediment and well aerated for vigorous coral growth. For this reason, corals thrive in positions exposed to wave attack from the open sea. Because muddy water prevents coral growth, reefs are missing opposite the mouths of muddy streams. Coral reefs are remarkably flat on top. They are exposed at low tide and covered at high tide.

There are three distinctive types of coral reefs—fringing reefs, barrier reefs, and atolls. *Fringing reefs* are built as platforms attached to shore (Figure 18.19). They are widest in front of headlands where wave attack is strongest. *Barrier reefs* lie out from shore and are separated from the mainland by a lagoon (Figure 18.19). Narrow gaps occur at intervals in barrier reefs. Through these openings, excess water from breaking waves is returned from the lagoon to the open sea.

Atolls are more or less circular coral reefs enclosing a lagoon but have no land inside. On large atolls, parts of the reef have been built up by wave action and wind to form low island chains connected by the reef. Most atolls are built on a foundation of volcanic rock that has subsided below sea level. (See Figure 13.6 and accompanying text.)

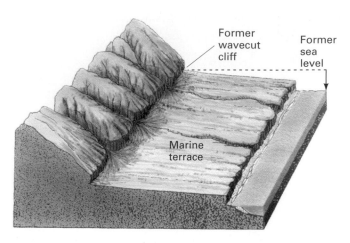

Former
wavecut
cliff

Former
sea
level

Marine
terrace

18.20 A marine terrace *A raised shoreline becomes a cliff parallel with the newer, lower shoreline. The former abrasion platform is now a marine terrace. (Drawn by A. N. Strahler.)*

Raised Shorelines and Marine Terraces

The active life of a shoreline is sometimes cut short by a sudden rise of the coast. When this tectonic event occurs, a *raised shoreline* is formed. If present, the marine cliff and abrasion platform are abruptly raised above the level of wave action. The former abrasion platform has now become a *marine ter-*

race (Figure 18.20). Of course, fluvial denudation acts to erode the terrace as soon as it is formed. The terrace may also undergo partial burial under alluvial fan deposits.

Raised shorelines are common along the continental and island coasts of the Pacific Ocean because here tectonic processes are active along the mountain and island arcs. Repeated uplifts result in a series of raised shorelines in a step-like arrangement. Fine examples of these multiple marine terraces are seen on the western slope of San Clemente Island, off the California coast (Figure 18.21).

Rising Sea Level

As we noted in our interchapter feature, *A Closer Look: Eye on Global Change 3.2 • The IPCC Report of 2001,* global warming will result in a rise of sea level estimated at 9 to 88 cm (3.5 to 34.6 in.) between now and 2100. Some of the rise is due to the simple thermal expansion of the upper layers of the ocean, which will grow warmer. The remainder is contributed by the melting of glaciers and snowpacks as air temperatures rise. Sea-level rise will have effects ranging from displacement of estuaries to enhanced coastal erosion. Depending on the amount of rise, some low-lying islands will disappear along with their inhabitants. The causes and effects of sea level rise are documented more fully in our interchapter feature, *A Closer Look: Eye on Global Change 18.1 • Global Change and Coastal Environments.*

18.21 A raised shoreline *Marine terraces on the western slope of San Clemente Island, off the southern California coast. More than 20 terraces have been identified in this series. The highest has an elevation of about 400 m (about 1300 ft).*

WIND ACTION

Transportation and deposition of sand by wind is an important process in shaping certain coastal landforms. We have already mentioned coastal sand dunes, which are derived from beach sand. In the remainder of this chapter, we investigate the transport of mineral particles by wind and the shaping of dune forms. Our discussion also provides information about dune forms far from the coast—in desert environments, where the lack of vegetation cover allows dunes to develop if a source of abundant sand particles is present.

Wind blowing over the land surface is one of the active agents of landform development. Ordinarily, wind is not strong enough to dislodge mineral matter from the surfaces of unweathered rock, or from moist, clay-rich soils, or from soils bound by a dense plant cover. Instead, the action of wind in eroding and transporting sediment is limited to land surfaces where small mineral and organic particles are in a loose, dry state. These areas are typically deserts and semiarid lands (steppes). An exception is the coastal environment, where beaches provide abundant supplies of loose sand. In this environment, wind action shapes coastal dunes, even where the climate is humid and the land surface inland from the coast is well protected by a plant cover.

Erosion by Wind

Wind performs two kinds of erosional work: abrasion and deflation. Loose particles lying on the ground surface may be lifted into the air or rolled along the ground by wind action. In the process of *wind abrasion,* wind drives sand and dust particles against an exposed rock or soil surface. This causes the surface to be worn away by the impact of the particles. Abrasion requires cutting tools—mineral particles—carried by the wind, while deflation is accomplished by air currents alone.

The sandblasting action of wind abrasion against exposed rock surfaces is limited to the basal meter or two of a rock mass that rises above a flat plain. This height is the limit to which sand grains can rise high into the air. Wind abrasion produces pits, grooves, and hollows in the rock. Wooden utility poles on windswept sandy plains are quickly cut through at the base unless a protective metal sheathing or heap of large stones is placed around the base.

The removal of loose particles from the ground is termed **deflation.** Deflation acts on loose soil or sediment. Dry river courses, beaches, and areas of recently formed glacial deposits are susceptible to deflation. In dry climates, much of the ground surface is subject to deflation because the soil or rock is largely bare of vegetation.

Wind action moves mineral particles when they are in a dry state and unprotected by a vegetation cover. These conditions are found in deserts and semiarid regions of the world, as well as on sandy shorelines.

Wind deflation can produce blowouts and help form desert pavement—a surface armor of coarse particles that reduces further deflation.

Wind is selective in its deflational action. The finest particles, those of clay and silt sizes, are lifted and raised into the air—sometimes to a height of a thousand meters (about 3300 ft) or more. Sand grains are moved only when winds are at least moderately strong and usually travel within a meter or two (about 3 to 6 ft) of the ground. Gravel fragments and rounded pebbles can be rolled or pushed over flat ground by strong winds, but they do not travel far. They become easily lodged in hollows or between other large grains. Consequently, where a mixture of size of particles is present on the ground, the finer sized particles are removed and the coarser particles remain behind.

A landform produced by deflation is a shallow depression called a **blowout.** The size of the depression may range from a few meters (10 to 20 ft) to a kilometer (0.6 mi) or more in diameter, although it is usually only a few meters deep. Blowouts form in plains regions of dry climate. Any small depression in the surface of the plain, especially where the grass cover has been broken or disturbed, can form a blowout. Rains fill the depression and create a shallow pond or lake. As the water evaporates, the mud bottom dries out and cracks, leaving small scales or pellets of dried mud. These particles are lifted out by the wind.

Deflation is also active in semidesert and desert regions. In the southwestern United States, playas often occupy large areas on the flat floors of tectonic basins (see Figure 16.30b). Deflation has reduced many playas several meters in elevation.

Rainbeat, overland flow, and deflation may be active for a long period on the gently sloping surface of a desert alluvial fan or alluvial terrace. These processes remove fine particles, leaving coarser, heavier materials behind. As a result, rock fragments ranging in size from pebbles to small boulders become concentrated into a surface layer known as a **desert pavement** (Figure 18.22). The large fragments become closely fitted together, concealing the smaller particles—grains of sand, silt, and clay—that remain beneath. The pavement acts as an armor that effectively protects the finer particles from rapid removal by deflation. However, the pavement is easily disturbed by the wheels of trucks and motorcycles, exposing the finer particles and allowing severe deflation and water erosion to follow.

Dust Storms

Strong, turbulent winds blowing over barren surfaces lift great quantities of fine dust into the air, forming a dense, high cloud called a **dust storm.** In semiarid grasslands, a dust storm is generated where ground surfaces have been stripped of protective vegetation cover by cultivation or grazing. Strong winds cause soil particles and coarse sand grains to hop along

18.22 **Desert pavement** *A desert pavement is formed of closely fitted rock fragments. Lying on the surface are fine examples of wind-faceted rocks, which attain their unusual shapes by long-continued sandblasting.*

the ground. This motion breaks down the soil particles and disturbs more soil. With each impact, fine dust is released that can be carried upward by turbulent winds.

A dust storm approaches as a dark cloud extending from the ground surface to heights of several thousand meters (Figure 18.23). Typically, the advancing cloud wall represents a rapidly moving cold front. Within the dust cloud there is deep gloom or even total darkness. Visibility is cut to a few meters, and a fine choking dust penetrates everywhere.

SAND DUNES

A **sand dune** is any hill of loose sand shaped by the wind. Active dunes constantly change form under wind currents. Dunes form where there is a source of sand—for example, a sandstone formation that weathers easily to release individual grains, or perhaps a beach supplied with abundant sand from a nearby river mouth. Dunes must be free of a vegetation cover in order to form and move. They become inactive

18.23 **Eye on the Landscape** **Dust storm** *A cloud of fine dust sweeps across this savanna plain in eastern Kenya.* **What else would the geographer see? ...Answers at the end of the chapter.**

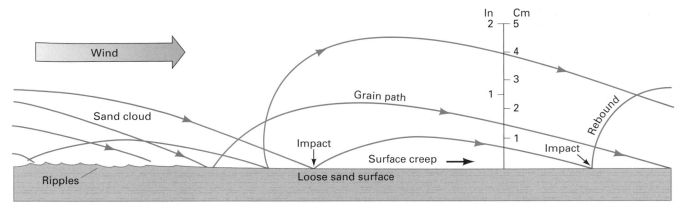

18.24 Saltation *Sand particles travel in a series of long leaps. (After R. A. Bagnold.)*

when stabilized by a vegetation cover or when patterns of wind or sand sources change.

Dune sand is most commonly composed of the mineral quartz, which is extremely hard and largely immune to chemical decay. The grains are beautifully rounded by abrasion (see Figure 11.12). Figure 18.24 shows how sand grains are moved by strong winds—in long, low leaps, bouncing after impact with other grains. Rebounding grains rarely rise more than half a centimeter above the dune surface. Grains struck by bouncing grains are pushed forward, and, in this way, the surface sand layer creeps downwind. This type of hopping, bouncing movement is termed *saltation.*

> The barchan dune is a crescent-shaped heap of sand that moves across a flat, pebble-covered plain. The points of the crescent are directed downwind.

Types of Sand Dunes

One common type of sand dune is an isolated heap of free sand called a *barchan,* or *crescentic dune.* This type of dune

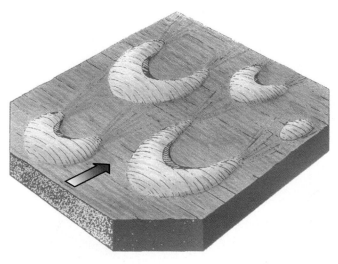

18.25 Barchan dunes *The arrow indicates wind direction. (Drawn by A. N. Strahler.)*

has the outline of a crescent, and the points of the crescent are directed downwind (Figure 18.25). On the upwind side of the crest, the sand slope is gentle and smoothly rounded. On the downwind side of the dune, within the crescent, is a steep dune slope, the *slip face.* This face maintains a more or less constant angle from the horizontal (Figure 18.26a), which is known as the *angle of repose.* The slip face is oversteepened slightly by the accumulation of individual wind-carried sand grains until it becomes unstable and the outermost layer of sand on the face slips down the dune slope, restoring the angle of repose. For loose sand, this angle is about 35°.

Barchan dunes usually rest on a flat, pebble-covered ground surface. The life of a barchan dune may begin as a sand drift in the lee of some obstacle, such as a small hill, rock, or clump of brush. Once a sufficient mass of sand has formed, it begins to move downwind, taking on the crescent form. For this reason, the dunes are usually arranged in chains extending downwind from the sand source.

Where sand is so abundant that it completely covers the solid ground, dunes take the form of wave-like ridges separated by trough-like furrows. These dunes are called *transverse dunes* because, like ocean waves, their crests trend at right angles to the direction of the dominant wind (Figure 18.26b). The entire area may be called a *sand sea* because it resembles a storm-tossed sea suddenly frozen to immobility. The sand ridges have sharp crests and are asymmetrical, the gentle slope being on the windward and the steep slip face on the lee side. Deep depressions lie between the dune ridges. Sand seas require enormous quantities of sand, supplied by material weathered from sandstone formations or from sands in nearby alluvial plains. Transverse dune belts also form adjacent to beaches that supply abundant sand and have strong onshore winds.

Wind is a major agent of landscape development in the Sahara Desert. Enormous quantities of reddish dune sand have been derived from weathering of sandstone formations. The sand is formed into a great sand sea, called an

a...Migrating barchan dunes *This aerial view shows a large barchan dune moving from right to left. At its apex is a smaller barchan dune that is overtaking it.*

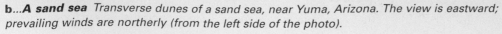

b...A sand sea *Transverse dunes of a sand sea, near Yuma, Arizona. The view is eastward; prevailing winds are northerly (from the left side of the photo).*

c..*Coastal blowout dune* This coastal blowout dune is advancing over a coniferous forest, with the slip face gradually burying the tree trunks. Pacific coast, near Florence, Oregon.

d...*Coastal foredunes* Beachgrass thriving on coastal foredunes has trapped drifting sand to produce a dune ridge. Queen's County, Prince Edward Island, Canada.

erg. Elsewhere, there are vast flat-surfaced sheets of sand that are armored by a layer of pebbles that forms a desert pavement. A surface of this kind in the Sahara is called a *reg.*

Some of the Saharan dunes are elaborate in shape. For example, the *star dune* (heaped dune) is a large hill of sand whose base resembles a many-pointed star in plan. The Arabian star dunes remain fixed in position and have served for centuries as reliable landmarks for desert travelers. The star dune also occurs in the deserts of the border region between the United States and Mexico.

Another group of dunes belongs to a family in which the curve of the dune crest is bowed outward in the downwind direction. (This curvature is the opposite of the barchan dune.) These are termed *parabolic dunes.* A common type of parabolic dune is the *coastal blowout dune,* formed adjacent to beaches. Here, large supplies of sand are available, and the sand is blown landward by prevailing winds (Figure 18.27*a*). A saucer-shaped depression is formed by deflation, and the sand is heaped in a curving ridge resembling a horseshoe in plan. On the landward side is a steep slip face that advances over the lower ground and buries forests, killing the trees (Figure 18.26*c*). Coastal blowout dunes are well displayed along the southern and eastern shore of Lake Michigan. Dunes of the southern shore have been protected for public use as the Indiana Dunes State Park.

On semiarid plains, where vegetation is sparse and winds are strong, groups of parabolic blowout dunes develop to the lee of shallow deflation hollows (Figure 18.27*b*). Sand is caught by low bushes and accumulates on a broad, low ridge. These dunes have no steep slip faces and may remain relatively immobile. In some cases, the dune ridge migrates downwind, drawing the dune into a long, narrow form with parallel sides resembling a hairpin in outline (Figure 18.27*c*).

Another class of dunes, described as *longitudinal dunes,* consists of long, narrow ridges oriented parallel with the direction of the prevailing wind (Figure 18.28). These dune ridges may be many kilometers long and cover vast areas of tropical and subtropical deserts in Africa and Australia.

> **Parabolic dunes are bowed outward in the downwind direction—the opposite of barchan dunes. They include coastal blowout dunes and hairpin dunes.**

GEODISCOVERIES **Types of Dunes.** Interact with a chart of sand dune types organized by wind, sand supply, and amount of vegetation to see photos of common types of dunes. An animation.

Coastal Foredunes

Landward of sand beaches, we usually find a narrow belt of dunes in the form of irregularly shaped hills and depressions. These are the *foredunes.* They normally bear a cover of beachgrass and a few other species of plants capable of survival in the severe environment (Figure 18.26d). On coastal foredunes, the sparse cover of beachgrass and other small plants acts as a baffle to trap sand moving landward from the adjacent beach. As a result, the foredune ridge is built upward to become a barrier standing several meters above high-tide level.

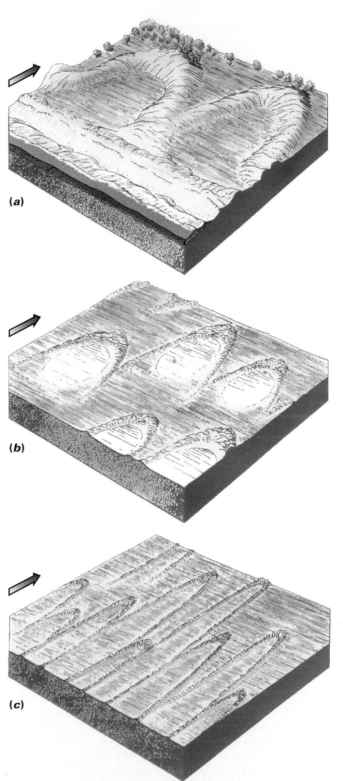

(a)

(b)

(c)

18.27 Three types of parabolic dunes *The prevailing wind direction is the same for all three types. (a) Coastal blowout dunes. (b) Parabolic dunes on a semiarid plain. (c) Parabolic dunes drawn out into hairpin forms. (Drawn by A. N. Strahler.)*

18.28 Longitudinal dunes *Longitudinal dunes run parallel to the direction of the wind. (Drawn by A. N. Strahler.)*

Foredunes form a protective barrier for tidal lands that often lie on the landward side of a beach ridge or barrier island. In a severe storm, the swash of storm waves cuts away the upper part of the beach. Although the foredune barrier may then be attacked by wave action and partly cut away, it will not usually yield. Between storms, the beach is rebuilt, and, in due time, wind action restores the dune ridge, if plants are maintained.

If the plant cover of the dune ridge is reduced by vehicular and foot traffic, a

---

Coastal foredunes form a protective barrier against storm wave action that keeps waves from overwashing a beach ridge or barrier island.

Loess is a deposit of wind-blown silt that may be as thick as 30 m (about 100 ft) in some regions of North America. It forms highly productive but easily eroded soils.

---

blowout will rapidly develop. The new cavity can extend as a trench across the dune ridge. With the onset of a storm that brings high water levels and intense wave action, swash is funneled through the gap and spreads out on the tidal marsh or tidal lagoon behind the ridge. Sand swept through the gap is spread over the tidal deposits. If eroded, the gap can become a new tidal inlet for ocean water to reach the bay beyond the beach. For many coastal communities of the eastern United States seaboard, the breaching of a dune ridge with its accompanying overwash may bring unwanted change to the tidal marsh or estuary.

LOESS

In several large midlatitude areas of the world, the surface is covered by deposits of wind-transported silt that has settled out from dust storms over many thousands of years. This material is known as **loess**. (The pronunciation of this German word is somewhere between "lerse" and "luss.") It generally has a uniform yellowish to buff color and lacks any visible layering. Loess tends to break away along vertical cliffs wherever it is exposed by the cutting of a stream or grading of a roadway (Figure 18.29). It is also very easily eroded by running water and is subject to rapid gullying when the vegetation cover that protects it is broken. Because it is easily excavated, loess has been widely used for cave dwellings both in China and in Central Europe.

The thickest deposits of loess are in northern China, where a layer over 30 m (about 100 ft) thick is common and a maximum thickness of 100 m (about 300 ft) has been measured. This layer

18.29 Wind-transported silt *This thick layer of loess in New Zealand was deposited during the Ice Age. Loess has excellent cohesion and often forms vertical faces as it wastes away.*

covers many hundreds of square kilometers and appears to have been brought as dust from the interior of Asia. Loess deposits are also of major importance in the United States, Central Europe, Central Asia, and Argentina.

In the United States, thick loess deposits lie in the Missouri-Mississippi Valley (Figure 18.30). Large areas of the prairie plains region of Indiana, Illinois, Iowa, Missouri, Nebraska, and Kansas are underlain by loess ranging in thickness from 1 to 30 m (about 3 to 100 ft). Extensive deposits also occur in Tennessee and Mississippi in areas bordering the lower Mississippi River floodplain. Still other loess deposits are in the Palouse region of northeast Washington and western Idaho.

The American and European loess deposits are directly related to the continental glaciers of the Pleistocene Epoch. At the time when the ice covered much of North America and Europe, a generally dry winter climate prevailed in the land bordering the ice sheets. Strong winds blew southward and eastward over the bare ground, picking up silt from the floodplains of braided streams that discharged the meltwater from the ice. This dust settled on the ground between streams, gradually building up a smooth, level ground surface. The loess is particularly thick along the eastern sides of the valleys because of prevailing westerly winds. It is well exposed along the bluffs of most streams flowing through these regions today.

Loess is of major importance in world agricultural resources. Loess forms the parent matter of rich black soils (Mollisols, Chapter 10) especially suited to cultivation of grains. The highly productive plains of southern Russia, the Argentine pampa, and the rich grain region of north China are underlain by loess. In the United States, corn is extensively cultivated on the loess plains in Kansas, Iowa, and Illinois, where rainfall is sufficient. Wheat is grown farther west on loess plains of Kansas and Nebraska and in the Palouse region of eastern Washington.

The thick loess deposit covering a large area of north-central China in the province of Shanxi and adjacent provinces poses a difficult problem of severe soil erosion. Although the loess is capable of standing in vertical walls, it also succumbs to deep gullying during the period of torrential summer rains. From the steep walls of these great scars, fine sediment is swept into streams and carried into tributaries of the Huang He (Yellow River). The Chinese government has implemented an intensive program of slope stabilization by using artificial contour terraces (seen in Figure 18.31) in combination with tree planting. Valley bottoms have been dammed so as to trap the silt to form flat patches of land suitable for cultivation.

Induced Deflation

Induced deflation is a frequent occurrence when short-grass prairie in a semiarid region is cultivated without irrigation. Plowing disturbs the natural soil surface and grass cover, and in drought years, when vegetation dies out, the unprotected soil is easily eroded by wind action. Much of the Great Plains region of North America has suffered such deflation, experiencing dust storms generated by turbulent winds. Strong cold fronts frequently sweep over this area and lift dust high into the troposphere at times when soil moisture is low. The "Dust Bowl" of the 1930s is an example.

Human activities in very dry, hot deserts contribute measurably to the raising of high dust clouds. In the desert of northwest India and Pakistan (the Thar Desert bordering the Indus River), the continued trampling of fine-textured soils by hooves of grazing animals and by human feet produces a dust cloud that hangs over the region for long periods. It extends to a height of 9 km (about 30,000 ft).

GEODISCOVERIES **Web Quiz.** Take a quick quiz on the key concepts of this chapter.

A LOOK AHEAD This chapter has described the processes and landforms associated with wind action, either directly or through the medium of wind-driven waves. The power source for wind action is, of course, the Sun. By heating the Earth's surface in a nonuniform pattern, the flow of solar energy produces pressure gradients that cause wind. The Sun also powers the last active landform-making agent of erosion, transportation, and deposition on our list—glacial ice. By evaporating water from the oceans and returning that water to the lands as snow, solar power creates the bodies of solid ice that we distinguish as mountain glaciers and ice sheets.

18.30 Map of loess distribution in the central United States *(Data from Map of Pleistocene Eolian Deposits of the United States, Geological Society of America.)*

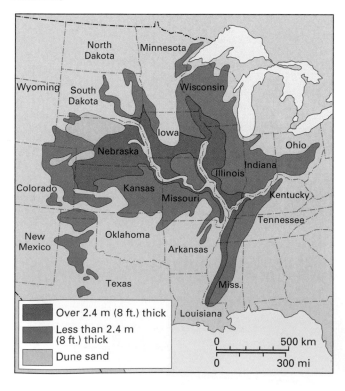

Legend:
- Over 2.4 m (8 ft.) thick
- Less than 2.4 m (8 ft.) thick
- Dune sand

0   500 km
0   300 mi

18.31 Slope stabilization in China *A succession of contour terraces, cut into thick loess and covered by tree plantings, is designed to prevent deep gullying and loss of soil. Arched entrances to cave dwellings can be seen at lower left and lower right. Grain fields on the flat valley floor occupy surfaces of thick sediment trapped behind dams. Shanxi Province, near Xian (Sian), People's Republic of China.*

Compared to wind and water, glacial ice moves much more slowly but is far steadier in its motion. Like a vast conveyor belt, glacial ice moves sediment forward relentlessly, depositing the sediment at the ice margin, where the ice melts. By plowing its way over the landscape, glacial ice also shapes the local terrain—bulldozing loose rock from hillsides and plastering sediments underneath its vast bulk. This slow but steady action is very different from that of water, wind, and waves, and produces a set of landforms that is the subject of our last text chapter.

GEODISCOVERIES **Web Links.** This chapter's web links let you visit sites of coastal erosion from San Diego to the Carolinas. Explore dunes and deserts to see wind in action.

In Review | Landforms Made by Waves and Wind

- This chapter has described the landforms of waves and wind, both of which are indirectly powered by the Earth's rotation and the unequal heating of its surface by the Sun. Waves act at the **shoreline**—the boundary between water and land. Waves expend their energy as *breakers,* which erode hard rock into **marine cliffs** and create *marine scarps* in softer materials.

- **Beaches,** usually formed of sand, are shaped by the swash and backwash of waves, which continually work and rework beach sediment. Wave action produces **littoral drift,** which moves sediment parallel to the beach. This sediment accumulates in bars and sandspits, which further extend the beach. Depending on the nature of *long-shore*

currents and the availability of sediment, shorelines can experience **progradation** or **retrogradation.**

- Tidal forces cause sea level to rise and fall rhythmically, and this change of level produces *tidal currents* in bays and estuaries. Tidal flows redistribute fine sediments within bays and estuaries, which can accumulate with the help of vegetation to form *salt marshes.*

- Coastlines of **submergence** result when coastal lands sink below sea level or sea level rises rapidly. Scenic *ria* and *fiord coasts* are examples. Coastlines of **emergence** include *barrier-island coasts* and *delta coasts.* **Coral-reef** coasts occur in regions of warm tropical and equatorial waters. Along some coasts, rapid uplift has occurred, creating *raised shorelines* and *marine terraces.*

- Global sea level is predicted to rise sharply in the twenty-first century due to both volume expansion of warmer sea water and increased melting of glaciers and snowpacks. Future rises may be very costly to human society as estuaries are displaced, islands are submerged, and coastal zones are subjected to frequent flooding.

- Wind is a landform-creating agent that acts by moving sediment. **Deflation** occurs when wind removes mineral particles—especially clay and silt, which can be carried long distances. Deflation creates **blowouts** in semidesert regions and lowers playa surfaces in deserts. In arid regions, deflation produces **dust storms.**

- **Sand dunes** form when a source, such as a sandstone outcrop or a beach, provides abundant sand that can be moved by wind action. *Barchan dunes* are arranged indi-

vidually or in chains leading away from the sand source. *Transverse dunes* form a sand sea of frozen "wave" forms arranged perpendicular to the wind direction. *Parabolic dunes* are arc-shaped—*coastal blowout dunes* are an example. *Longitudinal dunes* parallel the wind direction and cover vast desert areas. Coastal *foredunes* are stabilized by dune grass and help protect the coast against storm wave action.

- **Loess** is a surface deposit of fine, wind-transported silt. It can be quite thick, and it typically forms vertical banks. Loess is very easily eroded by water and wind. In eastern Asia, the silt forming the loess was transported by winds from extensive interior deserts located to the north and west. In Europe and North America, the silt was derived from fresh glacial deposits during the Pleistocene Epoch. Human activities can hasten the action of deflation by breaking protective surface covers of vegetation and desert pavement.

Key Terms

shoreline, p. 598
coastline, p. 598
coast, p. 598
bay, p. 598
estuary, p. 590
marine cliff, p. 600

beach, p. 604
littoral drift, p. 604
progradation, p. 605
retrogradation, p. 605
submergence, p. 607
emergence, p. 607

delta, p. 608
coral reef, p. 611
atolls, p. 611
deflation, p. 613
blowout, p. 613
desert pavement, p. 613

dust storm, p. 613
sand dune, p. 614
loess, p. 619

Review Questions

1. What is the energy source for wind and wave action?
2. What landforms can be found in areas where bedrock meets the sea?
3. What is littoral drift, and how is it produced by wave action?
4. Identify progradation and retrogradation. How can human activity influence retrogradation?
5. How are salt marshes formed? How can they be reclaimed for agricultural use?
6. What key features identify a coastline of submergence? Identify and compare the two types of coastlines of submergence.
7. Under what conditions do barrier-island coasts form? What are the typical features of this type of coastline? Provide and sketch an example of a barrier-island coast.
8. What conditions are necessary for the development of coral reefs? Identify three types of coral-reef coastlines.
9. How are marine terraces formed?
10. What is deflation, and what landforms does it produce? What role does the dust storm play in deflation?
11. How do sand dunes form? Describe and compare barchan dunes, transverse dunes, star dunes, coastal

blowout dunes, parabolic dunes, and longitudinal dunes.
12. What is the role of coastal dunes in beach preservation? How are coastal dunes influenced by human activity? What problems can result?
13. Define the term *loess.* What is the source of loess, and how are loess deposits formed?

A Closer Look:
Eye on Global Change 18.1 • Global Change and Coastal Environments

1. Review the observed and predicted changes in global climate that will impact coastal environments.
2. Identify the global change factors that will affect coastal erosion and describe their impacts.
3. How have human activities induced land subsidence in wetlands? Why are wetlands of delta coasts particularly at risk?
4. What impact will global climate change have on coral reefs?
5. Why is global warming expected to cause coastal recession of arctic shorelines?

Visualizing Exercises

1. Describe the features of delta coasts and their formation. Sketch and compare the shapes of the Mississippi and Nile deltas.
2. Take a piece of paper and let it represent a map with winds coming from the north, at the top of the page. Then sketch the shapes of the following types of dunes: barchan, transverse, parabolic, and longitudinal.

Essay Questions

1. Consult an atlas to identify a good example of each of the following types of coastlines: ria coast, fiord coast, barrier-island coast, delta coast, coral-reef coast, and fault coast. For each example, provide a brief description of the key features you used to identify the coastline type.

2. Wind action moves sand close to the ground in a bouncing motion, whereas silt and clay are lifted and carried longer distances. Compare landforms and deposits that result from wind transportation of sand with those that result from wind transportation of silt and finer particles.

Eye on the Landscape

18.5a Retreating shoreline The sediments exposed in the bluff were laid down by streams fed by melting stagnant continental ice sheets at the end of the Ice Age. Because the ice melted irregularly, the deposits are not very uniform, and the exposed bedding **(A)** gives that impression. Note also the many large blocks of rock present within the deposits. They were let down from melting ice and were too large to be moved by the streams laying the sediments. A large lag deposit **(B)** of these stones remains at the water's edge, where it is being worked by waves. Deposits of continental ice sheets are covered in Chapter 19.

18.8 Sandspit The freshness of the sand here **(A)** indicates that Monomoy Point is growing very rapidly. The sand is supplied by the erosion of marine cliffs at Nauset Beach to the north. Note the overwash channels **(B)** that are cut through the vegetated sand dunes by the high waters and high surf of severe storms. To the upper left is the town of Chatham **(C),** its low hills formed from rock debris shed by melting ice sheets during the Ice Age. The coastline has the "drowned" look of a coastline of submergence, with its many lakes and bays. See this chapter for more details.

18.23 Dust Storm Savanna vegetation is shown nicely in this photo **(A)**. It consists of scattered trees with an understory of shrubs and grasses (here in a brown and dormant stage during the dry season). Although the tree in **(B)** appears to be dead, it may be a small-leaved acacia in silhouette. Acacia is a plant genus that includes many common species of semiarid environments. Savanna vegetation is described in Chapter 9.

A CLOSER LOOK

Eye on Global Change 18.1 | Global Change and Coastal Environments

Global climate change over the remainder of the twenty-first century will have major impacts on coastal environments.[1] The changes include increases in sea-surface temperature and sea level, decreases in sea-ice cover, and changes in salinity, wave climate, and ocean circulation.

What changes have already occurred? According to the 2001 report of the Intergovernmental Panel on Climate Change, the global heat content of the ocean has been increasing since at least the late 1950s, and the increase in sea-surface temperature between 1950 and 1993 was about half that of the land-surface temperature. Sea level rose between 10 and 20 cm (4 and 8 in.). Sea-ice cover in the spring and summer of the northern hemisphere has decreased by 10 to 15 percent since the 1950s. After 1970, El Niño episodes, which affect ocean circulation as well as severe storm tracks and intensities, became more frequent, more intense, and more persistent than during the past 100 years.

What changes are in store? Between 1990 and 2100, global average surface temperature will increase 1.4 and 5.8°C (2.5 and 10.4°F), and if the present pattern persists, average sea-surface temperatures will account for one-third of that elevation. Sea level will rise from 9 to 88 cm (3.5 to

34.6°F), depending on the scenario. Snow and ice cover will continue to decrease, and mountain glaciers and icecaps will continue their retreat of the twentieth century. Tropical cyclone peak wind and peak precipitation intensities will increase, and El Niño extremes of flood and drought will be exaggerated.

Coastal Erosion

These changes are bad news for coastal environments. Let's begin with coastal erosion. Most coastal erosion occurs in severe storms, when high winds generate large waves and push water up onto the land in storm surges. Global warming will increase the frequency of high winds and heavy precipitation events, thus amplifying the effects of severe storms. More frequent and longer El Niños will increase the severity and frequency of Pacific storms on the North American coast, leading to increased sea-cliff erosion along southern

California's south- and southwest-facing coastlines. During opposing La Niña events, Atlantic hurricane frequency and intensity will increase, with higher risk of damage to structures and coastal populations.

How will the rise in sea-level impact coastlines? Studies of sandy shorelines, which account for about 20 percent of the global coastline, have shown that over the past 100 years or so, about 70 percent of these shorelines have retreated and 10 percent have advanced, with the remainder stable. Sea-level rise enhances coastal erosion in storms, but in the long term, its effect is to push beaches, salt marshes, and estuaries landward. In an unaltered landscape, the migration of these features landward and seaward with the rise and fall of sea level over thousands of years is a natural process without significant ecological impact. However, it is a serious problem when the rise is rapid and

See *Climate Change 2001: The Scientific Basis, Contribution of Working Group I to the Third Assessment Report of the Intergovernmental Panel on Climate Change*, IPCC, Cambridge University Press, 2001, and *Climate Change 2001: Impacts, Adaptation, and Vulnerability, Contribution of Working Group II to the Third Assessment Report of the Intergovernmental Panel on Climate Change*, IPCC, Cambridge University Press, 2001, which are used as the basis for this discussion.

Coastal erosion *Wave action has undermined the bluff beneath these two buildings, depositing them on the beach below.*

A new inlet *Storm waves from Hurricane Isabel breached the North Carolina barrier beach to create a new inlet, as shown in this aerial photo from September, 2003. Notice also the widespread destruction of the shoreline in the foreground, with streaks of sand carried far inland by wind and wave action. As sea level rises, ocean waves will attack barrier beaches with increasing frequency and severity.*

example, some models predict doubled rates of sea-level rise for portions of the eastern United States, North American Pacific coast, and the western North American arctic shoreline.

Subsidence and Sea-Level Rise

Land subsidence is a contributing factor to the impact of sea-level rise. In an unaltered environment, rivers bring fine sediment to the coastline that settles in estuaries and is also carried by waves, currents, and tides into salt marshes and mangrove swamps. As the fine sediment accumulates, it slowly compacts, forming rich, dense layers of silt and clay mixed with fine organic particles. However, many coastlines are now fed by rivers that have been dammed at multiple points on their courses, which reduces that amount of fine sediment brought to the coast. Without a constant inflow of new sediment, coastal wetlands slowly sink as the older sediment that supports them compacts. This subsidence increases the effects of sea-level rise. Note also that estuaries are affected by changes in river flows as a result of changes in the frequency of severe precipitation events and summer droughts.

Delta coasts are especially sensitive to sediment starvation and subsidence. Here, rates of subsidence can reach 2 cm/yr (0.8 in./yr). The Mississippi has lost about half of its natural sediment load, and sediment transport by such rivers as the Nile and Indus has been reduced by 95 percent. Extracting ground water from deltas also increases subsidence. The Chao Phraya delta near Bangkok and the old deltas of the Huang and Changjing rivers in China are important examples.

According to recent estimates, sea-level rise and subsidence could cause the loss of as much as 22 percent of the world's coastal wetlands by the 2080s. Coupled with losses directly related to human activity, coastal wetlands could decrease by 30 percent. This level of reduction would have major effects on commercially important

the coastline is developed. Beaches disappear and are replaced by sea walls. Salt marshes are drained to reduce inland flooding. Estuaries become shallower and more saline. In this way, the most productive areas of the coast are squeezed between a rising ocean and a water's edge that is increasingly defended.

It is also important to realize that sea-level rise will not be uniform. Modifying factors of waves, currents, tides, and offshore topography can act to magnify the rise, depending on the location. For

Mississippi delta marshland *With rising sea level and increasing subsidence, marshlands of many river deltas are endangered. Shown here is a marshland of the Mississippi delta in Louisiana, near the river's southwest pass.*

fish and shellfish populations, as well as on other organisms comprising the marine food chain.

Coral Reefs

Coral reefs, like coastal wetlands, perform important ecological functions, such as harboring marine fish and nursing their progeny. They are highly biodiverse, with some reefs containing more major plant and animal groups than rainforests. They also serve as protective barriers to coastlines that reduce the effects of storm waves and surges. However, more than half of the total area of living coral reefs is thought to be threatened by human activities ranging from water pollution to coral mining.

How will coral reefs be affected by global change? It appears that simple sea-level rise will not be a factor because healthy coral reefs are able to grow upward at a rate equal to or greater than projected sea-level rise. However, the increase in sea-surface temperature that will accompany global

warming is of major concern. Many coral reefs appear to be at or near their upper temperature limits. When stressed, for example by a rise in temperature, many corals respond by "bleaching." In this process, they expel the algae that live symbiotically inside their structures, leaving the coral without color. However, the algae are necessary for the continued survival of the coral. The bleaching may be temporary if the stress subsides, but if permanent, the corals die. Major episodes of coral bleaching have been associated with the strong El Niños where water temperatures were increased by at least 1°C (1.8°F). During the very strong El Niño of 1997–1998, the Indian Ocean experienced a major coral bleaching event that was especially prominent on Australia's Great Barrier Reef.

Another concern is the effect of increased atmospheric CO_2 levels on corals. With higher concentrations of atmospheric CO_2, more CO_2 dissolves in sea water, causing

the water to become slightly less alkaline. This in turn shifts the solubility of calcium carbonate, $CaCO_3$, making it less available to the corals to use in building their skeleton structure. Whether this will create yet another source of stress for coral reefs is still the subject of scientific study.

High-Latitude Coasts

Many pristine stretches of arctic shoreline are threatened by global warming. In these regions, the shoreline is sealed off for much of the year by sea ice. The shoreline is also buttressed by permanent ground ice that bonds unconsolidated sediment into a rocklike mass, much like the calcium carbonate or quartz cement of a sedimentary rock. This frozen ground is resistant to wave action and thus helps to protect the shoreline from erosion. In some areas, massive ice beds underlie major portions of the coastline.

With global warming, the shoreline is less protected by these

Bleached anemones *These anemones, observed in the shallow waters of the Maldive Islands, exhibit bleaching—a process in which coral animals expel symbiotic algae as a response to stress. The bleaching can be fatal.*

mechanisms. Sea ice melts earlier and returns later, increasing the season for wave action. Greater expanses of open sea allow larger waves to build. Ground ice thaws to a greater depth, releasing more surface sediment and allowing waves to scour the shore more deeply. Near-shore sediments, stored in cliffs or bluffs, thaw as well, releasing them to shoreline

processes. And, recall from our interchapter feature, *A Closer Look: Eye on Global Change 7.3 • Regional Impacts of Climate Change on North America* that global warming will be especially severe at high altitudes. Rapid coastal recession under wave attack is already reported for many ice-rich coasts along the Beaufort Sea.

It is apparent that global climate change will have major impacts on coastal environments, with very broad implications for ecosystems and natural resources. It will take careful management of our coastlines to reduce those impacts on both human and natural systems.

Arctic shoreline *Pristine arctic shorelines, such as this beach on the coast of Spitsbergen Island, Svalbard archipelago, Norway, will be subjected to rapid change as global climate warms. Thawing of ground ice will release beach sediments and the early retreat of sheltering sea ice will expose the shoreline to enhanced summer wave attack. The yellow flowering plant in the foreground is the bog saxifrage.*

An icefall from the front of the Hubbard glacier, Russell Fiord Wilderness, Alaska, hurls tons of seawater high in the air.

19 | GLACIAL LANDFORMS AND THE ICE AGE

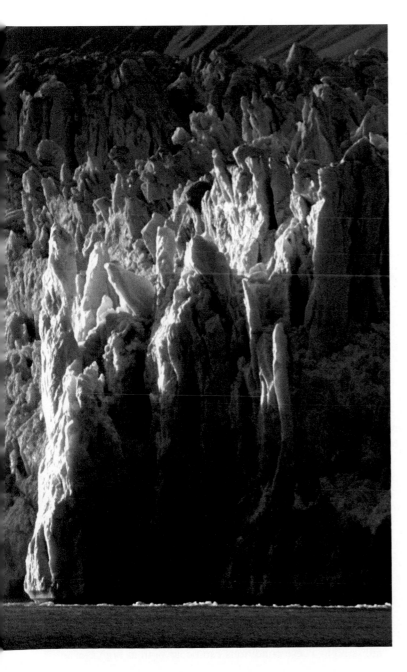

. . . .
PUTTING YOU IN THE PICTURE

Glacial ice, flowing slowly and majestically under the influence of gravity, is a powerful geomorphic agent that creates many types of distinctive landforms. Perhaps the best way to appreciate the power of glaciers is to visit one. Imagine yourself on an ocean cruise along the inland passage from Vancouver to Juneau with the ultimate destination of an Alaskan tidewater glacier. Here's what you might experience:

The huge cruise ship moves silently and effortlessly between the two steep, forest-covered slopes. The green walls of spruce and hemlock glide by slowly, the spires of the forest giants fading into the low ceiling of gray clouds overhead. Tiny droplets of drizzle cool your face as you lean against the rail, observing the somber scene. The trees seem almost close enough to reach out and touch. Below you, the ship's bow parts the gray-green water with little resistance, providing only a low rushing noise that barely breaks the stillness. Ahead, the sea and forest merge, fade, and then blend into the clouds and fog.

So this is Alaska! The travel brochure showed your ship cruising in a crystal-blue channel past magnificent vistas of snow-capped peaks, but so far the trip has provided only low clouds, fog, and conifer-clad slopes. The weather may soon change, however. The forecast calls for slow clearing later in the day, about the time that your ship will reach Glacier Bay. This steep-walled fiord is a drowned valley that was once filled with a huge tongue of glacial ice. Now, however, it is filled only with sea water and small drifting ice fragments released by the many streams of glacial ice that enter the bay along its 100 km (60 mi) length.

Soon you notice a change in the ship's rhythm. A graceful curving turn, and you leave Icy Strait to enter the mouth of Glacier Bay. Miraculously, the overcast skies have yielded to a blue and white patchwork of sky and cloud, and the sun has appeared. Your ship moves slowly down the narrow passage leading to the Grand Pacific Glacier. To either side are low, rocky peaks, sculpted by the ice into stark angular shapes composed of points and edges. Ahead are the high peaks of the St. Elias Mountains, entirely capped with white.

As the glacier comes into view, the ship slows further and approaches the steep ice face carefully. It is fractured into tall, vertical columns with step-like horizontal facets at the top. The color of the glacial ice is what strikes you most. Beneath a top white layer of decaying ice and snow, the ice is a bright greenish-blue. The color is so intense that the ice seems to glow from within. Above the clear aqua of the ice are the grays and browns of the rocks, the white of the snow-capped peaks, and the blue and white patchwork of sky. Below is the gray-green of the water, dotted with white ice fragments of many shapes and sizes.

The ice is also noisy. It groans, screeches, clicks, and pops. A loud crack startles you, then reverberates against the walls of the fiord. A monumental column of ice breaks free and falls, as if in slow motion. A great splash wells upward as it breaks the surface of the water. Next to the huge ice front, the bulk of the cruise ship seems very small. Suddenly, you connect the force of the moving ice with the shaping of the vast fiords that have contained your small ship on its passage. The power that carved these huge, water-filled canyons is awesome indeed.

If you live in a region that was covered by ice during the last Ice Age, the evidence of glaciation is all around. From ponds formed by the melting of buried ice blocks to the great hills of sediments dumped by glacial ice sheets at their margins, the action of glaciers has drastically modified much of the landscape of northern regions. In this chapter, you will learn about how glaciers create unique landforms like these. ■

GLACIAL LANDFORMS AND THE ICE AGE

In this chapter we turn to the last of the active agents that create landforms—glacial ice. Not long ago, during the Ice Age, much of northern North America and Eurasia was covered by massive sheets of glacial ice. As a result, glacial ice has played a dominant role in shaping landforms of large areas in midlatitude and subarctic zones. Glacial ice still exists today in two great accumulations of continental dimensions—the Greenland and Antarctic Ice Sheets—and in many smaller masses in high mountains.

The glacial ice sheets of Greenland and Antarctica strongly influence the radiation and heat balance of the globe. Because of their intense whiteness, they reflect much of the solar radiation they receive. Their intensely cold surface air temperatures contrast with temperatures at more equatorial latitudes. This temperature difference helps drive the system of meridional heat transport that we described in Chapters 3 and 5. In addition, these enormous ice accumulations represent water in storage in the solid state. They figure as a major component of the global water balance. When the volume of glacial ice increases, as during an ice age, sea levels must fall. When ice sheets melt away, sea level rises. Today's coastal environments evolved during the rising sea level that followed the melting of the last ice sheets of the Ice Age.

GLACIERS

Most of us know ice only as a brittle, crystalline solid because we are accustomed to seeing it in small quantities. Where a great thickness of ice exists, the pressure on the ice at the bottom makes the ice lose its rigidity. That is, the ice becomes plastic. This allows the ice mass to flow in response to gravity, slowly spreading out over a larger area or moving downhill. On steep mountain slopes, the ice can also move by sliding. Movement is the key characteristic of a *glacier,* defined as any large natural accumulation of land ice affected by present or past motion.

Glacial ice accumulates when the average snowfall of the winter exceeds the amount of snow that is lost in summer by ablation. The term **ablation** means the loss of snow and ice by evaporation and melting. When winter snowfall exceeds summer ablation, a layer of snow is added each year to what has already accumulated. As the snow compacts by surface melting and refreezing, it turns into a granular ice and is then compressed by overlying layers into hard crystalline ice. When the ice mass is so thick that the lower layers become plastic, outward or downhill flow starts, and the ice mass is now an active glacier.

Glacial ice forms where temperatures are low and snowfall is high. These conditions can occur both at high eleva-

When snow accumulates to a great thickness, it can turn into flowing glacial ice. Alpine glaciers form in high mountains, while ice sheets form on continental interiors at high latitudes.

19.1 Eye on the Landscape An alpine glacier Aerial view of the Grand Plateau Glacier, Saint Elias Mountains, Glacier Bay National Park, Alaska. The dark stripes are medial moraines. **What else would the geographer see? ... Answers at the end of the chapter.**

tions and at high latitudes. In mountains, glacial ice can form even in tropical and equatorial zones if the elevation is high enough to keep average annual temperatures below freezing. Orographic precipitation encourages the growth of glacial ice. In high mountains, glaciers flow from small high-elevation collecting grounds down to lower elevations, where temperatures are warmer. Here the ice disappears by ablation. Typically, mountain glaciers are long and narrow because they occupy former stream valleys. These **alpine glaciers** are a distinctive type (Figure 19.1).

In arctic and polar regions, prevailing temperatures are low enough that snow can accumulate over broad areas, eventually forming a vast layer of glacial ice. Accumulation starts on uplands that intercept heavy snowfall. The uplands become buried under enormous volumes of ice, which can reach a thickness of several thousand meters. The ice then spreads outward, over surrounding lowlands, and covers all landforms it encounters. This extensive type of ice mass is called an **ice sheet.** As already noted, ice sheets exist today in Greenland and Antarctica.

Glacial ice normally contains abundant rock fragments ranging from huge angular boulders to pulverized rock flour. Some of this material is eroded from the rock floor on which the ice moves. In alpine glaciers, rock debris is also derived from material that slides or falls from valley walls onto the ice.

Glaciers can erode and deposit great quantities of sediment. *Glacial abrasion* is a glacial erosion process caused by rock fragments that are held within the ice and scrape and grind against bedrock (Figure 19.2). Erosion also occurs by *plucking,* as moving ice lifts out blocks of bedrock that have been loosened by the freezing and expansion of water in

19.2 Glacial abrasion This grooved and polished surface, now partly eroded, marks the former path of glacial ice. Cathedral Lakes, Yosemite National Park, California.

joint fractures. Abrasion and plucking act to smooth the bed of a glacier as glacial flow continues through time. Rock debris brought into a glacier is eventually deposited at the lower end of a glacier, where the ice melts. Both erosion and deposition result in distinctive glacial landforms.

ALPINE GLACIERS

Figure 19.3 illustrates a number of features of alpine glaciers. The illustration shows a simple glacier occupying a sloping valley between steep rock walls. Snow collects at the upper end in a bowl-shaped depression, the **cirque.** The upper end lies in a zone of accumulation. Layers of snow in the process of compaction and recrystalliza-tion are called *firn.*

The smooth firn field is slightly bowl-shaped in profile. Flowage in the glacial ice beneath the firn carries the ice downvalley out of the cirque. The rate of ice flow is accelerated at a steep rock step, where deep crevasses (gaping fractures) mark an ice fall. The lower part of the glacier lies in the zone of ablation. In this area, the rate of ice wastage is rapid, and old ice is exposed at the glacier surface. As the ice thins by ablation, it loses its plasticity and may develop deep crevasses. At its lower end, or terminus, the glacier carries abundant rock debris. As the downward-flowing ice melts, the debris accumulates.

Although the uppermost layer of a glacier is brittle, the ice beneath behaves as a plastic substance and moves by slow flowage (Figure 19.4). Like stream flow, glacier flow is most rapid far from the glacier's bed—near the midline and toward the top of the glacier's surface. Alpine glaciers also move by basal sliding. In this process, the ice slides downhill, lubricated by meltwater and mud at its base.

A glacier establishes a dynamic balance in which the rate of accumulation at the upper end balances the rate of ablation at the lower end. This balance is easily upset by changes in the average annual rates of accumulation or ablation, causing the glacier's terminus to move forward or melt.

Glacial flow is usually very slow. It amounts to a few centimeters per day for large ice sheets and the more sluggish alpine glaciers, but as fast as several meters per day for an active alpine glacier. However, some alpine glaciers experience episodes of very rapid movement, termed *surges.* A surging glacier may travel downvalley at speeds of more than 60 m (about 200 ft) per day for several months. The reasons for surging are not well understood but probably involve mechanisms that increase the amount of meltwater beneath the ice, enhancing basal sliding. Most glaciers do not experience surging.

> Cirques are rounded rock basins that contain the heads of alpine glaciers. They form high on glaciated peaks.

GEODISCOVERIES Glacier Mass Balance. View this animation to visualize how an alpine glacier gains mass in its upper regions and loses mass in its lower regions.

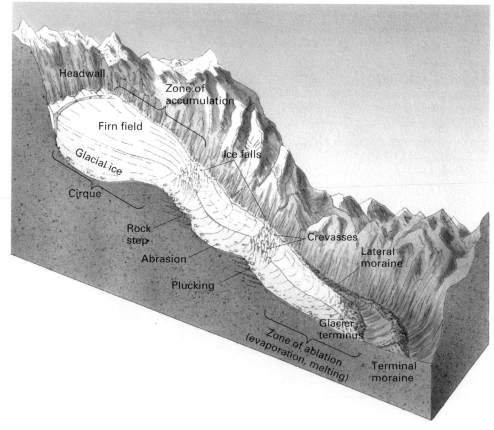

19.3 Cross section of an alpine glacier *Ice accumulates in the glacial cirque, then flows downhill, abrading and plucking the bedrock. Glacial debris accumulates at the glacier terminus. (After A. N. Strahler.)*

Headwall

Zone of accumulation

Firn field

Glacial ice

Cirque

Ice falls

Rock step

Crevasses

Abrasion

Lateral moraine

Plucking

Glacier terminus

Zone of ablation (evaporation, melting)

Terminal moraine

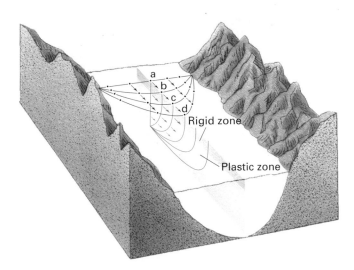

19.4 Motion of glacial ice *Ice moves most rapidly on the glacier's surface at its midline. Movement is slowest near the bed, where the ice contacts bedrock or sediment.*

Landforms Made by Alpine Glaciers

Landforms made by alpine glaciers are shown in a series of diagrams in Figure 19.5. Mountains are eroded and shaped by glaciers, and after the glaciers melt, the remaining landforms are exposed to view. Diagram *a* shows a region sculptured entirely by weathering, mass wasting, and streams. The mountains have a smooth, rounded appearance. Soil and regolith are thick.

Imagine now that a climatic change results in the accumulation of snow in the heads of the higher valleys. An early stage of glaciation is shown at the right side of diagram *b*, where snow is collecting and cirques are being carved by the grinding motion of the ice. Deepening of the cirques is aided by intensive frost shattering of the bedrock near the masses of compacted snow. At a later stage (center), glaciers have filled the valleys and are integrated into a system of tributaries that feed a trunk glacier. Tributary glaciers join the main glacier smoothly. The cirques grow steadily larger. Their rough, steep walls soon replace the smooth, rounded slopes of the original mountain mass. Where two cirque walls intersect from opposite sides, a jagged, knife-like ridge, called an *arête,* is formed. Where three or more cirques grow together, a sharp-pointed peak is formed. Such peaks are called *horns.* Where opposed cirques have intersected deeply, a pass or notch, called a *col,* is formed. On the left side of the diagram, a portion of the landscape is drawn as unglaciated. This portion retains its rounded forms and V-shaped valleys.

A ridge or pile of rock debris left by glacial action that marks the edge of a glacier is termed a **moraine.** A *lateral moraine* is a debris ridge formed along the edge of the ice adjacent to the trough wall (Figure 19.3). Where two ice streams join, this marginal debris is dragged along to form a narrow band riding on the ice in midstream (Figures

> Alpine glaciers, descending through preexisting valleys, excavate wide, U-shaped glacial troughs. When the glaciers retreat, meltwater streams can fill trough floors with sediment.

19.1, 19.5*b*), called a *medial moraine.* At the terminus of a glacier, rock debris accumulates in a *terminal moraine,* an embankment curving across the valley floor and bending upvalley along each wall of the trough (Figure 19.6).

Glacial Troughs and Fiords

Glacier flow constantly deepens and widens its rock channel, so that after the ice has finally melted, a deep, steep-walled **glacial trough** remains (Figure 19.5*c*). The trough typically has a U-shape in cross-profile (Figure 19.7). Tributary glaciers also carve U-shaped troughs, but they are smaller in cross section and less deeply eroded by their smaller glaciers. Because the floors of these troughs lie high above the level of the main trough, they are called *hanging valleys.* Streams later occupy the abandoned valleys, providing scenic waterfalls that cascade over the lip of the hanging valley to the main trough below. High up in the smaller troughs, the bedrock is unevenly excavated, so that the floors of troughs and cirques contain rock basins and rock steps. The rock basins are occupied by small lakes, called *tarns* (Figure 19.5*c*). Major troughs sometimes hold large, elongated trough lakes.

GEODISCOVERIES **Hanging Valleys.** Watch alpine glaciers grow and coalesce to carve U-shaped valleys, then retreat to expose hanging valleys. An animation.

Many large glacial troughs now are filled with alluvium and have flat floors. Aggrading streams that issued from the receding ice front were heavily laden with rock fragments so that the deposit of alluvium extended far downvalley. Figure 19.7 shows a comparison between a trough with little or no fill (*b*) and another with an alluvial-filled bottom (*c*).

When the floor of a trough open to the sea lies below sea level, the sea water enters as the ice front recedes. The result is a deep, narrow estuary known as a **fiord** (Figure 19.7*d*). Fiords are opening up today along the Alaskan coast, where some glaciers are melting back rapidly and ocean waters are filling their troughs. Fiords are found largely along mountainous coasts between lat. 50° and 70° N and S (Figure 19.8). On these coasts, glaciers were nourished by heavy orographic snowfall, associated with the marine west-coast climate ⑧.

As large, distinctive features in areas of rugged terrain, glaciers are readily viewed from the perspective of space. *Focus on Remote Sensing 19.1* • *Remote Sensing of Glaciers* shows some spectacular images of glaciers acquired from Earth orbit. One of the images uses a special radar imaging technique to portray the motion of an ice stream.

GEODISCOVERIES **The Cascade Range Interactivity.** Tour the mountains and glaciers of the Cascade Range and view the impact of volcanic activity on glacial activity.

GEODISCOVERIES **Satellite Imagery and Glaciers Interactivity.** Examine satellite images to identify the features of glaciers and icebergs from Iceland to Mount Kilimanjaro. View two short movies of the formation of icebergs.

19.5 Landforms produced by alpine glaciers *(a) Before glaciation sets in, the region has smoothly rounded divides and narrow, V-shaped stream valleys. (b) After glaciation has been in progress for thousands of years, new erosional forms are developed. (c) With the disappearance of the ice, a system of glacial troughs is exposed. (Drawn by A. N. Strahler.)*

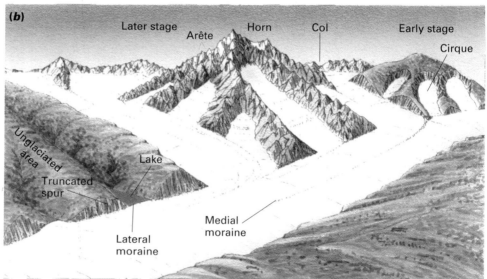

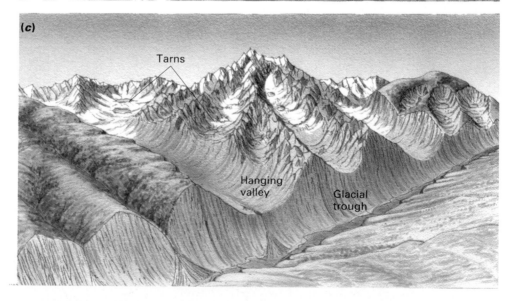

19.6 Alpine terminal moraine *A terminal moraine, shaped like the bow of a great canoe, lies at the mouth of a deep glacial trough on the east face of the Sierra Nevada. Cirques can be seen in the distance. Near Lee Vining, California.*

19.7 Development of a glacial trough *(a) During maximum glaciation, the U-shaped trough is filled by ice to the level of the small tributaries. (b) After glaciation, the trough floor may be occupied by a stream and lakes. (c) If the main stream is heavily loaded, it may fill the trough with alluvium. (d) Should the glacial trough have been deepened below sea level, it will be occupied by an arm of the sea, or fiord. (Drawn by E. Raisz.)*

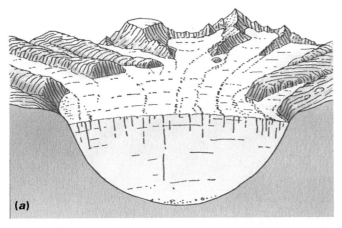

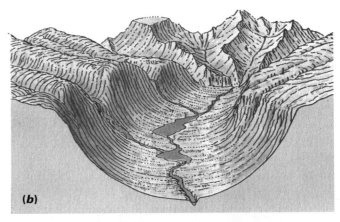

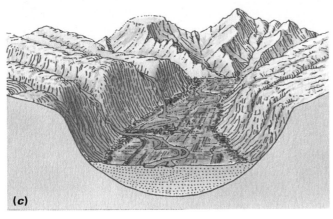

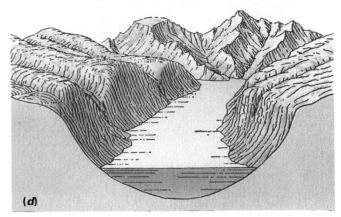

Focus on Remote Sensing | 19.1

Remote Sensing of Glaciers

Because glaciers are often found in inaccessible terrain or in extremely cold environments, they are difficult to survey and monitor. Satellite remote sensing provides an invaluable tool for studying both continental and alpine glaciers in spite of these difficulties.

Some of the world's more spectacular alpine glaciers are found in South America, along the crest of the Andes in Chile and Argentina, where mountain peaks reach as high as 3700 m (about 12,000 ft). Image (*a*) is a true-color image, acquired by astronauts aboard the International Space Station in December 2000 of Cerro San Lorenzo (San Lorenzo Peak). The peak itself is a glacial horn. Leading away from the horn to the south is a long, sharp ridge, or arête. To the left of the peak is a cirque, now only partly filled with glacial ice. These features were carved during the Ice Age, when the alpine glaciers were larger and filled the now-empty glacial

troughs behind the ridge to the right.

Northwest of Cerro San Lorenzo lies the San Quentin glacier, shown in ASTER image (*b*), acquired on May 2, 2000. This color-infrared image was acquired at 15-m spatial resolution and shows the glacier in fine detail. The snout of the glacier ends in a shallow lake of sediment-laden water that drains by fine streams into the Golfo de Penas at lower left. Note the low, semicircular ridge a short distance from the lake—this is a terminal moraine, marking a stand of the ice tongue in the recent past. A high cloud partly obscures the southern end of the snout and nearby coastline. The intense red color indicates a thick vegetation cover.

The world's largest glacier is, of course, the ice cap that covers nearly all of Antarctica. At the edges of the ice cap are outlet glaciers, where glacial flow into the ocean is quite rapid. Image (*c*) shows the Lambert Glacier, one of

the largest and longest of Antarctica's outlet glaciers. The image was acquired by Canada's Radarsat radar imager. Because this type of radar system can see through the clouds, it is ideal for mapping a large area in a short period of time. It also allows the measurement of the velocity of glacier flow by comparing paired images acquired at different times (in this case, 24 days apart) using a technique called radar interferometry. The image uses color to show the velocity. Brown tones indicate little or no motion, and show both exposed mountains and stationary ice. Green, blue, and red tones indicate increasing velocity. Velocity and direction are also shown by the arrows superimposed on the image. Glacial flow is most rapid at the left, where the flow is channeled through a narrow valley, and at the right, where the glacier spreads out and thins to feed the Amery Ice Shelf.

Andean alpine glacial features H, horn (San Lorenzo Peak); A, arête; C, cirque; T, glacial trough. (Courtesy NASA.)

(*a*)

San Quentin Glacier, Chile   *The San Quentin Glacier as imaged by ASTER. (Image courtesy NASA/GSFC/MITI/ERSDAC/JAROS and U.S./Japan ASTER Science Team.*

Lambert Glacier, Antarctica   *The Lambert Glacier as imaged by Radarsat during the 2000 Antarctic Mapping Mission. (Image courtesy Canadian Space Agency/NASA/Ohio State University, Jet Propulsion Laboratory, Alaska SAR Facility.)*

19.8 A glacial trough *Geirangerfjord, Norway, is a deeply carved glacial trough occupied by an arm of the sea.*

(about 13,000 ft) at maximum. At some locations, ice sheets extend long tongues, called outlet glaciers, to reach the sea at the heads of fiords. From the floating edge of the glacier, huge masses of ice break off and drift out to open sea with tidal currents to become icebergs. An important glacial feature of Antarctica is the presence of great plates of floating glacial ice, called *ice shelves* (Figure 19.10). Ice shelves are fed by the ice sheet, but they also accumulate new ice through the compaction of snow.

GEODISCOVERIES **Greenland's Glaciers.** This video features dramatic aerial views of the glaciers and fiords of Greenland.

19.9 The Greenland Ice Sheet *Contours show elevations of the ice sheet surface. (Based on data of R. F. Flint, Glacial and Pleistocene Geology, John Wiley & Sons, New York.)*

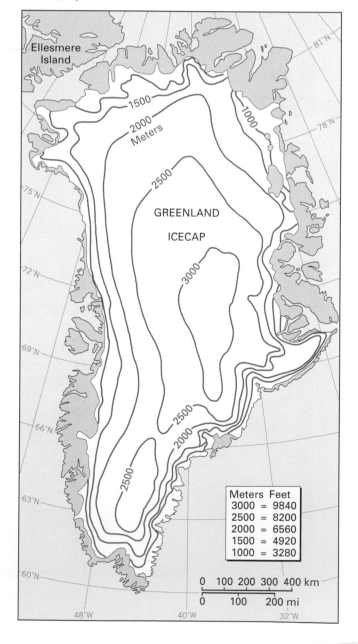

ICE SHEETS OF THE PRESENT

In contrast to alpine glaciers are the enormous ice sheets of Antarctica and Greenland. These are huge plates of ice, thousands of meters thick in the central areas, resting on land masses of subcontinental size. The Greenland Ice Sheet has an area of 1.7 million sq km (about 670,000 sq mi) and occupies about seven-eights of the entire island of Greenland (Figure 19.9). Only a narrow, mountainous coastal strip of land is exposed. The Antarctic Ice Sheet covers 13 million sq km (about 5 million sq mi) (Figure 19.10). Both ice sheets are developed on large, elevated land masses in high latitudes. No ice sheet exists near the north pole, which is positioned in the vast Arctic Ocean. Ice there occurs only as floating sea ice.

The surface of the Greenland Ice Sheet has the form of a very broad, smooth dome. Underneath the ice sheet, the rock floor lies near or slightly below sea level under the central region but is higher near the edges. The Antarctic Ice Sheet is thicker than the Greenland Ice Sheet—as much as 4000 m

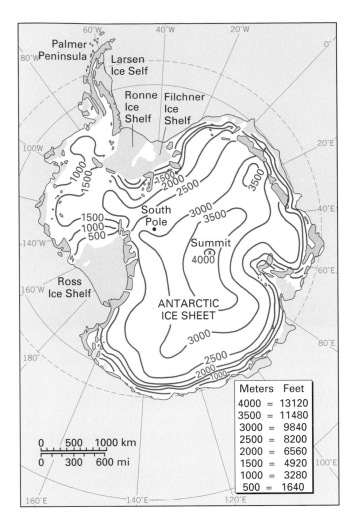

19.10   The Antarctic Ice Sheet and its ice shelves
Contours show elevations of the ice sheet surface. (Based on data of American Geophysical Union.)

19.11   Sea ice A Landsat image of a portion of the Canadian arctic archipelago. An ice cap on a land mass is visible in the center of the photo, with exposed mountainous ridges on the uncovered portions of the land mass. A branching glacial trough, now a water-filled fiord, is seen in the lower part of the image. In the upper left are huge chunks of free-floating sea ice.

SEA ICE AND ICEBERGS

Free-floating ice on the sea surface is of two types—sea ice and icebergs. *Sea ice* (Figure 19.11) is formed by direct freezing of ocean water. In contrast, *icebergs* are bodies of land ice that have broken free from glaciers that terminate in the ocean. Aside from differences in origin, a major difference between sea ice and icebergs is thickness. Sea ice does not exceed 5 m (15 ft) in thickness, while icebergs may be hundreds of meters thick.

Pack ice is sea ice that completely covers the sea surface. Under the forces of wind and currents, pack ice breaks up into individual patches called ice floes. The narrow strips of open water between such floes are known as *leads*. Where ice floes are forcibly brought together by winds, the ice margins buckle and turn upward into pressure ridges that often resemble walls of ice. Travel on foot across the polar sea ice is extremely difficult because of such obstacles. The surface zone of sea ice is composed of fresh water, while the deeper ice is salty.

Sea ice is formed by freezing of ocean surface water and is rarely thicker than 5 m (16.4 ft). Icebergs are floating chunks of glacial ice and can be hundreds of meters thick.

When a valley glacier or tongue of an ice sheet terminates in sea water, blocks of ice break off to form icebergs (Figure 19.12). Because they are only slightly less dense than sea water, icebergs float very low in the water. About five-sixths of the bulk of an iceberg is submerged. The ice is composed of fresh water since it is formed from compacted and recrystallized snow.

GEO*DISCOVERIES* **Calving of an Iceberg.** View the calving of an iceberg in a historic video from the last century.

THE ICE AGE

The period during which continental ice sheets grow and spread outward over vast areas is known as a **glaciation.** Glaciation is associated with a general cooling of average air temperatures over the regions where the ice sheets originate. At the same time, ample snowfall must persist over the growth areas to allow the ice masses to build in volume.

When the climate warms or snowfall decreases, ice sheets become thin-

19.12 Iceberg *Penguins enjoy an outing on an iceberg off the coast of Antarctica near Elephant Island.*

ner and cover less area. Eventually, the ice sheets may melt completely. This period is called a *deglaciation.* Following a deglaciation, but preceding the next glaciation, is a period in which a mild climate prevails—an **interglaciation.** The last interglaciation began about 140,000 years ago and ended between 120,000 and 110,000 years ago. A succession of alternating glaciations and interglaciations, spanning a period of 1 to 10 million years or more, constitutes an *ice age.*

Throughout the past 3 million years or so, the Earth has been experiencing the **Late-Cenozoic Ice Age** (or, simply, the **Ice Age**). As you may recall from Chapter 12, the Cenozoic Era has seven epochs (see Table 12.1). The Ice Age falls within the last three epochs: Pliocene, Pleistocene, and Holocene. These three epochs comprise only a small fraction—about one-twelfth—of the total duration of the Cenozoic Era.

A half-century ago, most geologists associated the Ice Age with the Pleistocene Epoch, which began about 1.6 million years before present. However, new evidence obtained from deep-sea sediments shows that the glaciations of the Ice Age began in late Pliocene time, perhaps 2.5 to 3.0 million years ago.

At present, we are within an interglaciation of the Late-Cenozoic Ice Age, following a deglaciation that set in quite rapidly about 15,000 years ago. In the preceding glaciation, called the *Wisconsinan Glaciation,* ice sheets covered much of North America and Europe, as well as parts of northern Asia and southern South America. The maximum ice advance of the Wisconsinan Glaciation was reached about 18,000 years ago.

> An ice age includes cycles of glaciation, deglaciation, and interglaciation. The Earth is presently in an interglaciation within the Late-Cenozoic Ice Age.

Glaciation During the Ice Age

Figures 19.13 and 19.14 show the maximum extent to which North America and Europe were covered during the last advance of the ice. Most of Canada was engulfed by the vast Laurentide Ice Sheet. It spread south into the United States, covering most of the land lying north of the Missouri and Ohio rivers, as well as northern Pennsylvania and all of New York and New England. Alpine glaciers of the western ranges coalesced into a single ice sheet that spread to the Pacific shores and met the Laurentide sheet on the east. Notice that an area in southwestern Wisconsin escaped inundation. Known as the Driftless Area, it was apparently bypassed by glacial lobes moving on either side.

In Europe, the Scandinavian Ice Sheet centered on the Baltic Sea, covering the Scandinavian countries. It spread south into central Germany and far eastward to cover much of Russia. In north-central Siberia, large ice caps formed over the northern Ural Mountains and highland areas farther east. Ice from these centers grew into a large sheet covering much of central Siberia. The European Alps were capped by enlarged alpine glaciers. The British Isles were mostly covered by a small ice sheet that had several centers on highland areas and spread outward to coalesce with the Scandinavian Ice Sheet.

At the maximum spread of these ice sheets, sea level was as much as 125 m (410 ft) lower than today, exposing large areas of the continental shelf on both sides of the Atlantic Basin. The shelf supported a vegetated landscape populated with animal life, including Pleistocene elephants (mastodons and mammoths). The drawdown of sea level explains why the ice sheets shown on our maps extend far out into what is now the open ocean.

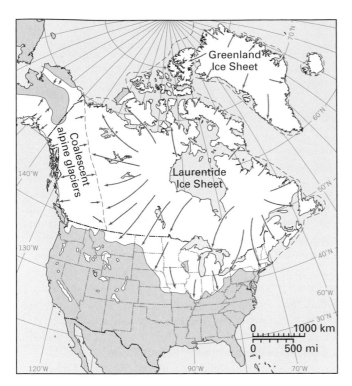

19.13 Maximum glaciation in North America
Continental glaciers of the Ice Age in North America at their maximum extent reached as far south as the present Ohio and Missouri rivers. Note that during glaciations sea level was much lower. The present coastline is shown for reference only. (Based on data of R. F. Flint, Glacial and Pleistocene Geology, John Wiley & Sons, New York.)

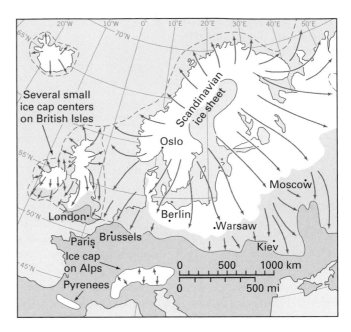

19.14 Maximum glaciation in Europe *The Scandinavian Ice Sheet dominated Northern Europe during the Ice Age glaciations. As noted in Figure 19.13, the present coastline is far inland from the coastline that prevailed during glaciations. (Based on data of R. F. Flint, Glacial and Pleistocene Geology, John Wiley & Sons, New York.)*

South America, too, had an ice sheet. It grew from ice caps on the southern Andes Range south of about latitude 40°S and spread westward to the Pacific shore, as well as eastward, to cover a broad belt of Patagonia. It covered all of Tierra del Fuego, the southern tip of the continent. The South Island of New Zealand, which today has a high spine of alpine mountains with small relict glaciers, developed a massive ice cap in late Pleistocene time. All high mountain areas of the world underwent greatly intensified alpine glaciation at the time of maximum ice sheet advance. Today, most remaining alpine glaciers are small ones. In less favorable locations, the Ice Age alpine glaciers are entirely gone.

GEODISCOVERIES **Last Ice Age.** This animated map shows the retreat of continental ice sheets and coalescing alpine glaciers after the last glaciation. Watch as antarctic ice shelves and arctic sea ice also shrink.

The weights of the continental ice sheets, covering vast areas with ice masses several kilometers thick, exerted downward forces on the crust, causing depressions of the crust of hundreds of meters at some locations. With the melting of the ice of the last glaciation, the crust began an *isostatic rebound* that is still going on today at some locations. Uplifted marine terraces provide the primary evidence for this recent upward motion.

> Although the largest ice sheets spread from northern hemisphere centers in Canada, Scandinavia, and Siberia, South America and New Zealand also developed ice sheets.

LANDFORMS MADE BY ICE SHEETS

Landforms made by the last ice advance and recession are very fresh in appearance and show little modification by erosion processes. It is to these landforms that we now turn our attention.

Erosion by Ice Sheets

Like alpine glaciers, ice sheets are highly effective eroding agents. The slowly moving ice scraped and ground away much solid bedrock, leaving behind smoothly rounded rock masses. These bear countless grooves and scratches trending in the general direction of ice movement (see Figure 19.2). Sometimes the ice polishes the rock to a smooth, shining surface. The evidence of ice abrasion is common throughout glaciated regions of North America and may be seen on almost any hard rock surface that is freshly exposed. Conspicuous knobs of solid bedrock shaped by the moving ice are also common features (Figure 19.15). The side from which the ice approached is usually smoothly rounded. The lee side, where

19.15 A glacially abraded rock knob *Glacial action abrades the rock into a smooth form as it rides over the rock summit, then plucks bedrock blocks from the lee side, producing a steep, rocky slope. (Copyright © A. N. Strahler.)*

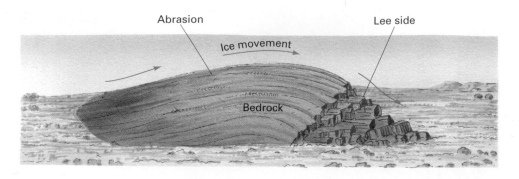

the ice plucked out angular joint blocks, is irregular and blocky.

The ice sheets also excavated enormous amounts of rock at locations where the bedrock was weak and the flow of ice was channeled by the presence of a valley trending in the direction of ice flow. Under these conditions, the ice sheet behaved like a valley glacier, scooping out a deep, U-shaped trough. The Finger Lakes of western New York State are fine examples (Figure 19.16). Here, a set of former stream valleys lay largely parallel to the southward spread of the ice, and a set of long, deep basins was eroded. Blocked at their north ends by glacial debris, the basins now hold lakes. Many hundreds of lake basins were created by glacial erosion and deposition over the glaciated portion of North America.

Deposits Left by Ice Sheets

The term **glacial drift** includes all varieties of rock debris deposited in close association with glaciers. Drift is of two major types. *Stratified drift* consists of layers of sorted and stratified clays, silts, sands, or gravels. These materials were

> The term *glacial drift* describes all types of rock debris deposited in close association with glaciers. *Stratified drift* includes sediment laid by water, while *till* is deposited directly by ice.

deposited by meltwater streams or in bodies of water adjacent to the ice. **Till** is an unstratified mixture of rock fragments, ranging in size from clay to boulders, that is deposited directly from the ice without water transport. As the glacial ice melts in a stagnant marginal zone, the rock particles it holds are lowered to the solid surface beneath, where they form a layer of debris (Figure 19.17). This *ablational till* shows no sorting and often consists of a mixture of sand and silt, with many angular pebbles and boulders. Beneath this residual layer there may be a basal layer of dense *lodgment till,* consisting of clay-rich debris previously dragged forward beneath the moving ice. Where till forms a thin, more or less even cover, it is referred to as *ground moraine.*

Over those parts of North America formerly covered by Late-Cenozoic ice sheets, glacial drift thickness averages from 6 m (about 20 ft) over mountainous terrain, such as New England, to 15 m (about 50 ft) and more over the lowlands of the north-central United States. Over Iowa, drift thickness is from 45 to 60 m (about 150 to 200 ft), and over Illinois it averages more than 30 m (about 100 ft). In some places where

19.16 Eye on the Landscape Finger Lakes *The Finger Lakes region of New York is shown in this photo taken by astronauts aboard the Space Shuttle. The view is looking toward the northeast. The lakes occupy valleys that were eroded and deepened by glacial ice.* **What else would the geographer see? ... Answers at the end of the chapter.**

(a)

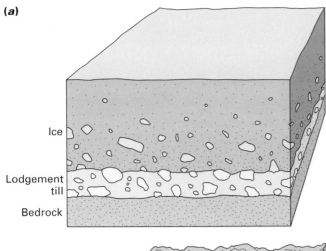

Ice

Lodgment till

Bedrock

(b)

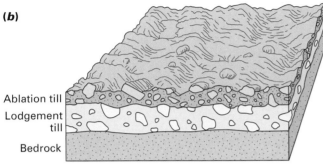

Ablation till

Lodgment till

Bedrock

19.17 Glacial till *(a) As ice passes over the ground, sediment and coarse rock fragments are pressed into a layer of lodgment till. (b) When the overlying ice stagnates and melts, it leaves a residual deposit of ablation till. (Copyright © A. N. Strahler.)*

deep stream valleys existed prior to glacial advance, as in parts of Ohio, drift is much thicker.

To understand the form and composition of deposits left by ice sheets, it will help to examine the conditions prevailing at the time of the ice sheet's existence. Figure 19.18*a* shows a region partly covered by an ice sheet with a stationary front edge. This condition occurs when the rate of ice ablation balances the amount of ice brought forward by spreading of the ice sheet. Although the ice fronts of the Ice Age advanced and receded in many minor and major fluctuations, there were long periods when the front was essentially stable and thick deposits of drift accumulated.

MORAINES The transportational work of an ice sheet resembles that of a huge conveyor belt. Anything carried on the belt is dumped off at the end and, if not constantly removed, will pile up in increasing quantity. Rock fragments brought within the ice are deposited at its outer edge as the ice evaporates or melts. Glacial till that accumulates at the immediate ice edge forms an irregular, rubbly heap—the *terminal moraine.* After the ice has disappeared (Figure

———
Moraines are built of rock debris deposited at the edges of a melting glacier or ice sheet. Terminal moraines mark the limits of glaciation.
———

19.20*a*), the moraine appears as a belt of knobby hills interspersed with basin-like hollows, or kettles, some of which hold small lakes. The name *knob-and-kettle* is often applied to morainal belts.

Terminal moraines form great curving patterns. The outward curvature is southward and indicates that the ice advanced as a series of great *ice lobes,* each with a curved front (Figure 19.19). Where two lobes come together, the moraines curve back and fuse together into a single *interlobate moraine* pointed northward. In its general recession accompanying disappearance, the ice front paused for some time along a number of positions, causing morainal belts similar to the terminal moraine belt to be formed. These belts are known as *recessional moraines* (Figure 19.20*a*). They run roughly parallel with the terminal moraine but are often thin and discontinuous.

OUTWASH AND ESKERS Figure 19.18 shows a smooth, sloping plain lying in front of the ice margin. This is the *outwash plain,* formed of stratified drift left by braided streams issuing from the ice. The plain is built of layer upon layer of sands and gravels.

Large streams carrying meltwater issue from tunnels in the ice. These form when the ice front stops moving for many kilometers back from the front. After the ice has gone, the position of a former ice tunnel is marked by a long, sinuous ridge of sediment known as an *esker* (Figure 19.20*b*). The esker is the deposit of sand and gravel laid on the floor of the former ice tunnel. After the ice has melted away, only the stream-bed deposit remains, forming a ridge. Many eskers are several kilometers long.

DRUMLINS AND TILL PLAINS Another common glacial form is the *drumlin,* a smoothly rounded, oval hill resembling the bowl of an inverted teaspoon. It consists in most cases of glacial till (Figure 19.20*c*). Drumlins invariably lie in a zone behind the terminal moraine. They commonly occur in groups or swarms and may number in the hundreds. The long axis of each drumlin parallels the direction of ice movement. Drumlins are typically steeper at the broad end, which faces oncoming ice. The origin of drumlins is not well understood. They seem to have been formed under moving ice by a plastering action in which layer upon layer of bouldery clay was spread on the drumlin.

Between moraines, the surface overridden by the ice is covered by glacial till. This cover is often inconspicuous since it forms no prominent landscape feature. The till layer may be thick and may obscure, or entirely bury, the hills and valleys that existed before glaciation. Where thick and smoothly spread, the layer forms a level *till plain.* Plains of this origin are widespread throughout the central lowlands of the United States and southern Canada.

MARGINAL LAKES AND THEIR DEPOSITS When the ice advanced toward higher ground, valleys that may have

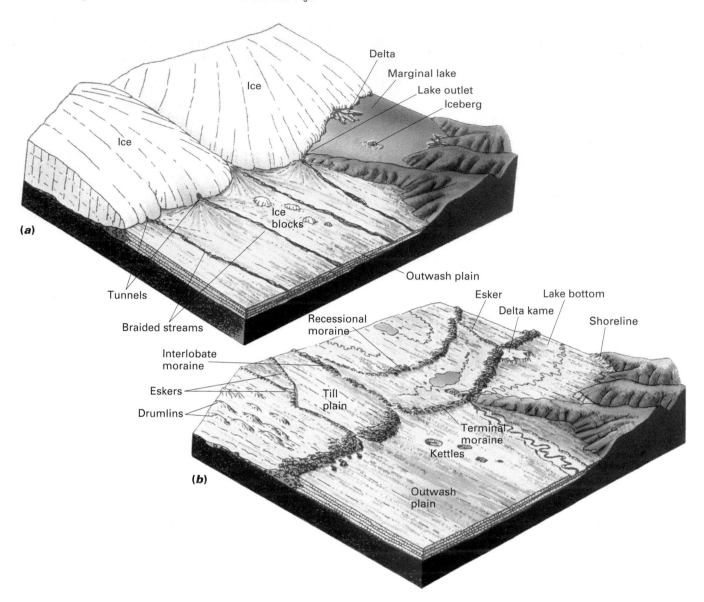

19.18 Marginal landforms of continental glaciers *(a) With the ice front stabilized and the ice in a wasting, stagnant condition, various depositional features are built by meltwater. (b) The ice has wasted completely away, exposing a variety of new landforms made under the ice. (Drawn by A. N. Strahler.)*

opened out northward were blocked by ice. Under such conditions, marginal glacial lakes formed along the ice front (see Figure 19.18a). These lakes overflowed along the lowest available channel between the ice and the rising ground slope, or over some low pass along a divide. Streams of meltwater from the ice built *glacial deltas* into these marginal lakes.

When the ice withered away, the lakes drained, leaving a flat floor exposed. Here, layers of fine clay and silt had accumulated. Glacial lake plains often contain extensive areas of marshland. The deltas are now curiously isolated, flat-topped landforms known as *delta kames,* composed of well-washed and well-sorted sands and gravels (Figure 19.20d).

PLUVIAL LAKES During the Ice Age, some regions experienced a cooler, moister climate. In the western United

States, closed basins filled with water, forming pluvial lakes. The largest of these, glacial Lake Bonneville, was about the size of Lake Michigan and occupied a vast area of western Utah. With the warmer and drier climate of the present interglacial period, these lakes shrank greatly in volume. Lake Bonneville became the present-day Great Salt Lake. Many other lakes dried up completely, forming desert playas. The history of these pluvial lakes is known from their ancient shorelines, some as high as 300 m (about 1000 ft) above present levels.

Environmental Aspects of Glacial Deposits

Because much of Europe and North America was glaciated by the Pleistocene ice sheets, landforms associated with the

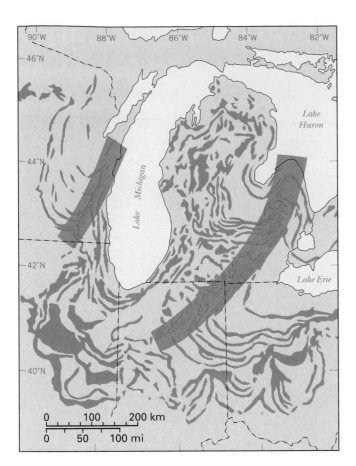

19.19 Map of Midwest moraines *Moraine belts of the north-central United States have a curving pattern left by ice lobes. Some regions of interlobate moraines are shown by the color overlay. (Based on data of R. F. Flint and others, Glacial Map of North America, Geological Society of America.)*

fertility is enhanced by a blanket of wind-deposited silt (loess) that covers these plains (Chapter 18).

Stratified drift deposits are of great commercial value. The sands and gravels of outwash plains, deltas, and eskers provide necessary materials for both concrete manufacture and highway construction. Where it is thick, stratified drift forms an excellent aquifer and is a major source of ground water supplies (see Chapter 15).

INVESTIGATING THE ICE AGE

A great scientific breakthrough in the study of Ice Age glacial history came in the 1960s. First, scientists learned how to measure the absolute age of certain types of water-laid sediments by means of ancient magnetism. The Earth's magnetic field experienced many sudden reversals of polarity in Cenozoic time, and the absolute ages of these reversals have been firmly established. Second, techniques were developed to take long sample cores of undisturbed fine-textured sediments of the deep ocean floor. Within each core, scientists could determine the age of sediment layers at various control points by identifying magnetic polarity reversals. By further studying the composition and chemistry of the layers within the core, a record of ancient temperature cycles in the air and ocean could be established.

Deep-sea cores reveal a long history of alternating glaciations and interglaciations going back at least as far as 2 million years and possibly 3 million years before present. The cores show that in Late-Cenozoic time more than 30 glaciations occurred, spaced at time intervals of about 90,000 years. How much longer this sequence will continue into the future is not known, but perhaps for 1 or 2 million years, or even longer.

Figure 19.21 presents a plot of global temperature, shown as a difference from present temperature, going back to about 800 thousand years ago. Each valley represents a glacial period and each peak an interglacial. The figure clearly shows five distinct glaciations and four interglacials since about 500,000 years ago. Before that time, the record shows more frequent glacial cycles that are somewhat less extreme.

Possible Causes of the Late-Cenozoic Ice Age

What caused the Earth to enter into an Ice Age with its numerous cycles of glaciation and interglaciation? Three causes seem possible. First is a change in the placement of continents on the Earth's surface through plate tectonic activity. Second is an increase in the number and severity of volcanic eruptions. Third is a reduction in the Sun's energy output.

Perhaps the answer lies in plate tectonics, through the motions of lithospheric plates following the breakup of Pangea. Recall from Chapter 12 that in

ice are of major environmental importance. Agricultural influences of glaciation are both favorable and unfavorable, depending on preglacial topography and the degree and nature of ice erosion and deposition.

In hilly or mountainous regions, such as New England, the glacial till is thinly distributed and extremely stony. Till cultivation is difficult because of countless boulders and cobbles in the clay soil. Till accumulations on steep mountain or roadside slopes are subject to mass movement as earthflows when clay in the till becomes weakened after absorbing water from melting snows and spring rains. Along moraine belts, the steep slopes, the irregularity of knob-and-kettle topography, and the abundance of boulders hinder crop cultivation but are suitable for use as pasture.

Flat till plains, outwash plains, and lake plains, on the other hand, can sometimes provide very productive agricultural land. Bordering the Great Lakes, fertile soils have formed on till plains and on exposed lakebeds. This

> Three factors have been proposed to explain why the Earth has entered the Late-Cenozoic Ice Age: a change in the placement of the continents, increased volcanic activity, and a reduction in solar energy output.

a...*Recessional moraine* The lower left portion of this aerial scene from Langlade County, Wisconsin, shows a recessional moraine covered with forest vegetation. Note the bumpy, irregular topography of sediments piled up at the former ice edge. To the upper right is the now-cultivated outwash plain of sediments laid down by rivers and streams draining the melting ice front.

b...*Esker* The curving ridge of sand and gravel in this photo is an esker, marking the bed of a river of meltwater flowing underneath a continental ice sheet near its margin. Kettle-Moraine State Park, Wisconsin.

c...Drumlin This small drumlin, located south of Sodus, New York, shows a tapered form from upper right to lower left, indicating that the ice moved in that direction (north to south).

d...Kame This tree-covered hill, rising above the surrounding plain, is a kame—a deposit of sand and gravel built out from the front of a retreating ice sheet, possibly as a delta accumulating in a short-lived lake. As the ice melted and the lake drained, the deposit lost its lateral support and slumped down under the force of gravity, forming a hill of roughly conical shape.

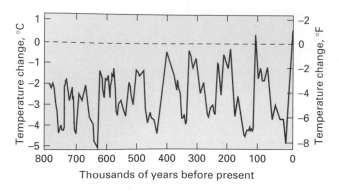

19.21 Global temperatures of the Ice Age *This record of the Earth's global surface temperature, expressed as a difference from present temperature, shows glaciations and interglaciations to 800,000 years before present. (Copyright © D. Reidel Pub. Co., 1984, used by permission.)*

Permian time, only the northern tip of the Eurasian continent projected into the polar zone. But as the Atlantic Basin opened up, North America moved westward and poleward to a position opposite Eurasia, while Greenland took up a position between North America and Europe.

The effect of these plate motions was to bring an enormous land-mass area to a high latitude and to surround a polar ocean with land. Because the flow of warm ocean currents into the polar ocean was greatly reduced, or at times totally cut off, this arrangement was favorable to the growth of ice sheets. The polar ocean was ice-covered much of the time, and average air temperatures in high latitudes were at times lowered enough to allow ice sheets to grow on the encircling continents. Furthermore, Antarctica moved southward during the breakup of Pangea and took up a position over the south pole. In that location, it was ideally situated to develop a large ice sheet. Some scientists have also proposed that the uplift of the Himalayan Plateau, a result of the collision of the Austral-Indian and Eurasian plates, could have modified weather patterns sufficiently to trigger the Ice Age.

The second geological mechanism suggested as a basic cause of the Ice Age is increased volcanic activity on a global scope in late-Cenozoic time. Volcanic eruptions produce dust veils that linger in the stratosphere and reduce the intensity of solar radiation reaching the ground (Chapter 3). Temporary cooling of near-surface air temperatures follows such eruptions. Although the geologic record shows periods of high levels of volcanic activity in the Miocene and Pliocene epochs, their role in initiating the Ice Age has not been convincingly demonstrated on the basis of present evidence.

Another possible cause of the Ice Age is a slow decrease in the Sun's energy output over the last several million years, perhaps as part of a cycle of slow increase and decrease over many million years' duration. As yet, data are insufficient to identify this mechanism as a possible basic cause. However, research on this topic is being stepped up as new knowledge of the Sun is acquired from satellites that probe the Sun's atmosphere and monitor its changing surface.

Possible Causes of Glaciation Cycles

What timing and triggering mechanisms are responsible for the many cycles of glaciation and interglaciation that the Earth is experiencing during the present Ice Age? Although many causes for glacial cycles have been proposed, we will limit our discussion here to one major contender called the **astronomical hypothesis.** It has been under consideration for about 40 years and is now widely accepted.

The astronomical hypothesis is based on well-established motions of the Earth in its orbit around the Sun. Recall from Chapter 1 that the Earth's orbit around the Sun is an ellipse, not a circle, and that we refer to the point in the orbit nearest the Sun as perihelion, and the point farthest as aphelion. Presently, perihelion occurs around December 5 and aphelion around July 5. Astronomers have observed that the orbit slowly rotates on a 108,000-year cycle, thus shifting the absolute time of perihelion and aphelion by a very small amount each year. In addition, the orbit's shape varies on a cycle of 92,000 years, becoming more and less elliptical. This changes the Earth–Sun distance and therefore the amount of solar energy the Earth receives at each point of the annual cycle.

The Earth's axis of rotation also experiences cyclic motions. The tilt angle of the axis varies from about 22 to 24 degrees on a 40,000-year cycle. The axis also "wobbles" on a 26,000-year cycle, moving in a slow circular motion much like that of a spinning top or toy gyroscope.

> According to the astronomical hypothesis, the timing of glaciations and interglaciations is determined by variations in insolation produced by minor cycles in the Earth's orbit and the Earth's axial rotation.

As a result of these cycles in axial rotation and solar revolution, the annual insolation experienced at each latitude changes from year to year. Figure 19.22 shows a graph of summer insolation received at 65° N latitude for the last 500,000 years as calculated from these cycles. The graph is known as the Milankovitch curve, named for Milutin Milankovich, the astronomer who first calculated it in 1938. The dominant cycle of the curve has a period of about 40,000 years, but note that every second or third peak seems to be higher. Peaks at about 12,000, 130,000, 220,000, 285,000, and 380,000 years ago have been associated with the rapid melting of ice sheets and the onset of deglaciations, as revealed by other dating methods involving ancient ice cores and deep lake sediment cores. Most scientists studying climate change during the Ice Age now agree that cyclic insolation changes are the primary factor explaining the cycles of glaciation of the Ice Age.

The actual mechanisms by which insolation changes cause ice sheets to grow or to disappear are unclear. The

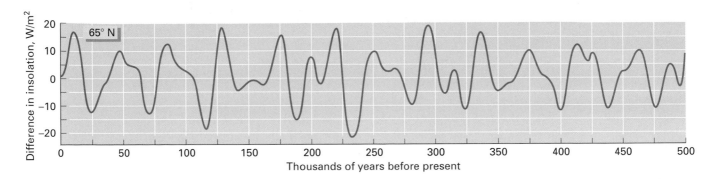

19.22   The Milankovitch curve *The vertical axis shows fluctuations in summer daily insolation at lat. 65° N for the last 500,000 years. These are calculated from mathematical models of the change in Earth–Sun distance and change in axial tilt with time. The zero value represents the present value. (Based on calculations by A. D. Vernekar, 1968. Copyright © A. N. Strahler.)*

entire subject is so complex that it is difficult for even a research scientist to grasp fully. Interactions between the atmosphere, the oceans, and the continental surfaces (including the ice sheets) are numerous and closely interrelated with many threads of cause and effect. Changes that occur in one Earth realm are fed back to the other realms in a most complex manner.

Holocene Environments

The elapsed time span of about 10,000 years since the Wisconsinan Glaciation ended is called the *Holocene Epoch.* It began with a rapid warming of ocean surface temperatures. Continental climate zones then quickly shifted poleward, and plants soon became reestablished in glaciated areas.

Three major climatic periods occurred during the Holocene Epoch leading up to the last 2000 years. These periods are inferred from studies of changes in vegetation cover types as observed in fossil pollen and spores preserved in glacial bogs. The earliest of the three is known as the Boreal stage and was characterized by boreal forest vegetation in midlatitude regions. There followed a general warming until the Atlantic stage, with temperatures somewhat warmer than today, was reached about 8000 years ago (–8000 years). Next came a period of temperatures that were below average, the Subboreal stage. This stage spanned the age range –5000 to –2000 years.

Through the availability of historical records and of more detailed evidence, the climate of the past 2000 years can be described on a finer scale. A secondary warm period occurred in the period A.D. 1000 to 1200 (–1000 to –800 years). This warm episode was followed by the Little Ice Age, A.D. 1450–1850 (–550 to –50 years). During the latter, valley glaciers made new advances and extended to lower elevations. More recent temperature cycles are discussed in Chapter 3.

Within the last century, global temperatures have slowly increased and are projected to increase more rapidly for at least the next 100 years. What will be the effect of global warming on the existing continental ice sheets and ice shelves of Greenland and Antarctica? *Eye on Global Change 19.2 • Ice Sheets and Global Warming* discusses the possibilities.

Cycles of glaciation and interglaciation, as well as the lesser climatic cycles of the Holocene Epoch, have proceeded without human influence for millions of years. They demonstrate the power of natural forces to make drastic swings from cold to warm climates, and they confound our efforts to understand human impact on climate.

GEODISCOVERIES **Web Quiz.** Take a quick quiz on the key concepts of this chapter.

A LOOK AHEAD   Our chapter has focused on the processes that construct glacial landforms on an individual or local scale, showing how flowing ice and meltwater leave distinctive signatures on the landscape. At regional and continental scales, we have examined the pattern of landscape features from finger lakes to the systems of moraines that mark the former presence of moving ice. We have also documented the pattern of expansion and contraction of continental and alpine glaciers in response to the climate change of the glacial and interglacial periods of the Ice Age.

The group of chapters we have now completed has reviewed landform-making processes that operate on the surface of the continents. These have ranged from mass wasting to the erosion and deposition brought about by glacial ice. The great variety and complexity of landforms we have described are not difficult to understand when each agent of denudation is examined in turn.

Human influence on landforms is felt most strongly on surfaces of fluvial denudation because of the severity of surface changes caused by agriculture and urbanization. Landforms shaped by wind and by waves and currents are

Eye on Global Change | 19.2

Ice Sheets and Global Warming

What effects will global warming have on the Earth's ice sheets? The Antarctic Ice Sheet holds 91 percent of the Earth's ice. If it were to melt entirely, the Earth's mean sea level would rise by about 40 m (about 200 ft). Additional water could be released by the melting of the Greenland Ice Sheet, which holds most of the remaining volume of land ice. Although global warming will accelerate glacial melting and thinning of the ice at the edges of ice sheets, increased precipitation, held by warmer air over the ice sheets, will likely produce a net growth in ice sheet thickness. Thus, it seems most unlikely that global warming will melt these ice sheets completely, unless the warming is much greater than anticipated. However, there may be other factors at work than snow buildup and marginal melting in the case of individual ice sheets.

In 1998 NASA researchers repeated measurements of the height of the southern half of the Greenland Ice Sheet that were originally made in 1993 using a laser altimeter mounted on an aircraft. They discovered that marginal thinning had reduced the volume of the ice sheet by about 42 km^3 (about 10 mi^3) in that five-year period. The thinning was primarily on the eastern side of the Ice Sheet. On the western side, melting was more in balance with new snow accumulation. The loss of this ice volume is not large enough to have much effect on global sea level. But a substantial flow of fresh meltwater into the ocean could influence the thermohaline circulation of the northern Atlantic (see Chapter 5), triggering an ocean cycle of several centuries' duration that would bring very cold winter weather to Europe.

At the other pole, recent attention has focused on the Western Antarctic Ice Sheet, shown in the map to the right. Much of this vast expanse of Antarctic ice is "grounded" on a bedrock base that is well below sea level—that is, a large portion of the ice sheet rests directly on deep

bedrock without sea water underneath. Attached to the grounded ice sheet are the Ross, Ronne, and Filchner ice shelves, which are underlain by sea water. They are also grounded at some points where the shelves enclose islands and overlay higher parts of undersea topography. At present, the grounded ice shelves act to hold back the flow of the main part of the ice sheet.

Geophysicists regard this as an unstable situation. A rapid melting or deterioriation of the ice shelves, perhaps in response to global warming, would release the back pressure on the main part of the ice sheet, which would then move forward and thin rapidly. With a reduced thickness, reduced pressure at the bottom of the ice would allow sea water to enter, and soon most of the sheet would be floating in ocean water. The added bulk would then raise sea level by as much as 6 m (about 20 ft).

A key feature of the Western Antarctic Ice Sheet is the presence of a number of ice streams within the

sheet. Ice in these streams flows at a much more rapid rate than in the surrounding ice mass, probably because geothermal activity under the ice streams provides enough heat to melt the ice at the base. This creates a liquid bottom layer that lubricates the ice motion. The ice streams blend gradually into the ice shelves, providing a main source for their supply of ice.

The flow of the ice streams is essential to maintaining the ice shelves. If these streams slowed, the ice shelf might retreat, which could release the unstable western ice sheet, producing catastrophic flooding. In 2002, Drs. Ian Joughin and Slawek Tulacyzk reported in the journal *Science* that the ice streams feeding the Ross Ice Shelf are getting thicker and flowing more slowly. They attribute the change to gradual thinning of the ice sheet since the end of the last glaciation, a situation that allows cold Antarctic temperatures to penetrate to the base of the ice and freeze the liquid bottom layer. If the slowing of the ice

West Antarctic Ice Sheet *A map of Antarctica showing the Western Antarctic Ice Sheet. (Adapted with permission from C.R. Bentley, Science Vol. 275, p. 1077. Copyright © American Association for the Advancement of Science.)*

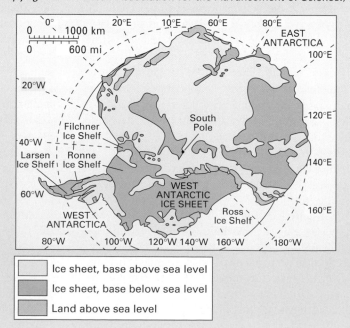

streams continues at the present rate for another 70 to 80 years, it would stop altogether, denying the West Antarctic Ice Sheet an influx of ice about equal to the average annual flow of the Missouri River. However, ice flow into other parts of the West Antarctic Ice Sheet seems to be speeding up, even as the ice streams feeding the Ross Ice Shelf are slowing. Whether this increasing flow will offset the effects of slowing Ross Shelf ice streams is not known.

Either way, new evidence from fossil shoreline deposits suggests that a portion of the Antarctic ice sheet collapsed into the ocean as recently as 14,200 years ago. In response, sea level rose about 20 m (65 ft) in a period of about 500 years. This rate is about 20 times larger than the slow rise of sea level measured today and about 4 times larger than the average rate at which sea level rose following the end of the last glacial period.

Meanwhile, the climatic warming of the past few decades has caused some ice shelves to thin and fracture more easily. The four MODIS images below document the disintegration of the Larsen B ice shelf during the austral summer in 2002. This ice shelf is located along the eastern side of Antarctic Peninsula, and the B portion was contained within the northernmost part of the shelf. Over a period of 35 days, 3250 km^2 (1254 mi^2) of floating ice, an area about 20 percent larger than Rhode Island, fractured and collapsed into thousands of individual icebergs. The sheet was about 220 m (720 ft) thick, and freed a volume of about 720 billion metric tons (792 billion tons) of ice. The collapse was the largest single event in a 30-year history of decline of the Larsen ice shelf, which has lost an area of about 13,500 km^2 (about 5200 mi^2) since 1974.

Collapse was apparently triggered by the formation of extensive melt-water ponds on the top of the shelf, a response to a particularly warm summer in a climate that has warmed by about 2.5°C (4.5°F) since the 1940s. Apparently, meltwater fills fractures in the ice, creating pressure at the bottom of the crack that causes the fracture to grow. Meltwater ponds have now been observed on the much larger Larsen C ice shelf, located to the south, and many scientists believe that it will be the next to collapse in the coming decades.

The possible effects of climate change on global ice sheets are far from certain. At best, we can hope that human-induced global warming will result in slow, progressive changes to which human civilization can readily adapt.

31 Jan 2002

23 Feb 2002

Breakup of the Larsen B ice shelf as seen by MODIS These four MODIS images document the disintegration of the Larsen B ice shelf during the Austral summer of 2002. (NASA.)

3 Mar 2002

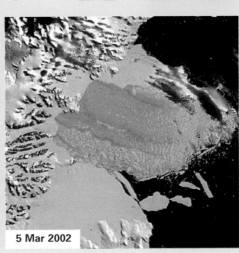

5 Mar 2002

also highly sensitive to changes induced by human activity. Only glaciers maintain their integrity and are thus far largely undisturbed by human activity. Perhaps even this last realm of nature's superiority will eventually fall prey to human interference through climate changes induced by industrial activity.

Our closing Epilogue dramatizes four areas of ongoing conflict between the human species and its natural environment—sea-level rise from climatic warming, population pressures, rainforest clearing, and development in earthquake-prone areas. As the human presence continues to impact our planet's natural systems, such conflicts will become increasingly important to resolve.

GEODISCOVERIES **Web Links.** This chapter's web links are rich in photos of glaciers and glacial landforms from Alaska to Antarctica. Go exploring!

In Review   Glacial Land Forms and the Ice Age

- Glaciers form when snow accumulates to a great depth, creating a mass of ice that is plastic in lower layers and flows outward or downhill from a center in response to gravity. As they move, glaciers can deeply erode bedrock by abrasion and plucking. The eroded fragments, incorporated into the flowing ice, leave depositional landforms when the ice melts.

- **Alpine glaciers** develop in **cirques** in high mountain locations. Alpine glaciers flow downvalley on steep slopes, picking up rock debris and depositing it in *lateral* and *terminal* **moraines.** Through erosion, glaciers carve U-shaped **glacial troughs** that are distinctive features of glaciated mountain regions. They become **fiords** if later submerged by rising sea level.

- **Ice sheets** are huge plates of ice that cover vast areas. They are present today in Greenland and Antarctica. The Antarctic Ice Sheet includes *ice shelves*—great plates of floating glacial ice. Icebergs form when glacial ice flowing into an ocean breaks into great chunks and floats free. *Sea ice,* which is much thinner and more continuous, is formed by direct freezing of ocean water and accumulation of snow.

- An ice age includes alternating periods of **glaciation,** *deglaciation,* and **interglaciation.** During the past 2 to 3 million years, the Earth has experienced the **Late-Ceno-** zoic Ice Age. During this ice age, continental ice sheets have grown and melted as many as 30 times. The most recent glaciation is the *Wisconsinan Glaciation,* in which ice sheets covered much of North America and Europe, as well as parts of northern Asia and southern South America.

- Moving ice sheets create many types of landforms. Bedrock is grooved and scratched. Where rocks are weak, long valleys can be excavated to depths of hundreds of meters. The melting of glacial ice deposits **glacial drift,** which may be stratified by water flow or deposited directly as **till.** Moraines accumulate at ice edges. *Outwash plains* are built up by meltwater streams. Tunnels within the ice leave streambed deposits as *eskers.* Till may be spread smooth and thick under an ice sheet, leaving a *till plain.* This may be studded with elongated till mounds, termed *drumlins.* Meltwater streams build *glacial deltas* into lakes formed at the ice margin and line lake bottoms with clay and silt. When the lakes drain, these features remain.

- Several factors have been proposed to explain the cause of present ice age glaciations and interglaciations. These factors include ongoing change in the global position of continents, an increase in volcanism, and a reduction in the Sun's energy output. Individual cycles of glaciation seem strongly related to cyclic changes in Earth–Sun distance and axial tilt.

Key Terms

ablation, p. 630	moraine, p. 633	interglaciation, p. 640	till, p. 642
alpine glacier, p. 631	glacial trough, p. 633	Late-Cenozoic Ice Age,	astronomical hypothesis,
ice sheet, p. 631	fiord, p. 633	p. 640	p. 648
cirque, p. 632	glaciation, p. 639	glacial drift, p. 642	

Review Questions

1. How does a glacier form? What factors are important? Why does a glacier move?
2. Distinguish between alpine glaciers and ice sheets.
3. What is a glacial trough and how is it formed? What is its basic shape? In what ways can a glacial trough appear after glaciation is over?
4. Where are ice sheets present today? How thick are they?
5. Contrast sea ice and icebergs, including the processes by which they form.
6. Identify the Late-Cenozoic Ice Age. When did it begin? What was the last glaciation in this cycle? When did it end?

7. What areas were covered with ice sheets by the last glaciation? How was sea level affected?
8. What are moraines? How are they formed? What types of moraines are there?
9. Identify the landforms and deposits associated with stream action at or near the front of an ice sheet.
10. Identify the landforms and deposits associated with deposition underneath a moving ice sheet.
11. Identify the landforms and deposits associated with lakes that form at ice sheet margins.
12. What cycles are known to affect the amount of solar radiation received by polar regions of the Earth?
13. What is the Milankovitch curve? What does it show about warm and cold periods during the last 500,000 years?

14. How have environments changed during the Holocene Epoch? What periods are recognized, and what are their characteristics?

Eye on Global Change 19.2 • Ice Sheets and Global Warming

1. What process seems to be offsetting the rate of melting of ice sheets as climate warms? Where has it been observed?
2. Why is the Western Antarctic Ice Sheet regarded as unstable? What is the role of ice streams in maintaining the present size of the ice sheet?
3. What change has recently been observed in the flow of ice streams into the Ross Ice Shelf? What are the implications?
4. Describe the recent fate of the Larsen B ice shelf and its causes.

Visualizing Exercises

1. What are some typical features of an alpine glacier? Sketch a cross section along the length of an alpine glacier and label it.
2. Refer to Figure 19.10, which shows the Antarctic continent and its ice cap. Identify the Ross, Filchner, and Larsen ice shelves. Use the scale to measure the approximate area of each in square kilometers or miles. Consulting an atlas or almanac, identify the state or province of the United States or Canada that is nearest in area to each.

Essay Questions

1. Imagine that you are planning a car trip to the Canadian Rockies. What glacial landforms would you expect to find there? Where would you look for them?
2. At some time during the latter part of the Pliocene Epoch, the Earth entered an ice age. Describe the nature of this ice age and the cycles that occur within it. What explanations are proposed for causing an ice age and its cycles? What cycles have been observed since the last ice sheets retreated?

Eye on the Landscape

19.1 Alpine glacier This alpine glacial landscape shows many of the glacial landforms and features described in this chapter. In the near distance are sharp peaks, or horns **(A)**, and knife-edge ridges, or arêtes **(B)**. In the middle foreground is a bowl-shaped cirque **(C)** that no longer bears glacial ice, although the glacier from the adjacent cirque spills into the empty cirque across a low pass (col). Glacial flow features are especially evident, including medial moraines **(D)**, lateral moraines **(E)**, and crevasses **(F)** that open as the ice falls across a rock step.

19.16 Finger Lakes The Finger Lakes of western New York State have been called "inland fiords" for their resemblance to the fiords of glaciated regions. (Fiords are discussed in this chapter.) As explained in our main text, the lakes were eroded from preexisting stream valleys by ice action during the multiple continental glaciations of the Ice Age. The two largest lakes in the center of the image **(A)** are Cayuga Lake (upper) and Seneca Lake (lower). The pattern of agricultural fields in the center and upper left part of the image **(B)** marks the intensive agricultural development of the Lake Erie lowlands and foothills of the Appalachian Plateau, which are mantled with productive soils of glacial origin (Udalfs; see Chapter 10). To the south, at the bottom of the image **(C),** the terrain becomes more dissected, with more pronounced valleys and ridges, as it slopes upward to the higher elevations of the plateau. Stream dissection of the landscape was covered in Chapter 16.

A crowded street in Hong Kong during the lunch hour.

NEWS FROM THE FUTURE

Our text began with a feature describing a trip you might take as a lunar astronaut, traveling home from the Moon to Earth in 2050. What will life be like in the middle of the century? Imagine turning on a futuristic television set and watching the news for June 26, 2050. It might go something like this.

"Good evening, America, and welcome to the Nightly News. This is Dan Rogers in Washington. Tonight's big stories are from the environment. First, we'll go to Galveston, where the story is the flooding from the first storm of the season, Hurricane Alfred. Here's our correspondent, Lorraine Jackson, on the scene. Lorraine, what's it like there now?"

"Thanks, Dan. The storm has slackened off in the last few hours, but the system of dams and pumps they have here has worked, at least for now, to keep the floodwaters out of the center of the city. As you can see, the rain is still falling and the winds are still strong. But the real problem with this storm has not been the wind and rain. Alfred is one of the weaker storms to reach the Texas coast in the past several hurricane seasons. The problem is with the ocean flooding that this coastal outpost endures when a storm like Alfred passes close by.

"The ocean dikes have been taking a terrible beating from the wave action. Here's some shots of the waves breaking on the dikes that we got earlier. All that wave water spilling over the dikes has to be pumped out, and fast. We understand from the local authorities that several smaller dikes west of the city were breached this morning, adding to the floodwaters. Apparently, several subdivisions out there are well under water now. There was a scare when the power went out earlier in the day, and one of the huge backup generators supplying power to the pumps refused to start. But the other generators are keeping up with the load of the pumps."

"When the citizens of this Texas city decided 30 years ago to fight against the rise in sea level rather than move inland like most other beach communities, they knew that the battle against the ocean would be costly and could eventually be a losing one. But for now, the valiant city of Galveston seems to be holding its own, Dan."

"Lorraine, what about the death toll?"

"So far, Dan, the authorities have not reported any deaths from the storm, although there were some injuries in the evacuation. We had a report that one of the huge buses they use for evacuations hit the rear end of another bus, but only the driver and two passengers were injured. Apparently, the accident didn't slow down the river of huge vehicles streaming across the viaduct to the mainland. As I reported this morning, last night's evacuation went pretty smoothly. The residents here have been through so many evacuations in the last few years that they are all familiar with the emergency routine."

"Thanks, Lorraine. That is relatively good news."

Climatic change may raise sea level, enhancing the ability of hurricanes to destroy coastal settlements. Here, Hurricane Alicia lashes the Texas coast at Galveston.

"Our next story marks a momentous event for the human race—the birth of the 7 billionth citizen of Earth. For the story, we go to Beijing, to our correspondent Li Feng Sun. Where are you, Feng Sun?"

"Dan, I'm here in the corridor outside the maternity ward in this small birthing center in a suburb west of Beijing, waiting word about the birth of Zhu Peng, destined to be the world's 7 billionth citizen. Of course, we're not precisely certain that baby Zhu Peng will be the world's 7 billionth citizen, but scientists have predicted that in precisely four minutes and fourteen seconds, the Earth's population will reach 7 billion. They also tell us that the 7 billionth citizen is most likely to be Chinese.

"Economists and population planners have been marking the event as a real milestone. Before the turn of the century, they projected that the world's population would be over 9 billion by 2050. You may remember some years ago the many predictions that the plans for sustainable world development would crash along with populations of Africa and Southeast Asia, which were decimated by the AIDS epidemic. China was only little impacted because AIDS spread quite slowly here, and because of China's crash program to inoculate its entire population with the AIDS vaccine shortly after it was developed. That left this huge country to continue its slow population growth coupled with rapid economic growth fueled by this country's vast natural and human resources. The result is the success story we're all familiar with—China's economy surpassing the economies of Europe, the Americas, and finally the East Asian trading block of Japan, Taiwan, Korea, and Singapore."

"Feng Sun, I hear some chanting in the background. Are those demonstrators?"

"That's right, Dan. The militant arm of the Chinese Green party has mounted a demonstration here. In fact, we have one of the leaders here, Huang Chung, ready to talk with us. Huang Chung, what are the demonstrators here for?"

"Well, Feng Sun, we're protesting this event because we don't think the world needs any more people. Every consumer requires more food and uses more resources. We've already cut down almost half of the world's forests. Global warming has made the deserts spread and our cropland become less productive. We all know that global warming was generated by consumers demanding products and lifestyles that depend on fossil fuel..."

"Feng Sun, I hate to break in, but we've got an interrupt here. Apparently, there's been a breakthrough on the biodi-

As progressively larger areas of the Earth's surface are developed, the potential for damage from extreme natural events, such as earthquakes, increases. This interchange on the Golden State Freeway, Los Angeles, was destroyed in the Whittier Narrows Earthquake of 1987.

versity talks at the U.N. For the story, let's go to Maria Remarquez in New York. Maria?"

"Hi, Dan. We've just gotten word here that the rainforest nations will back down from their threat to withdraw from the biodiversity treaty. Apparently, the U.S., the European Union, and Chinese-East Asian bloc have agreed to make some of the payments demanded for the use of the rainforest genetic materials that the rainforest nations contend were stolen from them by biotechnology companies.

"Here to tell us about it is Professor Kate Carver of New York's City University. Professor Carver, why is this agreement important?"

"Well, Maria, because with this agreement in place, we can go ahead with the plan to set up rainforest preservation zones, perhaps as early as next year. The rainforest ecosystems are our most complex ecological communities, and they hold the greatest diversity of life of all habitats on Earth. They are a reservoir of genetic material that is irreplaceable, and they need to be protected as vast areas forever. Without these genetic reserves, we'd be missing many of our cures for diseases ranging from cancer to AIDS.

"You know, Maria, I might also point out that this agreement is good for the environment in another way. The money will be used by the rainforest nations to stimulate the use of nonpolluting technologies for sustainable development. That is, the funds will be helping these nations promote more use of solar power, wind power, and methane gas production. In this way, they will reduce their reliance on old-fashioned fossil fuels and with it the release of carbon dioxide that produces climate change."

"Thanks for that perspective, Professor. It looks like a win for the environment here at the United Nations this evening, Dan."

"And thanks for that fine story, Maria. For our next story, remember that it was exactly one month ago when the disastrous El Cajon earthquake struck Los Angeles. We go now to Pasadena for a report on the cleanup and rebuilding. Our reporter with the story is Keith Mancini. Keith?"

"It was early on a Sunday morning just one month ago when Angelinos were thrown from their beds by the violent shaking that devastated so much of Los Angeles. It was the largest earthquake to hit Southern California in more than a century, measuring magnitude 8.1 on the Richter Scale, flat-

High biodiversity is a feature of equatorial rainforests, such as this example in the Datum River Gorge, Sabah, Borneo.

tening thousands of buildings, and rendering thousands more unusable. The death toll, estimated at over 16,000 with more than 100,000 injured, was also by far the largest in this century for an American natural disaster.

"Today Los Angeles is still digging out. The magnitude of the task ahead is mind-boggling, Dan. The electric freeway system is virtually closed for all but a few segments. Nearly every viaduct and bridge experienced some damage, and engineers are struggling to inspect them all for safety and set the priorities for repair. Most of the city's skyscrapers are still unoccupied, since structural repairs are expected to take many more months to complete. In the hardest-hit areas containing old masonry buildings, almost nothing was left standing. Now that the searches for casualties are over, bulldozers and dump trucks are removing the debris.

"In the Long Beach area, the cleanup is beginning from the fires that started in the oil processing plants and spread to the chemical factories. The toxic compounds carried by the smoke and ash contaminated a huge area. It has taken several weeks for the National Guard to replace their cordon of troops and vehicles with the fencing and barbed wire that will keep looters out while the area is being detoxified, which is expected to take six to nine months.

"Meanwhile, homeless residents are flocking to the tent cities constructed of portable geodomes now being set up by the National Guard. The demand increases daily as troops and local authorities evict inhabitants still trying to live in the dangerous, crumbling buildings. The geodome cities at least provide shelter, hot food, and sanitation for the thousands of displaced residents, luxuries that are not easy to come by here.

"But the amazing thing, Dan, is the dedication of these residents to rebuilding their city. Everywhere you go in this vast metropolis, there is activity. People are pulling together *to rebuild their homes, their businesses, and their lives. There's a real 'can-do' spirit here, and L.A. should emerge from this tragedy all the stronger for it."*

"Thanks, Keith, for that fine report. It won't be easy for the folks in Los Angeles in the weeks and months ahead, but at least they know that the rest of the nation is pulling for them.

"And, that's it for the top news stories today. Stay with us for the local report, coming up after these messages."

PERSPECTIVE ON THE NEWS FROM THE FUTURE

This news report dramatizes some of the present concerns about the environment that have arisen in our survey of physical geography. The first news story calls attention to the sea-level rise that is predicted to accompany global warming. The latest predictions are that by the year 2100 global temperature will increase by 1.4°C to 5.8°C (2.5 °F to 10.4°F). Sea level is expected to rise by 9 to 88 cm (3.5 to 34.6 in.).

The problem with rising sea level is not so much with day-to-day levels, but rather the levels that occur when tides combine with storms to produce intense wave action on low-lying coasts. The Republic of Maldives, which is a nation of 1190 small islands, would be entirely submerged by a rise of 2 m (6.6 ft). Even with a rise of only 1 m (3.3ft), the country could be wiped out by a severe storm surge.

Sea-level rise is just one of the possible effects of climatic warming. Even though the extent of warming is uncertain, scientists have concluded that warming would bring not only warmer temperatures, but also more global precipitation. However, this precipitation increase will not be evenly distributed. Computer models predict that high latitudes will experience more precipitation, while midlatitude continental interiors will experience drier summers. These types of changes would have important effects on crop growth, shifting the varieties and types of crops grown within large regions. Increased irrigation could also be needed.

Because the effects of climatic warming could be so far-reaching, scientists have managed to alert the public about the danger of continued increases of CO_2 and other gases that contribute to global warming. At the 1992 Earth Summit in Rio de Janeiro, most of the world's nations agreed in principle on a treaty to reduce human impact on climate. The industrialized countries pledged to reduce the levels of greenhouse gases they release, thus slowing the rapid increases in atmospheric CO_2, methane, chlorofluorocarbons, and nitrous oxide (N_2O) that have been measured. At subsequent meetings in Kyoto, Buenos Aires, and Marrakesh, specific reduction targets were hammered out and agreed upon. Hailed as the "strongest environmental treaty that's ever been drafted," it called for a group of industrialized nations, including Russia, Canada, Japan, Australia, and the European Union, to reduce emissions of greenhouse gases to levels that are 5 percent lower than those of 1990.

United States President George W. Bush rejected the treaty, however, leaving the United States on the sidelines of this pioneering effort to fight human-induced global change.

Another action of the Rio Earth Summit was the adoption of a treaty on biodiversity, which is the subject of the third news story. In the treaty, nations pledged to protect the genetic resources of their plant and animal populations by shielding the populations from extinction. Forest preservation was addressed as a need as well. The low-latitude rainforests cover only about 7 percent of the Earth's surface, but they contain over half of the world's species. They are especially rich in insect species and flowering plants. Plants of these regions are a particularly valuable resource. They have provided most of the species on which humans rely for food. Many highly effective medical drugs are produced from these plants.

Not only are low-latitude rainforests valuable resources for human exploitation, but they are also very complex ecosysystems that have evolved over millions of years. Many environmentalists believe that humans have a responsibility to preserve our planet's natural systems and maintain their diversity. It is encouraging that the world's nations have recognized the importance of ecological resources such as the low-latitude rainforests and are working toward their preservation.

The last future news story, about an earthquake in Los Angeles, demonstrates the impact of natural disasters on human activities. The story is only slightly exaggerated—an earthquake of magnitude 8.1 on the San Andreas fault would most certainly have devastating effects on a nearby city the size of Los Angeles.

By nature, the human species has a short-term outlook, preferring to prepare for dangers that are likely to occur within a time span of a few years to a few decades. Many natural processes work on far longer time scales, however. Although a major earthquake on the San Andreas fault may not happen more than once every few generations, there were probably tens of thousands of severe earthquakes on that fault in the Los Angeles region during the Ice Age, with hundreds of these occurring since the last advance of glacial ice. Although infrequent in human terms, these rare events have shaped much of the Earth's landscape. For the geologist or physical geographer trained in Earth processes, the evidence of these past events is everywhere.

Earthquakes, floods, and tropical storms are not new phenomena. What is new is that human civilization has come to dominate most areas of the planet, so that these natural occurrences now have major impacts on human societies in the regions in which they occur. Taken in the aggregate, they become a factor of global change.

The event of the second future news story, which dramatizes the birth of the 7 billionth citizen of Earth, probably has the most important implications. It is actually quite an optimistic scenario, for present estimates of the world population in 2050 are closer to 9.5 billion. The story refers to future population crashes in Africa and Southeast Asia produced by the AIDS epidemic that now rages throughout the world, and advances the idea that China will be impacted less severely than other developing nations. Whether this future will come to pass is uncertain. But in any event, the human population will continue to increase until either it regulates itself or destroys itself.

Why is population growth so important? Humans are the most powerful force transforming the surface of the Earth today. About 15 to 20 percent of the world's forest area has been cleared since human civilization began to exploit forest resources. In the last 300 years, humans have increased the area of cropland by 450 percent. Populations of the largest urban areas have increased 25 times in that same time span. These changes have directly influenced the global energy balance, the hydrologic cycle, and the dynamics of the atmosphere, with effects that are unknown in the long term.

Recognizing these trends, the nations of the world have come together in an effort to promote sustainable development. Under this policy, the needs and aspirations of present and future generations are met without impacting the ability of future generations to satisfy their needs. The idea is to focus on social and economic progress that is compatible with the environment. The concept draws on the premise that human knowledge, sophisticated technology, and access to resources are now so well developed that they can be used to allow developing countries to increase the well-being of their populations in a way that does not damage the environment. In this effort, much help and cooperation is required from developed nations, to provide not only the funds to stimulate sustainable development, but also the technological base that will be required.

There are now some hopeful signs that the long-continued increase of human population will slow and eventually stop. Annual global population growth peaked in the mid-1990s, and average family size has decreased from about 6 per woman in 1960 to about 3 today. Recent projections show the Earth's total population starting to level off at the middle of this century, reaching a peak around 11 billion by 2075, then remaining level or decreasing slightly from 2075 to 2100. Other studies of the economic impact of population growth have noted that technological innovation seems to naturally lead to increasing use of technologies that have a smaller environmental impact. Although the citizens of underdeveloped countries will want and need to advance their standard of living, their consumption will perhaps be less damaging to the environment. These recent trends in population and resource utilization can be expected to ease the transition from environmental exploitation to sustainable development in many world regions.

The social and economic aspects of continued population growth and policies such as sustainable development are far beyond the scope of physical geography, but they are concerns of which every responsible citizen of our planet must be aware. This book has provided a background and context on the workings of the Earth and the environment that we, as authors, hope will be valuable to you, its readers, as you face the challenges of world citizenship in the twenty-first century.

Appendix

1

THE CANADIAN SYSTEM OF SOIL CLASSIFICATION*

Canada has evolved a unique soil classification system that is especially suited to its own soils. Because Canada is located entirely poleward of 40° north latitude, tropical and equatorial soil types are simply absent from Canada. Moreover, nearly all of Canada experienced glaciation during the last Ice Age. Ice sheets and glaciers largely removed preexisting soils, replacing them with unsorted glacial debris, transported sands and gravels, and lake bottom deposits. As a result, the Canadian system emphasizes young soils of cold regions in more detail than do other systems.

The Canadian System of Soil Classification is a natural system in which the classes are based on properties of the soils themselves and not on interpretations of the soils for various uses. Thus, the classes are concepts based on generalization of soil properties observed in the field. In distinguishing among higher divisions, the system uses properties or combinations of properties that reflect processes of soil formation. The soils brought together in a single soil class are thus seen as the product of a similar set of dominant soil-forming processes resulting from broadly similar climatic conditions.

Soil classification systems typically use the *soil order* as the highest-level grouping. In the Canadian system, the next subdivision is the *great group*. Soil orders and great groups are often distinguished by the presence of a *diagnostic horizon*. Each diagnostic horizon has some unique combination of physical properties (color, structure, texture) or chemical properties (minerals present or absent). The two basic kinds of diagnostic horizons are (1) a horizon formed at the surface and called an *epipedon* (from the Greek word *epi*, meaning "over" or "upon") and (2) a subsurface horizon formed by the removal or accumulation of matter. In our descriptions of soil orders, we will refer to a number of diagnostic horizons.

SOIL HORIZONS

Table A1.1 provides a listing and description of the major horizons recognized by the Canadian Soil Classification System. Also described are subhorizons, which are identified with lowercase letters and attached to a horizon capital letter. The nature and order of horizons and subhorizons found in the soil profile are the main properties used to determine the soil order and great group classification of a soil.

SOIL ORDERS

The Canadian System of Soil Classification includes ten soil orders:

Chernozemic	Cryosolic	Regosolic
Brunisolic	Gleysolic	Vertisolic
Luvisolic	Organic	
Podsolic	Solonetzic	

*We are indebted to Professor O. W. Archibold of Saskatchewan University for help in preparing this appendix. Throughout this section numerous sentences and phrases are taken verbatim or paraphrased from the following work: Canadian Agricultural Services Coordinating Committee, Soil Classification Working Group, *The Canadian System of Soil Classification,* 3rd ed., 1998, NRC Research Press, Ottawa, 187 pp. Table A1.1 and Figure A1.1 are also compiled from this source. Used by permission of Agriculture and Agri-Food Canada. Reproduced with the permission of the Minister of Public Works and Government Services Canada 2004.

Table A1.1 | **Horizons and Subhorizons of the Canadian System of Soil Classification**

Organic Horizons

O	Organic horizon developed mainly from mosses, rushes, and woody materials (e.g., peat).
L	Organic horizon characterized by an accumulation of organic matter derived mainly from leaves, twigs, and woody materials in which the organic structures are easily discernible.
F	Same as *L*, above, except that the original structures are difficult to recognize.
H	Organic horizon characterized by decomposed organic matter in which the original structures are not discernible.

Mineral Horizons

A	Mineral horizon found at or near the surface in the zone of leaching or eluviation of materials in solution or suspension, or of maximum *in situ* accumulation of organic matter, or both.
B	Mineral horizon characterized by enrichment in organic matter, sesquioxides, or clay; or by the development of soil structure; or by change of color denoting hydrolysis, reduction, or oxidation.
C	Mineral horizon comparatively unaffected by the pedogenic processes operative in *A* and *B* horizons. The processes of gleying and the accumulation of calcium and magnesium and more soluble salts can occur in this horizon.

Subhorizons (Lowercase suffixes)

b	Buried soil horizon.
c	Irreversibly cemented pedogenic horizon. Also known as a hardpan.
ca	Horizon of secondary carbonate enrichment in which the concentration of lime exceeds that in the unenriched parent material.
cc	Horizon containing irreversibly cemented pedogenic concretions.
e	Horizon characterized by the eluviation of clay, Fe, Al, or organic matter alone or in combination.
f	Horizon enriched with amorphous material, principally Al and Fe combined with organic matter; reddish near upper boundary, becoming yellower at depth.
g	Horizon characterized by gray colors, or prominent mottling, or both, indicating permanent or intense chemical reduction.
h	Horizon enriched with organic matter.
j	Used as a modifier of suffixes *e, f, g, n,* and *t* to denote an expression of, but failure to meet, the specified limits of a suffix it modifies.
k	Denotes presence of carbonate as indicated by visible effervescence when dilute HCl is added.
m	Horizon slightly altered by hydrolysis, oxidation, or solution, or all three to give a change in color or structure, or both.
n	Horizon in which the ratio of exchangeable Ca to exchangeable Na is 10 or less, as well as the following distinctive morphological characteristics: prismatic or columnar structure, dark coating on ped surfaces, and hard to very hard consistency when dry.
p	Horizon disturbed by human activities, such as cultivation, logging, and habitation.
s	Horizon of salts, including gypsum, which may be detected as crystals or veins or as surface crusts of salt crystals.
sa	Horizon with secondary enrichment of salts more soluble than Ca and Mg carbonates; the concentration of salts exceeds that in the unenriched parent material.
ss	Horizon containing slickensides—shear surfaces that form when one soil mass moves over another.
t	Illuvial horizon enriched with silicate clay.
u	Horizon that is markedly disrupted by physical or faunal processes other than cryoturbation.
v	Horizon affected by disruption and mixing caused by shrinking and swelling of the soil mass.
x	Loamy subsurface horizon of high bulk density and very low organic matter content; when dry, it is hard and seems to be cemented. Also known as a fragipan.
y	Horizon affected by cryoturbation as manifested by disrupted or broken horizons, incorporation of materials from other horizons, and mechanical sorting.
z	A frozen layer.

Cross sections of soil types and associated horizons are shown in Figure A1.1, and a generalized map of soil regions of Canada is presented in Figure A1.2. A set of soil profile photos in Figure A1.3 illustrates the range of variation among soil orders of the Canadian system. The soil orders are presented in the order of their importance and areal extent within Canada.

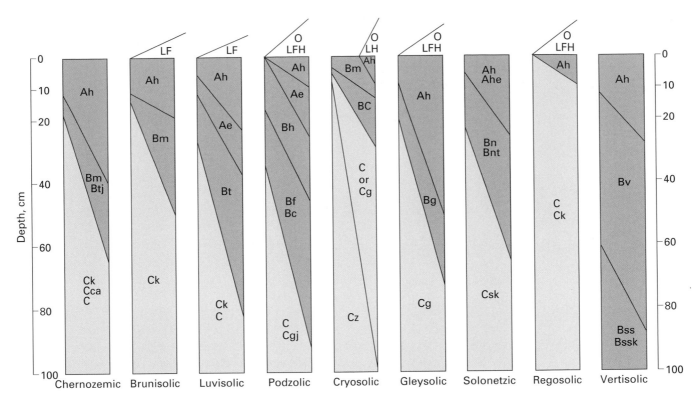

A1.1 Soil profile diagrams *Representative schematic profiles of nine of the ten orders of the Canadian System of Soil Classification. Slanting lines show the range in depth and thickness of each horizon. (The horizon planes are approximately horizontal within the pedon.) See Table 21.3 for an explanation of symbols.*

Chernozemic Order

Soils of the *Chernozemic order* have surface horizons darkened by the accumulation of organic matter from the decomposition of grasses and forbs of grassland communities or of grassland-forest communities. Chernozemic soils develop under a wide range of drainage conditions. The major area of Chernozemic soils is the cool, subarid to subhumid interior plains of western Canada (Figure A1.2). Most Chernozemic soils are frozen during some period each winter, and the soil is dry at some period each summer. The associated climate is typically the semiarid (steppe) variety of the dry midlatitude climate ⑨.

Figure A1.1 diagrams a typical profile of a Chernozemic soil. Soils of the Chernozemic order must have an *A* horizon (typically, *Ah*) in which organic matter has accumulated. The *A* horizon is at least 10 cm thick, and its color is dark brown to black. An eluviated *Ae* horizon may be present. Typically, the *B* horizon is slightly altered and may show a prismatic structure (*Bm*). The *C* horizon often has lime accumulation (*Cca*). The Chernozemic soil profile in Figure A1.4 shows a dark brown *A* horizon overlying a light brown prismatic *Bm* horizon and a *Cca* horizon with lime accumulation.

Brunisolic Order

The central concept of the *Brunisolic order* is that of soils under forest having brownish-colored *Bm* horizons (Fig-

ures A1.1, A1.3*b*). Most Brunisolic soils are well to imperfectly drained and typically lack the degree of horizon development found in other soil orders. They occur in a wide range of climates and vegetation covers, including boreal forest; mixed forest, shrubs, and grass; and heath and tundra. Compared to the Chernozemic soils, the Brunisolic soils show a weak *B* horizon of accumulation attributable to their moister environment. Brunisolic soils lack the diagnostic podzolic *B* horizon of the Podzolic soils, in which accumulation of clays and oxides in the *B* horizon is strongly developed.

Luvisolic Order

Soils of the *Luvisolic order* generally have light-colored, eluvial horizons (*Ae*) and illuvial *B* horizons (*Bt*) in which silicate clay has accumulated (Figures A1.1, A1.3*c*). These soils characteristically develop in sandy loam to clay base-saturated parent materials under forest vegetation in subhumid to humid, mild to very cold climates. Luvisolic soils evolve through the suspension of clay in the soil solution near the soil surface, downward movement of the suspended clay with the soil solution, and deposition of the translocated clay at a depth where downward motion of the soil solution ceases or becomes very slow.

Luvisolic soils occur throughout Canada, with the largest area occuring in the central to northern interior plains under deciduous, mixed, and coniferous forest (Figure A1.2).

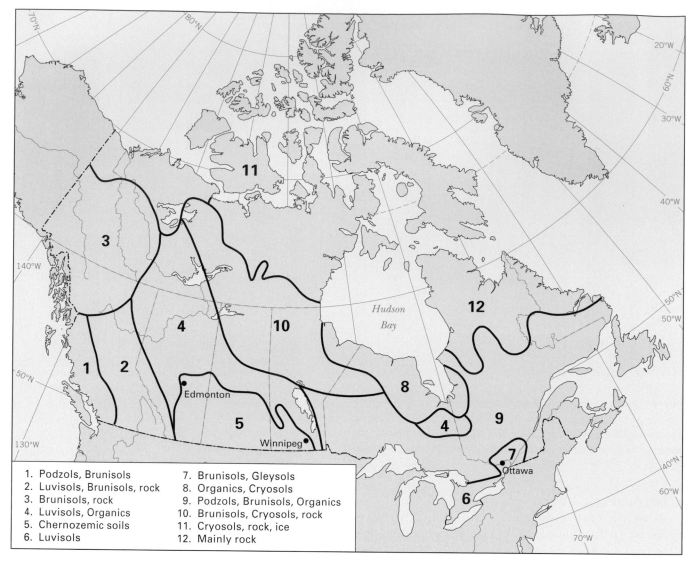

A1.2 Soil regions of Canada *Generalized map of soil regions of Canada. (Courtesy of Land Resources Research Institute, Agriculture Canada.) (Illustration is taken from Fundamentals of Soil Science, 7th ed., by Henry D. Foth, John Wiley & Sons.)*

Podzolic Order

Soils of the *Podzolic order* have *B* horizons characterized by accumulation of an amorphous material composed mainly of humified organic matter in varying degrees with Al and Fe. Podzolic soils occur under forest and heath vegetation in cool to very cold humid to very humid climates. Podzolic soils are generally distinguished by organic surface horizons and a light-colored eluvial horizon (*Ae*). Most Podzolic soils have a reddish brown to black *B* horizon (*Bh*) with an abrupt upper boundary (Figures A1.1, A1.3*d*).

Cryosolic Order

Soils of the *Cryosolic order* occupy much of northern Canada, where permafrost remains close to the surface of both mineral and organic deposits. Cryosolic soils predominate north of the tree line, are common in the subarctic for-

est area in fine-textured soils, and extend into the boreal forest in some organic materials and into some alpine areas of mountainous regions (Figure A1.5*a*). Cryoturbation (intense disturbance by freeze–thaw activity) of these soils is common, and it may be indicated by patterned ground features such as sorted and nonsorted nets, circles, polygons, stripes, and earth hummocks (see Chapter 14). A typical Cryosolic profile is diagrammed in Figure A1.1. Note the presence of organic *L*, *H*, and *O* surface horizons and the thin *Ah* horizon. Figure A1.5*b* shows a Cryosolic soil with marked flow structures.

Gleysolic Order

Soils of the *Gleysolic order* have features indicating periodic or prolonged saturation with water and chemically reducing conditions in which oxygen is absent. They com-

CHERNOZEMIC ORDER

A Black Chernozem,
   prairie provinces

BRUNISOLIC ORDER

B Melanic Brunisol,
   Quebec

LUVISOLIC ORDER

C Gray Luvisol,
   prairie provinces

PODZOLIC ORDER

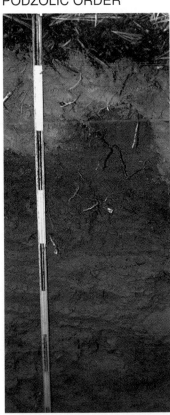

D Humo-ferric Podzol,
   Atlantic provinces

GLEYSOLIC ORDER

E Gleysol, Atlantic
   provinces

ORGANIC ORDER

F Organic Fibrisol,
   prairie provinces

A1.3 Soil profiles of selected Canadian soil orders *(Agriculture and Agri-Food Canada.)*

A1.4   Chermozemic soil profile *A Black Chernozem soil profile from southern British Columbia. Chernozems are characteristic of semiarid prairie grasslands. They are rich in organic matter and highly productive in wet years. (Agriculture and Agri-Food Canada.)*

monly occur in patches among other soils in the landscape. Gleysolic soils are usually associated with either a high ground water table at some period of the year or temporary saturation above a relatively impermeable layer. Some Gleysolic soils may be submerged under shallow water throughout the year. The profile diagrammed in Figure A1.1 has a thick *Ah* horizon. The underlying *Bg* horizon is grayish and often is marked by *mottles*—spots or blotches of varying color. Mottling is clearly visible in Figure A1.3*e*.

Organic Order

Soils of the *Organic order* are composed largely of organic materials. They include most of the soils commonly known as peat, muck, or bog soils. Organic soils contain 17 percent or more organic carbon (30 percent organic matter) by weight. Most Organic soils are saturated with water for prolonged periods. They occur widely in poorly drained areas in regions of subhumid to humid climate and are derived from vegetation that grows in such sites. However, one group of Organic soils consists of leaf litter lying directly over rock or coarse rock fragments. Soils of this group may occur on steep slopes and may rarely be saturated with water. An organic soil profile is shown in Figure A1.3*f*.

Solonetzic Order

Soils of the *Solonetzic order* occur on saline parent materials in some areas of the semiarid to subhumid interior plains. They have *B* horizons that are very hard when dry and swell to a sticky mass of very low permeability when wet. Typically, the Solonetzic *B* horizon has a prismatic or columnar macrostructure that breaks into hard to extremely hard, blocky peds with dark coatings (*Bn* subhorizon, shown in Figure A1.1). Solonetzic soils occur in association with Chernozemic soils and to a lesser extent with Luvisolic and Gleysolic soils. Most Solonetzic soils are associated with a vegetation cover of grasses and forbs.

Regosolic Order

Soils of the *Regosolic order* have weakly developed horizons. This may be due to any number of factors: youthfulness of the parent material as, for example, recent alluvium; instability of the material, such as colluvium on slopes sub-

A1.5   Cryosolic soil order *Cryosols are soils of permafrost terrains. (a) Permafrost and Cryosols underlie many boreal forest landscapes, such as this one in Yukon Territory. (b) A Turbic Cryosol profile from this region. Note the flow structures, formed by frost heaving and solifluction. (Agriculture and Agri-Food Canada.)*

A1.6   Regosolic soil profile   Regosols are weakly developed soils of recently deposited material. This profile shows silty river alluvium from the Atlantic provinces. Horizon development is generally lacking, although the upper 20 cm of the profile appears slightly lighter in color. (Agriculture and Agri-Food Canada.)

ject to mass wasting; nature of the material, as in nearly pure quartz sand; or climate, such as dry cold conditions. Regosolic soils occur in a wide range of vegetation and climates but often are of limited extent. The profile diagrammed in Figure A1.1 has only a thin humic A horizon (Ah) and a surface horizon of organic materials. Figure A1.6 shows a Regosol on silty river alluvium.

Vertisolic Order

Soils of the *Vertisolic order* occur in parent materials rich in clays that expand strongly when wet and then shrink greatly when dry. Deep cracks form in the soil, and material from the upper part of the soil profile fills the cracks. In this way, Vertisolic soils are self-mixing and lack distinctive horizons. The surface may show a Chernozemic-like A horizon or may have features diagnostic of the Gleysolic order. The B horizon below is often mottled. The lower B horizon typically shows *slickensides* (Bss)—shear surfaces that form when one soil mass moves over another (Figure A1.1). The major area of occurrence is in the cool, subarid to subhumid, grassland portion of the interior plains of western Canada. The Vertisolic order was only recently recognized as occurring in Canada and is not included in the soil regions map in Figure A1.2.

CLIMATE DEFINITIONS AND BOUNDARIES

The following table summarizes the definitions and boundaries of climates and climate subtypes based on the soil-water balance, as described in Chapter 15 and shown on the world climate map, Figure 7.6. All definitions and boundaries are provisional.

Ep   Water need (potential evapotranspiration)
D   Soil water shortage (deficit)
R   Water surplus (runoff)
S   Storage (limited to 30 cm)

Group I: Low-Latitude Climates

1. Wet equatorial climate ①
Ep ≥ 10 cm in every month, and
S ≥ 20 cm in 10 or more months.

2. Monsoon and trade-wind coastal climate ②
Ep ≥ 4 cm in every month, or
Ep > 130 cm annual total, or both, and
S ≥ 20 cm in 6, 7, 8, or 9 consecutive months, or, if
S > 20 cm in 10 or more months, then Ep ≤ 10 cm
   in 5 or more consecutive months.

3. Wet-dry tropical climate ③
D ≥ 20cm, and
R ≥ 10 cm, and
Ep ≥ 130 cm annual total, or Ep ≥ 4 cm in every
   month, or both, and
S ≥ 20 cm in 5 months or fewer, or minimum
   monthly S < 3 cm.

4. Dry tropical climate ④
D ≥15 cm, and
R = 0, and
Ep ≥ 130 cm annual total, or Ep ≥ 4 cm in every
   month, or both.

Subtypes of dry climates (④, ⑤, ⑦, and ⑨)
   s Semiarid subtype (Steppe subtype) At least 1
      month with S > 2 cm.
   a Desert subtype
      No month with S > 2 cm.

Group II: Midlatitude Climates

5. Dry subtropical climate ⑤
D ≥ 15 cm, and
R = 0, and Ep < 130 cm annual total, and
Ep ≥ 0.8 cm in every month, and
Ep < 4 cm in 1 month.
(Subtypes ⑤a and ⑤s as defined under ④.)

6. Moist subtropical climate ⑥
D < 15 cm when R = 0, and
Ep < 4 cm in at least 1 month, and
Ep ≥ 0.8 cm in every month.

7. Mediterranean climate ⑦
D ≥ 15 cm, and
R ≥ 0, and
Ep ≥ 0.8 cm in every month, and storage index
   > 75%, or P/Ea × 100 < 40%. (Subtypes ⑦a and
   ⑦s as defined under ④.)

8. Marine west-coast climate ⑧
D < 15 cm, and
Ep < 80 cm annual total, and
Ep ≥ 0.8 cm in every month.

9. Dry midlatitude climate ⑨
D ≥ 15 cm, and
R = 0, and
Ep ≤ 0.7 cm in at least 1 month, and

Ep > 52.5 cm annual total.

(Subtypes ⑨a and ⑨s as defined under ④.)

10. **Moist continental climate** ⑩

   D < 15 cm when R = 0, and

   Ep ≤ 0.7 cm in at least 1 month, and

   Ep > 52.5 cm annual total.

Group III: High-Latitude Climates

11. **Boreal forest climate** ⑪

52.5 cm > Ep > 35 cm annual total, and

Ep = 0 in fewer than 8 consecutive months.

12. **Tundra climate** ⑫

   Ep < 35 cm annual total, and

   Ep = 0 in 8 or more consecutive months.

13. **Ice sheet climate** ⑬

   Ep = 0 in all months.

Appendix

3 | TOPOGRAPHIC MAP SYMBOLS

USGS
science for a changing world

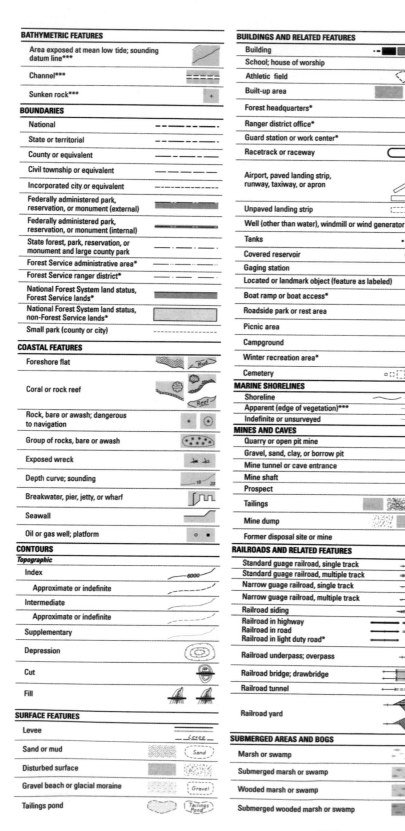

BATHYMETRIC FEATURES

Area exposed at mean low tide; sounding datum line***

Channel***

Sunken rock***

BOUNDARIES

National

State or territorial

County or equivalent

Civil township or equivalent

Incorporated city or equivalent

Federally administered park, reservation, or monument (external)

Federally administered park, reservation, or monument (internal)

State forest, park, reservation, or monument and large county park

Forest Service administrative area*

Forest Service ranger district*

National Forest System land status, Forest Service lands*

National Forest System land status, non-Forest Service lands*

Small park (county or city)

COASTAL FEATURES

Foreshore flat

Coral or rock reef

Rock, bare or awash; dangerous to navigation

Group of rocks, bare or awash

Exposed wreck

Depth curve; sounding

Breakwater, pier, jetty, or wharf

Seawall

Oil or gas well; platform

CONTOURS

Topographic

Index

Approximate or indefinite

Intermediate

Approximate or indefinite

Supplementary

Depression

Cut

Fill

SURFACE FEATURES

Levee

Sand or mud

Disturbed surface

Gravel beach or glacial moraine

Tailings pond

BUILDINGS AND RELATED FEATURES

Building

School; house of worship

Athletic field

Built-up area

Forest headquarters*

Ranger district office*

Guard station or work center*

Racetrack or raceway

Airport, paved landing strip, runway, taxiway, or apron

Unpaved landing strip

Well (other than water), windmill or wind generator

Tanks

Covered reservoir

Gaging station

Located or landmark object (feature as labeled)

Boat ramp or boat access*

Roadside park or rest area

Picnic area

Campground

Winter recreation area*

Cemetery

MARINE SHORELINES

Shoreline

Apparent (edge of vegetation)***

Indefinite or unsurveyed

MINES AND CAVES

Quarry or open pit mine

Gravel, sand, clay, or borrow pit

Mine tunnel or cave entrance

Mine shaft

Prospect

Tailings

Mine dump

Former disposal site or mine

RAILROADS AND RELATED FEATURES

Standard guage railroad, single track

Standard guage railroad, multiple track

Narrow guage railroad, single track

Narrow guage railroad, multiple track

Railroad siding

Railroad in highway

Railroad in road

Railroad in light duty road*

Railroad underpass; overpass

Railroad bridge; drawbridge

Railroad tunnel

Railroad yard

SUBMERGED AREAS AND BOGS

Marsh or swamp

Submerged marsh or swamp

Wooded marsh or swamp

Submerged wooded marsh or swamp

ROADS AND RELATED FEATURES

Please note: Roads on Provisional-edition maps are not classified as primary, secondary, or light duty. These roads are all classified as improved roads and are symbolized the same as light duty roads.

Primary highway

Secondary highway

Light duty road

Light duty road, paved*

Light duty road, gravel*

Light duty road, dirt*

Light duty road, unspecified*

Unimproved road

Unimproved road*

4WD road

4WD road*

Trail

Highway or road with median strip

Highway or road under construction

Highway or road underpass; overpass

Highway or road bridge; drawbridge

Highway or road tunnel

Road block, berm, or barrier*

Gate on road*

Trailhead*

RIVERS, LAKES, AND CANALS

Perennial stream

Perennial river

Intermittent stream

Intermittent river

Disappearing stream

Falls, small

Falls, large

Rapids, small

Rapids, large

Perennial lake/pond

Intermittent lake/pond

Dry lake/pond

Narrow wash

Wide wash

Canal, flume, or aqueduct with lock

Elevated aqueduct, flume, or conduit

Aqueduct tunnel

Water well, geyser, fumarole, or mud pot

Spring or seep

TRANSMISSION LINES AND PIPELINES

Power transmission line; pole; tower

Telephone line

Aboveground pipeline

Underground pipeline

VEGETATION

Woodland

Shrubland

Orchard

Vineyard

GLACIERS AND PERMANENT SNOWFIELDS

Contours and limits

Formlines

Glacial advance

Glacial retreat

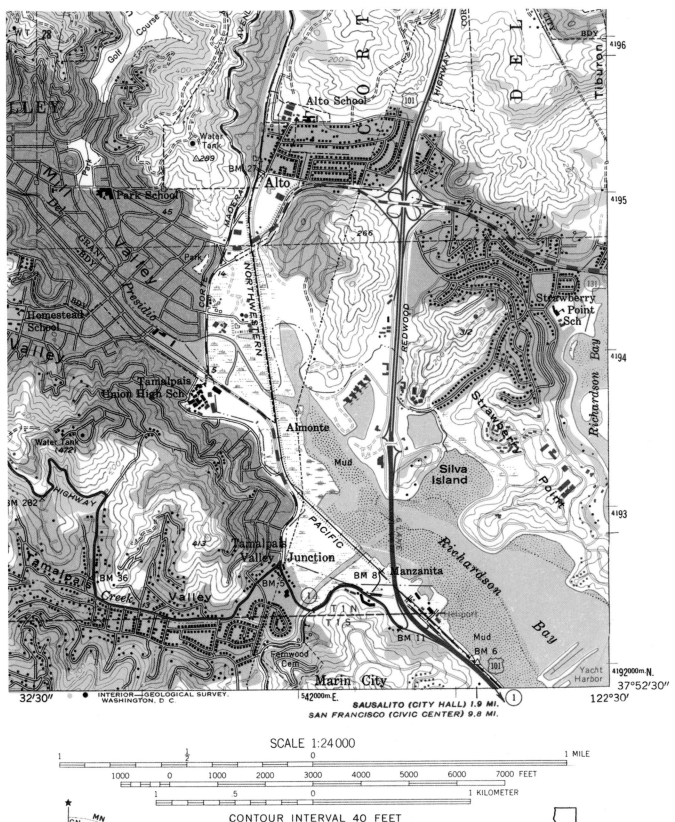

SAUSALITO (CITY HALL) 1.9 MI.
SAN FRANCISCO (CIVIC CENTER) 9.8 MI.

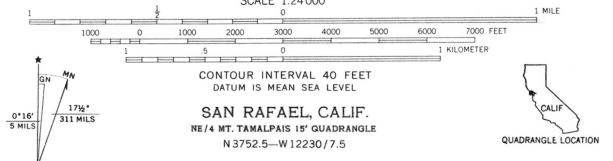

SCALE 1:24 000

CONTOUR INTERVAL 40 FEET
DATUM IS MEAN SEA LEVEL

SAN RAFAEL, CALIF.
NE/4 MT. TAMALPAIS 15' QUADRANGLE
N 3752.5—W 12230/7.5

QUADRANGLE LOCATION

CONVERSION FACTORS

Metric to English

Metric Measure	Multiply by*	English Measure
LENGTH		
Millimeters (mm)	0.0394	Inches (in.)
Centimeters (cm)	0.394	Inches (in.)
Meters (m)	3.28	Feet (ft)
Kilometers (km)	0.621	Miles (mi)
AREA		
Square centimeters (cm^2)	0.155	Square inches (in^2)
Square meters (m^2)	10.8	Square feet (ft^2)
Square meters (m^2)	1.12	Square yards (yd^2)
Square kilometers (km^2)	0.386	Square miles (mi^2)
Hectares (ha)	2.47	Acres
VOLUME		
Cubic centimeters (cm^3)	0.0610	Cubic inches (in^3)
Cubic meters (m^3)	35.3	Cubic feet (ft^3)
Cubic meters (m^3)	1.31	Cubic yards (yd^3)
Milliliters (ml)	0.0338	Fluid ounces (fl oz)
Liters (l)	1.06	Quarts (qt)
Liters (l)	0.264	Gallons (gal)
MASS		
Grams (g)	0.0353	Ounces (oz)
Kilograms (kg)	2.20	Pounds (lb)
Kilograms (kg)	0.00110	Tons (2000 lb)
Tonnes (t)	1.10	Tons (2000 lb)

English to Metric

English Measure	Multiply by*	Metric Measure
LENGTH		
Inches (in.)	2.54	Centimeters (cm)
Feet (ft)	0.305	Meters (m)
Yards (yd)	0.914	Meters (m)
Miles (mi)	1.61	Kilometers (km)
AREA		
Square inches (in^2)	6.45	Square centimeters (cm^2)
Square feet (ft^2)	0.0929	Square meters (m^2)
Square yards (yd^2)	0.836	Square meters (m^2)
Square miles (mi^2)	2.59	Square kilometers (km^2)
Acres	0.405	Hectares (ha)
VOLUME		
Cubic inches (in^3)	16.4	Cubic centimeters (cm^3)
Cubic feet (ft^3)	0.0283	Cubic meters (m^3)
Cubic yards (yd^3)	0.765	Cubic meters (m^3)
Fluid ounces (fl oz)	29.6	Milliliters (ml)
Pints (pt)	0.473	Liters (l)
Quarts (qt)	0.946	Liters (l)
Gallons (gal)	3.79	Liters (l)
MASS		
Ounces (oz)	28.4	Grams (g)
Pounds (lb)	0.454	Kilograms (kg)
Tons (2000 lb)	907	Kilograms (kg)
Tons (2000 lb)	0.907	Tonnes (t)

* Conversion factors shown to 3 decimal-digit precision.

GLOSSARY

This glossary contains definitions of terms shown in the text in italics or boldface. Terms that are *italicized* within the definitions will be found as individual entries elsewhere in the glossary.

A horizon *mineral* horizon of the *soil*, overlying the *E* and *B horizons*.

ablation a wastage of glacial ice by both *melting* and *evaporation*.

abrasion erosion of *bedrock* of a *stream channel* by impact of particles carried in a stream and by rolling of larger *rock* fragments over the stream bed; abrasion is also an activity of glacial ice, waves, and *wind*.

abrasion platform sloping, nearly flat *bedrock* surface extending out from the foot of a *marine cliff* under the shallow water of breaker zone.

absorption of radiation transfer of *electromagnetic energy* into heat *energy* within a *gas* or *liquid* through which the radiation is passing or at the surface of a *solid* struck by the radiation.

abyssal hills small hills rising to heights from a few tens of meters to a few hundred meters above the deep ocean floor.

abyssal plain large expanse of very smooth, flat ocean floor found at depths of 4600 to 5500 m (15,000 to 18,000 ft).

accelerated erosion *soil erosion* occurring at a rate much faster than *soil horizons* can be formed from the parent *regolith*.

accretion of lithosphere production of new *oceanic lithosphere* at an active *spreading plate boundary* by the rise and

solidification of *magma* of basaltic composition.

accretionary prism mass of deformed trench *sediments* and ocean floor *sediments* accumulated in wedge-like slices on the underside of the overlying plate above a plate undergoing *subduction*.

acid action solution of *minerals* by acids occurring in *soil* and *ground water*.

acid deposition the *deposition* of acid raindrops and/or dry acidic dust particles on vegetation and ground surfaces.

acid mine drainage sulfuric acid effluent from *coal* mines, mine tailings, or spoil ridges made by *strip mining*.

acid rain rainwater having an abnormally low *pH*, between 2 and 5, as a result of air pollution by sulfur oxides and nitrogen oxides.

active continental margins continental margins that coincide with tectonically active plate boundaries. (See also *continental margins, passive continental margins*.)

active layer shallow surface layer subject to seasonal thawing in *permafrost* regions.

active pool type of pool in the *biogeochemical cycle* in which the materials are in forms and places easily accessi-

ble to life processes. (See also *storage pool*.)

active systems *remote sensing* systems that emit a beam of wave *energy* at a source and measure the intensity of that *energy* reflected back to the source.

actual evapotranspiration (water use) Actual rate of *evapotranspiration* at a given time and place.

adiabatic lapse rate (See *dry adiabatic lapse rate, wet adiabatic lapse rate*.)

adiabatic principle the physical principle that a *gas* cools as it expands and warms as it is compressed, provided that no heat flows into or out of the gas during the process.

adiabatic process change of temperature within a *gas* because of compression or expansion, without gain or loss of heat from the outside.

advection fog *fog* produced by *condensation* within a moist basal air layer moving over a cold land or water surface.

aerosols tiny particles present in the *atmosphere,* so small and light that the slightest movements of air keep them aloft.

aggradation raising of *stream channel* altitude by continued *deposition* of *bed load*.

air   a mixture of *gases* that surrounds the Earth.

air mass   extensive body of air within which upward gradients of temperature and moisture are fairly uniform over a large area.

air pollutant   an unwanted substance injected into the *atmosphere* from the Earth's surface by either natural or human activities; includes *aerosols, gases,* and *particulates.*

air temperature   temperature of air, normally observed by a *thermometer* under standard conditions of shelter and height above the ground.

albedo   percentage of downwelling solar *radiation* reflected upward from a surface.

albic horizon   pale, often sandy *soil horizon* from which *clay* and free iron oxides have been removed. Found in the profile of the *Spodosols.*

Alfisols   *soil order* consisting of *soils* of humid and subhumid climates, with high *base status* and an *argillic horizon.*

allele   specific version of a particular gene.

allelopathy   interaction among *species* in which a plant secretes substances into the soil that are toxic to other organisms.

allopatric speciation   type of *speciation* in which populations are geographically isolated and gene flow between the populations does not take place.

alluvial fan   gently sloping, conical accumulation of coarse *alluvium* deposited by a *braided stream* undergoing *aggradation* below the point of emergence of the channel from a narrow *gorge* or *canyon.*

alluvial meanders   sinuous bends of a *graded stream* flowing in the alluvial deposit of a *floodplain.*

alluvial river   *stream* of low *gradient* flowing upon thick deposits of *alluvium* and experiencing approximately annual overbank flooding of the adjacent *floodplain.*

alluvial terrace   bench-like landform carved in *alluvium* by a *stream* during *degradation.*

alluvium   any stream-laid *sediment* deposit found in a *stream channel* and in low parts of a stream valley subject to flooding.

alpine chains   high mountain ranges that are narrow belts of *tectonic activity* severely deformed by *folding* and thrust-ing in comparatively recent geologic time.

alpine debris avalanche   *debris flood* of steep mountain *slopes,* often laden with tree trunks, limbs, and large boulders.

alpine glacier   long, narrow, mountain *glacier* on a steep downgrade, occupying the floor of a trough-like valley.

alpine permafrost   *permafrost* occurring at high altitudes equatorward of the normal limit of *permafrost.*

alpine tundra   a plant *formation class* within the *tundra biome,* found at high altitudes above the limit of *tree* growth.

amphibole group   *silicate minerals* rich in calcium, magnesium, and iron, dark in color, high in *density,* and classed as *mafic minerals.*

amplitude   for a smooth wave-like curve, the difference in height between a crest and the adjacent trough.

andesite   *extrusive igneous rock* of diorite composition, dominated by *plagioclase feldspar;* the extrusive equivalent of *diorite.*

Andisols   a *soil order* that includes *soils* formed on volcanic ash; often enriched by organic matter, yielding a dark soil color.

anemometer   weather instrument used to indicate *wind* speed.

aneroid barometer   *barometer* using a mechanism consisting of a partially evacuated air chamber and a flexible diaphragm.

angle of repose   natural surface inclination *(dip)* of a *slope* consisting of loose, coarse, well-sorted *rock* or *mineral fragments;* for example, the *slip face* of a *sand dune,* a *talus slope,* or the sides of a *cinder cone.*

annuals   plants that live only a single growing season, passing the unfavorable season as a seed or spore.

annular drainage pattern   a stream network dominated by concentric (ring-like) major *subsequent streams.*

antarctic circle   *parallel of latitude* at $66\frac{1}{2}°$S.

antarctic front zone   frontal zone of interaction between antarctic *air masses* and polar air masses.

antarctic zone   *latitude* zone in the latitude range 60° to 75°S (more or less), centered on the *antarctic circle,* and lying between the *subantarctic zone* and the *polar zone.*

anticlinal valley   valley eroded in weak *strata* along the central line or axis of an eroded *anticline.*

anticline   upfold of *strata* or other layered *rock* in an arch-like structure; a class of *folds.* (See also *syncline.*)

anticyclone   center of high *atmospheric pressure.*

aphelion   point on the Earth's elliptical orbit at which the Earth is farthest from the Sun.

aquatic ecosystem   *ecosystem* of a *lake, bog,* pond, river, *estuary,* or other body of water.

Aquepts   *suborder* of the *soil order Inceptisols;* includes Inceptisols of wet places, seasonally saturated with water.

aquiclude   *rock* mass or layer that impedes or prevents the movement of *ground water.*

aquifer   *rock* mass or layer that readily transmits and holds *ground water.*

arc   curved line that forms a portion of a circle.

arc-continent collision   collision of a volcanic arc with *continental lithosphere* along a *subduction* boundary.

arctic circle   *parallel of latitude* at $66\frac{1}{2}°$N.

arctic front zone   frontal zone of interaction between arctic *air masses* and polar air masses.

arctic tundra   a plant *formation class* within the *tundra biome,* consisting of low, mostly herbaceous plants, but with some very small stunted *trees,* associated with the *tundra climate* ⑫.

arctic zone   *latitude* zone in the latitude range 60° to 75°N (more or less), centered about on the *arctic circle,* and lying between the *subarctic zone* and the *polar zone.*

arête   sharp, knife-like divide or crest formed between two *cirques* by alpine glaciation.

argillic horizon   *soil horizon,* usually the B *horizon,* in which *clay minerals* have accumulated by *illuviation.*

arid (dry climate subtype)   subtype of the dry climates that is extremely dry and supports little or no vegetation cover.

Aridisols   *soil order* consisting of soils of dry climates, with or without *argillic* horizons, and with accumulations of *carbonates* or soluble salts.

artesian well drilled well in which water rises under hydraulic pressure above the level of the surrounding *water table* and may reach the surface.

aspect compass orientation of a *slope* as an inclined element of the ground surface.

association plant-animal community type identified by the typical organisms that are likely to be found together.

asthenosphere soft layer of the upper *mantle*, beneath the rigid *lithosphere*.

astronomical hypothesis explanation for glaciations and interglaciations making use of cyclic variations in the form of solar *energy* received at the Earth's surface.

atmosphere envelope of gases surrounding the Earth, held by *gravity*.

atmospheric pressure pressure exerted by the atmosphere because of the force of *gravity* acting upon the overlying column of air.

atoll circular or closed-loop *coral reef* enclosing an open *lagoon* with no island inside.

atomic mass number total number of *protons* and *neutrons* within the nucleus of an atom.

atomic number number of *protons* within the nucleus of an atom; determines element name and chemical properties of the atom.

autogenic succession form of *ecological succession* that is self-producing—that is, results from the actions of plants and animals themselves.

autumnal equinox *equinox* occurring on September 22 or 23.

average deviation difference between a single value and the mean of all values, taken without respect to sign.

axial rift narrow, trench-like depression situated along the center line of the *mid-oceanic ridge* and identified with active seafloor spreading.

axis of rotation center line around which a body revolves, as the Earth's axis of rotation.

B horizon mineral *soil horizon* located beneath the A *horizon*, and usually characterized by a gain of *mineral matter* (such as *clay minerals* and oxides of alu-

minum and iron) and organic matter *(humus)*.

backswamp area of low, swampy ground on the *floodplain* of an *alluvial river* between the *natural levee* and the *bluffs*.

backwash return flow of *swash* water under influence of gravity.

badlands rugged land surface of steep *slopes*, resembling miniature mountains, developed on weak *clay* formations or clay-rich *regolith* by fluvial erosion too rapid to permit plant growth and soil formation.

bar low ridge of *sand* built above water level across the mouth of a *bay* or in shallow water paralleling the shoreline. May also refer to embankment of sand or gravel on floor of a *stream channel*.

bar (pressure) unit of pressure equal to 10^5 Pa *(pascals)*; approximately equal to the pressure of the Earth's *atmosphere* at sea level.

barchan dune *sand dune* of crescentic base outline with a sharp crest and a steep lee *slip face*, with crescent points (horns) pointing downwind.

barometer instrument for measurement of *atmospheric pressure*.

barrier (to dispersal) a zone or region that a *species* is unable to colonize or perhaps even occupy for a short time, thus halting *diffusion*.

barrier island long narrow island, built largely of beach *sand* and dune sand, parallel with the mainland and separated from it by a *lagoon*.

barrier reef *coral reef* separated from mainland *shoreline* by a *lagoon*.

barrier-island coast *coastline* with broad zone of shallow water offshore (a *lagoon*) shut off from the ocean by a *barrier island*.

basalt *extrusive igneous rock* of *gabbro* composition; occurs as *lava*.

base flow that portion of the *discharge* of a *stream* contributed by *ground water* seepage.

base level lower limiting surface or level that can ultimately be attained by a *stream* under conditions of stability of the Earth's crust and sea level; an imaginary surface equivalent to sea level projected inland.

base status of soils quality of a *soil* as measured by the presence or absence of *clay minerals* capable of holding large numbers of *bases*. Soils of high

base status are rich in base-holding *clay minerals;* soils of low *base status* are deficient in such minerals.

bases certain positively charged *ions* in the *soil* that are also plant nutrients; the most important are calcium, magnesium, potassium, and sodium.

batholith large, deep-seated body of *intrusive igneous rock*, usually with an area of surface exposure greater than 100 km² (40 mi²).

bauxite mixture of several *clay minerals*, consisting largely of aluminum oxide and water with impurities; a principal ore of aluminum.

bay a body of water sheltered from strong wave action by the configuration of the *coast*.

beach thick, wedge-shaped accumulation of *sand, gravel,* or cobbles in the zone of breaking waves.

beach drift transport of *sand* on a beach parallel with a *shoreline* by a succession of landward and seaward water movements at times when *swash* approaches obliquely.

bearing direction angle between a line of interest and a reference line, which is usually a line pointing north.

bed load that portion of the *stream load* moving close to the stream bed by rolling and sliding.

bedrock solid *rock* in place with respect to the surrounding and underlying *rock* and relatively unchanged by *weathering* processes.

bedrock slump *landslide* of *bedrock* in which most of the *bedrock* remains more or less intact as it moves.

bioclimatic frontier geographic boundary corresponding with a critical limiting level of climate stress beyond which a *species* cannot survive.

biodiversity the variety of biological life on Earth or within a region.

biogas mixture of methane and *carbon dioxide* generated by action of anaerobic bacteria in animal and human wastes enclosed in a digesting chamber.

biogeochemical cycle total system of *pathways* by which a particular type of *matter* (a given element, compound, or ion, for example) moves through the Earth's *ecosystem* or *biosphere;* also called a *material cycle* or *nutrient cycle*.

biogeographic region region in which the same or closely related plants and animals tend to be found together.

biogeography the study of the distributions of organisms at varying spatial and temporal *scales,* as well as the processes that produce these distribution patterns.

biomass dry weight of living organic matter in an *ecosystem* within a designated surface area; units are kilograms of organic matter per square meter.

biome largest recognizable subdivision of *terrestrial ecosystems,* including the total assemblage of plant and animal life interacting within the *life layer.*

biosphere all living organisms of the Earth and the environments with which they interact.

biota plants and animals, referred to collectively; a list of plants and animals found at a location or in a region.

bitumen combustible mixture of hydrocarbons that is highly viscous and will flow only when heated; considered a form of petroleum.

bituminous sand (See *bitumen.*)

blackbody ideal object or surface that is a perfect radiator and absorber of *energy;* absorbs all radiation it intercepts and emits radiation perfectly according to physical theory.

block mountains class of mountains produced by block faulting and usually bounded by *normal faults.*

block separation separation of individual joint blocks during the process of *physical weathering.*

blowout shallow depression produced by continued *deflation.*

bluffs steeply rising ground slopes marking the outer limits of a *floodplain.*

bog a shallow depression filled with organic matter, for example, a glacial lake or pond basin filled with *peat.*

Boralfs *suborder* of the *soil order Alfisols;* includes Alfisols of *boreal forests* or high mountains.

boreal forest variety of *needleleaf forest* found in the *boreal forest climate* ⑪ regions of North America and Eurasia.

boreal forest climate ⑪ cold climate of the *subarctic zone* in the northern *hemisphere* with long, extremely severe winters and several consecutive months of zero *potential evapotranspiration (water need).*

Borolls *suborder* of the *soil order Mollisols;* includes Mollisols of cold-winter semiarid plants *(steppes)* or high mountains.

braided stream *stream* with shallow channel in coarse *alluvium* carrying multiple threads of fast flow that subdivide and rejoin repeatedly and continually shift in position.

breaker sudden collapse of a steepened water wave as it approaches the shoreline.

broadleaf deciduous forest *forest* type consisting of broadleaf *deciduous trees* and found in the *moist subtropical climate* ⑥ in parts of the *marine west-coast climate* ⑧. (See also *midlatitude deciduous forest.*)

broadleaf evergreen forest *forest* type consisting of broadleaf *evergreen trees* and found in the wet equatorial and tropical climates. (See also *low-latitude rainforest.*)

Brunisolic order a class of *forest soils* in the Canadian soil classification system with brownish *B horizon.*

budget in flow systems, an accounting of *energy* and *matter* flows that enter, move within, and leave a system.

bush-fallow farming agricultural system practiced in the African *savanna woodland* in which *trees* are cut and burned to provide cultivation plots.

butte prominent, steep-sided hill or peak, often representing the final remnant of a resistant layer in a region of flat-lying *strata.*

C horizon *soil horizon* lying beneath the *B horizon,* consisting of *sediment* or *regolith* that is the *parent material* of the soil.

calcification accumulation of *calcium carbonate* in a soil, usually occurring in the *B* or *C horizons.*

calcite mineral having the composition *calcium carbonate.*

calcium carbonate compound consisting of calcium (Ca) and carbonate (CO_3) *ions,* formula $CaCo_3$, occurring naturally as the mineral *calcite.*

caldera large, steep-sided circular depression resulting from the explosion and subsidence of a *stratovolcano.*

canyon (See *gorge.*)

capillary action process by which *capillary tension* draws water into a small opening, such as a *soil* pore or a *rock joint.*

capillary tension a cohesive force among surface molecules of a *liquid* that gives a droplet its rounded shape.

carbohydrate class of organic compounds consisting of the elements carbon, hydrogen, and oxygen.

carbon cycle *biogeochemical cycle* in which carbon moves through the *biosphere;* includes both *gaseous cycles* and *sedimentary cycles.*

carbon dioxide the chemical compound CO_2, formed by the union of two atoms of oxygen and one atom of carbon; normally a gas present in low concentration in the *atmosphere.*

carbon fixation (See *photosynthesis.*)

carbonates (carbonate minerals, carbonate rocks) *minerals* that are carbonate compounds of calcium or magnesium or both, i.e., *calcium carbonate* or magnesium carbonate. (See also *calcite.*)

carbonic acid a weak acid created when CO_2 gas dissolves in water.

carbonic acid action chemical reaction of *carbonic acid* in rainwater, *soil water,* and *ground water* with *minerals;* most strongly affects carbonate minerals and *rocks,* such as limestone and marble; an activity of *chemical weathering.*

cartography the science and art of making maps.

Celsius scale temperature scale in which the *freezing* point of water is 0° and the boiling point is 100°.

Cenozoic Era last (youngest) of the *eras* of geologic time.

channel (See *stream channel.*)

chaparral sclerophyll scrub and dwarf *forest* plant *formation class* found throughout the coastal mountain ranges and hills of central and southern California.

chemical energy *energy* stored within an organic molecule and capable of being transformed into *heat* during metabolism.

chemical weathering chemical change in *rock-forming* minerals through exposure to atmospheric conditions in the presence of water; mainly involving *oxidation, hydrolysis, carbonic acid action,* or direct solution.

chemically precipitated sediment *sediment* consisting of *mineral matter* precipitated from a water solution in which the matter has been transported in the dissolved state as *ions.*

chernozem   type of *soil order* closely equivalent to *Mollisol;* an order of the Canadian Soil Classification System.

Chernozemic order   a class of grassland *soils* in the Canadian soil classification system with a thick *A horizon* rich in organic matter.

chert   *sedimentary rock* composed largely of silicon dioxide and various impurities, in the form of nodules and layers, often occurring with *limestone* layers.

chinook wind   a *local wind* occurring at certain times to the lee of the Rocky Mountains; a very dry *wind* with a high capacity to evaporate *snow.*

chlorofluorocarbons (CFCs)   synthetic chemical compounds containing chlorine, fluorine, and carbon atoms that are widely used as coolant fluids in refrigeration systems.

cinder cone   conical hill built of coarse *tephra* ejected from a narrow volcanic vent; a type of *volcano.*

circle of illumination   great circle that divides the globe at all times into a sunlit *hemisphere* and a shadowed hemisphere.

circum-Pacific belt   chains of andesite *volcanoes* making up mountain belts and *island arcs* surrounding the Pacific Ocean basin.

cirque   bowl-shaped depression carved in *rock* by glacial processes and holding the *firn* of the upper end of an *alpine glacier.*

clast   rock or mineral fragment broken from a parent *rock* source.

clastic sediment   *sediment* consisting of particles broken away physically from a parent *rock* source.

clay   *sediment* particles smaller than 0.004 mm in diameter.

clay minerals   class of *minerals* produced by alteration of *silicate minerals,* having plastic properties when moist.

claystone   *sedimentary rock* formed by lithification of *clay* and lacking *fissile* structure.

cliff   sheer, near-vertical *rock* wall formed from flat-lying resistant layered *rocks,* usually *sandstone, limestone,* or *lava* flows; may refer to any near-vertical rock wall. (See also *marine cliff.*)

climate   generalized statement of the prevailing weather conditions at a given place, based on statistics of a long period of record and including mean values, departures from those means,

and the probabilities associated with those departures.

climatic frontier   a geographical boundary that marks the limit of survival of a plant *species* subjected to climatic stress.

climatology   the science that describes and explains the variability in space and time of the heat and moisture states of the Earth's surface, especially its land surfaces.

climax   stable community of plants and animals reached at the end point of *ecological succession.*

climograph   a graph on which two or more climatic variables, such as monthly mean temperature and monthly mean precipitation, are plotted for each month of the year.

closed flow system   flow system that is completely self-contained within a boundary through which no *matter* or *energy* is exchanged with the external environment. (See also *open flow system.*)

cloud forest   a type of low evergreen rainforest that occurs high on mountain slopes, where *clouds* and *fog* are frequent.

clouds   dense concentrations of suspended water or ice particles in the diameter range 20 to 50 μm. (See also *cumuliform clouds, stratiform clouds.*)

coal   *rock* consisting of hydrocarbon compounds, formed of compacted, lithified, and altered accumulations of plant remains *(peat).*

coarse textured (rock)   having *mineral* crystals sufficiently large that they are at least visible to the naked eye or with low magnification.

coast   (See *coastline.*)

coastal and marine geography   the study of the geomorphic processes that shape shores and coastlines and their application to coastal development and marine resource utilization.

coastal blowout dune   high *sand dune* of the *parabolic dunes* class formed adjacent to a beach, usually with a deep *deflation* hollow *(blowout)* enclosed within the dune ridge.

coastal forest   subtype of *needleleaf evergreen forest* found in the humid coastal zone of the northwestern United States and western Canada.

coastal plain   coastal belt, emerged from beneath the sea as a former *conti-*

nental shelf, underlain by *strata* with gentle *dip* seaward.

coastline (coast)   zone in which coastal processes operate or have a strong influence.

coefficient of variation   in statistics, the ratio of the standard deviation to the mean.

cognitive representation   in the *representation* perspective of *geography,* mental mapping of spatial relationships as they are experienced by humans.

col   natural pass or low notch in an *arête* between opposed *cirques.*

cold front   moving weather *front* along which a cold *air mass* moves underneath a warm air mass, causing the latter to be lifted.

cold-blooded animal   animal whose body temperature passively follows the temperature of the environment.

cold-core ring   circular eddy of cold water, surrounded by warm water and lying adjacent to a warm, poleward-moving *ocean current,* such as the Gulf Stream. (See also *warm-core ring.*)

colloids   particles of extremely small size, capable of remaining indefinitely in suspension in water. May be mineral or organic in nature.

colluvium   deposit of *sediment* or *rock* particles accumulating from overland flow at the base of a *slope* and originating from higher slopes where *sheet erosion* is in progress. (See also *alluvium.*)

community   an assemblage of organisms that live in a particular *habitat* and interact with one another.

competition   form of interaction among plant or animal *species* in which both draw resources from the same *pool.*

component   in flow systems, a part of the system, such as a *pathway,* connection, or flow of *matter* or *energy.*

composite volcano   volcano composed of layers of ash and lava. (See also *stratovolcano.*)

compression (tectonic)   squeezing together, as horizontal compression of crustal layers by *tectonic* processes.

condensation   process of change of *matter* in the gaseous state *(water vapor)* to the liquid state (liquid water) or solid state (ice).

condensation nucleus   a tiny bit of solid *matter (aerosol)* in the *atmosphere* on which *water vapor* condenses to form a tiny water droplet.

conduction of heat   transmission of *sensible heat* through *matter* by transfer of *energy* from one atom or molecule to the next in the direction of decreasing temperature.

cone of depression   conical configuration of the lowered *water table* around a well from which water is being rapidly withdrawn.

conformal projection   *map* projection that preserves without shearing the true shape or outline of any small surface feature of the Earth.

conglomerate   a *sedimentary rock* composed of pebbles in a matrix of finer *rock* particles.

conic projections   a group of *map projections* in which the *geographic grid* is transformed to lie on the surface of a developed cone.

consequent stream   *stream* that takes its course down the slope of an *initial landform*, such as a newly emerged *coastal plain* or a volcano.

consumers   animals in the *food chain* that live on organic matter formed by *primary producers* or by other *consumers*. (See also *primary consumers, secondary consumers*.)

consumption (of a lithospheric plate)   destruction or disappearance of a subducting *lithospheric plate* in the *asthenosphere*, in part by *melting* of the upper surface, but largely by softening because of heating to the temperature of the surrounding *mantle rock*.

continental collision   event in *plate tectonics* in which subduction brings two segments of the *continental lithosphere* into contact, leading to formation of a *continental suture*.

continental crust   crust of the continents, of felsic composition in the upper part; thicker and less dense than *oceanic crust*.

continental drift   hypothesis, introduced by Alfred Wegener and others early in the 1900s, of the breakup of a parent continent, *Pangea*, starting near the close of the *Mesozoic Era*, and resulting in the present arrangement of *continental shields* and intervening *ocean-basin floors*.

continental lithosphere   *lithosphere* bearing *continental crust* of *felsic igneous rock*.

continental margins   (1) Topographic: one of three major divisions of the ocean basins, being the zones directly adjacent to the continent and including the *continental shelf, continental slope,* and *continental rise*. (2) Tectonic: marginal belt of continental crust and lithosphere that is in contact with *oceanic crust* and *lithosphere*, with or without an active plate boundary being present at the contact. (See also *active continental margins, passive continental margins*.)

continental rise   gently sloping seafloor lying at the foot of the *continental slope* and leading gradually into the *abyssal plain*.

continental rupture   crustal spreading apart affecting the *continental lithosphere*, so as to cause a *rift valley* to appear and to widen, eventually creating a new belt of *oceanic lithosphere*.

continental scale   scale of observation at which we recognize continents and other large Earth surface features, such as ocean currents.

continental shelf   shallow, gently sloping belt of seafloor adjacent to the continental shoreline and terminating at its outer edge in the *continental slope*.

continental shields   ancient crustal *rock* masses of the continents, largely *igneous rock* and *metamorphic rock*, and mostly of *Precambrian age*.

continental slope   steeply descending belt of seafloor between the *continental shelf* and the *continental rise*.

continental suture   long, narrow zone of crustal deformation, including underthrusting and intense *folding*, produced by a *continental collision*. Examples: Himalayan Range, European Alps.

continuous permafrost   *permafrost* that underlies more than 90 percent of the surface area of a region.

convection (atmospheric)   air motion consisting of strong updrafts taking place within a *convection cell*.

convection cell   individual column of strong updrafts produced by atmospheric *convection*.

convection current   in *plate tectonics*, a stream of upwelling *mantle* rock that rises steadily beneath a spreading plate boundary.

convection loop   circuit of moving *fluid*, such as *air* or water, created by unequal heating of the *fluid*.

convectional precipitation   a form of *precipitation* induced when warm, moist air is heated at the ground surface, rises, cools, and condenses to form water droplets, raindrops, and eventually, rainfall.

convergence   horizontal motion of air creating a net inflow; causes a rising motion when occurring at the surface or a sinking motion when occurring aloft.

converging boundary   boundary between two crustal plates along which *subduction* is occurring and *lithosphere* is being consumed.

coral reef   rock-like accumulation of *carbonates* secreted by corals and algae in shallow water along a marine shoreline.

coral-reef coast   *coast* built out by accumulations of *limestone* in *coral reefs*.

core of Earth   spherical central mass of the Earth composed largely of iron and consisting of an outer liquid zone and an interior solid zone.

Coriolis effect   effect of the Earth's rotation tending to turn the direction of motion of any object or *fluid* toward the right in the northern *hemisphere* and to the left in the southern *hemisphere*.

corrosion   erosion of *bedrock* of a *stream channel* (or other *rock* surface) by chemical reactions between solutions in stream water and *mineral* surfaces.

cosmopolitan species   *species* that are found very widely.

counterradiation   *longwave radiation* of atmosphere directed downward to the Earth's surface.

covered shields   areas of *continental shields* in which the ancient *rocks* are covered beneath a thin layer of sedimentary *strata*.

crater   central summit depression associated with the principal vent of a *volcano*.

crescentic dune   (See *barchan dunes*.)

crest   in describing water waves, the highest point of the wave form.

crevasse   gaping crack in the brittle surface ice of a *glacier*.

crude oil   liquid fraction of *petroleum*.

crust of Earth   outermost solid shell or layer of the Earth, composed largely of *silicate minerals*.

Cryaquepts   great group within the soil suborder of *Aquepts*; includes Aquepts of cold climate regions and particularly the *tundra climate* ⑫.

Cryosolic order a class of *soils* in the Canadian soil classification system associated with strong frost action and underlying *permafrost*.

cryoturbation movement of mineral particles of any size by freezing and thawing of ice.

cuesta *erosional landform* developed on resistant *strata* having low to moderate *dip* and taking the form of an asymmetrical low ridge or hill belt with one side a steep slope and the other a gentle slope; usually associated with a *coastal plain*.

cultural energy *energy* in forms exclusive of solar *energy* of *photosynthesis* that is expended on the production of raw food or feed crops in agricultural *ecosystems*.

cumuliform clouds *clouds* of globular shape, often with extended vertical development.

cumulonimbus cloud large, dense *cumuliform cloud* yielding *precipitation*.

cumulus cloud type consisting of low-lying, white cloud masses of globular shape well separated from one another.

cutoff cutting-through of a narrow neck of land, so as to bypass the *stream flow* in an *alluvial meander* and cause it to be abandoned.

cycle in flow systems, a closed flow system of *matter*. Example: *biogeochemical cycle*. (See also *closed flow system*.)

cycle of rock change total cycle of changes in which *rock* of any one of the three major *rock* classes—*igneous rock, sedimentary rock, metamorphic rock*—is transformed into *rock* of one of the other classes.

cyclone center of low *atmospheric pressure*. (See also *tropical cyclone, wave cyclone*.)

cyclonic precipitation a form of *precipitation* that occurs as warm moist air is lifted by air motion occurring in a *cyclone*.

cyclonic storm intense weather disturbance within a moving *cyclone* generating strong winds, cloudiness, and *precipitation*.

cylindric projections group of *map projections* in which the *geographic grid* is transformed to lie on the surface of a developed cylinder.

data acquisition component component of a *geographic information system* in which data are gathered together for input to the system.

data management component component of a *geographic information system* that creates, stores, retrieves, and modifies data layers and *spatial objects*.

daughter product new *isotope* created by decay of an *unstable isotope*.

daylight that period of the day during which the Sun is above the horizon at a particular location.

daylight saving time time system under which time is advanced by one hour with respect to the *standard time* of the prevailing *standard meridian*.

debris flood (debris flow) stream-like flow of muddy water heavily charged with *sediment* of a wide range of size grades, including boulders, generated by sporadic torrential rains upon steep mountain watersheds.

decalcification removal of *calcium carbonate* from a *soil horizon* as *carbonic acid* reacts with *carbonate mineral matter*.

December solstice (See *winter solstice*.)

deciduous plant *tree* or *shrub* that sheds its leaves seasonally.

declination of Sun latitude at which the Sun is directly overhead; varies from $-23^1/_2°$ ($23^1/_2°$ S lat.) to $+23^1/_2°$ N lat.

décollement detachment and extensive sliding of a *rock* layer, usually *sedimentary*, over a near-horizontal basal *rock* surface; a special form of low-angle thrust *faulting*.

decomposers organisms that feed on dead organisms from all levels of the *food chain*; most are microorganisms and bacteria that feed on decaying organic matter.

deep sea cone a fan-shaped accumulation of undersea *sediment* on the *continental rise* produced by sediment-rich currents flowing down the *continental slope*.

deficit (soil water shortage) in the soil water budget, the difference between *water use* and *water need*; the quantity of irrigation water required to achieve maximum growth of agricultural crops.

deflation lifting and transport in *turbulent suspension* by wind of loose particles of *soil* or *regolith* from dry ground surfaces.

deglaciation widespread recession of *ice sheets* during a period of warming global climate, leading to an interglaciation. (See also *glaciation, interglaciation*.)

degradation lowering or downcutting of a *stream channel* by *stream erosion* in *alluvium* or *bedrock*.

degree of arc measurement of the angle associated with an *arc*, in degrees.

delta *sediment* deposit built by a stream entering a body of standing water and formed of the *stream load*.

delta coast *coast* bordered by a *delta*.

delta kame flat-topped hill of *stratified drift* representing a glacial *delta* constructed adjacent to an *ice sheet* in a marginal glacial lake.

dendritic drainage pattern *drainage pattern* of tree-like branched form, in which the smaller streams take a wide variety of directions and show no parallelism or dominant trend.

denitrification biochemical process in which nitrogen in forms usable to plants is converted into molecular nitrogen in the gaseous form and returned to the atmosphere—a process that is part of the *nitrogen cycle*.

density of matter quantity of mass per unit of volume, stated in kg m^{-2}.

denudation total action of all processes whereby the exposed *rocks* of the continents are worn down and the resulting *sediments* are transported to the sea by the *fluid agents*; includes also *weathering* and *mass wasting*.

deposition (atmosphere) the change of state of a substance from a *gas (water vapor)* to a *solid* (ice); in the science of *meteorology*, the term *sublimation* is used to describe both this process and the change of state from solid to vapor. (See also *sublimation*.)

deposition (of sediment) (See *stream deposition*.)

depositional landform *landform* made by *deposition* of *sediment*.

desert biome *biome* of the dry climates consisting of thinly dispersed plants that may be *shrubs*, grasses, or perennial *herbs*, but lacking in *trees*.

desert pavement surface layer of closely fitted pebbles or coarse *sand* from which finer particles have been removed.

desertification   (See *land degradation*.)

detritus   decaying organic matter on which *decomposers* feed.

dew-point lapse rate   rate at which the dew point of an air mass decreases with elevation; typical value is 1.8°C/1000 m (1.0°F/1000 ft).

dew-point temperature   temperature of an *air mass* at which the air holds its full capacity of water vapor.

diagnostic horizons   *soil horizons,* rigorously defined, that are used as diagnostic criteria in classifying *soils.*

diffuse radiation   solar radiation that has been *scattered* (deflected or reflected) by minute dust particles or cloud particles in the *atmosphere.*

diffuse reflection   solar *radiation* scattered back to space by the Earth's *atmosphere.*

diffusion   the slow extension of the range of a *species* by normal processes of dispersal.

digital image   numeric representation of a picture consisting of a collection of numeric brightness values (pixels) arrayed in a fine grid pattern.

dike   thin layer of *intrusive igneous rock,* often near-vertical or with steep *dip,* occupying a widened fracture in the surrounding *rock* and typically cutting across older *rock* planes.

diorite   *intrusive igneous rock* consisting dominantly of plagioclase feldspar and pyroxene; a *felsic igneous rock.*

dip   acute angle between an inclined natural *rock* plane or surface and an imaginary horizontal plane of reference; always measured perpendicular to the *strike.* Also a verb, meaning to incline toward.

diploid   having two sets of chromosomes, one from each parent organism.

discharge   volume of flow moving through a given cross section of a stream in a given unit of time; commonly given in cubic meters (feet) per second.

discontinuous permafrost   *permafrost* that underlies from 10 to 90 percent of the surface of a region.

disjunction   geographic distribution pattern of *species* in which one or more closely related species are found in widely separated regions.

dispersal   the capacity of a *species* to move from a location of birth or origin to new sites.

distributary   branching *stream channel* that crosses a *delta* to discharge into open water.

diurnal   adjective meaning "daily."

divergence   horizontal motion of air creating a net outflow; causes a rising motion from below when occurring aloft.

doldrums   belt of calms and variable winds occurring at times along the *equatorial trough.*

dolomite   carbonate mineral or *sedimentary rock* having the composition calcium magnesium carbonate.

dome   (See *sedimentary dome*.)

drainage basin   total land surface occupied by a *drainage system,* bounded by a *drainage divide* or watershed.

drainage divide   imaginary line following a crest of high land such that overland flow on opposite sides of the line enters different *streams.*

drainage pattern   the plan of a network of interconnected *stream channels.*

drainage system   a branched network of *stream channels* and adjacent land *slopes,* bounded by a *drainage divide* and converging to a single channel at the outlet.

drainage winds   *winds,* usually cold, that flow from higher to lower regions under the direct influence of *gravity.*

drawdown (of a well)   difference in height between base of cone of depression and original water table surface.

drought   occurrence of substantially lower-than-average *precipitation* in a season that normally has ample precipitation for the support of food-producing plants.

drumlin   hill of glacial *till,* oval or elliptical in basal outline and with smoothly rounded summit, formed by plastering of till beneath moving, debris-laden glacial ice.

dry adiabatic lapse rate   rate at which rising air is cooled by expansion when no *condensation* is occurring; 10°C per 1000 m (5.5°F per 1000 ft).

dry desert   plant *formation class* in the *desert biome* consisting of widely dispersed xerophytic plants that may be small, hard-leaved or spiny *shrubs,* succulent plants (cacti), or hard grasses.

dry lake   shallow basin covered with salt deposits formed when *stream* input to the basin is subjected to severe *evaporation;* may also form by evaporation of a saline lake when climate changes; see also *salt flat.*

dry midlatitude climate ⑨   dry climate of the *midlatitude zone* with a strong annual cycle of *potential evapotranspiration (water need)* and cold winters.

dry subtropical climate ⑤   dry climate of the *subtropical zone,* transitional between the *dry tropical climate* ④ and the *dry midlatitude climate* ⑨.

dry tropical climate ④   climate of the *tropical zone* with large total annual *potential evapotranspiration (water need).*

dune   (See *sand dune*.)

dust bowl   western Great Plains of the United States, which suffered severe wind deflation and soil drifting during the drought years of the middle 1930s.

dust storm   heavy concentration of dust in a turbulent *air mass,* often associated with a *cold front.*

E horizon   soil mineral horizon lying below the *A horizon* and characterized by the loss of *clay minerals* and oxides of iron and aluminum; it may show a concentration of *quartz* grains and is often pale in color.

Earth's crust   (See *crust of Earth*.)

earth hummock   low mound of vegetation-covered earth found in *permafrost* terrain, formed by cycles of *ground ice* growth and melting (see also *mud hummock*).

earthflow   moderately rapid downhill flowage of masses of water-saturated *soil, regolith,* or weak *shale,* typically forming a step-like terrace at the top and a bulging toe at the base.

earthquake   a trembling or shaking of the ground produced by the passage of *seismic waves.*

earthquake focus   point within the Earth at which the *energy* of an *earthquake* is first released by rupture and from which *seismic waves* emanate.

easterly wave   weak, slowly moving trough of low pressure within the belt of *tropical easterlies;* causes a weather disturbance with rain showers.

ebb current   oceanward flow of *tidal current* in a *bay* or tidal stream.

ecological succession   time-succession (sequence) of distinctive plant and animal communities occurring within a given area of newly formed land or land cleared of plant cover by burning, clear cutting, or other agents.

ecology science of interactions between life forms and their environment; the science of *ecosystems.*

ecosystem group of organisms and the environment with which the organisms interact.

edaphic factors factors relating to soil that influence a terrestrial ecosystem.

El Niño episodic cessation of the typical *upwelling* of cold deep water off the coast of Peru; literally, "The Christ Child," for its occurrence in the Christmas season once every few years.

electromagnetic radiation (electromagnetic energy) wave-like form of *energy* radiated by any substance possessing heat; it travels through space at the speed of light.

electromagnetic spectrum the total *wavelength* range of *electromagnetic energy.*

eluviation soil-forming process consisting of the downward transport of fine particles, particularly the *soil colloids* (both mineral and organic), carrying them out of an upper *soil horizon.*

emergence exposure of submarine landforms by a lowering of sea level or a rise of the crust, or both.

endemic species a *species* found only in one region or location.

endogenic processes internal Earth processes that create *landforms,* such as *tectonics* and *volcanism.*

energy the capacity to do work, that is, to bring about a change in the state or motion of *matter.*

energy balance (global) balance between *shortwave* solar *radiation* received by the Earth-atmosphere system and *radiation* lost to space by *shortwave* reflection and *longwave radiation* from the Earth-atmosphere system.

energy balance (of a surface) balance between the flows of *energy* reaching a surface and the flows of energy leaving it.

energy flow system *open system* that receives an input of *energy,* undergoes internal energy flow, energy transformation, and energy storage, and has an energy output.

Entisols *soil order* consisting of mineral soils lacking *soil horizons* that would persist after normal plowing.

entrenched meanders winding, sinuous valley produced by *degradation* of a *stream* with trenching into the *bedrock* by downcutting.

environmental temperature lapse rate rate of temperature decrease upward through the *troposphere;* standard value is 6.4 C°/km (3 F°/1000 ft).

epipedon *soil horizon* that forms at the surface.

epiphytes plants that live above ground level out of contact with the soil, usually growing on the limbs of *trees* or *shrubs;* also called "air plants."

epoch a subdivision of geologic time.

equal-area projections class of *map projections* on which any given area of the Earth's surface is shown to correct relative areal extent, regardless of position on the globe.

equator *parallel of latitude* occupying a position midway between the Earth's poles of *rotation;* the largest of the parallels, designated as *latitude* 0°.

equatorial current westward-flowing *ocean current* in the belt of the *trade winds.*

equatorial easterlies upper-level easterly air flow over the *equatorial zone.*

equatorial rainforest plant *formation class* within the *forest biome,* consisting of tall, closely set broadleaf *trees* of evergreen or semideciduous habit.

equatorial trough atmospheric low-pressure trough centered more or less over the *equator* and situated between the two belts of *trade winds.*

equatorial zone *latitude* zone lying between lat. 10° S and 10° N (more or less) and centered upon the *equator.*

equilibrium in flow systems, a state of balance in which flow rates remain unchanged.

equinox instant in time when the *subsolar point* falls on the Earth's equator and the *circle of illumination* passes through both poles. *Vernal equinox* occurs on March 20 or 21; *autumnal equinox* on September 22 or 23.

era major subdivision of geologic time consisting of a number of geologic periods. The three *eras* following *Precambrian time* are *Paleozoic, Mesozoic,* and *Cenozoic.*

erg large expanse of active *sand dunes* in the Sahara Desert of North Africa.

erosional landforms class of the *sequential landforms* shaped by the removal of *regolith* or *bedrock* by agents of erosion. Examples: *gorge,* glacial *cirque, marine cliff.*

esker narrow, often sinuous embankment of coarse gravel and boulders deposited in the bed of a meltwater *stream* enclosed in a tunnel within stagnant ice of an *ice sheet.*

estuary *bay* that receives fresh water from a river mouth and saltwater from the ocean.

Eurasian-Indonesian belt mountain arc system extending from southern Europe across southern Asia and Indonesia.

eustatic referring to a true change in sea level, as opposed to a local change created by upward or downward *tectonic* motion of land.

eutrophication excessive growth of algae and other related organisms in a *stream* or *lake* as a result of the input of large amounts of nutrient *ions,* especially phosphate and nitrate.

evaporation process in which water in liquid state or solid state passes into the vapor state.

evaporites class of *chemically precipitated sediment* and *sedimentary rock* composed of soluble salts deposited from saltwater bodies.

evapotranspiration combined water loss to the atmosphere by *evaporation* from the *soil* and *transpiration* from plants.

evergreen plant *tree* or *shrub* that holds most of its green leaves throughout the year.

evolution the creation of the diversity of life forms through the process of natural selection.

exfoliation (See *unloading.*)

exfoliation dome smoothly rounded *rock* knob or hilltop bearing *rock* sheets or shells produced by spontaneous expansion accompanying *unloading.*

exogenic processes *landform*-making processes that are active at the Earth's surface, such as erosion by water, waves and currents, glacial ice, and wind.

exotic river *stream* that flows across a region of dry climate and derives its *discharge* from adjacent uplands where a *water surplus* exists.

exponential growth increase in number or value over time in which the increase is a constant proportion or percentage within each time unit.

exposed shields areas of *continental shields* in which the ancient basement *rock,* usually of *Precambrian* age, is exposed to the surface.

extension (tectonic) drawing apart of crustal layers by *tectonic activity* resulting in *faulting.*

extinction the event that the number of organisms of a *species* shrinks to zero so that the species no longer exists.

extrusion release of molten *rock magma* at the surface, as in a flow of *lava* or shower of volcanic ash.

extrusive igneous rock *rock* produced by the solidification of *lava* or ejected fragments of *igneous rock (tephra).*

Fahrenheit scale temperature scale in which the *freezing* point of water is 32° and the boiling point 212°.

fair weather system a *traveling anticyclone,* in which the descent of air suppresses clouds and precipitation and the weather is typically fair.

fallout *gravity* fall of atmospheric particles of *particulates* reaching the ground.

fault sharp break in *rock* with a displacement (slippage) of the block on one side with respect to an adjacent block. (See also *normal fault, overthrust fault, strike-slip fault, transform fault.*)

fault coast *coast* formed when a *shoreline* comes to rest against a *fault scarp.*

fault creep more or less continuous slippage on a *fault plane,* relieving some of the accumulated strain.

fault plane surface of slippage between two Earth blocks moving relative to each other during faulting.

fault scarp cliff-like surface feature produced by faulting and exposing the *fault plane;* commonly associated with a *normal fault.*

fault-line scarp erosion scarp developed upon an inactive *fault* line.

feedback in flow systems, a linkage between flow paths such that the flow in one *pathway* acts either to reducē or increase the flow in another *pathway.*

feldspar group of *silicate minerals* consisting of silicate of aluminum and one or more of the metals potassium, sodium, or calcium. (See also *plagioclase feldspar, potash feldspar.*)

felsenmeer expanse of large blocks of *rock* produced by *joint* block separation and shattering by *frost action* at high altitudes or in high latitudes; from the German for "rock sea."

felsic igneous rock *igneous rock* dominantly composed of *felsic minerals.*

felsic minerals (felsic mineral group) *quartz* and *feldspars* treated as a mineral group of light color and relatively low *density.* (See also *mafic minerals.*)

fetch distance that wind blows over water to create a train of water waves.

fine textured (rock) having *mineral* crystals too small to be seen by eye or with low magnification.

fiord narrow, deep ocean embayment partially filling a *glacial trough.*

fiord coast deeply embayed, rugged coast formed by partial *submergence* of *glacial troughs.*

firn granular old *snow* forming a surface layer in the zone of accumulation of a *glacier.*

fissile adjective describing a *rock,* usually *shale,* that readily splits up into small flakes or scales.

flash flood flood in which heavy rainfall causes a stream or river to rise very rapidly.

flocculation the clotting together of colloidal mineral particles to form larger particles; it occurs when a colloidal suspension in fresh water mixes with sea water.

flood *stream flow* at a stream *stage* so high that it cannot be accommodated within the *stream channel* and must spread over the banks to inundate the adjacent *floodplain.*

flood basalts large-scale outpourings of basalt *lava* to produce thick accumulations of *basalt* over large areas.

flood current landward flow of a *tidal current.*

flood stage designated stream-surface level for a particular point on a *stream,* higher than which overbank flooding may be expected.

floodplain belt of low, flat ground, present on one or both sides of a *stream channel,* subject to inundation by a *flood* about once annually and underlain by alluvium.

flow system a physical *system* in which *matter, energy,* or both move through time from one location to another.

fluid substance that flows readily when subjected to unbalanced stresses; may exist as a *gas* or a *liquid.*

fluid agents *fluids* that erode, transport, and deposit *mineral matter* and organic matter; they are running water, waves and currents, glacial ice, and *wind.*

fluvial landforms *landforms* shaped by running water.

fluvial processes geomorphic processes in which running water is the dominant *fluid* agent, acting as *overland flow* and *stream flow.*

focus (See *earthquake focus.*)

fog cloud layer in contact with land or sea surface, or very close to that surface. (See also *advection fog, radiation fog.*)

folding process by which *folds* are produced; a form of *tectonic activity.*

folds wave-like corrugations of *strata* (or other layered *rock* masses) as a result of crustal *compression.*

food chain (food web) organization of an *ecosystem* into steps or levels through which *energy* flows as the organisms at each level consume *energy* stored in the bodies of organisms of the next lower level.

forb broad-leaved *herb,* as distinguished from the grasses.

forearc trough in plate tectonics, a shallow trough between a *tectonic arc* and a continent; accumulates *sediment* in a basin-like structure.

foredunes ridge of irregular *sand dunes* typically found adjacent to *beaches* on low-lying *coasts* and bearing a partial cover of plants.

foreland folds *folds* produced by *continental collision* in *strata* of a *passive continental margin.*

forest assemblage of *trees* growing close together, their crowns forming a layer of foliage that largely shades the ground.

forest biome *biome* that includes all regions of *forest* over the lands of the Earth.

formation classes subdivisions within a *biome* based on the size, shape, and structure of the plants that dominate the vegetation.

fossil fuels naturally occurring hydrocarbon compounds that represent the altered remains of organic materials enclosed in *rock;* examples are *coal, petroleum (crude oil),* and *natural* gas.

fractional scale (See *scale fraction.*)

freezing change from liquid state to solid state accompanied by release of *latent heat,* becoming *sensible heat.*

freezing front location at which freezing is occurring in the *active layer* of *permafrost* during the annual freeze-over; fronts may move downward from the top or upward from the bottom.

fringing reef *coral reef* directly attached to land with no intervening *lagoon* of open water.

front surface of contact between two unlike *air masses.* (See also *cold front, occluded front, polar front, warm front.*)

frost action *rock* breakup by forces accompanying the *freezing* of water.

gabbro *intrusive igneous rock* consisting largely of pyroxene and *plagioclase feldspar,* with variable amounts of *olivine;* a *mafic igneous rock.*

gas (gaseous state) *fluid* of very low density (as compared with a liquid of the same chemical composition) that expands to fill uniformly any small container and is readily compressed.

gaseous cycle type of *biogeochemical cycle* in which an element or compound is converted into *gaseous* form, diffuses through the *atmosphere,* and passes rapidly over land or sea where it is reused in the *biosphere.*

gene flow speciation process in which evolving populations exchange *alleles* as individuals move among populations.

genetic drift *speciation* process in which chance mutations change the genetic composition of a breeding population until it diverges from other populations.

genotype the gene set of an individual organism or *species.*

genus a collection of closely related *species* that share a similar genetic evolutionary history.

geographic grid complete network of *parallels* and *meridians* on the surface of the globe, used to fix the locations of surface points.

geographic information system (GIS) a system for acquiring, process-ing, storing, querying, creating, and displaying *spatial data;* in the *representation* perspective of *geography,* the use of GISs to represent and manipulate spatial data.

geographic isolation *speciation* process in which a breeding population is split into parts by an emerging geographic barrier, such as an uplifting mountain range or a changing *climate.*

geography the study of the evolving character and organization of the Earth's surface.

geography of soils the study of the distribution of soil types and properties and the processes of soil formation.

geologic norm stable natural condition in a moist climate in which slow *soil erosion* is paced by maintenance of *soil horizons* bearing a plant community in an equilibrium state.

geology science of the solid Earth, including the Earth's origin and history, materials comprising the Earth, and the processes acting within the Earth and upon its surface.

geomorphic factors *landform* factors influencing *ecosystems,* such as slope steepness, slope aspect, and relief.

geomorphology science of Earth surface processes and *landforms,* including their history and processes of origin.

geostrophic wind *wind* at high levels above the Earth's surface blowing parallel with a system of straight, parallel *isobars.*

geyser periodic jet-like emission of hot water and steam from a narrow vent at a geothermal locality.

glacial abrasion *abrasion* by a moving *glacier* of the *bedrock* floor beneath it.

glacial delta *delta* built by meltwater streams of a *glacier* into standing water of a marginal glacial lake.

glacial drift general term for all varieties and forms of *rock* debris deposited in close association with *ice sheets* of the *Pleistocene Epoch.*

glacial plucking removal of masses of *bedrock* from beneath an *alpine glacier* or *ice sheets* as ice moves forward suddenly.

glacial trough deep, steep-sided *rock* trench of U-shaped cross section formed by *alpine glacier* erosion.

glaciation (1) general term for the total process of glacier growth and *landform* modification by *glaciers.* (2) single episode or time period in which *ice sheets* formed, spread, and disappeared.

glacier large natural accumulation of land ice affected by present or past flowage. (See also *alpine glacier.*)

Gleysolic order a class of *soils* in the Canadian soil classification system characterized by indicators of periodic or prolonged water saturation.

global radiation balance the energy flow process by which the Earth absorbs shortwave solar radiation and emits longwave radiation. In the long run, the two flows must balance.

global scale scale at which we are concerned with the Earth as a whole, for example in considering Earth–Sun relationships.

gneiss variety of *metamorphic rock* showing banding and commonly rich in *quartz* and *feldspar.*

Gondwana a *supercontinent* of the Permian *Period* including much of the regions that are now South America, Africa, Antarctica, Australia, New Zealand, Madagascar, and peninsular India.

Goode projection an equal-area *map projection,* often used to display areal thematic information, such as *climate* or *soil* type.

gorge (canyon) steep-sided *bedrock* valley with a narrow floor limited to the width of a *stream channel.*

graben trench-like depression representing the surface of a crustal block dropped down between two opposed, infacing *normal faults.* (See also *rift valley.*)

graded profile smoothly descending profile displayed by a *graded stream.*

graded stream *stream* (or *stream channel*) with *stream gradient* so adjusted as to achieve a balanced state in which average *bed load* transport is matched to average bed load input; an average condition over periods of many years' duration.

gradient degree of *slope,* as the gradient of a river or a flowing glacier.

granite *intrusive igneous rock* consisting largely of *quartz, potash feldspar,* and *plagioclase feldspar,* with minor amounts of biotite and hornblende; a *felsic igneous rock.*

granitic rock general term for *rock* of the upper layer of the *continental crust,* composed largely of *felsic igneous* and *metamorphic rock; rock* of composition similar to that of *granite.*

granular disintegration grain-by-grain breakup of the outer surface of coarse-grained *rock,* yielding *sand* and gravel and leaving behind rounded boulders.

graphic scale *map* scale as shown by a line divided into equal parts.

grassland biome *biome* consisting largely or entirely of *herbs,* which may include grasses, grass-like plants, and *forbs.*

gravitation mutual attraction between any two masses.

gravity gravitational attraction of the Earth upon any small mass near the Earth's surface. (See also *gravitation.*)

gravity gliding the sliding of a *thrust sheet* away from the center of an *orogen* under the force of *gravity.*

great circle circle formed by passing a plane through the exact center of a perfect sphere; the largest circle that can be drawn on the surface of a sphere.

greenhouse effect accumulation of heat in the lower *atmosphere* through the absorption of *longwave radiation* from the Earth's surface.

greenhouse gases atmospheric gases such as CO_2 and *chlorofluorocarbons (CFCs)* that absorb outgoing *longwave radiation,* contributing to the *greenhouse effect.*

groin wall or embankment built out into the water at right angles to the *shoreline.*

gross photosynthesis total amount of *carbohydrate* produced by *photosynthesis* by a given organism or group of organisms in a given unit of time.

ground ice frozen water within the pores of *soils* and *regolith* or as free bodies or lenses of solid ice.

ground moraine moraine formed of till distributed beneath a large expanse of land surface covered at one time by an ice sheet.

ground water *subsurface water* occupying the *saturated zone* and moving under the force of *gravity.*

growth rate (of a population) rate at which a population grows or shrinks with time; usually expressed as a percent or proportion of increase or decrease in a given unit of time.

gullies deep, V-shaped trenches carved by newly formed *streams* in rapid head-ward growth during advanced stages of *accelerated soil erosion.*

guyot sunken remnant of a volcanic island.

gyres large circular *ocean current* systems centered upon the oceanic subtropical *high-pressure cells.*

habitat subdivision of the environment according to the needs and preferences of organisms or groups of organisms.

Hadley cell atmospheric circulation cell in low latitudes involving rising air over the *equatorial trough* and sinking air over the *subtropical high-pressure belts.*

hail form of *precipitation* consisting of pellets or spheres of ice with a concentric layered structure.

half-life time required for an initial quantity at time-zero to be reduced by one-half in an exponential decay system.

hanging valley stream valley that has been truncated by marine erosion so as to appear in cross section in a *marine cliff,* or truncated by glacial erosion so as to appear in cross section in the upper wall of a *glacial trough.*

hazards assessment a field of study blending *physical* and *human geography* to focus on the perception of risk of natural hazards and on developing public policy to mitigate that risk.

haze minor concentration of *pollutants* or natural forms of *aerosols* in the atmosphere causing a reduction in visibility.

heat (See *latent heat, sensible heat.*)

heat island persistent region of higher air temperatures centered over a city.

hemisphere half of a sphere; that portion of the Earth's surface found between the *equator* and a pole.

herb tender plant, lacking woody stems, usually small or low; may be *annual* or *perennial.*

herbivory form of interaction among *species* in which an animal (herbivore) grazes on herbaceous plants.

heterosphere region of the *atmosphere* above about 100 km in which *gas* molecules tend to become increasingly sorted into layers by molecular weight and electric charge.

hibernation dormant state of some vertebrate animals during the winter season.

high base status (See *base status of soils.*)

high-latitude climates group of climates in the *subarctic zone, arctic zone,* and *polar zone,* dominated by arctic *air masses* and polar air masses.

high-level temperature inversion condition in which a high-level layer of warm air overlies a layer of cooler air, reversing the normal trend of cooling with altitude.

high-pressure cell center of high barometric pressure; an *anticyclone.*

Histosols *soil order* consisting of *soils* with a thick upper layer of organic matter.

hogbacks sharp-crested, often sawtooth ridges formed of the upturned edge of a resistant *rock* layer of *sandstone, limestone,* or *lava.*

Holocene Epoch last *epoch* of geologic time, commencing about 10,000 years ago; it followed the *Pleistocene Epoch* and includes the present.

homosphere the lower portion of the *atmosphere,* below about 100 km altitude, in which atmospheric *gases* are uniformly mixed.

horse latitudes *subtropical high-pressure belt* of the North Atlantic Ocean, coincident with the central region of the Azores high; a belt of weak, variable winds and frequent calms.

horst crustal block uplifted between two *normal faults.*

hot springs springs discharging heated *ground water* at a temperature close to the boiling point; found in geothermal areas and thought to be related to a *magma* body at depth.

hotspot (biogeography) geographic region of high biodiversity.

hotspot (plate tectonics) center of intrusive *igneous* and *volcanic* activity thought to be located over a rising *mantle plume.*

human habitat the lands of the Earth that support human life.

human geography the part of *systematic geography* that deals with social, economic and behavioral processes that differentiate *places.*

human-influenced vegetation vegetation that has been influenced in some way by human activity, for example, through cultivation, grazing, timber cutting, or urbanization.

humidity general term for the amount of *water vapor* present in the air. (See also *relative humidity, specific humidity*.)

humification *pedogenic process* of transformation of plant tissues into *humus*.

humus dark brown to black organic matter on or in the *soil*, consisting of fragmented plant tissues partly digested by organisms.

hurricane *tropical cyclone* of the western North Atlantic and Caribbean Sea.

hydraulic action *stream erosion* by impact force of the flowing water upon the bed and banks of the *stream channel*.

hydrograph graphic presentation of the variation in *stream discharge* with elapsed time, based on data of stream gauging at a given station on a stream.

hydrologic cycle total plan of movement, exchange, and storage of the Earth's free water in gaseous state, liquid state, and solid state.

hydrology science of the Earth's water and its motions through the *hydrologic cycle*.

hydrolysis chemical union of water molecules with *minerals* to form different, more stable mineral compounds.

hydrosphere total water realm of the Earth's surface zone, including the oceans, surface waters of the lands, *ground water*, and water held in the *atmosphere*.

hygrometer instrument that measures the *water vapor* content of the *atmosphere*; some types measure *relative humidity* directly.

ice age span of geologic time, usually on the order of one to three million years, or longer, in which glaciations alternate with interglaciations repeatedly in rhythm with cyclic global climate changes. (See also *glaciation, interglaciation*.)

Ice Age (Late-Cenozoic Ice Age) the present ice age, which began in late Pliocene time, perhaps 2.5 to 3 million years ago.

ice lens more-or-less horizontal layer of *segregated ice* formed by capillary movement of soil water toward a *freezing front*.

ice lobes (glacial lobes) broad tongue-like extensions of an *ice sheet*

resulting from more rapid ice motion where terrain was more favorable.

ice sheet large thick plate of glacial ice moving outward in all directions from a central region of accumulation.

ice sheet climate ⑬ severely cold climate, found on the Greenland and Antarctic *ice sheets*, with *potential evapotranspiration (water need)* effectively zero throughout the year.

ice shelf thick plate of floating glacial ice attached to an *ice sheet* and fed by the ice sheet and by *snow* accumulation.

ice storm occurrence of heavy glaze of ice on solid surfaces.

ice wedge vertical, wall-like body of ground ice, often tapering downward, occupying a shrinkage crack in *silt* of *permafrost* areas.

ice-wedge polygons polygonal networks of *ice wedges*.

iceberg mass of glacial ice floating in the ocean, derived from a glacier that extends into tidal water.

igneous rock *rock* solidified from a high-temperature molten state; *rock* formed by cooling of *magma*. (See also *extrusive igneous rock, felsic igneous rock, intrusive igneous rock, mafic igneous rock, ultramafic igneous rock*.)

illuviation accumulation in a lower *soil horizon* (typically, the *B horizon*) of materials brought down from a higher horizon; a soil-forming process.

image processing mathematical manipulation of digital images, for example, to enhance contrast or edges.

Inceptisols *soil order* consisting of soils having weakly developed *soil horizons* and containing weatherable *minerals*.

induced deflation loss of *soil* by wind erosion that is triggered by human activity such as cultivation or overgrazing.

induced mass wasting *mass wasting* that is induced by human activity, such as creation of waste *soil* and *rock* piles or undercutting of *slopes* in construction.

infiltration absorption and downward movement of *precipitation* into the *soil* and *regolith*.

infrared imagery images formed by *infrared radiation* emanating from the ground surface as recorded by a remote sensor.

infrared radiation *electromagnetic energy* in the *wavelength* range of 0.7 to about 200 μm.

initial landforms *landforms* produced directly by internal Earth processes of *volcanism* and *tectonic activity*. Examples: *volcano, fault scarp*.

inner lowland on a *coastal plain*, a shallow valley lying between the first *cuesta* and the area of older *rock* (oldland).

input flow of *matter* or *energy* into a system.

insolation interception of solar *energy (shortwave radiation)* by an exposed surface.

inspiral horizontal inward spiral or motion, such as that found in a *cyclone*.

interglaciation within an *ice age*, a time interval of mild global climate in which continental *ice sheets* were largely absent or were limited to the Greenland and Antarctic ice sheets; the interval between two glaciations. (See also *deglaciation, glaciation*.)

interlobate moraine *moraine* formed between two adjacent lobes of an *ice sheet*.

International Date Line the 180° *meridian of longitude*, together with deviations east and west of that meridian, forming the time boundary between adjacent *standard time zones* that are 12 hours fast and 12 hours slow with respect to Greenwich standard time.

interrupted projection projection subdivided into a number of sectors (gores), each of which is centered on a different central meridian.

intertropical convergence zone (ITCZ) zone of convergence of *air masses* of *tropical easterlies (trade winds)* along the axis of the *equatorial trough*.

intrusion body of *igneous rock* injected as *magma* into preexisting crustal *rock*; example: *dike* or *sill*.

intrusive igneous rock *igneous rock* body produced by solidification of *magma* beneath the surface, surrounded by preexisting *rock*.

inversion (See *temperature inversion*.)

ion atom or group of atoms bearing an electrical charge as the result of a gain or loss of one or more electrons.

island arcs curved lines of volcanic islands associated with active *subduc-*

tion zones along the boundaries of *lithospheric plates.*

isobars lines on *map* passing through all points having the same *atmospheric pressure.*

isohyet line on a *map* drawn through all points having the same numerical value of *precipitation.*

isopleth line on a *map* or globe drawn through all points having the same value of a selected property or entity.

isostasy principle describing the flotation of the *lithosphere,* which is less dense, on the plastic *asthenosphere,* which is more dense.

isostatic compensation crustal rise or sinking in response to unloading by *denudation* or loading by sediment deposition, following the principle of *isostasy.*

isostatic rebound local crustal rise after the melting of *ice sheets,* following the principle of *isostasy.*

isotherm line on a *map* drawn through all points having the same air temperature.

isotope form of an element with a unique *atomic mass number.*

jet stream high-speed air flow in narrow bands within the *upper-air westerlies* and along certain other global *latitude* zones at high levels.

joints fractures within *bedrock,* usually occurring in parallel and intersecting sets of planes.

Joule unit of work or energy in the metric system; symbol, J.

June solstice (See *summer solstice.*)

karst landscape or topography dominated by surface features of *limestone* solution and underlain by a *limestone cavern* system.

Kelvin scale (K) temperature scale on which the starting point is absolute zero, equivalent to –273°C.

kinetic energy form of *energy* represented by *matter* (mass) in motion.

knob and kettle terrain of numerous small knobs of *glacial drift* and deep depressions usually situated along the *moraine* belt of a former *ice sheet.*

knot measure of speed used in marine and aeronautical applications equal to one

nautical mile per hour (1 kt = 0.514 m/s = 1.15 mi/hr).

lag time interval of time between occurrence of precipitation and peak discharge of a *stream.*

lagoon shallow body of open water lying between a *barrier island* or a *barrier reef* and the mainland.

lahar rapid downslope or downvalley movement of a tongue-like mass of water-saturated *tephra* (volcanic ash) originating high up on a steep-sided volcanic cone; a variety of *mudflow.*

lake body of standing water that is enclosed on all sides by land.

laminar flow smooth, even flow of a *fluid* shearing in thin layers without *turbulence.*

land breeze local wind blowing from land to water during the night.

land degradation *degradation* of the quality of plant cover and *soil* as a result of overuse by humans and their domesticated animals, especially during periods of *drought.*

land mass large area of *continental crust* lying above sea level (base level) and thus available for removal by *denudation.*

land-mass rejuvenation episode of rapid fluvial *denudation* set off by a rapid crustal rise, increasing the available *land mass.*

landforms configurations of the land surface taking distinctive forms and produced by natural processes. Examples: hill, valley, plateau. (See also *depositional landform, erosional landforms, initial landforms, sequential landforms.*)

landslide rapid sliding of large masses of *bedrock* on steep mountain slopes or from high *cliffs.*

lapse rate rate at which temperature decreases with increasing altitude. (See also *dry adiabatic lapse rate, environmental temperature lapse rate, wet adiabatic lapse rate.*)

large-scale map *map* with *fractional scale* greater than 1:100,000; usually shows a small area.

Late-Cenozoic Ice Age the series of *glaciations, deglaciations,* and *interglaciations* experienced during the late *Cenozoic Era.*

latent heat heat absorbed and held in storage in a *gas* or *liquid* during the processes of *evaporation,* or *melting,* or *sublimation;* distinguished from *sensible heat.*

latent heat transfer flow of *latent heat* that results when water absorbs heat to change from a *liquid* or *solid* to a *gas* and then later releases that heat to new surroundings by *condensation* or *deposition.*

lateral moraine *moraine* forming an embankment between the ice of an *alpine glacier* and the adjacent valley wall.

laterite rock-like layer rich in *sequioxides* and iron, including the minerals *bauxite* and *limonite,* found in low latitudes in association with *Ultisols* and *Oxisols.*

latitude arc of a *meridian* between the *equator* and a given point on the globe.

Laurasia a *supercontinent* of the Permian *Period,* including much of the region that is now North America and western Eurasia.

lava *magma* emerging on the Earth's solid surface, exposed to air or water.

leaching *pedogenic process* in which material is lost from the *soil* by downward washing out and removal by percolating surplus soil water.

leads narrow strips of open ocean water between ice floes.

level of condensation elevation at which an upward-moving parcel of moist air cools to the *dew point* and *condensation* begins to occur.

liana woody vine supported on the trunk or branches of a *tree.*

lichens plant forms in which algae and fungi live together (in a symbiotic relationship) to create a single structure; they typically form tough, leathery coatings or crusts attached to *rocks* and *tree* trunks.

life cycle continuous progression of stages in a growth or development process, such as that of a living organism.

life form characteristic physical structure, size, and shape of a plant or of an assemblage of plants.

life layer shallow surface zone containing the *biosphere;* a zone of interaction between *atmosphere* and land surface, and between atmosphere and ocean surface.

life zones series of vegetation zones describing vegetation types that are encountered with increasing elevation, especially in the southwestern U.S.

lightning an electric *arc* passing between differently charged parts of a *cloud* mass or between the cloud and the ground.

limestone nonclastic *sedimentary rock* in which *calcite* is the predominant *mineral,* and with varying minor amounts of other minerals and *clay.*

limestone caverns interconnected subterranean cavities formed in *limestone* by *carbonic acid action* occurring in slowly moving *ground water.*

limnology study of the physical, chemical, and biological processes of lakes.

limonite mineral or group of *minerals* consisting largely of iron oxide and water, produced by *chemical weathering* of other iron-bearing minerals.

line type of *spatial object* in a *geographic information system* that has starting and ending *nodes;* may be directional.

liquid *fluid* that maintains a free upper surface and is only very slightly compressible, as compared with a *gas.*

lithosphere strong, brittle outermost *rock* layer of the Earth, lying above the *asthenosphere.*

lithospheric plate segment of *lithosphere* moving as a unit, in contact with adjacent lithospheric plates along plate boundaries.

littoral drift transport of *sediment* parallel with the *shoreline* by the combined action of *beach drift* and *longshore current* transport.

loam soil-texture class in which no one of the three size grades *(sand, silt, clay)* dominates over the other two.

local scale scale of observation of the Earth in which local processes and phenomena are observed.

local winds general term for *winds* generated as direct or immediate effects of the local terrain.

loess accumulation of yellowish to buff-colored, fine-grained *sediment,* largely of *silt* grade, upon upland surfaces after transport in the air in *turbulent suspension* (i.e., carried in a *dust storm*).

logistic growth growth according to a mathematical model in which the *growth rate* eventually decreases to near zero.

longitude *arc* of a parallel between the *prime meridian* and a given point on the globe.

longitudinal dunes class of *sand dunes* in which the dune ridges are oriented parallel with the prevailing wind.

longshore current current in the breaker zone, running parallel with the *shoreline* and set up by the oblique approach of waves.

longshore drift *littoral drift* caused by action of a *longshore current.*

longwave radiation *electromagnetic energy* emitted by the Earth, largely in the range from 3 to 50 μm.

low base status (See *base status of soils.*)

low-angle overthrust fault *overthrust fault* in which the *fault plane* or fault surface has a low angle of *dip* or may be horizontal.

low-latitude climates group of climates of the *equatorial zone* and *tropical zone* dominated by the subtropical high-pressure belt and the *equatorial trough.*

low-latitude rainforest evergreen broadleaf forest of the wet equatorial and tropical climate zones.

low-latitude rainforest environment low-latitude environment of warm temperatures and abundant *precipitation* that characterizes rainforest in the *wet equatorial* ① and *monsoon and trade-wind coastal* ② climates.

low-level temperature inversion atmospheric condition in which temperature near the ground increases, rather than decreases, with elevation.

low pressure trough weak, elongated *cyclone* of clouds and showers resulting from surface *convergence* generated by *divergence* aloft.

lowlands broad, open valleys between two *cuestas* of a *coastal plain.* (The term may refer to any low areas of land surface.)

Luvisolic order a class of *forest soils* in the Canadian soil classification system in which the *B horizon* accumulates *clay.*

mafic igneous rock *igneous rock* dominantly composed of *mafic minerals.*

mafic minerals (mafic mineral group) *minerals,* largely *silicate minerals,* rich in magnesium and iron, dark in color, and of relatively great density.

magma mobile, high-temperature molten state of *rock,* usually of *silicate mineral* composition and with dissolved *gases.*

manipulation and analysis component component of a *geographic information system* that responds to spatial queries and creates new data layers.

mantle *rock* layer or shell of the Earth beneath the *crust* and surrounding the *core,* composed of *ultramafic igneous rock* of *silicate mineral* composition.

mantle plume a column-like rising of heated *mantle rock,* thought to be the cause of a *hotspot* in the overlying *lithospheric plate.*

map a paper representation of space showing point, line, or area data.

map projection any orderly system of parallels and meridians drawn on a flat surface to represent the Earth's curved surface.

marble variety of *metamorphic rock* derived from *limestone* or dolomite by recrystallization under pressure.

marine cliff *rock* cliff shaped and maintained by the undermining action of breaking waves.

marine scarp steep seaward *slope* in poorly consolidated *alluvium, glacial drift,* or other forms of *regolith,* produced along a coastline by the undermining action of waves.

marine terrace former *abrasion platform* elevated to become a step-like coastal *landform.*

marine west-coast climate ⑧ cool moist climate of west coasts in the *midlatitude zone,* usually with a substantial annual *water surplus* and a distinct winter *precipitation* maximum.

mass number (See *atomic mass number.*)

mass wasting spontaneous downhill movement of *soil, regolith,* and *bedrock* under the influence of *gravity,* rather than by the action of *fluid* agents.

massive icy beds layers of ice-rich sediment, found in *permafrost* regions, formed by upwelling *ground water* that flows to a freezing front.

material cycle a closed matter flow system in which matter flows endlessly, powered by energy inputs (See also *biogeochemical cycle.*)

mathematical modeling using variables and equations to represent real processes and systems.

mathematical and statistical models in the *representation* perspective of *geography*, the use of mathematical and statistical models to predict spatial phenomena.

matter physical substance that has mass and density.

matter flow system total system of *pathways* by which a particular type of *matter* (a given element, compound, or ion, for example) moves through the Earth's *ecosystem* or *biosphere*.

mean annual temperature mean of daily air temperature means for a given year or succession of years.

mean daily temperature sum of daily maximum and minimum air temperature readings divided by two.

mean monthly temperature mean of daily air temperature means for a given calendar month.

mean velocity mean, or average, speed of flow of water through an entire stream cross section.

meanders (See *alluvial meanders*.)

mechanical energy *energy* of motion or position; includes *kinetic energy* and *potential energy*.

mechanical weathering (See *physical weathering*.)

medial moraine long, narrow deposit of fragments on the surface of a *glacier*; created by the merging of *lateral moraines* when two glaciers join into a single stream of ice flow.

Mediterranean climate ⑦ climate type of the *subtropical zone*, characterized by the alternation of a very dry summer and a mild, rainy winter.

melting change from solid state to liquid state, accompanied by absorption of *sensible heat* to become *latent heat*.

Mercator projection conformal *map projection* with horizontal parallels and vertical meridians and with *map scale* rapidly increasing with increase in *latitude*.

mercury barometer *barometer* using the Torricelli principle, in which *atmospheric pressure* counterbalances a column of mercury in a tube.

meridian of longitude north–south line on the surface of the global *oblate ellipsoid*, connecting the *north pole* and *south pole*.

meridional transport flow of *energy* (heat) or *matter* (water) across the *parallels of latitude*, either poleward or equatorward.

mesa table-topped *plateau* of comparatively small extent bounded by *cliffs* and occurring in a region of flat-lying *strata*.

mesopause upper limit of the *mesosphere*.

mesosphere atmospheric layer of upwardly diminishing temperature, situated above the *stratopause* and below the *mesopause*.

Mesozoic Era second of three geologic eras following *Precambrian time*.

metamorphic rock *rock* altered in physical structure and/or chemical *(mineral)* composition by action of heat, pressure, *shearing* stress, or infusion of elements, all taking place at substantial depth beneath the surface.

meteorology science of the *atmosphere*; particularly the physics of the lower or inner atmosphere.

mica group aluminum-silicate *mineral* group of complex chemical formula having perfect cleavage into thin sheets.

microburst brief onset of intense *winds* close to the ground beneath the downdraft zone of a *thunderstorm* cell.

microcontinent fragment of *continental crust* and its *lithosphere* of subcontinental dimensions that is embedded in an expanse of *oceanic lithosphere*.

micrometer metric unit of length equal to one-millionth of a meter (0. 000001 m); abbreviated μm.

microwaves waves of the *electromagnetic radiation* spectrum in the *wavelength* band from about 0.03 cm to about 1 cm.

midlatitude climates group of climates of the *midlatitude zone* and *subtropical zone*, located in the *polar front zone* and dominated by both tropical *air masses* and polar air masses.

midlatitude deciduous forest plant *formation class* within the *forest biome* dominated by tall, broadleaf deciduous *trees*, found mostly in the *moist continental climate* ⑩ and *marine west-coast climate* ⑧.

midlatitude zones latitude zones occupying the *latitude* range 35° to 55° N and S (more or less) and lying between the *subtropical zones* and the *subarctic (subantarctic) zones*.

midoceanic ridge one of three major divisions of the ocean basins, being the central belt of submarine mountain topography with a characteristic *axial rift*.

millibar unit of *atmospheric pressure*; one-thousandth of a bar. *Bar* is a force of one million dynes per square centimeter.

mineral naturally occurring inorganic substance, usually having a definite chemical composition and a characteristic atomic structure. (See also *felsic minerals, mafic minerals, silicate minerals*.)

mineral alteration chemical change of *minerals* to more stable compounds upon exposure to atmospheric conditions; same as *chemical weathering*.

mineral matter (soils) component of *soil* consisting of weathered or unweathered mineral grains.

mineral oxides (soils) secondary *minerals* found in *soils* in which original minerals have been altered by chemical combination with oxygen.

minute (of arc) 1/60 of a degree.

mistral local drainage wind of cold air affecting the Rhone Valley of southern France.

Moho contact surface between the Earth's *crust* and *mantle*; a contraction of Mohorovic, the name of the seismologist who discovered this feature.

moist continental climate ⑩ moist climate of the *midlatitude zone* with strongly defined winter and summer seasons, adequate *precipitation* throughout the year, and a substantial annual *water surplus*.

moist subtropical climate ⑥ moist climate of the *subtropical zone*, characterized by a moderate to large annual *water surplus* and a strongly seasonal cycle of *potential evapotranspiration (water need)*.

mollic epipedon relatively thick, dark-colored surface *soil horizon*, containing substantial amounts of organic matter *(humus)* and usually rich in *bases*.

Mollisols *soil order* consisting of *soils* with a *mollic horizon* and high base status.

monadnock prominent, isolated mountain or large hill rising conspicuously above a surrounding *peneplain* and composed of a *rock* more resistant than that underlying the peneplain; a *landform* of *denudation* in moist climates.

monsoon and trade-wind coastal climate ② moist climate of low latitudes showing a strong rainfall peak in the season of high Sun and a short period of reduced rainfall.

monsoon forest *formation class* within the *forest biome* consisting in part of deciduous *trees* adapted to a long dry season in the *wet–dry tropical climate* ③.

monsoon system system of low-level *winds* blowing into a continent in summer and out of it in winter, controlled by *atmospheric pressure* systems developed seasonally over the continent.

montane forest plant *formation class* of the *forest biome* found in cool upland environments of the *tropical zone* and *equatorial zone*.

moraine accumulation of *rock* debris carried by an *alpine glacier* or an *ice sheet* and deposited by the ice to become a *depositional landform*. (See also *lateral moraine, terminal moraine*.)

morphology the outward form and appearance of individual organisms or *species*.

mountain arc curving section of an *alpine chain* occurring on a *converging boundary* between two crustal plates.

mountain roots erosional remnants of deep portions of ancient *continental sutures* that were once *alpine chains*.

mountain winds daytime movements of air up the *gradient* of valleys and mountain slopes; alternating with nocturnal *valley winds*.

mucks organic *soils* largely composed of fine, black, sticky organic matter.

mud *sediment* consisting of a mixture of *clay* and *silt* with water, often with minor amounts of *sand* and sometimes with organic matter.

mud hummock low mound of earth found in *permafrost* terrain, formed by cycles of *ground ice* growth and melting, with center of bare ground; vegetation may occur at edges (see also *earth hummock*).

mudflow a form of *mass wasting* consisting of the downslope flowage of a mixture of water and *mineral* fragments (*soil, regolith,* disintegrated *bedrock*), usually following a natural drainage line or *stream channel*.

mudstone *sedimentary rock* formed by the lithification of *mud*.

multipurpose map *map* containing several different types of information.

multispectral image image consisting of two or more images, each of which is taken from a different portion of the spectrum (e.g., blue, green, red, infrared).

multispectral scanner *remote sensing* instrument, flown on an aircraft or spacecraft, that simultaneously collects multiple *digital images (multispectral images)* of the ground. Typically, images are collected in four or more spectral bands.

mutation change in genetic material of a reproductive cell.

nappe overturned recumbent *fold* of *strata*, usually associated with *thrust sheets* in a collision *orogen*.

natural bridge natural *rock* arch spanning a *stream channel*, formed by cutoff of an *entrenched meander* bend.

natural flow systems flow systems of *energy* or naturally occurring substances that are powered largely or completely by natural power sources.

natural gas naturally occurring mixture of hydrocarbon compounds (principally methane) in the gaseous state held within certain porous *rocks*.

natural levee belt of higher ground paralleling a meandering *alluvial river* on both sides of the *stream channel* and built up by *deposition* of fine *sediment* during periods of overbank flooding.

natural selection selection of organisms by environment in a process similar to selection of plants or animals for breeding by agriculturalists.

natural vegetation stable, mature plant cover characteristic of a given area of land surface largely free from the influences and impacts of human activities.

needleleaf evergreen forest *needleleaf forest* composed of evergreen tree species, such as spruce, fir, and pine.

needleleaf forest plant *formation class* within the *forest biome,* consisting largely of needleleaf *trees*. (See also *boreal forest*.)

needleleaf tree *tree* with long, thin or flat leaves, such as pine, fir, larch, or spruce.

negative exponential mathematical form of a curve that smoothly decreases to approach a steady value, usually zero.

negative feedback in flow systems, a linkage between flow paths such that the flow in one *pathway* acts to reduce the flow in another pathway. (See also *feedback, positive feedback*.)

net photosynthesis *carbohydrate* production remaining in an organism after *respiration* has broken down sufficient carbohydrate to power the metabolism of the organism.

net primary production rate at which *carbohydrate* is accumulated in the tissues of plants within a given *ecosystem;* units are kilograms of dry organic matter per year per square meter of surface area.

net radiation difference in intensity between all incoming *energy* (positive quantity) and all outgoing energy (negative quantity) carried by both *shortwave radiation* and *longwave radiation*.

neutron atomic particle contained within the nucleus of an atom; similar in mass to a *proton,* but without a magnetic charge.

nitrogen cycle *biogeochemical cycle* in which nitrogen moves through the *biosphere* by the processes of *nitrogen fixation* and *denitrification*.

nitrogen fixation chemical process of conversion of *gaseous* molecular nitrogen of the *atmosphere* into compounds or *ions* that can be directly utilized by plants; a process carried out within the *nitrogen cycle* by certain microorganisms.

node point marking the end of a *line* or the intersection of lines as *spatial objects* in a *geographic information system*

noon (See *solar noon*.)

noon angle (of the Sun) angle of the Sun above the horizon at its highest point during the day.

normal fault variety of *fault* in which the *fault plane* inclines *(dips)* toward the downthrown block and a major component of the motion is vertical.

north pole point at which the northern end of the Earth's *axis of rotation* intersects the Earth's surface.

northeast trade winds surface *winds* of low *latitudes* that blow steadily from the northeast. (See also *trade winds*.)

nuclei (atmospheric) minute particles of solid *matter* suspended in the *atmosphere* and serving as cores for *condensation* of water or ice.

nutrient cycle (See *biogeochemical cycle.*)

O₁ horizon surface *soil horizon* containing decaying *organic matter* that is recognizable as leaves, twigs, or other organic structures.

Oₐ horizon *soil horizon* below the O₁ horizon containing decaying *organic matter* that is too decomposed to recognize as specific plant parts, such as leaves or twigs.

oasis desert area where *ground water* is tapped for crop irrigation and human needs.

oblate ellipsoid geometric *solid* resembling a flattened sphere, with polar axis shorter than the equatorial diameter.

occluded front weather *front* along which a moving *cold front* has overtaken a *warm front*, forcing the warm *air mass* aloft.

ocean basin floors one of the major divisions of the ocean basins, comprising the deep portions consisting of *abyssal plains* and low hills.

ocean current persistent, dominantly horizontal flow of ocean water.

ocean tide periodic rise and fall of the ocean level induced by gravitational attraction between the Earth and Moon in combination with Earth *rotation*.

oceanic crust crust of basaltic composition beneath the ocean floors, capping *oceanic lithosphere*. (See also *continental crust.*)

oceanic lithosphere *lithosphere* bearing *oceanic crust*.

oceanic trench narrow, deep depression in the seafloor representing the line of *subduction* of an oceanic *lithospheric plate* beneath the margin of a continental lithospheric plate; often associated with an *island arc*.

oil sand (See *bituminous sand.*)

old-field succession form of *secondary succession* typical of an abandoned field, such as might be found in eastern or central North America.

olivine *silicate mineral* with magnesium and iron but no aluminum, usually olive-green or grayish-green; a *mafic mineral*.

open flow system system of interconnected flow paths of *energy* and/or *matter* with a boundary through which that *energy* and/or *matter* can enter and leave the system.

organic matter (soils) material in *soil* that was originally produced by plants or animals and has been subjected to decay.

Organic order a class of *soils* in the Canadian soil classification system that is composed largely of organic materials.

organic sediment *sediment* consisting of the organic remains of plants or animals.

orogen the mass of tectonically deformed *rocks* and related *igneous rocks* produced during an *orogeny*.

orogeny major episode of *tectonic activity* resulting in *strata* being deformed by *folding* and faulting.

orographic pertaining to mountains.

orographic precipitation *precipitation* induced by the forced rise of moist air over a mountain barrier.

oscillatory wave type of wave that generates a oscillating motion of mass as the wave passes through the medium; water waves are of this type.

outcrop surface exposure of *bedrock*.

output the flow of *matter* or *energy* out of a system.

outspiral horizontal outward spiral or motion, such as that found in an *anticyclone*.

outwash glacial deposit of stratified drift left by *braided streams* issuing from the front of a *glacier*.

outwash plain flat, gently sloping plain built up of *sand* and gravel by the *aggradation* of meltwater *streams* in front of the margin of an *ice sheet*.

overburden *strata* overlying a layer or *stratum* of interest, as overburden above a *coal* seam.

overland flow motion of a surface layer of water over a sloping ground surface at times when the *infiltration* rate is exceeded by the *precipitation* rate; a form of *runoff*.

overthrust fault *fault* characterized by the overriding of one crustal block (or *thrust sheet*) over another along a gently inclined *fault plane*; associated with crustal *compression*.

ox-bow lake crescent-shaped lake representing the abandoned channel left by the *cutoff* of an *alluvial meander*.

oxidation chemical union of free oxygen with metallic elements in *minerals*.

oxide chemical compound containing oxygen; in *soils*, iron oxides and aluminum oxides are examples.

Oxisols *soil order* consisting of very old, highly weathered *soils* of low *latitudes*, with an oxic horizon and low *base status*.

oxygen cycle *biogeochemical cycle* in which oxygen moves through the *biosphere* in both *gaseous* and *sedimentary* forms.

ozone a form of oxygen with a molecule consisting of three atoms of oxygen, O_3.

ozone layer layer in the *stratosphere*, mostly in the altitude range 20 to 35 km (12 to 31 mi), in which a concentration of *ozone* is produced by the action of solar *ultraviolet radiation*.

pack ice floating *sea ice* that completely covers the sea surface.

Paleozoic Era first of three geologic *eras* comprising all geologic time younger than *Precambrian time*.

Pangea hypothetical parent continent, enduring until near the close of the *Mesozoic Era*, consisting of the *continental shields* of *Laurasia* and *Gondwana* joined into a single unit.

parabolic dunes isolated low *sand dunes* of parabolic outline, with points directed into the prevailing *wind*.

parallel of latitude east-west circle on the Earth's surface, lying in a plane parallel with the *equator* and at right angles to the *axis of rotation*.

parasitism form of negative interaction between *species* in which a small species (parasite) feeds on a larger one (host) without necessarily killing it.

parent material inorganic, *mineral* base from which the *soil* is formed; usually consists of *regolith*.

particulates *solid* and *liquid* particles capable of being suspended for long periods in the *atmosphere*.

pascal metric unit of pressure, defined as a force of one newton per square meter (1 N/m²); symbol, Pa; 100 Pa = 1 mb, 10^5 Pa = 1 bar.

passive continental margins continental margins lacking active plate boundaries at the contact of *continental* *crust* with *oceanic crust*. A passive margin thus lies within a single *lithospheric plate*. Example: Atlantic continental margin of North America. (See also *active continental margins, continental margins.*)

passive systems electromagnetic remote sensing systems that measure radiant *energy* reflected or emitted by an object or surface.

pathway in an *energy flow system*, a mechanism by which *matter* or *energy* flows from one part of the system to another.

patterned ground general term for a ground surface that bears polygonal or ring-like features, including stone circles, nets, polygons, steps, and stripes; includes *ice wedge polygons*; typically produced by *frost action* in cold climates.

peat partially decomposed, compacted accumulation of plant remains occurring in a *bog* environment.

ped individual natural *soil* aggregate.

pediment gently sloping, rock-floored land surface found at the base of a mountain mass or *cliff* in an arid region.

pedogenic processes group of recognized basic soil-forming processes, mostly involving the gain, loss, *translocation*, or transformation of materials within the *soil* body.

pedology science of the *soil* as a natural surface layer capable of supporting living plants; synonymous with *soil science*.

peneplain land surface of low elevation and slight relief produced in the late stages of *denudation* of a *land mass*.

perched water table surface of a lens of *ground water* held above the main body of ground water by a discontinuous impervious layer.

percolation slow, downward flow of water by *gravity* through *soil* and subsurface layers toward the *water table*.

perennials plants that live for more than one growing season.

peridotite *igneous rock* consisting largely of olivine and pyroxene; an *ultramafic igneous rock* occurring as a *pluton*, also thought to compose much of the upper *mantle*.

periglacial in an environment of intense *frost action*, located in cold climate regions or near the margins of *alpine glaciers* or large *ice sheets*.

periglacial system a distinctive set of landforms and land-forming processes that are created by intense *frost action*.

perihelion point on the Earth's elliptical orbit at which the Earth is nearest to the Sun.

period of geologic time time subdivision of the *era*, each ranging in duration between about 35 and 70 million years.

permafrost *soil, regolith*, and *bedrock* at a temperature below 0°C (32°F), found in cold climates of arctic, subarctic, and alpine regions.

permafrost table in *permafrost*, the upper surface of perennially frozen ground; lower surface of the *active layer*.

petroleum (crude oil) natural *liquid* mixture of many complex hydrocarbon compounds of organic origin, found in accumulations (oil pools) within certain *sedimentary rocks*.

pH measure of the concentration of hydrogen *ions* in a solution. (The number represents the logarithm to the base 10 of the reciprocal of the weight in grams of hydrogen *ions* per liter of water.) Acid solutions have pH values less than 6, and basic solutions have pH values greater than 6.

phenotype the morphological expression of the *genotype* of an individual. It includes all the physical aspects of its structure that are readily perceivable.

photoperiod duration of daylight on a given day of the year at a given *latitude*.

photosynthesis production of *carbohydrate* by the union of water with *carbon dioxide* while absorbing light *energy*.

phreatophytes plants that draw water from the *ground water table* beneath *alluvium* of dry *stream channels* and valley floors in desert regions.

phylum highest division of higher plant and animal life.

physical geography the part of *systematic geography* that deals with the natural processes occurring at the Earth's surface that provide the physical setting for human activities; includes the broad fields of *climatology, geomorphology, coastal and marine geography, geography of soils*, and *biogeography*.

physical weathering breakup of massive *rock (bedrock)* into small particles through the action of physical forces acting at or near the Earth's surface. (See also *weathering*.)

phytoplankton microscopic plants found largely in the uppermost layer of ocean or lake water.

pingo conspicuous conical mound or circular hill, having a core of ice, found on plains of the *arctic tundra* where *permafrost* is present.

pioneer plants plants that first invade an environment of new land or a *soil* that has been cleared of vegetation cover; often these are annual *herbs*.

pioneer stage first stage of an *ecological succession*.

place in *geography*, a location on the Earth's surface, typically a settlement or small region with unique characteristics; in the *viewpoint* perspective of *geography*, a focus on how processes are integrated at a single location or within a single region.

plagioclase feldspar aluminum-silicate *mineral* with sodium or calcium or both.

plane of the ecliptic imaginary plane in which the Earth's orbit lies.

plant ecology the study of the relationships between plants and their environment.

plant nutrients *ions* or chemical compounds that are needed for plant growth.

plate tectonics theory of *tectonic activity* dealing with *lithospheric plates* and their activity.

plateau upland surface, more or less flat and horizontal, upheld by resistant beds of *sedimentary rock* or *lava* flows and bounded by a steep *cliff*.

playa flat land surface underlain by fine *sediment* or evaporite minerals deposited from shallow lake waters in a dry climate in the floor of a closed topographic depression.

Pleistocene Epoch *epoch* of the *Cenozoic Era*, often identified as the *Ice Age*; it preceded the *Holocene Epoch*.

plinthite iron-rich concentrations present in some kinds of *soils* in deeper *soil horizons* and capable of hardening into rock-like material with repeated wetting and drying.

plucking (See *glacial plucking*.)

pluton any body of *intrusive igneous rock* that has solidified below the surface, enclosed in preexisting *rock*.

pocket beach *beach* of crescentic outline located at a *bay* head.

podzol type of *soil order* closely equivalent to *Spodosol;* an order of the Canadian Soil Classification System.

Podzolic order a class of *forest* and heath *soils* in the Canadian soil classification system in which an amorphous material of humified organic matter with Al and Fe accumulates.

point *spatial object* in a *geographic information system* with no area.

point bar deposit of coarse bed-load *alluvium* accumulated on the inside of a growing *alluvial meander.*

polar easterlies system of easterly surface winds at high *latitude,* best developed in the southern *hemisphere,* over Antarctica.

polar front *front* lying between cold polar *air masses* and warm tropical *air masses,* often situated along a *jet stream* within the *upper-air westerlies.*

polar front jet stream *jet stream* found along the *polar front,* where cold polar air and warm tropical air are in contact.

polar front zone broad zone in midlatitudes and higher latitudes, occupied by the shifting *polar front.*

polar high persistent low-level center of high *atmospheric pressure* located over the *polar zone* of Antarctica.

polar outbreak tongue of cold polar air, preceded by a *cold front,* penetrating far into the *tropical zone* and often reaching the *equatorial zone;* it brings rain squalls and unusual cold.

polar projection *map projection* centered on Earth's *north pole* or *south pole.*

polar zones *latitude* zones lying between 75° and 90° N and S.

poleward heat transport movement of heat from equatorial and tropical regions toward the poles, occurring as *latent* and *sensible heat transfer.*

pollutants in air pollution studies, foreign matter injected into the lower *atmosphere* as *particulates* or as chemical pollutant *gases.*

pollution dome broad, low dome-shaped layer of polluted air, formed over an urban area at times when winds are weak or calm prevails.

pollution plume (1) the trace or path of pollutant substances, moving along the flow paths of *ground water.* (2) trail of polluted air carried downwind from a pollution source by strong winds.

polygon type of *spatial object* in a *geographic information system* with a closed chain of connected *lines* surrounding an area.

polypedon smallest distinctive geographic unit of the *soil* of a given area.

polyploidy mechanism of *speciation* in which entire chromosome sets of organisms are doubled, tripled, quadrupled, etc.

pool in flow systems, an area or location of concentration of *matter.* (See also *active pool, storage pool.*)

positive feedback in flow systems, a linkage between flow paths such that the flow in one *pathway* acts to increase the flow in another *pathway.* (See also *feedback, negative feedback.*)

potash feldspar aluminum-silicate *mineral* with potassium the dominant metal.

potential energy *energy* of position; produced by *gravitational* attraction of the Earth's mass for a smaller mass on or near the Earth's surface.

potential evapotranspiration (water need) ideal or hypothetical rate of *evapotranspiration* estimated to occur from a complete canopy of green foliage of growing plants continuously supplied with all the *soil water* they can use; a real condition reached in those situations where *precipitation* is sufficiently great or irrigation water is supplied in sufficient amounts.

pothole cylindrical cavity in hard *bedrock* of a *stream channel* produced by *abrasion* of a rounded *rock* fragment rotating within the cavity.

power source flow of *energy* into a *flow system* that causes *matter* to move.

prairie plant *formation class* of the *grassland biome,* consisting of dominant tall grasses and subdominant *forbs,* widespread in subhumid continental climate regions of the *subtropical zone* and *midlatitude zone.* (See also *short-grass prairie, tall-grass prairie.*)

Precambrian time all of geologic time older than the beginning of the Cambrian Period, i.e., older than 600 million years.

precipitation particles of *liquid* water or ice that fall from the *atmosphere* and may reach the ground. (See also *convec-* *tional precipitation, cyclonic precipitation, orographic precipitation.*)

predation form of negative interaction among animal *species* in which one species (predator) kills and consumes the other (prey).

preprocessing component component of a *geographic information system* that prepares data for entry to the system.

pressure gradient change of *atmospheric pressure* measured along a line at right angles to the *isobars.*

pressure gradient force force acting horizontally, tending to move air in the direction of lower *atmospheric pressure.*

prevailing westerly winds (westerlies) surface winds blowing from a generally westerly direction in the *midlatitude zone,* but varying greatly in direction and intensity.

primary consumers organisms at the lowest level of the *food chain* that ingest *primary producers* or *decomposers* as their *energy* source.

primary minerals in *pedology (soil science),* the original, unaltered *silicate minerals* of *igneous rocks* and *metamorphic rocks.*

primary producers organisms that use light *energy* to convert *carbon dioxide* and water to *carbohydrates* through the process of *photosynthesis.*

primary succession *ecological succession* that begins on a newly constructed substrate.

prime meridian reference *meridian* of zero *longitude;* universally accepted as the Greenwich meridian.

product generation component component of a *geographic information system* that provides output products such as maps, images, or tabular reports.

progradation shoreward building of a *beach, bar,* or *sandspit* by addition of coarse *sediment* carried by *littoral drift* or brought from deeper water offshore.

proton positively charged particle within the nucleus of a atom.

pyroxene group complex aluminum-silicate *minerals* rich in calcium, magnesium, and iron, dark in color, high in density, classed as *mafic minerals.*

quartz mineral of silicon dioxide composition.

quartzite *metamorphic rock* consisting largely of the mineral *quartz*.

quick clays *clay* layers that spontaneously change from a solid condition to a near-liquid condition when disturbed.

radar an active *remote sensing* system in which a pulse of radiation is emitted by an instrument, and the strength of the echo of the pulse is recorded.

radial drainage pattern stream pattern consisting of *streams* radiating outward from a central peak or highland, such as a *sedimentary dome* or a *volcano*.

radiant energy transfer net flow of radiant *energy* between an object and its surroundings.

radiation (See *electromagnetic radiation*.)

radiation balance condition of balance between incoming *energy* of solar *shortwave radiation* and outgoing *longwave radiation* emitted by the Earth into space.

radiation fog *fog* produced by radiation cooling of the basal air layer.

radioactive decay spontaneous change in the nucleus of an atom that leads to the emission of *matter* and *energy*.

radiogenic heat heat from the Earth's interior that is slowly released by the *radioactive decay* of *unstable isotopes*.

radiometric dating a method of determining the geologic age of a *rock* or *mineral* by measuring the proportions of certain of its elements in their different isotopic forms.

rain form of *precipitation* consisting of falling water drops, usually 0.5 mm or larger in diameter.

rain gauge instrument used to measure the amount of *rain* that has fallen.

rain shadow belt of arid climate to lee of a mountain barrier, produced as a result of adiabatic warming of descending air.

rain-green vegetation vegetation that puts out green foliage in the wet season but becomes largely dormant in the dry season; found in the *tropical zone,* it includes the *savanna biome* and *monsoon forest*.

raised shoreline former *shoreline* lifted above the limit of wave action; also called an elevated *shoreline*.

rapids steep-*gradient* reaches of a *stream channel* in which *stream* velocity is high.

recessional moraine *moraine* produced at the ice margin during a temporary halt in the recessional phase of *deglaciation*.

reclamation in *strip mining,* the process of restoring *spoil* banks and ridges to a natural condition.

recombination source of variation in organisms arising from the free interchange of *alleles* of genes during the reproduction process.

recumbent overturned, as a folded sequence of *rock* layers in which the *folds* are doubled back upon themselves.

reflection outward scattering of *radiation* toward space by the *atmosphere* and/or Earth's surface.

reg desert surface armored with a pebble layer, resulting from long-continued *deflation;* found in the Sahara Desert of North Africa.

regional geography that branch of *geography* concerned with how the Earth's surface is differentiated into unique *places*.

regional scale the scale of observation at which subcontinental regions are discernible.

regolith layer of *mineral* particles overlying the *bedrock;* may be derived by *weathering* of underlying bedrock or be transported from other locations by *fluid* agents. (See also *residual regolith, transported regolith*.)

Regosolic order a class of *soils* in the Canadian soil classification system that exhibits weakly developed *horizons*.

relative humidity ratio of *water vapor* present in the air to the maximum quantity possible for *saturated air* at the same temperature.

relative variability ratio of a variability measure, such as the average deviation, to the mean of all observations.

remote sensing measurement of some property of an object or surface by means other than direct contact; usually refers to the gathering of scientific information about the Earth's surface from great heights and over broad areas, using instruments mounted on aircraft or orbiting space vehicles.

remote sensor instrument or device measuring *electromagnetic radiation* reflected or emitted from a target body.

removal in soil science, the set of processes that result in the removal of material from a *soil horizon,* such as surface erosion or *leaching*.

representation a perspective of *geography* that concerns developing and manipulating tools for the display and analysis of spatial information.

representative fraction (R.F.) (See *scale fraction*.)

residual regolith *regolith* formed in place by alteration of the *bedrock* directly beneath it.

resolution on a *map,* power to resolve small objects present on the ground.

respiration the oxidation of organic compounds by organisms that powers bodily functions.

retrogradation cutting back (retreat) of a *shoreline, beach, marine cliff,* or *marine scarp* by wave action.

retrogressive thaw slump slump and flowage of overlying *sediment* occurring where erosion exposes ice-rich *permafrost* or massive *ground ice* to thawing.

reverse fault type of *fault* in which one fault block rides up over the other on a steep *fault plane*.

revolution motion of a planet in its orbit around the Sun, or of a planetary satellite around a planet.

rhyolite *extrusive igneous rock* of *granite* composition; it occurs as *lava* or *tephra*.

ria coastal embayment or *estuary*.

ria coast deeply embayed *coast* formed by partial *submergence* of a *land mass* previously shaped by fluvial *denudation*.

Richter scale scale of magnitude numbers describing the quantity of *energy* released by an *earthquake*.

ridge-and-valley landscape assemblage of *landforms* developed by *denudation* of a system of open *folds* of *strata* and consisting of long, narrow ridges and valleys arranged in parallel or zigzag patterns.

rift valley trench-like valley with steep, parallel sides; essentially a *graben* between two *normal faults;* associated with crustal spreading.

rill erosion form of *accelerated erosion* in which numerous, closely spaced miniature channels (rills) are scored into the surface of exposed *soil* or *regolith*.

rock   natural aggregate of *minerals* in the solid state; usually hard and consisting of one, two, or more *mineral* varieties.

rock terrace   terrace carved in *bedrock* during the *degradation* of a *stream channel* induced by the crustal rise or a fall of the sea level. (See also *alluvial terrace, marine terrace.*)

rockslide   *landslide* of jumbled *bedrock* fragments.

Rodinia   early *supercontinent,* predating *Pangea,* that was fully formed about 700 million years ago.

Rossby waves   horizontal undulations in the flow path of thc *upper-air westerlies;* also known as upper-air waves.

rotation   spinning of an object around an axis.

runoff   flow of water from continents to oceans by way of *stream flow* and *ground water* flow; a term in the water balance of the *hydrologic cycle.* In a more restricted sense, runoff refers to surface flow by *overland flow* and channel flow.

Sahel (Sahelian zones)   belt of *wet–dry tropical* ③ and *semiarid dry tropical* ④ climate in Africa in which *precipitation* is highly variable from year to year.

salic horizon   *soil horizon* enriched by soluble salts.

salinity   degree of "saltiness" of water; refers to the abundance of such ions as sodium, calcium, potassium, chloride, fluoride, sulfate, and carbonate.

salinization   precipitation of soluble salts within the *soil.*

salt flat   shallow basin covered with salt deposits formed when stream input to the basin is evaporated to dryness from the basin of a *lake*; may also form by evaporation of a saline lake when climate changes; see also *dry lake.*

salt marsh   *peat*-covered expanse of *sediment* built up to the level of high tide over a previously formed tidal mud flat.

salt water intrusion   occurs in a coastal well when an upper layer of fresh water is pumped out, leaving a saltwater layer below to feed the well.

salt-crystal growth   a form of *weathering* in which *rock* is disintegrated by the expansive pressure of growing salt crystals during dry weather periods when *evaporation* is rapid.

saltation   leaping, impacting, and rebounding of sand grains transported over a *sand* or pebble surface by *wind.*

sample standard deviation   in statistics, the square root of the average squared deviation from the mean for a sample.

sample statistics   numerical values that give basic information about a sample and its variability.

sand   *sediment* particles between 0.06 and 2 mm in diameter.

sand dune   hill or ridge of loose, well-sorted *sand* shaped by *wind* and usually capable of downwind motion.

sand sea   field of *transverse dunes.*

sandspit   narrow, finger-like embankment of *sand* constructed by *littoral drift* into the open water of a *bay.*

sandstone   variety of *sedimentary rock* consisting largely of mineral particles of sand grade size.

Santa Ana   easterly *wind,* often hot and dry, that blows from the interior desert region of southern California and passes over the coastal mountain ranges to reach the Pacific Ocean.

saturated air   air holding the maximum possible quantity of *water vapor* at a given temperature and pressure.

saturated zone   zone beneath the land surface in which all pores of the *bedrock* or *regolith* are filled with *ground water.*

savanna   a vegetation cover of widely-spaced *trees* with a grassland beneath.

savanna biome   *biome* that consists of a combination of *trees* and grassland in various proportions.

savanna woodland   plant *formation class* of the *savanna biome* consisting of a *woodland* of widely spaced *trees* and a grass layer, found throughout the *wet–dry tropical climate* ③ regions in a belt adjacent to the *monsoon forest* and *low-latitude rainforest.*

scale   the magnitude of a phenomenon or system, as for example *global scale* or *local scale*; in the *viewpoint* perspective of *geography,* a focus on examining a phenomenon at different scales.

scale fraction   ratio that relates distance on the Earth's surface to distance on a *map* or surface of a globe.

scale of globe   ratio of size of a globe to size of the Earth, where size is expressed by a measure of length or distance.

scale of map   ratio of distance between two points on a *map* and the same two points on the ground.

scanning systems   *remote sensing* systems that make use of a scanning beam to generate images over the frame of surveillance.

scarification   general term for artificial excavations and other land disturbances produced for purposes of extracting or processing *mineral* resources.

scattering   turning aside of radiation by an atmospheric molecule or particle so that the direction of the scattered ray is changed.

schist   foliated *metamorphic rock* in which mica flakes are typically found oriented parallel with foliation surfaces.

sclerophyll forest   plant *formation class* of the *forest biome,* consisting of low sclerophyll *trees* and often including sclerophyll woodland or *scrub,* associated with regions of *Mediterranean climate* ⑦.

sclerophyll woodland   plant *formation class* of the *forest biome* composed of widely spaced sclerophyll *trees* and *shrubs.*

sclerophylls   hard-leaved evergreen *trees* and *shrubs* capable of enduring a long, dry summer.

scoria   *lava* or *tephra* containing numerous cavities produced by expanding gases during cooling.

scrub   plant *formation class* or subclass consisting of *shrubs* and having a canopy coverage of about 50 percent.

sea arch   arch-like *landform* of a rocky, cliffed coast created when waves erode through a narrow headland from both sides.

sea breeze   local wind blowing from sea to land during the day.

sea cave   cave near the base of a *marine cliff,* eroded by breaking waves.

sea fog   *fog* layer formed at sea when warm moist air passes over a cool ocean current and is chilled to the *condensation* point.

sea ice   floating ice of the oceans formed by direct *freezing* of ocean water.

second of arc   1/60 of a minute, or 1/3600 of a degree.

secondary consumers   animals that feed on *primary consumers.*

secondary minerals in *soil science, minerals* that are stable in the surface environment, derived by *mineral alteration* of the *primary minerals*.

secondary succession *ecological succession* beginning on a previously vegetated area that has been recently disturbed by such agents as fire, flood, windstorm, or humans.

sediment finely divided *mineral matter* and *organic matter* derived directly or indirectly from preexisting *rock* and from life processes. (See also *chemically precipitated sediment, organic sediment.*)

sediment yield quantity of sediment removed by *overland flow* from a land surface of given unit area in a given unit of time.

sedimentary cycle type of *biogeochemical cycle* in which the compound or element is released from *rock* by *weathering,* follows the movement of running water either in solution or as *sediment* to reach the sea, and is eventually converted into *rock.*

sedimentary dome up-arched *strata* forming a circular structure with domed summit and flanks with moderate to steep outward *dip.*

sedimentary rock *rock* formed from accumulation of *sediment.*

segregated ice lenses, wedges, or veins of ice occurring as free masses in *soil* or *regolith* of *permafrost* terrain.

seismic sea wave (tsunami) train of sea waves set off by an *earthquake* (or other seafloor disturbance) traveling over the ocean surface.

seismic waves waves sent out during an *earthquake* by faulting or other crustal disturbance from an *earthquake focus* and propagated through the solid Earth.

semiarid (steppe) dry climate subtype subtype of the dry climates exhibiting a short wet season supporting the growth of grasses and *annual* plants.

semidesert plant *formation class* of the *desert biome,* consisting of xerophytic *shrub* vegetation with a poorly developed herbaceous lower layer; subtypes are semidesert scrub and *woodland.*

sensible heat heat measurable by a *thermometer;* an indication of the intensity of *kinetic energy* of molecular motion within a substance.

sensible heat transfer flow of heat from one substance to another by direct contact.

sequential landforms *landforms* produced by external Earth processes in the total activity of *denudation.* Examples: *gorge, alluvial fan, floodplain.*

seral stage stage in a *sere.*

sere in an *ecological succession,* the series of biotic communities that follow one another on the way to the stable stage, or *climax.*

sesquioxides oxides of aluminum or iron with a ratio of two atoms of aluminum or iron to three atoms of oxygen.

shale fissile, *sedimentary rock* of *mud* or *clay* composition, showing lamination.

shearing (of rock) slipping motion between very thin *rock* layers, like a deck of cards fanned with the sweep of a palm.

sheet erosion type of *accelerated soil erosion* in which thin layers of *soil* are removed without formation of rills or *gullies.*

sheet flow overland flow taking the form of a continuous thin film of water over a smooth surface of *soil, regolith,* or *rock.*

sheeting structure thick, subparallel layers of massive *bedrock* formed by spontaneous expansion accompanying *unloading.*

shield volcano low, often large, dome-like accumulation of basalt lava flows emerging from long radial fissures on flanks.

shoreline shifting line of contact between water and land.

short-grass praire plant *formation class* in the *grassland biome* consisting of short grasses sparsely distributed in clumps and bunches and some *shrubs,* widespread in areas of semiarid climate in continental interiors of North America and Eurasia; also called *steppe.*

shortwave infrared *infrared radiation* with wavelengths shorter than 3 μm.

shortwave radiation electromagnetic *energy* in the range from 0.2 to 3 μm, including most of the *energy* spectrum of solar radiation.

shrubs woody *perennial* plants, usually small or low, with several low-branching stems and a foliage mass close to the ground.

silica silicon dioxide in any of several mineral forms.

silicate minerals (silicates) *minerals* containing silicon and oxygen atoms, linked in the crystal space lattice in units of four oxygen atoms to each silicon atom.

sill *intrusive igneous rock* in the form of a plate where *magma* was forced into a natural parting in the *bedrock,* such as a bedding surface in a sequence of *sedimentary rocks.*

silt *sediment* particles between 0.004 and 0.06 mm in diameter.

sinkhole surface depression in *limestone,* leading down into *limestone caverns.*

slash-and-burn agricultural system, practiced in the *low-latitude rainforest,* in which small areas are cleared and the *trees* burned, forming plots that can be cultivated for brief periods.

slate compact, fine-grained variety of *metamorphic rock,* derived from *shale,* showing well-developed cleavage.

sleet form of *precipitation* consisting of ice pellets, which may be frozen raindrops.

sling psychrometer form of *hygrometer* consisting of a wet-bulb thermometer and a dry-bulb thermometer.

slip face steep face of an active *sand dune,* receiving sand by *saltation* over the dune crest and repeatedly sliding because of oversteepening.

slope (1) degree of inclination from the horizontal of an element of ground surface, analogous to *dip* in the geologic sense. (2) any portion or element of the Earth's solid surface. (3) verb meaning "to incline."

small circle circle formed by passing a plane through a sphere without passing through the exact center.

small-scale map *map* with *fractional scale* of less than 1:100,000; usually shows a large area.

smog mixture of *aerosols* and chemical *pollutants* in the lower atmosphere, usually found over urban areas.

snow form of *precipitation* consisting of ice particles.

soil natural terrestrial surface layer containing living matter and supporting or capable of supporting plants.

soil colloids mineral particles of extremely small size, capable of remaining suspended indefinitely in water; typically, they have the form of thin plates or scales.

soil creep extremely slow downhill movement of *soil* and *regolith* as a result of continued agitation and disturbance of the particles by such activities as *frost action,* temperature changes, or wetting and drying of the soil.

soil enrichment additions of materials to the *soil* body; one of the *pedogenic processes.*

soil erosion erosional removal of material from the *soil* surface.

soil horizon distinctive layer of the *soil,* more or less horizontal, set apart from other soil zones or layers by differences in physical and chemical composition, organic content, structure, or a combination of those properties, produced by soil-forming processes.

soil orders those eleven *soil* classes forming the highest category in the classification of soils.

soil profile display of *soil horizons* on the face of a freshly cut vertical exposure through the *soil.*

soil science (See *pedology.*)

soil solum that part of the *soil* made up of the A, E, and B *soil horizons;* the soil zone in which living plant roots can influence the development of soil horizons.

soil structure presence, size, and form of aggregations (lumps or clusters) of *soil* particles.

soil texture descriptive property of the *mineral* portion of the *soil* based on varying proportions of *sand, silt,* and *clay.*

soil water water held in the *soil* and available to plants through their root systems; a form of *subsurface water.*

soil water balance balance among the component terms of the *soil water budget;* namely, *precipitation, evapotranspiration,* change in soil water storage, and water surplus.

soil water belt *soil* layer from which plants draw *soil water.*

soil water budget accounting system evaluating the daily, monthly, or yearly amounts of *precipitation, evapotranspiration,* soil water storage, water deficit, and water surplus.

soil water recharge restoring of depleted *soil water* by *infiltration* of *precipitation.*

soil water shortage (See *deficit.*)

soil water storage actual quantity of water held in the *soil water belt* at any given instant; usually applied to a soil layer of given depth, such as 300 cm (about 12 in.).

solar constant intensity of solar radiation falling upon a unit area of surface held at right angles to the Sun's rays at a point outside the Earth's *atmosphere;* equal to an *energy* flow of about 1400 W/m^2.

solar day average time required for the Earth to complete one *rotation* with respect to the Sun; time elapsed between one *solar noon* and the next, averaged over the period of one year.

solar noon instant at which the *subsolar point* crosses the *meridian of longitude* of a given point on the Earth; instant at which the Sun's shadow points exactly due north or due south at a given location.

solids substances in the solid state; they resist changes in shape and volume, are usually capable of withstanding large unbalanced forces without yielding, but will ultimately yield by sudden breakage.

solifluction tundra (arctic) variety of *earthflow* in which *sediments* of the *active layer* move in a mass slowly downhill over a water-rich plastic layer occurring at the top of *permafrost;* produces solifluction terraces and solifluction lobes.

solifluction lobe bulging mass of saturated *regolith* with steep curved front moved downhill by *solifluction.*

solifluction terrace mass of saturated *regolith* formed by *solifluction* into a flat-topped terrace.

Solonetzic order a class of *soils* in the Canadian soil classification system with a B horizon of sticky *clay* that dries to a vary hard condition.

solution a *weathering* process in which minerals dissolve in water; may be enhanced by the action of *carbonic acid* or weak organic acids.

sorting separation of one grade size of *sediment* particles from another by the action of currents of air or water.

source region extensive land or ocean surface over which an *air mass* derives its temperature and moisture characteristics.

south pole point at which the southern end of the Earth's *axis of rotation* intersects the Earth's surface.

southeast trade winds surface *winds* of low latitudes that blow steadily from the southeast. (See also *trade winds.*)

Southern Oscillation episodic reversal of prevailing barometric pressure differences between two regions, one centered on Darwin, Australia, in the eastern Indian Ocean, and the other on Tahiti in the western Pacific Ocean; a precursor to the occurrence of an *El Niño* event. (See also *El Ñino.*)

southern pine forest subtype of *needleleaf forest* dominated by pines and occurring in the *moist subtropical climate* ⑥; typically found on sandy soils of the Atlantic and Gulf Coast coastal plains.

space in the *viewpoint* perspective of *geography,* a focus on how places are interdependent.

spatial data information associated with a specific location or area of the Earth's surface.

spatial object a geographic area, *line* or *point* to which information is attached.

speciation the process by which *species* are differentiated and maintained.

species a collection of individual organisms that are capable of interbreeding to produce fertile offspring.

specific heat physical constant of a material that describes the amount of heat energy in joules required to raise the temperature of one gram of the material by one Celsius degree.

specific humidity mass of *water vapor* contained in a unit mass of air.

spit (See *sandspit.*)

splash erosion *soil erosion* caused by direct impact of falling raindrops on a wet surface of *soil* or *regolith.*

spodic horizon *soil horizon* containing precipitated amorphous materials composed of organic matter and *sesquioxides* of aluminum, with or without iron.

Spodosols *soil order* consisting of *soils* with a *spodic horizon,* an *albic horizon,* with low *base status,* and lacking in *carbonate* materials.

spoil *rock* waste removed in a mining operation.

spreading plate boundary *lithospheric plate* boundary along which two plates of *oceanic lithosphere* are undergoing separation, while at the same time new lithosphere is being formed by accretion. (See also *transform plate boundary*.)

stable air mass *air mass* in which the *environmental temperature lapse rate* is less than the *dry adiabatic lapse rate*, inhibiting convectional uplift and mixing.

stack (marine) isolated columnar mass of *bedrock* left standing in front of a retreating *marine cliff*.

stage height of the surface of a river above its bed or a fixed level near the bed.

standard meridians *standard time* meridians separated by 15° of *longitude* and having values that are multiples of 15°. (In some cases meridians are used that are multiples of $7\frac{1}{2}°$.)

standard time system time system based on the local time of a *standard meridian* and applied to belts of *longitude* extending $7\frac{1}{2}°$ (more or less) on either side of that meridian.

standard time zone zone of the Earth in which all inhabitants keep the same time, which is that of a *standard meridian* within the zone.

star dune large, isolated *sand dune* with radial ridges culminating in a peaked summit; found in the deserts of North Africa and the Arabian Peninsula.

statistics a branch of mathematical sciences that deals with the analysis of numerical data.

steppe semiarid grassland occurring largely in dry continental interiors. (See also *short-grass prairie*.)

steppe climate (See *semiarid (steppe) dry climate subtype*.)

stone polygons linked ring-like ridges of cobbles or boulders lying at the surface of the ground in *arctic* and *alpine tundra* regions.

storage capacity maximum capacity of *soil* to hold water against the pull of *gravity*.

storage pool type of pool in a *biogeochemical cycle* in which materials are largely inaccessible to life. (See also *active pool*.)

storage recharge restoration of stored *soil water* during periods when *precipitation* exceeds *potential evapotranspiration (water need)*.

storage withdrawal depletion of stored *soil water* during periods when *evapotranspiration* exceeds *precipitation*, calculated as the difference

between *actual evapotranspiration (water use)* and *precipitation*.

storm surge rapid rise of coastal water level accompanying the onshore arrival of a *tropical cyclone*.

strata layers of *sediment* or *sedimentary rock* in which individual beds are separated from one another along bedding planes.

stratified drift *glacial drift* made up of sorted and layered *clay, silt, sand*, or gravel deposited from meltwater in *stream channels*, or in marginal lakes close to the ice front.

stratiform clouds clouds of layered, blanket-like form.

stratopause upper limit of the *stratosphere*.

stratosphere layer of *atmosphere* lying directly above the *troposphere*.

stratovolcano *volcano* constructed of multiple layers of *lava* and *tephra* (volcanic ash).

stratus *cloud* type of the low-height family formed into a dense, dark gray layer.

stream long, narrow body of flowing water occupying a *stream channel* and moving to lower levels under the force of *gravity*. (See also *consequent stream, graded stream, subsequent stream*.)

stream capacity maximum *stream load* of solid matter that can be carried by a *stream* for a given *discharge*.

stream channel long, narrow, trough-like depression occupied and shaped by a *stream* moving to progressively lower levels.

stream deposition accumulation of transported particles on a *stream* bed, upon the adjacent *floodplain*, or in a body of standing water.

stream erosion progressive removal of mineral particles from the floor or sides of a *stream channel* by drag force of the moving water, or by *abrasion*, or by *corrosion*.

stream flow water flow in a *stream channel*; same as channel flow.

stream gradient rate of descent to lower elevations along the length of a *stream channel*, stated in m/km, ft/mi, degrees, or percent.

stream load solid matter carried by a *stream* in dissolved form (as *ions*), in *turbulent suspension*, and as *bed load*.

stream profile a graph of the elevation of a *stream* plotted against its distance downstream.

stream transportation downvalley movement of eroded particles in a *stream channel* in solution, in *turbulent suspension*, or as *bed load*.

strike compass direction of the line of intersection of an inclined *rock* plane and a horizontal plane of reference. (See also *dip*.)

strike-slip fault variety of *fault* on which the motion is dominantly horizontal along a near-vertical *fault plane*.

strip mining mining method in which *overburden* is first removed from a seam of *coal*, or a sedimentary ore, allowing the coal or ore to be extracted.

structure (of a system) the pattern of the pathways and their interconnections within a flow system.

subantarctic low-pressure belt persistent belt of low *atmospheric pressure* centered about at lat. 65°S over the Southern Ocean.

subantarctic zone *latitude* zone lying between lat. 55° and 60°S (more or less) and occupying a region between the *midlatitude zone* and the *antarctic zone*.

subarctic zone *latitude* zone between lat. 55° and 60° N (more or less), occupying a region between the *midlatitude zone* and the *arctic zone*.

subduction descent of the downbent edge of a *lithospheric plate* into the *asthenosphere* so as to pass beneath the edge of the adjoining plate.

sublimation process of change of ice (solid state) to *water vapor* (*gaseous state*); in *meteorology*, sublimation also refers to the change of state from water vapor (liquid) to ice (solid), which is referred to as *deposition* in this text.

submergence inundation or partial drowning of a former land surface by a rise of sea level or a sinking of the *crust* or both.

suborder a unit of *soil* classification representing a subdivision of the *soil order*.

subsea permafrost *permafrost* lying below sea level, found in a shallow offshore zone fringing the arctic seacoast.

subsequent stream *stream* that develops its course by *stream erosion* along a band or belt of weaker *rock*.

subsolar point point on the Earth's surface at which solar rays are perpendicular to the surface.

subsurface water water of the lands held in *soil, regolith,* or *bedrock* below the surface.

subtropical broadleaf evergreen forest a formation class of the *forest biome* composed of broadleaf evergreen *trees;* occurs primarily in the regions of the *moist subtropical climate* ⑥.

subtropical evergreen forest a subdivision of the *forest biome* composed of both broadleaf and needleleaf evergreen *trees.*

subtropical high-pressure belts belts of persistent high *atmospheric pressure* trending east–west and centered about on lat. 30° N and S.

subtropical jet stream *jet stream* of westerly winds forming at the *tropopause,* just above the *Hadley cell.*

subtropical needleleaf evergreen forest a *formation class* of the *forest biome* composed of needleleaf evergreen *trees* occurring in the *moist subtropical climate* ⑥ of the southeastern U.S.; also referred to as the *southern pine forest.*

subtropical zones *latitude* zones occupying the region of lat. 25° to 35° N and S (more or less) and lying between the *tropical zones* and the *midlatitude zones.*

succulents plants adapted to resist water losses by means of thickened spongy tissue in which water is stored.

summer monsoon inflow of maritime air at low levels from the Indian Ocean toward the Asiatic low pressure center in the season of high Sun; associated with the rainy season of the *wet–dry tropical climate* ③ and the Asiatic monsoon climate.

summer solstice solstice occurring on June 21 or 22, when the *subsolar point* is located at 23 1/2°N.

Sun-synchronous orbit satellite orbit in which the orbital plane remains fixed in position with respect to the Sun.

supercontinent single world continent, formed when *plate tectonic* motions move continents together into a single, large land mass. (See also *Pangea.*)

supercooled water water existing in the liquid state at a temperature lower than the normal *freezing* point.

surface the very thin layer of a substance that receives and radiates energy and conducts heat to and away from the substance.

surface energy balance equation equation expressing the balance among *heat* flows to and from a surface.

surface water water of the lands flowing freely (as *streams*) or impounded (as ponds, *lakes,* marshes).

surges episodes of very rapid downvalley movement within an *alpine glacier.*

suspended load that part of the *stream load* carried in *turbulent suspension.*

suspension (See *turbulent suspension.*)

suture (See *continental suture.*)

swash surge of water up the *beach* slope (landward) following collapse of a *breaker.*

symbiosis form of positive interaction between *species* that is beneficial to one of the species and does not harm the other.

sympatric speciation type of *speciation* in which speciation occurs within a larger population.

synclinal mountain steep-sided ridge or elongate mountain developed by erosion of a *syncline.*

synclinal valley valley eroded on weak *strata* along the central trough or axis of a *syncline.*

syncline downfold of *strata* (or other layered *rock*) in a trough-like structure; a class of *folds.* (See also *anticline.*)

synthesis a perspective of *geography* that focuses on putting together ideas from different fields and assembling them in new ways.

system (1) a collection of things that are somehow related or organized; (2) a scheme for naming, as in a classification system; (3) a flow system of *matter* and *energy.*

systematic geography the study of the physical, economic, and social processes that differentiate the Earth's surface into *places.*

systems approach the study of the interconnections among natural processes by focusing on how, where, and when natural systems are linked and interconnected.

systems theory body of knowledge explaining how systems work.

taiga plant *formation class* consisting of *woodland* with low, widely spaced *trees* and a ground cover of lichens and mosses, found along the northern fringes of the region of *boreal forest climate* ⑪; also called cold woodland.

tailings (See *spoil.*)

talik pocket or region within *permafrost* that is unfrozen; ranges from small inclusions to large "holes" in permafrost under *lakes.*

tall-grass prairie a *formation class* of the *grassland biome* that consists of tall grasses with broad-leaved *herbs.*

talus accumulation of loose *rock* fragments derived by fall of *rock* from a *cliff.*

talus slope slope formed of *talus.*

tar sand (See *bitumen.*)

tarn small *lake* occupying a *rock* basin in a *cirque* of *glacial trough.*

tectonic activity process of bending (*folding*) and breaking (faulting) of crustal mountains, concentrated on or near active *lithospheric plate* boundaries.

tectonic arc long, narrow chain of islands or mountains or a narrow submarine ridge adjacent to a *subduction* boundary and its trench, formed by *tectonic processes,* such as the construction and rise of an *accretionary prism.*

tectonic crest ridge-like summit line of a *tectonic arc* associated with an *accretionary prism.*

tectonics branch of *geology* relating to tectonic activity and the features it produces. (See also *plate tectonics, tectonic activity.*)

temperature gradient rate of temperature change along a selected line or direction.

temperature inversion upward reversal of the normal *environmental temperature lapse rate,* so that the air temperature increases upward. (See also *high-level temperature inversion, low-level temperature inversion.*)

temperature regime distinctive type of annual temperature cycle.

tephra collective term for all size grades of solid *igneous rock* particles blown out under gas pressure from a volcanic vent.

terminal moraine *moraine* deposited as an embankment at the terminus of an *alpine glacier* or at the leading edge of an *ice sheet.*

terrane continental crustal *rock* unit having a distinctive set of lithologic properties, reflecting its geologic history, that distinguish it from adjacent or surrounding *continental crust.*

terrestrial ecosystems *ecosystems* of land plants and animals found on upland surfaces of the continents.

tetraploid having four sets of chromosomes instead of a normal two sets.

thematic map *map* showing a single type of information.

theme category or class of information displayed on a *map.*

thermal erosion in regions of *permafrost,* the physical disruption of the land surface by melting of *ground ice,* brought about by removal of a protective organic layer.

thermal infrared a portion of the *infrared radiation wavelength* band, from approximately from 3 to 20 μm, in which objects at temperatures encountered on the Earth's surface (including fires) emit *electromagnetic radiation.*

thermal pollution form of water pollution in which heated water is discharged into a *stream* or *lake* from the cooling system of a power plant or other industrial heat source.

thermistor electronic device that measures (air) temperature.

thermocline water layer of a lake or the ocean in which temperature changes rapidly in the vertical direction.

thermokarst in arctic environments, an uneven terrain produced by thawing of the upper layer of *permafrost,* with settling of *sediment* and related water erosion; often occurs when the natural surface cover is disturbed by fire or human activity.

thermokarst lake shallow *lake* formed by the thawing and settling of *permafrost,* usually in response to disturbance of the natural surface cover by fire or human activity.

thermometer instrument measuring temperature.

thermometer shelter louvered wooden cabinet of standard construction used to hold *thermometers* and other weather-monitoring equipment.

thermosiphon device that pumps heat from the ground, keeping *permafrost* from thawing.

thermosphere atmospheric layer of upwardly increasing temperature, lying above the *mesopause.*

thorntree semidesert *formation class* within the *desert biome,* transitional from *grassland biome* and *savanna biome* and consisting of *xerophytic trees* and *shrubs.*

thorntree-tall-grass savanna plant *formation class,* transitional between the *savanna biome* and the *grassland biome,* consisting of widely scattered *trees* in an open grassland.

thrust sheet sheet-like mass of *rock* moving forward over a *low-angle overthrust fault.*

thunderstorm intense, local convectional storm associated with a *cumulonimbus cloud* and yielding heavy *precipitation,* also with lightning and thunder, and sometimes the fall of *hail.*

tidal current current set in motion by the *ocean tide.*

tidal inlet narrow opening in a *barrier island* or baymouth *bar* through which *tidal currents* flow.

tide (See *ocean tide.*)

tide curve graphical presentation of the rhythmic rise and fall of ocean water because of *ocean tides.*

till heterogeneous mixture of *rock* fragments ranging in size from *clay* to boulders, deposited beneath moving glacial ice or directly from the *melting* in place of stagnant glacial ice.

till plain undulating, plain-like land surface underlain by glacial *till.*

time cycle in flow systems, a regular alternation of flow rates with time.

time zones zones or belts of given east–west *(longitudinal)* extent within which *standard time* is applied according to a uniform system.

topographic contour *isopleth* of uniform elevation appearing on a *map.*

tornado small, very intense wind vortex with extremely low air pressure in center, formed beneath a dense *cumulonimbus cloud* in proximity to a *cold front.*

trade winds (trades) surface winds in low *latitudes,* representing the low-level airflow within the *tropical easterlies.*

transcurrent fault *fault* on which the relative motion is dominantly horizontal, in the direction of the *strike* of the fault; also called a *strike-slip fault.*

transform fault special case of a *strike-slip fault* making up the boundary of two moving *lithospheric plates;* usually found along an offset of the *mid-*

oceanic ridge where seafloor spreading is in progress.

transform plate boundary *lithospheric plate* boundary along which two plates are in contact on a *transform fault;* the relative motion is that of a *strike-slip fault.*

transform scar linear topographic feature of the ocean floor taking the form of an irregular scarp or ridge and originating at the offset *axial rift* of the *mid-oceanic ridge;* it represents a former *transform fault* but is no longer a plate boundary.

transformation (soils) a class of soil-forming processes that transform materials within the soil body; examples include *mineral alteration* and *humification.*

translocation a soil-forming process in which materials are moved within the soil body, usually from one horizon to another.

transpiration evaporative loss of water to the *atmosphere* from leaf pores of plants.

transportation (See *stream transportation.*)

transported regolith *regolith* formed of *mineral matter* carried by *fluid* agents from a distant source and deposited upon the *bedrock* or upon older regolith. Examples: floodplain silt, lake clay, beach sand.

transverse dunes field of wave-like *sand dunes* with crests running at right angles to the direction of the prevailing *wind.*

traveling anticyclone center of high pressure and *outspiraling* winds that travels over the Earth's surface; often associated with clear, dry weather.

traveling cyclone center of low pressure and *inspiraling* winds that travels over the Earth's surface; includes *wave cyclones, tropical cyclones,* and *tornadoes.*

travertine carbonate mineral matter, usually *calcite,* accumulating upon *limestone cavern* surfaces situated in the *unsaturated zone.*

tree large erect woody *perennial* plant typically having a single main trunk, few branches in the lower part, and a branching crown.

trellis drainage pattern *drainage pattern* characterized by a dominant parallel set of major *subsequent streams,* joined at right angles by numerous short tributaries; typical of *coastal plains* and belts of eroded *folds.*

tropic of cancer   *parallel of latitude at* 23 1/2°N.

tropic of capricorn   *parallel of latitude at* 23 1/2°S.

tropical cyclone   intense *traveling cyclone* of tropical and subtropical *latitudes,* accompanied by high *winds* and heavy rainfall.

tropical easterlies   low-latitude wind system of persistent airflow from east to west between the two *subtropical high-pressure belts.*

tropical easterly jet stream   upper-air *jet stream* of seasonal occurrence, running east to west at very high altitudes over Southeast Asia.

tropical high-pressure belt   a high-pressure belt occurring in tropical latitudes at a high level in the *troposphere;* extends downward and poleward to form the *subtropical high-pressure* belt, located at the surface.

tropical zones   *latitude* zones centered on the *tropic of cancer* and the *tropic of capricorn,* within the latitude ranges 10° to 25° N and 10° to 25°S, respectively.

tropical-zone rainforest   plant *formation class* within the *forest biome* similar to *equatorial rainforest,* but occurring farther poleward in tropical regions.

tropopause   boundary between *troposphere* and *stratosphere.*

tropophyte   plant that sheds its leaves and enters a dormant state during a dry or cold season when little *soil water* is available.

troposphere   lowermost layer of the *atmosphere* in which air temperature falls steadily with increasing altitude.

trough   in describing water waves, the lowest part of the wave form.

tsunami   (See *seismic sea wave.*)

tundra biome   *biome* of the cold regions of *arctic tundra* and *alpine tundra,* consisting of grasses, grass-like plants, flowering *herbs,* dwarf *shrubs,* mosses, and *lichens.*

tundra climate ⑫   cold climate of the *arctic zone* with eight or more consecutive months of zero *potential evapotranspiration (water need).*

tundra soils   soils of the arctic *tundra climate* ⑫ regions.

turbulence   in *fluid* flow, the motion of individual water particles in complex eddies, superimposed on the average downstream flow path.

turbulent flow   mode of *fluid* flow in which individual *fluid* particles (molecules) move in complex eddies, superimposed on the average downstream flow path.

turbulent suspension   *stream transportation* in which particles of *sediment* are held in the body of the *stream* by turbulent eddies. (Also applies to *wind* transportation.)

twilight   solar *radiation* from below the horizon that is scattered toward the ground by the *atmosphere* to provide illumination after the Sun has set or before it has risen.

typhoon   *tropical cyclone* of the western North Pacific and coastal waters of Southeast Asia.

Udalfs   suborder of the *soil order Alfisols;* includes Alfisols of moist regions, usually in the *midlatitude zone,* with deciduous forest as the natural vegetation.

Udolls   suborder of the *soil order Mollisols;* includes Mollisols of the moist soil-water regime in the *midlatitude zone* and with no horizon of *calcium carbonate* accumulation.

Ultisols   *soil order* consisting of *soils* of warm soil temperatures with an *argillic horizon* and low *base status.*

ultramafic igneous rock   *igneous rock* composed almost entirely of *mafic minerals,* usually *olivine* or *pyroxene group.*

ultraviolet radiation   *electromagnetic energy* in the *wavelength* range of 0.2 to 0.4 μm.

unloading   process of removal of overlying *rock* load from *bedrock* by processes of *denudation,* accompanied by expansion and often leading to the development of *sheeting structure.*

unsaturated zone   *subsurface water* zone in which pores are not fully saturated, except at times when *infiltration* is very rapid; lies above the *saturated zone.*

unstable air   air with substantial content of *water vapor,* capable of breaking into spontaneous *convectional* activity leading to the development of heavy showers and *thunderstorms.*

unstable isotope   elemental *isotope* that spontaneously decays to produce

one or more new isotopes. (See also *daughter product.*)

upper-air westerlies   system of westerly *winds* in the upper *atmosphere* over middle and high latitudes.

upwelling   upward motion of cold, nutrient-rich ocean waters, often associated with cool equatorward currents occurring along *continental margins.*

Ustalfs   suborder of the *soil order Alfisols;* includes Alfisols of semiarid and seasonally dry climates in which the *soil* is dry for a long period in most years.

Ustolls   suborder of the *soil order Mollisols;* includes Mollisols of the semiarid climate in the *midlatitude zone,* with a horizon of *calcium carbonate* accumulation.

valley winds   air movement at night down the *gradient* of valleys and the enclosing mountainsides; alternating with daytime *mountain winds.*

variability   measure of the variation in a series of observations that center around a mean.

variation   in the study of evolution, natural differences arising between parents and offspring as a result of *mutation* and *recombination.*

varve   annual layer of *sediment* on the bottom of a *lake* or the ocean marked by a change in color or texture of the sediment.

veins   small, irregular, branching network of *intrusive rock* within a preexisting *rock* mass.

verbal description   in the *representation* perspective of *geography,* the use of written or oral text to describe geographic phenomena.

vernal equinox   *equinox* occurring on March 20 or 21, when the *subsolar point* is at the *equator.*

Vertisols   *soil order* consisting of *soils* of the *subtropical zone* and the *tropical zone* with high *clay* content, developing deep, wide cracks when dry, and showing evidence of movement between aggregates.

viewpoint   a unique perspective of *geography* that considers where and how phenomena occur and how they are related to other phenomena nearby and far away.

visible light   *electromagnetic energy* in the *wavelength* range of 0.4 to 0.7 μm.

visual display   in the *representation* perspective of *geography*, tools such as *cartography* and *remote sensing* that display spatial information visually.

void   empty region of pore space in *sediment*; often occupied by water or water films.

volcanic bombs   boulder-sized, semi-solid masses of *lava* that are ejected from an erupting *volcano*.

volcanic neck   isolated, narrow steep-sided peak formed by erosion of *igneous rock* previously solidified in the feeder pipe of an extinct *volcano*.

volcanism   general term for *volcano* building and related forms of *extrusive igneous* activity.

volcano   conical, circular structure built by accumulation of *lava* flows and *tephra*. (See also *shield volcano, stratovolcano*.)

volcano coast   *coast* formed by *volcanoes* and *lava* flows built partly below and partly above sea level.

warm front   moving weather *front* along which a warm *air mass* is sliding up over a cold *air mass*, leading to production of *stratiform clouds* and *precipitation*.

warm-blooded animal   animal that possesses one or more adaptations to maintain a constant internal temperature despite fluctuations in the environmental temperature.

warm-core ring   circular eddy of warm water, surrounded by cold water and lying adjacent to a warm, poleward moving ocean current, such as the Gulf Stream. (See also *cold-core ring*.)

washout   downsweeping of atmospheric *particulates* by *precipitation*.

water gap   narrow transverse *gorge* cut across a narrow ridge by a *stream*, usually in a region of eroded *folds*.

water need   (See *potential evapotranspiration*.)

water resources   a field of study that couples basic study of the location, distribution, and movement of water with the utilization and quality of water for human use.

water surplus   water disposed of by *runoff* or percolation to the ground water zone after the *storage capacity* of the *soil* is full.

water table   upper boundary surface of the *saturated zone;* the upper limit of the *ground water* body.

water use   (See *actual evapotranspiration*.)

water vapor   the *gaseous* state of water.

waterfall   abrupt descent of a *stream* over a *bedrock* step in the *stream channel*.

waterlogging   rise of a *water table* in *alluvium* to bring the zone of saturation into the root zone of plants.

watt   unit of power equal to the quantity of work done at the rate of one joule per second; symbol, W.

wave cyclone   *traveling cyclone* of the midlatitudes involving interaction of cold and warm *air masses* along sharply defined *fronts*.

wave height   in describing water waves, the height of the wave as measured from the top of the *crest* to the bottom of the *trough*.

wave length   in describing water waves, the length of the wave from from *crest* to crest or *trough* to trough.

wave period   in describing water waves, time in seconds between successive *crests* or successive *troughs* that pass a fixed point.

wave-cut notch   *rock* recess at the base of a *marine cliff* where wave impact is concentrated.

weak equatorial low   weak, slowly moving low-pressure center (*cyclone*) accompanied by numerous convectional showers and *thunderstorms;* it forms close to the *intertropical convergence zone* in the rainy season, or *summer monsoon*.

weather   physical state of the *atmosphere* at a given time and place.

weather system   recurring pattern of atmospheric circulation associated with characteristic weather, such as a *cyclone* or *anticyclone*.

weathering   total of all processes acting at or near the Earth's surface to cause physical disruption and chemical decomposition of *rock*. (See also *chemical weathering, physical weathering*.)

west-wind drift   ocean drift current moving eastward in zone of *prevailing westerlies*.

westerlies   (See *prevailing westerly winds, upper-air westerlies*.)

wet adiabatic lapse rate   reduced *adiabatic lapse rate* when *condensation* is taking place in rising air; value ranges between 4 and 9°C per 1000 m (2.2 and 4.9°F per 1000 ft).

wet equatorial climate ①   moist climate of the *equatorial zone* with a large annual *water surplus*, and with uniformly warm temperatures throughout the year.

wet-dry tropical climate ③   climate of the *tropical zone* characterized by a very wet season alternating with a very dry season.

wetlands   land areas of poor surface drainage, such as marshes and swamps.

Wilson Cycle   *plate tectonic* cycle in which continents rupture and pull apart, forming oceans and *oceanic crust*, then converge and collide with accompanying subduction of *oceanic crust*.

wilting point   quantity of stored *soil water*, less than which the foliage of plants not adapted to *drought* will wilt.

wind   air motion, dominantly horizontal relative to the Earth's surface.

wind abrasion   mechanical wearing action of wind-driven *mineral* particles striking exposed *rock* surfaces.

wind vane   *weather* instrument used to indicate *wind* direction.

winter monsoon   outflow of continental air at low levels from the Siberian high, passing over Southeast Asia as a dry, cool northerly *wind*.

winter solstice   solstice occurring on December 21 or 22, when the *subsolar point* is at 23 1/2°S.

Wisconsinan Glaciation   last *glaciation* of the *Pleistocene Epoch*.

woodland   plant *formation class*, transitional between *forest biome* and *savanna biome*, consisting of widely spaced *trees* with canopy coverage between 25 and 60 percent.

Xeralfs   suborder of the *soil order Alfisols*; includes Alfisols of the *Mediterranean climate* ⑦.

xeric animals   animals adapted to dry conditions typical of a *desert* climate.

Xerolls   suborder of the *soil order Mollisols;* includes Mollisols of the *Mediterranean climate* ⑦.

xerophytes   plants adapted to a dry environment.

zooplankton   microscopic animals found largely in the uppermost layer of ocean or lake water.

PHOTO CREDITS

Cover Chris Noble/Photographer's Choice/Getty Images.

Prologue Pages 2-3 and 4 (top): Courtesy NOAA; Page 4 (bottom): Jacques Descloitres, MODIS Land Rapid Response Team, Courtesy NASA, Visible Earth.; Page 5 (top): Earth Satellite Corporation/Photo Researchers; Page 5 (bottom): Courtesy NASA; Page 6: Courtesy NOAA. Page 8: Pierre Longnus/Liaison Agency, Inc./Getty Images; Page 10 (top): David Olsen/Weatherstock; Page 10 (bottom left): T.A. Wiewandt/DRK Photo; Pages 10-11: Larry Ulrich/DRK Photo; Page 11 (top left): Michael Fogden/DRK Photo; Page 12 (top): Courtesy USGS; Page 11 (right): Fletcher & Baylis/Photo Researchers; Page 12 (bottom): ORBIMAGE (c) Orbital Imaging Corporation and SeaWiFS Project, NASA/Goddard Space Flight Center.; Page 13: Selected graphic image supplied courtesy of Environmental Systems Research Institute, Inc. (c) 2000, Environmental Systems Research Institute, Inc.; Page 17 (top left): Science Photo Library/Photo Researchers; Page 17 (top right): Michael Collier/DRK Photo; Page 17 (center): Michael Fogden/DRK Photo; Page 17 (bottom left): Mark Newman/Bruce Coleman, Inc.; Page 17 (bottom right): Dave Kaup/Reuters/Corbis;

Chapter 1 Pages 22-23 and 24: (c)Ron Watts/Black Star; Page 25 (top left): PLI/Science Photo Library/Photo Researchers; Page 25 (top right): Courtesy NASA; Page 25 (bottom right): Richard L. Carlton/Photo Researchers; Page 29: (c)National Maritime Museum, Greenwich, London; Page 39: Fred Hirschmann.

Chapter 2 Pages 50-51 and 52: Peter Hendrie/The Image Bank/Getty Images; Page 54: Courtesy Daedalus Enterprises, Inc. & National Geographic Magazine; Page 65: Courtesy NASA.; Page 69: Courtesy NASA; Page 71 (top left): Simon Fraser/Science Photo Library/Photo Researchers; Page 71 (top right): Stephen J. Krasemann//DRK Photo; Page 71 (center left): Galaxy Contact/Explorer/Photo Researchers; Page 71 (bottom right): Stephen J. Krasemann//DRK Photo; Page 72: Joe Flores, Southern California Edison/NREL; Page 79: Courtesy NASA, compiled and annotated by John E. Estes and Leslie W. Senger; Page 80: Courtesy Geonex/Chicago Aerial Survey, Inc.; Page 81: SAR image courtesy of Intera Technologies Corporation, Calgary, Alberta, Canada; Page 82: A. H. Strahler; Page 83 (all): A. H. Strahler; Page 84 (top right): Photo courtesy of Eastman Kodak Company; Page 84 (bottom): A. H. Strahler;.

Chapter 3 Pages 86-87 and 88: Michael Melford/The Image Bank/Getty Images; Page 90 (left): Environmental Analytical Systems; Page 90 (right): (c) Steve McCutcheon/Alaska Pictorial; Page 93 (left): Tom Bean/DRK Photo; Page 93 (right): Jeremy Woodhouse/DRK Photo; Page 95 (left and right): Courtesy NASA/EPA. Provided by Dr. Dale Quattrochi, Marshall Space Flight Center; Page 97: George Wuerthner Photography; Page 99: Christi Carter/Grant Heilman Photography; Page 112: Shawn Henry/SABA.

Chapter 4 Pages 118-119 and 120: Paul A. Zahl/National Geographic Society; Page 125: Arthur N.Strahler; Page 129 (top left): (c) Darryl Torckler/Stone/Getty Images; Page 129 (top right): (c)Kees van den Berg/Photo Researchers; Page 129 (bottom left): (c)Trevor Mein/Stone/Getty Images; Page 129 (bottom right): (c)Larry Ulrich, Trinidad, CA; Page 130: (c)Ron Sanford/Stone/Getty Images; Page 131 (top right): University of Wisconsin Space Science and Engineering Center; Page 131 (bottom left): Courtesy NASA. Image produced by M. Jentoft-Nilsen, F. Hasler, D. Chesters, and T. Neilsen.; Page 132: (c)Larry West/Bruce Coleman, Inc.; Page 133: Arthur N.Strahler; Page 137: Warren Faidley/Weatherstock; Page 138: (c)Nuridsany et Perennou/Photo Researchers; Page 139: (c)John H. Hoffman//Bruce Coleman, Inc.; Page 144 (left): Data received by the Canada Centre for Remote Sensing. Image provided courtesy of RADARSAT International.; Page 144 (right): David R. Frazier/Photo Researchers; Page 146: (c) John S. Shelton, La Jolla, California; Page 149: (c)Jim Strawser/Grant Heilman Photography.

Chapter 5 Pages 150-151 and 152: (c) Joe Sohm/Photo Researchers; Page 155: Courtesy Taylor Instrument Company and Wards Natural Science Establishment, Rochester, New York; Page 158: P.F. Bentley; Page 159 (top right): James Stevenson/Science Photo Library/ Photo Researchers; Page 159 (bottom left): Arthur N.Strahler; Page 173: Courtesy NASA; Page 176: Courtesy Otis B. Brown, Robert Evans, and M. Carle, University of Miami, Rosenstiel School of Marine and Atmospheric Science, Florida, and NOAA/Satellite Data Services Division; Page 177 (top left and right): Courtesy Otis B. Brown, University of Miami, and Gene Carl Feldman, NASA/Goddard Space Flight Center; Page 177 (bottom): Courtesy Steven R. Hare, International Pacific Halibut Commission. Adapted and updated from Mantua et al, 1997, *Bulletin American Meteorological Society* 78:1069-1079.

Chapter 6 Pages 184-185 and 186: NOAA Environmental Visualization Program; Page 189: Steve Pace/Envision; Page 191: The Image Bank/Getty Images; Page 196: (c)Keith Brewster/Weatherstock; Page 197: Christopher Smith/Enid News & Eagle/Liaison Agency, Inc./Getty Images; Page 198: Courtesy NASA; Page 199: Courtesy NASA; Page 202 (top): Courtesy NOAA; Page 202 (bottom): Courtesy NASA. Images and rendering by Marit Jentoft-Nilsen; Page 203 (top): Courtesy NASA, SeaWiFS Project Office; Page 203 (bottom): Courtesy NASA, Earth Observatory, Natural Hazards.; Page 206: (c)Robert Holland, Stuart, FL; Page 207: NOAA, Advanced Very High Resolution Radiometer.

Chapter 7 Pages 212-213 and 214: (c)Chris Brown/SABA; Page 235: (c)Will & Deni McIntyre/Photo Researchers; Page 237: (c)Boyd Norton; Page 239: Alain Nogues/Corbis Sygma; Page 242 (top): Frans Lanting/Minden Pictures, Inc.; Page 242 (center): Michael Fogden/DRK Photo; Page 242 (bottom): Walter Schmidt/Peter Arnold, Inc.; Page 243 (top): Joel Bennett/Peter Arnold, Inc.; Page 243 (bottom): Art Wolfe/Photo Researchers; Page 247: (c)Fred Hirschmann; Page 248: Arthur N.Strahler; Page 252 (top): Porterfield-Chickering/Photo Researchers; Page 252 (bottom): (c)D. Cavagnaro//DRK Photo; Page 253 (top): Tom McHugh/Photo Researchers; Page 253 (bottom): Arthur N. Strahler; Page 254: David Muench Photography; Page 255: (c)Tony Craddock/Stone/Getty Images; Page 257: (c)Porterfield/Chickering/Photo Researchers; Page 260: R. N. Drummond; Page 262: Warren Garst/Tom Stack & Associates.

Chapter 8 Pages 278-279 and 280: Frans Lanting/Minden Pictures, Inc.; Page 282: Michio Hoshino/Minden Pictures, Inc.; Page 283 (top): Marc Epstein/DRK Photo; Page 283 (bottom): Manoj Shah/Stone/Getty Images; Page 294: Michael P. Gadomski/Photo Researchers; Page 295 (top): (c)Josef Muench; Page 295 (bottom): Dennis Sheridan; Page 296: (c)Kevin Schafer; Page 297 (left): Larry Ulrich/DRK Photo; Page 297 (right): Tom Till/DRK Photo; Page 299: Gregory G. Dimijian/Photo Researchers; Page 301: Tom Brakefield/DRK Photo; Page 302 (top and bottom): MODIS Land Team/C. Justice/L. Giglio/J. Descloitres/NASA; Page 303 (top and center): Robert Simmon, NASA, GSFC; Page 303 (bottom): ORBIMAGE (c) Orbital Imaging Corporation and SeaWiFS Project, NASA/Goddard Space Flight Center.; Page 305 (left and right): Alan H. Strahler; Pages 308 and 309 (all): Michael P. Gadomski/Photo Researchers; Page 310 (left): Richard Parker/Photo Researchers;

Page 310 (right): Wendy Neefus/Animals Animals/Earth Scenes; Page 311 (left): Lewis Kemper/DRK Photo; Page 311 (right): M.P. Kahl/Photo Researchers; Page 314 (top): Jonathan Klizas, Chatham, NJ; Page 314 (bottom): Art Morris/Birds as Art/Visuals Unlimited; Page 315: Kenneth W. Fink/Photo Researchers; Page 316 (left): S.W. Carter/Photo Researchers; Page 316 (right): Runk/Schoenberger/Grant Heilman Photography; Page 325 (all): R. Nemani and S.W. Running, University of Montana NTSG/Courtesy NASA; Page 326 (top left and right): ORBIMAGE/ Orbital Imaging Corporation and SeaWiFS Project,; Page 326 (bottom): MODIS Science Team/ NASA; Page 327 (top and bottom): MODIS Science Team/ NASA; Page 328: R. Nemani, University of Montana NTSG/ NASA; Page 329: NASA/NOAA.

Chapter 9 Pages 330-331 and 332: Philip Condit II/Stone/Getty Images; Page 334: (c)Steve McCutcheon/Alaska Pictorial; Page 340 (top): (c)M. Freeman//Bruce Coleman, Inc.; Page 340 (bottom): (c)Ferrero/Labat/Auscape International Pty. Ltd.; Page 341 (top left): Tom & Susan Bean, Inc.; Page 341 (bottom right): Michel Gunther/Peter Arnold, Inc.; Page 343: (c)Jacques Jangoux/Peter Arnold, Inc.; Page 344: (c) John S. Shelton, La Jolla, California; Page 346: (c)Kenneth Murray/Photo Researchers; Page 347: (c)Jake Rajs; Page 348: (c)Michael Townsend/Stone/Getty Images; Page 350 (left and right): Arthur N. Strahler; Page 352: (c)Annie Griffiths Belt/DRK Photo; Page 354: (c)Brian A. Vikander; Page 356 (top and bottom): Arthur N. Strahler.

Chapter 10 Pages 362-363 and 364: Sam Abell/National Geographic; Page 366: Courtesy R. B. Krone, San Francisco District Corps. of Engineers, U. S. Army; Page 368: R. Schaetzl; Page 373: Arthur N. Strahler; Page 375: (c)Erich Lessing/Art Resource; Pages 380 and 381 (all): Estate of Henry D. Foth; Page 382 (top): Alan H. Strahler; Page 382 (bottom): Soil Conservation Service; Page 383 (top): Estate of Henry D. Foth; Page 383 (bottom): William E. Ferguson; Page 385: Ric Ergenbright/Stone/Getty Images; Page 386: Robin White/Fotolex Associates; Page 387: R. Schaetzl; Page 388 (top): Courtesy Soil Conservation Service; Page 388 (bottom): M. Collier/DRK Photo; Page 393: D. Cavagnaro/DRK Photo; Page 394 (top): TASS/Sovfoto/Eastfoto; Page 394 (bottom): Leonard Lee Rue III/Bruce Coleman, Inc.; Page 395 (top): Mark Edwards/Peter Arnold, Inc.; Page 395 (bottom): Charlie Waite/Stone/Getty Images.

Chapter 11 Pages 396-367 and 398: G. Brad Lewis/GettyImages/Stone; Page 399: Roberto de Gugliemo/Photo Researchers; Page 402 (left and right): Ward's Natural Science Establishment; Page 403 (top): Travelpix/Taxi/Getty Images; Page 403 (bottom left and right): Ward's Natural Science Establishment; Page 404: A. N. Strahler; Page 406: Courtesy of Richard S. Williams, Jr., U. S. Geological Survey; Page 408: (c) Carr Clifton//Minden Pictures, Inc.; Page 409 (top): Andrew McIntyre/Columbia University ; Page 409 (bottom): A. N. Strahler; Page 410 (top and bottom): A. N. Strahler; Page 411 (top): Victor Englebert/Photo Researchers; Page 411 (bottom): Charles R. Belinky/Photo Researchers; Page 412: A. N. Strahler; Page 413: (c)Freeman Patterson/Masterfile; Page 415 (all): NASA/GSFC/MITI/ERSDA C/JAROS and U.S./Japan ASTER Science Team.

Chapter 12 Pages 420-421 and 422: Jacques Descloitres, MODIS Rapid Response Team/NASA Visible Earth; Pages 430 and 431: Copyright (c) 1995, David T. Sandwell. Used by permission; Page 444: NASA.

Chapter 13 Pages 450-451 and 452: (c) Galen Rowell/ Mountain Light Photography, Inc.; Page 454 (top): James Mason/Black Star; Page 454 (bottom): K. Hamdorf/Auscape International Pty. Ltd.; Page 455 (top): Greg Vaughn/Tom Stack & Associates; Page 457 (top): Kevin West/Liaison Agency, Inc./Getty Images; Page 457 (bottom): Werner Stoy/Camera Hawaii, Inc.; Page 459: A. N. Strahler; Page 460 (top): A. N. Strahler; Page 460 (bottom left): (c)Larry Ulrich; Page 460 (bottom right): Steve Vidler/Leo de Wys, Inc.; Page 462: Courtesy Pacific Gas & Electric Company; Page 464 (top): Image courtesy NASA/GSFC/MITI/ERSDAC/JAROS and U.S./Japan ASTER Science Team; Page 464 (bottom): Image courtesy NASA/JPL/NIMA; Page 465 (top): Image courtesy Ron Beck, EROS Data Center; Page 465 (bottom): ORBIMAGE (c) Orbital Imaging Corporation and SeaWiFS Project, NASA/Goddard Space Flight Center.; Page 467: A. N. Strahler; Page 468: James Balog/Black Star; Page 469: Georg Gerster/Photo Researchers; Page 470: Exelsior/Sipa Press; Page 474: G. Hall/Woodfin Camp & Associates; Page 475: Michael S. Yamashita/Corbis Images; Page 477: Digital Globe/HO/AFP/Getty Images.

Chapter 14 Pages 480-481 and 482: Handout/Malacanang/Corbis; Page 483: (c)Susan Rayfield/Photo Researchers; Page 484: A. N. Strahler; Page 485 (top): A. N. Strahler; Page 485 (bottom): Steve McCutcheon/Alaska Pictorial; Page 486: (c)Kunio Owaki/Corbis Stock Market; Page 487: (c)George Wuerthner; Page 488 (top): (c)David Muench Photography; Page 488 (bottom): Tom & Susan Bean, Inc.; Page 489 (top left and right): Alan H. Strahler; Page 489 (bottom): (c)Douglas Peebles Photography; Page 491: (c) John S. Shelton, La Jolla, California; Page 493: Courtesy Raymond Drouin; Page 494: Orlo E. Childs; Page 496: (c)AP/Wide World Photos; Page 497: A. N. Strahler; Page 498 (top): Courtesy Los Angeles County Department of Public Works; Page 498 (bottom): (c)Bill Davis/Black Star; Page 501: Courtesy Troy L. Pewe; Page 502: Stephen J. Krasemann/DRK Photo; Page 503: Steve McCutcheon/Alaska Pictorial; Page 504: Bernard Hallet, Periglacial Laboratory, Quaternary Research Center; Page 505: (c)Steve McCutcheon/Alaska Pictorial Service.

Chapter 15 Pages 510-511 and 512: Courtesy NASA, Space Imaging; Page 517: (c) Laurence Parent; Page 518: (c) John S. Shelton, La Jolla, California; Page 519: (c)Bruno Barbey/Magnum Photos, Inc.; Page 521: Tom Bean/Tom & Susan Bean, Inc.; Page 523: (c)M. Smith/Sipa Press; Page 524: David R. Frazier/Photo Researchers; Page 528: Jacques Jangoux/Peter Arnold, Inc.; Page 530 (top): (c)Dan Koeck/Liaison Agency, Inc./Getty Images; Page 530 (bottom left and right): NASA Earth Observatory, MODIS Rapid Response Team; Page 531 (top): Galen Rowell/Corbis Images; Page 531 (bottom): Michael Williams/Getty Images News and Sport Services; Page 532: (c)Tom Bean/DRK Photo; Page 536: (c)Tom Till Photography; Page 537: National Audubon Society/Photo Researchers; Page 541 (left and right): Courtesy of Worldsat International; Page 542 (top): Shepard Sherbell/SABA; Page 542 (bottom): Panos Pictures; Page 543: Dieter Telemans/Panos Pictures.

Chapter 16 Pages 544-545 and 546: (c) John Beatty/Stone/Getty Images; Page 548: Official U.S. Navy Photographs; Page 549: Tom Bean/DRK Photo; Page 550: (c)Joe Englander/Viesti Associates, Inc.; Page 551: Alan H. Strahler; Page 552: (c)Frans Lanting/Minden Pictures, Inc.; Page 555: Dick Dietrich/Dietrich Leis Stock Photo, Inc.; Page 557: Larry Dale Gordon/The Image Bank/Getty Images; Page 558: Jan Kopec/Stone/Getty Images; Page 559: Tom &

Susan Bean, Inc.; Page 560 (top): Courtesy NASA/GSFC/LARC/JPL, MISR Team; Page 560 (bottom): Courtesy NASA/GSFC/MITI/ERSDAC/JAROS and U. S. Japan ASTER Science Team; Page 561 (top): Courtesy NASA/GSFC/LARC/JPL, MISR Team; Page 561 (bottom): Courtesy NASA/GSFC/MITI/ERSDAC/JAROS and U. S. Japan ASTER Science Team; Page 562: F. Kenneth Hare; Page 563: NASA/Science Source/Photo Researchers; Page 564: (c)Albert Moldvay/Eriako Associates; Page 565: Breck Kent/Earth Scenes; Page 567: T. A. Wiewandt/DRK Photo; Page 570 (top): Michael Collier, Flagstaff, Arizona; Page 571 (top): Scott Cotter, Redmond, Oregon; Page 571 (bottom): (c) John S. Shelton, La Jolla, California.

Chapter 17 Pages 574-575 and 576: (c)Tom Bean/DRK Photo; Page 579: Larry Ulrich/DRK Photo; Page 580 (top): Earth Satellite Corporation; Page 580 (bottom): NASA/JPL; Page 581 (top and bottom): NASA Jet Propulsion Laboratory; Page 584: (c) John S. Shelton, La Jolla, California; Page 587: J.A. Kraulis/Masterfile; Page 590: Reni Burri/Magnum Photos, Inc.; Page 591 (top): Carr Clifton; Page 591 (bottom): Landiscor Aerial Information, Phoenix, AZ; Page 592 (top left): (c) John S. Shelton, La Jolla, California; Page 592 (center): (c)Larry Ulrich; Page 592 (bottom): Alex McLean/Landslides.

Chapter 18 Page 596-597 and 598: (c)Jake Rajs/Stone/Getty Images; Page 602 (left): Alex McLean/Landslides; Pages 602-603: Chad Ehlers/Stone/Getty Images; Page 603 (top): Arthur N. Strahler; Page 604: Steve Dunwell, Boston, MA; Page 605: Vie De Lucia/NYT Pictures; Page 607: David Muench Photography; Page 610 (top and bottom): Courtesy NASA; Page 611: David Hiser/Photographers Aspen; Page 612: (c) John S. Shelton, L Jolla, California; Page 614 (top): Tom & Susan Bean, Inc.; Page 614 (bottom): M. J. Coe/Animals Animals/Earth Scenes; Page 616 (top and bottom): John S. Shelton, La Jolla, California; Page 617 (top): (c)William E. Ferguson; Page 617 (bottom): J. A. Kraulis/Masterfile; Page 619: G. R. Roberts, Nelson, New Zealand; Page 621: Alan H. Strahler; Page 624: (c)Stephen Rose/Liaison Agency, Inc./Getty Images; Page 625: Stephen Crowley/New York Times Pictures; Page 626: C.C. Lockwood/DRK Photo; Page 627 (top): BIOS (P.Kobeh)/Peter Arnold, Inc.; Page 627 (bottom): Tui De Roy/Minden Pictures, Inc.;

Chapter 19 Pages 628-629 and 630: Michael Melford/The Image Bank/Getty Images; Page 631 (top): Fred Hirschmann; Page 631 (bottom): Carr Clifton; Page 635: (c) John S. Shelton, La Jolla, California; Page 636: Courtesy NASA; Page 637 (top): Image courtesy NASA/GSFC/MITI/ERSDAC/JAROS and U.S./Japan ASTER Science Team; Page 637 (bottom): Image courtesy Canadian Space Agency/NASA/Ohio State University/Jet Propulsion Laboratory, Alaska SAR Facility; Page 638: Floyd L. Norgaard/Ric Ergenbright; Page 639: Courtesy NASA; Page 640: (c)Wolfgang Kaehler; Page 642: Courtesy NASA; Page 646 (top): Tom & Susan Bean, Inc.; Page 646 (bottom): C. Wolinsky/Stock, Boston; Page 647 (top): Arthur N. Strahler; Page 647 (bottom): Tom & Susan Bean, Inc.; Page 651 (all): NASA Earth Observatory.

Epilogue Pages 654-655: (c) Russell Gordon/Odyssey Productions; Page 656: (c)Alicia Hurr/ Weatherstock; Page 657: (c)Tom McHugh/Photo Researchers; Page 658: (c)Frans Lanting/Minden Pictures, Inc.

Appendix Pages 665, 666 and 667 (all): Canadian Soil Information System (CanSIS), Agriculture and Agri-Food Canada; Page 671: Geological Survey, Washington, D. C.

INDEX

Note: Page references followed by "f" indicate illustrations; while "t" indicates tables.